THE COMPLETE GUIDE
TO THE
SOVIET UNION

THE COMPLETE GUIDE TO THE

SOVIET UNION

Victor and Jennifer Louis

"—and then travel makes life worth living too!"
N. Przhevalsky
whose name is borne by the wild horses of Mongolia
which he discovered in 1811

St. Martin's Press

NEW YORK

Design by ROBERT BULL DESIGN

Library of Congress Cataloging-in-Publication Data
Louis, Victor E.
    The complete guide to the Soviet Union / Victor and Jennifer Louis. — 3rd. ed., completely updated and expanded.
        p.   cm.
    Includes index.
    ISBN 0-312-05837-3 (hard cover). — ISBN 0-312-05838-1 (pbk.)
    1. Soviet Union—Description and travel—1970—Guide-books.
I. Louis, Jennifer M.   II. Title.
DK16.L7   1991
914.704'854—dc20   90-28549
                                                                                    CIP

First Edition: October 1991

10   9   8   7   6   5   4   3   2   1

AUTHORS' NOTE

Our publishers once again deserve our most grateful thanks for taking on the mammoth task of this new edition. They are not to blame for any inaccuracies that may have crept in; we accept full responsibility. Our sincere thanks also go to our own team of helpers and to the many friendly travellers who have put our material to the test.

EDITOR'S NOTE

Republics are to be found in the alphabetical guide (part 2) under the names of their capital towns. They are listed in the index in capital letters. Towns for which maps have been provided are marked *map* in the index.

All the information in the guide is as up to date as possible, although it has been hard to keep up with the rate of change since the introduction of "perestroika." There have been widespread changes in place names; moreover, the reopening of closed churches in the hundreds and the reestablishment of scores of monasteries is an ongoing process, requiring the incorporation of many significant changes as we write.

Ethnic disturbances and the possibility of strikes, which may upset travel plans, were unknown before. A variety of new travel possibilities may open up. There may even be alterations in the national boundaries. The publishers would be grateful for notice of any corrections for subsequent editions of the guide.

C O N T E N T S

INTRODUCTION   ix

PART ONE
GENERAL INFORMATION   1
History of Russia and of the Soviet Union   3
Public Holidays   5
The Russian Orthodox Church   6
What to Take   7
Climate and Clothing   7
Passports and Other Formalities   8
Money   8
Restaurants and Food   9
Entertainment   11
Shopping   11
Transport   12
Car Hire   12
Mail and Telephone Service   13
Photography   13
Foreign Embassies and Missions in Moscow   14
Foreign Travel Agencies in Moscow   16
Consulates Outside Moscow   17
Vocabulary   18
The Alphabet • Numbers • Telling the Time • Asking the Way
First Aid   23

PART TWO
ALPHABETICAL GUIDE TO THE TOWNS   27

Index   685

INTRODUCTION

We have been writing our guidebooks about the Soviet Union for many years now. This new edition of the misleadingly titled "Complete Guide" is much enlarged; to keep it within reasonable bounds, we have adhered to the list of places that Intourist recommends to foreign visitors.

The policy of "glasnost" (openness) has led to the opening of more and more places in the country but one still cannot go everywhere. There is a shortage of hotels and other tourist facilities and a feeling of shame about inviting guests into untidy parts of the national home. In addition, the Soviets are still reluctant to let foreigners see areas that have long been classified as security risks.

An increasing number of books have been written by those who have some experience of travelling in the country, who use their general knowledge and supply usually subjective descriptions of the Soviet Union. At the other end of the scale are the guidebooks put out by each town and city and by each museum and picture gallery. We have tried to find the golden mean between these two, keeping our personal feelings from intruding but attempting to provide practical advice and interesting information on the widely differing areas within the scope of this book.

It is impossible for any guidebook on the Soviet Union to be completely up to date, given the amount of reconstruction and new building. For example, we describe churches and mosques that serve as storehouses and museums, but by the time you visit, they may well have been rededicated and filled with worshippers. Small cafés, now taken over by co-operatives, rival the best state-run restaurants.

"Perestroika" and the political turmoil at the time of writing are resulting in widespread changes, which may even affect the national boundaries. Even the means of reaching the USSR are changing. An increasing number of Soviet cities have direct links with the outside world. There are car ferries and direct flights from Scandinavia to the Baltic countries. Alaska and Siberia are developing contacts. More crossing points to China and Finland are opening. But whatever your route, certainly the wide expanses of Europe and Asia now included in the USSR will continue to appeal to those in search of adventure.

VICTOR AND JENNIFER LOUIS
Moscow

PART ONE

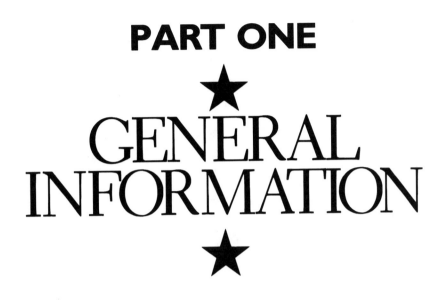

★

GENERAL INFORMATION

★

HISTORY OF
RUSSIA AND OF THE SOVIET UNION

The Soviet Union consists of 15 republics. The whole country is often referred to as Russia, but this is really the name of the largest of the republics, the Russian Federation. The Soviet Union consists mostly of the former territories of the Russian empire, and the history of the country as a whole is primarily the history of Russia. The other 14 republics are: the Ukraine, Byelorussia, Latvia, Lithuania, Estonia, Moldova, Georgia, Armenia, Azerbaijan, Kazakhstan, Uzbekistan, Tadzhikistan, Turkmenistan and Kirghizstan. The country, which is the largest in the world, occupies one-sixth of the world's land mass, 22,402,202 square kilometres (about 8,600,000 square miles). The population numbers 287,000,000 (1989), the third-largest population in the world, following China and India. Moscow time (3 hours ahead of GMT) is adhered to by the Moscow part of the Soviet Union, while the western part of the country (Estonia, etc.) is 2 hours ahead. During the summer months, Summer Time is observed, 1 hour earlier than standard time.

Facts and Figures from the Country's History

800–882: The formation of the first Russian state dates from this time. In the south a Slav tribe known as the Polyane founded the Kievan state, with its centre called Kiev, after Prince Kii of the Polyane. In the north was the state of Novgorod: when in 862 Norsemen, led by the Vikings Rurik, Sineus, and Truvor, were invited by the Novgorod Republic to come and restore order, one of them, Rurik, became the first of the Rurikids to rule in Russia. Their reign lasted until the 17th century.

882: Oleg, Rurik's successor, conquered Kiev and thus united both the states.

988: Prince Vladimir of Kiev introduce Christianity into Russia.

1169: Kiev began to decline in importance. Prince Andrei of Vladimir attacked and conquered Kiev and proclaimed Vladimir (800 km/500 miles northeast of Kiev) the new capital.

1224: Russia's first encounter with the advance army of Genghis Khan took place, and this was, in fact, the beginning of the Tatar invasions.

1237–1242: The Tatars, under Baty Khan, conquered Russia and established in the Volga steppes the rule of the Golden Horde, to which all Russia became vassal and paid tribute.

1380: Dmitri Donskoi (Demetrius of the Don), Grand-Prince of Muscovy, won a considerable battle against the Tatars. The Grand-Princedom of Muscovy had by this time gained power over most of the other principalities by acting as tax collector for the Tatars. Although Dmitri Donskoi's battle was not decisive, the Tatar grip on the country was loosened condiderably.

1462–1505: Ivan III of Muscovy laid the foundations of the future Russian empire when, between 1465 and 1488, he annexed the rich and strong city of Novgorod with its vast territories, defied the Tatars by refusing to pay them further taxes, and routed the Golden Horde's armies sent against him. This ended the 250-year-long Tatar oppression. Ivan III married Sophia, niece of the last Byzantine emperor, considered himself heir to the Byzantine empire, and after the fall of Constantinople in 1453, adopted their arms of the double-headed eagle, which remained the arms of the Russian empire until 1917.

1533–1584: The reign of Ivan IV (known as "the Terrible"). In 1547 Ivan assumed the title of Tsar (the word is derived from "caesar") of All the Russias. To Ivan IV goes the credit of building a powerful and united Russian state; during his reign the last of the independent principalities disappeared from the map of Russia. Ivan IV received his nickname for his severe persecution of the boyars (barons) who possessed great influence in government. In 1552 and 1557 respectively, the Tatar kingdoms of Kazan and Astrakhan were conquered. In 1582 the Russian conquest of Siberia began.

1598–1613: The Time of Troubles. When Feodor I, Ivan IV's son, died, ending the Rurik dynasty, 15 years of turmoil followed. Feodor I was succeeded by his brother-in-law, Boris Godunov, who died mysteriously in 1605. Boris Godunov had been opposed by two false Dmitris, each claiming in turn to be Ivan the Terrible's youngest son, Dmitri, who had died in 1591. Both imposters were supported by the Poles. Organised government collapsed, and a disastrous civil war ensued. In 1613 Kosma Minin, a Russian meat merchant, and Prince Pozharsky gathered an army of volunteers and finally drove the Poles from the country.

1613–1645: Mikhail Romanov's reign; he was elected tsar by the Land Assembly (Zemsky Sobor), thus founding the Romanov dynasty.

1682–1725: The reign of Peter I (the Great). Until 1696 he ruled jointly with Ivan V; afterward he was sole ruler of Russia. Peter I was one of the most outstanding statesmen and warriors in Russian history; he may rightly be called the "Enlightener of Russia," for he introduced Western customs, culture, and technical achievements to his backward country. He also extended Russian domination to the southern shore of the Caspian Sea, won access to the Baltic, reorganised the national economy, and founded a new army and Russia's first large fleet. In 1721 he assumed the Imperial title.

1730–1740: The reign of Anna Ivanovna; daughter of Ivan V, half-brother to Peter I.

1741–1761: The reign of Elizaveta Petrovna, daughter of Peter I.

1762–1796: The reign of Catherine II (the Great), widow of Peter III. Catherine's reign is notable for the extension of Russian territory after the three partitions of Poland, for victorious wars with Turkey, and for the acquisition of the Crimean and Danubian principalities. During this period Russia became a great power.

1796–1801: The reign of Paul I, son of Catherine II. Paul was unpopular with the nobility and was assassinated in his palace.

1801–1825: The reign of Alexander I, son of Paul. Alexander was the founder of the Holy Alliance and the principal figure in the coalition that defeated Napoleon. In 1812 Napoleon invaded Russia, with disastrous consequences. After the defeat of Napoleon, Alexander I became the most powerful sovereign in Europe. During his reign, Georgia, Azerbaijan, Bessarabia, Finland, and Poland were added to the Russian empire.

1825–1855: The reign of Nicholas I, third son of Paul. During the short interregnum caused by Alexander I's sudden death, a group of aristocratic officers made the first attempt by the military to overthrow the autocracy of the tsars and to change the system of serfdom. This rebellion took place on 14 December 1825, and the rebels were accordingly known as the Decembrists. The uprising was promptly suppressed, and its leaders were hanged or sent to Siberia; but the very fact of its occurrence served as a powerful impetus for the further development of liberal thought in Russia, although its immediate effect was to produce a period of intense persecution and affirmation of the autocratic powers of Tsar Nicholas.

1855–1881: The reign of Alexander II, son of Nicholas. In 1861 the tsar issued a decree for the emancipation of the serfs, making possible industrial expansion. The Caucasus was conquered, and in 1877–1878 the war with Turkey was won, resulting in the liberation of Bulgaria.

1881–1894: The reign of Alexander III, son of Alexander II. Russia acquired lands in Central Asia.

1894–1917: Nicholas II served as the last Russian tsar. In 1905 the first Russian revolution culminated in armed insurrections in the cities and countryside but was severely suppressed; it nevertheless loosened the tsar's control over the country. A constitution of a kind was granted. In February 1917, in the third year of World War I, another revolution began in Russia. On 2 March Nicholas abdicated, and soon a provisional government was formed. It existed till October. On 25 October (7 November, new style) the Bolsheviks (Communists) led by Lenin seized power and the Soviet state was established. Nicholas and all his immediate family were executed in July 1918 at Ekaterinburg (now Sverdlovsk) in the Urals.

1918: The Soviet government moved from Petrograd (Leningrad) to Moscow, which once again became the capital of Russia. The country was in a critical situation, as the young republic had to contend with the opposition of the White Russians (counterrevolutionaries) and with foreign intervention.

1918–1922: Civil war.

1924: Lenin died, and the Soviet leadership passed to Stalin.

1941–1945: War with Germany, known in Russia as the Great Patriotic War.

1953: Stalin died, and collective leadership was instituted.

1953–1964: Nikita Khruschev held power.

1964–1983: Leonid Brezhnev ruled.

1985: Mikhail Gorbachev elected Secretary General of the Communist party's Central Committee. "Perestroika" initiated.

1990: Institute of Presidency approved by the Special Congress of People's Deputies. Mikhail Gorbachev elected the first president of the USSR by the congress. The Communist party relinquished its monopoly on political power. An amendment to the constitution provided for the existence of other political parties.

PUBLIC HOLIDAYS

1 January: New Year's Day

8 March: International Women's Day

1–2 May: International Labour Day, celebrated with parades and demonstrations

9 May: Victory Day

7 October: Constitution Day (1977)

7–8 November: October Revolution Day, so called because the revolution took place on 25 October 1917, according to the old Julian calendar, which differs from the Gregorian calendar by 13 days. This holiday, regarded as the National Day, is also celebrated with military parades and demonstrations.

The Soviet Union also observes 23 February as Soviet Army and Navy Day, Lenin's birthday on 22 April, and other days for the air force, tank corps, railway men, etc.

THE RUSSIAN ORTHODOX CHURCH

The Eastern Orthodox church is the second-largest body of organised Christians in the world. It consists of a number of independent and self-governing churches, among them the churches of Russia and Georgia and the autonomous churches of Estonia and Latvia, which are independent except that the appointment of their chief bishops requires the sanction of the church of Russia.

When in 988–989 Russia adopted Orthodoxy, the religion already had a thousand-year history, and so the books, doctrine, music and paintings, monastic system, and even the architectural style were adopted as they were. They were regarded as an integrated whole, already as perfect as possible, as the name "Orthodox" even then conveyed—it means "that which guards and teaches the right belief" and allows for no alteration. The rigidity and conservatism of the Russian church was enhanced by centuries of threat from enemies of other faiths. The only change has been the translation of the Greek texts into old Slavonic. In general, language has never been a problem: as the Russian church spread, so the Arabian and Tatar peoples had suitable translations made for them and the peoples of the north, right across Siberia, were provided for in their turn.

As is to be expected, different parts of the country and different periods of history have produced variations of the form of ecclesiastical architecture, but it is still safe to say that most Russian Orthodox churches are built on a rectangular plan and have five domes, with the largest in the middle. If the church is in a good state of preservation, the domes may be gilded, painted silver or some bright colour, and surmounted by a Greek cross. The belfry, which has no clock, is generally a separate structure standing nearby, but it may also serve as an entrance tower, and be linked to the church by a refectory.

Inside the church the sanctuary is separated from the main body of the building by the iconostasis, a screen with sacred pictures (icons) painted on it. The icons may be richly decorated and have a lamp burning before them. Slender wax candles, which are on sale in the church, are also placed before them by the faithful. Of the three doors leading through the iconostasis, the central one, known as the Holy Door, is used by priests only. The language used during the services is Church Slavonic.

There are no seats in the church, and although the services are long, the congregation remains standing. The very stance is an act of worship. If, as a visitor, you get tired feet, you will not be the first to complain. In 1656 the Archdeacon of Aleppo wrote pathetically, "As for the Muscovites, their feet must surely be of iron." The singing, which is always unaccompanied but in which the congregation readily joins, is led by the choir, dressed in ordinary clothes and usually standing out of sight.

The head of the church is the Patriarch of Moscow and All Russia.

Although the Russian Orthodox church is quite separate from the Soviet state, a government council has been set up to maintain relations between the state and the religious bodies. This is the Council for Religious Affairs, which has its headquarters in Moscow.

"Tserkov" or "khram" means "church"; "sobor" means "cathedral." The following are the more usual names of churches in Russia.

Church of . . .

the Annunciation—Blagoveschenskaya
the Epiphany—Bogoyavlenskaya
the Transfiguration—Preobrazhenskaya
the Elevation of the Cross—Krestodvizhenskaya or Vozdvizhenskaya
the Deposition of the Robe—Rizopolozheniya
the Resurrection—Voskresenskaya
the Ascension—Voznesenskaya
the Nativity of the Virgin—Rozhdestva Bogoroditsi
the Immaculate Conception—Zachatievskaya
the Presentation of the Virgin—Vvedeniya
the Purification of the Virgin—Sreteniya
the Apparition of the Virgin—Znamenskaya
the Intercession of the Virgin—Pokorovskaya
Our Lady of All Sorrows—Skorbyaschenskaya
the Assumption—Uspenskaya
the Holy Trinity—Troitskaya

Many churches are dedicated to favourite saints, and those to St. Nicholas, SS. Peter and Paul, St. George, SS. Boris and Gleb, St. Vladimir, St. Dmitri, SS. Cosmo and Demian, and St. Sergei are easily recognisable by their Russian names. More difficult are St. John the Baptist (Ioanna Predtechi), St. John the Divine (Ioanna Bogoslova), St. John Chrysostom (Ioanna Zlatousta), the prophet Elijah (Ilyi Proroka), and the Myrrh-Bearing Women (Zhon Mironosits).

WHAT TO TAKE

It is worth every tourists's while to consider packing certain items that they will not find readily available in Russia, for instance, stain remover, air freshener, ballpoint refills and razor blades. Tourists should also remember to bring any medicines they normally take, e.g., analgesics, indigestion tablets, laxatives, to avoid having to look for a Russian substitute. Women should bring a supply of cosmetics.

Children will probably ask if you have any coins, matchboxes, stamps, or badges to exchange with them.

CLIMATE AND CLOTHING

The climate in the European part of Russia is moderately continental. Moscow's temperature averages 18.5°C (65°F) in July. The best weather is between May and September, but thunderstorms are likely during very hot spells. The autumn may be cold and wet, or there may be an Indian summer. Moscow's winter begins in mid-November, and snow and frosts are likely to last until the thaw at the beginning of April. Leningrad, being on the coast, has a milder, wetter climate than Moscow; Kiev, being farther south, is generally warmer.

The average July temperatures are as follows:

	°CELSIUS	°FAHRENHEIT
Kiev	19.3	67
Leningrad	17.5	64
Lvov	18.7	66
Minsk	17.5	64
Odessa	22.1	72

In summer light clothing will be sufficient, but tourists should bring at least one warm outfit. Evening dress will not be necessary, nor any formal dress or suit for visiting restaurants or theatres in the evening.

Tourists planning a winter visit are advised to bring a heavy fur or sheepskin coat, a fur hat, a warm scarf, boots, and gloves. A spare sweater and woolen socks may be necessary.

PASSPORTS AND OTHER FORMALITIES

To enter and leave the Soviet Union, a foreigner must have a valid national passport and Soviet entry visa. Before a visa can be issued, the applicant must have proof that accommodation has been reserved through Intourist.

It is forbidden to bring the following into the Soviet Union:

a. arms and ammunition

b. narcotics

c. printed matter, films, photographs, etc., of a pornographic nature

Items of value (watches, pearls, jewellery, foreign currency) must be declared and registered on entry to the country to ensure they are being taken out when you leave. A camera, movie or video camera, wireless, typewriter, or musical instrument may be included in one's luggage, and it is permitted to purchase an additional camera in the Soviet Union to take out of the country.

It is forbidden to take out of the Soviet Union:

a. arms and ammunition

b. precious works of art such as paintings, sculptures, and rugs

Antiques (including furniture, icons, and musical instruments) may be taken out only with the permission of the Ministry of Culture, on payment of 100 percent duty on the value of the article.

MONEY

The Russian rouble is divided into 100 kopeks. There are notes for 1, 3, 5, 10, 25, and 100 roubles; copper coins for 1, 2, 3, and 5 kopeks, and nickel coins for 10, 15, 20, and 50 kopeks and for 1 rouble. 1 and 2 kopeks are very useful to have for use in the local automatic telephone kiosks; 15 kopeks are needed for calls between cities.

On entering the country, tourists must declare the amount of foreign currency they bring in. They should be careful to save the certificate they are given, as it must be shown on leaving the Soviet Union. At the end of your visit, the roubles you have left will be changed back into your own currency, provided you save all your bank receipts to show how much money you have changed. No roubles are allowed to be taken in or out of the country, although naturally you can take small change with you as souvenirs.

RESTAURANTS AND FOOD

The times of Russian meals can catch you off guard. The hearty breakfast may not last until the substantial three-course dinner at 4 P.M., and when you know your schedule for the day, it might be wise to have coffee and a sandwich at midday. An advantage of the late-afternoon meal is that it fits in well with evening theatre performances.

We have learned to take emergency rations, including a small immersion heater, coffee, tea, sugar, powdered milk, biscuits, chocolate, and a couple of tins of sardines or luncheon meat. Fresh fruit purchased en route is always a good standby, and a visit to the market makes a break from the usual tourist sights.

Cafés usually close at 10 or 11 P.M.; restaurants at 11 or 11:30 P.M., although diners are not admitted during the half-hour before closing time. "Intourist" restaurants and a few others have their menus printed in several languages. Usually not all dishes have prices beside them; those not marked are not available on that particular day.

Recommended Russian food:

> *ikra*—black caviar (remember to ask for toast [*tost*] and butter [*maslo*])
> *krasnaya ikra*—red caviar (excellent with sour cream [*smetana*])
> *salat iz svezhikh agoortsov so smetanoy*—cucumber salad with sour cream
> *borshch*—beet soup
> *shchi*—cabbage soup
> *rassolnik*—hot soup, usually of pickled vegetables
> *akroshka*—cold soup with a *kvass* base (very refreshing; portions of soup are large, but one may ask for a half portion)
> *syomga s limonom*—smoked salmon with lemon
> *beef-Stroganov*—beef stewed in sour cream (*smetana*), with fried potatoes
> *kotleta po Kiyevski*—chicken Kiev: fried rolled breast of chicken (beware of the melted butter inside, which is liable to squirt)
> *pirozhki*—savoury fried or baked rolls with various fillings
> *bliny*—small pancakes, eaten with caviar, fish, melted butter, or sour cream
> *aladi*—crumpets, eaten with jam, as well as the accompaniments listed for bliny
> *pyelmeni*—meat dumplings
> *stakan kiselya*—dessert of thickened fruit juice (cranberry is the best)
> *gooryevskaya kasha*—semolina with various dried fruits
> *marozhnoye*—ice cream, eaten year-round; try "assorti" in a special ice-cream parlour.

Wines and Spirits

All alcoholic drinks must be ordered in grams or by the bottle.

Small glass—100 g
Large glass—200 g
Small bottle (2/3 regular size)—500 g (0.5 litre)
Normal bottle—750 g (0.75 litre)

Vodka: Certainly the most popular drink in Russia, the favourite brands are Stolichnaya, Russkaya, and Starka. There are other kinds too, including Petrovskaya (caraway flavour), lemon vodka, Okhotnichya (hunters') vodka, and Gorilka s'pertsem (Ukrainian vodka with peppers in it).
Wine: The best wine comes from the Crimea and the Caucasus. Here are the names of some good Georgian table wines:

Dry white—Tsinandali or Gurdzhani
Medium-dry white—Tvishi or Tetra
Dry red—Mookoozani or Saperavi
Medium-dry red—Khvanchkara (Stalin's favourite), Odzhaleshi, or Kindsmaraooli

Champagne:

Dry—Sookhoye
Medium-dry—Polusookhoye
Sweet—Sladkoye
Red (not pink) medium-dry—Tsimlyanskoye

There are Russian equivalents to port (portvein), Madeira (madera), and vermouth (vermoot). In general there is a wide choice of wine from Eastern Europe.
Brandy and Liqueurs: The best brandy comes from Armenia (Armyanski Cognac). Most liqueurs have French names, but the resemblance to the originals may be slight.
Mineral Water: The most common mineral waters are Narzan and the slightly salty Borzhomi. Fresh water is seldom served at the table, unless requested.
Fizzy fruit drinks include "Limonad" and various others—orange, cherry, apple, and pear. Sometimes Pepsi-Cola or orange-flavoured Fanta may also be available.
Outside in the street, you may buy a glass of "kvass" (fermented rye-bread water) or plain soda water.

In case the salt or sugar has been left off your breakfast tray or you wish to buy some fruit at the market, here is a short list of food items with their approximate pronunciation:

Bread—hlyeb
Water—voda'
Boiled water—keepyatok
Milk—malako'

Butter—ma'sla
Cheese—syir
Eggs—yaitsa
Yoghourt—kifir'
Sour cream—smetana
Salt—sol
Sugar—sa'khar
Cold sausage—kolbasa'
Ham—vetcheena'
Tea—chai
Coffee—ko'fye
Apples—ya'bloki
Pears—groo'shi
Grapes—veenograd'
Lemon—leemon'
Strawberries—kloobni'ka
Cucumbers—agoortsi'
Tomatoes—pamido'ri
Wine—veeno'
Beer—pee'vo
Soft fruit—ya' godi
Fruit—froo'kti
Sweets—kanfye'ti
Chocolate—shokolad'

ENTERTAINMENT

Visitors to Russia should apply to the service bureau of their hotel for tickets for shows; the sooner this is done, the greater the chance of obtaining tickets. The majority of theatre and circus performances are at 7 P.M., concerts at 7:30 P.M. Most performances end by 11 P.M. On Sundays there are matinees. Tourists may learn whether or not they have tickets only on the day of the performance.

There are no nightclubs, bars, or pubs open to the general public, but some large hotels have foreign-currency bars that stay open late.

SHOPPING

The larger cities now have foreign-currency shops just as the leading Intourist hotels have foreign-currency souvenir kiosks. In Moscow and Leningrad, they go under the general title of "Beryozka" (birch tree) shops. Here one may purchase souvenirs and other items for convertible currency considerably cheaper than in the ordinary shops, where they may also be difficult to find. It is definitely advisable, before paying roubles for items such as furs or silverware, to check whether they are available in the foreign-currency shops.

There are no prestige shops; the prices are the same for identical articles whether they are bought in Red Square or in a Siberian village store. All the shops are state-run with fixed prices.

In most of the shops it is necessary first to pay at the cash desk and then take the receipt to the sales-person and exchange it for what you have chosen. Self-service shops are run just the same as in the West.

TRANSPORT

The most popular form of transport in the largest cities is the underground Metro. The fare is 15 kopeks for any distance, and this is also the price of tickets on buses, trolley buses, and trams in Moscow.

Taxis have a chequered pattern on their doors and, when available for hire, show a green light in the corner of the windshield. You can catch a taxi in the street, or at a taxi stand, or call for one by telephone. It costs 40 kopeks to hire a taxi, and then the charge is 40 kopeks per kilometre; waiting costs 4 roubles per hour. There are also taxi services which ply to and fro along certain routes; these are called "marshrootnoye" taxis, and the charge is 25 kopeks for any distance along the route.

CAR HIRE

Foreign tourists may hire cars or coaches from Intourist with or without the services of a driver. The cost of hired transport is in addition to the cost of the tour.

A rent-a-car system for tourists travelling on Intourist itineraries or within individual cities is available in Brest, Erevan, Kharkov, Kiev, Kishinyov, Leningrad, Lvov, Minsk, Moscow, Odessa, Sochi, Sukhumi, Tbilisi, and Yalta. Cost depends on the make of the car, the period of rental, and the number of kilometres covered. Rental rates include:

- Insurance of the driver for third-party liability
- Car insurance (driver's liability for damage to car through his own fault is limited to 120 roubles; the liability for damage may be completely discharged on payment of an additional sum of money)
- Car delivery to and collection from hotels
- Car servicing

The cost of gasoline and car washing is not included in the rental charges. Gas is sold for coupons, which may be purchased at Intourist service bureaus for roubles. Car-washing facilities are available at service stations and payable in roubles.

Cars may be delivered to any town on the auto-routes where Intourist service is available. Collection of hired cars is made on the same terms as delivery.

Chauffeur-driven cars are available for hire in the following cities: Brest, Erevan, Kharkov, Kiev, Kishinyov, Krasnodar, Kursk, Leningrad, Lvov, Minsk, Moscow, Odessa, Orel, Sochi, Sukhumi, Tallinn, Tbilisi, Tver, Vladikavkaz, and Yalta. Rental rates for chauffeur-driven cars include:

- Driver's board and lodging
- Servicing and car washing
- Gasoline and oil

Chauffeur-driven cars may be delivered to any town on the auto-routes where Intourist service is available. Delivery to and collection from a town in which car-rental services are not provided is charged at the same rates as the delivery and collection of self-driven cars.

Chauffeur-driven coaches are hired out to groups of tourists provided the group has paid for Intourist services along the entire route, for the entire term of the rental. Chauffeur-driven coaches are available for hire in any town on the auto-routes where Intourist service is available and may be used for tours on Intourist itineraries and Intourist-organised excursions in and around the towns. The cost of hire includes:

- Driver's board and lodging
- Gasoline and oil
- Servicing and car washing
- Parking space for coach
- Delivery and collection of coach

MAIL AND TELEPHONE SERVICE

Any mail to be forwarded to a large city should be addressed care of Intourist, in that city, USSR. The more information on the envelope, the better, e.g., John Brown, from England, arriving Moscow, 2 July. Intourist will hold it for you to collect. Usually mail from European countries takes 3–10 days, from the United States and Canada, a week or more. The address must be legible.

Most Intourist hotels have automatic telephones in each room. One should usually dial 8 before the local number; frequent regular buzzing means the line is busy. With nonautomatic telephones, you should ask the operator for "gorod" and wait for a continuous buzzing sound before you dial. If you cannot manage to say room numbers in Russian, you may use English or French very slowly, number by number. In case of emergency, ask the operator for "service bureau" or "administrator."

To use phones in kiosks or booths, put a 2-kopek coin or two 1-kopek coins in the slot, lift the receiver, wait for a continuous buzzing, and then dial. 10-kopek coins also serve in an emergency, as do U.S. dimes.

Long-distance calls from a hotel must be ordered through the service bureau; they may take an hour to come through. Otherwise, one should go to a long-distance telephone office ("peregovornyi punkt"); there one might be asked to pay for 3 or 5 minutes of conversation in advance.

PHOTOGRAPHY

Photographs, movies, and videos may be taken during your visit, but you must obtain permission from the administration of factories, railway stations, and government offices before taking pictures there.

FOREIGN EMBASSIES AND MISSIONS IN MOSCOW

(and Consulates if located at a different address)

COUNTRY	ADDRESS	TELEPHONE	
Afghanistan	Sverchkov Per. 3/2	928	5044
Algeria	Krapivinsky Per. 1A	200	6642
Consulate	Ul. B. Spasskaya 12	280	4774
Angola	Ul. Olof Palme 6	143	6324
Argentina	Ul. Sadovo-Triumfalnaya 4/10	299	0367
Australia	Kropotkinsky Per. 13	246	5012
Austria	Starokonyushenny Per. 1	201	7317
Bangladesh	Zemledelchesky Per. 6	246	7900
Belgium	Stolovy Per. 7	203	6566
Consulate	Khlebny Per. 15	290	5328
Benin	Uspensky Per. 4a	299	2360
Bolivia	Lopukhinsky Per. 5	201	2508
Brazil	Ul. Gertsena 54	290	4022-26
Bulgaria	Ul. Mosfilmovskaya 66	147	9000
Burkina Faso	Ul. Meschanskaya 17	971	0620
Burundi	Uspensky Per. 7	299	7200
Cape Verde	Ul. B. Spasskaya 9	208	0856
Cambodia	Starokonyushenny Per. 16	201	4736
Cameroon	Ul. Vorovskove 40	290	6549
Canada	Starokonyushenny Per. 23	241	5882
Chad	Rublyovskoye Chaussée 26, Kv. 20–21	415	4139
China	Leninskiye Gory, Ul. Druzhby 6	143	1540
Colombia	Ul. Burdenko 20	248	3042
Congo	Kropotkinsky Per. 12	246	0234
Costa Rica	Rublyovskoye Ch. 26, Kv. 58-59	415	4042
Côte d'Ivoire	Molochny Per. 9/14	201	2400
Cuba	Ul. Mosfilmovskaya 40	147	4312
Cyprus	Ul. Gertsena 51	290	2154
Czechoslovakia	Ul. Yuliusa Fuchika 12/14	251	0540-46
Denmark	Per. Ostrovskovo 9	201	7860
Ecuador	Gorokhovsky Per. 12	261	5544
Egypt	Skatertny Per. 25	291	6283
Equatorial Guinea	Kutuzovsky Pr. 7/4, Kor. 5, Kv. 37	243	9611
Ethiopia	Orlovo-Davydovsky Per. 6	230	2036
Finland	Kropotkinsky Per. 15/17	246	4027
France	Ul. Dimitrova 45/47	236	0003
Consulate	Kazansky Per.	236	0003
Gabon	Ul. Vesnina 16	241	0080
Germany	Ul. Bolshaya Gruzinskaya 17	252	5521
Ghana	Skatertny Per. 14	202	1870-71
Greece	Ul. Stanislavskovo 4	290	2274

COUNTRY	ADDRESS	TELEPHONE	
Guinea	Pomerantsev Per. 6	201	3601
Guinea-Bissau	Ul. B. Ordynka 35	231	7928
Guyana	2-Kazachy Per. 7	230	0013
Hungary	Ul. Mosfilmovskaya 62	143	8611-15
Iceland	Khlebnyi Per. 28	290	4742
India	Ul. Obukha 6-8	297	0820
Indonesia	Ul. Novokuznetskaya 12	231	9549-51
Iran	Pokrovsky Bld. 7	227	5788
Iraq	Ul. Pogodinskaya 12	246	5506-13
Ireland	Grokholsky Per. 5	288	4101
Israel	Ul. B. Ordynka 56	238	1346
Italy	Ul. Vesnina 5	241	1533-36
Jamaica	Ul. Dobryninskaya 7, Kv. 70-71	237	2320
Japan	Kalashny Per. 12	291	8500-01
Consulate	Sobinovsky Per. 5a	202	8303
Jordan	Per. Sadovskikh 3	299	9564
Kenya	Ul. B. Ordynka 70	237	3462
Korean PDR	Ul. Mosfilmovskaya 72	143	6249
Republic of Korea	Ul. Gubkina	938	2802-08
Kuwait	3-Neopalimovsky Per. 13/5	248	5001
Laotian PDR	Ul. B. Ordynka 18/1	233	2035
Lebanon	Ul. Sadovo-Samotechnaya 14	200	0022
Libyan AJ	Ul. Mosfilmovskaya 38	143	0354
Luxembourg	Khruschevsky Per. 3	202	2171
Madagascar	Kursovoi Per. 5	290	0214
Malaysia	Ul. Mosfilmovskaya 50	147	1514
Mali	Ul. Novokuznetskaya 11	231	0655
Malta	Ul. Dobryninskaya 7, Kv. 219	237	1939
Mauritania	Ul. B. Ordynka 66	237	3792
Mexico	Ul. Schukina 4	201	4848
Mongolia	Ul Pisemskovo 11	290	6792
Consulate	Spasopeskovsky Per. 7/1	241	1548
Morocco	Per. Ostrovskovo 8	201	7395
Mozambique	Ul. Gilyarovskovo 20	284	4007
Myanmar	Ul. Gertsena 41	291	0534
Namibia (SWAPO)	Ul. Konyushkovskaya 28, Kv. 10	252	2471
Nepal	2-Neopalimovsky Per. 14/7	244	0215
Netherlands	Kalashny Per. 6	291	2999
Consulate	Ul. B. Ordynka 56	238	2732
New Zealand	Ul. Vorovskovo 44	290	1277
Nicaragua	Ul. Mosfilmovskaya 50, Kor. 1	938	2701
Niger	Kursovoy Per. 7/31	290	0101
Nigeria	Ul. Kachalova 13	290	3783/85/ 87
Norway	Ul. Vorovskovo 7	290	3872
Oman	Per. Obukhab	928	8268

COUNTRY	ADDRESS	TELEPHONE	
Pakistan	Ul. Sadovo-Kudrinskaya 17	250	3991
Palestine	Kropotkinsky Per. 26	201	4340
Peru	Smolensky Bld 22/14, Kv. 15	248	7738
Consulate	Smolensky Bld 22/14, Kv. 11	248	2766
Philippines	Karmanitsky Per. 6	241	0563/65
Poland	Ul. Klimashkina 4	255	0017
Portugal	Botanichesky Per. 1	230	2435
Qatar	Korovy Val 7, Kv. 197–198	230	1577
Romania	Ul. Mosfilmovskaya 64	143	0424
Rwanda	Ul. B. Ordynka 72	237	4626
Senegal	Ul. Donskaya 12	236	2040
Sierra Leone	Ul. Paliashvili 4	203	6200
Singapore	Per. Voyevodina 5	241	3702
Somali DR	Spasopeskovskaya Pl. 8	241	8624
South Africa (ANC)	Ul. Konyushkovskaya 28, Kv. 9	252	3295
Spain	Ul. Gertsena 50/8	202	2161
Sri Lanka	Ul. Schepkina 24	288	1651
Sudan	Ul. Vorovskovo 9	290	3993
Sweden	Ul. Mosfilmovskaya 60	147	9009
Switzerland	Per. Stopani 2/5	925	5322
Syria	Mansurovsky Per. 4	203	1521
Tanzania	Ul. Pyatnitskaya 33	231	8146
Thailand	Eropkinsky Per. 3	201	4893
Togo	Ul. Schuseva 1	290	6599
Tunisia	Ul. Kachalova 28/1	291	2858
Turkey	Vadkovsky Per. 7/37	972	6500
Uganda	Per. Sadovskikh 5	251	0060-62
United Arab Emirates	Ul. Olof Palme 4	147	6286
United Kingdom	Nab. Morisa Toreza 14	231	8511-12
United States	Novinsky Bld. 19/23	252	2451-59
Uruguay	Lomonosovsky Pr. 38	143	0401
Venezuela	Ul. Ermolovoy 13/15	299	9621
Vietnamese DR	Ul. B. Pirogovskaya 13	245	0925
Yemen	2-Neopalimovsky Per. 6	246	1531
Yugoslavia	Ul. Mosfilmovskaya 46	147	4106
Zaire	Per. N Ostrovskovo 10	201	7664
Zambia	Pr. Mira 52a	288	5001
Zimbabwe	Serpov Per. 6	248	4367

FOREIGN TRAVEL AGENCIES IN MOSCOW

AGENCY	ADDRESS	PHONE	
AMERICAN EXPRESS	Ul. Sadovo-Kudrinskaya 21a	254	2111
BARRY MARTIN	Mezhdunarodnaya-2, Room 940	253	2940
BALKANTOURIST	Kuznetsky Most 1/8	292	3125

AGENCY	ADDRESS	PHONE	
BUSINESS TOUR	Mezhdunarodnaya-2, Office 701	255	0584
CEDOK	4-Tverskaya Yamskaya 35/39	258	8932
DER-REISEN		203	8395
EUROPÄISCHES	Ul. B. Spasskaya 12	280	6438
EXPRESS-BOYD		203	2675
IBUSZ	Ul. Medvedeva 5	299	8010
INATOURS		253	1529
KALEVA	Hotel Intourist, Kom. 801	203	6108
NUR-TOURISTIK		203	5397
OLYMPIA-REISEN		263	0057
ORBIS (Poland)	Ul. Tverskaya 56, Kv. 88	250	1780
THOMSON HOLIDAYS		203	4025

CONSULATES OUTSIDE MOSCOW

Baku:

Iranian	Baku 370001, Bouniad Sardarof 4	92	6143
Iraqi	Ul. Khagani 9	93	8283

Batumi:

Turkish	Prospect Svobody 8	339	09

Irkutsk:

Mongolian	Ul. Lapina 11	24	2370

Kiev:

Bulgarian	Ul. Hospitalnaya 1	225	5119
Cuban	Bethersky Per. 5	216	2930
Czech	Yaroslavov Val 34	212	0210
German	252054 Kiev, Ul. Chkalova 84	216	6794
Hungarian	Ul. Reiterskaya 33	212	4094
Mongolian	Ul. Kotsyubinskovo 3	216	8891
Polish	Yaroslavov Val 12	224	8040
Romanian	Ul. Mihail Kochubinski 8	24	5261
U.S.	Ul. Florentsiya 9		

Leningrad:

Bulgarian	W.O., Ul. Ryleyeva 27	273	7347
Chinese	W.O., 3-Liniya 12	218	1721
Cuban	Ul. Ryleyeva 37	279	0492
Czechoslovak	Smolensky Rayon, Ul. Tverskaya 5	271	0459
Finnish	Ul. Chaikovskovo 71	273	7321/25
French	Moika Nab. 15	314	1443
German	Ul. Petra Lavrova 39	273	5598
Hungarian	Ul. Marata 15	312	6458
Italian	Pl. Teatralnaya 10	312	2896

Japanese	Nab. reki Moiki 29	312	1133
Mongolian	Saperny Per. 11	272	5472
Polish	Ul. 5-Sovietskaya 12	274	4331
Swedish	V.O., 10th line, No. 11	218	3525-29
U.S.	Ul. Petra Lavrova 15	274	8235

Lvov:
| Polish | Ul. Ivana Franko 10 | 72 | 3949 |

Minsk:
Bulgarian	Bronevoy Per. 3	22	5500
German	Ul. Sakharova 26	33	0752
Polish	Omsky Per. 6	33	1313

Nakhodka:
| Japanese | Ul. Lunacharskovo 9 | 56 | 371 |
| Korean DPR | Ul. Vladivostokskaya 1 | 55 | 310 |

Odessa:
Bulgarian	Ul. Posmitnovo 9	66	2015
Cuban	Ul. Tomasa 7/9	25	1469
Indian	Ul. Kirova 31	22	4333
Vietnamese Mission	Pr. Shevchenko 23B	63	4211

Syktyvkar:
| Bulgarian | Ul. Babushkina 10 | 23 | 544 |

Tashkent:
Afghan	Ul. Gogolya 73	33	9180
Cuban	Ul. Timiryazeva	35	0777
Indian	Ul. A Tolstova 5	33	3782
Libyan	Ul. Engelsa 95	35	6211
Mongolian	Ul. Gogolya	33	9847

VOCABULARY

The Alphabet

Vowels

Russian	English	Pronounced
a	a	as a in "father" (when in a stressed syllable) or as u in "up"
я	—	as ya in "yard"
э	e	as e in "pet"
e	—	as ye in "yet"

и	i	as i in "hit"
ы	—	as e in "me" pronounced with a strong Midland accent
о	o	as o in "hot"
ё	—	as ya in "yacht"
у	u	as u in "pull"
ю	—	as u in "union"

Consonants

б	b	as b in "box"
д	d	as d in "dog"
ф	f	as f in "fish"
г	g	as g in "go"
х	kh	as ch in "loch"
ж	zh	as s in "pleasure"
к	k	as k in "king"
л	l	as l in "like"
м	m	as m in "man"
н	n	as n in "nimble"
п	p	as p in "pin"
р	r	as r in "arrow"
с	s	as s in "miss"
т	t	as t in "take"
в	v	as v in "vat"
з	z	as z in "zebra"

Double Consonants

ц	—	as ts in "eats"
ч	—	as ch in "chair"
ш	—	as sh in "ship"
щ	—	as shch in "cash cheque"

Accent Letters

ь		soft sign (in transliterated words)
ъ		hard sign
й		short i (as "y" in "guy")

Numbers

1	один	udeen'
2	два	dva
3	три	tree
4	четыре	chyety'rye
5	пять	pyat
6	шесть	shest
7	семь	syem

8	во́семь	vo'syem
9	де́вять	dye'vyat
10	де́сять	dye'syat
11	оди́ннадцать	udeen'atsut
12	двена́дцать	dvyenat'sut
13	трина́дцать	treenat'sut
14	четы́рнадцать	chetyr'natsut
15	пятна́дцать	pyatnat'sut
16	шестна́дцать	shestnat'sut
17	семна́дцать	syemnat'sut
18	восемна́дцать	voysemnat'sut
19	девятна́дцать	dyevyatnat'sut
20	два́дцать	dvat'sut
21	два́дцать один	dvat'sut udeen
22	два́дцать два	dvat'sut dva
30	три́дцать	treet'sut
40	со́рок	so'rok
50	пятьдеся́т	pyatdyesyat'
60	шестьдеся́т	shestdyesyat
70	се́мьдесят	syemdyesyat
80	во́семьдесят	vo'syemdye syat
90	девяно́сто	dyevyano'sto
100	сто	sto
200	две́сти	dvye'sti
300	три́ста	tree'sta
400	четыреста	chety'ryesta
500	пятьсо́т	pyatsot
600	шестьсо́т	shestsot'
900	девятьсо́т	dyevyatsot'
1000	ты́сяча	ty'syacha

Telling the Time

To tell the time, one must always state the number of hours first and then the number of minutes. (There is a second way of telling the time in Russian that is more complicated grammatically: 8:20 would be literally "twenty minutes of the ninth.") The simple method given here will be perfectly adequate.

In the evening, especially when giving the times of film performances, train departures, etc., Russians tend to use the 24-hour system (saying 18:45 for 6:45 P.M.).

What is the time?
кото́рый час?
kato'ryi chas?

It is 1 o'clock, 2 o'clock
час, два часа́
chas, dva chasa'

It is 5 past 3 (P.M.)
три часа́ пять мину́т, пятна́дцать ноль пять
tree chasa'pyat minoot' or *pyatnat' sut nol pyat*

It is 20 to 5
четы́ре часа́ со́рок мину́т, шестна́дцать со́рок
chety' chasa'so'rok minoot' or *shestnat'sut so'rok*

It is 12 o'clock midday, midnight
по́лдень, по́лночь
pol'dyen, pol'noch

A.M.	утра́	*utra*
P.M.	ве́чера	*vye'chera*
This morning	сего́дня у́тром	*syevod'nya oot rom*
This afternoon	сего́дня днём	*syevod'nya dnyom*
This evening }	сего́дня ве́чером {	*syevod'nya*
Tonight		*vye'cherom*
Night	ночь	*noch*
Tomorrow evening	за́втра ве́чером	*zav'tra vye'cherom*
Tomorrow morning	за́втра у́тром	*zav'tra oot'rom*
The day after tomorrow	послеза́втра	*poslyezav'tra*
Yesterday	вчера́	*vchera'*
The day before yesterday	позавчера́	*pozavchera'*
Last night	вчера́ но́чью	*vchera'noch'yu*
Early	ра́но	*ra'no*
Late	по́здно	*poz'dno*
How long?	как до́лго	*kak dol'go?*
An hour	час	*chas*
A minute	мину́та	*minoo'ta*
Half a moment	мину́точку	*minoo'tochku*
In a moment	сейча́с	*sichas'*

Asking the Way

Would you please tell me . . .
скажи́те пожа́луйста
skazhee'tye pazhal'sta . . .

where there is a grocer's, baker's, market, chemist's here?
где здесь продма́г, бу́лочная, ры́нок, апте́ка?
gdye zdyes prodmag', boo'lochnaya, ry'nok, aptye'ka?

where there is a restaurant, café, cafeteria here?
где здесь рестора́н, кафе́ столо́вая?
gdye zdyes restoran', kafay', stalo'vaya?

cinema, theatre, park, museum, church?
кино́, теа́тр, парк, музе́й, це́рковь?
kino', tyea'tr, park, moozei', tser'kov?

where there is a lavatory here?
где здесь убо́рная?
gdye zdyes ubor'naya?

Highway	шóссе	*sho'sai*
Road	доро́га	*daro'ga*
Street	у́лица	*oo'litsa*
Square	пло́щадь	*plosh'chad*
Lane	пересу́лок	*pyeryeoo'lok*
Dead-end	тупи́к	*tupik*
Town	го́род	*go'rod*
Village	село́	*syelo*
Village	дере́вня	*dyerev'nya*
House	дом	*dom*
Sea	мо́ре	*mo'rye*
Black Sea	Чёрное	*chor'noye*
	море	*morye*
Turning	поворо́т	*pavarot'*
To the left	нале́во	*nalye'va*
To the right	напра́во	*napra'va*
Straight on	пря́мо	*prya'ma*
Here	сюда́	*syuda'*
There	туда́	*tuda'*
Back	наза́д	*nazad'*
Forest	лес	*lyes*
Field	по́ле	*po'lye*
River	река́	*reka'*
Lake	о́зеро	*o'zyero*
Hill	гора́	*gara'*

Who speaks English, French, German here?
кто здесь говори́т по-англи́йски, по-францу́зски, понеме́цки?
kto zdyes gavareet' panglee'ski, pafrantsoos'ki, panimyets'ki?

May I have an interpreter?
мо́жно попроси́ть перево́дчика?
mozh'no papraseet' perevod'chika?

We are tourists from England, America, France, Germany, Italy.
Мы тури́сты из Ангдии, Аме́рики, Фра́нции, Герма́нии, Ита́лии.
my tooris'ti iz an'glii, ame'riki, fran'tsii, germa'nii, ita'lii.

We are going to the town of . . .
Мы е́дем в горо́д . . .
my ye'dyem v gorod' . . .

We have come from the town of . . .
Мы е́дем из го́рада . . .
my ye'dem iz go'roda . . .

I do not understand Russian.
Я не понима́ю по-русски
ya ne panima'yu paroos'ki.

What is this called in Russian?
как э́то называ́ется по-ру́сски?
kak e'to nazyva'yetsa paroos'ki?

Yes	да	*da*
No	нет	*nyet*
Thank you	спаси́бо	*spasi'bo*
Please	пожалуйста	*pazhal'sta*
Hello	здра́вствуйте	*zdrav'st-vuytye*
Good-bye	до свида́ния	*dasvidanya*
Good	хорошо́	*kharasho'*
Bad	пло́хо	*plo'kho*
Much, many	мно́го	*mno'go*
Little, few	ма́ло	*ma'la*
When?	когда́	*kagda?*
Where?	где?	*gdye?*
Why?	почему́?	*pachimoo'?*
Quickly	бы́стро	*by'stra*
Slowly	ме́дленно	*myed'lenna*
I	я	*ya*
He	он	*on*
She	она́	*ana'*
We	мы	*my*
You	вы	*vy*

FIRST AID

In the Soviet Union medical care is free of charge, and tourists who fall ill during their trip are also entitled to free medical care. In case you are unwell, notify an Intourist representative and a doctor will be called immediately. There is no charge for the doctor's visit, but the patient pays for any medicines according to standard prices.

There are first-aid posts and hospitals at regular intervals along the Intourist routes, and in Moscow there is a special clinic that cares for foreign tourists. Its address is Gruzinsky Per. 3, Kor, 2, telephone number 254 2344, home calls 254 4326. Its staff includes qualified doctors and nurses, and there are X-ray, physiotherapy, dental, and other departments.

Vocabulary

I feel ill
Я пло́хо себя́ чу́вствую.
ya plo'kho syebya' choo'stvuyu

I have a head-, ear-, tooth-, stomach-ache, sore throat.
У меня болит голова, ухо, зуб, живот, горло.
u myenya' baleet' galava', oo' kho, zoob, zhivot', gor' lo

I have a cough, cold, influenza.
У меня кашель, насморк, грипп.
u myenya' ka' shyel, na' smork, grip

I have diarrhoea, constipation.
У меня понос, запор.
u myenya' panos', zapor

I have broken my arm, my leg.
Я сломал руку, ногу.
ya slamal roo' ku, no' gu

I have burnt my hand, my leg, my finger.
Я обжёг, руку, ногу, палец.
ya abzhog rooku, no' gu, pa' lyets

I have sprained my ankle.
У меня растряжение ноги.
u myenya' rastyazhe' niye naghee'

I have a blister.
Я натёр себе ногу.
ya natyor' sibye' no' gu

I have a rash, a swelling.
У меня сыпь, опухоль.
oo myenya' syp, o' pukhol

She is very tired.
она очень устала.
una o' chyen usta' la

He has a temperature.
У него температура.
oo nyevo' temperatoo' ra

What is the matter with you?
На что вы жалуетесь?
na shto vy zhaloo' yetyes?

Where is the hospital?
где здесь больница?
gdye zdyes balni' tsa?

Call an ambulance.
Позовите скорую помощь.
pazovi tye sko' ruyu po' moshch

It is necessary to call a doctor immediately.
нýжно срóчно позвáть врача.
noozh na sroch na pazvat' vracha'

I have lost my appetite.
У меня прóпал аппетит.
u myenya' propal' apeteet'

Fainting fit	óбморок	*ob'marok*
Infection	инфéкция	*infek'tsiya*
Burn	ожóг	*azhog*
Inflammation	воспалéние	*vospale'niye*
Sprain	вывих	*vy'vikh*
Convulsion	сýдорога	*soo'daraga*
Fracture	перелóм	*pyerelom*
Inoculation	привúвка	*priveev'ka*
Anaesthetic	наркóз	*narkoz*
Dressing	перевязка	*pyerevyaz'ka*
Injection	укóл	*ukol'*
Nurse	медсестрá	*myedsyestra'*
Medicines	лекáрства	*lekar'stva*
An aspirin	áспирин	*as'pirin*
First-aid kit	перевязочные средства	*pyerevya'zochnyye sryedstva*
Castor oil	касторка	*kastor'ka*
Disinfectant	дезинфицирýющее срéдство	*dizinfitseeroo'yushcheye sryed'stvo*
Epsom salts	англúйская соль	*anglee'skaya sol*
Iodine	йод	*yod*
Ointment	мазь	*maz*
A pill	пилюля	*pilyoo'lya*
Quinine	хинúн	*khineen'*
A bandage	бинт	*bint*
Cotton-wool	вáта	*va'ta*

PART TWO

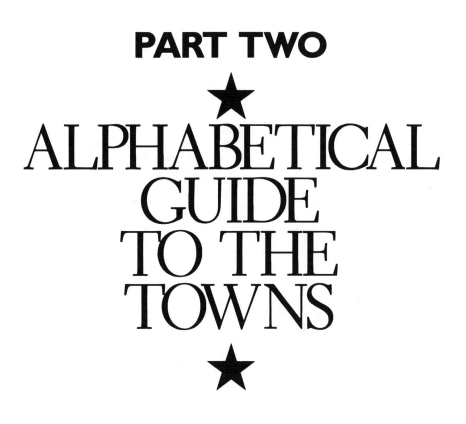

★

ALPHABETICAL GUIDE TO THE TOWNS

★

ABAKAN

Abakan is the administrative centre of the Khakas Autonomous Region.

KHAKASIA

The Khakas Autonomous Region is situated in the southwest of Krasnoyarsk Territory in the left-bank part of the Minusinsk basin, bounded by the Kuznetsk Alatau and Western Sayan Mountains. The state of Khakasia was formed in 840 B.C. It conducted a brisk trade with China and the countries of Central Asia, exchanging furs for silk and cotton fabrics, metal articles, and other goods.

In the 13th century, Khakasia was devastated by the Mongols. A considerable part of its population was killed, while others took to the forests. Their irrigation canals were destroyed, agriculture ceased, and trade came to a standstill. During the last five centuries, Khakasia has been the home of various Sayan nomad tribes. Until the 18th century, when the region was joined to Russia, the inhabitants, who were partly Turkicised Samoyeds, comprised a conglomerate of different tribes, and they were known either by the names of those tribes or by the geographical names of the Minusinsk or Abakan Tatars. They did not form a single nation until the 1920s. Now they are Turkic-speaking Orthodox people, and the name Khakas was adopted as a revival of the mediaeval name of the Kirghiz, who once inhabited the Minusinsk basin, which is thought to derive from the Chinese Ha-gias, which is how these peoples were described in the Chinese annals.

The Russians who came here in the 17th century settled predominantly along the right-bank part of the country, where the town of Minusinsk now stands. They preferred agriculture to hunting for furs. In the mid-18th century, the mining of copper and gold started in the Kuznetsk Alatau and Western Sayan Mountains, and in 1771–72 the botanist Peter Pallas (1741–1811) listed 77 species of plants growing here. Russian colonisation of the area in the 18th and even more in the 19th centuries was conducive to Khakasia's transition to a settled way of life. However, cattle and sheep raising remained the most important branch of the Khakas economy, in spite of the development of a mining industry prior to the 1917 revolution. The process of settlement of the area and the development of its natural resources were accelerated by the construction of the Trans-Siberian railway.

In 1930 the Khakas achieved national autonomy, and the Khakas Autonomous Region was formed. Two urban settlements have emerged: Abakan, now the centre of the region, and Chernogorsk.

Present-day Khakasia is one of southern Siberia's more important centres of lumbering and mechanised agriculture and is a well-developed industrial region. The main industries are mining and smelting, coal, iron ore and nonferrous metals. There is an important food-processing industry linked to its agriculture, and its economy is well balanced.

Khakasian culture is also well developed. In 1924–25 the Khakas people obtained their own written language based on the Cyrillic alphabet. Illiteracy has been almost totally eliminated. There are many schools and libraries in the Region. Khakasia has 200 houses of culture and clubs, a professional drama company, a broadcasting system, and a television centre.

Abakan Population—154,000

Abakan is the administrative centre of the Khakas Autonomous Region. Most of the population is now Russian, with Khakas in the minority. The town spreads over the Abakan Steppe on the left bank of the Abakan River, where it is navigable, 4 km (2 miles) from its confluence with the Yenisei, on the site of the small village of Ust-Abakanskoye. There is a microclimate in this part of the Yenisei valley, and melons can be grown in the summer.

In the 3rd and 4th centuries, this region was part of the Chinese Han empire. It is possible that the residence of one of the Han viceroys was located near the present town of Abakan, where some remnants of Chinese-style buildings dating from the 1st century B.C. have been found. Ust-Abakanskoye was founded as a Russian fort in 1707, grew into a village, and obtained town status in 1931.

The appearance and subsequent development of Abakan is intertwined with the construction of the Achinsk-Minusinsk railway line, which linked the area with the rest of Siberia in 1925. Abakan is further joined to the Tuva Autonomous SSR by road.

It is sensibly planned, and none of the new buildings are disproportionately large. It is divided by straight streets that are wide and clean and lined by shrubs and avenues of poplars. Walking along Lenin Prospect is like being in a garden. When we visited Abakan in September, there were so many flowers that nobody minded the little bull-calf happily grazing in a bed of marigolds on the airport roundabout. In town there is a well-tended municipal park and a square in front of the House of Soviets.

Abakan accounts for a quarter of the region's industry. The town is surrounded by deposits of natural minerals, which are used by local enterprises. There is a machine-building plant and footwear and garment factories. New branches of industry connected with the processing and utilisation of Tuvan asbestos and nonferrous metals are also developing. Abakan is also a centre of highly developed agriculture. The city has meat-packing and dairy plants, a juice and wine-making factory, a grain elevator, a flourmill, a bakery, and a large poultry farm on the way to the Yenisei. Abakan is also the cultural centre of Khakasia. There are several specialized secondary schools; a research institute of the Khakas language, literature, and history; and pedagogical and medical institutes. Some of the blocks of flats are linked by closed galleries for winter use.

Local Museum, Vokzalnaya Street 96 (a new building is under construction). Open 10–6; closed

Mon. and the last day of each month. There are the familiar ice-age skeletons of mammoths and woolly rhinoceros here, but unusual are the clay death masks, which remained from funeral pyres of the past. Of particular interest is the collection of prehistoric carved stone stellae, 2,000 years older than the statues on Easter Island. Some are carved with pictures like those of the North American Indians, even having different faces, one above the other, as on a totem pole. An archaeologist called Albert Lipsky found about 40 of them in the Minusinsk Steppe and brought them here. More recent ethographical material shows yurts and costumes richly decorated with mother-of-pearl, including highly prized shirt buttons, and with cowrie shells.

Lenin Statue, Pyervomaiskaya Square. Also here are the local government and regional administrative buildings, and it is here that local parades take place in May and November.

War Memorial and Eternal Flame, Pobedy Square, at the end of Lenin Prospect.

Union Monument, in front of the railway station. This commemorates the 250th anniversary of the union between Khakasia and Russia.

Zoo. The collection includes 70 species of animals and birds that live in Siberia and the Soviet Far East.

Town Park, Lenin Prospect 53

Stroitel Stadium, Chkalova Street 41

Torpedo Stadium, Gavan Street 1, in the north-eastern part of the town, by the big park

Racecourse, Kirov Street 18

Lermontov Drama Theatre, Schetinkin Street 14, on Pyervomaiskaya Square. Pyotr Schetinkin (1885–1927) was a Civil War hero.

Skazka (fairy-tale) Puppet Theatre, Karl Marx Street 5

Turist Hotel, in the square at the end of Schetinkin Street. This tall building is built on a Y-shaped plan.

Khakasia Hotel and Restaurant, Lenin Prospect 88; tel. 637–02. There is a souvenir kiosk in the hotel and the local Intourist office is here too. tel. 37–16.

Abakan Hotel, Lenin Prospect 59; tel. 630–26

Kantegir Hotel, near the airport

Abakan Restaurant, Lenin Prospect 65

Khakasia Restaurant, Schetinkin Street 15

GPO, Lenin Prospect

Long-distance Telephone, Schetinkin Street 20

Aeroflot Town Office, Chertyagasheva Street 104; tel. 634–85

Airport Enquiries, TEL. 630–54

Railway Station, Vokzalnaya Street 21

Central Department Store, Pushkin Street 127

Ametist Jewellery Shop, Lenin Prospect

Intourist organises a number of excursions from Abakan, to Minusinsk, Shushenskoye, and the Sayano-Shushensk Hydropower Station.

Minusinsk Population—75,000

This lies east of Abakan across the Yenisei, to the left of the road on the way to Shushenskoye. It was originally a Kazakh settlement, and its name means "my share" (meaning my share of the territory being divided). A reminder of the pride the people took in their horses is shown in the way that local harnesses are still richly decorated in brass. The older part of the town lies across the river Minusa, while the newer part is on the Abakan side. Some of the wooden houses share a common stone wall with their neighbours. As well as having carving around their windows, some have unusual decorations on the insides of the shutters.

Church, in the main square, near the museum. This is a wide, spreading building with a small silver dome and another on the belfry. Inside it is light and bright, and the arches are decorated in patterns reminiscent of a Buddhist temple. Open for services.

Martyanov Local Museum, open 11–6; closed Mon. and Tues. Nikolai Martyanov (1844–1904) organised the collection, and the building was financed by local contributions. Lenin used the library when he was in exile in Sushenskoye. Of particular interest is the winter garden, housing the ancient stone stellae from the steppes, mostly erected as memorial stones, the well-preserved hieroglyphics have been decyphered to give us strangely touching and poetic biographical mementoes from long ago. Martyanov sent a sample exhibit to the Paris Exhibition of 1900 and was awarded a silver medal. In the revolutionary part are some photographs of how the town used to look.

"House 73" is where Lenin's comrades-in-arms, G. Krzhizhanovsky and V. Starkov, lived during their period of Siberian exile. Lenin visited here for a meal in the dining room on the ground floor and to see in the New Year in 1899 in the sitting room upstairs. Both are furnished as they were at the time. Open 11–6; closed Mon. and Tues.

Schetinkin Statue, on the right on Oktyabrskaya Street. The Civil War hero is portrayed in a scarf and fur hat.

Tagarsky Restaurant, named after a local lake and resort

Minutka Café, Gagarin Street 197

It is 85 km (53 miles) from Abakan to the village of Shushenskoye, where Lenin spent his years of Siberian exile from 1897–1900. Excursions there take 7 hours.

The road runs over the broad, rolling, grassy hills of the steppe, where herds of horses graze. There are stretches of pine woods and signs showing the way to a number of Pioneer camps. The road crosses the river Nichka and then the Lugavka, which flows through the sand dunes. There are more pine woods on the northern slopes of the hills, and after a short climb over the watershed that marks the end of Minusinsky Region, a fine view opens out. On the maps the route looks like a mountain road, but it is very gentle country. Much is under the plough, and rows of birches and poplars serve as windbreaks. The only other trees in the stretches of steppe are those growing in the gullies or along the river.

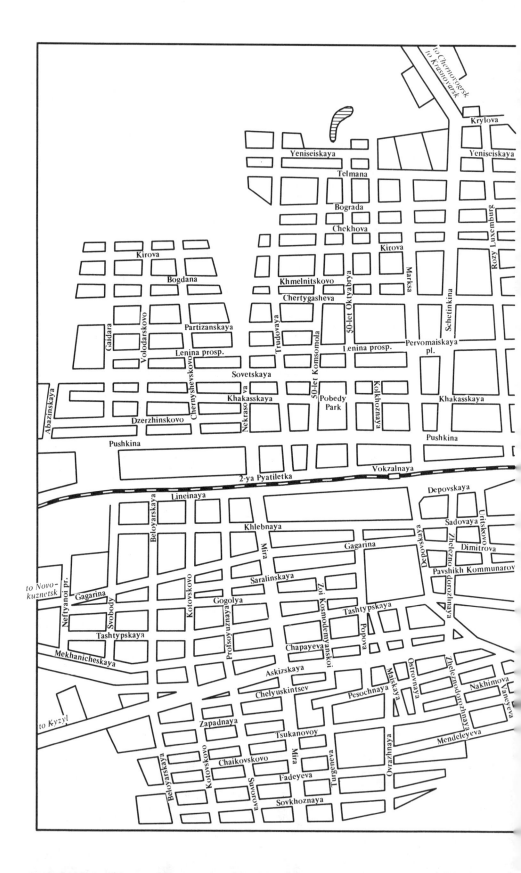

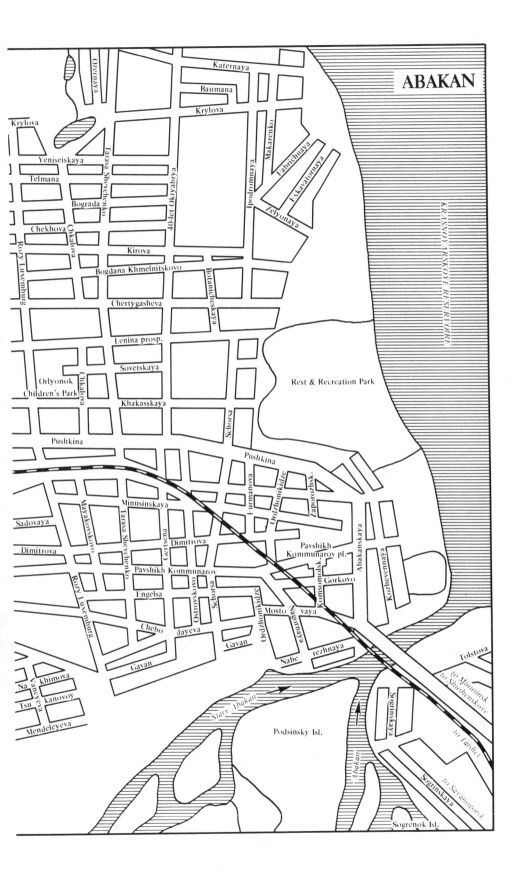

Shushenskoye Population—18,000

Founded by the Russians in 1728 as a fortified settlement on the banks of the river Shush where it flows into the Yenisei, by the end of the 19th century this village was, like others in the area, a place of exile for political prisoners such as the Russian Social Democrats. The village was large, with several streets, rather dirty, dusty—nothing out of the ordinary. It stood in the steppe; there were no gardens or indeed any vegetation at all. Surrounding the village was an accumulation of manure, which was never spread over the fields, but thrown out at the back; in order to leave the village, one almost always had to walk through a certain amount of manure. Off to one side was what the peasants grandly referred to as "the wood," which was in fact no more than a poor little de-forested coppice, lacking even proper shade.

Shushenskoye is particularly well known because Lenin was exiled here in 1897 for revolutionary activities, and it was he who wrote the above description of the place. When he disembarked from the St. Nicholas on 30 April of that year, he was billeted upon a peasant called Zyryanov. The house was square with four rooms, following the typical plan of larger peasant dwellings known as cross-shaped because of the layout of the dividing walls inside.

While he was in Shushenskoye, Lenin wrote a number of theoretical works. In spite of the fact that he was far away and newspapers took 17 days to arrive from St. Petersburg, letters 35 days, he maintained a lively correspondence with revolutionary friends throughout the country. It was here that he completed "The Development of Capitalism in Russia," which he had begun in prison in St. Petersburg, and wrote more than 30 other works. It was here too that his idea to publish the Marxist newspaper "Iskra" was born. He was helped greatly by the members of his family, who kept him informed of all that was taking place in Russia and abroad.

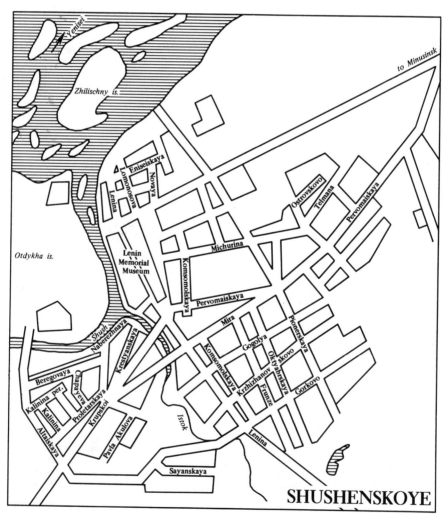

SHUSHENSKOYE

His fiancée, Nadezhda Krupskaya, had been exiled to Ufa Region in 1896 for her own revolutionary activity, and Lenin succeeded in obtaining permission to have her transferred to Shushenskoye to get married. She arrived in May 1898, and her mother, Elizaveta Vasilievna, who volunteered to go into exile with her, came too and stayed. The wedding took place in the local church on July 10. As Zyryanov could spare no more than a single room, they moved into another peasant house, belonging to the widow of a corn merchant named Petrov, where they could have three rooms. This stood right on the bank of the river Shush, and they stayed here until the end of Lenin's exile in 1900. Apart from Lenin's original writing, the couple together completed numerous translations, including material on trade unions by Sidney and Beatrice Webb.

Memorial plaques were put up on both the houses in 1938 following a government decision on the matter, and Nadezhda Krupskaya showed how the rooms were to be furnished. She provided many of their original items, including luggage hampers and Lenin's own pen, but was not well enough to come to Shushenskoye for the opening of the museum. A further government decision led to the opening of the *Lenin Siberian Exile Museum* in April 1970. The museum complex occupies a territory of 6 hectares (15 acres) and includes a reconstruction of the part of Shushenskoye around the small holdings of Zyryanov and Petrova, looking as it did when Lenin was here except that it is now uninhabited. All in all, 29 buildings of the total 267 houses that stood here in 1897 were restored. Apart from Zyranov's and Petrova's houses, they include a tavern and homes typical of a poor peasant, a more wealthy peasant, and a landowner. The village administration building has been reconstructed, as has the prison with three cells and a bathhouse inside a palisade next door, a rich merchant's shop stocked with all sorts of goods from haberdashery to hardware, and the houses where other revolutionaries lived in exile. There was neither a school nor a hospital at the time. It is unusual to see wooden houses now that are roofed with planks of wood instead of the ubiquitous iron sheeting or corrugated asbestos. Besides the houses, the yards also form an important part of the museum. There are wells, barns, and bathhouses, and they demonstrate various small-holding activities such as bee-keeping and threshing, while the gardens are planted with vegetables. Nadezhda Krupskaya planted a little flower garden in Petrova's yard and made a shady seat with hops growing over it. The flowerbed is planted annually as it used to be with pansies, viscaria, mignonette, sweetpeas, and Billy Button daisies. There is also an exposition devoted to Lenin's revolutionary activities. The little memorial by the embankment of the river Shush marks a grave that was there before the museum was opened. The statue of Lenin by Petrova's house is by Tomsky. The museum is open daily from 9–4:30.

Modern Shushenskoye consists of up-to-date blocks of flats, the House of Soviets, a hotel, and a post office, among other buildings. A grand looking club with a columned portico stands in the square in place of the church, which was demolished in 1930. The main local industry is a dried-milk factory and the production of a variety of souvenirs. 50,000 tourists come here each year.

Café, in the square beside the club, opposite the museum.

Souvenir Shop, beside the museum

There are three natural sights of interest in the vicinity of Shushenskoye. Excursions there take 2–2.5 hours including transport.

Crane's Mountain (Zhuravlinaya gorka), 4 km (2 miles) from Shushenskoye

Sandy Mountain (Peschanaya gorka), 5 km (3 miles) from Shushenskoye

Lake Perovo, 10 km (6 miles) from Shushenskoye

Sayano-Shushensk Hydropower Station (GES) is 140 km (87 miles) from Abakan. The route there leads along the valley of the Yenisei and into the Sayansk Hills. A picnic lunch is provided in the taiga.

ABKHASIA

See Sukhumi, p. 505.

ABRAMTSEVO

This estate lies 72 km (45 miles) to the north of Moscow, a little to the west of Yaroslavskoye Chaussée.

Intourist organises excursions here from Moscow. The museum is open 11–5:30; closed Mon., Tues., and 30th or last day of each month.

First mentioned as Obromkovo Pustosh and later known as Abramkovo, situated on the river Vorya close to the Troitse-Sergiyeva Lavra and to the monastery of Khotkovo, this site was ideal for the growth of the estate that was to become so spiritually close to the indigenous, patriarchal traditions of Russian culture. The house at Abramtsevo was built in the 1770s and from 1843–59 was the home of the Slavophile writer Sergei Aksakov. Eminent writers and actors, including Gogol, Turgenev, and Schepkin, visited him there, and it is mentioned in many of their letters.

In the spring of 1870, the estate was purchased by the wealthy industrialist and art connoisseur Savva Mamontov (1841–1918). He shared his interests in arts and crafts with his wife, Elizaveta (1847–1908), and their home became a meeting place and refuge for artists and actors. Repin, Serov, Vasili Polenov (1844–1927) and his sister Elena (1850–98), Victor Vasnetsov, Antokolsky, Korovin, Nesterov, Mikhail Vrubel, Chaliapin, Stanislavsky, and Maria Yermolova were all guests there, among other remarkable contemporaries whose work Mamontov admired. They were united by their recognition of the richness of their country's cultural heritage and their belief that Russian arts would undergo a renaissance through a revival of national traditions. Abramtsevo became famous for the neo-Russian style, and by the end of the 1870s the basis of the Abramtsevo artistic circle was established. Members set great value upon native art and architecture, which were being threatened with extinction by rapid industrial expansion. The sculptor Antokolsky wrote of their aims: "What we wish to see in art are sagas, fairy tales, dramas, the history of the past, and the events of the present."

The homely interior of Abramtsevo and its picturesque surroundings appear in many celebrated pictures by the artists who stayed there. An example is Nesterov's painting, now in the Tretyakov Gallery, "The Young Sergei."

In 1896–98 Vrubel was invited to decorate Alexei Morózov's house in Moscow, where his Faust and Mephistopheles panels were used. He was perhaps the most outstanding artist in the group, and the most individual. Although indebted to both the neo-Russian and the art nouveau styles, his treatment of surfaces anticipated the cubists, and his association with the World of Art society and the symbolists made him a natural link between the decor of Mamentov's Private Opera and that of Diaghilev's Ballets Russes.

September 1881 saw the foundation of the Church of Spas Nerukotvornyi (meaning the Saviour not made by hands) near the house. It was designed by Victor Vasnetsov in the best traditions of 14th-century Novgorodian architecture. The iconostasis was designed and executed by Repin and Vasili Polenov, and Antokolsky assisted with the other decorations. The church was consecrated the following year and was used regularly until the revolution. When Mamontov's second son, Andrei, died in 1891, he was buried in a chapel designed by Victor Vasnetsov and Polenov, built beside the church. Vasnetsov also built the Russian fairy-tale "Hut on Hen's Legs" in the park. In 1885 the carpenter's shop for making carved furniture and souvenirs was organised, and in 1889 the pottery was founded with Vrubel's active participation.

The museum is laid out to describe the two eras of the house, the first rooms telling of the time when it was owned by Aksakov and the last showing it as it was after 1870 when it was an active arts centre. There are a number of portraits and paintings in the museum as well as colourful majolicas by Vrubel.

ABRAU-DURSO
See Novorossiisk, p. 392.

ADLER
See Sochi environs, p. 494.

AGARTSIN
See Erevan environs, p. 137.

AINAZHI
See Riga, p. 451.

ALA-ARCHA RAVINE
See Bishkek, p. 80.

ALIBEKSY GLACIER
See Kislovodsk, p. 240.

ALMA-ATA
Alma-Ata is the capital of the Kazakh Soviet Socialist Republic.

KAZAKHSTAN
Area: 1,064,000 sq miles, Population—16,538,000, of which 40.8 percent are Russian, 36 percent Kazakh, 6.1 percent Ukrainians; the remainder includes Tatars and Uzbeks

Kazakhstan is situated in the middle of the Eurasian continent. It stretches west almost to the river Volga and the Caspian Sea and eastwards to the Altai Mountains. In the southeast it borders China. Its capital is Alma-Ata, and other major towns are Chimkent, Karaganda, Petropavlovsk, Semipalatinsk, Akmolinsk, and Uralsk.

The climate is mostly continental and dry, so the country is mainly steppe and semidesert with forests covering no more than 5 percent of the territory. There is black earth in the north, and in the southeast are some places with a comparatively mild climate.

Kazakhstan is very rich in minerals, including gold, coal, iron ore, copper, and several other nonferrous metals. The principal industries are coal, iron, and copper mining, oil extraction and processing, engineering, and chemical industries, which have been developing since the 1950s. Local agriculture is concerned with growing rice, cotton, and fruit in the south, while in the north cattle breeding and wheat growing are predominant. This country was one of the major areas to be developed during the 1953–56 virgin lands campaign.

After the death of Genghis Khan, the strength of the Mongols diminished, and a new khanate called Ak-Orda (the White Horde) was established, covering all the territory from the Aral Sea to the river Ishym. Its rulers were the descendants of Genghis Khan and known as "ak-seuk" ("white bone") while their subjects, "black bones," were the local cattle-breeding nomads, people of Mongolian and Turkic origin. The nomads were known as Kazakhs, and although they belonged to a variety of tribes, they all spoke the same Turkic language. The name Uzbek was reserved for the military aristocracy, who were more inclined to a settled way of life.

By 1500 the Uzbek khan Sheibani had captured all Central Asia, but the rolling steppe land to the north remained in the hands of the Kazakhs, and three khanates were formed there. They were continually threatened by the Uzbeks but retained their independence. In 1594 the Kazakh khan Tevekkel sent envoys to the Russian tsar to request help. The fighting continued over the years, and succeeding khans sought Russian protection. Khan Abdulkhair of the Lesser Horde submitted to Russian domination in 1730, but it was not until 1738 that the Empress Anna Ivanovna finally agreed to accept full responsibility. The decision was followed by the construction of fortresses and defence lines manned by Russian military units.

In the early 19th century, Russia refused to support the Kazakh khans, and as their power weakened and the Hordes were divided among sultans, Russian encroachment increased. The sultanates of Khiva and Bokhara maintained a strong resistance, and the Kazakh sultans followed their example and sought their support. The tsarist forces moved from their outposts into the steppes, where they formed their own Cossack villages. Kazakhstan was fully incorporated into the Russian state after the defeat of the Kokand khanate in 1864–65. Thereafter the influence of Russian culture upon Kazakhstan grew stronger. The Uzbeks, by contrast, had their own literary tradition, but the nomadic Kazakhs retained an oral tradition and their writers and scholars were keen to learn from Russia. At the time of the Russian famine of 1891–92, large numbers of Russian peasants wended their way eastward along the route of the newly laid Siberian railway track and settled in Kazakhstan. In fact they arrived in such numbers that the population of Kazakhstan rose by 30 percent at the time. The opening of the railway line between Russia and Central Asia faciliated the growth of trade, and Kazakh meat and dairy products were able to reach foreign markets. In return an increasing number of foreign investments were made in Kazakh industry. There were still, however, periods of unrest, and several Kazakh uprisings; that of 1916 led by a Bolshevik called Amangeldy Imanov was particularly violent. Tsarist troops were diverted from suppressing it completely because of the revolution that broke out in Petrograd in February 1917.

In 1920 the Kirghiz Autonomous Republic was set up in the region; in 1925 the area was enlarged and renamed the Kazakh Autonomous Republic; and in 1936 it became the Kazakh Soviet Socialist Republic.

Souvenirs from Kazakhstan include pottery vases, silk chiffon scarves, and holders for tea-glasses, all decorated with traditional local designs. A few words in Kazakh:

hello	salem
I am a tourist	men tourist
thank you	rakhmet
yes	ya
no	zhok
good	zhaksy
bad	zhaman
I don't understand	men tsusinbaimen
please fetch me an interpreter	magan tilmash kerek
good-bye	hosh bolinyz
how do you do?	hal kalai

Alma-Ata (Verny until 1921) Population—1,128,000
Alma-Ata, since 1929 capital of the Kazakh Soviet Socialist Republic, lies to the south of the Kazakh Steppe, at 650–950 m (2,100–3,100 ft) above sea level in the foothills of the snowcapped Zailiysky Alatau range. China is 300 km (185 miles) away to the south across the mountains. On either side of Alma-Ata flow the Bolshaya Almaatinka and the Malaya Almaatinka rivers. In summer the temperature may rise to 40°C (104°F), and the winter extreme is −34°C (−28.1°F), although temperatures are usually milder. The town is famous for its Aport apples, which sometimes weigh 500 g (18 oz) each; Alma-Ata literally means "father of apples."

Nomads lived on this site in the centuries before Christ. According to the reports of a 7th-century Chinese traveller and of Marco Polo who came this way in the 13th century, there was a town here which they referred to as Almalyk and Almatu. It was of some commercial importance in the 13th and 14th centuries but was laid waste by the Tatars and never recovered. The area often changed hands among different nomadic tribes, and at the beginning of the 18th century, it was conquered by the Kalmyk commander Galdan Tseren. It thus became part of the Kalmyk state ruled by Dzhungarsky Khan until 1757, when it became part of Kokand khanate.

In 1853 a Russian military unit headed by Peryemyshalsky explored the valleys of the Almaatinkas. The following year a military fortress was built on the site of ancient settlements at a strategic point where routes from Central Asia to Siberia and West China crossed. It was called Zailiiskoye and had 2,500 inhabitants. There were barracks, two houses for officers, and a storehouse, all surrounded by a sand rampart. A year later it was renamed Verny ("reliable"). Soon after the decisive battle between the Kokand khan and the Russian units in 1860, Cossack and Tatar settlements sprang up beside the fortress. In 1867 Verny, by this time with a population of 6,000, was declared a town and was given a coat-of-arms: a shield entwined in a garland of apple branches with fruit: on its upper part was a fortress; on the lower, a cross and a crescent, symbolising the coexistence of Muslims and Christians under military authority. During the next 30 years, many Russian and Ukrainian families were encouraged to make their homes here, and in 1870, by a special order of General Kolpakovsky, who served as governor at that time, every householder was obliged to plant at least five trees along his part of the street. Today Alma-Ata is appropriately known as the Garden City.

In 1887 all but one of the town's 1,788 houses were destroyed by an earthquake. It was then decreed that only single-storey houses of wood should be built, except in the centre, where a few two-storey buildings were allowed. Thus, when the next earthquake occurred in 1911, the damage was not so disastrous as before. One of the more important streets at this time was Kolpakovsky Prospect, lined by the best and most important buildings in town.

In the 1890s Verny began to be used as a place of exile for political prisoners, and it was they who were behind some of the political demonstrations and strikes in 1905–7. It is recorded that the town

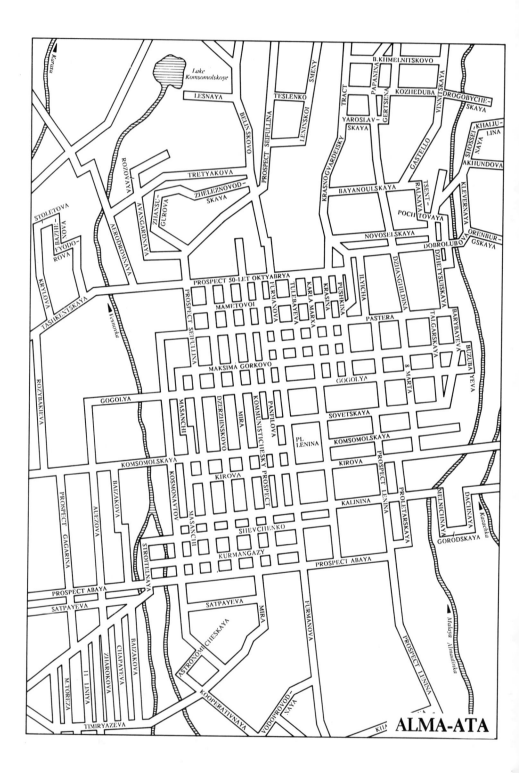

ALMA-ATA

council in 1915 turned down a proposal to install more street lamps because "respectable citizens stay at home after dusk."

After the 1917 revolution, Verny was included in the Turkestan Soviet Republic, and in 1921 its name was changed to Alma-Ata. It became the capital of Kazakhstan (instead of Kzyl-Orda) in 1929 and thereafter developed rapidly, especially with the completion of the Turksib (Turkestano-Sibirskaya) railway, which had been started in 1927.

Komsomolskaya Street crosses the city from east to west, dividing it roughly in half. There are many educational establishments along its 10-km (6-mile) length. At its intersection with the main street, Kommunistichesky Prospect, is the civil and business centre, as well as the local film studios. Alma-Ata's largest buildings are in the blocks nearby, lining Kirov, Vinogradov, Mira, and Kalinin streets. The tallest building of all, which towers above the others, is the *new Government House*. This five-storey (40-m/131-ft) building designed by Rubanenko is decorated with granite and marble. In Revolution (formerly Brezhnev) Square in front of it, where parades and demonstations take place, is a 7-m (23-ft) *Lenin Monument* by Evgeni Vuchetich. Opposite stands the *old Government House*, built by Ginzburg in the 1930s in the constructivist style, which was soon to be adversely criticised and officially frowned upon. There are, however, some other buildings in Alma-Ata of the same period and style. This building now accommodates some faculties of the university. *Kirov State University* (founded in 1934) has several faculties and is attended by 14,000 students, with another 3,000 taking correspondence courses. There are 15 other higher-educational establishments in addition to the university.

The old Kolpakovsky Prospect is now *Lenin Prospect* and still one of the main streets of the city, with the Kazakhstan Hotel and state and party buildings, and other modern buildings, especially where it crosses Abai Prospect and Revolution Square.

Kommunistichesky Prospect is a 4-km (2-mile) avenue that connects the railway station with the upper part of the city. Many government buildings and offices are located here. All new buildings are designed to be earthquake-proof. The *Kazakh Academy of Sciences*, Shevchenko Street, which crosses Kommunistichesky Prospect, was founded in 1946 and supervises the work of more than 20 research institutes. The architect of its main building was Schusev.

Gorky Street (formerly Trade Street) is the site of most of the shops. The old market square, at the crossing with Pushkin Street, has been rebuilt, still incorporating the market, as the *Alma-Ata Shopping Centre*.

Alma-Ata is beautifully located with snowy peaks rising up in the background and verdant greenery along the straight, wide streets, with little "aryks" (irrigation canals) flowing beside them.

Over 10 million trees have been planted here since the city was founded.

The town is laid out rather like a chessboard. 3–5 km (2–3 mile) avenues run from north to south, and in the extreme south, they begin to climb uphill, so that every block is 4 m (13 ft) higher than the one before it. There are typical Siberian wooden houses, white-walled Ukrainian houses, and the mud-brick houses of Asia. People spend most of the time outdoors. There are old houses at Furmanova Street 99 and 162. The newest parts of Alma-Ata are the suburbs in the southwest and the northwest.

The city's industry includes food, tobacco, engineering, textiles, leather, printing, and film-making. Among the souvenirs offered for sale are attractive vases and scarves decorated with traditional national designs. There is a Champagne factory in Gogol Street.

The following religious buildings are all open for services:

St. Nicholas's Cathedral, Kalinin Street 46. Built in 1914.

Church of Our Lady of Kazan, Malaya Stanitsa
Church of the Intercession, Dzerzhinsky Street.
Mosque, Pushkin Street 16
Synagogue, Proletarskaya Street 48

Other places of interest are *Alma-Ata City Museum*, 28 Panfilov Guardsmen Park. The museum is housed in the domed Ascension Cathedral, erected in 1907 by Andrei Zenkov (1863–1935). It claims to be the second-tallest wooden building in the world; the six storeys of the belfry are all separate, and the whole is 54.5 m (179 ft) high and built without a single nail. The interior was painted by Nikolai Khludov (1865–1934). Open 10–7, closed Tues.

Central Museum of Kazakhstan, Samal Mikrorayon 44, near Revolution Square. Open 10:30–5, closed Tues.

Kasteyev Kazakhstan State Museum of Fine Arts and Art Gallery, Satpayeva Street 30a. Abilkhan Kasteyev (1904–73) was a Kazakh artist, known for his historical and revolutionary themes, as well as for his landscapes and portraits. The 15 halls of the museum exhibit over 15,000 works of Kazakh, Russian, Soviet, and Western artists. There are also rare works by Chinese and Indian artists on display. Open 11–7, closed on the last two days of each month.

Union of Painters' Art Exhibition Hall, Panfilov Street 92. Open 11–7, closed Mon.

Shoqan Valiqan-uli Archaeology, History and Ethnography Museum, Lenin Prospect 44. Called Chokan Valikhanov in Russian, Shoqan Shingisuli Valiqan-uli (1835–65) was an outstanding orientalist, historian, ethnographer, traveller, and scholar. The museum is attached to a scientific research institute and is housed in the ground floor of a 3-part block of flats. Open 10–5, closed Mon., Sat., and Sun.

Kazakh Folk Instruments Museum, on the east side of 28-Pantfilovtsev Park, opposite the memorial. The museum is located in a house dating back to the 19th century, which is rare in Alma-Ata. It is equipped with tape recorders so that visitors can hear the sound of each musical instrument. Open 10–7, closed Mon. and Tues.

Combat Glory Museum, Proletarskaya Street 24

Natural History Museum, Shevchenko Street 28

Public Health Museum, Furmanov Street 92a. In a fine old building known as Vernen House, the museum is open 9–6, closed Mon.

Geological Museum, Kalinin Street 65

Mukhtar Auezov Memorial Museum, Tulyebayev Street 185. The local writer Mukhtar Auezov (1897–1961) lived and worked in this house during the last years of his life. The city theatre is named for him. Open 10–5, closed Fri. and Sat.

Shoqan Valiqan-uli Statue, Shevchenko Street, in front of the Academy of Sciences. (For information on Valiqan-uli, see above, Archaeology Museum.)

Qunanbay-uli Statue, Abaya Prospect. Abay Qunanbay-uli (1845–1904) (Abai Kunanbayev in Russian) is the Kazakh poet and composer who is honoured as the founder of the Kazakh literary language. The opera house bears his name.

Amangeldi Iman-uli Equestrian Statue, in a garden off Kommunistichesky Prospect. Amangeldi Iman-uli (1873–1919) was a local hero who led the national independence campaign in 1916. He later became a Communist. The statue by Askar Sarydzha was unveiled in 1950.

Civil War Heroes Monument, 50-lyetya Oktyabrya Square

Bokin Monument, Karl Marx Street, at the entrance to Panfilov Park. Tokash Bokin (1890–1918) was a leader of the national liberation movement who was killed in the Civil War. He was a translator and compiled the first Kazakh-Russian dictionary. It had 1,802 words and was published in 1913. The monument was sculpted in grey granite by Abishev in 1980.

Yemelev Monument, at the crossing of Lenin Prospect and Gogol Street. Lukian Yemelev (1894–1919) was a young revolutionary who was killed in 1919. His monument, in cast iron on a granite pedestal, was sculpted by Mergenov in 1961.

Mikhail Frunze Monument, Dzerzhinsky Park. Civil War hero Mikhail Frunze lived in Verny from 1896–1904.

Maxim Gorky Monument, Gorky Recreation Park, at the end of Gorky Street

Furmanov Monument, Furmanov Street. Dmitry Furmanov (1867–1926) was a Soviet writer and Civil War hero who lived part of his life in Alma-Ata.

Felix Dzerzhinsky Monument, Dzerzhinsky Street

Kirov Monument, Komsomolskaya Street

Vinogradov Bust, in a small garden at the crossing of Vinogradov and Dzerzhinsky streets, just in front of the Russian Drama Theatre. Pavel Vinogradov (1889–1932) was head of the first Bolshevik

organisation in this area, and he lived in Alma-Ata after his retirement. This bronze bust on a red granite pedestal was sculpted by Urmanche in 1956.

Djandosov Monument, at the crossing of Djandosov and Gagarin streets. Uraz Djandosov (1899–1939) was an educationalist and Communist party activist of Kazakhstan. The cast-iron bust was unveiled in 1969.

Panfilov Monument, Panfilov Street. Major-General Panfilov was sent from Alma-Ata to help defend Moscow in 1941. Twenty-eight men withstood an attack by 50 enemy tanks and were justly awarded the title Heroes of the Soviet Union.

Lugansky Bust, Kommunistichesky Prospect, in front of the Town Hall. Major-General Sergei Lugansky (1918–77) was a pilot who became a national hero during World War II.

Eternal Glory Monument, with eternal flame, Panfilov Park. The figures of soldiers rush forward in all directions, backed by the red battlements of Moscow's Kremlin wall.

Abai Opera and Drama Theatre, Kalinin Street 112. The company was founded in 1934 and the designer Prostakov, had the theatre built in 1941 with favourite Kazakh colours and ornaments used for the decor. It can seat 1,250.

Auezov Kazakh Drama Theatre, Abai Prospect

Lermontov Russian Drama Theatre, Abai Prospect 43

Uigur and Korean Music and Drama Theatre, Dzerzhinsky Street 83

Youth Theatre, Kommunisticheskaya Prospect 21

Circus, Abai Prospect 50. The building resembles a yurt.

Philarmonia Concert Hall, Kirov Street 158. The Kurmangazi Orchestra of National Instruments gives concerts here.

Lenin Palace, at the crossing of Lenin and Abai prospects. It can seat 3,000 and is also used for political meetings and artistic performances. Its wide façade overlooks a pool with fountains.

Central Stadium, Mechnikova Street. This stadium can seat 35,000.

Exhibition of People's Achievements, Satpaev Street. Besides the 10 exhibition pavilions, there is Dostyk Restaurant on the grounds, a cinema, and a shop. Open 9–6, closed Tues.

Artificial Lake, near the airport. The construction of this lake was finished in 1961. Now it is popular recreation area with bathing beaches and places where boats can be hired.

Gorky Park, Gogol Street, in the eastern part of the city, on the right bank of the Malaya Almaatinka. Here is the Aral Restaurant, some cafés, and a restaurant serving Kazakh national food. Here too boats can be hired. There is a dance hall, Spartak Stadium, an open-air theatre, and a children's railway called the small Turksib Railway. The park covers 7 hectares (17.5 acres). The oldest part of it was planned as a public garden in 1866. The beautiful central avenue is over a mile long.

Zoo, Klevernaya Street 126. The zoo, which is near Gorky Park, was founded in 1937 and covers a territory of 20 hectares (50 acres).

Children's Park, Kalinin Street, in Pine Park. There is a newly built House of Pioneers here.

Eduard Baum Grove was laid out by Eduard Baum (1850–1921), an outstanding dendrologist, in 1892, along with many other parks and gardens.

Botanical Gardens, in the foothills of the Zailiisky Alatau. The gardens, 850–900 m (2,790–2,950 ft) above sea level, were laid out in 1932.

Otrar Hotel and Restaurant, Gogol Street 65; tel. 33–0002. This is an Intourist hotel and there is an Intourist office here; tel. 33–0026.

Kazakhstan Hotel and Restaurant, Lenin Prospect 52

Alma-Ata Hotel and Restaurant, Kalinin Street 85. There is a souvenir shop here.

Zhetysu Hotel and Restaurant, Kommunistichesky Prospect 55; tel. 39–2807

Alatau Hotel, Kirov Street 142

Turkestan Hotel and Restaurant, Pasteur Street, at the corner of Pushkin Street; tel. 33–3417

Kazakhsky Aul (village) Intourist Camping Site, 25 km (16 miles) from Alma-Ata, near the Sports Complex; tel. 68–89–59. The accommodations are in yurts, the round, portable huts used by the nomads.

Kazakhstan Restaurant, Lenin Prospect 52

Tien-Shan Restaurant, Mendeleyev Street 36

Issyk Restaurant, Panfilov Street 133

Zhuldys (star) Café Restaurant, Panfilov Guardsmen Park

Aul Restaurant, on the summit of Mount Kok-Tyube, reached by cablecar from the Lenin Palace of Sports. It serves Kazakh national cuisine.

Samal Restaurant, on the Medeo Highway

Dzhaylyau Restaurant, on the Medeo Highway

Bank, Panfilov Street

GPO, Kirov Street 134

Kazakhstan Shop, Lenin Street 40

Souvenirs, Furmanov Street 80

Beryozka (foreign-currency) Shop, Furmanova Street 80. Open 10–7.

Intourist organises excursions up the Maloye Alma-Altinskoye Ravine.

Observatory, in Malo-Almatinskoye Uscheliye (Ravine), 12 km (7 miles) from Alma-Ata. This was founded in 1946 and is the largest astronomical centre in the Soviet Union.

Medeo Skating Rink, 22 km (14 miles) from the city, up in the mountains on the left bank of the Malaya Almaatinka. "Medeo" comes from Medeu, the name of a nomad who used to winter in this place. This skating rink, 1,640 m (5,380 ft) above sea level, is used for international competitions, and the surrounding slopes are used for skiing in winter and for climbing in summer.

Lake Issyk used to be a beauty spot outside Alma-Ata, 1,800 (5,906 ft) above sea level and encircled by steep slopes densely covered with Tien Shan spruce, until one day in July 1963 a landslide caused it to disappear entirely. Today Kazakh hydrologists have drawn up a plan to restore the lake by building a dam across the breach where the water poured out. The future basin will serve as a mud trap, calculated to retain over 12,000,000 cubic metres of mud and stones.

Dzhambul Jabay-uli Memorial Museum, 90 km (56 miles) from Alma-Ata. Dzhambul Jabay-uli (1846–1945) was a well-known folk bard who came from a nomad family and wrote patriotic poetry. During the last years of his life, he lived in this house. His mausoleum is nearby.

ALMALYK
See Tashkent, p. 543.

ALUPKA
See Yalta environs, p. 665.

ALUSHTA
See Yalta environs, p. 653.

AMANAUZ
See Kislovodsk, p. 240.

AMAN-KUTAN
See Samarkand, p. 467.

AMBERD FORTRESS
See Erevan environs, p. 132.

ANANURI
See Georgian Military Highway, p. 146.

ANAU
See Ashkhabad, p. 46.

ANDIZHAN Population—293,000
Andizhan is the principal town of the Andizhan region in the southeastern part of Fergana Valley. It stands on the river Andizhan-Sai, 7 km (4 miles) from the Great Fergana Canal. In the Andizhan and Alamyshik hills are deposits of oil and gas. The climate is extreme continental.

This is one of the most ancient towns of the Fergana Valley, and there are many legends about the origin of its name. Some say that it derives from that of Prince Afrasiab's daughter, Adinazhana. Others say that "andi" (Indians) used to live in this area, and this is supported by the ancient cemetery called Indi-Mazari near the town. It is also possible that Andi was the name of the founder of the settlement in the 1st century B.C. while "-dzhan" means his soul. There is a legend that a caravan passing this way was attacked by bandits who killed 10 people, and that the name comes from "un dzhan" (10 souls). More scientific sources hold that an Uzbek tribe called Andi settled here and gave the place its name. The town was called Andukan from the 4th century until the 7th century, when it became known as Andizhan. In 1469 Sultan

Omar-Sheikh wrote of it as Andagan in his book "Zafarnam."

The Great Silk Road, which linked East and West, crossed the river of Andizhan-Sai, and at this point caravanserais were built, as were forges. As the settlement grew, agriculture and crafts developed, until it became a sizeable and important commercial centre. In the 8th and 9th centuries, the area was ruled by Arabs. Then Andizhan became part of the Samanid state, and in the 11th century, it was included in the Karakhanid state. It remained the capital of Fergana Valley until the 13th century. Along with the rest of Central Asia, Andizhan was conquered by the Mongols, and in the 14th century, still an important economical and political centre, it became part of Tamerlane's empire.

In the Middle Ages, during the reigns of Omar-Sheikh and his son Zakhriddin Mukhammed Babur, Andizhan reached the peak of its development and once again became capital of Fergana Valley. Zakhriddin Mukhammed Babur (1483–1530) was an outstanding 15th-century statesman, scientist, and poet who conquered India and founded the Great Mogol empire. In his book "Baburname," he wrote that in Maverannakhr (the lands between the rivers Syr-Darya and Amu-Darya) "there is no fortress except Samarkand and Kesh (modern Shahr-i Sabz) as strong as that of Andizhan." The town itself was encircled by mighty walls with three gates, and by two moats. The fortress of Ark-ichi, in the centre of the town, also had its own moat. (The remains of Ark-ichi are on Krasnoarmaeyskaya Street.) To the southwest of the fortress was a bazaar surrounded by buildings of the ruler's palace (urdu), medressehs, and mosques.

Around Andizhan lay the estates of civil servants. Many poets, writers, and scientists inhabited the town. Culture and science flourished, and the prominent 15th-century musician Khodzha Yusuf was surnamed Andizhanets because he lived here.

Andizhan was also respected as a commercial centre, and the Chinese referred to all the merchants of Fergana Valley as Andizhans. Due to the hot and cold sulphur and ferrous springs, the area became a popular place for cures. It was also a place of pilgrimage. Here was the grave of Khazret Ayub Paigambar, allegedly the prophet of Jove, who was cured of leprosy by the waters, and also that of Kuteibe-bin-Muslim, the 8th-century Arab conqueror of Central Asia who brought Islam here and was killed in 715 by his own warriors.

In 1593 Andizhan was ruled by the Sheibanids and remained the most important town of Fergana Valley. At the end of the 16th century, the Sheibanid state disintegrated, and in 1710 the Kokand khanate was founded. Till 1876 Andizhan was part of the Kokand khanate, being the residence of the ruler of Andizhan.

In the 1870s Russia began to advance into Central Asia, and in August 1875 General Skobelev led a march into the Fergana Valley. The Russians met strong resistance from the soldiers of Sherali-

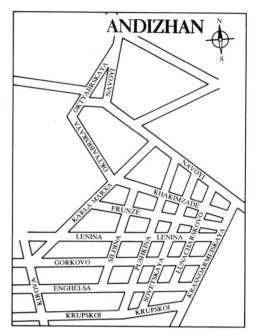

khan, ruler of Andizhan, who formed the bulwarks of the valley's defence. In October 1875 General Trotsky's troops were rebuffed, and in January 1876 Skobelev attacked Andizhan once again. It was bombarded on 8 January and subsequently surrendered. The capture of Andizhan meant that the Kokand khanate was also under Russian control. The Fergana region was established, and Andizhan became the regional centre.

The town was divided into Russian and Asian sections, with the Russian part lying to the southeast and 12 m (40 ft) above the local part. The Asian part was no different from any other settlement of the time. In the north it was crossed by the Andizhan-Sai Canal, which led from the Kara-Darya. The town contained 283 mosques, and its multinational population included Uzbeks, Dungans, Jews, Tatars, Tadzhiks, and Armenians. In 1880–83 the wall between the two parts of the town was destroyed, and the moats filled in.

In 1898 a significant popular uprising took place in the town. As early as 1895, Ismail Khan Tore from Andizhan was arrested in Auliye-Ata (Dzhambul), where he was collecting funds to finance a holy war (ghazawat) to be waged by his disciples. Three years later another revolt broke out in Andizhan and quickly spread to the districts of Osh, Namangan, and Marghilan. Leading the revolt was an ishan (religious leader) of the Sufi Brotherhood of the Naqshbandi, Mohammed-Ali-Kalfa, also known as Madali or Dukchi-Ishan. He was an astonishing figure. Born not far from Marghilan, he was 42 on the eve of the outbreak of the revolt and had gained a reputation for wisdom, holiness, and charity, which spread throughout Fergana. With the help of his disciples, he had by 1889 erected a medresseh and two mosques, and he accumulated a library (though he himself had never learned to read). He also built a minaret of clay without a brick foundation, and in reply to misgivings expressed by some of his followers, he said that the minaret would be held up by his prayers. However, in 1897 it collapsed, killing 5 men, but by this time the ishan had gained such a hold on his followers that no one questioned his judgment, and they quickly erected a new minaret. He planned to restore the former khanate of Kokand at Namangan with his 14-year-old nephew as khan. To defeat the Russian troops, he gave his followers toothpicks, which he said would, if thrust into their "tyubiteikas" (skullcaps), make them invulnerable to iron and bullets and cause the Russian guns to shoot water. He assured them that when he waved his right hand all the enemies on his right would fall; all those on his left, at a wave of his left hand. On the night of 17 May, a great white horse and a golden sword would be sent from heaven to carry the ishan into battle. Rumours spread among the people that the ishan would be aided by the Turkish sultan, the emir of Afghanistan, and even by the English, who had allegedly supplied arms. These, however, were hidden in the mountains, as the toothpicks would be enough. On 17 May 1898, following the 7 o'clock evening service, the ishan, clad in a green robe, appeared on the white horse before his 2,000 men. "In the name of almighty God—to the Holy War," he cried from the saddle and marched on Andizhan. But Russian retaliation was immediate, and the toothpicks did not help. Madali's men were routed in front of the walls by the 20th Line Battalion. 18 of the ishan's warriors were left dead, and the entire action took no more than 15 minutes. The ishan was captured the following day and hanged with his 5 lieutenants. 15 other participants of the rebellion were executed later.

The year 1898 saw both the suppression of the uprising and the construction of the railway that made Andizhan an important junction. The town developed rapidly, growing to absorb the nearby villages of Sarakui and Ravat. Many factories and plants belonging to Russian, local, and foreign owners were built. By the turn of the century, the population of the town had reached 40,000.

The area is subject to earthquakes, and Andizhan suffered many. That of 1902 was especially severe and ruined the palaces and other interesting buildings. 11,000 local and 161 European-type buildings were ruined, and 4,662 lives were lost. In planning the new town, two sections were given over to parks, one of 2.9 hectares (7 acres), now Pushkin Park, and the other of 3.7 hectares (9 acres), now Krupskaya Park. The type of housing changed so that more buildings were of wood or brick (instead of mud-brick) while public buildings and the homes of prominent citizens were designed to withstand earthquakes.

The Russian revolution of 1917 brought revolutionary fervour to Central Asia, and in December 1917 Soviet power was established in Andizhan.

The Civil War that followed and lasted until 1924 was devastating for the town. Present-day industry mainly started to develop during the years of World War II, when some factories and plants were moved here from Moscow, Leningrad, and other major cities. Industry is now represented by machine building, chemistry, cotton ginnery, and various branches of the food industry. There are 4 research institutes in Andizhan.

Dzhami Medresseh and Mosque, Oktyabrskaya Street. It was built with money donated by local inhabitants in 1883–90. During the earthquake of 1902, the medresseh suffered great damage and was renovated in 1903–8 by Usta Yusuf-all Musayev (1869–1947), a prominent local artist.

Local Museum, Alisher Navoi Prospect 111. There are 15,000 items on display.

Atheism Museum, Shakhristanskaya Street 101. This museum was founded in 1967.

Akhunbabayev Musical Drama Theatre, Oktyabrskaya Street 149. It was founded in 1919 and named after Yuldashbai Akhunbabayev, the first president of Uzbekistan.

Akhunbabayev Summer Theatre, in Alisher Navoi Park

Lola Puppet Theatre, Navoi Prospect 2

Babur Library was founded in 1907. There are 250,000 books, including some that are very rare.

Civil War Heroes Monument, in Pushkin Park

Navoi Park, Navoi Prospect. This was laid out on the site of the local ruler's estate. There is an avenue with busts of heroes of the Soviet Union, an obelisk to the heroes of the revolution and a Civil War Memorial Complex. There is also a popular amusement park.

Builders of the Great Fergana Canal Monument

Andizhan Hotel and Restaurant, Oktyabrskaya Street 241, tel. 55–73

Uzbekistan Restaurant, Lenin Street 29

Shark Restaurant, Oktyabrskaya Street 236

GPO, Sovietskaya Street 232

ANGREN
See Tashkent, p. 543.

APSHERON
See Baku, p. 60.

ARKHANGELSKOYE PALACE MUSEUM
See Moscow environs, p. 361.

ARMENIA
See Erevan, p. 121.

ASHKHABAD
Ashkhabad is the capital of Turkmenistan.

TURKMENISTAN, TURKMENIA
Turkmenistan has a population of 3,534,000. There are people of 70 different nationalities here, with Turkmens making up 68.4 percent of them. The rest include 12.6 percent Russians, 8.5 percent Uzbeks, and 2.9 percent Kazakhs, as well as Armenians, Baluchi, and Kurds. The Turkmens orig-

inated from Caucasian cattle-breeding tribes (Parthenians, Marshans, Dakhi, Massagets, and Irkhans) who lived in the steppes and from Turkic nomads of Mongolian stock who came from the east in the 7th century. In the Middle Ages, they were known as Khorossan people.

Turkmenia is the southernmost republic of the Soviet Union. Its borders extend to Iran and Afghanistan. The greater part of its territory is taken up by the vast Kara-Kum (black sands) Desert, and the majority of the population lives in oases stretching along the rivers and canals. Water has always been a problem in these parts, but the situation has been alleviated to a great extent by the building of the Kara-Kum Canal, which already runs 1,200 km (750 miles). There are wide-scale experiments in progress in distilling fresh water from the Caspian, using nuclear energy, but in the meantime fresh water is still shipped across the Caspian Sea from the Caucasian coast to the Turkmeni port of Krasnovodsk, and in many parts of the republic, people rely on traditional methods of collecting snow and rainwater.

Present-day Turkmenistan was once the site of the powerful states of Parthia, Bactria, Khorezm, and Margiana. There were prosperous towns and cities where outstanding scholars, poets, and architects lived and worked. The course of history was suddenly changed in the 13th century by the devastating invasion of Genghis Khan.

Between the 17th and 19th centuries, Turkmenistan was fought for by Persian shahs, Khivan khans, the emirs of Bukhara, and the rulers of Afghanistan. In the 19th century, it became part of the Russian empire. Soviet rule was proclaimed here in 1917, but in 1918 the region was occupied by British troops. Civil war lasted until 1920, and in February 1925 the Turkmeni Soviet Socialist Republic was formed.

The climate here is very hot and dry. The average temperature for July is 29°C (84°F). In winter the sky is usually clear, but sometimes the temperature drops in the northern regions to −29°C (−20°F). Depending upon the geography, above-zero temperatures usually last from 193–276 days each year. The mountains encircling Turkmenia are considered young, and earthquakes are frequent. The most powerful tremors registered (10 on the Richter scale) occurred in 1895 in the Krasnovodsk area and in 1948 in the capital, Ashkhabad. In less than a minute the capital was completely devastated.

The traditional dwelling of the nomadic Turkmen tribes was the "yurta" or "kara-oi," a collapsible tent formed by an intricate wooden framework covered with rush mats and felt. Inside the yurta were laid gaily coloured rugs, and the walls were hung with tapestry and woven bags where clothes and household utensils were kept. Although today most people live in brick houses with a covered terrace on the shady side, the yurta is still very much in evidence. It is often set up near the house as a summer dwelling.

Following ancient tradition, the Turkmens greatly enjoy organising a festival called a "toi" to mark a wedding, the birth of a child (formerly only the birth of a boy baby, but now girls are honoured too), harvest time, and other family and social events. The guests to a toi are given refreshments and are entertained by horse racing, wrestling bouts, and other games.

National dishes include "kara-chorbe" (peppery meat soup) and "fitchi" (meat pies). As in the other republics of Central Asia, "chok-chai" (green tea) is drunk after meals, but there are also some pleasant local wines, for there is a wine factory in Ashkhabad. "Yasman-salik" is a very sweet sherry-type wine, which won a gold medal in Belgrade in 1956. Among others worthy of recommendation are "Kara-uzyum" and "Ter-bash".

National costumes are now giving way to European dress, but many men still wear red or crimson robes over a white shirt and high, shaggy sheepskin hats or smaller ones of astrakhan. The women wear a long sack-dress and narrow trousers trimmed with a band of embroidery at the ankle. The headdress is decorated with coins and pendants, and their national silver jewellery is very striking, especially the heavy bracelets and brooches set with semiprecious stones.

Mosques where services are held can be found throughout the republic. The Turkmens have followed Islam since the 10th century. They belong to the Sunnite sect of Mohammedanism and are led by Iman-Khatib of the Talhatan-Baba mosque, who represents the Ecclesiastical Board of Moslems in Central Asia and Kazakhstan. Many still make the traditional pilgrimage to Mecca, to the Kaaba Temple.

Oil is Turkmenia's basic source of wealth. The republic holds third place in USSR oil production, after the Russian Federation and Azerbaijan. But its fame comes from its rugs, which are exported to over 50 countries and are admired by all visitors. Turkmeni carpet weaving involves truly artistic workmanship. It is said here, "Spread out your rug, and I will read your heart." Often known in Europe as Bukhara rugs, Turkmenian rugs are richly coloured, as a rule in different shades of red. The designs, which are strictly geometrical, vary from tribe to tribe. The republic is also famous for astrakhan pelts (called "karakul" here) and for its horses. The annual output of pelts is the largest in the Soviet Union: 1,200,000. Particularly valued are the pure white ones, which have a moiré effect and look pearly in the sunlight. Strange as it may seem, it is the severe desert conditions and particularly the scantiness of water and fodder that ensure the high quality of karakul. Local pelts are said to retain their qualities for as long as 50 years. Turkmenian horses have long been exported to the east and to Europe, and the Ashkhabad Stud Farm continues the tradition. The Argamak (Akhal-Teke) strain, directly descended from the ancient Oriental horses, is particularly beautiful and has great endurance. It was used to breed Arabian, English, and Persian horses, among others.

A nomadic way of life does not leave much

opportunity for schooling, and it is recorded that before 1917 only seven out of every one thousand Turkmen were literate. Today illiteracy has been almost completely overcome. The Turkmen used to write in Arabic and then changed to Latin letters before changing again, this time to Cyrillic, in 1930; the Turkmeni alphabet includes five extra letters.

Some words in Turkmeni:

hello	salam
I am a tourist	men turist
please	bash uthtene
thank you	sag bol
yes	hova
no	yok
good	govi
bad	ervet
I don't understand	men dushemok
please fetch an interpreter for me	manya dilmachi chagerung
good-bye	hosh sag bolin
how do you do?	kaiplering nakhili

ASHKHABAD Population—398,000
Between 1921 and 1924, Ashkhabad was known as Poltoratsk, and then it resumed its former name, about which the following legend is told.

Once upon a time, there was a young girl called Amu, meaning "desirable," and a boy called Ashik, meaning "love." The ill-fated young couple made Allah angry, and so he turned the girl into a river and the young man into a city, soon to be called Ashik-abad or Ashkhabad, "city-in-love." A desert lay between them, and the lovers never had a chance to meet. Ashkhabad suffered from thirst, but Amu, whose water overflowed, was powerless to help her beloved.

The story is frequently retold today, now that the Kara-Kum Canal brings the waters of the Amu-Darya to Ashkhabad. A Turkmeni proverb says: "Water is more precious than diamonds," and the people relate that when all the peoples of the world were awaiting the gifts of God, they themselves had an abundance of sun and fertile earth but were unlucky with water. Throughout the centuries they have had to strive with Allah for their right to have water. The new canal runs for nearly 1,200 km (750 miles) past once desolate places with such names as Cursed-by-God and No-Road.

The city of Ashkhabad stands in the centre of the Akhal-Teke Oasis. On the northern side, the Kara-Kum Desert borders the city, and to the south the Kopet-Dag Mountains form an encircling amphitheatre. The climate here is of the dry, continental type, with autumn the most pleasant season. Summer temperatures average 40–45°C (104–113°F) in the shade, and 60–70°C (140–158°F) or even higher in the open, making it the hottest place in the Soviet Union. There is no rain at all during the summer months. The population of the city is 48 percent Turkmeni.

In the vicinity is Pessengik-depe, a settlement from the Neolithic era, 6 millenium B.C. making it the second-most ancient settlement in the world.

Ashkhabad was founded in 1881 by the Russians on the site of a village also called Ashkhabad. The place was taken without a single shot by Russian general Mikhail Skobelev (1843–82) and for many years served as a Russian military stronghold in the area. Its coat-of-arms shows a camel with 1881 above and 1892 below. The first civilians to settle were Russian traders and retired servicemen. Other ethnic groups included Persians, Armenians, and Jews. It is recorded that in 1886 every second man was a member of a merchant family. The population grew rapidly with the construction of the railway but halted for a short time in 1892 because of an epidemic of cholera. Trade with Persia stimulated business, and Ashkhabad stood on the cross-roads of the trade routes. A considerable proportion of Soviet-Iranian trade still goes through this city, which lies 40 km (25 miles) from the Iranian border.

It was the railway workers who were responsible for the strikes here in 1905–7, and soon after the 1917 revolution, in December of that year, Soviet power was established. This was overthrown, and the city was run by Muslim nationalists and anti-Bolshevik representatives, who were known as the Trans-Caspian Government; the British at that time supported the anti-Bolshevik forces in Ashkhabad. Soviet power was restored in 1919, and the city was renamed Poltoratsk in honour of Commissar Pavel Poltoratsky, who was shot during the revolt. The following year the city was made the centre of the Turkmenia region, becoming the capital of Turkmenia in 1924.

The fortress in the centre became the focal point of the new town; it used to stand on the small hill behind the Turkmenistan Hotel, oppsite the museum. The military barracks had to be accommodated too, and radial streets were planned to fan out to the south, the southwest, and the west and also to run parallel to the railway line. The area of the city now measures nearly 6,000 hectares (2,500 acres). The distance across it from northeast to southwest is about 22 km (14 miles). The majority of the population lives in the hilly southwestern sector, while the north is mostly occupied by offices, colleges, and factories. Following the earthquake in 1929, the Institute of Anti-Seismic Construction has played an important role in the growth of the city. Builders now use a great deal of reinforced concrete, and one building incorporates springs in its foundations. A terrible 9-point earthquake with its epicentre only 25 km (16 miles) southeast of the city occurred on the night of 5 October 1948. This quake ruined the city, especially the houses made from mud bricks and roofs of mud. The local museum was one of the only 12 buildings to remain standing. After the earthquake factories were moved to the suburbs, and new houses were designed to withstand future earthquakes. New buildings sprang up along the original city street plan because trees and drainage channels had not been disturbed.

The city is now twice the size it was before the

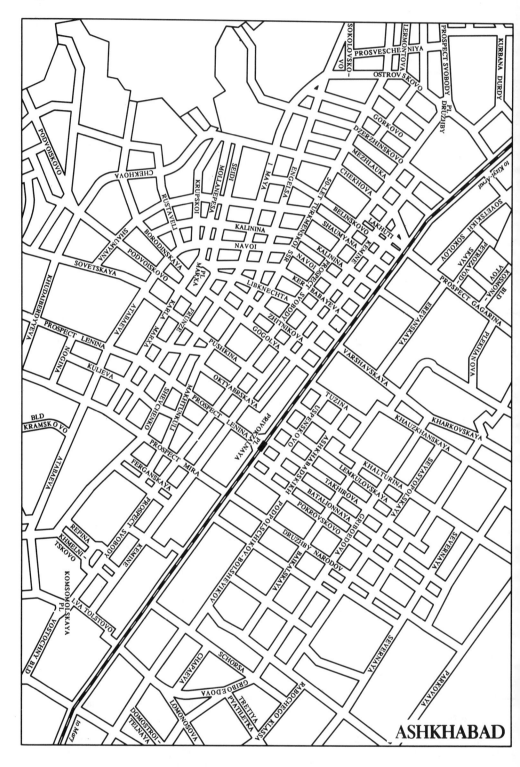

ASHKHABAD

earthquake. There are 50 industrial enterprises, producing food, carpets, glass, and machinery. Gorky University was founded in 1960. 10,000 students attend it or the agricultural and medical institutes and other colleges in the town. This is a considerable achievement when one realises that, before the revolution of 1917, not a single Turkman had higher education. The local Academy of Sciences controls 12 research institutes. Its main building is a large block on Gogol Street.

The Communist Party Headquarters on Karl Marx (formerly Bolshaya Officerskaya) Street is decorated with traditional local designs and a fine bas-relief by Ernst Neizvestny). In *Karl Marx Square* (formerly known as Skobelev Square), a fountain and flowerbeds are being laid out, following the designs of local carpets. The buildings around this square include the Town Hall, Aeroflot's offices, the Turkmeni Ministry of Culture, the main bank, and the central library. From here streets radiate to the centre of the city and to the suburbs. Gogol Street crosses the city's three main streets, 1-May and Engels streets and Svobody Prospect. The *offices of the Supreme Soviet and the Council of Ministers*, decorated with traditional designs, stand on Gogol Street near the Turkmenistan Hotel, and opposite is the *Khudozhestvenny Cinema*.

St. Nicholas's Church (Russian Orthodox), at the cemetery

Fine Art Museum, Svobody Prospect 84. Open 11–7; closed Tues. The collection was founded in 1939, and now the 6,000 exhibits include paintings, sculpture, and graphics by local, Russian, and foreign artists. There are examples of local craftsmanship, perhaps the most interesting of which are the carpets. The pride of the museum is an enormous carpet of 192 sq m (2,067 sq ft), made as a curtain for Moscow's Bolshoi Theatre. There is also a collection of Eastern works of art.

Local Museum, Svobody Prospect. Open 11–5; closed Thurs.

Turkmenian History Museum, Shevchenko Street 1, in the former residence of the governor-general. Open 10–6; closed Mon.

Art Exhibition Hall, 1-May Street 4. Open 10–6; closed Mon.

Kerbabayev Literary House-Museum, Khivali Babyev Street 3. This was the home of the poet Berdy Kerbabayev (1894–1974).

Carpet Factory and Museum, Liebknecht Street 23, at the crossing with Svobody Prospect. Here about 200 workers are trained and employed to produce what are known throughout the world as Bukhara carpets. In fact every Turkmeni tribe had its own carpet ornament, and these are faithfully reproduced today. Most popular of all have always been the Tekke carpets, but the name Bukhara was used to describe them because they were marketed there. Many of the local girls working here wear their national dress. The sharp curved knife they use for cutting the wool is called a "kesser." The museum is on the first floor. Among the exhibits are reversible carpet portraits. Local souvenirs manufactured here include tiny carpets, carpet chair seats, handbags, and other articles, all woven in authentic designs.

Economic Achievements Exhibition, Atabayeva Street. Open 11–5:30; closed Mon.

Lenin Monument, in Lenin Garden. The bronze statue of Lenin pointing to the east by Tripolskaya was begun at the time of Lenin's funeral in Moscow in 1924 and unveiled in 1927. The unusual pedestal is decorated with carpet patterns executed in majolica tiles by Nazarov. Inside the pedestal is the Lenin Museum.

Mahtum Quli Monument, near the Fine Art Museum. Mahtum Quli (1733–1782), also known as Azadi Oghli Fragi, was a poet and philosopher and founder of Turkmeni classical literature. He pleaded for unity among the warring Turkmeni tribes and maintained a hostile attitude toward the local religious leaders. The monument by Victor Popov was unveiled in 1970. The inscription on the pedestal reads, "Mahtum Quli will always be remembered by his descendants; he was indeed the mouth of the Turkmen people."

Kemine Monument, Ferganskaya Street. Mamed-veli Kemine (1770–1840) was a Turkmen satirical poet.

War Memorials, in the garden between Universitetskaya and Karl Marx squares. One is dedicated to soldiers of World War II and the other to revolutionary fighters.

Mollanepes Turkmenian Drama Theatre, Kemine Street 79. The building is embellished with local designs and colours.

Mahtum Quli Opera and Ballet Theatre, Engels Street 9. This theatre was founded in 1941.

Pushkin Russian Drama Theatre, 1-May Street 19. It was founded in 1926.

Philharmonic Society, Oktyabrskaya Street 3. This comprises a choir, a dance ensemble, and an orchestra of national instruments. The concert season lasts from May till October.

Ashkhabad's oldest park is the one with the longest name: the *Twentieth Anniversary of the Founding of the Young Communist League Park*, Svobody Prospect 69. Here there is a summer theatre, a disco club, a restaurant, an amusement arcade, and a sports area.

Kirov Park, Svobody Prospect

Soviet Army Officers' Park, in front of the university

Botanical Garden, Timiryazev Street 16. This garden was founded in 1930 and now contains about a thousand different species of trees and shrubs. There are Victoria waterlilies, cacti, and palms. Opposite is the Kalinin Agricultural Institute.

Sad Keshi Botanical Garden, 1-May Street

Republic Stadium, opposite the wine factory

Turkmenistan (Intourist) Hotel and Restaurant, Gogol Street 19; tel. 58–35

Ashkhabad Hotel and Restaurant, Svobody Prospect 74; tel. 57393

Oktyabrskaya (Intourist) Hotel and Restaurant, Prospect Svobody 67

Gulistan Restaurant, 1-May Street 8. The restaurant is on the first floor, while the ground floor is run as a café. "Gulistan" means "the country of flowers," and the same name is carried by a new shopping centre built of concrete in national "girikh" style.

Gorka Shashlik Bar, on the small hill behind the Turkmenistan Hotel. This is in the open air. There are tearooms at all the markets.

Bank, Svobody Prospect 73

Telephone and Telegraph Office, Engels Street 18

GPO, at the crossing of Karl Liebknecht and Mopr streets. Liebknecht Street is in the centre of the main shopping area. Here are:

Department Store, at the crossing with 1-May Street 15

Beryozka Gift Shop, Engels Street 30

Altyn (jeweller's), Kerbabayeva Street 27

Central Bookshop, Engels Street

Paintings and Objets d'Art, 1-May Street and Karl Marx Street 14

Taxi Stand, in front of the Mahtum Quli Opera and Ballet Theatre

Water Sports Park, 15 km (9 miles) out of Ashkhabad. The fine beaches here date from the completion of the third section of the Kara-Kum Canal on 12 May, 1962.

Intourist organises a variety of excursions from Ashkhabad. These include a chance to visit a yurta, to try on Turkmen national dress, and to go camel riding. There are also excursions to see the Kara-Kum Canal and Firyuza Ravine and to visit Anau, Nisa, and Bakharden, all described below.

Kara-Kum Canal

The idea of using the waters of the river Amu-Darya to irrigate the Kara-Kum Desert was conceived in the 18th century. Long ago the river had flowed into the Caspian Sea, and so some Turkmen went to St. Petersburg to ask the help of Peter the Great in turning the river back to its ancient bed.

Projects were drawn up in 1906, 1908, and 1912, but they were never realised. The 1952 project of Igor Boltenkov was divided into five stages. It began from the Amu-Darya at Mukry to the river Murgab at Mari, then led to the river Tezhen, then flowed beyond Ashkhabad to Geok-Tepe, and the fourth part reached Kazanzhyk in 1981. The canal now runs for 1,200 km (750 miles); when the fifth section is completed it will be about 1,340 km (833 miles) long. Four reservoirs have been built in its vicinity, and the canal is navigable for 800 km (almost 500 miles).

Anau

12 km (7 miles) to the southeast of Ashkhabad is Anau, a valuable trip for those interested in old civilisations. The name derives from Abi-Nau, meaning "new water." The site was inhabited from the 3rd to the 1st centuries B.C. Excavations began

in 1904 when an American archaeologist, R. Pempelli, launched an expedition. The site includes a great wall and a ditch, as well as clay pillars. The remains of ancient towns are scattered between the mountains and the railway line. The remains of a mausoleum stand on one of the slopes; it is supposed to have been built by a great-grandson of Tamerlane. The mausoleum is to be restored. Excavations have revealed that one of the embankments near the mausoleum was erected in the 3rd century B.C. immediately after the decline of Alexander the Great's empire. Some bejewelled skeletons of children were found in a nearby cemetery.

A mosque was built here in 1455 by Khan Abdul Qasim-Babir. The story of its foundation is that a dragon went to the town for help. There he met two woodcutters, and they set off together to free another dragon that was pinned down by a log. When he was freed he gave them two rich jewels, and they used the money to build the mosque. Two red and yellow dragons were depicted on the façade, and they were regarded as sacred beasts. The mosque was destroyed by the earthquake of 1948, but is to be rebuilt. In the meantime the location is still hallowed as the site of the grave of Sheikh Dzhemaletdin. Childless couples bring children's clothes here as an offering, and baby dolls are swaddled and left in tiny hammocks slung between two sticks.

Nisa

Nisa, known locally as Nusai, is 16 km (10 miles) to the northeast of Ashkhabad near the village of Baguir in a picturesque valley watered by a mountain spring. It is the legendary and enigmatic capital of the Parthian state which was founded in the 3rd century B.C. under Tiridate I and reached prosperity under Mithridates I (171–138 B.C.). With its possessions stretching to Syria in the west and India in the east, it rivaled the power of Rome. The army of the Roman commander Crassus, which had put down the slave uprising led by Spartacus, suffered an utter defeat after confronting the Parthian troops, with 20,000 dead and 10,000 prisoners exiled to Merv (then Margiane). Sometimes the capital was called Parthinisa or, by the Greeks, Nisaya. But during the reign of Mithridates, it was renamed Mithridatokert. It grew on the site of a family estate. The town itself spread over 18 hectares (45 acres), with the citadel in its southern part. This was surrounded by a wall 7 km (4 miles) long and reinforced by 43 rectangular towers.

Inside the fortress were administrative buildings, barracks, and many dwellings. In the northern part stood the royal palace, a fortified castle, its audience hall about 400 sq m (4,305 sq. ft.) with 3-m (10-ft)-thick colour-washed walls; it was also decorated with half-columns of brick. The upper parts of the walls were painted dark red and decorated with wooden columns. There were statues, presumably of the king and the queen, made of clay, in niches created between these columns; the statues were as high as 2.5 m (8 ft). The floor was covered with luxurious carpets and according to the famous historians Strabon and Pliny, Parthia was renowned for its carpets. Another sizeable building in the northern part of the Mithridatokert was most probably used as a place for honouring the deceased. It consisted of 12 rooms with the ceiling supported with pillars. This site archaeologists call Old Nisa. Around it is the settlement of New Nisa, which also has the remains of a fortress with powerful walls flanked with towers. There was only one entrance to the fortress, and it still exists today. In the northwestern part one can see the ruins of the necropolis of the nobility of Parthia along with a religious complex. The traces of the necropolis were damaged badly during the 1948 earthquake, but nevertheless the remains of an artisan's quarter can be seen. It was here that beautiful china was excavated with markings of the Chinese Ming dynasty. In the southern part of the site were some administrative and other buildings, including storehouses for wine and grain.

In the 6th century B.C. Nisa was taken by the Arabs without any resistance on the part of the inhabitants, and starting from the 10th century A.D. it suffered from local strife. In those times, however, its silk and cotton fabrics were greatly renowned. In the 11th–12th centuries, it was the second major town of the area after Merv, and bathhouses of that period have survived. These had an underground heating system, and the walls were decorated with waterproof colours; Mukhammed ibn-Mukhameddon Nisevi was a local artist who was especially famous.

In 1221 Nisa was devastated by the Mongol invasion led by Genghis Khan, and in 1384 it was overrun by Tamerlane.

An Oriental historian wrote that "beautiful Nisa has always been desired by somebody," and all through the 16th–17th centuries, when fierce battles took place on the territory of present-day Turkmenia, Nisa's development suffered continuously. By the beginning of the 19th century, the town no longer existed. The area was inhabited by the Tekins, and in the 1820s the village of Baguir was founded.

The hill of Novaya Nisa can be seen from this village. The pits to the right of the road are the traces of Sardova—a large mediaeval artisans' quarter where glass, metal, and ceramics handicrafts have been found.

Baba-Alimes Mazar is a shabby mud house. Judging by the inscription, it belonged to the daughter of Seyid Akhad, son of Emir Mukhammed Salami. She died in August 1417. In contrast to the outside, her carved monument is splendid, with the remains of the tomb made of dark stone and a tall octangular column with a cupola known as a "chiragkhana." Nearby is a large slab with a hollow the shape of a horseshoe. People say it is the track of Duldul, a magic horse that belonged to the Arab Khalif Khazret-Ali. There are many legends about Duldul, which are mostly connected with horse breeding. People bring their horses to the stone and circle it 7 times for luck.

A gentle slope leads up the hill to the old settlement of Nisa; the ruins of the citadel show what a powerful stronghold it once was.

A path leads to the Abu-Ali Dakkak Mausoleum, which is an octangular structure of fire-brick covered with a cupola. There is a large tomb inside, called locally "sagana." Abu-Ali was mentioned in mediaeval records as Dakkak, meaning "cloth-fuller." He lived in Nisa in the 10th-11th centuries, when he built with his own means Khanaka Seravi ("khanaka" means a house for the members of the Sufi fraternity); here lived Sheikh Akhmed-i Nazyr, who was famous in those times. The remains of the khanaka can be seen 300 m (300 yds) from Novaya Nisa. There is also a legend about Abu-Ali. Allegedly he was a 7-year-old athlete who lived in the times of the Arabian conquest. Khazret Ali took him into battle, where the boy perished near Nisa. After the victory over the "unfaithful," Khazret Ali ordered the domed tomb to be erected over the lad's grave.

Namazga Mosque's ruins date back to the 12th century; the walls are made of the local Kopet-Dag stone. In this outskirt mosque, the inhabitants of Nisa and nearby villages celebrated two Muslim feasts, Kurban and Fitr. The mosque has suffered greatly both from the passing of time and from earthquakes.

Firyuza Ravine

Firyuza Ravine is about 18 km (11 miles) from Ashkhabad. The river Firyuzinka flows along by the road in the ravine, and the road leads to the settlement of Firyuza, 39 km (24 miles) from Ashkhabad. It is from the settlement that the ravine takes its name, and there is a legend about the place.

Long ago in these mountains there lived a gardener by the name of Bakharly. He had 7 sons and 1 beautiful daughter, whose name, Firyuza, meant "turquoise." When Firyuza was 14 years old, a neighbouring king asked her to marry him, but she refused. The king sent his soldiers to carry her away, but the 7 brothers fought to save her for 2 long days. Finally, on the third day, the last of the brothers was killed, whereupon Firyuza took up a dagger and stabbed herself. Over their tomb there grew up a great plane tree with 8 trunks.

Maral Restaurant, in Firyuza Ravine

Lake Kov-Ata

This lake is 78 km (48 miles) from Ashkhabad, in the direction of Krasnovodsk. At the 78-km mark, turn left and go 6 km (4 miles) farther. The lake lies underground and is the largest of its kind in the Soviet Union.

The entrance to the cave in which the lake lies is on a high slope. It has a vast arch of 5 m (16 ft). A 10-m (33-ft) flight of 262 concrete steps leads down, and the cave itself makes a great impression; it is 230 m (252 yd) long and 20 m (66 ft) high and filled with the strong smell of sulphur. At a depth of 52 m (171 ft) is Lake Kov-Ata (meaning "father of caves"), with its mirrorlike transparent water spreading over 2,500 sq m (2,990 sq yd). It is 13 m (43 ft) deep, and legends give it curative powers. The water is rather salty and maintains a steady temperature of 33°–37°C (91°–99°F). Analyses have shown that there are over 30 chemical elements in the water, and it is biologically active too. Certainly bathers find that all fatigue disappears.

Many insects live in the cave, and the bat colony numbers about 150,000.

Ozero Café, near the lake

Bakharden

Bakharden is a town 20 km (12 miles) beyond the turning to the lake, 110 km (68 miles) from Ashkhabad on the river Arvaz. It is famous for its carpets.

(Intourist also organises day trips from Ashkhabad to Mari (q.v.), formerly known as Merv.)

ASKANIA NOVA
See Kherson, p. 208.

AZERBAIJAN
See Baku, p. 52.

AZOV Population—87,000
Intourist organises trips here by boat from Rostov-on-Don.

Azov, one of the oldest towns in the lower reaches of the Don, is situated 40 km (25 miles) from Rostov on the left bank of the river, near the mouth.

Azov is 900 years old. It was originally founded by the Greeks in the 3rd century B.C. and called Tanais (after the old name of the Don). Through Tanais the Greeks conducted a brisk trade with the Orient and the Urals and exported grain. In the mid-3rd century A.D. it was destroyed by the Huns. In the 10th–11th centuries, Azov was part of the Tmutarakan princedom of Kiev Rus.

According to literary and historical sources, during the seizure of a Polovets settlement that existed at that time on the territory of present-day Azov, a Polovets khan, Azup, was killed, and from that time the town was known to the Russians as Azov, although the Tatars called it Azak.

In the 13th century, the southern regions of Russia were subjected to frequent raids by the Tatars, and Azak was the major trade centre of the Golden Horde. At the same time, Italian and Genoese merchants also came to these regions and founded commercial ports along the shores of the Black Sea and the Sea of Azov. They reconstructed ancient Tanais, which was situated on the outskirts of Azak, and called it Tana. During excavations on the territory of Azov, a marble tombstone was found with an inscription dedicated to Giacomo Cornaro, Venetian consul in Tana in 1362. Tana became a lively commercial centre, through which Oriental goods from Persia, India, and China, furs and precious stones from the Urals, and slaves from the southern steppes of Russia were brought to Western Europe. Tana even established contacts with Ryazan and Muscovy through the Oka inland waterway. It occupied the territory of the present Suvorovskaya, Genuezskaya, and Sovietskaya streets and that where the fish cannery is now situated. Azak occupied almost all of the territory of present-day Azov, excluding its eastern and western outskirts.

With the invasion by Tamerlane in 1395, Tana and Azak were mostly destroyed. The constant warring between Muscovy and the Tatars hindered the Genoese traders, who found themselves behind Tatar lines and were forced to seek other means of exporting their goods east, usually through Syria. With the conquest of Constantinople by the Turks in 1475, the trade significance of Tana fell, since the Turks prohibited all foreigners conducting trade in their territory.

In the 15th century, Russians fleeing from the repressive Moscow government and slaves escaping from the Azov slave markets began settling in the lower reaches of the Don. Thus the first Cossack settlement appeared here. Muscovy, in its efforts to colonise the black earth areas, supported the Russian runaways against the Turks. The Don Cossacks played a major role in gaining Azov for Russia. In 1551 Ivan the Terrible aided the Cossacks against the Turks by sending there an ataman (military leader) with troops. That same year the Turkish sultan complained to his ally, the Nogai leader Samail Mirza, that "the Cossacks of Ivan the Terrible laid Azov under tribute and forbade it to drink water from the Don."

During the 1620s and 1630s, the Don Cossacks with their Zaporozhye counterparts made a number of devastating raids on the Crimea and Turkey and almost reached Constantinople. On one of their raids in 1625, they invaded Azov, seizing one of its towers and destroying another. In 1637 Turkey became embroiled in a war with Persia, and the Nogai army went to the Crimea. A number of Don Cossacks, aided by some of their compatriots (who were nominally Polish subjects) wanted to seize the opportunity to take the town of Azov in another of their regular raids against the Turks. Azov was in a strategic position that would give the Russians a foothold on the Black Sea, and it was offered to the tsar of Muscovy. There was deliberation for some time, but the fortifications were dilapidated and expensive to repair, and in addition it would have been too advanced a post for the Russians to hold at that time. Moreover, Russia, weakened by her unsuccessful war against Poland (1632–34), was afraid to strain relations with Turkey and the Crimean khanate and tried to restrain the Cossacks' activity. All the same, in April 1637 the Cossacks attacked Azov "mounted and on ships." The battle for Azov continued for 2 months, after which the town surrendered. But to keep Azov, Russia needed additional troops, which she could not provide at that time. For the Turks the loss of Azov meant the loss of a major springboard for their struggle against the Russians, since the Azov and Black seas ceased to be within the bounds of the Ottoman Empire. So, after completing their war against Persia in 1638, the Turks attempted to besiege Azov from the sea. In 1641 a large Turkish army approached Azov and laid siege to the town for 112 days, but the Cossacks stood firm, and the Turkish army withdrew. On 9 October 1641, the Cossacks went to Moscow to report their victory and to ask the tsar to incorporate the town into the Russian state. However, the Russian government, fearing the Turks, refused to protect Azov, and the following April it was recaptured by the Turkish army.

By the beginning of Peter the Great's reign, Russia badly needed an outlet to the Azov and Black seas in the south and to the Baltic in the northwest. Peter undertook his first march upon Azov in the summer of 1695. He mustered an army of 31,000, and himself took part in the campaign under the name of artillery commander Pyotr Alexeyev. The commander-in-chief was his old friend, Patrick Gordon, a Scotsman in his service who had taught him military tactics. The Russians' first attack was unsuccessful, owing to the defection of a Dutch gunner, Jacob Jensen. During the battle Peter had also realised that it would be impossible to capture Azov without a strong naval fleet. He founded his main shipyards near Voronezh, but shipbuilding went on in many other parts of the country as well. At the same time, Peter started training a large army.

In May 1696 a huge Russian fleet appeared at the walls of Azov, Peter the Great sailing in the warship "Principium," which he had built himself along Dutch lines. This time Azov was besieged both from the land and from the sea. On 28 July the Turks opened the gates of Azov and surrendered. Azov was taken chiefly through the skill of Gordon, and the tsar made a triumphant entry into Moscow, bringing the wretched traitor-gunner with him; the Turks had been obliged to hand Jensen over, even though he had become a Muslim. After the triumphal procession, he was executed.

Later Austrian engineers supervised the reconstruction of Azov's fortified walls and bastions. The Azov campaign was the first page of Russia's future military glory. The soldiers and sailors who took part in the taking of Azov later crushed the Swedes near Poltava and then the Swedish fleet in the Battle of Gangut. These successes led to Russia becoming a world power. However, in 1711, after Peter the Great's unsuccessful Pruth campaign, she was forced to return Azov and the surrounding region to Turkey.

On 19 June 1737, the next Russian siege of Azov was crowned by success, for the town was taken by storm. However, according to the Belgrade Peace Treaty, the Turks demanded that the Azov fortifications be demolished, and Russia began building a stronghold near the city of Cherkassk.

After the routing of Tatar and Turkish armies from the Ukraine and the Azov region, the Russians undertook new measures to defend their lands from raids. They started a campaign against the Turks for Azov. On 6 March 1769, the Don Cossacks, having crossed the Don over the ice, captured Azov, but to keep it, Russia again needed a strong fleet. The Azov flotilla was built at the Rogozhin shipyards near the town. It took an active part in the 1768–74 Russo-Turkish War and formed the foundation of Russia's Black Sea fleet. Russia's success in this led to the signing of the Treaty of Kuchuk-Kainarji in 1774, according to which Azov was joined to Russia. To strengthen the Russian position in the Azov region further, Alexander Suvorov, commander of the Kuban Corps and hero of the Seven-Year and Russo-Turkish wars of 1768–74, came to the fortress of Dmitry Rostovsky (now Rostov-on-Don) and Azov. In 1783 the long years of Russo-Turkish wars (against Turkey and the Crimean Khanate) were crowned with Russian victory and the liberation of the southern part of the country from foreign domination.

With the beginning of the Crimean War of 1853–56, Azov's importance as a marine stronghold rose once again. In July 1855 an English naval vessel, the "Jasper," ran aground in the Strait of Taganrog, trying to enter the mouth of the Don. The Cossacks set it on fire and captured its flag and 2 guns. However, with the end of the Crimean war, Azov lost its significance and became a small, provincial town. There are still a number of thatched cottages in the villages on the way to the town. They are roofed with reeds from the reed beds of the Don estuary.

After the 1917 revolution, Azov became industrialised. It boasts the country's largest fish cannery, a shipyard, a forging and automatic equipment plant, and a factory producing baby foods.

III-International Square overlooks the river and the valley. Below it are beaches, boating centres, and a park. There is a Lenin monument in the centre of the square and the Solnechnaya Hotel and Restaurant form the eastern side. On the opposite side of the square from the Chaika Café, Dzerzhinsky Street runs past the Pioneer Palace to the old ramparts, where there is a vaulted arch which served as gates in its time. Here is the Krepostnoy Val Café, with old-style decor and special cuisine to delight the tourist palate.

The ramparts of *Azov fortress* stretch for hundreds of metres. They are 5–15 m (16–49 ft) high and 10–25 m (33–82 ft) wide at the foundation. The entrance arch is toward the eastern end, and recently the remains of the other, the arch of Troitskiye (Trinity) Gates, has been found. These ramparts of Azov fortress were built by the Turks in the 16th–17th centuries and were slightly reconstructed in the 18th century during Peter the Great's time.

Local History Museum, Moskovskaya Street 38. Open 11–6; closed Mon. This was opened in 1960 in the old town hall building, which itself dates from 1892. Another old house is that where Alexander Suvorov stayed in 1778.

Powder Store, Lermontov Street. Open 10–6, daily. In 1770 there was a wooden building here, but in 1779 the brick one was constructed to replace it.

The Powder Cellar, built at the beginning of the 18th century. This solid, 11-m (36-ft) building goes as deep as 5 m (16 ft) into the ground. The cellar has recently been partly restored. Here is a diorama showing the assault of the Turkish fortress by Peter the Great's troops.

The remains of a dilapidated wall, called the *Genoese Wall* and dating back to the 14th century, can be seen at Genuezskaya Street. It is here that the marble tombstone of Giacomo Cornaro, a Venetian counsul in ancient Tana, was found. The tombstone is now kept in the Novocherkassk Don Cossack History Museum.

Airmen's Monument, Moskovskaya Street. This 10-m (33-ft) monument with a propeller in front commemorates the deeds of the pilots of the 248th Squadron who defended the Don region in World War II.

Naval Ship Monument, Moskovskaya Street, below the ramparts, beyond the arch at the pier. Commemorating Soviet seamen killed during the Second World War. This ship took part in the landing of Caesar Kunikov's group on Malaya Zemlya near Novorossiisk.

Lenin Monument, III-International Square

Solnechnaya (Sunny) Hotel and Restaurant, III-International Square 12

Kazachok Restaurant, Mira Street 6

Molodyozhnoye (youth) Café

Krepostnoy Val Café, at the end of Dzerzhinsky Street, by the arch under the ramparts

Chaika Café, III-International Square

GPO, Karl Marx Street 22

Bank, Karl Marx Street 2

Azov Department Store, III-International Square 3

BAIKAL, LAKE

See Irkutsk, p. 165.

BAKHARDEN

See Ashkhabad, p. 48.

BAKHCHISARAI

Intourist organises excursions here from Yalta, 125 km (78 miles) away, with lunch in Simferopol, and also direct from Simferopol, 40 km (25 miles) away.

Bakhchisarai, "The Palace of Gardens," lies on the river Churyuk-Su ("rotten water"). On the outskirts of Bakhchisarai at Ashlam-Dere, tombs from the 8th–7th centuries B.C. were found, belonging to the Taurs. Taurs, Scyths, Sarmaths, Alans, and Greeks lived here. They lived by agriculture and vine growing. In the 14th century, when the area was taken over by the Golden Horde, the Eski-Yurt settlement appeared here. One of the Golden Horde's officer's mausoleums still exists. With the proclamation of the Crimean khanate in the mid-15th century, Khan Khadzhi-Girei transferred his residence from Solkhat (now known as Stary Krym) to Kyrk-Or (now Chufut-Kale). The new capital, Bakhchisarai, in the valley below the fortress, was first mentioned in 1502. Bakhchisarai remained the capital until the last khan, Shagin-Girei (Gehan-

Ghiri), abdicated in 1783. The unlucky khan was confined to Kaluga, near Moscow, then left for Turkey at his own request and later fell victim to an arrow on the island of Rhodes, where he had been banished by the Turks for yielding to Russian pressure.

In 1824 it is recorded that the Tatars in Bakhchisarai were under another sort of pressure. A Scottish missionary by the name of the Rev. Mr. Carruthers, who had spent some years studying the local languages, "proceeds with the greatest zeal and success in converting the Tartars to Christianity. A great number of them have been baptised by him. Colonies are to be established for these converts, and divine service will be performed in the Tartar language." The town's economy declined sharply after the Crimea became part of the Russian empire. In the late 1850s, after the Crimean War, many of the inhabitants emigrated, and in 1897 the mayor reported that Bakhchisarai had become one of the poorest places in the Crimea.

Up until the end of the last war, it remained mainly a Tatar town, but after the deportation of the Tatars, the town gradually began to lose its Oriental look, and apart from the single mosque, which is now part of the museum, nothing is left of the 32 mosques and 3 medressehs that stood here 100 years ago, at the height of the town's prosperity.

Bakhchisarai is divided into the old part and the new; only the main street is partly built up with new houses. Present-day industry includes a cement works, a wine factory, and milk-bottling plant.

Khan's Palace (Khan-Serai), Rechnaya Street 139. Open 9–5; closed Tues. The palace was founded in 1532–51, built by slaves and craftsmen from Iran and Turkey in the 16th–18th centuries. It now houses the local history and archaeology museum. Of the palace the Russian poet Pushkin wrote,

All silent now those spacious halls,
And courts deserted, once so gay
With feasters thronged within their walls,
Carousing after battle fray.
Even now each desolated room
And ruined garden luxury breathes,
Gold listens, shrubs exhale perfume.
The shattered casements still are there
Within which once, in days gone by,
Their beads of amber chose the fair,
And heaved the unregarded sigh

The complex consists of a number of buildings, including the harem, now inhabited by waxworks. The Fruit Room was designed by a Persian artist, Omar, in the 18th century. There is a pleasant garden and a falcon tower. During its history the palace was partly burned and robbed, but it was rebuilt for Catherine the Great's 3-day visit in 1787, and was again restored in 1837 for Nicholas I to see. This restoration, however, was not well done, and only in 1900 was additional work on the palace carried out with consideration for the past; not simply for Oriental style.

In the palace is the famous *Fountain of Tears*, built in 1756, which inspired Pushkin and the Polish poet Mickiewicz. Its story is as follows:

Khan Krim-Girei was well known for his cruelty; it was he who ordered the death of all the boys of his family who stood higher than the hub of his chariot wheel and were his potential rivals. People said that instead of a heart he had a lump of wool. However, when he fell in love with a slave girl called Delarai, he realised that he had indeed a living heart. Delarai could not return his love and soon died of sorrow.

Krim-Girei grieved deeply; he asked the Persian craftsman, Omar, to "make a stone that will continue my grief through the centuries, that will cry as only a man's heart can." Omar thought that if the stony heart of the khan could weep, then so could a stone, and he made a marble fountain and carved flower petals with a human eye in the centre from which would fall heavy drops like human tears, day and night till the end of time. Omar carved a marble snail on the fountain too, to symbolise the khan's doubt of the use of his life to him—or of his laughter and sadness, his love and his hatred.

On the palace grounds there is a mosque with two minarets that was used by the townsfolk and was built in 1740. Next to it is the cemetery of Khan Girei's dynasty including many tombstones of the Crimean khans, the Rotonda Mausoleum of Mengli-Girei and other mausoleums of the 17th–18th centuries. Next to the cemetery is the palace bathhouse of 1533.

Hotel and Restaurant, Lenin Street 93

Restaurant, in the town

Restaurant, on the road to Simferopol

Cheburechnaya, opposite the entrance to the palace. "Chebureki" are local meat pasties.

GPO, Pochtovaya Street 18

Telegraph and Telephone, Lenin Street 75

Beside the main road, near Bakhchisarai, are a number of round domes. There are 15th–18th-century mausoleums in the old Tatar cemetery.

Bakhchisarai's local museum is responsible for 14 ancient cave towns in the vicinity. Uspensky-Peschernyi Monastery and Chufut-Kaleh are probably of the greatest interest.

Uspensky-Peschernyi Monastery is about 2 km (1 mile) from Bakhchisarai, past the village of Staroselye on the road to Chufut-Kaleh. It is also known as Panhagia, from the Greek "pan"—whole—and "hagios"—saint. The road there is fairly good. This is a cave monastery, located in the mountainside and no longer inhabited. In it are the Cathedral of the Assumption of the Virgin, and 4 churches dedicated to SS. Constantine and Helen, St. Mark, St. George, and St. Innocent of Irkutsk. The monastery existed before the Turks came to the Crimea, and there is a legend attached to its foundation.

Once upon a time a dragon appeared in the mountains and devoured many of the villagers and their cattle. The rest fled down into the valley and in despair prayed to the Virgin Mary to help them. Then a strange light appeared upon one of the heights and shone there for 3 or 4 days. The sheerness of the cliff face made it impossible to climb, so 84 steps were cut in the rock. At the top was found an icon of Our Lady with a lamp burning before it, and nearby the fearful dragon lay dead. The people carried the icon down to the valley in gratitude—but it returned to its former position of its own accord; after several attempts to move it, it was decided to found a church there on the cliff top, and so a cave was dug and dedicated to the Virgin, and soon a monastery grew up around it. The icon's fame spread far and wide, and it was revered not only by the Crimean Greeks, but also by the Tatars and even the Turkish khans.

The monastery was active until the Russians came to the Crimea, but when the Crimean Greeks were transferred to the Sea of Azov in 1778 they took the icon with them, and the monastery lost much of its magnetism. It was, however, rebuilt in 1850, and the churches reopened; it is recorded that as many as 20,000 pilgrims used to come for the festival of the Dormition every August. Visitors can climb up the 84 steps cut in the cliff and get a good view of Bakhchisarai and the old Jewish cemetery known, like the cemetery at the foot of Jerusalem's Mount of Olives, as the Valley of Jehosophat.

Chufut-Kaleh

3 km (2 miles) from Bakhchisarai is Chufut-Kaleh, an uninhabited fortified mediaeval cave town on a high limestone plateau (558 m / 1830 ft above sea level) with steep slopes which fall away precipitiously to the southeast. There is plenty of room to park cars at the Uspensky-Peschernyi Monastery (see above) and from there the walk to Chufut-Kaleh is a little over a mile. The path leads to a nut grove, at the end of which is a fountain, and from here up the mountain to the gate of Chufut-Kaleh.

Possibly the most interesting of all the cave towns, it is also the easiest to access. A *fortress* was built in A.D. 10 known from the 13th century as Kyrk-Or (meaning forty fortifications) and later as Chufut-Kaleh. The fortress and the town were well known in the 14th century, and by the 16th century the town covered 18 hectares (45 acres) and consisted of 400 houses while the population numbered 5,000. A mosque was built, using the stones from the fallen basilica, but the mosque itself later fell into ruins. It is said that one of the Chufut-Kaleh caves was the site of the khan's tribunal and a gaol for prisoners of importance. It is known that the Polish hetman (leader) Potocki was incarcerated in Chufut-Kaleh in 1648, and that from 1660 the Russian governor and military leader, Vasily Sheremetyev, languished in captivity there, as did the Russian prince Andrei Romodanovsky in the late 17th century.

The place, however, is most famous for having been the headquarters of the Jewish sect called the

Karaites. These are disciples of the letter of the Law of Moses, adhering to Judaism without accepting the Talmud and other holy Jewish books nor the traditions of the Elders. Their name appears to have derived from the Hebrew "qara," meaning "to read," because of the way they study their Bible. They were also found in Russia, Poland, and Egypt, and today about 10,000 of them live near Tel-Aviv. But the Karaite Jews here, having long been under the domination of their Tatar neighbours, adopted much of the costume, language, and customs of the Tatars. Their tongue is Karaim, and although a member of the Turkic group, the language has been written in Hebrew characters since the 16th century. This place was first used by them in the 17th century, and in the mid-19th century was visited by the traveller Laurence Oliphant, who was later to spend much time and energy attempting to establish a Jewish state in Palestine. Oliphant tells how, as the community prospered and their honesty became a byword, they began to leave their mountain home for more convenient places to carry on business. By the time the last family left in 1852, there were said to be about 2,000 Karaite Jews, including a number of wealthy merchants, living in Evpatoria on the western coast of the Crimea. For many years, however, Oliphant says, the Karaite Jews from Chufut-Kaleh made a point of ensuring that when they died they would be laid to rest, like their ancestors, in the Valley of Jehosophat.

Today Chufut-Kaleh is a dead city, a town of silent streets and ruined houses. The remains of the two synagogues can be seen, and in the centre is a *mausoleum* built in Moorish style in 1437. This was erected by Khan Taktamish for his beautiful daughter, Dzhanike-Hanym. The tragedy of her death, according to Turkish history books, began in 1392 when Tamerlane conquered the Crimea. The valiant young prince who was sent to rule the area fell in love with the Tatar princess and asked Tamerlane to restore the Crimea to her father if he might ask her hand in marriage instead. Both Tamerlane and the old khan agreed, but the latter broke his part of the bargain. He retreated to the impregnable fortress of Chufut-Kaleh with his daughter and, after leaving her there, went off to stir up a revolt of his nobles against Tamerlane, hoping to free his lands from the powerful conqueror. When the happy prince returned to join Dzhanike-Hanym, the officer in charge refused her request to hand over the command of the fortress to her lover, and the garrison was divided in its loyalty. Fighting broke out and the prince was wounded. When the princess rushed to his aid, they were both stabbed in the confusion and died there together in each other's arms. The fighting ceased immediately, and the general remorse was only increased when Khan Taktamish returned to see the results of his perfidy. There was nothing left for him to do but build a mausoleum for the young couple.

Leaving the town, Oliphant went down to the bottom of the valley "to the well of delicious water which supplies the inhabitants. . . . At this well is usually stationed a man who fills the water-skins borne by donkeys to their master above, both the consigner and the consignee being probably too old to accompany these sagacious animals on the numerous trips which are, nevertheless, so essential to the comforts of the inhabitants."

Opposite the monastery on the slope of the plateau where Chufut-Kaleh is situated, there is a cemetery for those who fell in the Crimean War and quite near the monastery is another for World War II soldiers who died of their injuries in the nearby military hospital.

BAKU

Baku is the capital of the Azerbaijan Republic.

AZERBAIJAN

Area: 33,400 sq. miles, Population—7,029,000, of which 78.1 percent are Azerbaijanis, who are Turkic-speaking people, 7.9 percent Russians, and 7.9 percent are Armenians

Azerbaijan is situated in eastern Transcaucasia. Its capital is Baku, and other large towns include Gyandzha and Sumgait.

The country used to be the stronghold of the magians, or fire worshippers. They had temples here and tended perpetual flames, and from this the place got its name, for "azer" means "fire."

In the 3rd century A.D., it fell under Persian domination; after 641 A.D. the Moslems invaded it; and in the 8th century it was conquered by the Arabs. From the 11th century it was under the Seljuk Turks, until it was overrun by the Mongols, under Genghis Khan, in the 13th century and Tamerlane in the 14th.

In the 15th century, the area consisted of several Turkic-speaking Azerbaijan states, and for the next 300 years it was the object of rivalry between Persia and Turkey. In 1723–35 part of the country belonged to Russia, but it became part of the Russian empire only in 1828, after the Russo-Persian War.

Soviet power was established in Azerbaijan after the Russian revolution of 1917 but was followed for a short time by a parliamentary republic, which existed until 1920. Then, with the help of the Red Army, Soviet power was re-established, and Azerbaijan joined the Transcaucasian Soviet Federative Republic until, in 1936, upon the abolition of the federation, it became a Union Republic of the USSR.

Local dishes include "doga," which is a soup of rice, peas, herbs, and sour milk, and "bozartma," which is mutton stew. Attractive souvenirs are the shawls with bright designs printed on fine woolen material.

Turkey changed its alphabet from Arabic to Latin letters in 1926, but in Azerbaijan the change was not made until 1929. The second change, to the Cyrillic alphabet, was made in 1940. At school, children have the opportunity to study Turkish, Arabic, and Persian.

Here are a few words of Azerbaijani:

hello	salaam aleihum
I am a tourist	man turistam
please	buyurun
thank you	sakh olun
yes	bali
no	khe-ish
good	yakhshi
bad	pees
I don't understand	basha dushmuram
please fetch me an	mana tardzhumachi
interpreter	charurun
good-bye	alvida
how do you do?	nedzhsineez

Baku (In Azerbaijani: Baky)
Population— 1,757,000
Capital of the Azerbaijan Republic, the name of the city of Baku comes from the Persian "bad-kubé,"meaning a squall blown up by mountain winds.

Baku, on the shore of the low-lying Caspian, is 17 m (56 ft) below sea level. The town rises up from the seashore, forming an amphitheatre on the southern coast of the peninsula of Apsheron and the western coast of the Caspian Sea. The region is naturally treeless, the climate dry, and strong northerly winds (khazri) blow frequently. Most of the newer buildings are placed to lessen their exposure to the wind. The summer is warm, with an average temperature in July and August of 26°C (79°F), and the short winter is mild, with an average January temperature of 3°C (38°F).

Local naphtha springs have been known here for many hundreds of years. Although the first written record of a town on this site dates from the 9th century, some historians consider it was in fact founded in the 5th or 6th century during the rule of the Persian Sasanid dynasty. Some say that there was a city called Gagara on the site not later than the 4th century. The area belonged first to the Arabs, second to the Shirvan khans, then to the Turks from 1583–1606, next to the Persians under whom the Baku khanate was founded in 1747, and from 1806 it became Russian. (It had in fact been subject to Russia before, between 1723 and 1735, but was returned to Persia).

The real development of the town started in 1859 with the transfer of the regional centre from Shemakha to Baku. The ancient capital had suffered from an earthquake once again, and this made a good excuse for the authorities in Baku to take on the responsibilities of regional government. At the turn of the century, Baku was one of the fastest-growing towns in the world. From 4,500 people in 1826, the population reached 156,000 in 1903 and 215,000 in 1910, which was a larger increase than the populations of Paris, London, or New York during the same time. The oil fields started to be exploited in the 1870s, and at the beginning of this century the Apsheron Peninsula held an important place in the world's oil production. Besides the Azerbaijanis who flocked to the rapidly developing oil industry, there were large numbers of Russians and Armenians as well. Foreign capital was freely available to help obtain oil for the oil lamps of Europe, long before the internal combustion engine was taken seriously. Most of the refineries and the oil trade were in foreign hands. So were the largest plants—the Nobel petroleum works and the Rothschild oil refinery. In 1901 Baku supplied almost half of the world's oil, and by 1903 Russia was the world's largest producer, with the Baku oil field far the most important source of supply.

The workers' living conditions, however, ranked last on the list of priorities. Before the revolution Baku was the scene of active revolutionary work. A series of strikes between 1903 and 1907 led to the signing of the first agreement in Russia between workers and oil industrialists. In 1914 nearly 50,000 workers went out on strike. Soviet power was established in 1917, and in April 1918 the Baku Council of People's Commissars was set up as the official government body. The following year the course of the Civil War led to the formation of the anti-Bolshevik Azerbaijan Republic, run by the Mussavat Muslim Party (which was pan-Islamic and pro-Turkish and supported by British and Turkish troops).

The British interest here was primarily to prevent Russian sale of arms and other military equipment to the Persians, Kurds, and other peoples hostile to the British and threatening the security of the North-West Frontier, but it was also important to prevent the Germans from reaching the oil fields of Baku. Major General L. C. Dunsterville arrived in Baghdad from India, having been appointed to organise local sympathisers into a fighting force under the leadership of British, Canadian, Australian, New Zealand, South African, and Russian officers and 1 Persian officer. However, before they could reach Baku, the Treaty of Brest-Litovsk ceded large areas of Trans-Caucasia to Turkey. Turkey then began to claim more of the region through the Moslem inhabitants there, but Germany feared such Turkish expansion would hinder her own designs upon Baku and the oil fields. The Georgians welcomed the Germans as protection against the Turkish advance. General Bicharakov, commander of the Red Army in the Caucasus, brought about a coup d'etat in Baku on 26 July 1918, whereby the Bolshevik members of the government resigned and the new Centro-Caspian government sought British aid. 26 of the Soviet commissars were arrested and transported across the Caspian Sea, detained in a town prison, and then executed in the Karakum Desert near Krasnovodsk.

In 1920 the town was retaken by the Red Army. The remains of the 26 commissars were exhumed and brought back to Baku to be interred, where the memorial stands today.

The population of the city is principally Azerbaijani, Russian, and Armenian. The Azerbaijani language is very similar to Turkish, but today the Cyrillic alphabet is used.

Baku's present prosperity is still chiefly due to oil. Since 1935 it has been obtained from the seabed by building artificial islands in the open sea.

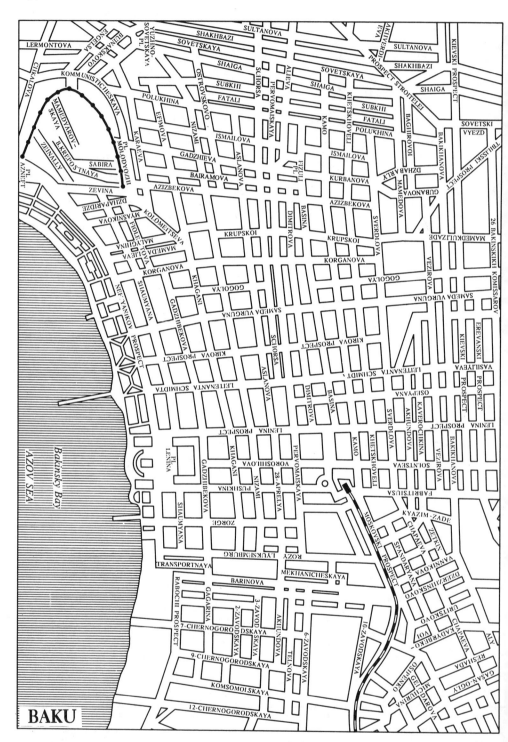

BAKU

During World War II, the German authorities hoped to seize the oil fields, which were supplying the Soviet forces, and the Battle of Stalingrad was largely a battle for Baku. An oil pipeline now runs from Baku to the port of Batumi on the Black Sea coast.

Baku is itself one of the largest ports in the USSR. It is about 350 km (217 miles) from the Iranian port of Enzeli (formerly Pekhlevi), and Soviet ships sail to and fro about 4 times a month, the one-way trip taking about 18 hours.

The town's industry is primarily dependent on oil; there are refineries, cracking plants, and engineering works. Beside these, however, there are flourishing chemical, food, leather goods, and printing industries, and a French-built factory producing prefabricated houses. Baku has become a pleasant place to live since determined efforts were taken to control the industrial pollution, and its modernisation has included the construction of the underground railway.

The city is rich in a variety of buildings dating from the different periods of its history. The oldest of these include the fortress, the palace, and the mosques. More recently, since it was incorporated into Russia in 1806, there have been a succession of architectural styles. A great stimulus to the city's development followed the earthquake of 1859; before that date the area had been administered from the town of Shemakha, but then Baku became the capital, and consequently a whole series of public and private buildings were constructed. The most impressive of these were built at the end of the 19th and the beginning of the 20th centuries, by which time Baku had become rich from oil and from the growth of business activity.

In an attempt to satisfy their clients' tastes, the architects drew upon the traditions of Moorish and Gothic, baroque and classical styles, and sometimes even mixed them all together in what became known locally as "roofless Renaissance" style. Art nouveau elements were also included. The local architects were particularly impressed by the buildings of Cordoba, the Moorish khalifate, and Cairo. The local architect Ter-Mikelov was responsible for a number of them: the Muslim Magomayev Azerbaidzhan State Philarmonia, built as the Assembly Rooms in neo-classical style, and the art nouveau building of a bank, now used by the Azerbaijani Znanie Society. Some of the private houses were certainly designed to outdo a neighbour's mansion. The size and unusual appearance of a house served to demonstrate the wealth and importance of its owner.

Government House is an imposing 12-storey building with 1,000 rooms. It stands on the north side of the bay, where there were once goods depots. It was designed by Rudnev and Munts and also houses the local ministries. The large, but strangely misnamed, *Central Square* in front of it is used for parades and festivities. From here a popular promenade runs all the way back to the centre. Here the busiest places are *Zabaidke* and

Kommunisticheskaya (formerly Nikolayevskaya) streets, and the old central square, popularly known as Parapet, has become *Karl Marx Garden*. It was always a popular place to take the air, and this has been maintained now that, along with Nizami (formerly Torgovaya) Street, it has been made into a pedestrian precinct. It is certainly a very pleasant area to wander through. Nearby is the Armenian church of *St. Grigori the Enlightener*, built in 1863 and open to all passersby who want to drop in and light a candle. The old buildings in this central part of the city have been carefully restored. The impressive houses that were constructed at the turn of the century, reflecting their owners' new-found wealth, are still to be seen in along Kommunisticheskaya, Nizami, and Korganovo streets. The streets near the fortress are interesting too. The parallel streets leading down to Myasnikova (formerly Milyutinskaya) Embankment and Malygina (formerly Gorchakovskaya) Street were built up with banks, imposing offices, private homes and hotels at the end of the last century. Similar are the streets leading toward the Oriental-looking railway station.

In the 1920s leading Soviet architects, such as the Vesnin brothers and Schusev, built a number of houses in constructivist style, which are known as Baku constructivism. Many houses built in this style may still be seen today, for instance, the *Intourist Hotel*, the *Physiotherapy Institute* and the *Press Palace*. They are easily identified by their modernistic appearance.

The Azerbaijan Academy of Sciences is at 10 Kommunisticheskaya Street. Known as the Ismailia Palace, it was built in 1908–13 by the architect I Ploshko in a Venetian Gothic style reminiscent of that of the Doge's Palace in Venice, at the behest of oil millionaire Musa Nagiev, in memory of his son. At that time it was used by a charitable society. The same architect built another imposing house in French Gothic style in 1911–12 at Polukhina (formerly Persian) Street 6 with a library panelled in wood in Gothic style. It used to be known as Mukhtarov Palace, but now it is the *Palace of Happiness* where marriages are registered. No. 13 on the same street was built by K. Skurevich in 1898–99 as the *Rothschild office*. Baku is also the location of *Kirov University*, a *Conservatoire*, 91 scientific research institutes including the renowned *Petroleum Institute*, and a polytechnical institute with 5 faculties and 3000 students. 70,000 other students study in Baku too, though not all are engaged full time. The *Akhundov Library* in a new building on 26-Baku-Commissars Street has 3 million books. It is named after Mirza-Fatali Akhundov (1812–78), a philosopher, dramatist, and poet. Of Pushkin's death he wrote:

The heart where nightingales his genius
    sang
Is covered now with naught by thorny sloe.
      —trans. Olga Moisseyenko

Akhundov was one of the best-educated men of his day and the initiator of realism in Azerbaijani literature.

On Nizami Street stands one of Baku's largest structures, a *skyscraper block of flats*. It was built in the 1930s when a great deal of building was going on. There was more after the Second World War. Gadzhiev Street is an old street that has been completely reconstructed so that it is now double its former width. It ends in Dmitrov Square and was the first street in Baku to be built according to a single architectural plan. There are many other new buildings to see, including the *Pyotr Montin Settlement*, just outside Baku.

The Town Hall on Kommunisticheskaya Street was built in 1870 as the Duma building. There is an attractive clock over the entrance, and the coat-of-arms of Baku is used as a motif on the walls. The building now used as the *House of Pioneers* was built in the early 20th century by a rich merchant. After the demolition of part of the town wall nearest to the Caspian in 1860 there was room for the construction of the Alexander Embankment. Renamed Neftyanikov (oilworkers) Prospect, this is now one of the main streets of the city. It runs from the centre around the bay close to the sea, and beside it is a *chess pavilion* built in the same style as a pavilion at the World's Fair in Brussels. Farther along the avenue, beside the sea, is a *parachute tower*, 73 m (240 ft) high. Finally the street leads to the new part of the town, where the modern hotels and government buildings are.

Sabunchinsky Railway Station (unofficially called Sabunchinka), Lenin Prospect. It was completed in 1926 when the local railway line was electrified, being one of the first stations in the country to be built for a new, electrified system. The architect Bayev was responsible for the mixture of many styles topped by a minaret; the effect is of a typically Oriental eclectic style.

Icheri Shekher (inner city), the old town, is partly surrounded by walls. About 130 years ago, the whole of Baku was contained within the citadel. The walls, built between the 12th and 16th centuries, have been reconstructed several times, but some of the original carved ornament remains. The last time the walls were used to defend the city was in 1826, when the Persian army was at the gates. The walls were restored in 1953–54. Originally they were double, and in some places they measure 15 m (49 ft) on the outside, while on the inside the highest point is 5 m (16 ft). Part of the wall was demolished to make room for caravanserais. The *Multani* (known as the Indian) *Caravanserai* still exists at Gala Street 12 (about 50 m/yds from the Maiden's Tower, see below). It was built in the 17th century, and on the opposite side of the street, at No. 9, is the 14th-century *Bukhara Caravanserai*, built around an octagonal courtyard and with the original archways now blocked to provide living accommodations.

In the southern part of the citadel and only about 50 m/yd from the caravanserais is *Kiz-Kalasyi* (Maiden's Tower). This massive structure (29 m/

95 ft high, 16–16.5 m/52–54 ft in diameter, and with walls 5 m/16 ft thick at the bottom and at least 4 m/13 ft thick at the top) dates from the first half of the 12th century. It is believed to have been built by Sultan Masud as part of the city's early fortifications. The foundations, however, may be much older, 5th or 6th century. Its base must once have been washed by the waves of the sea, but the waters have now retreated about 500 m/yds. Once the tower consisted of 8 floors, and a flight of 116 steps led to the top. On the western side, an ancient inscription on the stone reads: "Kube Masud bin Daud" (the tower of Masud, son of David). On the eastern side, a rectangle of wall projects. About a hundred years ago, the sea came up to the foot of the tower, and for several years, until 1909, it was used as a lighthouse.

The name the Maiden's Tower comes from the legend that a certain khan of Baku wished to marry his own daughter. The girl tried in vain to dissuade him and then had the idea of asking her father first to build a tower, hoping that by the time it was completed he would have changed his mind. However, when the tower was ready the khan came one stormy night to claim his bride, who threw herself in desperation into the sea below.

Bakikhanov House, Gala Street 46. This imposing house was built by an 18th-century merchant. Other separate buildings of interest in the citadel include the remains of the *Mirza Akhmed Mosque* (1345) at Voyannaya Street 6, the disused *Gadzhi Bami Mosque* (16th century) at Maly Krepostnoi Pereulok 8, and the *Djouma Mosque and Bathhouse*. The *Synikh Kala Minaret*, the oldest building in Baku, which belonged to a mosque of the same name, is near the Maiden's Tower and on the sea side of the palace. Its name means "ravaged," and it was built in 1077–78 "by the order of Seyad-ed-Din, son of Mohammed I"; it has been restored recently. The *Mohammed Mosque*, which now stands next to the minaret, was built much later.

Shirvan Shah's Palace, or the Palace of the Khans, stands high in the old part of the town at Zamkovy Pereulok 76. The best way to get there is via Kommunisticheskaya Street 4. Turn here along 3-Kommunistichesky Pereulok and climb up the steps under the coat-of-arms on the old fortress wall. At the top keep straight ahead and then turn right along Zamkovy Pereulok. The palace complex is open 10–5 daily.

It is surrounded by the citadel wall, and there is a good view over the town. The 5 wells on the territory were dug long before the palace was built, and through the years the various buildings were designed to create intimate, shady courtyards between them. In the 15th century, Khalil-Ulla I (1417–62), a ruler of the Derbent dynasty of Shirvan shahs, built a mosque here as well as a family mausoleum, the palace, and a court of justice. The main building of the palace is 2 storeys and built of finely finished stone. The exact date of its construction is not known, but originally it had 52 rooms, 27 downstairs and 25 above. The shah lived upstairs, while the servants' quarters and the storage rooms were below. The palace has been reconstructed several times, and now there are 16 upper rooms. It houses part of the Baku Museum.

Divan-Khane, the court of justice, is a small 15th-century, octagonal pavilion in the centre of a square courtyard, galleried on the sides, to the right as one comes out of the main building. To the left is the intricately carved main portal with hexagonal medallions inscribed in Arabic. One has the general Moslem creed and the other the Sheid version. The pavilion is surrounded on 3 sides by 20 columns. The inner portal to the central chamber is decorated in a pattern taken from local flora. Beside this is an Arabic inscription from the Koran which says, "God said glory to him and blessing, and God called peace and blessing to the house and leads in the right way whomsoever he wishes. Those who do good will be good and with surplus, nor dust nor disgrace will cover their faces. They will be inhabitants of Heaven where they will dwell forever." Over all 6 doors, "Ali" is written in Arabic inside hexagonal medallions. The holes in the inside wall were for pegs from which carpets were hung.

The hole in the centre of the floor of the pavilion was supposedly used at the time of executions, when the victim's head dropped through it into a channel and floated out to sea; the body was given to relatives. The chamber below is now dry. Some historians think that Divan-Khane was used as a reception hall or state council chamber. At any rate it was never completed, although other doorways were prepared for carving.

In the courtyard are relics of masonry and stone sepulchres and on the opposite side of the pavilion from the main portal a steep stone stair leads up to a small, blue-domed chamber.

On the other side of the palace more steps lead down to the *Dervish Mausoleum* or *Seid Yahiya Bakuvi Mausoleum*, another octangular building on the palace territory. It was built in 1464 over the grave of the court scientist, astrologer, doctor, and mathematician. It consists of a ground floor and an underground chamber. Inside, part of the ancient decor remains: black and red drawing inlaid on a surface of white stucco. The windows have carved stone gratings. The outside walls are built of alternate wide and narrow layers of limestone, giving an effect of lightness, surmounted by an octangular pyramid.

Next to the mausoleum are the foundations of the small *Kegubade Medresseh*, where Said Yahiya Bakuvi worked and taught. The little octagonal pool on the other side of the mausoleum was constructed sometime between the 13th and 15th centuries.

Lower down still in a pleasant fountained courtyard is the *Shah's Mausoleum*, or "turbe," built in 1435–36 with a beautiful arch over the entrance. Inscriptions indicate that it was constructed on the orders of Khalil-Ulla and built by an architect called Mohammed Ali. Nearby is the shah's subterranean reservoir known as the Ovdan, its water brought from a long way away by underground pipes. Beside the mausoleum is the *Shah's Mosque*, with 2 stone domes of different sizes. Inside, jars were set high into the walls to improve the acoustics, just as they were in some early Russian churches. The minaret, which stands 22 m (72 ft) high, was built in 1441–42, also by Shah Khalil-Ulla, as indicated by the inscription under its balcony. Through a gate across the courtyard are the remains of the shah's bathhouse.

The Murad Gates, built in 1385, are the gates leading to the palace from the northeast. The attractive portal is decorated with stalactites and stone carvings, but the purpose of the construction is not clear. Possibly it was intended as the magnificent entrance to a house that was never completed. The gates are closed, and one has to go around the outside of the walls to see the decorations.

Mosques are usually named for those who donated the money for their construction. Two that are still in use in Baku are the *Taza-pir* and *Azhdarbek mosques*. Taza-pir Mosque is at Akhindova Street 7. "Taza" means "new," and this was built in 1906 from money donated by a woman named Nabad Khanum. It has two minarets and is used by the Shiite Muslims. Azhdarbek Mosque is at Samed Virgun Street 58. Built in 1911 with a large green dome and a minaret, it is used by both the Shiites and the Sunnites.

Muhammed, Djuma, and Lesghi mosques, in the citadel

Gadji Sultan Ali Mosque, Polukhina Street

Church of the Nativity of the Virgin (Russian Orthodox), Ketskhoveli Street 205

Church of St. Gregory the Enlightener (Armenian Gregorian), Efima Saratovtsa Street 27. Built in 1863.

Armenian Church of Our Lady, Menzhinskova Street 11, near the Virgin Tower. Built in the 18th century.

Lutheran Church, built following the design of St. Elizabeth's Church in Marburg, Germany, the earliest German church to be built in purely Gothic style. It was constructed from 1235–83 over the tomb of St. Elizabeth of Hungary, who died in 1231 at age 24. The Baku church has been reopened as a concert hall for organ music.

Synagogue, Gogol Street

History of Azerbaijan Museum, Malygina Street 4. The building was designed by I. Goslavksy in the Mauritanian style popular in Cordoba and constructed from 1893–1902. It used to belong to the oil millionaire Tagiyev, and the city art collection was once housed here. The collection of historical exhibits dates from 1896. Open 11:30–6; closed Fri.

Archaeology and Ethnographical Museum, open 10–6.

Carpet and Applied Art Museum, in the Old Town, at Asafa Zeinally Street 49. Open daily, 10:30–5:30. This museum, opened in 1972, claims to be the first of its kind in the world. Particularly beautiful is one small carpet woven in natural colours.

Rustama Mustafayev Art Museum, Chkalova Street 9. This national art collection contains works from the 18th century to the present day, as well as examples of Russian and Western European art (mostly copies). There are also carpets, embroidery, and china. The building was originally constructed for the oil millionaire Gugasov in 1876. On the first floor is the Eastern Room, decorated in red and gold, with an Arabic inscription that is a quotation from the Koran. It was used as a chapel and as a guest room for eastern visitors. Open 10:30–6; closed Mon.

Art Gallery, Gadzhibekov Street 27

Nizami Literary Museum, Kommunisticheskaya Street 33. The museum is housed in a building specially erected for the Museum of the History of Azerbaijani Literature, and between the columns are sculptures of outstanding Azerbaijani writers. Part of the exhibit is dedicated to Khagani ("Regal") Shirvani (Afsaladdin Ibrahim ibn-Ali Nadjar) (1120–94), the court poet whose dissatisfaction with the Shirvanshahs led to his imprisonment and self-imposed exile in Tabriz. The museum itself bears the name of another poet and thinker, Nizami Ganjevi (1141–1209), whose real name was Ilias ibn-Yusif Ogli and whose works are well known in Eastern literature. The pseudonym Nizami means "the one who strings syllables." Many of his poems have been translated into European languages. In one of them he describes how Baku welcomed Alexander the Great. He is especially famous for his 5 long poems forming the Khamsa, which has 30,000 couplets. When his beloved wife, Afrak, died, he mourned her deeply but felt his poetry benefited from the experience.

> Nizami's style resembles a charger with a
> bridle—a light leather strap,
> And my grief is a hard, heavy stirrup, but
> how perfectly gallops my steed!
> —Trans. OLGA MOISSEYENKO

The museum contains manuscripts, miniatures, and carpets. Open 11:30–5; closed Thurs.

Djabarly Theatre Museum, Karayev Street 24. It is named for Djafar Djabarly (1899–1934) who was the founder of Soviet Azerbaijani drama. The house where he lived has also been opened as a museum (see below).

Vurgun's House, Myasnikova Street 4. Samed Vurgun Yusif ogly Vekilov (1906–56) was a poet and playwright who wrote of the commissars mentioned above:

> I recall how the British shot our men from
> Baku—
> Those twenty-six commissars, brave men
> and true . . .
> —Trans. TOM BOTTING

Lenin Museum, Neftyanikov Prospect 123a. Open 12–5; closed Mon. The next 3 museums are also run by the Lenin Museum.

"Nina" Underground Printing-house Museum, Iskrovskaya Street 102. Open 11–7; closed Mon. The printing press here went into action in 1901, and its revolutionary pamphlets and leaflets were distributed all over Russia.

Kirov's Flat, Khagani Street 18. This is where Sergei Kirov (1886–1934), one of the leading Bolsheviks, lived from 1921–25, during the time of his work in Baku. Open 11–7; closed Mon.

Azizbekov's Flat, Montina Street 105. This was the birthplace of Meshadi Azizbekov (1876–1918). He was a leading local Bolshevik and 1 of the 26 commissars shot in 1918. Open 11–7; closed Mon.

Azim-zade's Flat, Pyervomaiskaya Street 157. Azim-Aslan ogly Azim-zade (1880–1943) was a Soviet painter known as the founder of Azerbaijani realist drawing.

Gadjibekov's House, Ketskhoveli Street 67. Uzeik Gadjibekov (1885–1948) was the Soviet composer and public figure known as the founder of Azerbaijani opera.

Byul-Byul Memorial Flat

Djabarly's House, Gamid Sultanov Street 44. Djafar Djabarly (1899–1934) was the founder of Soviet Azerbaijani drama.

Zardabi Natural History Museum, Lermontov Street 3. There is a good collection of local fauna here. Open 8–2; closed Mon.

Nizami Monument, Nizami Square. The 6-m (20-ft) bronze statue of the local 12th-century poet (mentioned above under the Nizami Literary Museum) is by F. Abdurakhmanov and was unveiled in 1949. The granite pedestal is decorated with bronze bas-reliefs illustrating his works.

Fisuli Monument, Fisuli Square. Muhammed Fisuli (1498–1556) was a poet who wrote in Azerbaijani, Arabic, and Persian and used the full range of style known to Oriental literature in the Middle Ages. This monument was unveiled to mark the 400th anniversary of his death.

Akhundov Monument, Karayeva Street. This is the same Mirza-Fatali Akhundov after whom the library is named. P. Sabsai designed the monument in 1928.

Natavan Statue, Dzhaparidze Street. Khurshid-Banu Natavan (1830–97) was a poetess who founded a literary circle in her native Shusha for all the progressive poets of her time. Much of her verse reflects her grief at the loss of her young son from tuberculosis.

> Through my tears your image I always see.
> You dried up so soon, O, my cypress tree!
> —Trans. DORIAN ROTTENBERG

This statue, the only monument to a woman in Baku, shows the poetess seated with a pencil in her hand.

Sabir Monument, in Sabir garden on Kommunisticheskaya Street, in front of the Academy of Sciences. Mirza-Alekper Sabir (1862–1911) was a folk poet and satirist, much influenced by the revolution of 1905. He was born and lived all his life in Shemakha, but in 1910 he came to Baku to teach languages. Of the workers of Baku he wrote:

But the wheel of fortune's turning in a new way nowadays;
The working men begin to think they're human nowadays.

Samed Vurgun Statue, in the square at the crossing of 28-April and Pushkin streets

Karl Marx Monument, Lenin Prospect

Monument to the 26 commissars of Baku, in the garden in 26-Bakinskikh Komissarov (formerly Stock Market) Square. The British are usually blamed for the deaths of these men, shot in 1918. Tripolskaya was the sculptress and Pavlevich the architect of the monument, which was unveiled in 1923. There is an eternal flame here and a red granite monument on the right, bearing the inscription: "Here lie the brave fighters for communism, 26 Baku commissars evilly shot on 20 September 1918 by hirelings of the imperialists." The square is further decorated with busts of the 4 most famous of the commissars—Shaumyan, Azizbekov, Dzhaparidze, and Fioletov—created by Sabsai in 1928.

Azizbekov Monument, Commemorating 1 of the 26 Baku commissars and unveiled in 1978. (See Azizbekov's Flat.)

Lenin Monument, Lenin Square

Djabarly Monument, in Sambuchinsky Railway Square. Djafar Djabarly (1899–1934) was the founder of Soviet Azerbaijani drama.

Kirov Monument, in Kirov Park, on the hillside above the town to the west. It stands by the exit from the funicular railway, which runs up to the park from the town below. Sergei Kirov, a well-known Bolshevik who was assassinated in Leningrad in 1934, was head of the local Communist party organisation from 1921–25. The statue by P. Sabsai was unveiled in 1939.

Narimanov Monument, Yuzhno-Sovietskaya Square. Nariman Nadzhaf ogly Narimanov (1871–1925) was a Soviet statesman.

Sorge Monument, Samed Vurgun Street. Richard Sorge (1895–1944) was a famous Soviet intellegence agent of World War II. He came to the USSR in 1924, worked as press attache at the German Embassy in Tokyo before the war, then as a German correspondent in Tokyo, was arrested in 1941, and was hanged in Japan.

Dzerzhinsky Monument, Dzerzhinsky Park

Krasin Monument, Krasin Street. Leonid Krasin (1870–1926) was the same age as Lenin and one of his sparring partners through the years leading up to the revolution. He was invaluable in helping to organise the Soviet economy and served as his country's ambassador, twice in London and once in Paris.

Azi-Aslanov Monument, Kirov Park. Major-General Azi-Aslanov was a Hero of the Soviet Union who fell in World War II.

Mekhti Gusein-zade Monument, at the crossing of Bakikhanov and Djafar Djabarly streets. Mekhti Gusein-zade was a German POW who escaped to join the Yugoslavian and Italian resistance movements. He was made a Hero of the Soviet Union.

Caspian Sailors' Monument, 8-Bailovsky Pereulok

World War II Memorial, at the crossing of Gadzhibekova and Sorge streets

Liberated Azerbaijan Monument, Sverdlov Street

Uz Gadjibekov Monument, at the crossing of Dmitrov and Lt. Schmidt streets. His house is now a museum, listed above.

The impressive *fountain* near the Intourist Hotel and the entrance to the funicular railway depicts a character from one of Nizami's stories. It is Bakhramshah, who is shown killing a dragon, which had prevented people from reaching a spring of fresh water.

Azizbekov Academic Drama Theatre, Fizuli Square. The company was founded in 1873, but the impressive columned building is quite new.

Akhundov Opera and Ballet Theatre, Nizami Street 95

Vurgun Russian Drama Theatre, Khagani Street 7

Children's Summer Theatre, Primorksy Park

Magomayev Philharmonic Concert Hall, Kommunisticheskaya Street 2. Built in 1912 in neo-classical style by G. Termikelov.

House of Folk Art, Myasnikova Street 3

Kurbanov Musical Comedy Theatre, Azerbaijana Street 8. Built in 1883 and formerly the home of the G. Tagiev Theatre.

Gadzhibekov Conservatoire, Dmitrova Street 98. The building of the conservatoire was specially constructed for the purpose in 1941.

Shaiga Puppet Theatre, Prospect Neftyanikov 36

Circus, Samed Vurgun Street

Kirov Park, Lermontov Street 9, on the slopes above the west side of the town. Maxim Gorky said that the view over the bay from this point was better than that from Naples, and a few years later, at the end of the 1930s, a park was opened here. The centre of the park is best reached from a point near the Intourist Hotel by the funicular railway, opened in 1960, which rises 100 m (328 ft) over a distance of 500 m/yds. (It operates from 7 A.M. till 11 P.M. but is closed Mon. until 3 P.M.) Located in the park are an open-air theatre, sports facilities, cafés, an abandoned tearoom, and the *Druzhba Restaurant*, with an excellent view over the bay. There is also the statue to Kirov and a monument to Major-General Azi Aslanov.

Nizami Garden, Rabochi Prospect 57. This park was formerly known as Nobel Park and surrounded Villa Petrolea.

Dzerzhinsky Park, Chapayev Street 37

Lenin Stadium, Dzerzhinsky Street 20. The stadium was built in 1953 and can seat 50,000. Near it is the Palace of Sport and the Baku Children's Railway.

Hippodrome Racecourse, Nadj. Narimanov Street

Botanical Garden, Patamdarskoye Chaussee 4. This garden was founded in 1935 and covers a territory of 16 hectares (40 acres).

The city bathing beach is near Government House.

Zoo, Saraikina Street 2

Azerbaijan Hotel, Restaurant and Bar, Lenin Prospect 1; tel. 98–9842.

Moscow Hotel, Restaurant and Bar, Mekhty Goussain Street 1a; tel. 39–4048. This is also an Intourist hotel, with a foreign-currency bar.

Intourist Hotel, Restaurant and Bar, Neftyanikov Prospect 63; tel. 92–1265

Tourist Hotel, Chapayev Street 2

Baku Hotel, Darwin Street 9

Metro Restaurant, at the crossing of Gogol and Nizami streets

Shirvan Restaurant, Kirov Prospect 15

Gulistan Restaurant

Caravansarai Restaurants, Bashennaya Street 11, in the old town, just above the Maiden's Tower. These two 14th- and 15th-century caravanserais stand opposite each other, and the restaurants have been built in their cellars.

Gyz-galasy (Maiden's Tower) Café, in the centre of town in Primorsky Park beside the Caspian. This decorative Oriental building stands opposite the real Maiden's Tower.

Bank, Kirov Prospect 17

Consulate General of the Islamic Republic of Iran, Bonyardi Sardarof Street 4; tel. 92–6143

In Azerbaijan the foreign-currency shops are called "Chinar" (plane tree).

Chinar Foreign-Currency Shop, Prospect Neftyanikov 103

Chinar Foreign Currency Shop, in the Azerbaijan Hotel

General Department Store, Ali Bairamova Street 5

Oriental Bazaar Shopping Centre, Moskovsky Prospect

Carpet Shops, Gorky Street 1 and Zevina Street 11

Gift Shop, Nizami Street 20

Souvenirs, Kolomiitsieva Street 8

Books, Yefimova Street 46, Bashennaya Street 8/10, and Voroshilov Street 1

Camera Shop, Kommunisticheskaya Street 21

Jewellers, Zevina Street 11 and Nizami Street 28

Paintings, Nizami Street 18

Central Market, Samed Vurgun Street 73

Public Bathhouse, Schorsa Street 130

Taxi Stands, Aznefti Square, Molodyozhi Square, and the central railway station

In the southwest part of Baku Bay, about 250 m/yd from the shore on a small island, can be seen the ruins of a mediaeval fortress. Archaeologists excavated some stones with inscriptions that indicate that it was built in 1234. There is a legend that this is the remains of the town of Sabail, now lying at the bottom of the sea.

Intourist organises a number of excursions from Baku, including those to the seaside resort of Zagulba, the carpet factory at Nardaran, the archaeological site of Kobystan, and the towns of Sumgait, Kuba, and Shemakha.

Apsheron Peninsula

Apsheron Peninsula (in Russian, Apsheronsky Poluostrov) is an eastern extension of the Caucasus Mountains running into the Caspian Sea. All the Apsheron Peninsula used to be guarded by towers, and signals of fire or smoke were visible from one to the other.

The surface of the peninsula consists of a gently undulating plain, partly traversed by ravines and characterised by its salty lakes. Vineyards and tea plantations are features of the regional economy, but the peninsula is especially noted for its oil-bearing strata, and the workings extend into the sea. The northern part of the peninsula is occupied by the Apsheron resorts, Mardakyan, Shuvelyan, Buzovna, Bylgiya-Zagulba, Pirshagi, and Turkyany being the best known. *Zagulba* (40 km/25 miles) from Baku is the site of the Intourist bathing beach. There are neurological and cardiological sanatoria in this area, and sea bathing is recommended to both types of patients, being particularly beneficial in conjunction with the fresh sea air. The average temperature of the water in May is about 19°C (66°F) and in August, 27°C (80.6°F). In this resort area are many orchards and plantations with fine grapes as well as wonderful beaches of golden sand.

In Apsheron there are a number of *castles* which belonged to different feuding families. These castles have played a strategic role over the years.

Travelling from Baku in a northeasterly direction, as if going to the airport; continue past the oil wells to the *Yesenin Museum*, located on the left of the road, in the Dendrarium. The original garden belonged to a millionaire. The Russian poet Sergei Yesenin came to Baku in 1924 and wrote here. He became very fond of the town and the people. Yesenin came again in 1925 and wrote his "Ballad of 26" (referring to the 26 commissars) in May of that year. He committed suicide in Leningrad on 28 December 1925. The bas-relief of Yesenin beside the road was made in 1972.

Kulustan Restaurant, on the right of the road

Mardakyan

40 km (25 miles) from Baku. The road leads past the 19th-century *Khanbaba bathhouse*. The hot bathing rooms were at the back, and the dirty water drained out under the walls. The front room had a cold pool. Nearby is the *Almas-zade or Heidar Mosque*, built in 1893 by a rich man concerned with fishing. This is to be used as a museum, among the exhibits being stones found in Mardakyan bearing prehistoric carvings including pictures of deer, people, and tigers.

From the bathhouse, turn left into the centre of the settlement for the 14th-century *square tower* in a walled enclosure. The tower itself is a rectangular structure, 22 m (72 ft) high, with semicircular bastions at the corners and measuring 7–10 m (25–32 ft) along each wall. It has 5 floors, and the interior is mostly wooden. It is surrounded by walls 20–25 m (22–27 yd) long and 7 m (23 ft) high, all supposedly built in the 14th–16th centuries. Big jars were sunk into the ground to store food. There were 30 such jars for grain, and 2 wells for water. Stone steps adjacent to the walls lead up to a tower. The tower was restored from 1954 to 59.

Go back to the bathhouse and straight on to find the *round tower*, also with a surrounding wall. This is situated 2–2.5 km (about a mile) from the sea in the western part of Mardakyan.

Two Arabic inscriptions on slabs of stone, one of which used to be above the entrance and the other on one side, are on display in the Hermitage Museum in Leningrad. They say: "The fortress was built by Shirvan Shah Kesranid Gershasp, son of Farukh-zade I, son of Menuchekhr II [in] the month of Murdad, the 600th year [i.e., 1232] by architect Abd-al-Medzhid, son of Masud."

The round tower is 15.5 m (51 ft) high, with an exterior diameter of 7.6 m (25 ft) and an interior diameter of 4.2 m (14 ft). The entrance inside is 7 m (23 ft) up, with a retractable ladder. It has 3 floors, each roofed with a hemispherical cupola and connected by a staircase.

Tuba-Shakh Mosque carries the date of 1481–82 and the name of the donor, a certain Tuba-Shakh. There is another inscription near the spiral staircase leading to the roof, which has the date of 1372 and the name of the donor, Khadzha Bakhakh-din, which, according to scientific sources, belongs to a more ancient mosque in the nearby village of Buznova.

Nardaran

On the way to Nardaran is the *Mamedierov Monument*, commemorating 1 of the 26 commissars who was born nearby, and the *Azizbekov Monument*.

Nardaran is 40 km from the centre of Baku. This is sand-dune country, and there are deep drifts of sand in the yards and lanes. In the northern part of the village is another *round 14th-century tower* inside a vast yard, 560 sq m (67 sq yd) surrounded with fortified walls and not yet fully restored. It is 12.5 m (41 ft) high and 6.2 m (20 ft) in diameter. Its walls are 1.6 m (5.2 ft) thick and their circumference is 22.4 m (73 ft). The surrounding wall is 5.5 m (18 ft) high in some places. An Arabic inscription on the tower said that it was dedicated to Mother Hura Bereke in 1301, but some interpret this to mean Barakat ("generous"). Another inscription gave the name of the builder, Mahmud ben Sa'd. It has 3 storeys with vaulted ceilings, and the floors are connected by a spiral staircase. There was a well in the ground floor linked to a system of underground water pipes, while the 2 upper storeys were used for defence. Near the tower was a shrine or "pir" with the grave of a saint, built in 1363. Also inside the walls was: the *khan's bathhouse*, built in 1388 by Gushtasif, son of Musa, a

caravanserai of the Persian shah Abbas II (1660), with a well-preserved inscription of a poem and stone rings for tethering horses; *Abbas II Mosque*, built in 1662–63, *Shakh Suleiman's Mosque*, built in 1686; and the *khan's summer cottage*, which dated back to the 15th century and was a small structure. It stood 2 km (1 mile) from the seashore in the northeastern part of the village. In the vineyard, there were some additional buildings, 2 wells, and a swimming pool. The cottage was crowned with a cupola like that of a mosque. There were underground passages at a depth of 2–4 m (6–13 ft) between the tower, the shrine and the khan's residence.

Indzhes enet Carpet Factory, Tourists are shown the process of the manufacture of handmade carpets.

Surakhany (Surakhani)

About 26 km (16 miles) northeast of the centre of Baku. In this village stands a *fire worshippers' temple*, said to have been founded in the 13th century and restored in the 17th, and the *Monastery of Atesh-Gede*, founded by Indians who traded in this area. The museum is open 11:30–6, daily.

Fire worship was fundamental to 2 religions. First was that of the Parsees, disciples of the Iranian prophet Zoroaster, a faith founded in the 6th century B.C. and practised in Persia before the rise of Islam. Zoroaster influenced the other major Western religions, namely Judaism, Christianity, and Islam. According to the legends, he was viewed as a model for priests, warriors, and agriculturists as well as being a skillful craftsman and healer.

The second fire-worshipping religion was that of the Hindu brahmins (Brahma, Vishnu and Siva worshippers), who especially honoured cows. They burned their dead in fire, having first poured clarified butter over them, and threw the ashes into the river.

The pentagonal monastery is a single-storey building with sides 40 m (44 yds) long. It is surrounded by a 5-m (16-ft)-high wall. Inside the spacious yard stands the temple, an open square structure, with sides 6 m (6.5 yd) long, and consisting of 4 stone columns connected by arches and roofed by a cupola. Pipes were built into the columns, and gas burned above the temple as well as from the central well. The fire worshippers used to burn their dead over the flame. The inside part of the temple rises .75 m (2.5 ft) above the yard. In the middle there was a hollow, which used to be a 10-m- (33-ft)-deep well, and an eternal flame burned there; that was the most sacred place. Above the gates was a special room for visitors, from which a stone staircase leads down into the yard. There used to be other guest rooms along the insides of the surrounding wall. In 1746 an English traveller by the name of Gunway visited this temple and described it. Now there is an iron gas pipe inside each column, and there is a flame at each corner, but none now over the roof of the temple. There is an inscription on the northern wall in Hindi, and others over the entrance of each monastic cell in Hindi and Farsi. In these cells in the 18th and the beginning of the 19th centuries lived Hindu fire worshippers and their disciples. They spent their time in prayer, facing the fire, and imposed all sorts of disciplines upon themselves: they fasted, remained standing or wandered with their arms up year-round, losing the use of their hands. Most of them were naked. In 1825 there were 25 Hindus here, but by 1860 only 1 was left and soon he died too.

In the middle of the 19th century, there were 3 wells in the yard: a water well, a fire well, and a small 1-m (3.3-ft)-deep well. There was also a large stone on which the Hindu fire worshippers once put the bodies of the deceased; they poured clarified butter over them and burned them in the fire, which came from the fire well. The monastery was abandoned in 1887, though the gas is still burning and the buildings are kept up.

Roman Castle, on top of a hill, is a polygonal structure; its walls, 7–8 m (23–26 ft) high, come close to the slopes of the hill. The corners and the middle of the eastern wall are fortified with round towers. Its rectangular "donzhon" (tower) is 13 m (43 ft) high and is similar to that in Mardakyan. The 4 storeys of the "donzhon" are connected with a staircase. The castle dates back to the 13th century. It looks very much like mediaeval European castles. A village stretches over the eastern slope of the hill; there is an ancient mosque and a cemetery with old tombs.

Sumgait Population—231,000

Sumgait, on the northern shore of the Apsheron Peninsula at the mouth of the river Sumgait and 40 km (25 miles) northwest of Baku, became a town in 1949. Light and textile industries, machine building, chemical (superphosphates) and metallurgic, particularly aluminum, industries are developed here. There is also a synthetic rubber plant. Foreign visitors may go there if they gain permission.

It was founded as a satellite town of Baku with the establishment on the Apsheron Peninsula of metallurgical and chemical industries and has grown into a modern, European-looking town, spic and span, with a busy atmosphere.

The town stretches along the seashore with eight-storey blocks closest to the sea and five-storey ones behind. Nizami Street is particularly good looking with its three-storey blocks mostly faced with local stone. The main thoroughfares are Mira Street and Lenin Prospect; they have trees planted in the middle and run parallel to each other down to Samed Vurgun Embankment, which curves along beside the sea, and Primorsky Park, a popular place for a stroll. The park is planted with cypress, weeping willows, poplar, and pine, and there are sheep and hens there too.

Lenin Monument, Lenin Prospect
Nariman Monument, Druzhba Street
Local Museum
26 Baku Commissars' Memorial, with an eternal flame

Hotel and Restaurant, at the crossing of Mira and Narimanov streets, in the *Trade Center*, which also comprises the garage, the department store, and the market
Hotel for Sportsmen, on the waterfront
Sumgait Restaurant, Samed Vurgun Street
Bahar Restaurant, Druzhba Street
Dzheiran Sashlik Bar, on the left of Mira Street
GPO, Lenin Prospect 14
Market, on the left of Mira Street

Neftyaniye Kamni (Oil Rocks) Population—6,000

This is the only town in the world built on piles in the open sea. It is about 45 km (28 miles) from the Apsheron Peninsula in the Caspian Sea. "Black gold" was discovered under the water in an underwater chain of ancient rocks, hence the name of the city. It was founded in 1949 when the first wells were sunk. The founder, Mikhail Kaveroshkin, perished in a storm, and there is a bust to him in the town.

Kobystan

60 km (37 miles) to the south of Baku. On one of the cliff faces of Mt. Beyukdash is carved a Latin inscription from the first century A.D. that is unique in that it is the most easterly inscription in that language to have been discovered. There is, besides, a great range and variety of carvings here, the earliest dating from the Stone Age and the most recent from the Middle Ages. There are scenes showing hunting, harvesting, and dancing among a total of about 4,000 drawings. Open 10–5.

Kuba Population—21,000

In northeastern Azerbaijan, 170 km (106 miles) from Baku, beyond Sumgait.

Archaeological data suggest that Kuba was known in the 7th century. Founded on the river Gudial-Chai in the 15th century (Sov. Enc.) 616 m (2,021 ft) above sea level in the foothills of the Greater Caucasian Range, on the northeastern slopes of Mt. Shakhdag, it was probably called Kudial until the 17th century. A khanate was founded here in the 18th century by Nadir Shah. It was semi-independent from Persia, and in 1782 the local khan, Fateli-Khan (1736–89), signed a trade agreement with Russia. The khanate was subsequently annexed by Russia and abolished entirely in 1806.

It is 28 km (17 miles) from the Khachmas railway station.

The main street is Lenin Street.

The town is the centre of an orchard region, particularly famed for its apples. Local industry includes a cannery and here also is the *Azerbaijan Institute of Fruit-Growing, Viticulture and Subtropical Plants*. There is a factory of microelectric engines. Traditionally, Kuba has also been a centre of carpet making; Kuba carpets are considered the best in Azerbaijan.

Khadji-Baba Akhun Mosque, Sovietskaya Street 62. Founded in 1910 and open for services.

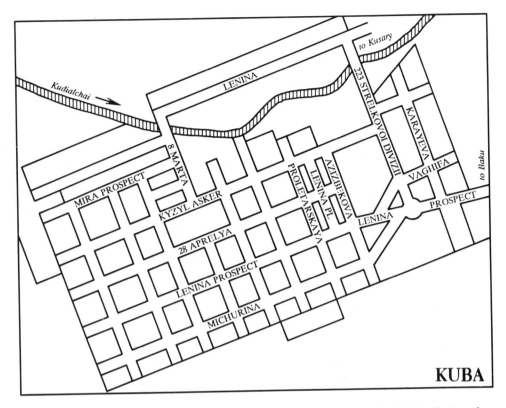

Sakini-Khanum Mosque, built in 1820.

Ardebin Mosque, Sovietskaya Street. Built in the 20th century and now closed.

Local Museum, Sovietskaya Street 12. Open 10–7. Dedicated to the poet, linguist, scientist, and local enlightener Abbaskuli-Aga Bakikhanov (Abas-Kuli-Aga Kudsi Bakikhanov) (1794–1847). The museum was formerly his house.

Djuma Mosque, Central Square. Built in 1806. Open as an annex of the local museum.

Bathhouse, Sovietskaya Street. Built in the 19th century.

Mausoleum, in the cemetery. Built in the 19th century.

Lenin Statue, in the square by the bus station, on the way into town

Volna Hotel, Lenin Street

Gulustan Restaurant, on the right of the road at the entrance to the town

Bag-Ban Restaurant, to the left of the Lenin Street

Kebab Khana, on the left of the central square

Filling Station, on the left of the main road

Shemakha Population—60,000

This town lies a little to the right of the main road, 128 km (80 miles) inland from Baku. Now the administrative and cultural centre of the district, Shemakha is thought by some historians to stand on the site of the ancient town of Kamekhiya. The name of Shemakha perhaps derives from the Arabic "Sham" (Damascus) and "akhi" (brother), so that it would mean "like Damascus," a logical description to have been used by people coming from Syria. It is located 750 m (2,461 ft) above sea level in a seismatic area and has suffered continually from earthquakes. That of 1671–72 was exceptionally severe, and others occurred in 1859, 1895, and 1902.

Ptolemy in his "Guide to Geography" in the 2nd century A.D. referred to the place as Kmakhia, but the historic foundation of the town is traditionally attributed to the period of the Sasanian kings of the 3rd century A.D., particularly to King Yazdegerd. It has in any case been known since the 5th–6th centuries and enjoyed its heyday from 9th–16th centuries, when it was the residence of the shahs of Shirvan. Its importance grew when it rose to become the trade, religious, political, and the cultural centre of the area. It minted its own coins and produced painted pottery, copper tableware, weapons and woven carpets; the fame of its silk spread far and wide. It flourished particularly under the 12th-century Kesranid rulers, Menuchekhev II and Akhsitan I. Its fame as one of the largest trading centres of Transcaucasia spread to Europe and Russia, and travellers to the Orient who visited the place called it Scamachia or Samagi. Hagani (c. 1120–99), a classic poet of Azerbaijan, said that it "eclipsed Bukhara's splendour."

A terrible earthquake in 1176 caused the shahs to transfer their residence to Baku; the setback, however, was no more than temporary. A turning point came at the end of the 15th century, when the army of the shah of Shirvan was defeated in battle against that of Shah Esmail of Persia. Shirvan was thereafter a vassal of the Safavid shahs of Persia.

It maintained its de facto independence until 1537, when Shah Tahmasp (1524–76) appointed his brother as governor of the province of Shirvan. The shah was instrumental in encouraging the weaving of carpets and of raising it to the level of a state industry.

This was also the time when the Ottoman Empire rose to full power, and in the 1580s Sultan Suleiman the Magnificent took over Azerbaijan. Turks began to move in, settle, and fortify the town. The fortress walls around Shemakha were built in 1583. The English explorer and merchant Anthony Jenkinson praised the town highly, as did a certain Geoffrey Deckett. The walls were interspersed with towers and within were caravanserai, a fine palace, and a number of mosques. It had become a stopover through which passed most of the diplomatic, political, and trade missions between Persia and Russia. Its fortifications, however, were fully justified, as there were Turkish wars against Safavid Persia during the reigns of Murat III (1574–95) and Murat IV (1629–40). In 1607 Shah Abbas (1587–1629) besieged Shemakha and ordered the fortress walls to be pulled down. But, in spite of the instability of the times, the German traveller, scientist, and diplomat Adam Oelshlager (Olearius) was able to write in 1636 that about 30,000 citizens had made their homes within the walls.

From the 18th century, the town was the capital of the Shemakha khanate, but there came a sudden end to the town's prosperity in 1734 when Nadir Shah of Persia descended upon it and caused the survivors of his wrath to move to a site near Akhsu, which was called New Shemakha. At one point all 3 neighbouring powers of Turkey, Russia, and Persia were struggling for possession of Azerbaijan at the same time. After the death of Nadir Shah in 1747, a number of separate khanates were set up in the area, including the khanate of Shemakha. The last khan of Shemakha chose a fortress on Mt. Fitdag for his residence, and by the beginning of the 19th century, Shemakha was no more than a ruined and neglected town. The remains of the khanate of Shemakha were united with Russia in 1806 as a result of the Russo-Persian War of 1805–13, and this was confirmed by the Treaty of Gulistan of 1813.

In 1820 some people began to move into old Shemakha again, but the town had to be rebuilt. Hardly any important ancient monuments had survived. Russian military engineers laid the plans, and construction began in earnest after 1824. There is an obvious influence of Russian classic style, especially in the architecture of the public buildings. In 1846 Shemakha was declared the provincial centre, and Azerbaijan's first theatre was built here. The town that had suffered so from its enemies in the past was never free from the threat of earthquakes. Its newfound importance was soon to

SHEMAKHA

be lost when in 1859 yet another earthquake caused the governor to transfer his offices to the safety of Baku. Much of what was left was destroyed by another earthquake in 1902. Now only the old fortress wall, which once protected the residence of the Shirvan shahs, remains.

Shemakha was the birthplace of the poets Afsaladdin Khagani (1120–99), Imameddin Nasimi, Seiazim Shirvani (1835–88) and Mirza-Alekper Sabir (Tair-zade) (1862–1911). Also born here were the geographers Gadzhi Zeinal-Abdin Shirvani and Gamidi Shirvani.

The town is a major agricultural centre and has 25,000 hectares (62,500 acres) of vineyards watered from a system of 34 reservoirs. The surrounding area has long been famous for its wine; there is even a story that it was from here that the vine was imported to France, and thus it is from this stock that the world's most famous wines have developed. In the town are a number of wine factories producing wines, including Matrasa, Kagor, and appropriately, Shemakha.

Another factory makes building materials, but it is the *Shemakha Carpet Workshop* that is of the greatest importance here. The handwoven Shirvan rugs are usually made entirely of wool, and their designs often contain elements similar to those used in the rugs of neighbouring Daghestan and Kurdistan. There are Azerbaijan carpets in the Vatican, in the Victoria and Albert Museum in London, and in the art galleries of New York; there is a good selection in the carpet museum in Baku. The workshop is the centre of the local carpet industry; it supplies carpet makers in the surrounding villages, and collects their finished carpets for sale. Some of the designs were used in the 12th century, but each craftsman adds his own personal touch.

Juma Mosque, Gubkina Street 41. Founded in the 10th century, this is now built of yellow stone with battlements and 4 small minarets. The original was constructed with mortar of sand and egg. It was heavily damaged by fire at the beginning of the century.

Local Museum, in the Juma Mosque

Sabir's House, Shirvani Street, near the mosque. The folk poet and satirist Mirza-Alekper Sabir (Tair-Zade) (1862–1911) was much influenced by the revolution of 1905. He was born and lived most of his life in Shemakha, but in 1910 he went to Baku to teach Persian and Azerbaijani. There is a gold-painted bust in front of this, a pink-washed, 2-storey house. The room downstairs is the original building; the upstairs part was added as a museum to house the display of photographs and documents. Open 10–6, daily.

Intourist organises visits to one of the state wine farms where there is a *wine-tasting hall*. Lunch is provided at the *Banovsha ("violet") Restaurant*.

Sabir Statue, in front of the teacher-training college

Stadium

Park

Shemakha Hotel, tel. 92–307

Restaurant, on the left on the way out of town

Filling Station, to the right of the road just beyond the town

Gulistan Fortress, 1.5 km (1 mile) on foot out of town, in a hollow on the upper slopes of the hill. This was the site of the Shirvan shahs' palace. It was built in the 11th–12th centuries, and the walls run for a total length of 45 m/yd. There is a secret underground passage leading to it, and the entrance is on the eastern side, 32 m (105 ft) up the mountain slope. Some historians believe that the fortress was named for the daughter of the Sasanid shah, Anushirvan.

There is a good view of the surrounding area and the nearby villages from the fortress. 8 km (5 miles) to the southwest is Klakhany, where there are 10 half-ruined mausolea dating from the 17th–18th centuries. In addition to the mausolea, some Armenian churches can also be seen in the villages below. There is also a good view from the more easily accessible Yeddi-Gyumbez cemetery (see below), looking north and leftward toward the town.

Medresseh and Kalakhana, drive southwest of Shemakha to the medresseh and from there, southeast to Kalakhana

Shakhanda Cemetery, the cemetery nearest to town. It is the oldest, but not the largest. Sciazin Shirvani's grave is here.

Shemakha Reservoir, with its dam below the town, to the the the southwest

Yeddi-Gyumbez ("seven cupolas") Cemetery, to the west of the town, beyond the reservoir. From here, looking down on the town, the Juma Mosque is visible, with yellow stone walls and battlements. In the cemetery on the crest of the hill are the 7 18th–19th-century octagonal mausolea from which the cemetery takes its name. 3 are well preserved, and the others are under reconstruction. They were damaged in 1905 during fighting between the Armenians and Azerbaijanis. It was a strategic vantage point for battling. Also here, up at the top of the hill beyond the trees, are the octagonal Adji-Khan Gumbezi mausoleum (1763) and the Eddi-Gumbez mausoleum (1810).

Pir Dere Kos (Pedrakos) Mausoleum, ruins on the top of another hill near the fortress

Sundhi, 18 km (11 miles) to the northeast of Shemakha. A "mausoleum cemetery" just above the dam of the reservoir.

Diri Baba Mausoleum, 30 km (19 miles) from Shemakha, on the road to Baku. Built in the 15th century.

Yashar, at the crossing of 26-Komissar Street and 8-Marta Street

Astrophysical Observatory, at Resedkhana, in the mountains about 8 km (5 miles) north of Shemakha. The road goes through the village of Chukhuryud and Kirovka on the way to a settlement inhabited by scientists. Beside the road and between the 2 villages is a hydrogen sulphide spring. The observatory stands at a height of 1,440 m (4,724 ft) above sea level on the foothills of Mt. Pirkuli. The mirror telescope made by the firm of Karl Zeiss of Germany is housed in a silver tower 8 storeys high. It is so powerful that if it were to be turned upon the city of Leningrad from where it stands, a single candle flame could be seen.

BURANA
See Bishkek, p. 80.

BASHKORSTAN
See Ufa, p. 583.

BATUMI Population—136,000
Batumi is the capital of the Ajar (Atchar) Autonomous Republic; the Ajars are Muslim Georgians who were forced to adopt Islam. The city lies along the shore of a deep bay on the eastern shore of the Black Sea and is an important resort. It has a warm, damp, subtropical climate with an average annual temperature of 14.6°C (58.1°F.) (August: 23.2°C/73.8°F; January: 6.4°C/43.5°F). The bathing season lasts from April till November.

The place was first mentioned by Pliny (23–78 A.D.) as Bathus. The settlement was on the left bank of the river Bat (from which derives the Georgian name Bat-om-i). The Greeks understood it as "badus" (deep), although the river itself is not and never has been so. It is also said that "batus" means stone; the riverbed is certainly very stony. Today the river is called Korolis-Tskali.

In ancient times the part of the Black Sea coast near Batumi, a land of legendary wealth, was called Colchis, "land of the sun." The mythical Argonauts sailed here to find the Golden Fleece (see Sukhumi for more of the story, or read "the Jason Voyage" by Tim Severin for a modern version). The Romans came as early as the 4th century B.C., and Bathus was the site of a Roman encampment. In the 4th century A.D., a state called Lazika was formed here, but after the fall of the western Roman Empire, it was subject to Byzantium. In the 6th–

7th centuries, the area saw unremitting struggles between Byzantium and Persia.

From the 10th century, Ajaria was part of Georgia, but from the second half of the 15th century, the Turks began trying to annex this area. It was captured in 1547, when the Turks destroyed the churches, virtually eradicated Christianity, and converted the local population to Islam. The local landlords in particular had to convert in order to protect their property. The majority of the Ajarians, who are a western branch of the Karveli group of Georgians, have been Muslims since the 17th century. They are Sunni Muslims of the Hanafi school, more often found in the countryside than in Batumi itself. The Ajarians use some Turkish words in their vocabulary. Today nearly half the local population is Georgian, one-third is either Russian or Ukrainian, and the rest are Armenians and Greeks.

In 1878, after the Russian victory in the Russo-Turkish War and after the Congress of Berlin, Batumi and its adjoining area, having been dominated by the Turks for 300 years, were placed under Russian authority. At that time Batumi was a small, poor village with but 2,000 inhabitants. Trade was at a standstill and the port of little significance. However, between 1878 and 1886, it operated as a Free Port, was linked by rail to the rest of the country in 1883, and by the end of the 19th century, it had grown considerably, both as a city and as a port. It gained further importance at the beginning of the 20th century when an oil pipeline linked it with Baku and thus with the oil export trade.

In 1918 the Turks seized the city but had to abandon it almost immediately. It was under British occupation for more than a year. In 1921, with the advent of Soviet power, Batumi became the capital of the Ajarian Autonomous Republic.

There is no architectural centre of the city. Of the 3 main squares, Lenin Square is officially the central one. Beyond it lie the fishing, freight, and passenger ports, with the building of the former Customs House nearby. The square is used for public holiday demonstrations, but it is located in the suburbs. The railway station is right in the middle of Batumi, and Rustaveli Street is the real heart of the place. The Russians built some administrative buildings here, as well as some mansions typical of the last century and the beginning of this, both of which are easily distinguished. The governor's residence, at the corner of Kirov and Rustaveli streets, is now a maternity hospital. Part of the old town can still be seen, but it has lost its Oriental quality. Many new houses have sprung up among the old single-storey buildings. Rustaveli Street and Stalin (formerly Mariisky) Prospect lead up to the dolphinarium, as does the old embankment, with smart hotels built at the turn of the century and the wooden resort building, the "kurzal," now used by the army. In 1884 these buildings stood on the waterfront with the seashore right opposite them. Now, a hundred years later, the sea has receded, and a marine park has been planted

with gardens and an esplanade. Dynamo Stadium and an amusement park are also on the sandy, level ground here.

Besides the work connected with the port, local industries today include oil refining, the manufacture of machinery for the food industry, woodworking and furniture manufacture, tobacco, and some food industries. It is also an important curative resort with a number of specialised sanatoria. There is a pedagogical institute and a marine school.

St. Nicholas's Cathedral, Telmann Street 20. This blue and white building dates from 1865, when it was designed as a Greek church. Today services are held in both Georgian and Russian.

Roman Catholic Church, Shaumyan Street 55. Built in stone in 1907 with twin towers and decorated with dolphin gargoyles.

Church, 31-Dekabrya Street

SS. Nino and Andrei Church, a Georgian church built in 1895.

Troitskaya Church, at the cemetery

Synagogue, 8-Marta Street

Mosque, Chkalova Street, not far from St. Nicholas's Cathedral, behind an 8-storey building. It is open for services.

Mosque, on the seafront

Castle, to the left of the road on the way to Batumi from the north, not far from the mouth of the Korolis-Tskali River. These ruins of Queen Tamar's Castle stand a bit back from the sea now but must once have been on the coast.

Ajaria Museum, Dzhincharadze Street 4, in the former treasury building. The museum was founded in 1908, and among its 70,000 exhibits are unique archaeological finds. In the ethnographical section on the ground floor is an interesting exhibition of national costumes. Open 10–7.

Architecture Museum, on the way out of town to the north, near Queen Tamar's Castle.

Revolution Museum, Gorky Street 7. Displayed here is the equipment of an underground printing shop and the portraits and personal belongings of local revolutionaries. Open 10–6; closed Mon.

Military Museum, Gogebashvili Street, near the war memorial by the sea

Stalin's House, Sulaberidze Street

Planetarium, Sverdlov Street 26. Housed in the disused Armenian church.

Dolphinarium and Oceanarium, Ninoshvili Street 37. 50 different kinds of fish are kept here, besides Caspian Sea seals and turtles from the Indian Ocean. Open daily 10–6. Except on Mondays, from May till November, three 30-min. performances a day are given in the dolphinarium.

Exhibition Hall, Lenin Prospect

Chavchavadze Monument, Teatralnaya Square. Ilya Chavchavadze was an outstanding 19th-century Georgian writer and public figure. The monument was sculpted by Elgudzha Amashukeli and unveiled in 1988.

Obelisk, 31-Dekabrya Street. Erected in honour of Batumi's first Social-Democrat conference, chaired by Stalin on 31 December 1901.

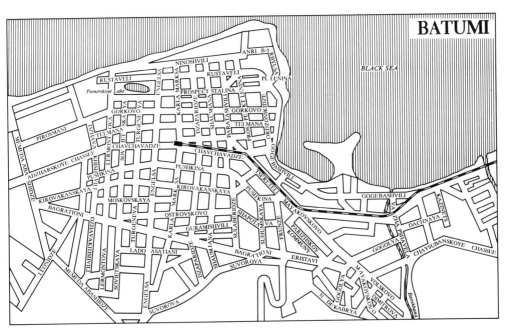

BATUMI

Strike Monument, Frunze Street. This obelisk commemorates the strike of 1902.

Lenin Monuments, Henri Barbussa Street, by the dolphinarium, and on Dzhaparidze Street

Civil War Memorial, on Lenin Square, by the port. Here is a carved column marking the common grave of those who lost their lives fighting in the Civil War in Ajaria.

War Memorial, Gogebashvili Street, by the sea. Glory Obelisk and an eternal flame commemorate those who fell during World War II.

War Memorial, 31-Dekabrya Street. To those who gave their lives in the Second World War.

Tabidze Bust, Stalin Prospect. This monument in the form of a gigantic head commemorates poet Galaktion Tabidze (1892–1959).

Chavchavadze Drama Theatre, Rustaveli Street 1. Built with a grand, 8-columned portico in 1951–52 to seat 650 people.

Summer Theatre, in Primorsky Park, Ninoshvili Street 2. This theatre was built in Georgian style in 1948.

Philharmonia Concert Hall, Stalin Prospect

Circus, Baratashvili Street

Dynamo Stadium and Sports Complex, Henri Barbusse Street. The stadium has seats for 20,000, and here too is the open-air swimming pool and the Gantiadi Water Sports Centre. The bathing beaches begin nearby and stretch right along to the dolphinarium and beyond.

Yacht Club, Primorskoye Ozero

Children's Yacht Club, Engels Street 4

Primorsky Park, Ninoshvili Street 2. This was formerly called City Boulevard and runs beside a long, wide beach. There is a restaurant here, and the Summer Theatre. Magnolias, palms, and other subtropical trees have been planted.

Young Pioneers' Park, Engels Street 4. This is laid out beside a lake where schoolchildren crew a ship. The park extends for 18 hectares (45 acres) and contains a considerable collection of local flora and fauna. The first few trees were planted here in 1881 by Alexander II, and the park was called Alexandrovsky Park. At the entrance to the park is a sculpture commemorating the first local female pilot, Gogitidze, and a bust of a test pilot named Dzinacharadze.

Intourist Hotel and Restaurant and Minutka Café, Ninoshvili Street 11; tel. 22–229; Intourist office: TEL. 21–902.

Batumi Hotel, Ninoshvili Street

Medea Hotel, Karl Marx Street

Moryak Hotel, Lermontov Street

Meskheti Hotel This 18-storey hotel opened in 1986.

Restaurant, in Primorsky Park

There are various small cafés in the city where Georgian dishes can be found; recommended is "khachapuri" (cheese pie), which is available fresh in the morning, as Georgians like it for breakfast.

Bank, Lenin Street and Oktyabrsky Prospect 27

Turkish Consulate General, Stalin Prospect 8; tel. 33909

Department Store, Chavchavadze Street 1

Tsitsinatela Foreign-Currency Shop, in the Intourist Hotel

Art Salon, Rustaveli Street 10

Bookshops, Stalin Prospect 25 and Dzhaparidze Street 23

Market, Chavchavadze Street

The coastal area, which stretches for about 35 km (22 miles) between Batumi and Kobuleti, is known as the resort area. There are many sanatoria and private houses here. There is a good motor road, and the local railway also links them with Batumi. Beside the road, on a hill on the right near the bridge over the river Korolis-Tskali, stand the ruins of a mediaeval tower known here as Queen Tamar's Castle (see above).

Intourist's excursions from Batumi include trips to the botanical garden in Zelyoni Mys, the tea plantation at Chakva, and a trip up into the mountains to the village of Khala.

Makhindzhauri

6 km (4 miles) from Batumi. The name means "place of the maimed" and refers to the torture that the Turks inflicted upon the Georgian Christians as they forced here to accept Islam. There is a good beach here, with Marine Park behind it. There are also mineral springs and a number of rest homes and sanatoria.

Makhindzauri Café

Zelyoni Mys (Georgian: Mtsvane Kontskhi)

Intourist organises excursions here, 9 km (6 miles) from Batumi. The name means "green cape." This resort is 72 m (236 ft) above sea level and is famous for its *Botanical Garden*, which is the largest in the country. It was founded in 1912 by the botanist Prof. Andrei Krasnov (1862–1914) with plants from all the continents and has a most comprehensive collection of subtropical flora. His dream was to turn the place into a garden-exhibition, with areas such as a Mexican boulevard or a Chilean town planted with date and coconut palms, where Creole women in the taverns would serve tourists liqueurs distilled from local fruit. Among other ideas, he wanted a few Negro families and pygmies from the mountains of New Guinea to settle here. Krasnov also hoped to build a Chinese house on the top of the hill.

While working here in the garden, Professor Krasnov hurt his leg, and it turned gangrenous. He died at the age of 52 and was buried near the Japanese Garden, on the hill overlooking the sea. Professor Krasnov died in 1914, but the garden continued to grow. Since 1925 it has also become an important scientific research centre, and in 1930 the 16th Party Congress ordered the subtropical region of the Caucasus to be turned into a Soviet Florida and California—meaning that it should be the most important area for the growing of citrus fruits. The garden now stretches for 5 km (3 miles) along the coast, covers 113 hectares (283 acres), has 1,500 varieties of trees, and is divided into 9 different sections, including Transcaucasian, Australian, New Zealand, Himalayan, Sino-Japanese, North American, South American, and Mediterranean. The Japanese Courtyard is worthy of special attention.

In 1962, marking the centenary of his birth, a monument was set up on his grave with the inscription: "To the Founder of this Garden—Krasnov.'" The bust was made by his granddaughter, Krasnova-Vertinskaya.

Abkhazia Restaurant
Café, by the entrance to the Botanical Garden.

Chakva

Chakva is 18 km (11 miles) northeast of Batumi, by the river Chakvis-Tskali and on the way to Kobuleti. Intourist organises excursions here from Batumi.

Lenin Tea Planation. The first tea plantation was laid out here in 1883 by a retired engineer named Solontsev, who reaped his first harvest two years later. The first commercial planting was made in 1885. Tea bushes were brought from Hankow in China, and a group of Chinese tea specialists led by Lao Zhon Zhau were invited to assist. The first real crop was harvested in 1894.

Citrus fruits and bamboo are also grown here, and tung trees for the oil that is extracted from their seeds for use in the manufacture of paints, varnishes, and linoleum. From May until October there are tours of the local tea factory. There is also an Institute of Tea and Subtropical Cultures.

Ulybka Proshlovo ("smile of the past") Restaurant, down toward the sea and the Chakva Tourist Centre. An Intourist restaurant with Ajari decor and cuisine.

Tsikhis-Dziri

Tsikhis-Dziri is 19 km (12 miles) from Batumi, just beyond Chakva. It stands on a cape rising 70–92 m (230–302 ft) above sea level.

In 523 A.D. the Byzantine emperor Justinian ordered a fortress be built here on the top of a high rock; it was called Petra, and a Byzantine garrison was sent to man it under the leadership of the local King Tsate, who was a convert to the Christian faith. It stands at the northern end of Tsikhis-Dziri; the present name means "foundations of a fortress," and the ruins are very picturesque. The place was at one time called Justinian's Town, and excavations carried out in 1962 helped to discover more about it. In some places there were 2 or 3 storeys underground, and it was the centre of a system of underground tunnels. The southern side has survived best, and visitors enjoy climbing up the slopes to it, especially in the evening when they can watch the sunset. Tsikhis-Dziri was a very real stronghold, not only because of the fortress but because of its natural position. The Russian army failed to pass through this way as they marched on Batumi during the campaigns of 1829 and 1877–87. The cape divided this part of the coastline into north and south beaches; the southern beach is wider and is covered with small pebbles.

Tsikhis-Dziri has some of the most important citrus plantations in the country, and the main road twists through them. The orange and lemon trees growing on the terraces near the fortress were planted in 1934, and there is an enormous greenhouse where lemons are picked year-round.

The slopes of *Tsihis-Dziri Gorge* are covered with what remains of the ancient forest of Colchis, and there is a 17-m (56-ft) waterfall. Another favourite spot to walk to is *Sergeyev Kamen* ("Sergei's stone"), with this name written on it.

The Nauka (Science) Sanatorium now occupies a house built on the cape in 1909 by an engineer called Skarzhinsky. He copied a castle he had seen in Naples, and palm trees from the Canary Islands were planted in the park.

Khala

This village is 27 km (17 miles) from Batumi, inland in the mountains above Chakva. Intourist organises excursions here, but only in good weather. In Khala there is the opportunity to enjoy the scenic walk to the waterfall on the river Chakvis-Tskali. As one of its tributaries flows down from the slopes of Mt. Chakvistavi, the rainiest place in the Soviet Union, the waterfall is impressive whatever the weather.

BAUSKA

See Riga, p. 448.

BEGOVAT

See Tashkent, p. 543.

BELGOROD-DNESTROVSKY Population—56,000

Intourist organises day trips here from Odessa.

As one enters the town, there is a sign with a bunch of grapes, which are of more than economic importance to this ancient town. A legend has been told in connection with Romaneshty, centre of the Moldavian wine industry, but it is appropriate here too. Once, when the fortress was under siege, the defenders were threatened with starvation. However, the storks, which had their nests on the tops of the towers, flew in with bunches of grapes in their long beaks and the warriors' lives were saved.

The place was originally known as Tiras when it was colonised by the Milesians of ancient Greece. It is one of the oldest towns on the Black Sea coast and has probably changed its name more often than any other town on earth. In the 6th century B.C., there was a Phoenician colony, Ofiusa. At the time of Herodotus, 5th century B.C., on the site of Ofiusa, there was a town called Tyrus. It was inhabited by the Tiriti, who in 300 B.C. were conquered by the Daks, who in turn were conquered by the Romans, who called Tyrus Alba Julia. The Roman rule ended with Attila entering Bessarabia. Then came the Anti, who called it Turis. The Polovtsi called it Akliba, the Slavs called it Belgorod (meaning "white town"), and the Greeks called it both Levcopolis and Asprocastron at the same time. The Venetians, who monopolised the trade on the Black Sea, renamed Belgorod Mon Castro or Mavrocastron, after the Fourth Crusade in 1204 when Constantinople was sacked. In the 15th century, the town was in the hands of the Genoese, and they built a fortress here in 1548. The Magyars called the town Ferievar, and the Moldavians, Cetetea Alba. It changed hands several times, until in 1503 the Turks took it and held it for 300 years, calling it Akkerman. It has had 13 names altogether.

It was in 1420 that the Turkish army first reached the walls of the town, but their attack was only half-hearted as their sultan was at the same time engaged in a protracted war with Byzantium. In August 1484 Sultan Bajazet II made a more determined attack upon the fortress. He called it the Key to Galicia and Poland, and he enlisted the help of Khan Mengli-Girei of the Crimea. The fighting lasted 15 days, until on 16 August the fortress was taken, and the Turks devastated the city. They renamed it Akkerman at this time and built a mosque in place of a Russian Orthodox church.

During the subsequent 300 years, the Zaporozhye Cossacks retook the fortress on several occasions, but they could never hold it long, as the Turks were superior in strength. Turkey declared war on Russia in 1768, and during the campaign Field Marshal Suvorov gained a resounding victory near Rymnik, earning him the title count of Rymnik, but the Treaty of Iasi of 1791 still allowed Akkerman to remain in Turkish hands. While the city was held for three months by the Russians, its military commander was Mikhail Kutuzov, and it was he who in 1812 signed the Treaty of Bucharest for the Russians, by which all lands between the Dniester and the Danube, including Akkerman, became Russian.

In 1821, while Pushkin was in exile in Kishinyov, he was granted permission to visit Akkerman and stayed there with Colonel Andrei Nepenin, commander of the garrison. There is a memorial plaque on the little white house at the corner of Gorky and Pushkin streets where he lived. It is said that he also spent a night in one of the fortress towers, which accordingly bore his name. His friend, the Polish poet Adam Mickiewicz, also visited Akkerman. The place had by this time become a provincial centre and had its own coat-of-arms; a grapevine on a red field.

At the corner of Shvabskaya and Pervomaiskaya streets stands an old building where the Akkerman Convention of 1862 was signed, confirming the clauses of the 1812 Treaty of Bucharest. According to the convention, Russia received the right of unhindered trade in all regions of the Turkish Empire, while its merchant fleet gained the right of free passage in all waters belonging to the Ottoman Empire.

After the reunion with Russia, this area was first resettled by the Zaporozhye Cossacks. Later 23 German and 83 Bulgarian settlements were organised. Russian fugitive serfs also settled here. For this purpose they had to acquire the passport of some deceased Akkerman resident; so it was that many of these peasants were 100 or 130 years old according to their new passports. Because of this they were called "the immortal residents of Akkerman."

In March 1918 Bessarabia, again including Akkerman, was occupied by Rumania. It remained part of Rumania until 28 June 1940, when the Soviet army entered Bessarabia. On 21 July 1941, Belgorod-Dnestrovsky was occupied by German troops and was under German occupation until

August 1944. To commemorate the 20th anniversary of the city's liberation from the enemy, a monument was erected in the city park and unveiled on 9 May 1965. An eternal flame burns near the monument.

There is a People's Drama Theatre, a youth theatre, and a puppet theatre. Among its educational establishments is a music school, founded in 1940.

Industry includes the manufacture of cardboard, building materials, furniture, light bulbs, clothing, and footwear, but food industries predominate. There are a fish cannery and plants making wine, juice, and meat and dairy products.

Previously it was very difficult to get to Belgorod-Dnestrovsky even from the regional centre of Odessa. The ferry across the saltwater estuary ("liman") operated only in summer, and in winter the city could be reached only by a roundabout way by rail through Tiraspol, Bessarabskaya, and Arzys.

The fortress, the most impressive monument in the town, was built in 1438 by Stephan II. Originally it had 26 towers, 12 of which were used for storage while the rest were just for show and for reinforcing the walls. There were 3 gates, 2 leading to the liman and the third to an open field. The bridge over the moat was 7 sazhen (49 ft) wide. There were 2 round towers, and in 1620 at the side of 1, on a chain was kept the Polish crown of Hetman Stanislaw Koniecpolski, which had been captured by the Turks.

There is a story attached to *Devichya Bashnya, the Maiden's Tower*. There once lived a very cruel princess called Tamara, daughter of the Moldavian ruler Alexander Dobry (Kind). She took advantage of his absence with his soldiers to rob the local population, even holding up travellers on the highway. Then she declared that she wished to build a monastery and levied taxes upon her countrymen. Instead of a monastery, however, she built a strong fortress with many towers and from this stronghold she continued raiding the populace. When Alexander returned from his campaigning, he saw what had happened and vowed that his daughter should be walled up alive in a tower to pay for her misdeeds. He cursed his daughter and at the moment of his cursing, she fell into a deep and lasting sleep. In that state she was walled into a tower, and it is said that she would awaken only if a knight came to release her by taking her misdeeds upon himself and her as his wife. But no one came, and the Devichya Bashnya remains with its legend.

Just in front of the fortress is an excavation of ancient Tira.

Apart from the fortress, Belgorod-Dnestrovsky has two other examples of mediaeval architecture—the Armenian and Greek churches. The *Armenian Church of Our Lady*, opposite Kutuzov Street, was built in the 14th century, when the Armenians resettled here. It is executed with columns in the style of an ancient Roman basilica and appears with the passing of the centuries to have sunk halfway down into the ground. 12 steps

lead down into it. Tombstones with ancient inscriptions are built into the walls. The tiny *Greek Church of Our Lady* was built later, in the 15th and 16th centuries. It is opposite Leona Pavlova Street 10. Both churches stand on the high bank of the saltwater estuary (liman) near Portovaya Street.

Voznesenskaya (Ascension) Church, Ismailskaya Street 72. This white church with a belfry is open for services.

St. Nicholas's Church, by the cemetery at Ismailskaya Street 79. It is distinguishable by its blue dome, was built in the 1860s and is open for services.

Synagogue, Kirov Street 29. No longer in use.

Local Museum, Pushkin Street 19. Open 10–6. The nine halls contain material on local history from the time of ancient Tira.

Avanguard Stadium, at the corner of Pervomaiskaya and Michurin streets

Vasily Ryabov Obelisk, in a square on Shevchenko Street. Vasily Ryabov was a hero of the 1905 Russo-Japanese War, and the monument was paid for by local donations.

Lenin Monument

War Memorial Obelisk and Eternal Flame, at the end of Shevchenko Street

Hotel, Shevchenko Street 48

Byely Parus Restaurant, Ismailsky Street 60

Yuzhny Restaurant, Komsomoloskaya Street 25

Restaurant, at the railway terminal

In an up-to-date guidebook there is certainly room for old legends, but in moderation. Why there should be so many associated with Belgorod-Dnestrovsky, it is hard to say. The other two legends are both about freshwater springs which bubble out beside the liman and flow into it. There are quite a number of these springs, and some are said to be holy. That nearest the town is called *Paraskovia Krinitsa (Paraskovia's Spring)*.

Once upon a time there was a girl named Paraskovia, as wise as she was beautiful, and she was taken captive by the Turks. She was remarkable for the strength both of her will and of her Christian faith. She was sent to join Uzun-Pasha's harem but refused to accept Islam. She was imprisoned, and when the pasha threatened to kill her, an angel came to her rescue. Such was the pasha's astonishment that he was dumbfounded and unable to move, and Paraskovia used this opportunity to slip out of the door, passing the guards unnoticed as she fled down to the liman. When the pasha came to himself, he sent his guards to catch the fugitive, but just as they drew level with her, she vanished into thin air, and from the place where she had last stood beside the liman, a spring of clear water burst forth. The Turkish soldiers turned to stone, but the stones in time weathered away and now only the spring remains.

Another spring beside the liman near the Greek church in the suburbs of the town is known as the *Holy Spring of Ioan Suchavsky* (John of Suceava). In years gone by it was revered as one of the holiest places in Bessarabia. Long ago there was a rich

Orthodox merchant by the name of Ioan living in Trebizond, on the southern shore of the Black Sea. While sailing in Bessarabia, he quarrelled with the ship's captain, a Roman Catholic by faith. The captain, angered by his failure to convert Ioan to Catholicism, vowed when they reached land to hand him over to the local ruler, who was a fire-worshipping Persian, saying that Ioan was interested in taking the Persian's faith. The ruler was furious with Ioan's repeated refusal to abandon Orthodoxy and condemned him to the torture of being drawn by a wild horse. The terrified animal finally came to a halt by a spring of water, and that night over the martyr's body there appeared a pillar of fire with burning lamps and the figures of 3 elders, robed in white and singing. Much alarmed by reports of this vision, the ruler allowed local Christians to bury the body there, by the spring. The captain's conscience, however, gave him no rest, and he wanted to steal the remains of his victim. He went at night to disinter him but was prevented by a priest, who had been warned of the impending crime by Ioan himself in a dream. After this the remains were removed and kept for 70 years in the safety of a church. In 1402 they were transferred to *Suceava Chapel* by Alexander the Kind, and another chapel was built over the spring. The marble slab inscribed in Greek which has lain on the martyr's grave was kept there.

BELORUSSIA

See Minsk (Byelorussia), p. 320.

BELTSY (Romanian: Baltsi) Population—160,000

The town stands at the confluence of the Reut and Reutsel rivers, which flood the district in the spring and autumn and give the town its name, meaning "bog."

Its first mention goes back to 1421, when, during the reign of Alexander the Kind of Moldavia, it entered into the possession of Princess Mazowieckaja, sister of Prince Wladislaw II of Lithuania. Beltsy was at that time insufficiently fortified to withstand the frequent raids of the Tatar khan Girei.

In 1711 Peter the Great made his way through Beltsy during his Prut campaign. He liked the look of the place and decided to make it one of the Russian army's headquarters.

When Moldavian sovereign Alexander Gika finally succeeded in driving the Tatars away, he presented the fertile lands along the Reut and Reutsel rivers to the Iasi Monastery and to the three rich Moldavian merchant brothers, Alexander, Konstantin, and Iordaku Panainte. In the 1750s Beltsy became known for its fair. The ancient coat-of-arms has a horse's head on it, indicating that horse and cattle dealing made up much of the business.

Until 1812, when Bessarabia was reunited with Russia, Beltsy belonged to a Rumanian nobleman called Catarjiu. The place was designated a town in 1818 when Alexander I stayed here.

By the end of the last century, the population had grown to 20,000, and local industry included 3 candle factories, a mill, and a distillery. A significant part of local trade centered upon 46 taverns and pot-houses. In 1894 Beltsy was linked to the expanding railway system. It had one of the most thriving Jewish communities in the area, and this remained true right up till the Second World War. Much of the town remains from those days, and there are whole streets lined with solid little single-storey town houses, discreetly decorated with plasterwork.

Today it is Moldova's third-largest town (after Kishinyov and Tiraspol), and it is an important road and railway junction. Local factories produce electrical equipment, oil, and fat and process meat and furs. Lenin Boulevard is refreshingly green and pleasantly planted.

Nikolayevsky (St. Nicholas's) Cathedral, Leningradskaya Street, just off Lenin Square. It was built in 1791 as an Armenian church, by the Austrian architect Weismann at the time that the Panainte family, who intended to form a town, invited 300 Armenian merchants to move here from Galicia. Local authorities refused permission for the Armenians to settle here, and the church was used by the local Catholic community. The cathedral is painted blue and white and has always been open for services. Formerly it was just a church but was elevated to the rank of cathedral only when SS. Konstantine and Helena's was desecrated.

Armenian Church, Leningradskaya Street 78. Like Nikolayevsky Cathedral, this church was built for the Armenians who never came. The Panaintes converted it for Orthodox use, and it was consecrated in 1804. Of interest is the cross on the iconostasis, based on a 2-headed snake, and the iconostasis itself, painted by Evstafiy. It was Prince Potyomkin (1739–91), who once lived in Iasi, who recognised Evstafiy's artistic talent and, at his expense, sent him to study at the Vienna Academy of Arts. The church is now used as a gymnasium.

Roman Catholic Church

Local Museum, Lenin Street 55. In the most impressive white building of the Cathedral of SS. Konstantine and Helena, which was built in 1934 by the distinguished Rumanian architect Gabrilescu (also responsible for the house on Volodarsky Street now occupied by a research institute). The museum is open 10–7; closed Mon.

Lenin Monument, Lenin Street

Kotovsky Monument

Obelisk. In memory of World War II heroes.

Tank Monument, in Victory Square. This was unveiled on the occasion of the 25th anniversary of the town's liberation.

Russian Drama Theatre, Lenin Street 14; tel. 2–20–83

House of Culture, Dostoyevsky Street 19

Oktyabr Hotel, Pioneer Street 1; tel. 2–33–66

Oktyabr Hotel Annex, Dostoyevsky Street 26; tel. 2–35–63

Moldavia Hotel, Dostoyevsky Street 12

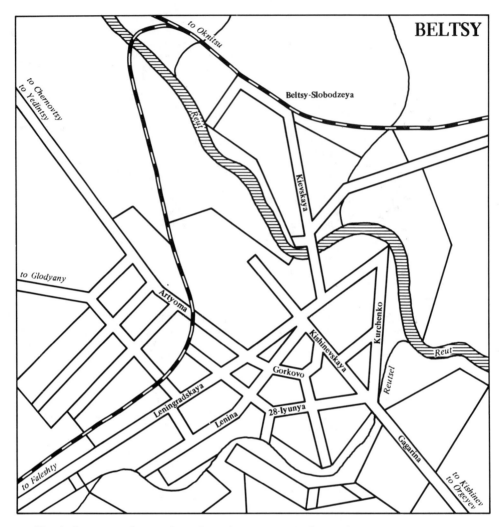

BELTSY

Oktyabr Restaurant, Pioneer Street 1, in the Oktyabr Hotel

Nistru (Dniester) Restaurant, Lenin Street 52

Yubileiny Restaurant, Pobedy Prospect 72

Mioritsa Restaurant, Ivan Franko Street

Department Store, Lenin Square.

GPO, Leningradskaya Street. Located in an imposing building in art nouveau style.

The road leading out of Beltsy toward Odessa passes a statue of a woman greeting people coming from the other way. She holds the traditional bread and salt in her hands. There is a dual carriageway here.

BENDERY (Rumanian: Tighina; Turkish: Bendery) Population—130,000

Intourist organise tours here from Kishinyov.

This town is situated in the former Roman province of Dacia. Dacia was conquered in A.D. 105 when Trajan was emperor. To commemorate the event, the Trajan Column was erected in Rome in A.D. 113, decorated with bas-reliefs illustrating episodes in the Dacian campaign. Two earth walls along the river Prut, the Upper and the Lower, end several kilometres east of Bendery, and are still called the Trajan Walls.

In the Slav chronicles, the town was known as Tungati, meaning the town of the Danube Slavs. In the 15th century, Prince Vitovt of Lithuania built a fortress here and named it Tigin. Then the town was occupied by the Genoese, who in the 16th century built an eight-towered fortress. When the Ottoman Empire was at the height of its power, Sultan Suleiman I (the Magnificent) occupied Tigin and renamed it Bender, which means "I want" in Turkish, although there is another meaning—"the fortified post" or "gates." Bendery was made into a Turkish province for non-Muslims. In 1708 the Genoese fortress was extensively enlarged with stone gateways, drawbridges, a deep moat, and lower fortifications along the Dniester.

Charles XII stopped near Bendery in 1709 after

his defeat at Poltava. However, the Dniester flood-waters caused him to move to the nearby village of Varnitsa, where he pitched his camp and stayed until 1712, calling the site New Stockholm. The Ukrainian Hetman Mazepa (1644–1709) who had advocated an independent Ukraine, fighting against Peter I and openly siding with Charles XII during the Northern War, escaped with the Swedish army after Poltava and died here, anathematized by the church. Charles XII was offered money by Sultan Ahmet III in 1712 so that he might make his way safely back to Sweden, but he refused and decided to resist the Turks. With only his general staff and 300 soldiers, he took on an opposing force of 20,000 Tatars and 6,000 Turks. When he was left with but 60 brave supporters, they locked themselves in his house and refused to surrender. The Turks set fire to the house, and still the courageous king and his men fought on; but at last he was taken prisoner and sent to the Baltic city of Stralsund, then belonging to Sweden. Bendery's coat-of-arms, however still shows per fess sable double-headed eagle with the Swedish lion couchant below.

Bendery became Russian after that, and the fortress was abandoned in 1897. It is now used by the army and closed to the public. During the Civil War, the soldiers of the 58th Avignon Regiment of the 30th French Infantry Division who were here were the first members of the Entente Army who refused to take sides. Like Kishinyov, Bendery was later under Rumanian rule and passed back to Russia in 1940.

Bendery is now a large river port and railway centre and, as a textile town, serves as the industrial heart of Moldova, its industry concerned with the production of cotton and silk fabric, food, electrical apparatus, and cables. There are also mechanical repair works and a shipyard for river vessels. The new 5-storey buildings of the *town hall, bank, and post office* are on Lenin Street, the main thoroughfare, formerly known as Karusina Street. It leads down to the Dniester, right to the port.

Preobrazhensky (Transfiguration) Cathedral, Lazo Street, by the market. Built from 1825–34.

A *regimental church* was built in 1912 inside the fortress to commemorate the victory over Napoleon.

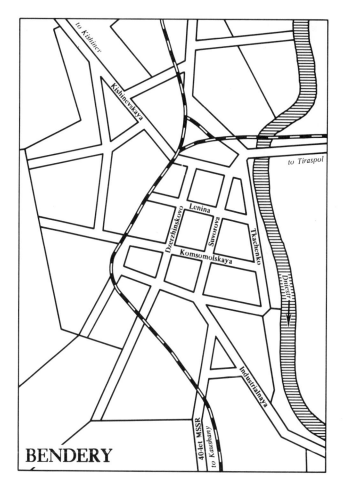

BENDERY

Synagogue, Suvorov (formerly Mikhailovskaya) Street

Local Museum, Dzerzhinsky Street 38. Open 11–6; closed Wed.

Picture Gallery, Kommunisticheskaya Street 77. Open 10–6; closed Mon.

55th Podolsk Regiment Obelisk, on the right of the Kishinyov-Odessa road. Built in memory of the 55th Podolsk Regiment, which defeated the Turks in 1806. From that time the regiment made its headquarters in Bendery and went from here to fight the French. The obelisk, which is surmounted by an eagle, was unveiled in 1912 to mark the centenary of the victory of 1812. It was moved to its present site in 1968.

Tkachenko Monument, near the Palace of Culture in the square on Lenin Street. Pavel Tkachenko was a hero of the revolution. The monument was sculpted by Epelbaum and Marchenko.

Monument to Soviet Power, above the river

Dzerzhinsky Monument, Dzerzhinsky Street

Black Fence Memorial, by the level crossing that connects the central part of the town with the suburb of Khomutyanovka. In February 1918 a number of revolutionary workers were shot here by the "black fence" (a concrete wall dividing a railway workshop) by the Rumanian army, which had occupied the town.

Lenin Statue, Lenin Square

War Memorial, Geroyev ("heroes") Square. There is an eternal flame by the common grave of 2,000 soldiers. At the entrance to the square, a marble plaque is inscribed, "Bare your head! Here lie the ashes of those who gave their lives for your happiness."

Open-air Theatre

October Park, along the river Dniester. This park has a recreation area.

Moldavia Hotel and Restaurant, Lenin Street

Nistru (Dniester) Hotel and Restaurant, Lenin Street 38, above the river; tel. 40–26

Nistru Hotel Annex, Lenin Street 50; tel. 31–51

Victoria Hotel

Prieteniya ("friendship") Hotel and Restaurant, opposite the river port

Fet-Frumos Restaurant, Lenin Street 6

Sputnik Café, Lenin Street 33

GPO, Suvorov Street

Filling Station, near the fortress (open 7 A.M.– 8 P.M.) and on the right of the road into town from Kishinyov

Charles XII Obelisk, in the nearby village of Varnitsa. Leave Bendery by Suvorov Street in the direction of Kishinyov. Cross the railway bridge and turn left. Pass the eagle monument and a filling station, both on the left, and go straight on past the roundabout onto Engels Street. In Varnitsa drive on after the level crossing as far as Lenin Street 58, where there is a war memorial and a grocer's shop ("Alimentara"). Turn right and go past the school, right again at the end, then make the first

left onto Dzerzhinsky Street, and turn left again down Fedko Street.

The obelisk is now in the garden of the last house on the left, No. 5. The owner has extended his territory to include that part of Svedsky ("Swedish") Hill where the monument stands but allows visitors in. The 2-m (6-ft) obelisk was built in grey stone by the Rumanians to mark the place where the king stayed until 1712, before his battle with the Turks, and it is inscribed "Carol XII" and the date, 1709–1711. Even today this spot is known as Swedish Camp.

It was in Varnitsa also that Mazepa died, and although anathematised, he was buried near the church that stands on Frunze Street. His body was, however, exhumed while the Russians were approaching.

BEREZHANY (Polish: Brzezany) Population— 13,500

This district centre in the Ternopol Region is situated on either bank of the Zlota ("golden") Lipa river and on the shore of the lake formed by the river.

First mentioned in 1375, Berezhany was given by the king of Poland to a Russian military governor by the name of Nikolai Sinyavsky in 1530; and at the same time the area was granted Magdeburg Law. Sinyavsky founded a castle here in 1534, and the construction work continued for 20 years. The castle, in the form of an irregular pentagon, was encircled by high walls with 3 towers. The inscription on Sinyavsky's tombstone says that the castle was designed to ensure a happy life for Russia and safety from her enemies. Berezhany was at that time inhabited by Armenians and Jews as well as Poles and Ukrainians. In 1649 the castle was besieged by the Tatars, and they burned the place down before they retreated.

In 1772 Berezhany fell under Austro-Hungarian rule. After the fall of the Austro-Hungarian empire in 1918, Berezhany became part of the Western Ukraine, and from 1920 till 1939 it was part of Poland. In 1802 a lycee was founded in the town.

Berezhany was the birthplace of the Ukrainian poet and public figure Markian Shashkevich (1811–43). He graduated from the local lycee in 1810 and was the first Ukrainian poet to write in his native tongue. His poems praise the struggle of the Ukrainians against the Tatars and the Poles. Also born here was the Ukrainian writer Andrei Chaikovsky, a close friend of another well-known writer, Ivan Franco (1856–1916).

Local industry comprises a branch of the Ternopol furniture factory and a glass factory.

Troitskaya (Trinity) Church. Behind this there used to be an 18th-century Armenian church and a 15th-century synagogue.

Roman Catholic Church, built in the 15th century.

Town Hall, in the market place. Built in 1811.

Lime Tree Avenue. This was planted in the 18th century and leads to the village of Raj, where a hunting castle with 4 towers was built in Renaissance style.

BISHKEK

Bishkek is the capital of Kirghizstan.

KIRGHIZSTAN

Population: 4,291,000, 47.9 percent of which are Kirghiz, belonging racially to the southern Siberian Mongoloids, while their language is related to the Turkic group. There are 25.9 percent Russians, as well as many other nationalities—the Uzbeks (12.1 percent) and the Ukrainians (3.1 percent) being the next most numerous.

Kirghizstan is one of the smallest republics in the Soviet Union; its territory is less than 1 percent of the total territory of the USSR. It shares its southern borders with China and is very mountainous. Almost half lies at more than 3,000 m (9,843 ft) above sea level. Highest of all is Pik Pobedy (Victory Peak) which soars to 7,439 m (24,406 ft) above sea level. Almost 6,600 sq km (2,548 sq miles) of Kirghizstan's territory are perpetually covered with snow and ice, the source of rivers that empty either into the Aral Sea or into the lakes Balkhash and Taryma. The climate is extremely varied. The mountains are dry, and subtropical areas are found lying beside zones of temperate climate and very cold regions. Kirghizstan has many lakes; most of them are small, except Issyk Kul (Warm Lake), which is one of the largest in the USSR. It is 182 km (113 miles) long and 58 km (36 miles) wide, and in places as much as 702 m (2,303 ft) deep. The mountain slopes are lush with walnut, apple trees, barberry, and pistachio. There is also the wild nut of Kirghizstan, which is found nowhere else in the world.

The Kirghiz tribes came very long ago to the Tien-Shan mountains from the upper reaches of the Siberian river Yenisei. They soon discovered that their new territory was not very peaceful because it was crossed by the east-west trade routes and many other nations wished to control it. The Kirghiz had to fight newcomers from China, Central Asia, and the Arab potentates. They also suffered from the Mongol invasions. Until the end of the last century, the Kirghiz tribes were headed by feudal lords, "manaps," who claimed descent from a famous khan and led a nomadic life. A saying is still used today: "My home is round my campfire, my pasture round my horse's tether." In 1855 Boromei Bekmuratov, chief of the Begu tribe, which roamed the area east of Issyk Kul, was the first to become dependent on the Russian empire. The other tribes were still ruled by the Kokand khanate (now Uzbekistan). When the Russian troops entered this region, they attacked the Kokand fortresses one by one until, by 1870, northern and central Kirghizstan became part of the Russian empire. After the 1917 revolution, the establishment of Soviet power in this area was assisted by the poor settlers who had come from Russia and the Ukraine. In 1926 the Kirghiz Autonomous Republic was set up, and 10 years later it was declared a Union state.

The distribution of the population is very uneven. The majority live in the valleys, which cover only one-sixth of the area, while only 2 percent live in the mountains. Considerable efforts have been made in the past few decades to bring civilisation to the mountains, but many age-old customs still survive. One of the greatest problems is the status of women, which is officially equal to that of the men but in reality is far from it. Moslem influence is still very strong. Early marriages and payment, called "kalym," from the bridegroom are still practised.

The mountains here are rich in nonferrous ores, which has led to significant industrial development. Kirghizstan is the prime source of mercury and antimony in the country. The latter is so pure that it is respected as a standard on the international market. The republic also has great resources of hydroelectric power. The river Naryn, one of the republic's many waterways, has a potential of 35.6 billion kilowatts per hour. There is construction work in progress on a whole chain of power stations. The communication problem is very acute, for it often happens that 2 neighbouring districts only a dozen miles apart are entirely cut off from each other by impenetrable mountains.

Folk games and contests are very popular in Kirghizstan. There is "zhamby-atmai," an archery contest; "kuresh," which is free-style wrestling; and apart from "at-chabysh" (horse racing), there are a number of other diversions designed to test the skill of horsemen. "Kuz-kuumai" is a horse race in which a "bride" gallops away from her "groom," who has to catch her and receives a kiss as his reward. "Oorarrysh" is wrestling on horseback, and "tyin engmei" entails picking up coins from the ground at full gallop. These occasions bring in crowds of people dressed in national garments, which consist of a padded coat, felt boots with leather overshoes, and a white felt hat with black flaps. Married women often wear the "echelek," a great white turban made from a scarf 15 m (16 yd) long.

National dishes of Kirghizstan include "sharpo" (mutton and potato soup), "manti" (thin-skinned dumplings filled with peppery meat and onions), "besh-barkam" (spaghetti and mutton), "tukachi" (flat bread rolls), and "konina" (horse meat).

A few words of the Kirghiz language:

hello	salaam matszbe
I am a tourist	bis tourist
thank you	rakhmat
yes	oh-a
no	dzho
good	yakshe
bad	dzhaman
I don't understand	men bil bame
Please fetch me an interpreter	maga kotormochu kerek
good-bye	koshkolumus
how do you do?	kandaysys

Bishkek (Pishpek till 1926; Frunze till 1991)
Population—616,000

The capital of Kirghizstan is situated 750 m (2,460 ft) above sea level in the valley of the river Chu, which flows down from the Tien-Shan Mountains. It is also irrigated by 2 smaller rivers, the Ala-Archa and the Alamedin. The city stretches 20 km (12 miles) from north to south and 16 km (10 miles) from east to west, but as it stands at a point where the valley slopes considerably, there is a difference of as much as 200 m (656 ft) in the level of the southern and the northern suburbs. The northern districts of the town are crossed by the Great Chuisky Canel, built in the war years of 1941–45. New construction always takes into account the area's liability to suffer up to a 9-point earthquake.

The climate here is extreme continental. It was once −38°C (−37°F) in January, and it has reached 43°C (109°F) in July. The hot, dry weather starts in May, and the moderate temperatures of autumn make this a particularly good time of year for a visit. It averages 322 sunny days per year.

The earliest settlements grew up in the valley along the old caravan route from China, known as the Silk Road. Remains of a fairly prosperous trading settlement of the 8–12th centuries A.D. which now carry the name of Kyzyl-Askerskoye Gordische ("settlement") have been found on the site of present-day Bishkek. 10th-century travellers said that the route was so densely populated that "cats could walk the rooftops all along the valley." At that time the Kirghiz people moved into the valley en masse. There is a legend about the origin of the people of Kirghizstan.

Once upon a time a town stood on the banks of a large river. The ruler of the town had 40 maiden daughters. Once a "divana" (a madman) wandered along the streets of the town, and as he went he kept repeating, "Ana-el-khak, mana-el-khak," meaning "this is God and this is God." With the first part of the phrase, he pointed to the skies and with the second to himself. The town's theologians considered this blasphemy and condemned him to be burned to death. His ashes were thrown into the river, but the water foamed and hissed, saying "Ana-el-khak, mana-el-khak." At the same time, the 40 maidens were bathing in the river. They drank the water, and all became pregnant. They were ashamed and went to live up in the mountains. There they gave birth to 40 sons, who grew up to found the family of "Kyrk kyz" (or Kirkghiz), meaning "40 girls."

In the 13th century, the dwellings of the valley suffered greatly from the nomadic Mongols, and for almost the next 600 years the valley changed hands among different nomadic tribes.

In the early 19th century, Kirghizstan was taken by the khan of Kokand, and among the fortresses built by the order of Madali Khan (1821–42) was that of Pishpek. The name is said to come from the tool that the nomad women use to whip up kumys ("mare's milk"). It is a small wooden stick with a little wheel on the end. The story goes that when a nomad family had moved on, someone left

her pishpek behind. When in 1825 it was decided to build a fortress in that very place, the forgotten pishpek was found and the name, Pishpek, was given to the fortress.

It was built in 1846 in the northeast of the town to protect the tax collectors from the Kirghiz tribes. The *fortress*, covering 6 hectares (15 acres) was built of clay with gates in the western wall only. Inside among other things there was a prison pit ("zindan"). Until 1858 the fortress had one 7-m (23-ft) wall surrounded by a moat and fortified with towers. With the beginning of the Russian advance upon Central Asia, another defending wall was erected. It was first stormed by the Russians headed by Colonel Zimmerman in 1860, then again in 1862, and it was finally ruined in 1866. As it had not been built of stone, nothing remains of it today except a small clay hill near Karpinsky Street with the name of Kuznechnaya Krepost ("blacksmiths' fortress") because blacksmiths used to live on the nearby street, now called Pravda Street.

Russian peasants soon settled here, and a posting station was opened in 1870. By that time there were up to 50 Russian families there. The Ukrainians who moved in a little later brought with them the Ukrainian look, which many of the whitewashed houses have even today. After 2 years there were 500 people living there. Although the settlement stood on the road between Tashkent and Verny (now Alma-Ata), it was more like a large village than anything else.

This settlement on the right bank of the Alamedin was called Lebedinovka ("swan"). After the collapse of the Kokand khanate in 1878, a Russian military settlement was founded, and Pishpek became an administrative and trading centre of local importance. It was proclaimed the principal town of the district, instead of the very swampy Tokmak, 60 km (37 miles) east of Pishpek. It was badly damaged by the flooding of the Chu in 1878, but the Russian generals wanted it to become one of their strongholds in Central Asia. Military men drew up the plans for the new city, which were rather primitive and architecturally uninspired. In 1883 a thousand Chinese Muslim refugees, known as Dungans, came from China to settle, so the population of the town of 6,361 in 1897 was indeed multinational. It was considered to be the first European-type town in Kirghizstan. The present-day Lenin Prospect was called Kupecheskaya ("merchants") Street because the wealthiest people used to live there; modern Sovietskaya Street was Bazarnaya ("market") Street, and Frunze Street used to be Sudeiskaya ("court") Street. The inhabitants were mostly connected with agriculture, rice and melons in particular. 2 tanneries and a brewery were built. The town was also renowned for its local Swiss-type cheese.

A single-class parochial school had opened in the town in 1879. In 1908 a Russian-Turkish school was opened, which helped to encourage the local use of Russian. The first cinemas to open were the Meteor and the Mars in 1911. When the Eddison Cinema with 400 seats opened in 1914,

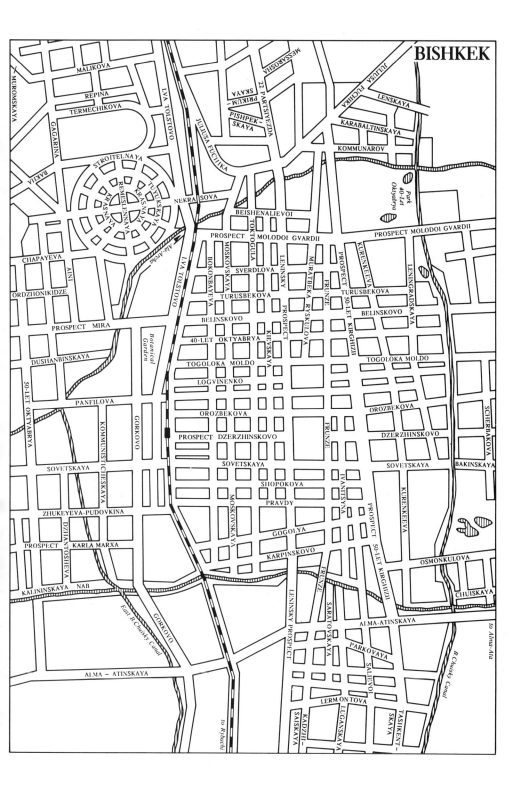

clubs were formed there and literary-musical evenings were organised. The first scientific establishment was the meteorological station.

By the outbreak of the First World War the
population had risen to 15,000, the majority being
Russian, as is still the case today. Soviet power was
established in 1918, and Pishpek's importance as
an administrative centre was increased in 1924
when it was linked by rail to the rest of the country.
Its name was changed in 1926 to Frunze, after
Mikhail Frunze (see below). After the formation of
the Kirghiz republic in 1936, Frunze was made
the capital, sizeable building projects were undertaken, and the Kirghiz population increased as
workers moved into the young city. Many impressive buildings were put up at the end of the 1920s
and the beginning of the 1930s. Two of them are
now occupied by the *Presidium* (Respublikanskaya
Square) and the *Russian Drama Theatre* (in Dubovy Park). Some were designed in the constructivist style, which was later criticised and banned
entirely. Local industry began with Interhelpo, an
industrial cooperative venture organised by Czechoslovakian Communist workers in 1925. 1,500
Czech mechanics arrived with their families and
industrial equipment as part of the Interhelpo plan.
Their first job was to build a power station. The
plan lasted until 1943, after which time their enterprises were taken over by the state. The situation
was further improved when evacuated factories,
particularly from Odessa and Rostov-on-Don, were
set up here during World War II. The city was
renamed Bishkek in 1991. Now local industry includes the manufacture of agricultural machinery,
textiles, food, and tobacco products, and Bishkek
is the major industrial centre of Kirghizstan and
the second in Central Asia after Tashkent. The
local brewery is among several constructed by
builders from Leningrad. New projects include a
stud farm, a meat-processing plant, and a garment
factory.

Bishkek is well planned, and the square blocks
are set off by rows of poplar and plane trees throughout the city. In summertime the smaller houses
can hardly be seen through the foliage, and it is
estimated that a fifth of the city's area is taken up
by gardens, parks, and orchards. All the streets that
run from north to south have a wonderful panoramic view onto the snowy sunlit peaks of the
Kirghiz Mountains. Because of their trees, some
of the streets, particularly Lenin and Dzerzhinsky,
would be best described as boulevards, and in fact
the latter, laid out in 1883, was originally called
Boulevard Street. Part of it was planted by schoolchildren in 1902, and the trees have been allowed
to mature unhindered. Dzerzhinsky Boulevard,
which is 100 m (109 yds) wide, runs northward
from Railway Street to a point near the Great
Canal. On it, in the centre, stands the eye-catching
new building of the *House of Government* (also the
work of builders from Leningrad) and the *Council
of Ministers*. Here also is *Dubovy Park*. The *Vladimir Mayakovsky Women Teachers' Training College* on Dzerzhinsky Boulevard is quite unusual in

the Soviet Union as it is only for girl students. It
was founded in 1952 because of a serious lack of
women entering the teaching profession in Kirghizstan. It was organised on a residential basis, for
non-Russian nationals only, and when it became
clear to the country people with their strong Muslim background and traditions that their daughters
would be in safe hands, there was little difficulty
in filling the places. Now native teachers return to
their distant villages to staff the schools there.
(Other teachers' training colleges in the city cater
to students of both sexes, of any nationality.)

Respublikanskaya Square, where the *Kirghiz
Theatre* also stands, is the place where demonstrations are held. The central street (formerly Grazh-
danskaya—"citizen") is called XXII Partsyezda
Street after the 22nd Party Congress, and Sovietskaya Street is the principal shopping street. Bishkek
is the home of a number of institutes and of *Kirghizstan State University* (Belinskovo Street 101),
which dates from 1951 and is named for the 50th
anniversary of the founding of the Soviet state. The
city maintains close ties with Leningrad and sends
many students to study there.

Voskresensky (Resurrection) Church, Lenin
Street 479. Built in 1946–47 and open for services;
the entrance is from the side street.

Church, 50-Years-of-Kirghizstan Street

Synagogue, Lenin Street 290

Mosque, Gogol Street 53. Built in the 1930s.

Historical Museum, Pushkin Street 78. Open
10–7; closed Tues. It was built in 1926–27 to house
the Central Executive Committee of Kirghizstan
and was the first 2-storey building in Bishkek. Later
the Historical Museum, the first to open in Kirghizstan, moved in. Beside the main entrance are
stone slabs, which were worked in the 6th–10th
centuries.

Lenin Museum, Al-Ato Square, Sverdlov
Street. Part of the town was completely cleared to
make room for this modern building. Inside, much
use was made of marble and bronze, and the ceilings are decorated with unusual frescoes. The windows overlook the square with a statue of Lenin.
Open 10:30–7; closed Mon. Behind it is the building of the *Supreme Soviet* in what used to be the
old Government House.

Frunze Museum, Frunze Street 64. Mikhail
Frunze (1885–1925), the Bolshevik revolutionary
and Civil War commander, was born here while
his father had a job as the first medical worker in
Pishpek. The house where he lived until he was 7
years old was preserved in 1967 by enclosing it in
a modern three-storey building. On the third floor
is a display illustrating Frunze's revolutionary activities. Open 10–6; closed Mon.

Fine Arts Museum, Sovietskaya Street 196.
Founded in 1974 and housed in a new, modern
building. There is a collection of classical Russian
paintings (including Repin, Vereschagin and Falk)
and works of modern local artists (e.g., Chuikov
and Akibekov) to be found here. The museum also
has national handcrafted garments, carpets, yurts,
and all the appropriate equipment, including har-

nesses, as well as jewellery and silver bracelets. Open 11–6; closed Mon.

Sculpture Museum, in the open air in Dubovy Park

Zoological Museum, Pushkin Street 78. Open 10–6; closed Mon. Among the rare animals and birds on display are the red wolf and the griffon.

Exhibition Centre of Kirghizstan, Mir Prospect, in the outskirts of Bishkek at the foot of the mountains. Open 9–6; closed Mon. It was first opened in 1948 and now covers a territory of 150 hectares (375 acres). The entrance was designed by Lysenko and built in 1974.

Karl Marx and Friedrich Engels Monument, in the central avenue of the town garden (the western part of Dubovy Park)

Revolution Fighters Monument, Sovietskaya Prospect, near the Sports Palace. This sculpture by Tyrgunby Sadykov is a group with the figure of a woman on a column to one side; unveiled in 1977.

Memorial Obelisk, in the centre of Dubovy Park. This 11-m (36-ft) structure commemorates the Red Guards who perished in 1918, during the Civil War, establishing Soviet power in Pishpek. It was unveiled in 1960 following a design by Lyublinsky.

Young Communist Monument, Molodoy Gvardi Boulevard. This monument, dedicated to the Young Communists of the 1920s by Komsomol members of the 1960s, was made by Pusyrevsky and unveiled in 1963.

Lenin Monument, in Dubovy Park. By Neroda and Veryuzhsky; unveiled in 1948. (There is another statue of the founder in Bishkek by Kibalnikov, Sadykov, and Protkov, and a third in front of the Lenin Museum.)

Maxim Gorky Monument, 40-Lyet-Oktyabra Street, in a small park

Ivanitsin Monument, Dzerzhinsky Prospect. Alexei Ivanitsin (1870–1925) was a revolutionary and one of the organisers of the first Bolshevik groups here.

Dzerzhinsky Statue, Dzerzhinsky Prospect. The 6-m (20-ft) figure is by Sadykov.

Fucik Monument, in Julius Fucik Garden, Trudovaya Street. In 1930 Julius Fucik (1903–43), Czech journalist and public activist, came to Bishkek as head of a Czechoslovak delegation. The monument was unveiled in 1981.

Toktogul Satylganov Monument, Sovietskaya Street, in front of the Opera and Ballet Theatre. Toktogul Satylganov (1864–1933), known affectionately here as Toko, was a famous Kirghiz poet, composer, and philosopher. The 4-m (13-ft) monument by Gapar Aitiev was unveiled in 1974.

Togolok Moldo Monument, in Togolok Moldo Park. Togolok Moldo was the pseudonym of the local "akyn" (poet and song writer) Baiyimbet Abdrakhmanov (1860–1942). The monument by Olga Manuilova was unveiled in 1948.

Panfilov Monument, in Panfilov Park, Panfilov Street. By Olga Manuilova and erected in 1944. General Ivan Panfilov (1893–1941), who lived and worked in Bishkek as military commissar of the Republic in 1938–41, was a hero of World War II, killed in the battle for Moscow. The division he led is known for its brave part in the defence of Moscow in 1941.

Hero Avenue starts from Molodoy Gvardi Boulevard. It was laid out in 1975 and is lined by busts of World War II heroes.

World War II Monument, in Dubovy Park. Unveiled in 1970; created by Askar Isayev. An eternal flame is nearby.

Talgat Begeldinov Bust, Lenin Prospect, opposite the GPO. Talgat Begeldinov was a hero-pilot of World War II (b. 1922). The bust is by Abakumov and was unveiled in 1950.

Dzhoomart Bokombayev Bust, Dzerzhinsky Prospect. Dzhoomart Bokombayev (1910–44) was a local poet who perished tragically in a car accident during the shooting of a film. The bust by Olga Manuilova was put up in 1948.

Muratali Kurenkeyev Bust, Moskovskaya Street. This bust was also created by Olga Manuilova. Muratali Kurenkeyev (1865–1949) was a local composer famous for his performances on Kirghiz folk instruments, such as the kiyak and the choor.

Druzhba Monument, Panfilov Street, not far from the Kirghiz Drama Theatre. This 30-m (98-ft) monument by Sadykov was unveiled in 1974 to commemorate the 100th anniversary of the unification of Russia and Kirghizstan.

Slava ("glory") Monument, in Central Square, opposite the building of the Central Committee of the Communist party. It was erected in 1974 to honour the Kirghiz achievements within the Soviet economy.

Maldybayev Opera and Ballet Threatre, Sovietskaya Street 169. The building was erected in 1955 by Laburenko and can seat about 1,000.

Krupskaya Russian Drama Theatre, Krasnooktyabrskaya Street, Dubovy Park. The Permanent Russian Theatre was founded in 1935 by a group of graduates from a Moscow theatre college. Friendship Avenue runs from the theatre.

Kirghiz Drama Theatre, Panfilov Street 273. The new building was opened in 1970.

Puppet Theatre, Lenin Prospect 168. Founded in 1938.

Satylganov Kirghiz Philharmonia Concert Hall, Lenin Prospect, on Sovietskaya Square. The new building was designed in Moscow by Pechenkin and opened in the capital of Kirghizstan in 1980. The sculpture of "Manas" in front of the building was designed by Sadykov and unveiled in 1981. Manas is the hero of a Kirghizstan epic, a trilogy of 500,000 lines, telling of the Kirghiz fight for independence.

Circus, Ivansitsin Street 119. The fine modern building can seat 2,000 people.

Karagachevaya Grove, in the northern suburbs. This covers 230 hectares (575 acres). The oaks, maples, and poplars were planted in 1881 by Alexey Fetisov, a friend of Mikhail Frunze's father and a famous botanist who imported many of the plants from abroad, including the Champani vines from

France. There is a slab of pink granite in the middle of the grove to commemorate the scientist. The grove is a popular amusement ground with 2 lakes, Komsomolskoye and Pionerskoye.

Dubovy ("oak") Park, Krasnooktyabrskaya Street. This park was also created by Fetisov, who had it planted in 1898. It was a popular place for promenading among the nobility. The cathedral in the park is used now by the Fine Arts Museum as an exhibition hall, and there is also an open-air Sculpture Museum.

Druzhba ("friendship") Park, stretches from 50-Lyet-Oktybrya Street southward to Chuisky Canal and from Mira Prospect eastward to Asanbay Canal. It covers 500 hectares (1,250 acres). Some of the trees are planted so that, from above, they read as a commemoration of the 50th anniversary of the revolution.

Julius Fucik Garden, Trudovaya Street. The first trees in the park were planted by Julius Fucik himself in 1930, when he visited Bishkek.

The Botanical Garden was founded in 1938 and now covers over 130 hectares (325 acres). 540 specimens of flora are planted here, including a fine collection of 400 sorts of roses.

Hippodrome Racecourse, on the outskirts of the southwestern part of the town

Panfilov Stud Farm, Fucik Street

Ala-Too (Intourist) Hotel and Restaurant, Dzerzhinsky Prospect 1; tel. 22–6341. Intourist office: tel. 22–6442.

Tien-Shan Hotel and Restaurant, at the crossing of Panfilov and XXII-Partsyezda streets

Kirghizstan Hotel and Restaurant, Sovietskaya Street 181

Ak-Sai Hotel, Ivanitsin Street 117

Spartak Hotel, Togolok Moldo Stret 17

Pishpek Hotel and Restaurant, Dzerzhinsky Prospect 21

Sayakat Hotel, Dushanbinskaya Street 8a

Kirghizstan Restaurant, Orozbekova Street 62

Susamyr Restaurant, Toktogula Street 257

Ak-Suu Restaurant, Dzerzhinsky Prospect 2

Seyil Restaurant, Dzerzhinsky Prospect 37

Druzhba Restaurant, at the crossing of Ivanitsin and Shopokov streets

Son-Kul Café, Dzerzhinsky Prospect, near the building of Kirghizstan's first printing works

Lenin Sports Palace, Togolok Moldo Street. Built in streamlined modern style in 1974 to seat 3,000. All kinds of conferences and performances take place here.

Sparta Stadium, Togolok Moldo Street 17. Seats 25,000.

Bank, Al-Ato Square, Sverdlov Street, opposite the Lenin Museum. The building is in Oriental style, with a golden cupola, resembling a mosque.

GPO, Dzerzhinsky Prospect

Beryozka (foreign-currency) Shop, Lenin Prospect 243

Department Store, Lenin Prospect 152

Korabl Shop. A grocer's shop with a silhouette like a ship.

Art Salon, Belinskovo Street 57

Markets, Ivanitsin Street 105, Shapkova Street, and the crossing of Sovietskaya and Frunze streets

Manas Airport, 30 km (19 miles) from the city. This bears the name of the Kirghiz epic hero.

Intourist organises out-of-town excursions to Ala-Archa Ravine and to the Burana Tower.

Ala-Archa Ravine

This ravine is in the Ala-Too Mountains, 42 km (26 miles) from Bishkek. The Ala-Archa is a clear mountain river in a stony bed. There is an alpine camp here in a picturesque glade at a height of 2,100 m (6,890 ft) above sea level, and it is a good place for gliding.

Burana

The ancient tower of Burana is 80 km (50 miles) from Bishkek. In the valley of the river Chu used to be the ancient town of Balasagun. It fell into ruin in the 16th century, but in the 11th–12th centuries, it was a very important administrative and cultural centre of Central Asia. Here lived and worked Khadji Yusuf Balasagun, author of "Kudatgu Bilik" ("How to Become Happy"), a handbook for Oriental rulers, well known in Egypt and on the Volga.

There were a number of Muslim mosques in Balasagun and its suburbs in the 10th–12th centuries. 6 km (4 miles) from Balasagun in the settlement of Kirmirau there was one with an 11th-century minaret, but only the minaret has survived. It is called the *Burana Tower*. The word "burana" most probably comes from "monara," meaning minaret. The mosque became dilapidated, and by the 16th century, a legend had sprung up that the minaret was either a guardtower or part of a castle where in the olden days a khan had hidden his daughter to protect her from the bite of a scorpion, from which it had been predicted that she would die. Nevertheless, his precautions were in vain, as there was a scorpion in a basket of fruit brought to her. Another legend says that she was hidden from her suitors.

The Burana minaret is surrounded by a mud-walled rampart enclosing an area of 34 hectares (88 acres), and a small river runs to the east of it. The museum area was established in 1977 and is open daily, 10–6. Archaeological excavations are still in progress. The minaret is 21.6 m (71 ft) in height, standing on a base of 3.45 m (11 ft). Its diameter at the bottom is 8.85 m (29 ft) and at the top, 5.90 m (19 ft). Only 55 steps of the long staircase have survived, but they can still be used. The minaret is made of solid cubic bricks, measuring 25 cm (9.8 in) square; the exterior is decorated with the same bricks, reminiscent of the decoration of the mausoleum of Ismail Samani in Bukhara and typical of Central Asian architecture of the 10th–11th centuries. The inscriptions in Arabic are unfortunately illegible. 20 m/yd to the north is a 10-m (33-ft) hill, which is all that remains of the ancient mosque. There was also a Muslim cemetery here.

Lake Issyk-Kul
This lies about 150 km (93 miles) from Bishkek. It is a salt lake fed by about 50 small rivers. Some travellers have compared it to Lake Geneva for the dark sapphire colour of its water, although it is many times larger and the surrounding mountains even grander than the Alps. The water is heated by volcanic activity, and the lake never freezes over.

BOGOLUBOVO
See Vladimir, p. 636.

BOLSHOI DUB
See Kursk, p. 264.

BORODINO
Intourist organises excursions here from Moscow, 112 km (70 miles) away. The museum and battle-field territory are open 10–6; closed Wed. and the last day of each month.
This little village gave its name to the famous 15-hour battle between the French and Russian armies on 26 August 1812. It saw fighting again during the Second World War, after which, it is recorded, only two houses remained standing.
Rozhdestvenskaya (Nativity) Church, up on the hill, dates from 1701 and is the only building in the vicinity to have witnessed the battle of Borodino. It suffered heavy damage in World War II but was fully restored in 1961–63.
Spasa-Nerukotvornovo Chapel, a beautiful building in Empire style with a high-columned portico, was erected in 1820 in memory of General Alexei Tuchkov by his widow on the place where he met his death. It later served as a mausoleum for members of the Tuchkov family.
Spaso-Bogoroditsky Convent was also founded by General Tuchkov's widow. It was completed in 1838; recently there have been major repairs to the eroded limestone of the walls.
Convent Hotel, across the road from the convent. It was here that Tolstoy stayed in the autumn of 1867 when he visited Borodino while writing "War and Peace."
Borodino Museum. The first exhibits of the museum were collected by P. Bogdanovich, the local stationmaster, and were displayed in the railway station building in 1902. The present building was constructed in 1912 to commemorate the 100th anniversary of the battle; it was destroyed during the Second World War and reconstructed and re-opened at the end of the war. The collection included guns, pictures, and personal relics. There is an electrified model of the battlefield and sketches that Franz Roubaud made for the Borodino Panorama in Moscow. In front of the building are busts of the Russian generals, Mikhail Barclay de Tolly (1761–1818) and Pyotr Bagration, made by Azgur in 1948. Open 10–6. Near the museum is a car park, kiosks, and a restaurant.
Borodino Battlefield was selected by Kutuzov, who wrote in his report to Moscow, to Tsar Alexander I: "This is one of the best positions one could find on a flat terrain. . . . It would be ideal if the enemy were to attack us here. I should then have high hopes of victory." The site is hilly and criss-crossed by rivulets and brooks flowing into the river Koloch. The Smolensk road, along which Napoleon's Grande Armée was advancing toward Moscow, ran through the village of Borodino. Kutuzov deployed his troops along the high bank of the river to form his right flank, while the left ran along with thick forest and undergrowth to the rear. The total length of the Russian position was about 8 km (5 miles) but Napoleon's army was forced to attack across a narrow strip of land, which excluded all chances of manoeuvering.
The day before the battle, the icon of the Virgin Mary saved from Smolensk was carried through the Russian camps to hearten the soldiers. On the same day, 2 visitors came to Napoleon's camp, the first bringing a new portrait of the little king of Rome to please his father and the second, less welcome, bringing news that Marshal Marmont's army had met with defeat at the battle of Salamanca.
Fighting began at Borodino at 6 o'clock on the morning of 26 August and was unusual for its fierceness and heavy losses. It turned into a desperate struggle for position, without room for either side to manoeuvre. Napoleon exclaimed: "These Russians let themselves be killed like machines. . . . They are citadels that have to be demolished with cannon."
By the end of the day the great losses on both sides amounted, it was estimated, to over 100,000 killed and wounded. Marshal Ney received the title of Prince de la Moskowa (from the nearby Moskva river) in recognition of the valour he had displayed. Russian casualties were very heavy, but their situation was less serious than that of the Grande Armée, far from base. Prince Bagration, however, was mortally wounded here. The result was indecisive; both armies claimed the victory, and Napoleon entered Moscow upon the strength of it. Ultimately events proved that the battle had drastically changed the course of the war and led to the Russian victory.
The battlefield is kept as a historic site, and the previous appearance of the landscape will be restored by the growth of recently planted trees and bushes. Electric power cables have been laid underground, and a total area of above 110 sq km (42 sq miles) falls within the protected territory.
Many of the defences built in 1812 have been preserved: the Shevardino redoubt, the Bagration flèches, Maslov's fortifications, and a number of French batteries. Most of the monuments erected on the battlefield were built in 1912 to mark the 100th anniversary of the battle. Some are dedicated to the Russian leaders and others to whole regiments. Many of them were financed by money donated by Russian soldiers and army officers, especially those whose forebears took part in the historic battle.
One of the monuments was erected by the French. About 150 m/yd east of Shevardino redoubt (reconstructed in 1912) stands the grey granite obelisk to the soldiers of Napoleon's army. It is

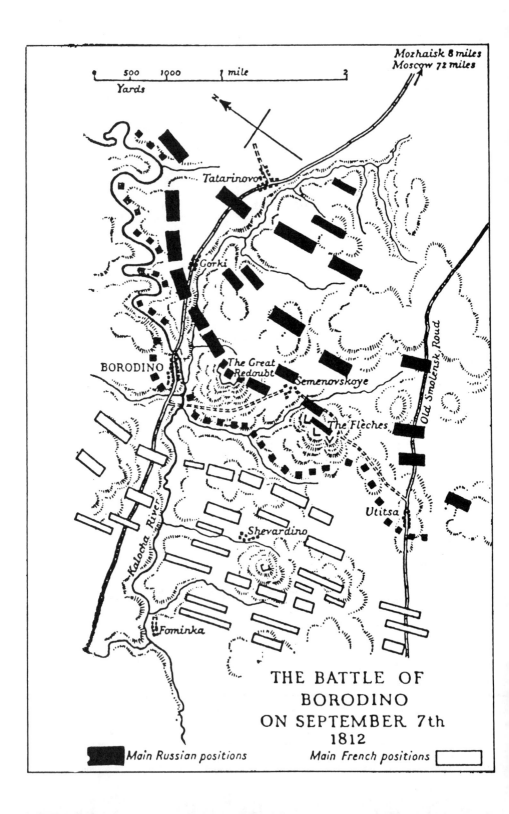

THE BATTLE OF
BORODINO
ON SEPTEMBER 7th
1812

Main Russian positions   Main French positions

crowned with a bronze eagle. The inscription on it reads; "Aux Morts de la Grande Armée," and it was built with money collected in France in 1912.

Just outside the convent fence stands a monument to the Russian grenadiers bearing a quotation from Lermontov's poem "Borodino":

And we kept our vow of loyalty
In Borodino Field.

On the top of a hill, near Rayevsky's battery, is the grave of perhaps the best-known Russian hero of the battle, the general of infantry Prince Pyotr Bagration (1765–1812), who was fatally wounded here and taken to Prince Golitsyn's estate of Simy, near Vladimir, where he died 17 days later. After 27 years had passed and upon the initiative of his aide-de-camp, the poet and partisan Denis Davydov, the mortal remains of the prince were transferred to Borodino and duly interred here on 26 August 1839. There is a good view from here across to the village of Borodino.

In the village of Gorki, back along the road toward Moscow, *Kutuzov's monument* stands high above the road, exactly where he and his staff were watching the battle throughout that fateful day. The obelisk of pale pink granite is topped by an eagle, and on the side of the column is a bas-relief showing Kutuzov at the command post during the battle. Above it are carved the words: "The enemy is rebuffed at all points." The monument, designed by Colonel-Engineer Vorontsov-Velyaminov, was erected in 1912.

Granite tombstones beside the monuments of the 1812 war mark the common graves of Soviet soldiers who fought and died here during World War II. New monuments are planned, bringing the total to about 360.

BORZHOMI

27 km (17 miles) from Khashuri is Georgia's largest mountain balneological spa. Its name consists of two words, "burdzhi" and "omi," meaning respectively "fortress" and "war" and connected with the battles that took place here.

The greater part of Borzhomi is situated along the Kura Valley, which was previously called Mtkvaris-Kheoba but was so difficult for Russians to pronounce that it was changed into Borzhomi Gorge (which is really the valley of the Kura River). A subtropical balneological and forest resort is situated 800–850 m (2,625–2,780 ft) above sea level, while some parts of it are even higher, along the narrow gorges of the Borzhomula and Gudzhare-tistskali rivers, tributaries of the Kura. It covers 612.6 hectares (1,530 acres). Stretching up the mountain slopes west of the resort is the *Borzhomi State Nature Reserve*, almost entirely covered with thick woods and 14,300 hectares (36,000 acres) in area.

Borzhomi mineral waters are of a single kind, with an average mineralisation of 6–7 g/l (about .2 oz/qt) and a temperature varying from 19.4°–

37°C (66.9°–98.6°F). The water can be used for drinking or for baths. Prior to bottling, Borzhomi water is fed along a pipeline to a plant where it is carbonated.

The Borzhomi curative mineral springs have been known to people from times long past. Due to its wonderful natural beauty, the Georgian queen Tamar called it "the pearl of her crown" and spared no means to embellish it. This is evidenced by the ruins of numerous architectural monuments scattered in the vicinity. The first mention of Borzhomi Gorge can be found in the Armenian historical chronicles, since it was once part of greater Armenia and was known as Tayastan. Later it was subjected to a devastating Turkish invasion, as a result of which many architectural monuments of Armenian-Georgian style were destroyed and of which we can only judge by the ruins remaining in the Borzhomi Gorge. Then it was under Persian rule, followed by a new Turkish invasion in the 17th century, when it was cut off from Georgia altogether. The Alkhatsikhe region, of which Borzhomi was a part, was joined to Russia in 1828 after a raid by the Russian general Prince Ivan Paskevich (1782–1856) against the Persians.

After joining Russia, the Borzhomi Gorge attracted the attention of the Russian Caucasus Administration because of its rich forests and its mineral springs. The importance of Borzhomi mineral waters and their curative effects were known long ago, but they became widely known only after the almost miraculous healing by Dr. Amirov, of the Georgian Grenadier Regiment, of a young girl, Yekaterina Golovina, daughter of General Yevgeni Golovin (1782–1858), Russian commander-in-chief in the Caucasus. The sick girl was completely cured of a gynaecological problem and became a walking advertisement for the Borzhomi waters. Much was done in Borzhomi in the time of Prince Mikhail Vorontsov (1782–1856), who replaced General Golovin. In 1871 the spa was visited by Tsar Alexander II, who presented Borzhomi, together with all the surrounding forest, arable land, and waters, to Grand-Duke Mikhail (1832–81), son of tsar Nicholas I, who ran it as his own estate. At that time Borzhomi was known as the Caucasian Vichy because its waters had the same curative effect as Vichy Grande Grille. Borzhomi claimed to be superior to world-famous spas such as Baden-Baden, Wiesbaden, and Karlsbad (now Karlovy Vary).

Borzhomi has 3 parks: Mineral (or Kurortny) Park, Ordzhonikidze Park, and 26-Bakinskikh Komissarov Park. The first, *Mineral Park*, stretches along the Borzhomka River gorge, where two Borzhomi mineral springs are situated. The first of these is called *Yekaterinensky*, in memory of Yekaterina Golovina, so surprisingly cured by its waters, and the second bears the name of *Yevgen-yevsky*, after her father. Engineer Major-General Yevgeny Espekho faced the springs with stone and put glass covers over them. Yevgenyevsky Spring is located at the entrance to the park, on a little island in the river Borzhomka, connected with the bank by a small bridge. Yekaterinensky Spring is situated in the middle of a long covered gallery, located higher along the Borzhomka. The water of the Yevgenyevsky Spring slightly resembles seltzer water and has a temperature of 22.5°C (72.5°F). The Yekaterinensky Spring water is distinguished by a higher temperature; however, both kinds of water have the same curative properties. Near the springs are bathhouses. In this park Russia's first electric power station was built in 1899, using the 152-m (300-ft) waterfall on the river Borzhomka. The building is still there, all its equipment intact but no longer used. At the entrance to the park is the lower station of the cablecar system, which links it to the plateau above.

The next park, *Ordzhonikidze Park*, was first named Remertovsky Park, in honour of D. A. Remmert, who contributed much to the development of the spa at Borzhomi. The park is situated at the confluence of the river Borzhomka and the Kura. It is beautifully planned and has many wide shady avenues.

The third park, *26-Bakinskikh Komissarov Park* (formerly Vorontsovsky Park), is situated on a plateau above the Borzhomi Gorge and stretches along the Kura, Gudzharatis-Tskhali ("black river"), and the Borzhomka. The plateau is about 150 m (500 ft) above the rivers. From here a beautiful view of the surroundings of Borzhomi can be seen. The air is pure and easy to breathe, and it is locally said, "He who breathes Borzhomi air, breathes health."

On the right side of Olginsky Bridge, which spans the Kura not far from its confluence with the Borzhomka, and higher up in the mountains, stands the elaborate *palace of Grand-Duke Sergei Mikhailovich*.

There were many elegant houses on Ordzhonikidze Street along the Borzhomka River. They were of different styles—Gothic, in the form of Swiss chalets, and so on. However, the most interesting of them was *Firuze*, at Ordzhonikidze Street 48, which belonged to a Persian consul and was richly decorated with Armenian and Georgian ornamentation; it now houses part of a sanatorium.

The main wealth of the spa, the Borzhomi mineral water, is used at home and abroad. The mild Borzhomi mountain climate is conducive to the treatment of various ills—gastric, liver, and gall bladder, metabolic and cardiovascular.

Tbilisi Hotel and Restaurant, Borzhomskaya Street 6; tel. 23160

Borzhomi Hotel and Restaurant, Baratashvili Street 1; tel. 22445

Local History Museum, Tchaikovsky Street 5. Open 10–5; closed Mon.
The museum building belonged in the 1880s to the manager of the imperial estates. In front of the museum is a bust to the poet Akaki Tsereteli.

Tchaikovsky Monument, Kirov Street
Lenin Monument, Rustaveli Street
Sergo Ordzhonikidze Monument
Paliashvili Monument. Zakhary Paliashvili (1871–1933) was a famous artist.

Tsintsinatela Gift Shop, on the left, across the suspension bridge
GPO, Kirov Street 103

Borzhomi has a summer tourist centre and a winter mountain-skiing station. The most interesting walks to be taken from Borzhomi are those "beyond the bridges," up along the Borzhomi River and passing the waterfall, to the power station, up to the Sadger sulphuric springs, to the 26-Kommissars Plateau, to Torkoye Plateau, to Likany and Likany Monastery, and to the Petre-Tsikhe and Gogias-Tsikhe fortresses.

Likany

About 3 km (2 miles) from Borzhomi along the main road to Akhaltsikhe is the small village of Likany, famous for its *palace*, which belonged to Grand-Duke Nikolai Mikhailovich. It is very elegant, built in Renaissance style after the Florentine palazzos. It was designed by Nikolai Benoit and executed by the architect Bilfeld. Its façade is decorated with several precious Japanese and Chinese vases, marble statues, and a bronze group depicting two eagles fighting over a hare. The palace stands in a vast park with a pond. The park was founded in 1892 and is rightly considered one of the best landscaped parks in Georgia. The palace is now a sanatorium. For a long time it was a VIP guest house, and Stalin stayed here for the last time in 1952, the year before his death.

On the right bank of the Kura, almost opposite the Likany Palace, are the *ruins of the Petris Tsikhe* fortress. From these ruins opens a beautiful view of Likany Gorge, encircled by the Vakhansky Ridge and of its summit, Lomis-Mta ("the lion's hill"). On the left bank of the Kura, on top of a hill, almost over Borzhomi, are the ruins of the 16th-century *fortress of Gogias-Tsikhe*. Both fortresses are often mentioned in Georgian folk songs and legends. It is locally said that once they were two formidable palaces belonging to two brothers. A bloody feud existed between them. Once they decided to put an end to the quarrel and make up. They threw a huge party with plenty of food and wine. Everybody thought that the feud had come to an end and rejoiced. However, one of the brothers let slip a careless word, and they took up their daggers once again and killed each other. The guests started to fight as well, and there were no survivors. Since then both fortresses have been deserted and now lie in ruins.

About 6 km (4 miles) from Borzhomi, along the Akhaltsikhskoye Highway, in a thick forest, stands the *Green Monastery*, consisting of a church and a belfry. Near the monastery is a spring of pure cold water.

A bit further up along the Likany Gorge one reaches the Lomis-Mta Mountain, from which opens up a beautiful view of the Main Caucasian Ridge, Rlbrus from one side and Kazbek from the other, as well as of the summits of Ushba, Tetnulda, and Dykh-Tau. Below stretch the green valleys of Imeretia and the Surami Pass.

The road to Bakuriani starts by following the Gudzharetistskali River. A narrow-gauge electric railway runs beside the road from Borzhomi to Bakuriani, 1,700 m (5,577 ft) above sea level. About 10 km (6 miles) along the way stands *Dabsky Monastery*, built of stone slabs covered with cunningly carved ornaments. According to the inscription on the church, it was built in 1175 in the time of King Georgi III, father of Queen Tamar. Not far from the monastery is the 61-m (200-ft) *Dabsky Waterfall*. In the forests surrounding Bakuriani are the little villages of Tsagveri, Tsemi, and Tba.

Tsagveri

Tsagveri is famous for its mineral springs, pure mountain air, and abundance of cherries and raspberries. The ferrocarbonic content of the Tsagveri mineral waters is as good as those of Pyromont, Spa, and Wildugen. At the entrance to the village is a laboratory researching plant protection.

From Tsagveri eastward along the Gudzharetistskali River, the road leads to *Timotisubani (St. Timothy's) Monastery*. Among its ruins stands a huge demolished church, built, as legend has it, in the time of King Vakhtang Gorgoslan (446–49). It is the size of Sioni Cathedral in Tbilisi. It is said locally that in the time of enemy invasion all the monastery treasures were kept here, and the local population also took refuge in the church.

The main road leads southeast from Tsagveri, through Libani to Bakuriani.

Bakuriani

A mountain skiing resort and one of the Soviet centres of this sport, Bakuriani is situated 37 km (23 miles) from Borzhomi at a height of over 1,829 m (6,000 ft) above sea level. In its sunshine and moderate temperature, Bakuriani equals the famous high-mountain resorts of Europe, including Davos. One of its advantages is its location, in a hollow between the mountains, safely protected from winds and at the same time exposed to the ultraviolet rays of the sun. The population of Bakuriani consists of Ukrainians, who were resettled there in the time of Prince Vorontsov, as well as Georgians and Ossetians. Bakuriani is famous for its wonderful natural surroundings, of which a Russian doctor once said, "In such a place all worldly sorrows and tribulations cease, and the miraculous landscape fills one's soul with quiet, strengthens it, and raises the spirits."

At present Bakuriani is a popular winter sports resort. Though the facilities for all types of winter sports are rather limited, there are still ski jumps, a cableway to Kokhta Mountain, special mountain ski routes, and sporting centres. Winter skiing in general is excellent.

Intourist organises 2-day tours to Bakuriani from Tbilisi, 200 km (124 miles) away.

Health-building sports camp, in Sun Valley
Tourist Centre and Hotel
Children's Sanatorium
Intourist Hotel
Botanical Gardens with Subalpine Flora

Fox-breeding Farm
There are interesting excursions that can be made from Bakuriani. There is a road up to the *Pass* (2,454 m/8,051 ft) *and summit of Tskhra-Tskharo* ("nine brothers" in Georgian), which is 2,711 m (8,858 ft) above sea level and has fine views of the South-Georgian Plateau and the Central Caucasian Mountains, especially at sunrise. From here is a descent to Lake Tabatskuri in the hollow between the high (up to 2,550 m/8,202 ft) volcanic mountains. The lake itself is 2,000 m (6,562 ft) above sea level and has beautiful small bays and peninsulas. The surrounding mountains are covered with subalpine and alpine pastures and in summer are bright with flowers. The lake is about 14 sq m (5.5 sq miles) in area, its average depth, 15 m (49 ft), while the maximum depth reaches 40 m (131 ft). It is of volcanic origin, is fed by subterranean springs, and abounds with trout and other fish.

Another tourist route, which requires special permission for foreigners from either Tbilisi or Moscow, goes from Borzhomi southward beyond Likany and Chitakhevi to Akhaltsikhe.

Situated on an inaccessible cliff near the road is *Atskuri Fortress*, which for many centuries blocked the way of enemies trying to invade Borzhomi Gorge.

Akhaltsikhe

Founded in the 10th–11th centuries, it was until the 16th century one of the most important places in Georgia. Captured by the Turks, it grew into the largest slave market, to which the Lezghins brought Christian slaves. The town, which was one of the most important Turkish strongholds in the region, flourished upon the slave trade. There was a rich Armenian church here, with a vast collection of parchment manuscripts embellished with miniatures. The local artisans were famous for their filigree silver work. The old part of the city, Babat, with a mediaeval fortress, is preserved to this day. There are many historical monuments in the vicinity of Akhaltsikhe.

Safarsky Monastery is situated on the picturesque steep bank of Uravelis-Tskhali. It is an interesting monument of early Christian times, built in the 13th–14th centuries. Of its 12 churches, only 3 remain. The main church is *St. Savva's*, and nearby is the *Church of the Assumption*. The monastery was last reconstructed in 1893.

To the east of Akhaltsikhe, along the Kura valley, can be seen a number of ancient monuments. The road passes Minadze, Rustavi, and Aspindze to reach the *Khertvissi Fortress*, at the confluence of the Paravani River and the Kura. It is said to have been founded in the 4th century B.C. Worth mentioning is *Tsundi Church*, built in the 12th century, in Rustaveli's time. Not far from here, in the depth of the gorge, is the large *Kumurdo Cathedral* (built in 964), and V*aniskvabebi cave monastery*.

Tmogva Fortress is 15 km (9 miles) south of

Khvertissi, still following the Kura. This ancient stronghold was considered inaccessible in its time. It was destroyed by earthquakes in the 11th and 13th centuries and restored in 1350. The remains of the caravanserais that are found here testify to the fact that it was here that the trade route passed from India to Europe.

After several kilometres and after crossing the Kura, the road comes to one of the most remarkable monuments of ancient Georgian culture, the *Vardzia "palace of roses") cave complex*. This mammoth monastery was built during the 12th–13th centuries in the time of George III and his daughter Queen Tamar. The steep cliffs stretch for several kilometres; in them, across a 500–m (550–yd) façade are 7–10 tiers of caves, serving both religious and secular purposes. These caves could accommodate about 200,000 people at once, and the majority of the residential quarters were built at the same time, following a single pattern. In front of an open loggia-like portico, linked by arches running sideways with the others at the same level, was a main living room and a small storeroom at the far back. There are about 550 caves, including several churches, and halls for ceremonial and residential quarters. The two-tier walls of the main, Uspensky, church are covered with frescoes of high artistic mastery. Among them are portraits of Georgi III and Queen Tamar. As legend has it, Vardzia was one of the queen's favourite residences. Tamar Palace consists of several hundred caves of different sizes. The most interesting is the large hall of the Queen's Council, with a niche for the throne and stone benches. Next to it is a small domestic chapel connected to the hall by a door and a small cell, through the window of which Queen Tamar liked to follow divine services without being seen.

An interesting detail of this cave-city is its elaborate water supply system, capable of bringing in 160,000 litres (qt) of fresh water a day.

BRATSK Population—255,000
The history of the old town of Bratsk goes back to 1631. The settlement emerged on the land of the Buryats, whom the Russian cossacks called "Brat" (brother); hence the name Bratsk. Formerly a quiet town in the Siberian taiga, where the winters are extremely cold, Bratsk changed beyond recognition during the 1960s.

There is a large aluminum plant here, and the town is now well known as the site of a hydropower station, which was the largest in the world when it was completed in 1964. It stands on the river Angara, 600 km (372 miles) downstream from Irkutsk. The high dam is 127 m (417 ft) high and almost 5 km (3 miles) long. 20 aggregates of 225,000 kilowatts produce 4,500,000 kilowatts, and between 22 and 24 billion kilowatt-hours annually.

Bratsk is also a port on the huge Bratsk reservoir, which was formed from the confluence of Oka, Iya, and Angara rivers and was completed in 1965. It is 570 km (354 miles) long, the largest artificial lake in the world. On the shore is the largest Pioneer camp in Siberia; it is open year-round and can take 1,300 children at a time. Besides hydroelectricity, Bratsk is the centre of an important timber and iron-ore area. The Bratsk forestry complex processes about 7 million cu m of timber annually, another world record.

Uspenskaya (Assumption) Church. This wooden church was built in 1979 and is open for services.

Local Museum, Komsomolskaya Street 38. Open 10–6.

Evenkiiskoye Stoibische Open-air Museum. It contains an ethnographical collection depicting the way of life of the Evenki. Open June–Sept. 10–5; closed Mon. the seminomadic Evenki are fur trappers, fishermen, and reindeer breeders. Their pagan religion is known as Shamanism.

Puppet Theatre, Podbelskovo Street

Taiga (Intourist) Hotel and Restaurant, Mira Street 35; tel. 439–78

Bratsk Hotel and Restaurant, Deputatskaya Street 32

Pursei Department Store, Naimushina Street

Gift Shop, Kirov Street. Open 11–8.

Intourist organises 2-hour excursions into the deep forest of the taiga, only 15 km (9 miles) from the centre of the city of Bratsk.

BREST (Brezesc nad Bugiem) Population—258,000
The border town of Brest, perhaps the most important of all entry points to the Soviet Union, is also the gateway to Byelorussia, described under Minsk, its capital city.

Formerly known as Brest-Litovsk, Brest stands on the right bank of the river Mukhavets (Muchawiec), at the point where it flows into the river Bug (pronounced "boug"). It was founded by monks, who were the first to bridge it and to build several houses among the birch trees on the island there. Their settlement was called Berestje, from the Russian word for birch bark. The first written records describe it as a fortress on a small island by the bridge over the Bug. The site was only recently located by archaeologists who had pieced together all the available evidence. Berestje Archaeological Preserve contains the excavated remains of the old town with traces of old buildings. A number of household utensils and items made by local craftsmen have been unearthed, and many of these are now on display in the local museum.

Brest has been known as a fortified town since 1017. From then onward it was frequently fought over by the Poles, Lithuanians, and Russians. In 1240 it was completely devastated by the Tartars, but it was already rebuilt by 1275, upon the order of Prince Vladimir of Volhynia. It became Lithuanian in 1319, Polish in 1569, Russian in 1795, and again Polish from 1919 until 1939. In 1596 the council that established the Uniate Church met here. These Christians, also known as the Greek Catholics, acknowledge the pope as their head but retain the Russian Orthodox order of service; they have been in communion with Rome since the Union of Uzhgorod of 1646 (see Transcarpathia). When Brest became Russian in 1795, its position on the western border of the country increased its strategic and trade importance. It was decided to build a really strong fortress here, but this plan was delayed because of the Napoleonic Wars, and only in 1830 did Nicholas I approve a plan for the proposed fortress. Prince Vladimir's pentagonal castle was demolished in 1831, and the town itself was transferred in 1833 to a site 5 km (3 miles) to the east. Between 1838 and 1842, this whole area was under construction. The fortress and its outer defences were situated on 4 islands on the river Bug. Surrounding the whole structure was an earth wall 10 m (33 ft) high. The central citadel had a 2-storey barrack square, 1.8 km (1 mile) in circumference, with walls 2 m (6 ft) thick, which could hold over 12,000 soldiers. During its history the stronghold was reinforced several times, particularly in 1911–14.

The Treaty of Brest-Litovsk was signed on 3 March 1918. By this treaty Russia gave up large territories in the west, including the Baltic provinces and the Ukraine, and was obliged to demobilise the army. The treaty was annulled by the armistice between Germany and the Western powers, signed in November 1918. Poland again occupied her eastern territories, including the area beyond Brest, but in September 1939, as the Nazi forces took over Poland from the north, west, and south, the Soviet army regained the eastern part of the country. During these events, the Brest fortress no longer played its strategic role, serving simply as the quarters for the local garrison.

When in 1941 Germany invaded the Soviet Union, there were no more than 2 regiments there, with many women and children who were members of their families. The 4-hectare (10-acre) territory of the fortress was shelled both by 500 cannon and from the air. It withstood the German attack for about a month, when all the surrounding area had capitulated and the German front line had advanced far to the east. The town is honoured in Russia as the place where the war broke out, and in 1965 it was proclaimed a "hero-fortress" in recognition of the valour displayed.

The large *memorial complex* designed by Alexander Kibalnikov was unveiled in 1971. It is impressive, although not perhaps to every foreign tourist's taste, and tends to detract from the historical impact of the fortress itself. It is, however, satisfying in its stark grandeur to Russian visitors and in keeping with the Orthodox tradition of pompes funèbres (funeral pomp). It consists of old buildings, preserved ruins, and new sculptures. The entrance is from Moskovskaya Street, through an arch in the form of a star, cut into a massive block of concrete. The way from here to the citadel on Central Island is paved by reinforced-concrete slabs; a bridge crosses the Mukhavets and leads to the Ceremonial Square, where there is room for 25,000 people to gather. Beyond the square, granite slabs cover the ashes of 833 defenders of the fortress. There is a *museum* on Central Island in commemoration of the brave stand, since described in many books and poems. The museum is open 10–6; closed Mon.

Today Brest is a major transportation centre. 5 railway lines meet there, and it is the frontier town on the Moscow–Warsaw line. It is also stands on the Dnieper-Bug Canal. It has various food and light industries, and there are teachers' training and civil engineering colleges in the town.

Local Museum, Lenin Street 34, in the building of a Roman Catholic church, which dates from 1856. Open 11–6; closed Mon.

Brestje Archaeological Preserve, on the island in the Bug. Open 11–6; closed Mon. and Tues.

Svyato-Semynovskaya Church (also known as Simeon Stolpnik Church), on the main road at the crossing of Moskovskaya and Karl Marx streets. Open for services.

St. Nicholas's Church, Mickiewicz Street. Built in 1910, it houses the local archives.

St. Afanasi Church, Moskovskaya Street, near the Intourist Hotel. St. Afanasi was once abbott of Brest. The church dates from 1654 and is open for services.

Lenin Monument, Lenin Square, at the crossing of Pushkin and Lenin streets

Mickiewicz Monument. The Polish poet Adam Mickiewicz (1798–1855) lived in the town.

Border Guards Monument, Lenin Street. This commemorates the Soviet border guards who lost their lives defending the town in 1941.

Liberation Monument, at the crossing of 17th September and Gogol streets

Lenkomsomol Drama Theatre, Lenin Street 21

Puppet Theatre, Lenin Street 56

Park of Culture, Lenin Street

Spartak Stadium

Intourist Hotel and Restaurant, Moskovskaya Street 15; tel. 51–071. Intourist office, tel. 51–152.

Bug Hotel and Restaurant, Lenin Street 2; tel 64–453

Belarus Hotel and Restaurant, Shevchenko Bld. 150; tel. 64–166

Camping Site, on the territory of the fortress; tel. 66–213

Brest Restaurant, Pushkinskaya Street 20

Cafeteria, at the fortress. Open 10–6.

GPO, Moskovskaya Street 10

International Telephone, Lenin Street 32

Department Store, Sovetskaya Street 16

Souvenirs, Shevchenko Bld. 170

Service Station, Spokoynayay Street 17

Filling Station, Kamenetsky Chaussee and Moskovskaya Street

Intourist organises excursions from Brest to Belovezhskaya Puscha (see below) and to Kobrin (q.v.).

Belovezhskaya Puscha (Polish: Puszsza Bialowieska)
The village is located 60 km (37 miles) to the north-west of Brest off the main road. One of the oldest nature reserves in the world, Belovezhskaya Puscha occupies an area of 130,000 hectares (325,000 acres), of which 75,000 (187,500) are in the the Soviet Union, the rest being Polish. It spreads northward from Kamanets. The round stone battlemented *tower* ("wieze" in Polish) was built by an architect called Olesko in 1276 for Prince Vladimir Vasilkovich, who had decided to found a town here since Brest was so often subject to destruction. The 30-m (98-ft) tower was built of brick, with walls 2.5 m (8 ft) thick, and because it was whitewashed, it was called byelaya or biala, meaning "white." It is an interesting example of local 13th-century architecture and now contains a museum with many historical documents, including those telling of the Battle of Grunwald (1410) against the Teutonic knights, in which Byelorussians also took part.

Perhaps it was the tower that gave Belovezhskaya Puscha its name. The reserve stretches northward to the village of Kamenyuki, and within its bounds can be found 285 representatives of the animal kingdom and 900 species of plants. There are deer, wild boar, aurochs, and elk, but the real pride of the reserve is the mighty bison. In 1921 there were none left here, and indeed only 26 European bison existed at all in the world. 3 were brought here from 1921 to 30 from Germany and Sweden, and by 1941 there were already 17. However, after World War II, part of the reserve, together with all the bison, went to Poland. 5 animals were returned in 1945; by 1952 there were 16; and now the population is more than 80.

There is a *museum and hotel* here. Excursions into the reserve are made only by car, but near the museum are enclosures where visitors can observe bison, tarpans (wild horses), red deer, roe deer, and wild boar. Open 9–5:30; closed Tues. (The ticket office is closed for lunch 1–2.) Since 1957 the reserve has also been used as a state hunting ground.

BUKHARA Population—224,000

The inhabitants of this ancient city are mainly Uzbeks, but there are many Tadzhiks, Russians, and Jews, and as many as 16 other nationalities. Most of the inhabitants speak 3 languages: Uzbek, Tadzhik (which resembles Farsi or Persian), and Russian.

Although archaeological excavations trace the story of Bukhara back to the 1st century A.D., it has in fact been known since the 2nd century B.C., when travellers visited it. Some of them gave its name as Poo Kho, and others called it Noo Me. This confusion lasted for hundreds of years, so that the 10th-century historian Narshakhi wrote that Bukhara had more names than any other city at that time. It was the Chinese and the Uighurs who at that time called it Bukhar, meaning "the temple of idols," but today some Russian scientists think

that its name is derived from the Sanskrit "bihara," meaning "monastery."

According to legend, Prince Seyavush of Persia came to Bukhara, married the khan's daughter, and built the fortress known as the Ark. Certainly the whole Bukhara region was under Persian rule between the 6th and 4th centuries B.C. From the time that Alexander the Great conquered Persia in 329 B.C. until the 2nd century B.C., the lands were under Greek rule.

During the first 5 centuries A.D., Bukhara was part of a number of different states in turn, including Kushan and the Epithalites' or White Huns' States under Atilla, Scourge of God (406–53), and was one of the most important centres of both trade and culture in Central Asia. Its trade connections linked it with Persia, India, and China, among other countries.

In 709, after a bloody struggle, the Arabs seized Bukhara, and their rule was notable for the series of revolts against them. The movement of the Men in White, led by a certain Moukanna, was the longest lasting of these uprisings, and legend tells that at the moment of their defeat, while surrounded by their oppressors, the rebels threw themselves into a great fire, together with their leader.

In the 9th century, the Samanid family rose in power. Originally they had been the governors appointed by the Arabs, but they became a powerful land-owning family. Ismail Samani was the first of the dynasty that ruled Bukhara from 874 to 999. Under the Samanid's rule, Bukhara became the capital of a vast feudal state, embracing nearly the whole territory of Central Asia. In the 10th century, Bukhara was famed as the centre of culture. Among the enlightened citizens of Bukhara were the poet Abul Hassan Rudaki and the physician and philosopher Abu-Ali Ibn Sina (otherwise known as Avicenna, 980–1037). Rudaki, who died in 941, said that Bukhara was better than Baghdad. The Karakhanids ruled Bukhara from 999 till 1141 and the Kara-Kitays from 1141 till 1206. Monuments dating from the first period are the Arslan-Khan Minaret (which, with the Amir and the Mir-i-Arab Medressehs, is part of the Kalan Mosque ensemble), the Maghak-il Attari Mosque, the Namazgoh Mosque, and the Chashma-Ayub Tomb.

After 1206 Bukhara belonged to the powerful state of Khorezm but in 1220 was overrun by the Mongols of Genghis Khan. The city was razed to the ground and its inhabitants enslaved. By the second half of that century, Bukhara had gradually recovered, so that when Marco Polo visited it he called it "the city of high grandeur."

In 1370 Bukhara fell under the jurisdiction of Tamerlane (also known as Tamberlaine or Timur) and lost its political importance to Samarkand, which Tamerlane had chosen as his capital.

The Saybanids' dynasty began in 1506, and by the end of the 16th century, Bukhara had become the capital of the state that came to be called the khanate of Bukhara. The period brought back flourishing trade, and the city acquired the appearance that it preserved until the 1919 revolution. It was

surrounded by a wall about 12 km (7 miles) long, 5 m (16 ft) thick and 10 m (33 ft) high.

In 1595 a new dynasty, the Ashtarkhanids (who were descendants of the rulers of Astrakhan) came to power, and by the end of their rule in the 18th century, Bukhara had lost much of its economic and cultural importance. When in 1740 the Persian Shah Nadir captured Bukhara, he appointed a local landlord, Mohammad Rahim, as his governor. The latter proclaimed himself emir and founded Bukhara's last dynasty, the Mangids (1753–1920). Under Mangid rule, Bukhara turned from the centre of local culture to the centre of religious obscurantism and political reaction. In theological Moslem literature, it was called Bukhara-y-Sherif (holy Bukhara).

In the 1860s and 1870s, the tsarist government started its attempts to take over Bukhara. In 1868 the Russian general Kaufman defeated the emir's army after a short struggle, and Bukhara became a Russian protectorate. In subsequent years the slave trade was abolished, telegraph and post offices were built, and between 1877 and 1888 the first railway was laid from Krasnovodsk to Samarkand. Schools and hospitals were built near the railway stations, but life was not very bright. In Bukhara they complained, "only air is untaxed." At the beginning of the 20th century, a political movement called "Djadidizm" was formed. "Djadid" means "new" in Arabic, and the party was similar to the liberal Young Turkey movement in Turkey during the same period.

In 1919 an uprising against the emir was led by the Communist party, who called for help, and in September 1920 Red Army troops took the city after 4 days' fighting. Bukhara was declared a republic. It joined the Soviet Union in 1924 and became a regional centre of Uzbekistan.

More than 30 of the architectural monuments of the ancient city of Bukhara are considered to be of national importance. They belong to all periods, from the 9th century up to the present day. The *Charud Canal*, running through the city roughly from east to west, used to supply as many as 85 "hauzes" or reservoirs, which formed the water-supply system of Bukhara. With the passing of the years, the level of the city rose, and so the canal was constantly raised and relined; all the same it now appears to flow at the bottom of a deep rift in many places. In the past, the hauzes were used for drinking water and for washing in; they were rife with bacteria and extremely unwholesome. Now only 5 of the original 20 largest hauzes remain, and of these, 2 are empty. They are 10 m (33 ft) deep and were built in 1620. The water was usually changed every 2 weeks.

The wall of the city is earthen, 8 m (26 ft) high and 12 km (7 miles) in circumference. It was first built in the 15th–16th centuries but was constantly being damaged and rebuilt. The *Tali-Pach Gate* is the only one of the 11 to survive. It has been restored.

New Bukhara is growing up around the old mud houses. Every year new streets are lined with prefabricated 4-storey houses. Ulyanova and Khamza streets are the central thoroughfares of the new town. A special housing complex is being built to provide new accommodations for the inhabitants of the old town.

Local industry is mainly cotton ginning and the manufacture of silk textiles, Astrakhan fur, food products, and components for prefabricated buildings. It is interesting to pay a visit to the *Gold-Embroidering Factory*, Detsky Pereulok 4. 240 workers are employed here, and one can inspect the articles they produce—gowns, shoes, and "tub-eteiki" (national skullcaps). These items are on sale in local shops as well as in Moscow. The factory itself is the largest of a small number of similar enterprises that exist in the Soviet Union. Visits may also be made to the fur factory.

The donkeys that are to be seen wandering about the streets of Bukhara in fact belong to no one in particular. They are rounded up once a week and taken out to the surrounding villages by the truck load. The villagers use them to bring their goods to market, particularly to the busy Sunday markets, and then abandon them and return home by more modern means of transport.

The Ark is the oldest structure in Bukhara. It is the city fortress, parts of which are at least 2,000 years old. It now forms the main section of the local museum, open 9–5; closed Wed. It is situated on an artificial hill 16–20 m (52–66 ft) high and covers more than 2.4 hectares (6 acres). The wall surrounding it has been rebuilt several times, and the existing one is believed to have been erected about 200 or 300 years ago. Until the Arab invasion, the Ark served as the residence of the governors of the city. Several times during the 12th–14th centuries, various invaders ruined it, and its present form dates from the 16th century. The ceremonial entrance is protected by two pillarlike towers connected by a gallery above, in which the emir's musicians and the city guards usually lived. The big leather lash that usually hung on the walls as a symbol of the emir's power had once, according to tradition, belonged to the Persian warrior Rustam, the same that Matthew Arnold tells of in his poem "Sohrab and Rustam."

All the buildings inside the fortress are from the 17th–20th centuries, during the time the emirs used it as their residence, together with their ministers and members of the nobility. The entrance to the citadel is by way of a long, covered gallery, flanked by rooms on both sides. Some of these were used for storing water, while others served as prison cells. The *Djuma Mosque* with a carved wooden porch was built in 1919. The narrow street leading from the mosque runs to a small cupola called *Charsu* over the entrance to Salam-Khana (court of greetings), the emir's reception hall and the highest point of the citadel. From here doors lead onto a balcony overlooking the Registan. To the right of Charsu were the stables, and in fact Charsu is in the paved Mews' court. It contains the "saganah" (tomb) supposed to be that of the founder of the fortress, Prince Seyavush.

To the left of Charsu is *Kurynish-Khana*, the place where the emirs were crowned and where they received foreign ambassadors. In *Chyl Duktaron* in the northern part of the fortress forty girls were, according to legend, tortured and thrown into a well at the command of Emir Nasroulla.

Zindan, Kolkhoznaya Street. Formerly the emir's prison, this was built in the 18th century. There are prison cells, some of which are below ground. The prisoners were given their food from above. There was a deep pit for special offenders, where the emir kept specially bred vermin and reptiles to torture his prisoners. Stoddart and Connolly, the two British officers sent in 1843 to offer British assistance against Russian incursions, spent many months in one of the cells as well as the pit. Nearby is the place where they were beheaded. Zindan now forms part of the Bukhara Museum, and there are two dummy prisoners at the bottom of the pit. Open 9–5; closed Tues.

In front of the Ark lies the square called the *Registan* (with Marx Street as its address), across from which stands the *Bolo Haus* ("near-the-pool") *Mosque*. This was usually visited on Friday by the emirs when they came to Bukhara, and valuable carpets were laid between it and the ark especially for the occasion. Founded in 1712, the mosque was rebuilt at the beginning of the 18th century and enlarged in 1917. It is characterised by 20 wooden columns.

Behind the mosque, on the site of an old cemetery, is *Kirov Park*, in which some of the oldest monuments of Bukhara are to be found. On the road to the park, a little to the southwest of the Registan, are two medressehs (Muslim theological colleges), now standing on either side of the street, but still called *Kosh* ("*double*") *Medresseh* because they stand so close. The effect is very imposing. *Modari-Khan* ("Khan's mother"), to the east, was built in 1566 and *Abdullah Khan*, to the west, in 1589. The latter is the grander and more richly decorated of the two, and it is distinguished by its architectural originality. The first was built by Abdullah Khan for his mother, and the second was built for him by his own son.

In Kirov Park the *Ismail Sanami Mausoleum* (built between 892 and 907) is a cube-shaped building with a hemispherical cupola resting on four archways. 4 smaller cupolas around the larger one give the whole structure an appearance of lightness. It became almost completely buried and so survived the ravages of Genghis Khan. The walls are 1.8 m (6 ft) thick, which partly accounts for the fact that the mausoleum is still standing after over 1,000 years. Some restorations were carried out in 1934. An interesting point is that it has no main façade—all 4 sides are identical, each containing a lancet arch over an entrance. The gallery running around the top of the outer walls has 40 window openings. The walls themselves, both inside and out, are decorated with ornamental terra-cotta; the decorations seem to change several times during the day, depending upon the angle at which the sun's rays strike them, and they appear most effective of all by moonlight. This feature of the building is architecturally unique.

Chronicles testify that the mausoleum was built by the founder of the Samanid dynasty, Ismail Samani, in honour of his father, and that later Ismail himself was buried here. For centuries the Muslim mullahs fostered the illusion that Ismail Samani was alive and helping his people. There were 2 openings in the tombstone inside the mausoleum, one for questions and requests and another for answers supplied by the mullahs.

Also in Kirov Park, Lenin Street, and not far from the Ismail Samani Mausoleum, is the 12th-century *Mazaar-Chashma-Ayub*. The 4 parts of the rectangular structure were all built at different times and crowned by cupolas of different design. The northern and southern sides of the monument are particularly interesting. Inside the mazaar is an ice-cold spring. Legend has it that long ago, before the foundation of the city and in a year of terrible drought, Job came to these parts. The people were dying of thirst, but when Job struck the earth with his staff, a spring of water started to flow, hence the name Chashma-Ayub ("spring of Job").

Maghak-Attari Mosque, Frunze Square, opposite the open-air cinema. The name of this mosque indicates that once this was the place where medicinal herbs were sold. It was founded no later than the 9th century but has been rebuilt many times, in the 12th, 16th, and 20th centuries. The building appears to have sunk down 6 m (20 ft) into the earth, but in fact the ground level has risen with the passage of time, as in usual in places that have been inhabited for many centuries. In the 1930s archaeological excavations revealed 5 layers of floors, helping to prove that it was the site of a 5th-century fire-worshippers' temple, before the arrival of Islam. At a depth of more than 10 m (33 ft) were found signs of a Buddhist monastery, which helped to identify the date of the foundation of Bukhara as 1st century A.D.

The southern portal (pishtak) of the mosque is a masterpiece of Oriental architecture, with many different styles, including carved alabaster, turquoise tiles, and polished brick. Its small finely carved columns make it particularly beautiful.

The Kalan ("*great*") *Mosque*, Kolkhoznaya Street, by the market. This is the city's principal mosque and together with the Great Minaret and the Mir-i-Arab Medresseh forms an architectural ensemble sometimes called the Bukhara Forum. It was built in 1514 on the site of a 12th-century Karakhanid mosque and is one of the oldest and, after Bibi Khanum in Samarkand, the second-largest mosque in Central Asia. The cupola is higher than any other structure in Bukhara except the Great Minaret and gives the mosque its second name, Kok-Gumbar ("blue dome"). The mosque has 7 entrances and covers an area of 9,906 sq m (106,627 sq ft). It is a so-called open mosque, and the gallery of the courtyard is roofed by 288 cupolas, supported by 208 pillars. It can take a congregation of 10,000 in the courtyard, under the gallery, and on the roof.

The Kalan Minaret, near the centre of town, is linked to the Kalan Mosque by a stone arch. Kalan was also the name of one of the rulers of the Karakhanid dynasty. The minaret was built in 1127 by Arslan-Khan and, at 46.5 m (153 ft) high, is the tallest structure in Central Asia. It is pillar-shaped, tapering slightly at the top, and is of terra-cotta laid on a thick alabaster solution. Inside is a spiral staircase of 104 steps, leading up to a rotunda with 16 archlike openings. The belt of light blue enamel at the top is 16th century.

In the past, on Fridays, 4 muedzins called the faithful to prayer. Their call was relayed by the muedzins of 200 other Bukhara mosques. The minaret also served as a watch tower and as a beacon for smoke signals to guide approaching merchant caravans. When Genghis Khan reached the centre of Bukhara, he halted his horse in front of the minaret for a long time and put his finger to his mouth in a gesture of amazement; then he ordered the city to be entirely destroyed with the exception of the minaret. The legend attached to the two marble plaques fixed to the minaret near the top is that in the 16th century two men on two different occasions managed to climb the minaret using a hammer and awl, and when they had each fixed their plaque, they came safely down again.

During the period of the Mangid dynasty, criminals were thrown from the top of the minaret, but the practice ceased with the abolition of slavery in 1868. In general the treatment of wrongdoers was extremely cruel. As late as 1829 it is recorded that the punishment for "murder, revolt, forgery, treason, adultery and drunkenness" was death by beating on the back of the head until the victim lost consciousness. Thereafter his throat was cut, he was hanged, taken down, beheaded, and the severed head nailed up by the ears for a period of 3 days, while the body was handed over to his relatives. At the end of the 19th and the beginning of the 20th centuries, the minaret was called Manari-Kalan, the Tower of Death. In September 1920 the establishment of Soviet power was declared from the top of the minaret.

Many legends about its origin have arisen during the minaret's 800 years of existence. One says that the architect laid foundations based on a solution of clay, camels' milk, eggs, and bulls' blood. He then disappeared, only returning after 2 years when the solution had hardened considerably. Another legend says that the architect asked to be buried nearby, in a place situated as far from the minaret as the height of the building itself. Tourists are still shown his grave. Recent restoration works have included cleaning the 10-m (33-ft) foundation of layers of mud.

The *Mir-i-Arab Medresseh*, Kolkhoznaya Street, near the market, stands opposite the Kalan Mosque. It was built in 1534 and takes its name form the Sheik Abdulla from Yemen, whose nickname was Mir-i-Arab and who is buried here along with many of his numerous relatives. The room in which they lie is richly decorated. Mir-i-Arab's tomb is the large one in the window recess. Another interesting one is that with a wooden cover instead of a tombstone. It marks the grave of Mir-i-Arab's pupil, Obaidolla-Khan Sheibanid.

The medresseh is one of the few in Central Asia to be serving its intended purpose as a Moslem theological training college. It was closed in 1925 but was reopened in 1946, permission for this being granted by the state as a token of gratitude to Soviet Islam for its valuable part in the war effort. The students study religion, Islamic law, and Arabic and usually return home to preach. There are about 400 mosques still operating in the USSR, and as many as 30 students graduate from the medresseh each year. There are now 80 students following a 7-year course, part of their studies being in Arabic. The building consists of two storeys of arched cloisters around a central courtyard. Each archway leads into a small cell, which serves either as a classroom or as accommodation for 4 students; traditionally the classrooms should be on the ground floor and the students' rooms above. Before the 1917 revolution, the medressehs were the only schools in Bukhara.

Ibn-Sein (Avicenna) Library is behind the medresseh, on 40-Let Oktyabrya Street, next to the Intourist Hotel. It was built in 1914 as the Kalan Medresseh (or the Emir Medresseh). Now it contains 150,000 books and a good collection of ancient manuscripts.

Ulug-Beg Medresseh, just up Kolkhoznaya Street, under the archway. This medresseh was built in 1417. It is rectangular with a courtyard and a wide portal serving as an entrance, over which there was once a library (Ketab-Khana). The medresseh was built by a Persian architect called Ismail for Ulug-Beg, the famous astronomer and administrator. It was completely rebuilt in 1583 and has been restored many times since. The decorations are of a scientific and mainly astronomical character, owing to Ulug-Beg's proclivities. A wooden plaque on the gate bears the inscription: "It is the duty of every true Moslem, man and woman, to strive after knowledge." The decorative tiles have been restored recently. Soviet scientists spent much time trying to find out their chemical composition, and finally the secret of their production was discovered. A small factory was founded in Bukhara to produce exactly the right enamel for their restoration.

Abdulaziz-Khan Medresseh, Kolkhoznaya Street, stands facing the Ulug-Beg Medresseh and forms an architectural ensemble with it. It has a summer mosque in the courtyard, and the winter mosque is in the western corner of the entrance passage. Both are richly decorated with majolica, glazed tiles, brick mosaic, and carved marble. On the facings of the walls are various paintings of animals and also of Chinese motifs, bearing witness to the fact that in the 17th century trade relations existed between China and Bukhara. The left part of the façade and the right part of the courtyard appear lacking in decoration. This is because, before the medresseh was really completed, Abdulaziz-Khan was overpowered, and the work, begun in 1652, ceased. Inside the medresseh is the Sharbat-khan Bar which serves cold drinks.

Kukeldash Medresseh, Lab-i-Hauz Square. This is one of the largest and grandest medressehs in Central Asia. The facing has much in common with that of Abdulaziz-Khan Medresseh, built 10 years later. The entrance door is made of carved wooden planks fastened with wooden pegs, and inside the courtyard is a fine portal of blue, green, and white brick. The building contains 160 cells (hudjras) and today houses the local record office.

Lab-i-Hauz Square itself is of interest to the visitor for it is still one of Bukhara's liveliest marketplaces and one of the most attractive spots in the city. It is so called because of the large pool in the centre, which has been there since 1620. "Hauz" means "pool," and the name of the square, "over-the-pool." The ensemble of buildings around the square was completed under the Ashtarkhanid dynasty. On the same side of the square as the Kukeldash Medresseh is the *Yr-Nazaar-Ilchei Medresseh*, which was named for the Bukharan ambassador to Catherine the Great and was built at her expense. On the west side of the square is the *Lab-i-Hauz Mosque* (1611) and the *Khanigah* ("*prayer house*") *of Divan Beg*. Opposite is the

Nadir Divan Beg Medresseh, built in 1631 as a caravanserai and then rebuilt as a medresseh, which accounts for its having no mosque. On its façade and right wing it bears an effigy of the mythological Semurg bird and a deer. There is a tearoom in the courtyard.

The Chahar-Minar Medresseh, built in 1807, belongs to a much later period than most of the other ancient monuments of Bukhara, and in style it resembles an Indian mosque. Its name means "4 minarets," but in fact the 4 towers are not true minarets. They are nevertheless very imposing, being covered with cornflower blue and dark blue bricks and crowned with blue cupolas. The cupolas, just as those of many of the other buildings in Bukhara, are topped with special spikes to encourage storks to build their nests there. These birds have been nesting in Bukhara for a thousand years or more, one of the few places in Central Asia that they favour.

In the 15th century, a number of buildings connected with the commercial life of the city appeared in Bukhara. Among them were 5 cupolas constructed at the crossroads on Shah-Restan, the main shopping street. Inside the cupolas were little shops, and the cupolas themselves were called after the trade they housed. Still in existence are the grey domes of the *Taq-i-Sarrafon* (at the crossing of Sovietskaya and Lenin streets), where the money changers did business, the *Taq-i-Talpakfurushon* (Pushkin and Frunze streets), where skullcaps were and are still sold, and *Taq-i-Zargaran*, the goldsmiths' bazaar, which used to be the centre of the whole trading area.

To the south of the city on Kirov Street is *Namazgoh Mosque*, its name meaning "the place of prayer." It was built in the 12th century on the site of an estate with a rich orchard and a zoo, as an out-of-town mosque of the type constructed for great religious holidays when the city mosques could not house all the faithful. It was redecorated in the 14th century with horizontal majolica plates bearing bright blue, navy, and white inscriptions in Arabic. The cupola-crowned gallery was added in the 16th century. The architecture of the main entrance is similar to that of the Maghak-i-Attari Mosque, and the west wall is attractively decorated in terra-cotta and blue majolica.

In the eastern part of Bukhara, just beyond the railway station at Lenin Street 180, are two more buildings of interest. The larger, a *mausoleum and mosque* built in the 13th or 14th century, is connected with the name of Saifuddin Bukharzi, a Moslem theologist who died in 1262. It consists of 2 rooms, one for prayer and one with the tomb. The walls of the building and the cupola, both of which were cracking, have been reinforced with iron. Nearby is another *mausoleum* which stands over the grave of a Mongol noble, Buyan Quli Khan, a descendant of Genghis Khan, who was killed in Samarkand in 1358. It is lavishly decorated, being faced both inside and out with terra-cotta in bright blue, navy, violet, and white. The imposing portal on the eastern side is richly decorated so that it appears to be covered with stone lacework. The mausoleum was completely restored in 1926.

There used to be 360 mosques in Bukhara. Now only 3 are open for services. The best one to visit is *Hodja-Zai-Edin Mosque*, Vodoprovodnaya Street 5.

Synagogue, Tsentralnaya Street 20. According to local tradition, the Bukharan Jews came originally from Shiraz in the time of Tamerlane, and indeed he may have brought some of them with him from Baghdad. They wear traditional costumes on feast days and have some special customs of their own. Their native language is either Tadzhik or Uzbek.

History Museum and Local Museum, Karl Marx Street 1. Open 9–5; closed Wed.

Decorative and Applied Arts Museum. Open 9–5; closed Wed.

Art Museum. Open 9–5; Closed Tues.

Handicraft Museum, Karl Marx Street 2. Open 9–5; closed Wed.

Lenin Monument, in front of the Intourist Hotel

Frunze Monument, in Frunze Park. General Mikhail V. Frunze was the old-time communist whose troops defeated the last emir.

Revolution Obelisk, on Revolution Square, in front of the railway station. Dedicated to those who died in 1920.

Music and Drama Theatre, Teatralnaya Street 3

Summer Branch of the Music and Drama Theatre, Lenin Street 61, opposite Lab-i-Hauz

Puppet Theatre, Gazovikov Street 1

Stadium, Shevchenko Prospect

Eshlik Sport Complex, Pablo Nerudy Street 9/1

Bukhoro Intourist Hotel and Restaurant, 40-Let-Oktyabrya Street 8; tel. 31–104. Intourist office: tel. 31–033.

Intourist Hotel and Shark ("eastern") Restaurant, Lenin Square; tel. 22–76

Bukhara Restaurant, Frunze Square

Branch of the Bukhara Restaurant, Kirov Street

Chorsy Restaurant and Tearoom, near Lab-i-Hauz

Café, Lenin Street 84

Ice Cream Parlour and Tearoom, Frunze Square

Sharbat-khan Bar, Abdul-aziz Khan Medresseh, Kolkhoznaya Street. Cold drinks are served here.

Shashlik Bar, in a small garden near the Intourist Hotel

Beryozka Foreign Currency Shop, Navoi Prospect 17

Bank, Lenin Street 41

Taxi stands, Kukeldash Square and at the railway station

Char-Bakir ("our girls") Medresseh, 7 km (4 miles) from town. This medresseh was built in the 16th–17th centuries. One can reach the top of the building through a side entrance, and from there is a good panoramic view. The ancient cemetery nearby was the burial place of prominent Bukharans. There are two mosques on the ground floor of the medresseh. Char-Bakir can be reached by car.

The Setori-y-Mahi-Hasa Palace (also known as Mahasa) lies 14 km (9 miles) to the north of Bukhara. It was built in 1911–12 as a summer residence by the last of the emirs, Said-Alim-Khan, a despotic gentleman who had 100 wives (some even say 450). He ruled from 1911–20 and died in Afghanistan in 1946. The artificial style of the palace resulted from a mixture of the poorer features of Central Asian architecture and elements introduced by the Europeanised tastes of the emir. European influence is apparent in all the details of the construction of the single-storey, L-shaped building. Interesting are the Summer Room, with stained-glass windows, the Ministerial Room, painted in colours that were mixed with egg, and the large white Ceremonial Hall, with mirrored-walls.

Today the palace forms part of the Bukhara Museum and is used as a rest home. Peacocks stroll in the park, and the local inhabitants like to point out the little stone pavilion from which they say the emir could watch his womenfolk bathing in the large pool below. The smaller palace nearby was built by Ahad Khan, the last emir's father, who ruled from 1885 to 1910. It retains all the elements of the old national architectural style. Now it houses a lung sanatorium for children.

BURYATIA

See Ulan-Ude, p. 590.

BYELORUSSIA

See Minsk, p. 320.

BYURAKAN

See Erevan, p. 133.

CESIS Population—20,000

This Latvian town, on either bank of the river Gauja, was formerly known as Wenden. It is 93 km (58 miles) from Riga on the road to Pskov and is a regional centre.

It was first mentioned by Henry Litovsky (1180–1259) in the Livonian Chronicle, but Latgale Fortress already stood on Riekstu ("nut") Hill in the 11th century. In 1207–9 the site was used for the building of a new fortress, which was to serve also as a monastery and a residence for Volkquin (1209–36), the second of the Grand-Masters of the Brethren of the Sword. From 1237 onward it was occupied by the Masters of the Teutonic Order (the Brethren of the Cross). Hermann Balk took up residence in 1239, but the best known of the Masters was Walter von Plettenberg (1494–1535), who considerably enlarged the castle. It was he who built the Western Tower, which remains today. Cesis was proclaimed a town in 1323, and at the end of

the 14th century, it was incorporated into the Hanseatic League.

During the Livonian War (1558–83) between the Russians and Poles, the city was seized by the Poles in 1561; in 1577 the castle garrison blew themselves up rather than fall into the hands of Ivan the Terrible. It was retaken by the Poles in 1578 after a particularly bloody battle, and in 1583 the castle became the residence of Bishop Patricius Nidecki (d. 1587), appointed by King Stephen Batory of Poland. The king gave Cesis the same rights as the city of Riga with regard to trade along the river Gauja and the minting of its own coinage.

The Swedish-Polish War of 1600–1629 saw Cesis changing hands, finally being taken by King Gustav II of Sweden. It suffered a disastrous fire in 1671 and further damage during the Northern War of 1700–1721, finally being incorporated into Russia. The town was presented as private property to Ernst Biron by Empress Anna in 1730 and to Count Bestuzhev-Ryumin in 1747 by Empress Elizabeth. The fire of 1748 left little but ruins of the castle, but they stood undisturbed in the park, which belonged to the estate of the local landlord, Count Sievers. Count Bestuzhev-Ryumin forbade any house building after the fire, and town status was only restored in 1759. The castle was purchased by Count Sievers in 1777, and it remained in the hands of his family until the 1920s. The railway connection with Riga was opened in 1889.

During the Civil War period, Cesis was under German occupation from February 1918 till May 1919 when it was joined to the rest of Latvia. Latvia as a whole became part of the Soviet Union in 1940.

Lenin Square is in the centre of the town, and from here Gagarin Street leads to the railway station.

St. John the Baptist's Church, Tornja Street 2. Built in Roman-Gothic style in 1281–84 by Vilekin von Endorp, Master of the Brethren of the Sword. After dedication it served as a house church for members of the Livonian Order. The 65-m (213-ft) spire was added in 1853 by Marius Sarum, and the church itself was restored in 1900. Inside are some remains of the tombstone of Walter von Plettenberg. The painting over the altar was made by Johann Koehlers in Paris in 1858 and depicts the Crucifixion. The painting was a gift from Count Sievers; there are copies of it in St. Isaac's Cathedral in Leningrad, in St. Stephen's in Vienna, and in St. Martin's in Riga. The entrance to the church is the same height above sea level as the cock on the top of the spire of St. Peter's Church in Riga. The organ was installed in 1907.

Orthodox Church, in the northwestern part of October Park. Built in Byzantine style in 1845.

History and Art Museum, Pils Street 9, in New Castle (Lademacher Tower). Outside there is an ethnographical section, showing wooden peasant architecture and also methods of spinning and weaving in the villages in the last century.

Castle, near Pils Street and October Park. The

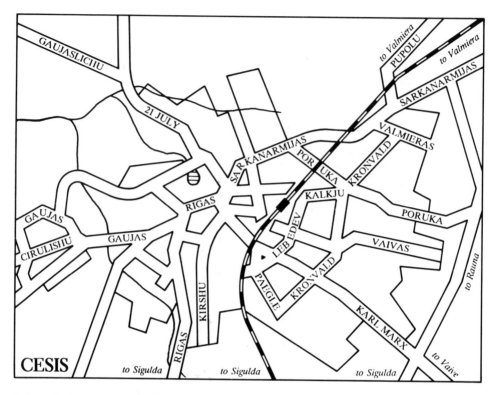

CESIS

to Sigulda   to Sigulda   to Sigulda

Lademacher Tower was restored by Count Sievers, and reopened as New Castle. Of special interest is the late-Gothic reticulated vaulting of the Grand-Master's room in the tower. There is a good view over the town from the top of the tower, as well as of the surrounding hilly countryside.

Ratusha (Town Hall), Rigas Street 7. It was built in 1767.

In addition to the town hall, there are a number of other *old houses* in Cesis. These include that at Rigas Street 24, which was built at the beginning of the 18th century; it was purchased in 1767 by Harmonia, the town musical society, and later housed the first cinema in Cesis. No. 47 on the same street is known as the *Princesses' House*; it was used in the 18th century by society ladies expelled for their misdemeanours from St. Petersburg. Also of the 18th century is No. 12 Pioneru Street and No. 6 Gaujas Street, which was a technical school between 1892 and 1895. Today the *Technical School* is at No. 6 Skolas Street (built in 1789). No. 27 Komjaunatnes street (1762) is the hospital, and No. 60 on the same street is a school-sanatorium; it was built in 1882 by Kampe as a grammar school, and so it remained until 1915. 19th-century buildings include Nos. 37 and 39 Valnu Street and No. 51 Rigas Street, which used to be the posting station. The *Cesu alus Brewery* at 21-July Street 11 was founded in 1878.

Turkish Tombs, Imanas Street. 26 Turks captured in the Russian-Turkish War of 1877–78 were buried here. The granite monument was installed by the town council in 1880.

Lenin Statue, Lenin Square. Sculpted by Janson, it was unveiled in 1959.

Liberators' Monument, in Pobedy ("victory") Park. Dedicated to the soldiers who liberated the town in World War II, it was sculpted by Janson in 1946.

October Park, near Padomjus Street and the castle. The park was laid out in 1812 by Count Sievers. There is an open-air song platform and many sculptures and a pond with the Fisherman Fountain, by Jansons (1961).

Pobedy Park. Founded in the 19th century. There are crimson water lilies in the pond here.

Stadium, Poruka Street

Tervete Hotel and Café, Lenin Square 1; tel. 22–851

Tervete Hotel Annex, Rigas Street 21; tel. 22–347

Cesis Restaurant, Uzvaras Boulevard 1

Department Store, Uzvaras Square

Market, Uzvaras Square

Rauna (formerly Ronneburg)
23 km (14 miles) east of Cesis on the river Rauna is the village of Rauna.

The village was conquered by the Knights of the Livonian Order in the 13th century. From 1420 it served as the winter residence of the archbishops of Riga. In 1536 the village was destroyed by the knights but was rebuilt and granted town status in 1590. During the Northern War, it was all but razed to the ground. In the 19th century it began to recover.

Church. Built in 1262. Here are the extensive *ruins of the castle* built by Archbishop Albert of Riga in 1262.

Tanisakaln, on the left bank of the river Rauna. This is the site of a 6th century town.

CHAKVA
See Batumi, p. 68.

CHARDZHOU (Formerly Chardjui; from 1924 to 27, Leninsk-Turkmensky) Population—161,000
Chardzhou is the largest city in the middle reaches of the Amu-Darya River, and after Ashkhabad, the second largest in the Turkmen Republic. It is situated where the Transcaspian Railway crosses the river and is also a railway junction, as the line to Kungrad in Kara-Kalpakia starts here.

Near present-day Chardzhou is the settlement of Komsomolsk, previously known as Old Chardzhou and from the 3rd century B.C. as Amul (also Amuye, Amuy and Amu), the town that gave its name to the river Amu-Darya (darya in Turkmen, Tadzhik, and Uzbek means "big river," and in Persian, "sea"). Ancient geographers, Strabon and Gueradot among them, called the Amu-Darya the Araks and Oks (Oxus), and Oriental historians call it Djeikhun ("wild"). The river is 1,415 km (880 miles) long and flows into the Aral Sea. It is extremely important for irrigating the desert areas of Central Asia and was considered one of the targets in the Russian advance upon this region.

The settlement had, in the 1st–4th centuries A.D., been a part of the state of Kushan. In 1972, during excavation work, unique figurines of local idols made with great skill, belonging to that period, were found here, along with sculptures of more ancient times, one even belonging to the 3rd millennium B.C. They are exhibited in the local museum. The caravan routes to Khorezm, Bukhara, Merv, and Iran passed this way, and the town stood upon the Silk Road, as some of the Chinese silk went through Amul on its way to the cities of the Mediterranean. There was a fortress here that belonged to the khan of Bukhara, which watched over the river crossing to prevent nomad tribes from endangering faraway Bukhara. The fortress was surrounded by a wall of reinforced clay, and its 4 gates were under constant guard; now there is nothing left but mounds and half-demolished walls. Amul was devastated by Genghis Khan in 1221, and it only recovered in the 14th century.

Chardzhou (Chardjui) is a relatively recent name, first mentioned in literature in the 16th century. It come from "chakhar jui," meaning "4 streams." The new town grew with the construction of the Transcaspian Railway, which reached the left bank of the Amu-Darya in November 1866, the territory having been given to the Russian government by the emir of Bukhara. It was at first no more than a military settlement, but 2 years later the first town plans were drawn up, and a large cotton-ginning plant was built in 1910. Russian Chardjui, as it was then called, was inhabited by Russians, Armenians, and Jews, in addition to the Turkmens. (In 1911 there were 8,000 Russian civilians here, not to mention the military personnel.) The original wooden railway bridge was replaced by an iron one in 1901; at 1.6 km (1 mile) in length, it was the longest bridge in Russia at the time and in fact the third longest in the world. Even now it is one of the largest in the country.

Chardzhou became an industrial town even before the 1917 revolution, when as many as 18 different plants and factories were nationalised. Now it is one of the major industrial and cultural centres of Turkmenia. The town has been fully reconstructed, and only a few old buildings remain. In the centre, the former residence of the local "bek" (ruler) and the former grammar school are now used as party and government offices. Another building bears a memorial plaque stating that in 1891 Fyodor Chaliapin, the great Russian bass, stopped here and gave a concert. Educational establishments include the Lenin Pedagogical Institute.

The town is both an important railway and road junction and the centre of the Amu-Darya Shipping Line. Local enterprises process agricultural products, cotton, Astrakhan skins, and raw silk. There are metal-working plants, a shipyard, and motor and locomotive repair shops. The chemical industry, especially superphosphate production, is probably the most important of all, having become well developed since oil and gas deposits were discovered in the vicinity, and a large petrochemical plant has been founded. Intourist organises visits to the silk factory, the Astrakhan fur factory, and other places of particular interest. Turkmenia's only teacher-training college is in Chardzhou.

Chardzhou is known for its melons. The best variety is called Gulyaby, which means "juice of roses" in Turkmen. It is said that, in the old days, these melons were sent by caravan in special lead containers or in copper pots to Baghdad and India. Another variety is known as Kary-kyz, meaning "old maid" because of its rough, wrinkly rind.

SS. Peter and Paul Russian Orthodox Church, in the cemetery

Local History Museum, Shaidakov Street 35, in a former Persian mosque, which was built in 1901. There is an excellent collection of local jewellery and carpets here. Open 10–6, closed Tues.

Lenin Monument

Obelisk, in front of the railway station. It commemorates the awarding of the Order of Red Banner of Labour to Chardzhou in 1928.

World War II Memorial, Druzhba Park. There is an eternal flame here.

Seidi Music and Drama Theatre, Gagarin Street 47

Amu-Darya Hotel and Restaurant, Lenin Street 14; tel. 2434

Chardjou Hotel, Shaidakova Street 36; tel. 1388
Polyet ("flight") Hotel and Restaurant, at
Chardzhou Airport

Intourist organises excursions into the desert.
Repetek Desert Nature Reserve, 70 km (43
miles) from Chardzhou, is used for scientific research. It covers 35 hectares (88 acres) in the Karakum Desert and was founded in 1912 by V.
Dubyansky (1871–1962), of the Russian Geographical Society. In the 18th century the poet Seidi
wrote:

All the land before you is poor,
A desert!

and so it looked once again when it was laid waste
in 1918 during the Civil War, but it was restored
in 1925 and is now staffed by 22 scientists. There
are examples here of the flora and fauna of Turkmenia. The desert plants are interesting in that the
lack of minerals and water may cause root systems
to go down as deep as 7–8 m (23–26 ft), while they
may stretch horizontally for 25–30 m (27–33 yds).
With the introduction of irrigation in the 1960s,
trees and shrubs were planted, and an experimental
dendropark has developed. There are also examples
of flora growing naturally in the desert without
irrigation. *Repetek Herbarium* has local collections
dating from 1899, as well as collections from the
desert regions of the United States that were presented by the American national herbarium.

Local fauna includes the Siberian marmot, the
jerboa, thousands of different insects (among them
the tarantulas, which block up their tunnels against
the noonday heat), and 20 kinds of reptiles. There
are tortoises and the "*varan*," a giant 1.5-m (5-foot)
lizard also known as the desert crocodile, which is
the Soviet Unions' largest reptile. Repeteksky Desert is also the home of more than 100 species of
birds, 25 of which nest here.

In 1979 Repetek was also proclaimed a bio-
spheric reserve for the study of shifting sands. In
1912 it was the only such scientific desert station
in the world, but in 1979 the work that had been
carried out here since the earliest years was incorporated into an international research programme.

The museum was established in 1927 and
brought up to date in 1976. Most exhibits reflect
the natural history of the reserve, but there are also
some archaeological finds on display. The treasure
of 104 silver coins that was found near Repetek
railway station in 1933 is kept in the Hermitage
Museum in Leningrad. Repetek has an history of
its own, for where Repetek railway station is now,
in the 9th–10th centuries there stood a large caravansarai. Its name perhaps came from the Arabic
"Rupshatah," but in the middle of the 10th century, it was called Jubba ("deep well") Hamad.
Kenik Café

Not far from the town is a *monument* to the
memory of a holy Mohammedan by the name of
Shah-i-Mordona.

At the side of the road leading toward Kerki
stands the 11th-century *Ashtan-baba mausoleum*;
the name means "holy man's tomb." The local
saint was called "the saint from Shakh's Square";
however, the tomb contains the remnants of two
holy brethren and their wives, and it is really a
whole complex of structures, consisting of mausolea, a mosque, a "ziaratkhana" (room for saying
memorial prayers), covered and open corridors,
and a courtyard. It is said that the walls of these
structures kept collapsing until clay and water were
brought from Mecca to be mixed with the local
stone. Supposedly from then on they have stood
firm, and no wonder, for the walls were built with
bricks in pairs. The complex was first reconstructed
in the 14th century, when the cupola's pediment
had become dilapidated; in the 17th century, the
10-cupola hall was rebuilt, and in the 19th century
a corridor with a portal entrance was added. The
ensemble is surrounded by an ancient cemetery.

CHEGEMSKOYE RAVINE
See Nalchik, p. 378.

CHERKASSY Population—290,000
The town, a port on Kremenchug Reservoir, stands
on the steep right bank of the river Dnieper.

Founded in the 13th century and first mentioned in 1394, it was the capital of the Ukrainian
hetmans (commanders in chief) from 1386 to
1649. In 1591 Hetman Krishtof Kosinsky led a
Cossack uprising, and his men were joined by peasants and a number of townsfolk. The rebels destroyed several large estates and stormed the fortress
at Kiev, where they seized cannon, guns, and gunpowder. They were defeated in 1593 by the united
forces of the Polish gentry. Kosinsky declared that
he would stop fighting, and moved with his Cossacks down to the delta of the Dnieper. Shortly
afterward he reappeared near Cherkassy at the head
of 2,000 men, and at the same time the Cossacks
appealed to Tsar Fedor Ivanovich of Moscow to
accept them as his subjects. The tsar agreed, but
the Cossacks were again defeated at Cherkassy, and
Kosinsky himself was killed in battle.

The town was the headquarters of Hetman Bogdan Khmelnitsky. Under him the Ukrainian Cossacks and numbers of peasants had risen against
Polish rule and, with the temporary assistance of
the Crimean Tatars and the backing of the Orthodox Church, had scored several victories. It was
from Cherkassy that Khmelnitsky sent his first message to Moscow on 8 June 1648, appealing for help
and suggesting that the Ukraine be incorporated
into Russia. With the desertion of the Crimean
khan however, Khmelnitsky's position weakened,
and in 1651 he wrote again asking for Russian
assistance. He became a vassal of Tsar Alexei Mikhailovich in 1654.

Cherkassy was the centre of further disturbances

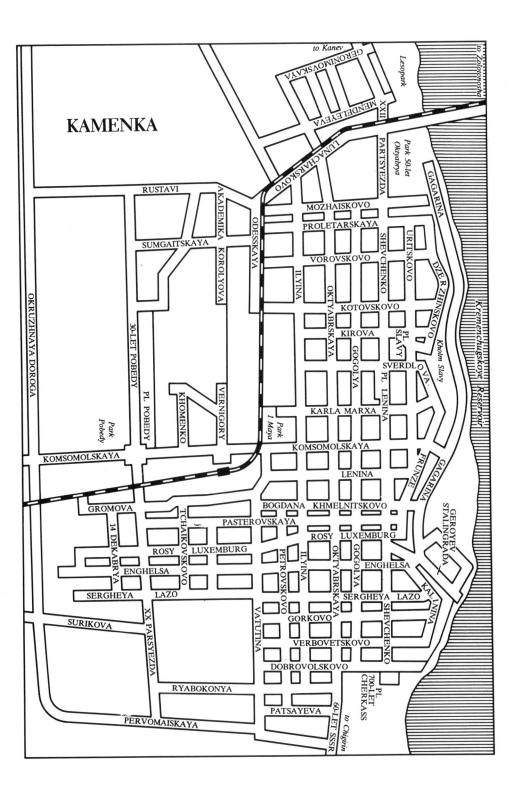

KAMENKA

in 1768, when the large-scale Koliyivschina Uprising took place. The rebels this time were chiefly peasants, armed for the most part with nothing more than wooden stakes ("kol" in Russian—hence the name of the movement). The rebellion began near Cherkassy, at Motroninsky Monastery, and soon spread to the western Ukraine, as far as Lvov. By the end of July 1768 it had been put down, and the rebels were severely punished.

Cherkassy became a town in 1795. The town plan is a neat grid of streets. The old coat-of-arms used to bear a horse on a red field with an angel with a sword on a blue field in the top left corner.

The poet Taras Shevchenko was born in this area, in the village of Morintsy on 9 March 1814. He was buried near Kaniv on the bank of Dnieper. He visited the town twice, in 1845 and 1859. The castle was built in 1849. There was an agricultural exhibition in Cherkassy in 1908. In December 1943 the battle to liberate the town from the Nazis lasted almost a month.

In 1954 the town became a regional centre. The local railway junction is of importance. Local industry includes the Petrovsky machine-building plant, working for the food industry. Light industry is represented by the Artificial Fibre Plant, the Frunzesugar factory, and a photographic and telegraphic equipment works. There is a polytechnical institute and a medical school.

Of the 4 old houses of interest that remain in the town, two are on Uritsky Street; the *Former Slavyanskaya Hotel* (early 20th century) is at 229, and the *former Commercial Bank* (1914), which is at 251, now houses a printing works. The *old town hall* (1907–12) is at Lenin Street 3, and *another building* dating from 1905–10 is at Shevchenko Street 287. The central street of the town, lined with modern buildings, is Shevchenko Boulevard, and there are more new buildings along 30-Let-Pobedy Street. One of the main thoroughfares is named for a local called Moisey Uritsky, one of the leading Bolsheviks during the revolution.

Church, Oktyabrskaya Street

Nativity of the Virgin Church, Zhovtneva Street 374. This is housed in the refectory of the former Onufri Monastery (built in 1906). Inside are the relics of St. Makarius, which were brought here from the fortress church of the Holy Trinity before the latter was demolished.

Local Museum, Slavy Steet 5. The museum was founded in 1985. The pride of the collection is the flags of the regiment that fought the Turks at the Battle of Shipka in Bulgaria in the last century.

Diorama Museum

Shevchenko Museum, at the crossing of Uritsky and Sverdlov streets

Art Gallery, Sverdlov Street 32

Planetarium, Sverdlov Street 14

Shevchenko Statue, Boulevard Street

Bust of Lenin, Lenin Square

War Memorial, Hill of Glory. A huge statue of the Motherland marks the common grave of 14,000 war dead. This was unveiled in 1975 to mark the 30th anniversary of VE-Day. The hill was originally the site of the fortress and of Troitsky Cathedral.

Fighter Plane Monument, Komsomolskaya Street, on the left on the way in

Shevchenko Music and Drama Theatre, Shevchenko Street 234

Puppet Theatre, Lenin Street 4

Philharmonia House Concert Hall, Uritsky Street 194

Lenkomsomol Stadium

Pyervovo Maya Park, Ilina and Komsomolskaya streets

50th Anniversary of October Revolution Park, on the hills overlooking the Dnieper

The *long beaches of Sosnivka and Sokirne* stretch for many kilometres along the Dnieper.

Tourist Hotel and Restaurant, Sosnovskaya Street 4, tel. 790–41

Zhovtnevo Hotel and Restaurant, Frunze Street 145

Cherkassy Hotel and Restaurant, Lazerev Street 4

Intourist Office, Lazerev Street 6; tel. 21–902

Shopping Centre and Department Store, Shevchenko Street 207

Ukrainian Souvenirs, Komsomolskaya Street 59

Yunost Shop, Shevchenko Street 224

Market, Komsomolskaya Street 61

The *airport* lies to the left of the main road on the way into town from the south. The main roads outside the town are lined with poplars and acacias.

Sosnovka

3 km (2 miles) from Cherkassy, 116 m (381 ft) above sea level.

There are a number of sanatoria here, mainly caring for patients with tuberculosis.

In the centre of the resort is a *park* of 25 hectares (63 acres), with a concert stage, dance floor, boat-hiring station, and bathing beach.

Intourist organises excursions from Cherkassy to Kaniv (q.v.; 82 km/51 miles one way; the trip lasts about 8 hours and the sights including Uspensky Cathedral, the Gaidar Museum and Shevchenko's grave) and to Uman (q.v.), as well as to the following places.

Kamenka

60 km (37 miles) one way; the trip lasts about 6 hours.

Standing on either side of the river Tyasmin, Kamenka was founded in the 18th century. In the 19th it belonged to the Davydov family. Pushkin visited it in the early 1820s. From 1862 and over a period of 20 years, Tchaikovsky came to Kamenka every summer to stay with his sister and wrote while he was here. It was in Kamenka that he first staged "Swan Lake," using an amateur company.

The village was granted town status in 1956.

Church. Built by the local congregation in 1988.

Pushkin and Tchaikovsky Museums, in the Green House, formerly part of the Davydov family residence. In fact, along with the mill and the grotto, this is the only part to have survived over the years. The museums cover the visits of the poet and later the composer to Kamenka.

Kamenka Hotel and Café, Pushkin Street 54; tel. 21464

Korsun-Shevchenkovsky

90 km (56 miles) one way; the trip lasts 10 hours.

Founded in 1032 on the river Ros by Yaroslav the Wise to guard the southern borders of Kiev Rus, it was granted town status in 1938. All through its history, the Russian Civil War included, Korsun changed hands among different warring factions. It was known simply as Korsun until 1944, when it was renamed after having been the site of one of the largest battles on the Russian-German front in the Second World War.

Korsun was occupied and served as a Nazi bridgehead between Belaya Tserkov and Kirovograd. About 3,000 townsfolk were shot while it was in German hands. Marshal Zhukov engineered the encirclement of 100,000 enemy troops, uniting the 1st and 2nd Ukrainian Fronts. These met near the village of Olshana on 31 January 1944, and the battle began. On 8 February the Soviet side proposed that the Germans should surrender, but the offer was rejected, and the slaughter continued for 25 days, the town itself being retaken by the Soviet army on 14 February. This, however, was not before the Nazis had destroyed the hydropower station, the railway station, and the hospital. The German defeat came on 17 February, when 55,000 soldiers were killed and 18,200 prisoners of war were taken.

and Korsun-Shevchenkovsky became the central town of Cherkasskaya Region. There are machine building and mechanical plants here, and it is a railway junction.

Museum of the Battle of Korsun-Shevchenkovsky (1944), in the impressive 18th-century palace that belonged to the Lopukhin-Demidov family. Pyotr Lopukhin was minister of justice. The palace served as the family's summer residence from 1883–89. Taras Shevchenko visited it, and there is a chestnut tree that bears his name on the grounds. After the revolution the palace was turned into a holiday home, and during the Second World War, it owed its survival to being used as a German military hospital. The museum was opened in 1945 and displays documents and weapons from the time of the battle.

Gate-Tower, on one of the islands in the river Ros. Dates from the 18th century.

Shevchenko Monument

Lenin Monument

Korsun-Shevchenkovsky Battle Memorial Complex. It opens with a monument symbolising the encirclement of the enemy.

Battle Heroes' Avenue, in the centre of the town

5th Guard Tank Army Monument

Avengers' Monument

War Memorial, Rezany Yar. Commemorating those shot here by the Nazis.

Korsunsky Units' Monument. Erected in memory of the fallen from the 5th Air, the 2nd Tank, and the 5th Guard Cavalry Corps.

Stele, at the entrance to the town

Hotel, Shevchenko Street 51; tel. 225–70

GPO, Shevchenko Street 21

In the town itself, along the surrounding roads and in the nearby villages are many monuments commemorating the local victory.

Shevchenkovo

116 km (72 miles) from Cherkassy.

Formerly known as the village of Kirillovka, this is where the poet Shevchenko lived as a child. In 1914 his relatives planted an oak tree here to commemorate the 100th anniversary of his birth.

Shevchenko Museum

Morintsy

124 km (77 miles) from Cherkassy.

The Ukrainian poet Taras Shevchenko was born in this village in 1814.

Local Museum

Ukrainian Ethnographical Museum

Shevchenko Monument, on the site of Shevchenko's home. Unveiled in 1956.

CHERKESSK

Intourist organises excursions this way from Kislovodsk up to Teberda and Dombai.

Cherkessk, formerly Batalpashinsk, is the capital of the Karachay-Cherkess Autonomous Region.

KARACHAY-CHERKESS AUTONOMOUS REPUBLIC

The region is 14,200 sq km (5,500 sq miles) in area and consists of lowland steppe in the north, where grain is grown, and the foothills of the Caucasus Mountains in the south, where livestock is kept. Lumbering is carried on in the mountains. Through the region flows the Kuban River. It has a population of 369,000, mostly Russians, Cherkess (still also known as Circassians, but they call themselves Adigai) and Karachays, but also some Abaza and Nogai Tatars. Of the 2 major towns, Cherkessk in the lower land to the north is the Cherkess centre, and Karachayevsk, farther up in the hills, belongs to the Karachay.

From the 10th century, the Karachay area was inhabited by cattle breeders. There were also a number of people of different Caucasian nationalities escaping persecution, who found refuge in this area and were assimilated into the basic Karachay population. The peoples inhabiting this territory began to develop some sort of unity in the 13th–14th centuries, and in 1557 the lower area was joined to Russia as part of Ivan the Terrible's sphere of influence. The Karachay, however, became in 1733 dependent upon the princes of Kabarda, a protectorate of Turkey. They fought the Russians, who were expanding southward toward the Caucasus, at the beginning of the 19th century, but when the Russo-Turkish Peace Treaty of 1812 placed the boundary between the two countries along the Kuban River, Karachay on the right bank came officially under Russian influence. Then, in 1828, Russia decided to advance farther; when General Emmanuel had taken Kart-Dzhurtu, he said, "The Thermopylae of the Northern Caucasus is taken, the stronghold of Karachay at the foot of Elbrus is destroyed." There were local revolts in Karachay, especially when in 1873 some of the population were forced to move to Turkey.

Local culture was Islamic, and medressehs were the only source of education until the first European-type school was opened in 1877. Even so, before the revolution, 96 percent of the population was illiterate. When the area came under Kuban Cossack jurisdiction, the local population was not even recruited into the army, and there was much talk before the First World War about their having equal rights with the Cossacks.

During the Civil War, it changed hands and, when the Kuban area was reformed in June 1918 into the short-lived Kuban Black Sea Soviet Socialist Republic, it became part of that republic. But in August 1918 it was taken by counterrevolutionary Cossacks. Local nobles, landlords, and Muslim leaders organised a national committee under Hamzat-Hadji Urusov. They were, in the name of national liberation and self-determination, to create a local government. The counterrevolutionary General Wrangel sent General Kelich-Girai and Colonel Mirzakul Krimshakhmalov to Karachay from the Crimea, and until November 1920 they were in charge of the local nationalist and pan-Islamic elements.

In March 1920 the Red Army entered Batalpashinsk (now Cherkessk), and the area became part of the Mountain Peoples' Republic in January 1921. It was renamed the Karachay-Cherkess Autonomous Region in 1922 and in 1926 was divided into separate parts for the Cherkess and the Karachay peoples. In World War II, the area was in enemy hands. Following its liberation, the Karachay, the indigenous Turkic-speaking population, were sent to the Asian part of the USSR, accused of collaboration with the Germans (just like the Balkars of the Kabardino-Balkar Autonomous Region, farther along on our journey). The decree on their rehabilitation in 1957 allowed them to return home.

Cherkessk Population—113,000
Cherkessk, the former Cossack village of Batalpashinskaya and then the town of Batalpashinsk, is the capital of the Karachay-Cherkess Autonomous Region. It is situated on the upper reaches of the river Kuban where it flows from the mountains. It changed its name many times: in 1931 to Sulimov, back to Batalpashinsk in 1935, to Yezhovo-Cherkessk in 1937, which was almost its final name, but the first half was dropped in 1939 after the purge of Nikolai Yezhov, the notorious commissar for internal affairs. Its first name of Batalpashinsk was given in memory of the crushing defeat that the Russian troops, under Major-General Ivan Gherman, dealt to the 25,000-strong Turkish army of the Anatolian military leader Batal-Pasha in 1790. Batal Pasha himself was taken prisoner and spent 9 years in captivity in Russia. To strengthen the area, a stronghold was built in 1804 and named after the conquered Batal-Pasha.

The first Cossack settlers came here in 1825, and by 1860 Batalpashinsk, because of its sizeable population, became a district centre. Its industry was limited to all sorts of handicrafts, while the main occupation of the villagers was grain growing. After the establishment of Soviet power here in 1920, Batalpashinsk started developing rapidly and by 1926 became the administrative centre of an autonomous region.

Cherkessk was badly damaged in the war, with all its industry completely destroyed. At present it is the major industrial centre in the region, with chemical, metal-working, timber, light, and food industries. It is also a cultural centre and boasts a teachers' training college, technical schools, a research institute, and a nursing school.

Local History Museum, Lenin Street
Kuban Hotel and Restaurant

From Cherkessk begins the Sukhumi Military Highway, which runs across the Klukhor Pass (2,820 m/9,250 ft) to Abkhazia and the Black Sea. It stretches for almost 270 km (168 miles) and is one of the most beautiful routes in the Caucasus. Along it one travels through all the seasons of the year and all the climatic and vegetation zones from the tropics to the Arctic.

Ust-Djiguta
A Russian village, it has construction works for producing cement and gypsum.

Sary-Tyuz
A Karachay village. Passing it, the road runs across a bridge to the left bank of the Kuban, where it forks; take the left fork leading southward.

Ordzhonikidzevsky
A miners' settlement, named after the well-known Georgian revolutionary and Party functionary.

Memorial Museum to the defenders of the Caucasian passes in 1942; it was here that Field Marshal von Kleist's army was stopped. An eternal flame burns at a common military grave. The vertical concrete slabs to be found in the valley symbolise antitank barricades, and the slabs with a narrow horizontal slit represent the vision-slits of a bunker. The monument was erected in 1968 by the Georgian architects Davitaya and Chikovani.

Opposite the memorial, across the Kuban, is the village of Khumara and next to it, on a mound, excavation works are being carried out on an 8th-century *fortress*, the walls of which in some places are 6 m (20 ft) thick. It is 1,900 m (more than a

CHERKESSK

mile) long, and it once blocked entrance to the valley.

Imeni Kosta Khetagurova (formerly Georgievsko-Ossetinskoye)

The village is an old Ossetian town situated at the foot of the picturesque Mt. Shoan. The classic Ossetian poet, Kosta Khetagurov, lived here. He died in 1906 and was buried in the centre of the village, where a *monument* was erected in 1959 by sculptor Dzangiev. His grave has since been removed to Vladikavkaz, capital of Ossetia.

I didn't know happiness,
But I'm prepared to give up freedom
Which I cherish as happiness
For the possibility to pave the way to
          freedom
For my people.

Near the village are quaint-looking rocks called "diabas." On a flat terrain of rock is a grove of a rare berry-bearing yew tree. A church may be seen on the southern spur of the side ridge.

St. George's Church. Built in the 10th century and reconstructed in the 1800s. A steep road that runs past the ruins of St. George's Monastery leads to it. Christianity came here from Abkhazia, where the new faith was adopted in the 4th century. The missionaries of Patriarch Nicholas the Mystic of Constantinople (901–925) came here over the mountain pass.

Karachayevsk Population—15,000

Until 1943, it was called Mikoyan-Shakhar; then till 1957 Klukhory. Now the town is called Karachayevsk, after the Karachay people inhabiting it.

Karachayevsk was founded at the confluence of the Kuban and Teberda rivers in 1926, when the region was separated from the Karachay-Cherkess Autonomous Region. Situated on the left slope of the foothills of the Great Caucasus Mountains, 870 m (2,850 ft) above sea level, it has a mild and sunny climate. The village is horseshoe-shaped, at the foot of the surrounding mountains, and divided into 3 districts: left-bank, right-bank, and central, all connected by bridges. Multistoreyed houses are being built along new, straight streets, surrounded by shady parks and gardens.

Karachayevsk is the industrial and cultural centre of the upper part of the region. In the suburbs are light and food industries and also coal, lead, and zinc mines as well as stone quarries. There is a teacher-training college in the village.

Seid Khalidov Monument. Seid Khalidov was a national hero.

Nizhnyaya Teberda (formerly Senty)

Nizhnyaya Teberda was founded in 1875, when the poor peasants of Higher Teberda became short of plots of land. Another name for this village was Karakulkabak ("village of black slaves").

Former Transfiguration Convent. On the left river bank stands the 10th-century Transfiguration Church of great historical value. A specially built road leads up to it; the church was partially restored in 1896, at the time of the opening of the convent, and contains the remains of frescoes believed to be of Byzantine origin. Not far to the northwest of the church, is a stone mausoleum dating probably to the 10th century.

St. Agafor the Martyr's Church was built in the late 19th century. The convent, which used to have 170 nuns, is now closed.

The end of this route, up to Teberda and Dombai, is described under Kislovodsk (see page 239).

CHERNIGOV Population—296,000

Intourist organises excursions here from Kiev.

This ancient town was first mentioned in records dating from 907, but its founding was actually much earlier. Its name, according to legend, is derived from that of a certain Black Prince, "cherny" meaning "black." It stands upon the river Desna, of which a tributary, the Strizhen, divides the town.

In 992, a few years after this part of the country was converted to Christianity, a bishop was established here and soon the bishopric was second in importance only to Novgorod. Chernigov became the capital of a princedom, and it was at this time that Spaso-Preobrazhensky Cathedral was founded by Prince Mstislav on the site of a pagan temple. The territory of the princedom was very large, stretching as far as the boundaries of the Moscow and the Vladimir regions.

The town lost its importance after being sacked by the Tatars in 1239. At first the inhabitants defended themselves bravely by rolling big boulders down the steep bank of the Desna upon the heads of the invaders. Chernigov's last prince, Mikhail Vsevolodovich, was taken prisoner, and along with a faithful follower called Fedor, he died a martyr's death. They were both canonised, and in 1572, upon the order of Ivan the Terrible, their bodies were carried to Moscow and laid to rest in the Kremlin's Arkhangelsky Cathedral.

Subsequently Chernigov changed hands several times and was under Polish-Lithuanian rule for 328 years. The churches, which have survived successive wars and the passage of the years, tell the history of the place; some were converted into Roman Catholic churches and then back again to Russian Orthodox.

In 1941 the town was heavily bombed and most of the present-day buildings and the abundant trees and gardens date from after the war. The town planners did their best to preserve what they could of ancient Chernigov, and a notable achievement is the boulevard planted along the line of the old earth wall, which until the 18th century surrounded the Kremlin, Detinets. Strategically placed cannons serve as decorations on the boulevard. Lenin Street, where most of the adminis-

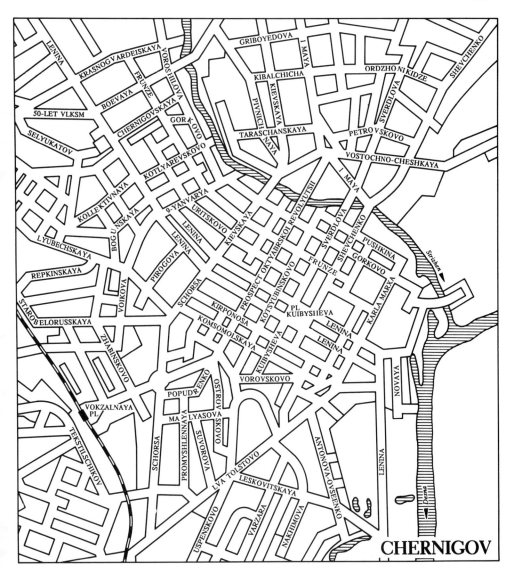

CHERNIGOV

trative buildings are located, was completely new, laid out across the ruins. Shevchenko Street extends from the wide expanse of Kuibyshev Street.

Local industry includes the production of up to 25,000 pianos annually and a variety of textiles and synthetic fibres; the textile mills are mostly in the Shovkograd region of the town.

Spaso-Preobrazhensky Cathedral, inside the Kremlin area, is one of the country's oldest stone buildings. It was designed in 1030 as a cathedral and is still most impressive. It also served as princely sepulchre; Prince Mstislav, his wife, Anastasia, their son, and a number of other princes were buried here. The original cathedral has been rebuilt and embellished many times, and the present building is a 1792–98 reconstruction with an icon-

ostasis of the same date. This, like most of Chernigov's churches, is open as a museum, 10–5:30; closed Thurs.

The yellow building with a 6-column portico near the approach to the cathedral used to be the governor's residence, built in 1803; it is now a polytechnical college.

Near the cathedral stands SS. *Boris and Gleb Cathedral* (1123), originally part of the monastery of the same name. The cathedral was burned in 1511 and taken over and rebuilt by a Dominican monastery. At about this time a silver idol was unearthed nearby. It was melted down and the silver used to make a pair of altar gates, depicting in very fine work Isaiah on the left and David on the right. The gates are now in Gdansk (Danzig).

During World War II the church was again ruined, but it has since been rebuilt.

A little farther on stands a *belfry*, which suffered from fire during the last war but was restored in 1954. Adjoining the belfry is the *Collegium*, which dates from 1702, when the education problem was recognised as being in urgent need of solution, and many schools and "collegia" were built. It stood within the monastery walls until the monastery closed. The original building was later added to and now houses the town archives.

Pyatnitskaya Church (Church of St. Paraskeva), Bogdan Khmelnisky Square, behind the theatre. This was founded in the 12th century but was almost completely destroyed when it received a direct hit during a World War II raid. It was rebuilt in 1962.

Voskresenskaya Church and Belfry (1722), Komsomolskaya Street, in the old part of the town, near the market. The belfry is a copy of that in the Kirillovsky Monastery in Kiev. The church is open for services.

St. Catherine's (Ekaterininskaya) Church (1715), Lenin Street, standing near the road on the way into the town from Kiev. It was built as a memorial by Colonel Yakov Lizogub, hero of the storming of the Turkish fortress in Azov. The colonel's own house, built in the 1680s, is inside the Detinets territory. It is open as a museum 10–6; closed Wed. The colonel himself was buried in the family crypt in the cathedral of Eletsky Monastery (see below).

The war left only a few old buildings of interest in Chernigov. Among those are a *bank* on 25-Anniversary Street 16, at the end of the garden on Kuibyshev Square, located in the former magistrate (late 19th century), which once also served as a prison and then as a police station; an old red-and-white brick hospital at Lenin Street 36, now a *polyclinic*; a *printing works* with a tall tower at Lenin Street 34; and the *original post office* building at Lenin Street 38.

History Museum, Revolyutsii Street 16. Open 10–6; closed Wed. There is a good collection of Cossack arms here; among the icons, note the 17th-century Our Lady of Elets from Uspenskaya Church in the local Eletsky Monastery.

Kotsyubinsky Museum, Kotsyubinsky Street 3. Open 10–6. Mikhail Kotsyubinsky (1864–1913) was a famous Ukrainian writer and translator. He lived here from 1898 until his death. He was buried nearby on Boklin Hill.

Troitsky Monastery, Lev Tolstoy Street, opposite No. 111. The monastery's principal building is Troitsky Cathedral, built in baroque style in 1679–85. Beside it, to the south, stands V*vedenskaya Refectory Church (1677)*. The belfry and the entrance gate were built later, in 1775, to complete the ensemble. Near the cathedral stands a *monument* to the poet Balkar, the pseudonym used by Leonid Glibov (1827–93).

A short walk down the narrow path from Troitsky Monastery leads to *Ilyinskaya Church* at Uspensky Street 33. This marks the entrance to the

Antoniev Caves, where there are 3 underground *churches* dedicated to SS. Antonia, Feodosia, and Mikola.

Eletsky-Uspensky Monastery, Proletarskaya Street, to the southeast of the town. *Uspenskaya Church* was founded by the local Great Prince Svyatoslav in 1060 after a vision of an icon of the Virgin appeared there in a fir tree ("el" in Russian), and it is from this word that the monastery took its name. It was ruined by Baty Khan in 1240, along with the town of Chernigov. Following its restoration in 1445, it was again demolished, but this time by the Poles in 1579 and 1611. The Jesuits and monks of the Dominican Order settled in the remains of the buildings in 1624, but it was only 25 years before Bogdan Khmelnitsky drove them out, allowing the Orthodox monastery to revive once more. The church was restored again in 1960 and now appears as it did in 1679. The iconostasis and some of the frescoes are still under restoration. The original icon was lost in 1611, but a copy of it was brought to Chernigov market in 1676, where it was purchased and presented to the church. It is this wonder-working 17th century icon of Our Lady that now hangs in the local history museum.

The belfry stands 36 m (118 ft) high, and both this and the other buildings of the monastery date from the 17th century.

Opposite the entrance to the monastery is the *Black Grave*, one of the many barrows in this area. It is thought to be a 10th-century prince's burial mound.

Art Gallery, Lenin Street 51

Historical Museum, in what used to be the governor's house, Gorky Street 4

Kotsubinsky House Museum, Kotsubinsky Street 3. Mikhail Kotsubinsky (1864–1913) was a Ukrainian writer and public figure who died in Chernigov and was buried here on Lev Tolstoy Street.

Pushkin Monument, Kotsubinsky Park. Also in the park are 16th–18th-century guns.

Bogdan Khmelnitsky Monument, Bogdan Khmelnitsky Square

Taras Shevchenko Monument, in Kotsubinsky Park

Kotsubinsky Monument, Kotsubinsky Street

Civil War Memorial, Kotsubinsky Street

Popudrenko Monument, in the garden by the Regional Council building. Popudrenko was a partisan leader and local hero. The memorial marks his grave.

War Memorials, in the Kremlin and on Pobeda Square

Hill of Glory and Grave of the Unknown Soldier, Lev Tolstoy Street

Tank Monument, Schors Street, opposite the prewar railway station building

Shevchenko Music and Drama Theatre, Kuibysheva Square

Concert Hall, Lenin Street 15

Puppet Theatre, Komsomolskaya Street 11

Gagarin Stadium

Grodetskaya Hotel and Restaurant, Lenin

Street 68; tel. 274–23. This is a 15-storey building.

Ukraina Hotel and Restaurant, Lenin Street 33

Desna Hotel and Restaurant, Kuibysheva Street 1

Sport Hotel, Shevchenko Street 61

Kolos Hotel, Krasnogvardeiskaya Street 17

Siversky Restaurant, Rokosovsky Street 15

Stary ("old") Chernigov Restaurant, Prospect Oktyabrskoy Revolutsii 137

Druzhba ("friendship") Restaurant, Lenin Street 49

Polesiye Restaurant, Lenin Street 32

GPO, Lenin Street 28

Druzhba Souvenir Shop

CHERNOVTSY (Ukrainian: Chernovtsi; Romanian: Cernauti; Austrian: Czernauz; German: Czernowitz) Population—260,000
The town stretches for 12 km (7 miles) along the banks of the river Prut. The whole territory is famous for its beech trees (pronounced "bouk" in Russian), and from these it gets its alternative name of Bukovina.

The town's name was first recorded in 1408, its ancient coat-of-arms depicts an open gateway, and it was founded at the beginning of the 15th century near another small town, Chern, only the remains of which are to be seen today. Earlier, in the 10th and 11th centuries, the territory was part of Kiev Rus, and in the 12th and 13th centuries, the territory was part of the Volyn princedom. In the first half of the 13th century, the place was invaded by Tatars and Mongolians, who stayed there for over 100 years. From the middle of the 14th century, it was a part of the state of Moldavia, so that from the 16th century onward it was indirectly under Turkish rule.

A local legend recalls how settlers made their homes near the Turkish Well, under the rule of a powerful pasha. He lived comfortably, rejoicing in the fine air of the fir and beech forests, and all the same fell victim to the charms of a young girl who came each morning to the well for water. Her eyes were deep and clear as a mountain tarn at dawn and her figure as slender as a young spruce, but beneath her thin robe her heart fluttered with alarm, for the pasha watched her closely. At last he could restrain himself no longer. "Be my wife," he pleaded, "you will be the most beautiful of all my wives. You shall be a princess." Her eyebrow rose as swift as startled birds, her eyes widened in fear, and in a moment she had fled. The next day the angry pasha ordered the girl's father to send his daughter to join the harem. When she failed to appear, the pasha in fury forbade the people to draw water from the well and waited to see whether their thirst would prevail over their pride. It was not long before the girl came forward. The pasha took a step toward her, his arms outstretched, but she, with a look of scorn, avoided him, darted to the well, and threw herself in. The well was never used again.

After the Russian-Turkish peace treaty of 1774, the territory passed to Austria. Chernovtsy became a town in 1786 and the capital of Bukovina in 1849.

The area went to Rumania in 1918 and finally to Russia in 1940, after which it was united with the Ukrainian Republic.

The face of the town reflects its origin, and walking through the streets around the central square, one can easily imagine oneself in Austria, Germany, or Czechoslovakia. Many of Chernovtsy's buildings were designed by Austrian architects. Those in Tsentralnaya Square date mostly from the 19th century, though the municipal Party building, attractively decorated with sculptures and multicoloured mosaics, was built in 1901 as a savings bank. The town's main street, Lenin (formerly High) Street, is one of the oldest in the town, although the two large churches, Vozdvizhenskaya at No. 20 and Troitsky (Trinity Cathedral) which is now used as an exhibition hall, were built in the 19th century. Kobylyanskya Street runs next to Lenin Street and also leads into Tsentralnaya Square. Here Zoya Kosmodemyanskaya Cinema is in the building of the Polish House while opposite the former German House is now the Ukrainian Cinema. Russkaya Street, which runs out of Tsentralnaya Square for a distance of 6 km (4 miles), is also very old but again most of the buildings date from the 19th century. They include the Uspenskaya (Assumption) Church. St. Nicholas's Cathedral was completed only in 1939. There are many other interesting buildings to be seen as one walks around the town. Boarding School No. 1 at Gorky Street 23 was once a teachers' training college. The building belonging to the Medical Institute in Theatre Square used to be the Hall of Trade and Commerce, and its façade is suitably decorated with coloured plaques of tools and instruments. School No. 1, at the corner of the same square, where Ivan Franko Street joins it, was built as a grammar school and had the Rumanian poet, Mihai Eminescu (1850–89), as a pupil; he spent his youth in Chernovtsy and wrote his first works here, many of which are about Bukovina. There are administrative offices in the old law court buildings with lions by the steps on Radyanska Street, and the Regional Party Committee uses the former residence of the Austro-Hungarian representative. The way down to the old town is along Henri Barbusse Street, past the building of a synagogue, now closed, and leading to the railway station, constructed in art nouveau style in 1908.

The University, University Street, was built as the residence of the bishops of Bukovina in 1864–78 in mixed Romanesque and Byzantine style, at a cost of more than 1.5 million golden roubles. It stands in a park, and the main building faces the imposing entrance archway. The ground floor was used for administrative purposes, and there were monks' cells. Also on the first floor was a lavish marble hall designed for the reception of important guests. The two-storey building on the right with a clocktower was also used by monks, but later a museum of ecclesiastical art was opened here. The university was founded in 1875, and the church building now serves the students as a digital-computing laboratory. The university suffered some war

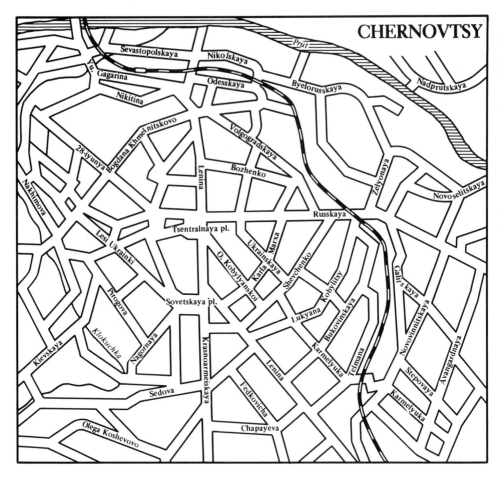

damage but has been fully restored. In the park immediately behind the main building stands a monument to the architect Josef Hlavka (1831–1908). Hlavka was born in the small Czechoslovakian town of Prsesice and became famous both as an architect and a scientist. He was the founder of the Czech Academy of Literature and Art and also of the Prague Technical Institute.

Chernovtsy's main industries are connected with food, textiles, and machine building. The population includes many Ukrainians and Jews. One can even hear Yiddish spoken on the streets, unusual in large Soviet towns.

St. Nicholas's Cathedral, Russkaya Street 35. Built in 1939, this 5-domed cathedral, with 4 of its cupola drums constructed as spirals, owes its exotic appearance to its being a copy of the royal church in the Romanian town of Curtea de Arges. Open for services.

St. Paraskeva Church, Zankovetskaya Street 13. Designed by Pavlovsky in the mid-19th century, it is now newly painted and serves as a storehouse.

Church of St. Nicholas, Volgogradsky Street. Built of wood in 1607, this is the oldest church in Chernovtsy.

Vozdvizhenskaya (Holy Cross) Roman Catholic Church, Lenin Street 20. Built in 1830s and reconstructed in 1910.

Jesuit Church, Kirov Street. The sharply pointed, tapering spires reach upward to the sky, and when there is heavy low cloud drifting just above, the whole edifice appears to be falling. It is said that once catastrophe appeared so imminent that the market-women, bargaining in the nearby square, fled for their lives, and it was several hours before they dared return to their stalls.

Grey Gothic-style Church, just off the beginning of Shevchenko Street. It now houses the city archives.

Uspenskaya (Assumption) Greek Catholic Church, Russkaya Street 20. Built at the end of the 19th century.

Troitsky (Trinity) Romanian Orthodox Cathedral, Lenin Street. Built in 1844, it now serves as an exhibition hall.

Lutheran Church, Ryazanskaya Street. Used as the House of Teachers.

Armenian Church, Ukrainskaya Street 32. Built in 1869–75 in Gothic style of red brick by Hlavka (who was also responsible for the university) but with a typical Armenian roof to the tower. There is fine stained glass in the windows and art nouveau murals on the interior walls. Both the pulpit and the altar are in place, although the church itself is used as a storehouse.

Synagogue, Yanko Belits Street, near the park. This synagogue is open for services. A more imposing building with a patterned frieze high on the walls and locally known as "the temple" stands at the corner of Ryazanskaya and 28th-June streets and houses the *Zhovten (October) Cinema*.

Rathaus, Tsentralnaya Square. This building dates from 1843–47 and is used now by the Local Executive Committee.

Local Museum, Kobylyanskaya Street 28. Open 10–5:30; closed Wed.

Art Gallery, Ivan Franko Street 15

Fedkovich Literary Museum, in the same building as the local Museum. Yuri Fedkovich (1834–88) was a Ukrainian writer who lived in Chernovtsy for some time.

Kobylyanskaya Literary Museum, Dmitrov Street 5. The Ukrainian writer Olga Kobylyanskaya (1861–1942) lived here for more than 50 years. Open 10–6; closed Tues.

Planetarium, Gorky Street 12. The planetarium stands in the grounds of the local museum.

Folk Architecture Museum, in the suburbs. This open-air museum opened in 1986.

Lenin Monument, Tsentralnaya Square. Sculpted by Oleinik and Vronsky.

Olga Kobylyanskaya Monument, Theatre Square

Victory Obelisk, Radyanska Square. It is in this square that parades and mass meetings take place. The 22-m (72 ft) granite obelisk designed by Petrashevich was unveiled in 1946 to commemorate the victory of World War II.

Tank Monument, Gagarin Street. This tank on a stone block was the first to enter the town on the occasion of its liberation in 1944 and is dedicated to the soldiers of the First Ukrainian Front.

War Memorial, Kalinin Park. This obelisk commemorates the officers who fell here during World War II. Here also is the common grave of Soviet and Czech soldiers.

Kobylyanskaya Ukrainian Music and Drama Theatre, Teatralnaya Square 1. This theatre was built in 1904–5 by the Viennese architects Fellner and Helmer, who also designed the opera houses in Vienna and Odessa. The façade is decorated with figures from Greek mythology, and set into niches are busts of Goethe, Schiller, and Beethoven, among others. The interior is mainly in baroque style.

Philharmonia Concert Hall, Philharmonia Square 10. Built in 1876–77, this hall has served the singers Enrico Caruso and Paul Morgano and the French violinist Jacques Thibault. Franz Liszt spent a whole week in Chernovtsy but gave his 2 concerts in the Moldavia Hotel, which has not survived.

Kalinin Park, Dzerzhinsky Street 1. This park, opened in the 1830s, is the town's largest. It contains an open-air theatre seating 2,000, and at the entrance to the park stands a monument to Kalinin, which was unveiled in 1956.

University Botanical Garden, Fedkovich Street 11, near Kalinin Park. This garden was founded in 1877 and now covers 3.7 hectares (9.25 acres).

Dynamo Stadium, Leningradskaya Street 1

Bukovina Stadium is part of a sports complex, including a swimming pool and volleyball and basketball courts.

Bukovina Intourist Hotel and Restaurant, Lenin Street 14; tel. 3–8274

Kiev Hotel and Restaurant, Lenin Street 46

Ryadyanska Hotel, Universitetskaya Street 34

Verkhovina Hotel and Café, Tsentralnaya Square 7

Dniester Hotel, Kobylyanskoy Street

Cheremosh Hotel and Restaurant, Komarov Street 13a. There is a Kashtan foreign-currency shop here.

Dniester Restaurant, Kobylyanskoy Street 5

Teatralny Restaurant, Kotlyerevskovo Street 26

Zatyshok Restaurant, Zelyonaya Street 6

Dorrestoran Restaurant, Yuri Gagarin Street

Zelyonaya Dubrava Restaurant, out of town. Ukrainian national cooking and folk music.

Podlisok Restaurant, at the camping site

Chernovtsy Hotel and Camping Site, Moskovskoy Olimpiady Street 3, 3.5 km (2 miles) east of Chernovtsy; tel. 2–5496. There are a restaurant, café, post office, service station, filling station, and bathing beach. Open June–October.

Intourist Office, Lenin Street 141; tel. 38–047.

GPO, Pochtovaya Street

Kashtan Foreign-Currency Shops, 50-Let-Oktyabrya Prospect and in the Cheremosh Hotel

Central Department Store, Lenin Street

Art Salon, Kobylyanskaya Street 23

Gift Shop, Kobylyanskaya Street 18

Arts and Crafts, Teatralnaya Square. The town is famed for its woodcarving.

Service Station, Novoselitskaya Street 8a

Filling Station, Maurice Thorez Street 33a

Gora Tsetsino, 7 km (4 miles) out of town. On the top of this mountain, which is 541 m (1,775 ft) high, are the remains of a 14th-century fortress.

Gorecha

This is a suburb of Chernovtsy, situated on the high right bank of the river Prut. The remains of a *monastery church* stand here. It was built in 1767 with money donated by Catherine the Great, and there are some frescoes to be seen inside.

By the river down below there is a sandy *bathing beach*.

Intourist organises excursions from here to Vashkovtsy, Kamenets-Podolsky (q.v.), and Khotin (q.v.).

Vashkovtsy

70 km (43 miles) from Chernovtsy. Vashkovtsy is a village in the Bukovina area.

Garas Folk Arts Museum, Chekhov Street 2.

The house of decorative artist G. A. Garas and his wife, E. P. Garas, has been turned into a museum.

CHIMGAN
See Tashkent, p. 543.

Chimkent Population—396,000
Chimkent, which literally means "green city," is in the far south of Kazakhstan, lying on the ancient bed of the river Sairam-Su at the foot of the southwestern branch of the Tien Shan Mountains and the Ugamsky chain. The town is irrigated by the rivers Badam and Koshkar-Ata. The climate here is of an extreme continental type.

The city grew from being a small military settlement near Sairam, an ancient town of Central Asia and an important administrative and trade centre renowned for its ceramics. Chimkent stood 12 km (7 miles) from Sairam but was in fact part of its fortified outskirts. Local rebellions and the constant raids of various Turkic and Arab nomadic tribes devastated Sairam, and after it fell entirely, Chimkent began to revive due to its convenient geographical position at the crossing of routes leading from Semirechye to Central Asia, China, and India. Semirechye is the Russian translation of the Turkic "Dzhety-su" or Seven Rivers, and is a geographical and historical region in Central Asia between Lake Balkhash and the upper course of the river Naryn. In the 15th–17th centuries, Chimkent played an important role in southern Kazakhstan.

During the Russian advance to Central Asia, General Mikhail Chernyayev, moving from the eastern sector of the Russian front, attempted to seize Chimkent, but he was beaten off by stout resistance and strong reinforcements led by the tough Mullah Alim Qul. Finally at the third attempt, Chimkent fell to the Russians in September 1864, when 3,170 dead were left in the field.

Chimkent was a typical Central Asian town, divided into Russian and local quarters. The town library is named after Pushkin and the town garden after General Chernyayev. The trade of the town was mostly in the hands of Uzbeks. As in most Central Asian towns, industry was represented by a cotton gin and a brewery, but there was also the Ivanov and Savinov Pharmaceutical Plant, founded in 1885, which used a species of wormwood that grows wild in the vicinity. The coat-of-arms of Chimkent depicts vert a flowering branch of wormwood argent to reflect the importance of this industry. At that time picturesque Chimkent attracted considerable numbers of tourists, many of whom came for a course of treatment with kumys ("mare's milk").

Now Chimkent is a large industrial town with a well-developed lead industry and a large machine-building plant, as well as a cotton-ginning plant, a brewery, a dairy and brickworks, and a large astrakhan fur factory, which exports 3 million pelts annually; there is also a scientific research institute on Lenin Square, which studies astrakhan production. Pharmacology is highly developed, based on the santonin works founded at the end of the 19th century. The recreational facilities include a children's railway.

The earth walls opposite the hotel are all that is left of a very old stronghold. From Bazaarnaya Street a road leads to the old town. The former *Governor's Residence* is on 8-March Street. Modern buildings line Lenin Prospect.

The remains of the 19th-century *fortress* can still be seen on the hill.

Astrakhan-making Museum, Lenin Square 3, on the 5th floor of the Astrakhan Institute. Open 9–6; closed Sat. and Sun. The museum demonstrates the selection of new breeds of sheep and has on display a great variety of samples of the finest skins and of clothes made from them.

Kazanskaya Church, Moskovskaya Street 5. Open for services.

St. Nicholas's Cathedral. Built in 1914.

Mosque, Amangeldi Street 29. This was built in 1890.

Local Museum, Sovietskaya (formerly Nikolayevskaya) Street 23. Open 10–7, closed Mon. The museum features national costumes and tools, stone idols dating from the 9th and 10th centuries and Turkic tents or "yurts."

Lenin Statue, Lenin Square

Bust of Kuibyshev, Sovietskaya Street, by the Voskhod Hotel

Shanin Drama Theatre, Lenin Prospect. Shanin (1892–1938) was a local theatre director who had a great influence on modern Kazakh national drama.

Puppet Theatre, in Pioneer Park

Philarmonia Concert Hall, Sovietskaya Street 9. Built in 1930.

Zoo

Hippodrome Racecourse

Central Park, Sovietskaya Street 26

Spartak Sport Complex, Kommunistichesky Prospect 44

Voskhod (Intourist) Hotel and Restaurant, Sovietskaya Street 1; tel. 37817

Chimkent Hotel, tel. 226–83

Turist Hotel, tel. 227–22

Yuzhnaya Hotel, tel. 206–98

Kainar ("spring") Restaurant, in the recreation area on the outskirts of the town

Solnechny Restaurant, in nearby village of Vaninovka

Ak-su ("white waters") Restaurant, 18 km (11 miles) from Chimkent

Department Store, Kommunisticheskaya Street

Intourist organises excursions from Chimkent to Mashat Ravine, the Michurin State Farm, to Turkestan (q.v.) and Kentau (see Turkestan).

Mashat Ravine, 40 km (25 miles) from Chimkent, with a river of the same name

Aul Restaurant, 45 km (28 miles) from Chimkent, just before reaching the village of Tamerlanovka. Here tourists can enjoy national dishes and ride horses and camels.

Hodji Mukan Manaitposov Museum, Pochtovaya Street 6. Hodji Mukan was a famous wrestler

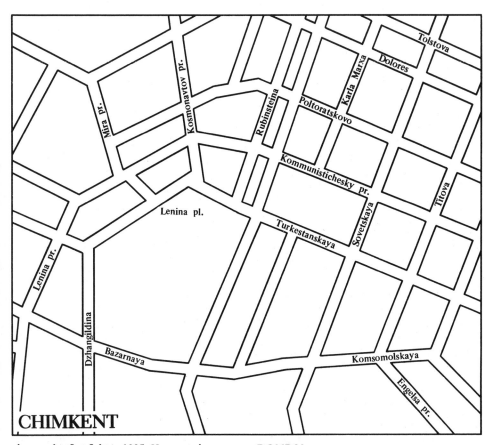

CHIMKENT

who won his first fight in 1895. He rose to become world champion and earned 48 gold and silver medals. In the museum is a stone that he broke across his chest and a model of the fighter plane that he bought with his own money.

Michurin State Farm, 70 km (43 miles) northeast of Chimkent. The farm has fine orchards and vineyards, and there is an opportunity for wine tasting. The excursion takes four hours.

CHIRCHIK
See Tashkent, p. 543.

CHUCHKHUR FALLS
See Kislovodsk, p. 240.

CHUFUT-KHALEH
See Bakhchisarai, p. 51.

CRIMEA
See Simferopol, p. 474.

DAGOMYS
See Sochi environs, p. 487.

DILIJAN
See Erevan environs, p. 136.

DOMBAI
See Kislovodsk, p. 240.

DONETSK Population—1,110,00
Known as Yuzovka until 1924 and then as Stalino until 1961.
None yet brought the Donbas to its knees,
Nor will any ever bring it down.
— PAVEL BESPOSCHANDY

Donetsk, on the river Kalmius, is the central city of the Donbas region and is often called the Miners' Capital. After Kiev and Kharkov, it is the Ukraine's third-largest city.

The Donbas (taking its name from its location in the basin of the Don) covers a total area of 1,860 sq km (718 sq miles) and stretches 110 km (68 miles) from east to west and 50 km (31 miles) from north to south. There are good deposits of anthracite and steam coal in comparatively thin seams. The Russian scientist Dmitry Mendeleyev (famous for his periodic table) spent 3 months in the Donbas in 1888 and wrote: "I was struck by the inexhaustible richness of the area, surpassing anything I have ever seen, not only in Russia but in Europe and America as well." It has proved to be the most important coal basin in the European part of the USSR, and geologists have found coal to a depth of 1,800 m (5,906 ft). In 1957 it was estimated that there were 240,620 million tons.

In 1721 Peter the Great showed interest in the news of a clerk, Grigory Kapustin, that coal was to be found in the area, but things moved slowly. The area was taken from the Crimean Tatars in 1739, and mining began only in 1798. There were settlements on the site of Donetsk at the end of the 18th century, but the first mine was not opened there until 1820, and the date of the foundation of the city is regarded as 1869.

It rapidly grew into an industrial centre after the establishment in 1871 of a metallurgical plant by the Welshman John Hughes (1814–89), who started his career as a blacksmith. In 1869 with capital of £300,000 and the sanction of the Russian government, he founded the New Russian Metallurgical Company in London. Subsequently, still with no knowledge of Russia or of the Russian language, he organised a new factory in the sparsely populated country north of the Sea of Azov. The equipment shipped from Britain was put ashore at Taganrog, the nearest port, and teams of oxen were used for the final stage of the journey. Some experts and skilled workers came from England, but the majority were from the provinces of northern Russia. *The Church of St. David and St. George* was built for the Welsh and the English to use, and even today on Leninskaya Street are some typical English houses of red brick called the "three- and four-rouble houses" because that was the rent charged for them.

The settlement was called Yuzovka after Hughes. The fortunate combination of pit-coal, iron ore, and manganese ensured its prosperity, but the development was strange to Russian eyes. It was described as a "town of weeping blast furnaces whose tears are molten metal," and the numerous chimneys were reminiscent of a forest after a fire, with the blackened treetops still smoking. It was also noted for its strikes, which occurred repeatedly after 1874. The Bolsheviks were later to find support among the local workers. A railway connection added to Yuzovka's affluence, and the expanding village grew into a town by 1917.

The town's boundaries encompass over 40 villages where miners live. Some of them—Kalinovka, Vetka, Putilovka, Larinka, Zakop, and Standart—are linked with the centre of town, but most of them have their own clubs and social establishments. New blocks of flats, factories, and institutes have taken the place of the old huts. One of the largest regions of the town bears the name of the village of Yuzovka.

Donetsk was under enemy occupation from October 1941 to September 1943. It was heavily damaged, and almost all the administrative buildings were destroyed. Nevertheless, both the town and the mines were restored by 1950, and the coal output is now 3 times that of the whole of Russia in 1913. This one city produces more metal today than the whole country did then. It is often called the "city of metal and coal," and indeed there are about 50 coal mines right in the city itself. The

oldest of all, *Tsentralno-Zavodskaya*, is near Dzerzhinskaya Square. (Factories and mines are not described in this guide; they can be visited only by special arrangement through Intourist.) Donetsk is a twin city of Sheffield, England.

Artyoma is the name of the main street. Its 10-km (6-mile) length connects the Metallurgical Factory with the railway station. It is the busiest and the most attractive street of the city, and the administrative buildings of the town hall and the local party committee are here, as well as the polytechnical Institute, the best hotels, Lokomotiv Stadium, and the best shops and cafés. The new Pushkin and Mayakovsky prospects, together with Universitetskaya Street, are also impressive. Shevchenko Boulevard runs for 5 km (3 miles), connecting the centre of the town with Cheryomushki, a new residential area that has grown rapidly since 1959. The complex of *Lenin Square* was finished only in 1955. The new buildings of the *House of Soviets*, the *Drama Theatre*, and the *Concert Hall* stand on the site of older buildings, among them the prerevolutionary "English Club." The imposing *fountain* in the centre of the square is illuminated after dark. Parallel to Artyoma is Universitetskaya Prospect, running from the city garden. Along it are the *University buildings, the House of Architects, the Palace of Sports*, and the new *Intourist Hotel*. Donetsk's numerous parks and gardens improve the look of the city, but their more practical purpose is to help freshen the smoke-laden air. This industrial town takes the greatest pride in the annual display of flowers in the city park. The first display was arranged in 1956.

Plans for future construction in Donetsk spread over 20 years. The city is to cover 400 sq km (154 sq miles), with offices, theatres, etc. in the centre, surrounded by the residential areas, each a separate and independent suburb. Underground springs will be used for forming lakes with beaches and boating stations within the city limits.

The suburbs of Donetsk have already met those of Makeyevka, another quickly growing industrial centre (see below), 13 km (8 miles) from Donetsk, and soon the 2 towns will merge.

Apart from the local coal mining and metallurgy, there are important machine-building and chemical industries. Factories produce mining equipment and agricultural machinery, and there are light and food industries. Since 1959 local industry has run on natural gas piped from Stavropol in the North Caucasus. Donetsk has polytechnical, medical, and commercial institutes as well as a number of scientific research institutes. The university opened in 1964.

St. Nicholas's Church, near Lenin Street

Local Museum, Chelyuskintsev Street 189a. Open 10–5, closed Tues. Sections include the natural history of the Donbas, archaeology (including stone figures of the 8th–13th centuries), and the history of the Donbas.

Art Museum, Pushkin Boulevard 35. Open 10–6; closed Wed.

Planetarium, Artyom Street

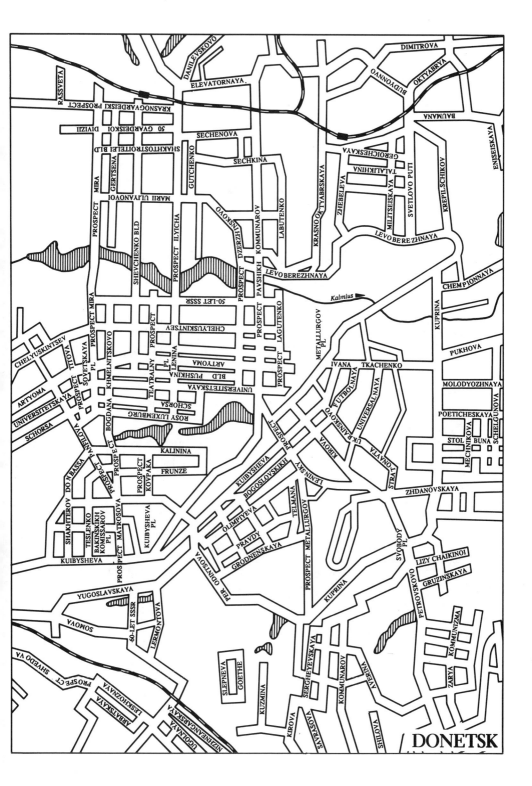

DONETSK

Nikita Khruschev's House, Kirov Street 90. The Khruschev family lived here in 1912. It was in Donetsk in the early 1920s that Khruschev began his political career.

Lenin Monument, Lenin Square

Flerovsky Obelisk, Flerovsky Garden. Vasily Bervi–Flerovsky (1829–1918) was a sociologist and philosopher who lived and died in Donetsk.

Dzerzhinsky Bust, Dzerzhinsky Garden

Shevchenko Monument, Shevchenko Boulevard. The monument by Vronsky and Oleinik was unveiled in 1955. The upper part of the pedestal is decorated with a bronze bas-relief depicting the heroes of the poet's work. He himself is also shown here, reading his poetry to the Russian writers Chernyshevsky and Dobrolyubov.

Fighters for Soviet Power Monument, Pogibshikh Kommunarov Garden. Unveiled in 1957.

Monument to Stratonauts, on the way to the city park. The 2-m (7-ft) statue of a pilot marks the burial place of 4 pilots (Batenko, Stobun, Ukrainskii, and Kuchumov) who died after an accident with a stratospheric balloon in 1938. The statue by Belostotski was unveiled in 1953.

Col. Franz Grinkevich Monument, in the garden beside the opera and ballet theatre. The colonel's soldiers made the monument themselves, pulling the T-34 tank up into position unaided and cementing it there on the pedestal. Also in this garden is the grave of Lieutenant-General Kuzma Gurov (1901–43), marked by his bust.

Opera and Ballet Theatre, Artyom Street 82

Artyom Drama Theatre, Artyom Street 74

Concert Hall, Posticheva Street. Here is the only Czechoslovakian organ in the Ukraine. The hall seats 600.

Puppet Theatre, Artyom Street

Circus, Lenin Prospect 2

Shakhter ("miner") Stadium. Opened in 1949, with room for 50,000.

Lokomotiv Stadium, Chelyuskintsev Street 48

Druzhba Sports Hall. With seats for 5,000.

Khimik Swimming Pool, Smolyanka

Botanical Garden

There are 16 ponds within the city, but locals are most proud of the *city reservoir* in the valley of the river Kalmius. There are sports grounds here and a bathing beach.

Druzhba Hotel and Restaurant, Universitetskaya Street 48; tel. 34–076. Intourist office: tel. 91–1996.

Ukraina Hotel and Restaurant, Artyom Street 88. This 10-storey building is the city's tallest.

Donbas Hotel and Restaurant, Artyom Street 80

Oktyabr (October) Hotel, Posticheva Street. This was formerly the Great Britain Hotel.

Shakhtyor Hotel and Restaurant, Titov Prospect 5

Troyanda ("rose") Restaurant, Artyom Street

Kalmius Restaurant, Makeyevskoye Chaussée

Moskva Restaurant, Artyom Street 71

Metallurg Restaurant, Artyom Street, by the garden

Sport Restaurant, Universitetskaya Street

Otdykh ("rest") Café, Pavshikh Kommunarov Square

Sputnik Café, by Avtovokzal

Beryozka Café, Lenin Square

GPO and Telegraph Office, Artyom Street 72

Bank, Artyom Street 38

Kashtan (foreign-currency) Shop, Postyshev Street 129

Ukrainian Souvenirs, Universitetskaya Street 30

Bookshops, Artyom Street 79 and 125

Department Store, Artyom Street 34

Art Salon, Artyom Street 127

Taxi Stands, Theatre Square and Central Square

Intourist organises excursion from here to Slavyanogorsk (q.v.), about 175 km (108 miles) away.

DRUSKININKAI
See Vilnius, p. 617.

DUBOSEKOVO
See Moscow environs, p. 361.

DUSHANBE Population—595,000
Dushanbe is the capital of Tajikistan

TAJIKISTAN
Population—5,112,000. The Tajiks account for 58.8 percent of the population and are the oldest inhabitants of the region. Other nationalities living here include 22.9 percent Uzbeks, 10.4 percent Russians, Tatars, and Ukrainians.

The country is almost entirely mountainous, and the Soviet Union's highest peaks are to be found here, in the Pamirs—Mt. Kommunism (formerly Mt. Stalin) (7,495 m/24,589 ft) and Mt. Lenin (7,134 m/23,406 ft). To the south of Mt. Kommunism lies Fedchenko Glacier, 71.2 km (44 miles) in length, the longest continental ice river in the world. Almost all the greatest rivers of Central Asia also flow through the republic, and Tajikistan is the region most liable to earthquakes in the USSR.

The country has three climatic belts; in the lowlands it is hot and dry, while in the cooler foothills there is more rain, and in the mountains there is little precipitation but the average temperature is below freezing. The mean temperature for January varies from −1°C (30°F) in the north to 3°C (37°F) in the south. In the month of July it is 23°C (73°F) to 30°C (86°F), respectively. The wild life is similarly varied. In the southern lowlands, tigers, deer, and many kinds of waterfowl are to be found. In the higher plateaus are antelopes and huge lizards about 1.5 m (5 ft) long, and in the Pamirs live bears and wild sheep.

The Tajiks are a very old people. Their ancestors lived here in the state of Sogdiana at the beginning of the 1st century B.C. The Tajiks come from Iranian stock, but the name only appeared in the 8th century A.D. when the country was conquered by the Arabs. 2 centuries later the Turks took it over. Part of the Tajik territory was incorporated into the Russian empire in 1895, when an Anglo-Russian commission fixed the northern frontier of Afghanistan on the river Pyandj and separated the Russian and Indian empires by an Afghan corridor. Soviet power was finally established here in 1920, at the end of the Civil War in Russia. In 1929 it was proclaimed an autonomous republic and received statehood within the USSR.

Tajiks differ in appearance from the other peoples of Central Asia. Dark-eyed, dark-haired, and suntanned, they have European features. High in the Pamirs one meets blue-eyed, blond Tajiks who speak a slightly different language. They are descendants of the native population who escaped the Mongolian conquest in the inaccessible mountains. The Tajiks are a people of poets and sages. Their respect for the elderly is equalled only by their love for children. The republic has one of the highest birth rates in the Soviet Union. They also show a great fondness for birds, as these are considered a symbol of happiness.

Unlike the rich and fertile valleys, the regions of the Pamirs are still very mysterious. Even primitive civilisation was late in reaching this out-of-the-way corner of the world, and today people still live according to the older customs and superstitions of their forbears. A local legend says that 2 angels lowered the sheep from heaven to help people make a living here, and for a long time everything about a sheep was held sacred. A fallen sheep was even mourned like a human being. Dairy products are still the staple foods. There is, however, a good local pea soup called "shurpo-nakhud," and their recommended minced beef is "kima-tajikist."

Pamir dwellings have very intricate wood carvings. A project is under way to resettle mountain folk in the lowlands where they can enjoy more comfort. But not all of the locals are willing to leave their present homes, in spite of the difficulties they face living there. The Pamir roads are open to traffic only for 3 months of the year.

Beautiful pottery and ceramics have been made in Tajikistan since the earliest times. There are all kinds of pottery for household use, decorative kinds and some that is simpler for wedding festivals (called "toi," which used to last, with short intervals, for over a month, and attracted crowds of guests). Tajik embroidery is also famous. One needs only to look at the skullcaps the men wear. It is the custom for a bride to embroider a skullcap for her groom. Women have fine embroidery on their dresses too.

Tajikistan plays an appreciable part in the Soviet economy. The finest fibre cotton is grown here, and uranium and polymetallic ores are mined. A unique power station is being built on the Vakhsh River, near the town of Nurek. The name of the river means "turbulent," and there is a legend of a Tajik boy called Nur who fell in love with a girl but was told she would marry him only if he could tame the Vakhsh. He tried to do it with boulders, but it only swirled and foamed the more. At last

he threw an enormously big rock into the river, but that only made it angrier still, so he admitted defeat. However, for his brave attempt, the small settlement on the banks of the Vakhsh was called Nurek after him, and now it is the site of one of the world's largest hydropower stations. The station has the highest concrete dam in the world—300 m/984 ft—but apart from that, erecting it in a zone of frequent earthquakes made it a particularly difficult engineering feat. Nurek is 70 km (43 miles) from the capital.

A few words of Tajik:

hello	salom
I am a tourist	man turist
please	markhamat
thank you	rakhmat
yes	kha
no	nahz
bad	bad (yes, it's true!)
I don't understand	man namefakhmam
please fetch me an interpreter	marhamat ba man tarjimonro taklif namyed
good-bye	haier (or) hai
how do you do?	akhvoli shumo chi tavr

Dushanbe (Dyushanbe till 1929; Stalinobad till 1961) Population—595,000

Dushanbe is the capital of Tajikistan, situated in the Gissar Valley, beside the river Dushanbinka, a tributary of the Varzob (Vakhsh). "Dushanbe" in Tajik simply means "second night," which is the third day of the eastern week and falls on Monday. It was so called because of the big weekly market that was held on Mondays, and the old name was revived in 1961.

The town lies on the same latitude as Spain and Portugal and is about 846 m (2,776 ft) above sea level. The climate is continental; in summer the temperature rises to 40°C (104°F), and in winter it falls to −20°C (−4°F). The system of reservoirs now under construction around the capital is expected to lower the summer temperature to about 33°C (91°F). For almost half the year there is no rain, and there is unlikely to be any during the months of August and September, which is the time of the fruit harvest. The rainy season starts at the end of October and finishes at the end of May.

The site has been inhabited since ancient times. Local archaeologists have found pottery dating from the 2nd century B.C. to the 13th century A.D. A 7th-century Buddhist temple was excavated in the Adjinatepe ("evil spirit") Hill with a 12-m (39-ft) statue of Buddha, the tallest ever found in the Soviet Union. The paint on it is well preserved, and the broken head, found nearby, is to be restored. With the statue were many other smaller figurines of similar date. From the 16th century, the area belonged to the khanate of Bukhara and was known as Eastern Bukhara. First mentioned in 1676 by Khan Balkh-khan Subkhankul Bekhadur in his letter to the Russian tsar Fyodor with

DUSHANBE

a proposal for contacts between the two states, it was then a poor town with a half-ruined mud fortress in the centre. The present town was formed from 3 villages. Sari-Asiya became the northern part of the town, Shakhmansur the southern part, and Dushanbe the centre. The latter was the largest of the 3; it had 500 houses and was known for the colourful bazaar held there every Monday. The town was practically ruined in the middle of the 19th century during the reign of Ismail-khan, due to his regular raids on Dushanbe, but was rebuilt by inhabitants.

In 1920–21 Dushanbe was the residence of the emir of Bukhara, Seid-Alim-khan, who escaped here from Bukhara itself, because Dushanbe was an important strategic point, a crossroad of caravan routes leading to other settlements of eastern Bukhara. The town was entirely ruined during the Civil War, and when it was made the centre of an autonomous republic in 1924 it had only 42 houses, with a civil population numbering 242. At that time only 4 of the new capital's houses had wooden floors, and the street lighting consisted of one oil lamp on Bazaar Square. Hyenas and jackals used to roam nearby and could be heard howling during the night.

The town grew rapidly during the 1930s. The population rose from 5,600 in 1926 to 82,500 in 1939. In 1929 it was proclaimed the capital of the newly formed Tajik Republic, renamed Stalinobad, and was linked by rail with the rest of the country.

There are now food and textile industries here, with silk and cotton mills, as well as machine and metal industries. There are 9 large educational establishments in the city, including the University (1948). Here also is the Tajik Academy of Sciences, founded in 1951.

The main thoroughfare, *Lenin Prospect*, is nearly 15 km (9 miles) long and runs north from Privokzalnaya Square, in front of the railway station. The most important buildings are on Lenin Prospect itself or its vicinity; their names are mostly prefaced by the word "new," as far as the local people are concerned. Lenin Prospect is crossed by many smaller streets, and some of those parallel to it look like green tunnels, as the foliage from the trees on either side meet overhead.

Aini Square, the first through which Lenin Prospect runs from the station end, is named for the founder of Soviet Tajik literature, Sadriddin Murad Khoja Zada Aini (1878–1954). He was the first president of the local academy of sciences, and *Aini Monument* was erected with money donated by UNESCO; it was sculpted by Eldarov and unveiled in 1978. *Dushanbe Hotel* also stands here. A number of the institutes of the academy are situated on Aini Street, which runs out of the square. Also near the square is the *Vatan ("motherland")* *Cinema*, built in national style, and farther on is a 3-storey building of the *University*, founded in 1948.

In *Lenin Square* is a monument to Lenin that was unveiled in 1960 and the *25th Anniversary*

Obelisk, bearing the republic's coat-of-arms and commemorating the founding of Soviet Tajikistan. Around the square are the impressive *Government House* and other offices and ministries, including *Communication House* and the *Djami Cinema*.

Putovskova Square is surrounded by the local *Communist party headquarters* and the *Drama Theatre* and the *Palace of Congresses* is in a park nearby. Lenin Prospect then runs into Sari-Asiya ("northern village"), the one-time village that forms the northern suburbs of the town. Here is the newly planned *Aini Park*, where a small rotunda resembling a mausoleum shelters the grave of Aini.

800 Lyet Moskvy Square is notable for its fountains. There is a *hotel and the Opera Theatre* here. A little farther along Lenin Prospect is *Firdawsi Library*, with over 1 million books and ancient manuscripts. Abul Qasim Firdawsi (b. 934–41, d. ca. 1020) was a Persian poet, the 1,000th anniversary of whose birth was celebrated in 1934.

Shamaisur Mosque, Vasifi Street 1. Built in the 19th century.

Sari Osnob Mosque, Ozodi-Zanon Street 124. Built in the 19th century.

Karamishkar Mosque, Lermontov Street 20

Khaji Yakub Mosque, Shodmoni Street 58. This is the largest mosque in Dushanbe and was built in the 19th century.

St. Nicholas's Russian Orthodox Cathedral, Druzhbi Narodov Prospect 58. Built in 1946.

St. Joseph's Roman Catholic Church, Titov Street 10. Built in 1978.

Baptist Chapel, Repin Street, Proyezd No. 1

Synagogue, Dekhkanskaya Street, near the Tajikistan Hotel

Bekhzad Local History Museum and Fine Art Museum, Aini Street 31. Local handicrafts are included among other exhibits here. Kemaleddin Bekhzad (b. ca. 1455, d. 1535–36) was an outstanding miniatures painter and illustrated handwritten books, including those by Saadi and Nisami. His influence spread to Azerbaijan and Iran. Open 11–5, closed Mon.

Ethnographical Museum of the Peoples of the Orient, Putovsky Street 7. Closed Mon. The collection of 10,000 items shows the customs of the Orient from ancient times till the present. The scale models of palaces are especially worth seeing. The collection was started by the outstanding ethnographer and linguist Mikhail Stepanov in the 1920s. The carved entrance door of the museum was made by Khamdamov.

Aini House Museum, Khamze Hakim-Zadeh Street 1

Exhibition of National Economic Achievements, Lomonosov Street 162. This was opened in 1967.

Sadriddin Aini Memorial Complex, Aini Square. This was unveiled in 1978 to commemorate the 100th anniversary of the founder of Tajik literature. The ensemble by Eldarov and Agaronov is composed of several structures: "Liberation," "The Victory of Soviet Power," and the mournful "Odina," with the figure of Aini dominating.

Rudaki Monument, Rudaki Square. Abu Rudaki was an outstanding Bukharan poet (875–941).

Obelisk to the 25th Anniversary of Soviet Tajikistan, Lenin Square

Victory Monument, Pobedy Square. Commemorates World War II victory.

War Memorial, in Pobedy Park. There is a Wall of Glory here and an eternal flame.

Aini Opera and Ballet Theatre, Lenin Prospect 28, 800-Lyet Moskvy Square

Lakhuti Tajik Drama Theatre, Lenin Prospect 86. Founded in 1929 and named after the local poet Abdulkasim Lakhuti (1887–1957).

Mayakovsky Russian Drama Theatre, Lenin Prospect 76. Founded in 1937.

Cinema Concert Hall, Cheslav Putovsky Street. This seats 2,670.

Open-Air Theatre (Zelyeny Teatr), Frunze Park

Circus, Karabayeva Street 2

Lenin Park was laid out in the 1920s in the centre of the town and covers 3 hectares (7.5 acres). Here is *Lenin Monument* and *Civil War Heroes Memorial* with an eternal flame. There is also a popular amusement ground with the *Lyeto ("summer") Restaurant*.

Komsomol Park and Lake, Putovskova Street. The construction of this artificial lake began in 1939 but was suspended during the war. There is a beach, a boating station, a restaurant and zoo in the park.

Pobedy ("victory") Park. A 600-m (656-yd) cableway takes 3 minutes to reach the park.

Frunze Stadium, Putovskovo Street 28

Dynamo Stadium, Shevchenko Street 27

Botanical Garden, Karamova Street. This garden was laid out in 1934.

Shapkin Racecourse, Novi Posyelok

Tajikistan Hotel and Restaurant, Kommunisticheskaya Street 22; tel. 27–4393. Intourist office: tel. 27–4973.

Farogat Restaurant, opposite the Tajikistan Hotel

Dushanbe Hotel and Restaurant, Lenin Street 7

Vakhsh Hotel and Restaurant, Lenin Prospect 26/2

Pamir Restaurant, Kirov Street 21a

Khisor ("rest") Restaurant, near Komsomol Lake

Rokhat ("leisure") Tearoom, Lenin Prospect 84. The tearoom is decorated in national style.

GPO, Lenin Prospect 52

Bank, Lenin Square 23/2

Beryozka (foreign-currency) Shop, Lenin Prospect 70

Arts and Crafts, Lenin Prospect 89. Open 11–5, closed Mon. There is pottery on sale here and, among other things, traditional tobacco horns.

Department Store, Lenin Prospect 83

Markets, Putovskova Street 5, Lakhuti Street 12

Mavlono Yakub Carkhi Mosque (Mausoleum), 10 km (6 miles) from Dushanbe. Built in the 18th century.

Intourist organises a 4-hour excursion to Guissar and day trips from Dushanbe to Varzobskoye Ravine and Nurek.

Guissar

Guissar lies 30 km (19 miles) from Dushanbe. In the 14th–15th centuries, it was the residence of the Turko-Mongol rulers, and a complex of religious buildings was founded here, but in the 17th century it fell into decay. The bek of Guissar resided here in the days of the emirate of Bukhara. Remains of the mausoleum, 2 mosques, and a fortress of later date have survived. *Guissar-Darvaza* (fortress gates) of the 18th–19th centuries are at the foot of the Guissar Fortress. A pandus with powerful rotund towers by its side leads to the arch entrance. Beyond are domed guard rooms. *Makhdumi-Azam Mausoleum* dates to the 15th–16th centuries. It is an asymmetrical structure, since the burial vault and the prayer room were built first, and the cross-shaped domed hall was erected later. *Madressah-i Kukhna* was built in the 16th–17th centuries with a mosque in its right wing. Another religious institution, *Madressah-i Nau*, dates to the 17th–18th centuries, but only part of it has survived.

Varzob Ravine

Varzob Ravine is 56 km (35 miles) from Dushanbe. The excursions here take 7 hours, including time for a picnic lunch.

At the 17-km mark on the highway along the turbulent river Varzob, to the left of the road, is *Chor Bed ("weeping willow") Tea House* in local style, and farther on, at the 27-km mark, is the *Nassimi Kukhsor ("mountain breeze") Restaurant*, where European and Tajik dishes are served. The view of the snow-capped Guissarsky Mountains, which are part of the Pamirs, is very beautiful. Amid this fine scenery stands in the ravine a hydropower station built in 1937; there are beaches, and boats can be hired on the reservoir.

A little farther along in the same direction, a side road branches off to *Khodzha-Obi-Garm*. This is a health resort, which lies between 1,740 and 1,960 m (5,709–6,430 ft) above sea level. The rivers Obi-Mazar and Obi-Kalandio form picturesque waterfalls. It is said that long ago a mountain dweller by the name of Khodzha noticed the curative powers of the local springs and of the steam that issued from under the ground, and he began curing people from these resources. But his brothers envied his enterprise, lured him to the mountain top, and threw him down. The local people considered him a saint and called the place and springs after him.

The health resort was founded here in 1935, particularly to treat cardiological and gynaecological diseases with the waters, which have a low mineral content and a temperature of 65°–96°C (149°–205°F), and with the hot radon steam, found nowhere else in the Soviet Union. There is a restaurant here.

Nurek Population—40,000

Nurek lies 75 km (47 miles) to the south of Dushanbe. The road to it runs between cotton fields,
orchards, and vineyards and twists up to Chor-
magzak Pass (1,610 m/5,282 ft above sea level),
from whence there is a good view over the Nurek
Valley.

Nurek is an entirely new town, built in 1960
on the bank of the turbulent mountain river
Vakhsh. It was founded for those working on the
Nurek Hydropower Station and its 300-m (984-ft)
dam, the highest in the world. With its output of
2.7 million kilowatt-hours, it is one of the most
powerful in the world. Another hydropower station
on the Vakhsh, the "second Nurek," has a capacity
of 3.6 million kilowatt-hours.

The main street, lined with tall buildings, is
Lenin Street. *Elektron* is the name of a very up-
to-date cinema, and there is a building college here
and a branch of the Dushanbe Polytechnical Institute.

Intourist Office, Kalyuzhnik Street 1; tel. 93–
362

Kurgan-Tube Population—59,100

This town is 100 km (62 miles) south of Dushanbe.
Until the 19th century, Kishlad Kurgan-Tube was
the centre of the Kurgan-Tube region of the Bukhara emirate.

The ruins of *Lyagman Fortress* (10th–13th centuries) stand on the bank of the river Vakhsh.

World War II Memorial

Tigrovaya Balka ("tiger ravine"), at the place
where the river Vakhsh flows into the Pyandzh.
There is subtropical jungle here and a nature reserve with decorative flamingo and Persian otter,
among other creatures.

DZHAMBUL (Auliye-Ata till 1936, Mirzoyan
from 1936 to 38) Population—310,000

The town, which is situated in the valley of the
river Talas 545 km (339 miles) from Alma-Ata and
2,140 m (7,021 ft) above sea level, was first mentioned as Taraz in 568 A.D. when Zemarkh, the
envoy of Emperor Justinian of Byzantium, visited
it and described a stone bridge across the river.
Excavations in 1936 and 1938 showed that on the
site of present-day Dzhambul was a rectangular
settlement that covered 14 hectares (35 acres). The
citadel was on the northern side, and in this area
part of the water-supply system, pavement, and
canals have been found. Now this district of the
modern town is called Zeleny Bazar, meaning
"green market." One of the most interesting finds
was the baths with their carved plaster decorations,
roofs with many cupolas, and a hot-water system
beneath the floor.

Taraz stood on one of the silk roads from China
to Rome, and caravans from Shasha (Tashkent)
passed this way, making it the economic and cultural centre of the area. The Buddhist priest Suan
Tsian, who visited Taraz from China in 680, described Dzhambul as a sizeable commercial centre

with a circumference of 2.5 km (1.5 miles). The
Chinese said that it had its own coinage from the
8th century. In 751 there was a decisive battle between the Chinese and the Arabs, and when the
Arabs finally captured Dzhambul in 898 after a
long siege, Islam was established throughout Central Asia. Their victory incidentally led also to the
Chinese secret of paper making spreading to the
Mediterranean. The Arab geographer Makdisi
wrote of Taraz at the end of the 10th century as
being a large, fortified town with many gardens and
numerous plantations. It flourished as the capital
of the Karakhanid state but was captured by the
soldiers of Shah Mohammed of Khorezm and then,
in 1219, ruined by Tatars led by Ghengis Khan.
When the ancient caravan route lost its importance, many trade centres, Taraz included, fell into
decay.

At the end of the 18th century, the Kokand
khans built a fortress near the ruins of Taraz and
called it Auliye-Ata. The first settlers were from
the town of Namangan. Russians took the fortress
in 1864, following the formation of Turkestan. The
roads from Tashkent to other strategic places in this
area such as Verny and Pishpek (known today as
Alma-Ata and Frunze) passed through Auliye-Ata,
and military personnel, their families, and civil
servants, were among the first European settlers.
The town grew into a market for cattle and wool.
It was also renowned for its stud farm.

Dzhambul was renamed in 1936 after Dzhambul Dzhabayev (Jumbili Jabay-uli) (1846–1945), a
Kazakh folk bard who since the revolution wrote
many poems about socialist construction in Kazakhstan and the gallantry of Soviet soldiers.
Dzhambul was awarded a state prize in 1941.
Today new streets and squares have covered the
caravansarais and workshops of old Taraz. The
streets follow a radial plan and the small irrigation
canals (aryks) form a network throughout the town,
contributing to the abundant greenery. Factories
for superphosphates and sugar as well as for building materials and food products also operate in
Dzhambul.

Within the town limits there are interesting
mausolea. That of *Kara-khan* is said to have been
built in the 11th century on the grave of the founder
of the Karakhanid dynasty and was once an object
of pilgrimage. The mausoleum was reconstructed
in 1906 and is now a museum, complete with maps
of old Taraz. The museum is open 9–2 and 3–6;
closed Tues. Another, smaller "mazar" (the local
word for mausoleum) is a 13th-century structure
called *Daud-bek*, which serves as the tomb of a
Mongolian vice-regent. There is also *Tek-Turmaz
Mausoleum* and *Shakh-Mansur Mausoleum*, belonging to a 14th-century Mongolian khan's vice-
regent in Taraz. Shakh-Mansur is a well-preserved,
domed mausoleum on 4 pillars connected by
arches.

Local Museum, Kommunisticheskaya Street
91. Open 10–7; closed Mon. It contains a valuable
collection of archaeological finds from ancient

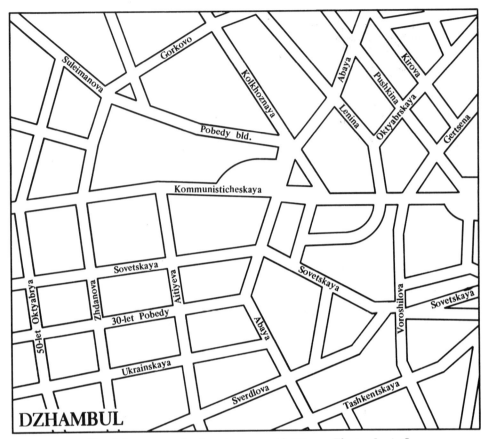

DZHAMBUL

Taraz and the old Uzbek cemetery. In the ethnographical section on the 3rd floor is a yurt and a collection of national costumes. Nearby is the *Gallery of Ancient Monuments*, with sculptures up to 2 m (7 ft) high. The pieces are made of pink and grey granite or sandstone and are covered with images of people, their implements and scenes from their daily lives. This sculpture has proven to be of great value in the study of the Turkic tribes that inhabited southern Kazakhstan over a thousand years ago.

Mausoleum, Taraz Street 2. This used to have a minaret beside it. Inside are stone idols found in the vicinity of Dzhambul.

Davud-beg Mausoleum and Tomb. From the 13th century. Davud-beg was also known as Tsanmanozr, and his tomb was a place of pilgrimage.

Yady-Kadir Mosque and Minaret, Furmanova Street. Built in 1912.

Bathhouse, Voroshilov Street. It dates from the beginning of the 19th century.

Koshmambetov Bust, Abai Street, near the Central Square. Karimbai Koshmambetov (d. 1930) was a local revolutionary and statesman.

Lenin Monument

Dzhambul Monument

Civil War Heroes Obelisk, Kommunisticheskaya Street

Abai Drama Theatre, Lenin Square
Lenin Park, Abaya Street
Stadium
Taraz Hotel and Restaurant, Trudovaya Street 25; tel. 3–15–55
Dzhambul Hotel and Vesna Restaurant, Kommunisticheskaya Street
Tyulipan Restaurant, Sovietskaya Street 103
Kuyuk Restaurant, 35 km (22 miles) from the town on the Kuyuk Pass. Decorated in national style.
GPO, Lenin Square
Souvenirs, at the crossing of Abaya and Sovietskaya streets

Intourist organises excursions to Golovachevka and to the Michurin State Farm.

Golovachevka

This small village is 18 km (11 miles) to the west of Dzhambul. To the left of the main road there is a grove with the *Babadja-Khatun Mausoleum* in the middle of it. The construction of the mausoleum dates back to 11th-century reign of the Karakhanids. No legend has survived about this burial vault, but judging by the inscription, it was erected on the grave of a woman distinguished enough to be worthy of the honour. This is a very rare occurrence in a Muslim country, where women were considered the lowest of the low. The mausoleum, the tallest in Central Asia, is a cubic structure with walls over 1 metre thick. The entrance, the highest part of the mausoleum, has a frieze decorated with terra-cotta tiles. An inscription in Arabic reads: "This is an imposing tomb called Babadji-Khatun." The name of the builder, which followed, has not survived. The mausoleum has a rare tent-style roof. The architecture of that period was influenced by nomadic customs, and the mausoleum itself is reminiscent of a tent. It is considered the prototype of many mediaeval Central Asian buildings.

Further on in the grove, on the left, is the 12th-century *Aishi-Bibi Mausoleum*. As legend has it, Aishi-bibi, daughter of the famous poet and scientist Khakim-Ata, was betrothed to Kara-khan, ruler of Taraz. The date of the wedding was appointed, but Kara-khan was away, fighting his enemies, and was late for the wedding. So Aishi-bibi left her home in Tashkent and set out to find her betrothed. On the way she fell ill and died without reaching Taraz. On learning the news, Kara-khan hurried to the place, buried his beloved, and erected this mausoleum to commemorate her. The western wall with its entrance and half-ruined columns and the ruins of the northern and southern walls are all that have survived, but it is supposed to have been a domed mausoleum. It has unique carved terra-cota tiles. At the top of the corner tower of the western wall are the words "autumn, clouds, a beautiful world." The whole structure is very elegant, reminiscent of an Oriental carpet.

Michurin State Farm

This is 107 km (66 miles) from Dzhambul and 3 km (2 miles) from the main road. The farm's land is planted with orchards and vineyards, and it harvests 6,000 tons of grapes a year. Its factory takes more from other nearby farms, processing 10,000 tons annually. It also handles 10,000 tons of apples and produces juice as well as table and sparkling wines. There is an opportunity for wine tasting at the factory.

Bust of Michurin

War Memorial, with an eternal flame.

DZHVARI

See Tbilisi environs, p. 544.

DZINTARI

See Riga, p. 445.

ECHMIADZIN

See Ereven environs, p. 128.

ELBRUS

See Nalchik, p. 380.

ELEKTRENAI

See Vilnius, p. 616.

EREVAN

Erevan is the capital of Armenia.

ARMENIA

The name of the republic in Armenian is Ayastan. It covers an area of 29,800 sq km (11,503 sq miles), and the population of 3,283,000 is 89.7 percent Armenian and the rest Azerbaijani, Russian, and Kurd. It is situated in the south of central Transcaucasia, and its principal towns are the capital, Erevan, and Leninakan.

The Armenians are one of the most ancient peoples in the world. In the 8th–7th centuries B.C., the Hay tribe conquered the Armens and, later, other Urartu tribes, hence the two names of the country, Hayastan (their own name for it) and Armenia (as it was known to the Greeks, Persians, and Romans). Sometimes the Armenians refer to it as Ayastan-Karastan, meaning Armenia, country of stones; this is an apt name as one-third of the territory is rocky and arid.

During the country's 3,000 years of history, it has known heroic ups and downs. Once its might was compared to that of ancient Rome, but later on it became the most backward province of Persia. Its position on the main trade route between east and west was the main reason for its being constantly conquered and reconquered, and then regaining its independence. In 519 B.C. the Armenians were conquered by Persia and in 334 B.C. by Alexander the Great. In 189 B.C. the country regained its independence, and by the middle of the 1st century B.C. it became one of the most powerful states in the Near East, especially during the reign of Tigranes II (95–56 B.C.), when Armenian territory stretched from the Caucasus Mountains down to the Mediterranean. Tigranes was finally defeated by Pompey, and his country fell under Roman rule.

The country became Christian in 301 A.D., following the conversion of Tridates III by St. Gregory the Enlightener, but at the end of the 4th century, Armenia was divided between Persia and Byzantium. In 628 it was conquered by the Arabs. It was only in 886 that Armenian independence was regained, to last for another 160 years.

From the middle of the 11th century, Armenia was invaded and conquered successively by the Seljuk Turks, the Mongols, and Tamerlane. Among the more peaceful visits was that of Marco Polo in 1271. In the 16th century, it was a bone of contention between Persia and Turkey and was always under the rule of one or the other.

In 1826, as a result of the Russo-Persian War, eastern Armenia became part of the Russian empire. A revival of national feeling at the end of the 19th century was halted by the massacres of 1894–96. Then and during World War I, when the Young Turks junta was aided by the Germans, 1,500,000 Armenians (half the small country's population) lost their lives. Many escaped death only by fleeing abroad. At the present there is a steady trickle of Armenians returning to their country, and many repatriates have settled in the suburbs of Erevan on Norka Hill.

After the Russian revolution of 1917, Armenia first became part of the Transcaucasian Federation (which soon disintegrated), and after that was ruled by the Dashnaktsutyun Party, which advocated Armenian independence, until in 1920 it became part of the Transcaucasian Federal Republic of the USSR. Soviet power was established in December 1920, and although there was a revolt in February 1921, the Soviets were never challenged after April of that year. Since 1936 Armenia has been a Union Republic of the USSR.

Soviet Armenia lays claim to Turkish Armenia. This includes the holy mountain of Ararat and in spite of the fact that it is no longer theirs, the Armenians are proud to depict it on their coat-of-arms. It is said that when the Turks protested this, saying that the mountain was on Turkish territory, the Soviet reply was that although the Turkish symbol was the crescent, surely it did not mean that they laid claim to the moon. The highest mountain in Armenia is the 4-peaked Mt. Aragats (4,016 m/13,176 ft). One of the leading Soviet observatories was built here in 1946, in the village of Byurakan.

The Armenian alphabet was composed in the 4th century A.D. by Maesrob Mashtotz and is still in use today. Armenia had its own university in the Middle Ages.

Some words and phrases of modern Armenian:

hello	voghdzuyin
I am a tourist	yes tourist em
please	khntrem
thank you	horhakalutyun
yes	ayi-ye
no	votch
good	lav
I don't understand	yes chen haska-noom
good-bye	tsertesootyun
how do you do?	barev dzez

Many modern buildings in Armenia contain traditional architectural elements, and frequent use is made of classic decorative designs carved into the stonework. Often they are built of the same pink tufa or dark-grey basalt that has been used through the ages.

There are over 2,500 buildings and other monuments of historical interest in Armenia, and the church architecture especially deserves attention. The earliest churches were basilical, with a nave, or a nave flanked by two aisles. Gradually the central stone cupola was introduced, and the ground plan changed to cruciform. The 5th–7th centuries were a golden age of ecclesiastical building. Many forms of churches, besides basilical, were tried, including circular and polygonal. Typical of most churches is the stone cupola on a circular or polygonal drum, surmounted by a conical top. These churches were bare, even to the point of being austere, with the only decorations being sculpted friezes around the windows.

In the 9th–11th centuries, when the monasteries were founded, decoration gradually became more apparent. The conical roof of the cupola became corrugated, bas-reliefs and high reliefs were introduced, including those featuring animals as well as purely formal designs. In addition, the first frescoes graced the walls. Most important of all innovations was the pointed arch, first used in 1001 in the Cathedral of Ani. The churches retained their simple lines, but a large narthex, or porch, was built in front. Through the years the monastic buildings increased in number and complexity but always showed a remarkable geometric sense. They housed libraries and schools and were vital centres of learning and art until the Mongol invasion.

New ecclesiastical buildings appeared only in the 17th century, when they tended to return to the basilical style with the central cupola but now adding an open gallery and a belfry to the western façade. At this time belfrys were also added to the older churches, not always harmoniously. The arabesques in the designs of the stonework patterns and the use of alternating red and black stone show the influence of Moslem art.

The inventiveness and skill of the Armenian stonemasons had long been known far and wide. In 806–11 Oton Matdsrydi built St. Germain-des-Pres and the belfry of Charlemagne's palace in Aachen. Armenian influence spread farther when the Crusades began since the road to Jerusalem lay through Armenia. Later, when the Mongols descended from the east, Armenian workers themselves emigrated westward. In Milan Armenians were called upon to repair the dome of St. Sophia in Constantinople and to build the church of San Satiro. In 1221 St. Trophime in Arles had its main entrance restored by an Armenian mason, and many other churches and cathedrals in France not only bear witness to the popularity of the Armenian style but were actually signed with the special trademarks of Armenian masons. In particular one may mention Sainte-Chapelle in Paris, where in 3 medallions illustrating the story of Noah's ark, the silhouette of Zvartnots cathedral appears complete in every detail.

Today the churches of the Balkan countries display ample evidence of Armenian work. The French archaeologist François Choisy theorizes that the Armenian style of decoration using elaborated interlace carving, accompanied by flowers and leaves, spread along the Dniester and the Vistula to Scandinavia, and thence to Scotland, Ireland, and Normandy, where it was reflected in Romanesque ornament.

Erevan (Yerevan) Population—1,200,000
One of the legends about the derivation of the name Erevan is that it comes from the Armenian "ereval" (or erevangal), meaning "it appears," and was what Noah shouted when he first saw land after the flood, before landing on Mt. Ararat. The story however, gives no explanation as to why Noah shouted in Armenian. Historians have suggested that Erevan was the centre of the Eri tribe.

Erevan is the capital of Armenia and is divided into 2 parts by the river Razdan, which flows down from Lake Sevan. The hilly plateau on the right bank of the river was long completely untouched and has only recently been included in the growing city. The highest part of Erevan stands 1,043 m (3,422 ft) above sea level. Its highest temperature is 40°C (104°F) in summer and its lowest is −20°C (−40°F) in winter.

Mt. Ararat, which the Armenians hold sacred, can be seen from Erevan, although it is on Turkish territory. It stands 5,156 m (16,916 ft) high.

Erevan's founding is lost in the mists of the past. Archaeologists have made some amazing finds just outside the city on Arinberd Hill. The name means "bloody hill," and over the centuries much bitter fighting has taken place here. It is also fairly certain now that this region was the site of Erebuni. Stone slabs have been found in different places in the vicinity, all bearing the same inscription, "Arghishtis, son of Menua, founded the town of Erebuni to the glory of the land of Bianili and to instill fear into his enemies. I have settled 6,600 prisoners from the land of Khatti and the land of Tsupani here."

In the 8th century B.C., Erebuni was an important centre of the Urartu kingdom. It traded actively with Egypt, Greece, and Rome. Among the many items discovered here is an amulet of the Egyptian god Bas, dragon-slayer, guardian of the sleeping, and of female beauty; as well as 68 large ceramic jars (about 2 m/6.5 ft tall), which were used to store grain and wine. Of even greater interest are the ruins of an elegant palace surrounded by a double defence wall. The gateway has been found, and inside are the remains of a temple-tower and a hall in which 30 mighty pillars of pine, rose each from a basalt pedestal. Some of the timber is so well preserved that it could be used today. Parts of the fortress, including the guardhouse, were reconstructed by 1968 to celebrate the 2,750th anniversary of its foundation.

The first written mention of Erevan in Armenian was in the 7th century. In 1387 the town was attacked by Tamerlane's hordes, and from 1500 it had military importance as a frontier town between the rivals Persia and Turkey. The Turkish army occupied it in 1554, and in 1639 the country of Armenia was divided between Turkey and Persia. Erevan fell in the eastern section and so was under Persian rule. Later still, the town changed hands again, and the Turks held it for 10 years. In 1735 the Persians moved back again.

One of the principal aims of the Russo-Persian wars of 1804–13 and 1826–29 was the capture of the Erevan khanate, but the Russian army only moved in in 1827. A special thanksgiving service was held in St. Petersburg, and the keys and flags of the captured fortress were displayed in procession along the streets of the Russian capital. Erevan was the administrative centre and was also of strategic importance.

It was still a typical Asian town with labyrinthine streets and mud-brick houses. Tsar Nicholas I, who visited Erevan in 1837, called it a "clay pot." The first town planning and reconstruction took place in the 1850s. One of the reasons for the rebuilding given by the local authorities was that the twisty streets "make police observation difficult." The best buildings were those put up along Astafyevskaya Street, now Abovyan Street.

The most important item of local industry became the production of vodka and wine. Shustov's famous Russian brandy was produced here, and the production of spirits made up 90 percent of Erevan's industry. The city is still famous for its brandy, perhaps the best in the country. The city's industrial production is now worth 10 million roubles a day.

Erevan itself grew as thousands of Armenians came flocking in as refugees after the Turkish massacres during World War I. In December 1918 representatives of the Entente came to Erevan, and it was recorded that an order was given to move the clocks 50 minutes forward so that local time would correspond to that adhered to by the British fleet. Major-General L. C. Dunsterville, head of the British mission to the Caucasus, also issued an order that the signs in the streets be written in English.

The city's most interesting streets are *Lenin and Ordzhonikidze prospects. Abovyan and Teryan streets* are among the most fashionable, with many theatres, cinemas, hotels, and shops. The centre of Erevan is *Lenin Square*, built as an architectural whole using the Armenian national style of architecture. The most impressive building is *Government House*, designed by academician Alexander Tamanyan, who was also responsible for planning the reconstruction of Erevan in 1924. The clock on the top of Government House chimes the hours and the quarters. Other buildings here are *Trade Union House*, the *post office*, the *Armenia Hotel*, and the *historical museum*. The fountains in the large pool in front of the history museum play to music and changing coloured lights each evening during the summer.

On Lenin Prospect, opposite the History of Erevan Museum, stands the largest *department store*. The building is of an interesting national design, devised by architects Agababyan and Arakyelyan. To the right of Lenin Prospect is the *Komitas Conservatoire*, founded in 1923 and named after the composer Komitas (1869–1935), whose real name was Sogomon Sogomonyan. Looking right along Lenin Prospect to the east, one can see the *Matenadaran Library* on the hillside. There is another good view of the library, along Yuzhny Prospect, from the *50 Years of Soviet Power Monument*.

On the left bank of the river Razdan, on the city side of Victory Bridge, are the Ararat wine cellars, designed by Rafael Israelyan and tastefully decorated with bas-reliefs of ancient wine jars. On the other side of the bridge is the *Ararat brandy distillery*, built in national architectural style by Markaryan in 1953. The *Victory Bridge* itself was built in 1945 by architects Ovnanyan, Mamidzanyan, and Asatryan.

Barekamutsyan ("friendship") Street is in one of the newest areas and is lined with impressive buildings, such as those of the *Supreme Soviet*, the *Academy of Sciences*, and the *House of Architects*.

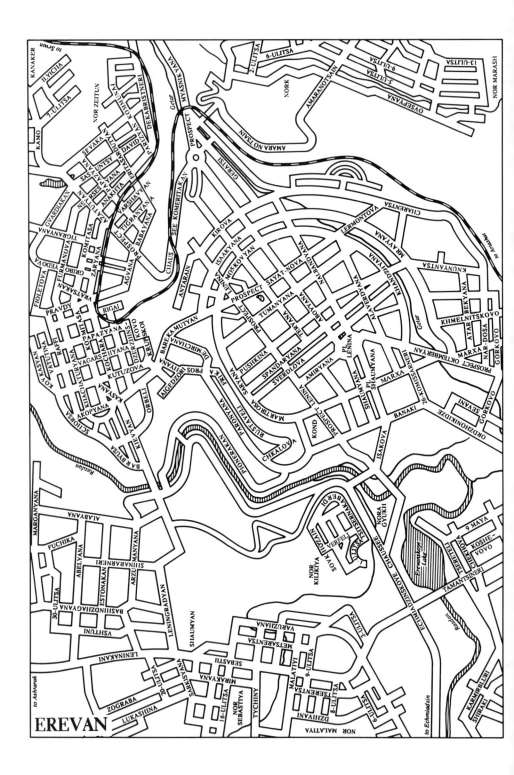

EREVAN

Another rapidly developing part is the Nork region; this is where many immigrants have settled, and it is linked with Kirov Street down below by a funicular railway.

Of the most recent modern buildings in the city, those that catch the eye include the *Palace of Youth* (known as the Corn Cob), *Armenian Contemporary Art Museum* (6 interlocking drums), and the *central post office* (a tall white skyscraper). The underground railway (Metro) links Lenin Square with the railway station in one direction and Druzhba Square in the other. The Druzhba station end is especially well planned, with shops and cafés.

St. Sarkis Church, near Victory Bridge. Built in the 19th century.

St. Oganes's Church, Konda region. Also of 19th-century construction.

Mosque, Lenin Prospect. This was built in the 1660s.

Baptist Church, Nardosa Street 90

Historical Museum, Lenin Square. This museum was founded in 1921 and includes archaeological, ethnographical, and numismatic departments. It has a good display of items discovered in excavations, the oldest of which come from the most ancient town on Soviet territory, Urartu (8th–7th centuries B.C.) and includes the bronze shields of the kings of Urartu. A special hall is devoted to the excavation of Dvin, Armenian capital from the 10th–13th centuries. Among samples of local craftsmanship are 15th–17th-century monastery doors of carved woodwork and a 17th-century throne of the Catholicos, head of the Armenian church. There are also a number of other ecclesiastical items, musical instruments, and carpets. Open 9–4:30; closed Mon.

Revolution Museum, Lenin Square, in the same building as the Historical Museum. This museum was opened in 1960 to commemorate the 40th anniversary of the establishment of Soviet power in Armenia. It illustrates the revolutionary movement in the country before the revolution and the progress after 1920. Open 10:30–4:30; closed Mon.

Erebuni Museum, Erebuni Street 38, at the foot of the hill where the citadel stood. Open 9:30–5; Wed. 11–4:30; closed Mon. Erebuni is the old name for Erevan, and this museum shows the story of the earliest history of Erevan, which was founded on the Hill of Arinberd in 782 B.C. by King Argishtis I of Urartu. A portrait of the king is carved over the museum entrance.

History of Erevan Museum, Lenin Prospect 12, opposite the market. Located in the 17th-century Persian mosque, this museum is divided into 2 departments, pre- and post-revolutionary. It contains Persian arms and flags that were captured here, keys to the town fortress as well as other excavated items. In this building also are the Erevan Planetarium and the Armenian Natural History Museum. Open 11–7; closed Mon.

Matenadaran Library of Ancient Manuscripts, Lenin Prospect 111. This is one of the largest storage places of its kind in the world. It contains over 13,000 items, some of which are 15,600 years old. The building was specially designed in 1959 by the architect Grigoryan. Statues of 6 Armenian philosophers grace the façade and seated at the entrance is a large figure of Mesrob Mashtotz, who created the Armenian alphabet. Most of the manuscripts are of Armenian origin from the 6th to 8th centuries. There are works of historians, mathematicians, astronomers, and philosophers, but there are also manuscripts from Persia and the Arab countries as well as others written in Latin and Greek. Some ancient Greek works are known today only because the Armenian translations survived; one example is Xenon's "Tractate on Nature," which is illustrated by delightful miniatures. There is a book of the gospels written on parchment in 887 and a book of sermons weighing 32 kg (more than 70 lb), which needed 607 calves' skins to complete and which was transcribed in 1205. Here too is the oldest manuscript in Europe to be written on paper, dating from 971.

The nucleus of this collection (and the library's name, which means "manuscript store") came from Echmiadzin Library in 1920, but items from other monasteries and from private collections were added. Open 9:30–4:30; closed Sun. and Mon.

Charentz Literature and Art Museum, Spandaryan Street 1. Here are the personal archives of a number of famous Armenian writers (including those of the poet Eghishe Charentz, after whom it is named) and an exhibition about the Armenian theatre since 53 B.C. Open 11–4:30; closed Wed. (The street is named after Suren Spandaryan, disciple and comrade-in-arms of Lenin.)

Armenian Picture Gallery, Abovyan Street 2 (in the same building as the Historical Museum, but with the entrance from the side). This gallery was opened in 1921 and ranks among the best in the country, after those of Moscow and Leningrad. There are about 16,000 works of art, dating from the early Middle Ages until the present day. There is a section displaying porcelain and a special hall with 17th–19th century east European art. There are paintings by Tintoretto, Rubens, Van Dyck, Jordaens, Delacroix, Courbet, and Fragonard. There is also a fine collection of etchings. Open 10:30–7; closed Mon. Also housed in the gallery is a small *Theatrical Museum*.

Modern Art Museum, Lenin Prospect 7. Shows the work of young Armenian artists. Open 11–6.

Children's Picture Gallery, Abovyan Street 20. Open 10:30–5:30; closed Mon.

Armenian Folk Art Museum, Abovyan Street 64. Open 11–5:30; closed Mon.

Armenian Natural History Museum, Lenin Prospect 12. This is in the building of a 17th-century Persian mosque; here also are the History of Erevan Museum and the Erevan Planetarium. Open 11–5:30; closed Tues.

Karapetyan Geological Museum, Abovyan Street 10. Open 11–3 on Tues. and Fri. only.

Planetarium, Lenin Prospect 12. It is in a 17th-century Persian mosque; here also are the History of Erevan Museum and the Armenian Natural History Museum.

Armenian Economic Achievements Exhibition, Shiraki Street 43. Open 9:30–5:30; closed Tues.

World War II Museum, Akhtanak Park, inside the base of the Mother Armenia monument. Open 11–4; closed Mon.

Khachatur Abovyan Museum, Kanaker Street 2. Open 11–5; closed Mon. The museum is in the house of Khachatur Abovyan (1805–48), author and ethnographer, who created the modern Armenian literary language. He was born in the village of Kanakir and as a child studied at the seminary at Echmiadzin. His chance to better himself came when he was able to accompany a visiting professor from Dorpat (now Tartu in Estonia) University to the top of Mt. Ararat. The professor helped him enter Dorpat University, and after graduation he taught in Triflis. From 1843 he was a school inspector in the Erevan region. One day in 1848, he left his home, never to return; he was lost without trace.

Strangely enough, the same tragic disappearance almost befell the statue in front of his house. It was commissioned in 1913 from Andreas Ter-Marukyan in Paris, and then lay, ready and packed but completely forgotten, in a warehouse for 20 years. It was finally delivered in 1935. Another statue of him stands in Abovyan Street.

Tumanyan Museum, Moskovyan Street 40. Hovannes Tumanyan (1869–1923) was a famous Armenian poet and classical author. The museum was built in 1953 to commemorate the 30th anniversary of his death. The wide flight of steps leading up to the museum has as many steps as there were years of his life. Open 12–7; closed Mon.

Spendiarov Museum, Nalbandyan Street 21. Alexander Spendiarov (also known as Alexander Spendaryan) was a composer.

Saryan Museum, Saryan Street 3. Martiros Saryan (1880–1972) was a well-known Armenian landscape artist who studied in Moscow between 1897 and 1903. His style was much influenced by Cézanne and other French postimpressionists. The museum contains nearly 1,000 of his works, painted during the past 60 years, and is sometimes called the Second Armenian Picture Gallery. Open 12:30–8; closed Thurs. The house and garden next door still belong to the Saryan family, and his son lives there.

Avetik Issahakyan Museum, Plekhanova Street 20. Avetik Issahakyan (1875–1957) was a poet whose first collection was published in 1897. In 1911 he emigrated, but after his return in 1936 he continued to write and is remembered as he is portrayed in the statue on Abovyan Street, slowly walking the streets he loved, leaning on his long cane. The museum is in his house. Open 11–5:30; closed Wed.

Charentz Memorial Museum, Lenin Prospect 17. The poet Eghishe Charentz (1897–1937) lived here on the second floor, and his flat is now a museum. He was shot during the purge of 1937 and was later rehabilitated.

Demirchyan Memorial Museum, Abovyan Street 29. Derenik Demirchyan (1877–1956) was a writer of historical novels.

Statue of David of Sassun, by the railway station. The equestrian statue is of David, a legendary hero immortalised in a national epic, on his magic steed, Dzhelali. The bowls into which water is trickling are specially symbolic of the Armenian people's anger, which will rise and overflow if the freedom and happiness of their country is endangered, at which point David will intervene to crush the enemy. In this statue, David is portrayed as being just about to strike with his sword. The statue by Ervand Kochar stands 12.5 m (41 ft) high on a basalt rock. It was unveiled in 1959.

Vartan Mamikonyan Monument. This statue of the 5th-century hero was also created by Kochar.

Sayat-Nova Monument, in a garden in front of a music school named for him on Lenin Prospect. Arutin Sayadyan (1712–95) was the poet's real name. Arutunyan's portrait of him was unveiled in 1962.

Abovyan Monument, in a small garden at the end of Abovyan Street. The statue of Khachatur Abovyan is by Stepanyan and Tamanyan.

Tumanyan and Spendaryan Monuments, in front of the State Opera House. The monuments to Hovannes Tumanyan, the classical author, and to the composer Alexander Spendaryan are by Sarkisyan and Chubaryan.

Nalbandyan Monument, Nalbandyan Street. Michael Nalbandyan (1829–66) was known as a philosopher, poet, scientist, and revolutionary, and the monument was created by Nikolai Nikogosyan.

Issahakyan Monument, Semi-Circular Boulevard. Avetik Issahakyan was sculpted by Bagdasaryan.

Lenin Statue, Lenin Square. This statue by Sergei Merkurov (who studied under Rodin in Paris in 1909) is of copper with a pedestal of polished Armenian granite. Its total height is 18.5 m (61 ft), and it was unveiled in 1940. In the boulevard behind the monument, 2,750 fountains represent the 2,750 of Erevan's history (celebrated in 1968). In their midst burns an eternal flame to the memory of the heroes of the revolution.

Shaumyan Monument, Shaumyan Square, on the other side of the fountains. Stepan Shaumyan (1878–1918) was an Armenian communist and at one time chairman of the Baku Council. He was the leader of the 26 commissars who were shot, and the statue depicts the moment of his death. It was sculpted in pink granite by Merkurov, stands 3.5 m (11 ft) high, and was unveiled in 1931.

Myasnikyan Bust. There are 4 stelae behind the bust and, behind them, a garden with fountains.

Soviet Armenia Monument, Akhtanak Park. This basalt monument, unveiled in 1970 to commemorate the 50th anniversary of the establishment of Soviet power in Armenia, was designed by

Sarkis Gurzadyan and Jim Torosyan. There are 3 terraces, the lowest serving as a platform for the Erevan-Sevan railway line, the second with a fine view over Erevan and the Ararat Valley for observation purposes, and the third crowned by a rectangular column, 50 m (164 ft) high and bearing on each of its 4 sides the ancient Armenian symbol for eternity. Next to the column stands a block, 30 m (98 ft) square, with a polished stone slab bearing commemorative inscriptions. The Northern Cascade sweeps down from the foot of the column with a waterfall and flights of steps to Tumanyan Street.

Genocide Victims Memorial, overlooking Tsitsernakaberd Park, reached by a long walk from the Sport and Concert Complex. The architects Sashur Kalashyan and Artur Tarkhanyan and the sculptor Hovannes Khachatryan were responsible for the 3 parts of this moving tribute to those who died in the slaughter of 1915, when over one million Armenians perished at the hands of the Turks. The Avenue of Mourning is 110 m (110 yds) long and 10 m (10 yds) wide and is paved with smooth basalt. The wall along the left side bears illustrations in high relief of episodes in the massacre. The avenue leads to the open-air Mausoleum, where 12 stone buttresses form a circle, their sloping sides giving the whole the impression of a truncated pyramid. The buttresses bend in grief, and between them 12 flights of steps lead down to the sunken place 20 m (22 yds) in diameter that they encircle. In the centre burns an eternal flame, and the silence is broken only by funeral music by the Armenian composers Komitas and Yekmalian. The interior surfaces of the buttresses have inscriptions in Armenian, Russian, English, French, Spanish, German, and Arabic, all relating the story of the massacre. Visitors are able to read about it for themselves in this quiet place, rather than listen to the spoken explanation of a guide.

Beyond the mausoleum rises a sharply pointed 40-m (131-ft) black stone spire. It is formed of 2 parts, the larger outside enfolding a second spike, like a shoot of young grass. It is highlighted with lamps inside and symbolises eternal life and brotherhood. From here there is a splendid view of Erevan etched on the grey background of Mt. Ararat, sacred to all Armenians.

Gukasyan Monument, near Abovyan Garden. Gukas Gukasyan was the founder of the Armenian Young Communist League. The sculpture by Sarisyan was unveiled in 1935.

Victory Monument, in Akhtanak Park. This impressive statue of a woman holding a drawn sword is of forged sheet-copper and stands 56 m (184 ft) high on a base of Armenian tufa stone. The architect of the latter was Rafael Israelyan and the sculptor was Ara Arutyunyan. There is a museum inside the base, and on the first floor is the grave of an unknown soldier and an eternal flame. There is an Order of Victory on the main façade, and the emblems of all the regiments of the Soviet army are depicted on the stones.

Stepanyan Monument, in Kirov Children's Park. Nelson Stepanyan was a World War II veteran, twice Hero of the Soviet Union.

Hands of Friendship, On Semi-Circular Boulevard. These marble hands were sent to Erevan as a token of friendship from Catarra in Italy in 1962.

Saryan Monument, near the Opera Theatre. Martiros Saryan was a famous Armenian artist. The monument by Levon Tokmajyan and Artur Tarkhanyan was unveiled in 1986.

Spendiarov Opera and Ballet Theatre, Lenin Prospect 54. This theatre has 1,200 seats. The lake near it was designed by Gevork Mushegyan and, appropriately known as Swan Lake, is the home of black and white swans.

Sundukyan Drama Theatre, Karmir Banaki Street 6. Gabriel Sundukyan (1825–1912) was the founder of Armenian realist drama. This building designed by Rafael Alaverdyan was built in 1966, and the foyer is decorated with a panel by Martiros Saryan. Performances here are in Armenian.

Stanislavsky Drama Theatre, Abovyan Street 7. In this theatre the performances are in Russian.

Erevan Drama Theatre, Isakyaan Street 28

Musical Comedy Theatre, Shaumyan Street 4

Mikoyan Youth Theatre, Moskovskaya Street 35

Chamber Theatre, in a building below Matenadaran

Large Philharmonic Hall, Lenin Prospect 54. The hall seats 1,400.

Small Philharmonic Hall, Abovyan Street 1

Circus, 26-Kommisars Street 5

Tsitsernakaberd Sport and Concert Complex. So high up that it really needs those escalators leading up past the fountains at the entrance. Opened in 1983.

Racecourse, in the village of Verkhny Charbakh. Racing is on Sundays at 3 P.M.

Razdan Stadium, in Razdan Gorge, by the river. This is Armenia's largest stadium, with seats for 75,000.

Republican Stadium, Gnuti Street 65. This one can seat 20,000.

Zoo, Avanskoye Chaussée, 2 km (1 mile) from Erevan. The zoo covers an area of 28 hectares (70 acres) and is open from 8:30–7. The popular elephant Vova came here from Britain, and his keepers are proud of his linguistic skill. He understands English, German, Russian, and Armenian and can obey more than 20 commands in these 4 languages.

Botanical Garden, Avanskoye Chaussée, 3.5 km (2 miles) northwest of Erevan. This park covers 105 hectares (262 acres) and is open 9–5.

Akhtanak (Victory) Park, Kanakev Chaussée. These gardens cover 70 hectares (175 acres) of hilly territory. The Victory Monument, which can be seen from the city and which was built by Rafael Israelyan, is 35 m (115 ft) high. It used to be topped by an enormous 16-m (52-ft) statue of Stalin, but this was demolished and replaced by one of a woman with a sword. The monument is decorated with stone carving in national style and inside it is the Modern Armenia Exhibition.

Komitas Park, Ordzhonikidze Prospect 130. In
the park is a pantheon of outstanding figures in the
world of Armenian literature and art, including
the composer Komitas, poet and translator Ioanes
Ioannisyan, architectural historian Toros Toro-
manyan, actor Hovannes Abelyan (1874–1934),
and Shirvan-Zade.

Komsomol Park, Marx Street 227

26-Komissarov Park, Shaumyan Street 2

Armenia (Intourist) Hotel and Restaurant,
Amiryan Street 1; tel. 52–5393. Intourist office:
tel. 56–0781. Both this hotel and the 2 following
have foreign-currency bars and restaurants with national dishes.

Ani Hotel and Restaurant, Sayat-Novy Prospect 19; tel. 52–3961

Dvin Hotel and Restaurant, Paronyan Street
40; tel. 53–6343. There is a floor show here.

Arabkir Hotel and Restaurant, Komitas
Street 54

Sevan Hotel and Restaurant, Shaumyan Street
10; tel. 536343. There is a floor show here.

Masis Restaurant, Krasnoarmeiskaya Street.
Masis is the Armenian name for Mt. Ararat.

Egnik ("deer") Restaurant, Spandaryan Square

Ararat Restaurant, Sverdlov Street 3

Aragil ("stork") Restaurant, in Victory Park

Zephyr Café, Kievskaya Street

Armenia Café, Lenin Square

Lyre Café, Komitas Street

Anait Café, Nalbandyan Street

Garni Shashlik Bar, Nork region

Cocktail Bar, Abovyan Street 24, in the Armenia Hotel

Foreign-Currency Shops, Amiryan Street 3 and
Sayat-Nova Street 20

Souvenirs, Abovyan Street 24, in the Armenia
Hotel

Shirak Hotel, a 14-storey building in the centre
of town

Intourist organises many interesting excursions
from Erevan, except those to Kumairi. The nearest
trips are those to Zvartnots and Echmiadzin (22
km/14 miles), Metsamor (50 km/31 miles), Oktem-
bryan (70 km/43 miles), Oshakan (35 km/22 miles),
Amberd (70 km/43 miles), and Garni-Gueghard
(38 km/24 miles). Kumairi (q.v.) is 147 km (91
miles) to the west.

Other day trips starting from the main road
northwards, toward Tbilisi, can be made to Tsakhkadzor (70 km/43 miles), Lake Sevan (70 km/43
miles), Dilijan (120 km/75 miles), and Sanahin,
Aghpat, and Odzun (250 km/155 miles).

The monastery of Noravank lies to the east of
Erevan.

Echmiadzin lies 15 km (9 miles) to the west of
the city; Zvartnots is just 2 km (1 mile) before Echmiadzin, but as it is on the left of a dual roadway,
it is perhaps better to visit it on the return journey.

Leave Erevan via Echmiadzin Street in a
southwesterly direction, passing the wine factory
built by German prisoners-of-war and crossing the

bridge with the brandy factory standing opposite
and up the steps. This is also the way to Erevan
Airport. The road passes Erevan Sea on the left
and the 15-Kvartal region (known locally as Bang-
ladesh) on the right.

Echmiadzin Population—30,000

The Middle Araxes valley has a number of ancient
sites that at different periods of Armenia's chequered history served as her capital. Chief among
these is today's Echmiadzin, no longer a capital
but still, since the 14th century, the residence of
the Supreme Catholicos of the Armenian Church.
At the end of the 3rd century B.C. a settlement
called Vardlesavam was established here. Later its
name was changed to Vagarshapat, but the story
of Echmiadzin really has its beginnings in Rome.
When the Roman emperor Diocletian was seeking
a bride, he chose as fairest in the land a Christian
girl called Rhipsime. She refused him because he
was a pagan and fled to Armenia with a number
of other Christians. They sought refuge in the vineyards of Vagarshapat and preached their religion
there. Tridates III was Armenia's ruler at that time,
and the Roman emperor asked him to send Rhipsime back, but Tridates himself was also eager to
marry the beautiful maiden. Again she refused, for
he too was a pagan. In anger he had her and her
friends driven from the palace grounds and stoned
to death. This, however, is not the end of the story,
for Tridates went out of his mind and believed
himself to be a wild boar. Help was sought from a
certain prisoner named Gregory, who not only
cured the tsar's madness but also converted him to
Christianity. Thereupon this was adopted as the
state religion, and chapels were built to commemorate the untimely deaths of Rhipsime and Gayane,
one of the girls martyred with her.

On the eastern outskirts of the town of Echmiadzin, opposite a wine factory, stands *Rhipsime
Cathedral* (618 A.D.), so that you pass it on the
right on your way to Shogakat Cathedral (see
below). A small chapel was built to mark the place
where Rhipsime was executed in the 4th century,
but this was pulled down at the beginning of the
7th century on the order of Catholicos Komitas,
and the present cathedral was built instead. It is a
classical example of an Armenian church, roofed
in stone and with a central cone. The red stone
belfry is under restoration, and one of the old bells
is to be rehung. The marble tombs by the entrance
door belong to 2 Catholikoses. Inside a small, sloping passage leads down from the left of the altar to
the crypt where Rhipsime's tomb is, under the side
altar in the northeastern corner of the cathedral.
The old mud wall in front of the cathedral remains
from a fortress. The cathedral itself is open for
services.

Shogakat Cathedral, a little farther west from
Rhipsime Cathedral; turn right onto Dmitrova
Street from Myasnikyan Street. Built in 1694, also
to commemorate the virgin martyrs and replacing
a 7th-century church. Although built much later
than the other cathedrals, it is nevertheless one of

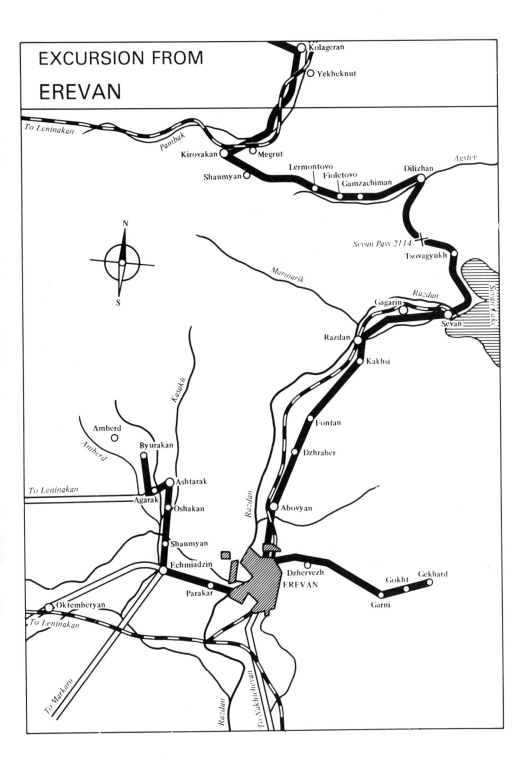

EXCURSION FROM

EREVAN

the finest examples of Armenian ecclesiastical architecture. Shogakat means "ray" and is derived from the story that a ray of light was said to have fallen on the broken bodies. Like Rhipsime Cathedral, there are again 2 marble tombs in the porch, and a bell is also to be rehung in the belfry. It is also open for services.

Gregory, later canonised and thereafter known as St. Gregory the Enlightener, and Tsar Tridates III literally had to fight to convert the people from paganism. Very often the splendid new churches were built over pagan temples to gods of fire, water, and other popular deities. It is said that St. Gregory had a vision of Christ descending to the earth, and on the spot he struck with a golden hammer, an image of a church appeared. It was in this place in 303 A.D. that St. Gregory founded Echmiadzin Cathedral, its name meaning "the Descent of the Only Begotten," to commemorate the conversion of the tsar and his people.

The cathedral stands to the right of the main road, Araratyana Street, in the centre of the town. Under the main altar is a room containing a fire-worshipping altar from pagan times. Other traces of paganism can be found in some of the rites of the Armenian church. For example, it is still customary to make sacrifices, and in the inner courtyard of Echmiadzin Cathedral, there is a place where sheep, lambs, cocks, and doves used to be slaughtered, but this spot has now been transferred to Gayane Cathedral.

The original stone building of the cathedral, which had wooden partitions inside, was burned and later rebuilt in 483 by Prince Vagan Mamikonyan. It has been rebuilt and indeed remodelled repeatedly since then, but the present ground plan dates from the 7th century. The 17th-century murals were painted by Nagash Ovnatan. The main altar used to be a 4th-century one of wood, but the present marble altar was installed in 1955. The 18th-century mother-of-pearl throne was a gift from the Armenian community in Izmir, Turkey, while the wooden one was presented by Pope Innocent XII. The belfry over the main entrance to the cathedral was constructed in 1653, and the sacristy, now housing the treasury and open as a museum, was added behind the choir in 1869.

The monastic museum was built in 1869 and is indeed a real treasury of church vessels, silver and gold work, jewellery, and embroidery. The museum also lays claim to a number of sacred relics, including a piece of the Cross, a piece of Noah's ark in a golden case, relics of St. Gregory the Enlightener and of the first Catholicos who died in the 4th century, and the lance that pierced the body of Christ, long preserved in Gueghard Monastery (see below, p. xxx.). Also in the museum are illuminated manuscripts and miniatures and a famous collection of coins.

The monastery pond was made in the mid-19th century and is 6 m (20 ft) deep. It was used for irrigation but now serves as a vast pool for water sports, including water polo and boating. Other monastery buildings surround the cathedral.

The old seminary (chemaran) stands inside the monastery wall, to the right. It was built in 1874 as the first seminary in Armenia. Among its better-known graduates are the poet Avetik Isahakyan, the composer Komitas, and the statesman Anastas Mikoyan. The building is now used as a school, which is known as the Mikoyan School. The seminary itself has been housed since 1945 in the 1908 building that used to be the manuscript library. It is attended by 40 students, who follow a 6-year course. Other important buildings include the printing works, offices, and behind the cathedral, the episcopal palace, built at the beginning of this century but decorated with stonework using classic motifs. The Supreme Catholicos, Vazgen I, resides here. His palace has an impressive throne room with finely ornamented walls and ceilings, but it is not open to the public.

Gayane Cathedral is in the southern part of the town, near the monastic pond and dominating the ecclesiastical cemetery. Beyond the main cathedral, turn right from Araratyana Street onto Komeritmiutyan Street. Gayane Cathedral was built in A.D. 630 and, like Rhipsime Cathedral, stands on the site of a commemorative chapel. In 1652 restoration work was carried out, and in 1683 a gallery was added in front of the entrance, to house the tombs of the monks, but its simplicity is unspoiled. Opposite the entrance is a sacrificial block with 2 holes to collect the blood of the lambs and birds still slaughtered there today.

Mariyan-Astvatsatsin (Virgin Mary) Church, behind the shopping centre

Ioanes Ioannisyan House Museum, in a quiet garden behind the shopping centre. Open 10–5; closed Sun. The poet and translator Ioanes Ioannisyan (1864–1929) was born here. He came from a peasant family, but when he was 12 years old he set out for Vladikavkaz and from there went by train to Moscow, where he finished his schooling. He returned and was married in St. Mary's Church, just near his home. There is a bust of Ioannisyan in the garden.

The 25-m (82-ft) *obelisk* commemorates the Russian-Persian war of 1827 and bears the inscription: "In memory of Russian and Armenian soldiers killed in battle and as a token of Russian-Armenian friendship."

Monument to Genocide Victims of 1915

World War II Memorial, to the right of Myasnikyan Street. Commemorating townsmen who lost their lives, the complex includes an eternal flame, an obelisk, and a bas-relief.

Komitas Bust, to the right of Myasnikyan Street

Restaurant, on the 4th floor of the shopping centre

Vagarshapat Café, opposite Rhipsime Cathedral

Tsitsernak (foreign-currency) Shop. Open 10–6; closed Mon.

Echmiadzin Shopping Centre, to the right of Myasnikyan Street

Today in Echmiadzin there are a dozen or so industrial enterprises, producing plastics, agricultural machinery, and wine and canning fruit.

Zvartnots

13 km (8 miles) from Erevan, and 2 km (1 mile) east of Echmiadzin. The village lies on the left of a dual roadway and is easier to visit on the return journey from Echmiadzin. Located here is the site of the 3-storey circular Cathedral of St. Gregory, built in 641–661 by Catholicos Nerses III Shinogh. The building collapsed as the result of an earthquake in 930 and was never restored, but now rebuilding plans are under way, and the first floor has already been reconstructed. 4 semicircular apses form the inner wall, and there was a crypt under the altar. There are traces of other square buildings and rooms surrounding the cathedral.

The historian Moses of Khorene mentioned in his writings that construction of the original cathedral was almost completed by the time of a visit by the Byzantine emperor Konstantine III in 652. Konstantine was present when the cathedral was consecrated, and he was so struck by the beauty of the building that he ordered the architect Ioann to accompany him to Constantinople to build a similar edifice there. Ioann, however, died on the course of journey, but he is depicted on the richly decorated outer walls of Zvartnots Cathedral. It was certainly reputed to have been more beautiful than any church then in existence; perhaps in proof of this, in the Sainte-Chapelle in Paris, there is a stone relief that shows Noah's ark and the flood, with Mt. Ararat and Zvartnots Cathedral in the background.

In 1901–4 the architect Tormanyan made a study of the ruins and constructed a model of the original cathedral. This can now be seen in the *museum*, which was organised to the south of the ruins in 1938. Also on display in the museum are items discovered during excavations on this site. Other ruins here belong to the Palace of the Catholicos. The large *pool* on the eastern side of the territory was used for adult baptisms, while behind the chancel apse stands the monolithic *stone font*, which was reserved for infants. There still exists a well 49 m (161 ft) deep with its sides faced with stone.

Tormanyan's Bust, by the ruins

Zvartnots Café. Open in summer only.

Metsamor

This is 55 km (34 miles) from Erevan, beyond Echmiadzin along the Oktemberyan road, to the northeast of Lake Aigerlich. The two Metsamor Hills, about 28 m (92 ft) high, stand in the flat and, in some places, boggy valley of the river Metsamor (Sevdzhur). This was the ancient home of the Armenian tribe and so is regarded as the birthplace of the Armenian people.

In 1965 an archaeological expedition discovered a Bronze Age settlement here, probably the centre of a mining industry. In addition, 5 cultural layers of the 3rd–1st centuries B.C. were unearthed as well as finds dating from the 12th–13th centuries A.D., 23 copper-smelting furnaces and an ancient observatory were found, and it is supposed that there was a town here.

Local Museum. The archaeological finds are on display here.

Oktemberyan (Until 1932, Sardarabad; pronounced Sardarapat in Armenian) Population— 30,000

Situated 70 km (43 miles) from Erevan, beyond Echmiadzin and to the west of Lake Aigerlich, in the foothills of Mt. Aragats. The road there runs through level plain with poplars, fields, and canals; the mountains are on either side. At the beginning of this century, Sardarapat was no more than a village of 500 inhabitants.

Its rapid development was due to its favourable situation at the crossing of the railway line and the main road. Local industry is mainly concerned with the processing of agricultural produce; local factories make wine, brandy, vegetable and fruit juices, and geranium-oil perfume. There are also machine-building and cotton-ginning plants. Oktemberyan was proclaimed a town in 1947.

The Sardarapat Steppe (now called the Armavir Steppe) was the site of the Battle of Sardarapat in May 1918. Ottoman Turkey was dissatisfied with the territories ceded to it according to the Treaty of Brest-Litovsk. While negotiations were in progress in Batumi between Turkey and Transcaucasia, Turkish forces launched a 3-pronged attack. From 22 until 26 May, Armenian civilians joined the ranks of the Armenian Army Corps and together fought the Turks in defence of Erevan, the last town still held by the Armenians. The Armenian victory at Sardarapat, despite the defenders being outnumbered 2 to 1, put an end to the Turkish territorial claims, and the Republic of Armenia was organised (although it remained in existence for only 2 years). A peace treaty was signed between Turkey and Armenia on 4 June 1918, a week after the battle.

The *memorial park* was laid out in 1968 to commemorate the 50th anniversary of the Battle of Sardarapat. It covers 20 hectares (50 acres) on the level ground on the left bank of the Araks where the battle took place. To reach the park, cross the railway line and go southward, toward Ararat. The two winged bulls at the entrance to the park symbolise the firmness and strength of the Armenian forces. A 35-m (115-ft) belfry with 12 bells symbolises the call to battle. The arches are designed like the tombstones of mediaeval warriors, and between 10 and 5 the bells chime at each hour, playing mediaeval Armenian melodies. Above the fountain at the base of the belfry is the inscription: "Immortal glory to those sons who lost their lives defending their motherland!" The 5 stone eagles standing in an impressive line symbolise the soldiers, and behind the last of them is the outline of Mt. Ararat. They lead to a curved, red wall, 7 m (23 ft) high and 55 m (60 yds) long, covered with bas-reliefs depicting episodes in the battle.

Through an arch in the wall a path leads on to the *Ethnographical Museum*, open 11–4:30; closed Mon. The museum, surely among the most beautiful structures of the twentieth century, was designed by Rafael Israelyan, who is known for the care with which he places each stone. It was opened in 1978 and is well worth a visit, for its architecture and layout as well as for the items on display. From inside, 2 windows facing in opposite directions look out onto the 2 mountains—Ararat to the south and Aragats to the north. It is only 7 km (4 miles) to the Turkish border from here and 43 km (27 miles) to Ararat.

Ashtarak

This town, formerly Agagatsont, is 35 km (22 miles) from Erevan, in a northwesterly direction. The landscape on either side of the road along the southern foothills of Mt. Aragats is semidesert, but now irrigation systems are changing its appearance. New villages with vineyards and orchards have appeared in recent years.

The name Ashtarak means "tower," perhaps referring to a temple-tower of a cult of dragons that existed here in pre-Christian times. It is one of the most ancient settlements in Armenia, with numerous historical monuments and its own traditions. It was the birthplace of Nerses Ashtarakets (1770–1857), an outstanding political and social activist, influential in uniting Armenia with Russia.

The town remained a green spot while the rest of the area was still treeless and arid. The oldest part of Ashtarak is hidden by thick gardens on the high right bank of the river Kazakh. Traffic used to cross the river by a 3-arched bridge of tufa, which was built in the 17th century, but now there is a new bridge 1 km (about .5 mile) below it, allowing the town to spread onto the left bank of the Kazakh ravine. Ashtarak has long been known as a centre of viniculture and wine making. Wines produced by local factories have won several gold medals and first prizes at international contests, particularly the Oshakan and Ashtarak sherry-type wines.

Pokaberd Fortress was first mentioned in the 9th century. The ruins of the fortress walls on the western side date from the 10th–11th centuries.

Tsiranavor ("crimson") Church (Church of Our Lady), on the bank of the river Kazakh. This basilica dates to the 5th century. It is divided into 3 naves by the 4 columns inside. The building used to be surrounded by towering walls, and it served as a fortress. Services were held in the church until the roof collapsed in 1815. Today it is in a very dilapidated state.

Karmarvor Chapel (Red Chapel), in the southeastern part of town. Built in the 7th century, this small (6 by 7.5 m/7 by 8 yd) mausoleum with its unique helmet-shaped roof has its original tiles still in place. An inscription running along its walls tells of the villagers who donated money for its construction and about the difficulties encountered in building a canal, and another nearby house which has not survived. There are many of the carved

stelae known as "khachkars" around the chapel, and the territory is surrounded by a wall dating from 1325. *The Canal* is from the 12th century.

Spitakavor Chapel (White Chapel), near Tsiranavor Church, on the bank of the river Kazakh. Built in the 13th century. Among the khachkars surrounding the building, the most interesting is *Tsak-Kar* (Holy Stone). The inscription on it explains that it was set up by a priest in 1268. From it a road leads to *Mugninsky Monastery*, 2 km (1 mile) away.

Marine (Mariam) Church, in the northwestern part of town. It was built in 1281. Neglected for many years, it was restored in 1838, at which time the belfry was added. Further restoration began in 1907, as well as the foundation of another, larger church beside it. The new wall rose to a height of 4 m (13 ft), but the project was never completed.

13th-century Bridge. Only ruins remain.

Mugninsky Monastery, near the town. Built in the 17th century.

Perch Proshyan House-Museum was the home of Perch Proshyan (Ovanes Ter-Arakelyan; 1837–1907), an Armenian writer who was born and lived here.

Sagmosavank, near the town. Built in the 13th century.

Ovannavank, near the town. From the 5th–13th centuries.

Oshakan

A little downstream from Ashtarak but already linked to it by new buildings is the village of Oshakan.

Oshakan was the home of Mesrob Mashtotz (361–440), a monk from Echmiadzin who in A.D. 404 invented the Armenian alphabet, which is still in use today. During the 35 years of his life Mashtotz was engaged in translations (including that of the Bible), and organised and taught in Armenian schools. His grave, known as the Translator's Grave, is in the crypt of a church, which was rebuilt in the 19th century. The crypt over his grave is now a memorial museum.

Memorial Obelisk, just outside Oshakan. This is made of basalt and is in the form of an open book, upon which the Armenian alphabet is carved. It was erected in 1962 to commemorate the invention of the Armenian alphabet in A.D. 404.

Morik (Mavriky) Pillar is from the 7th century.

The Five-arched Bridge was built across the river Kasakh in 1706.

Obelisk, on the common grave of Russian and Armenian soldiers killed in 1827, during the Russian-Persian war.

Amberd Fortress is 40 km (25 miles) from Erevan, past Ashtarak along the main road toward Kumairi, then following a right turn at Agarak, into the valley of the river Amberd. The asphalt road passes the village of Byurakan, where the astrophysical observatory is. 3 km (2 miles) from Byurakan is Antarut, the name meaning "forestry." It got its name from the very beautiful oak forests here. The fortress is 10 km (6 miles) beyond Byurakan, but the road stops before it gets there, and the last 3 km (2 miles) of the climb must be made on foot.

Byurakan
The name means "1,000 springs." Byurakan is situated on the beautiful southern slopes of Mt. Aragats, more than 3,000 m (9,840 ft) above sea level. The *astrophysical observatory* here belongs to the Armenian Academy of Sciences. It was built in 1946.

Amberd Fortress
Amberd Fortress stands upon the southern slope of Mt. Aragats, at a height of 2,300 m (7,546 ft) above sea level. It is an outstanding example of Armenian secular architecture and, as it was protected by thick walls and placed almost inaccessibly on the crags overlooking the 2 deep ravines of Arshakhyan and Amberd, it rebuked nearly every attack launched upon it during more than 7 centuries.

The fortress is believed to have been founded in the 7th century A.D. during the rule of the Kamsarakan princes. It was rebuilt 4 centuries later by Vakhram Vachutian Pakhlavuni, one of Armenia's most famous warriors. He added thick stone walls and 3 bastions along the ridge of the Arkhashyan ravine, where there were no natural defences. The church inside the fortress was built at the same time, as is proved by the date, 1026, inscribed over its door.

Later on, Amberd was taken over by Armenia's ruling princes, the Bagratids, and made into their most important forepost against enemies from the south. It was taken in the 11th century by the Seljuk Turks, but in 1200 Zahare Mkharadzeli, who served Queen Tamara of Georgia, drove out the Turks and flew Tamar's banner from the main bastion of the fortress. In the 13th century, Amberd was taken by the Mongol invaders and ravaged by a fire, which must have raged over the entire territory surrounding it.

Apart from the remains of the walls and towers and the church, there are the ruins of a bathhouse and parts of a secret passage and a water-supply system to be seen.

Garni
It is 28 km (17 miles) in a northeasterly direction from Erevan to Garni, and 6 km (4 miles) further along the same road to Gueghard. Leave Erevan along Tbiliskoye Chaussée, following the signs to "Gekhard" (sic).

The main road reaches the high bank of the river Azat, a short but rapid and noisy tributary of the Araks. Garni *fortress* was built in the 3rd century B.C. on its triangular plateau. It is one of the most famous fortresses of ancient Armenia and is mentioned by Tacitus. It was virtually impregnable, and a number of Armenian kings took refuge here during their civil wars.

Garni was first destroyed by the Romans in the year A.D. 59. However, Tridates I defeated the Romans and then travelled to Rome to receive a crown from Nero and a compensation of 150 million dinars. It is said that the proud king refused to part with his sword, as was demanded by etiquette in the presence of the Roman emperor. He restored the fortress and on a plateau high above built the *Temple of the Sun*, which was completed in A.D. 66; a Greek inscription found during excavations says that the king built a palace for his queen and restored the citadel in the 11th year of his reign. 50 m/yd northwest of the temple are the remains of the *royal baths* (1st–3rd centuries A.D.). These were in Roman style and had separate rooms with cold, warm, and hot water, while a system of ceramic pipes circulated hot air under the floors. A priceless piece of mosaic flooring has been discovered in the baths. Multicoloured local stones were crushed and set into patterns featuring sea gods, fish, and mythological creatures. On one piece of mosaic (almost 3 sq m/32 sq ft) are the figures of Oceanus and Thalassa (the sea). Above their heads, a Greek inscription reads: "We worked without pay." Its meaning is still uncertain; some ascribe it to the artists, who were proud to work for art's sake, while others explain it as a comment upon the work of those at sea.

After their conversion to Christianity at the beginning of the 4th century, the Armenian rulers used the temple as their summer residence, and it was known as the Cool Palace. King Khosrov often stayed here, as this valley was his favourite hunting ground. Garni was again destroyed when the Arabs conquered Armenia but was rebuilt at the beginning of the 10th century. Its final destruction came in 1638 during the Turkish invasion, and then a violent earthquake in 1679 buried what remained of it.

Since excavations were started here in 1949, the fortress walls and 14 towers have been unearthed. Among the mediaeval buildings of Garni are the *ruins* of a circular, 4-altared church (7th century) and houses of the 12th–17th centuries. Reconstruction work upon the temple was completed in 1976, and now it stands, once again surrounded by 24 Ionic columns.

Gueghard
6 km (4 miles) farther along the same road from Garni. First called Airivank, or the Monastery of the Caves, the history of this place probably goes back to pre-Christian times, but nothing has survived from then except perhaps the small cave-chapel to the west of the monastery.

The present buildings here date from the 10th–13th centuries, when the *monastery* was renamed Gueghard, meaning "lance" in Armenian. The name comes from the legendary lance, said to be the one used to pierce the body of Christ, which was long kept here but is now in the museum of Echmiadzin Cathedral. Besides the main church with its impressive narthex, and the other monastic buildings, there are 3 churches here cut into the solid rock. The main church is the oldest building in the complex. It was constructed in 1215 and belonged to the princes Ivane and Zahare Mkharadzeli. They were brave and talented warriors who served Queen Tamara of Georgia. They won most of Armenia back from the Seljuk Turks, were crowned kings of Armenia, and established the Zakharides dynasty. The most interesting buildings date from a few years later, after Prince Prosh had purchased Gueghard from the Zakharides.

Avazan Church (1283) is carved right into the rock and is an incomparable work of art. It leads to a rectangular portico, believed to have served as the Proshyan family mausoleum, and then to another church deeper in the rock. In 1288 a columned portico was carved in the upper part of the rock. One large bas-relief is thought to be the Proshyan coat-of-arms; it depicts the head of an ox with two lions tied to ropes, while between the lions is an eagle with a lamb in his claws. Other bas-reliefs represent the sun, a mythical bird called Sirin with the head of a woman, and figures stemming from the folk art of pagan times. Connoisseurs say that the rock churches are best seen when the sun is directly above the window in the cupola; then the stone figures come to life and begin to move, the lions show their teeth, and the eagle spreads his wings. They are, however, very impressive at any time of day.

Inside the rock church to the northwest of the main building, a clear spring wells up from the ground; it is said that in pre-Christian times this was the site of a temple to the god of water.

Along the southern and eastern walls of Guegh-

ard Monastery, high above the valley, are *mediaeval communal buildings* and dwellings, which are well preserved. The monastery withstood all manner of assaults over a period of 700 years. Its walls stood firm and in times of danger sheltered many scholars, so that it was revered throughout Armenia as one of the country's greatest spiritual and cultural centres.

Other excursions from Erevan go northward along M-24, the main road toward Tbilisi. They take in Tsakhkadzor, Sevan and Lake Sevan, Dilijan, Agartsin and Goshavank, and from Dilijan: Kirovakan, Uzunlar (Odzun), Sanahin, and Akhpat. Noravank Monastery lies to the east of Erevan.

Tsakhkadzor

Tsakhkadzor ("valley of flowers") is situated 70 km (43 miles) from Erevan and 3 km (2 miles) from Razdan, in Marmarik Valley (the river Marmarik is a tributary of the river Razdan).

The remains of *Kecharis Monastery*, typical of 11th–13th-century monasteries, is situated at the edge of some woods. The church nearest the road, *St. Gregory's* (with a flattened dome) dates from 1033, and beside it stands the small 11th-century *Church of St. Nshan*, with its cone-roof intact. The largest building is *St. Lusavorich Cathedral* (katoghike), founded in 1003, but now without its dome. The refectory that was added to the entrance in the 12th–13th centuries has wine jugs carved over a narrow window. Behind St. Gregory's are several carved stone monuments and tombs. A little

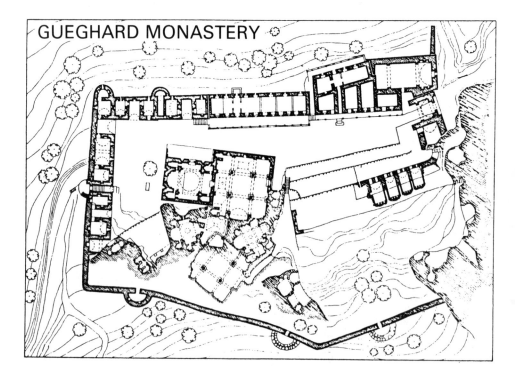

GUEGHARD MONASTERY

way off, farther up the road, is the *Arutyuna (Resurrection) Church*, built in 1220 by Asan and Ruzukan. There are intricate plaited carvings around the windows and an interesting pie-crust trim at the vertical corners of the walls.

Tsakhkadzor is a popular place for skiing, with rest homes, Young Pioneer camps, facilities for both winter and summer sports, and cablecars going up to the top of Mt. Tehenis. Tsakhkadzor has been used for Olympic training and is one of the most important sports centres in the country.

"Giving the Sun as a Present" (Daryaschaya Solntse) Monument

Sevan

The town of Sevan is 75 km (47 miles) from Erevan.

It was formerly a village known a Elenovka. Like Semyonovka just before the lake, it was founded by a group of Molokans in the late 19th century. These people were driven from the central part of Russia at the beginning of the 19th century for their heretical beliefs. They were ordered to settle permanently in the lands beyond the Caucasus mountains. They were mainly occupied with raising potatoes, grain, sunflowers, and cattle.

It stands at the 204-km mark and is a lakeshore resort. It is 1,900 m (6,230 ft) above sea level and enclosed by the Tsamkaberdsky and Gegamsky ranges.

In 921 Ashot II Erkat led his Armenians to victory over Arab invaders in a battle at Sevan.

Airavank Monastery, built on a rocky cape close to the water. Although the date of its foundation is unknown and it is 25 km (16 miles) distant from Sevan Monastery, it resembles the latter in many respects.

Ruins of 9th-century Fortress

Sevan Hydrometeorological Observatory

Monument. To Civil War victims.

Akhtamar Intourist Hotel and Restaurants, high on a cliff, up to the left, overlooking the lake. This has a carpark and three good restaurants. The place is famed for "ishkhan" (king trout), a variety of salmon-trout found only in Lake Sevan. There is another good restaurant nearer the monastery, which is appropriately called *Ishkhan Restaurant*.

Sevan (Intourist) Motel and Restaurant, 75 km (47 miles) from Erevan; tel. (822230) 4213

Motel, on the lake shore. Opened in 1986.

Cafés. Many and various

Motorboats. Near the hotel, boats can be hired for trips on the lake or for fishing for the same fine trout that is served in the restaurants.

Service Station and Filling Station, by the motel

Lake Sevan

70 km (43 miles) northeast of Erevan. Lake Sevan, or Gokcha, is often called Armenia's pearl. It is certainly a lake of great beauty and has served as the theme for many songs and poems. Gorky likened it to a piece of the sky amidst the mountains, and the Armenian writer Marietta Shaginyan

(1888–1981) called it a "blue flame." It lies 1,916 m (6,286 ft) above sea level and is surrounded by high ranges. To the northeast are the Arenguniysky and Sevansky ranges (2,500 m/8,200 ft); to the southwest, the Gegamsky (3,600 m/11,810 ft); to the south, the Vardenissky (2,800 m/9,190 ft); and to the northwest, the Pambaksky Range. It is one of the largest mountain lakes in the world. It is 75 km (47 miles) long and avearges 25 km (16 miles) wide. In fact, there are really 2 lakes, Large Sevan and Small Sevan, connected by a strait 8.5 km (5 miles) wide. 28 rivers run into it, but only the Razdan flows out. The water is fresh and the lake navigable. A variety of fish live in it, including trout.

On the southeastern shore of the lake, near the village of Zod, gold has been found. There were gold mines here from the 5th century on.

The name Sevan comes from the Urartu word "siunn" or "shana," meaning "the country of the lake," and in biblical times it was also called the Sea of Gegham or Gekcha.

King Argishtis I of Urartu, ruler of Tushpatown, decided to seize the enigmatic lake country of Siunna for himself. He heard from his priests that a giant bowl of water was hidden in the Gegham Mountains and that the country there was inhabited by rich tribes who had fine cattle and innumerable horses. In addition it was said that their horses were sea-horses, far superior to ordinary steeds, and able to cover a 3-month journey in a single day, fly, and even give wise advice. Kiehuni, the fortress of the cattle breeders, stood on a hill and was surrounded by thick walls. There were many varied urban buildings around the fortress. Most were spacious, housing families of 30 or 40 persons each. The surprise attack mounted by the Urartu warriors met with no resistance. They destroyed the houses and killed many people, but took no time to search the town carefully. A variety of armaments, household utensils, jewellery, and even carts buried alongside their owners in the cemetery were never found.

To commemorate this victory, the ruler of Urartu ordered an inscription to be made, listing all his titles and victories. This monument was discovered 2,800 years later in the village of Lchashen, which stands on the site of Kiehuni.

Later Rusa I also visited the town with his warriors. He built 2 new towns and 2 fortresses here, also leaving an inscription which was deciphered 2,600 years later. When the waters of Lake Sevan rose and covered the ancient towns and fortresses, the wealth of the cattle breeders, as well as all traces of the early invaders were lost.

In recent years Lake Sevan lost much of its water because of the number of power stations and irrigation canals built on the river Razdan, which is fed by the lake. The receding waters left parts of the bottom of the lake exposed, and digging revealed evidence of much human activity. Since 1951 archaeological excavations have resulted in a number of important discoveries, including fortresses, burial grounds, and whole settlements, as well as a wealth of ancient treasure dating from the early 3rd millenium B.C. to the end of the 11th century. These include carts and chariots, wooden articles, and ceramics. The wooden items are of particular interest, as these decay unless they are kept either perfectly dry or completely immersed in water, as these were. Some of the vessels are covered with fine drawings, coloured in 3 unfaded shades, which resemble Etruscan ware.

The oldest items, which were found about 5 m (16 ft) below the ruins of houses, were shiny black vessels with finely carved decorations (the secret of how the colour was produced has yet to be solved), spiral bracelets made of copper, rings, and millstones. All these have been dated as from the Aeneolothic period, 2,500 B.C.

Today, to save Lake Sevan from drying out further, a tunnel is being drilled in the basalt rocks to divert the waters of the river Arpa into the lake.

Urartu remains have also been discovered along the lake shores, including some ancient inscriptions. It is here that the name of "Suinia," meaning "lake" or "basin," was found inscribed. Some think "Sevan" came from this, while others think it came from the monastery built of black tufa; called Sev Vank ("black monastery") in Armenian. The road following the line of the lake shore, stretches east out to the peninsula where *Sevan Monastery* is situated.

In 862 Armenia was ruled by Ashot I Bagratuni, founder of the Bagratids dynasty. At that time Armenia was a part of the Arab khalifate, whose power was only imposed in collecting taxes. Local princes appointed by Arab vice-regents were the actual rulers. Ashot I was given the title of "prince over princes" and was only later crowned king. The monastery is one of the surviving monuments of his time. It was built in A.D. 874 upon the special order of the king and his daughter, Mariam. The princess, who was married to Prince Gabur of Syunia, was a faithful believer. Although at that time Armenia was part of the Arab khalifate, the monastery is free from the slightest influence of Arabian architecture. It was built as a fortress on an island at the northwest corner of the lake. As it was always such a safe place, all the most precious and ancient ecclesiastical books and documents were collected and stored. It is recorded that when, in the last century, the Katolikos Simeon wanted to inspect the library, the abbot was so ashamed of the tattered and faded collection that he allowed only the best and cleanest copies to be shown to his superior, loading the rest onto a boat and sinking it into the lake. Gradually the waters of the lake receded, so now the monastery stands on a high peninsula. Originally there were 3 churches, all built in the usual cruciform pattern with a central cupola. The larger of the 2 that survive, both built of blackish stone, is *Arakelots' (Holy Apostles') Church*. A wooden porch built on the western side and embellished with uniquely carved wooden pillars now stands in the Historical Museum in Erevan. Carved by the builders around the drum of the church appears the first written record of local history. The church itself is built of unpolished slabs of stone, while the octagonal drum, the cornices, and decorative borders are finely finished. The smaller church is *St. Karapet's*.

Above the monastery, nearer the top of the hill, is *Astavatsatsin Church*, larger than the monastery church and built of more carefully worked stone.

Parvana Restaurant, by the highway at the beginning of the path leading onto the peninsula where the Holy Apostles' Church stands.

Ishkhan ("trout") Restaurant, to the right of the turn to the church.

Dilijan Population—16,000
This resort town, 120 km (75 miles) from Erevan, is situated where 3 beautiful valleys meet, by the Agstev at the point where it is joined by 2 tributaries, the Golovinka and the Dilijanskaya, and from here a road leads through to Kirovakan. There are many curative mineral springs in the vicinity, some similar to those at Vichy in France and some particularly useful in the cure of intestinal diseases and metabolic disorders. The climatic conditions are said to be even better than those at Davos for the treatment of lung diseases.

The territory covered by the town is large and includes the village of Papanino, farther along the Agstev, on the left bank where there are some sanatoria. 2 other villages upstream, Bldan and Shamakhyan, also are considered part of the town. The route through the town goes along Myasnikyan Street. There were armed rebellions here in May and November 1920.

About 6 million bottles of the local mineral water, called "Dilijan," from Bldan are sold each year. Besides the bottling plant, there are factories here for making furniture and carpets.

Local Museum, Myasnikyan Street 28. Open 10–5:30; closed Mon.

Dilijan Hotel and Restaurant, Maxim Gorky Street

Melnitsa ("mill") Restaurant serves Armenian food.

OVK Restaurant, Myasnikyan Street

Café, near the lake. Swans make it even more attractive.

Djukhtakvank Monastery, leave Dilijan via Papanino and go 3 km (2 miles) along the road toward Kirovakan. The monastery, which is empty, was built in the 13th century and consists of the Church of St. George and Church of Our Lady. Its name means "pair" because opposite, on the other side of Bldan Ravine, are the ruins of another monastery, *Matosavank*, dating from the 10th–13th centuries. Here are the remains of a church and a library, both in an abandoned state. Below in the valley are springs, one of which is called Ttoo-Djur, meaning "bitter water."

Garun ("spring") Restaurant, on the way out of town, toward Sevan

Agartsin Hotel and Restaurant, at the 60-km mark, just at the beginning of the Sevan Pass.

The restaurant is known for its good national cuisine.

Agartsin

8 km (5 miles) from Dilijan; a little to the north of the town a left turn leaves the main road and leads through the wooded valley of the Agartsin to a clearing where the ancient buildings of *Agartsin Monastery* stand.

The Armenians say that if there are woods, mountains, and mineral springs in paradise, then paradise must look like the surroundings of Dilijan, and the most picturesque spot near Dilijan is indisputably *Agartsin Gorge*, perhaps loveliest in early autumn, with the last of the summer flowers, and the leaves just beginning to change. The Armenian composer Khachatur Taronatsi chose to live and work here in the 12th century. The monastery, which was the cultural centre of mediaeval Armenia, was no small settlement, judging by the surviving evidence. There are ruins of a kitchen by the refectory and of several little chapels on the territory. There are also a number of khachkars in the long grass; one standing by the southern wall is inscribed "King Smbat" and next to it is one commemorating King Gaghik. As a whole, the complex is a classic excample of mediaeval Armenian architecture. The principal building, *Surb Astvatsatsin (Cathedral of Our Lady)*, founded in 1071 and rebuilt in 1281 with lavish decorations of carved stone, is typical of Armenian ecclesiastical architecture of the period. It is almost an exact copy of the small family *Church of St. Stepanos* standing nearby, which was built of blue basalt in 1244 and has a sundial on is southern wall. *St. Gregory's Church* dates from the 11th century and is probably the oldest building here. It was built of rough-hewn white limestone, following the traditions of secular architecture, repeating and developing the elements of a peasant house. Although it is plain outside, the interior is richly decorated, and symmetry has been sacrificed to make each window frame and arch more beautiful than its neighbour. According to an inscription, Prince Ivane Mkharadzeli added the entrance at the end of the 12th century or the beginning of the 13th. The small basilica nestling against the northern side of the church dates from the 13th century. The architectural characteristics of St. Gregory's appear even more strongly in the *refectory*, beyond the wall, which is generally considered the building most worthy of note in Agartsin. It was built by a talented architect called Minas in 1248, who departed from the usual contemporary style of small buildings with room for only a relatively small number of people at a time. Outside, its lines, excecuted in smooth stone, are simple and unpretentious, but inside its 2 connected halls are splendidly spacious with an ingeniously designed roof support. The impression of space is not due to the height or length of the building (it is no more than 20 m/65 ft long) but, unlike St. Gregory's, to its uncluttered lines and the absence of all decoration inside.

Agartsin was in the territory belonging to the princes Ivane and Zahare Mkharadzeli. Legends tell of vast treasure hidden somewhere in the monastery walls and in the surrounding rocks, one of which is even known as Treasure Rock.

Agartsin Composers' Rest Home, at the southern end of Dilijan, on the right. The buildings can be seen from the main road. Among its visitors have been Shostakovich, Khachaturyan, and Benjamin Britten.

Goshavank

19 km (12 miles) north of Dilijan, and 11 km (7 miles) beyond Agartsin.

The village of Gosh lies beyond Krasnoselsk, a little off the main Erevan-Tbilisi road. It is 1,250 m (4,100 ft) above sea level and in its centre is *Nor-Ghetik Monastery* or *Goshavank (Gosh Academy)*, which was founded by Mkhitar Gosh (1133–1213), an Armenian ruler who was also a politician, thinker, and poet, the author of the first Armenian book of law and of a number of fables and parables. In the 13th century, the academy grew so that the monastery became a major Armenian cultural centre. From here historians, musicians, and theologians graduated. The main building is the *Astvatsatsin Church (Church of the Virgin)*, built by Gosh in 1191–96. On its southern side is another church, built in 1208–41 and dedicated to St. Gregory the Illuminator, but perhaps better known still is the tiny *Chapel of St. Gregory*, built by Prince Gregor Tkha in 1237. He much admired the churches and palaces of the ancient Armenian capital of Ani (now in Turkey), and so he made sure that the stone portal and arches of this chapel were most richly decorated and that, in spite of its diminutive size, it gave the impression of a much larger, 2-storey structure. On the other side of the Church of the Virgin is a 13th-century *library* with a cross-vaulted roof to which a belfry was added in 1291. Other buildings include a *small chapel* dedicated to Rhipsime. (For the legend about her, see Echmiadzin above.)

There are a number of large memorial stones (khachcars) on the site made by the master Pavghos, whose own grave is here. These always include a cross in their carved design and were used to commemorate such events as victories and the laying of a foundation as well as the deaths of individual people. One khachkar in particular, which Pavghos made in 1231 and which stands on a pedestal by the entrance to the main church, is considered to be his best and indeed one of the finest examples of its kind in the country.

The main road from Dilijan for Kirovakan (40 km/25 miles) is also the way to Tumanyan, Uzunlar, Alaverdi, Sanahin, Akhpat, and Akhtala. Akhpat is a total distance of 250 km (155 miles) from Erevan. Leave Dilijan via Kalin Street.

The road to Kirovakan goes through Fioletovo, Gamzachiman, Lermontovo, and im. Shumyana, and the first part runs beside a newly built railway line.

Fioletovo

This is in an agricultural area, known for growing the big, round cabbages that make good sauerkraut.

Mayakovsky's House. The family of the poet Vladimir Mayakovsky lived here at the end of the 19th century.

Lermontovo

There is a fox-fur farm here.

Kirovakan (Until 1935, Karaklis) Population— 107,000

Kirovakan is situated 1,350 m (4,430 ft) above sea level, at the confluence of the rivers Pambak, Vanadzoriget, and Tandzut. It is the republic's third-largest city (after Erevan and Leninakan). It was renamed after Sergei Kirov (1886–1934), who had taken an active part in establishing Soviet power in the Caucasus after the revolution of 1917. "Akan" is the Armenian word for "city."

Goshavank has been inhabited since ancient times. Stone sarcophagi of the Bronze and early Iron Ages (9th–8th centuries B.C.) have been found along the banks of the Tandzut within the city limits.

At the turn of the century there were about 3,000 inhabitants and all engaged in agriculture and a variety of crafts. In both May and November 1920 there were armed uprisings here. When Armenia's first hydropower station was built not far from Karaklis in 1934, the chemical industry began to develop rapidly. It mostly produces fertilisers. There are also machine-building and textile industries and an artificial-filament plant.

Today, there is almost nothing left of the old city. The main thoroughfare is Agayana Street. Lenin Prospect crosses Kirov Square and leads to the bridge over the Tandzut, connecting the centre with the Dimats region. Karl Marx Street runs parallel to Lenin Prospect, and the railway station is down below. The administrative buildings on Kirov Square were built as a group, and there is a pond with swans here. On Shaumyan Square there is an artificial lake.

Church of Our Lady, Tumanyan Street

Local Museum and Picture Gallery, Lenin Prospect 52

Applied Art Museum, open 10–5; closed Mon.

Zoryan House-Museum. It commemorates the writer Stepan Zoryan (Rostom) (1867–1919).

Botanical Garden, in the valley of the river Vanadzor. 620 different species of trees and shrubs have been collected on a territory of 13 hectares (32 acres).

Lenin Monument

Shaumyan Monument, Shaumyan Square. This bas-relief commemorates Stepan Shaumyan, the leader of a commune in Baku.

Kirov Monument

Eternal Flame, part of the World War II memorial

Drama Theatre

Gugark Hotel and Restaurant, Lenin Prospect at Kirov Square

Erevan Restaurant, Shaumyan Square

Kirovakan Restaurant, on the right of Erevanskoye Chaussée, on the way in from Dilijan

Market, Karl Marx Street

From Kirovakan the road northeast to Alaverdi follows first the valley of the Pambak through Mergut. A right turn leads to a bridge over the Pambak and on through Vaagnadzor and Dzoraget to Tumanyan, which is 24 km (15 miles) from Kirovakan. There are a number of tunnels on the way.

Ekheknut

There is a group of mediaeval buildings here.

Tumanyan (Formerly Dsekh) Population—5,000

The outstanding Armenian poet Ovanes Tumanyan spent his childhood in this village.

There is a factory here that produces refractory materials, using minerals mined locally. Not far from here, on the river Debed, Dzorages, Armenia's first large hydropower station with a capacity of 25,000 kw, was built in 1932.

From the northern outskirts of the village there begins a slope up to the Martsiget Gorge.

Tumanyan House-Museum, 1 km (.5 mile) to the right of the main road. This 2-storey house is where Ovanes Tumanyan (1869–1923) lived. Behind it stands the local school, and in its garden is a bust of the writer sculpted by Urartu.

Return to the main road to continue the journey to Alaverdi.

Kolageran

There are a number of examples of mediaeval architecture in the vicinity, including churches, fortresses, and khachkars.

The road now enters the valley of the Debed and goes on through Kachagan.

Danushavan

There was a settlement here in the Middle Ages. There remains a fortress, churches, sepulchres, and khachkars.

Odzun

Sometimes known as Uzunlar, this village stands high up on the Lori Plateau, to the west above Alaverdi, and at a distance of 8 km (5 miles) from the town by the zigzag road that makes the ascent. The local collective farm is engaged in horticulture and cattle breeding.

Odzun Church is a domed basilica dating from the 6th–7th centuries. It has a nave and two aisles, and the central dome is surrounded by a gallery on the north, west, and south sides.

To the north of the church stands an unusual tomb with elegant columns with very fine carving on all four sides. These tell the story of how Christianity came to Armenia, with representations of King Tridates with a hog's head and Gregory the

Enlightener, and even the 4th-century Rhipsime Chapel in its original form, this latter of great interest to students of early Christian architecture in Armenia.

There are also a number of khachkars here.

Alaverdi Population—20,000

Alaverdi is one of Armenia's oldest industrial centres. It is situated on the steep slopes of Mt. Lalvar above the left bank of the turbulent river Debed, a tributary of the Kura. Following the slope it forms a gigantic staircase, with the lowest step by the river being 750 m (2,460 ft) above sea level and the highest point 1,300 m (4,265 ft) above sea level.

The town is an old centre of the copper industry. In the second half of the 18th century, gold and silver were also mined here. In 1905–6 Spandaryan organised strikes of the copper smelters here, and there was an armed uprising in 1920. Today Alaverdi is the Soviet Union's third-most important copper-producing centre, after the Urals and Kazakhstan. There are also chemical plants, and so local industry combines two production cycles, metallurgical and chemical. The most important products are electrolytic copper and copper sulphate, the latter for export.

Alaverdi was the birthplace of Sayat-Nova (1712–91), a classic Armenian poet whose real name was Arutun Sayadyans and who wrote in three languages, Armenian, Georgian, and Azerbaijani, at the court of King Erakli II of Georgia. He had to leave because of intrigues and became a priest at the Armenian church in Gori. After the death of his wife, he took his vows and became a monk of the monastery at Haghpat (see below). He died when Tbilisi was stormed by the troops of Aga Muhammed Khan. Also born here, in Sanahin (see below) were the brothers Anastas (statesman) and Artyom (airplane designer) Mikoyan.

Besides Armenians, there were also Azerbaijanis here, and about 10 percent of the population is Greek, descendants of the Anatolian Greeks who migrated here from Turkey about 200 years ago.

Sanahin Bridge, over the Debed. This is 800 years old and has a single arch 18 m (20 yd) in length. There are stone lions guarding either end. It links the old and new parts of Alaverdi.

The forests surrounding the town abound in wild fruit bushes and trees. The local residents gather over 1,000 tons of such fruit each year, including wild apples, pears, and plums.

Debed Hotel, in Rabochi Posyolok, across the bridge and up the road.

Sanahin

This village is now part of Alaverdi. The road from the town to the monastery crosses the river Debed by the *Sanahin Bridge*. It was built in 1234, and its single span is 18 m (20 yd) long. Behind the bridge and the road that is cut through a steep cliff opens up a panoramic view of the monastery against the background of Mt. Chatyn-Dag.

Sanahin Monastery, open 10–4:30; closed Mon. The word Sanahin in Armenian means "this one is more ancient than that one," and refers to an ancient rivalry with the neighbouring Akhpat (Haghpat) Monastery. The construction of Sanahin Monastery spread over 450 years. The date of its foundation is not known, but Gregory the Enlightener is said to have raised a cross on the site of the future monastery at the beginning of the 4th century.

At the beginning of the 10th century, when the Shahinshah Ashot II (the Iron) restored order in the country, a period of intensive construction began. The monastery was founded during the reign of Ashot's brother, King Abas I. Although the building work can be divided into 13 different periods, it still forms a harmonious whole around the central *Astavatsatsin Church (Church of the Virgin)*, built in 951 by fugitive monks who had fled to the mountains from persecution by the king. Less immense structures built on small hills at some distance from the monastery only serve to emphasise its size and dramatic impact. After the completion of Astavatsatsin Church, a larger copy was built in 967–972 with money donated by Queen Khosrowanuch and her sons, Kyurike and Smbat, whose sculptured portraits decorate the eastern wall of the church. The new church was called *Amenaprkich Church (Church of Our Saviour)*. The space between the churches was roofed over and used as an academy with 6 aisles. Both the academy here and that at Haghpat (see below) were founded by the great 11th-century scholar Ovanes Imastaser. It was here that the Armenian philosopher, the monk Grigor Magistros Pakhlavuni (990–1058), gave his lectures. In 1051 he translated Euclid's "Elements" into Armenian, almost 70 years before the Latin translation was made from the Greek. In 1063 a square library with a vaulted roof was built, connected with Astvatsatsin Church by a gallery. The beautiful entrance arch was built by Princess Granush, King David's daughter. The plaque on the wall commemorates the writer Sayat-Nova (see Alaverdi, above). The small, round church at the southeast corner of the library was added in 1885. Sanahin is notable for its secular structures; besides the library and the academy, there were a number of houses inside the walls for the monks to live in.

St. Gregory's Church, to the east of Astvatsatsin Church. This was built in 1061 and reconstructed in 1652, while the towerlike belfry dates from the 13th century.

St. Arutyun's Church

There are several family *burial vaults and khachkars* (memorial stones) on the territory of Sanahin Monastery. One of the finest of these stands at the end of Amenaprkich Church. Another commemorates Grigor Tutevordi (d. 1184?). The burial vaults include those of the Spesalars family and of the Mkharadzelis, Prince Zahare and his father and grandfather. Also buried here was General Prince Moses Argutinsky-Dolgoruky (1798–1855), who fought in Daghestan.

St. Sarkis's Chapel, in the northeastern part of the village

St. Karapet's Chapel, in the western part of the village

The village has a 12th-century *fountain* roofed by a stone tent with banks along its walls.

Mikoyan Museum, was the home of the airplane designer Artyom Mikoyan (1895–1978). It was opened as a museum to commemorate both brothers in 1982, and in front of it stands a *bust* of Artyom and a MiG plane, mounted as a monument.

Akhpat (Haghpat)

This village is 7 km (4 miles) from Alaverdi, 1,000 m (3,280 ft) above sea level. Leave Alaverdi through the new part of town, going downhill, over the bridge and to the right, past the old Sanahin Bridge. Turn right over the next road bridge, left along the river following the signs, and the old fortress is on the right.

Haghpat Monastery, open 10–4:30; closed Mon. This monastery is one of the finest mediaeval architectural complexes in Armenia. It was founded in 976, 10 years after the main churches of Sanahin Monastery, in the reign of Abas I Bagratuni. It stands on a high plateau surrounded by mountain slopes, and its construction continued for 300 years. The ramparts around it date from 1120 and 1246, and the original entrance is on the eastern side of these, through an old arch surmounted by a cross.

Inside the walls are 4 churches, 2 with large porches known as narthexes built on the front, a refectory, a library (with its roof under the earth of the mountain slope), a bell tower, and many tombs and memorial stones. The belfry was built in 1245, and the refectory also dates from the 13th century. The main church is *Surb-Nshan (Holy Cross)*, built between 967 and 991. It has an enormous domed interior, and the inside walls are covered with sculptured ornamentation, frescoes, and inscriptions, but they have suffered serious damage. There are high-relief decorations on the outside walls as well. It is believed to have been built by Trdat, the famous architect who was also responsible for the cathedrals at Ani (Once the Armenian capital, but now on Turkish territory). The narthex of Surb-Nshan's was built in 1201 and is unusual in that its roof consists of 2 systems of intersecting arches, like a great curved frame for playing tic-tac-toe. Inside is a tomb of the Bagratid family. North and south of this narthex are 2 small churches dedicated to the *Virgin* (11th–12th century) and *St. Gregory* (1005). A vaulted gallery connects the Sub-Nshan Church with the great narthex erected in 1257 by Bishop Hamazasmp. This building was intended as a seminary. In the northern part of the monastery are 3 13th-century mausolea of Kurd princes, all designed like tiny churches.

Outside the walls is a well-preserved *fountain* (1258), the façade of which consists of a triple arcade surmounted by a pediment. It is fed by a stream, which flows down from Mt. Lusisar.

As at Sanahin, there was an academy here founded by the great 11th-century scholar Ovanes Imastaser. He also chose to make his home at Haghpat. The monks of Haghpat collected a rich library with all that had ever been written in Armenian, and also with copies of manuscripts from other libraries. The jars sunk into the library floor were used to store precious manuscripts, but at any threat of invasion the library was hidden in local caves. In the 12th–13th centuries, the monastery was the centre of Armenian manuscript work and was also famous for its "book miniatures." The most famous miniature painter was Markar. The Haghpat illustrated gospels were copied in many other monasteries. Many Armenian miniature artists abandoned the generally accepted traditions of ecclesiastical art and portrayed birds with human faces.

The Haghpat and Sanahin manuscripts were last hidden in the local caves in the 11th century, and they lay there undisturbed until they were discovered in the late 18th century. Unfortunately many of the manuscripts had become rotten or had petrified over the years. To make matters worse most of the manuscripts were burned by Deacon Petros, who built a 4-m (12-foot) bonfire of them. The treasures that have survived are now in the Matenadaran in Erevan.

Among the monks of Haghpat was Sayat-Nova (1712–91), a classical Armenian poet (see Alaverdi, above).

On the eastern outskirts of the village is the *Maiden's Desert (Kusanats Anapat) Church*, built in the 13th century.

The Church of the Virgin (Dzhgrashen), on the western outskirts of the village. Built in 1195.

Kayan-Berd Fortress, near Akhpat, on the plateau between the ravines of the rivers Debet and Zhivan. Built by Ioann, Bishop of Haghpat Monastery, this "eyrie" was detroyed by the Mongols.

Ancient history apart, it is on record that there was an uprising of local peasants in 1903.

Akhtala

This is 15 km (9 miles) farther along the road from Haghpat toward Tbilisi, but on the other side of the river Debed. Return to the main Alaverdi-Tbilisi road first. This is a popular place to come for a summer holiday in the mountains.

To reach the 10th-century monastery go into the centre of the town, cross the river and the railway, and turn right to follow the zigzag road upward. The green stones show the rich copper deposits (see Alaverdi). There is a 10th-century *fortress* and *monastery* buildings of the 12th–13th centuries up on the promontory jutting out into the river valley. The green stones have been incorporated in the fortress walls. The ruins of a big *tower* stand by the entrance arch, and there is a smaller arch to the right.

The beautiful *Church of St. Gregory* was built in the 10th Century, rebuilt in the 13th century, and is famous for its frescoes, which have been carefully restored. Its outside walls are wonderfully decorated with carved stonework. It has a porch and a second small church built onto the western side.

Noravank-Gladzor

Intourist organises excursions here from Erevan.

Noravank Monastery is near the village of Amagu, not far from *Ekhegnadzor*, and is east of Erevan and due south of Lake Sevan. Ekhegnadzor stands upon the site of the ancient university of Gladzor, once known as the "second Athens." Science, history, philosophy, astronomy, and mathematics were studied here. There was a rich library and schools of art and painting.

Noravank was founded in the 13th century, during the reign of the Orbelian family, as the residence of the bishop of Syunik. It became an important religious centre, closely connected with the university and library at Gladzor. Its name means Nor Academy.

The oldest building in the monastery complex was a church dedicated to St. Karapet in the 9th century, but it is in ruins. A new *St. Karapet's Church* was built inside it in 1221–27, and to the entrance of this large refectory building was added in 1261. The *refectory*, however, seems to have collapsed during an earthquake, for in 1321 a new roof was built. This is in the form of a stone tent, imitating the wooden roof of a peasant home, quite unlike any other Armenian building of the same type.

St. Gregory's Church was built onto the northern wall of St. Karapet's in 1275. It was designed by Siranes and used by Prince Orbelian as a family mausoleum.

The memorial church of *St. Astvatsatsin (Church of the Virgin)* was founded by Burtel Orbelian and so is also called Burtelashen. The ground floor was a burial vault, while upstairs was a memorial temple. It stands to the southeast of the other churches and was completed in 1339. Its architect was Momik, an artist who had created beautiful miniatures in the studios of Gladzor in 1302.

The refectory and the Church of St. Astvatsatsin are in the best state of preservation. Most interesting are the deep stone carvings over their western windows and doors. The tympanum of the refectory portal carries a carving of the Virgin and Child, while there is a representation of God the Father over the upper window. The western wall of St. Astvatsatsin's is decorated with cantilever steps rising over the lower door with its tympanum carving of the Virgin and Child with the archangels Michael and Gabriel. The steps lead up to the portal of the memorial temple, over which is carved a figure of Christ with St. Peter and St. Paul.

There are a number of khachkars (memorial stones, commemorating dates and occasions as well as people) on the monastery territory, the most valuable being one that was made in 1308 by Momik; it is entirely covered by fine carving.

The monastery was surrounded by a wall. Inside in the northwest and the southwest corners are the remains of 18th-century residential and service buildings, while outside to the east, there are 2 *chapels*, dating from the 14th and 17th centuries.

ESSENTUKI Population—87,000

Intourist organises excursions here from nearby Pyatigorsk and Kislovodsk.

This spa, with salt and alkaline springs, lies off the main Intourist road, almost immediately after Pyatigorsk, in a valley fed by 2 streams, the Bugunty and the Essentuchok.

There are several legends explaining the origin of the name Essentuki. One of them says that a sickly child was born into the family of a prince from the ancient town of Burhustan. The child was absolutely bald, and the parents decided to take him to the miracle-working sulphuric springs near present Pyatigorsk. Making a short stop in the steppe, they bathed him in one of the mineral springs. The next day, hair started to grow on the child's head. The spring got the name Essen-tyuk, which in Karachai means "live hair."

Essentuki spa is younger than its neighbours, Pyatigorsk and Kislovodsk. It was founded in 1798 as a military settlement. When Dr. Friedrich Haaz came to this region in 1810, he was told by a local Cossack about a mineral spring that existed in the nearby steppes and which was the horses' favourite drinking spot. The spring was called the Horses' Spring, but now it is known as Haaz-Ponomarevsky.

The place continued to be known as a Cossack settlement until the late 1880s, when it began to be developed as a spa.

There are 16 springs yielding a total of 500,000 litres (110,000 gallons) of water daily. The springs are cold and either carbonic ferruginous or alkaline. The best are No. 17 and No. 4, both of which have a high degree of mineralisation. The water cures here are augmented with mud baths and recommended for the treatment of digestive and metabolic disorders. Intourist organises courses of treatment lasting 26 days.

The main street, Internationalnaya (formerly Kursovaya) Street, runs down from the railway station and leads to the old town centre, a square, unofficially known as "Pyatachok," meaning "5-kopeck coin" and indicating its originally small size and its liveliness. It is the real heart of the spa but has grown in size, is newly paved, and laid out with flowerbeds.

There are still some old, balconied houses on the street, for example Nos. 14 and 16. The old Metropole Hotel is now the Mayak, with a souvenir and gift shop on the ground floor, and a fine, modern drama theatre stands opposite the entrance to the park.

The old part of Essentuki park was laid out in 1849 on a territory of 40 hectares (100 acres). Just inside is the old theatre, and nearby stands a *pavilion*, where the water from springs Nos. 17, 4, and 20 is used for drinking in summer. The pavilion was built by the English architect Upton in English Gothic style in 1847–48 and is the oldest building of the spa. Spring No. 17 is open 7–10,

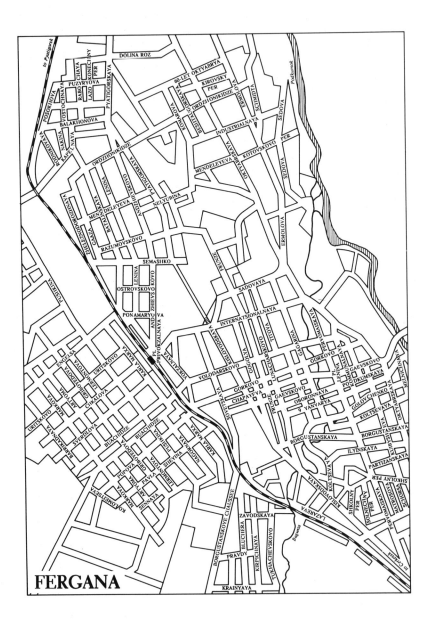

FERGANA

12–3:30, and 5–8 so that one can drink before meals. When it was discovered over 100 years ago, it was called the "pearl of Caucasian mineral waters, and the pride of the motherland." The temperature of its waters is about 13°C (56°F). Behind the theatre is the main bathhouse supplied by these springs. There is a memorial plaque here with the dates of their discovery.

Farther to the right is the *mechanical therapeutical department* housed in an ancient pavilion, formerly known as the Zander Institute, after Dr. Zander from Sweden. The department gave very successful treatment to wounded soldiers during World War II.

An asphalted avenue, Alkalichesky Prospect, leads down through the park. To the right, opposite the theatre, and with birch trees in front of it, is the building of the *Lower Baths* with 34 bathrooms. Further on, to the left of the avenue, is the summer pavilion of spring No. 4 and on the right-hand side is its winter pavilion. This spring is less mineralised than No. 17 and has a temperature of 10°–12°C (50°–54°F).

The avenue next leads to the domed and columned *Pavilion No. 1*. To the right is a pile of stones with the local emblem of an eagle killing a serpent, and to the left, on the slopes of Alkali Hill, is a sculpture of a Russian peasant seated with a drinking cup in his hand, probably commemorating the Cossack who was the first to show the mineral springs to Dr. Haaz in 1810. Above him can be seen a semicircular colonnade, from which there is a good view across to Mashuk and Pyatigorsk. Farther on, the path leads past flowerbeds to stone steps and a small bridge. The big building of a sanatorium, one of the oldest in Essentuki and formerly a restaurant, is situated here.

Near by with a fountain in front, are the Upper (*formerly Nikolayevskiye*) Baths, built in 1898 and then called after the last Russian tsar, Nicholas II. This has 60 bathrooms, each bath being of solid marble. Not far away along another avenue are other baths, which are used only in summer.

The avenue now runs to the centre of the park, where there is a *concert platform* and a *library*. The metal column with a figure of a dove on it marks the place where the water of spring No. 17 was first tapped. A little aside from this, an avenue of palms leads back to the entrance. 3 walks begin from the eastern gates of the park. The first is 1,820 m (just over a mile) in length and is a gentle slope climbing upward 23.5 m (77 ft); the second, more hilly than the first, is 2,515 m (a little over 1.5 miles) and rises 42.4 m (139 ft.) The third walk is 2,436 m (1.5 miles), and steeper still, going up 61.8 m (202 ft).

In the northern part of Essentuki is another park on higher ground, *Komsomolosky Park*, originally known as the English Park. From here opens out a beautiful view of Elbrus, Mashuk, and Beshtau mountains and of the Podkumok river valley.

Semashko Mud Baths (former Alexeyevskaya), Semashko Street. These baths were built in 1913–15 by academician Shreter and are named for Dr. Nikolai Semashko, Soviet comissar of health from 1918 till 1930. The building is in the style of ancient Greek public buildings, decorated with bas-reliefs, lions, columns and two statues, of Aesculapius, the Greek god of medicine and healing, and his daughter, Hiygea, goddess of health.

Local Museum, Kislovodskaya Street 5. Open 10–5:30; closed Tues.

Memorial Obelisk, in front of the railway station. This small obelisk is dedicated to those who fell during the revolution.

St. Nicholas's Church, Lenin Square

Theatre, in the park

Not far from Essentuki, the *Byeli Ugol ("white coal") power station*, one of the oldest in Russia, was built on the river Podkumok. There is good bathing in the lake here.

Essentuki Hotel and Restaurant, Karl Marx Street 26

Mayak ("lighthouse") Hotel, Internatsionalnaya Street 3. This was formerly the Metropole Hotel.

Kavkaz Restaurant, Internatsionalnaya Street 26

Vstrecha Restaurant, Oktyabrskaya Street, on the right. There is a floor show here in the evenings.

Olympia Resturant. There is a floor show here in the evenings.

Zastava Restaurant serves European cuisine.

Parus ("sail") Restaurant

Bank, Kislovodskaya Street 5

GPO, Kislovodskaya Street 18

Department Store, Internatsionalnaya Street 11

Bookshop, Internatsionalnaya Street 5

Filling Station, on the right, on the way into town

ESTONIA
See Tallinn, p. 525.

FERGANA
Fergana is the largest city in the fertile Fergana Valley.

FERGANA VALLEY
Although the valley is unusually thought of as being in Uzbekistan, parts of Tajikistan and Kirghizia also run into it. It is an almond-shaped valley, situated at a height of 300 m (980 ft) above sea level in its western part and 1,000 m (3,280 ft) in the east. It is about 300 km (186 miles) long and a maximum of 140 km (87 miles) wide, covering a territory of 52,000 sq km (20,000 sq miles) with mountains on all sides except for a pass in the west. The Tien-Shan Mountains lie to the east and the Pamir-Alayas to the south. The major river of the valley is the Syr-Darya, which is formed by the confluence of the Naryn and Kara-Darya. The valley is often referred to as "the pearl of Central Asia" because it is one of the main cotton, silk, and fruit-growing districts in the Soviet Union. Within the valley are reserves of oil, gas, and coal. The average temperature in January is −3°C (27°F), and the valley has all types of Central Asian landscapes.

In 1868–71 the largest canal in the valley at

that time was dug; it was 85 km (53 miles) long. In the years of World War II, the Southern Fergana Canal was dug between the towns of Fergana and Marghilan. It was 93 km (58 miles) long and added 53,000 hectares (132,000 acres) of irrigated land to the valley's total. Other canals include the Great Fergana Canal, named after Usman Yusupov, and the Great Andizhan Canal, constructed in 1970. (Usman Yusupov [1900–1966] was a Party Official and an Uzbek political figure.) In the Fergana Valley there are 32 ancient architectural monuments and 85 archaeological places worth seeing. Among them the 11th–12th-century Uzgensky mausolea and minaret are under reconstruction.

Fergana (Formerly Noviy Marghilan; Skobelev from 1907–24) Population—200,000
The town of Fergana was founded in 1877, the year after the Russians took the area. Fergana stands 580 m (1,903 ft) above sea level, with a good view to the south of the snow-covered Alaya Mountains. It is on the edge of an oasis and is watered by the Marghilan-sai, a branch of the river Shakhimadan, which has its source in the nearby mountains.

Fergana was founded as the centre of the region, and its site included the territory of 2 villages, Yar-Mazar and Chim. Being only about 10 km (6 miles) from the ancient town of Marghilan, it was called Noviy ("new") Marghilan and was an entirely Russian town, having 7,000 Russians among its 11,000 population at the time. In 1907 it was renamed in honour of General Mikhail Skobelev (1843–82), who made his name campaigning in Central Asia and later in Turkey. The city was given its present name in 1924 (after the 1917 revolution).

The original town plan followed the same lines as the new parts of Tashkent and Samarkand. The first building was the *fortress*, which still stands behind the impressive modern building of the Party Committee. There were barracks nearby. From the fortress three long streets radiated to the northwest and the west. The first settlers were encouraged to plant trees for shade and orchards, and the tradition continued. By the turn of the century, there were about 4,000 inhabitants, but then, with the construction of the railway in 1899, the town began to grow more rapidly. It is now the industrial and cultural centre of the valley. Textiles and food production are the most important industries, but there is also an oil refinery and chemical factories. There is a teachers' training college too, housed in the old building of the boy's grammar school; a plaque describes how it served as Frunze's headquarters in 1918–20 during the Civil War.

In the Central Square is a many-tiered *fountain*. The main thoroughfare is Karl Marx Street, which leads toward Marghilan and then runs on farther as the road to Kokand. Along Karl Marx Street (formerly Abramovsky Prospect) and Lenin (formerly Gubernatorskaya) Street, a number of old houses can still be seen. The building on the corner of 1st-May and Lenin streets was formerly a girl's school, built in the 1880s. At Karl Marx Street 48 is the formerly Officers' Club.

Mosque, Pamirskaya Street
St. Sergius's Church, Krupskaya Street 8
Local Museum, 1st-May Street 18. Opened in 1896. Open 9–6; closed Mon.
Obelisk, Karl Marx Street. It is on the common grave of soldiers who fell in the Fergana Valley, fighting for Soviet power.
War Memorial and Eternal Flame, Karl Liebknecht Street. Commemorating local soldiers who died during World War II.
Lenin Monument, Pushkin Street, in front of the building of the Party Committee
Gorky Russian Drama Theatre, Karl Marx Street 36. The building dates from 1882 and was formerly the Governor's House.
Uzbek Music and Drama Theatre, Karl Marx Street 36
Spartak Stadium, Kommunistov Street
Gorky (formerly Gubernatorsky) Park, Lenin Street 29
Komsomolskoye Lake, 25 Lyet Oktyabrya
Fergana (Intourist) Hotel and Restaurant, Kommunistov Street 29; tel. 42–528.
Hotel and Restaurant, Kommunistov Street 35
Dustlik Hotel & Restaurant
Markhabo Restaurant, Pushkin Street 1
Fergana Restaurant, Lenin Street 9
Bakhor Restaurant, Individualnaya Street
Intourist Office, Kommunistov Street 27; tel. 43–097
GPO, Marx Street 5
Mysl Bookshop
Market, Dzerzhinsky Street

Intourist organises excursions to Marghilan (see p. 314), Hamzaabad, and Kokand (see p. 247).

Hamzaabad
52 km (32 miles) to the south of Fergana. Formerly known as Shakh-i-mardan, this is a pleasant health resort with mineral springs up in the mountains, 1,550 m (5,085 ft) above sea level, reached by driving up the river valley. On the way is the village of Vuadil (literally "open heart"), about 25 km (16 miles) from Fergana, which used to be a recreation place of the nobility.

Its bazaar is on the former site of the khan's garden. The ancient *Muslim cemetery* is interesting, with its enormous plane trees. The hollow of one of them can house a card-table and 4 chairs. According to the legends, at one time there was a big town here that devastated by the "mugal" people, who in turn were later conquered by the Muslims. The first settlers of Vuadil were the Mugi tribe, who have left burial hills. Local people find coins with engravings also left by this tribe.

The village of Shakh-i-mardan has always been very popular, as the tomb of the holy Shakh-i-mardan was said to be here. Khalif Ali, who was very popular in Central Asia, was named Shakh-i-mardan (literally "the king of the people"). There is a *teahouse* here, and 8 km (5 miles) away is another picturesque spot known as the Blue Lake.
Hamza Memorial Museum, on the place where

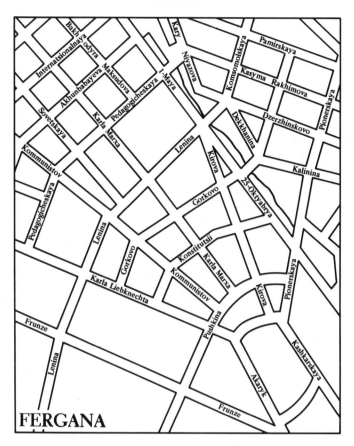

FERGANA

the poet was murdered in 1929. Open 9–6; closed Mon. Ham̲a Hakim-zade Niyazi (1889–1929) is regarded as the founder of modern Uzbek literature. At the age of 16, he began to write poems, revolutionary songs, and plays, which were the first in the Uzbek tongue. He was murdered in Shakh-i-mardan, subsequently renamed for him as Hamzaabad, and his tomb is here.

Hamza's Tomb can be reached by driving up a steep and winding road from the resort, or by climbing a flight of stone steps. On the mausoleum overlooking the town were inscribed these lines of his as an epitaph:

> The happiness of bright, new life
> Soon across the world will bloom,
> Will be our joy for ever more:
> Just grief lies hidden in the tomb.

Also at the top of the hill is a *memorial* to those who fell in the Civil War, dated December 1921, an eternal flame, and a statue.

FERGANA VALLEY
See Fergana, p. 143.

FIRYUZA RAVINE
See Ashkhabad, p. 47.

FLYONOVO
See Smolensk, p. 486.

GAGRA
See Sukhumi environs, p. 515.

GARNI
See Erevan, p. 133.

GATCHINA
See Leningrad environs, p. 298.

GHELATI MONASTERY
See Tskhaltubo, p. 576.

GEORGIA
See Tbilisi, p. 544.

THE GEORGIAN MILITARY HIGHWAY
Intourist runs excursions northward from Tbilisi and Pasanauri to Vladikavkaz and from Vladikavkaz south as far as Kazbegi.

The highway runs north from Tbilisi to Vladikavkaz, capital of Northern Ossetia, through the Caucasus Mountains. It connects Georgia with the Northern Caucasus, running 207 km (129 miles) between Tbilisi and Vladikavkaz. It starts at Geroyev Square in Tbilisi and ends at Geroyev Square in Vladikavkaz.

It is divided into 2 parts, the hilly southern part and the mountainous northern part. The southern part of the road winds up the valleys of the Kura and the Aragvi until it reaches its highest point, Krestovy Pass (2,379 m/7,805 ft above sea level). Being the lowest of the Caucasian passes, it is still much higher than the St. Gothard (2,112 m/6,929 ft), the Simplon (2,009 m/6,591 ft), and the St. Bernard (2,188 m/7,178 ft) passes in the Alps, and Somport (1,632 m/5,354 ft) in the Pyrenées.

In its mountainous section, the road crosses 5 mountain ridges: the Main Caucasian, Side, Rocky, Pasture, and Forest. It descends the Terek Valley from Baidarskoye Gorge down into the Khevskoye, Daryal, and Balta gorges.

The route now followed by the Georgian Military Highway has been known since time immemorial. A testimony to this is the description of the road by the Greek historian and geographer Strabo, who lived in the 1st century B.C. In his book on Iveria (the ancient name of Georgia), Strabo noted that this mountainous path that served as a trade channel between Europe and Asia was very difficult and dangerous. Its economic importance in the 12th century, the time of Georgia's greatest political might, caused new towns to appear along it, Zhinvali, for instance. However, for Georgia this was not only a trade route. It was also important for the defence of the region. In the Middle Ages, Georgia suffered numerous invasions from Persia and Turkey, so many watchtowers were built along the way. With the Tatar invasion of the 13th century, the road lost its importance.

At the end of the 17th century, diplomatic relations were established between Georgia and Russia. Then renewed threats from Persia and Turkey forced the Georgian king Erekle II to seek help from Russia, and the route revived from the time the Russians first appeared in the North Caucasus. In 1768 the Russian army under Count Todleben was sent this way through the mountains to help the Georgians against the Turks. The very size of his force, and particularly the presence of the guns, made his passage through the Daryal Gorge and Krestovaya Pass unique. "Todleben," wrote one Russian general, "went up the Terek . . . and down the Aragvi. He had nothing but the beds of those rivers for a road and to have got his artillery over them was an astonishing feat." After the unification of Georgia and Russia in 1801, it became important to have a reliable route to Georgia as the easiest connection between the two countries. The Russian Military Administration was charged with the building of the road, hence its name, and construction went ahead with the help of "iron and powder." The first to supervise it was the veteran of the Napoleonic War General Alexei Yermolov (1772–1861), who had been appointed commander-in-chief of the Russian troops in the Caucasus by Alexander I. The work in the Daryal Gorge lasted over 5 years. The Terek was spanned by bridges, and by 1817 the whole length was already

open to the public. On top of Mt. Krestovaya is a stone cross put up by Yermolov in 1824. At the time General Yermolov was justly called the builder of the Russian Simplon. Many Russian writers and artists travelled along the new road, among them Pushkin, Lermontov, Tolstoy, Repin, Mayakovsky, and Gorky. Pushkin described the Daryal Gorge in his "Journey to Erzrum" in 1829, and Lermontov gives a picture of it in his famous poem "The Demon." In 1863 the road was turned into a highway and was considered one of the best in Russia. In 1911 it was opened to motor traffic, and the journey took 14 hours in one direction.

From Mtskheta at its southern end, the Georgian Military Highway climbs slowly up the valley of the Aragvi through a region of vineyards and orchards. Up on the slopes on either side appear from time to time the first of the ancient towers, churches, and castles, mementoes of the importance of this route in the past.

Zhinvali
In the vicinity of this village are the remains of a *7th-century town* and a *castle* called Bebris-Tsikhe.

Ananuri
The name means "holy mother," and the village stands among the woods beside the river Arkala at the 138-km mark. On the right is an *18th-century fortress*, and within its walls stands the *Assumption Church*, built in 1689. There is a fine carved cross on the outside of the west wall, and inside some 17th- and 18th-century frescoes remain. The iconostasis, of Muscovite workmanship, dates from the 19th century. Nearby is the 16th century *Bteba Church*, and the small buildings up the hill, to the left as one goes through the entrance gate, were *bathhouses*. Below is a ridged-domed *Armenian Church* of the 19th century.

The fortress, built by Eristav Georgy (Eristav being the title of a hereditary ruler of the Aragvi Gorge) in 1704, was intended to control the main road leading from Georgia to the Northern Caucasus via the Daryal Gorge and to defend the approaches to Mtskheta and Tbilisi. In 1739 Eristav Shanche of the region along the river Ksan quarreled with the Ananuri Eristav and, with the help of the warlike Lezghins, besieged the fortress. Exceptionally bloody battles occurred, and barricades were made of corpses. Still, the outcome of the battle would have been uncertain if not for a woman who showed the enemy the water duct along which water was supplied to the besieged. The fortress was taken by a storm. Eristav Georgy, with his family, tried to take refuge in an old church. However, the church was set afire, and all inside perished in the flames.

Among Persian writers, Ananur was known as Kara-Kalkan-Kala ("the fortress of black shields"), because the Moslems called the members of the Khevsur tribe Kara-kalkans, meaning black shields.

Beyond Ananuri the vineyards and orchards continue. There are many mineral springs with

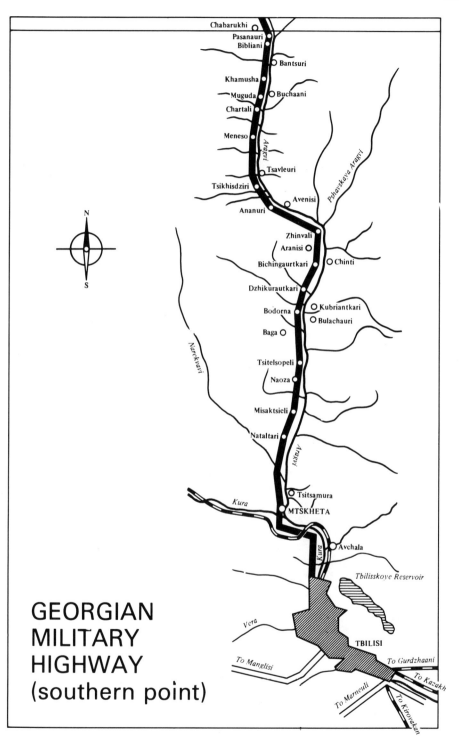

Chabarukhi
Pasanauri
Bibliani

Bantsuri

Khamusha
Muguda
Buchaani
Chartali

Meneso

Tsavleuri

Tsikhisdziri
Avenisi
Ananuri

Zhinvali
Aranisi
Bichingaurtkari
Chinti

Dzhikurautkari

Kubriantkari
Bodorna
Bulachauri
Baga

Tsitelsopeli

Naoza

Misaktsieli

Nataltari

Tsitsamura
MTSKHETA

Kura

Narekvavi

Aragvi

Pshavskaya Aragvi

Aragvi

Kura

Avchala

Tbilisskoye Reservoir

Vera

TBILISI

To Manglisi
To Gurdzhaani
To Kazakh
To Marneuli
To Kirovakan

GEORGIAN
MILITARY
HIGHWAY
(southern point)

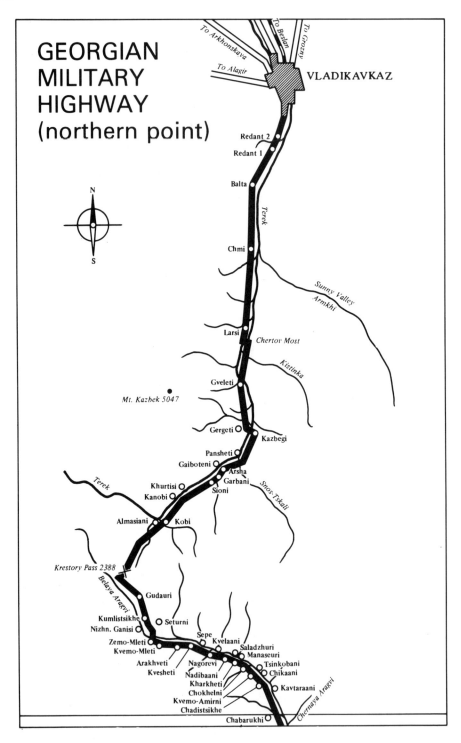

GEORGIAN MILITARY HIGHWAY
(northern point)

N
S

To Arkhonskaya
To Beslan
To Grozny
To Alagir

VLADIKAVKAZ

Redant 2
Redant 1
Balta

Terek

Chmi

Sunny Valley
Armkhi

Larsi
Chertov Most

Kistinka

Gveleti

Mt. Kazbek 5047

Gergeti
Kazbegi

Pansheti
Gaiboteni
Arsha
Garbani
Khurtisi
Sioni
Kanobi

Snos-Tskali

Terek

Almasiani
Kobi

Krestory Pass 2388

Belaya Aragvi

Gudauri

Kumlistsikhe
Seturni
Nizhn. Ganisi
Sepe
Kvelaani
Zemo-Mleti
Kvemo-Mleti
Saladzhuri
Manaseuri
Arakhveti
Nagorevi
Tsinkobani
Kvesheti
Nadibaani
Chikaani
Kharkheti
Chokhelni
Kavtaraani
Kvemo-Amirni
Chadistsikhe
Chernaya Aragvi
Chabarukhi

ASHKHABAD–A view of the Ernst Neizvestny facade.

ASHKHABAD–Melons in the market in mid-winter.

DUSHANBE–The central square.

BAKU–Nighttime view over the city and bay.

BREST–Brest Fortress, rebuilt in 1838–42 and now part of the Memorial Complex.

KHIVA–A view over the old part of the city.

KAMENETS-PODOLSKY–Long an impregnable fortress, the cliffs and walls still command respect.

EREVAN–The Spendiarov Opera and Ballet Theatre overlooks Swan Lake in the Armenian capital.

KHARKOV–Distinctive with its red-and-white, neo-Byzantine style horizontal stripes, Annunciation (blagoveschensky) Cathedral was consecrated in 1901.

water similar to that found in Essentuki. The road still runs along the right bank of the Aragvi.

Pasanauri

It is 81 km (50 miles) from here to Tbilisi. From Pasanauri Intourist organises excursions to Vladi-kavkaz. In old Persian, Pasanauri means "holy height."

The 19th-century Church is closed.

Gorky Monument, by Kratsashvili. Maxim Gorky journeyed along the Georgian Military Highway in 1891.

Intourist Hotel & Restaurant, beside the main road, Lenin Street 60; tel. 444. There is an Intourist office here.

Aragvi Hotel and Restaurant, on the right, beyond Pasanauri

GPO, on the left

The town is 1,014 m (335 ft) above sea level, in a narrow valley at the confluence of the Black and White Aragvi rivers. An interesting natural phenomenon occurs here, in that the waters of the two rivers do not mix for some distance, until the village of Bibliani. The dark water of the Black Aragvi keeps to the left side of the stream and the light-coloured White Aragvi stays on the right.

At the mouth of the Black Aragvi, 5 or 6 km (3 or 4 miles) from Pasanauri, is a place locally called *"Devis' Dishes."* Here the traces of an ancient workshop for making troughlike vessels from whole pieces of rock were discovered. The huge size of these vessels gave the population grounds to believe them to be the work of legendary giants called Devis.

Handos Khevi

Up in the valley of the Black Aragvi live 3 tribes of Caucasians that have puzzled ethnologists for many years. They are the Khevsurs (mentioned above), the Tishins, and the Pshavs. These tribes are still thought by some to be descendants of the Crusaders, because even as late as the 1930s some of the families still possessed unusual national costumes. These costumes are decorated with a large white or coloured cross and consist of chain-mail shirts, helmets with chain-mail, and broad-swords. The shields bear inscriptions in Latin letters as, for instance, "Vivat Stephan Batory" (a Polish king), "Souvenir," "Genoa," "Vivat Hussar," and "Sol-lingen." Some have images of eagles and crowns. Linguists, however, have discovered that the tribes belong to the Kartli peoples.

The Khevsurs are good hunters and are famed for their kindness and hospitality. The greatest dishonour is to beat a child or insult a guest. Even if the offender is the host's own brother, he still risks his life if breaking some of these codes. From times immemorial all 3 tribes were subject to the Georgian tsars and formed the cream of the Georgian army. They consider themselves Christians, although their beliefs are rather confused.

Beyond Pasanauri the road follows the valley of the White Aragvi.

Kvesheti

In the 19th century, the residence of the governor-general of the mountain peoples and a posting station were situated here. Travellers who had already crossed or who were preparing to cross Krestovy Pass usually spent the night here. The local population is engaged in sheep breeding and cattle raising. Large farms have been organised here, with power from the Zhinvalsky and Misaktsielsky hydropower stations.

Mleti

This village is at the 95/106-km mark and stands at a height of 1,412 m (4,635 ft). From here the road rises steeply as the Zemo-Mletsky Spusk (descent) begins, which zigzags 640 m (2,100 ft) up the mountains in 6 great bends. It is built on the sheer rocks on the left bank of the Aragvi and is a rare example of skillful engineering. In some places the outside of the road runs on a high supporting wall, and there are 18 sharp corners. The road was built between 1857 and 1861, following the project of Colonel Boleslaw Statkovsky (1825–98) and under his personal supervision.

It crosses a bridge over the White Aragvi and runs along the edges of precipices to Kumlis Tsikhe. There is probably no place along the whole length of the highway that can compare with this, both for its beauty and for its sudden contrasts as it leaves the joyful southern valleys of Georgia behind and enters Gudauri. It climbs above the Gudar Abyss (500 m/1,642 ft) and affords a good panoramic view over the southern mountains. Then it winds in zigzags through heaps of rock known as the Stone Chaos, and tourists begin to feel themselves entering a severe, cold mountain world.

Now the road climbs to the 74-km mark and Krestovy Pereval (Cross Pass) (2,388 m/7,837 ft), the highest point on the road, marked by an *obelisk* with the inscription "Krestovy Pass." The name Krestovy derives from the brown stone cross that Major David Kananov, then governor of this region, erected on the old road to mark the pass. Now the cross is a bit higher up and to the left of the main road. A French traveller, Gambat, who was consul in Tbilisi at Yermolov's time, did not understand the meaning of Krestovaya Gora and turned it into Mont Saint-Christophe. It is so called in some French and even Russian geography books on the Caucasus.

The pass used to be so dangerous that sometimes people preferred to get out of their carriages and walk, and it is recorded that a certain foreign ambassador was so frightened that he asked to be blindfolded and was then led through by the hand. When the bandage was taken from his eyes, he fell down on his knees to thank God for his survival. From here there is a wonderful panorama of the Caucasus. The alpine meadows of Cross Pass are used as pastures by the surrounding farms. To the right is the old part of the road, where at a distance of about a kilometre (.5 mile) one can see a *cross* of red stone, which was, according to legend, placed there by King David the Builder (grandfather of Queen Tamar) and repaired by General Yermolov in 1824. The tops of the mountains Nepis-Kalo (3,536 m/11,604 ft) and Shvidt-Dzma (7 Brothers) (3,150 m/10,341 ft) can be seen, among others. At the foot of Krestovaya Mountain is the small Chertovaya Ravine. According to Lermontov, this name, like that of the bridge farther on, derives from the Russian word "cherta" (border) and marks the place where the Georgian border once was.

In the 10-km (6-mile) Baidarsky Gorge, the road now starts the descent of the Main Caucasian Ridge. The gorge is known for its avalanches of rock and snow, and between the 72- and the 68-km marks, there is a series of special galleries to protect the road. Until there was a railway connection with Tbilisi, the highway had to function year-round, and special workers were employed to keep it clear of snow in winter.

At the 65-km mark, near Almasiani (Upper Kobi), the highway turns right from the river Terek, which flows out of the Trusovskoye Gorge.

Kobi

Kobi lies at 1,932 m (6,340 ft) above sea level by the 64-km mark, at the junction of 4 ravines: Khevsky, Ukhatsky (to the right of the road), Trusovsky (to the left of the road), and behind, Baidarsky. It is believed that the river Baidarka, from which Baidarsky Gorge got its name, was marked as river Shtasavali on the 18th-century map drawn by Prince Vakhushti. It received its present name from that of an Ossetian, Bidarov, who lived here in the time of the Georgian king Erekle II, for rendering help to those travelling along this difficult stretch of road.

Small church, on the right
Cafeteria, on the right

Kazbegi

This is only 47 km (29 miles) from Vladikavkaz and was known in the 19th century as Stepan-Tsminda.

The first description of Mt. Kazbek, which the Russians seemed not to have noticed before, was made by a Russian ambassador to Georgia, Mikhail Tatischev, in 1604, when he passed it travelling along the Terek. In the Ossetian language, Mt. Kazbek is called the Mountain of Christ. According to a legend, the top of the mountain is inaccessible and God himself dwells on the summit. Anyone approaching it will be stopped by unseen forces or by a terrible storm. In spite of the legends, members of the London Alpine Club (Tucker, Moore, and Douglas Freshfield) managed to climb from the southeast slope to the top of the mountain in June 1886. From 1900 onward the Russian mountaineer Mrs. Preobrazhenskaya made the ascent 9 times, obviously finding it a pleasant walk. In 1913, at a height of 3,962 m (13,000 ft), the ruins of a church with a cross on the top were found.

The village of Kazbegi is the centre of the ethnographical district of Khevi. Its former name Stepan-Tsminda, according to a local legend, derives from that of a certain monk, Stepan, who advised transferring the old village, situated near the Beshenaya Balka ("mad ravine"), a little to the south, thus saving it from the regular avalanches of snow. Beshenaya Balka is known for the turbulence of its streams during the rainy seasons, when they smash everything that stands in their way. The new name of the village came from "ka-zibeg," the local border guards whose duty it was to see to the roads and bridges. The village was the birthplace of the Georgian writer Alexander Kazbegi (1848–93).

Church, in the main square of Kazbegi. This was built in 1801 in Roman style and belonged to a local family.

Kazbegi Local Museum, on the main square. Open 10–6; closed Mon. The museum occupies the house where the writer Alexander Kazbegi lived. It contains a section devoted to him and also to the history, economy, and natural resources of the Khevi region. Arms and national costumes are also on display, as well as a hat and tobacco pipe that belonged to Pushkin. There is a statue of Kazbegi in the square, which was unveiled in 1960, and nearby is his grave, with a tombstone carved out of solid marble in the shape of two-peaked Mt. Kazbek. Alexander Kazbegi was of a princely line, and it is said locally that the mountain was called after his family.

Pushkin Statue, to the left of the road.

Intourist Hotel and Restaurant, tel. 2436. There is an Intourist office here.

Kazbegi Restaurant, on the main road on the right

Department Store

On the mountain slope is the village of Gergeti and the *Tsminda Samebo (Holy Trinity) Church.* It was apparently built in the 12th century in the time of Queen Tamar, on the spot where it was believed the apostle Andrew erected a cross. It was built with particular attention to the surrounding mountains and to snowy Kazbek itself. The Georgian historian Tsarevich Vakhushti refers to this church as a monastery, which is corroborated by the numerous caves around it that once served as monks' cells. In times of danger, according to Vakhushti, the church was a storehouse for the treasures of Mtskheta and even St. Nina's cross was kept there. The Tsminda Samebo church was described by Pushkin in his poem "Monastery on Kazbek." A treasure trove was discovered on the territory of the village, consisting of copper vessels, bronze figurines, and silver bowls dating back to the 6th–7th century B.C.

The fine mountain pastures here encouraged the breeding of sheep, which leads the local economy. The place is also famous for its deer hunters and mountain guides.

Farther along, the highway winds down through Dariyalskoye Uschelye (Daryal Gorge), or the "Gate of Alani," Dar-y-Alan, in old Persian. According to Pliny, the Caucasian Gates (Porta Caucasia, also erroneously called Portae Caspiae) were here. They were of wood, plated with iron, and closed the mouth of the 8-km (5-mile) gorge, the rocky sides of which tower perpendicularly to a height of 1,798 m (5,900 ft).

One cannot help but be impressed by this stretch. Some have said that this is not a road but a thrilling fairy tale; the narrow, curiously shaped rift is like a gigantic grave, and the traveller feels like a poor, helpless creature at the bottom. Everything in the ravine is dim, and the southern sky looks like a narrow blue ribbon high above. The Daryal Gorge has been compared to the banks of the Rhine, where similar romantic castles perch on the rocks. At the 33/34-km mark are the ruins of the early 19th-century Daryal *fortress*, which was built of pinkish stone, with round towers at each corner to defend the Daryal Ravine against the enemy. Halfway down the ravine on a small rock up on the right are the *ruins of Tamar's Castle*, which has, however, nothing to do with the famous Georgian Queen Tamar (1184–1212).

Finally the highway crosses the bridge over the Terek known as Chertov Most, marking the border between Georgia and Northern Ossetia. (These republics are described under their respective capitals, Tbilisi and Vladikavkaz.) The name has often been translated as Devil's Bridge, but it is more likely derived from the word for "mark," referring to its position on the boundary.

GIDIGICH, LAKE
See Kishinyov, p. 234.

GOLOVACHEVKA
See Dzhambul, p. 120.

GOLUBIYE OZYORA
See Nalchik, p. 380.

GORI Population—65,000
Intourist runs overnight trips to Gori from Tbilisi, 98 km (61 miles) away by road.

The town is in the geometrical centre of Georgia and stands on the left bank of the Kura River, at the point where it is joined by the Leakhvi and the Ludzhudi. The exact date of its foundation is unknown. In Georgian chronicles it is first mentioned during the reign of Queen Tamar (1184–1212). According to another source, an Armenian historian, Mathew of Edess, Gori was founded by King David the Builder in 1123 and settled by Armenians who sought asylum and protection from their enemies in Georgia. However, the town's location, on the way to Imeretia, confirms the fact that Gori fortress existed here long before the Armenian settlement. in the 16th century, the town was captured by the Turks and then changed hands among the Persians, Turks, and Georgians. In 1801 it was joined to Russia and became a district centre.

At present Gori is the administrative centre of a large agricultural district with food and light industrial production. There is a textile factory and a fruit cannery there. The local white wine, Atenuri, can only be drunk in Gori, as it travels badly. There are many cultural and educational institutions including a branch of the Georgian Polytechnical Institute, a teachers' training college, and a drama theatre. A large park with venerable trees stretches along the Leakhvi River.

The ruins of the Goris-Tsikhe, Gori's fortress, are a specimen of mediaeval defence architecture. The name Gori itself means "hill" in Georgian, referring to that upon which the fortress stands. An acropolis stood here in the 1st century B.C. A fortress also stood here, and the existing ruins, where some frescoes remain, date from the 12th century. There is a church within the walls. In 1123 it was inhabited by the refugee Armenians. In the 16th century, the Turks captured the fortress, along with Gori itself, and then it continually changed hands among the Turks, the Persians, and the Georgians until it was taken by Russia in 1801. It was restored in 1900 but suffered considerably in the earthquake of 1920. There is a model of this fortress in the History Museum and the castle can be well viewed along the length of Lenin Street.

Near the fortress are the *ruins of the Armenian Church of St. Stephan*, founded in the 12th century, restored in the 17th century, and destroyed by the earthquake of 1920.

Synagogue, Chelyuskintsev Street

Amilakhvari Palace, at the end of Lenin Street. This fine old blue house was formerly the home of the Amilakhvari family.

Stalin's House Museum, Stalin Prospect, in the garden in the centre of the town. Open 9–6; closed Mon. Joseph Stalin was born in Gori on 21 December 1879, and spent his childhood until 1893 in this house. His father, Vissarion Dzhugashvili, was a local cobbler. The museum was opened in 1939 and is in the form of a special pavilion, which was built to protect the hut where Stalin was born. All the surrounding buildings were demolished.

Stalin Museum, just beside the house-museum. Open 9–6; closed Mon. This contains documentary material telling the story of Stalin's career, both political and military. There is a most unusual sepulchre-hall to frame his bronze death-mask. The museum was built in 1957 and was closed between 1962 and 1964.

Local History Ethnography Museum, Lomauri Street 7. Open 9–5; closed Mon. This is housed in the domed *Roman Catholic Church of the Dormition* and in the building beside it. Catholic monks were active in their missionary work in Georgia from the 13th century, but this church was built in 1806 and the house next door belonged to it as well. The museum contains an interesting archaeological collection, and the stones from the ancient acropolis prove that the town has at least 2,400 years of history behind it. Alexandre Dumas visited here, as did Edouard Manet. A lithograph by Manet shows a view of the castle above the town.

Eternal Flame and Museum of Military Glory, Stalin Prospect 19

House of Pioneers, Lenin (formerly Tsar) Street 3. In the building of the seminary where Stalin studied from 1888–94.

Chavchavadze's Bust, Chavchavadze Street.

Prince Alexander Chavchavadze (1784–1846) was a Georgian poet and statesman, whose daughter, Nina, married Griboyedov.

Baratashvili Monument, Baratashvili Street. Nikolai Baratashvili (1816–45) was a poet.

Stalin Monument, Stalin Square. This is now the only big monument to Stalin in the whole of the Soviet Union.

Victory Monument. Sculpted by Amashukeli.

Georgian Drama Theatre, Chavchavadze Street 24. In front of the theatre building is a bust of Georgi Eristavi (1811–64), founder of Georgian drama.

Youth Theatre

Intourist Hotel and Restaurant, Stalin Street 26; tel. 23–091. The hotel was built in 1957, at the same time as the Stalin Museum. The same pattern of parquet flooring is in both buildings. Intourist office: tel. 23–588.

Kartli Hotel and Restaurant, Lenin Street

Khachapuri Parlour, at the corner of Lenin and Baratashvili streets

Department Store, Stalin Street

Gift Shop, Stalin Street

Bookshop, Chavchavadze Street 55

GPO, Stalin Prospect 15

Bank, Lenin Street 50

Filling and Repair Station, out of town, on the road leading to Tbilisi. There is also a *Service Station* up on the left, on the way into town.

Uplis-Tsikhe

This cave town is 10 km (6 miles) from Gori, along a very bad road. Also known as the Troglodite Town, this was inhabited in pre-Christian times. Some scientists say it belongs to the period of Persian and Parthian influence in Georgia. The name means "Uplis castle." Uplis was the son of the founder of Mtskheta, the ancient capital of Georgia, and was said to be a direct descendant of Japhet. The caves of this town rise up in tiers. Streets, a marketplace, swimming pools, and houses of different sizes can be recognised. Some of the caves look very much like churches. Also underground is the *Palace of Tamar*. There is no evidence that Tamar actually lived there, but the Georgians are fond of calling anything unusually splendid after her.

The following out-of-town excursions are not on Intourist's list.

Goris-Dzhavari (Cross of Gori) Monastery, 3 km (2 miles) from the town centre, on a hill above the right bank of the river Kura.

The 16th-century church is dedicated to St. George. The legend of its foundation is as follows. Queen Tamar was hunting in this region, when her favourite falcon flew away and settled on the top of the mountain, where the monastery now stands. In dismay she asked that the man in her party who loved her best should swim across the Kura and recapture the bird for her. The river was in full spring flood, and the young men hesitated

to show their loyalty, but at last one plunged in. He reached the opposite bank, caught the falcon and began to swim back again, but halfway across he encountered difficulties and it seemed that he would drown. Tamar prayed to St. George for help, promising to found a monastery if her prayer were answered. Apparently it was, for she later founded the monastery on the mountain top where her falcon had alighted.

At the end of the last century, it was a tradition of the cathedral that those women who wanted either a husband or a child should put an iron chain weighing more than 50 kg (more than 100 pounds) around their necks, and if they were then able to walk around the building 3 times, their misfortunes would be over.

Ateni

The cathedral of Atensky Sioni (Athenian Sion) is 12 km (7 miles) from Gori on the way to Ateni. Leaving the town, cross the river and go to Zhidistavi, then turn right.

The drive up the valley of the river Tana to the cathedral is beautiful. To start with, the road passes through vineyards and orchards of apple trees, quinces, figs, and walnuts. On the left, across the river, stands a wine factory. Then the scenery becomes wilder, as the road leads deeper into the mountains. Although there are 3 places along the way where mountain streams flow over the road, the surface is good.

The village of Ateni stands on the site of a town founded in the 2nd century B.C. Above the road can be seen the *ruins of the Sativis-Tsikhe Monastery*, standing 274 m (900 ft) above the river.

St. George's Church, above Ateni on the left

Atenski Sioni Cathedral was built by Bagrat IV (1027–72) and is considered to be one of the best examples of 11th-century architecture. The walls are covered with carving and have marble columns and good frescoes.

GORKI LENINSKIYE

See Moscow environs, p. 362.

GUEGHARD

See Erevan environs, p. 133.

GUISSAR

See Dushanbe, p. 118.

HAGHPAT MONASTERY

See Erevan environs, p. 140.

HAMZAABAD

See Fergana, p. 144.

IRKUTSK Population—626,000

This city is situated among beautiful scenery on, and half-encircled by, the river Angara and its tributary, the Ushakovka, at the point where the Irkut joins them. It is unevenly divided by the Angara, the oldest and the largest part being on the right side. It is practically in the centre of Siberia, 5,042 km (3,133 miles) from Moscow and 65 km (40 miles) west of Lake Baikal, where the Angara begins. It has plenty of sunshine, even more sunny days than the Caucasian resorts. It is dry, with snow in winter. Its extreme climate is tempered by its proximity to the lake. There are warm springs nearby. This couplet in its praise dates from 1846:

Our Irkutsk, a splendid city, is indeed a gift
    of God
Although freezing cold in winter and in
    summer monstrous hot.

The hottest days in July are preceded by a cool morning mist, which lies over the river and over Lake Baikal. When this lifts, the temperature in the city may become uncomfortable, but it is always much cooler by the lakeside. The summer flowers appear about 6 weeks later than the same species in Moscow.

Chekhov, who was here in 1890, wrote: "Of all the towns of Siberia, the best is Irkutsk. It is a superior city, absolutely intelligent. Theatre, museum, city garden with music, good hotels . . . absolutely European!" One of the names by which it is known in contemporary literature is the pearl of Siberia.

The Irkutsk area, of which the city is the centre, is equal in size to the territory of pre-war Germany, plus Austria, Switzerland, and Italy. Its gold-mining industry is the largest in the Soviet Union. The Trans-Siberian Railway runs through Irkutsk, linking it with Moscow, 5,031 km (3,126 miles) to the west, and with Vladivostok, 4,141 km (2,573 miles) to the east.

The region has long been inhabited by hunters and fishermen. In Glazkovskoye, on the outskirts of the city, a burial site was found with items made of copper and brass. It dates back to the 17th–13th centuries B.C. Irkutsk was founded in 1652 as a Cossack encampment by a nobleman, Ivan Pokhabov. He had come to collect the fur tribute from the Buryats, who inhabited the country on either side of Lake Baikal. He built a stronghold on Dyachy Island, in the Angara by the mouth of the Irkut. 9 years passed before the local Buryat tribesmen were subdued, and only then, in 1661, was a fort built on the mainland, on the right bank of the river, opposite the mouth of the Irkut. It was at first known as Yandashevsky Ostrog, and its site was just about where the 2 big white churches stand today. It was strengthened in 1671, and 4 corner towers were added. The chronicles mention that in 1682 there was a wooden church inside the fortress, but this was burned down in 1716.

Irkutsk became a town in 1686 and after another 10 years was granted the coat-of-arms of argent a panther, running on green grass holding a sable in its jaws. From Irkutsk the Yakutsk Tract led northward, and trade grew with Yakutsk and Dauria.

The signing of the first Treaty of Nerchinsk in 1689 was followed by increased commercial contacts with China and Mongolia. The city's first chime of bells was installed in the Sergiyev Tower in 1698. The first school in Eastern Siberia was opened in 1725 by the order of Peter the Great. It was in *Voznesensky Monastery*, 6 km (4 miles) from the town. The main purpose of the school was to train Mongolian-speaking interpreters and to prepare missionaries to convert the Mongols and Buryats to Christianity. In 1736 Irkutsk became a provincial capital, and it was made capital of Eastern Siberia in 1822. Although linked by the Angara to the Yenisei, this area was nevertheless remote from the rest of Russia, and the local authorities often acquired immense power. The reputations of the governors of Irkutsk were not always the best. Peter the Great in 1721 ordered that Governor Prince Matvei Gagarin, governor of Siberia from 1711–21, be hanged for abuses of power and "unheard-of theft." He was accused of punishing and then pardoning just for monetary gain. His carriage wheels were of silver, and his horses were shod with silver and gold. One of the ceilings of his house was decorated with an aquarium filled with exotic fish. Gagarin, among other governors of Siberia, tried to establish vice-royalty. He was even suspected of planning to sever Siberia from Russia and proclaim its independence. At his inauguration in 1782, Governor-General Koshkin stood on the imperial throne and received homage from all the different tribes of Siberia, and he served bulls roasted whole at his great parties. Governor-General Speransky helped to improve the situation when he instituted proceedings for gross embezzlement against the 2 previous governors-general and 48 lesser officials.

As Russian territory expanded eastward, it stood at the gateway to the trans-Baikal region. In the 1750s a new school opened, teaching geodesy, navigation, and Japanese. Those who failed their examinations were sent into the army. It was notable for having 80- and 90-year-olds among its pupils. There were 100 pupils by 1781, and in 1789 Catherine II presented it with a library and arranged that teachers should be sent from St. Petersburg. In 1784 the merchant-explorer Grigory Shelekhov established a fur-trading post on Kodiak Island off the Alaskan coast. A Russian-American company was founded by Paul I in 1799 and given a monopoly on hunting and mining on the North American seaboard north of 55 degrees north.

From 1798 Irkutsk was important for its place on the Russian trade route to China and Mongolia known as the Tuva Tract when furs, hides, silk, and tea passed this way. In 1792, with the first attempts to establish regular trade relations with Japan, a special Japanese school was opened. Among the teachers was a Lutheran from Saxony called Ivan Bekker and a Japanese sailor called Nikolai Kolotygin. He had been shipwrecked on Kamchatka, and when he arrived in Irkutsk he converted to Orthodoxy and was christened Nikolai. He took a Russian surname, learned Russian, bought a house, married a Russian girl, and brought up a

IRKUTSK

family. When Russia received the left bank of the river Amur and the territory as far as the Pacific Ocean after the Peking Treaty of 1860, the Amur Gates were erected with the inscription: "The Road to the Great Ocean."

The town was a place of exile from the 17th century onward. One of the earliest to be banished here was Alexander Radischev (1749–1802), whose death sentence for his revolutionary writings was commuted to 10 years' banishment in Siberia.

In spite of the traffic passing through, in the early 19th century, Irkutsk still looked more like a large, dirty village than the "capital of Siberia," as it claimed to be. After rain, a number of streets were impassable, and the mud never dried. The houses were built at all angles to the roads "as if they wanted to watch what was going on in the street or recessed as though trying to find a private retreat." Cows wandered through the mud along with packs of dogs, and sometimes ducks were able to swim by. In 1808, however, the village look

became a thing of the past as Nikolai Treskin took over the post of governor. The squares were raised and dried, and the streets were filled in by prison labour. There was no professional engineer to oversee the work; instead an exiled convict by the name of Gushya took full responsibility. He even devised an official uniform for himself, and he and his workers were known as Gushya's Brigade. He terrorised the householders, especially when their wooden buildings failed to conform to the new street plan. If a corner or a wall stuck out too far, he would have it chopped off, causing some half-sawn-off rooms to be left open to the elements, sometimes for years. By 1822 there were 15,000 citizens and 2,000 houses in Irkutsk.

Some participants in the 1825 (Decembrists') revolt were sent here and played an important role in the development of the town. In 1851 a Siberian department of Russian Geographical Society was organised. The department thoroughly researched the Siberian and Far Eastern territories. It was then that gold was discovered to the north and the east of Irkutsk. This attracted crowds of people, and the Siberian Klondike began. In 1864, the first telegram was sent from Irkutsk to St. Petersburg from the governor-general to the palace with New Year's greetings.

After the Polish uprising of 1863, 18,000 Poles were sent to Siberia from their own country. Part of their number settled in Irkutsk. Among them were doctors, teachers, and artists, who added to the cultural development of the town. They included the zoologists B. Dybowski and V. Godlewski, the geologists I. Cherski and A. Chekanowski, the archaeologist N. Witkowski, and artists Wronski and Zenkowski. Skilled workers and technical specialists from Warsaw and other big Polish cities also shared their knowledge with local Siberians. The Poles gave lessons in music and foreign languages, and the far-away, provincial town turned quite suddenly into something like a European cultural centre, with an unusually high percentage of intellectuals. It was even called the Paris of Siberia.

Those who had participated in the uprising of 1863 were allowed to return home only after 20 years had passed. By that time large numbers had settled down properly and had married Siberians, so they stayed on with no thought of leaving. There are still many families in Irkutsk with Polish names, but they have been completely assimilated.

By 1885 exiles constituted one-third of the local population. Among the Marxists who were sent to Irkutsk in the 1890s was Leonid Krasin, a well-known communist who later became commissar for foreign trade. Between 1922 and 1926, he was twice ambassador to Britain and once to France. Later still the exiles included Stalin and Dzerzhinsky. Another well-known communist sent here was Sergei Kirov, in 1909. Mikhail Frunze was banished to the village of Manzurka, in the Irkutsk area, in 1914, and Vyacheslav Molotov followed him in 1915. Valerian Kuibyshev was sent to the village of Tutura. All of these managed to escape. Although electricity and water supplies were laid down at the very beginning of this century (the first power station was built in 1910, and the streets were lit then), in 1912 the town's budget for public utilities was almost entirely spent on prison construction.

The Great Siberian Railway was built as far as Irkutsk in 1898, but for the 7 years until the round-Baikal line was completed, trains crossed the lake in a specially equipped icebreaker, the Baikal. The ship had been built in England, brought here in sections, and reassembled on the lake. She was 4,200 tons, 88 m (289 ft) long and 17 m (56 ft) wide, the second-largest icebreaker in the world at the time. After the completion of the railway Irkutsk began to grow rapidly. In 1897 the town had 51,473 inhabitants; by 1919, 90,800. In 1910 there were 18,187 houses in Irkutsk, all but 1,190 were built of wood.

During the Civil War, there was exceptionally bitter fighting here. The town changed hands and was held by the counterrevolutionaries, but it was here that Admiral Kolchak met his end. Alexander Kolchak (1870–1920) called himself the Supreme Ruler of Russia, but he was betrayed along with his prime minister, Viktor Pepelyayev, and shot on 7 February. As it was winter, it was impossible to dig graves for them, so the bodies were pushed under the ice of the frozen river. At this time a great part of Russia's gold was recaptured from the Czech ex-prisoners-of-war at Irkutsk. There were 29 railway truckloads of gold in 1,678 sacks and 5,143 boxes and, in addition, a further 7 truckloads of platinum and silver. After the Civil War, the reconstruction of the town was delayed until 1924.

Irkutsk's importance as a railway junction has increased, until now nearly one-fifth of the local workers are employed by the railways. Timber, grain, building materials, and other goods transported on the Angara pass through Irkutsk, and it has become a centre for gold trans-shipment and fur purchasing. Thousands of sable skins, of every possible shade between black and red, are collected and stored here. The best variety is the Barkuzin sable from the thick forests of the Baikal area. The first direct Moscow–Irkutsk flight took place in 1929, and now the city's air traffic is also considerable.

Besides being both the administrative centre of the region and the chief cultural centre of Eastern Siberia, Irkutsk is also the home of a special branch of SOAN (the Siberian Department of the Academy of Sciences), which was established to deal with the scientific problems of the industrialisation of Eastern Siberia. It is the second-largest branch after that in Novosibirsk. Its 30 research institutes include those of geochemistry, the earth's crust, plant physiology and biochemistry, power engineering, economics, and geography. Most of these are situated in an academic township on the left bank of the Angara. The Limnological Institute on the shore of Lake Baikal is the oldest of all Siberia's academic institutes. It makes a special study of the lake in all its aspects. Numerous expeditions set out from here annually to the remotest parts of the area. It was local geologists who found the important diamond fields in Vilnya.

The 7 local higher educational establishments take 20,000 students. Chief among these is the University on Gagarin Boulevard. This was founded in 1918 as the first university in Siberia. Besides having faculties of physics, mathematics, chemistry, geology, philology, geography, and law, it also trains Buryat-Mongolian- and Russian-speaking teachers for East Siberian schools. There are separate colleges for mining, economics, agriculture, medicine, teacher training, and foreign languages, with polytechnical and engineering colleges planned for the near future. The scientists of the academic institutes work in close collaboration with the staff of the university and the other local educational establishments.

Local industries produce heavy machinery for the mining and metal industries, machine tools, mica, soap, flour, and macaroni, among other things. There are also plants for tea packing, agricultural machinery repairs, and woodworking, besides a number of brickyards and timberyards. Electrical power comes from the 66,000-kilowatt station, which was built on the Angara in 1959, and from Bratsk.

The city truly reflects the past, and the words of an eminent local called Shelgunov might be addressed to today's visitor: "Irkutsk: as England gave birth to London and France Paris, so Siberia produced Irkutsk. She is her pride, and to miss seeing Irkutsk is to miss Siberia."

Many of the impressive old buildings still standing were put up between 1830 and 1890, including the *town hall*, the *theatre* (1897), the *banks*, and the *museum* in Moorish style. There were plenty of well-to-do merchants in Irkutsk until as late as the 1880s, because it was they who were the principal owners of the famous Lena goldfields, and naturally part of their wealth was spent on the construction of public buildings. These included schools, hospitals, workshops, orphanages, museums, theatres, and art galleries. They also helped to finance exploration and the development of the Amur region. Few Russian towns can equal Irkutsk in this respect. An example of the buildings is the *Central Telegraph Office*, which belonged to the goldmine owner Nemchinov; it was reconstructed in the 1920s. On the records is the great 2-day fire of 1870, when much of the town, including 10 churches, burned down. Local inhabitants compared the catastrophe with the last days of Pompeii. One big bell melted from the heat and turned into a large lump of copper on the ground. About 105 stone and 3,418 wooden houses were destroyed. A museum, libraries, and important archive documents were also lost, and no more than 35 stone and about 3,000 wooden houses remained in the town.

Wooden houses, typical of old Siberia, can still be seen on Krasnogvardeiskaya Street as well as in many other places. There are several in the park at the crossing of Dekabrskikh Sobytii and Sovietskaya streets, and the one at Gagarin Boulevard 16 is especially decorative. *Shubin's House* at Lapin Street 23 dates from the 18th century. Those less spectacular are gradually disappearing and making room for new buildings.

The historical and modern centre of the city is around the asphalt expanse of *Kirov Square*, and it is a logical place to start a walking tour of the city. The garden with a large fountain was once the territory of the mainland fortress. Spassky Church is also on the fortress site. From here Lenin (formerly Zamorskaya, and later Amurskaya) Street leads eastward. The name change to Amurskaya came about after the signing of the Russo-Chinese Treaty of Aigun in 1858, when the border was redrawn to follow the line of the Amur river. Upon Governor-General Muravyov's return to Irkutsk after the signing, Triumphal Gates were built on Zamorskaya Street, and when he received the title of Amursky, the street was renamed too.

Spassky Church is now run as part of the *Local*

Museum, while *Bogoyavlenye Cathedral*, which stands to the right and nearer the river, serves as an art gallery in conjunction with the Art Museum. The Catholic church beside it is now a concert hall. Kirov Square used to be called Cathedral Square before Tikhvinsky Cathedral was blown up. Then it was renamed III-International Square and in 1935 called Kirov Square in honour of the Soviet revolutionary and statesman Sergei Kirov (Kostrikov), who had lived in Irkutsk in 1908–9 on his way back from exile in Tomsk. Here now is the *World War II Memorial*, where schoolchildren form a guard of honour that changes half-hourly while music plays. There are government buildings around it. As one walks down the street, away from the river, there is a hotel on either side. The *Sibir Hotel* on the right was built in 1933 in constructivist style. Opposite is the *Geographical Department of Irkutsk University*, in the former building of the State Bank. Next to it is the *Art Museum*. The old brick building on the right is part of the city orphanage, built in 1873 by the industrialist Bazanov and now used as an eye clinic and an ear-nose-throat hospital. The street goes on to cross the busy thoroughfare of Karl Marx (formerly Bolshaya) Street at the point where there is a *garden* and a *statue of Lenin*. Farther on, on the left, is the old *Social Club*, designed in 1891 by Rassushin; from 1941 it was used by the company of the Musical Comedy Theatre until their new building was opened in 1986. On the right is the *Almaz Restaurant* and up on the left *Krestovozdvizhenskaya Church*, open for services. Here too is the newly built *Musical Comedy Theatre*.

A second recommended walk starts in the area at the far end of Karl Marx Street with the *Decembrists' Museum* in Trubetskoy's house (closed on Tuesdays). The establishment of the fortress in the Kirov Square area was certainly the beginning of the story of Irkutsk, but the arrival of the Decembrists was very important for the social and cultural growth of the town. A fortress is a fortress, but the oldest real street in Irkutsk is that now called *Dekabrskikh Sobytii*, and a visit to the nearby *Decembrists' church* and *Prince Volkonsky's house* put history well in perspective. From there walk southward along Karl Marx Street, which really starts even farther from the river with *Kuibyshev's statue*. In the 19th century, this street was lined with rich mansions and shops, and still the best shops and cafés are here, together with a rich variety of old buildings. These include the *Grand Hotel* (now the Rodnik sports shop), built of brick and plaster in neo-Renaissance style by Kuznetsov in 1903. The tiled building of the *Hotel Moderne* now houses an art college, and *Dunayeva House* is where Chekhov stayed. No. 47, the *House of Officers*, was built by Kudelsky in 1878 as Kalygina Palace. The red and white building with steps at the entrance at No. 43 was Kalygina's house and is now the Pioneer Cinema. The large, grey building was the railway headquarters while the building of Polyclinic No. 2 used to belong to the Russo-

Asiatic Bank. No. 28 is the *Post Office*. There are *banks and shops*, and Uritsky (formerly Pesterovskaya) Street leads down to the left to the local *market* (formerly the corn exchange). The *Natural History Branch of the Local Museum* is in an exbookshop with a globe high on the façade. Printing works adjoin it. Beyond the *Arctica Restaurant* comes the crossing with Lenin Street and the garden with the statue of Lenin, and then the *Drama Theatre* on the left. At the end on the left, by the embankment, is the *Local Museum*, once used by the Geographical Society and with names of the famous outside including Bering (of the Straits) and Humboldt (of the Current). The *University Library* on the right side is in the White House, formerly the governor-general's residence. Behind it is a *monument* to fighters for soviet power, commemorating the Civil War fighting that took place all around the White House.

Cross over now to *Conqueror's of Siberia Obelisk* and onto Gagarin Boulevard, the right embankment of the Angara with *gardens* in both directions. Along to the left a bridge leads from the garden onto an island, which is a recreation area with a boating station. Farther upstream is the dam of the Irkutsk Reservoir, with a motor road leading across the river. Following along the embankment in the opposite direction, to the right, tall, modern buildings overlook the river. Irkutsk is in fact in a seismic zone, and it is only in recent years that builders have been able to put up houses more than 4 storeys high. On the right now is the *Gold Institute*. The local gold-melting laboratory was opened in 1871, and it worked upon all kinds of ore research. The marble plaque was affixed to the new, grey building of the *Institute of Non-Ferrous and Precious Metals* in 1971. Ingots used to be sent from here under armed guard to the State Bank at a time when 70 percent of Russia's gold came from Siberia. Next on the right is the *Intourist Hotel*. The wide bridge over the river was completed in 1936, replacing a pontoon bridge. It leads to the railway station on the left bank of the Angara. Behind it is the new town with Irkutsk's Akademgorodok, where the scientists live and work.

Znamensky Convent is some distance from the centre of the city. It is of brick and was founded in 1762, when Peter the Great presented it with a much-treasured silver-bound Bible, which is used for special services. It is one of the 3 Orthodox churches still used in Irkutsk. A prelate has his headquarters here. The main *Cathedral*, dedicated to the Apparition of Our Lady, was built in 1757, and the iconostasis and frescoes were restored in 1950. It is now the cathedral church of Irkutsk and the centre of an extremely large bishopric. Within the convent walls as you approach, a low iron fence encloses the grave of Yekaterina Trubetskoy, the first Decembrist wife to follow her husband into exile from St. Petersburg. Buried with her, among other little children, is their infant son Volodya, with his memorial reading, "Of such is the Kingdom of Heaven." The Decembrist wives lost many babies, and not only here. Maria Volkonskaya left her year-old son in St. Petersburg with relatives and only learned later of his death. Here too are the graves of some of the Decembrists—Bechasny, Mukhanov, Panov—and also Grigory Sheleknov, known as the Russian Columbus and the conqueror of Russian America (Alaska) because he founded the first Russian settlements in North America and in the Aleutian Islands in 1783. He died in Irkutsk in 1795. Nearby, near Radischev Street, is a *monument* marking the grave of historian Afanasii Schapov (1830–75).

The suburb of Znamenskoye was the start of the Yakutsk Tract. It was also the site of Irkutsk prison. The area is now called Maratovskoye.

Voznesensky Monastery used to stand 5 km (3 miles) from Znamensky, near the place where the new bridge is today. There is nothing left now except the old hotel. In 1725 a Mongolian School was opened in the monastery.

Spasskaya (Our Saviour's) Church, Sukhe Bator Street 2, near the eternal flame and beside the Angara. Founded in 1706, this 2-storey stone church is Irkutsk's oldest building. Its construction lasted for 10 years. The mural on the eastern end dates from the building's earliest years, for it was painted in 1710. On the southern wall is a Veronica. The church is open as a branch of the *Local Museum*, having changing exhibits on ethnography. We saw a display of Gerasimov's reconstructions of portraits from skulls, stone-age art, archaeological finds from the 1981 excavations for the Bratsk hydropower station, human skeletons in hollowed-out tree trunks that were used as coffins. Upstairs is a variety of forest and hunting equipment, embroidery, carving, and silverwork, much resembling that of the North American Indians, but belonging to 15 different Siberian nationalities—Buryat, Evenk, Yakut, Tuva, Tofalari, Tatar, Yukagiri, Koryaki, and Itelmeni among them. Open 10–6; closed Tues.

Bogoyavlensky (Epiphany) Cathedral, Nizhne Naberezhnaya Street. Built in 1725. Used as a picture gallery with changing exhibits. There is a good collection of icons. Open 11–7; closed Mon. and Tues.

Krestovozdvizhenskaya (Elevation of the Cross) Church, Sedova Street. Built in Siberian baroque style in 1758, decorated with some fine stonework, and still in use.

Troitskaya (Trinity) Church, 5-Armii Street 8. Built in 1775 and now used as a planetarium.

Grigory Neokesariisky Church, at the crossing of Gorky and 5-Armii streets, next to the Troitskaya Church. The church is large, white-painted, and used as a library. Behind it is a 2-storey wooden building that is a kindergarten. It used to be the kindergarten part of Bazanov's orphanage but was damaged by fire, restored in 1882, and moved here in 1920. At that time it still had some stained glass in its windows.

Preobrazhenskaya (Transfiguration) Church, Timiryazeva (formerly Preobrazhenskaya) Street

56–58, near Prince Volkonsky's house. This church was built in 1798 and is under restoration; it can be distinguished by its green roof and spire. Timiryazeva Street is one of the few streets that was not damaged by the fire of 1879.

Entry to Jerusalem Church (1835), Bortsov Revolutsii Street 15

Catholic Church, near Kirov Square. This spired church stands on the site of an earlier wooden one. It was designed by the Polish architect Tamulewicz in 1883 and built with money donated by the Polish exiles who were sent to Irkutsk after the uprisings of 1831 and 1863. It was restored in 1978, and an organ was installed by an East German firm. The acoustics are very good, and it is now used for organ concerts.

Church of Our Lady of Kazan, Barrikad Street 34. This church has been closed and is now used by a school of cinemechanics.

Innokentievskaya Church, farther from the centre of Irkutsk. Open for services.

Vladimirskaya Church, Dekabrskikh Sobytii Street

Mikhail Arkhangel Church, Innokentievsky Street. This white church is some distance from the centre of town, in Novo-Leninsky Raion.

Local Museum, Karl Marx Street 2, in a red brick building opposite the White House. Open 10–6; closed Tues. Founded in 1782, the museum has departments of natural resources and of history. Ethnographical material depicts the old way of life of the Evenki, the Yajuts, and the Buryats, the indigenous peoples of Eastern Siberia. The building was designed by Rozen in 1883 for the Geographical Society and completed in 1891. The names of eminent geographers and explorers can be seen in the panels decorating the walls.

The White House, Gagarin Boulevard 24. This house, built in 1804 probably after a project by Giacome Quarenghi, was known as "the gem of Irkutsk." Its portico and 6 Corinthian columns marks it as an example of Russian empire style. It used to be the governor-general's residence, was the venue of the Siberian Geographical Society when it was organised in 1851, and at the time of the revolution, it served as the Bolshevik headquarters. Today it houses the university's scientific library. After climbing the governor-general's stairs, one may visit the high-ceilinged reading room above, which used to be his ballroom. 3 crystal and blue glass chandeliers are still in place, and the windows high up are where the musicians used to be.

Decembrists' Museum, Dzerzhinsky Street 64. Open 10–6; closed Mon. This is a branch of the Local Museum and is in the attractive, wooden house in typical 19th-century empire style that belonged to Sergei Trubetskoy (1790–1860), a colonel of the Preobrazhensky Regiment and influential in the Decembrist Northern Society. He was sentenced to hard labour in Siberia in 1826, and after his release in 1839, he lived in Oyek in the province of Irkutsk. Trubetskoy moved with his family to Irkutsk in 1845, and it was here that his wife and

several of their children died. He lived here until the amnesty of 1856, when he left for Moscow to live the final years of his life.

Volkonsky's House, Volkonsky Street 12, opposite the Agricultural Institute and not far from the Decembrists' Museum. Open 10–6; closed Mon. & Tues. This belonged to the Decembrist Sergei Volkonsky and his wife, Maria. They did much for the theatrical development of Irkutsk, for they staged performances in their home which were attended by the Decembrists and other residents of the town. The large house is in a courtyard, complete with a coachhouse, a stable, and a servants' house with attics over them. A well and 2 barns are also inside the enclosure. Among the interesting exhibits in the house are some pieces of Maria Volkonskaya's own bead embroidery. The house was opened as a museum in 1985, 160 years after the Decembrists' revolt. Apart from the restoration of the Decembrists' church, local Decembrist coverage is being extended by moving the wooden house of Kuznetsov here. The Volkonskys stayed in this house on their way east, and again on their return, while their own house was being built.

Dunayeva House, Fourier Street 1. This blue and white 2-storey house is where Anton Chekhov took rooms from 4–11 June 1890, during his visit to Irkutsk. There is a plaque on the building façade to commemorate his visit. The street is named after the same Charles Fourier (1772–1837) whose social theories based on domestic agricultural associations were, after his death, briefly put into practice in the United States at Brook Farm in Massachusetts.

Kirov's House, Stepan Khalturin Street. Sergei Kirov lived here illegally after the failure of the 1905 revolution, and here, in 1909, he carried on party work in secret.

Regional Art Museum, Lenin Street 5. Open 11–7; Sat. and Sun. 12–8; closed Tues. The collection began with 250 pictures that belonged to Mayor Vladimir Sukachev before the revolution and with others from the merchant Sibiryakov. Russian art is well represented. There is a portrait of Governor-General Muravyov-Amursky, looking a little like Harold Wilson. Anatolsky's sculpture "Ivan the Terrible" stands at the entrance. There are a number of old copies of Western masters, as well as several originals.

The Museum of the Biological and Geographical Institute has a good display of the flora and fauna of Lake Baikal.

Mineralogical Museum, in the Polytechnical Institute, Lermontov Street 83. Open 9–4; closed Sun. A good display of the mineral wealth of Siberia.

Planetarium, 5-Armii Street 8. In the building of the Troitskaya (Trinity) Church, built in 1775.

Obelisk to the Conquerors of Siberia, Gagarin Boulevard. This stands on the original granite base of a statue sculpted by Bach of Tsar Alexander III, which was erected to mark the completion of the Great Siberian Railway. It was unveiled in 1909, and the first inscription read: "To the Founder of the Great Siberian Railway." The statue was removed in 1920, and an obelisk of identical weight and made of Finnish granite was put up in 1964. On the various sides of the pedestal are the ancient coats-of-arms of Irkutsk, Krasnoyarsk, Yakutsk, and of all Siberia, and high-reliefs of Yermak, Count Speransky, and Governor-General Muravyov-Amursky.

Revolutionary Fighters' Monument, behind the White House. This monument designed by Ryashentsev stands on the common grave of the 153 Red Army soldiers who lost their lives defending the building in December 1917. It was unveiled in 1965.

Civil War Memorial, Kommunarov Street. A statue of 3 partisans with a flag.

Lenin Statue, in the garden at the crossing of Lenin and Karl Marx streets, opposite the Labour Palace. By Tomsky, and unveiled in 1952.

Lenin Monument, at the crossing of Karl Marx and Proletarskaya streets

Gorky Bust, Gorky Street

Kuibyshev Monument, in the northern part of Karl Marx Street, where it crosses Frank-Kamenetsky (formerly Myasnoryadskaya) Street

War Memorial Complex, Kirov Square. Commemorating citizens of Irkutsk who lost their lives in World War II. Of the 200,000 who joined up, 79,000 never returned. Here too are the names of the 37 heroes who came from the Irkutsk region. The complex includes an eternal flame, which was lit from the Tomb of the Unknown Soldier in Moscow. Schoolchildren provide a guard of honour, which changes regularly to a musical accompaniment.

Beloborodov's Bust, Trud (formerly Ivanovskaya) Square. General Afanasi Beloborodov was born in the Irkutsk region and was twice decorated as a Hero of the Soviet Union.

T-34 Tank, Sovietsky Square, at the crossing of Dekabrskikh Sobytii and Sovietskaya streets, on the way into the town from the airport. Commemorating the tank columns that were formed to serve in World War II, using money collected by Siberians. It is known as Irkutsk Komsomolets.

Gagarin's Bust

Okhlopkov Drama Theatre, Karl Marx Street 14. Built by Shreter in 1894–97.

Musical Comedy Theatre, Sovietskaya Street, just beyond Krestovozdvizhenskaya Church. The modern building was completed in 1986.

Youth Theatre, Lenin Street 13, in what was formerly the Central Hotel

Philharmonia Concert Hall, Dzerzhinsky Street 2

Organ Concert Hall, Sukhe-Bator Strcet 1, in the building of the former Catholic church (1884). Open September–June on Fri., Sat., and Sun.

Circus, Proletarskaya Street 13, on Trud Square, opposite the Central Telegraph building. Built in 1965 with seats for 1,745, and open from September till May.

Khudozhestvenny Theatre. Formerly the Yard-joglu Theatre, built by the Greek merchant Yardjoglu to house a greengrocer's and a dairy.

Stadium, Lenin Street

Park, Bortsov Revolutsii Street 15

The Children's Railway. In Irkutsk it is called the Small East-Siberian Line.

Intourist Hotel and Restaurant, Gagarin Boulevard 44; tel. 91–353; for rooms, dial 296 + room no. There is an Intourist office here (tel. 44–686) and a *Beryozka (foreign-currency) Shop* (as well as at Irkutsk Airport).

Angara Hotel and Restaurant, Ul. Sukhe Bator 7; tel. 46–065

Sibir Hotel and Restaurant, Lenin Street 18, opposite the Geography Department of the University. This was built in 1933 in constructivist style.

Gornyak Hotel, Lenin Street 21

Baikal Restaurant, Bogdan Khmelnitsky Street 1

Arctica Restaurant, Karl Marx Street 46

Almaz ("diamond") Restaurant, Lenin Street 46

Post Office, Karl Marx Street 28

Bank, Karl Marx Street. Built by Kolenovsky in art nouveau style.

Mongolian Consulate General, Lapina Street 11; tel. 44–2370

Aeroflot, Gorky Street 29

Shopping Centre, by the market, at the end of Chekhov Street

Khudozhnik Art Shop, Karl Marx Street

Gifts, Karl Marx Street 35

Souvenirs, Karl Marx Street 23

Market, Chekhov Street. Here the sight of frozen milk on a stick, unwrapped and for sale, is quite common.

Intourist organises visits to the Fur Centre as well as yachting and trips on motorboats and steamers, picnics in the Siberian taiga, and excursions to Lake Baikal.

Lake Baikal

The trip to Lake Baikal takes 8 hours; the road is good and one way takes about an hour and a half. The lake is about 65 km (40 miles) from town. It is possible to go by bus and return on a 45-min. journey by boat (hydrofoil).

The road there goes along the right bank of the Angara, eastward, where the old railway used to run to the ferry quay. It was moved to the left bank before the Irkutsk hydropower station reservoir flooded the Angara for 70 km (43 miles) upstream to its source in Baikal. The road runs through green forests and little villages, crossing small rivers that drain their boggy valley into the Angara.

The *Museum of Wooden Architecture* is at the 47-km mark on the road to Baikal. It is small by comparison with others of its kind in the Soviet Union, but the woods are pleasantly cool in the heat of summer. The cows relish the shade too. The territory of 50 hectares (125 acres) is divided into 3 sections with a Russian village, a Buryat settlement, and a camp such as the nomadic Evenks used to have. Among the wooden buildings are 3 cunningly equipped 18th–19th century peasant houses and a windmill, brought from villages later submerged by the Bratsk and Ust-Ilim reservoirs. The houses have bathhouses and low, wide doors to keep the warmth in and admit sledges. All the wooden farm tools, kitchen utensils, and spinning and weaving equipment is like that used by the first settlers here. There are also the guardtower with a double-headed eagle on top and the chapel from Ilim gaol, were the revolutionary writer Alexander Radischev was exiled. Open June–September, 10–4.

Beyond the museum, on the lake shore, the road swings northward. At the point where the Angara takes its source from the lake, the *Shaman Stone* (see legend below), revered as sacred by the Buryats, stands in midstream.

Listvyanka

This is an unpretentious little wooden village on either side of a small river at the point where it flows into Lake Baikal. The village stretches for 4 km (2 miles) along the lake shore. Anton Chekhov was delighted by the local landscape, comparing it to Switzerland and the Crimea. The *Church of St. Nicholas* (Kulikova Street) is up one of the valleys where the houses spread back from the lake. There is an embankment under construction and a lakeside road.

Museum, in the building of the Limnological Institute, by the lake. There is a model of an icebreaker built in 1899 by Sir K. G. Armstrong Witworth and Co. of Newcastle. Baikal is not without its dramas. In 1862 17,000 head of cattle drowned with the flooding when Tsaganskaya Island was formed. The earthquake of 1959 measured 9 degrees on the Richter scale in the lake. There are plans to build a large aquarium here.

Two *monuments* commemorate the dead of the Civil War and World War II

Baikal (Intourist) Hotel and Restaurant, up the slope, 500 m/yd from the lake shore; tel. 9396–234. The restaurant is closed 4–6. There is a *Beryozka foreign-currency shop* here.

Baikal Restaurant, by the shore

Intourist Office, tel. 96–331

Boat trips are available.

Lake Baikal lies 450 m (1,476 ft) above sea level. Its name possibly derives from the Turkic or Yakut "bai-kul" (rich lake), or perhaps from the Mongolian "baigaal" (great water). The latter theory is supported by the fact that Buryats living in the area called the lake Baigaal-Dalai, meaning "water reservoir as big as the sea." It is described in the words of an old song, hardly great literature but nonetheless popular:

Holy Baikal—glorious sea,
An old fish barrel—my glorious ship.
Ho, North Wind, stir the waves for me,
And hasten a brave lad's ship.

The "brave lad" is a fugitive convict, working his way westward, back to freedom.

The crescent-shaped lake is the deepest in the world; it measures 1,620 m (5,314 ft) in the deepest part and is only seconded by Lake Tanganyika's 1,435 m (4,708 ft). 636 km (395 miles) long and varying between 24 and 80 km (15 and 50 miles) in width, Baikal contains 5,513 cubic miles of water, so much so that if no more water flowed in and the river Angara continued to flow out at its fairly constant rate of 1,982 cu m per second, the supply would last for 500 years.

The river Angara, itself a tributary of the Yenisei, is in fact the only outflow, while the lake is fed by 336 rivers and streams. An old legend relates that Baikal had 337 daughters, as quiet and obedient as any father could wish, with the exception of one, the headstrong Angara, who fell in love with Yenisei. Baikal forbade their marriage, and so the young couple eloped. As they fled, Baikal hurled after them the great Shaman Stone, which stands where river Angara leaves Lake Baikal.

Olkhon is the largest of the lake's 22 islands. Storms are frequent and violent, and earthquakes still occur here. The 190 sq miles of the Gulf of Proval was formed only 100 years ago. The water of the lake is very cold and freezes over in December. The surrounding mountains may already be snow-covered in October.

Perhaps the most interesting feature of Baikal is its flora and fauna. It is believed that most of the indigenous species originally came from the sea. Because there are seals and saltwater types of fish among them, the local fishermen still say that there is an underground tunnel linking the lake with the Arctic Ocean, although this theory has been scientifically disproved. Altogether 1,700 different types of animals and plants are to be found in the waters (compared with only 400 in Lake Tanganyika), and of these, more than 1,000 are not to be found anywhere else in the world. Another feature of the lake is that it is free of plankton; instead of being able to see 2–3 m (7–10 ft) down into the water, as is usual, it is possible to see down to a depth of 40 m (131 ft).

A local delicacy, besides the famous Siberian "pelmeni," is the Baikal "omul," a species of salmon exclusive to this lake.

ISTRA

Intourist organises excursions here from Moscow.

In 1636 the first wooden Voskresenskaya Church was built here beside the river Istra, and the village that later grew up was also so named.

In 1656, on the picturesque site of the village of Rogozha, the New Jerusalem Monastery was founded upon the order of Patriarch Nikon (1605–81), who was greatly struck by the beauty of the place. He wanted to reproduce the Church of the Holy Sepulchre in Jerusalem, his idea being to build such a grand complex that it would prove the greatness of the Russian Orthodox Church. After the fall of the Byzantine Empire in Constantinople, he believed the Russian church to be the only repository of true Christianity.

The history of the little village of Voskresenskaya that grew into the town of Istra was intimately connected with the great monastery upon its outskirts from the time that Patriarch Nikon used to stay here for the night on the way to the construction site. Later many hotels were built to accommodate the constant flow of monks and pilgrims. Its main street, the Moscow Volokolamsk road, led toward the monastery. The present-day Lenin and Pyervomaiskaya streets are part of the old trade route to the capital.

During the last war, the town was almost entirely devastated. At Pyervomaiskaya Street 4, the stone pillars of a gateway bearing a memorial plaque are all that remain of the house where Anton Chekhov once lived. When his brother Ivan took a teaching job here in 1880, he was given such a spacious house that all the family joined him. Brother Mikhail wrote, "As a writer Anton Chekhov needed impressions, and he began drawing them for his themes from the surrounding life in Voskresenskoye—he immersed himself wholly in it. As a future physician he needed medical practice, and he found it here too." Indeed Chekhov practised in the local hospital as a young doctor in 1883–84, and it was here that the idea of "The Three Sisters" was born. What was later known as "the house of the three sisters" belonged to the Mengalev sisters, but it has disappeared. The Chekhov house burned down in 1941. There is a *bust* of the playwright nearby.

Some 2-storey houses survived by a miracle in the central square, and one now serves as the local post office. Opposite is the new *town hall*, designed by Alexei Schusyev. As a war memorial there is a *fighter plane monument* with a map of the Soviet troop movements in the area in November 1941.

Restaurant, near the central square

Ogonyok Café, on the left at the entrance to the town

Voskresensky Novo-Yerusalimsky Monastery, Sovietskaya Street 2. To reach the monastery, drive on out of Istra for another 2 km (1 mile) to a point where the main road makes a turn to the left. Just here the entrance to the monastery stands straight ahead. There is a carpark to the right, and toilets below ground a little farther, on the left. The territory of the monastery is open 10–6; closed Mon. and the last Friday in the month. The museum inside is open 10–6; closed Mon.

The monastery, on the site of the one-time Kremlin, itself resembles a fortress with its lofty walls. Patriarch Nikon was so enchanted by the landscape here that he thought it the very spot to re-create Jerusalem's Church of the Holy Sepulchre and the Garden of Gethsemane. Russian historians are of the opinion that the description in the Bible of King Solomon's fantastically sumptuous temple influenced those responsible for the design of the monastery, the granite cathedral symbolising the power of the Russian patriarch. Some also see the influence of Florentine architects, especially of Bernardino Amico, whose blueprints published in 1624 could have been available to his Russian colleagues. The decorative work was in the hands of the Byelorussian craftsman Pyotor Zaborsky, and the principal decoration of the cathedral lay in the use of multicoloured tiles; as many as 50,000 were required. The Peacock's Eye frieze was designed by Stepan Polubes. The monastery buildings were surrounded by a wooden wall in 1664.

Ironically, it was Patriarch Nikon's power that almost prevented the cathedral from being completed. For many years he enjoyed the highest confidence of Tsar Alexei Mikhailovich, leader of both church and state, and was his spiritual adviser and his friend. However, he demanded more and more privileges for the church and behaved so independently that eventually the nobles accused him of trying to steal away the prerogatives of the tsar. They had him formally deposed in 1666 and exiled to the faraway Ferapontov Monastery, northwest of Vologda, where he spent 15 years. Construction came to a halt as soon as he left and was only resumed in 1679.

Voskresensky (Resurrection) Cathedral was planned in 3 parts—the "underground" church of SS. Konstantin and Helena, the cruciform cathedral with a single golden dome, and the Great Rotunda, a church built upon a circular plan such as that of the Church of the Holy Sepulchre in Jerusalem and other similar buildings constructed by the Knights Templars. On the southern side, there stood a 7-tiered belfry. All was completed and consecrated in 1685, but in 1723 the rotunda roof collapsed, and 3 years later the cathedral was destroyed by fire. In 1740 Empress Elizabeth, daughter of Peter I, entrusted the reconstruction of the monastery to Archimandrite Ambrosii Zertis-Kamensky. The work took many years and was supervised first by Rastrellii and later by the architect Karl Blank, Kazakov being among those who joined in the work. It was finished in 1761, during the reign of Catherine II, the stone rotunda being replaced by a wooden one supported by 18 columns and reaching a height of 67 m (220 ft).

Immediately beneath the Great Cupola stands *the Chapel of the Holy Sepulchre*, but a number of other small churches and chapels are also inside the main building, including that of *St. John the Baptist*, where Patriarch Nikon was buried in 1681. A flight of 33 steps leads down to the crypt.

The Rozhdestvenskaya (Nativity) Refectory Church was built on the site of earlier stone buildings in Moscow baroque style in 1686–92, with money donated by Princess Tatiana Mikhailovna; it stands to the west of the cathedral. The arcade on the eastern façade of the adjoining Tsar's Chambers dated from the 18th century, when it was designed by Kazakov and put up to strengthen the lower parts of the walls, the pilasters being added in the mid-19th century. The carved stone decorations around the upper windows are typical of the 17th century. Adjoining this to the south is the single-storey hospital (1698) with the *Three-Saints Church*. On the other (northern) side of Rozhdestvenskaya Church are the *Archimandrite's Chambers*, built in 1750 on 17th-century foundations. The complex now houses the *Moscow Regional Museum*, founded in 1920. There is a picture gallery with portraits of the 17th and 18th centuries, a collection of porcelain, and details of the history and the restoration of the monastery.

Other buildings of interest within the compound include the *smithy* and *malthouse* (1690–94) near the entrance gate, against the northern wall, and *Princess Tatiana Mikhailovna's palace*, a single-storey building dating from the end of the 17th century.

In 1690–97, 40 years after the foundation of the monastery, the wooden walls and towers of 1664 were replaced by stone ones, 1 km (.6 mile) in circumference and 10 m (33 ft) high. They have the familiar features of military fortresses, but in fact these were only decorative. There are 8 towers, and each bore the name of the towers defending Jerusalem, among them Gethsemane, Zion, David's Tower, Elizabeth, and Damascus. Apart from Elizabeth Tower, all are alike and stand 19 m (62 ft) high, their silhouettes echoing that of the cathedral rotunda. The Gethsemane and Damascus towers flank the Holy Gates leading into the monastery. The 3 arches of the entrance gates are surmounted by the *Church of the Entry-into-Jerusalem*, built in 1690–97 in a unique variation of the Moscow baroque style by the serf-architect Yakov Bukhvostov, who was also responsible for the walls and towers. Included in the gate building are guardrooms and the abbot's quarters.

The monastery suffered severely from enemy occupation during World War II, and upon their retreat on 10 December 1941, the Germans blew up the cathedral, belfry, walls, and towers. Restoration work has been carried out upon all the edifices with the exception of the belfry. The towers of the surrounding walls, the entrance Gate-Church and the Underground Church are complete, and work is in progress on the great rotunda roof, which is to have its original appearance. The final piece of restoration will be the rebuilding of the mighty belfry. Standing in the grounds is the 100-pood (1 ton 12 cwt) *Three-Saints Bell*, designed by Brother Paisi and cast on 21 January 1666 by Brother Sergei Turchaninov. The figures upon it represent Vasili the Great, Grigori Bogoslov, and John Zlatoust, and the decorative work is very like that used upon the cathedral itself.

After visiting the inside of the monastery, it is worthwhile to walk around the outside of the walls, turning to the left from the Holy Gates and following them round, above the little river Zolotyshka. On the far side, a small path leads down from the Elizabeth Tower toward Mt. Helion and the Gardens of Gethsemane. The birch grove was planted in the 19th century, and beyond on the right, to the northwest of the monastery, is Patriarch Nikon's *Hermitage*, built in 1658 near the river. There are 3 floors with living accommodation, service quarters, and a little church and belfry. Nikon's cell was the small one with a stone bed, upstairs on the flat roof.

A little farther from the monastery, to the north-west, above the steep bank of the river Istra, is a collection of wooden buildings forming the *Architectural and Ethnographical Museum* of the Moscow region. Designed to represent a Russian village of the 17th–18th centuries, the various buildings have been brought together from different parts of the region. There is a church of 1647, Bogoyavleniya Church from Semyonovskoye in Pushkinsky region (17th century), a reconstruction of a chapel from Sokolniki near Chekhov, Kokorin's House from Vykhino in Lyuberetsky region, which once served as an inn (end of the 18th–beginning of the 19th century), a peasant house of 1827, a 19th-century windmill, which used to stand in Kochemlevo beside the river Vorya (crossed by the Yaroslavskoye Chaussée), a wooden well, barns, and many other buildings, some of them richly decorated with carved wood. Open 10–6; closed Mon. and the last Fri. of the month.

ITKOL
See Nalchik, p. 381.

IVANETS
See Minsk, p. 325.

IVANOVO Population—483,000
Known from 1871–1932 as Ivanovo-Voznesensk, this textile town lies 287 km (178 miles) northwest of Moscow and is probably best visited between April and August. It is situated on either side of the river Uvod, a tributary of the Klyazma, and 65 km (40 miles) distant from the Volga. The little river runs through it from the northwest to the southeast, dividing the town into 2 parts; on the right is the older part, formerly the village of Ivanovo, and on the left is what was once the village of Voznesensk. This left part dates from 1844 and took its name from the special Ascension Day (Vozneseniya) church parade; a church of the same name was later built there. Voznesensk was incorporated into Ivanovo together with other nearby villages when it was declared a town in 1871.

Ivanovo was first mentioned in 1561, when Ivan the Terrible gave it to the princely family of Temrukovich-Cherkassky because he married the Kabarda princess Maria. The first linen mills were founded in the vicinity by the order of Peter the Great in 1710, and in 1741, when one of the local princesses married into the well-known Sheremetiev family, Ivanovo and the mills passed to the Sheremetievs. Count Peter Sheremetiev in fact never lived here, but he did seek refuge in Ivanovo for a short time in 1771 to avoid catching the plague. In those early days much of Ivanovo's production went to England, which was interested in Russian linen. The flax was and is grown locally. They made "Flemish cloth" and sailcloth. Russian sailcloth was as essential to the Royal Navy as hempen cord, ships' timbers, and Russian tar and masts. Later on weaving mills and textile-printing factories were opened, until by the middle of the 19th century, the locality was known as the Russian Manchester. Until the abolition of serfdom in 1861, not only the workers but many of the factory owners as well were Count Sheremetiev's serfs. In fact, Ivanovo owes its development as a textile centre largely to the activity in the 1740s of 2 serf factory owners named Grachev and Butrimov.

The damage caused in Moscow by fires in 1812 was an important factor in Ivanovo's further growth; other villages nearby benefitted from Count Sheremetiev's policy whereby he permitted the construction of factories in Ivanovo itself only on the condition that should the owners leave the village, the property would pass to the Sheremetiev family. Machinery had begun to be used here from 1826,

and the first steam-powered machinery was installed in 1832, so the rate of development was considerable, and naturally many people preferred to build their factories outside the village boundary. Thus the neighbouring villages, particularly Voznesensk on the opposite side of the river, began to expand rapidly in the 1840s.

The town is also known for its revolutionary activities, including strikes in 1883, 1885, and during the 1905 revolt. Mass meetings were organised at that time in a field just outside the town, by the river Talka, a tributary of the Uvod. During the 72-day strike of 1905, when more than 30,000 local

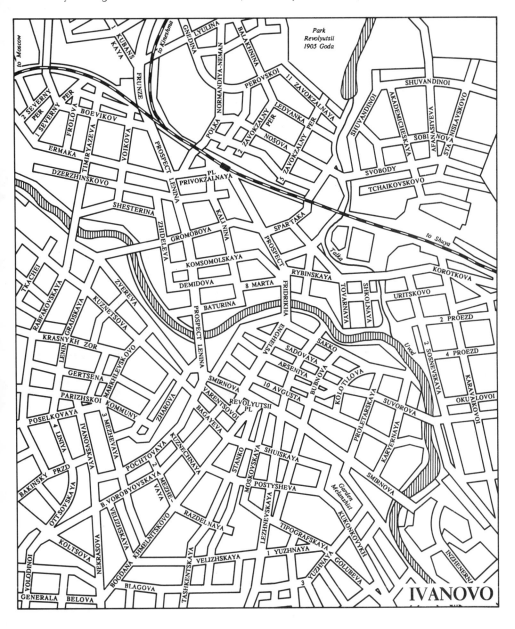

textile workers came out, the first Soviet (meaning "council") of Workers' Deputies was established in Ivanovo. Apart from the demand for economical improvements (an 8-hour day instead of 11 or 12 hours), they also had political aims. Over 15,000 workers gathered in the field by the Talka, but eventually mounted Cossacks from Astrakhan were called in to disperse the crowd, which they did in a brutal fashion. Ivanovo was then beseiged for a full week, but finally concessions were made; the working week was shortened by an hour, and there was a 15 percent pay increase. After the 1917 revolution, Ivanovo was called "the third proletarian capital of the Soviet Republic" after Leningrad and Moscow, and many of its streets still bear the names of local Bolsheviks, such as Afanasiev, Gromoboya, and Stanko streets. The strike tradition continued, for there was another as late as 1932.

Ivanovo was never properly planned. Local architects explain that the winding river Uvod dictated the form the town has taken. Many sections are still more like villages than parts of a town. Among the older buildings can be seen some put up in the 1920s and 1930s in constructivist style. These include the building of the bank, the "horse-shoe" building at Gromoboya Street 13, and the apartment house on Lenin Prospect (formerly Alexandrovskaya Street), known locally as "the ship" because of its shape (there is a grocery shop on the ground floor, but higher up the balconies all along its length give the impression of decks). Rapid housing construction began in the 1950s and is still going on, particularly in the southeastern part of the town where Tekstilschikov ("textile workers") and Stroitelei ("builders") prospects run parallel to each other, each of which are lined with new buildings.

Local industry is still mainly concerned with textiles. There are also clothing factories, textile and food factories, a piano factory, and a variety of machine-building plants, including those for turf cutting. The machine-building industry is among the best in the country, and its production is exported to many parts of the world. The university was opened in 1974, based upon the existing pedagogical institute. 6 other institutes include those specialising in medicine and textiles.

Preobrazhensky (Transfiguration) Cathedral, Kolotilova Street 39. This large white church with green roofs was built in 1892 and is open for services.

Uspenskaya (Assumption) Church, Frunze Street 7; go along Lenin Prospect and over the railway bridge, and the church is on the left, behind the trees. Wooden buildings are not too difficult to dismantle and rebuild on a new site. The construction of this one is quite typical, but it has been moved twice. It started out in the 17th century as part of Pokrovsky Monastery. Then in 1817 it was transferred to Uspenskoye Cemetery, finally being brought to its present site in 1904. The nearby belfry is of 20th-century construction.

Vvedeniye Church, at the crossing of Spartak and Engels streets. This big red-brick church with 5 fat domes and a priest's house beside it was built in 1909. Today the archives are kept here.

Ilinskaya Church, Koltsovaya Street. This church has columns and a cupola topped by 5 little domes, while the belfry has Gothic arches. It was built in 1842 as part of his private estate by a merchant called Alexander Lepetov.

Old Believers' Prayerhouse, Engels Street 41. This was originally a textile mill built in the 1780s for Osip Sokov, who made chintz. It was later converted by architect Mauricelli into a prayerhouse, which accounts for the apse looking onto the street.

Kazanskaya Old Believers' Church, Lenin Prospect. This is a 17th-century wooden church. When visiting, remember that women are required to wear long sleeves and to have their heads covered, and also that anyone daring to stand with his hands behind his back will have his hands bound through all eternity, or so they say.

Local History-Revolutionary Museum, Baturin Street 6/40. Open 11–6; closed Mon. The collection includes some items from Burylin's collection of rarities (see below), such as the Universal Clock, which was made to order for Count Alba by Albert Billeter in Paris in 1873 and purchased at an auction in 1912. It was repaired in 1943.

Ivanovo Chintz Museum. Open 11–6; closed Mon. This is connected by an underground tunnel to the smaller *Burylin's House,* across the street. In 1915 Dmitri Burylin, a factory owner, art collector, and local millionaire, built a museum for his own collection in memory of his grandfather, who had founded the family factory in 1812. (Burylin's own house faces the museum and another that he owned is beside it.) He called his museum "Industry and Art with Antiques and Rarities" and willed it to the town, but when in 1918 it was taken over anyway, he became its first curator. *The Weaving Museum* is the only one of its kind in the country, and its pride is its international textile collection, with over a million samples of 17th–20th-century production. On one of the ceilings is a portrait of Burylin dressed in Oriental costume.

Art Gallery, Lenin Prospect 33. Open 11–6; closed Tues. This was once a grammar school building. The gallery was opened in 1960, the collections being based on paintings confiscated after the revolution.

Artists' Exhibition Hall, Lenin Prospect 45

Schudrov's House, 10th August Street 36a. Built in the 17th century for Prince Cherkassky, this is one of the town's oldest buildings. It now bears the name of the last private owner, Osip Schudrov.

Grachov's House, Kolotilova Street 43. Efim Grachov was one of the richest serf-peasants, and in 1793 he bought his freedom for what was then an astronomical price, 135,000 roubles. His mansion was built in the 1790s and is now used as a House of Pioneers.

Count Sheremetiev's Office, Krutitskaya Street 3. Built in the early 19th century. The family held land here from 1743 until the revolution.

Prorokov's House, Prorokov Street. Open 11–6;

closed Tues. Boris Prorokov (b. 1911) was an artist who lived in this house until he was 17.

Bubnov's House, 3-International Street. This museum is dedicated to the memory of the revolutionary Andrei Bubnov, who was born here.

Frunze's Study, Rabfakovskaya Street 6. Mikhail Frunze (1885–1925), the military leader, was involved in revolutionary activity in Ivanovo in 1905. After the revolution (1918–19), he worked here in the regional party organisation.

Pyervy Soviet Museum, Sovietskaya Street 27–29. Open 11–6; closed Mon. This is located in a specially constructed building, which stands next to the small one where the first soviet met during the strike of 1905. The exhibit includes a diorama 40 m (44 yd) long and 8 m (26 ft) high and an interesting miniature of Miss Hellot attributed to Gainsborough. The textile machine made by Platt Bros. and Co. Ltd. of Oldham in 1882 is one of many that operated in the local mills.

Local Library, Engels Street 10. This modern building has a roof in the shape of a butterfly cake.

Varentsova Statue, Lenin Prospect. In 1892 Olga Varentsova (1862–1950) organised the first Marxist groups in Ivanovo. Her statue was sculpted by Anikushin and unveiled in 1980.

Afanasiyev Statue, Engels Street 16. Fyodor Afanasiyev (1859–1905) was a revolutionary, popularly known as Otyets ("father"), and one of the leaders of the 1905 strike. The stone statue is by Shmelev.

Krasnaya ("red") Talka Memorial, Svobody Street, beside the river Talka, on the site of the mass meetings during the strike of 1905. This impressive complex was sculpted with decorative shields, stone bas-reliefs, busts of local heroes, and an eternal flame by Mikhailenok to commemorate the first revolution of 1905–7. There is a separate bas-relief in memory of Fyodor Afanasiyev (see above), who was shot here during one of the mass meetings. The complex was unveiled in 1957. The nearby *Red Talka textile mill* was built in 1927, decorated with a mosaic panel of revolutionaries' portraits.

Revolutionary Fighters' Monument, in Revolution Square. This imposing stone memorial on a grassy hill was sculpted by Ryabichev and unveiled in 1975. It has two figures and a dropped flag; there is also an eternal flame.

Monument, in a park on 10-August Street. It marks the grave of 30 workers killed during a demonstration on 10 August 1915.

Young Revolutionaries of the Textile Area, Railway Square. This decorative composition includes the head of a young woman with her hair blowing in the wind. It was sculpted by Kolesnikov and unveiled in 1977.

Lenin Statue, Lenin Square. This was sculpted by Fridman and unveiled in 1956.

Frunze Monument, in the Town Garden, on Lenin Prospect. The sculptor of the statue in military uniform was Neroda, and it was unveiled in 1957.

Drama Theatre, Engels Street 58, beside the river Uvod. It was built in 1940 and reconstructed in 1979.

Musical Comedy Theatre, Krasnoi Armii Street 8/2. There is also an amateur symphony orchestra and 2 choirs here.

Puppet Theatre, Kuznetsova Street 59

Circus, Lenin Prospect. The building dates from 1979.

Stepanov Park, Yermaka Street. This park was opened in 1936 and has a dance hall, a planetarium, and a boating station, as well as an open-air theatre.

Pobeda Park, beside the river Talka

1905 Park

Textilschik Stadium, Yermaka Street 49

Sovietskaya Hotel and Rossia Restaurant, Lenin Prospect 65, opposite the Art Gallery; TEL. 725–47. This is an Intourist hotel.

Tsentralnaya Hotel and Moskva Restaurant, Engels Street 1/25; tel. 281–22

Ivanovo Hotel and Sever Restaurant, Karl Marx Street 46; tel. 76–545

Tourist Hotel and Restaurant, Naberezhnaya Street 9; tel. 76–519

Ivanovo Restaurant, Lenin Prospect 11

Intourist Office, Naberezhnaya Street 6; tel. 78–558

GPO, Lenin Prospect 17

Bank, Krasnoi Armii Street 10/1. Built in constructivist style in 1928 by academician Vesnin.

Souvenirs, Lenin Prospect 2/4 and Krasnoy Armii Street 4/2

Textiles, Lenin Prospect 100. This is a place to buy fabric as souvenirs and gifts.

Art Salon, Lenin Prospect 100

Department Store, Engels Prospect 89

Druzhba Bookshop, Pushkin Street 45

Market, B. Khmelnitskovo Street (the road leading out of town), on the right

Novotalitsa

Novotalitsa is an ancient village on the outskirts of Ivanovo, on the bank of the river Verguza.

Tsvetayev's House. Professor of history Ivan Tsvetayev (1847–1913) was the founder of the Pushkin Fine Arts Museum (formerly the Alexander III Museum) and father of the Russian poetess Marina Tsvetayeva (1894–1941). Marina Tsvetayeva followed her husband, Sergei Efron, abroad in 1921 and lived in Paris from 1926 onward. Then she returned to Russia in 1939, to discover that her husband, who had become a double-agent in France, had already been shot. After a period of hopeless misery she committed suicide.

This thing called homesickness! A fable
That was exploded long ago!
Because for me it does not matter
Where to be completely so
Alone . . .

The house was built about 150 years ago by Ivan Tsvetayev's father and remains unchanged.

*   *   *

In what is now the Ivanovo region, a number of centres of miniature painting developed—Kholui, Mstera and, perhaps the best known of all, Palekh. Intourist runs excursions there, which take 6 hours; the village is 65 km (40 miles) from Ivanovo.

Shuya

On the way to Palekh, Shuya stands on the left bank of the river Teza, a tributary of the Klyazma.

Filling Station, on the right on the way into the town

Shuya derives its name from the old Russian word "shuya," meaning the left. There are not many historical mentions of Shuya; the first says that it was given to one of the descendants of the prince of Suzdal, who got his name, Shuisky, from it. The Shuisky family is known from 1402 and was prominent in the 16th–17th centuries. In 1539 Shuya fell victim to the invasion of the Crimean khan Safa-Girei. In 1548 Ivan the Terrible awarded Shuya to a nobleman, Ignat Golokhvatov, who during the reign of Tsar Vasily Ivanovich (father of Ivan the Terrible), was Russian envoy to the Crimean khan. In the Time of Troubles in 1609–10, Shuya was devastated by the Poles, but the townsfolk drove them out.

Shuya is closely connected with the Russian military leader Dmitry Pozharsky, to whom belonged the villages of Kuryanovo, Kurdyakovo, and others nearby. Thanks to its geographic position, Shuya was one of the more important strongholds of the state Moscow Rus. It was surrounded by deep moats and high earth walls, the remains of which can still be seen. Shuya conducted a brisk trade with Yaroslavl, through which Moscow Rus maintained her trade ties with England in the 16th century, and in the 17th century a shop belonging to an English firm was opened here. The predominant industry was linen weaving. The first linen factory was set up in 1755 and the first cotton mill in 1834.

The leading industry in Shuya today is the textile industry; flax is still much in evidence. There are a machine-building plant and an accordion-making factory too. There is also an embroidery workshop here, which has restored church embroidery and from which work has been sent to England, the United States, France, and other countries. In 1957 its products were exhibited at the international fair in Brussels.

Shuya is also a major cultural centre of the region, with its school, technical schools, colleges, theatres, and stadiums.

Melnichnoye Church, to the left, beyond the railway line. This blue-domed church is clearly visible from the centre of town, although it is really 3 km (2 miles) outside, in the village of Melnichnoye. It is in good condition and open for services.

Pokorovskaya (Intercession of the Virgin) Church, Soyuznaya Square. Built in 1754, it is now in a dilapidated state.

Kresto-Vozdvizhenskaya Church, at the end of Teatralnaya Street

Voskresensky (Ascension) Cathedral, on the central square. There are two buildings, the old and the "new." The little single-storey church with porticoes built in 1756 down near the river was too small, so a second, larger one was built higher up in 1798. The cathedral's belfry stands on the other side of Teatralnaya Street. Construction began upon it in 1810, under the guidance of an Italian architect, Mauricelli (also responsible for a prayerhouse in Ivanovo). However, in 1819, when three storeys had been built, it collapsed. It was finally completed in 1832 with 4 storeys and a spire rising to 104 m (341 ft) by a peasant architect from Vladimir called Mikhail Savvateyev.

Red-brick Church. Built in 1883.

Local Museum, Lenin Square, opposite the post office. Open 10:30–4.

Frunze Museum, Torgovaya Street 11. Open 10:30–5:30; closed Mon. The Soviet military leader and Civil War hero lived in Shuya at 1-Nagornaya Street 87 in 1905.

Hospital, Soyuznaya Square, opposite Pokrova Church. Built in 1841.

Lenin Monument, Lenin Square

Frunze Monument, Frunze Square. This was put up in 1927.

Hotel, Belovo Street

Stolovaya Restaurant, Soyuznaya Square

GPO, Lenin Square 4

Souvenirs, Lenin Square

Trading Arcade, Malakhia Belova Street

Filling Station, on the left, on the way out of Shuya, toward Palekh.

On the outskirts of Shuya in the place called Likhushino was an estate belonging to Boris Pestel, a brother of the Decembrist Pavel Pestel.

Nikolo-Shartomsky Monastery, in Pupki, 12 km (7 miles) to the north of Shuya. The monastery took its name from the river Shartoma, which is now called the Shakhma. The first mention of the monastery dates from 1425. In the 16th century, it was a family burial place of descendants of the princes of Suzdal, the Gorbatyi-Shuisky family. The best known of the family was Prince Alexander Gorbatyi-Shuisky, who was Ivan the Terrible's comrade-in-arms during the seizure of Kazan, where he was then appointed governor. In 1564 he was executed by the tsar, together with his young son Ivan, for his friendship with Prince Kurbsky, who then fled to Lithuania. At the beginning of the 17th century, the monastery fell victim to Polish invasion; then it was plundered by robbers, and in 1645 its wooden buildings were burned down. The most ancient of its remaining churches is St. Nicholas's Cathedral, built in 1651. The 5-domed cathedral is built in Russian-Byzantine style. Beside it is a 4-tier belfry. Another church is the Kazanskaya (Our Lady of Kazan) Winter Church, built in 1678. Rather a gloomy building, it was previously the monastery storehouse. The third of the remaining churches is the small Grigoriya Akragantiiskovo (St. Gregory of Akragas) refectory church. Beside the monastery's low walls, Nikolskaya fair was held before the 1917 revolution.

Dunilovo
17 km (11 miles) from Shuya. The village already existed in the 16th century. In 1535 it was mentioned in the will of Prince Mikhail Gorbatyi-Shuisky, who bequeathed it to his wife, Anna. In 1608 a fierce battle against the Poles took place nearby. In 1632 the Uspensky (Assumption) Convent was here, but it was closed in 1764. The only church of the convent now preserved is the *Blagoveschenskaya (Annunciation) Church*, on a steep bank of the river Teza, built in Russian-Byzantine style in 1675. As legend has it, the nun Yelena, formerly Yelena Lopukhina, wife of Peter the Great, used to come here from Suzdal. In 1704 Fyodor Lopukhin, Peter the Great's father-in-law, built the summer Pokrovskaya (Intercession of the Virgin) Church in Dunilovo. In the winter Pokrovskaya Church, built in 1742, there is a locally made carved wooden icon of St. Nicholas the Wonder-Worker.

In nearby Krasnoarmeiskoye village are 2 churches, *Trinity*, built in 1784, and *St. Michael's*, built in 1797. The latter was transformed into a school. Beside it is a belfry.

Palekh Population—6,000
Palekh is an urban settlement in the Ivanovo region, 65 km (40 miles) southeast of Ivanovo, situated along either bank of the river Paleshka. It is one of the oldest villages in the region. Local church chronicles say that Palekh used to belong to the Paletskys through the side of the family that descended from Rurik. In the 15th century, when the Paletskys died out, Palekh became national property. In the first quarter of the 17th century, it was presented to Ivan Buturlin, of Ivan the Terrible's retinue, for his military deeds and remained in the Buturlin family until 1861.

In the 16th–17th centuries, when icon painting became widespread in the Vladimir-Suzdal monasteries, a number of centres of this art form developed in what is now the Ivanovo region—Kholui, Mstera, and perhaps the best known, Palekh.

Palekh frescoes and icons of the turn of the 17th century were famous for their artistry and craftsmanship and were considered to be the best examples of Russian icon painting. Following the Stroganov school, they were renowned for the original decorative ornamentality of their composition and for the harmony of their bright colours. The free use of gold and the small size of the icon itself were also typical. However, from the 18th century onward, there was a distinct, gradual decline in this once great art. By the beginning of the 19th century, icon painting here had degenerated into a craft devoid of any artistic significance. The Russian writer Anton Chekhov wrote sadly of this decline. He inherited his love for icons from his mother, who lived here in her early youth and was a connoisseur of the art. The Palekh masters were also engaged in icon and fresco restoration work in Russian churches and monasteries.

The 1917 revolution confronted the icon painters with the task of reviving their craft on a new creative foundation. The wealth of experience and tradition, accumulated throughout centuries and handed down from father to son, was too good to waste. In 1923, 7 former icon painters founded a Workshop of Old Painting, where modern Palekh painting developed. It did not happen all at once. The artists tried different types of material before they began basing their work on the familiar small lacquered papier-mâché boxes of Fedoskino and later started the production of their own lacquered boxes. The characteristic Palekh boxes are painted black and have on this background pictures resembling in form and character the early 17th-century icons of the Stroganov school. This return to the ancient Russian icon as a source of inspiration was quite logical in former icon painters, since ancient Russian frescoes and icons were based on methods of decorative painting evolved throughout the ages. It was precisely upon this essentially decorative art that the Palekh masters based their work. Using the technique of ancient Russian painting, they work with distemper (colour dissolved in egg yolk mixed with vinegar). The purity and transparency of shades and the delicacy of the colour layer in their work is astounding. The superb artistry is accentuated by the fragile web of gold and silver ornament framing the painting and compositionally introduced as the thinnest and lightest of dots and lines. This technique naturally led to artistic success in themes borrowed from Russian folk legends, tales, and songs.

Fame soon came to Palekh. In the first years of the new workshop's existence, its articles were displayed at international fairs in Paris, Venice, New York, and Berlin and were much admired. The Palekh artists kept expanding. They began illustrating books, painting murals, and designing sets and costumes for plays. They took part in the reconstruction of the Moscow Kremlin cathedrals and painted murals in the Young Pioneer Palaces in Leningrad, Sverdlovsk, Ivanovo, and Yaroslavl. Maxim Gorky, who closely watched the art of Palekh painters, wrote: "It could hardly be imagined that through this most conservative of crafts, icon painting, the Palekh artists . . . would come to their highly qualified modern mastery, which evokes admiration even among people spoiled by versatility of painting."

In 1935 an art studio was organised here that now produces 600–650 articles a month. There is also an art school in the village that trains new artists in Palekh miniature work.

Palekh is also famous for its embroidery. The Palekh embroideresses invented a new kind of satin-stitch. Their work has been displayed at many Russian as well as international exhibitions.

Today the Palekh artists have many new themes for their miniatures, such as country life, military exploits, and historical scenes. Besides fairy tales, they are also inspired by favourite works of Russian classic writers—Pushkin, Lermontov, Nekrasov, Gogol, Chekhov, and Gorky.

Present-day Palekh is the administrative and cultural centre of a vast agricultural area. Apart from cultural institutions, it has a flax-processing plant, a dairy, a brickworks, and the embroidery workshop. The river Paleshka has been dammed to form a reservoir known as the Palekh Sea.

Ilyinskaya (St. Elijah's) Church, Gorky Street. This was built in 1790.

St. Nicholas's Church. Built in 1796

Museum of Applied Art (Old Palekh Museum), in Krestovozdvizhensky (Elevation of the Cross) Church, on the left, behind a small pond. The large church was built in 1762–74 for summer use as part of a monastery. The architect, Yegor Dubov, used the old Russian style of the 17th century. The 19th-century frescoes on both the outside and the inside walls were executed by local artists in collaboration with the Sapozhnikov brothers. There is also an ornate gilded iconostasis, and the collection of prerevolutionary art includes 18th-century icons by local painters. Open 10–5; closed Mon. Below the belfry there is a small church, which was used in winter.

Ivan Golikov's House. Ivan Golikov (1886–1937) was a skilled artist and teacher and is considered the founder of the tradition of Palekh miniatures. His bust is in the garden behind his house.

New Palekh Museum, in a red brick building at Bakanov Street 34. This is the Soviet part of the Palekh collection. Open 10–5; closed Mon. and the last Fri. of each month.

Artists' Workshop, in the red brick buildings at Lenin Street 31. The original workshop is on the left of the main road.

Vikhrev's Grave, behind the church. Yefim Vikhrev (1901–35) was a local writer who devoted himself entirely to the subject of Palekh painting and who died here, in the village.

World War II Memorial

Palekh Restaurant, to the left of the main road. Located in a new building, decorated with carving on the outside and Palekh murals inside.

IZBORSK

See Pskov, p. 430.

JURMALA

See Riga, p. 445.

KABARDINO-BALKAR AUTONOMOUS REPUBLIC

See Nalchik, p. 377.

KAKHETIA

See Telavi, p. 552.

KAKHOVKA

See Kherson, p. 208.

KAMENETS-PODOLSKY Population—103,000

Intourist organises day trips here from Khmelnitsky, 100 km (62 miles) away, and from Chernovitsy 75 km (47 miles) away.

This is an extraordinarily lovely old town situated on either side of the winding ravine through which the river Smotrich flows at the base of precipitous grey cliffs. The loop of the river almost surrounded the old town, and the fortress guards the narrow causeway to it. St. George and the dragon are featured on its coat-of-arms.

Some scholars think that Kamenets was built near the ancient Dacian town of Klepidava or Petrodava, particularly as "petros" and "kamen" both mean "stone." It was first mentioned in 1062 in an Armenian chronicle. About 20,000 Armenians came to serve in the army of Prince Izyaslav of Russia against the Polovtsy tribes. After the battles they settled in Kiev, Kamenets-Podolsky, and other towns instead of returning home. In the 12th century, it was part of the principality of Galic-Volyn, suffered badly from attacks by the Turks, Tatars, and Lithuanians, and at the end of the 14th century, it passed into Polish hands. It became a centre of Roman Catholicism, with establishments of the Dominicans, Franciscans, and Trinitarians appearing. As a frontier town, it was well fortified, the original wooden walls being replaced by stone in the 14th century. The first detailed description of the town was that made by Afanasi Nikitin from Tver, who was the first Russian merchant to travel to India and who lived here in the middle of the 15th century. Russia's first printer, Ivan Fyodorov, stayed here in 1577 on his way to Turkey. Kamenets-Podolsky fortress was besieged by the Turks in 1621, and the Polish historian Piasecki recounts how the Sultan Oman turned to his vizier when he saw how badly things were going, and asked who had built the fortress. He was told "God Himself!" and in turn replied "Then let God take it, if He so wishes!" and ordered a retreat.

The Turks returned in strength, crossing the Dniester near Khotin with an army of 150,000 in August 1672. The town was well fortified, but the garrison was weak and lacked food, and the women of the town were so frightened that they came to the fortress to ask the commander, Nikolai Potocki, to surrender, hoping that the Turks would then spare their lives and those of their families. The seige had lasted 2 weeks when Potocki agreed, and the triumphant Sultan Mahomet IV, remembering how Mehmet II had entered St. Sophia's in Constantinople after its fall in 1453, rode his horse right into the cathedral. The Turks held the town for 27 years, during which time all the churches were looted and much gold, silver, and precious stones taken away. Crosses and bells were removed, icons were used to pave the muddy streets, churches were turned into mosques, and corpses were exhumed and carried out of the town. Only 4 churches were left, including the Armenian one.

With the second division of Poland in 1793, the left-bank Ukraine became part of Russia and

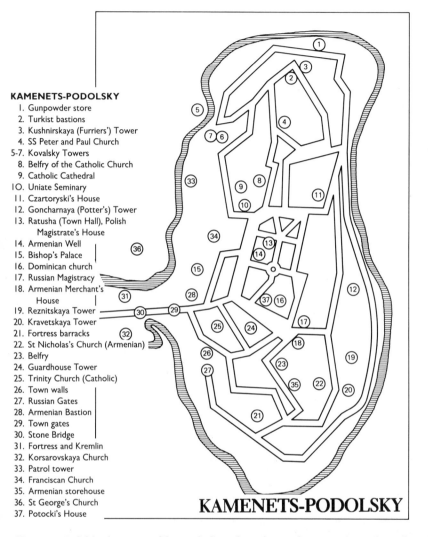

KAMENETS-PODOLSKY

1. Gunpowder store
2. Turkist bastions
3. Kushnirskaya (Furriers') Tower
4. SS Peter and Paul Church
5-7. Kovalsky Towers
8. Belfry of the Catholic Church
9. Catholic Cathedral
10. Uniate Seminary
11. Czartoryski's House
12. Goncharnaya (Potter's) Tower
13. Ratusha (Town Hall), Polish
    Magistrate's House
14. Armenian Well
15. Bishop's Palace
16. Dominican church
17. Russian Magistracy
18. Armenian Merchant's
    House
19. Reznitskaya Tower
20. Kravetskaya Tower
21. Fortress barracks
22. St Nicholas's Church (Armenian)
23. Belfry
24. Guardhouse Tower
25. Trinity Church (Catholic)
26. Town walls
27. Russian Gates
28. Armenian Bastion
29. Town gates
30. Stone Bridge
31. Fortress and Kremlin
32. Korsarovskaya Church
33. Patrol tower
34. Franciscan Church
35. Armenian storehouse
36. St George's Church
37. Potocki's House

KAMENETS-PODOLSKY

Kamenets-Podolsky the centre of the newly formed province of Podolsk. Among the outstanding figures from the world of literature and art to stay in the town was the Ukrainian poet Taras Shevchenko, in 1846. Today among the local educational establishments are teachers' training, agricultural, and civil engineering colleges. The botanical garden has 2,800 species of plants from all over the world.

Local industry includes machine building, building materials, beer, tobacco, textiles, clothing, and food products.

Kamenets-Podolsky rivals the Ukrainian cities of Kiev and Lvov for the number of interesting buildings that have survived. The fortress set high on the rocky cliffs is a uniquely beautiful example of mediaeval architecture. The museum was organised in 1890 and has 3 main parts, the fortress, the cathedral, and the town hall. Tickets for all these places are sold in the cathedral but the fol-

lowing description begins logically with the fortress, which played such an important part in the history of the old town and which stands at its entrance.

The Turkish Fortress, Papina Street 1. So called since the Turkish occupation of 1672. It was built of wood in the 10th–13th centuries and first mentioned in documents in 1374. The fortress was rebuilt in stone with earthen walls surrounding it in the middle of the 16th century by Iov Pretvich. It is in the form of a protracted polygon with 11 towers. Inside the Western Gates on the left is *Pope's Tower*, named after Pope Julius II, who contributed toward the cost of its construction. The tower is also called Karmalyukova, after a Ukrainian national hero, Ustin Karmalyuk, who led peasant uprisings in the 19th century. He was imprisoned several times and sent to Siberia but always managed to escape. He was kept prisoner here, in this fortress, from 1818–23, when it served as a jail for political prisoners held by the tsarist authorities.

He was killed in the Ukraine in an ambush in 1835. Since he had been such a wanted man, his assassin was granted a special audience with Emperor Nicholas I, receiving a golden ring with the imperial insignia. Karmalyuk was buried in Litichev (just beyond Medzhibozh, see Khmelnitsky), and the plaque to his memory was unveiled here in 1958.

The *Black Tower* to the right of the gates contains a well shaft, 56 m (184 ft) deep and 6 m (20 ft) wide. The *Soldiers' Monument* in the castle yard is a World War II memorial. The museum in the fortress contains much of interest about the town's varied history, including armour, old pictures, and a letter from the sultan.

The five-arched *Turkish Bridge* connecting the fortress with the old town was built in the 14th–17th centuries. It was faced with stone during the Turkish occupation, and its name dates from that time. The road leads through the 16th-century City Gates and inside bears left, passing the central square and Rathaus and going back to the cathedral.

Petropavlovskaya (SS. Peter and Paul's) Cathedral, Karl Marx Street 20. The cathedral was founded in the 15th century. When it was taken by the Turks in 1672, it was turned into a mosque, and the richly decorated Muslim pulpit is still in place. A minaret was built onto one of the chapels, and in 1756, after the Turks had been driven out of Kamenets-Podolsky, the Poles placed a bronze statue of the Virgin on top of the minaret against the background of the crescent, symbolising the victory of Christianity over Islam. A new main altar was built in the middle of the 18th century, other premises were added, and an episcopal throne and an organ were installed. The square-towered belfry was built in the 15th–18th centuries, and there is a triumphal arch beside the cathedral. The building has housed various museums since 1930 and now serves as the Museum of Atheism. Open 10–5:30; closed Mon.

Ticket to all branches of the local museum are on sale here, and the cathedral itself serves as a concert hall for organ music, at 12 noon on Saturdays, 12 noon and 6 P.M. on Sundays, and at 12 noon daily during the summer.

On the way to the central square one passes the 18th-century building of the *Uniate Seminary*.

Rathaus, Tsentralnaya Square 1. Formerly the Polish Magistracy. Built in the 16th century, it has a sharply pointed spire and is decorated with the coat-of-arms of Podolia in the form of a shining sun. There is also a plaque dated 1754 inscribed to the effect that it was put up "in gratitude for the restoration of this territory."

The clock, which was installed in the tower in 1818, was made by Fyodor Polyanski of Lvov. The building was ruined during World War II but restored in 1956 and now serves as a picture gallery and exhibition hall. Nearby is the *Armenian Well*, dug 40 m (131 ft) deep in 1638 and filled in at the end of the 19th century. The building was restored in 1956.

Also near the Rathaus is the 16th-century *Dominican Church*, built on the site of a wooden church founded in 1370. *Potocki's House* (16th century) where the commander lived and the *Commander's House* is now a sewing factory. The building of the *Russian Magistracy* also dates from the 16th century; the Russian community obtained the right to self-government in 1658, but this was withdrawn in 1670, and the Polish magistracy was solely responsible for the town. This building was given to Predtechensky (John the Baptist's) Church and served as a seminary. From here the road leads into the old *Armenian quarter* of the town. There is a 17th-century trading centre, a belltower and triumphal arch (16th–18th centuries), storehouse, and St. Nicholas's Church, built in 1389 by the Armenians and of strategic importance because of its high stone walls. The belfry was built at the end of the 18th century.

Turning back toward the old city gate, the way into the town from the Turkish bridge, there are parts of the town wall and the Russian Gates (16th–18th centuries). Ukrainians who refused to accept Catholicism had to live in the southwestern part of the town, and they built their own line of defence against the Tatars, restored in 1960. The *Trinitarian Church* (18th century) is within the walls, on the way down to the bridge.

The *Armenian Bastion* (16th century), on the other side of the city gate, was so called not because of its position, for it is some distance from the Armenian quarter, but because it was manned by Armenians. The *Bishop's Palace* was built in 1753, and the *Franciscan Church* (16th–18th centuries) at Muzeiny Prospect 6 was once part of a monastery and is now used as a cotton mill.

From the western part of the town, the *Lookout Tower* commands a view across to the fortress and upon *St. George's Church* (1861) on the other side of the river. Other towers and bastions still stand at strategic points around the town. Most northerly are the *Turkish Bastion* of the 17th century and *Kushnirskaya Tower*, Bazarnaya Square 1, its name deriving from the word for the furriers who lived and worked in this part of town, who donated part of the money for its construction and helped to maintain and man it. Its other name, Stephan Batory Tower, commemorates that Polish king's order to build it in 1585. It formed a continuation of the fortifications of the Polish Gate, which looked to the northwest, toward Poland, and was restored in 1785 by Stanislas Augustus and again in 1958. The long passage leading to the tower was known as Windy Gates from the time in 1711 when Peter the Great's hat was blown off there. He was returning from his Pruth campaign against the Swedes. A stone plaque in the arch of the passage tells of the foundation of the tower.

SS. Peter and Paul Church, back toward the centre, on Karl Marx Street. Dates from the 15th–16th centuries. A number of old frescoes were discovered during restoration work.

Potter's Tower was built in 1538 as an important part of the eastern wall, reinforced to the southeast by the *Reznitskaya and Kravetskaya ("tailor's")* towers.

Guardhouse Tower was built in 1667 and restored in 1783.

The Barracks in the southern part of the town were built as a supplementary accommodation to the fortress in 1760. Vladimir Dahl, best known for his work as a lexicographer, served here as a doctor at the beginning of the 19th century.

Kazematna Tower, Radyanska Square, was built as a guard house in the 17th century.

Czartoryiski's House, Kirov Street 7, was built in the 16th century and belonged to a wealthy Polish family.

Galil Pasha's House (17th century) was the home of a Turkish ruler. Beside the main house, there is a harem and an underground prison.

Kazanskaya Church was built in the first half of the 18th century as the cathedral church of the Carmelite Convent but used after 1878 by the Uniate Church.

Vozdvizhenskaya (Elevation of the Cross) Church, or Korsarovskaya Church, in the valley of the Smotrich, below the fortress. Built of wood in 1799 in the tent-roofed style that was popular in the Carpathians.

The *teacher's training college* building was built in 1831–33. It was first used as a Jesuit seminary and then, until 1917, as a boys' school.

War Memorial, near the local Party building. Dedicated to heroes of the revolution and Civil War.

Tank Monument, Tankisty Park. This was one of the first tanks to enter the town at the time of its liberation in 1944 and commemorates those who lost their lives in World War II.

Urals Soldiers' Monument, in the park on Starobulvarny Spusk. In memory of the soldiers from the Urals who helped defend the town.

Smirnov Monument, Kirovsky Park. M. S. Smirnov was a hero of the Second World War.

Botanical Garden, Leningradskaya Street 78. Opened in 1930, it covers 25 hectares (63 acres).

Lenin Park, Shevchenko Street. There is a monument to Lenin here and an open-air theatre.

Stadium, Lenin Prospect 13

Ukraina Hotel and Restaurant, Leningradskaya Street 42

Chervone Podillya Hotel, Shevchenko Street 33

Stara Fortetsya Restaurant, Skhidni Boulevard, beside a 16th-century tower in the Old Town

Tourist Restaurant, to the left of the road, soon after leaving the town on the way to Vinnitsa

Yunost Café, Pushkin Street 40

GPO, Shevchenko Street 23

Department Store, Kirov Street 3

Filling Station, Zhvanetskoye Chaussée 36, beyond the town, at the 128-km mark, on the left

A recommended out-of-town Ukrainian restaurant is *Rossia Restaurant*, in the town of Letichev, 40 km (25 miles) from Kamenets-Podolsky.

KAMENKA
See Cherkassy, p. 99.

KANIV Population—25,000
(Russian: Kanev)

Intourist organises excursions here from Cherkassy, 82 km (51 miles) away, which takes about 8 hours, as well as excursions from Kiev.

Kaniv was founded by Yaroslavl the Wise in 1144 as a strong fortress near Kiev on the right bank of the river Dnieper, 732 km (455 miles) upstream from its mouth.

In the ancient chronicles it is mentioned as a well-fortified town on the southern border of Kievan Rus. Like Vitachiv, it was a point where the local garrison waited for boats with Byzantine goods to arrive and then escorted them safely to Kiev. As a border town, it was a place where the Polovtsi princes met to work out their relations. In 1239 it was taken by the army of Baty-Khan and was even the residence of the Tatars for a short time, but they ruined it before they left. In the 14th century, it belonged to Lithuania, and later to Poland. The town was the seat of the first Cossack hetmans, Ostap Dashkovich and Baida Vishnevetski. Many episodes of the Cossacks' wars are connected with this place.

The central square is called *Lenin Square*. There is a monument to Lenin, and the town's most important buildings, including the Dnipro Hotel, the GPO, and the Local Party Committee, are here. A local hydropower station was built in the 1970s.

The town's chief claim to fame is that 4 km (2 miles) away is the burial place of Taras Shevchenko (1814–61), who is often simply called Kobzar, which is Ukrainian for "bard." The site is known as the *Kaniv State Taras Shevchenko Museum-Reserve*. It is open 9–6; closed Mon.

In 1845 Shevchenko was visiting friends in nearby Pereyaslavl. He fell ill, and expecting to die, he wrote his well-known Testament (Zapovit) in which he asks to be buried on the high bank of the Dnieper:

> When I die, pray, bury me
> In my beloved Ukraine,
> My tomb upon a grave mound high
> Amid the spreading plain,
> So that the fields, the boundless steppes,
> The Dnieper's plunging shore
> Mine eyes might see, and my ears hear
> The mighty river roar.
> —Trans. JOHN WEIR

He recovered from his illness, visited Kaniv in 1859, and thought of settling here, but his plans never materialised. He died in St. Petersburg in March 1861 and was buried there. Shortly after the funeral, his friends, carrying out his last wish, brought his remains to Moscow by train and then to Kaniv by road. His brother, Varfolomei, at last found the right place on Mt. Chernecha, where Taras was reburied in May 1861, on the beautiful slopes of the right bank of the Dnieper. The Ukrainian writer Nechui-Levitsky said of the spot,

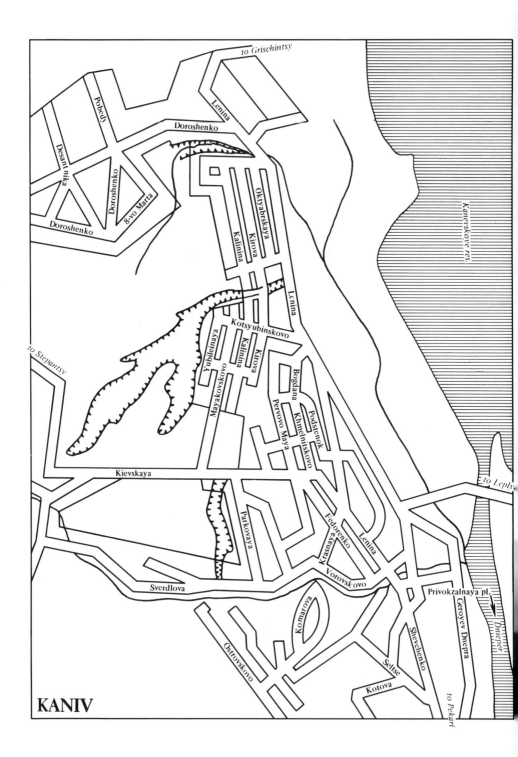

KANIV

"Those who have seen this wonderful place once will never forget it."

At first the grave was planned by the poet's friend, an artist called Chestakhovsky, who made a "kurgan," an earth hill walled by stone, with a big oak Cossack cross on the top. In 1883 the grave was enlarged, reinforced, and a new cast-iron cross was erected. The hill-grave reached 6 m (20 ft) in height, and a winding flight of 342 steps lead to the top. In 1914, on the 100th anniversary of Shevchenko's birth, it was forbidden to hold any kind of demonstration on the hill. In 1924 the cross was removed, and Shevchenko's bust was installed instead. The remains of the cross are still nearby. The following year a competition was organised for designing a monument, and the new bronze statue by Manizer was set up on a dark-grey granite pedestal in 1939, on the 125th anniversary of the poet's birth. The whole monument stands 17.5 m (57 ft) high.

In the 2-storey literary museum, documents (including the decisions of the World Peace Council and of UNESCO to commemorate the 150th anniversary of the poet's birth), pictures, and sculptures connected with Shevchenko, copies of his publications, and some of his watercolours are displayed in 10 halls. The museum was also opened in 1939.

The grave and the surrounding area of 1,360

Druzhba ("friendship") Park. 250 young oaks were planted here in 1961–64 on the 150th anniversary of his birth.

Uspensky (Assumption) Cathedral, Lenin Street 62, on Dnieper Hill. Also known as Yurevsky Cathedral, this was built in 1144, but its form has altered over the years. During a battle in 1678, the cathedral was the last stronghold in town. The Tartars and Turks brought straw and set fire to it, burning the building and the people inside. It is now plastered, decorated in classical style, and painted white, but part of the old brickwork is left to view on the west wall. A number of Cossack hetmans (leaders) lie buried by the walls of the cathedral. Inside the building is now the Museum of Decorative and Applied Art.

Arkadi Gaidar Library-Museum, Lenin Street 78. Open 9–6. Arkadi Gaidar (Golikov; 1904–41) is a popular children's writer. He died as a war correspondent and is buried here in the town. His grave is marked by a monument in Memorial Park, in the centre of Kaniv.

Museum of Ukrainian Decorative Folk Art, Lenin Street 62. Open 9–6; closed Tues.

Monuments to Lenin

Lensky's Grave, Memorial Park. Alexander Lensky (1847–1908), being the illegitimate son of Prince Gagarin, was known until 1897 by his mother's name of Vervitsiotti. He was a classical actor and drama teacher, closely connected with Moscow's Maly Theatre, where he worked from 1876 until his death, when he held the position of director.

Yadlovsky's Grave, on the way up the hill to Shevchenko's grave. Ivan Yadlovsky was the caretaker of Shevchenko's grave, and the first museum was in his own small house, which he built in 1884 and where he lived for 50 years.

Koshevoi Memorial Plaque, Lenin Street 64. Oleg Koshevoi (1926–43) was a pupil at this school in 1939–40. During the German occupation, he was one of the leaders of the underground Young Communist organisation. He was caught, executed, and posthumously made a Hero of the Soviet Union.

Koshevoi Bust, in Memorial Park, near the school

Tarasova Hora ("Taras's hill") Hotel and Restaurant, near Shevchenko's grave

Stadium, Energetikov Street 18

Dnieper Hotel and Restaurant, Lenin Street 48

Ukraina Restaurant, Lenin Street 20

Roden Restaurant, Lenin Street 12

Topolya Restaurant, Dnieprovskaya Street 13

GPO, Lenin Square

Department Stores, Lenin Street 18 and Koshevovo Street 2

KARABIKHA
See Yaroslavl, p. 673.

KARACHAY-CHERKESSK AUTONOMOUS REPUBLIC
See Cherkessk, p. 101.

KARAGANDA Population—614,000
Karaganda is the second-largest city in Kazakhstan after Alma-Ata. It is situated on a plateau, 660–650 m (1,970–2,130 ft) above sea level. In summer the temperature may rise to 40°C (104°F), and the lowest winter temperature is −40°C (−40°F).

The city derives its name from a species of yellow desert acacia called karagannik. In 1833 a young Kazakh hunter called Appak Baizhanov found coal here quite by chance. After setting fire to a bush, to his great surprise, what he thought was a stone burned as well. Soon a local ruler, Iglik Utepov, sold the territory to a merchant called Ushakov for 250 roubles and 10 horses. In 1856 the first 115 tons of coal were excavated. Somewhat later, copper works were founded. In 1904 Carnot, a Frenchman and son of President Carnot, rented the Karaganda mines, but in 1907 they became the property of "Spasskiye Mednye Rudy Company," organized in London by one J. Herbert. The biggest copper deposit was at Spassky and was also bought by a Briton, John Lesley Urquhart. At the same time a narrow-gauge railroad was built here.

In 1918 the mines and the plant were nationalised, and a new railroad was built. From 1929 the extraction of coal increased greatly, and the city began to grow. In 1934 it already had a population of more than 100,000, and that year it received city status. During World War II, many enterprises from occupied territories were evacuated to Karaganda, and a number of present-day plants developed from them. These include machine-building, food, and light industries. Spassky copper refinery proved unproductive and was closed down. Its territory was occupied by a prison camp for invalids until it was closed in the 1950s. Now Karaganda produces over 50 million tons of coal a year.

There are several satellite towns near Karaganda, including Saran, Churbai-Nura, and Dolinsk. There is a community of Volga Germans, and their neat houses stand out among the local dwellings. Sovietsky Prospect is the main thoroughfare, while Lenin Prospect is older and built up with three- and four-storey pink-washed buildings. The centre of the town continues to be embellished with new administrative buildings, sports structures, and apartment houses.

Presvyatoy Bogaroditsy (Our Lady) Church, in Mikhailovka

Mosque

Lutheran Church

Mennonite Church. There have been Mennonites here since 1957; the congregation numbers about 500.

Besides the churches mentioned above, there are also Catholic, Baptist, and Seventh-Day Adventist churches in Karaganda.

Local Museum, Kirov Street 38. Open 10–7, closed Tues. Contains a display of local handicrafts and everyday items; also some interesting stone carvings.

Exhibition Hall, Sovietsky Prospect 33

Lenin Monument, Sovietskaya Square

Old Lenin Monument, Kosenko Street

Miner's Glory Monument, Sovietskaya Square

Abdirov Monument, Nurken Abdirov Proyezd. Nurken Abdirov was a Hero of the Soviet Union, killed during World War II.

Kostenko Obelisk, Amangeldy Street. Kostenko was a prominent statesman, and one of the founders of contemporary Karaganda.

Stanislavsky Russian Drama Theatre, Mira Boulevard 19

Seifullin Kazakh Drama Theatre, Mira Boulevard 19. Named after Saken Seifullin (1894–1939), a poet and statesman.

Musical Comedy Theatre, Sovietsky Prospect 322

   Youth Theatre, Sovietsky Prospect 56

   Miners' Palace, Sovietsky Prospect 32

   Circus, Sovietsky Prospect 60

   Shakhtyor Stadium, Sovietsky Prospect

   Kazakhstan Hotel and Restaurant, Sovietsky Prospect 49; tel. 57–5554. Service bureau: tel. 57–7012. Intourist office: tel. 57–7017.

   Karaganda Hotel, tel. 57–7025

   Zarya Hotel, Sovietsky Prospect; tel. 51–2042

   Tsentralny Hotel, tel. 57–2333

   Aeroflot Agency, tel. 54–2424

   Orbita Restaurant

   Bank, Sovietsky Prospect 19

   Gift Shop, Sovietsky Prospect 28

Intourist organises excursions from Karaganda to Temirtau and Shakhtinsk.

Temirtau (Samarkandsky till 1945) Population—212,000

30 km (19 miles) from Karaganda. Intourist brings visitors here to see the sports complex, the park, and the aquarium.

In translation Temirtau means "iron hill." In 1934 a dam and a reservoir were built here on the river Kura, where the settlement of Samarkandsky soon sprang up and a metallurgical plant was constructed. Soon after, the settlement spread to include other villages and to become one of the largest metallurgical centres of Kazakhstan. In 1945 it was renamed Temirtau, simultaneously receiving the status of a town. Temirtau has a hilly landscape, with a ridge of high hills to the south and the reservoir to the north. The main thoroughfare is Lenin Street, and the newest parts of the town are Sotsgorod and Vostok.

It has coal, metallurgical, and chemical industries.

Lenin Monument, Lenin Square, between Sotsgorod and Vostok

War Memorial, in Sotsgorod. There is an eternal flame here, commemorating those who fell in the Second World War.

German Drama Theatre, in the old town. This is the only German-language theatre in the country.

Metallurgists' Palace, Lenin Square

Children's Park. Here is the Vostok children's cinema, a games pavilion, and an aquarium.

Sports Complex, Lenin Square. The facilities include the largest swimming pool in Kazakhstan.

Aquarium

GPO, Lenin Square

Shakhtinsk Population—65,000

50 km (31 miles) from Karaganda. The tours here are for those connected with the coal-mining industry. The mines are 3–5 km (2–3 miles) outside the town. Shakhtinsk emerged in 1956 as a settlement of coal miners. In 1961 it became a satellite town of Karaganda. There are coal and chemical industries.

KARAGOL, LAKE
See Yalta, p. 661.

KARA-KUM CANAL
See Ashkhabad, p. 46.

KARELIA
See Petrozavodsk, p. 418.

KAUNAS (Formerly Russian Kovno)
Population—423,000
Intourist organises excursions here by bus frm Vilnius, 100 km (60 miles) away.

Kaunas is situated where the River Niemen (Nyamunas) joins the Neris (Vilya). It is the second-largest town in Lithuania and one of 4 to have served as the capital.

As legend has it, in the 1st century B.C. a Roman called Patrithian Palemon was prosecuted by the Emperor Nero and had to leave his country and seek a new home in the north. Accompanied by 500 noblemen, he reached the mouth of the Nyamunas, found a favourable place, and settled there. He had 3 sons, one of whom, called Kunas, travelled up the Nyamunas and founded a town, which took its name from his own, hence Kaunas.

Linguists presume that in ancient Lithuanian there was a word "kaunus" or "kaunas," meaning "lower". In the old chronicles, the place was called Caonia, Cawonia, and Cowna. It was first mentioned in documents in 1280. During the 14th century, the town was invaded several times by the Teutonic Knights. Over the years it was reduced to ashes no less than 13 times.

In 1408 the town received the Freedom of Magdeburg, which gave it self-government and other privileges. It became the hub of Lithuania's export trade; the Hanseatic League had warehouses here, and there was a trading centre for other merchants. The town, together with the rest of Lithuania, fell into Polish hands in 1569. In the 16th century in Kaunas, there were builders' workshops united in guilds; the bricklayers' and carpenters' guilds had as many as 50 members.

In 1537 a terrible fire damaged the town. It is recorded that Sigizmund the Old freed the townspeople from the taxes that had to be paid into the royal treasury and in 1540 gave them other privileges as well. Great attention was paid to the planning of Kaunas. In June 1542 the civic authorities signed a contract to build the town hall and in July it was founded. Kaunas was a busy centre for the surrounding countryside. Markets and fairs, elections, executions, and feasts were all held there. The lands around were given only to the most prominent citizens, and nearby estates were occupied by representatives of Dutch, English, German, and other merchants.

The town remained in Polish hands until the Third Partition of Poland in 1795, when it passed to the Russian empire. Gradually the Lithuanian language was suppressed, and trading only took place in Russian, although in the 16th and 17th centuries, there had been trading stations run by the Dutch, English, Prussians, Swedes, and Venetians, with an annual trade turnover of one million ducats.

Napoleon's army passed through the town twice in 1812. Napoleon stayed in a Carmelite convent built in 1685, which stood on Lenin Street, but he is also supposed to have lodged in a number of private houses. He surveyed the town from the top of a nearby hill before giving orders to his 600,000 men. In the battle, Kaunas was badly damaged, and only 3,000 inhabitants remained alive. In 1842 Kaunas became a provincial capital with a governor.

By 1914 nearly half the population of 88,000 was Jewish. The Germans occupied the town in 1915–18 and again in 1941–44. After the Polish occupation of the ancient Lithuanian capital of Vilnius in 1919, Kaunas became the de facto capital of the country till 1939, when Vilnius was returned to Lithuania. During these years a number of impressive buildings were put up, such as the *Land Bank*, the *Seim government building* (1930—now the Philharmonia Concert Hall), the central *post office* (1932), the *public library*, and the impressive building of the *Art Museum* and the *Historical Museum* (1936). In 1940 Kaunas became Soviet with the rest of Lithuania. The population of the city is 80 percent Lithuanian.

There is an excellent view over the town from a nearby hill, which is still known as *Napoleon's Hill*. It is 43 m (141 ft) high. According to a story, Napoleon stood here to observe his army crossing the river. A small funicular railway runs up to the higher parts of the town.

Kaunas spreads widely along the banks of its 2 rivers, and some districts are quite a distance from each other and from the centre. The latter can be divided into the Old Town, with its narrow streets near the confluence of the Nyamunas and the Neris, and the New Town, with Laisves Allée and other broad straight streets in the hollow to the east of the ancient castle. It is pleasant to wander about the Old Town to see the mediaeval houses and romantic corners, the old warehouses, and Napoleon's House.

There are 5 institutes in Kaunas including a medical college. The largest of these establishments is the Polytechnical Institute, with about 10,000 students. It was founded in 1951 after Kaunas University was reorganised. (The country's university is now in Vilnius.) There are also a number of scientific research institutes and a Catholic seminary.

Many new apartment houses have been built recently in the centre of the town, along Pergale Embankment, and on the outskirts, on Jaunoji Gvardija Street, as well as in the districts of Vilijampole, Petrasiunai, and Panemune.

The town has light and food industries as well as metal and woodworking industries.

Part of the original town walls with a tower have survived in the town garden. They were erected in 1670–80. The wall was 9 m (30 ft) high and stretched from north to south between the Nyaris and the Nyamunas. The round tower is made of brick, and during the restoration work it was covered with a cone-shaped tiled roof.

A number of the town's Roman Catholic churches were converted for Russian Orthodox use in the 19th century. One of them was dedicated to St. Nicholas by special order of the Russian tsar Nicholas I after he escaped drowning in the Nieman in 1853.

Church of Vytautas, Aleksotas Street 1, in the Old Town, is the largest Roman Catholic church in Lithuania, and one of the first brick buildings. It stands down by the bank of the Nyamunas, is

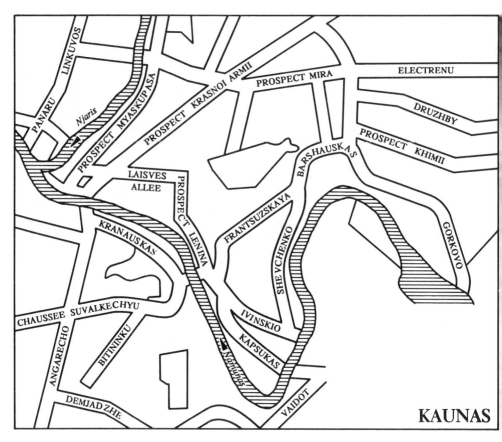

KAUNAS

dedicated to SS. Peter and Paul, and is the oldest church in the town. It was built by Grand Duke Vytautas in 1400 of red brick in Gothic style. Legend has it that he wished to commemorate his safety after his army was defeated by the Tatars in a battle by the river Vorskla in 1399. In this battle his dreams of conquering Moscow and of destroying the Golden Horde also perished. According to other sources, Vytautas erected this church when King Jogailo appointed him ruler of Lithuania, and it was designed for use by Christians from other lands. The church belonged at one time to Augustinian monks. It was devastated many times by Swedes, French, and Germans. At the end of the 19th century, a system of strong buttresses was installed, which helped the building to withstand floods. During the 1946 flood, the water reached the mark of 2.9 m (8 ft) above the crypt. There is an octangular tower in the centre of the western façade, and the windows are of stained glass. The interior is very simple Gothic, and there is an organ. The church is open for services.

Kaunas Basilica, Vilniaus Street 26. Built in 1412, also, so it is said, by Prince Vytautas. It was a Gothic structure, 30 m (98 ft) in height. It has a single 55-m (180-ft) tower and somehow looks unfinished. Originally Gothic in design, it was practically destroyed in the wars of 1655–60 and

1701 and in 1732 by a great town fire. It was partially restored in 1770 and in 1775 reconstructed by Italian builders in baroque style; now only the windows remain Gothic. At the end of the 19th century, it became the principal Catholic church of Jemaitis episcopasy. There are precious works in the basilica, large pictures by Elviro Andriolli as well as works by Lithuanian artists.

St. Yurgius (George) Roman Catholic Church, Papiles Street 7/9, beside what remains of Kaunas castle. In 1471 Great Prince Kazimieras gave permission to the monks of the Bernardine Order to build a church and a monastery at the confluence of the Nyamunas and the Neris. When the townspeople saw a real fortress being erected, they protested to the king, but the monks defended their right to build as they wished, and the construction of the monastery was completed in 1504. Later it was badly damaged by several fires and restored at the end of the 16th century, in 1688, and most particularly in 1927. The Lithuanian-Gothic-style church has a baroque interior with 6 altars lavishly decorated with icons and sculptures. The U-shaped building of the monastery joins the church on its southern side. It now serves as a Museum of Atheism.

St. Michaloyus (Nicholas) Roman Catholic Church, Pakalnes Street 8. The building was erected in the northern suburbs of the town in the 15th century and enlarged in the 16th century. The belfry dates to the 18th century. The church suffered neither fire nor devastation, and Gothic, Renaissance and baroque styles blend beautifully together. The sacristy of the church is particularly worthy of attention.

Carmelite Convent, Lenin Street. This was built in 1685, and Napoleon may have stayed here when he passed through Kaunas in 1812.

St. Anthony's Catholic Church, Baranauskas Allée, by the Polytechnic Institute in Zelyonaya Gora, 16th Division. This is all a new area of the town and is known as the Song Region; someone starts to sing, and all the neighbors join in the chorus.

Church of SS. James and Phillip, behind Lenin's statue in Lenin Square (also formerly called Market Square), off Lenin Street

Lutheran Church and Hall of Germonius, Snitko Street

St. Joseph's Church, Lincovos Square, Paneru Street

St. Michael's Church, Klozela Street

Resurrection Roman Catholic Church, Aukstashia Street 4

Dominican Church, now the Confluence Cinema

Carmelite Church, Gediminas Street 1. This twin-towered church was built in baroque style in the shape of a cross in 1685–95.

Orthodox Church, Lenin Street. One of the four Russian Orthodox churches open for services.

Old Believers' Church, Shirvintu Street, on Zelyoni Gora

Ogel Yakob Choral Synagogue, Ozeskienes Street 13. Built in the early 19th century.

Tatar Mosque, Tataryu Street. This is not very old and now houses a reading room and children's library.

Karaliskoji Karcema, Vilnius Street 22. After a fire in 1743, this 2-storey asymmetrical house, said to be without a single right angle in all its construction, was rebuilt in Gothic style in stone. It is known locally as the Royal Tavern.

Rotuses Aikstes, Town Hall Square, formerly Market Square, the heart of the Old Town. The square has been extensively restored, and now there are a number of small shops selling souvenirs and ceramics, a beer-hall and café with a restaurant upstairs in the guild hall, and a chemist's shop. On the west side of the square is the Hunter's Inn Restaurant.

Town Hall, The spender spire of the white town hall soars in the middle of the square. It looks so proud and graceful that the citizens call it the white swan. It was built as a church in 1556 by the Litunanian architect Khoinovsky. It was rebuilt as a royal residence in 1771 by architect Mateker upon the order of Stanislav August, the new tower reaching a height of 53 m (174 ft), rivalling that of the Jesuits' basilica. Since then the town hall has reflected late baroque and early classical styles. In the 19th century, it was turned into an accommo-

dation for receptions, and later a theatre moved in. Now it serves as a palace for wedding ceremonies.

House No. 29 on the square consisted of 2 parts. Till 1625 it belonged to a chemist, Gannus Mantus. In the 18th century, the owners of the house, who were close relatives of members of the town council, ran a post office here. In 1972 the house was restored. The western part of it is 16th-century Gothic style, and the corner part, which suffered greatly from fires, is Renaissance. There is still a post office on the ground floor. The courtyard of the house is very picturesque and is a favourite spot for making films.

Masalsky Palace, No. 22 on the square. Prince Masalsky erected the palace in 1640. The 2-storey building and Holy Trinity Church are encircled by a high stone wall. From Traku Street there are wonderful early baroque gates. The eastern façade is especially beautiful. Its fronton is completed with a semicircular design of a 3-petalled wildflower, finely forged in the 17th century. The architecture of the palace is greatly influenced by Renaissance ideas from Italy and the countries of central Europe.

Holy Trinity Church, No. 22 on the square. It was under construction between 1634 and 1703. The main entrance is unusual in that it is in a side wall, in the tower. The church is in Gothic style, and during the long years of construction, fragments of earlier structures were included. The church is now used by the Catholic seminary.

Zabel Palace, No. 10 on the square, was built in the 17th century on the base of houses from the 15th–16th centuries and rebuilt in 1800 by architect Dekern in classical style. The interior of the palace houses the justly popular *Hunter's Inn Restaurant*.

The *Jesuit complex* on the southern side of the square has monastery buildings on the left and their college on the right. The Jesuits' Church (Nos. 7, 8, and 9) was built in the 17th century. Jesuit monks appeared in Kaunas in 1642. They owed their strong position in the town to the Koyaloviches family, which owned part of the square. The historian Albert Koyalovich-Viyukas and his brothers donated their property to the Order, and from 1647 there was a Jesuit college in the house. The twin towers of the church, under construction in 1666, were to have been taller than the spire on the town hall, and there was legal conflict over the matter for a period of 20 years, but the Jesuits lost their argument. A great fire in 1732 damaged the uncompleted building. At the end of the 18th century, the Jesuit Order was disbanded, and in 1806 their college (on the right) was reorganised as a local school. In 1819–23 the Polish poet Adam Mitskevich lived and worked here. Now the building houses an ordinary school which bears his name. It is built in baroque style.

The Consistorium, Pyargales Krantine ("embankment") 3. The first Reformist Church had been standing on Rotushes Square since the 16th century, but the advocates of the new religion were finally driven out of the square by the Jesuits. They then founded this new building, beyond the southern bounds of Rotushes Square. In 1683 a small stone church in late Renaissance style was built adjoining the consistorium.

SS. *Peter and Paul Basilica*, at the corner of Valaciaus and Vilniaus Streets, just outside the northeast corner of the square, behind the King's Post Office. It was founded in the 15th century and is in Gothic style, built of red brick. The basilica is open for services, as are 11 other Catholic churches, including those in Shantzi Region and in Panemuni, on Vaidoto Street.

Kaunas Castle, Aleksotas Street 6. The remains of the 14th-century castle can still be seen at the confluence of the Neris and the Nyamunas. It is divided from the rest of the town by a moat. It used to cover a territory of 1 hectare (2.5 acres). The first castle on the site was ruined by the Teutonic Knights in 1362, and a new one was built in 1384 in the course of 6 weeks, when 60,000 people and 80,000 horses were employed for the job. A canal was dug, so that the castle stood upon a small island. It was named Ritters-Werder. It was taken back by the Lithuanians in October of the same year. It had 9-m (30-ft) walls that were 3.5 m (11 ft) thick, and 4-storeyed towers stood at the corners. In the 15th century, it was used for receptions and audiences. The castle was badly damaged by the flooding of the river Neris in 1611 and during the 17th–18th century wars, and eventually the southeastern tower was the only one to remain standing. It was from the top of this that the freedom flag flew at the end of World War II. Some reconstruction work was done in the 1950s, and now the southeastern tower houses a branch of the *Historical Museum*, open 11–6; closed Tues. and the last day of each month. A park was laid out around the castle, and in 1975 a *monument* by R. Antonis was unveiled here depicting a musician playing a folk instrument called the kankles.

In the Old Town there are a number of old houses besides those around the town hall. The most famous is the *House of Perkunas*, Aleksotas Street 6, down by the bank of the river, opposite the Church of Vytautas and behind the Jesuits' church. Perkunas was the god of thunder and lightning, the Thor of the ancient Lithuanians. This is a 15th-century red-brick building in the style known as "flaming Gothic," which stands on the site of Perkunas's temple. (It was after the completion of this building that St. Anne's in Vilnius was constructed.) In 1634 the Jesuit Order was using the building as a chapel, and in the 18th–19th centuries, it was rebuilt as a theatre, then a school, then an inn. Now there is another branch of the *Historical Museum*.

Petranskas House and Museum, This old house used to be the Italian Embassy.

Napoleon's House, Kuzmos Street 67. The southern façade is in Renaissance style, and the northern in classical style. It was built in the 16th–18th centuries, and Napoleon is said to have stayed here in 1812.

Patsus Palace, Museiyaus Street 13. The 17th-century councellor Krishtupas-Zugmantas Patsus of Lithuania built this luxurious 2-storey palace on the base of devastated 16th-century houses. Count Khrapovnitsky bought it in the 18th century and made some changes in its baroque architecture. In 1910 the building passed to poet Maironis, and the palace was later restored as both an architectural and a historical monument. Now it houses the *Lithuanian Literature Museum*.

Pazaislio Cloister is in Pazaislis pine wood on a peninsula in the Kaunas Sea. It was founded in 1664 by Councellor Patsas, and at the beginning the construction was undertaken by an Italian architect, Ludovic Fredo, following the design of Bielany Convent, 8 km (5 miles) west of Cracow, but he died in 1682 without having completed his masterpiece. The main church was to have a tall façade decorated with pilasters and set between 2 towers, and with a square belltower behind. The Italian brothers Carlo and Pietro Putini finished the construction in 1719, by which time the church had cost "8 barrels of gold to build." Now it is one of the most beautiful baroque monuments in the USSR. It is lavishly decorated with frescoes and sculptures by Italian artists, including Giovanni Merli and Michelangelo Palloni de Campi. The interior of the church is set off with marble brought from Cracow in Poland.

The monastery changed hands between Catholic and Orthodox monks and suffered greatly when Napoleon's army retreated in 1812. During World War I, when there was a military hospital there, part of the precious frescoes perished, and many works of art and a brass bell were taken to Germany in 1919. After World War I, the nuns of the Order of St. Casimir made it their convent. Now the building houses a branch of the *Ciurlionis Art Museum*.

President's Palace, Dzerzhinsky Street. Now the House of Teachers.

Historical Museum, K. Donelaitis Street 64. Open 11–6; closed Tues. and the last day of each month. There is a small garden around the museum, and here is the Book-Peddler sculpture by Zikaras, commemorating the times when the Lithuanian language was suppressed. Many people come here to listen to bell-ringing concerts given by the Kupryavichus family.

Stained-glass and Sculpture Gallery, Bilyunas Street 14, at the end of the Laisves Street. This is housed in the large white-and-gold SS. Peter and Paul Cathedral, originally built in 1895 for Catholic use but converted to serve as a Russian Orthodox church for the local garrison. It is now a branch of the *Ciurlionis Art Museum*. Open 12–6; closed Mon. Organ and chamber music concerts are also held here.

Art Gallery, Donelaichio Street 16. Open 12–6; closed Mon.

Literature Museum, Rotushes Square 13, near the Town Hall. In front of the museum there is the poet *Maironis Monument* by Iokubonis.

Lithuanian Literature Museum, in Patsus Palace, Museiyaus Street 13

Museum of Atheism, in St. Yurgius (George) Roman Catholic Church at Papiles Street 7/9, beside the remains of Kaunas castle

Zoological Museum, Laisves Allée 106. Laisves means "freedom"; it used to be called Nikolayevskaya Prospect and then Stalin Street. The buildings are now painted in their original colours.

Petrs Cvirka Memorial Museum, Donelaichio Street 13 (a branch of the Literature Museum). Cvirka (1909–47) was a writer who lived in the cellar of this house. His bust, sculpted by Palis, stands in the garden.

Salomeya Neris Memorial Museum, Vilnyales Street 7 (another branch of the Literature Museum). The famous Lithuanian poetess Bachinskaite-Buchene (1904–45) spent most of her life in Kaunas and was buried in the garden of the Historical Museum. There is a monument by Buchas marking her grave.

Ciurlionis Art Museum, S Neries Street 45. Open 10–6; closed Mon. and the last Tues. of each month. Mikalojus Ciurlionis (1875–1911) was both an artist and a musician. He tried to transmit sounds and melodies by means of paint. There is a good collection of Ciurlionis's own works here and much folk art, which includes some unusual bark sculptures. The 100th anniversary of Ciurlionis's birth was celebrated both in the Soviet Union and elsewhere on UNESCO initiative. Concerts of his music are given in the gallery. The sculptural group "Kings" is by Vildzhunas. (There is another branch of the museum in Pazaislio Cloister (see above), in Pazaislis pine wood by Kaunas Sea.

Zhmuidzinavicius House-Museum, S Neris Street 45 (a branch of the Ciurlionis Art Museum). Open 12–6, closed Mon. Beside the works of Prof. Antonas Zhmuidzinavicius (1876–1966), the famous Lithuanian landscape painter, there is his collection of devils, which now numbers over 500 items, made of glass, wood, or fabric.

Drama Theatre, Laisves Allée 71. This is the oldest theatre in Lithuania. It was founded in 1920 and in 1925 was united with an opera group and called the State Drama Theatre.

Musical Theatre, Laisves Allée 91. Founded in 1940.

Puppet Theatre, Laisves Allée 87a. Opened in 1960. It has received many international prizes and is a member of UNIMA—the puppet theatres' international organisation.

Kaunas Philharmonia Concert Hall, Tolstoy Street 5

Perkunas Sculpture, in the Old Town. By Antonis.

Holiday Sculpture. By Antonis.

Rebels Monument. By Daugvilene.

Lenin Monument, in Lenin Prospect. By Petrulis.

Dzerzhinsky Bust. Felix Dzerzhinsky (1877–1926), the well-known revolutionary, began his professional revolutionary work here. He published an underground newspaper here in 1897. The bust was made by Bogdanas.

Vincas Mickevicius-Kapsukas Bust. Vincas Mickevicius-Kapsukas (1880–1935) was head of the Lithuanian communist government in 1919.

Montvila's Bust, in Vytautas Park. Vytautas Montvila (1902–41) was a poet who was shot by the Nazis.

Four Communists' Monument, Lenin Prospect. This has memorial plaques to Karolis Pozela, Juozas Greifenbergeois, Kazys Giedrys, and Rapolas Garnas, who were shot on 27 December 1926, after the coup d'état by the Iron Wolf organisation. There is also a tank here, the first one to enter the town in 1944.

Zoo, Sixteenth Divizijos Pl. 21, is in the valley of the river Guirstupis. It was founded in 1938, and now there are over 2,500 specimens of fauna.

Botanical Garden, Botanikos Prospect 6, in the suburban region of Kaunas called Freda. The garden was founded here in 1923 in the park that had belonged to the landowner Godlevsky. He had also built a small palace in classical style. The estate also includes the stables, a storehouse, a wine cellar, and a bridge.

Stadium

Palace of Sports

Dainava Sports and Cultural Complex

Vytautas Park. In the park are 300-year-old oaks, Lithuania's national tree, and a bust of the poet Vytautas Motvila.

Baltiya Hotel and Restaurant, Lenin Prospect 71

Lietuva Hotel and Restaurant, Daukantas Street 21

Nyamunas Hotel and Restaurant, Laisves Allée 88

Metropolis Restaurant, Laisves Allée 44 (formerly the Metropole Café)

Hunter's Inn Restaurant, Town Hall Square

Bialyastok Restaurant, Lenin Street

Gintaras ("amber") Restaurant, Liepos Street 21

Pasaka Children's Restaurant, Laisves Allée

Tulpe Café, Laisves Allée 25. This used to be known as Conrad's, and the best cakes in Kaunas are sold here.

Egle Café

Medsiotoju Uzeiga ("hunters' inn"), Rotuses Street 10, near the Town Hall

Department Store, Laisves Allée, opposite the Tulpe Café

GPO, Laisves Allée 74

There are a number of places to visit in the vicinity of Kaunas; among them are IX *Fort Museum*, Zhemaitiskoye Chaussée, 6 km (4 miles) from the centre of town. This is a branch of the Historical Museum, founded in 1959. Open 10–6; closed Tues. and the last Mon. of each month. IX Fort was a fortress in Kaunas's defence system. The Nazis turned it into an international death camp but gave it the innocent-sounding name of Enterprise No. 1005-B. Nearly 80,000 people were tortured, killed, and buried here in a common grave during the years of German occupation. They came from Algeria, Austria, Belgium, Czechoslovakia, Monaco, and the Netherlands. The testimonies of survivors made a formidable indictment against the Nazis. A second part of the museum was opened in 1985 to mark the 40th anniversary of the liberation of Lithuania. A memorial complex, including a *Monument to the Victims of Fascism* (1985), has been installed in the field where mass executions took place.

Azhuolynas ("oak grove") and *Panemune*, with pine forests and beaches. The annual song festival is held here on a special stage in a leafy valley called the Valley of Songs, along Barshanskas Street.

In Mickiewicz Valley is a stone with the initials "A.M.—1823" and a few lines from a poem. Adam Mickiewicz was a famous Polish poet who worked from 1819–23 as a teacher in Kaunas, at school No. 9. He described this valley as the most beautiful in the world.

Kaunas Sea was formed 12 km (7 miles) up the river Niemen when the hydropower station was built in 1955–60. It is 64 sq km (25 sq miles) in area. The power station has 4 aggregates of 22,500 kilowatts each.

Before the valley was flooded, 45 villages were moved. Near the largest village of Rumsiskes, 23 km (14 miles) from Kaunas, the *Lithuanian Ethnographical Museum* was founded in 1966. Open 10–7, closed last Mon. of each month. This open-air museum covers a territory of 1,800 hectares (4,500 acres) and displays interesting examples of folk architecture and the customs and habits of the 4 main Lithuanian ethnographical regions. The exhibits reflect the life of Lithuanian peasants and artisans in the 18th–20th centuries; concerts by ethnographical ensembles are held here.

KAZAKHSTAN

See Alma-Ata, p. 34.

KAZAN

Kazan is the capital of the Tatarstan.

TATARSTAN

Established in 1920, this was one of the first autonomous republics. It covers an area of 67,858 sq. km (26,200 sq. miles) in the east of European Russia and is rich in natural gas and oil. It is in the Middle Volga basin, around the confluence of the Volga and the Kama rivers.

In the 10th century, the Bulgarian Volga state was here, but it was ruined by the Tatars in 1236, in the time of Khan Batyi. Their town of Bulgar was burned down, and in the 15th century the Kazan khanate was formed in the same territory, with Kazan as its capital.

The history of the republic and its people is closely connected with the capital, Kazan. The present-day location of the republic more or less corresponds to the boundaries of the Bulgar state and the Kazan khanate. Many tatars live in nearby Bashkorstan, and there were plans after the revo-

lution for a Tatar-Bashkir republic, but they never materialised; the organisers, headed by Mirza Sultan-Galiyev (in charge of the All-Russian Muslim Movement) had visualised this republic with a Muslim Communist party and Muslim administration. There were also hopes in 1917 to establish a Tatar-Bashkir national state (Idel-Ural), as a state within a state, but nothing came of this either.

During the Civil War, a train was sent here from Petrograd loaded with the imperial Russian treasure, consisting of gold bricks valued at that time at £65 million (or $325 million). The capture of Kazan, only 800 km (500 miles) from Moscow, seriously threatened the success of the revolution. Counterrevolutionary troops captured the train and passed the gold reserve over to Admiral Kolchak, then leader of the White forces in Siberia.

The Turkic-speaking Sunnite Muslims are also known as Kazan or Volga Tatars. Since 1782 their religious leader (Mufti) has had his headquarters in Ufa. They make up less than half the population of the republic, the rest being Russians and a variety of minority groups.

Kazan Population—1,095,000

Sing to me, O harp, all about Kazan . . .
          —DERZHAVIN

Kazan has been called "the Beauty of the East" and is sometimes called the virtual capital of Russian Islam. It stands on the left bank of the Volga, near the point where it is joined by the Kazanka. The central part of the town stands on hills which are 60–90 m (195–295 ft) above sea level. The climate is continental, and the summer temperature averages 22°C (71.5°F).

The Tatar word "kazan" means "cauldron." The first Kazan was founded some 45 km (28 miles) away from here in the second half of the 13th century by Tudai-Menghe, Khan of the Golden Horde (also known as Kazan-Khan). It was later known as Iske-Kazan (Old Kazan), but no trace of it can be found. Legend has it that while one of Tudai-Menghe's servants was preparing a bath for his master, he dropped a golden cauldron into the river, and the new town was later founded nearby.

In the 14th century, Kazan became the capital of the principality and in the mid-15th, when it had already been transferred to its present position, of the Kazan khanate. The new site was better both geographically and strategically. There are a number of Tatar legends connected with the construction of the new town. One of these tells of a rich man from old Kazan who often visited his apiaries in the forest near Jilan-Tau ("snake hill") and who usually took his daughter with him. When this young lady got married, she lived in old Kazan and had to go quite a distance to the Kazanka for water. She blamed the founder of the town for his bad planning. Ali-Bei, ruler of Kazan, learned of her complaints and sent for her. She told him that the founder of the town, who had water brought to him by servants, could not have realised how difficult

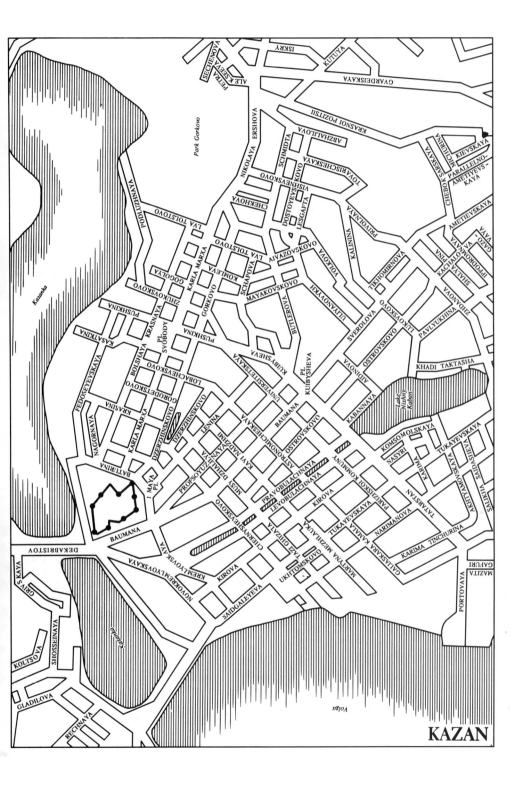

KAZAN

it would be for the poor women, especially those expecting babies, to carry jars of water up the hill. The woman told Ali-Bei about the advantages of a place near the mouth of the Kazanka where her apiaries were situated. The khan replied that Jilan-Tau was notorious for the great number of snakes there and that the place near the mouth of the Kazanka was inhabited by wild boars. The woman argued that both snakes and boars could be dealt with by wizards.

As it happened, the khan himself was dissatisfied with the position of his town, so he sent his son with 2 nobles and 100 warriors to the mouth of the Kazanka to search for a better site for the town and gave them sealed instructions, to be opened the moment they agreed about the site. When they were agreed, the instructions were opened, and the nobles read the khan's order to bury one member of their party alive where the future city was to be built. Lots were cast, and it fell to the khan's son to die, but the servants hid him and buried a dog instead. When the khan came to inspect the site, he was grieved to learn of his son's fate, but his servants soon told him the truth. Although he was much relieved, he still regretted that his command had not been obeyed and remarked sadly: "This means that our new city and kingdom will eventually fall into the hands of the enemies of our true religion, whom we call unholy dogs."

In the autumn a wizard drove all the snakes into a certain place and gave orders that wood and straw be piled around them. This was done, and the following spring all the snakes were burned. However, a dragon survived on Jilan-Tau and long held the whole area in terror, until it too was killed by a wizard. Probably it is to this legend that Kazan owed its coat-of-arms, which first appeared at the beginning of the 17th century. The final version of the design, argent a black dragon with red wings under the golden crown of Kazan, was approved in 1730.

After the disintegration of the Golden Horde, Kazan became the centre of a "new Horde," an independent khanate. In the period between 1445 and 1477, Kazan troops made frequent incursions into Russian lands, attacking Murom, Galich, Vladimir, and other cities. In 1487, in a massive retaliation campaign, Russian troops under Ivan III entered Kazan and put a pro-Russian khan, Mohammad Emin, on the throne.

At the end of the 15th and the beginning of the 16th centuries, the economic ties between Kazan and Russia grew considerably. Kazan had a population of about 30,000. The city centred around the high, oak-walled Kremlin, inside which stood stone-built mosques, mausolea, and the khan's palace.

Kazan was the centre of a typical feudal Muslim state, where internal strife resulted in frequent changes of khans. In the 1520s anti-Russian tendencies gradually developed, the policies of Mohammad Emin were forgotten, and in 1521 a pro-Turkish group placed Sahib-Ghirey, a brother of

the Crimean khan, on the Kazan throne. Kazan became a tool in the hands of the Turkish sultan and his vassal, the Crimean khan, in their struggle against Moscow. Sahib-Ghirey and his successor, Safa-Ghirey, made several raids into Russian territory.

In self-defence Russia waged 2 unsuccessful campaigns (in 1547–48 and 1549–50), and finally the Russian fortress of Sviyazhsk (see below) was built near Kazan. The people living on the right bank of the Volga refused to serve Kazan and swore allegiance to Moscow. An uprising in Kazan in 1551 brought the pro-Russian Shah-Alei to the throne, but he lacked the support of his chief vassals, and in the early spring of 1552, they asked the Russian tsar, Ivan IV (the Terrible), to make Kazan a Moscow protectorate. Before negotiations were complete, a pro-Turkish group once more seized power and closed the city gate. They invited Prince Yedigher of Astrakhan to take the Kazan throne. The Russian army attacked in the summer of 1552 with an army of 150,000, and by 25 August the city was surrounded. The siege lasted for a month, until Russian engineers mined the city walls and, on 2 October, blew them up in 2 places. The fortress fell after fierce fighting. That same year Ivan the Terrible organised the rebuilding of the fortress, sending the best masons from Pskov to do the work. At the same time, churches were built where the mosques had stood, and Ivan proclaimed, "Let the unbelievers accept the true God as new subjects of Russia, and let them with us praise the Holy Trinity for ever and ever, Amen." In 1555 the first archbishop of Kazan, St. Guryi, arrived from Moscow with instructions to "convert the Tatars by love and not force." Altogether about 20,000 Tatars became Christian under Ivan the Terrible, but most resented the idea, and those in Kazan who refused to accept Christianity were forbidden to live within the city walls.

Due to this, by the second half of the 16th century, Kazan was much changed. The Tatars had been moved out of the centre of the town, and their places had been taken by Russians. The Tatar regions were Zabulachye and Zabakanye, on the far side of Lake Kaban, where Narimanova, Tukayevskaya (formerly Ekaterininskaya), Kirov (formerly Moskovskaya), Parizhskoi Kommuny, and Tatarstan streets are today. The centre of Kazan had become a military settlement. In 1593 Tsar Feodor Ioannovich ordered that all Tatar mosques inside the city of Kazan be destroyed. Kazan became a centre for converting non-Christians to Orthodoxy; converts were given a cross, a shirt, shoes, a hat, 1.50 roubles, and 50 kopeks for each of their children. All sorts of other privileges were offered, and some priests managed to attract thousands of people. But sometimes the priests were short of funds and failed to keep their promises. The converts became so infuriated that the priests had to seek military protection. In general, in the 17th and 18th centuries, Kazan served as a stronghold of government troops against rebellious peasants. In 1612 volunteers went from Kazan to help Minin and Pozharsky's forces liberate Moscow from the Poles. They took with them their own icon of Our Lady from the convent of the same name. The wonder-working icon was reputed to have been found buried in the earth, and one of the convent's churches was specially built to mark the spot. After the victory in Moscow, it was generally believed that the good fortune was due to Our Lady of Kazan, as the icon was called. In gratitude the royal family, the Romanovs, built a church in Moscow dedicated to Our Lady of Kazan. The icon was held in great veneration and was claimed to have helped stop the spread of the city fire of 1737. St. Petersburg's Kazan Cathedral was built to house the icon in the 19th century.

In the late 17th century, Kazan was gripped by plague, and in 1672–74 terrible fires burned down many houses. In 1708 Kazan was declared the centre of the province of the same name, and soon all the trade and industry of eastern Russia focussed upon it. The first organised industry in Kazan itself appeared at the order of Peter the Great. In 1718 the Volga-Caspian Admiralty was established, and a shipyard was founded, which built 342 ships for the Persian campaign. During this period the wool and leather industries also developed. Peter, who visited Kazan in 1722 on his way down to Astrakhan, thought of it as a trade centre between Siberia, China, and Persia. He inspected the town thoroughly and without hesitation gave a badly run government-owned textile mill to an efficient private mill-owner. In spite of the policy of religious freedom followed earlier, the Tatars were now forced to adopt Christianity at swordpoint. After the fire of 1742, Archbishop Luka Konashevich of Kazan accused the Tatars of starting the blaze and obtained permission from Elizaveta Petrovna to destroy all Tatar mosques, no matter where they stood. 418 mosques were demolished, and after 1744 not a single one built in the 17th or early 18th century remained. The restrictions were lifted by Chatherine the Great, and the first new mosque was built in 1766. This was the Mardzhani Mosque on Nasiri Street, and in general most of the 18th-century mosques are on this street. The Tatars were also allowed to reopen their schools, and after all the efforts, less than 10 percent of the Tatar population were baptised. When the empress visited the town in 1767, she wrote of it: "There is no doubt that town is the first in Russia after Moscow," but times were still far from peaceful. In 1774 it was seized and burnt by Pugachev, Cossack leader of a popular revolt.

The first provincial Russian grammar school had been opened in Kazan in 1759, run as a branch of Moscow University. In 1804 Kazan's own university was opened. For 19 years, from 1827 until 1846, the famous Russian mathematician Nikolai Lobachevsky (1793–1857) was rector here; it was he who pioneered modern non-Euclidean geometry. At this time the Department of Oriental Languages was opened. In the 1840s the University of Kazan was an important scientific centre and a centre of progressive social thought in the Volga basin and the Urals. In the late 1840s, one of the first underground groups in Russia was established here. For years the University of Kazan was considered the centre of liberal ideas in eastern Russia, especially after 1866, when a former student, Karakozov, made an unsuccessful attempt upon Tsar Alexander II's life. At the end of the 19th century, the first Marxist groups appeared in Kazan, and Maxim Gorky called it his "spiritual birthplace." Lenin, who was at that time studying at the university, was an active member of the group and was sent down for taking part in student riots in 1887.

The famous Russian singer Feodor Chaliapin was born here in 1873. He travelled the world over but said, "There are many wonderful towns in the world but Kazan is the very best."

Before the 1917 revolution, the Bolsheviks were both strong and influential in Kazan. Soviet power was established here on 26 October 1917, at the same time as the uprising in Petrograd. In March 1918 Tatar nationalists established their short-lived Trans-Bulak Republic (so called because the Tatar population of Kazan lived near the little river Bulak). On 6 August 1918, Kazan was seized by the Czech Legion, the ex-prisoner-of-war troops assisting the counterrevolutionaries on their way westward from Siberia. Theirs was only a small force, but along with the city they captured the Imperial Gold Reserve, which was in Kazan for safekeeping. Soviet power was nevertheless re-established on 10 September. In 1920 the Tatar Autonomous Republic was formed, with Kazan as its capital; in 1990 the republic was renamed Tatarstan.

Today Kazan stretches 20 km (12 miles) from north to south. It is one of the Volga basin's largest industrial centres, with sizeable chemical, engineering, food, leather, and fur industries. Local products include photographic film, typewriters, and synthetic rubber, and more than half of Russia's furs are processed in Kazan.

There is a conservatoire, a local branch of the Academy of Sciences, and a number of scientific and research institutes, including those connected with the republic's oil and gas fields. Kazan is also an important transport centre, with an airport, a big railway junction, and a river port.

It is best to start a sightseeing tour of Kazan with the *Kremlin*. It is possible to climb the Spassky tower, and from the northern side of the Kremlin is a good panoramic view. The town still falls naturally into 2 parts: there is the central town with the Russian population, Orthodox churches and belltowers, hotels and impressive buildings; and the Oriental Zabulachnoye region, mainly populated with Tatars.

Many of the fine old houses of Kazan were built by Thomas Petondi (1794–1874), the son of an Italian architect who settled in Russia. There are also a number of buildings by Mikhail Korinfsky (1788–1851); he was partly responsible for the Kazan University building.

In front of the Kremlin's Spassky Gate is *First-*

of-May Square (formerly Ivanovskaya, called after Ivanovsky Monastery, which stood opposite the Kremlin). Situated similarly to Moscow's Red Square, it was also the heart of the city. There is a *customs house* here. In January 1775, when Pugachev was executed in Moscow, gallows were erected here in front of the Spassky Gate, and Pugachev's portrait hung there before it was burned. From the Kremlin, *Lenin (formerly Voskresenskaya) Street* leads toward the *university*, and *Bauman Street*, farther to the right, is the main shopping centre.

Much farther to the left of Lenin Street, *Karl Marx Street* runs through Svobody Square and onwards to Gorky Park. Karl Marx Street, with the surrounding district, is perhaps the most interesting part of Kazan from both an artistic and a historical point of view. It was formerly known as Arskaya because it was the ancient road to Arsk, one of the older towns of the Kazan khanate. It was reconstructed and widened in 1768, and then, with the construction of the 3 churches along its length, it was renamed successively Vizdvizhenskaya, Pokrovskaya, and Gruzinskaya. Where it crosses Mislavskovo Street, a bit of 19th-century Kazan has been preserved, with *4 houses in Russian classical style*. One of these wsa the Ecclesiastical School where Kayum Nasyrov (1825–1905), known as the Tatar Lomonosov, taught Russian. No. 10, built in 1808–11, used to be the First Public School; now it is the Aviation Institute. *Svobody ("freedom") Square*, surrounded with impressive buildings, both old and new, is now the city's central square. Outstanding among them is the *House of Officers* (formerly the House of Nobles), built in the style of a Florentine palazzo in 1845–48. *St. Barbara's Church*, with a tiered belfry, dates from the late 19th century.

Zabulachnoye, the Tatar part of the city, is on the other side of Bauman street beyond Lake Kaban. It included the area of Narimanova, Tukayevskaya, Kirova, Parizhskoi Kommuny, and Tatarstan streets. Apart from the mosques, there are a number of *houses* that belonged to merchants, especially along *Kayum Nasiri Street*. Nos. 5 and 11 are decorated wtih national Tatar motifs. Also with interesting decor is *No. 67 Tukayevskaya Street*, which belonged to the rich Apanayev merchant family. *No. 74* on the same street was designed by Amlong in art nouveau style with local motifs. *No. 42 Kirov Street* is another with a mixture of local styles. Besides the old houses, there are several new ones, as for example those in *Hadi Taktash Street*, near Lake Kaban.

To describe the *Kremlin* in detail, the walls, at the end of the 15th and the beginning of the 16th century, consisted of a double stockade of thick oaken logs, with the space between them filled with earth and stones. Inside was the khan's palace and 5 mosques, the main one, Kul-Sherif, with 8 minarets. There was also a medresseh and a mausoleum. During the Russian siege of 1552, the wooden walls were burned down and blown up. In 1556 Ivan the Terrible sent 200 masons from Pskov

to "break the stone and build a new stone town in Kazan." Part of the wall was built of limestone, but the remains of the oak logs were only replaced in the 17th century by a red brick wall. The architect Postnik, who was later responsible for the famous St. Basil's Cathedral on Red Square in Moscow, was in charge of the reconstruction. 13 towers were built, and a bridge over the moat linked the fortress to the town.

When Giles Fletcher visited Russia in 1588–89, he mentioned the fortress of Kazan among the 4 he considered able to withstand any serious siege. However, through the years the walls and towers of the Kremlin were damaged many times by fire, and each time the reconstruction was different. Now the walls are 2-storeyed. The lower part is 4–5 m (13–16 ft) thick. The 8 towers remaining of the original 13 are: the Spassky Gate (with an electric clock), Preobrazhenskaya and Nameless Towers, the Tainitskaya and Pyatnitskaya Gates, and Konsistovskaya, Southeastern, and Southwestern Round Towers. Spassky Tower is 44 m (144 ft) high and crowned by a 2.6-m (9-ft) bronze star. It took its name from the big icon of Our Saviour that hung in the niche over the gate. Tainitskaya Tower, the northern entrance to the Kremlin, got its name from the secret ("tainy") passage under it to a source of fresh water.

Inside the Kremlin, entering through the Spassky Gate, the white 3-storey building on the right, in the southeastern corner of the Kremlin, used to be a military guardhouse. Many of the buildings in the Kremlin, of little architectural interest, are now used by governmental and administrative offices. The Administrative Building and the Ecclesiastical Consistory (now housing the Ministry of Health), which stretch out in a long line from the Spassky Gate, were built in the 1780s. The former barracks, where the Cadet School is now, dates from 1840.

The *Annunciation Cathedral* stands on the site of a mosque destroyed by Ivan the Terrible. It was founded by him on the day of his triumphant entry into Kazan. As ordered the small wooden church was built in 3 days to commemorate the victory and to symbolise the triumph of Christianity over Islam. Between 1556 and 1561, at the same time as the Kremlin walls and towers were being rebuilt, the master masons from Pskov, Postnik and Ivan Shiryai, were responsible for an edifice of white limestone slabs, typical of the architecture of Pskov and Novgorod. It was later reconstructed many times, a refectory being added in 1841, and the ruined frescoes being overpainted again and again after fires. The most recent one was painted in 1870. The most valuable icons, including a 16th-century icon of the apostle Paul, are now in Kazan Art Gallery. Now only the eastern part of the cathedral remains unaltered. Nearby is the former *Archbishop's Palace*, built in the 19th century.

A little farther on, on the site of the Khan's Palace, and separated from the Annunciation Cathedral by a small garden, is the former *Governor's*

House, built in 1845–48 by Konstantin Thon (who also built the Grand Kremlin Palace in Moscow). It now houses the Council of Ministers and the Supreme Soviet of Tatarstan. The single-domed 18th-century church, *Soshestviye Svyatovo Dukha*, was restored in 1859, after the time of the construction of the palace, and linked to it by a covered gallery.

Queen Suyum-Bike's Tower, next to the church and to the left of the palace, is perhaps the most interesting structure in the Kremlin. It has served as a symbol of Tatar nationalism. It stands 57 m (118 ft) high and has 7 storeys. The first 3 are cubes, while the upper storeys are octagonal. The top of the tower has tilted over 1.5 m (5 ft), and the lean is quite noticeable. Before the revolution there was a double-headed eagle on the top. The date of construction is unknown, but it is supposed to have been built in the 17th century as a watchtower. It closely resembles Moscow Kremlin's Borovitsky Tower, which dates from that period.

There are plenty of other theories about its history. Some historians think it was the minaret of a large mosque, which was converted into the Russian Orthodox Vvedenia Church after the Russian conquest and later used as a gunpowder depot. Others think that it was built entirely by the Russians or alternatively by Tatar prince Mur-Alei, who was ambassador to Moscow during the negotiations with Ivan the Terrible. Other historians have come to the conclusion that at least the first 3 storeys were built by the Tatars long before, some saying that part was the remains of the khan's palace or that under the tower a saint lies buried, from whose skull flows a spring of water. One of the least likely theories is that the tower was built by Queen Suyum-Bike and was called after her.

Suyum-Bike was the wife of 3 successive Tatar khans. Folk legends depict her as a wise and beautiful woman who lived in luxurious, royal surroundings and yet suffered much misery, finally falling into the hands of her enemies and seeing her kingdom collapse. She was the daughter of the Nogai Tatar prince Usuf. At 13 she was married to the 15-year-old Tatar Kazan-Khan Yen-Alei. His immaturity made him a weak ruler, and his nobles plotted against him and killed him. She then married Khan Safa-Ghirey, who died in a drunken fight, leaving her with 2 baby sons. Finally, she was forced to marry Shah-Alei, whose pro-Moscow policies displeased her. She prepared some poisoned food and an enchanted shirt for him, but he gave the food to a dog, and the shirt was put upon a condemned criminal. Both died immediately. In 1551 Shah-Alei sent his wife and elder stepson to Moscow, where they died.

Although it seems that the tower was built nearly a century and a half after Suyum-Bike died, it may have been called after her because perhaps the site was formerly that of a mosque that she had built. Certainly the legend that she jumped to her death when the army of Ivan the Terrible came to Kazan has no historical foundation.

A copy of the tower can be seen near the Len-ingradskaya Hotel in Moscow, forming the façade of the Kazan railway station.

Zilantov-Uspensky Monastery, in Kirov District, near the railway line, on a high hill. Here are the remains of a monastery founded by Ivan the Terrible in 1552. It was flooded in its former location and transferred here, 3 km (2 miles) from the centre of the city. The hill is called Zilantov Hill, Zilant being the name of a mythical dragon who hid here. Uspenskaya Church was built in 1625 in Pskov-Novgorod style.

Cathedral of SS. Peter and Paul, Dzhalilya Street 17. The merchant Mikhlyaev built this church in 1723–26 to commemorate Peter the Great's visit to Kazan. Peter stayed in his house and rewarded him with broadcloth factories. The cathedral and the nearby 6-storey belltower dominate the city. Both were designed in baroque style by a Florentine architect, the beautiful belltower being called "the Song of Songs" by a Moscow art critic. The cathedral consisted of an upper and a lower church. The upper church is well preserved, but the lower one has been reconstructed several times and now houses a planetarium. Both the cathedral and the belltower are decorated with patterns of vine leaves, peaches, pears, and flowers, and inside are fine tiles depicting white and yellow flowers on a blue background. A refectory adjoins the western end of the cathedral, and the belltower served as the Mikhlyaev family burial place.

Mikhlyaev's House, Dzhalylya Street, near the cathedral. Built in the 18th century and now known as Dryablov's House, after the last owner.

Ecclesiastical Seminary, Dzhalylya Street, next to Mikhlyaev's House. Built in the 18th–19th century and now housing the Geological Faculty of Kazan University.

Ioanno-Predtechensky Monastery, Profsoyuznaya Street 1. Founded in 1564 by St. Gherman, archbishop of Kazan. It twiced burned down during its history and was restored in 1819. Inside it is Vvedenskaya Church (1652) and a belfry.

St. Nicholas's Church was built in 1634 and reconstructed in 1870.

St. Nicholas's Cathedral, Bauman Street 5. The cathedral was built in 1885 and contains a miracle-working icon of St. Nicholas. Both this and the Pokrovskaya Church (1703) nearby are open for services.

Yaroslavl Martyrs' Cemetery Church was built in 1760.

Pokrovskaya Church, Bauman Street 5. Familiarly known as St. Nicholas Nissky ("low"), because in 1885 the taller St. Nicholas's Cathedral was built next to it.

Bogoyavlenskaya (Epiphany) Church, Bauman Street. Founded in the late 16th century. The present church was built in 1731 with 5 domes, but now there is only 1. Its original tent-roofed belfry was replaced by that in pseudo-Russian style in 1898. It is 61.73 m (203 ft) high (only 6 m/20 ft lower than Notre-Dame de Paris) and serves as a focal point in the city's architecture.

Bogoroditsky Convent, near the Kremlin, on

Krasina Street. It was founded in 1579, but all the buildings that remain were constructed in the 19th century. The hospital was built in 1803–7, St. Nicholas of Tula church in 1810–16, and the Gate-Church of St. Sophia in 1815, reconstructed in 1858. The 2-storeyed Nastoyatelsky House dates from 1832. Rozhdestva Cathedral was destroyed in the 1930s. It was from this convent that the icon of Our Lady was taken to Moscow in 1612.

There are a number of other monasteries and churches in the city, all closed.

Apanayevskaya Mosque, Nasiri Street 29. Built in the 1760s.

Mardzhani Mosque, Nasiri Street 17. Built in 1766, it was called Mardzhani after Shigabutdin Mardzhani, a mullah and outstanding Oriental scholar, who first established the date of its construction. The national Tatar motifs in the decoration show some influence of contemporary Russian baroque style. It is open for services.

Main Mosque, Kirov Street 74. Built in the mid-19th century by Peske. The minaret was taken down in 1930.

Azimovsky Mosque, Fatkulli Street 15. Built in the late 19th century in Moorish style.

Zabakannaya Mosque, Taktash Street 26. Also known as the Old Mosque, this was built on the site of an old wooden mosque at the beginning of the century by Pechnikov in art nouveau style.

Tatar State Museum, Lenin Street 2. Open 10–5. The collector Likhachev was responsible for the opening of the original local museum in 1895. Now there are departments of history and natural history. Of interest in the former is a coach used by Catherine II in 1767 and a desk that belonged to the classical poet Gavril Derzhavin (1743–1816), who lived in Kazan, Derzhavin's wife's harp, a New Testament dated 1606, and a collection of national costumes.

Kazan Art Gallery, Karl Marx Street 54. Open 10–6; closed Mon. The house was built at the beginning of the century by Mufke for the local commander-in-chief. It contains both Russian and Tatar work. The most valuable icons from the Kremlin churches are here, including the 16th-century apostle Paul.

Gorky Museum, Gorky Street 10. Open 10–7, closed Tues.

Lenin Museum, Ulyanovykh Street 58. Open 11–6, closed Mon. Lenin lived here with the rest of the family in 1888–89, when he was permitted to return to Kazan after being sent down to the village of Kokushkin (see below), 40 km (25 miles) away, for participation in student riots.

Kamal Museum, Ostrovsky Street 15. Open 10–4, closed Fri. Here the Tatar writer, Sharif Kamal (1884–1942), whose real name was Baigildeyev, lived between 1928 and 1942. On display are his personal belongings, books, etc.

Kazan University, Lenin Street 18. The university was founded in 1804, and the buildings were constructed in the 1820s and the 1830s by architects Pyatnitsky and Korinfsky. 4 museums are supervised by the university:

Ethnographical Museum, open 10–4, closed Sun.

Zoological Museum, open 4–5, closed Sun. Founded in 1838. (Special permission required.)

Auditorium Museum, open 10–5:30, closed Sun. Lenin attended this university from August till December 1887. On view is auditorium No. 7 of the law faculty, reconstructed following photographs taken in the 1890s.

Geological Museum, Lenin Street 4, entrance from Dzhalila Street. Open 8–4, closed Sun.

Planetarium, Dzhalilya Street 21, in the lower church of the Cathedral of SS. Peter and Paul.

Industrial and Agricultural Exhibition, Orenburgsky Trakt. Open in summer only from 10–6, closed Mon.

Town Hall, Lenin Street 1, in First-of-May Square, on the left of Spasskaya Tower

Gostiny Dvor, Lenin Street 2, on the right side of the street. The old trading centre, founded in 1800, was reconstructed after the fire of 1842.

Shopping Arcade (Passage), Lenin Street 19. Built by Rush in 1880 and formerly called Alexandrovsky Passage. (Pronounce Passage in French, and it will be right.)

The former House of Nobles, Svobody Square. This was built in the 1840s, and there is a commemorative plaque saying that Soviet power was declared here on 26 October 1917. The building is now the House of Officers.

Derenkov's House, Kuibyshev Street 13. This is where Maxim Gorky lived and worked in 1886–87. The house belonged to the baker, Derenkov, and the actual bakery where Gorky was employed is in a cellar.

Lenin Library, Lenin Street 33, in Ushkov Mansion. Built in 1910 by architect Mufke for factory owner Ushkov as a wedding present for Zinaida Ushkova, a relative of his, each room was decorated in a different style. The entrance is Japanese, the hall Empire, the room next to it Moorish, the study is an imitation grotto, and the dining room is Gothic.

Monument to Russian Warriors, who fell capturing Kazan in 1552. The monument has been on an island since the Volga was dammed lower downstream and can best be seen from the northern part of the Kremlin. A combination of Egyptian pyramid and classic Greek forms, this was built in 1823 by Alferov; it stands 20 m (66 ft) high and inside is the *Spasa Nerukotvornovo Church*.

Lobachevsky Monument, near the main building of the university. Nikolai Lobachevsky (1793–1857) was a great Russian mathematician who pioneered modern non-Euclidean geometry and who was rector of this university for 19 years. The bust by Dillon was unveiled in 1896.

Leo Tolstoy Monument, in a garden on the corner of Marx Street and Tolstoy Street, near a house where the writer lived when he was a university student here. The bust was designed by Pinchuk.

Chaliapin Memorial, Kuibyshev Street 14. There is a commemorative plaque on the house where the famous singer Fyodor Chaliapin (1873–1938) was born.

Bauman Monument, Ershova Street, in front of the Veterinary Institute. Nikolai Bauman (1873–1905) studied at this institute before he began his career as a professional revolutionary in Kazan.

Ulyanov Statue, in front of the university. This monument depicts Lenin as a student, when he was known by his real name of Ulyanov. The statue is by Tsigal and was unveiled in 1954.

Lenin Monument, Svobody Square. Yatsyno was the sculptor of this statue, which was unveiled in 1954. Together with the pedestal, it stands 12 m (39 ft) high.

Kirov Monument, Marx Street, near the former Industrial College from which Kirov graduated. Sergei Kirov (1886–1934) was another famous revolutionary.

Tukai Monument, near Lake Kaban. Gabdulla Muhammed Tukai (1886–1913) was a poet. This statue by Akhun, Kerbel, and Pisarevsky stands 10 m (33 ft) high and was unveiled in 1958.

Ershov Monument, Ershov Garden. Nikolai Ershov was a young Bolshevik who headed the uprising in Kazan in 1917. The sculptor was Novoselov.

Stolyarov Monument, in a garden on Tsetkina Street. This bust of the Kazan-born Second World War pilot, twice decorated as a Hero of the Soviet Union, is by Mukhina.

Revolutionary Heroes' Monument, with an eternal flame; unveiled in 1967

Musa Dzhalil Monument, First-of-May Square. Musa Dzhalil (1906–44) was a local poet whose real name was Zalilov. He died in a Nazi concentration camp and was proclaimed a Hero of the Soviet Union. This bronze statue by Tsigal stands 7-m (23 ft) high.

Musa Dzhalil Opera and Ballet Theatre, Svobody Square. The theatre company was founded in 1939 after the graduation of performers from a special Tatar Studio in the Moscow Conservatoire. The building was designed by Gainutdinov and Skvortsov in 1956 and seats 1,025 people.

Kamala Tatar Drama Theatre, by Lake Kaban. This theatre is named for the Tatar playwright Galiasgar Kamal (1879–1933), whose real name was Kamaletdinov. The building, resembling a snow-white sailing boat, was completed in 1986.

Kachalov Russian Drama Theatre, Bauman Street 48. One of the oldest theatres in the country—the first performance in Russian was presented in 1804. The theatre is named for Vasily Kachalov (1875–1948), a famous Russian actor who began his career here in 1897 and who played at the Moscow Arts Theatre from 1900.

Lenkomsomola Youth Theatre, Ostrovskovo Street 10

Puppet Theatre, Lukovskovo Street 21

Conservatoire Concert Hall, Svobody Square. The organ was built by the Czech firm Riger Kloss.

Circus, Kremlyovskaya Street 2. Built in 1967 by Pechuyev to seat 2,400. It is sometimes called the Flying Saucer because of its shape. There is certainly no other similar circus building in the whole of Europe.

Gorky Park, Ershova Street

Central Recreation Park, formerly called Russian Switzerland

Lenin Stadium, Kremlyovskaya Damba

Spartak Stadium, Tukayevskaya Street 30

Zoo and Botanical Gardens, Taktasha Street 112. This was founded as a botanical garden in 1834; the zoo was transferred here in 1931.

Kazan Hotel and Restaurant, Bauman Street 9/10; tel. 20091. The Intourist office is in Room 212; tel. 32–0145.

Tatarstan Hotel and Restaurant, Sverdlov Street 2; tel. 32–6979

Volga Hotel and Restaurant, Said Galiyev Street 1a; tel. 32–1894

Soviet Hotel, Universitetskaya Street 7

Akcharlak Restaurant, Ershova Street 5. Floor show from 7 P.M.

Torgovy Tsentr Restaurant, Kirov Street 2. Tatar cuisine.

Molodyozhny Tsentr Restaurant, Dekabristov Street 1.

Vostok ("east") Restaurant, Kuibysheva Square 13. Tatar cuisine. Floor show from 7:30.

Mayak ("lighthouse") Restaurant, Dekabristov Street 185/17

Parus ("sail") Restaurant, on a houseboat anchored near Lenin Bridge

House of Tatar Cuisine, Bauman Street 31/32

Torgovy Trade Centre Restaurant, Kirov Street 2

Molodyozhny Youth Centre Restaurant, Dekabristov Street 1. There is a disco bar here.

Milk Bar, Bauman Street 58

Bank, Bauman Street 37

Shopping Centre, Kirov Street 2

Bookshop, Bauman Street 19

Gifts, Bauman Street 13

Art Salon, Dzerzhinskovo Street 27

Jeweller's, Bauman Street 58

Kizichesky-Vvedensky Monastery, Dekabristov Street, 3 km (2 miles) north of Kazan. Founded by Metropolitan Bishop Adrian of Kazan in 1687 (before he became patriarch of Moscow). The only church to survive is the St. Vladimir Gate-Church, over the Holy Gates. It was built in 1690.

Voznesensky-Yerusalimsky Monastery, 7 km (4 miles) to the south, by Dalny Kaban Lake. Here, from the monastery, remain Voskresensky Cathedral and refectory, St. Tikhon Amafutsky Gate-Church, and monks' cells dating from the 17th–18th centuries. The palatial house was built in 1781 upon the order of Catherine the Great as the archbishop of Kazan's country house and called Novy Yerusalim (New Jerusalem).

Lebazhye ("swan") Lake is a popular recreation place 10 km (6 miles) from the town. The *Beryozka (birch tree) Café* is there.

Volgo-Kama Reserve, 30 km (19 miles) along Gorky Chaussée, east of the village of Vasilyevo. The dendrarium here has 200 species of trees.

Raifsky Bogoroditsky Monastery, inside the Volgo-Kama Reserve (see above), 12 km (7 miles) from the railway station and 18 km (11 miles) from Sviyazhsk (see below). Founded in the 17th century by Lake Raifskoye and the river Sumka by a monk called Filaret from Chudov Monastery. It was built with 5 churches by masons from Istra. Nearby is a *War Memorial* to Red Army soldiers who were shot here in 1918 by counterrevolutionaries.

Sviyazhsk

30 km (19 miles) from Kazan, this town was founded as Ivangorod by the Russians on 24 May 1551 with the help of the Chuvash and the Tatars. Ivan the Terrible commanded that it be built with the utmost speed after he had failed to conquer Kazan for lack of a military base nearby. The timbers for the towers and other buildings were prepared in Uglich in the Upper Volga region and then shipped downriver to the construction site on a hill near the mouth of the Sviyaga. The fortress was built within a month, with 18 towers around the 2.5-km (1.5-mile) surrounding walls. Inside, in addition to the buildings needed by the army, was Trinity Cathedral and Rozdestvenskaya Church. Later the coat-of-arms of Sviyazhsk reflected the story of the building of the fortress, for it depicted "a wooden town on ships on the Volga."

The site proved a good one. Within 15 years a proper town had grown by the fortress. It is often compared to Novgorod, Pskov, Vladimir, and Suzdal. The Sviyazhsk fortress had 2- and 3-storey towers with battlements. The main tower was crowned by a clock that chimed the hours. There are a number of buildings from the 16th–18th centuries still standing. When the Kuibyshev hydropower station was built, the waters rose, leaving the hill as a picturesque island.

Assumption Cathedral (16th century) was built on the hill of Stolovaya Gora, with the rivers Sviyaga and Schuka at its foot, near the Sviyaga's confluence with the Volga. It was built by Posnik Yakovlev, who was also responsible for St. Basil's Cathedral in Moscow. It has recently been restored to all its former beauty and splendour. It looks particularly fine from the river.

Uspensko-Bogoroditsky Monastery was founded in 1555 by St. Gherman, later Metropolitan Bishop of Kazan. Uspensky Cathedral was built in 1556–60 but was reconstructed several times during its existence. It has several interesting frescoes; the only one to survive completely intact is from the 16th century. The *St. Nicholas Refectory Church* (1555–56) has some fragments of frescoes inside. The belfry was built somewhat later than the church. *St. Gherman's Church* dates from the end of the 18th century. There is little left of it, but the baroque windows are there among the other monastery buildings. In the mid-19th century, some of the buildings were used as an ecclesiastical school and as the archbishop's quarters.

*Ioanna Predtechensky (John the Baptist) Con-*vent was founded at the end of the 16th century in the centre of the town. After the fire of 1753, it was transferred to its present location, next to the 2 surviving buildings of the abandoned Troitsko-Sergiev Monastery (which used to be under the protection of the Troisko-Sergiyevsky Lavra in Zagorsk), and at that point it began to be called Troitsko-Sergiev Convent as well. *Trinity Cathedral* is the oldest church in Sviyazhsk. It was built in 1551 of prefabricated parts and shipped here along with the timbers for the fortress. It was restored in 1742, and then in 1821 it was given a stone foundation, panelled on the outside and painted. Inside, interesting icons and holy gates still remain. *St. Sergius's Church* (dedicated to Sergi Radonezhsky) was built in 1605. There is a belfry nearby and also the quarters of the mother superior. The 2-storey refectory in the southeastern corner of the grounds was built in 1890. The convent grew rich enough to build the big brick *Church of Our Lady of All Sorrows* in 1896–1906. The architect, Malinovsky, used the pseudo-Byzantine style popular at the time.

The Church of SS. Constantine and Helena, on the riverbank, was built in the mid-16th century, together with its belfry. There are a number of other churches in the town, but this one is particularly beautiful in its setting.

Most of the *houses* in the town date from the end of the 19th century, the older ones having been reconstructed.

Civil War Memorial, in the centre of the island. This commemorates the 36 Communists shot by the Czechs in 1918. Sviyazhsk was important during the Civil War in the struggle for the Volga and Kazan. Kazan was taken by the Czechs on 6 August, and then Leo Trotsky, as commissar of war, came to Sviyazhsk by train. He built the 5th Army out of separate military units, so that it was probably the best of all the 16 armies raised during the Civil War. On 28 August the Whites under Kappel tried to destroy Sviyazhsk, but failed and withdrew, and on 10 September the Volga Flotilla together with the 5th Army took Kazan.

Kokushkino

This village along the river Ushnya is 45 km (28 miles) from Kazan.

Lenin Memorial Museum, in an annex on the estate that used to belong to Lenin's grandfather, Alexander Blank, a retired doctor. The museum consists of 5 rooms, including the one Lenin used when he was a student at Kazan University in 1887, before he was exiled. The museum was opened in 1939.

KAZBEGI

See Georgian Military Highway, p. 156.

KEMERI

See Riga, p. 447.

KENTAU

See Turkestan, p. 579.

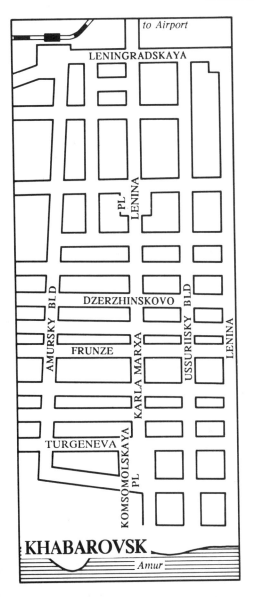

to Airport

LENINGRADSKAYA

PL. LENINA

AMURSKY BLD   DZERZHINSKOVO   USSURIISKY BLD

FRUNZE   KARLA MARXA   LENINA

TURGENEVA   KOMSOMOLSKAYA PL.

KHABAROVSK

Amur

KHABAROVSK Population—601,000

The town is named for Yerofey Pavlovich Khabarov, a Russian explorer who made several expeditions to the region of the river Amur in the middle of the 17th century. With a group of 70 hunters, he conquered the area beside the river, and in recognition of this, he received the honourable title "Son of a Boyar." On the occasion of his second expedition, he took 138 people and 3 guns with him to help him subdue the local tribes. He achieved this largely by wholesale slaughter of the inhabitants and by devastating their land.

Long ago it was supposed that this part of the country rested on the backs of 3 great whales. Today

they are hardly discernible, but the city of Khabarovsk does in fact stand upon the "backs" of 3 long hills that lie side by side as they drink forever the waters of the Amur. The hills and the generous width of the streets both add to the town's pleasant appearance.

Khabarovsk stands on the right bank of the Amur at the point where its tributary, the Ussuri, flows into it and where the Trans-Siberian Railway crosses it. It is 769 km (478 miles) by rail from Vladivostok, and its average annual temperature is only half a degree above freezing ($-26°C/-15°F$ in winter; $26°C/78.8°F$ in summer). The majority of the population is Russian, but there are also some Ukrainians and Koreans.

It was founded in 1858 as a military outpost by Count Muravyev, governor of Eastern Siberia. At one time it was a trading centre for sable pelts, but it grew into a sizeable town and replaced Nikolayevsk-on-Amur as capital of the Maritime Province in 1880. The opening of the railway connection with Vladivostok in 1897 proved of great importance in the development of the town's economy. It soon became the main transit point for cargos to and from China, Manchuria, and the Upper and Lower Amur. The description, "3 hills, 2 holes, and 40,000 briefcases," summed up neatly both its geographical features and its flourishing business at the beginning of the 20th century.

During the Civil War, from April until October in 1920, Khabarovsk was occupied by the Japanese army, but between 1918 and 1922 it was mainly held by the White Russians. From 1926 to 1938, it was the capital of the whole of the Soviet Far East. Now it is the largest city and the main transport and political centre east of Lake Baikal. It is also the biggest industrial and cultural centre of the Soviet Far East and covers an area of over 300 sq km (116 sq miles).

Local industry includes ship repairing, engineering, oil refining, and the manufacture of food products. Also prepared here are medicines from the ginseng, magnolia vine, and eleutherococcus plants, which are native to the region. There are 7 high educational establishments. Local research institutes include the Institute of Oceanography.

The Amur Cliff is a huge rock on the bank of the river, and there is a good view from the top. *Lenin Square*, covering nearly 5–6 hectares (14 acres), is the focal point of Khabarovsk. It was the scene of revolutionary meetings and demonstrations by striking workers before the establishment of Soviet power, and parades and demonstrations on public holidays are still held there. On either side of the large statue of Lenin are stands for 2,500 people.

2 parks, the Amur Steamship office, and the regional library face onto *Komsomolskaya Square*, and from it a wide flight of steps leads down to the river embankment. The library, founded in 1894, contains 1,200,000 books, including the best collection of literature on the Russian Far East. The main shopping street of the city, *Karl Marx Street*,

begins in Komsomolskaya Square. No. 23 Karl Marx Street, once the Merchants' Duma, is now the Palace of Pioneers.

Khristorozhdestvenskaya (Nativity) Church, Leningradskaya Street 65. This church was built at the beginning of this century and is open for services.

Local Museum, Schevchenko Street 21. Open 10–6; closed Mon. The museum was founded in 1896, and the stone tortoise in front of the building weighing 6.5 tons has been there since that date. The exhibits illustrate the region's history, geography, geology, and natural history. On the first floor are interesting costumes and items of handicraft made by the primitive peoples of the north and of Kamchatka which are worth seeing. On the second floor is an exhibition showing progress in Soviet time. On the wall of the building is a memorial plaque to Vladimir Arsenyev (see below), who worked here for many years. Under a protecting roof outside in the garden is the 20-m (66-ft) skeleton of a whale caught in 1891.

Fine Arts Museum, Frunze Street 45. Open 10–7; closed Mon. There are some good icons, Russian classical paintings, including some by Repin, Shishkin, and Levitan, a West European section including a Rembrandt etching, a Rubens drawing, and a painting by Monet, and a collection of Chinese and Japanese works of art, besides paintings and drawings by Soviet artists.

Fadeyev Literary Museum, Open 11–6; closed Mon.

Arsenyev's House, Arsenyev Lane 9. Vladimir Arsenyev (1872–1930) was an ethnographer who explored the Far East and wrote many books about its flora and fauna. His house is marked by a memorial plaque (as is the Local Museum).

Narodny Dom ("people's house"), Pushkin Street 37. This house was built in 1899 to mark the centenary of Pushkin's birth.

Tower, beside the Amur. Here, in 1918, a number of Hungarian and Austrian prisoners-of-war were shot. They were musicians who refused to play the imperial Russian anthem.

Khabarov Monument, Vokzalnaya Square. Yerofey Khabarov was responsible for bringing the first Russian settlers to the river Amur in 1649. He reported to the government that "by the Amur is much goodly arable land and meadow and fishing and all kinds of virtues." The monument by A. Milchin was unveiled in 1958, when the city celebrated its centenary.

Pushkin Monument, Karl Marx Street 64, in front of the main building of the Pedagogical Institute.

Nevelskoy Monument, at the crossing of 2 walks in the city park. Admiral Gennadi I. Nevelskoy (1813–76) was exploring the Russian Pacific coast when he discovered that Sakhalin was in fact an island.

Volochayevka Battle Museum, Volochayevka 1st Station. The 3-day battle of Volochayevka in February 1922 was a turning point in the Civil War in the Far East. The memorial building, which stands on Mt. Ijun-Koran where there was a White Russian fortress, was constructed in 1928 over the grave of 118 soldiers who fell in the battle. On the top of the building is a statue of a Red Army soldier brandishing his rifle above a barbed-wire entanglement.

Amur Sailors' Memorial, Vokzalnaya Square. The memorial in front of the railway station commemorates the detachment of 150 sailors who died here in 1920 during the Civil War.

Civil War Victims' Memorial, Chornorechenskoye Chaussée. The monument, easily seen from the road to the airport, was erected in 1953, over the ravine where mass executions took place.

Seryshev Monument, Seryshev Station. Stepan Seryshev was an eminent military leader during the Civil War of 1918–22. As commander-in-chief of the eastern front in 1922, he led the victorious attack on Volochayevka. His bust by A. Malinovsky was unveiled in 1958.

Civil War Heroes' Memorial, Komsomolskaya Square. The grey granite obelisk is crowned with a laurel wreath and a 5-pointed star. The 3 bronze figures on the pedestal form a group 7 m (23 ft) high, symbolising the revolutionary forces. The architect was Professor Barsh, the sculptor Faidysh-Krandievsky, and the work was unveiled in 1956.

Lenin Monument, Lenin Square. The metal monument on its granite pedestal was created in 1925 by Manizer.

Soldiers' Tombstone, Lenin Square. This marks the grave of four soldiers killed in a Russian-Chinese conflict in 1929 concerning the ownership of the eastern end of the Trans-Siberian Railway. The tombstone, decorated with laurels, banners, and a star, was set up in 1950.

A second *monument to Lenin* stands in the city park, marking the spot where the city was supposed to have been founded.

Arsenyev Monument, in the city park

Drama Theatre, Dzerzhinsky Street 44. The building, the auditorium of which seats 840 people, was completed in 1959.

Musical Comedy Theatre, Karl Marx Street 64. Opened in 1926.

Youth Theatre, Karl Marx Street 10. The theatre was opened in the former Merchants' Hall in 1945.

Philharmonia Concert Hall, Shevchenko Street 7

Circus, Leo Tolstoy Street 20

City Park, Komsomolskaya Street. The park stretches along the high rocky bank of the Amur, with a view across the valley to the Khakhtsir Mountains. Chekhov was enchanted with the view and wrote: "I wish I could stay and live here forever." In the park are a summer theatre, cinema, sports facilities, and a children's playground. A flight of steps leads down to the river embankment.

Gagarin Park, Krasnorechenskoye Chaussée

Children's Park, Karl Marx Street 69. Here are 8 hectares (20 acres) of woodland with an open-air theatre and playgrounds.

Children's Railway, Zheleznodorozhny Rayon.

The Small Far Eastern Railway runs from Karl Marx Street near the Agricultural Research Institute at No. 143 to a vegetable farm in the suburbs and back again in a 3,400-m (2-mile) circle. The railway operates four days a week. It was opened in 1958 as part of the town's centenary celebrations.

Lenin Stadium, Serysheva Street. Designed by M. Sorokin and opened in 1957, the stadium, which seats 25,000, stands on a territory of 34.2 hectares (85.5 acres). The complex also includes a football field, tennis courts, gymnasia, a Palace of Sports seating 6,000, and a heated open-air pool, which is used year-round.

Botanical Garden, Volochayevskaya Street 71. On an area of 11.5 hectares (nearly 29 acres), the collection of 1,300 trees and shrubs is claimed to represent all the types that grow in the Soviet Far East. The garden belongs to the Far East Institute of Forestry Research, which has done much to improve forestry in the Far East.

Intourist Hotel and Restaurant, Amursky Boulevard 2, by Lenin Stadium; tel. 33–7634. This is a 13-storey building, and the local Intourist office is here; tel. 33–6395.

Amur Hotel and Restaurant, Lenin Street 49; tel. 33–5043.

Tsentralnaya (Intourist) Hotel and Restaurant, Pushkin Street 52; tel. 33–6731.

Dalni Vostok (Far East) Hotel, Karl Marx Street 20; tel. 33–1434. Hotel residents should dial 9 before the town number they require.

Sever ("north") Hotel, Volochayevskaya Street 108; tel. 33–1434.

While in a Khabarovsk restaurant, one should try the "ukha," which is fish soup of Siberian salmon and ruffe.

Ussuri Café, Karl Marx Street 34

Dalni Vostok Café, Karl Marx Street

Bank, Karl Marx Street 44

GPO, Karl Marx Street 24

Central Telegraph Office, Lenin Square

Beryozka (foreign-currency) Shop, Amursky Boulevard 14

Department Store, Karl Marx Street 23

Central Bookshop, Karl Marx Street 37

Taxi Stands, on Vokzalnaya Square and Komsomolskaya Square by the Department Store, by No. 1 Grocery Store at Karl Marx Street 13, and by the Amur and Sever hotels. To call a taxi, dial 33–1958.

Khabarovsk Airport is only 9 km (6 miles) out of town, and there are two more hotels, a new restaurant, and another Beryozka foreign-currency shop there also.

On the outskirts is the bowl-shaped aerial of the Orbita television station, which receives programmes from Moscow via the Molniya satellite. Intourist organises boat trips on the river Amur.

KHAKASIA
See Abakan, p. 29.

KHALA
See Batumi, p. 69.

KHAMZAABAD
See Fergana (Hamzaabad), p. 144.

KHARKOV (Pronounced *"harkoff"*)
Population—1,611,000

The city is built on a plateau in the midst of the black earth region of the Ukraine. 3 rivers flow through it, the Lopan, the Udy, and the Kharkov. Although it probably took its name from the river Kharkov, legend records that a certain Cossack called Kharko or Khariton founded the place and lived here, fighting against the Crimean Tatars until he was drowned in the river Donets, and that it was called after him.

The first historic mention of Kharkov was made in 1655, when a group of Ukrainian settlers migrated from the banks of the Dnieper to a site at the confluence of the rivers Lopan and Kharkov. There people encircled their homes with an oaken stockade, and the following year Tsar Alexei Mikhailovich of Moscow decreed that Voin Selifontov should be the governor of the independent province of Kharkov. The simple stockade grew into a regular wooden fortress, part of the defence line built to protect Russia's southern border, particularly from the Crimean Tatars. A second stockade, about 1 km (.6 miles) in length and with 10 towers, a deep moat, and a rampart, was built to surround the first. Underground passges led from the centre of the fortress to the rivers Lopan and Kharkov and to the forest region where Shevchenko Park is now. The residents received the right to hold annual fairs in 1659, and the marketplace where these were held is now the central Soviet Ukraine Square. The economic growth was paralleled by the strategic importance of the fortress, and records of 1663 state that it was armed with 12 cannon, 402 cannonballs, and 8 kegs of gunpowder.

During the Cossack insurrection of 1656 Kharkov remained loyal to Alexei Mikhailovich, who in turn granted the town various privileges. These were subsequently confirmed by Fyodor, Ivan Alexeyevich, Sophia, and Peter the Great. In 1707 Kharkov was part of the Kiev province, and in 1709, when Peter the Great visited it as he made the rounds of his defence installations prior to the Battle of Poltava, he ordered the reconstruction and expansion of the fortress.

The town's cultural development was marked by the opening of Kharkov College in 1727, as an institution that was later to grow into university but which, during those early years, was connected with the names of two men in particular who were closely concerned with the problems of education in the Ukraine. They were Grigori Skovoroda (1722–94), a philosopher who spent most of his life as an itinerant teacher of morals and was one of the chief sources of modern Russian intuitivism, and Grigori Kvitka-Osnovyanenko (1778–1843), an author and playwright. By Catherine the Great's order of 1765, Kharkov became the capital of the Slobodsko-Ukrainian Region, and from 1767 the haphazard growth of the town was replaced by an orderly plan. In 1781 it was granted its own coat-

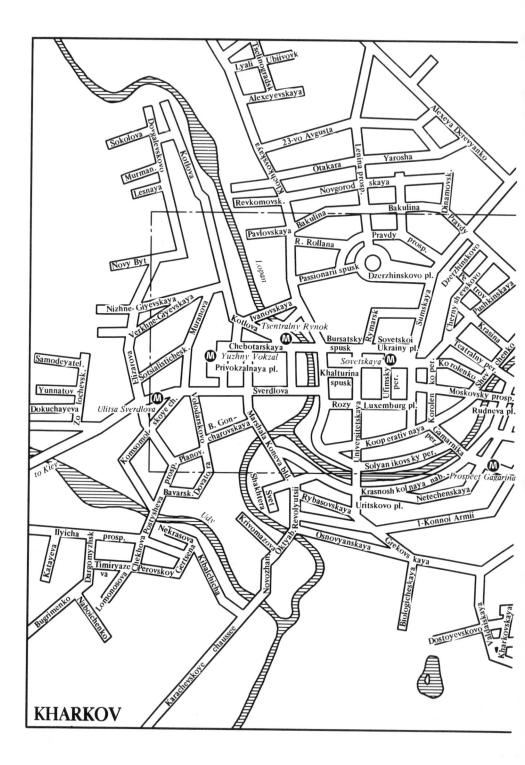

KHARKOV

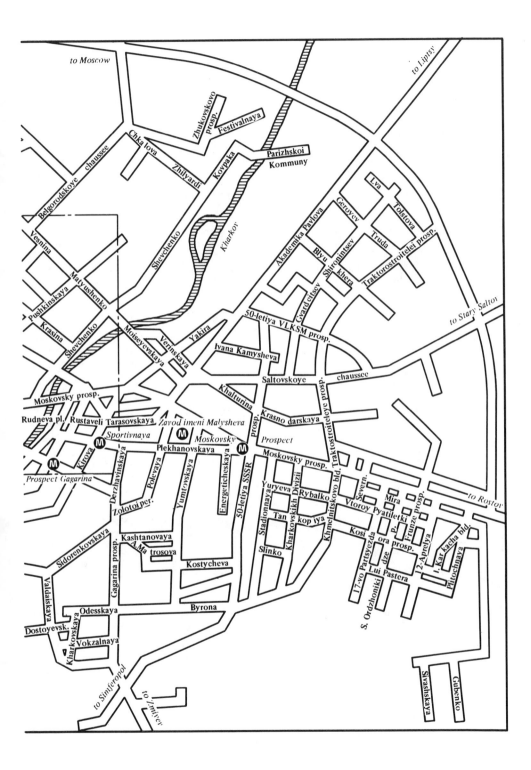

of-arms which signified Kharkov's importance as a trading centre. (The imperial crown was to be added in 1878). Toward the end of the century, when the Tatar menace was no longer, Kharkov lost its military-strategic value, but from then on the construction of the town proceeded according to a general plan, and the first public buildings began to make their appearance. 17 January 1805 saw the opening ceremony of Kharkov University, founded by scientist and public figure Vasily Karazin (1773–1842). Having left a letter in the palace at the time of the accession of Alexander I explaining his ideas and hopes for the future of Russia, he was then summoned to St. Petersburg to discuss educational problems. The tsar gave him permission to organise a university in Kharkov, and Karazin collected the necessary money to do so from the nobles and merchants of the town. It was housed in the governor's residence to start with. One of the best known names linked with the university is that of biologist Ilya Mechnikov.

In 1861 the town had a population of 50,000, but by the end of the century there were already 200,000. This increase was largely due to the economic development following the construction of the railways. Kharkov was an important junction and became the administrative centre of the great iron and coal-mining industries of the southern part of the country. Both Russian and foreign capital was welcomed, and the banks and apartment buildings that were founded at the turn of the century were as fine as those anywhere in Europe. Kharkov was no longer a provincial town, and Britain, France and Belgium were among the countries to open their consulates there. It remained the capital

of the Ukraine until 1934, when this honour was restored to ancient Kiev.

During the Second World War, the city changed hands twice, each time being left in ruins. Some of the buildings were even demolished by radio control, as for example Dzerzhinsky Square 17, which was at one time occupied by Nikita Khruschev. Before the Russian army retreated, 350 kg (770 lb) of explosive mines were hidden in this very desirable residence. Lieutenant-General Georg von Braun was head of the Kharkov garrison and commander of the 68th infantry division, and to make sure that he and his officers chose No. 17 as their quarters, other houses were made to appear to be mined. When they were comfortably settled in, a Russian radio signal from Voronezh on 14 November 1941 detonated the mines and blew up the building, killing the general together with members of his staff and security personnel.

Kharkov is still a major scientific centre. There are 23 higher educational establishments besides the university, including medical, teacher's training, polytechnical, and art schools, and there are besides as many as 57 research institutions. Kharkov is a sister town of both Bologna and Lille.

Industry includes locomotives, tractors, aircraft, agricultural and mining machinery and turbines, generators, electrical motors, and diesel engines. There are various light industries as well.

One of the oldest parts of the town is Universitetskaya Gorka. This was originally surrounded by a wooden palisade, and at the end of the 17th century, the first brick buildings were erected. The most interesting building of ancient Kharkov is *Pokrovsky (Intercession of the Virgin) Cathedral*. It

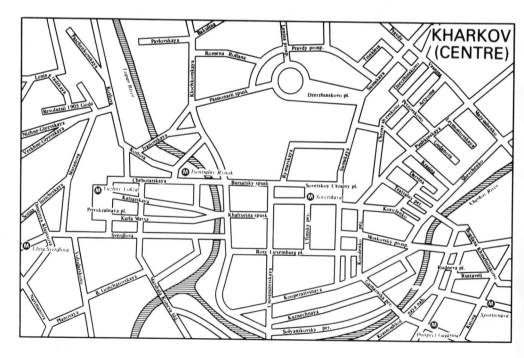

dates from 1689, when it was consecrated by Metropolitan Avraami, and it stands where the fortress used to be, on the steep bank of the Lopan. Its domes rise to a height of 40 m (131 ft), and its shape and proportions faithfully follow those traditional for the wooden churches of the Ukraine, making it a real architectural gem. The *Bishop's Palace* standing next to it was built in 1820–26 and now houses the Kharkov History Museum.

Across Universitetskaya Street rise the gilded domes of *Uspensky (Assumption) Cathedral*, with its tall belfry in the adjoining square. In 1670 a wooden cathedral of the same name stood here, but in 1733 was so badly damaged by fire that a new stone cathedral was designed by Yevlashev to replace it. It imitated the baroque style of the 5-domed St. Clement's Church in Moscow, and its iconostasis was designed by Rastrelli. It was completed in 1777. The original wooden belfry was unharmed by the fire, but it was decided to build a new one in its stead to commemorate the victory over Napoleon in 1812. Professor Vasilyev was charged with the construction, and he chose a traditional classical style. Work began in 1821, but the 82-m (269-ft) 5-tiered, many-columned structure was only finally completed by A. Thon and dedicated to St. Alexander Nevsky in 1844. Part of the delay occurred when Vasilyev submitted his plans to Mayor Lomakin. The mayor suspected that the overall height would be greater than that of Moscow's Ivan the Great Belfry, and Vasilyev promised to make the necessary alterations. Lomakin couldn't read blueprints in any case, but he believed the architect's assertions that the new belfry would be lower than Ivan the Great's. When the finished building turned out to be about 4 m (13 ft) taller than he had expected, it was too late to do anything about it. In 1862 a huge clock was installed that had been specifically made at the Borel Clock Factory in Paris.

A little farther down the hill, at Universitetskaya 16, stands the *Governor's Residence*. Construction began in 1766 under Ulyanov and Yaroslavsky, and in 1787 a reception hall was added because of the visit made to Kharkov by Catherine the Great. It was the first large civic building in Kharkov and now houses a corrspondence college. Provincial administrative buildings were founded in 1786 in the square just to the north of the residence. The project was by Quarenghi, but work was delayed due to the Russo-Turkish War and only finished in 1808.

The city's third great cathedral, *Blagoveschensky (Annunciation) Cathedral*, can be seen lower down and across the river. It is just northwest of Proletarskaya Square (formerly Sergiyevskaya Square) and with its tall belfry is easily seen from far away. It was built in 1881–1901 by Lovtsov, the neo-Byzantine style of red and white striped brickwork and the decorative motifs having been taken from St. Sophia's in Istanbul. The height of the belfry to the top of the cross is 80 m (262 ft), while the height of the main building is 59 m (194 ft). Nearly 7 million bricks were used during the construction, and there is room inside for a congregation of 4,000. The cathedral is open for services, and the interior is unusual both for the continuation of the neo-Byzantine theme and for the beauty of the stained-glass windows.

Behind the 2 older cathedrals stretches the square that was the heart of old Kharkov. It was the original market square and bore the names Nikolayevskaya and Tevelyova before being renamed *Soviet Ukraine Square*. At the end of the 19th century began the construction of a whole complex of impressive buildings, which were to be the financial centre of Kharkov, and indeed of the Ukraine. 3 on the eastern side of the square, the *Land Bank* at No. 28 (built in 1898 and now the Motor-Transport Technical School), the *Kharkov Commercial Bank*, and the *Volga-Kama Commercial Bank* (now the Puppet Theatre), were all-designed by academician Beketov. In 1891 he had first made daring use of metal and reinforced concrete in the building of the Korolenko Scientific Library, and he was eventually to be responsible for more than 25 of Kharkov's largest structures. Some of these were ruined during World War II, and Academician himself died when the city was occupied. The *Petersburg International Bank* (now a savings bank) was designed by Velichko, and the two commercial banks (now the Pedagogical Institute) at the corner of Soviet Ukraine Square and Korolenko Street were by Lidval. Kharkov's commercial centre was completed on the northern and southern sides of the square by Munz and Speigel's *Northern Bank* (now a library and medical institute) on the corner of Sumskaya, and by Tsaun's *Mutual Credit Society* (now housing the Tsentralny Restaurant). Verevkin's huge building of the Rossiya Insurance Society at the corner of Soviet Ukraine and Rosa Luxembourg squares dates from 1910, and in 1928–29 the shopping arcades (now the Children's World Store) and the Commodity Exchange (now the Art Institute) were built.

Leading away from the centre of the city in the direction of Moscow runs *Sumskaya Street*, with cafés, restaurants, shops, and old buildings on either side. There are 2- and 3-storey houses with classical-style façades typical of the early 19th century (Nos. 8, 16, 22, and 28, for instance), but more usual are those that are Renaissance in appearance. The Shevchenko Ukrainian Drama Theatre at Sumskaya 9, designed by Andrei Thon in 1841, is a good example.

Theatre Square links Sumskaya with Pushkin Street. It has been so called since the beginning of the 19th century when the town's first permanent theatre was opened here. The 18th-century classical-style building in the northeast part of the square was built as a warehouse by Yaroslavsky. The Florentine Renaissance–style building of the State Bank in the northwest part of the square dates from the end of the last century. In the garden in the centre of the square, the busts of Pushkin and Gogol were created by sculptor Edwards in 1904 and 1909, respectively. Another literary figure commemorated nearby is the Ukrainian writer Mikhail Kotsyubinsky (1864–1913); his monument stands in the garden at the crossing of Pushkin and Chernyshevsky streets.

Further up Sumskaya, at No. 17, stands the building of the Salamandra Insurance Society in strict classical style; it is still known by its original name. The 4-storey Renaissance-style houses on the opposite side of the street were built in 1906 and 1908 by Zagoskin brothers. Again on the left of Sumskaya, *Shevchenko Park* opens onto the street. Since 1935 an impressive statue of Shevchenko by Manizer and Langbard has stood near the entrance. The park was formerly known as University Garden, and at the end of the avenue that leads to the adjoining university buildings is a statue of the founder, Karazin. The House of Pioneers in the park was built in 1850 by Lvov and reconstructed in the 1950s. There is also a cinema-cum-concert hall that seats 2,000, and at the far end of the park is Kharkov Zoo, founded in 1895.

On the other side of the park, far from the historical heart of the city, lies the modern municipal centre. *Dzerzhinsky Square* was built between 1925 and 1930, when Kharkov was still the Ukrainian capital. The square, 750 m (820 yards) long and 350 m (380 yds) in width (making an area of 11 hectares or 27 acres) is one of the largest in the world. In 1925 work began on the huge building for the Department of Industry. It has 4,000 windows and 1,300 doors, and the glass required would have been sufficient for a 17-hectare (47-acre) greenhouse. It was designed by Serafimov, Kravets, and Zelger with Rottert as the engineer and is undoubtedly the most interesting structure in the square, being a fine example of the constructivist style predominant at the time. This was, according to the "Constructivist Manifesto" of 1927, "indissolubly bound up with the proletarian revolution and with the socialist construction of the Soviet system." The old understanding of an architect as a "façademonger" gave way to the architect as a social leader, providing the accommodation the workers would need to build "a new life, a new way of living." There are isolated examples of constructivist style in Moscow, Leningrad, and many other Soviet cities, but Dzerzhinsky Square in Kharkov was unique in that it was planned as a whole constructivist complex and even after the postwar rebuilding retains much of its original appearance. The *Department of Industry* building comprises 3 ferro-concrete structures, of which the centre one is 11 storeys high, united by covered passageways at sixth-floor level. When completed it was the country's first skyscraper, and the visiting French writer Henri Barbusse said it gave "the impression of an organised mountain." In 1929 the House of Cooperatives was built, and then between 1930 and 1935 the House of Planning, designed like the House of Industry by Serafimov but this time with the assistance of Zandberg-Serafimova. The International Hotel, built at the same time, was by Yanovitsky. At the beginning of the 1930s,

all the mass demonstrations and military parades were held in this square, but it suffered greatly during the German occupation and during the fighting. After the war, the House of State Industry was the first to be reconstructed. It now houses the editorial offices of newspapers, a scientific-technical library, the local television theatre and studios, and the local chamber of commerce. The reconstructed House of Planning is the home of Kharkov University and in front of it stands Kharkov Hotel, formerly the International and reconstructed by the original architect, Yanovitsky. The local Party building dates from 1954, and the Lenin monument was unveiled on 5 November 1963. From Dzerzhinsky Square runs *Lenin Prospect*, a relatively new street, begun before the war and now built up with modern buildings housing hotels, scientific institutes, and apartment blocks.

Moscow Prospect, which is the way from the centre toward Rostov-on-Don and the Caucasus, is the city's longest thoroughfare. In the oldest part are classical-style buildings of the early 19th century. The first square along it is *Rudnev Square*, named after Nikolai Rudnev, a hero of the Civil War whose grave is here. 2 buildings of interest are the Agricultural Institute, built along its northern side in 1877 in pseudo-Russian style by Mikhalkovsky, and the huge Renaissance-style building designed by Beketov; during the Civil War the latter served as Red Army headquarters. Before the revolution there were many foreign industrial enterprises along this street, among them the Gelferich-Sade and Melgose Plant, and the factories of Leitner, Bleichert, and Eichner. Farther out, the eastern part of the town is still mainly industrial, and the street runs past workers' houses, stadia, and parks.

To the west, *Karl Marx Street* leads through an area once known for its pleasant public gardens—Chateau de Fleurs, Tivoli, and Hermitage—to *Privokzalnaya Square*, with the building of the Southern Railway Administration built in 1912 by Dmitriyev and Kakinin and engineered by Rottert.

Pokrovksy Cathedral, Universitetskaya Street

Uspensky Cathedral and Belfry, Unversitetskaya Gorka

Blagoveschensky Cathedral, Engels Street

Three Saints' Church, Zaikovskaya Street. Built in 1915 and open for services. Part of the church is used by the Old Believers and contains some old icons.

Roman Catholic Church, Gogol Street

There are, besides those mentioned, a number of other churches, mostly of the 19th and 20th centuries, of no particular historical interest.

Historical Museum, Universitetskaya Street 10 and another nearby building. Open 9–6; closed Tues. The displays illustrate the past history of the city and the most recent development of its flourishing industry. Other sections are devoted to the Civil War and to World War II.

Fine Arts Museum, Sovnarkomovskaya Street 11. Open 10:30–6; closed Fri. This museum contains works by Repin, who was born nearby in

Chuguyev, including a copy of his "Zaporozhye Cossacks writing a letter to the Sultan." The museum has 19 halls, with the first section devoted to Russian and Ukrainian revolutionary art. It also shows icons of the Novgorod, Pskov, and other schools dating from the 16th century. The second section covers Soviet art.

Museum of Natural Sciences, in the university

Planetarium, Kravtsov Pereulok 13

Pushkin Monument, Teatralnaya Square. The monument was erected in 1904 and designed by B. Edwards.

Karazin Monument. This monument was bult in 1905 and designed by Andrioletti.

Gogol Monument, Sumskaya Street. This monument was erected in 1909; the author's autograph is on the lower part of the pedestal.

Kotsyubinsky Monument, in the garden at the crossing of Pushkinskaya and Chernyshevsky streets. Mikhail Kotsyubinsky (1864–1913) was a Ukrainian writer and revolutionary democrat.

Shevchenko Monument, Sumskaya Street, at the main entrance to Shevchenko Park. The 16.5-m (54-ft) statue and its base by Matvei Manizer were erected in 1935. The 16 subsidiary statues represent the history of the Ukrainian people.

Lenin Monument, Dzerzhinsky Square. The monument, by Oleinik and Vronsky, was unveiled in 1963.

Obelisk, Vosstaniya Square. This commemorates the armed uprising of Kharkov workers in December 1905.

Monument to Revolutionaries, Radyanska Square. Unveiled in 1957.

Monument to Fighters of the October Revolution, University Square. Marked by an urn and eternal flame.

Monument Marking the Proclamation of the Establishment of the Soviet Ukraine, Soviet Ukraine Square. The proclamation was made here in the House of Nobles in December 1917, but the original monument was destroyed during the Second World War. The existing 18-m (59-ft) monument of red granite was unveiled in 1975.

Rudnev Statue, Rudnev Square. Nikolai Rudnev (1894–1918) was a hero of the Civil War who was killed at the Battle of Tsaritsyno. He was buried in this square, and the monument by Volovik dates from 1959.

Postyshev Monument. Pavel Postyshev (1888–1940) was an outstanding Soviet statesman, and the monument by Korolkov was unveiled on 30 December 1977.

Eternal Glory Memorial, in Lesopark, at the entrance to the town from the north. A 13-m (43-ft) statue of a woman symbolising the Motherland stands over an eternal flame and the graves of those who fell in the Second World War; unveiled on 28 October 1977.

Lysenko Opera House, Rymarskaya Street 19

Musical Comedy Theatre, Karl Marx Street 28

Krupskaya Puppet Theatre, Krasin Street 3

Pushkin Russian Drama Theatre, Chernyshevsky Street 11

Regional Drama Theatre, Sverdlov Street 18

Shevchenko Ukrainian Drama Theatre, Sumskaya Street 9

Circus, Uritskovo Square 8

Philharmonia Concert Hall, Sumskaya Street 10

Ukraina Concert Hall, Shevchenko Garden. This modern building, seating 2,000, was opened in 1965.

Hippodrome Racecourse, 1-Travnya Square

Avangard Stadium, Plekhanovskaya Street 65

Dynamo Stadium, Dynamovskaya Street. There is a swimming pool at the stadium.

Spartak Swimming Palace, Botanicheskaya Street 9

Sports Palace, Stadionnaya Street 2

Zoo, Sumskaya Street 35

Gorky Park, Sumskaya Street 81. There is a monument to Gorky here and also a children's railway.

Botanical Gardens, Klochkovskaya Street 52 and Otaokara Jaros 12. The first mentioned was founded in 1804 and belongs to the university. The second, which is much larger, was laid out in 1962.

Hydropark, Zhuravlevka, Shevchenko Street. Here there is an island in the middle of the river Kharkov, as well as plenty of sandy bathing beaches.

Shevchenko Park, Sumskaya Street

Intourist Hotel and Restaurant, Lenin Prospect 21; tel. 32–0508. Intourist office: tel. 32–0512.

Kharkov Hotel, Restaurant, and Café, Trinkler Street 2

Spartak Hotel and Restaurant, Sverdlov Street 4

Mir Hotel and Restaurant, Lenin Prospect 27; tel. 32–2330

Tourist Hotel, Moskovsky Prospect 144

Druzhba Motel, Gagarin Prospect 185; tel. 52–0142

Lux Restaurant, Sumskaya Street 3

Teatralny Restaurant, Sumskaya Street 2

Dynamo Restaurant, in the Dynamo Stadium

Vareniki ("dumplings") Bar, Sumskaya Street 14. These small dumplings are a national Ukrainian dish. They may be filled with various things, including cottage cheese, potato, and fruit.

GPO, Privokzalnaya Square 1

Bank, Teatralnaya Square 1

Kashtan (foreign-currency) Shop, Lenin Prospect 32

Ukrainian Souvenirs, Moskovsky Prospect 1

Department Store, Rosa Luxembourg Street

Intourist organises excursions from Kharkov to Sokolovo and Skovorodinovka.

Sokolovo

Located 55 km (34 miles) from Kharkov, this was the site in 1943 of a battle in which the 1st Czech Battalion took part. There is a *war memorial*, the *grave* of Hero of the Soviet Union Otakar Jaros, and a *museum*. Open 9–6; closed Mon.

Skovorodinovka
70 km (43 miles) away, in the direction of Zo-
lochev. The Ukrainian philosopher and poet Grigori Skovoroda (1722–94) lived here for some years
on his estate; his grave is here too. The estate is
open as a *museum*, but special permission is required to make this trip, and it is best in the summer.

KHATYN
See Minsk, p. 325.

KHERSON Population—355,000
Intourist organises excursions here from Odessa.

The town stands on the high right bank of the
river Dnieper, about 24 km (15 miles) upstream
from where it empties into the Black Sea. In the
spring the river floods nearby to a width of 25 km
(16 miles) and forms numerous small rivers, so that
the area is known as Kherson's Venice. The population of the town is mainly composed of Ukrainians and Russians.

Scythian gold has been found in this area, and
there are tunnels under the fortress, which vary in
depth from 4 to 11 m (13 to 37 ft). It is believed
that these date from the time of the greatest activity
of Zaporozhye Cossacks. They were then used by
smugglers and finally served as emergency exits
from the fortress above.

A Russian fortress was built here in 1737 during
one of the many wars with Turkey but was soon
overrun by the Turks and demolished. The place
was remembered when, after the Treaty of Kucuk
Kaynarca (Kuchuk Kainarji) in 1774, Russia gained
access to the Black Sea and won for its ships the
same privileges as those already enjoyed by Britain
and France. In 1778 Prince Grigory Potyomkin,
favorite of Catherine II, who was then administer-
ing the lands acquired from Turkey, was ordered
to find a suitable place for a town and a shipyard.
"And I order this place to be called Kherson," wrote
Catherine. At that time she had an ambitious plan
to resurrect the Greek empire, and the name was
chosen after that of the ancient Greek colony of
Khersones, where Prince Vladimir of Kiev received
his baptism. (The ruins of the colony were later
found near Sevastopol in the Crimea and have been
excavated.) It was said that Catherine II wanted to
crown her grandson, who bore the Greek name of
Konstantine, in Khersones, and the only reason for
this not taking place was because the boy caught
measles when she travelled there. Prince Potyomkin chose the ruins of the old fortification as a
site for the town, and so Kherson was founded in
1778. (Where the old fortification, known as Alexander's Fort, used to be, there is now a grain elevator.)

The initial work on Kherson was conducted by
General Ivan Hannibal (1737–1801), grandfather
of the poet Alexander Pushkin. After a few years,
a fortress was constructed, as well as a large shipyard. Count Segur, French ambassador to the court
of Catherine II, noted after visiting Kherson that
the place for the town was ill-chosen, since the
shallow water prevented the docking of merchant
ships and the naval vessels built there could not
sail downriver for the same reason. Besides, the
place was unhealthy because of the swamps around
it.

All the same, building went ahead so quickly
that when Catherine the Great visited the town 8
years after its foundation she wrote: "There is a
mass of people, apart from the military, and they
speak all the languages of Europe." The speed of
Kherson's growth accelerated after Potyomkin's
idea of making it a free port was adopted.

The present-day Black Sea Fleet can trace its
origins back to the old shipyard. The 66-gun frigate
"Glory of Catherine" was completed here in 1783,
and Kherson itself was the fleet's first base. A monument to the first shipbuilders of Kherson stands
on the quay. It was unveiled in 1972. In 1783–84
the shipyard was run by the famous Russian admiral
Fyodor Ushakov (1744–1817), and it was from here
that in 1787 and 1792–94 the future generalissimo
Alexander Suvorov conducted operations against
the Turks.

In 1803 Kherson was designated the provincial
centre and grew in importance because it was the
point of export of corn and wool. It enjoyed the
unique advantages of being close to the Black Sea
and also beside a large navigable river. Through
Kherson Russia imported wines, fine fabrics, and
furniture from France. Russian merchants and foreign firms opened their offices here, and until the
foundation of other ports—Nikolayev and more
particularly Odessa—Kherson grew and prospered.
Then the new ports took a great deal of its trade,
and only after 1890, when the river had been deep-
ened, allowing ocean vessels to call, did Kherson
revive.

For a long time, the town's industries were of
secondary importance, but machine building became established at the end of the 19th century,
and now Kherson has a highly developed shipbuilding industry. There are also agricultural machinery factories (combine harvesters for maize are
their most important product) and sizeable food-
producing plants, among them the largest food cannery in the Ukraine. The textile combine, one of
the biggest in the whole country, covers an area of
100 hectares (250 acres) near the river Dnieper.
Altogether there are about 100 industrial enterprises. Part of the town's industry is located on
Quarantine Island, where there is also a variety of
sports facilties and boat-hiring stations.

Modern Kherson is one of the Ukraine's regional centres. New buildings line the main street,
Prospect Ushakova, which runs from the railway
station down to the river, as they do *Suvorova Street*
and *Pobedy Square*. *Prospect Ushakova* is divided
into two equal parts by *Svobody ("liberty") Square*,
and among the new buildings along its length still
stands the old 17th-century fire-watching tower.
Among Kherson's oldest buildings to have partly
survived are the *arsenal* built in 1784 and *Yekaterininsky (Catherine's) Cathedral*, founded in
1781. On the cathedral's premises are the graves

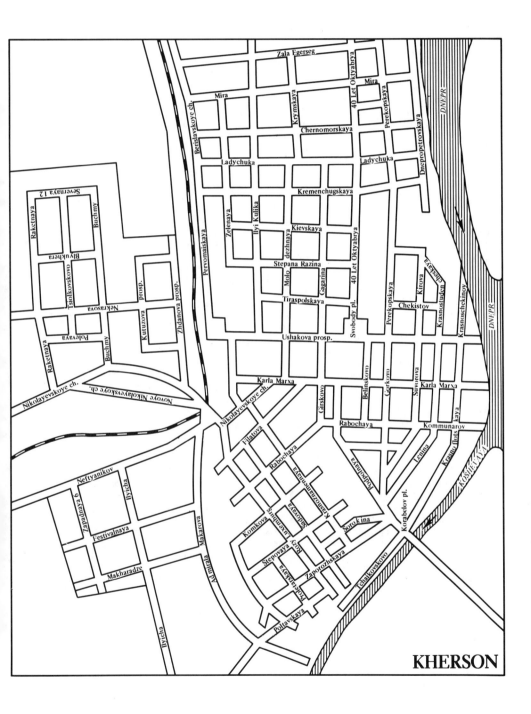

KHERSON

of the Russian soldiers killed during the Russo-Turkish War of 1787–91. The only streets of Kherson to be cobbled with stone (which is scarce in this swampy region) were the main ones, and the pavements were made of the volcanic lava used as ballast by ships coming from Italy.

Suvorov Street is closed to traffic. It used to be a market street in the old days, and now most of the ground-floor accommodation is used for shops. It is a popular place for strolling in the evening. On the corner of Lenin and Kommunarov streets are the impressive buildings of the old *Duma* ("town hall"), built in 1906 and now used as the Art Museum. Also here is the old law court (1893). Another venerable thoroughfare that has retained its importance is *Perekopskaya Street*, which runs beside the Dnieper for 12 km (7 miles). Some old aristocratic mansions remain here, including the 2-storey house formerly used by the governor. It is marked by a plaque commemorating the revolutionary events that took place here. Among the town's larger establishments are the *Lieutenant Schmidt Naval School* (1834), housed in an impressive building decorated with anchors, the *Krupskaya Pedagogical College* (1917), and the *Tsuryupa Agricultural College* (1874), in front of which there is a large, modern bust of Alexander Tsuryupa (1870–1928). He was a former student here, a professional revolutionary, and Lenin's colleague, who organised the first Marxist group in Kherson in the 1890s. After the 1917 revolution, he held a number of ministerial posts. In Kherson are also branches of the Odessa Technical Institute (a grey building) and the Nikolayevsk Shipbuilding Institute.

Kherson was occupied by the Germans from August 1941 until March 1944, but after the war it was quick to recover. The town's holiday facilities are good, and it is said to have 300 sunny days a year. The fame of the local melons and watermelons is an additional attraction to visitors.

The Fortress, Perekopskaya Street 13, by the river, a little to the northwest of the town. It was abandoned as a military stronghold in 1835, but the earth walls and the Moskovskiye and the Ochakovskiye Gates are preserved as examples of 18th-century fortifications. The fortress well dates from 1785. Besides the building of the former arsenal, there also remains here the *Church of Our Saviour*, locally known as St. Catherine's, built by Starov in 1781. One of the inscriptions reads: "Dedicated to the Saviour of Mankind by Catherine II." The empress's favourite, Prince Potyomkin, was buried here, but her son, Paul I, ordered that the tomb be secretly opened in 1798. Potyomkin's remains were removed, and the vault resealed. There are a number of valuable icons in this church, 2 of which by the portrait-painter Vladimir Borovikovsky (1757–1825) are likenesses of Catherine II and Prince Potyomkin; she is represented as St. Catherine the Martyr and he as St. George. The building is now used as an exhibition hall, open 9–7:30, but Potyomkin's tomb is still there. The 6 sculptures set in niches in the outside wall are by Zamaryev (1758–1823). Most of the monuments and tombstones are of those who fell during the 1788 seige of the nearby Turkish fortress, Ochakov. The belfry was constructed in 1802.

Greco-Sofiiskaya Church, Krasnoflotskaya Street 11. This church is dedicated to the Nativity of the Virgin but is usually referred to as the Greek Church. Its iconostasis of carved walnut, made in Cyprus, is famous, although four rows of new icons have taken the place of the originals. The church was built in 1780 and is open for services.

Cathedral of the Holy Spirit (Svyatodukhovsky), Dekabristov Street 36. This cathedral is also open for services. It was built in 1836 and is often called Privoznaya ("brought-in") Church because it stood near the market where goods that had been brought into town were sold.

Uspenskaya Church was built in 1798 and now serves as a sports hall.

All Saints' Church, in a cemetery in Melnitsa Region, beyond Howard's Obelisk

Local Museum, Lenin Street 9. Open 10–5:30; closed Mon. Among other items are objects that belonged to the Scythians and Sarmatians from the ancient Greek colony-town of Olvia. A more modern treasure is the Key of the City of Potsdam, a Soviet army trophy.

Natural History Museum, Gorky Street 5. Open 10–5; closed Wed.

Shovkunenko Art Museum, Lenin Street 34, in the old building of the town council. Open 11–7; closed Fri. Alexei Shovkunenko (1884–   ) is a water-colourist, portraitist, and landscape artist.

Yuri Gagarin Planetarium, Kommunarov Street 14. Built in 1960.

Howard's Obelisk, Ushakov Prospect, protected by a circular wall in the middle of a building site. John Howard (1727–90) was an English philanthropist and prison-reformer who caught typhus while visiting a local hospital here and never recovered. The obelisk of grey granite was erected on the order of Alexander I in 1828 and bears a plaque saying: "Howard died on January 20th, 1790, in his 63rd year." In 1890, on the centenary of his death, a memorial plaque was affixed to the house at Suvorov Street 14, on the second floor where he used to live, but the building was demolished during recent replanning of the centre of the town. Howard was once mayor of Bedford, and there is a bust of him in Westminster Abbey.

Bust of Suvorov, Suvorov Street. The bust, a copy of an old one by Rukavishnikov, was unveiled in 1950. The two-storey house where the generalissimo lived between 1792 and 1794 stands at Suvorova Street 13.

Bust of Shevchenko, in the Oak Grove. The trees were planted in 1964 to commemorate the 150th anniversary of the poet's birth.

Ushakov Statue, Ushakov Prospect, in front of the red-and-white-painted technical college that bears his name. The statue of Admiral Ushakov by Kravchenko and Chubin was unveiled in 1957.

First Shipbuilders' Monument, on the embankment. Topped by a fine 3-master in full sail with a bas-relief below showing the shipbuilders at work.

Karl Marx Monument, in Marx Garden

Lenin Statue, Svobody Square

Dzerzhinsky Statue, Kirov Street

Cannon Monument, 13th-March Square. In honour of the Soviet soldiers who liberated Kherson from enemy occupation on 13 March 1944.

Tank Monument, in the Slavy ("glory") Park, on the bank of the river. This T-34 tank overlooks the Dnieper and commemorates the liberation of Kherson from Nazi occupation.

Tsuryupa Bust, Rosa Luxembourg Street. Alexander Tsuryupa was a Soviet statesman, and this powerful portrait of him is carved in granite.

Tomb of the Unknown Soldier with an Eternal Flame, in Glory Park

Musical and Drama Theatre, Gorky Street 7

Puppet Theatre, 40-Let-Oktyabrya Street 8

Philharmonia Concert Hall, Gorky Street 17

Yubileiny Cinema and Concert Hall, Perekopskaya Street 13. In a dramatic modern building shaped like a tiara.

Lenin Park, Ushakov Prospect. This is Kherson's oldest park. It was laid out at the end of the 18th century and known as Alexander Park. An ancient oak stands in the centre, and outside the main gate is a statue of Lenin

Slavy Park, on the bank of the river. There is the statue of a woman symbolising Glory as the centrepiece.

Lenkomsomol Park, Perekopsk Street, near the old fortress. The 19-m (63-ft) obelisk honours the first Young Communists of the town. There is an amusement area here and the *Otdykh* ("rest") *Café*.

On *Quarantine Island* is one of the oldest yacht clubs in the Ukraine, founded in 1907. Also on the island is a good bathing beach, just as there is on either bank of the river.

Fregat Hotel (Intourist) and Restaurant, Svoboda Square

Kiev Hotel and Restaurant, Lenin Square, Ushakov Prospect 43; tel. 62–937. The local Intourist office is here: tel. 22–619.

Pervomaisky Hotel and Kherson Restaurant, Lenin Street 26

Kiev Restaurant, Mirny Boulevard 1

Orbita Restaurant, Komkov Street 99

Dnieper Restaurant, at the seaport

Ogonyok ("little light") Café, Ushakov Prospect 30/1

Minutka Café, Suvorov Street 1/13

GPO, Gorky Street 54

Bank, Komsomolskaya Street 21

Telegraph Office, Druzhby Street 4

Department Stores, Ushakov Prospect 26/2 and 49

Central Bookshop, Svobody Square 1

Gramophone Record Shop, Suvorov Street 14

Jeweller's, Suvorov Street 22

Market, Belinskovo Street 19

Filling Station, near the market, Perekopsk Street

Not far from Kherson, but on the opposite side of the Dnieper, is the small holiday resort of *Tsuryupinsk*.

Hunting tours can be organised in the *Gavriilovsky Reserve*, 30 km (19 miles) from town (45 min. by speedboat). The reserve, which covers an area of 87,348 hectares (218,370 acres), was founded in the dry steppe and on the neighbouring islands in 1927 as a bird sanctuary. Today it is supervised by the Black Sea State Biosphere Reserve. There is a museum here and the Schmelgausen Zoological Institute. Now there are 620 different plants here, 25 mammals, 300 kinds of birds, 9 species of reptiles, and 5 amphibians.

Intourist organises excursions from Kherson to Novaya-Kakhovka, 75 km (47 miles) away, to Kakhovka, and to Askania-Nova 167 km (104 miles).

Novaya-Kakhovka Population—55,000

In 1959 the decision was made to build a new hydropower station on the river Dnieper, 10 km (6 miles) away from the old town of Kakhovka. So it was that on the site of the little village of Klyuzhevoye, where a few fishermen used to live, New (Novaya) Kakhovka was founded. Construction for the hydropower station began in 1951 and continued for 5 years, Novaya-Kakhovka being declared a town in 1952.

The gigantic reservoir, now known as the Kakhovka Sea, was not completely filled until 1957. It covers an area of 2,150 sq km (820 sq miles), has an average depth of 8.4 m (27 ft), and a maximum depth of 36 m (118 ft). The reservoir stretches from Novaya-Kakhovka to Zaporozhye and is used for the irrigation of the southern Ukraine and the northern part of the Crimea.

The hydropower station is of 312,000-kw capacity and supplies the Dnieper area and the Donbas coal-mining region. It is situated on the Dnieper rapids, 90 km (56 miles) upstream from the river mouth.

The town stands on the left bank, connected by rail and road via the dam with the opposite bank. It was built as an example of a new type of planning: the streets follow the sweep of the river and are lined with 2- and 3-storey houses. The residential, working, and shopping areas are on the higher ground, while the lower slopes leading down to the river are all parks. Wide stone steps lead down from the impressive Palace of Culture through the park to the river, where there is a bathing beach and a boating station.

The town's principal street is *Dneprovsky Prospect*, and the chief local industries are food production and electromachine building.

Local Museum and Art Gallery, Lenin Street 18. Open 10–6; closed Wed.

War Memorial, Dneprovsky Prospect. Commemorating those who fell in the Civil War and World War II.

Civil War Memorial, near the dam, on the Novaya-Kakhovka side

Lenin Monument, Central Square

Summer Theatre, in the park

Energia Stadium. Seats 5,000.

Druzhba ("friendship") Hotel and Restaurant, Dneprovsky Prospect 1; tel. 42–100

Tavrida Restaurant, Dneprovsky Prospect

GPO and Telegraph Office, Lenin Street 24

Bank, Dneprovsky Prospect 15

Kakhovka Population—30,000

Kakhovka lies on the left bank of the river Dnieper. It was founded in the 18th century on the site of the Tatar fortress of Islam-Kermen, built in 1492.

Its name came from that of the Kakhovsky family; General Kakhovsky, who participated in the Russo-Turkish wars, obtained the land after it became Russian in 1783.

The place soon developed into an important trading centre. Some 200,00 cartloads of Crimean salt were ferried annually across the Dnieper at this point. By the turn of the century, over 100,000 people came to the fairs here, and there was also a hiring fair for craftsmen, where up to 40,000 from the nearby provinces would gather to offer their skills.

Kakhovka was a centre of culture and the birthplace of the Armenian classical composer, Alexander Spendiarov (Spendiarian) (1871–1928).

Kakhovka was of greatest importance during the Civil War, for it was used as a bridgehead before the capture of the Crimea in 1920. The Crimean peninsula was the last stronghold of the anti-Bolshevik forces, and General Wrangel's army held out for 82 days before its findal defeat and evacuation to Constantinople. The poet Mikhail Svetlov wrote a song which became very popular:

Kakhovka, Kakhovka—my own trusty rifle,
Let the hot bullet fly free!
Irkutsk and Warsaw, Orel and Kakhovka
Steps through our great history!

After the revolution measures were taken to modernise the local farms, and in 1924 the first Fordson tractors to be bought from the United States were delivered here. Kakhovka's industry grew rapidly after the hydropower station was completed in 1955. Now the most important factory is that producing electro-welding equipment, but there is also some food production and car repairing.

Chapel, Pushkin Street 94

Local Museum, Lenin Street 12; open Tues., Thurs., and Sat., 10–7. Most of the exhibits illustrate the history of the attack on nearby Perekop in November 1920, which preceded the taking of the Crimea by the Red Army.

Pushkin's Bust, Pushkin Street. The poet visited Kakhovka in 1820, and the monument was unveiled in 1937.

Frunze Monument, on the embankment of the Kakhovka Sea, which is in fact a reservoir. Mikhail Frunze was a famous Bolshevik who was a commander on the southern front during the Civil War. The monument, with an inscription reading "From the inhabitants of Kakhovka," was unveiled in 1957.

Lenin Monument

Bust of Marshal Blucher, Karl Marx Street. Vasili Blucher (1889–1938) was a Civil War hero.

There is a *bathing beach* and a *boat-hiring station.*

Tavria Hotel and Kakhovka Restaurant, Karl Marx Street 138

Tourist Restaurant, outside the town, beside the road leading on to Novaya-Kakhovka.

GPO, Karl Marx Street

Bank, Karl Marx Street 118

Department Store, Lenin Street

Bookshop, Lenin Street

Filling Station, by the road leading out of the town

Askania-Nova

The village lies 23 km (14 miles) by a good side road from Chkalovo; take the sign-posted left turn. Askania-Nova is best known for its wildlife reserve.

Catherine the Great had in 1763 originated the plan to colonise the crown lands in the empty steppes with foreign settlers. Born a German princess, the daughter of Prince Christian August von Anhalt-Zerbst, it was logical that in later years preference should be given to a member of her own family. The territory of 50,000 hectares (125,000 acres) was purchased in 1828 by Duke von Anhalt-Kothen, and he founded a small settlement in 1841, naming it after his 700-year-old native estate of Askania in Germany, which in its turn, was called after Aeneas's son, Ascanius. The steppe was used for breeding sheep and horses. But the estate really became profitable after 1856, when it was sold to another German family, descended from the first wave of immigrants who had arrived 60 years earlier, under Catherine the Great. These were the Falz-Feins, who, with up to 400,000 sheep, became known as "sheep-breeding kings" in the southern Ukraine. Their vast estates were conveniently near Russia's main wool market in Odessa.

In 1863 Friedrich Falz-Fein was born at Askania-Nova, and it was he who in 1884 founded a little zoo, which he called the Tierpark. Soon he began to buy animals from different parts of the world—ostriches from Africa, emus from Australia, zebu and antelopes from India, as well as reindeer and other animals native to the Russian empire. In 1899 Falz-Fein acquired his first wild Przhevalsky horses from Mongolia, and from being a simple collection, the zoo took on scientific aims, the acclimatisation of animals and the preservation of rare species from extinction. In 1904 Falz-Fein was assisted by Professor Mikhail Ivanov (1871–1935). In 1914 Tsar Nicholas II drove up for a visit to Askania-Nova from the imperial palace at Livadia in the Crimea. He was so impressed with Falz-Fein's work that he made him a baron.

The animals thrived and multiplied, but wars took a heavy toll. During the Civil War most of the Germans fled. Any who remained were murdered. Baron von Falz-Fein himself died in Bad-Kissingen in 1920. The zoo's population was drastically depleted as warring armies killed and burned, and the carefully bred and valuable zebra hybrids were used to pull gun carriages. After the war Professor Ivanov was appointed as head of the livestock-breeding institute, and he was then responsible for breeding the Russian Rambouilet sheep, a fine-fleeced mountain merino variety, and also a new white pig, which was to do particularly well on the Ukrainian steppe. The Institute of Hybridisation and Acclimatisation was founded in 1932 and named for Ivanov. But once again war was to all but destroy the zoo, and in addition the trees of the botanical gardens were felled for firewood. After the German occupation (1941–43), when the scattered herds of bison, deer, gazelles, and antelope were rounded up from the steppe, it was found that only 20 percent of the animals were left. In addition all the scientific records were gone. The farmlands and gardens were arid and bare, and to create new windbreaks, truckloads of acorns were painstakingly planted in lines marked out by Caterpillar tractors.

In 1956 Askania-Nova was placed under the control of the Ukrainian Academy and renamed the Ukrainian Scientific Ivanov Research Institute. Its main work is now the domestication of valuable wild animals and cross-breeding them with other domestic animals. Today there are about 100 different species of animals and birds, including 4 kinds of zebra, 6 different antelopes, 3 types of ostrich, 5 kinds of swans, and both American and European bison. The animals are either cloven-hooved or members of the horse family belonging to the Przhevalsky horses. Animals and birds are transferred from here to other zoos in the Soviet Union, and exchanges are made with foreign zoos. The local hospital carries out useful experiments with antelope milk for curing ulcers and other diseases. Special permission is required to see the animals, living free on the open steppe.

Institute for Animal Hybridisation and Acclimatisation, founded in 1932. In front of the building stands a bronze bust of academician Ivanov who worked here for many years.

Natural History Museum and Askania-Nova Zoo, both open 8 A.M.–4 P.M.

Botanical Garden, open 9 A.M.–7 P.M. The garden was laid out between 1887 and 1902, when seeds and plants were brought in, mainly from Odessa and Riga. The landscaping was by Dufresne, a French gardener, and the territory covers 68 hectares (170 acres) including a beautiful lake with an island and a grotto of stone. There are 120 different trees and bushes that have been acclimatised on the dry Tavrida steppe, and the garden is rightly known as the emerald oasis.

At the entrance stands a *water tower* built in 1892–93 in Gothic style but no longer used. Here also is a granite *monument* to the 15 paratroopers shot against the wall on this spot in 1941.

Hotel and Restaurant, Chervonoarmeiska Street

Olen Restaurant

KHIVA Population—40,000

Intourist organises 6-hour day trips here from Urgench and it is best to see the desert after visiting the town.

Khiva is situated in the Khorezm Oasis, on the Palvan Canal and the left bank of the river Amu-Darya. To the south stretches the Karakum Desert and to the northeast the Kyzylkum Desert. The average temperature in January is − 5°C (23°F) and in July, 28.5°C (83°F). The irrigated area surrounding the city produces fruit, cotton, maize, and rice.

The history of Khiva begins with the legend of how Shem, son of Noah, lay asleep on a hill of sand and dreamed of a future city in that very place. He dug a well, which he named Kheivak and which can be seen in the northwest part of Ishan Qal'eh (the old city) today. Khiva is supposed to derive its name from that of the well.

Certainly Khiva was known in the 4th century B.C. as part of the state of Khorezm, when the Amu-Darya still flowed into the Caspian Sea and not into the Aral Sea as it does today. Recent excavations have disclosed ruins of grey walls, built of bricks similar to those used to line the fortress walls of Samarkand and other strongholds in south Turkestan in that same early period. In A.D. 712, along with the rest of Khorezm, Khiva fell under Arab domination. It was at this time that Abu Mohammed ibn Musa al Khwarizmi (783–850), a native of Khiva, wrote some of the first treatises on mathematics. The word "algebra" comes from his own "al-jabr." "Algorism," which means the Arabic system of numerals (1–9 with 0), is really a corruption of his own name. However, it was only in the 10th century that the first written account of the place itself was made, by two Arabian travellers and geographers, Istakhri and Makdisi. At that time it began to become an important port on the trade routes from China, India, and Iran to Bulgaria and Ryazan, Pskov and Novgorod on the way to the Baltic countries and the rest of Europe.

Khiva suffered severely in 1220 from Genghis Khan's Mongol invasion, and little of the city was left standing. By the 16th century, however, it had recovered sufficiently to become the capital of the khanate that was formed by Khan Ara-Muhammed in 1511. It grew to be the centre of Islam in Central Asia and had one of the most important slave markets in that part of the world. Its legendary magnificence provided the source for the Oriental saying: "I would give 2 sacks of gold to look at Khiva!" Its growing prosperity attracted the attention of both Iran and Bukhara, and there followed a long period when its possession was under hot dispute. It was for some time held as a province of Iran, but the Persians were driven out in 1741. It is on record that Khiva was ruled by 33 different

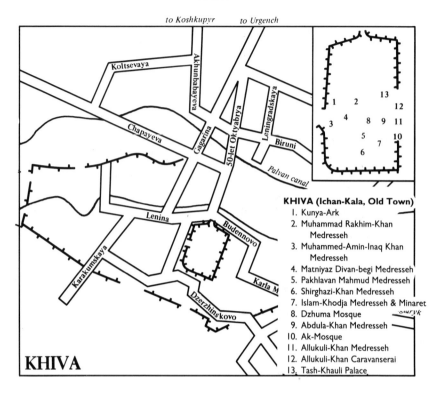

KHIVA (Ichan-Kala, Old Town)
1. Kunya-Ark
2. Muhammad Rakhim-Khan Medresseh
3. Muhammed-Amin-Inaq Khan Medresseh
4. Matniyaz Divan-begi Medresseh
5. Pakhlavan Mahmud Medresseh
6. Shirghazi-Khan Medresseh
7. Islam-Khodja Medresseh & Minaret
8. Dzhuma Mosque
9. Abdula-Khan Medresseh
10. Ak-Mosque
11. Allukuli-Khan Medresseh
12. Allukuli-Khan Caravanserai
13. Tash-Khauli Palace

KHIVA

khans during the course of the 18th century, finally being taken over by the Uzbek "Inaqs" (nobles). Inaq Iltuzer declared himself khan in 1804, and his family maintained possession of Khiva until 1920.

The Khivan khans kept themselves cut off from the infidel western world and found the position of the newly crowned Queen Victoria almost impossible to comprehend, even with the careful explanation provided by Captain Abbot in 1839–40. The interview with Khan Hazurut went as follows:

"Is your king really a woman?" he asked.

"She is."

The khan smiled, and all his satellites, as in duty bound, giggled.

"How," he inquired, "can she rule, being 'rooposh' (concealed)?"

"Our females, like those of the Turcumuns, are not concealed. The Queen of England has ministers who transact business for her."

"Are they women?"

"No, they are men. They receive their general instructions from the Queen and act accordingly."

The khan continued: "Do you always choose women as your kings?"

"No, we give preference to heirs male, but when there is a female and no male, rather than disturb the country by introducing a new family of claimants to the crown, we crown this female. One of the greatest of our kings was a woman."

"Is your king married?"

"No, she is very young."

"But will she marry?"

"Inshallah."

"And if she marry, does her husband become king?"

"By no means. He has no authority in the state."

Here there was some more smiling.*

Eventually it was a Russian force that brought this eastern city nearer the west, but it was much earlier than 1917 that the main Russian expeditions first came here. In 1717 Peter the Great had sent a military force under the leadership of Bokovich-Cherkassy to search for gold in the sands of the Oxus; few lived to tell the tale of how the Russians

*From "Narrative of a Journey from Heraut to Khiva, Moscow and St. Petersburg," 2 vols., by Capt. James Abbot. W.H. Allen and Co. Ltd., London, 1884.

were trapped and slaughtered and how Cherkassy himself was skinned, stuffed, and exhibited in the courtyard of the khan's palace. Another expedition under Perovsky set out in the winter of 1839, especially to avoid the summer heat, but instead of meeting with success, it became stuck in the snow in the desert. In 1873 Khiva was taken by the Russian army under Kaufman and was subsequently crippled by the indemnity that was imposed. In 1920 Khiva was made the capital of Khorezm and remained so until the state was incorporated into Uzbekistan in 1924.

Khiva long retained its eastern character. There was a large bazaar and, besides the 94 mosques, there were 63 medressehs in the city. Today the architectural ensembles are much better preserved than those of the more ancient cities of Bukhara and Samarkand and have a further advantage over them in that they were properly planned and completed. Although many of the buildings in Khiva were built comparatively recently, the architects made use of the best traditional designs of Central Asian architecture while they developed a new style in town planning. The layer of straw incorporated in some of the walls served the dual purpose of protection against rising damp and against damage from earthquakes. The sticks protruding from some of the towers indicated that the building was unfinished, in order to protect it from evil spirits. Much restoration was carried out before 1967, but it was then that the oldest part of the city was declared a "town-reserve" (like Suzdal, near Moscow) and restoration work began to be carried out scientifically, following the original plans. Today the projects include the laying of telephone and power lines underground and then the repaving of the streets with square bricks, just as they used to be, but the main street still bears Gagarin's names. The organisation in charge of the restoration work is buying up private houses to complete the complex of the city, but often people are unwilling to leave for the new apartments set up outside the ancient walls. So it is that half the town is a museum while the rest is still lived in.

All the monuments of greatest historical interest are located in *Ishan Qal'eh* (the inner city), which was surrounded by walls, of which some parts still remain. The walls are thought to have been built in the 5th–6th centuries. Where they are still intact they are over 2 km (1 mile) in circumference, stand 7–8 m (23–26 ft) high, and their thickness at the bottom is 5–6 m (16–20 ft).

Ishan Qal'eh covers 26 hectares (65 acres) and is crossed by 2 main streets; from north to south runs *Bukhara Street*, and *Marx Street* crosses it from east to west. At each end of the streets is one of Ishan Qal'eh's 4 gates.

The buildings of greatest interest are close together, and it doesn't matter in which order they are visited. If one starts at the site of the western gate (which was removed in 1924), where Marx Street enters Ishan Qal'eh, the first complex on the left is that of *Kunya-Ark*, the ancient citadel, founded in the 15th century. Its name means "old

palace fortress," and indeed it used to be the palace of the khans. Most of the remaining buildings date from the 17th century, when the palace stretched right along the western wall of Ishan Qal'eh. The *Kurnysh-Khana* (reception hall) has been restored since the Revolution. Its ceiling is decorated with paint made from mineral glue. In one of the walls is the niche where the khan's throne used to stand, but the throne itself is now in the armoury in the Moscow Kremlin. *Tosh-Khavli* (stone court), *the harem*, has been restored to its original appearance. There is also a *summer mosque* (the White Mosque), which now serves as a bookshop. It was built in 1838 and was notable for its decorative tiles, particularly the majolica work in the prayer niche in the southern wall. The khan's mint functioned in Kunya-Ark in 1806–25, and the building has been fully restored. On the left is a prison.

Besides these buildings put up by the khans of the last century, inside Kunya-Ark, on a small hill, are the ruins of the oldest part of the town, *Ashik-Baba*. Perhaps called after a certain Ak-shikh ("white sheik"), the clay tower that used to stand here was the place where the khans took refuge from their rebellious vassals. Certainly it is true that Shirghazi-Khan (1715–28) so feared for his life that he used to lock himself in the tower and kept it always ready for withstanding siege.

On the right side of the street opposite the citadel is the *Muhammed-Amin Khan Medresseh* and the colossal base of the unfinished *Kalta-Minar Minaret*, nearly 28 m (92 ft) high, built in 1851–55 and decorated with blue tiles. Kalta means "short," and there are different stories attached to it. It is said that construction work on the minaret ceased in 1855, either because the khan was killed in battle or because there was a disagreement between him and the architect responsible. The base of the minaret is 14.2 m (47 ft) in diameter, much larger than most minarets, and suggests that the finished structure was meant to be exceptionally tall. There is a story that the architect had agreed to build a similar minaret for the emir of Bukhara when this one was completed, but when the jealous Muhammed-Amin Khan learned of this, he ordered that the architect be thrown from the tower to his death. Another version says that the architect was to be imprisoned inside the minaret until it was finished, but he managed to escape and so the work was abandoned.

Close to the Kalta-Minar is the *Matiyez Divan-begi Medresseh* (1871), now serving as a restaurant, and the *Mausoleum of Seid Alauddin* (1310), which is the only monument in Khiva to have survived from the time of Mongol domination. Built by Emir Kullal, the mausoleum is of burnt brick and the tomb with elaborately decorated ceramic tiles, really beautiful.

Next are the *Kazi-Kalyan Medresseh* (1905) and the *Dzhuma Mosque*, which was first mentioned in the 10th century but was rebuilt in 1788. It is 55 m (180 ft) long and 46 m (151 ft) wide, with 2 holes in the roof to let in the light. The wooden ceiling inside is supported by 115 carved wooden columns standing 3.5 m (11 ft) apart. Today only 15 of the old pillars remain, but 3 of these date from the 11th century; the newer pillars are plain. It is said that the old pillars were brought here from a mosque in Kyata, the capital of Khorezm in the 10th century.

On the left side of the street after the citadel are the high walls of the Muhammed Rakhim-Khan Medresseh (1871). Close to it is the Arab-Khan Medresseh (1616).

At the crossing of Marx Street with Bukhara Street, to the right (the southern side), is the Mausoleum of Pakhlavan- (or Palvan-) Mahmud. Pakhlavan-Mahmud was the son of a furrier whose workshop stood on the site of the mausoleum. Pakhlavan means "mighty one," because he was very strong and generally respected and even had considerable influence over the khan. He was also a poet. When he died he was buried here, and he was later declared a saint; the mausoleum was built over his grave in the 14th century. Palvan-Ata was considered the guardian of the Khivan khanate, and his mausoleum was revered as a sacred shrine. It was rebuilt in 1810 by Mukhammad Rakhim-Khan after it had been used as the family mausoleum of the Kungrad khans. The tomb is now decorated with blue tiles with quotations from Pakhlavan's poetry. The doors are of carved ivory.

Just south of the mausoleum is the Shirghazi-Khan Medresseh (1718–19), built after a campaign by Shirgazi-Khan against the Persian city of Meshed during which he took 5,000 prisoners. The prisoners were enslaved, brought back to Khiva, and put to work to build this medresseh on the understanding that they would be freed when the building was complete. However, the khan delayed the completion and employed them for other construction work, whereupon they lost patience and murdered him there, in the medresseh. Later the medresseh became one of the most important in the whole of Khorezm and earned the name of Maskanfazylan, the House of the Learned.

To the east of the Shirghazi-Khan Medresseh is the Islam-Hoja Medresseh, with a minaret (1908) that, at 57 m (187 ft) high, is the tallest in Khiva; its base is 9.5 m (31 ft) in diameter. Islam Hoja, who built it, was the khan's minister. Now it serves as the Applied Art Museum. The Bogobouli Mosque (19th century) is nearby.

In the opposite direction, to the north of Marx street, along Bukhara Street, are the Muhamed-Amin-Inaq Medresseh (1765), the Dos-Alim Medresseh (1882), the Yusup-Yaszhaulibashi Medresseh (1906), the Musa-Turya Medresseh (1841), and the Emir-Turya Medresseh (1870). Bukhara Street ends with the northern gate, Bogcha-Darvaza, which is in the form of a covered passage 10 m (11 yd) long and 5 m (16 ft) wide. It is roofed with 2 cupolas, and on either side is a 10-m (33-ft) semicircular tower, joined together by a gallery.

Following Marx Street farther along toward the eastern gates of Ishan Qal'eh, on the right side, are the Abdullah-Khan Medresseh (1855), which is now used as the Natural History Museum. Abdullah-khan is known as the One-Day Khan. His life was cut short when he fell from his horse. Next comes the Ak-Mosque (1857) and the Anusha-Khan Bathhouse (1657); Anusha-Khan, son of Abul-gari-Khan, was presented with these baths by his father after having fought particularly valiantly in battle. The building is now deep in the ground, but the baths are open. Also on the same side of Marx Street is the Saidniyaz Sholiker-Bai Medresseh and Mosque (1835); the mosque is open for services.

To the left of Marx Street and along Lermontov Street, which run northward from it parallel with Bukhara Street, is the Kutlug-Murad-inaq Medresseh (1804–12). Kutlug-Murad-inaq had said that he wished to be buried in the medresseh he had built, but he chanced to die while he was in the outer city, Dishan-Qal'eh, and it was forbidden to carry dead bodies into Ishan Qal'eh. The problem was solved by pulling down part of the wall of Ishan Qal'eh near the eastern gate (the Pavlan-Darvaza Gate), so that the medresseh appeared to stand in Dishan-Qal'eh.

The Khodzhamberdibiya (or Khurdzhum) Medresseh (1683) is also on Lermontov Street and adjoining it is the Uch-avlya Mausoleum (16th century). Its name means "Three Saints' Mausoleum," and there is a legend that once 3 brothers feared that drought would ruin their crops, so they diverted some water from the irrigation channels in the khan's fields to their own small holding. They were sentenced to death, but at night they went out into the fields to pray to Allah, and immediately a heavy downpour of rain began, a rare occurrence in Khorezm. The khan's crops were spoiled because his fields had only just been watered, but the rain was just what was needed by the three brothers' fields, and they later yielded a good crop.

Local Museum, at the end of Marx Street, but still within the walls of Ishan Qal'eh and near the east gates, in the Palace of Allukuli-Khan (or Tash-Khauli, meaning "stone court") and in the former Allakuli-Khan Medresseh (1835). Open daily. It has been fully restored, and its main façade is most interesting architecturally and uses decorative majolica. Thousands of slaves were employed to build the palace. There were 163 rooms arranged around 3 large courtyards and 5 smaller ones, and the whole complex was surrounded by a high stone wall. Most of the inside walls are of burnt brick. The 3 ceremonial courts and some of the rooms are decorated wtih blue, white, and turquoise tiles and with carved wooden columns rising from carved marble bases; many of the doors are intricately carved. The 3 large courts are the blue-tiled Harem Court, Ishrari-Hauly (the reception court), and Arz-Hauly (the court of justice). The Harem Court had special accommodations for 4 of the many wives: the oldest, the most beautiful, the favourite, and the youngest. The Court of Justice has 2 gates, the main one and a second through which prisoners were led to trial.

Adjoining the palace is the *Allakuli-Khan Caravanserai*, built in 1835 and fully restored. It has 105 rooms and was an inn for travelling merchants. It now houses the *Museum of the Ancient Medicine of Khorezm*. Next to the caravanserai, built at the same time, are the buildings of the bazaar, mainly a long covered passage roofed with 14 cupolas, the central one rising high above the others.

The southern side of the Allakuli-Khan complex joins the *Palvan-Darvaza Gate*, rebuilt in 1806. This gate leading into Ishan Qal'eh is a passageway 60 m (66 yd) long, roofed by 6 cupolas. The small recesses in the walls were used as prison cells in the 17th and 18th centuries and later as trading stalls. There used to be a slave market to the right of the gate, and it is on record that runaway slaves were nailed to the gate by their ears. It was by this gate that the khan's edicts were read to the people.

Outside the walls of Ishan Qal'eh lies what was the poorer region of the city, known as Dishan Qal'eh. This was enclosed in the middle of the 19th century by walls with watchtowers and 10 gates.

Saidniyaz Sholiker Bai Mosque, by the East Gate. This mosque was built in 1835 and is open for services.

Local History and Revolutionary Museum, Gagarin Street 5; open 9–6; closed Mon. This museum is located in the former official residence of the late Seid Asphendiar Bogadur Khan. The palace, Khiva's first European-type building, was constructed in 1902 for the khan by his father, Muhammed Rahim Khan II. It was here that ambassadors were received. The impressive chandeliers in the reception hall were a present from the last Russian tsar, Nicholas II. The palace's small generator fed the building with electricity, and it was in fact the only place that was lit in the whole country. Among the exhibits is silk money, which was used here for some time in the 1920s. The Asphendiar family tomb was designed by the last khan for himself, his mother, and his son, but only his mother was buried there, as both he and his son died violent deaths and their bodies could not be laid in a holy place.

Opposite the local savings bank office, the khan used to receive complaints and petitions from his subjects. Close to the museum is the former *harem*, now a boarding school, and the *pavilion* where Asphendiar Khan was killed in 1918.

Applied Art Museum, in the Islam Hodja Medresseh. Carved wood and marble are among the exhibits here, and examples of carpet weaving are displayed. Open 9–6; closed Mon.

Natural History Museum, in the Abdullah-Khan Medresseh. Local flora and fauna, including desert species. Open 9–6; closed Mon.

Museum of the Ancient Medicine of Khorezm, in the Allakuli-Khan Medresseh, Marx Street. Particular attention is paid to the contributions of Ali-ibn-Sin and Abu-Al-Biruni. Open 9–6; closed Tues.

Al Khwarizmi Monument, by the West Gate.

Al Khwarizmi (783–850) was a mathematician who was born here (see above).

Lenin Statue, in front of the Local Museum

Khiva Hotel, in the building of a medresseh by the West Gate. It has a little minaret at each corner.

Hotel and Café, Gagarin Street 13

Khiva Restaurant, in Divan Begi Medresseh

Cafeteria, in the department store

Chaikhana Tearoom, in Ishan Qal'eh

GPO, Pochtovaya Street, in the building next to that formerly known as the Khan's Post Office. Standing opposite is the *Khan's Hospital*, built in 1912.

Sarai-Bazaar Shopping Centre, in the building of a caravanserai

Department Store, in the building of a medresseh

Souvenirs and Books, in the West Gate

Bookshop, in the White Mosque

Taxi. At the time of writing, it is recommended to keep the taxi from Urgench to make the return journey.

KHMELNITSKY Population 240,000

Known as Proskurov until 1954, this town was renamed after Ukrainian leader Bogdan Khmelnitsky, to commemorate the 300th anniversary of the Ukraine's union with Russia.

The town is situated in the fertile region of Podolia, where the river Ploskaya joins the river Bug.

It was first mentioned in writing in 1493. 400 years later, when Nicholas I was passing through the town one autumn day with 12 yoke of oxen to pull his carriage, he scarcely managed to get through the mud. Russian writer Alexei Kuprin was stationed in Proskurov late in the 19th century when he was serving as a junior officer with the 46th Dnieper Infantry Regiment. "The railway station," he wrote, "was the only place where people could go to enjoy themselves. They would even go there for a game of cards. The ladies went to wait for the passenger train to come in as a diversion in the depressing monotony of provincial life." He used his impressions and observations in his novelette "The Duel."

Today, besides many provincial buildings typical of the last century, there is an impressive new building of the House of Soviets in the town centre. The main thoroughfare, which is lined with new buildings, is *25-Zhovtneva Street*.

The town contains factories for machine building, food processing, and the manufacture of synthetic fur.

Pokrovskaya (Intercession) Church, Frunze Street 72. Among big buildings, it is reached through the archway of a large apartment house. It was built at the end of the 19th century and is open for services.

St. Mary's Church, Telmann Street 15

Local Museum, Liebknecht Street 38, a street lined with old houses. On display are paintings by the artist Georgi Vereisky (1886–1962), who was born in Khmelnitsky.

Vereisky Memorial Museum, Chervonoar-meiska Street 5. Open 10–7; closed Wed.

Bogdan Khmelnitsky Monument, Vokzalnaya Square

Shevchenko Monument, 25-Zhovtneva Street

Ostrovsky Monument. This memorial to Nikolai Ostrovsky (1904–36), writer and Civil War hero, was sculpted in 1964 by Vladimir Kornev using money donated by Young Communists. Ostrovsky was born in Shepetovka, about 60 km (37 miles) north of Khmelnitsky, and his house there is now a museum.

Tank Monument, 25-Zhovtneva Street. A World War II memorial.

"Work, Science and Space," Frunze Street. This modern sculptural composition stands among the new apartment houses.

Music and Drama Theatre, Gagarin Street 7, close to the House of Soviets

Puppet Theatre, Kotovsky Street 34

Dynamo Stadium, 25-Zhovtneva Street

Philharmonia Concert Hall, Kotovsky Street

Kotsubinsky Park and Franko Park have their main entrances on 25-Zhovtneva Street and lie beside the rivers.

Tsentralnaya Hotel and Restaurant

Podillya Hotel and Restaurant, Gagarin Street 5; tel. 6–4723

Druzhba Restaurant, 25-Zhovtneva Street. Khmelnitsky cutlets are a local specialty.

Ukraina Restaurant

Tourist Restaurant, just out of town, where the road forks, on the way to Vinnitsa.

Mriya Café, Frunze Street 82

Post Office, Lenin Street and 25-Zhovtneva Street 11

Department Store, 25-Zhovtneva Street 50

Gift Shop and Jeweller's, 25-Zhovtneva Street 31

Handicraft and Art Shop, Frunze Street 48

Filling Station, where the road forks, just out of town in the direction of Vinnitsa.

There are two recommended out-of-town Ukrainian restaurants:

Chaika Restaurant, Letichev (just beyond Medzhibozh, see below), 45 km (28 miles) from Khmelnitsky.

Rossia Restaurant, in the town of Dunayevtsi, 60 km (37 miles) from Khmelnitsky, on the road south toward Kamenets-Podolsky.

Intourist organises excurisons from Khmelnitsky to Vinnitsa via Medzhibozh, Letichev, and Shepetovka, and to Kamenets-Podolsky (q.v.) via Dunayevtsi.

Medzhibozh Population—4,000

Situated 35 km (22 miles) from Khmelnitsky on the road to Vinnitsa, it stands at the point where the Buzhenka flows into the river Bug, its position being reflected in its name—mezhbuzhye means "between the Buzhenka and the Bug." The small and typically Ukrainian settlement was founded long ago by the first Russian princes. In the 12th

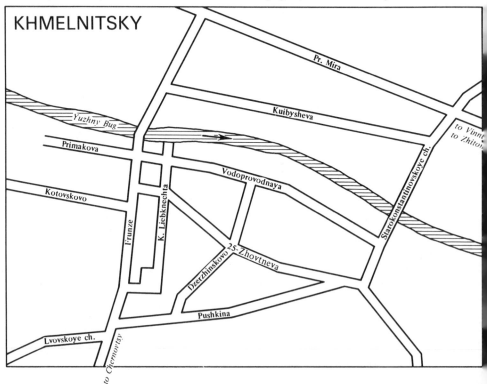

KHMELNITSKY

century, it was a large town of the princedom of Kiev and was mentioned in the chronicle of 1140 as Pozhye. Records tell how it was given to Prince Svyatoslav in 1146 and to Rostislav, son of Moscow's founder, Yuri Dolgoruky, in 1148. It changed hands many times after that until it became Lithuanian in the 14th century.

The 13th–14th century fortifications were replaced by a really strong castle in the 16th century, called Medzhibozh Fortress from 1516 onward. It stands on the hill above the river and was previously surrounded by a moat 6 m (20 ft) deep with a drawbridge leading to the castle. 3 of the 4 towers are still standing, the best preserved being that known as Skhidna, built on a rhomboid plan, which made it possible to shoot in all 4 directions. The castle withstood Mongol attacks on a number of occasions. In 1648 it was occupied by Cossacks under the leadership of Maxim Krivonos, and the Jews and Catholics in the town were put to death. In 1872 it was taken by the Turks and adapted to the Mohammedan faith, with a mosque and various Islamic sculptures inside the castle walls. The Poles captured it in 1699, and it was the property of Prince Czartoryjski's family for the latter part of the 18th century, being united with Russia in 1793. Catherine II's manifesto on the reunification of Podolia and the left-bank Ukraine under Russian rule was read aloud on the territory of the fortress. Russian soldiers were quartered in Medzhibozh from 1830.

Medzhibozh is a place held sacred by the Hasidic Jews. In 1736 the mystically inclined Israel ben Eliezer (c. 1700–1760), called the Ba'al Shem Tov or Basht (Master of the Good Name), settled here. He was already known as a healer, and now he dressed and lived very simply and taught in the marketplace, albeit with the strongest disapproval of the rabbinical leaders, that divinity could be found in the simplest human deeds. His charismatic character and clairvoyant powers made such a strong impression upon his followers that, although he left no writings, his discourses were recorded as the core of Hasidic literature, and his principles remained alive to give Judaism a new religious dimension.

Local Museum, inside the fortress. Open 9–7; closed Wed. There is restoration work in progress on the fortress.

Roman Catholic Church. 16th century. It is planned to open a panoramic exhibition in the church, showing the history of the town's defence against invaders.

Ioan Bogoslov Church, at the entrance to the fortress. Open for services.

St. Dmitry's Church can be seen across the river.

Obelisk, Zhovtneva Street. A memorial to fellow villagers who were killed during the Second World War.

Hotel, Shevchenko Street
Buzhok Restaurant, Zhovtneva Street
Uspenskaya Church
Troitskaya (Trinity) Church was built in 1632.

Letichev Population—10,000
The road from Medzhibozh runs over a bridge into Letichev, which was founded at the beginning of the 15th century, first mentioned in 1411 as a fortress and in 1429 as a settlement. From 1453 until the end of the 17th century, it was constantly under attack from the Tatars, particularly in 1516, 1558, and 1567. In 1598 the Polish nobleman Jan Potocki built a new stone castle in place of the old wooden fortress. It was reinforced with walls of stone and an outer palisade of oak to be proof against the Tatars. The wall and a single tower have survived. During Bogdan Khmelnitsky's warring against the Poles, the place suffered grievously from the Cossacks, the most dreadful attack being in 1777. In 1793 Letichev was united with Russia, and from 1796 it served as a regional centre. The coat-of-arms shows a wolf and was presented to the town by Stephan Batory in 1796. The wolf symbolises the river Volk (meaning "wolf") which runs through the town. The river is a tributary of the Yuzhny Bug.

St. Michael's Church was built in the 15th–16th centuries and open for services.

Uspenskaya (Assumption) Church, Lenin Street, the main throughfare. Built in 1546, rebuilt as a Catholic church in 1605 by Hetman Potocki, and restored in 1854. A wonder-working icon of the Virgin was brought to Letichev by Dominican monks at the end of the 15th century. It was taken to Lvov during the period of Bogdan Khmelnitsky's wars, returned to Letichev in 1723, and installed in this church. In 1778 Pope Clement XIV ordered by a special bull that the icon be crowned. The crown was brought from Rome, and the ceremony took place where the memorial column now stands. The pope also ordered the minting of a commemorative medal inscribed with Our Lady and St. Casimir.

Uspenskaya Church, Bellavina Street. Built in 1790.

Cemetery Church, dating from 1873. Ustin Karmalyuk (1787–1835), who led Ukrainian national uprisings in the 19th century, is buried in Letichev.

Synagogue, Bazarnaya Square, on the right
Local Museum, in the House of Culture
War Memorial, on the left of Bazarnaya Square. Dedicated to those who lost their lives in World War II.

Chaika Restaurant, 50-Zhovtneva Street, by the lake

Shepetovka Population—42,000
This lies 120 km (75 miles) north of Khmelnitsky.

Shepetovka was a settlement inhabited by steppe people. The high Scythian barrows covering rich burial mounds can still be seen around it. It was first mentioned in 1594. Shepetovka was destroyed more than once by war. In the 19th century, it was the site of a large fair, and the sugar industry gained in importance. Since it consisted mostly of wooden houses, it suffered from numerous fires. It was proclaimed a town in 1923.

Local industry includes machine building,

sugar making, and meat and dairy production. At present Shepetovka is a district centre and a large railway junction.

Ostrovsky Museum. Nikolai Ostrovsky (1904–36), a Civil War hero and outstanding Soviet writer, who first came to Shepetovka in 1911, when he was 7 years old. He visited again in 1924. Ostrovsky was paralysed and by 1929 blind, and had to dictate his famous novel "How the Steel Was Tempered." The story, about Pavel Korchagin, is partly a biography of the writer. It remained a best-seller for a decade after it appeared in the 1930s, and has been known as a favourite Soviet children's book. Ostrovsky died young from polyarthritis. His memorial museum was opened in 1946.

Ostrovsky Monument, on one of Shepetovka's central squares. This monument to the writer by Znoba was unveiled in 1970.

Kotik Monument. Valentin Kotik (1930–44) was a 13-year-old boy who acted as a scout for the partisans during the occupation. He was posthumously awarded the title of Hero of the Soviet Union.

Yubileiny Restaurant, in the town centre

KHOBI

See Sukhumi, p. 517.

KHOLMSK

See Yuzhno-Sakhalinsk, p. 676.

KHOSTA

See Sochi, p. 493.

KHOTIN Population—11,000
(Romanian: Chotin)

Intourist organises excursions here from Chernovtsy, 70 km (43 miles) away, as part of the trip to Kamenets-Podolsky.

The name of Khotin is thought to stem from that of the Dacian khan Khotizon, who, according to a legend, founded the town in the 8th century A.D. Russian chronicles, however, maintain that it derives from the Russian khotim ("we want"), which may have given the Turks the idea of renaming the Moldavian town of Tighin as Bendery (meaning "I want" in Turkish).

Archaeological finds in the vicinity date from the 3rd millennium B.C. to the 13th century, and later a trade route between Moldavia and Poland ran this way, linking up with Turkey and Persia. The present town stands on the right bank of the Dniester, but the mighty stone fortress is 2 km (1 mile) from the centre, on the northern outskirts of the town. It was founded in the 14th century by the Genoese to protect their trade route and became one of the strongest fortifications in eastern Europe in the Middle Ages. Although part of the principality of Moldavia, it changed hands several times over a period of 250 years, between the Moldavians, the Poles, and the Turks.

The Khotin Gospels now displayed in the manuscript section of Leningrad's Saltykov-Schedrin Library were copied in the 15th century. Khotin

was vital in protecting Northern Bukovina from Poland, but the Poles took it in 1538, destroying the southern part and the gate tower and partly demolishing the round tower in the southwest. The fortress was restored and enlarged in 1540–44, and the southern wall and a tower remain from that time. Trade flourished in the shadow of the mighty walls, and Khotin became renowned for its fairs. A clash of territorial interests between Turkey and Poland at the beginning of the 17th century gave rise to a series of Turko-Polish wars, the principal battle taking place here in 1621, when the Ukrainian Cossacks were asked to assist the Poles. An army of 40,000 was mustered and led to victory by Sagaidachny. The Battle of Khotin was featured in folk songs and was described by Russian, Polish, and Ukrainian writers as well as by Soviet authors and artists. In the subsequent peace treaty, Sultan Osman II of Turkey agreed that the Turkish-Polish frontier should follow the line of the Dniester, which meant that Khotin was once again Turkish. Russian-Turkish wars continued through the 17th–19th centuries, with Khotin changing hands 4 times. The castle was again reinforced in 1718, when it was held by the Turks, this time by French engineers. They designed a new fortress of earth and stone alongside the old structure.

Mikhail Lomonosov, poet and naturalist, wrote a special ode dedicated to the Russian victory at Khotin in 1739. The Turks were driven out for the last time in 1806, and the Treaty of Bucharest of 1812 declared Khotin a Russian town. Its economic development burgeoned as trade relationships were established with many Russian towns and the river port was enlarged.

From 1918 to 1940, Khotin was part of Romania. The use of either the Ukrainian or the Russian language was strictly punished, and the severity of the rule gave rise to the Khotin Uprising of 1919; the insurgents held Khotin for 10 days and British and French troops helped to restore order. During World War II, when Khotin was in occupied territory, many townspeople were shot and some hundreds were deported to Germany.

Local industry includes oil, food products, electrical goods, clothing, textiles, and souvenirs.

Castle, along Lenin Street and then Krepostnaya Street. The outer walls are stone-built, decorated with brickwork and now topped with earth. Apart from the ancient Genoese tower, there remain a partly demolished Turkish minaret and a deep well, now dry.

Nothing is left of the newer fortress except the *Alexander Nevsky Church,* which was built in 1835 for the Russian garrison and which has been restored. In the dungeons below the older structures, there were prisons where many people were tortured to death. In 1490–92 the participants of a peasant uprising led by a certain Mukha spent time in the dungeons before they were thrown down 60 m (197 ft) to their deaths from the top of the Northern Tower. The upper floor was used as a small church, and the interior walls still bear fragments of the 15th–16th-century frescoes. The castle walls are 5 m (16 ft) thick, and the largest of the towers is the Northern Tower. The other 4 are the Gate, Eastern, Commandant, and Southwestern Towers. Return to town along Krepostnaya and Lenin streets.

Pokrovskaya (Intercession) Church, Lenin Street 15

History and Revolution Museum, Lenin Street 17. Established in 1963; open 10–6; closed Mon.

Carpet Factory, 28th-June Street. Khotin rugs and carpets usually have geometrical designs. They are well known throughout the country.

Lenin Monument, in the town centre

Komsomol Monument, in the main square. This memorial to Khotin's Young Communists was unveiled in 1969. It is in the form of a column of red granite and bronze, designed by Flit and sculpted by Egorov.

Obelisk, Karl Marx Street. A World War II memorial

Soldiers' Grave, on Lenin Street, near the obelisk. This is the common grave of a number of Soviet soldiers.

Hotel, Lenin Street 72

Dnieper Restaurant, 28th-June Street 77

Stara Fortetsya Restaurant, in the main square

GPO, Komsomolskaya Street 58

KIDEKSHA
See Suzdal, p. 518.

KIEV
The city of Kiev is the capital of the Ukraine.

UKRAINIAN SOVIET SOCIALIST REPUBLIC

The Ukraine, known as Ukrayina in Ukrainian, is situated in the southwest of the European part of the USSR and shares its western frontier with Rumania, Hungary, Czechoslovakia, and Poland. After the Russian Federation, its population of 51,704,000 is the second-largest in the USSR, and in size it is the third-largest republic (after the Russian Federation and Kazakhstan), covering an area of 601,000 sq km (232,000 sq miles). 46 percent of the population is urban. The majority are Ukrainians (73.6 percent), then come Russians (21.1 percent), Jews (1.3 percent), and relatively small numbers of Byelorussians, Poles, Moldovans, and Bulgarians. By nationality the Ukrainians are Eastern Slavs, closely related to the Russians and Byelorussians.

Since the Kievan period of Ukrainian history, some distinctive features have developed in local speech. Now the Ukrainian language, which is similar to Russian and Byelorussian, is used. With the exception of Lvov, Russian is spoken mostly in the big cities.

The Ukraine was the cradle of the Kiev state. It was in Kiev that Christianity was introduced into Russia when Prince Vladimir had his subjects baptised in the river Dnieper in 988, in the stretch opposite the modern bathing beach. After the Tatar invasion and the decline of the Kievan state (13th–14th century) the Ukraine changed masters several times, being held by Russia and Poland. Then it was devastated by the Crimean Tatars. In the 16th century Ukrainian hatred rose against the Polish landlords, who were unpopular because they took the most fertile land for themselves and tried to introduce Catholicism. In 1654 the Cossacks, the most militant members of the Ukrainian population at the time, led by Hetman (Cossack military leader) Bogdan Khmelnitsky, won independence from Poland and established a state of their own, which occupied the central part of the present-day Ukraine. Then, as the new state could not possibly stand alone, it chose to unite with Muscovy, the agreement being signed at the end of 1654.

Nationalist feelings and demands for the autonomy of the Ukraine developed at the beginning of the 20th century. During the Civil War of 1918–22, the Ukraine was one of the most fiercely contested areas. It was under both German and White Russian occupation and had different nationalist governments. The Ukrainian Soviet Republic was first proclaimed in December 1917, and in 1922 it was one of the 4 original republics to form the USSR.

In 1939 the western part of the Ukraine was included in the republic, followed by Transcarpathia (formerly part of Hungary and Czechoslovakia) in 1945 and the Crimea (formerly part of the Russian Federation) in 1954.

The Ukraine can be divided into 3 soil and vegetation zones: (1) mixed forests on the Byelorussian boundary in the north; (2) wooded steppe with oak and beech forests; and (3) steppe. The zones are notable for their predominantly fertile black earth. The moderate continental climate is much warmer than that of central Russia, and the southern coast of the Crimea has a Mediterranean climate.

The Ukraine is highly developed both industrially and agriculturally. The main crops are wheat, barley, rye, oats, sugarbeet, and sunflowers. Between 1910 and 1914, the Ukraine yielded 80 percent of Europe's sugar. There are also many orchards. The main industries include engineering, metallurgy, coal mining, and chemicals. It is also very rich in natural deposits, which include coal, iron ore, natural gas, manganese, oil, and mercury.

Besides Kiev, the capital, the major cities are Kharkov, Lvov, Odessa, Donetsk, Dnepropetrovsk, and Lugansk.

Some words of Ukrainian:

Hello	dobri dyen
I am a tourist	ya tourist
please	bood laska
thank you	dyakooyoo
yes	tuk
no	nee
good	dobri
bad	poháno
I don't understand	ya ne razoomayoo

I need an inter-	meni potriben
preter	tolmach
goodbye	do pobáchenya

Kiev Population—2,600,000

The Ukrainian capital has long covered a series of wooded hills on the right bank of the river Dnieper.

> Away above me, towering high,
> Old Kiev guards her river.
> At the steep wood's foot doth Dnieper lie,
> His water rippling silver.

The city now has an area of over 75,000 hectares (187,500 acres), which also includes the industrial district of Darnitsa, which has grown up on the left bank of the river. This region is connected with the rest of Kiev by the Paton Bridge. In Darnitsa Forest, on the site of the Darnitsa concentration camp, a Memorial Complex by Malinovsky and Moskaltsev was unveiled in 1968.

Kiev is said to have got its name from the first prince of the Slav tribe, the Polyani, who lived in this area. He was called Ki, and with his brothers he founded the town at the end of the 5th century. In 864 Askold and Dir made themselves masters of the region, and the city-state of Kiev grew and prospered from 882 until 1169. Mostly due to the hilly site, the town's early development was unusual. It consisted of three separate settlements. The Upper City (Staro-Kiev) overlooked the Podol, meaning "low," which was the trading area close to the Dnieper. The third settlement was also on high ground above the river but set at some distance behind Staro-Kiev; this was Pechersk, where vast natural caves are to be found. Hermits lived in them first, and then the Monastery of the Caves was founded and used them. In spite of the divided layout of the town, Kiev was strong enough to become the capital of the country and the trading centre of eastern Europe. Situated on the navigable river Dnieper, Kiev had trading relations with the countries of western Europe and the Baltic as well as Armenia, Constantinople, and Arabia. Its importance gave rise to a Russian proverb, reminiscent of "All roads lead to Rome," saying, "Your tongue will lead you to Kiev," meaning you had but to ask the way.

But it was during the reign of Prince Vladimir (978–1015) that the Golden Age of Kiev began. In 988 Prince Vladimir introduced Christianity into Russia, but his choice of Christianity as the national religion was not an easy one. According to chronicles, he was a violent man, "insatiable in vice," and a fanatical heathen who had offered thousands of human sacrifices. But he was also a thinker, and although there is no record of his reasons for seeking a new religion, it is fairly clear that as an intelligent monarch he saw that the peoples who remained outside the world's great religions never achieved any degree of culture, civilisation, or political power.

The legend runs that Vladimir considered many religions before finally choosing Christianity. The Jewish faith was admirable, but the thought that its followers had been scattered throughout the earth for their sins distressed the Russian prince. He rejected Islam on the grounds that total abstinence was incompatible with survival in a cold climate. Roman Catholicism he could not accept because he himself would have become subservient to the pope. The emissaries Prince Vladimir sent to find out about the Greek Orthodox church reported on their return, "The Greeks led us to the edifices where they worship their God; and we knew not whether we were in heaven or on earth. For on earth there is no such splendour or beauty, and we are at a loss how to describe it. We only know that God dwells there among men, and their service is fairer than the ceremonies of other nations. We can never forget that beauty." Accordingly, Vladimir was baptized, married to Princess Anna, sister of the Greek emperor, and adopted Orthodoxy as the religion for the country as a whole. Mass baptism took place in the Dnieper, even though it was mid-winter, and Prince Vladimir was canonised for his part in the conversions.

The acceptance of Christianity brought Kiev into closer contact with Byzantium, and Kiev adopted both the autocratic government and the architecture of Constantinople.

There were many rival city-states, and constant wars raged between them. In 1169 Kiev gave way to the city of Vladimir, and the title of capital was lost (at this early date Moscow was still a small settlement of no consequence). After its early period of glory, Kiev fell into a decline. A series of fires devastated the city during the 12th century, and in 1240 it was plundered by the Tatars. An Italian traveller who visited Kiev 6 years later wrote that most of the churches had been burned and that only 200 houses remained. Kiev remained under the Tatar yoke until 1320 and was invaded again in the 15th century. It was also badly damaged by Lithuanian and Polish forces and was under Lithuanian rule from 1320 to 1455.

Kiev only recovered again after the unification of the Ukraine and Russia in 1654, when it was proclaimed that they "should be one forever." It then became a city of merchants. Many magnificent buildings were erected in the 17th and 18th centuries, a large number of them in baroque style, among them the Klovsky and the Maryinsky palaces. The city spread along the river, and its original 3 settlements were quickly surrounded by houses and other buildings, but it was not until the 19th century that Kiev was elevated to the status of provincial centre. The city's growth was temporarily halted by a series of fires, the most disastrous of which was in 1811. It raged for several days and Podol, the most densely inhabited part of Kiev, suffered particularly badly. This is one reason for the lack of ancient monuments in that region; the other is that it was an area never surrounded by adequate defences, which had always been subject to terrible devastation by invaders.

In May 1812 the general reconstruction of the

KIEV (Lavra; Monastery of the Caves)

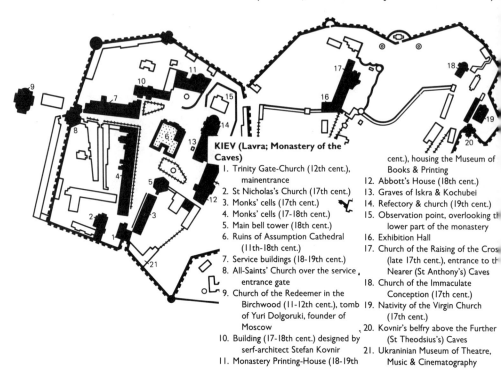

KIEV (Lavra; Monastery of the Caves)

1. Trinity Gate-Church (12th cent.), main entrance
2. St Nicholas's Church (17th cent.)
3. Monks' cells (17th cent.)
4. Monks' cells (17-18th cent.)
5. Main bell tower (18th cent.)
6. Ruins of Assumption Cathedral (11th-18th cent.)
7. Service buildings (18-19th cent.)
8. All-Saints' Church over the service entrance gate
9. Church of the Redeemer in the Birchwood (11-12th cent.), tomb of Yuri Dolgoruki, founder of Moscow
10. Building (17-18th cent.) designed by serf-architect Stefan Kovnir
11. Monastery Printing-House (18-19th cent.), housing the Museum of Books & Printing
12. Abbott's House (18th cent.)
13. Graves of Iskra & Kochubei
14. Refectory & church (19th cent.)
15. Observation point, overlooking the lower part of the monastery
16. Exhibition Hall
17. Church of the Raising of the Cross (late 17th cent.), entrance to the Nearer (St Anthony's) Caves
18. Church of the Immaculate Conception (17th cent.)
19. Nativity of the Virgin Church (17th cent.)
20. Kovnir's belfry above the Further (St Theodsius's) Caves
21. Ukrainian Museum of Theatre, Music & Cinematography

city began, and by the middle of the 19th century, the central part of Kiev had wide, well-planned streets with plenty of attractive buildings lining them. Kiev became modernised, and a number of factories were built on the other side of the Dnieper. The first of Kiev's annual contract fairs were held in 1889. These brought merchants to Kiev from all over Europe. By 1888 they found a telephone service in operation, while in 1892 the first trains in Russia (the second in Europe) began to run from the city. As well as being the administrative and economic centre of the southwest part of the Russian empire, Kiev was also the hub of the Ukrainian literary and national movement. By 1917 its population had reached half a million.

After the October Revolution and during the 1918–20 Civil War, Kiev was the seat of several transitory Ukrainian governments. It was occupied by the Germans for a short while in 1918. When the Ukraine joined the Soviet Union in 1922, Kharkov was made the capital; the seat of government was transferred to Kiev only in 1934.

In spite of severe damage during the Second World War, when 195,000 Kievans lost their lives, and despite the drastic rebuilding necessary after it, the 3 old divisions of the city still exist and have retained their individuality.

Kreschatik is the city's central street, and its busiest. In the old days, the site of the street was a deep, wooded valley crossed by ravines. It was known as Kreschata, meaning "crossed," and from this the street's present name is derived. The street is less than 2 km (1 mile) long, but over 350 buildings were destroyed in this part of Kiev during the war. Afterwards its width was doubled, and it was completely rebuilt. Very few of the old houses remain. No. 8 was the Petersburg Bank and was designed by Benois. No. 10 was the Volgo-Kama Bank, and No. 15 was, and still is, an arcade of shops. Both the latter were designed by Andreyev, and all three were built in 1911–14.

Kirov Street runs through the Staro-Kiev part of the city, between Kreschatik and the riverside parks. Here the building of the *Ukrainian Parliament* stands out, with its 6-columned portico and its great glass dome. It was built in 1939 and designed by Zabolotny. Next to it, behind ornamental iron railings, is the former Tsar's Palace, built in 1742 following Rastrelli's design but enlarged and reconstructed in 1870. It is used partly by the Supreme Soviet and partly as a guest house for important visitors to the Ukrainian capital. This area is still known by its ancient name of Lipki ("lime trees"). It used to be the old aristocratic quarter, and a number of ornately decorated noble mansions remain.

Volodimerska Street runs parallel to Kreschatik on the side farthest from the Dnieper. Most of the ancient monuments of Kiev are to be found here. Apart from the best known including the Golden

Gate and St. Sophia's Cathedral (see below), No. 54 is a fine *mansion* built in the 1850s by Beretti; it is now the seat of the praesidium of the Ukrainian Academy of Sciences. No. 57 was built as a pedagogical museum by Alyoshin in 1911 and reconstructed in 1939. The *university building*, No. 58, was designed by Beretti and constructed in 1837–42.

Apart from the usual forms of public transport, a *funicular railway* runs down from Volodimerska Girka to Podol. It was first built in 1905. Kievans are also proud to have the Soviet Union's third metro. It was opened in November 1960.

Kiev is unlike most of the ancient cities and towns of Russia in that there are no obvious remains of a Kremlin or a fortified citadel. The *Golden Gate* in the centre of the town, said to have been inspired by Constantinople's Golden Gate, is almost the only reminder of the way the city had to fight for its very existence. For many years there were only ruins here, 2 parallel walls built in 1037 by Yaroslav the Wise to support the main entrance arch into the earthen-walled city of Kiev. These were incorporated in reconstruction work, and now the arch is again surmounted by the small Church of the Annunciation.

St. Sophia's Cathedral (Sofiisky Sobor), Volodimerska St. 24. Open 10–6, closed Thurs. The cathedral, founded on the tomb of Dir, was dedicated in 1037 by Yaroslav the Wise in gratitude for the victory he gained on this site (then an open meadow outside the city walls) over the Pechenegi, an invading tribe from the east. It was here that the country's earliest historical chronicles were written and the first library organised.

The design of the cathedral was influenced by St. Sophia in Constantinople, but the Kievan cathedral also contains elements of early wooden architecture. When first built, the cathedral was a large 5-aisled building with an open gallery on 3 sides and 13 cupolas. The first Metropolitan of Kiev, Illarion, wrote of the cathedral in 1037, "This church has roused the astonishment and praise of all people around, and nothing like unto it can be found in the breadth of the land from east to west."

Interesting mosaics and frescoes are to be seen in the central part of the cathedral and in the main dome. The latter contains a mosaic representation of Christ the All-Ruler, the Pantokrator, not the realistic Christ of the Gospels, but a being very closely akin to the other two members of the Trinity. The archangels surrounding him are dressed in the costume of the imperial court at Byzantium and hold the symbols of the imperial office, the orb and standard. In the apse of the cathedral is the magnificent Virgin Orans, another symbolic figure in mosaic. She is neither the Queen of Heaven nor the Mother of God, but a symbol of the earthly Church interceding for mankind. Both the figure and the splendid golden background survived the ups and downs of the cathedral, so that a legend grew up about the wall's indestructibility, and the Virgin Orans became an increasingly important object of worship. Below the Virgin Orans are depicted the 12 apostles receiving the eucharist and below them are the Fathers of the Church.

In the cathedral's central aisle is a portrait of the family of Yaroslav the Wise and on the walls of the southern and northern towers are pictures of entertainment and hunting and battle scenes. In the northeastern part of the cathedral is a marble tomb where in 1054 Yaroslav the Wise was buried.

The cathedral was partly ruined by Tatars and Mongols and was further damaged while the Poles and Lithuanians were ruling the region. It was restored in 1636 and reconstructed at the beginning of the 18th century, when 6 new domes were added. The iconostasis was installed in 1754 and is the work of local craftsmen. After the unification of the Ukraine and Russia in 1654, it was in the cathedral that the Kievans pledged their oath of loyalty. It was also here that Peter the Great celebrated his victory over the Swedish army in 1709. The acoustics are magnificent—any opportunity to hear them put to the test is recommended.

Of the 18th-century buildings, the most outstanding is the 4-storey *belltower* near the main entrance. It was erected between 1744 and 1752 and is 78 m (256 ft) high. Also of interest is the *Zabrovsky Gate*, built in 1745 as the main entrance to the Metropolitan's house. It is decorated with elaborate detail and stucco ornament but has lost its original proportions, as the ground level has risen considerably during the past 200 years. The *Metropolitan's House* was built at the beginning of the 18th century in the Ukrainian baroque style. To the south of the cathedral is the *refectory*, built in 1722–30.

The wall surrounding the cathedral was built in the 1740s.

The Sophia Cathedral is now a museum, which also displays the architecture of the other old Russian towns of Novgorod and Chernigov and local archaeological finds. All its precincts are kept as an architectural and historical monument.

The Monastery of the Caves (Pecherskaya Lavra, after "peschera," meaning "cave"), Sichneve Povstannya Street 21. Every visitor to Kiev should certainly try to see this monastery, back in church hands again. It has been described as the place:

Where the darkness of the silent caves
Is livelier than the royal halls.

It was founded in 1051 by two monks, Antony and Theodosius, and through the centuries underground churches were built. In some cases the caves were natural, and then the monks themselves excavated further. Some of the members of the community lived their lives there underground, and when they died their bodies remained in the cells. Due to the temperature and the chemical properties of the soil, the bodies became mummified, and they are still to be seen. "The whole Orthodox world bows before the relics of the saints of the monastery; in times past and today, undiminished their blessing emanates upon all who come to their tombs in faith and love."

From the time of Peter the Great and throughout the 18th and 19th centuries, almost all the tsars and tsarinas came to Kiev and made lavish gifts to the Lavra, the other monasteries, and the churches of the city. The monastery became exceedingly wealthy; in the 18th century, it owned 13 smaller monasteries, 7 towns, 189 villages, and 3 glass factories.

The entrance gate is surmounted by the *Trinity Church*, which was built in 1108 and contains frescoes and a wooden iconostasis dating from the 18th century. The walls of the *Upper Monastery*, built between 1698 and 1701, run from this gateway.

Inside, a little way on from the entrance gate, a much smaller archway on the left leads through to an enclosed corner of the monastery grounds surrounding the *Church of St. Nicholas*, built in 1696 in Ukrainian baroque style and brought here from its original site over Askold's grave. It now serves as a lecture hall, but its appearance is good; it was restored in 1956–57, right up to its blue, star-bedecked dome.

The five-domed *All Saints' Church* by another gateway was built in the 17th century by the architect Aksamitov. The iconostasis dates from the end of the 18th century and the murals from 1906 (restored in 1973). The main court of the Upper Monastery centres around the *Cathedral of the Assumption (Uspensky Sobor)*, built in 1073–89. It was blown up during the Second World War but is now being rebuilt. Most of the surrounding houses date from the 18th century. In some of these houses were the printing works of the monastery, which printed its first book in 1617 and continued to function until the revolution. The architectural complex of the Upper Monastery is completed by the *belltower*, which was built in 1731–45 by St. Petersburg architect Shedel. At 96.5 m (317 ft), it is the highest belltower in Russia. The 4 tiers of the tower are all decorated with pillars and pilasters, and a flight of 374 steps leads to the top. Although the tower was constructed in comparatively recent times, there is nevertheless a legend about its construction. It is supposed to have been built by 12 brothers, who are now buried in the caves. During construction the tower sank slowly into the earth, thus obviating the use of ladders or scaffolding. When it was completed, it sprang out of the earth in a single night.

The way down to the caves leads past the *refectory church*, which was built in 1893 on the site of an older stone building. It was restored in 1956 and is used as a concert hall, while the actual refectory is a Museum of Atheism.

Near the walls of the refectory are the graves of the Cossack leaders Judge Kotchubei and Colonel Iskra, executed in 1708 by Ivan Mazepa because they informed Peter the Great of the Ukrainian hetman's plan to separate the Ukraine from Russia with the help of Charles XII of Sweden and the Zaporozhye Cossacks. Following Mazepa's own treachery, Peter the Great had their mortal remains transferred from their original graves to holy ground. Mazepa's ambitious plan was defeated the

following year when the Russian army won the Battle of Poltava.

A last diversion before going down to the caves is to walk onto a wide stone terrace on the right, which has a most impressive view over the wooded slopes, the wide river, the spreading suburbs of Kiev, and the countryside beyond.

The *Nearer Caves*, sometimes referred to as *St. Anthony's Caves*, contain 73 tombs and 3 underground churches. In the *Further Caves*, or *St. Theodosius's Caves*, there are 3 more churches and 47 tombs. They are quite separate from each other. The *Belfry of the Further Caves* was built in the 18th century by a serf-architect named Stefan Kovnir, who also designed one of the houses in the Upper Monastery.

From 1926 to 1964, the whole territory was open to the public as a museum, with monks caring for it and acting as guides. On entering the caves, visitors were asked to purchase a small candle instead of an admission ticket. Then the monks had to leave. Electric light was installed, and the insides of the caves were painted. The mummified bodies still had their names attached, but many of them were further described on antireligious plaques. In 1988 these holiest of shrines were returned to the Orthodox church as part of the millennial celebrations (since the adoption of Christianity by Prince Vladimir in 988). The most famous tomb of all is probably that of the chronicler Nestor, who died in 1115.

Historical Treasures of the Ukraine, a museum housed in the building of the monastery bakery. Open 10–5; closed Tues. The items on display date from the 6th to 19th centuries. There is jewellery and coins from the ancient Scythian settlements on the northern coast of the Black Sea as well as pieces of Greek and Roman origin. Here also is the best collection of coins belonging to Kiev Rus. Next door, in the former printing shop of the Lavra, is the *Museum of the History of Ukrainian Books and Printing*, open 10–6; closed Tues. The oldest manuscripts here date from the 12th century. Nearby also is the *Ukrainian Folk Art Museum*, open 10–5:45; closed Tues. Here are exhibits of the embroidery and other handicrafts of the 16th–20th centuries. The *Museum of Theatre, Music and Cinematography* (open 10–5:45; closed Tues.) is another rich collection within the old monastery walls.

A little to the north of the monastery stands the early 12th-century *Church of the Redeemer in the Birchwood (Tserkov Spas-na-Berestove)*. The eastern part dates from 1640–43 and contains frescoes of that time. The older part was formerly a sepulchre for the princes of Kiev, and in 1157 Prince Yuri Dolgoruki, who had founded Moscow 10 years earlier, was buried here. The grey marble tomb now commemorating him was intalled in 1947 to mark Moscow's 800th anniversary. It weighs 6 tons. The church is open as a museum.

Vydubetsy Monastery is situated on the higher bank of the river Dnieper, south of the Monastery of the Caves, and is part of the land belonging to the Academy of Sciences' Botanical Garden. This architectural complex was founded in 1070–77 by Prince Vsevolod, and there is a story attached to its unusual name. After the mass conversion of Kievans to Christianity, the powerful pagan idol Perun was thrown into the Dnieper. He was carved out of wood, but his head was silver and his beard was gold, and apparently the weight of the metal kept him underwater. For some time his distressed followers ran along the river bank shouting, "Vydubai, come out of the water, O God!" A mile farther down he did in fact rise to the surface, but there was much confusion and fighting on the bank as the newly baptised Christians were all for letting him continue his journey downstream. It was from the shouts of "vydubai" that the whole area was thereafter known as Vydubichi, as was the monastery.

The complex overlooks Vydubetsky Lake, which is used for boating in summer. The road runs uphill beside the walls and turns left at the top to reach the entrance gate. Inside and right across the enclosure, overlooking the lake, is *St. Michael's Cathedral* (1070–88). Only the western side, which has good fescoes, remained after a landslide in the 15th century, but the building has recently been reconstructed, as has the monastery well. *St. George's Church* (1696–1701) is a 5-domed masterpiece of Ukrainian architecture. The refectory dates from the beginning of the 18th century, and the belfry was built in 1730. Between St. Michael's and St. George's is the grave of Konstantin Ushinsky (1824–70), Russian teacher and educationalist.

Mikhailovsky-Zlatoverkhy Monastery (St. Michael-with-the-Golden Roof), Geroyev Revolutsii Street. The monastery was founded in 1051. Its cathedral, founded by Prince Svyatopolk in 1108, is Kiev's second-most important construction of this period, after Sofiisky Sobor. Part of a mosaic of the Last Supper remains.

St. Andrew's Church, Andreyevsky Spusk 33. Open, as a museum, 10–5:30; closed Thurs. This church was built in 1744–53 in baroque style by Rastrelli, renowned court architect of St. Petersburg and master of the baroque. It stands on Andreyevsky Hill, the highest point of old Kiev, overlooking Podol, the river, and the plain to the east. The site is said to have been chosen for the erection of a cross by the apostle Andrew himself, when he first preached the Gospel in Russia. There were Christian churches built at Kerch (Tanais) and Khersones by the Black Sea in the 1st century A.D., which were reputed to date from St. Andrew's missionary visit.

The church stands on a platform reached by a broad flight of steps. It was built at the command of Peter the Great's religious daughter, Elizaveta. It is outstanding for its perfect proportions as well as for the way in which it makes use of the hilltop upon which it stands. Today the domes are green with gilded trim, the walls decorated with blue and gold. Inside, the iconostasis is interesting; it was made under the guidance of portrait-painter An-

tropov, who was also responsible for the frescoes. The church was restored in 1982 to celebrate the 1,500th anniversary of the founding of Kiev.

Volodimersky Sobor (St. Vladimir's Cathedral), Shevchenko Boulevard 20. This cathedral with 7 cupolas was built in Byzantine style in 1863–96 by Beretti and Gernhardt to commemorate the 900th anniversary of Christianity in Russia. Sparro was another architect who participated in the church later. The completed building shows a diversity of styles, which resulted from frequent changes of plan. The original idea was to follow the lines of ancient Russian architecture. It is 49 m (54 yds) long, 28 m (31 yds) wide, and 50 m (164 ft) in height. The windows are framed with fine stone ornamentation. The walls bear some interesting murals in imitation of Byzantine style. The decorations were carried out under the supervision of Professor Prakhov, a specialist in the history of art, and include some paintings by famous artists, Vasnetsov and Nesterov among others. Vasnetsov's portrayal of the Virgin and Child breaks away from the traditional Russian icon interpretation. In the central aisle is a painting called "The Christening of Russia," showing Prince Vladimir and Princess Olga and the mass baptism taking place. The paintings were restored after the Second World War. It is worthwhile attending a service here to hear one of the best church choirs in the Soviet Union.

St. Kirill's Church, Frunze Street 103. Open, as a museum, 10–6; closed Thurs. This church was founded on the northern outskirts of Kiev in 1146 as the main church of St. Kirill's Monastery, itself founded in 1140 by Prince Vsevolod. It has been restored several times, and its shape dates from the 18th-century reconstruction by Beretti. The 12th-century frescoes were restored in the 1880s under the direction of Professor A. Prakhov, and Vrubel worked under him. Vrubel's murals show the weeping over Christ's coffin, and the iconostasis was painted by him too. His "Entry to Jerusalem" is through the main arch and up, on the immediate right. Upstairs, in the choir gallery, is the descent of the Holy Spirit upon the apostles, with the white of their clothing appearing in mother-of-pearl colours, just like the glazes Vrubel used on ceramics. Around the Holy Spirit mural are a number of panels with Old Testament prophets, judges, and kings.

St. Flor's Convent, Podol, Florivska Street 6/8. This convent dates from the foundation of the church of SS. Flor and Lavr near Kiselevka Hill in the 16th century. It was exceedingly prosperous at the end of the 18th century, but a disastrous fire in 1811 burned down most of the buildings. The *Church of the Ascension (Voznesenskaya Tserkov)* is still open for services. Opposite stands the 17th–18th-century refectory. The belltower was built between 1740 and 1821. The *Resurrection Church*, which is white with 6 columns, was built in 1824 by Melensky for the use of the hospital run by the sisters. It is now closed.

Convent of the Intercession (Pokrova), Bekhterevsky Pereulok 15, near Artyoma Street. The convent was founded in 1889, and in the same year the Pokrovsky Church was built. In St. Nicholas's Church, built in 1896–1911, is the wonder-working icon of Our Lady of Pochayev. Today the convent is the home of some 140 nuns and most of the buildings on the convent's territory are used by a state hospital.

There are two other churches in Podol, the *Bratskaya* or *Bogoyavlenskaya (Epiphany) Church* (1710), which is closed, and the ancient *Church of the Prophet Elijah*, which is open for services. It is said to have been built by Askold as the country's very first Christian church, but other sources attribute it to Olga, following her baptism in A.D. 957.

Novonikolayevskaya Roman Catholic Church, Chervonoarmeiskaya Street 75. Built in 1913 and restored recently. The organ was built by Riger-Closs of Czechoslovakia, and the church now serves as the House of Organ and Chamber Music; there are seats for 750.

Synagogue, Moskovskaya Street 29. The building was constructed in the mid-19th century and is still open for services. Nearby in Podol, at Yaroslavov Val 7, is the House of Actors, built in 1900 in Mauritanian style by Gorodetsky as a Karaim Kinass (temple). It was used as a cinema until 1982. Another good example of Gorodetsky's work is a building on Ordzhonikidze Street decorated with rhinoceroses and frogs.

The Academy of Free Sciences, established by the order of Peter the Great, built at the beginning of the 18th century and now state protected, used to house a branch of the State Public Library of the Ukrainian Academy of Sciences.

Kosoi Kaponir Museum, Gospitalnaya Street 24. Open 9:30–6; closed Mon. Kosoi Kaponir was built in 1844 as part of Novaya Pechorskaya Fortress. Half is underground, and the walls are of stone and brick. Instead of stretching out, parallel to the earthen rampart, it ran at an angle and so earned the name kosoi, meaning "slanting." It was first used as an armoury, but in the 1860s it served as a political prison. The exhibition tells of the history of the fortress in the 18th and 19th centuries and of the 1905–7 revolution in Kiev.

Museum of Oriental and Western Art, Repin Street 15. Open 10–6; closed Wed. The collection includes Byzantine paintings of the 6th and 8th centuries; Italian Renaissance art, including works by Bellini, Tiepolo, and Guardi; Flemish and Dutch art of the 15th to 18th centuries, including works by Frans Hals and Rembrandt; and works by Velasquez, Goya, Bouchet, and David.

Museum of Russian Art, Repin Street 11. Open 10–6; closed Thurs. The section of Russian art from the 12th to 17th centuries includes icons of the Novgorod, Moscow, and Stroganov schools. The 18th–19th century section contains works by Brullov, Ivanov, Shishkin, and Repin. The first quarter of the 20th century is represented by Vrubel, Serov, and Korovin, among others. Another section shows Soviet art. There is an interesting

collection of 18th–20th-century porcelain, glass, and crystal. The very imposing house was once the home of the Tereschenko family, sugar millionaires from Glukhov.

Museum of Ukrainian Applied Art, Kirov Street 6. Open 10–6; closed Fri. The museum was built under the supervision of academician Nikolayev in 1898–1900. It was supposed to resemble an ancient Greek temple, and the huge granite steps, over 17 m (19 yds) wide, which lead to the main façade have lions at each side. The 6-columned portico in antique style is decorated with a sculptured group called "The Triumph of Art." The first section of the museum is devoted to Ukrainian art of the 15th–19th centuries; the second section, to works by Soviet Ukrainian artists.

Historical Museum, Volodimerska Street 2. Open 10–6; closed Wed. The museum contains over 500,000 exhibits, dating from prehistoric times to the present day. Of particular interest are the sections on the Scythians and Kievan Rus. Here are examples of 17th- to 20th-century fabrics and 16th- to 19th-century handwork. There are also wood carvings, metalwork, and ceramics on view, all displayed to demonstrate Ukrainian artwork. Particularly interesting are the krashenki, intricately painted eggs to be exchanged at Easter time. Some rooms here are reserved for temporary art exhibitions. (A branch of the historical museum is also housed in the Monastery of Caves.)

Ukrainian World War II Memorial Museum, Sichneve Povstannya Street 33. Open 10–5; closed Mon. The gigantic female figure symbolising the Motherland that has dominated the high right bank of the Dnieper since 1981 stands on top of the museum. Also here are the names of the Heroes of the Soviet Union, engraved in gold on white marble.

Museum of the History of Kiev, Chekistov Street 8. Open 10–6; closed Fri. This museum was opened in 1982. It is housed in the Klovsky Palace, which was built in classical style in 1750–55 by Ilya Neyelov and Stefan Kovnir, but only fully completed in 1863.

Maryinsky Palace, Radyanska Square. Built in 1750–55 in baroque style by Michurin, from a project by Rastrelli. The wooden second floor was burned in 1819, but the palace was restored in the second half of the 19th century.

Lesya Ukrainka Museum, Saksaganskovo Street 97. Open 10–5; closed Thurs. Lesya Ukrainka (1871–1913), was a well-known Ukrainian poetess.

Shevchenko Museum, Shevchenko Boulevard 12. Open 10–6; closed Mon. The museum, which was opened in 1949, contains 28 halls with over 800 works of art by the poet Taras Shevchenko, who was trained at the St. Petersburg Academy of Arts. Also on display are editions of his literary works and a number of personal possessions.

Shevchenko's House, Shevchenko Lane 8a. Open 10–6; closed Fri. Shevchenko lived in this small house during the spring and summer of 1846. The display is very similar to that of the Shevchenko Museum and mostly includes his personal possessions and editions of his literary works. There is a bust of the poet in the garden.

Posting Station, Pochtovaya Square. Built in the 1850s in classical style as one of the first posting stations on the road from the Ukraine up to Moscow and St. Petersburg. It was in use until 1919 and consists of a post office (1846), a hotel, coach houses and stables, and a telegraph office of later date. Now being restored as a museum.

Lenin Museum, Leinisky Komsomol Square. Open 10–6; closed Mon.

Branch of the Lenin Museum, Volodimerska Street 67. Open 10–6; closed Mon.

Planetarium, Chelyuskintsev Street 17. This is housed in what was formerly a Roman Catholic church.

St. Vladimir Monument, in the park of Volodimerska Girka, at the northern end of the main street, Kreschatik. Overlooking the river is a statue of Prince Vladimir, erected in 1853. He is holding aloft a cross. The statue was cast in bronze by Klodt (famous for his horses on the Anichkov Bridge in Leningrad), after a design by Demut-Malinovsky. Prince Vladimir is shown in the dress of an ancient Russian warrior, standing bareheaded in thanksgiving as he gazes at the water of the Dnieper below, where he was instrumental in the mass baptism of his people. The statue is 4.5 m (15 ft) high and weighs about 6 tons. The unusual chapel-like pedestal is covered with cast-iron plates. On the pedestal above the bas-relief depicting the baptism of Rus is the old seal of Kiev. The height of the statue and pedestal together is 20.4 m (67 ft).

At the bottom of Volodimerska Girka is another *monument*, dating from 1802, commemorating the conversion of Russia to Christianity, sited where the mass baptism took place.

Magdeburg Law Column, in Pionersky Park, at the bottom of Volodimerska Girka. The granting of Magdeburg Law to any town gave it the right to self-government; it was granted to Kiev in 1499 and only abolished in 1835. This column, made by architect Milensky, was erected in 1802–8. It stands 23.1 m (76 ft) high.

Bogdan Khmelnitsky Monument, in the centre of Bogdan Khmelnitsky Square, opposite St. Sophia's Cathedral and near the spot where the Kievans took their oath of loyalty to Russia in 1654. Bogdan Khmelnitsky (1593–1657) was the Cossack hetman who freed the Ukraine from the Poles and later subjected it to the Moscow state. The equestrian statue was cast in bronze in St. Petersburg by Mikeshin in 1880 and transported to Kiev, where it was erected in 1888. The statue is 10.85 m (36 ft) high and so placed that it can be seen from 3 different directions. The mace Khmelnitsky holds is a symbol of his power as hetman, and it points to the north, toward Moscow.

Monument to Russia's First Library, in St. Sophia's Cathedral close. The library was founded by Yaroslav the Wise in the 9th century.

Skovoroda Monument, Red Square Garden.

Grigory Skovoroda (1722–94) was a Ukrainian enlightener, philosopher, and poet. The monument by Kavaleridze and Gnezdilov was unveiled in 1976.

Pushkin Monument, in front of the entrance to Pushkin Park. The bronze sculpture by Kovalyov stands 3.5 m (11 ft) high, and the total height of the monument is over 7 m (23 ft). The black granite pedestal carries the inscription: "To Pushkin from the Ukrainian people." The monument was unveiled in 1962.

Taras Shevchenko Monument, in the park bearing his name, in front of the university. The monument was unveiled in 1939 on the 150th anniversary of the poet's birth. It was designed by Manizer and is 6 m (20 ft) high. On the pedestal is a quotation from one of his most famous poems:

And in the great family,
The new, free family,
Do not forget me.
Remember me
With a kind, quiet word.

Nikolai Lysenko Monument, Teatralnaya Square. This monument to Nikolai Lysenko (1842–1912), founder of Ukrainian classical music, was designed by Kovalev and Gnezdilov and was unveiled in 1976.

Lenin Monument, Shevchenko Boulevard. The statue, designed by Merkurov, was unveiled in 1946. There is a more recent *monument* of granite in front of the Moskva Hotel on Kreschatik, an imposing structure with bronze statues in front and a series of terraced waterfalls leading down to the street.

Ivan Franko Monument, Franko Square, near the Ivan Franko theatre. The statue of the writer and public figure was unveiled in 1956.

Schors Monument, at the crossing of Shevchenko Boulevard and Kominterna Street. Nikolai Schors (1895–1919) was a Red Army commander who became a hero of the Civil War. The equestrian statue, which stands 6.5 m (21 ft) high, was made by Lysenko, Sukhodolov, and Borodai and unveiled in 1954. The upper end of the red granite pedestal bears a bronze cornice and a frieze depicting episodes from the history of the Red Army.

Arsenal Workers' Monument, at the crossing of Kirov and Sichneve Povstannya streets. The cannon mounted on a pedestal of red granite was unveiled in 1922 to commemorate the workers of the arsenal plant who fell during the Civil War of 1918–22. There is another *monument* to these workers in Radyansky Park; it takes the form of a red granite urn hung with crepe and standing on a black marble pedestal, which bears the inscription: "To the eternal glory of the fighters for freedom."

Askold's Grave and War Memorial, Sichneve Povstannya Street 33. These are in one of the most beautiful parts of Kiev, in the park that is also called

Askold's Grave. There used to be a wooden church dedicated to St. Nicholas over Askold's tomb, where, according to legend, Askold, Prince of Kiev, was buried in 882. This was moved to the upper part of the Lavra territory. In 1909–10 the architect Melensky built a rotunda here instead, which now houses a branch of the History Museum. In the upper part of the park, Park Slavy, near the rotunda, is the *Tomb of the Unknown Soldier of the Second World War*, and as a memorial there is a 27-m (89 ft) obelisk and an eternal flame. There is a *Heroes' Avenue*, and a collection of armaments, including a T-34 tank, airplanes, and a "katyusha" rocket launcher. Crowning the memorial is the gigantic 72-m (236-ft) statue of the Motherland, bearing a sword and shield by Borodai. The complex was completed in 1957. A good road runs through the park.

Vatutin Monument, in Radyansky Park, Kirov Street. General Nikolai Vatutin (1901–44) died, heavily wounded, in Kiev after the liberation of the city. The monument by Vuchetich was unveiled in 1948. The 4.7-m (15-ft) sculpture is of grey granite and stands over the general's grave. On the pedestal is an inscription reading: "To General Vatutin from the Ukrainian people."

Lesya Ukrainka Monument, in Lesya Ukrainka Square. The pediment stands 5 m (16 ft) high, and the sculptor was G. Kalchenko; it was unveiled in 1973, on the 60th anniversary of the death of the poetess.

Ostrovsky Monument, Vozdukhoflotsky Prospect. This monument to Nikolai Ostrovsky is by Karechko and Ignashenko.

Obelisk, Peremoghi Square. In honour of the hero-city of Kiev, this 40-m (131-ft) obelisk was unveiled in 1982 to commemorate her citizens' contribution toward victory in 1945; it is by Lashko and Semisyuk.

Foundation of Kiev Memorial, in Vitaly Primakov Park. It was created by Borodai to celebrate the 1,500th anniversary of the city's foundation in 1982.

Arch, in 1-Travnevy Park. Commemorates the unification of the Ukraine and Russia.

Shevchenko Opera and Ballet Theatre, Volodimerska Street 50. This building was designed in 1901 by Schretter. It seats 1,650. The company was formed in 1926.

Ivan Franko Ukrainian Drama Theatre, Franko Square 3. The theatre was built in 1898 and reconstructed in 1960.

Lesya Ukrainka Russian Drama Theatre, Lenin Street 5

Musical Comedy Theatre, Chervonoarmiiska Street 53/3

Youth Theatre, Rosa Luxemburg Street 15/17

Puppet Theatre, Rustaveli Street 13. This theatre, which can seat 316, was once a synagogue.

Philharmonia Concert Hall, Kirov Street 16. This was built in 1882 by Nikolayev as the Merchants' Hall.

Organ Music Concert Hall, Chervonoarmiiska Street 70

Zhvotnevii (October) Place of Culture, Zhvotnevoi Revolyutsii Street 1. This building was built by Beretti in 1838–42 as a school for the daughters of gentlemen. It has a classical colonnade and stands on a hilltop. It was restored and enlarged in 1953–57, and its hall, which can seat 2,000, is one of the largest in Kiev and is used for concerts.

Ukraina Palace of Culture, Chervonoarmiiska Street 85

Circus, Peremoghi Square 1. The circus was built in 1958–60 and can seat 2,100.

Cinerama, Rustaveli Street 19. Built in 1959, this was the first cinerama in the Soviet Union.

Hippodrome Racecourse, Sverdlovskaya Street 5

Dynamo Stadium, Kirov Street 3. Built in 1941 (but only opened in 1946, because of the war), at the foot of Mt. Cherepanova to accommodate 50,000 spectators. There is a *monument* here to the memory of the Dynamo soccer team, which was shot by the Nazis for winning. Since soccer grew in popularity, a second tier of stands was built above the first, so now there is room for 100,000. The stadium, described as one of the most beautiful in the world, stands, together with a sports complex that includes two training fields and a well-equipped health and physical fitness centre, in a park just off Kreschatik Street. To help visitors find their places, each sector of the stands has its own colour, and the entrance tickets are printed to match.

There are more than 160 municipal football fields and ice hockey rinks in Kiev, and in general the city's sports facilities are such that over 260,000 people can participate in one or another sport at a time. But there is no doubt that soccer is the big favourite, which is hardly surprising, when Kiev and this excellent stadium are the home of the outstanding Kiev Dynamo team, 8 times national champion and acknowledged leader of Soviet soccer.

Koncha Zaspa Olympic Training Centre

Tsentralny Stadium, Chervonoarmiiska Street 55. This occupies a territory of 53 hectares (130 acres), and the main stadium seats 60,000. Nearby is a *Palace of Sport*, opened in 1960, and locally known as Crystal Palace. With accommodation for 12,000, it is the largest covered arena in the Soviet Union.

Zoo, Brest-Litovskoye Prospect 80

Swimming Pool, Vozdukhoflotskoye Chaussée 32

Academy of Sciences Botanical Garden, Vydubetska Street 11. The garden is situated on the bank of the river Dnieper, to the south of the Monastery of the Caves, and it covers an area of 180 hectares (450 acres).

Fomin Botanical Garden, Kominterna Street 1. The garden lies behind the university and covers an area of 22 hectares (54 acres). It was laid out in 1841 on a stretch of wasteland, and its present name comes from a botanist who fought for its preservation just after the revolution.

Ukrainian Economic Exhibition, Sorokorichya Zhovtnya Prospect. This is a permanent exhibition in the southern suburbs of the city. It is laid out in grounds of 300 hectares (750 acres), more than half of which is parkland.

Kiev is lucky to have another beautiful stretch of natural parkland close to its centre. It runs along the hilly wooded slopes above the river. There are actually a number of parks here, but they run into each other imperceptibly. The most northerly is *Volodimerska Girka (Vladimir's Hill)*, where there is the *St. Vladimir Monument* and an open-air cinema seating 1,500. *Pionersky ("pioneer") Park* is reached by a flight of steps from Lenkomsomola Square and contains monuments, a cinema, and a concert platform. *1-Travnevy (First of May) Park* was laid out in 1747–55 as the tsar's park adjoining the palace. There is a bandstand with 2,000 seats, an open-air theatre, amusements, and the Cuckoo Restaurant. *Radyansky (Soviet) Park*, laid out in the 19th century, is opposite the tsar's palace and contains a children's village and a playground. The last of the parks is called *Askold's Grave* (see above).

Lower down, beside the river, runs *Park Lane*, which is closed to motor traffic on summer evenings, when it is usually crowded with pedestrians. In the autumn the local fruit and flower show is held here, near the statue of the horticulturist Michurin. Also on Park Lane is an open-air theatre with a seating capacity of 4,000. Its amphitheatre makes use of the 19th-century wall of Kiev fortress. Higher up the slope, but still in the park area, runs a good motor road with an excellent view across the river. One can get onto it by driving from the clover-leaf at Paton Bridge along the embankment road and taking the first large left fork up the hill.

Trukhanov Island, in the Dnieper, is reached by a suspension bridge for pedestrians, which was opened in 1957. It is Kiev's most popular bathing beach.

Pushkin Park, Brest-Litovskoye Chaussée. This park was opened in 1899 to mark the 100th anniversary of the poet's birth. There are groves of beech, pine, birch, and other trees.

Lenkomsomol Park, Brest-Litovskoye Chaussée. There is a monument to the Young Communists of the 1920s. Boats can be hired on the pond.

Babi Yar, out of the centre of the city, along Artemov Street, toward the television tower; just the other side of the tower, on the left of the main road, is a monument, unveiled in 1976 and dedicated to the "Victims of Fascism—1941–43." Babi Yar is the name of the wooded gully where a little stream flows down into the river Pochaina. It runs back from the road at this point and was the scene of gruesome mass murders during the time of the occupation of Kiev. Now planted with young birches, rowans, and firs and crisscrossed with winding footpaths, its very simplicity and silence are deeply moving.

Folk Architectural Museum, outskirts of Kiev, near Pirogova village. Open 10–6; closed Wed. Here on a territory of over 100 hectares (250 acres) is a collection of 400 old houses, mills, forges, and other structures, brought from all over the Ukraine. They are appropriately equipped and furnished, so

that the items on display number about 30,000.

Goloseyevo Forest, on the left of the main road leading to the Ukrainian Economic Exhibition. There are lakes and ancient trees, and also a 160-hectare (400-acre) park with sports grounds and an open-air theatre. In the summer a restaurant and a café are open here. The *Monument to the Defenders of Kiev* by Suvorov was unveiled in 1965.

Children's Railway, in the Syrets district of Kiev. The engine and 6 coaches run for 3 km (2 miles) along a track that was opened in 1953. The railway is staffed by schoolchildren.

Lyebed ("swan") Hotel and Restaurant, Peremoghi Square 6; tel. 74–3206

Dnipro Hotel and Restaruant, Kreschatik Street 1/2; tel. 91–4875, 29–7270

Moskva Hotel, Restaurant, and Café, Zhovtnevoy Revolutsii Street 4; tel. 41–9529

Intourist Hotel and Restaurant, Lenin Street 26, tel. 25–1121. Intourist office: tel. 25–3051. (There is another Intourist office, at Borispol Airport; tel. 26–7342.)

Slavutich Hotel and Restaurant, Entuziastov Street 1; tel. 555–9445

Rus Hotel and Restaurant, Gospitalnaya Street 4; tel. 20–5122

Mir Hotel and Restaurant, Goloseyevsky Forest

Leningradskaya Hotel and Restaurant, Shevchenko Boulevard 4; tel. 25–7101

Bratislava Hotel and Restaurant, on the left bank of the Dnieper

Kiev Hotel and Restaurant, Kirov Street 26/1

Ukraine Hotel and Restaurant, Shevchenko Boulevard 5; tel. 21–7584

Teatralny Hotel and Restaurant, Lenin Street 17; tel. 23–5045

Pervomaiskaya Hotel and Restaurant, Lenin Street 1/3; tel. 4–1015

Chaika ("seagull") Hotel, to the right, on the way into town from Zhitomir

Camping Site, just before reaching the city, on the Zhitomir road. There are a *service station* and a *filling station*, all to the right of the road.

Abkhazia Restaurant, Kreschatik 43

Dynamo Restaurant, Kirov Street 3, at the Dynamo Stadium

Metro Restaurant and Café, Kreschatik Street 42

Leipzig Restaurant, Volodimerska Street 30. Specialises in German dishes.

Khata Karasya Restaurant, in Svyatoshino, in the northwestern outskirts of Kiev. Specialises in Ukrainian cuisine.

Kureni Tavern, near the Dnieper River. Local dishes served under a thatched roof.

Poplavok ("fishing float") Restaurant, Naberezhnoye Chaussée

Priboy ("surf") Restaurant, Rechnoi Vokzal

Cuckoo Restaurant, 1-Travnevy Park

Riviera Restaurant, Park Lane

Kashtan (foreign-currency) Shops, Shevchenko Boulevard 2 and 6, Lesi Ukrainki Boulevard 26. Open 9–7.

GOP, Kreschatik Street 22

Main Department Store, Lenin Street 2, at the corner of Kreschatik Street

Podarki ("gift") Shop, Karl Marx Street 9 and Lesi Ukrainki Boulevard 5a

Ukrainian Handicrafts, Chervonoarmiiska Street 23 and Kirov Street 93

Perlina (jewellery shop), Kreschatik Street 21

Book Shop, Kreschatik Street 30

Bessarabka Covered Market, Shevchenko Boulevard. The building was designed by Gai and erected in 1910.

Market, Vorovskovo Street 17

Balkan and Balkantourist, Kreschatik Street, opposite the Dniepro Hotel

Czechoslovak Consulate General, Yaroslavov Val 34; tel. 229–7269

German Consulate General, ul. Chkalova 84; tel. 216–6794.

Hungarian Consulate General, Reiterskaya Street 33; tel. 212–4094

Polish Consulate General, Yaroslavov Val 12; tel. 224–8040

Rumanian Consulate General, Vyborgskaya Street 89; tel. 46–7118

Intourist organises motorboat trips on the Dnieper and Kiev Reservoir as well as excursions to Noviye Petrovniye, 18 km (11 miles) away, and to Kaniv, Chernigov, and Uman (all listed under their own names).

Noviye Petrovniye

This village was used as the headquarters of the 1st Ukrainian Front, just before Kiev was liberated in November 1943.

The *Museum* illustrates the battle for the liberation of the city. Pillboxes and observation posts have been preserved. Included in the excursion is a visit to the memorial at Babi Yar and to the diorama "The Battle for Kiev, Lyutezhsky Battlefield, 1943."

The 3-hour excursion takes place between 10 and 6.

KIRGHIZSTAN

See Bishkek, p. 75.

KIROVAKAN

See Erevan environs, p. 138.

KISHINYOV

Kishinyov is the capital of the Soviet Socialist Republic of Moldova

MOLDOVA (formerly Moldavia)

This republic of the Soviet Union is situated to the northwest of the Black Sea, on the Romanian frontier. It is 33,700 sq km (13,000 sq miles) in area and is divided by the river Dniester. Its population numbers 4,341,000, which is the highest average density in the USSR, for after Armenia it is the second-smallest republic. 22 percent of the Moldavian population lives in the towns. The people are mostly Moldavians (63 percent), but other nationalities include Ukrainians (14.2 percent), Russians (12.8 percent), Jews and Gagauz.

The Moldavians, once called the Volokhs by the Russians, speak a Romance language very similar to Romanian, but use the Cyrillic alphabet. As much as 40 percent of the language consists of words of Ukrainian origin. Anyone from Western Europe would be surprised at how much of the rest of the language they can understand, especially if they know the Latin roots. For example, the Zhok Dance Ensemble takes its name from the Latin *jocus* (joke).

The country has been inhabited since prehistoric times. It is supposed that the Moldavians are descendants of the ancient Thracians, and the Greeks, Romans, and Turks had colonies in the area and influenced the country for a considerable time. The Moldavian principality was formed in the 14th century by the Vlakhs, who emigrated here from the Carpathian Mountains. It achieved independence in about 1349 under Prince Bogdan. It expanded to include Bessarabia in the southeast and so was bounded by the Dniester, the Black Sea, and Transylvania. It was able to withstand pressures from Hungary and Poland, but after the death of Prince Stephen the Great in 1504, it was compelled to pay tribute to the sultan of Turkey. It was said that "Moldavia lay in the path of all misfortunes," and by the mid-16th century it was already a vassal-state of the Ottoman empire.

During the 18th century, Russian influence increased so that eventually Moldavia was under Russian protection. Austria claimed the northwestern part, known as Bukovina, and with the Treaty of Bucharest after the Russo-Turkish war of 1806–12 Bessarabia was annexed by Russia. From 1918 until 1940, Bessarabia was under Romanian rule, and a small autonomous Moldavian republic was created in 1921 within the Ukraine on the left bank of the river Dniester. The Soviet Union never accepted the annexation of Bessarabia, and in 1940 she demanded that the Romanian army leave Bessarabia within 4 days. Subsequently the union republic of Moldavia was formed, comprising both parts of the country.

Moldova's soil is fertile and the climate very mild compared with other parts of the Soviet Union, so that the country is mainly agricultural and grows wheat, maize, sunflowers, etc. In viniculture it ranks second in importance in the USSR.

The country's food and light industries are well developed; its mineral resources are only lignite and stone. The main towns are Kishinyov (capital), Beltsy, Tiraspol, and Bendery.

Useful expressions in Moldavian:

Hello	Norok
I am a tourist	ayoo sint tourist
please	poftim
thank you	mooltsoomesk
yes	da
no	noo
good	beene

bad	rayoo
I don't understand	noo intseleg
please fetch an in-	kemats ve rog
terpreter for me	con interpret
good bye	la revedere

Kishinyov Population—670,000
(Rumanian: Chisinau)

Intourist organises day trips here from Odessa.

The name Kishinyov is supposed to come from Kishla Noue (kishla meaning "sheepfold"), but there is an ancient word, kishinin ("spring") from which it may be derived. A third possibility is connected with its very early history: the first written mention of the town was made in 1420, and the place was the property of the Holy Sepulchre Monastery for many years, so it has been suggested that the name might have come from the Turkish word for "monastery village."

The city stands on the river Bik at the foothills of the Kodry Mountains. It has an average summer temperature of 20°–23°C (68°–74°F) and is warm in the autumn.

In 1812, when Moldavia was united with Russia, there were only 7,000 people living in Kishinyov. The population decreased again when, from 6–8 April 1903, there was a severe Jewish pogrom, but it has since increased greatly.

Kishinyov is divided into 2 parts, the old town with small winding streets down by the river Bik, and the new town, where the streets were properly planned, which occupies the upper part of the territory beginning from Lenin Prospect. *Lenin Prospect*, formerly called Alexandrovskaya Street, after Tsar Alexander II and then Moskovskaya Street, has been entirely rebuilt with new houses, but farther up, *Iskra Street* remains very much as it used to be, with small 1 and 2-storey houses, once the private mansions of merchants and businessmen.

Kishinyov was in Romanian hands from 1918 until 1940, and during World War II 76 percent of the residential buildings were destroyed.

In 1953 the 3.5 km (2-mile) Lenin Prospect was reconstructed, and office blocks of 3 and 5 storeys were put up. The bank building at No. 81 with a statue of Mercury (god of trade) on the façade was constructed at the end of the last century and now houses the State Bank. No. 83, now the local Party building, used to be the duma (town hall). The central part of the prospect, between Pushkinskaya Street and Gogolevskaya Street, was extended to 5 times its original width and was called Pobedy ("victory") Square. A monument to Lenin was erected, and it became the Red Square of Kishinyov, where parades and demonstrations take place. The new Moldovan government building is in this square. Postwar reconstruction was carried out according to a plan by the architect academician Schusev, himself a local citizen.

The suburbs of Kishinyov, especially Benderskaya, Novye Chekany, and Skuiyanskaya, have become the industrial regions of the capital, and account for half Moldova's industry. The food industry is the most important, but there are also factories for tobacco, textiles, clothing, electrical equipment, garden tractors, and machine building. Among the new parts of the city built in the suburbs after the war is a branch of the USSR Academy of Sciences (1961), some research institutes, Lenin University (1945) with 8 faculties and 7,000 students, medical, agricultural, and pedagogical institutes, and a conservatory.

Visitors are always pleased to see the original work of local craftsmen in the shops. The pottery, woodcarving, carpets, and metalwork of Moldova are known in many parts of the world.

Cathedral of the Nativity, Lenin Prospect, in a small park opposite the Lenin Monument in the city centre. The cathedral was built by Melnikov in 1836. The *Victory Arch*, which stands between Lenin Prospect and the cathedral, was designed by Zaushkevich and constructed using donations made by local citizens. Originally known as Holy Gate, the arch is decorated with 16 Corinthian columns and supports the town clock. The big bell weighs 7 tons and was cast from melted-down Turkish guns captured during the Russo-Turkish wars. It was only renamed "Victory" after World War II, when commemorative plaques were added. The cathedral now serves as an art exhibition hall.

As the cathedral building is now used for exhibitions, the church acting as *Kishinyov cathedral* is that opposite the Intourist Hotel, at Tkachenko Street 12, which has a belfry, one big dome and some smaller ones beside it. Services are held here daily, not only on Sundays and special church holidays as is usual.

Mazarakievskaya Church of the Nativity of the Virgin, Tulskaya Street 3, on an elevated site, in the old part of the town down by the river Bik. The green-roofed church, rebuilt in 1757, is named for Vaisily Mazaraki, a Greek Christian in the service of the Turkish sultan. At one time he was suspected of disloyalty to his master, but throughout his troubles his faith remained unshaken, and he vowed that if only his innocence could be proved he would show his gratitude by providing the money to build a church. This one that still bears his name owes its existence to Mazaraki's donation; it must have been a handsome gift, judging by the solid construction, for the walls of the church are 1.4 m (4.5 ft) thick. It is well seen from the bridge where Molodyozhny Prospect crosses the Bik.

SS. Konstantine and Helena, or Ryshkanskaya Church, Krutoy Pereulok, in the Ryshkanovka region of the city, across the river, to the left of the Molodyozhy Bridge. Built in 1777 on a hill above the left bank of the river Bik to serve as a cemetery church.

Blagoveschenskaya (Annunciation) Church, Koshevoi Street 10. Built in the Middle Ages, reconstructed in 1810 and again in 1979.

St. George's (Georgiyevskaya) Church, Bazhenova Street, below the hotel end of Lenin Prospect and farther downriver than the Mazarakievskaya Church. Built in 1819, it is now closed but can be distinguished by its pointed spire.

Byzantine-style Church, Pushkinskaya Street. A

KISHINYOV

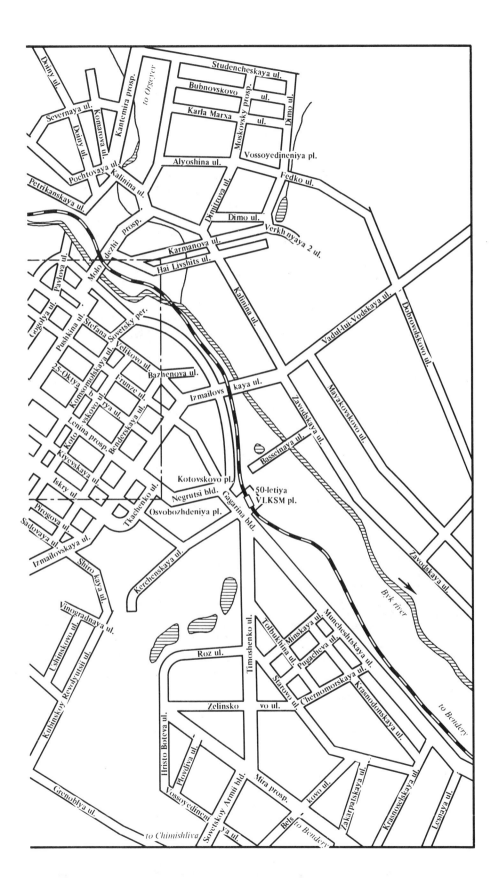

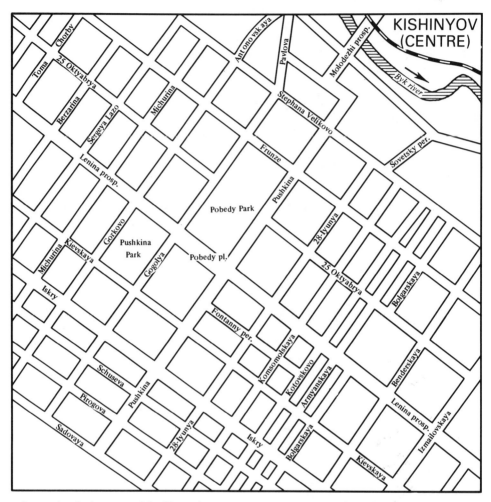

striking red-and-white striped building, this was originally designed as the chapel for the girls' school, which was in the building now used as the Party Museum at Kievskaya Street 115. The chapel is used as a concert hall at present.

St. Paraskeva's Church, just off Kolkhoznaya Street. This attractive small church was restored in 1979.

Roman Catholic Church, in the Polish cemetery

Synagogue, Yakimovsky Pereulok 8, near Armyanskaya Street. The building is 120 years old.

Local Museum, Pirogov Street 82. Open 10–6; closed Mon. The museum, founded in 1889, is located in a house built as a museum in 1905 in Mauritanian style; it has a good collection of carpets and national costumes and some interesting old maps.

Fine Arts Museum, Lenin Prospect 115. Open 11–6; closed Mon. The 5,000 exhibits are displayed in 14 halls, and they include Russian art dating from the end of the 18th to the beginning of the 20th century, and also Soviet, Moldavian,

West European (16th–19th centuries), and applied art. The West European section has examples of Italian, Dutch, Flemish, and German masters, including a print by Dürer. The building, constructed by the Viennese architect Henrich Lansky in 1903–5, was formerly the home of a rich local merchant named Hertz.

Moldavian History Museum, in a former school. Opened 1986

Archaeological Museum belongs to the Moldavian Academy of Sciences.

Literary Museum, Kievskaya Street 115. Open 10–6; closed Sat. and Sun.

Pushkin's House Museum, Antonovskovo Street 19. Open 11–7; closed Wed. Pushkin lived in exile in Kishinyov between 1820 and 1823, and it was here that he began to write "Eugene Onegin." In his poem "To Ovid," who was at that time believed to have been exiled here, he wrote, "with northern lyre filling deserts, here I wandered. . . ."

Moldavian Communist Party History Museum, Kievskaya Street 115. This was built by Bernardazzi as a girls' school in 1900. Yuri Bernardazzi worked as Kishinyov city architect for over 20 years. Open 10–7; closed Fri.

Iskra Museum, Iskra Street 66. Open 10–6; closed Fri. This is a branch of the Party History Museum. "Iskra" ("spark") was the name of the first Bolshevik newspaper, published illegally here in 1901–2 by the Social Democratic Party.

Kotovsky and Sergei Lazo Museum, Komsomolskaya Street 31. Open 10–5:30; closed Tues. These were heroes of the Civil War, both born in Moldavia.

Schusev Museum, Schusev Street 77. Alexander Schusev (1873–1949) was born here. He grew up to be an academician of architecture, with the Lenin Mausoleum in Moscow as one of his most famous works. The plan for the postwar reconstruction of Kishinyov was also his work.

Wine-tasting Hall, Kievskaya Street 70. In the building of a Greek church designed by Bernardazzi in 1895, in striped stonework like the Byzantine-style church on Pushkinskaya Street.

Planetarium, Lenin Prospect 164a

Stephan the Great Monument, at the entrance to Pushkin Park, where Gogol Street crosses Lenin Prospect. Stephan III was called "the Great," despite his small stature, for his victories over the Turks. He was Moldavian Gospodar (ruler) between 1457 and 1504, and during that time the country remained independent. This monument by Plamadeala was unveiled in 1927. The quotation from Russian historian Karamzin inscribed on the sides of the pedestal in both Russian and Moldavian reads: "Courageous in danger, resolute in disaster, unassuming in time of good fortune, . . . he was the wonder of all sovereigns and peoples, doing mighty deeds with paltry means."

Pushkin Monument, in Pushkin Park. Unveiled in 1885, in memory of his stay in Moldavia from 1820 till 1823, this bronze bust is by Opekushin, who designed the Pushkin Statue in Moscow. It was paid for by local donations.

Tolstoy's Portrait, in front of the Beryozka Shop at Lenin Prospect 6. Carved in red granite.

Obelisk and Chapel, Ryshkanovka. Here in April 1877 on the former racecourse, the manifesto of the declaration of war with Turkey was read. There was a parade of the Russian army, with detachments of Bulgarian volunteers among them. The obelisk was dedicated to these volunteers and bears the inscription: "In memory of the Bulgarian militia squads, organised in Kishinyov in 1876–77, who gallantly fought with the Russian army for Bulgaria's liberation from the Turkish yoke." The obelisk was executed by Dementiev, Novic, and Tsehanovich and unveiled in 1966. The chapel was built in 1882 in memory of the Russian army that liberated Bulgaria, Serbia, and Montenegro from the Turks. It has now been turned into a small museum of the event.

Karl Marx's Bust, in the garden where Gorky Street crosses Lenin Prospect. Sculpted in granite by Maiko.

Lenin Monument, Pobedy Square, just opposite the cathedral. This 12-m (39-ft) monument is by Merkurov and was unveiled in 1949 to mark the 25th anniversary of the foundation of the Moldavian republic.

Kotovsky Monument, Kotovsky Square. This equestrian statue by the Moldavian sculptors Dubinovsky and Kitaika was unveiled in 1954. The statue stands near the old railway office where the Civil War hero was arrested in 1906.

Gorky's Bust, in the garden by the Moldova Hotel, next to the Music and Drama Theatre

Soviet Power Monument, at the fork of Kotovskoye Chaussée and Dzerzhinsky Street. The figure of a worker on a 14-m (46-ft) column was unveiled in 1966 to commemorate the fighters for Soviet power. It was designed by Ponyatovsky, Maiko, and Fitov.

Komsomol Monument, Molodyozhi Prospect. This 15-m (49-ft) obelisk is crowned by the figure of a girl with a flaming torch. It was created by Dubinsky and Naumov and unveiled in 1959. During World War II this part of the town was the Jewish ghetto.

Liberation Monument, Pyatsa Elibereri. The figures of a soldier and a woman by Dubinovsky and Epelbaum stand at the foot of a 27-m (89-ft) obelisk topped by a palm branch. This was erected on 9 May 1965 to commemorate the 20th anniversary of the liberation of Moldavia.

Military Glory Memorial. This imaginative World War II memorial is in the form of 5 rifles standing watch over an eternal flame. There are soldiers' graves here and marble stelae engraved with particular incidents of the war. The memorial was unveiled on 9 May 1975 to mark the 30th anniversary of VE-Day.

Opera and Ballet Theatre, Lenin Prospect 152. The architect was A. Gorshkov. There are seats for 1,200.

Pushkin Drama Theatre, Lenin Prospect 79. All performances here are in Moldavian.

Chekhov Drama Theatre, 28-June Street 75. This theatre used to be a synagogue.

Concert Hall (Philharmonia), 25-October Street 78. Performances are given by symphony orchestras, the Doina choir, the Zhok National Dance Ensemble, and the Fluerash Orchestra of National Music.

Concert Hall for Organ Music, Lenin Prospect 81, in the building decorated with a figure of Mercury and lions, formerly a bank

Likurich ("glow worm") Puppet Theatre, Fontanny Pureulok 7

Intourist Concert Hall, Kerchenskaya Street 7

Circus, in a new building on the left at the top of Molodyozhi Bridge, near the church

Pushkin Park, in the centre of the town. This park is famous for its Writers' Walk, lined by 12 bronze busts of Romanian and Moldavian classical writers and opened in April 1958. The main gates of the park are on Lenin Prospect.

Komsomolskoye Ozero (Young Communist League Lake). Here there is a bathing beach and a boat-hire station. An impressive flight of 250 steps with waterfalls leads down to the water. In the park is an open-air theatre for 7,000 and also a parachute tower, a dance floor, and other attractions. There are two restaurants, the Otdykh ("rest") and Chaika ("seagull"), the latter on a floating raft. The park covers 96 hectares (240 acres).

Economic Achievements Exhibition, Zaozernaya Street 1, on the banks of Komsomolskoye Lake. Open 10–6; closed Mon. and Tues.

Rose Valley, in the southeastern suburbs of the city. There is a grove of trees here and Lenin Park laid out by a pond. A plantation of roses stretches out on the left side of the valley.

Botanical Gardens, Boyukansky Spusk, behind the Local Museum. The old park here covers 75 hectares (180 acres) and contains specimens of the entire flora of Moldova.

Respublikansky Stadium, Benderskaya Street. The stadium seats 30,000 people.

Intourist Hotel and Restaurant, Lenin Prospect 4; tel. 26–6054. Intourist office: tel. 26–2569. There is a disco bar on the 3rd floor.

Cosmos Hotel and Restaurant, Kotovsky Square 2; tel. 265–232

Kishinyov Hotel and Restaurant, Negruzzi Boulevard 7; tel. 313–23

Moldova Hotel and Restaurant, Lenin Prospect 7a, tel. 226–52

Strugurash Motel and Restaurant, Kotovskoye Chaussée 230; tel.. 53–2841. There is room here for 206 guests. *Bar, GPO, and filling station.*

Butoyash Restaurant, Kuibyshev Street 251, tel. 193–35. Decorated to look like a beer barrel.

Norok Restaurant, Gorky Street 20; tel. 336–09

Plovdiv Restaurant, Moskovsky Prospect 6; tel. 402–22

Tourist Restaurant, Molodyozhi Prospect 11a; tel. 294–68

Dniester Café, Komsomolskaya Street 56

Druzhba ("friendship") Café, Lenin Prospect 62. A national dish worth trying is a "mititeyi," small sausages containing spice and onions.

Foreign-Exchange Counter, Kishinyov Hotel, Negruzzi Boulevard 7.

GPO, Lenin Prospect 134

Kolkhozny Rynok, at the corner of Benderskaya Street and Lenin Prospect. This modern market in the centre of the town sells peasant ware and national handicrafts as well as food.

Department Store, Lenin Prospect 136, at the corner of Pushkinskaya Street

Podarki (gift shop), Komsomolskaya Street, at the corner of Lenin Prospect

Beryozka (foreign-currency) Shop, Lenin Prospect 6, next to the Intourist Hotel

Souvenirs, Lenin Prospect 64

Mertsishor Souvenirs, Lenin Prospect 132

Melodia (records), 28th-June Street 63

Moldavian Wine and Brandy, Lenin Prospect 67

Main Taxi Stands, Gogol Street, at the corner of Lenin Prospect; Zhukovsky Street, at the corner of Lenin Prospect; and by the hotels and the railway station

Service Station, Kotovskoye Chaussée 230 and on the right of the road into town from Chernovtsy

Filling Station, by the Strugurash Motel, Kotovskoye Chaussée 230

Intourist organises boat trips on the river Dnieper and out-of-town excursions to Vadu-Lui-Vode, Pushkino, and Lake Gidigich. Lake Gidigich is also known as the Sea of Kishinyov and is 12 km from the capital along the road to Pushkino. Tourists can also visit a wine-making farm or help with the fruit or grape harvest. Longer excursions include those to Bendery, Tiraspol, Beltsy, and to Odessa (200 km/124 miles) away, all of which are listed under their own names.

Vadu-Lui-Vode, a forest park recreation area with good bathing beaches beside the river Dniester, is 30 km (19 miles) from Kishinyov. To reach it, leave the city in a northerly direction via Prospect Molodyozhi, Kalinin Street, and Kantemir Prospect, past the racecourse and some recently planted parkland and out through vineyards. The route is well signposted and runs through the following towns.

Goyani

St. Mary's Church, to the left of the road; open for services. From here the road winds over treeless slopes down to the Dniester River.

Grushevo

Freshwater spring, on the left of the road

There is also a *church* up the hill on the left.

Vadu-Lui-Vode

War Memorial, in the main square

Restaurant

Dnestrovsky Park, in lush woodland, with a sandy bathing beach beside the river

Pushkino is 21 km (13 miles) from Kishinyov. Leave Kishinyov in a northwesterly direction, via Lenin Prospect and Kuibysheva Street, following the signs to Ungeni.

Lake Gidigich

12 km from Kishinyov. The reservoir here covers more than 1,000 hectares (2,500 acres) and is also known as the Sea of Kishinyov. Its waters are used to irrigate the region.

Filling Station, on the right of the main road

Strasheny

Strugurash Restaurant, on the left

Wine Bar, on the left

Turn left toward Nisporeni at the 35-km mark.

Vornichena

SS. Peter and Paul's Church, on the left side of Lenin Street. Built in 1914.

The next two villages are Lozovo and Mikleusheny. *Holy Trinity Church* can be seen in the distance on the left. It was built in the 19th century and is open for services.

Café, on the right of the road

Turn left to reach Pushkino in another 2 km (1 mile).

Pushkino Population—1,000

War Memorial, at the entrance to the village on the right

St. Nicholas's Church, on the hill behind the museum. From the early 19th century.

Restaurant

Pushkin Museum, up on the right, in the summer home of the Ralli family. It was here that Pushkin met the gypsies that are featured in his early poetry. A formal rose garden has been laid out on a terrace in front of the house with a statue of the poet, and the central path leads to a small wooden pavilion. The museum occupies 2 rooms only, the rest of the house serving as a library. Open April–October, 10–5; closed Mon.

KISLOVODSK Population—114,000

Intourist organises excursions here from Terskol and Stavropol.

This spa, one of the Mineralniye Vodi group, lies off the main road, to the right from Pyatigorsk; it is 20 km (12.5 miles) past Essentuki and 45 km (28 miles) from Pyatigorsk itself. The way in is via Pobeda Prospect.

Kislovodsk is 822 m (2,695 ft) above sea level and lies at the bottom of a mountain valley crossed by the rivers Olkhovka and Berezovka. The Russians came here at the end of the 18th century, and by the confluence of these 2 rivers they saw an unusual sight. A great fountain of sharp-tasting, aerated water gushed from the ground to the height of a man. Nearby were the remains of a well, and stone and wooden baths. This was the Narzan spring. It was often referred to as "cold boiling water," but the Russians called narzan "kislaya voda" (sour water), and that gave the name to the present spa of Kislovodsk. In the local language "narzan," originates from the words "nart," meaning giant, and "sano," drink, which after many centuries' corruption, became narzan, meaning "drink of the giants." The academician Pyotr Pallas (1768–1810) from Berlin worked extensively on the ethnology and natural history of Russia. He was one of the discoverers of the Caucasian mineral springs and as far back as 1793 indicated their great curative power. There are many old stories still told by the local mountain people about the legendary giants, the narts who derive their mighty strength from the springs so abundant in these parts. One of the legends about the origin of this wonderful drink ends with the following words, "If death is near, all you have to do is bathe in Narzan and you will live many long years. If your wounds are sore, bathe in Narzan and the pain will disappear."

When in 1803 the spas were organised in the Caucasus, a small settlement called Kislovodskoye was built here where soldiers lived with their families. There was no accommodation for patients who wanted to come here for cures. The first baths were built in 1812. During the early years, the local people made constant raids, and the military settlement was necessary to protect the patients, who hid themselves inside the fortress in time of danger.

The 2 mountain rivers, Berezovka and Olkhovka, which meet at the point where Narzan was discovered and which run through the spa, are also the subject of a folk tale. Prior to the arrival of the Russians, the Berezovka was called Elkusha, which in the Karachai language meant "eagle settlement," which tallies with the appearance of the wild, rocky Berezovskoye Gorge. The cold Olkhovka was called Kozada, meaning "steep ravine." After their confluence they both flow into the Podkumok River. The story tells how once upon a time a young man, Elkush, was in love with the beautiful Kozada, but she remained cold and unmoved by his love and hid herself in the gorge. Then one day he chased her far down into the valley, and they became one. Many romantic literary poems were written about Elkush and Kozada, and the Podkumok valley is itself very lovely, with rolling hills, chalk scree, and maples that turn fiery red in autumn.

Surrounded by forestless mountains, Kislovodsk is protected from all winds, and late summer and autumn are its best seasons. Winters are warm— in fact it has more sunny days in winter than Davos, and only 60 to 70 rainy days in the whole year. The average annual temperature is 10°C (50°F), and the average winter temperature, 2°C (35.5°F). The town is surrounded by terracelike slopes of hard limestone, which contain many caves.

There are 7 springs in Kislovodsk, the Narzan spring being the most famous of all in the region. It is the richest carbonic spring in the world. It is 818 m (2,683 ft) above sea level, and its temperature is 13°C (55°F). The spring has been known since the 18th century, and in 1848–58 a gallery was built in English Gothic style. The *Narzan Bathhouse* was built later, in the form of an Indian temple. In the centre of the town is a Narzan-bottling factory. The other springs in the town, including *Dolomite Narzan* and *Sulphate Narzan*, are of similar type. The volume of water yielded daily by the Kislovodsk springs is exceeded only by those of Pyatigorsk.

The waters here have been found most effective in the cure first and foremost of cardiological diseases. Those of the circulatory system are also treated, as are bronchial asthma and chronic (but nontubercular) diseases of the respiratory organs.

Narzan Sanatorium, which was formerly the Grand Hotel, stands at the corner of Karl Marx and 5-Anniversary-of-October-Revolution streets. There are other interesting buildings along Vokzalnaya Street, including the medical treatment block run by the Ministry of Defence. *Astronauts' House* on Uritsky Street is worthy of mention, and the administrative block of the *Dimitrov Sanatorium* on Lenin Prospect formerly belonged to the last tsar's mistress, the ballerina Kseshinskaya. *Chaliapin's dacha* is on Semashko Street near the railway station; it is now the administrative block

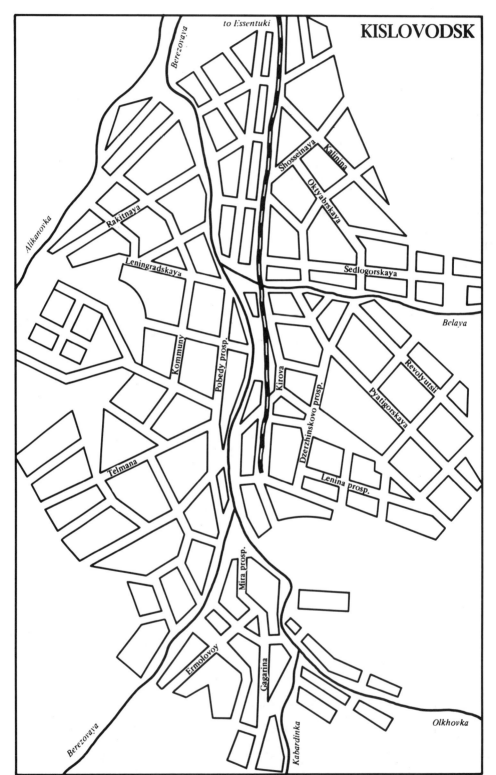

KISLOVODSK

to Essentuki

Berezovaya

Alikanovka

Rakitnaya

Shosseinaya

Kalinina

Oktyabrskaya

Leningradskaya

Sedlogorskaya

Belaya

Kommuny

Pobedy prosp.

Kirova

Revolyutsii

Dzerzhinskovo prosp.

Pyatigorskaya

Telmana

Lenina prosp.

Mira prosp.

Ermolovoy

Gagarina

Kabardinka

Berezovaya

Olkhovka

of the Semashko Sanatorium. The *Krugozor Boarding House* on Zhelyabov Street was built as a block of flats.

Local Museum, in Krepost Sanatorium (1803), Krepostnoy Pereulok 3. Open 10–6; closed Tues. Here you can see Alan skulls, elongated by having been bound with leather.

Music and Theatre Museum, in Gorky Theatre. Open 10–3; closed Sun.

Yaroshenko Museum, Yaroshenko Street 1. Open 11–7; closed Thurs. and Fri. Nikolai Yaroshenko (1846–98) was a prominent Russian painter, a member of the group known as the Wanderers. He lived in this house and died here in 1898. On display are over 50 of his original paintings and copies of others that are in the Tretyakov Gallery in Moscow. Nearby in a garden is a bust of the artist.

Sergo Ordzhonikidze Museum, in the Sergo Ordzhonikidze Sanatorium

Tsander Astronautics Museum, Ozyornaya Street, Komsomol Park. Open 10–6; closed Mon. and Tues.

Monument to Lermontov, Lermontov Square, in front of the Narzan Gallery. Built by Upton. The monument stands upon the site of the old Restoratsia, described by Lermontov in "Princess Mary."

Statue of Lenin, Kurortny Park.

World War II Memorial. An unusual memorial, with a statue of a kneeling woman and 3 cranes flying.

Gorky Theatre, in Verkhny Park, Krasnoarmeiskaya Street 5

Concert Hall, in Verkhny Park, Karl Marx Street, in the building of the old Kursal. Built in 1895.

Chaliapin's Cave was where Chaliapin liked to sing.

Circus, by the main road, on the left

Stadium, Pervomaisky Prospect 34, on the left side of the road leading into town

Kurortny Park, at the crossing of Dzerzhinsky and Lenin prospects. It was first laid out in 1823 on either side of the river Olkhovka. Additional planting was made in the 1830s and 1840s, and there is now a wide variety of shrubs and trees, including many of the shady, broad-leafed species. In the park are the Cascade Stairs. The main path leads to the Mirror Pool, filled by water from the Seven-Degree Spring (so called from its temperature, 7°C, or 44.6°F). The water then flows out from under a small pavilion in a steady stream. It is crystal clear and so much resembles molten glass that it is often called the Glass Stream. From the Glass Stream the path leads to Sosnovaya Gorka ("pine hill"), where there is a rosarium and an open-air stage. Farther along, shady avenues reach Krasnye Kamni (red stones), which are coloured by the iron content of the water and in some places eroded by the weather into strange mushroomlike shapes. A bas-relief of Lenin has been carved on one of the stones. A flight of steps runs down from this point to Lenin Prospect.

A legend is connected with Krasnye Kamni ("red stones"). Once upon a time there lived the beautiful Adiyukh, whose name in the Nart language meant "brighthanded." Adiyukh impersonated the moon in the local folklore. On a pitch-dark night, Adiyukh would stretch her hands out of the window, and everything around would be lit up with light more pleasant than sunlight. Adiyukh's husband used to come home at night, across a linen bridge over an abyss that led to their house on top of a mountain. At nights Adiyukh stretched her hands out to meet her husband, and he crossed the bridge safely. Once he ordered her not to look out of the window and not to stretch her hands out to meet him. As soon as Adiyukh heard the noise of her husband's horses, she wanted to light the way for him but remembered his orders and hid her hands behind her back. In pitch darkness her husband stumbled and fell into the depth of the abyss. Adiyukh shed so many tears that she could no longer see. She came down from her mountains and went to seek her husband's body among the cliffs. Blinded by tears, she stumbled over each cliff, wounding her hands on sharp stones and thorny bushes. Her blood stained the stones, and they have been called Krasnye Kamni ever since.

From here the path leads to another rocky terrace called Seriye Kamni ("grey stones"), standing at a height of 942 m (3,090 ft), 20 m (66 ft) higher than the Krasnye Kamni. From this point there is a good view of Kislovodsk, and in fine weather the summit of Elbrus can be seen. Farther on is Pervomaiskaya Polyana ("Mayday field"), a meadow surrounded by mountain slopes forming a natural amphitheatre with room for 60,000; it is occasionally so used. Nearby is Khram Vozdukha ("temple of air"), a pleasant little pavilion housing a library. Siniye Gory ("blue mountains") are a group of beautiful rocks which are already outside the park. They are so called because at sunset they assume a bluish colour. The spot commands a good view of Kislovodsk and Elbrus. At Siniye Gory is a small hill with a flat top. This is Krasnoye Solnyshko, a favourite place to watch the sun rise and set. It is said that long before the revolution an enterprising local opened a small restaurant here under the sign "Krasnoye Solnyshko Restaurant," where shashlyks and wine were served. The name was a success, and the place is now called after it. People with weight to lose are advised to walk on from this point, up to Maloye and Bolshoye Sedlo ("small and large saddle").

Verkhny ("upper") or Novy ("new") Park was laid out in 1902, joining onto the end of the old park. Verkhny Park is usually at its liveliest in the evening. Here are the Gorky Theatre, a cinema, and a concert platform that is acoustically unique: the floor of its stage contains a layer of broken glass to reflect the sound, and the shell-shaped roof is double-layered and itself resounds like a musical instrument.

Bathing beaches, on the shores of Kislovodsk Reservoir. The reservoir covers 70,000 hectares

(175,000 acres), and the sandy beaches stretch for 1.5 km (almost 1 mile).

Kavkaz Hotel (Intourist) and Druzhba Restaurant, Dzerzhinsky Prospect 24; tel. 391–84. Intourist office: tel. 53–409. There is a floor show in the restaurant from 8–9.

Narzan Hotel, Mir Prospect 14

Vilengrad Tourist Complex, by Kislovodsk Lake, tel. 513–44

Teatralny Restaurant, Kirov Prospect 2a. There is a floor show from 9–10.

Zarya ("dawn") Restaurant, Herzen Street

Chaika ("seagull") Restaurant, Pervomaisky Prospect 4

Khram Vozdukha ("temple of air") Restaurant, Verkhny Park

GPO, Krasnaya Street 3, Prospect Mira 19, and Pyervomaisky Prospect

Bank, Karl Marx Prospect

Elbrus Department Store, Pyervomaisky Prospect 27

Jewellers', Karl Marx Prospect

Syurpriz ("souvenirs"), Vokzalnaya Street 18/20

Intourist's shorter excursions from Kislovodsk include those up the beautiful Alikanovskoye Gorge, to Tersky Stud Farm, and to Kum-Bashi Pass. There are others to the neighbouring resorts of Pyatigorsk and Essentuki, and to Nalachik and Stavropol, all described under their own names.

Farther up into the mountains from Kislovodsk, Intourist organises a 480-km (298-mile) trip to Teberda and Dombai, via Cherkessk and Karachayevsk, which takes 13 hours. There are also long excursions to Golubiye Ozera and up to Elbrus, 440 km (274 miles), but these are described under Nalchik, as the journey is shorter from there.

Vilengrad Motel, 3 km (2 miles) from the centre of the town, beside Lake Kislovodsk, which covers 10 hectares (25 acres). Here there are facilities for bathing and boating. The *Tourist Restaurant* is nearby, and also a *service station, carwash*, and *filling station*.

The *Zamok ("castle") Motel* is 3 km (2 miles) farther on, 6 km (3.5 miles) from Kislovodsk. Here a 2-storey building built to resemble an old castle is used as an annex to the main motel; it also has the *Zamok Restaurant*, which specialises in Caucasian dishes. Its name was originally the Castle of Perfidy and Love, and this again was really the name of a much eroded rocky cliff that has the shape of a castle. The restaurant, which was opened here at the beginning of the century, had the same name, and now the motel has assumed the title. The story about the cliff is as follows.

Once upon a time, the daughter of one of the mountain princes fell in love with a simple shepherd boy. Her father was angry at this and betrothed her to a rich relative of his own. When the young couple learned of his plans, they decided to commit suicide by leaping from the cliff. The young man jumped first, and the girl was so terrified at the sight of his battered body that she thought better of her intention and returned home to marry the man of her father's choice. The cliffs alone were witness to the tragedy.

Medovyi Vodopad ("honey waterfall") is 10 km (6 miles) beyond the Zamok, following the same lovely road with gorge and valley landscapes. The name Medovyi came from the numerous swarms of wild bees that were abundant here a century ago. They lived in the cracks, crevices, and holes in the rocks. During the summer rains, the honeycombs were washed out by the water, and thick streaks of amber honey slowly poured down from the rocks. There are no bees here anymore; they died during one particularly severe winter. However, the waterfalls have been called medovye ("honey") ever since.

Lermontov Cliff is 4.5 (3 miles) from Kislovodsk, in the Olkhovka river gorge. This cliff is described by Lermontov in his "A Hero of Our Time" as the site of the duel between Pechorin and Grushnitsky. It is dangerous, as there are liable to be rock falls. About 430 m (500 yd) from here is the *Lermontov Spring*.

Dolina Narzanov ("Narzan Valley") is 33 km (20.5 miles) from Kislovodsk, up the valley of the river Beryozovaya and over into that of the Khasaum. It is so called because there are 17 Narzan-type springs here. And here is still another legend about the origin of the Narzan springs. It reminds one of the myth of Prometheus.

Once upon a time, on the snow-capped summit of Elbrus, there lived the formidable god Tha. He sowed fear among the Nart giants living around this mountain, but none dared to challenge him except for one young Nart who wanted to help his people. Against all odds, he climbed the mountain and felt the fierce breath of all-destroying Tha. "How dare you come here?" exclaimed the angered god. "Didn't you ever hear about me?" "Yes," said the brave lad, "I heard all about your evil deeds and came here to take revenge!" With these words he engaged Tha in battle. After a long and fierce fight, the evil Tha chained the young man to the icy wall in one of his caves. Every spring he visited the unfortunate lad to torment him more and more. The young man would sigh deeply and shed abundant bitter tears, which penetrated the thick walls of the mountains and appeared as the Narzan springs. So Narzan waters are the bitter tears of unfortunate Nart.

Kum-Bashi Pass is 60 km (37 miles) from Kislovodsk. The pass itself is at a height of 2,044 m (6,706 ft) above sea level, and from it open out fine views of the snow-capped peaks of the Central and the Western Caucasus mountains.

Tersky Stud Farm is 65 km (40 miles) from Kislovodsk. It is beautifully sited between the mountains Mashuk, Zheleznaya, Beshtau, and Zmeika and specialises in purebred Arabians. The annual auction takes place here in June.

At the start of the road from Kislovodsk up into the mountains to Teberda, the road runs through Stanitsa Suvorovskaya, named after Field-Marshal

Alexander Suvorov in recognition of his victory in the Crimean War. The road from Cherkessk until it reaches Teberda is described under Cherkessk (see p. 101).

Teberda

Intourist organises excursions here and on to Dombai from Stavropol.

Teberda is situated 1,350 m (4,430 ft) above sea level. It became a town in 1971. One of the possible derivations of the name is "teiriberdy," which means "godsent" in the Karachai language.

The region is known for its mild climate, dense forests of pine and silver fir, game, and alpine pastures. The Teberda valley is one of the most ancient routes connecting the rolling North Caucasian steppes with the Black Sea coast. As far back as the 1st century B.C., the Greek historian Strabo mentions this as part of the shortest trade route from the Black Sea coast through the Klukhor Pass.

The first building in Teberda was that of a 3-storeyed country house, built on the shore of Lake Karakel in 1883 by a Batalpashinsk town councillor, called Kuzovlyov for his sick wife; after her death it was given to a local charitable organisation. A settlement rapidly began to grow around Kuzovlyov's house, and it is now used as the Bolshevik Sanatorium. A mountaineering society was started in 1901–4. Its chairman, A. K. von Mekk, and a Swiss mountain climber, A. Fischer, climbed the difficult Teberda mountains for the first time. According to Fischer the Teberda-Dombai region surpassed the Western Alps in the beauty of its scenery, glaciers, forests, and vegetation.

The first tourist centre was opened here in 1926, and the tourist route across the ancient Klukhor Pass soon became very popular.

The Teberda valley climate, with lower atmospheric pressure, dry air, and considerable temperature fluctuations during the day, is typical of a mountain valley. The winter is moderately warm here, with many bright, windless days. It starts in mid-December, with January and February being the coldest months. The average winter temperature is − 2.3°C (28°F). Spring weather is unstable, with the recurrence of slight frosts and snowfalls. Summer usually starts in mid-June. It is not very hot, with the average temperature being 15.5°C (60°F). The long, sunny days of autumn are considered the best time of the year here. The average annual temperature is 8.1°C (46.6°F). The Teberda climate is curative for pulmonary diseases; because of this, there are 7 lung tuberculosis sanatoria, rest homes, and Pioneer camps here.

Teberda State Reservation. To preserve intact this unique beauty spot, the upper reaches of the Teberda River were proclaimed a state reservation in 1926. It now covers a territory of 83,400 hectares (208,500 acres). It is situated over 2,000 m (6,560 ft) above sea level. There are numerous high mountain lakes here, with cold, crystal-clear water. The landscape is typically alpine, with sharp peaks surrounding it, sheer rock faces, stone scree, and glaciers. The lower belt of the reservation is primarily

dark fir trees: Caucasian fir (abies) and Eastern fir as well as berry-bearing yew and deciduous trees such as beech, oak, hornbeam, and maple. There are 1,175 kinds of flowers, 186 of them unique to the Caucasus region. The animal kingdom of the reservation is very varied and includes chamois, Caucasian deer, European deer, wild pigs, and aurochs. Since 1937 there have also been plenty of squirrels, which were brought here from the Altai mountains; having changed their habitat, the squirrels have also changed the colour and texture of their fur. Wonderful trout live in the abundant rivers and in Lake Tunaly Kel. The many rare birds include the Alpine daw and the Caucasus ular.

Natural History Museum, in the reservation. Its collection tells not only of the flora and fauna of Teberda but also of its history. On display are archaeological finds of the Alans and other peoples inhabiting the region. Open daily, 8–5.

World War II Memorial, in the centre of the town

Obelisk to Victims of Fascism, at the entrance to Teberda, on the bank of the river Mukhu, on the site where Jews, patients of the local sanatoria, were shot dead during the occupation.

Teberda Hotel and Restaurant, in the centre of town; tel. 71–425

Teberda Restaurant in the centre of town.

Department Store, beside the hotel

The Teberda-Dombai road runs along the shore of Lake Karakel and follows the valley of the river Teberda.

The river Shumka flows into the Teberda from the left. At a height of 1,523 m (4,997 ft) above sea level it forms the *Shumka Waterfall,* with a drop of 12 m (39 ft).

The Baduk Lakes are 10 km (6 miles) from Teberda by bus or car, and then another 5 km (3 miles) on foot.

The Baduk Lakes are situated up to the west of the Teberda valley and were formed by a retreating glacier. The river Baduk is a tributary of the Hadjiby, and a legend exists about these names. The youth Hadjiby and a young girl called Baduk did not receive their parents' approval for their marriage, so they ran away into these mountains. Here they were caught, and for their disobedience the young man was tied to a rock in one ravine and the girl in another. From their tears, 2 rapid rivers were born.

The first lake lies at a height of 1,930 m (6,330 ft), among granite boulders. The waters of the river Baduk come bubbling up to the surface of the lake from an underground channel. The second lake is on the left of the path and is hardly visible from it. The third lake, which covers 2.6 hectares (6.5 acres), is situated in a forest at an altitude of 1,980 m (6,500 ft). Its clear, blue-green water in midsummer reaches a temperature of 10°C (50°F). Trout were introduced at the end of the 1960s.

The Teberda-Dombai road then crosses the southern outskirts of the village of Krasnaya Polyana. At the 15-km mark the road forks, and a right turn leads up the valley of the river Gonach-khir, while the way to Dombai is across the Gon-achkhir. To reach Klukhor Pass, follow the Gonachkhir valley, and then that of the Klukhor in a southeasterly direction for a total of 25 km (16 miles).

The Northern Shelter (Severny Priyut) is situated at a height of 2,040 m (6,690 ft). 5 km (3 miles) from it lies the warm Lake Tumanlykel, fit for bathing.

Lake Klukhor is situated on the footpath from the Northern Shelter to the pass. The river Severny flows out of Lake Klukhor.

World War II Memorials, by the lake and in its vicinity, are dedicated to soldiers killed during the defence of Klukhor Pass.

The Southern Shelter (Yuzhny Priyut) is free from snow from the beginning of July to mid-September. The path over it runs along a steep slope (4–5 hours on foot). In July and August, Intourist organises walking excursions well in advance, so that transport can be waiting on the other side.

Dombai Valley is situated in the upper part of the Teberda Reservation, 1,560 m (5,120 ft) above sea level. It is surrounded by mountains on all sides, and from it to the south opens up a beautiful panoramic view of the grandiose Main Caucasian Ridge, the snowy peaks of which rise to a height of 3,800–4,040 m (12,470–13,250 ft). The ridge serves as a border between Georgia and Russia, and Dombai is the heart of the Caucasus. Ine ("needle") Peak towers on the right, together with the Dju-guturlyuchata Crest. The first alpine camp was or-ganised here in 1935. In spite of the closeness of glaciers, the vegetation is very rich. In summer it is cool here, and in winter, mild with abundant snow. The environs are covered by dense fir forests, with an occasional birch or ash, and there is an abundance of flowers and berries.

Dombai Population—1,200

Intourist organises excursions here from Stavropol.

24 km (15 miles) from Teberda is Dombai, which means "buffalo" in Turkish. The village lies at the confluence of 3 rivers, the Dombai-Ulgen, the Alibek, and the Amnauz. There are 3 alpine camps, Combai, Belaly-kaya, and Krasnaya Zvezda. The whole recreation complex for tour-ism, alpinism, mountain skiing, and skating can accommodate 2,000 persons.

Cablecars and chairlifts run into the mountains. Russian Clearing is a favourite place for sunbath-ing, not only in the summer but in winter as well.

Dumbai Hotel and Restaurant, tel. 78–169

Gornye Vershiny Hotel, tel. 78–236. This hotel has a swimming pool, but meals are taken at the Dombai Hotel.

Crocus Hotel and Restaurant

Intourist Office, tel. 78–168

5 km (3 miles) from the village in Alibeck river valley is the Alibeck alpine camp.

Intourist organises a series of interesting alpine walks from Dombai:

Semyonov-Bashi. The lookout point is not far from Dombai but is a 5–6-hour climb to a height of 2,400 m (7,874 ft) above sea level—and there is no water on the way! Mount Semyonov rises to the northeast of Dombai, and the path up it runs through pine forest and alpine meadows. The pan-oramic view from its slopes over the valley and the surrounding mountains is excellent.

Alibeck Glacier. Farther up the valley from Dombai, this is the most easily accessible of the Main Caucasian Ridge glaciers. It descends deep into the valley, close to the fir forest, occupying an area of 9,750 sq m (11,660 sq yd). At its edge, among the rhododendrons, lies the picturesque greenish-blue Turiye ("aurochs") Lake, a favourite watering place of aurochs and chamois in the early morning or late evening.

Amnauz Ravine. Amnauz is one of the 3 rivers that meet at Dombai. Its valley runs up in a south-erly direction. The road to the ravine leads through a fir forest. The return distance on foot is 10 km (6 miles). Amnauz means "vicious mouth" or "big jaws," and the Amnauz Glacier and Amnauz-Baa-shi Mountain all share the name.

Chuchkhur Waterfalls. 7 km (4 miles) from Dombai by foot along the Dombai-Ulgen valley, the excursions there and back take 5–6 hours. Chuchkhur means "waterfall," and the water pours down from the smooth, grey slopes known as Barani Lby ("sheep's brows"), cliffs worn smooth by some ancient glacial action. The confluence of 2 streams, the Chuchkhur and the Ptysh, forms the river Dombai-Ulgen, which in translation means "the buffalo is killed." The main peak of this region bears the same name; its height is 4,047 m (13,278 ft).

Mussa-Achitara. The Mussa-Achitara Ridge runs parallel to the Main Caucasian Ridge and is considered the best point for seeing the mountain panorama. A cablecar takes one to a height of 2,500 m (8,200 ft), and then a footpath leads to the crest of the ridge, at a height of 3,030 m (9,940 ft). The distance to be walked is 6 km (4 miles), both ways.

Klukhor. Back toward Teberda, and then south-eastward up the valley of the Gonatskhir is Lake Klukhor and Klukhor Pass (described above).

Dzhamagatskiye Narzany. This excursion to the mineral springs of Dzamagatskiye Narzany starts some distance from Dombai, a little below Teberda, where a 3-hour walk follows the valley of the Dzhamagat up to the east. At a height of about 1,800 m (5,906 ft) above sea level, the 4 springs pour out about 26,000 litres (6,868 gal) of water a day, maintaining a steady temperature of 6°C (42.8°F).

KIZHI

Intourist organises excursions here by hydrofoil from Petrovodsk.

The island of Kizhi is situated near the edge of Lake Onega. Before the Slavs penetrated here, these parts were inhabited by Finnish tribes, in-cluding the Karels, the Ests, the Izhora, and the Ves. The shores of Lake Onega belonged to Nov-

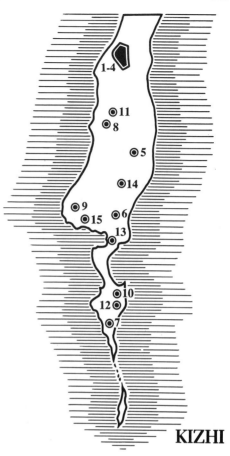

1 Preobrazhenskaya Church

2 Pokrovskaya Church

3 Bell Tower

4 Fence

5 Lazar Church

6 Lelikozero Chapel

7 Kavgora Chapel

8 Oshevnev's House

9 Yelizarov's House

10 Sergeyev's House

11 Two-storey Barn

12 Barn

13 Watermill

14 Windmill

15 Treshing Barn

KIZHI

gorod as early as the 9th century. The island's name derives from "kizha-suari," meaning "island of games," because there are grounds for believing it to have been the site of ritual sacrifices accompanied by song and dance in the pagan past. Christianity was slow to gain hold. Although it reached Novgorod in the 11th century, it only came to Karelia in 1227, when Prince Yaroslav Vsevolodovich, the father of Alexander Nevsky, sent priests to baptise the local population. However, paganism remained long after. In the 16th century, Archbishop Makary of Novgorod and Pskov wrote to Moscow that there were still all too many idols and pagan rituals in the north. One of the earliest missionaries in the Onega area was a Novgorod monk named Lazar (1286–1391), who was later canonised under the name of Lazar Muromsky (after Muromsky Island, now Much Island, in Lake Onega). The parish of Kizhi was founded in the middle of the 16th century. In 1769–71 Kizhi was the site of the largest peasants' revolt in Karelia.

Now there is a collection of different examples of peasant architecture here. There are houses, barns, and both a watermill and a windmill. The *house from the village of Oshenevo*, only 2 km (1 mile) from Kizhi, was built in 1876, and *Yelizarov's House* (1880) came from nearby Seredok. The latter

has no chimney and the smoke from the stove had to find its own way out. *Sergeyev's House* (1910) came from Logmurichi, 13 km (8 miles) outside Petrozavodsk.

The 3 *barns* are all of 19th-century construction. In the threshing barn, grain was dried as well as threshed. This barn came from Beryozovaya Selga, as did the *watermill* (1875), while the *windmill* is from Volkostrov. All the buildings were put together without nails, in the traditional style of wooden architecture in the north.

Preobrazhenskaya (Transfiguration) Church has 22 cupolas and was built in 1714. The cupolas rise up high in 5 tiers. The cupolas of the 1st, 3rd, and 5th tiers increase in size from bottom to top in a ratio of 1:1.5, thus emphasising the main feature of the church, the central octagonal. It has been called "an incomparable fairy tale of cupolas" and "a miracle of miracles." Some Russian artists consider it to be the ultimate in Russian church architecture and the equal of St. Basil's in Moscow's Red Square. Its total height is 37 m (121 ft).

The interior of the church is remarkable for its unusual iconostasis. It is curved, and the left and right ends follow the lines of the north and south walls, with the result that the light falls differently on the various parts of it and the effect changes with the time of day. The icons in the lowest row are perhaps the most interesting. There is one depicting Abraham and Sarah (third from the right), which is an excellent example of the colours typical of the icons of the north, making full use of rust-red and golden-toned ochres. The icon on the farthest left shows Zosima and Savatyi, founders of the monastery on Solovetsky Island in the White Sea, and that third from the left illustrates the life of St. George. The fourth from the left is of Elijah being carried away to heaven in the chariot, always a favourite theme for icon painters. The iconostasis was dismantled during the Second World War before the occupation and was reassembled in 1945 when the icons, all dating from the 17th and 18th centuries, were restored. The large, wooden cross was originally a wayside one.

Pokrovskaya (Intercession) Church was built in 1764. The 9 cupolas are each dedicated to a different saint, and there is a tenth over the altar.

The church's original iconostasis was lost, but the present one was put together in 1951 to display local icons painted in the 18th century, many of them older than the church itself. The beautiful colouring of "The Entry into Jerusalem" (sixth from the left) is worth noting, as is the realistic detail of the costumes and horses in "Flor and Lavr." The variety of the collection gives a good idea of the richness of northern icon-painting in the 17th and 18th centuries.

The palistrade surrounding the churches was restored in 1959, following old illustrations and the construction methods of existing wooden walls in other places in the north. The belfry was built in 1874.

The *Church of St. Lazarus* (1390) is the oldest in Karelia. It was built by Lazar Muromsky himself. It has a single dome and was brought here from the former Muromsky Monastery and restored in 1961.

The *Chapel of Michael the Archangel* (late 18th century) was brought here from the village of Lelikozero and restored in 1961.

The *Chapel of the Three Prelates* (17th century) was restored in 1962 after being brought here from the village of Kavgory.

KLAIPEDA Population—205,000
Intourist organises excursions here from Vilnius.

This is Lithuania's third-largest town. It was known as Memel until 1923, and then again when it was in German hands during the Second World War. It stands on either side of the narrow but deep river Danga and the channel by which the lagoon of Kursiu Marios and the river Nyemunas (Niemen) connect with the Baltic. An important river and seaport, Klaipeda remains icefree throughout the winter. In 1986 its importance increased with the opening of a railway and container ferry service, which bypasses Poland and goes to Mukran on the German island of Rugen.

It is one of the most ancient towns in Lithuania. There was a settlement here in the 7th century, and in 1202, with the backing of Pope Innocent

III, the Knights of the Sword, later to be called the Livonian Order, settled in the area. The local fortress (which stood where the Klaipeda Ship-repairing Yard is today) was seized and destroyed, and Memelburg Castle was built in its stead in 1252. From the south the Prussian-based Teutonic Order (the Knights of the Cross) reached northward in an attempt to link up with the Livonian Order. The Teutonic Knights had a jealously guarded monopoly on the collection of amber as it was washed up on the beaches after storms. There was a Lithuanian uprising in 1525–27, but the land along the Baltic shore continued to become increasingly German. From 1629–35 the Swedes were here, and in 1757 the Russians captured the town and held it for 5 years.

In 1807, after Napoleon had occupied Berlin, Frederick William III of Prussia (1770–1840) resided in Memel. It was here that he signed the act releasing the peasants from hereditary servitude and other important documents. Memel continued to grow as a seaport and as the area's commercial centre. It was a German city as far as language, customs, and allegiance were concerned, but nevertheless the rural population remained predominantly Lithuanian. An English traveller of the 19th century called Memel "the dullest of all the seaports in Europe" and said, "There is not anything in this place to detain a man's curiosity for 2 hours. The buildings are very wretched. The ships at the quay are the finest sight in Memel."

The town remained German until the end of the First World War, when it was taken from Germany by the Treaty of Versailles. The Entente gave France a mandate to govern the district, and in 1920 French troops arrived. The answer to the German protest was, "The allied and associated powers refuse to admit that the cession of the Klaipeda region might be contrary to the principle of nationality. The region in question has always been Lithuanian, the majority of the population is Lithuanian in regard to origin and language." The German Reich Commissar, Graf Lambsdorff, turned the area over to the French general Dominique Joseph Odry.

In 1923 the region was joined to Lithuania, but a new category of inhabitants developed, neither pro-German nor pro-Lithuanian, called Memellanders. After the Memel Statute (or the Klaipeda Convention) of 1924, the town was incorporated into Lithuania, and so it was that Lithuania gained its exit to the sea. Because a large part of the city was German, Klaipeda territory became an autonomous unit in Lithuania, a kind of state within a state. The administration of Memel-Klaipeda territory was in German hands. There were hopes to make Klaipeda a Free City, like nearby Danzig. Along with the political changes in Germany, a Nazi party appeared in Klaipeda. The Klaipeda Convention remained valid until 1939. After the Anschluss with Austria, annexing Sudentenland from Czechoslovakia, came Lithuania's turn. In March 1939 Lithuania had to sign a treaty in Berlin turning Klaipeda over to Germany. 6 hours before the signing, Hitler steamed into Memel aboard the battleship "Deutschland." He was accompanied by the "Graf Spee," the cruisers "Nurnberg," "Leipzig," and "Kol," and other craft, making a total of 40 men-of-war. Hitler reviewed a march past and said from the balcony of the city theatre that Memel would always belong to the Reich. So Lithuania lost her only seaport again.

The population, which had been 47,000 in 1931, fell to 13,000 after the Second World War. Now it keeps growing each year, and the boundaries are extending. The former remote outskirts of Rumpiske, Mazasis, and Kaimelis have now merged into the city.

Despite the fact that two-thirds of the houses were destroyed toward the end of World War II, particularly in 1944, the town still retains its Germanic appearance. Nevertheless, German tourists who have been here before can now hardly recognise it. Among other architectural monuments, a complex of 16th–18th-century houses and storehouses in the old part of the town has been proclaimed a historical reserve. Restoration work is still in progress. There are the remains of a castle and bastions of the 13th–18th centuries; also of architectural interest is the former town hall (Rathaus), the post building, the theatre, and the military barracks. The portal of old Luisenkirche survived the war and is now an arch for traffic to drive through.

The main thoroughfare is Mantas Street, and this is where the best shops are to be found. The broad Taika Avenue is also attractive, as are Kaunas and Debrecen avenues. The port has been extended to accommodate the considerable oil export. There is also a coal-grading complex. The fishing port is the home of a large deep-sea fishing fleet. There is a fish cannery, and fish processing is the main local industry, centered in Smelte. The Baltija Shipyard, specialising in trawlers and floating docks, is one of the largest in the Baltic. There is also a pulp and paper mill and a woodworking factory, and the town has long been known for its production of articles made from amber.

There is a polytechnical institute, a music school, and a seamen's school.

Catholic Church of Our Lady, Queen of Peace was built in 1957–60 by Baltrenas to hold a congregation of 3,000. Closed in 1961, it was shorn of its belfry (depcapitated, as they say) and converted into a concert hall.

Local Museum, Gorky Street 7

Watch and Clock Museum

Marine Museum, in Kopgalis Fortress, on Kursiu Nerija

Aquarium, in Kopgalis Fortress, on Kursiu Nerija

World War II Monument, Victory Square

Drama Theatre, Teatro Street 2. The theatre was founded in 1875 and is the oldest in Lithuania.

Concert Hall, in the Catholic church

Palace of Culture, Tarybu (Soviet) Square. Built in 1964.

International Seamen's Club

Mazvidas Park. Here is an open-air sculpture

exhibition with over 100 pieces of contemporary work.

Klaipeda Hotel and Restaurant, Melnikaite 12

Baltija Hotel, Monte Street 41. Herkus Monte was the leader of a 13th-century Lithuanian uprising against the Teutonic Knights.

Near Klaipeda are splendid white sandy beaches. They are backed by grass-covered dunes and then forest of pine, birch, and fir. Famous here is the unique spit called Kursiu Nerija (Kurische Nehrung in German), which is 98 km (61 miles) long and divides the lagoon, which is 400 m (437 yd) wide and called *Kursiu Marios* (Kurische Haff in German), from the Baltic Sea. Kursiu Nerija, real dune country, is protected as a landscape and nature reserve, the local fauna including elk. The sand is as fine as any in the Sahara Desert, and it is even known as the Northern Sahara. On Kursiu Nerija are the *remains of an 18th-century fortress* and the popular *resort* of Neringa.

Neringa Population—2,000

In 1961 the villages of Nida, Juodkrante, and Preile were united into a township and called Neringa. It is 50 km (31 miles) long.

Smiltyne (German: Sandkrug)

This village on Kursiu Nerija has been known since 1616. Until 1833 it was a post station on the road to Konigsberg. Before the Second World War, there was a casino here, and it is still Klaipeda's most popular beach.

Juodkrante (German: Schwarzort)

This is a fishermen's village, 18 km (11 miles) farther to the south.

Nida (German: Nidden)

This is another fishing village, 30 km (19 miles) beyond that, 50 km (31 km) from Klaipeda. It was founded in the 15th century. Now the old villas are used as holiday homes. Until 1933 the German writer Thomas Mann spent his summers in one of them.

Intourist also organises excursions from Klaipeda, northward up the coast to Palanga.

KLIN Population—100,000

Intourist organises trips here from both Moscow and Tver.

The name of this town, which stands on the river Sestra (sister), is first recorded in 1234. In 1482 it became part of Moscovy, and in 1572 Ivan the Terrible left it to his son, Ivan, after which it passed to the Romanovs. Klin was made a district town in 1785, and its coat-of-arms bears gules (red), that of Moscow above, while the lower part shows its importance on the post road between St. Petersburg and Moscow; it is argent (silver-white), a mounted courier sounding his horn. Klin has factories making synthetic fibre, glass, and thermometers.

Among the older buildings in the town is an arcade of shops and the administrative centre, Papivin Street 2-4, built in classical style at the turn of the 19th century by Semyon Karin. The 3 buildings in the administrative centre were the mayor's house, the treasury and a police station. Karin was also responsible for the post office building in Sovietskaya Square. The old 2-storey Empire-style hotel that stands nearby dates from the early 19th century.

Uspensky (Assumption) Monastery, Papivin Street 16a. The 16th-century church here is the oldest in the town. Although the monastery was closed in the late 18th century, the church was reconstructed in the 19th century in Empire style and restored in 1960.

Voskresenskaya (Resurrection) Church & Belfry, Sovietskaya Square. The local Kremlin stood here, but it was never reinforced with more than earthen walls. The church was founded in 1712 and built of brick, the work being financed by the congregation. It was in Moscow baroque style but has been considerably altered. The belfry, which stands apart, to the south-west of the church, was built in 1769 though the lower portion appears to be of considerably earlier date.

Tchaikovsky Museum, Tchaikovsky Street 48. Open 10–6; closed Wed., Fri., and last Mon. of each month. The composer Peter Tchaikovsky lived in this region from 1885 and 1893. He wrote of his affection for the place, "I have become so attached to Klin that I cannot imagine myself living anywhere else. . . . I am unable to do justice to the charm of the Russian village, the Russian landscape and the silence which I need most of all." He wrote his "6th (Pathetic) Symphony," the "3rd Piano Concerto," and the music for the "Nutcracker" and "Sleeping Beauty" ballets here.

After his death his brother, Modest, decided to make the house a museum, so it was first purchased from the owner by Tchaikovsky's servant, Alexei Sofronov, and then bought by Modest Tchaikovsky and the composer's nephew, V. Davydov. The brother died in 1916 and the house passed to the Russian Musical Society; it was protected by government charter, was restored in 1942, and became state property in 1944.

The 2-storey building is furnished and decorated as it was in the composer's lifetime, and contains his books, paintings, grand piano, and other personal possessions. Winners of the International Tchaikovsky Competition are allowed to play the Becker grand; Van Cliburn was the first to be so honoured. Modest Tchaikovsky wrote a 3-volume biography of his brother, and the material he collected for this purpose formed the basis of the Tchaikovsky archives now amounting to almost 50,000 items and still used for research.

The nearby *Concert Hall* with seats for 400 was built in 1963.

Hotel, Lenin Street 37, tel. 5313

Hotel, Sovietskaya Square 1/3

Yubileinyi Restaurant, Mira Street 58, tel. 6543

Kolos Restaurant, Teatralnaya Street 1/3, tel. 6406

Restaurant and Cafeteria, on the way out of town

Yunost Cafe, at the entrance to the town

Post Office, Sovietskaya Street 1/3

Filling Station and Service Station, beside the road on the way into town from Moscow

KOBRIN (Kobryn) Population—28,000

(Intourist organises excursions here from Brest.)

Kobrin, at the 52/1,002 km mark, stands on either side of the river Mukhavets. It was founded in the 11th century and in the 15th and 16th cen-

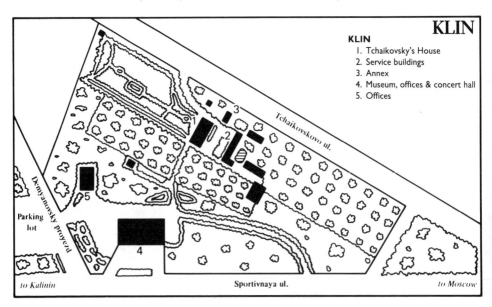

KLIN

KLIN
1. Tchaikovsky's House
2. Service buildings
3. Annex
4. Museum, offices & concert hall
5. Offices

to Kalinin Sportivnaya ul. *to Moscow*

turies served as the centre of the Princedom of Kobrin. The first recorded mention of the town was made in 1287 and during its history it changed hands between the Poles and the Lithuanians. On 18 August 1795, it was presented by Catherine II to Generalissimo Suvorov, and he ordered the construction of a wooden house for his personal use. It was in Kobrin that the Russians, on 15 July 1812, had their first victory over Napoleon. Romuald Traugutt, leader of the Polish insurrection against Russia in 1863, lived at Traugutt Street 10.

Local industry: consumer goods, food products, furniture, building materials. Of economic importance to Kobrin is the navigable 92.8-km (58-mile) Dnieper-Bug Canal, which links the Dnieper and the Vistula and runs near the town.

St. Alexander Nevsky Cathedral, on the main street. This dates from the 19th century.

Church of SS Peter and Paul, in the cemetery. This wooden church was built in the 15th century. Open for services.

Suvorov Military History Museum, Suvorov Street 16. (Generalissimo Suvorov lived in Kobrin March–April 1797 and February–March 1800.)

Victory Monument with an eagle on top, by the bridge. Unveiled in 1912 to commemorate the centenary of the victory over Napoleon. The inscription reads: "To the Russian warriors who won the first victory over the Napoleonic Army within the bounds of Russia—15th July, 1812" and refers to the taking of the first French detachment here. Next to the monument stand four mortars inscribed "No. 23 Finsong 1837."

World War II Monument, on the common grave of Soviet soldiers and civilians.

Suvorov Park, on the grounds of Suvorov's estate. The lime trees date from his time and there is a bust in his memory.

Byelorus Restaurant, Suvorov Street 33.

Kobrin Restaurant, on the main street, upstairs in the department store.

KOBULETI

Kobuleti is 33 km (21 miles) from Batumi. It stands only 10 m (33 ft) above sea level, and stretches for 10 km (6 miles) along the shore. It has an excellent beach of sand and fine pebbles, and in some places stretches up to 100 m (109 yds) wide. The water is shallow here, and is especially good for children. The beach is backed by pines and subtropical flora.

There was a sizeable town here in ancient times and trade contacts were maintained with Colchis and the cities of the Mediterranean. It was first mentioned in writing by the Italian missionary Archangelo Lamberti, who visited Georgia in 1633–49.

Kobuleti first became popular as a resort at the beginning of this century when many retired tsarist generals built villas here. Its value was much increased, however, with the draining of the malarial swamps in the vicinity. The local inhabitants are proud of the splendid view over the valley and say that it is a combination of the French Riviera and Switzerland. A nearby herbal institute has a plantation of medicinal herbs.

Lenin Street is the main thoroughfare. From

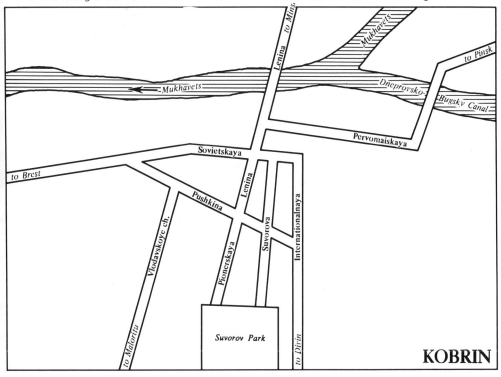

KOBRIN

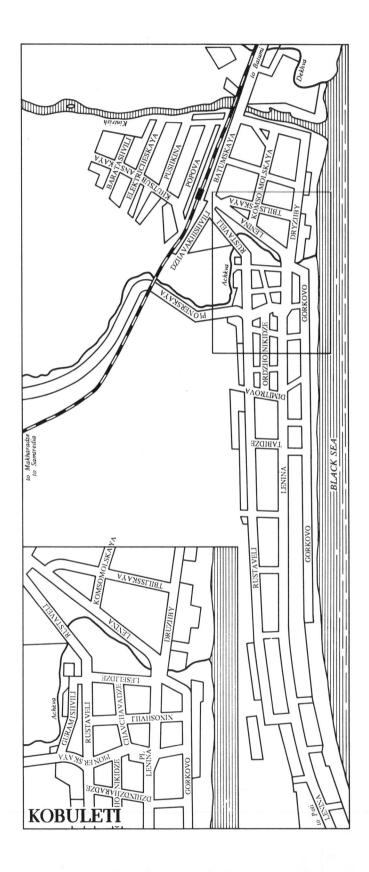

KOBULETI

Batumi, Batumskaya Street runs in as far as the railway station. From there Lenin Street runs out to the left towards the sea, and then makes a right turn to continue straight through the town. Rustaveli Street lies parallel to Lenin Street, but further inland.

Lenin Statue, on the square by the railway station

Threatre

Park

Gorizont (Intourist) Hotel, Lenin Street 291

Kolkheti Hotel & Restaurant, Lenin Street. This is an Intourist hotel.

Intourist Hotel, Lenin Street 283

Iveria Hotel, Lenin Street 281

Kobuleti Restaurant, Lenin Street

National Restaurant, in the village of Nakvi

Cafés & Snackbars, all along the length of the town

Intourist office, Lenin Street 285; tel. 4277

Telephone Office, Lenin Square

Intourist organises excursions from here to Tskhaltubo via Kutaisi.

KOKAND (also Khokand, Khovakend)
Population—185,000

Intourist organises excursions here from Fergana, 90 km/56 miles away.

Kokand (locally pronounced "kuk-kon") takes its name from the word "khukiyand i-lyatif," meaning joyful or pleasant. It stands in the fertile Fergana Valley on the river Sokh. It is 450 m (1,476 ft) above sea level and was first mentioned as a small settlement in the 10th century.

The Khanate of Kokand was, along with Bukhara and Khiva, one of the 3 restless khanates of Central Asia that lay at the borders of Russian lands in the 18th century. They were constantly at war with each other as well as with Persia, Afghanistan, and China, and suffered in addition from sporadic raids by the Kazakh and Turkmen nomads in the area. The Khanate of Kokand was the first of the three to be annexed by Russia while the others survived as vassal states.

The first Khan of Kokand, Abdul-Karim-bai Shakhrukh Beg, built not far from present-day Kokand the fortress of Eski-Kurgan from which the town grew. Kokand was founded in 1732 and its name dates from 1740. It lay on the ancient caravan route that connected the east and the west, and after the Chinese first entered Fergana Valley in 1758, and due to its convenient geographical position at the entrance to the Valley, Kokand became well known as a political and trade centre.

The Khanate of Kokand was founded in 1798, and the town rose to become its capital. One of the local rulers (begs), Alim-Khan, killed all his relatives and rivals, united under his rule some areas of the valley, and thereafter took in Tashkent, Chimkent, and Ura-Tyube. Alim-Khan was killed in 1817, but his brother Omar reigned till 1822. He patronized the arts and sciences. It was he who joined Turkestan (formerly Azret, Yassy) to the

Khanate and built some fortifications on the Syr-Darya. It was the construction of the latter that first caused friction with the Russians. In 1842, the Kokand Khanate was subdued by the Emirate of Bukhara, but retained a certain amount of autonomy.

Khudayar Khan, who ruled the Khanate 1843–75, was the last of the local Khans. He was a hunter, sportsman, and bon vivant. He used to enjoy organising dog fights but had to give it up as the owners besieged the palace ("urdu"), complaining of the loss of their dogs. When, during the Russian advance in 1866, the Kokand Khanate was cut off from the Emirate of Bukhara, Khudayar Khan was still recognised by the Russians.

In 1867, the governor-generalship of Turkestan was established with its headquarters at Tashkent and General Von Kaufmann was appointed as the first governor-general. Kokand at this time had a population of 80,000, a total of 600 mosques, and 15 medressehs, where about 15,000 students were enrolled. In 1868 the Emir of Bukhara declared a holy war against the Russians, but Russian troops headed by General Von Kaufmann entered the city. Bukhara was further humbled by the capture of Samarkand and the Khanate was reduced to a vassalage.

Peace treaties were concluded in 1868, which gave the Russians highly favorable trade terms. Russia and Kokand signed a commercial treaty in 1872. Khudayar, however, did not seize the opportunity of establishing a state of his own; rather he tended to rob his vassals, and rebellions broke out here and there. The relationship between Russia and Kokand remained good until 1875 when a rebellion broke out against both Khudayar Khan and the Russians. Khudayar had become very unpopular and was forced by the rebels to seek protection of the Russian army. Von Kaufmann took Kokand on 26th August, 1875. He proclaimed Khudayar's son, Nasr-Eddin, khan instead of his father, but his rule collapsed when the Russian troops withdrew, and he followed his father to Russia. General Skobelev was put in command and the following year the khanate was annexed by Russia on the grounds of domestic instability. It was only at this point that serfdom was abolished in the area.

The town of Kokand at this time was surrounded by a high wall of mud bricks, 19 km (12 miles) in length, with 12 gates and a moat. The streets leading from the gates met in Urdinskaya Square ("urdu" meaning palace). This was the Russian part of the town with the main thoroughfare being Rosenbachovsky Prospect (named after General N. O. Rosenbach, governor-general of Turkestan), later renamed Sovietskaya Street. It runs right through Kokand, and Skobelev Prospect leads to the railway station. There were 250 houses in the Russian part of the town and all the state buildings were concentrated here. The Orthodox Church of SS Helena and Konstantin was opened in the hall of the palace.

The Asian part of Kokand was typical, with its

mud houses, medressehs, and 248 mosques. Located here is the Dzhuma-mosque with an infamous tower in the middle of its courtyard from which criminals were thrown down to their deaths.

The town developed and the first cotton-ginning plant in Central Asia was built in Kokand in 1881, thus making the valley of Fergana the main cotton-ginning area. After Kokand became a railroad junction in 1898, its trade importance increased. The town developed into a banking and business centre, and Kokand's stock exchange committee had its representation in St. Petersburg. Because of the extent of its foreign trade relations, a customs office was organised in Kokand. Commerce was concentrated in the hands of the Bukharan Jews.

A hotel was built here before the revolution, and also the Russian-Asian Bank (the building still serves as a bank). A number of German firms had their offices in the town (Kraft's is now used by the army, while Schmidt's is a TB sanatorium). In 1917–18 Kokand served for 3 months as the capital of the anti-Bolshevik autonomous government of Turkestan. It suffered much damage from the Red Army in 1918.

Present-day Kokand has developed chemical (particularly fertilisers), machine-building, light, and food industries. It is also the centre of a renowned national pottery industry.

Local Museum, Sovietskaya Street 2, in the palace, inside Khudayar's Fortress. The fortress stands on a hill 12 m (39 ft) high and covers 3.9 hectares (9.75 acres). The khan's palace ("urdu") was built in 1871 for Khudayar-Khan. It has an impressive portal decorated with floral motifs and quotations from the Koran in white lettering on a blue background. It was a sizeable building, and the best architects and artists of the period took part in its construction, the chief architect being Mir Ubaidulla. The palace consisted of administrative, ceremonial, and dwelling sections; the decorative audience hall is especially worth seeing. It was built above a military parade ground and was ornamented with multicolored tiles. The museum was founded in 1924.

Medresseh-i-Mir (13th century)

Norbut bai Medresseh was built during the reign of Norbut bai in 1799 by an architect from Buhara. The walls of the medresseh are of brick.

Dzhuma Mosque was the major mosque. The ceiling is richly decorated and nearby there is a minaret with a cupola.

Dakhami-Shakhon Mausoleum was built in the 1830s as a family mausoleum for the Kokand khans. The builders tried to copy burial vaults of the 14th–15th centuries.

Madarikhan Mausoleum was erected in 1825. Its portal copies that of the Bibi-Khanym Mosque in Samarkand.

Nadira Tomb. Nadira Maknuna (1791–1842) was a local poetess and philosopher.

Mukimi Memorial Museum, Mukimi Street 77; Mukhamed Amin Hodja, known as Mukimi (1850–1903), was a local poet who spent almost

all his life in Kokand and so chose the pseudonym of Mukimi, meaning "steady."

Gulyam Literature Museum, Sovietskaya Street 69. Gafur Gulyam (Gulyamov), born in 1903, was a poet. There are 6 halls containing ancient manuscripts, as well as the books and other works by outstanding Uzbek literary figures connected with Kokand, such as Mukimi, Furkhat, and Hamza. Open 9–6; closed Mon.

Hamza Drama Threatre, Kirov Street 19. Named after Hamza Hakim-zade Niyazi (1889–1929), founder of Uzbek literature.

Mukimi Park, Sovietskaya Street 2

Furkhat Park, Kirov Street 2. Zakir-dzhan Furkhat (1858–1909) was an outstanding local poet who studied in Kokand.

Civil War Monument and Eternal Flame, in Oktyabrsky garden, in the centre of the town. Unveiled in 1965.

Kokand Hotel & Restaurant, Sovietskaya Street 29

GPO, Karl Marx Street 20

KOSTROMA Population—280,000

Kostroma is situated 300 km (186 miles) from Moscow, on the left bank of the river Volga, where it is joined by the Kostroma. The origins of its founding and name are shrouded in legend. There used to be a folk tradition among the peoples of the upper reaches of the Volga River to mark the beginning of summer. The young village girls staged what they called the funeral of Kostroma, the most beautiful young girl chosen from their midst. She was carried down to the river on a white plank to be bathed, but a rival group would capture her and throw her into the river, and pretend to be rejoicing over their victory while they were really grieving for her death. Then they all returned to a festival of song and dance. In cold weather Kostroma was replaced by an effigy made out of dry twigs and straw, which were probably called "kostroma" in the local dialect and hence the name of the town.

Kostroma was first mentioned in the ancient Russian chronicles in 1213, though the town probably existed before then, perhaps founded by Yuri Dolgoruki in 1152. For reasons of defence it first stood on the higher right bank of the river. The first mention of Kostroma is connected with the fratricidal war between the princes Konstantin of Rostov and Yuri, sons of Prince Vsevolod the Big Nest. In 1238, Kostroma was devastated by Tatar hordes and the townsfolk fled to the woods. Uspensky ("Assumption") Cathedral was founded by Prince Vasily the following year (and he himself was buried here in 1276). In 1246, after Kostroma had been rebuilt, the Great Prince of Vladimir gave the town to his youngest son, Vasily, youngest brother of Alexander Nevsky. It then became the centre of an independent princedom. Along with the whole of Rus, the princedom of Kostroma fell victim to the oppression of Golden Horde. In the summer of 1264, the townspeople of Kostroma won a battle at Svyatoye Ozero ("Holy Lake") against the Tatars. In 1271, Prince Vasily, surnamed the

Trough, inherited the title of Grand Prince of Vladimir, but he continued to live in Kostroma and died childless in 1276.

At the beginning of the 14th century Kostroma served as a hiding place for the Great Princes. In the first half of the 14th century it was joined to the Princedom of Moscow by Ivan Kalita. After that it became one of the strongholds of the Russian state in the Volga area, and an oaken kremlin was built.

During the invasion by the Tatar Khan Tokhtamysh, and after the Russian victory in the Battle of Kulikovo (1380), Dmitry Donskoi hid himself in Kostroma while gathering enough troops to start his campaign against the Tatar Khan Edigei. In 1408, Great Prince Vasily of Moscow hid here from Edigei's invasion. In 1433, Kostroma was also the hiding place for Great Prince Vasily Temny (Vasily the Blind) of Moscow during the attack on Moscow by his uncle, Prince Yuri of Galich. In 1448, the troops of Vasily Temny led by Prince Striga-Obolensky successfully defended Kostroma from the attack of Dmitry Shemyaka, the Prince of Galich who blinded Prince Vasily of Moscow.

During the Time of Troubles Kostroma took an active part in the struggle against False Dmitry and the Poles. In 1608 it was twice captured by Alexander Lisovsky's troops and devastated by them. In 1609, False Dmitri's followers locked themselves in Ipatiyevsky Monastery and 10,000 people besieged it for 6 months before it fell. In 1611, Kostroma took part in the popular movement against the Poles.

After the fall of the Godunovs, the monastery was taken over by another royal dynasty, the Romanov family.

In 1613 an All-Russia Council for the election of the new Russian Tsar met in Moscow. On 14th March that year the whole council, headed by the future Tsar's closest relative, the boyar Fedor Sheremetyev, came to the Ipatiyevsky Monastery in Kostroma, where the young boyar, Mikhail Romanov, together with his mother, a nun called Marfa, had come from their family estate of Diminino, 70 km (43 miles) from Kostroma. They were hiding from the Poles and numerous other groups of outlaws who were roaming Russia at the time. After a daylong display of "great anger and weeping," Mikhail finally consented to take the crown and thus became the first Tsar of the Romanov dynasty.

According to the legends, he was right to hide because there were Poles who were out for his blood even before his coronation. It is told how a Russian peasant, Ivan Susanin, gave his life to save that of the future Russian Tsar by promising to show the way through the woods to the Tsar's hiding place to Polish invaders; Susanin brought them instead into the midst of impassable thickets where, though he was killed, the Poles also perished. The gallantry and spiritual beauty of Ivan Susanin inspired Mikhail Glinka to write his famous opera "Ivan Susanin," which is also called "A Life for the Tsar."

On 19th March the newly elected Tsar left Kostroma for Moscow, from where he later sent rich gifts to the monastery; the Romanov family continued to consider the monastery their personal family sanctuary and regarded it their duty to afford it their protection.

In the mid-17th century Kostroma was Russia's third-largest town after Moscow and Yaroslavl.

In 1719, when Russia was divided into different provinces, Kostroma became a regional centre within the province of Moscow.

It was known as the "cradle of the Romanov dynasty" and was visited frequently by royalty, right up until the 1917 revolution. In 1767 the town welcomed Catherine the Great, who arrived by boat from Tver. In memory of her visit, Catherine the Great gave the town its first coat-of-arms, which depicts a boat sailing downriver under the imperial flag, all in natural colours. Most of the wooden structures burned in a great fire in 1773, as did also the kremlin and Uspensky ("Assumption") Cathedral. It was decided not to rebuild the kremlin, but the cathedral was completely restored in 1776–91 following a new design by the talented local architect Stepan Vorotilov. He added a 4-tiered belfry that dominated the skyline from the river side of the town until it was demolished in the 1930s. Kostroma was declared provincial centre in 1778 on the order of Pavel I. A new town plan with a fan-like arrangement of streets was approved in 1784. In subsequent years the town became a place of exile for Polish insurgents, and they helped Kostroma to adopt its European appearance. Also influential in this respect was governor Baumgarten, who did much to improve the town. One of the finest buildings, the Hauptwacht ("guardhouse") was commissioned by him.

In 1817 it was visited by the Great Prince Mikhail and in 1834 by Emperor Nicholas I. In memory of this visit a monument of Ivan Susanin by Denut-Malinovsky was unveiled; it was in the form of a tall column crowned with a bust of the young Tsar Mikhail with an expressive kneeling figure of Ivan Susanin. The pedestal was adorned by bas-reliefs depicting scenes of the hero's tragic death. (Later the monument was demolished, because it supposedly did not conform to the Soviet people's conception of Susanin's feat; a new one by Lavinsky was erected in 1967.)

In 1851 some Moscow flax traders decided to open mills here and Kostroma grew to become the "flax capital of the north," one of the principal products being sailcoth for the international market, much of which was purchased by the English navy. The 2 original mills are still standing.

The last visit to Kostroma by a reigning member of the Romanov family was that of Nicholas II in 1913, on the occasion of the celebrations marking the 300th anniversary of the founding of the dynasty.

Today, Kostroma stands on either side of the Volga and serves as an important river port. It is the centre of the flax industry, and with three specialised educational establishments and a research institute engaged in flax processing studies, it is the

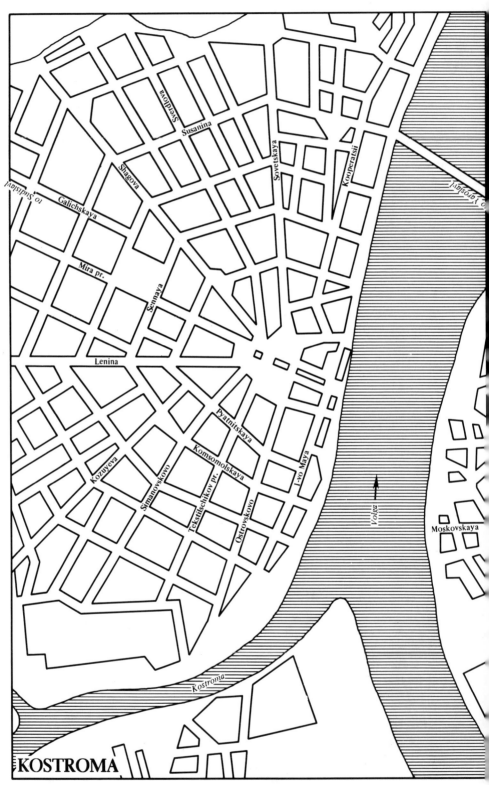

KOSTROMA

principal training centre for textile specialists. There are also metal-working and machine-building enterprises. The population of the town has more than doubled from 1939, when there were 120,000.

The historic Uspensky ("Assumption") Cathedral was demolished in the 1930s, and now nothing remains of the cathedral complex except for two 3-storey buildings.

Trade Arcades, in the old trade centre of Kostroma, near the city park. The arcades were built at the end of the 17th century. The architectural complex of Kostroma arcades, which took its final form by the beginning of the 19th century, is the oldest large town trade centre still to be found in Russia. It consists of more than a dozen buildings. Architects Vorotilov, Metlin, and Fursov took part in its construction. The last buildings to be built were the Tobacco Arcades, completed by Stasov in 1822.

Revolution Square, formerly Susanin Square, is one of the best squares in any provincial Russian town. Around it stand the Guard House, the Fire Tower, 19th-century administrative buildings, and the Borschov House. Today, it is the place where demonstrations, parades, and mass meetings take place.

Bogoyavlensky-Anastasinsky (Epiphany) Convent, Simonovskova Street. This was built as a monastery at the beginning of the 15th century by a monk named Nikita, a disciple of Sergius of Radonezh. Bogoyavlensky Cathedral was built in 1559–65 following the lines of the Uspensky Cathedral in Moscow. The monastery fell victim to Ivan the Terrible's rage; he suspected the clergy of Kostroma of being in sympathy with his cousin, Prince Vladimir Staritsky. Many people, including some of the builders of the cathedral, were executed upon the Tsar's order. In 1608, when Polish troops entered the town under Alexander Lisovsky, the monks and some of the Kostroma townsfolk hid themselves in the monastery. By the end of the 17th century Bogoyavlensky Monastery was a fortress that rivalled the Kostroma kremlin in strength.

In 1847, after another great fire, the monastery was closed and its half-burned buildings were given to the Anastasyin convent. The rich nuns restored Bogoyavlensky Cathedral in 1864–69, adding to its beautiful ancient form elements in pseudo-Russian style. Of great interest are the cathedral's interior frescoes by local painters.

One block of the original monks' cells remains, but of the walls with 6 towers that surrounded the monastery before the fire, only one tower is left, and this was reconstructed to serve as a belfry. The convent was closed in 1918 and since then the cathedral has served to house the Kostroma Regional Archives, one of the richest historical archives in the country.

Voskreseniya (Resurrection) Church-na-Debre is one of the finest examples of Russian 17th-century architecture. It was built in 1652 with the money of a rich merchant named Kirill Isakov near one of his own jetties. As legend has it, Isakov ordered a consignment of dyes from England but received in addition a barrel of pure gold. He reported the find to the London company, and they instructed him to "use the gold for charitable purposes." He accordingly donated it to the construction of this church, which was built on the site of a wooden church built at the turn of the 14th century by Prince Vasily (1248–76), who used to hunt in this area. According to another legend, Isakov was returning from England and was on open sea when his ship fell in a storm. He vowed that if his life was spared he would build a church. Either way, he built it, and the interesting carved stone entrance to the church includes, along with birds and other animals, the English lion and the unicorn.

At the northwestern end stands the *Tryokh Svyatitelei (Three Saints) Chapel*, dedicated to Vasily the Great, John the Divine, and Grigory (Bogoslov). The iconostasis of the chapel dates from ancient times. The oldest of the icons is that of the Fyodorovskaya Virgin (mid-13th century). Another treasure is the 15th-century Our Almighty Saviour, with which many local tales and legends are connected. It is a 2-sided icon; the front is covered with a decorative metal riza and cannot be seen, while the reverse shows the image of Paraskeva Pyatnitskaya painted in the pure and simple manner of old icon-painters.

In 1802 the *Znamenskaya Church* was erected beside the older building, later considered an act of vandalism by many architects because the styles clash so badly.

Ipatiyevsky Monastery, on the right bank of the little river Kostroma, at its confluence into the Volga. (On the way there the road passes Spassky and St. Nicholas's churches, and another small church just over the river, which is open 10–6.) Ipatiyevsky is one of the most interesting ancient architectural monuments of Kostroma. It was probably founded by Grand Prince Vasili of Vladimir in 1275. There is, however, a legend that it was founded in 1330 by a Tatar noble named Chet, who came from the Golden Horde to work for Prince Ivan Kalita of Moscow. He built the monastery on the site where he suddenly became ill, but in a dream he was promised a miraculous cure by the Virgin, who appeared before him together with the Apostle Philip and the holy martyr Ipati Gangrsky (who died in Asia Minor in the 9th century). Cured, Chet was baptised in Moscow under the name of Zakhary and became the founder of the Godunov family. The Godunov burial vault in the crypt once held more than 50 stone coffins. In 1382 Dmitry Donskoi visited the monastery with his son.

In the 16th century the monastery was patronised by Boris Godunov who built the Troitskaya (Trinity) Church here in 1586. The monastery was enriched by stone walls and within them were many valuable treasures, including the famous Ipatiyevskaya Chronicle, a document of priceless cultural worth as it is the main source of information about ancient Rus.

Troitsky Cathedral, was founded in 1590 and decorated with frescoes in 1595–96. It was here that the young Tsar Mikhail consented to accept the throne of Moscow in 1613. Following the destruction of the cathedral in 1649 by an explosion of gunpowder stored in the basement, it was restored in 1652 by Tsar Alexei and Archimandrite Hermogen following the design of Yaroslavl cathedral, typical of 17th-century churches.

The interior decorations were painted in the 17th–18th century under the famous Kostroma icon-painter Guri Mikitin who painted the interiors of many churches including the Archangel Cathedral in Moscow, the Danilov Monastery in Pereslavl-Zalessky, the Uspensky Cathedral in Rostov, and the Ilya Proroka (Elijah the Prophet) Church in Yaroslavl.

The northern gallery of the Troitsky Cathedral lost its frescoes completely in the 17th century. In the western gallery only part of the frescoes have survived. On the columns inside the cathedral there are portraits of many Russian princes and tsars, including Mikhail Romanov who was crowned here. In the southern part of the altar Chet is depicted being baptised by St. Ipathy. Most of the interior decorations still to be seen in the cathedral were done in 1912–13 during restoration work for the 300th anniversary of the Romanovs; the style of the painting was taken from the Church of Ilya Proroka in Yaroslavl.

The iconostasis of Troitskaya Cathedral is an interesting example of the 18th-century wood-carving. It was made in 1756–58 by Kostroma woodcarvers under Pyotr Zolotarev and Makar Bykov. Some of the icons of this cathedral are masterpieces of old-Russian icon-painting. There are burial places in the cathedral foundation. Boris Godunov's parents, Zakhary Chet (the founder of the monastery) and Ivan Susanin are buried here.

The cathedral was last constructed in 1835 after a fierce storm stripped the roofing off the domes; The southwestern sacristy was connected with the Rozhdestva Bogoroditsy (Nativity of the Virgin) Church.

To the east of the Troitsky Cathedral stands a 5-tiered belfry founded by Dmitri Godunov in 1603–05. The belfry has 19 bells, presented to the monastery by the Godunov family. The biggest, weighting 600 pounds, was presented to the monastery by Boris Godunov's mother. The belfry also has chimes of original design. Peter the Great had some of the bells removed and melted down to make cannon.

The so-called *Palaty Romanovykh* (Romanov's Palace) was built in the late 16th century. Originally a building with monks' cells, this was converted to royal use when Mikhail was proclaimed tsar. After the visit to the monastery by Tsar Alexander II in 1858, the palace was reconstructed in 17th-century style under court architect Richter. During the 300th anniversary celebrations of the Romanov family, Tsar Nicholas II also stayed here.

Other monastery buildings include the *Bishop's Palace* (1588), the *Refectory* (1640), the *Monks' Cells* (1758–59) and the *Candle Factory*. The column, with the names of all who donated money, was put up as a memorial on the monastery grounds in 1836.

The territory of the monastery was divided into 2 parts, which were called the Old Town and the New. Both parts are encircled by stone walls with towers, built in 1586–90 by the Godunov family. The New Town was added to the western side of the monastery in 1642–45, and the gate in the middle of its western wall, which is roofed with green tiles and called the Green Tower, was built in memory of Mikhail Romanov's departure to Moscow after his election to the throne; the gatechurch on top of the tower was dedicated to the Archangel Michael.

In 1767, to mark the arrival to the monastery of Catherine the Great, a new Yekaterininskiye Gate was built in the northern wall, which became the main entrance.

A new gate was made in the Water-Tower in the eastern wall of the monastery. The Gate-church of SS. Khrisanph and Darya, originally built in 1841 by Konstantin Ton, was completely rebuilt in 1862 by Grigoriev as a new Holy Gate.

The monastery was closed in 1918. Since 1946 it has housed a branch of Kostroma Regional Museum. In 1958 the monastery was proclaimed a historical-architectural museum preserve.

Museum of Wooden Folk Architecture, open-air, beside the monastery, near the river. This is the oldest museum of its kind in the country. It belongs to the local museum. *Preobrazhenskaya (Transfiguration) Church* (1628) from the village of Spas-Vezhi, 20 km (12 miles) from Kostroma, and the *bathhouses* (19th century) from Zharki, are built on stilts to protect them from the spring floods. The *Cathedral of the Virgin* (1552) comes from the village of Kholm and the *peasant houses* from Kologriv and Portyuk. The wooden shingles, used for roofing, are completely waterproof as they swell when wet; when dry, the ones on the church domes look like prickly fir cones when they open up.

Church of Ilyinskaya (St. Elijah) na-Gorodische, Dachnaya Street, beautifully sited in 1683–85 on the high right bank of the Volga.

Spasopreobrazhenskaya (Transfiguration) Church, Volgarei Street, also on the right bank of the Volga. A 5-domed church built in 1685–88. The interior frescoes date from the 17th century, and are similar to those of the Resurrection-on-the-Debre.

Church of Ioanna Bogoslova (St. John the Divine), in Trudovaya Sloboda, near the Ipatiyevsky Monastery. The church was built in 1681–87, with a low refectory that served as a winter church. The frescoes inside were painted in 1735 and again in 1885. The wooden iconostasis dates from 1770. The little openings in the roof of the belfry are unusual, as also the fine design of the iron railings (1765).

Church of Ioanna Zlatoust, Lavrovskaya Street. This 5-domed, baroque church with a refectory and a belfry dates from 1791.

Kostroma is known for its many brick houses

built in classic style in the 1830s, such as Akatov's House, the House of Nobles (Ostrovskovo Street 22), the Orphanage (at the corner of Pyatnitskaya and Vorovskovo streets), and Borschov's House (Ostrovsky Street); the latter belonged to General Borschov who fought in the War of 1812. Near it is a fine fire tower (1860), which is part of the fire station and still serves its original purpose.

Hauptwacht (guardhouse), near Lenin Street, near Borschov House. Built in 1826 by Fursov.

Kostroma Regional Museum, in Ipatiyevsky Monastery

Museum of Wooden Folk Architecture, open-air, beside Ipatiyevsky Monastery, near the river.

Art Gallery, Prospect Mira 5. This was built as a museum in 1913 to commemorate the 300th anniversary of the founding of the Romanov dynasty. There are icons upstairs and the paintings include some by Aivazovsky, Repin, and Chyesyakov.

Planetarium, Gornaya Street 14

Susanin Monument, in a garden in the centre of town, near the embankment. This is a new statue by Lavinsky, erected in 1967.

Ostrovsky Bust, in front of the Ostrovsky Theatre. This bust of Alexander Ostrovsky (1823–86) by N. Sarkisov was brought here from the playwright's estate in Schelykovo in 1967.

Kostroma was quite frequently visited by Ostrovsky; there is a pavilion on the bank of the Volga called Ostrovsky Pavilion where he liked to sit, enjoying the beautiful scenery. His play "The Storm" takes place in Kostroma.

Lenin Monument, in Lenin Park. In 1913, during the celebration of the 300th anniversary of the Romanov accession, the building of a monument was begun, dedicated to the Romanov family. Tsar Nicholas II, who was present when the foundation stone was laid, threw a handful of gold into its foundation. The pedestal of the monument designed by Adamson was built prior to February 1917, and the sculptures of the tsars were cast but not yet mounted in their places. After the revolution the sculptures were sent away to be melted down as non-ferrous metal scrap. During the celebrations of the 10th anniversary of the 1917 revolution, the citizens of Kostroma decided to erect a monument to Lenin on the empty pedestal. Money for the project was collected locally, and the monument was built by Listopad, Ivanova, and Lebedeva.

World War II Memorial & Eternal Flame, on the way out of town, in a park to the right of Prospect Mira.

Revolutionary Workers' Monument, unveiled in 1959, sculpted by Polyakov.

Novikov Bust, in a garden on Komsomolskaya Street. This bronze bust of Air Marshal Alexander Novikov (1900–76), twice Hero of the Soviet Union, was built by Vuchetich in 1958.

Ostrovsky Drama Theatre, Prospect Mira 9
Puppet Theatre, Ostrovsky Street 5
Hippodrome Racecourse
Concert Hall, Sovietskaya Street 64

Circus, Komsomolskaya Street 30
Kostroma Hotel, Sovietskaya Street 20
Tsentralnaya Hotel & Restaurant, Sovietskaya Street 2
Sever Restaurant, Prospect Mira 115
Volna Café, Tekstilshchikov Street
GPO, Sovietskaya Street 6

KRASNODAR Population—620,000
Until 1920 this was known as Yekaterinodar. It stands on the high right bank of the river Kuban (ancient Hypanis), which flows down north-west from Mt. Elbrus in the Caucasus and through the black-earth plain that is one of the Soviet Union's most important areas for growing wheat, sugar beet, and sunflowers, and which is often known as the "pearl of Russia."

It was founded in 1793 during the reign of Catherine II as a Cossack settlement and fortress protecting the Russian frontier. Ataman Zakhr Chepega brought a detachment of his men from the Dnieper and on 18th September, 1794, they used a wooden plough drawn by 12 oxen to mark out the first division of the future town; today's main thoroughfare, Krasnaya Street, follows this very line. The town that grew up was called Yekaterinodar and became the Cossack army's headquarters. The buildings at that time consisted largely of mud huts thatched with reeds and straw. A traveller at the beginning of the 19th century wrote that the huts reminded him of the military command "at ease," because they all faced different ways, some even having their backs to the streets. In 1860, it was made the capital of the Kuban Cossacks but 7 years later it was reorganised as a civilian town. At the end of the 19th century it began to develop rapidly, as did so many other towns, because of the railway connections; in the 1890s it was already a large transportion and trade junction. Krasnaya Street was lit by electricity in 1894, and in 1900 Yekaterinodar was the second Russian town to have trams. The mixture of ancient and modern prompted a traveller to write at the turn of the century: "Yekaterinodar looks like an old, torn, dirty winter coat on the back of which have been sewn strips of expensive velvet from Lyons."

In 1905, Yekaterinodar was the centre of the area's revolutionary activities. During the Civil War, Yekaterinodar served as a nucleus of anti-Bolshevik resistance, which meant the fighting went on here until 1920; later than in other places. There is a monument to the memory of those who lost their lives.

There are still remains of the earth wall of the fortress to be seen, and among the older buildings of interest are the Kuban (formerly the Central) Hotel built in 1911 by Kozlov and the Kuban Cinema at Krasnaya Street 27 (built in 1912 as a skating rink, and at that time the talk of the town).

Krasnodar became the regional centre in 1937, and as capital of the Kuban it grew rapidly. During the Second World War it was occupied by the Germans from August 1942, till February 1943,

254

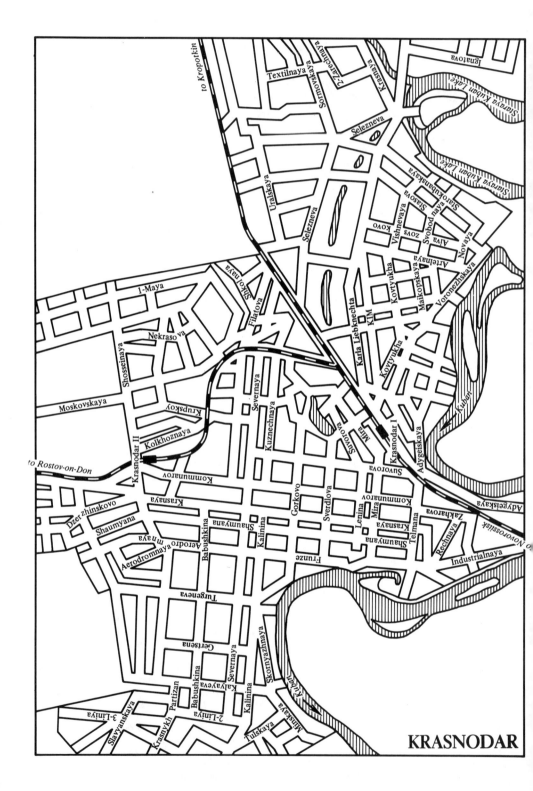

KRASNODAR

and an obelisk commemorates the liberation date. When the Germans retreated, they blew up or burned most of the principal buildings.

Local industry now produces machine tools, electrical measuring devices, chemicals, gas, cement, textiles, oil, and food products. There are medical, agricultural, teachers' training colleges, a polytechnical institute, as well as a number of research institutes dealing with agriculture, oil, and food products. Modern buildings now line the suburban streets, and along Krasnaya Street are the newest buildings of shops, a hotel, and a theatre.

St. Catherine's Cathedral, Kommunarov Street 52. Built in 1912.

St. George's Church, Severnaya Street. This was built in the 19th century as part of a convent and is locally called the Blue Church because of its colour.

Local Museum, Voroshilov Street 67. Open 10–5; closed Fri. The museum was founded in 1879 and it is now housed in what was once the home of a rich merchant family named Bogarsukov. The entrance porch supported by statues of seahorses leads to a series of elaborate halls. In the museum's courtyard there is a good collection of stone figures dating from Scythian times as well as Greek and Moslem monuments.

Lunacharsky Picture Gallery, Krasnaya Street 13. Open 10–6; closed Tues. In 1904 a local art collector, Fyodor Kovalenko (1866–1919), presented his collection to the town. West European art is represented downstairs by many old copies of famous works. The gallery is especially proud of its collection of 18th- and 19th-century miniatures and there are some good icons on display. The house itself is interesting, built at the turn of the century for Prince Sherdanov. The staircase is particularly fine and some of the halls upstairs have been used as a gallery since 1907.

Local Artists' Gallery, Krasnaya Street 9

Monuments to Lenin, Krasnaya Street and Zheleznodorozhnikov Square; unveiled in 1956

Liberators' Monument, Pobeda Square. To the soldiers who liberated the town in 1943.

Luzan Monument. Fyodor Luzan was a medical student who worked as a radio operator during the war. He drew enemy fire upon himself and then blew himself up, together with his portable transmitter and the Germans who discovered him. He was awarded the title of Hero of the Soviet Union for his gallantry.

Memorial Complex, Pamyati Geroyev Square. "To the Memory of Fallen Heroes."

Gorky Drama Theatre, Oktyabrskoy Revolutsii Square 2. Seats 830 people.

Musical Comedy Theatre, Krasnaya Street 40. Seats 830 people.

Concert Hall, Krasnaya Street 55

Puppet Theatre, Krasnaya Street 31

Circus, Shaumyan Street 147.

Gorky Park, Tehlmann Street 34. Opened in 1850 as the town garden. There are boat rentals by the pond. Other attractions include a small zoo.

40th-Anniversary-of-the-Revolution Park, TETS Region

May Day Park, in Roscha Region

Kuban Stadium, Zheleznodorozhnaya Street 49. This stadium can hold 38,000.

Dynamo Stadium, Krasnaya Street 174. This one has room for 12,000.

Hippodrome Racecourse, Rossiskaya Street 595. Open Sun., May–Sept.

Intourist Hotel & Restaurant, Krasnaya Street 109, tel. 5588-97. Intourist office; tel. 59-040. There is a Beryozka foreign-currency shop here.

Krasnodar Hotel & Restaurant, Gogol Street 52, tel. 49-01. The local Intourist office is here.

Kuban Hotel & Restaurant, Krasnaya Street 25

Yuzhny (south) Intourist Motel & Restaurant, Moskovskaya Street 40, tel. 5593-36.

Kavkaz Restaurant, Krasnaya Street 174

Kuren Restaurant, 40-Lyet-Oktyabrya Park

Aeroport Restaurant, 15 km (9 miles) from the town centre

Ogonyok Restaurant, Gorky Park, Tehlmann Street 32

Russky Chai Café, Oktyabrskaya Street

Mir (peace) café, Mir Street 29/11

GPO, Shaumyan Street 60

Bank, Ordzhonikidze Street 29, in an art nouveau building.

Telegraph Office, Sverdlov Street 64

Beryozka (tourists' foreign-currency shop), Krasnaya Street 109, in the Intourist Hotel.

Department Store, Mira Street 3

Izumrud Gift Shop, Krasnaya Street 75

Bookshop, Krasnaya Street 37

Intourist organises a 2-hour excursion by motorboat along the Kuban river and on the reservoir known as the Kuban Sea; another 2-hour visit to the Kuban Rice Farm; and a day trip to the city of Novorossiisk (q.v.) 141 km (88 miles) away, with a visit to the Abrau-Durso vineyards.

Kuban Sea, near the town. Named after the Kuban river, this reservoir 46 km (29 miles) long and 20 km (12 miles) wide covers an area of 33,000 hectares (82,500 acres). Construction began in 1973 and about 16,000 people from the villages and estates that were to be flooded were resettled beside the river Kuban in the newly built town of Teuchezhsk, named after a bard of the Circassians, who are the local population. (They are also known as Adyge, which accounts for the place being called Adygeisk in the beginning.) The reservoir holds 3,100 million cubic metres of water and will serve to irrigate 20,000 hectares (50,000 acres) of paddy fields.

KRASNOGORSK See Moscow environs, p. 361.

KUMAIRI (formerly Gyumri; 1837–1924 Alexandropol; 1924–1991 Leninakan) Population—120,000 (Intourist organises excursions here from Erevan.)

In December 1988 the earthquake in the Kumairi area affected a population of 700,000. Help came from all over the world and reconstruction began. However, this was slowed down by the tense situation between Armenia and neighbouring Azerbaijan.

The first settlement on the site of present-day Kumairi was in the Bronze Age, at the beginning of the 1st millennium B.C. This territory was part of the ancient Urartu state (part of present-day Armenia and Eastern Turkey). 8th-century Urartu chronicles mention the land of Eriakhi (today's Shirak—north-west of Armenia where Kumairi is now situated). According to the writings of the ancient Greek historian Xenophon, the Greek Army retreating from Persia in 401 B.C. reached the "large, rich and crowded town of Hyumnias" in Armenia, which is believed to have been situated on the site of modern-day Kumairi. However, according to the Armenian historian Gevond, in the 8th century the town changed hands between Turkey and Persia and experienced a period of decay. Under Turkish rule it was only mentioned as a village. The Turks called it Gyumri ("customs" in Turkish) since a caravan route from Kars to Erevan and Tiflis passed through it.

In 1804, the town of Gyumri was captured by Russian troops under the command of Prince Tsitsianov and became a Cossack settlement. In 1829–30 a large number of Armenian families from Eastern Turkey came here. A Russian immigration centre was situated in this Cossack settlement. In 1837, during the visit to Gyumri by Emperor Nicholas I, a fortress was built and the settlement received town status and was renamed Alexandropol in honour of Alexandra, Nicholas I's wife. The fortress retained its military importance until the capture of Kars by the Russians in 1878 during the 1877–78 Russo-Turkish War. At that time, Alexandropol became a major artisan centre of Transcaucasia, where one in every four men was engaged in some kind of craftmanship. In the late 19th century the town became a railway junction connecting Kars, Erevan, and Tiflis. Alexandropol developed rapidly and soon became one of the largest towns in Eastern Armenia, which in those days was superior even to Erevan. In 1912 its population was 30,000.

In 1920 Alexandropol became part of Turkey and in 1921, part of Armenia. In 1924, after Lenin's death, it was renamed Leninakan.

Before the 1988 earthquake Kumairi was a major industrial and scientific centre of Armenia, specialising in textiles. Restoration of the old houses and monuments which were only partly damaged is planned. The description below dates from before the earthquake.

Ruins of a round church and a chapel, built in the 5th century. Near the tourist centre.

Ruins of a bridge, over the river Akhurian, 13th century

Amenaprkich (Our Saviour in ancient Armenian) Cathedral, Maiskovo Vosstania Square. Built in the 19th century as a copy of one in Ani, the ancient capital of Armenia. Open for services.

Shiraka History Museum

Issahakyan's House. Avetic Issahakyan was a poet who lived here.

Garibshanyan's House, B. Garibshanyan was a revolutionary.

Philharmonic Concert Hall, Maiskovo Vosstania Square. In the building of a 19th-century church.

Railway Engine Monument, in front of the engine shed. This engine arrived in Alexandropol in 1899, and during the uprising in May 1920 it pulled the Vartan Zoravan armoured train, which took part in the fight for Soviet power in Armenia.

Obelisk, near the locomotive depot. The inscription reads, "The banner of the May Uprising was raised here in 1920."

May Uprising Monument, in a garden between Lenin and Maiskovo Vosstania squares. In memory of those who lost their lives during the 1920 uprising against the Armenian nationalist party.

Lenin Monument, Lenin Square. Sculpted by Merkurov in 1954.

Anniversary Monument, a bas-relief commemorating the 50th anniversary of the establishment of Soviet power in Armenia.

Ani Monument, commemorating the 1,000th anniversary of the foundation of Ani (now in Turkey).

Shaumyan Monument, Shaumyan was an Armenian revolutionary, an outstanding Trans-Caucasian commissar and president of the Baku "Sovnarkom."

Eternal Flame, Zvyozdy Square. A World War II memorial.

Armenian Drama Threatre, between Lenin and Maiskovo Vosstaniya squares. The theatre company was established in 1865, and the building was constructed in 1965.

Dvin Hotel & Restaurant,

Shirak Hotel,

Leninakan Hotel, Maiskovo Vosstaniya Square

Sevan Restaurant,

Marmashen Church Complex, 9 km (6 miles) from Kumairi. The most famous of the group of 10th–11th century churches is the elegant 10th-century Church of Vahram, built by Prince Vahram Pakhlavuni in 986–1029.

KURESSAARE (formerly Kingisepp)
Kuressaare is the capital of the island of Saaremaa.

SAAREMAA
Saaremaa (Sarema, Osel) is the largest island in the Moonsund Archipelago, which lies in the Baltic Sea at the entrance to the Gulf of Riga. The island is part of Estonia, and its territory is 2,700 sq km (1,010 sq miles). It is connected with its eastern neighbour, the island of Mukhu, by a causeway.

Saare-Ma is Estonian for "insular land." Its other name of Kure-Saare means "Island of the Courlanders." The island was occupied by King Valdemar II of Denmark (1170–1241), who was anxious to conquer the eastern Baltic region and convert the inhabitants to Christianity. In 1227 the Knights of the Sword took the island, and it was then placed under the bishopric of Saare-Laane. Johann von Munchhausen, the last bishop, sold the island to Denmark in 1559, and in 1645 it became Swedish under the Treaty of Bromsebro. It was incorporated into Russia with the rest of Livonia upon the signing of the Peace of Nistadt in 1721.

During World War II there were Soviet naval and air force bases on the island.

Kuressaare Population—13,000

Formerly known as Arensburg, then in 1917 Kuressaare, in 1952 it was renamed Kingisepp after Victor Kingisepp (1888–1922), an Estonian Communist who was born here. In 1990 its name was changed back to Kuressaare.

Foreign tourists can reach Kuressaare by air. The locals can also go by sea, or by car using the ferry over Suurbyain Strait on to Mukhu Island, and then the causeway.

Kuressaare is the only town on Saaremaa, or indeed on any of the islands in the archipelago. Its site has been inhabited since the 12th century. In the 13th century, a settlement began to grow around the castle that belonged to the bishop of Kuressaare. Many merchants fled to Arensburg during the Livonian War of 1559–83. Duke Magnus, who ruled Eastern Saaremaa, gave the settlement town status in 1563, and it became the administrative and commercial centre of the island in 1570, when its only competitor, Maazilinn (Zoneburg), on the island's northeastern shore and capital of Eastern Saaremaa, was razed to the ground. (Maazilinn is now the village of Maazi, near the causeway.)

Emperor Alexander I visited Arensburg in 1804.

In 1826 therapeutic mud was discovered in the Gulf of Kuressaare and in Lake Suurlakt ("bird's gulf"). The lake is 4 km (1.5 miles) northeast of Kuressaare and was formerly a gulf of the sea. The mud is beneficial in the treatment of nervous diseases and muscular and gynaecological ailments.

Most of Kuressaare's new buildings are 4 storeys high. There is a wood-working factory in the town, and branches of light and food industries, including a brewery and a bakery.

Castle of the Bishop of Kuressaare, Tallinn (formerly Lossi) Street. The castle was built in the course of 70 years in the 14th century as an administrative and military centre upon the order of the bishop of Saare-Laane. It is in Gothic style, and its ground plan is 42.5 m (46 yd) square. The 20-m (65-ft) walls of dolomite stone blocks are 3 m (10 ft) thick, and there is no other castle like it throughout the Baltic countries. Its only gate is on the northern side. The bishop's rooms were in the western part of the castle, while the southern part was taken up by a handsome chapel and a refectory. There were dining rooms and bedrooms in the eastern and northern parts of the building. Sturvolt Tower rises from the northwestern corner of the castle, and Pikk (Long) Hermann from the north-

eastern corner. Knights lived in Sturvolt Tower, while Pikk Hermann served as a prison. The castle was damaged during the Northern War (1700–1721) and was restored in 1904–12.

St. Lavrenti's Lutheran Church, was built in the 17th century and restored in classical style in 1835. There is a unique mid-14th-century "victim stone" with figures of fantastic animals.

St. Nicholas's Orthodox Church, Tallinn Street. Built in 1790 in classical style.

Town Hall, Tallinn Street. Constructed in 1654–70 in baroque style, and restored in 1969–73.

Town Weights and Measures Office, Tallinn Street 23, opposite the town hall. Built in 1663.

Warehouse, Komsomoli Street. This is still used for storage.

Rectory, at the crossing of 1-May and Pioneeri streets.

Customs House, Moskovskaya Street

Warehouse, Moskovskaya Street

Schmidt's Warehouse, at the beginning of Pikk Street

Kampenhausen's House, at the crossing of Oktooberi and Torni streets. Kampenhausen was a Livonian vice-regent.

Consulary House, Tallinn Street. Built in the 18th century.

Former Town School, Kyvera Street. From 1919–40 there was a seamen's school here.

School, Pikk Street. This used to be a grammar school.

Therapeutic Bathhouse, Kingisepp Street. There are a number of buildings here, but the wooden one was built in 1856.

Saaremaa Local Museum, in the mediaeval Kuressaare Castle. The museum was founded in 1865.

Kingisepp Museum, Kingisepp Street. Victor Kingisepp lived here.

Lutse Monument, on the grave of the Estonian cultural activist I. Lutse (1750–1842).

Sjuda Monument. P. Sjuda (1883–1920) was a composer.

Aavik's House. Philologist I. Aavik (1880–1973) lived here.

War Memorial, in the castle yard. Sculpted by Lembit Palm, it commemorates the heroes of the Second World War who liberated Kuressaare from enemy occupation.

Deyev Monument, in the park at the beginning of Lenin (formerly Uus) Street. Vladimir Deyev (1925–44) was a Hero of the Soviet Union.

Victims of Nazism Monument, near the castle. Sculpted by Matti Barik and Rikho Kuld and unveiled in 1965.

Heroes of Saaremaa Revolt Monument, on the central square (formerly Market Square). A Bolshevik rebellion against the Estonian provisional government took place on the island of Saaremaa in February 1919. The monument was made by Endel Taniloo and installed in 1963.

The Water Tower was built in 1970 to resemble a block of flats. (In fact people do live in the building too.)

Saaremaa Theatre
Town Park, laid out in 1861, is one of the most beautiful parks in Estonia.
Bird Sanctuary, on Lake Linnulakht
Kurzal. The concert and dancing hall of the resort was built in 1889.
Department Store
Restaurant, in the building of an old mill

Kaarma

A settlement 15 km (9 miles) from Kuressaare where dolomite stones are quarried.

There was a castle here in the 13th century, and in 1261 there was a bloody battle between the islanders and the Knights of the Livonian Order.

SS. Peter and Paul's Church was built in the 13th century and reconstructed in the 15th. Some 13th- and 15th-century frescoes remain on the interior walls. The 15th-century wooden sculpture of St. Joseph on the altar is by Klaus Sittoi.

Also there are the *ruins of a rectory and a warehouse.*

Karja

37 km (23 miles) northeast of Kuressaare.

The *Church* was built in 1335–40 in Gothic style. A 16th-century vestry was built onto the southern wall. There are unique frescoes on the interior walls and many stone figures with biblical themes in the church.

Angla

This village, just north of Karja, has a group of 4 windmills, dating from the beginning of the 20th century.

Kikhelkonna

At the western side of the island, 31 km (19 miles) from Kuressaare, its name means "parish."

There are traces of a prehistoric settlement here, and stones of the first century B.C. that have a religious significance.

Museum

The *church* was built in the 14th century and reconstructed in the 19th century. Near it stands a belltower, which was built in 1638 and restored in 1968.

The small islands in the bay off the coast and all the little inlets form part of the *Visandsky Bird Sanctuary*, set apart with the nesting grounds of a variety of sea birds. Its headquarters are on Visandi Island.

Viidumyaesky Nature Reserve

On the western part of the island, running parallel to the Pussa Canal. With its climate warmed by the Gulf Stream, a number of plants can grow on Saaremaa that are indeed rare for these latitudes of the Soviet Union. They include rattle-box, ivy, yew, broad-flowered rush, and white rowan.
Museum

KURGAN Population—360,000

Kurgan stands on Tsar's Hill beside the river Tobol.

Once a Tatar town stood upon this site. In the middle of the 17th century "a peasant named Timofei Nevezhin made his home here on the ruins of a former Tatar town because of the fertile, arable land. Since his farmstead was favourably situated, it was later turned into a frontier stronghold." So wrote Johan Falk (1725–74), a Russian scientist who worked in Siberia in 1782. 17th-century chronicles mention Timofei Nevezhin as the founder of Tsareva Sloboda (Tsar's Village, from the name of the hill) in the year 1662. The stronghold was isolated. The nearest Russian settlement was at Yalutorovsk, 3 or 4 days' journey away down the Tobol, to the north-east. The stronghold was raided more than once by nomadic tribesmen. In 1661 and again in 1662 it was set on fire, and its women and children taken prisoner. The Siberian authorities were anxious not to lose this frontier position, so arms and ammunition were dispatched to the stronghold, and a company of soldiers under Captain Stepan Ranchovsky garrisoned it.

The regions beyond the Ural Mountains were important to Russian development of Siberia. Russian peasants moved here to escape from their landlords and to till the rich farmlands for themselves. During the 16th and 17th centuries a mighty stream of Russian settlers passed this way, but eventually all the land was proclaimed to belong to the tsar and the peasants had to pay tithes. In 1710, upon the order of Peter the Great, the nobleman Vasili Tursky visited all the villages along the Tobol in turn and made the first census of the population. In Tsareva Sloboda 456 souls lived in 71 peasant holdings.

By the 1720s Tsareva Sloboda was already a major settlement on the Tobol, but it remained in military hands because of the continuing raids by the nomads. In 1773–75 it was one of the centres of the peasant revolt led by Emelian Pugachev. In 1774 the garrison of 951 soldiers, armed with 28 cannon, was the largest in the Tobol region. The kremlin, built of wood, had a moat, 8 bastions, and 2 gate towers. As the population grew, new rows of bastions and earth walls were erected. The first stone structure was the Troitskaya Church, built in 1777.

At this time another stronghold, called Kurganskaya Sloboda in the 18th century documents, was built to the south-west of Tsareva Sloboda, on the river Ui, a tributary of the Tobol. Tsareva Sloboda slowly lost its military importance. However, it remained a sizeable settlement, was renamed Kurgan in 1782, and 3 years later was granted town status. Its new coat-of-arms was 2 silver hills on a green background, one hill representing the one on which the town stood and the other symbolising that the town was surrounded by hills. From then on, besides soldiers, the population consisted increasingly of officials, clergy, craftsmen, and exiles. In 1786 the first town planning was undertaken.

The town's economy relied mainly on trade in meat and grain, and it supplied Tyumen, Tobolsk, and other towns along the Tobol. The fairs in Kurgan attracted merchants from Moscow, Ekaterinenburg (now Sverdlovsk), and other towns, as well

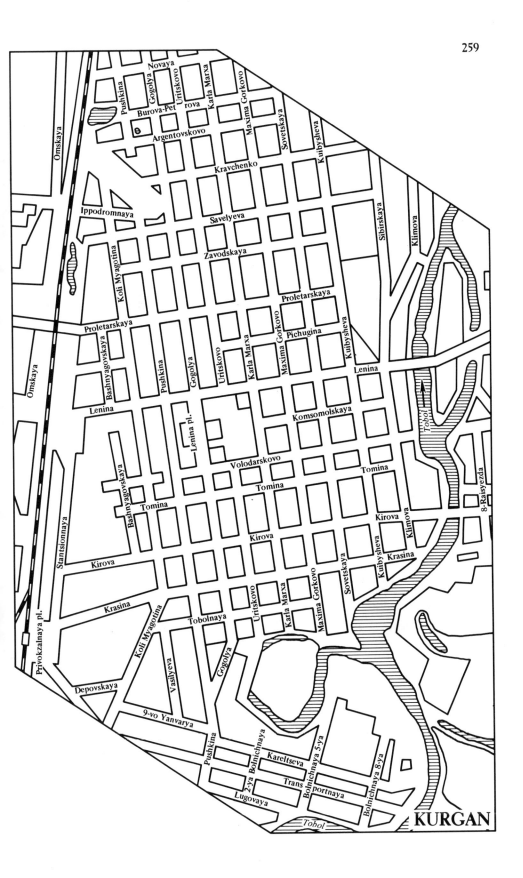

KURGAN

as from Central Asia and China. The archives in Tobolsk, however, show that there was a considerable quantity of counterfeit money in circulation in Kurgan, which brought the locals fabulous profits. It was one of the rich merchants, Berezin, who in 1845 built Kurgan's second stone church.

By the beginning of the 19th century the population had grown to almost 4,000, and there began a tendency to build houses along the bank of the river. The first proper streets were Beregovaya (now Klimov) and behind it Troitskaya (now Kuibyshev). By 1860 2 more streets had been added, running parallel to the first 2—Dvoryanskaya (now Sovietskaya) and Soldatskaya (now Gorky). In the centre of the town was Troitskaya Square, now a garden on Kuibyshev Street, and the largest buildings were the prison, the police station, and the churches.

The townsfolk of Tobolsk called Kurgan "Siberian Italy" because of the pleasant setting and the mild climate. On 5th July, 1837, the heir apparent, the future Tsar Alexander II, visited Kurgan accompanied by his tutor, the well-known Russian poet Vasili Zhukovsky.

Kurgan was a place of exile, starting with de Gravi, one of the Swedish officers who was banished after the defeat of the army of Charles XII at Poltava in 1709. De Gravi settled here and married, and at the beginning of the 19th century his son served in the Kurgan law court. The first Polish exile arrived in 1797, and the first Decembrist, I. Focht, in March 1830. He was followed by 12 Decembrists and their wives, and later the first participants in the Polish uprising of 1830. Soldiers who had taken part in the 1831 mutiny of the military settlements in Staraya Russa were also exiled here. During a period of 27 years the presence of the Decembrists did much to stimulate the cultural development of Kurgan. After he had completed his term of imprisonment at Petrovsky Zavod 1,000 km (600 miles) to the east in Siberia, Ivan Annenkov and his French wife, Pauline, were sent to Kurgan. The Naryshkins arrived in 1833 and the Svistunovs in 1838. M. Naryshkin played the guitar, whilie P. Svistunov was a talented cellist. They both contributed to the Decembrist music-making during their Siberian exile, as had also Rozen with his flageolet. Naryshkin purchased a house and a garden from a local official and it was in this house that the works of Beethoven and other classical composers were first played in Kurgan. Svistunov organised a series of concerts of classical music for the Kurgan public as well. N. Basargin came later (1842–46), and was an excellent chess player. Like N. Lorer, who lived here from 1833–37, Basargin was one of the Decembrists whose memoirs were to be published.

New buildings began to appear. Besides his church, the merchant Berezin built himself a fine mansion in 1868; it now houses the city archives. In the 1870s trade arcades were built in Troitskaya Square. In 1884 the Great Siberian Railway reached Kurgan, linking it with Ekaterinenburg in the north-west and Omsk in the south-east. After the construction of the railway, the town's population rapidly increased and more construction work was undertaken. The old cemetery was transformed into a town park, and in 1896 the foundations of the Church of St. Alexander Nevsky were laid nearby. The church was completed in 1902, and then the wasteland in front of it was laid out as Alexandrovskaya Square (now Lenin Garden).

At the beginning of the 20th century the wealthy merchants favoured a new style for the construction of their homes. A typical example is the house at the crossing of Klimova and Volodarskovo streets. It was built by Dunayev in 1906 with ornamental woodcarving and a balcony tower on the corner.

With a cheap and reliable means of transportation, the local merchants turned to export, especially shipments of grain, from Kurgan westwards to Ekaterinenburg, Chelyabinsk, Moscow, and St. Petersburg. Butter was also sold abroad, and by the beginning of the 20th century it had become the principal export item, going to England, Germany, and Denmark. The Union of Siberian Butter-Makers formed in 1907 was headed by Balakshin of Kurgan. However, there was foreign competition, both in the production and in the marketing of Kurgan butter, as well as other products. The Danish firm of Poulsen had opened its butter marketing office in 1896 and was joined the following year by Esmans. In 1907 Brull & Tegersen Company of Denmark opened a sausage factory, and Gamples of Austria a brewery. In 1912 an Englishman named Lonsdale founded the Union Company, with most of the shares in English hands. McCormicks was an American company with its offices in Troitskaya Street, while other Americans, Walter Wood and John Grieves, owned warehouses for agricultural machinery in Novo-Zapolnaya (now Gogol) Street. Singer sewing machines had their office on Kuibyshev Street. There were many warehouses here, too.

Besides Novo-Zapolnaya, other new streets were built up, always running parallel to the first—Skobelevskaya (now Marx), Zapolnaya (now Uritskovo), and Pushkinskaya streets—so that by 1914 the town already had 8 streets. Foreigners had considerable influence in the growth of the town and by 1919 9 of the 12 Kurgan butter-exporting companies belonged to them rather than to Russians. Among them were Randroops of England, Fients of Denmark, and Franz Dorfs of Germany.

During the Civil War, the Czech Legion, ex-prisoners-of-war on their way to getting back to fighting the Germans, became enmeshed in counter-revolutionary warfare. In June 1918 they captured Kurgan from the Red Army. It was a good place to be, with ample supplies of meat and dairy products and over 2,700 Czech officers and men stationed there. Soviet power was, however, reestablished the following year.

After the revolution, the sausage factory, Goldstone's tannery, and the brewery continued production under state management, and a machine-building plant was opened. During World War II the Gomel Agricultural Machinery Plant was evacuated to Kurgan and merged with the local ma-chine-building plant from the existing Uralselmash agricultural machinery plant. In 1941 the Cher-kassy wood-working factory was similarly relocated. Modern industry includes a bus factory, machine-building works, and various other branches of the food industry.

The old fire station, distinguished by its tower, stands at the crossing of Kuibyshev and Lenin streets. The wide expanse of Lenin Square is where parades and demonstrations take place on public holidays. It is surrounded by new build ings, as is also Railway Square, Festivalnaya Square, and the crossing of Krasina and Koli Myagotina streets.

St. Alexander Nevsky Church, Volodarskovo Street 42. Built in 1896–1902 and now housing the local museum.

Local Museum, Volodarskovo Street 42, in Alexander Nevsky Church

19th-century Wooden Building, Klimova Street 47

Decembrists' Museum, Klimova Street 80a, high above the river. The museum is in the fine house bought by the Naryshkins from a local of-ficial named Serebryakov. Naryshkin was a good gardener and the house was reconstructed to make it "the best in the whole town of Kurgan."

Rozen's House, Sovietskaya Street 67. The Bal-tic Baron Andrei Rozen and his wife, Anna, lived here as Decembrist exiles from 1832–37. They pur-chased the house from a local official named Ivanov. An extremely efficient and punctilious landowner, with a professional knowledge of ag-riculture, Baron Rozen had been in charge of the household economy in the Decembrist community in Chita, including the running of the kitchen gar-den. While in Kurgan he again took up vegetable growing and did modestly well. Tactful, even-tem-pered, sensible, he was a definite asset to any com-munity, and he was also skillful at playing the flageolet. His memoirs were published in the sec-ond half of the 19th century.

Burov-Petrov's House, Burova-Petrova Street 47. V. Burov-Petrov was a local activist for the establishment of Soviet power, a commissar and editor of the local Bolshevist newspaper, "Novy Mir."

Vasiliev Museum, Vasilieva Street 30. The poet S. Vasiliev (1911–75) was born in Kurgan.

Founders' Monument, Railway Square. Hon-ouring the founders of the town. Sculpted by Ko-zyrev and unveiled in 1964.

Karl Marx Monument, Krasin Street. Unveiled in 1968.

Krasin Monument, Krasin Street. L. Krasin (1870–1926) was a statesman and diplomat who was born in Kurgan. The monument was designed by Chernov and unveiled in 1978.

Pichugin's Bust, Koli Myagotina Street. D. Pi-chugin represented the peasants on the local coun-cil and was shot in 1918 during the Civil War. The bust by Kozyrev was unveiled in 1959.

Memorial to Fighters for Soviet Power, in Lenin Garden. Sculpted by Goloshapov and unveiled in 1969.

Obelisk, Lenin Garden. This commemorates the commissars of Kurgan. It was erected in 1921.

Burov-Petrov Obelisk, Pushkin Street. Designed by Korochkin.

Argentovskaya Monument, Kuibyshev Street. Komsomol member Natasha Argentovskaya was a local Civil War heroine who was killed in 1919. The monument by Kozyrev was unveiled in 1961.

Lenin Statue, in Lenin Square. Sculpted by Egorov and reconstructed in 1967.

Myagotin Monument, Koli Myagotina Street. Kolya was a Pioneer who was killed in 1932 during the collectivisation campaign. The monument by Kozyrev was unveiled in 1962.

Memorial Complex, Pushkin Street. Commem-orating local soldiers who fell in World War II. Reconstructed with an eternal flame in 1975.

Drama Theatre, Gogol Street 58

Gulliver Puppet Theatre, Kuibyshev Street 87

Philharmonia Concert Hall, Kuibyshev Street 55

Spartak Sports Palace, Gogol Street 135

Stadium, Kuibyshev Street

Kurgan Hotel (Intourist) & Restaurant

Moskva Hotel & Restaurant, Krasina Street 49; tel. 55-074

Tobol Hotel & Restaurant, Pichugina Street 9, in the oldest part of the town

Bank, Kuibyshev Street. This is still in an im-posing prerevolutionary bank building.

Horses may be rented from the local stud farm for pleasant rides along the banks of the river Tobol.

Ryabkova

This village is the home of the *Ilizarov Orthopedic Centre*, at Ulianov Street 6; tel. 33-321. The Re-search Institute of Orthopedics and Traumatology is headed by Professor Gavriil Ilizarov, who revo-lutionised medical treatment with the development of a device that helps increase the length of arms or legs by as much as 50 cm (19 inches).

Smolino

This village is 5 km (3 miles) to the south-west of Kurgan.

Orthodox church, open for services

Kuchelbeker's House, Wilhelm Kuchelbecker (1797–1846) was a school friend of Pushkin's, and a poet and literary critic who was exiled here as a Decembrist between 1845 and 1846. His log cabin has been preserved.

KURSK Population—424,000

The name Kursk comes from "kuropatka," the Rus-sian word for partridge, and 3 of these birds are pictured on the coat-of-arms. The town is situated on 2 hills on the right bank of the River Seim. It was founded in the 9th century and was first men-tioned in a document of 1032. The Mongols de-stroyed it in 1240; later it belonged to Lithuania for many years and it became important in trade in grain, linen, leather, and apples. It was eventually annexed to the principality of Moscow, and in the 16th century became another of the defence points on Russia's southern boundary.

At the beginning of the 18th century when the Russian border was moved still further south, Kursk fortress lost much of its importance. Administrative buildings were put up and in 1798 Kursk became a provincial capital. There are still many houses of typical 19th-century Russian architecture, among them the former *House of Nobles* at 4, Verkhne-Naberczhnaya Street and the manege or riding school (now a cinema) at 51, Dzerzhinsky (formerly Khersonskaya) Street. The building above the circus bears the date 1836–42. It was a school first of all, then served as barracks, and then it was rebuilt into a factory. Electrical instruments are made there now. An even older part of Kursk can be seen on Pionerov (formerly Troitskaya) and Zolotarevskaya streets; of a number of old merchants' houses, *Romodanovsky House* at Pionerov Street 6 was built in 1649–80 and opposite, at Gaidar Street 30, is *Lower Trinity Church* (1680), soon to be turned into a planetarium. Another memento of the past is the Old Water Tower beside the road leading out of Kursk towards the north. There might have been more old buildings to see had it not been for the fighting and enemy occupation here during the Second World War.

Lenin Street (formerly Moskovskaya) is the main thoroughfare and the road followed by motorists passing through the town. The best shops are here and it leads into Krasnaya (red) Square with the *hotel* and the impressive buildings of the *House of Soviets* (1948), the town hall, and the local economic council. The *monument to Lenin* by Manizer was unveiled in 1956. There are teacher training, medical, and agricultural institutes in Kursk and local factories produce electrical apparatus, synthetic fibre, rubber, glass, textiles, and food products. The Kursk region is famous for its nightingales and for its Antonovka apples that ripen at the end of September.

Sergievo-Kazansky Cathedral, Gorky (formerly Sergiyevskaya) Street 27. This impressive blue-and-white cathedral was built in 1752–78 following a project by Rastrelli and is the seat of the Bishop of Kursk and Belgorod. The double name of the church is the usual way of indicating that there are in fact two churches in one, being summer and winter premises. The low, vaulted church downstairs is dedicated to Our Lady of Kazan, while upstairs is the Church of St. Sergius Radonezhsky with a beautiful baroque interior and a carved and gilded iconostasis standing 18 m (60 ft) high. Both churches are open for services.

Mikhailovskaya Church, Mikhailovsky Pereulok, which is a left turn from Verkhnyaya Lugovaya Street. Built in 1762–67, the church is distinguished by its two thin spires, one belonging to the church and one to the belfry.

Church of the Miraculous Apparition of the Virgin Mary, 43 m (141 ft) high and built in 1816–28, it was formerly the cathedral church of Znamensky Monastery. The distinctive silver dome stands out clearly as one drives down Lenin Street. The round brick tower nearby that dates from the 1970s was part of the monastery wall. The church now houses the October Cinema. The church standing nearby in the grounds of the electrical instrument factory is Voskresenskaya, built in 1875.

Trinity Convent, Gorky Street 13. The bell tower and Upper Trinity Church (1695). The buildings are now used to house the local archives.

St. Nikita's Church, Karl Marx Street 8, on the way out of Kursk towards Moscow at the cemetery near Moskovskiye Vorota, the old northern entrance into the town. The church was built in 1786 and is open for services.

Roman Catholic Church, Marata Street 29, off Lenin Street, to the right just before the Kursk Hotel. This was built of red brick in 1892 and has been restored. Many Poles moved to Kursk in the 1860s, after the revolution in Poland, and this church is still known as the Polish church.

Church of St. Catherine the Martyr, Engels Street 7, on the left on the way into town from Kharkov

There are 3 more churches in Kursk that are all open for services—Ilyinskaya, Vvedenskaya, and Nikolaya Ugodnika.

Officers' House & Museum of the Battle of Kursk, Sonina Street, which runs up to the left from Kolkhoznaya Street. The building was originally the House of Nobles. The museum is open 11–5; closed Mon & Tues.

Local Museum, Lunacharsky Street 8. Open 11–7; closed Mon. & the last Thurs. of each month. This is housed in what used to be the Bishop's Palace (1826–53). Upstairs there is a collection of furniture with some unusual pieces including two armchairs and a table all joined together and a circular sofa with five seats back to back.

Moskovskiye Vorota, Karl Marx Street, on the way out of Kursk on the main road to Moscow. The name means Moscow Gates, and originally there was a triumphal arch here to commemorate the visit of Alexander I in 1823, but now only the gateposts remain.

Ufimtsev Museum, Semenovskaya Street 13. Anatoli Ufimtsev (1880–1936) was a Kursk-born inventor and aeroplane engine constructor. His first claim to fame was when in 1898 he blew up a supposed miracle-working icon in the cathedral of the Znamensky (Miraculous Apparition of the Virgin) Monastery with a time bomb. He was sent to Siberia and the monks set up a copy of the original icon in the hopes that it would also work miracles. Ufimtsev also built the windmill that stands beside his house. Today the house is used as a club for young technicians.

Picture Gallery, Sovietskaya Street 3

Dzerzhinsky Monument, Dzerzhinsky Square

Borovykh's Bust, in the park, is a memorial to the pilot, Andrei Borovykh, Kursk-born and twice made a Hero of the Soviet Union.

Pushkin Drama Theatre, Lenin Street 56

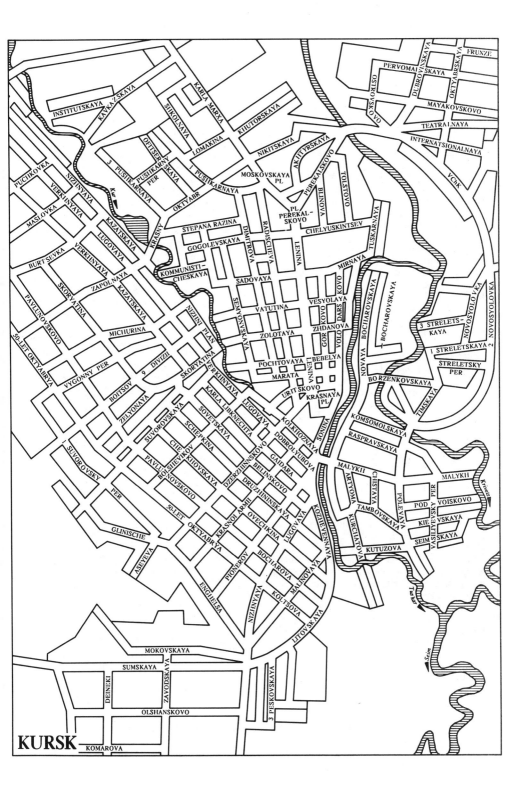

KURSK

Theatre, Dzerhzhinsky Street 51
Summer Theatre, Lenin Street, in the 1st May Garden opposite the Kursk Hotel
Puppet Theatre, Radischev Street
Circus, Sovietov Square
Trudovye Rezervy Stadium, Lenin Street 58. There are places for 17,000 spectators.
Solyanka Park, 300 m from the camping site beside the River Seim. Has facilities for fishing, bathing, and boats for rent.
Oktyabrskyaya Hotel & Restaurant, Lenin Street 72. The local Intourist Office is here; tel. 23-192.
Kursk Hotel & Restaurant, Lenin Street 2; tel. 274-38. An Intourist hotel with an office. There is also a courtyard carpark that is guarded at night.
Teatralnaya Hotel, Lenin Street 2; tel. 6-7084
Seim Restaurant, Engels Street 148, near the camping site
Voskhod Café, Lenin Street 4. Local delicacies include "kursky salat" (salad of chicken, butter and apple) and "govyadina-po-kursky" (rolls of beef stuffed with egg, rice, and butter and then deep-fried).
GPO & Telegraph Office, Krasnaya Square
Bank, Lenin Street 83. It was built in art nouveaustyle as the Nobles' and Peasants' Landbank. Kurk's coat-of-arms with the partridges can be seen on the facade.
Department Store, Lenin Street 12
Gifts, Krasnaya Square 2/4
Amethyst Jeweller's, Lenin Street 4
Bookshop, Lenin Street 11
Market, at the crossing of Dzerzhinsky Street and Verkhnyaya Lugovaya Street. Located just before the river crossing.
Filling Station, on the left on the way into town from the south and in the centre at Engels Street 3.
Repair Station, Karl Marx Street 31a
Solovyinaya Roscha (nightingale grove) Intourist Motel & Restaurant, Engels Street 142, in the southern part of Kursk, 200 m/yds off the main road, to the right; tel. 515-62.
Sosnovy Bor Camping Site, Engels Street 150 (just beyond the Motel), tel. 508-71. The tents and bungalows are in a pinewood forest. There is a buffet, self-service kitchen, post office, souvenir kiosk, international telephone, carwash, and repair trench. 300 m/yds from the camping site, beside the River Seim, is Solyanka Park with facilities for fishing, bathing, and boats for rent. Here, too, is the Sosenka Café.

Intourist organises a number of excursions from Kursk.

Aloykhin Nature Reserve, 18 km (11 miles). Professor Vasili Alyokhin (1882–1946) worked as a geobotanist at Moscow university. He was born near Kursk and specialised in the study of local flora. In 1907 he was the first botanist to classify the flora of the Streletsky and Kazatsky Steppes near Kursk.

The nature reserve was formed in 1935 and named after him. There are over 4,000 hectares (10,000 acres) that are particularly beautiful in spring and summer, when the colours of the 754 different species of plants and flowers change according to the season. There is a museum here.

Svoboda
This village 30 km (19 miles) from Kursk was the headquarters of the Central Front in 1943. The memorial complex includes a museum and a monument to Marshal Rokosovsky.

Yakovlevo
Kursk Battlefield Memorial, 110 km (68 miles) from Kursk

Zheleznogorsk (also Zelenogorsk) (see Vyoborg, p. 649) Population—85,000
This young town lies 150 km (93 miles) from Kursk. It was founded in 1962 when the Mikhailovsky mines went into operation and its youthful population has an average age of 28. The town is located at the 77/36 km mark where, on the right, there is a monument to the miners and a statue of an excavator head and the appropriate chemical symbol Fe.
There are large deposits of iron ore in the Central Russian Upland in the black earth belt. It is worked by the Kursk Magnetic Anomaly and has reserves of up to 200 billion tons. The KMA territory covers over 100,000 sq. km (38,600 sq. miles) in a strip about 600 km (375 miles) long and varying in width from 2 to 40 km (1 to 25 miles). Opencast methods are used in the Zheleznogorsk region since rich ore lies only 40 to 80 m (130 to 260 ft) below the surface. There are 2 large workings further along the main road.
Zheleznogorsk Hotel & Restaurant, Lenin Street 13; tel. 51-317
Filling Station, beside the main road, on the left

Bolshoy Dub (Also Bolshoi Dub)
A small village, a little beyond Zheleznogorsk, and 3 km (2 miles) to the south of the main Orel–Kiev road, through the woods from the 70/43 km mark.
In the village is a memorial complex dedicated to the Victims of Fascism. There are also graves, the sites of 14 cottages and cellars where 144 villagers were killed on 14th October 1942, an eternal flame, samples of earth from the country's Hero Cities, and a tragic statue of an oak tree, with the forlorn figures of a family standing by it. This statue symbolises the village.
Museum, open 10–7; closed Mon.

LENINGRAD Population—5,020,000
Leningrad is the second-largest city in the Soviet Union. From 1712, 9 years after its foundation by Peter the Great, until 1918 it was the capital of the Russian Empire. Originally named St. Petersburg

after its founder (who was affectionately called "Peter" by its inhabitants), it has since been twice renamed. In 1914, after the beginning of the war with Germany, its name was changed from the Germanic-sounding "Petersburg" to the Russian equivalent "Petrograd" ("grad" meaning city or town), and in 1924, after the death of Lenin, it was renamed Leningrad in his honour.

Situated on a flat plain at the mouth of the river Neva in the Gulf of Finland, the city covers an area of over 500 sq km (193 sq miles). There are 101 islands in Leningrad. Numerous canals, spanned by 620 bridges, take up one-sixth of the total area of the city. The Neva itself is 67 km (42 miles) long, 13 km (8 miles) of which are within the boundaries of the city. Its width in those stretches varies from 337 m (369 yds) to 592 m (647 yds).

Leningrad is undoubtedly among the best-planned and most attractive cities in the world, and has deservedly earned its many titles such as "Northern Palmyra" and "Venice of the North." The city is seen at its best in May and June, during the "White Nights," celebrated by so many poets, when only 40 minutes of semi-darkness occur in 24 hours. From the beginning the city layout conformed to strict planning under the personal direction of Peter I. Even today his planning is evident for, on the left side of the river, the 3 main streets converge at the golden-spired building of the Admiralty where the first shipyard used to be, while a series of canals form concentric semi-circles around it, flowing into the river on either side. The right bank of the main stream of the river is at this point formed by many islands. Spreading behind the Peter and Paul Fortress is Petrogradskaya Storona and nearer the sea is the expanse of Vasilyevsky Ostrov (island), where Peter I founded the Academy of Sciences and where Lomonosov, Popov, Mendeleyev, and Pavlov all worked. Peter's heirs and successors faithfully continued his work of constructing and embellishing the city, which now forms an admirable and harmonious ensemble of classical Russian architecture.

Moreover, there are few skyscrapers or very tall buildings to disturb this harmony, at least in the old central districts of the city, where 4- or 5-storey buildings predominate. In 1844 Nicholas I, wishing to stress the difference in station between the tsar and his subjects, decreed that all new buildings in St. Petersburg should be at least a "sazhen" (about 7 feet) lower than the Winter Palace. Only the churches, with their domes, spires, and crosses, rose higher than the palace. This tradition was enforced for many decades. The tallest landmark in Leningrad today is the new television tower, completed in 1962, which stands on the Petrogradskaya Storona. It rises to a height of 316 m (1,037 ft). Although it is taller than the Eiffel Tower, its total weight is calculated to be seven times lighter.

Since the Revolution, Leningrad has retained its position of importance in the spheres of administration, industry, trade, and the arts in the Soviet Union. It remains the administrative capital of the region of the same name, and is still one of the biggest sea ports in the country. Its strategic position on the Baltic makes it an essential link in trade and communication between the interior of the Soviet Union and Finland, the Baltic countries, and the West. It is also one of the most important industrial centres of the country, the main products being machinery, metals, ships, chemicals, electrical goods, and textiles. Besides the university, there are about 270 scientific research centres, over 40 institutes of higher education, a conservatory, 13 theatres, and 7 concert halls. The city boasts over 1,000 architectural and historical monuments, and immense artistic and cultural riches are housed in its 50 museums and 2,000 libraries. The largest of these is the Saltykov-Schedrin Library, which has a collection of over 13,000,000 books and manuscripts.

The climate is quite mild in comparison to the central regions of the Soviet Union, but tends to be rather damp and misty. The average temperature for the year is 4°C (39°F); for July it is 18°C (63°F) and for January −8°C (17°F). From mid-November to April the river is frozen.

Leningrad is a young city in comparison with many towns of the Soviet Union and Europe, but it has achieved an unprecedented historical significance. However, although St. Petersburg was only founded in the 18th century, the history of the area around the city goes back many centuries.

It is often said that St. Petersburg was founded in the midst of uninhabited swamps and forests. It is true that these did exist but the place was inhabited. The area around the mouth of the Neva, at the point where the Baltic Sea penetrates deepest on its eastern shore, was of importance long before the building of St. Petersburg. The earliest settlers appear to have been the Finns, and up to the time of Peter the Great the various parts of the Neva delta retained their Finnish names. The Finns were followed by the Swedes and the Novgorodian Russians, who built castles and founded settlements that changed hands several times during the long struggle for permanent possession, for this area soon became an object of heated dispute.

In the earliest times for which there is any record of this part of Russia, the Neva served as an artery of trade between Europe and Asia; according to Arabian and Persian chronicles, the Persians and even Indians received goods from the West along this route. It was the starting point for the great trade routes running from the Varangians to the Greeks, through the Volkhov and the Dnieper, and from the Varangians to the Arabs along the Volga. Evidence of this ancient traffic has been brought to light in discoveries of large numbers of Saxon and Arabian coins dug up in several places at the mouth of the Neva and on the shores of Lake Ladoga. Nestor, the 11th-century Russian chronicler, recorded that "the Neva served as a means of communication between peoples of the West and Novgorod through the Volkhov; by the Neva they went into the Varangian Sea, and by that sea to Rome." Thus for Novgorod, the most important Russian

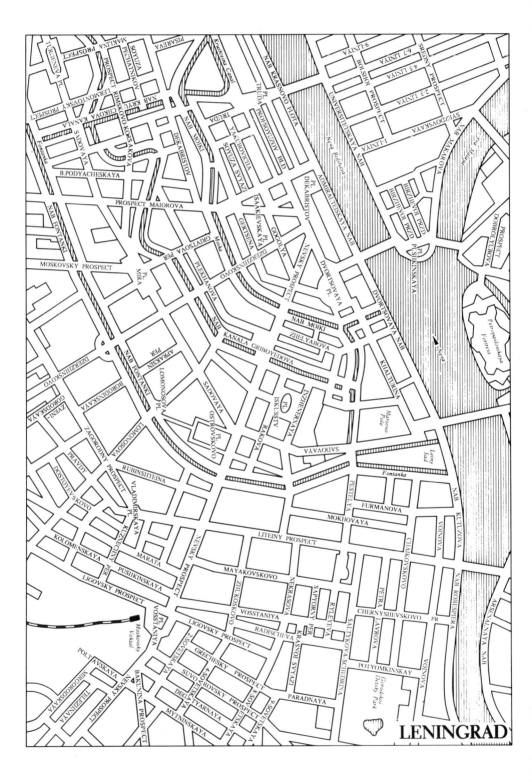

LENINGRAD

A fine Russian church.

Black Sea beach.

KIEV–The Trinity Gate-Church (1108) serves as the entrance to the famed Monastery of the Caves.

KIEV–An ornate house on Ordzhonikidze Street, designed by Gorodetsky at the turn of the century.

KIEV–St. Cyril's Church (12–18th century) showing Beretti's decorative 18th century facade.

KIEV–The Golden Gate, the main entrance to the city in 1037, has been entirely rebuilt to provide yet another momento of Kiev's past.

KIEV–The equestrian statue of Bogdan Khmelnitsky, the Ukrainian leader who was instrumental in uniting the Ukraine in 1654.

KIEV–The domes of St. Sophia's Cathedral and its bell-tower against a panorama of modern Kiev.

LENINGRAD–The spring thaw on the Neva, looking across to the slender spire of the cathedral in the Peter and Paul Fortress.

LENINGRAD–The gates of the courtyard of Yekaterininsky Palace at Pushkin, near Leningrad.

LENINGRAD–Lilacs bloom in the gardens by the mighty dome of St. Isaac's Cathedral.

LENINGRAD–View over the river Neva upon the old building of the Exchange (now the Central Naval Museum). It is a copy of the Temple of Paestum in Southern Italy and is flanked by the two Rostral Columns.

LENINGRAD–The landmark of the Admiralty's pointed spire set off by an elegant fountain in the garden below.

trading centre at this time, the Neva was a vital natural outlet to the Western sea, while on the other hand, for the seafaring Swedes, the Neva delta was the key to Ingermanland, the southern shore of the Gulf of Finland, where trade with the inhabitants of the spreading plain was being developed. Gradually, there was strife between Slavs and Scandinavians over the command of the Neva. In 1143 the Swedes, assisted by the Finns, attacked the Russians at Ladoga and were repulsed, but from that time the contest became serious and, in spite of several peace treaties, it went on intermittently for 600 years. The strife was finally put to an end in 1743 by the Treaty of Abo, which confirmed Russia's possession of the whole area of the Neva and the Gulf of Finland.

Besides the Swedes and the Danes on one hand, who began to approach through the Baltic provinces, the other most important contestants for this region were the Knights of the Teutonic and the Livonian Orders, who tried to extend their conquests into the Neva region. The struggle with these invaders took place in the south-western part of the present region of Leningrad and lasted about 400 years. The ostensible purpose of the knights, also known as the Brothers of the Cross and the Brothers of the Sword, was to spread Christianity, which meant Catholicism, among the "Baltic heathen and the Russian schismatics." They were joined in this purpose by the Swedes, who organised a holy crusade at the behest of Pope Gregory IX. The wishes of the pope were conveyed in a Bull to the Archbishop of Uppsala in 1237. This resulted in the famous battle of 1240 between the invaders and the inhabitants of Novgorod under the leadership of their Grand Duke Alexander. The Swedes, led by Jarl Birger, brother-in-law of King Erik of Sweden, encamped at the mouth of the Izhyora, a tributary of the Neva, were taken completely by surprise and were totally routed by the Russian forces who, according to legend, were inspired by a vision of the Russian saints Boris and Gleb. For this exploit Grand Duke Alexander was canonised under the name of St. Alexander Nevsky. One of the first things that Peter the Great did when he began the foundation of St. Petersburg was to have St. Alexander Nevsky made the patron saint of his new capital and build a magnificent monastery for the saint's remains.

In 1300 the Swedes established the castle of Vyborg and reappeared on the Neva. This time they built a fortified position, Landskrona, at the mouth of river Okhta in the Neva delta, but this fortress—the first attempt to establish a Swedish town within the limits of the present Leningrad—was soon foiled by the inhabitants of Novgorod.—In order to be able to defend themselves from these continual encroachments the Russians, in 1323, built a fortress at Ladoga, on a small island at the head of the Neva. However, during the succeeding 300 years, this fortress was continually taken and retaken by the Swedes. At last, at the end of the sixteenth and beginning of the seventeenth centuries, circumstances became particularly favour-

able for the Swedes. Novgorod had lost its independence to Moscow, and Russia's national power was greatly weakened by sedition and rivalry for possession of the throne. During this "Time of Troubles," the Swedes took advantage of the opportunity to settle themselves firmly on the Neva and Lake Ladoga. After the first Romanov came to the Russian throne, the Swedes, by the Treaty of Stolbova, signed on 27 February 1617, confirmed their possession and remained masters until the time of Peter the Great.

During this time the most important undertaking of the Swedes on the Neva was undoubtedly the founding of the settlement of Nyenshantz on the site of former Landskrona. A small fortress was first built on the right bank of the Neva in 1632, and a tiny, flourishing town soon grew up around it. Today, this site is the region of Leningrad called Okhta, which lies opposite the former Smolny Institute. In the 17th century the Smolny district was a colony of Russian tar distillers, from whom it derived its name ("smola" meaning tar or pitch). The colony was dependent upon Nyenshantz, both politically and economically, and came under the control of the Swedish authorities. There is evidence that the commercial community of Nyenshantz was a wealthy one: it carried on considerable trade with Lubeck and Amsterdam (during the summer of 1691 over 100 foreign vessels sailed up the Neva and discharged their cargoes, the goods probably being sent up the River Volkhov to Novgorod), and one of the town's merchants, named Frelius, was able to lend a large sum of money to Charles XII in his war against Russia. Besides the town itself some 45 villages and farmsteads are marked on Swedish maps from 1670, dotted over the area now occupied by Leningrad. There was good pastureland, an abundance of waterfowl, and plenty of game, including elk, in the surrounding woods. Many Swedish noblemen had extensive game reserves here. Thus, in pre-Petrine times, the region was far from being uninhabited swamp.

After his return from visiting England and Holland, Peter the Great began to turn his attention to the Neva. At that time Russia had no access to the sea, as Turkey still held the Black Sea. So it was of the utmost importance for the development of Russia's economic, technological, and cultural contacts with the West that she gain control of this area. Thus, after his unsuccessful attempt to wrest Narva from the grasp of the Swedes, Peter resolved to attack and capture Noteburg and Nyenshantz. In the autumn of 1702 he was successful in forcing the surrender of Noteburg: the key of the fortress, surrendered by the Swedish commandant, was nailed by Peter's orders to the top of the principal bastion, and the fortress itself was renamed Schlusselburg, from the German word for a key. In the following year Nyenshantz, too, was captured.

After the capture of Nyenshantz, Peter lost no time in beginning to carry out his project of establishing a commercial town in order to utilise the mouth of the Neva. Nyenshantz itself was not suited to the purpose as it was situated a little too far up the river. Therefore, a spot nearer the sea was selected, at the point where the Neva, before entering the Gulf of Finland, branches into 3 main channels, with several minor streams that form a number of islands. On the first of these islands—a very small one, known by the Finnish name of "Janni-saari" or Hare Island—Peter started the building of the fortress of St. Petersburg. Immediately behind Janni-saari was the large island called "Koivu-saari" or Birch Island, now the Petrogradskaya Storona (Petrograd Side), on which the first buildings outside the fortress were erected. On 16 May, 1703, only 16 days after the conquest of Nyenshantz, Peter the Great laid the foundation stone of the fortress and ordered a cathedral dedicated to the Apostles Peter and Paul to be built within the walls.

Wooden barracks and houses were rapidly put up to accommodate the troops from Nyenshantz and the chief officers and civil officials. For himself, Peter had a small hut built of logs, with only 3 rooms, just outside the fortress on the adjoining island of the Petrogradskaya Storona so that he could supervise the construction work. Peter disliked large and luxurious buildings, and the palaces which were built for him in St. Petersburg were all mere cottages in comparison with the magnificent structures raised by his successors. He preferred to give his money and attention to the commercial and military aspects of building the city. He resolved to ensure the safety of the city by fortifying the island of Kronstadt, some 29 km (18 miles) out in the Gulf, on Kotlin Island, and by constructing a mid-water fort to protect the navigable passage. Kronstadt in effect rendered the Peter and Paul Fortress redundant, but nevertheless it was reconstructed with more solid material some 6 or 7 years later. Its ramparts and 6 bastions were at first built of wood and earth, which were subsequently replaced by stone revetments and masonry.

Besides the construction of these fortifications, Peter gave the greatest attention to the building of the Admiralty and shipbuilding yards on the opposite side of the Neva. In fact, the left bank of the Neva, on which the principal quarter of the city eventually developed, was at first largely populated by shipwrights—Dutch and other foreign experts in naval construction—together with great numbers of workmen.

Estimates as to the precise number of workmen involved in the building of the new city vary enormously, but it is said that over 10,000 people died during the course of the operations (hence the melancholy saying that the town was "built on bones"). Workers were sent by force to St. Petersburg from all parts of the Empire and were employed in laying the first foundations in the marshes and digging the canals. In the unhealthy climate and under the terrible conditions of work, they died through disease and exhaustion. The mortality rate was further increased in the early days by frequent flooding: during Peter's reign there were no less than 7 floods, and it seems miraculous that the town was not washed away in its infancy. It was only the tenacity and determination of the tsar himself that ensured the eventual success of the city, for it appears that everyone else, nobleman and peasant alike, hated the place. Many of the soldiers and workmen deserted whenever the chance arose, but most were soon caught and dragged back. Nor could people be persuaded to come and live here, in spite of the fact that incentives were offered. Thus Peter was forced to resort to drastic measures. In 1710 he ordered 40,000 workmen a year for 3 years to be sent to St. Petersburg from the provinces and, with a view to attracting masons, he further commanded under penalty of banishment to Siberia that no stone buildings should be erected anywhere in the Empire except St. Petersburg. One of Peter's decrees, dated 26th May 1712, reads as follows: "1. One thousand of the best families of the nobility are required to build houses of beams, with lath and plaster, in the old English style, along the bank of the Neva from the Imperial Palace to the point opposite Nyenshantz. 2. Five hundred of the best-known merchant families and five hundred traders less distinguished, must build for themselves wooden houses on the other side of the river, opposite to the dwellings of the nobility, until the Government can provide them with stone houses and shops. 3. Two thousand artisans of every kind—painters, tailors, joiners, blacksmiths, etc.—must settle themselves on the same side of the river, right up to Nyenshantz."

Under such pressure the progress of the city was naturally very rapid. Within 8 or 10 years of its foundation there were a dozen streets and about 1,000 houses. The paving of the streets was begun in 1717 and in 1725 Peter ordered lamps to be put up, by which time the city already contained 75,000 inhabitants.

After Peter the Great's death, his widow, Empress Catherine I, and his grandson, Peter II, did nothing for the advancement of St. Petersburg. On the contrary, Peter II transferred his court to Moscow and entertained the idea of divesting St. Petersburg of its rank as capital. The mere attempt led thousands of people to desert the city, and before the next ruler who took up residence in St. Petersburg, the Empress Anna, could reinstall her court on the Neva, more compulsory measures had to be taken to bring back deserters. Then the city had to contend with an epidemic of incendiarism: in 1737 over 1,000 houses were destroyed by arson. Nevertheless, under Anna and her successor, the Empress Elizabeth, the town grew rapidly. Anna built the Admiralty Tower, with its gilded spire, and also began the Winter Palace; Elizabeth erected the Anichkov Palace. However, the real successor to Peter the Great, as far as the continuation of his building work was concerned, was Catherine II (the Great). Many of the finest buildings date from her reign (1762–96). On her invitation a number of well-known foreign architects came to St. Petersburg during this period and designed not only single houses but complete "architectural landscapes," in which all the buildings were regarded as parts of a great whole. It is largely owing to the encouragement of such building that the city, even today, has so many architecturally harmonious squares and streets.

Not without reason is Leningrad frequently called "the Cradle of the Revolution," for the whole history of the revolutionary movement in Russia is intimately connected with this city. The first strike broke out in St. Petersburg as early as 1749, in the form of a weavers' uprising, and thereafter the workers, students, and intellectuals of the city were always in the forefront of revolutionary activity. In 1825 the Decembrist uprising, an attempt by a group of officers of the Guards to overthrow the tsar and establish a constitutional form of government, broke out here but was quickly suppressed. Here too, in the 1870s and 1880s the Narodnaya Volya (People's Freedom) Group, which, on 1st March, 1881, succeeded in assassinating Tsar Alexander II, concentrated their terrorist activities. Here too, the first Marxist group of workers in Russia, the Northern Workers Association, was formed. On 9th January, 1905, the first Russian revolution received its bloody baptism here, when a huge demonstration of workers, led by the priest Father Gapon, was fired upon by the Imperial Guards in the square in front of the Winter Palace. After the ensuing strikes and disturbances, the tsar was forced to call a limited form of parliament, a consultative body called the State Duma. At this time too, the first Soviet (council) of workers and soldiers was formed in St. Petersburg, and Soviets subsequently sprang up all over the country.

By the outbreak of the First World War in 1914, the population of St. Petersburg, then renamed Petrograd, had reached 2 million, of whom approximately 250,000 were industrial workers. After the February revolution of 1917, which overthrew the monarchy and established a Provisional Government, Lenin returned to Petrograd from his exile abroad. Upon his arrival at the Finlyandsky (Finland) Station he was greeted by and he addressed a huge crowd of workers, soldiers, and sailors. Except for a short period in July/August when he went into hiding in Razliv and Finland, Lenin was constantly in Petrograd, planning the Bolshevik takeover of the government. On 25th October (or 7 November as it became when the calendar was revised), 1917 the Soviet government was proclaimed and the Red Guard of the Petrograd workers, with the help of the Baltic Fleet, broke down the resistance of the Provisional Government.

Naturally after the transfer of the seat of government to Moscow, the city's political significance to a certain extent diminished, but it continued its previous development as an industrial and commercial centre. In 1924 it was again the victim of serious flooding, but even this could not restrain its growth. Disaster again struck Leningrad during World War II, when the city was under siege by the Germans for almost 900 days. In August 1941 Nazi troops reached the outskirts of Leningrad and it became part of the front line. Food supplies ran short, water and electricity supplies were cut off,

fuel stocks ran out, and public transport came to a standstill. About 650,000 people died in Leningrad during the blockade and more than 10,000 buildings were destroyed or damaged by bombs or artillery fire. There are many war memorials in Leningrad. The most impressive is in Piscarevskoye Cemetery, where the blockade victims were buried in common graves. However, the blockade could not succeed in starving Leningrad into surrender, for a constant flow of lorries brought to Leningrad provisions, fuel, and ammunitions along the so-called road of life, laid across the ice of Lake Ladoga a few miles from the front line. In January 1943 the ring of the blockade was broken, and a year later a victory salute was fired over the city to celebrate its liberation. Leningrad was subsequently awarded the title "Hero City."

Work was immediately started on repairing the damage caused by the war. In 1948 Leningrad's industry reached its prewar level of production and soon thereafter surpassed it. In particular, electrical and electronic industries were developed here, and the technical level is especially high in these fields. The first atomic ice-breaker in the world, the 44,000 h.p. "Lenin," which can sail for more than a year without refuelling, was built here as was later the "Arctica."

Reconstruction and repair of the buildings damaged during the war was faithfully carried out, inspired by the past, and has now been completed. Much new building also went on, and there are many modern blocks of flats, such as those along Moskovsky Prospect, and even whole new residential regions, such as Avtovo.

Petrogradskaya Storona (Petrograd Side)

The name "Petrogradskaya Storona" applies to the part of Leningrad that includes the Zayachy, Petrogradsky, Aptekarsky, and Petrovsky islands. The Neva is at its broadest at the point where it divides the centre of the city, on its left bank, from the Petrogradskaya Storona, and it was here that the building of St. Petersburg began and it is here that the city's oldest building stands:

Peter and Paul Fortress (Petropavlovskaya Krepost). The fortress was founded in May 1703, and by the autumn of that year there were emplacements on the earth works round the fortress and 300 guns barred the Swedish fleet's approach to the site of the new city. In 1706 builders began to replace the original earth works with powerful brick fortifications according to the plans of Domenico Trezzini. The new walls were 12 m (40 ft) high and took 35 years to complete. However by the end of that century the brick had begun to look shabby in comparison with the other buildings erected on the banks of the Neva, and in the reign of Catherine II the walls were faced with granite slabs, which gave them the appearance they have today.

Gradually, as the fortress lost its military importance, it was used for other purposes, notably as a prison for political prisoners. Many of the most famous opponents of the tsarist regime were imprisoned here at one time or another. The first prisoner held here was Peter I's son, Alexei, who was tortured on his father's orders in 1718, and who died of his wounds. In 1790 the writer Alexander Radischev was imprisoned here before his exile to Siberia by Catherine II for writing about the horrors of serfdom and autocracy in his book "Journey from St. Petersburg to Moscow." After the Decembrist uprising of 1825, the leaders of the conspiracy were confined in the Alexeyevsky Bastion to await judgment: the majority were sentenced to many years of hard labour, but five were sentenced to death and executed outside the fortress, to the north of it, on 13th July, 1826. Throughout the nineteenth century the list of prisoners reads like a catalogue of the revolutionary movement in Russia: after 1849, members of the Petrashevsky Circle (which included Dostoyevsky) before their exile to Siberia; in the 1850s, the anarchist Mikhail Bakunin; in 1862, the writer Dmitri Pisarev and in July of the same year, Nikolai Chernyshevsky (who wrote his famous novel "What Is to Be Done?"); in 1866, Karakozov, who made an unsuccessful attempt on the life of Alexander II before his subsequent execution. In the 1870s and 1880s, the cells of solitary confinement in the Trubetskoy Bastion held many of the most prominent members of the "Zemlya i Volya" (Land and Liberty) and "Narodnaya Volya" (People's Freedom) groups, including Lenin's elder brother, Alexander Ulyanov. In January 1905 the writer Maxim Gorky was imprisoned here for issuing a revolutionary proclamation. In October 1917 the garrison of the fortress came over to the side of the revolutionaries, and the arsenal, containing nearly 10,000 rifles and large supplier of ammunition, was used to arm the insurrection. In 1924 the Peter and Paul Fortress was opened as a museum.

The fortress is entered through the outer *Ioanovskiye Vorota (the John Gate)* and the *Petrovskiye Vorota (the Peter Gate)*. The latter is of particular interest, as it is the only building in the fortress that has remained practically unchanged since it was first built. It was designed by Domenico Trezzini, built in 1717–18, and adorned with bas-reliefs by Konrad Osner representing the story of Peter confounding Simon the Sorcerer. In the niches are statues of Mars and Venus. In the centre of the fortress stands *Petropavlovsky Sobor (SS. Peter and Paul Cathedral)*. This is a domed building, in Dutch style, which was erected between 1712 and 1721, also by Trezzini. It was reconstructed by Rastrelli and Chevakinsky in 1750 after a fire, and again altered under Nicholas I. It is 64 m (70 yds) long and 30 m (33 yds) wide; the extremely slender gilded spire, which stands 120 m (394 ft) high, is crowned by an angel bearing a cross, the work of Rinaldi. The clock in the tower was brought from Cologne in 1760. Of particular interest inside the cathedral are the pulpit, rare in a Russian church, dating from the time of Peter the Great, and the carved and gilded wooden iconostasis made in the 1720s by carvers Ivan Telegin and Trifon Ivanov and artist Andrei Merkuryev.

This cathedral is the burial place of all the Russian tsars, from Peter I to Alexander III, with the exception of Peter II and Nicholas II. The imperial tombs are of white marble, with gilded eagles at the corners. The sarcophagi of Alexander II and his wife, however, are carved respectively of Altai jasper and red Ural quartz; the work on these tombs took 17 years.

To the right of the cathedral stands a small house, built by the architect Zomtsov in 1730 and adorned with a statue of a nymph holding an oar. It used to house a little boat belonging to Peter the Great—the so-called "Grandfather of the Russian Fleet."

To the west, opposite the cathedral, is *Monetny Dvor (the Mint)*. This was originally founded in 1724, but the present building by Voronikhin dates from the 19th century.

Also near the Cathedral stands the *Nevskiye Vorota (the Neva Gate)*, built by Lvov in 1787. It was through this gate that prisoners were led at night from the fortress dungeons to the granite Commandant's Wharf, to be sent to the Schlusselburg Fortress or to Lisy Nos (fox's nose), a remote spot on the shore of the Gulf of Finland, where the death sentences were carried out.

On the crownwork of the fortress is situated the *Arsenal*, the old building of which was established on the site of the former outer fortifications of the fortress in 1706. It now houses the *Military Museum*. This museum was founded by Peter the Great himself with the purpose of representing the whole history of weaponry, particularly in Russia. The collection has over 50,000 exhibits, including weapons (dating from the Paleolithic Age to the present day), military uniforms, and documents.

The park on the bank of the Kronverksky (crownwork) Sound was planted in 1845 and has since 1923 been called the *Lenin Park*. It stretches from the sound to Gorky Prospect, where the writer Gorky lived from 1914 to 1921 at No. 23. On the park side of the Prospect stands the *Lenin Komsomol Theatre*, built in 1939 but damaged during the siege and restored after the war. Next door (at 4, Lenin Park) is the *Planetarium*, opened to the public in 1959. Adjoining the Planetarium is a three-dimensional cinema and next, the Vulkan, the largest cinema in Leningrad, seating about 2,000. Further round to the west of the crownwork are the Zoological Gardens (founded in 1865), which have a collection of about 250 types of animals and birds.

On the opposite side of the fortress, on the Petrovskaya Naberezhnaya (Embankment), stands *Peter the Great's Cottage (Domik Petra Velikovo)*. This was built in 3 days in May 1703, in Dutch style, as the first house of the city. From here the tsar directed the building of St. Petersburg. As Peter lived in the cottage only in summer, it had no stone foundation, no stoves, and no chimneys. The cottage is about 12 m (40 ft) long and 6 m (20 ft) wide, and contains two rooms and a study. The doors and windows are all different sizes, and the biggest door is only 175 cm (5' 9"), while Peter was 198 cm (6' 6"). It is built of pine logs and painted to

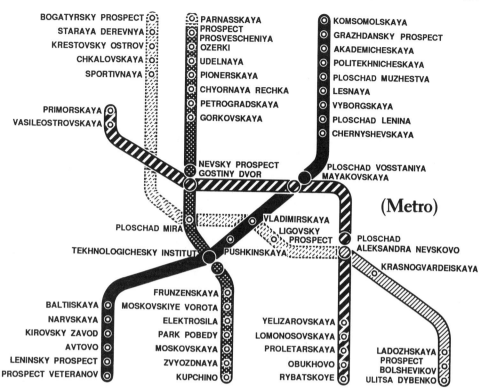

BOGATYRSKY PROSPECT
STARAYA DEREVNYA
KRESTOVSKY OSTROV
CHKALOVSKAYA
SPORTIVNAYA

PARNASSKAYA
PROSPECT PROSVESCHENIYA
OZERKI
UDELNAYA
PIONERSKAYA
CHYORNAYA RECHKA
PETROGRADSKAYA
GORKOVSKAYA

KOMSOMOLSKAYA
GRAZHDANSKY PROSPECT
AKADEMICHESKAYA
POLITEKHNICHESKAYA
PLOSCHAD MUZHESTVA
LESNAYA
VYBORGSKAYA
PLOSCHAD LENINA
CHERNYSHEVSKAYA

PRIMORSKAYA
VASILEOSTROVSKAYA

NEVSKY PROSPECT
GOSTINY DVOR

PLOSCHAD VOSSTANIYA
MAYAKOVSKAYA

(Metro)

PLOSCHAD MIRA

VLADIMIRSKAYA
LIGOVSKY PROSPECT

PLOSCHAD ALEKSANDRA NEVSKOVO

TEKHNOLOGICHESKY INSTITUT

PUSHKINSKAYA

KRASNOGVARDEISKAYA

BALTIISKAYA
NARVSKAYA
KIROVSKY ZAVOD
AVTOVO
LENINSKY PROSPECT
PROSPECT VETERANOV

FRUNZENSKAYA
MOSKOVSKIYE VOROTA
ELEKTROSILA
PARK POBEDY
MOSKOVSKAYA
ZVYOZDNAYA
KUPCHINO

YELIZAROVSKAYA
LOMONOSOVSKAYA
PROLETARSKAYA
OBUKHOVO
RYBATSKOYE

LADOZHSKAYA PROSPECT
BOLSHEVIKOV
ULITSA DYBENKO

resemble bricks, a device frequently employed in the city's early years to give hastily erected wooden structures the appearance of solid brick buildings. When the Summer Palace across the river was completed, Peter stopped using the cottage altogether and it was preserved only as an interesting historical relic. In 1784 Catherine II had a stone shelter built around it to protect it.

Inside the cottage is the boat in which the tsar saved the lives of some fishermen on Lake Ladoga in 1690. It is said to have been built by Peter himself. There is also an exhibition about Russia's victory in the Northern War and the early years of St. Petersburg.

The granite wharf on the embankment in front of the cottage is decorated with two mythical Shih Tsa (lion-frog) carvings, brought to St. Petersburg from Manchuria in 1907. There is a bronze bust of Peter I in the garden.

A little further along the embankment, near the Nakhimov Naval College, is moored the cruiser "Aurora," which fired a blank shot as the signal for assault on the Winter Palace on 7th November (24th October), 1917, the day observed annually as the Day of the October Socialist Revolution. The ship was built in 1900 and took part in the Russo-Japanese War of 1904–05. In October 1917 the crew went over to the side of the revolutionaries and took command of the ship. On instructions from the Revolutionary Military Committee, the "Aurora" sailed up the Neva to the palace. The gun that fired the shot and the radio room from

which Lenin's manifesto announcing the victory of the revolution was transmitted can still be seen, and the ship is open to the public.

Returning along Petrovskaya Embankment, past Peter the Great's cottage, one comes to *Revolution Square,* formerly called Troitskaya (trinity) Square. This is the oldest square of the city, for it was here that the first houses of St. Petersburg were built. Here too were the first harbour, the Exchange, the Customs House, and the market. The Troitsky Cathedral—built after the victory in the Battle of Poltava in 1710 and the place where Peter I took the title of Emperor in 1721—stood here. Today little remains of these very early buildings.

On the corner of Gorky Prospect stands *Kshesinskaya Palace,* which formerly belonged to the ballerina Matilda Ksheshinskaya, mistress of Nicholas II. This very elegant building, with its tiled facade, was built in 1902 by the architect A. I. Gogen. In 1917 the palace was the headquarters of the Bolshevik Party. It and the building next to it now house the *Museum of the October Revolution.*

Adjoining the palace is a mosque, built in 1912. It has two minarets and its grey stone is decorated with gaily coloured tiles. Krichinsky, the architect who designed it, took as his model Tamerlane's tomb in Samarkand, which dates from the beginning of the 15th century.

Here in Revolution Square begins one of the main thoroughfares of the city, *Kirovsky Prospect,* which runs through the Petrogradskaya Storona to the Kamennoostrovsky Bridge.

At No. 10 are the Lenfilm Studios, one of the most famous and important film studios in the country.

In Kirovsky Prospect there are several examples of early 20th-century Russian architecture using classical forms. One of these is No. 19, a stone-faced building designed by S. Minash.

Next to this house stands the oldest building in the street, No. 21. It was to this building that, in 1843, the *Tsarskoye Selo Lyceum*, a school for the sons of the gentry where Pushkin had been a pupil, was moved. It was then renamed the Alexandrovsky Lyceum.

A little further along, the street broadens into *Lev Tolstoy Square*. The local point of this square's architecture is a building known as "The House with the Towers." This strange building was erected in 1914, by Byelogrud; above a rough-stone and ceramic facade, its hexahedral towers rise high over the square, giving the impression of a medieval castle.

At No. 42 Kirovsky Prospect stands the Leningrad Soviet Palace of Culture, a building dating from 1934 and designed by Levinson and Munts.

Crossing the river Karpovka, one reaches the part of the Petrogradskaya Storona known as *Aptyekarsky Ostrov (apothecary island)*. It received this name in the time of Peter the Great, when, in 1713, a large plantation of medicinal herbs was laid out on the island and called the Apothecary's Garden. A hundred years later the plantation became a botanical garden. In 1931 the Botanical Institute, attached to the Academy of Sciences, was founded here. The institute has a Botanical Museum whose herbarium, with over 3 million samples, is one of the largest in Europe.

Continuing down Kirovsky Prospect one comes to a timber house (No. 62) which belonged to the architect A. Voronikhin. It was built in 1807–08, probably by the architect himself, and it was here, until his death in 1814, that he spent the last years of his life.

A little further along are the *Dzerzhinsky Gardens*. Here Kirovsky Prospect ends in a broad bridge (Kammenoostrovsky Most), which crosses the Malaya Kevka and leads to the *Kirovskiye Ostrova (Kirovskiye Islands)*. This is a collective name for the islands north of the Petrogradskaya Storona; they consist of Yelagin Island, Krestovsky Island, and Trudyaschikhsya (workers') Island, formerly called Kamenny (stone) Island.

The first island one comes to is the *Trudyaschikhsya*, which has an area of 103 hectares (260 acres). It was first owned by a leading statesman of Peter the Great's reign, Golovkin. He was succeeded by the Chancellor, Bestuzhev-Ryumin, who had thousands of serfs brought from the Ukraine to improve his estate here. These peasants settled around the island, thus founding those parts of the city now known as the Staraya Derevnya and the Novaya Derevnya (the old and new villages). During the 18th century canals were dug on the island, and their banks lined with limestone and granite. Many of the leading families among the gentry built magnificent summer houses and hunting-lodges here. On the eastern side of the island stands the *Kamennoostrovsky Dvoryets (palace)*, which was built for Paul I, who owned the island before his accession to the throne. The palace was probably designed by the distinguished 18th-century Russian architects Bazhenov and Felten, and the latter was certainly responsible for the design of the Maltese Chapel attached to the palace.

At No. 1, *Bekhterev Embankment* stands the former villa of Prince Dolgorukov, built in 1831–32 by Shustov in the shape of a domed cube.

The wooden building of the *Kamennoostrovsky Theatre*, which stands at No. 26 Bolshaya Nevka Embankment, was also the work of Shustov. It was erected within 40 days in 1827 and was restored later in the 19th century after damage by fire. This theatre was particularly popular for its performances during the summer season when the back walls were opened and the grove in which it stands was used as a natural backdrop.

The poet Pushkin was a frequent visitor to the island and he owned a house here that has not survived. It was replaced in 1913 by a mansion built for the senator Polovtsev by the architect Fomin. This building, in strict classical style, with rooms richly decorated with marble, Italian silk, moulding, and gilt and painted ceilings, is considered the most beautiful on the island.

On Krestovka Embankment stands *Peter the Great's Oak*, planted by the tsar in 1709, and nearby (at No. 2) is a villa built for the industrialist Vurgaft, again by Fomin. This and most of the other large mansions on the island were converted after the revolution into sanatoria and holiday centres.

Crossing the Srednaya (medium) Nevka, one comes to *Yelagin Island*, where there is a park of 95 hectares (230 acres). The island was first owned by Shafirov, a noted diplomat of the beginning of the 18th century, but in 1780 it passed into the hands of the nobleman Yelagin, whose name it still bears. Under his ownership, the marshy land was drained, and broad dykes, which still survive, were built to prevent flooding. In 1817 Alexander I purchased the island from Count Orlov, and gave the young but brilliant archietect Carl Rossi the task of building a palace there for his mother, the widow of Paul I. *Yelagin Dvoryets*, built between 1818 and 1826 in classical Russian style, was the result. It stands on a broad stone terrace, girdled with an elegant grille, and has 2 facades. The main one faces the park, which is laid out in English style, and is very impressive: a broad flight of steps decorated with lion carvings leads up to the 6-columned portico of the main entrance. The other facade overlooking the river is more restrained: its central section consists of the convex wall of the Oval Hall, beautifully proportioned columns, and an elegant frieze above the windows of the ground floor. Also outstanding are the colossal white marble vases with bas-relief groups of Nereids and Tritons, designed by Rossi himself. Of the surrounding buildings the semi-circular kitchen, the Pavilion (on the embankment of the Bolshaya Nevka), and the Musical Pavilion are also of interest.

The extreme western tip of the island, which runs out into the Gulf of Finland, the so-called Strelka, was replanned and laid out in 1927 by Ilyin. It has a terrace of pink marble with carved lions on stone pedestals. The rest of Yelagin Island is taken up by a park with various amusement and sports facilities. Celebrations are held in this park in June and July to see the white nights in and out.

The largest of the Kirovskiye Islands is *Krestovsky Island* with an area of 415 hectares (1037 acres). This is the sports centre of Leningrad, for in the western part of the island lies the huge *Kirov Stadium*, with a seating capacity of almost 100,000. It was built in 1950 mainly of earth; millions of cubic metres were raised from the bed of the Gulf of Finland to form the mound on which the stadium rests. The liquid mud was pumped through pipes to the construction site, where it was allowed to harden in the required shape. Also on Krestovsky Island is Victory Park, laid out in 1945 to celebrate and commemorate victory in World War II.

Continuing farther to the north of the Petrogradskaya Storona, through Novaya Derevnya and along Kolomyazhskoye Chaussee, one reaches the site where Pushkin fought the duel in which he was mortally wounded on 27th January, 1837. The spot is marked by an obelisk of pink granite.

The Strelka of Vasilyevsky Ostrov (Island)

This is the name given to the eastern tip of the island nearest to the Peter and Paul Fortress. It is the largest island in the Neva delta (8300 hectares/27,170 acres). Its principal fame now lies in the many institutes of higher education and research that are concentrated here.

The central position on the Strelka is occupied by the former *Exchange*, designed by Thomas de Thomon in 1810–16, and surrounded by 44 white Doric columns in imitation of the ancient temple at Paestum in southern Italy. The building stands on a massive, granite foundation, with a broad staircase leading up from a semicircular court to the main facade. On this facade (the eastern) stands a figure of Neptune in a chariot drawn by seahorses, with the Russian rivers Neva and Volkhov flowing round him. On the opposite pediment stand the goddess of seafaring, and the patron saint of trade, Mercury, surrounded by nymphs. One of the most beautiful views of Leningrad is obtained from the semicircular space between the columns. On the left-hand side is the spire of the cathedral in the Peter and Paul Fortress, and to the right, the former palaces along the Neva embankment.

The Exchange building now houses the *Central Naval Museum*.

In front of the Exchange stand two 32-m (105-ft) *Rostral Columns*, designed by Thomon in 1806 and decorated with beaks of galleys and figures of naiads. The figures at the foot of the columns personify Russia's commercial waterways, the Neva,

the Volkhov, the Volga, and the Dnieper. Besides being decorative, the columns also served as beacons for ships entering the commercial port between 1733 and 1885. Oil was poured into the copper cups at the top and, when it was lighted at dusk, the columns turned into gigantic flaming torches. Now on national holidays gas jets are lit and the heat from them can be felt by those standing nearby.

The ensemble of buildings here was later completed by the addition of warehouses on either side of the Exchange and the construction of the Customs House. Since 1886 the southern warehouse has accommodated the *Zoological Institute* and the *Museum of the Academy of Sciences*, and the northern warehouse is now the Academy's *Geological Museum*.

The *Customs House*, at 2a Naberezhnaya Makarova, is adorned with a severe portico and statues of Fortune and Mercury. From its dome, lookouts used to give signals of ships approaching port. The building now houses the Academy of Sciences, the Institute of Russian Literature, and the museum known as Pushkin House.

No. 3 Universitetskaya Naberezhnaya is the *Kunstkammer*, a massive 2-storey building with a tower, a protruding central section and arched facade built in baroque style in 1718–34 by Mattarnovi, Kiaveri, and Zemtsov. The upper part of the building used to be an astronomical observatory. It was here that the Academy of Sciences, planned by Peter the Great with the help of Leibniz and Christian von Wolff, first began its work, and its round conference hall still retains its original appearance. Here the great Mikhail Lomonosov worked from 1741–1765. However, the building was chiefly the home of Peter the Great's Kunstkammer, the first Russian natural science museum, which Peter referred to as his cabinet of "curiosities, rarities and monsters." His collection formed the basis of the *Museum of Anthropology and Ethnography*, which is housed here in the Kunstkammer. Also in the Kunstkammer is the *Lomonosov Museum*.

By the end of the 18th century, space in the Kunstkammer had become too cramped for the Academy, and a separate building was erected next door. The main building of the *Academy of Sciences* was completed between 1783 and 1788 and is one of the architect Quarenghi's greatest achievements. Its noble classical proportions are embellished only with a fine 8-columned portico and a double flight of steps down to the pavement.

Also on the embankment, but divided from the Academy building by the street called the Mendeleyevskaya Liniya, are the premises of the *University*, a group of 12 identical buildings designed by Trezzini in 1722–42 to house various government institutions. It was placed at the disposal of the university in 1819. Many brilliant and distinguished men in all fields of study were once students here, among them Mendeleyev, Popov, Pavlov, Turgenev, and Chernyshevsky.

Near the university is the 3-storey, red-and-

white building of the *Menshikov Palace*. It was built
as the first stone structure in St. Petersburg by the
architects Giovanni Fontana and Schedel for General Alexander Menshikov (1670–1729) in 1707,
when Peter the Great presented the whole of Vasilyevsky Ostrov to him so that he could build a
residence there. Menshikov was his close friend and
comrade-in-arms, and the first governor-general of
St. Petersburg, and indeed second in importance
only to the tsar. The building was relatively small
and homey, and Peter himself was very fond of
visiting there. Guests arrived by boat, and from the
riverside they climbed an oak staircase to the great
hall. From the window of the hall there is a beautiful view over the Neva. Menshikov had a splendid
gilded gondola that never failed to catch the eye of
passersby. (The gift of the island was withdrawn
again, however, in 1714).

From 1732 the building was used as a military
school by the First Cadet Corps and a long new
wing was added. The original Dutch tiles that line
a number of the rooms were covered with layers of
plaster and paint, and were thus preserved intact
until their recent discovery. The interiors all date
from the early 18th century and have been carefully
restored to their original appearance. The floors are
excellent examples of early parquet, and in the
room that belonged to Menshikov's wife is an oval
English table made of a single piece of precious
wood. The rest of the furniture also dates from the
early 18th century, and many pieces were previously in the Hermitage Museum with which this
is now affiliated. In the Shpalernaya Room hang
valuable tapestries with scenes from the "Odyssey."
This museum is well worth a visit for its 18th-
century interiors alone, not to mention its historical
importance. Intourist arranges tours for groups of
limited size; tickets should be obtained in advance.

Next to it on the embankment, and facing the
Neva, is the *Academy of Arts*, whose inner courtyard forms a circle set in a huge rectangle of surrounding buildings. The central section has a dome
and portal decorated with sculptures of Hercules
and Flora. When, in 1947, the Academy was
moved to Moscow, the Repin Institute of Painting,
Sculpture, and Architecture was accommodated
here.

The embankment in front of the Academy is
interesting for its classical quay with Egyptian
sphinxes, granite seats, and bronze torches. The
sphinxes are carved in pink granite, obtained from
the Aswan quarries nearly 3,500 years ago, and the
hieroglyphs on them eulogise the Pharaoh Ame-
nophis III, whose palace they once adorned. They
were bought by the Russian Government in 1831
and transported to St. Petersurg.

The Left Bank of the Neva

Much of the best architecture in Leningrad is
found on the banks of the Neva. Here there are
many squares and buildings, even complexes of
buildings, of great artistic and historical importance. Beginning at the eastern end of the em-

bankment is the whole complex of the *Smolny*.
Before the founding of the city the Swedish fort
Sabina stood on this site (facing the fortress Nyenshantz on the right bank of the river) and later there
arose a colony of tar distillers, from whom the
district derived its name. In the 18th century under
Peter the Great, Smolny Dvor (tar yard) was built
here to store tar for the ships being built further
downriver in the shipyards of St. Petersburg. In
1723, Smolny Dvor was moved to another part of
the city and a summer residence for the daughter
of Peter the Great, the Tsarevna Elizabeth, was
built in its place. When the main building of the
palace burned down in 1744, Elizabeth, now Empress, decided to found a convent here in which
to spend her last days. In 1748 the building was
begun to the designs of Rastrelli, in baroque style,
with the convent buildings grouped around the *Cathedral of the Resurrection*. This has 5 domes, the
central one of which is almost 80 m (262 ft) high
and is surrounded by 4 smaller differently shaped
domes. The whole group is reminiscent of early
Russian church architecture.

On her accession to the throne, Catherine II
decreed that a school for young ladies of noble birth
be founded in the convent, and at the same time
a house for widows was built next door to the convent. The plans for the latter were entrusted to the
architect Giacomo Quarenghi, and the building
was erected between 1806 and 1808 in strict classical style. Set well back from the street, its long
facade is relieved by two projecting wings and the
elaborate central part. Above the raised arcade of
the front entrance there is a portico of 8 Ionic
columns with a pediment and a loggia behind the
columns. The white-and-yellow facade has no
moulded ornaments at all, except for the capitals
of the flat pilasters. The interior decorations are
even more simple, but nonetheless impressive; particularly attractive is the enormous assembly hall,
which takes up the first and second floors of the
entire south wing.

When this building was completed, the school
(the Smolny Institute) was moved here, and the
occupants of the Widows' House were accommodated in the convent. In August 1917 the building
was taken over by the Petrograd Soviet and the
Central Executive Committee, and in October
1917, when the Revolutionary Military Committee
began working here, it became the headquarters of
the revolutionary forces. After the overthrow of the
Provisional Government the first Soviet Government was formed here. The room in which Lenin
lived and worked has been turned into a museum.

From the Smolny there is no through road
along the embankment, and so one must follow
the parallel Voinova Street. Here, at the junction
with Stavropol Street, stands one of the oldest
buildings in the city, built in 1714. In the early
years of St. Petersburg it was the home of the boyar
Kikin, who conspired with the Tsarevich Alexei in
a plot against Peter the Great. After the exposure
of the plot and Kikin's execution in 1719, the house
was given over to the collections of the Kunstkam-

mer, the first Russian science museum, founded by Peter. Entry was open to all, free of charge, and, to attract the public, all those who visited the museum were given refreshments including a glass of vodka. In 1727 the Kunstkammer was moved to another building, and this building now houses a children's club.

A little further on, on the opposite side of Voinova Street at No. 47, stands the *Taurida Palace (Tavrichesky Dvorets)* built in 1783–89 by Starov on the orders of Catherine the Great and presented by her to her favourite, Prince Potemkin of Taurida, after his conquest of the Crimea. The interior in particular was decorated with great splendour, but after Potemkin's death in 1791 the palace was resumed by the crown, and the mad Paul I, out of sheer hatred for Potemkin, had it turned into barracks. The famous Oval Hall with white marble columns was used as a stable. At the beginning of the 19th century, after Paul's death, the palace was restored by Rusca, and in 1906 it was slightly reconstructed so that it could be used for the sessions of the State Duma. It was here that, after the overthrow of the monarchy in February 1917, the Provisional Government was formed.

Behind the Taurida Palace lies the 30-hectare (75-acre) park, the *Tavrichesky Sad (Taurida Garden)* where, in the days of Catherine II, magnificent entertainments were given. Part of the park is now used as Leningrad's largest nursery garden.

Towards the end of Voinova Street, at No. 6, is a house where, from 1860–1870, the composers Rimsky-Korsakov and Mussorgsky lived. Here Mussorgsky worked on his opera "Khovanshchina." "Pictures from an Exhibition" was composed in 1874.

At the end of the street stands a house, faced entirely with marble, which used to belong to the uncrowned wife of Alexander II, Princess Yuryevskaya.

A right turn here leads onto *Kutuzov Embankment (Naberezhnaya Kutuzova)* and beyond the steeply arched bridge over the Fontanka lies a large park of nearly 12 hectares (30 acres).

Summer Garden (Lyetny Sad). On the side facing the Neva, the garden is enclosed by a fine wrought-iron railing, designed by Felten and erected in 1770–84. The pillars of greyish-pink granite, decorated with vases and urns, are linked with extremely delicate iron tracery work.

The garden itself was laid out in 1704–12 by Leblond in geometrically precise Franco-Dutch style. The avenues were lined with trimmed trees and the park was decorated with many fountains fed by the Fontanka. Peter the Great dreamed of making it a Russian Versailles and spared no expense in bringing rare trees and plants, and even sculptures, from all parts of Russia and Western Europe; for the Summer Garden he acquired an ancient statue of Venus (300 B.C.) discovered during excavations in Italy. Subsequently the statue was housed in the Taurida Palace—and hence became known as the Venus of Taurida—and it now stands in the Hermitage museum. There are now 79 statues in the Summer Garden, many of which have stood here for more than 200 years. The sculpture of "Peace and Plenty" was carved by special order of Peter the Great by P. Baratta in 1722 to be placed before the southern facade of the Summer Palace, and is an allegorical representation of the Russian victory in the Northern War (1700–21). Other statues are by such Italian masters as Bonazzo, Gronelli, and Tarzia. To the left of the main avenue stands a statue of the famous Russian fabler Ivan Krylov, a seated bronze figure sculpted by Klodt in 1856. On the granite pedestal are four bronze reliefs with animals and birds and other figures from his fables by A. Agin. Krylov himself loved to visit the garden as did many other writers, artists, and musicians, including Pushkin, Zhukovsky, Mussorgsky, and Repin. In the 18th and 19th centuries the garden was a centre of social and political life in St. Petersburg.

In the garden stands the unpretentious 2-storey building known as the *Summer Palace (Lyetny Dvoryets)*. Built in 1710–12 for Peter the Great in Dutch style by Domenico Trezzini, and decorated with statuary by Schluter, this palace was not usually inhabited, but rather was used during the festivities that took place in the garden. The layout of the 2 floors is identical: each has 6 halls, a kitchen, a corridor, and a servants' room. Particularly noteworthy are the kitchen (with its walls covered with Dutch tiles), the entrance hall (with a bas-relief in carved oak, representing Minerva, by Schluter), the Green Study upstairs, and the numerous blue-and-white tiled stoves. The paintings on many of the ceilings are still in very good condition.

Also very attractive are the Coffee House, built by Rossi in 1826 and with bas-reliefs by Demut-Malinovsky, and the *Tea House* by Charlemagne, 1827.

In the southern part of the garden stands a huge porphyry vase, presented in 1839 by Charles XIV of Sweden.

A little further along the Neva embankment, opposite Kirovsky Most (bridge), which leads to the Petrogradskaya Storona, is the small Suvorov Square. In the centre of it stands a monument to the 18th-century Russian general by the sculptor Kozlovsky, in which Suvorov is depicted as the god of war. An effective background for the statue is formed by the broad, open space of *Marsovo Polye* (Field of Mars), which borders the square on the southern side.

Marsovo Polye, now a beautiful 10-hectare (25-acre) park, was formerly used as a vast drilling ground where great military parades and splendid firework displays were held on special occasions. In the city's early years the site of the park was marshland, but Peter the Great had the whole area drained by two canals. When he had a palace built for his wife Catherine to the south of what is now the Field of Mars, the areas came to be called Tsaritsin Lug (Tsaritsa's Meadow). The park received its present name at the end of the 18th century or possibly at the beginning of the 19th, when the Suvorov statue was erected. For over 2 centuries the Field of Mars remained a completely bare stretch of land, without trees, bushes, or lawns. It was known for its dustiness in summer, and was often described as the "St. Petersburg Sahara." Now, however, it has been laid out with flowerbeds and avenues. In the very centre of the garden, where the walks meet, stands a massive quadrilateral block of granite, designed by Rudnev in 1919 as a monument to the victims of the February Revolution, where 180 revolutionaries lie buried here in a common grave. On the 8 stone blocks of the tomb are inscribed epitaphs in blank verse written by Lunacharsky. One of them reads:

By the will of tyrants
The nations were tearing at each other.
You rose, St. Petersburg toilers,
And were the first to wage a war
Of all the oppressed
Against all the oppressors, thus to destroy
The very seed of war itself.

In 1957, on the 40th anniversary of the October Revolution, an eternal flame was lit in the centre of the monument.

The Field of Mars is surrounded by a number of buildings of outstanding architectural interest. Almost the whole of the western edge of the park is taken up by the enormously long former barracks of the Pavlovsky Regiment. This was built by Stasov in 1817–20 after this regiment had distinguished itself against Napoleon in 1812.

In the south-east corner of the Field stands *Mikhailovsky Zamok (Mikhailovsky Castle)* or *Inzhinerny Zamok (Engineers' Castle)*, built at the close of the 18th century by Bazhenov and Brenna on the orders of Paul I. The building has an interesting history. Paul sought refuge here from the conspirators in his court, who were plotting against him, and ordered the castle to be constructed with secret passages, moats, and drawbridges. However, this was all to no avail; when he had lived here for little more than 12 days Paul was strangled by his own courtiers in the castle on 11th March, 1801. Subsequently a school for military engineers was opened in the castle, and since 1819 it has been known as the Engineers' Castle. Many famous men at one time or another studied here, among them the future writers Dostoyevsky and Dmitri Grigorovich (1822–99). The castle is also interesting from an architectural point of view, for each of its 4 facades was treated in a different way by the architects. The main, south, facade looking over a great square on which parades took place, is relieved by groups of Ionic columns supporting a pediment adorned with reliefs of historical scenes. The square entrance arch is framed by huge obelisks of dark stone and extending up all 3 storeys of the building. The north facade with its colonnade of pink marble faces the Summer Garden.

At the main entrance to the castle stands an equestrian *statue of Peter the Great*, cast in the reign of Elizabeth from designs by K. Rastrelli (father of the architect) and set up under Paul I, on whose orders the pedestal was inscribed with the words: "To great-grandfather from great-grandson—1800." The statue portrays Peter as a victorious general, and the pedestal is decorated with bas-reliefs in bronze by Kozlovsky, depicting the decisive battles of the Northern War (Poltava, 1709; and Cape Hango, 1714).

On the opposite corner of the Field of Mars, to the north-west, is *Mramorny Dvoryets (marble palace)*, built in 1768–85 from plans by Antonio Rinaldi and presented by Catherine II to Count Orlov. 32 kinds of marble were used for the facing and the interior decoration of the palace, which was carried out by the two best Russian sculptors of the day, Shubin and Kozlovsky.

At this point begins *Khalturin Street* in which there are several interesting buildings: No. 22-24, which is particularly old, dating from 1710, and No. 30, which used to belong to the Princess Golitsyna.

Parallel to Khalturin Street, along the river bank, runs *Dvortsovaya Naberezhnaya (palace embankment)*. No. 18 was built by Stakenschneider in the middle of the 19th century for a member of the tsar's family, and at No. 26-28 stands another ducal palace, built by Rezanov in 1867–72 in the style of a 15th-century Florentine palace. Further along, the embankment is crossed by *Zimnaya Kanavka (winter canal)*, dug in 1718 along the Old Winter Palace wall. On the corner stands the *Ermitazhny Teatr (hermitage theatre)*, completed by Giacomo Quarenghi in 1787 as a court theatre and now used as a lecture hall for the State Hermitage Museum. The hall is built in classical style in the form of an amphitheatre without boxes or stalls. It stands on the site of the former Winter Palace in which Peter the Great died in 1725.

The Hermitage Theatre is connected by a small, covered bridge to the building of the *Hermitage (Ermitazh)*. This itself consists of 3 separate but adjoining buildings: the oldest is the so-called *Small Hermitage*, a 2-storey pavilion that Catherine II had built by de la Mothe in 1764–67 to house her collections of paintings. It was named the Hermitage because it indeed served as a retreat for the empress from the vastness of the Winter Palace, and was a place where she could entertain artists and men of letters in more intimate surroundings than those provided by the palace. In 1775–84 another building, known as the Old Hermitage and notable for its interior decoration, was added by Felten, Director of the Imperial Academy. Here, in 1788, Quarenghi constructed the *Raphael Gallery*, an exact replica of the Raphael Gallery in Rome and now of particular interest as the original is in poor condition.

On the Khalturin Street side, the Old Hermitage adjoins the building of the *New Hermitage*, to which it is connected by corridors. This was constructed in 1839–52 by the architects Klenze and Yefimov on the orders of Nicholas I, and contains several points of interest, including the *Hall of*

Twenty Columns, with pillars of Karelian granite, and the white marble Roman courtyard. Its portico is supported by granite figures of the Atlantes.

From here opens up a splendid view of *Dvortsovaya Ploschad (palace square)*. This is the most impressive square in the city, designed to form one harmonious architectural whole. The oldest building is *Zimny Dvoryets (winter palace)*, a grandiose edifice in baroque style that stands on the northern side of the square. It was built in 1754–62 by Rastrelli, and after the fire of 1837, was reconstructed by Stasov and Bryullov to become the largest and most splendid building in St. Petersburg. Each of its 4 facades has a character of its own: the design of the eastern facade is a canopy of pylons, and its projecting wings form the main courtyard opening into the city towards the Admiralty; the northern facade, facing the Neva, is quieter in style but with a double tier of white columns, which give an impressive effect of light and shade; the main southern facade is richly decorated. The latter, looking onto *Palace Square*, has 3 arched entrances; the walls are of a light green colour, which sets off the white of the columns. The cornices and window mouldings, with their baroque cupids' heads, lions' faces, and scrolls, are intricately cast, and on the roof are 176 sculptural figures interspersed with vases. The whole building is of impressive size: it contains more than 1,000 rooms and reception halls, and has 1945 windows, 1786 doors, and 117 staircases. Many of the rooms, with their ornamentations of Russian semi-precious stones, such as malachite, jasper, and agate, afford unique examples of interior decoration. One of the richest in the palace is the Small Throne Room, with its beautiful panels and painted ceiling, its walls adorned with silver-embroidered velvet, consoles of coloured stone, parquet flooring of rare varieties of wood, silver chandeliers, and Peter the Great's throne.

Almost next door is the *Gallery of the 1812 Patriotic War*, the walls of which are almost entirely covered with 332 inset portraits of the generals who took part in the war. The majority of the portraits are by the English portrait-painter George Dawe, who painted them from life, as the subjects were commanded to appear in the artist's studio, each at an appointed day and hour. Adjoining the gallery is the *Georgiyevsky Hall*, or Large Throne Room, in which the tsar used to receive visitors; here too the first Russian parliament, the Duma, was opened in 1906. The parquet flooring (with an area of 800 sq. m) is composed of 16 different sorts of wood and its pattern repeats that of the ceiling. The balcony round the hall is supported by 48 Corinthian columns of pure white Italian marble, and the walls and balcony are faced with marble blocks. All the columns, as well as the 52 pilasters, have capitals of gilded bronze, and the decor is completed by 28 chandeliers and the bas-relief of Georgy Pobedonosets (St. George), patron saint of Russia. The throne, which is now in the Small Throne Room, also used to stand here. At the back of the hall there is now a large mosaic

map of the Soviet Union, made from stones and jewels from the Urals. Moscow, as the capital, is executed entirely in rubies. On the same floor is the Malachite Hall, so-called because all 8 columns, 8 pilasters, and 2 fireplaces are faced with dark green Urals malachite with a silky finish. More than 2 tons of malachite were used for the columns alone. The inlaid parquet floor is made of 9 different sorts of wood, including rosewood, ebony, mahogany, and palm. It was in this hall that the ministers of the Provisional Government gathered for conference on the eve of the October Revolution before being arrested by the revolutionary troops. The main white marble staircase of the palace, with its magnificent sculptures, gilding, painted ceiling, and moulding, is a masterpiece of 18th-century baroque.

In these buildings are housed Leningrad's world-famous collections of paintings and other priceless art treasures.

At the beginning of the 19th century the government decided to make Palace Square one complete architectural unit, and therefore bought up all the private buildings on the south side. In 1819 Carl Rossi was commissioned to design an administrative building, the *Glavny Shtab (General Headquarters)*, and the result was a severe classical building, almost totally devoid of decoration, completed in 1829. At one time it housed the offices of the Ministries of Finance and Foreign Affairs. The horseshoe-shaped facade centres on the Winter Palace and is broken by a large archway. This triumphal arch is surmounted by a bronze 6-horse victory chariot by Pimenov and Demut-Malinovsky, symbolising the victory of Russia over Napoleon in 1812. The 28-m (92-ft) arch is further decorated with coats-of-arms and martial figures, and is now called the Triumphal Arch of the Red Army.

In the centre of the square stands a triumphal column, *Alexandrovskaya Kolonna (Alexander's Column)*, which also commemorates the Russian victory of 1812. It was designed by Montferrand and erected in 1834 on the orders of Nicholas I in memory of Alexander I, and it bears the inscription, "To Alexander I from a Grateful Russia." The column of polished red Finnish granite stands 30 m (98 ft) high, weighs 600 tons, and was quarried out of a cliff in the Gulf of Finland, a task which took 3 years. It was brought to St. Petersburg on a specially constructed barge, and it took 2,000 soldiers, aided by a complicated system of pulleys, to raise it into position. After erection, the column was given its final polishing and crowned with the huge figure of an angel by Orlovsky representing the peace that was established in Europe after the victory over Napoleon. The base of the column is ornamented with coats-of-arms and bas-reliefs all of allegorical nature.

On the eastern side of the square are former barracks, built in 1840 by Bryullov for one of the Guards regiments.

The square itself was the scene of the massacre of "Bloody Sunday" in January 1905, and it was from here that the revolutionary troops and workers attacked the Winter Palace, then the headquarters of Kerensky's Provisional Government, in October 1917.

To the west of the Winter Palace lies the huge building of the *Admiralty*. This was founded originally in 1704 by Peter the Great as a fortress and shipyard, and was one of St. Petersburg's most important enterprises in those days. In the U-shaped yard opening on to the Neva, there were storehouses, workshops, and 10 large covered slipways. Here the large warships with which Peter founded and built his navy were built. The present building, also in a broad U-shape, dates from the years 1806–23 and was built to the designs of A. Zakharov. The central block is 150 m/yds long and each of the 2 wings, turned towards the Neva, are 65 m/yds in length; there are several porticos to relieve the monotony of such a huge facade. The building is also adorned with 56 sculptures and 11 large reliefs, all with the common theme of the sea or the Russian navy. The high relief sculpture over the arch of the main entrance, dedicated to the foundation of the navy, depicts Neptune presenting Peter the Great with a trident in the presence of Minerva and Mercury. This was the work of Terbenev. To the right and left are groups by Schedrin of 3 sea nymphs bearing the terrestrial globe, and at each of the 4 corners is a figure of a seated warrior, also by Schedrin. Over the gateway rises the Admiralty Tower, visible from almost all parts of the city. It is 70 m (230 ft) high, ending in a tapering gilded spire and surmounted by a weathervane in the form of a crown and ship.

From the west wing of the Admiralty stretches *Ploschad Dekabristov (Decembrists' Square)*, which takes its name from the conspirators, mainly tsarist officers, who, in December 1825, attempted a coup d'état and gathered here outside the Senate and the Council of State. In the centre of this grassy square stands the celebrated Peter the Great Monument, the work of French sculptor Etien Falconet, unveiled in 1782. It portrays Peter on horseback, his face turned to the Neva and his right hand pointing towards the scene of his labours. The horse is balanced on its hind legs and tail, while its hoofs trample on a writhing snake, said to be an allegorical representation of Sweden. Pushkin, in his poem "The Bronze Horseman," wrote of it:

There, by the billows desolate
He stood, with mighty thoughts elate,
And gazed.

Work on the statue took several years, and Falconet was aided in this by his pupil Marie Collot, who sculpted the head of the rider. The snake was the work of the Russian sculptor Gordeyev. The enormous solid block of granite that forms the pedestal weighs nearly 1,500 tons and was transported part of the way to St. Petersburg on an ingeniously constructed platform on wheels. The pedestal bears the inscription in Russian and Latin "Petro Primo Catharina Secunda 1782."

On the opposite side of the square from the Admiralty stand the twin buildings of the former *Senate* and the *Holy Synod*. The Senate House was designed in 1763; in 1829–34 it and the Synod were reconstructed by Rossi and connected by a gallery spanning the street between them. In the south-west corner of the square stands a former *manege*, or riding school, built by Quarenghi in 1804–07 and decorated with marble figures.

To the south of the square stands the magnificent structure of Leningrad's largest church, *St. Isaac's Cathedral*. With its impressive columned porticos, beautiful bronze sculpture, and golden dome, it took the French architect Auguste Montferrand over 40 years (1819–59) to build. He was assisted by Elson, responsible also for Prince Golitsyn's Crimean palace at Gaspra. Constructed of granite and marble, in the shape of a cross, it is 111 m (121 yds) long, 96 m (105 yds) wide, and has a total height of 110 m (361 ft). The enormous dome is visible from afar, and there is a magnificent view of the city and the river from here. (Permission is needed to take photographs.) The building, which can hold 14,000 people, is now a museum.

The main entrances on the north and south sides have beautiful porticos imitating those of the Pantheon in Rome. Each has 16 monolith columns of polished red Finnish granite, 16 m (52 ft) high and 2 m (7 ft) thick, with bronze bases and capitals. The columns are surmounted by pediments adorned with larger bronze reliefs, and above these are statues of the evangelists and apostles; the statues of angels at the corners of the roof are by Vitali. Altogether on the roof there are more than 350 sculpted decorations, some of them by Klodt.

The interior height of the dome from the floor is 82 m (269 ft), compared with St. Paul's in London (69 m/226 ft) and St. Peter's in Rome (123 m/404 ft). 562 steps lead to the top of the dome, and from the dome swings a pendulum weighing 54 kg (over a hundredweight), which moves round 13° each hour. The interior of the cathedral is decorated with nearly 200 valuable paintings, many of them by Bryullov, Bruni, and Bassin. The iconostasis, 68 m (223 ft) long, is of richly gilded marble, and has 33 large mosaics of saints; the Holy Door in the centre is the work of Vitali, flanked by columns veneered with malachite and lapis lazuli. The 4 colossal beaten bronze doors, richly adorned with sculptures by Vitali, each weigh 10 tons.

On the high-relief sculpture of the pediment on the western facade is depicted the figure of Montferrand holding a model of the cathedral.

St. Isaac's Square, on which the cathedral stands, contains buildings dating mainly from the 19th century. No. 9, however, in the north-west corner, was built in the 1760s for Myatlev, a friend of Pushkin, and the French philosopher Diderot lived here in 1773–34 during his stay in St. Petersburg.

On the opposite side of the square stands the building, decorated with lions, which until 1917 housed the War Office.

On the south side of the square, beyond *Siny Most (blue bridge)*, the broadest bridge in the city, which used to be used as a serf market, stands the former *Mariinsky Dvoryets (palace)*, built in 1839–44 by Stakenschneider for Maria, daughter of Nicholas I, and subsequently used for sessions of the State Council.

In 1859 a statue to Nicholas I by P. Klodt was erected at the southern end of the square. The tsar is represented on a prancing horse, and the sculpture has only 2 points of support (the hind legs). The pedestal is adorned with bronze trophies and 4 reliefs depicting memorable events in the tsar's rule. At the corners are allegorical figures of Faith, Justice, Wisdom, and Strength, which are portraits of the tsar's wife and daughters.

From the northern end of the square the *Bulvar Profsoyuzov (trade union boulevard)* runs westwards for almost half a mile to *Truda (Labour) Square*. In the early days of the city this square was one of the outlying districts adjoining the Admiralty Yard. However, upon the expansion of the city and particularly the shipbuilding activities, it became part of the central districts. Its increasing importance was marked by the building there in 1853–61 of a palace of Stakenschneider for the eldest son of Nicholas I. This palace is a monumental building on the eastern side of the square, surrounded by a fine railing on a granite pediment, which is now occupied by the Regional Trade Union Council.

On the opposite corner of the square, to the south-west, lies the triangular-shaped island known as *Novaya Gollandiya (New Holland)*. This is a man-made island, formed by the Moika, the Kryukov, and New Admiralty canals, which were dug in the reign of Peter the Great to connect the Admiralty with its subsidiary enterprises further along the embankment. Surrounded by water, Novaya Gollandiya was a useful place for storing inflammable materials, and as early as the 1730s timber for shipbuilding was stacked here. A whole complex of stone buildings were built for this purpose, and the project was entrusted to the architect Chevakinsky. In 1780 the buildings on the side of the Moika were completed, but the rest was not finished until the 1840s. In the center was built a dock, connected to the outer canals, which could accommodate 30 barges at one time for unloading. The subsidiary canal leading to the Moika is spanned by a beautifully decorative arch.

The street leading southwards from Truda Square brings one to the old *Most Potseluyev (Bridge of Kisses)*, decorated with granite obelisks. From here one can see, on the left, on the opposite bank of the Moika (at No. 94), a yellow building with white columns, which was formerly the palace of Prince Yusupov. Built at the end of the 18th century by Quarenghi, it was here, in one of the basements, that Yusopov and his fellow-conspirators killed Rasputin in 1916.

Beyond Most Potseluyev lies *Teatralnaya (theatre) Square*. The oldest building here is St. Nicholas's Cathedral, a splendid turquoise-and-white baroque building with a soaring belltower, erected in 1753–62 and decorated in traditional Russian style by Chevakinsky. It is open for services.

The square has long been a centre of entertainment in Leningrad (hence its name). As early as 1765 a wooden theatre was constructed here for performances by amateur companies, and in 1782 it was replaced by a brick building known as the Bolshoi (big) Theatre. In this, the largest theatre in Europe at that time, were performed operas, ballets, and plays. However, in 1886 the theatre closed down, and its premises were converted for use by the St. Petersburg Conservatoire, which had been founded in 1862 on the initiative of the composer Anton Rubinstein as the first higher musical institution in Russia. It is now known as the *Rimsky-Korsakov Conservatoire*, and its famous graduates include Tchaikovsky, Glazunov, Prokofiev, and Shostakovich.

Opposite the Conservatoire stands the building of the *Kirov State Theatre of Opera and Ballet*, formerly called the Mariinsky Theatre in honour of the Tsaritsa Maria, wife of Alexander II. Designed by the architect Kavos in 1860, this theatre was one of the most important centres of Russian opera and ballet. Both Fyodor Chaliapin and Anna Pavlova performed on its stage, and later Galina Ulanova started her career here followed more recently by Rudolf Nureyev and Mikhail Barishnikov.

In Teatralnaya Square stand monuments to *Glinka* (sculpted by Bakh in 1906) and *Rimsky-Korsakov* (Bogolyubov and Ingal, 1952).

Nevsky Prospect

This is the main street of the city and one of the oldest. It was built in 1710 to link the Admiralty Yard directly with the Great Novgorod Road leading to Novgorod. Beginning at the Admiralty building, it runs to the Moscow Railway Station and then stretches on further to the Alexander Nevsky Lavra (Monastery), covering a total of 4.5 km (2.5 miles).

Here, in tsarist times, were built all the largest banks, the best shops and the palaces of the nobility. *House No. 9*, on the corner of Gogol Street, was once the Wavelburg Bank, built in 1912 by Petryatkovich in imitation of the Doge's palace in Venice and the Medici Palace in Florence. Its granite facing stone was imported ready for building from Sweden.

In *Gogol Street*, house No. 13 was for a long time the residence of the composer Tchaikovsky, who died there on 25th October, 1893. No. 17 was occupied by the writer Gogol from 1833–36, and it was here that he wrote "The Inspector General" and "Taras Bulba." The next side-road is *Bolshaya Morskaya* (formerly Herzen Street), where Gogol lived in house No. 25 in 1840–41.

The part of Bolshaya Morskaya Street to the north of Nevsky Prospect was built by the architect Rossi straight along the Pulkovo meridian, and at noon on a sunny day one can check one's watch by it—the facades of the houses cast no shade.

No. 15 *Nevsky Prospect* is one of the oldest in
the street. It was built in 1768–71 by Kokorinov
for the chief of the St. Petersburg police, Chich-
erin, and is now a cinema. The elegant classical
building at No. 20 was once a Dutch Church, built
in 1837 by Jacquot, and is now a library.

On the corner of the Moika Embankment is
the white-columned *Stroganov Dvoryets* (palace),
built in 1752–54 by the architect Rastrelli, and one
of the best examples of Russian baroque.

No. 22–24 is the former Lutheran Church of
SS. Peter and Paul, built in Romanesque style by
the architect Bryullov in 1833–38. Almost opposite
stands the impressive *Kazan Cathedral*, which is
approached by a semi-circular colonnade of 136
Corinthian columns, modelled on that of St. Peter's in Rome. It was designed by Andrei Voronikhin (1706–1814) and at the time of its
construction in 1811 was the third-largest cathedral
in the world. It is 79 m (259 ft) high, 72 m (79
yds) long, and 55 m (60 yds) wide, built in the
shape of a Latin cross in Greek neoclassical style.
Huge bas-reliefs of biblical themes adorn the end
walls of the colonnade, and the niches of the facade
contain enormous statues of Russian warriors. The
small square in front of the main entrance is surrounded by beautiful ironwork, also designed by
Voronikhin. To the right of the entrance is the
tomb of Field Marshal Kutuzov, and on either side
hang the keys of the towns and cities he captured
during his campaigns. Nearby is a memorial to the
architect of the cathedral. The building takes its
name from the wonder-working icon of Our Lady
of Kazan, which used to be here but has now been
transferred to the Russian Museum. It is worthwhile going down into the crypt to see the exhibits
there. The cathedral was only open as a museum
for many years. In 1990 it was returned to the
church, and services are occasionally held.

In the square in front of the cathedral stand
statues designed by Orlovsky in 1831–32 of Kutuzov and General Barclay de Tolly, who led the
Russian army to victory in the 1812 campaign. At
their feet lie the banners of Napoleon's defeated
army.

On the corner of Nevsky Prospect and the Griboyedov Canal stands a building faced with polished granite, with a glass tower and a 3-m (10-ft)
glass globe, which was built in 1907 and which
formerly belonged to the Singer sewing machine
company.

On the left, some distance along the embankment, stands a church built in 1883–1907 by Par-
land on the spot where in 1881 Alexander II was
assassinated by members of the Narodnaya Volya
(People's Freedom) group. The church is in the
old Russian style, with ornate decorations, modelled on St. Basil's Cathedral in Moscow. It is
called the *Church of the Resurrection*.

No. 30 *Nevsky Prospect* was once owned by a
friend of Pushkin, Engelhardt, and later, in the
19th century, was used for concerts by the Philharmonic Society. Performers here include Berlioz, Wagner, Liszt, and Strauss. Today it is the

Small Hall of the Leningrad State Philharmonic
Society. Next door (*Nos. 32–34*) was formerly the
Roman Catholic Church of St. Catherine, built by
de la Mothe in 1763–64 in the shape of a Latin
cross. The pentagonal tower by Ferrari (1802) was
used originally as a firemen's watch-tower, then as
a semaphore station linking St. Petersburg with
such country residences as Tsarskoye Selo and
Warsaw. Between the Winter Palace and Warsaw
there were 149 such towers, all of them over 15 m
(49 ft) high.

Here the side street to the left, Brodsky Street,
links Nevsky Prospecy with Iskusstv (arts) Square.
The most striking building here is the large *Mikhailovsky Dvoryets (palace)* built in 1819–25 by
Rossi for Nicholas I's brother, the Grand Duke
Michael. The main building stands at the back of
a courtyard formed by subsidiary blocks. High iron
railings separate the courtyard from the square,
which is entered through 3 gates, decorated with
coats-of-arms. The palace stands on a socle and
there are arches under the protruding 8-columned
portico, which enabled carriages to drive straight
up to the palace doors. There is also a broad granite
staircase decorated with bronze lions. On both sides
of the portico, between the high oval windows of
the first floor there are elegant Corinthian pilasters.
Rossi is said to have likened the palace to the building of the Louvre in outward appearance. Decorative sculpture was much used on the facades and
interiors of the palace and the best artists of the
time collaborated in this work and that of painting
the ceilings and walls. The original decorations of
the vestibule, main staircase, and White Hall,
which has survived to this day, is one of the best
examples of the Russian classical interior. In 1890–
95 the palace was converted into the *State Russian
Museum*.

The painter Isaak Brodsky lived and worked in
Isskustv Square, at No. 3, in 1924–39, and after
his death his flat was turned into a museum.

Next door stands the *Maly (Small) Opera*, built
in 1833 by Bryullov, following Rossi's general project for the whole square. It was first called the
Mikhailovsky Theatre, and up to 1918 it was occupied on a more or less permanent basis by a
French drama company. After that date an opera
company worked here, and it was joined by a ballet
company in 1933. Lavrovsky was in charge of the
ballet in this theatre before he became the chief
choreographer at the Bolshoi Theatre in Moscow.

On the other side of the square, in a building
on the corner of Brodsky Street, originally erected
by Jacquot for the Dvoryanskoye Sobraniye (Assembly of Nobles) is the *Leningrad Philharmonic
Society*.

Back on Nevsky Prospect, No. 35 is the 230-m
(252-yd) frontage of *Gostiny Dvor department store*,
a 2-storey building with a row of arches and arcades
along each floor. It was built in 1761–85 by de la
Mothe, and numerous shops were turned into galleries forming a square, 1 km (0.6 miles) around.
The interior has now been reconstructed to form
the largest department store in the city. Opposite,

at Nos. 40–42, is the small but elegant former Armenian Church, built in the 1770s probably by Felten, and a little further down is another big arcade of shops, founded in 1848 and reconstructed in 1900, now turned into another large department store.

At the corner of Sadovaya Street is the *Saltykov-Schedrin Library*, built partly by Sokolov in 1796–1801 and partly by Rossi in 1828–32 and decorated with bas-reliefs and carvings of ancient orators, philosophers, and writers. It is one of the largest libraries in the world.

At this point Nevsky Prospect runs into Ostrovsky Square, on the south side of which stands the *Pushkin Drama Theatre*. It was built by Rossi in 1832 and, until the Revolution, it was called the Alexandrinsky Theatre in honor of Tsaritsa Alexandra, wife of Nicholas I. It was built by Rossi in 1832. The main facade is decorated with a 6-columned loggia raised above the ground floor, and the whole building is surrounded by a frieze of theatrical masks and garlands. The attic is crowned with a chariot of Apollo, executed by Pimenov. Southwards from the theatre runs an interesting street named after Rossi, who designed it in 1828–34. On either side lie identical buildings, painted yellow and decorated with white columns, their walls exactly the same height as the width of the street. The length of the street is exactly 10 times its width. In the centre of the gardens in Ostrovsky Square stands a statue of *Catherine II*, erected in 1873 by Mikyeshin. Round the base of the statue are grouped figures of distinguished persons from 18th-century Russia. On the eastern side of the square stands the *Anichkov Dvoryets*, built in 1741–47 according to the designs of Rastrelli, by order of the Empress Elizabeth for her favourite, Count Razumovsky. From Nevsky Prospect only the northern side, which is devoid of decoration, is visible; the front of the palace faces the Fontanka, as, at the time of its building, this embankment was a more fashionable area than Nevsky Prospect.

At the place where Nevsky Prospect crosses the Fontanka is the famous *Anichkov Most (bridge)*. The present bridge was built in 1839–41, with railings designed by Montferrand. It is chiefly noted for its statues of youths with horses by Peter Klodt; these were begun 10 years before the present bridge was completed. Originally there were 2 statues, each cast twice and placed at the 4 corners of the bridge. Then one pair was sent by Nicholas I to the King of Prussia as a present, and plaster casts, painted in imitation of bronze, were erected in their place. New casts were made, but in 1846 Nicholas again sent them away as a present, this time to the King of Sicily. In 1850 Klodt made 2 different statues to complete the set, and they were eventually erected on the bridge. They have stood here since then, except for a time during World War II, when they were buried in the nearby gardens for protection.

Most of the rest of Nevsky Prospect, from the Fontanka to Vosstaniya (uprising) Square, was built at the end of the 19th century, and there is little of very great architectural interest here. However, No. 68 was the residence of the famous Russian critic and writer Vissarion Belinsky in 1842–46, and he was often visited here by Dostoyevsky, Goncharov, and other well-known writers. In 1851 Turgenev lived in the same building.

The cross-road of Nevsky Prospect with Liteiny Prospect and Vladimirsky Prospect is one of the busiest in the city.

In Vosstaniya Square stands the *Moscow Railway Station* building, designed by Thon and opened in 1851, when trains started running between St. Petersburg and Moscow.

From the square it is just a little over half a mile to *Alexander Nevsky Lavra*. A "lavra" in Russian is a monastery of the highest order, one which is also the seat of a Metropolitan Bishop. There are only 4 of them in Russia, and the Alexander Nevsky Monastery was raised to this status in 1797. After the Monastery of the Caves in Kiev, it was the largest lavra in Russia. According to legend it stands on the spot where Grand-Prince Alexander won his great victory over the Swedes and the Teutonic Knights in 1240, although the battle was actually fought much higher up the Neva. Peter I built a small church on this spot in 1713, and in 1724 had the remains of St. Alexander brought here from Vladimir. In 1750 a silver sarcophagus was made in the St. Petersurg Mint for the remains of the saint; this was transferred to the Hermitage in 1922.

The lavra, which contained 11 churches and 4 cemeteries, as well as church offices, an ecclesiastical academy, and a seminary, is surrounded by a stone wall. The central entrance is adorned with an elegant *Gate-Chapel*, designed by Starov in 1783–85. Beyond this main entrance lie 2 of the cemeteries, known as necropoles, on either side. Admission to the cemeteries is by ticket. On the left is the 18th-century *Lazarevskoye Cemetery*, where Peter the Great's sister, Natalia Alexeyevna, was buried in 1716, soon after the foundation of the monastery. Also buried here are the scientists Lomonosov and Euler, and the architects Voronikhin, Rossi, and Zakharov. There are the tombs of some noble families, but more have been collected here for their artistic worth. *Tikhvinsky Cemetery*, on the right, contains the graves of many famous in the world of the arts—the fabler Krylov, the composers Glinka, Tchaikovsky, Mussorgsky, Rimsky-Korsakov, and Borodin, the architects Stasov and Klodt, the writer Dostoyevsky, and the poet Zhukovsky. The buildings of the lavra were designed by Trezzini, Starov, and others. The oldest part (1722) is the 2-storey building to the left of the main gate; here there are 2 churches. On the upper floor is the *Church of Alexander Nevsky*, and below it is the *Blagovescheniye (Annunciation) Church*. Here a marble slab set in the floor and bearing the simple inscription "Here lies Suvorov" marks the grave of that famous Field Marshal. Other monuments in the church were carved by such sculptors as Martos and Gordeyev. This building also houses the *Museum of Urban Sculpture*, where the original models of many of the works of art that decorate the city are on display. The *Troitsky Sobor (Trinity Cathedral)* was founded in 1724 by Peter I to house the remains of St. Alexander Nevsky, and was completed in 1778–90 by Starov. It is in classical style, with sculptures by Shubin. The *Mitropolichny Korpus* is a fine example of Russian Baroque, designed in 1756–59 by Rastorguyev.

Former Palaces, etc.

Peter & Paul Fortress, Revolutsii Square. Open 11–6; closed Wed. & the last Tues. of each month.
Peter I's Cottage, Petrovskaya Nab. 6. Open May–November, 10–6; closed Tues.
The *Summer Palace*, Nab. Kutuzova, Letny Sad *(Summer Garden)*. Open May–November, 11–6:30; closed Tues. and last Mon. of each month.

Art Museums

Hermitage, Dvortsovaya Nab. 4–6. Open 10–6; closed Tues. June–September open 10–5. The State Hermitage contains one of the largest and most valuable collections of paintings in the world, including priceless examples of works by the greatest Western European masters. Although it is often claimed that Catherine II was the creator of the Hermitage collections, several paintings that hang here today were in fact purchased earlier, in the reign of Peter the Great. Peter's interest in art was mainly of a practical nature; in particular he recognised the value of art as propaganda in his struggle for the modernisation of Russia, and this explains his predilection for the work of such Dutch painters as Adam Silo, who depicted the ships and shipyards of the Netherlands. However, we also know that in 1716 Peter purchased for the Hermitage one of its Rembrandts, "David's Farewell to Jonathan." Peter also began collections of Russian antiquities by issuing an order prescribing the careful preservation of all ancient objects found in the ground; as a result of this arose the Hermitage's Siberian collection, mainly gold objects.

It was Catherine II, however, who began collecting art, mainly Western, for its own sake, and on a large scale. She systematically bought up whole collections of paintings that came on to the market, such as that of Gotkowski, which comprised 225 pictures, including several Rembrandts, a Frans Hals, a Van der Helst, and two Gotzius. Her ambassadors throughout Europe, and particularly in Paris, were ordered to keep her constantly informed of interesting sales, and in 1769 she pulled off a major coup by acquiring for 180,000 roubles the collection of the recently deceased Count de Bruhl of Dresden. This contained many masterpieces: 4 paintings by Rembrandt, 4 Ruisdaels, 21 Wouwermans, 5 Rubens, and several Bellottos and Watteaus. One of the most remarkable collections in Europe was that of Sir Robert Walpole, and that in its entirety was sold to Catherine by his grandson, Horace Walpole; the loss to the British nation was appreciated all too late, and it

was after this that it was decided that a national British collection should be formed. It was Catherine too who had the actual buildings of the Hermitage constructed to house her collections of paintings, and she purchased so many pictures that the high walls were closely covered from the floor to the ceiling. On Catherine's death it was estimated that the Imperial collections totalled 3,926 pictures.

The process of collecting was continued, to a greater or lesser degree, by succeeding monarchs; Nicholas I in particular greatly expanded the collection and did much to rectify the preponderance of Dutch and Flemish paintings by purchasing works of the Spanish and Italian schools. Hitherto the collection had been an entirely private one, open only to a few privileged guests and visitors. It was Nicholas I who, in 1852, opened the Hermitage as a public museum, and at that time the Hermitage became an independent administration under the direction of curators, and the acquisition of paintings depended not on the individual caprices of the tsar, but rather on the decisions of a public body. Apart from works purchased abroad, the Hermitage also benefitted to a large extent from the collections of members of the Russian aristocracy who, following the fashion set by Catherine II, had become prodigious collectors of Western art. After the Revolution the private collections that remained in Russia, such as those of the Stroganov and Yusupov families, were all taken over by the State and they went to swell the Hermitage collection. Thanks to such discriminating collectors as Sergei Shchukin and Ivan Morozov, who both purchased and also commissioned works from contemporary artists such as Bonnard, Cezanne, Picasso, and Matisse, the Hermitage has one of the world's richest collections of Impressionist art, although many of these paintings have now been transferred to the Pushkin Museum in Moscow.

The exhibits in the Hermitage Museum fall into 7 main sections, and are subdivided into 40 smaller sections:

1. HISTORY OF RUSSIAN CULTURE

7–13th centuries	1st floor, rooms 5–10
17th–early 18th century	1st floor, rooms 13–18
(Includes a bronze bust and a wax mask of Peter the Great by Rastrelli)	
Malachite objects (early 19th century)	1st floor, room 19 (Malachite Hall)
Second half of 18th century	1st floor, rooms 20–34
Early 19th century	1st floor, rooms 35–9, 48
Russian Silverware (17th–20th century)	1st floor, room 60 (including the silver tomb of Alexander Nevsky made in St. Petersburg mint in 1750–3)
Russia's Heroic Military past	1st floor, rooms 65–7

1812 Patriotic war — 1st floor, room 67

Mosaic map of Soviet Union (in precious and semi-precious stones) — 1st floor, room 68 (St. George's Hall, or Small Throne Room)

2. HISTORY OF PRIMEVAL CULTURE
(Relics of primeval culture found on the territory of the USSR)

Scythian culture and art (7th–2nd century B.C.) — Ground floor, rooms 6–12

Culture and art of primeval nomads in the Altai area (Western Siberia) — Ground floor, rooms 15–21

3. HISTORY OF ORIENTAL CULTURE
(Within the Soviet Union)

Central Asia (6th century B.C.) — Ground floor, rooms 1–16

Caucasus (10th century B.C.–8th century A.D.) — Ground floor, rooms 17–22

4. ORIENTAL CULTURE AND ART
(Outside the Soviet Union)

Ancient Egypt (4000 B.C.–6th century A.D.) — Ground floor, rooms 1–12

Babylon and Assyria (4000–1000 B.C.) and Palmyra (2nd–3rd century A.D.) — Ground floor, rooms 13–17

Byzantium (4–15th century) — 2nd floor, rooms 39–40

Near and Middle East — 2nd floor, rooms 41–55

China (2000 B.C.–20th century) — 2nd floor, rooms 18–35

India (17th–20th century) — 2nd floor, rooms 36–38a

Japan (17th–19th century) — 2nd floor, room 26a

5. ANTIQUE CULTURE AND ART

Ancient Greece (8th–2nd century B.C.) — Ground floor, rooms 1–4, 8, 10

Greek colonies on the northern shore of the Black Sea (7th century B.C.–3 century B.C.) — Ground floor, rooms 5–7, 9, 10, and 21

Ancient Italy (7th–2nd century B.C.) — Ground floor, room 13

Ancient Rome (1st century B.C.–4th century A.D.) — Ground floor, rooms 11–12, 14–18

6. WEST EUROPEAN ART

Medieval European Applied Art (11th–15th century) — 1st floor, room 1

Italian Art (13th–18th century) — 1st floor, rooms 4–33. Room II has 2 paintings by Leonardo da Vinci, room 25 7 Titians, and room 26 several Veroneses and Tintorettos.

Spanish Art (16th–18th century) — 1st floor, rooms 34–5. El Greco and Velasquez are in room 35.

Dutch Art (15th–16th century) — 1st floor, rooms 37–40. Painting "The Fair," attributed to Peter Brueghel, and 2 drawings by Brueghel in room 39

Flemish Art (17th century) — 1st floor, rooms 41–4. In room 42 are most of the 42 paintings by Rubens that the Hermitage possesses, including "The Descent from the Cross," "Venus and Adonis," "Perseus and Andromeda," and "Union of Earth and Water." Room 43 contains many works by Van Dyck, including "The Holy Family," "Self Portrait," "Charles I of England," "St. Peter," and "Rubens with his son Albert."

Dutch Art (17th–18th century) — 1st floor, rooms 46–54. In room 46 are two Frans Hals, a Pieter de Hooch, several Ruisdaels, and a Hobbema. 21 works attributed to Rembrandt hang in room 50, including "The Holy Family," "Parting of David with Jonathan," "Portrait of Saskia as Flora," and "Descent from the Cross."

Belgian Art (18th–20th century) — 2nd floor, rooms 121–3

Dutch Art (19th century) — 2nd floor, rooms 124–5

German Art (15th–19th century) — 1st floor, rooms 55–60. Rooms 55–6 contain several woodcuts and engravings by Duerer, and paintings by Holbein.

	2nd floor, rooms 61–9. Room 64 was the Small Throne Room, also known as Peter's Hall.
Finnish Art (19th–20th century)	2nd floor, room 70
Austrian Art (18th–19th century)	2nd floor, room 71–3
French Art (15th–20th century)	1st floor, rooms 74–89a, 93–7. Room 80 contains several works by Poussin and room 85 by Watteau. Rooms 93–7 contain an exhibition of articles of applied art. 2nd floor, rooms 98–114. Rooms 111–14 contain works by Renoir, Monet, Pissaro, Sisley, Degas, Rodin, Cezanne, Gauguin, Bonnard, Matisse, Picasso, and Toulouse-Lautrec.
Swedish Art and Danish Art (18th century)	1st floor, rooms 90–2
English Art (17th–19th century)	1st floor, rooms 115–18. Works by Lely, William Hogarth, Godfrey Kneller, Reynolds, Gainsborough, and others.
History of Western European Arms (15th–17th century)	1st floor, room 36
Western European Silverware (17th–18th century)	1st floor, room 83
Western European Decorative China	1st floor, room 120

7. RUSSIAN AND FOREIGN MEDALS, BADGES AND ORDERS　2nd floor, room 2

Russian Museum, Inzhenernaya Street. 4/2. Open 10–6; closed Tues.

The museum, which is housed in the former Mikhailovsky Dvoryets (Palace), is the second largest depositary of Russian art after the Tretyakov Gallery in Moscow. It has about 300,000 exhibits in all, dating from the 10th century to the present day. They include priceless specimens of Russian 12th- and 13th-century icon painting by Rublev and Ushakov, and works by such well-known 18th- and 19th-century artists as Ivanov, Levitan, Repin, and Bryullov.

The post-revolutionary section of the collection is on show in the Benois Building, facing the Gri-

boyedov Canal, built in 1912–16 by Benois and reconstructed after extensive damage in World War II. On the walkway between buildings, windows look out upon Paolo Trubetskoy's equestrian statue of Alexander III, which used to stand in front of the Moskovsky railway station. In the second building in Hall 91 are paintings by Kandinsky and Malevich, and in Hall 92 Chagall, Petrov-Vodkin, and Goncharova. There is a permanent Boerich exhibition.

Museum of Urban Sculpture, Alexander Nevsky Square (Alexander Nevsky Lavra). Open 1 May–30 September, 11–7; Sat. & Sun. 11–8; Wed. 11–4; closed Thurs. 1 October–30 April, open 11–6; Wed. 11–4.

Brodsky Museum, Iskusstv Square 3. The museum is housed in the apartment where Isaak Brodsky lived and worked from 1924–39. 80 of his own paintings are on display, as well as his collection of paintings and sketches by other artists.

Historical Museums

Museum of the History of Leningrad, Naberezhnaya Krasnovo Flota 14. Open 11–4; Mon. & Fri. 1–7; closed Wed. The house was built by Glinka in 1826 for an English merchant, and later purchased by Count Rumyantsev (son of the field marshal). The museum was founded in 1918 and has many exhibits illustrating the history of Leningrad; among them are detailed models portraying such scenes as Nevsky Prospect in the middle of the 18th century, the transporting of the rock for the statue of the Bronze Horseman, and a fireworks display in the early years of the 18th century. Included here also is the story of the 1941–43 defence of the city during the Nazi blockade and the breaking of the blockade when the Soviet Army cut through south of Schusselburg. Among the more modern exhibits is a scroll presented to Leningrad by Franklin D. Roosevelt on behalf of the people of the United States of America in honour of the city's gallant stand during the blockade.

Smolny Cathedral & Lenin's Room, Proletarskoy Diktatury Square. Group sightseeing 10:15 & 3; closed Sat. & Sun.

Pharmacy Museum, Vasiliyev Island, 7th Liniya. Open as a chemist's shop as well as a museum.

Museum of the October Revolution, Kuibysheva Street 4 (Kshesinskaya Palace). Open 10–7 (June–August 10–6); Mon. & Fri. 12–7; closed Thurs. The museum contains over 5,000 exhibits pertaining to the October Revolution. They are displayed in 35 halls of the former ballerina Kshesinskaya's Palace and the house next door. Apart from the art nouveau staircase and stained-glass windows and a winter garden, little remains of the original decor of the Palace. A newly built entrance now links the two buildings.

Lenin Museum (Marble Palace), Khalturnia Street 5/1. Open 10:30–6:30; closed Wed.

Cruiser "Aurora", Petrovskaya Naberezhnaya. Open 11–5; closed Wed. & Sat.

Military Museum, Peter and Paul Fortress.

Central Naval Museum, Pushkinskaya Square 4, Vasiliyevsky Island. Open 10.30–5; closed Tues. The museum is housed in the building of the former Exchange. The collection was started by Peter the Great in 1709, who ordered models of ships to be kept here. It now has about 200,000 exhibits, amongst them a 3,000-year-old dugout canoe and Peter the Great's boat, which was the foundation of the Russian navy.

Museum of Artillery History, Lenin Park 4. Open 11–6; Mon. 11–3; Sun. 10.30–6; closed Thurs.

Suvorov Museum, Saltykov-Schedrin Street 41b. Open 11–7; closed Wed. The building was constructed in 1904 by Gogen with money collected by public subscription. It has nearly 4,000 exhibits pertaining to the 18th-century general—his personal belongings, documents, and trophies captured by the Russian army during his campaigns. The building was badly damaged during World War II and after it reopened, the right wing was used for World War II memorabilia.

Narva Triumphal Gate Museum, Stachek Square. The gate was created by Vasily Stasov in 1834 in honour of the Russian victory over Napoleon in 1812.

Scientific Museums

Kunstkammer (Museum of Anthropology and Ethnography), Universersitetskaya Naberezhnaya 3. Open 11–5; closed Fri. & Sat. The building of the Kunstkammer was the first home of the Academy of Sciences in the reign of Peter the Great. The collection of the Museum of Anthropology and Ethnography developed from art works that Peter purchased in Holland in 1716; these were predominantly of Chinese and Indian origin. Added to these were anatomical specimens and a collection of "monsters," mostly freak human and animal embryos. Also on display are Peter I's surgical instruments, porcelain, lacquerwork, bronzes, wood-, stone-, and ivory-carvings, and a large globe made in 1754. The collection has since grown into one of the biggest anthropological museums in the country.

In the same building is the *Lomonosov Museum*. Mikhail Lomonosov worked here from 1741–65 and the exhibition includes documents and relics relating to his life and many-sided work in science, history, philology, and literature.

State Ethnography Museum, Inzhenernaya Street 4/1. Open 10–5; closed Mon.

Zoological Museum, Universitetskaya Naberezhnaya 1. Open 11–5; closed Mon.

Geological Museum, Naberezhnaya Makarova 2. Open 11–5; closed Mon. & Sat.

Arctic & Antarctic Museum, Marat (formerly Malaya Vladimirskaya) Street 24a. Open Wed.–Sat. 11–7. Housed in St. Nicholas's Old Believers' Church, built in 1828–80, but used as a museum since 1934. The Arctic display is downstairs and the Antarctic, including Captain Scott's sled presented by the Polar Arctic Institute of Cambridge, England, in 1956, upstairs. The collection ranges over history, geography, science, and art and is of the widest interest.

Railway Museum, Sadovaya Street 50. Open 11–5.30; closed Fri. & Sat. The collection includes models of the earliest examples of railway engines, some from England. There is also much about the development of the St. Petersburg–Moscow railway.

Literary, Musical, Theatrical Museums

Literary Museum (Pushkin House), Naberezhnaya Makarova 2. Open 11–5.30; closed Mon. & Tues. The museum is housed in the Customs House. The collection includes rare ancient manuscripts, first editions, archives, letters, and a unique collection of recorded folk lays, legends, and songs on phonographs. The museum exhibits give a broad picture of the development of Russian literature from the first edition of the ancient Russian "Lay of Igor's Host" to the present day, and there are also displays of a number of personal articles that belonged to Russian writers such as Tolstoy, Chekhov, Dostoyevsky, Gogol, and Blok.

Nekrasov Memorial Museum, Ostrovskovo Square 6. Open 12–7; closed Mon. & Tues.

Russian Opera Museum, Graftio Street 2b, 2nd floor, in Fyodor Chaliapin's flat. Open 11–6; closed Mon. & Tues. There are family rooms and others for concerts of recorded music.

Exhibition of Musical Instruments, Isaakievskaya Square 5. Open 12–6; closed Tues.

Saltykov-Schedrin Library, Nevsky Prospect. One of the largest libraries in the world. Of particular interest are the old collections that include ancient Slavonic and Russian manuscripts (including the 11th-century "Ostromirovo Gospel"), West European editions printed before 1500, the original manuscripts and papers of Peter the Great and Suvorov, the letters of Catherine de Medici and Henry IV, and 6,814 volumes of Voltaire's personal library.

House-Museums

Pushkin's Flat, Nab. reki Moiki 12. Open 11–6; Mon. 11–4; Thurs. & Sat. 1–8; closed Tues. The poet Alexander Pushkin lived here with his wife and young children from 1836 until he died on 29th January, 1837, from wounds incurred during a duel. Large numbers of mourners came here to pay him tribute. His flat is kept as it was during his lifetime and there are many of his personal belongings amongst the exhibits. His bust, by Didikin, is in the courtyard garden, through the archway, beyond the entrance to the museum.

Rimsky-Korsakov's Flat, Zagorodny Proyezd 28, Apt. 30; the block of flats stands inside the courtyard. Open 11–6; closed Mon. & Tues. Concerts of recorded music are given in the first rooms, and further on are the family rooms.

Dostoyevsky's Flat, Kuznechny Per. 5/2, just

behind Kuznetsky Market. Open 10.30–6.30. Documents and photographs on the 1st floor; family flat on 2nd floor.

Lenin's Flat, Serdobolskaya Street 1, Apt. 20. Open 11–5; Tues. 11–4; closed Wed. This is only one of eleven museums in the many Leningrad places that Lenin visited or lived in. It is on the 4th floor, and he hid here for 17 days before discarding his disguise. The little 3-room flat has some photographs and documents, and his landlady's living room and his, both furnished under the landlady's supervision, as they used to be.

Chaliapin's Flat, Graftio Street 2b, 2nd floor. Open as the Russian Opera Museum 11–6; closed Mon. & Tues. The opera singer Fyodor Chaliapin (1873–1938) lived here until he left for Paris in 1922. He liked the Kustodiev portrait so much that he took it with him, but in 1968 his daughters presented it to the museum. There are family rooms and others for concerts of recorded music.

Blok's Flat, Dekabristov Street 57. Open 11–6; closed Wed. The 2nd-floor flat that belonged to his mother now contains documents and photographs. The 4th-floor flat was Blok's home, now perfectly restored, even the wallpaper. The tablecloth and firescreen in the sitting room were embroidered by his mother, and the pink silk lampshade was made by his wife, Mendeleyev's daughter.

Kirov's Flat, Kirov Prospect 26–28. Closed Wed. The cloakroom is on the 5th floor and the flat on the floor below. Sergei Kirov (1886–1934), the Communist leader who for some time headed the Leningrad Party organisation, lived here from the time he arrived from Baku to take over the administration until his assassination. There are photographs and documents, and also rooms furnished as they used to be. Some rooms are decorated with his hunting trophies, and others with his tools, clothing, and hunting equipment.

Gardens

Botanical Gardens, Professora Popova Street 2. Open in summer 9–5; Fri. 9–2; closed Sat. In winter 11–3; Fri. 11–2; closed Sat.

Zoological Gardens, Lenin Park 1. Open daily May–August 10 A.M.–10 P.M.; September–April 10–5.

Planetarium, Lenin Park 4. Open 3–8; Sun. 12–8; closed Wed.

Churches

St. Nicholas's Cathedral, Kommunarov Square 3. This cathedral was built in 1753–62 by Chevakinsky. It is open for services.

Church of the Transfiguration, Radischev Square 1. The architect of this church was Stasov. Open for services.

Church of St Vladimir or (Church of the Assumption), Petrogradskaya Storona, Blokhina Street 16. Open for services.

Kazan Cathedral, Kazanskaya Square 2. Open for sightseeing, 11–6, and occasionally for services.

St. Isaac's Cathedral, Isaakievskaya Square. Open as a museum 10–5; closed Wed.

Alexander Nevsky Monastery, Alexander Nevsky Square. Open 1 May–30 September: Mon., Tues. & Fri. 11–7, Sun. 11–8, Wed. 11–4; 1 October–30 April: 11–6, except Wed. 11–4.

Cathedral of the Resurrection, Smolny

Church of the Resurrection, north side of Nevsky Prospect

Baptist Church, Bolshiokhtinsky Prospect 5

Roman Catholic Church, Kovensky Pereulok 7

Synagogue, Lermontovsky Prospect 4. Built by Baron Ginsburg in 1882–96.

Mosque, at the beginning of Kirovsky Prospect. Open Fri.

Statues and Monuments

Peter the Great (The Bronze Horseman), Dekabristov Square

Peter the Great, Inzhenerny (Mikhailovsky) Zamok

Catherine II, Ostrovskovo Square. By Mikeshin in 1873

Nicholas I, Isaakyevskaya Square

Pushkin, Iskusstv Square. Sculpted by Anikushin in 1957.

Pushkin, Pushkin Square. By Opekushin, 1884

Pushkin, Novaya Derevnya

Rimsky-Korsakov, Teatralnaya Square

Glinka, Teatralnaya Square

Krylov, Lyetny Sad

Griboyedov, Zagorodny Prospect, Vitebsky Railway Station. By Lishev in 1959.

Suvorov, Suvorov Square. This monument, designed by Kozlovsky in 1809, shows the Russian general as the god of war.

Chernyshevsky, Moskovsky Prospect. By Lishev, 1947.

Lenin, by the Finland Railway Station. This monument by Yevsyev, 1926, is perhaps the best of the many of Lenin, who is shown standing on an armoured car.

Kirov, at the entrance to the Kirov Stadium, Krestovsky Island. Pinchuk designed this monument in 1950.

Moscow Triumphal Gates, Moskovsky Prospect. These gates were built by Stasov in 1833–38.

Narva Triumphal Gates, Stachek Prospect. These gates were planned by Quarenghi and reconstructed by Stasov in 1827–34. They commemorate those who defended the country in the 1812–14 war. The arch is decorated with allegorical figures of Glory and with inscriptions enumerating the Guards' Regiments that had distinguished themselves during the war, and the places where decisive battles had been fought.

War Memorial, Serafimovsky Cemetery. This memorial, unveiled in 1965, is dedicated to the memory of the defenders of Leningrad.

Piskarevskoye Memorial Cemetery, Nepokorennykh Prospect 9. There is a war memorial by the main gate, and also in the cemetery are 2 pavilions with a museum showing life in Leningrad during

World War II. At the end of the avenue of graves is a sculpture by Isayeva and Taurit, of a woman symbolising the Motherland.

Literatorskiye Mostki (Necropolis at the Volkov Cemetery), Rasstannaya Street 30; closed Thurs.

Theatres

Kirov Theatre (Opera & Ballet), Teatralnaya Square 1

Maly Opera Theatre, Iskusstv Square 1

Pushkin Drama Theatre, Osrovsky Square 2. Modern and classical drama.

Gorky Drama Theatre, Nab. Fontanki 65. This building was constructed in 1879 by the architect Fontan. Maxim Gorky was responsible for the foundation of the present theatre company in 1919.

Comedy Theatre, Nevsky Prospect 56. This theatre has the reputation for being one of the best comedy theatres in the country.

Lensoviet Theatre, Vladimirsky Prospect 12

Lenin Komsomol Theatre, Lenin Park 14

Youth Theatre, Zagorodny Prospect 46. This theatre was founded in 1921 by A. Bryantsev.

Musical Comedy Theatre, Rakova Street 13. Opened in 1929, this was the only theatre in Leningrad that gave performances throughout World War II, even during the siege of Leningrad.

Puppet Theatre, Nekrasovoy Street 10. Performances for adults at 7 P.M.; for children at 11 A.M. and 3 P.M.

Marionettes, Nevsky Prospect 52

Theatre of the Music and Drama Institute, Mokhovaya Street 35

Shostakovich Concert Hall, Brodskovo Street 2.

Small Philharmonia Concert Hall, Nevsky Prospect

Oktyabrsky Concert Hall, Ligovsky Prospect 6

New Concert Hall, Lenin Square 1

Chamber Music Theatre, Moika Embankment 94

Glinka Kapella (Choir Hall), Moika Naberezhnaya 20. The building was constructed in 1880 by L. Benois, but the choir itself was founded by Peter the Great in 1713. Glinka and Rimsky-Korsakov performed here, as did other famous musicians.

Circus, Nab. Fontanki 3. This building was designed by Kennel in 1876. Performances begin at 8 P.M.

Sports Facilities

Kirov Stadium, Krestovsky Island. The green slopes of a 16-m (52-ft) hill near the shore hide Leningrad's main soccer field from view.

Lenin Stadium, Yuri Gagarin Prospect 8. The sports complex here includes an All-Purpose Hall with seating for 25,000.

Yubileiny Sports Palace, Dobrolyubov Prospect

Yachting Centre, on a spit of land projecting into the sea

Hotels

(Those marked * have Beryozka foreign currency shops.)

*Astoria (Intourist)**, Bolshaya Morskaya (formerly Herzen) Street 39; tel. 212-3605

Baltyiskaya, Nevsky Prospect 57; tel. 277-7731

*Evropeiskaya (Intourist)**, Brodskovo Street 1/7; tel. 312-4149

*Karelia (Intourist)**, Tukhachevskovo Street 27/2; tel. 226-3238

Kievskaya, Dnepropetrovskaya Street 49; tel. 316-0456

Ladoga, Shaumyana Prospect 26; tel. 221-5728

*Leningrad (Intourist)**, Vyborgskaya Nab. 5/2; tel. 542-9123

*Moskva (Intourist)**, Alexander Nevsky Prospect 2; tel. 274-2051

Neva, Tchaikovsky Street 17; tel. 278-0505

*Oktyabrskaya**, Ligovsky Prospect 10; tel. 277-6330

Oktyabrskaya, annex 1, Ligovsky Prospect 43/45; tel. 277-7281

Oktyabrskaya, annex 2, Vosstaniya Street. 2; tel. 277-7812.

*Pribaltyiskaya (Intourist)**, Korablestroiteley Street 14; tel. 356-0263

*Pulkovskaya (Intourist)**, Pobedy Square 1; tel. 264-5109

Rechnaya, Obukhovskoy Oborony Prospect 195; tel. 276-3196

Rossia, Chernyshevskovo Prospect 11; tel. 296-7649

*Sovetskaya**, Lermontov Prospect 43; tel. 259-2552

Sportivnaya, Khalturina Street 24; tel. 211-7653

Sputnik, Morisa Toreza Prospect 34; tel. 552-8330

Tourist, Sevastyanova Street 3; tel. 298-5831

Vyborgskaya, Torzhkovskaya Street 3; tel. 246-9141

Yuzhnaya, Rasstannya Street 2b; tel. 316-9738

Zanevskaya, Stakhanovtsev Street 14; tel. 221-8014

Zarya, Kurskaya Street 40; tel. 316-8398

Olgino Intourist Hotel, Motel & Camping Site, Primorskoye Chaussee 5 (18 km/11 miles north of Leningrad); tel. 238-3453. There is a service station, filling station, and a Beryozka foreign currency shop here.

Intourist office, Isaakiyevskaya Square 11; tel. 214-6420. Intourist provides other out-of-town accommodation on the coast north of Leningrad at Dyuny in Sestroretsk (41 km/25 miles) away, and at Repino (44 km/27 miles).

Restaurants

Baku (Caucasian food), Sadovaya Street 12; tel. 311-2751

Evropeiskaya, Brodsky Street 1/7; tel. 210-3481

Restaurant on the Fontanka, Fontanka Embankment 77

Fregat (old Russian dishes from Peter the

Great's time), Bolshoy Prospect 39/14, Vasilyevsky
Island; tel. 213-4923

Kavkazsky, Nevsky Prospect 25; tel. 311-4526

Kronwerk, on board a ship moored by the Peter
and Paul Fortress, Mytninskaya Nab. 3; tel.
232-8620

Leningrad, Vyborskaya Nab. 5/2; tel. 542-9155

Meridian, Pobedy Square 1; tel. 264-5810

Metropol, Sadovaya Street 22; tel. 310-2272

Moskva, Nevsky Prospect 49; tel. 314-4085

Moskva (in hotel), A Nevsky Square 2; tel.
274-9503

Neva, Nevsky Prospect 46; tel. 210-3667

Sadko (Russian cuisine), Brodskovo Street 1/7;
tel. 210-3667

Severny, Sadovaya Street 12

Turku, Pobedy Square 1; tel. 264-5024

Universal, Nevsky Prospect 12

Volkhov, Liteiny Prospect 28; tel. 273-2262

Shops

Beryozka (foreign currency) Shops, Nevsky Prospect 9, Herzen Street 26, Morskaya Naberezhnaya
15 (on Vasilievsky Island), at the Hermitage Museum, at the Palace of Furs and at Pulkovo Airport.

Beryozka (foreign currency) Groceries, Baltyiskaya Street 2/4

Gostiny Dvor (department store), Nevsky Prospect 35, between Sadovaya and Dumskaya streets

Dom Torgovli (department store), Zhelyabova
Street 21/23

Passage Department Store, Nevsky Prospect 48

Dom Knigi (books), Nevsky Prospect 28

Novinok (Novelties) Shop, Nevsky Prospect 23

Gift Shop, Nevsky Prospect 26

Souvenirs, Nevsky Prospect 100

Gramplastinki (records), Nevsky Prospect 32/34

Service

Intourist, Isaakievskaya 11; tel. 214-6420

Bank, Brodskovo Street 2

Ingosstrakh (Insurance), Kalyaeva Street 17

GPO, Soyuza Svyazi Street 9

Central Telegraph Office, Soyuza Svyazi
Street 14

International Telephone Exchange, Bolshaya
Morskaya (formerly Herzen) Street 3/5

Service Station, 1-Staroderevenskaya Street 5;
tel. 229-2231

Bulgarian Consulate General, VO, Ryleyeva
Street 27; tel. 273-7347

Chinese Consulate General, VO, 3-Liniya 12;
tel. 218-1721

Czechoslovak Consulate General, Smolensky
Raion, Tverskaya Street 5; tel. 271-0459

Finnish Consulate General, Chaikovskovo
Street 71; tel. 273-7321/25

Hungarian Consulate General, Marata Street
15; tel. 312-4658

Japanese Consulate General, Nab. reki Moiki
29; tel. 312-1133

Mongolian Consulate General, Saperny Per.
11; tel. 272-2688

Polish Consulate General, 5-Sovietskaya Street
12; tel. 274-4331

Swedish Consulate General, No. 11, 10th Line;
tel. 218-3526

United States Consulate General, Petra Lav-
rova Street 15; tel. 274-8235

Intourist organises boat trips on the rivers and
canals of Leningrad, and also out-of-town excursions from Leningrad to the imperial palaces at
Petrodvorets (including the Cottage Museum), Lomonosov, Gatchina, Pushkin, and Pavlovsk and
northwards to Repino (to Repin's estate of Penaty)
and the Lenin Memorial Museums at Razliv.

Petrodvorets

Komintern Street 2. Can be reached by road or by
boat from Leningrad. It is about 34 km (21 miles)
west of Leningrad on the low, southern shore of
the Gulf of Finland. The buildings are open 10.30–
5; closed Mon. & the last Tues. of each month.

Petrodvorets was founded by Peter the Great,
who gave it the German name Peterhof, in commemoration of the victory of the Russian army over
the Swedes at Poltava and the gaining of an outlet
to the Baltic.

Petrodvorets is mainly famous for its system of
fountains that begins 21 km (13 miles) away on the
Ropshinskiye Heights. It was Peter the Great's intention to make Petrodvorets the Russian equivalent of Versailles; he himself drafted the original
layout of the park and gave numerous instructions
on the decoration of the pavilions and the design
of the fountains.

Over 4,000 soldiers and peasants dug canals for
the fountains, which altogether use nearly 30,000
litres (7,500 gallons) of water each second. The
system was designed by hydro-engineer Tuvolkov,
and the water supply is sufficient to enable the
fountains to work 10–12 hours out of every 24.

The Grand Palace was begun in 1715–24 according to plans by Le Blond, but its modest dimensions could not hold the large imperial court.
It was reconstructed and enlarged for the Tsaritsa
Elizabeth by Rastrelli in 1746–51. The main building has 3 storeys and is connected to the wings by
galleries. The facade is 268 m (293 yds) long and
at the eastern corner of the palace is a church built
in rococo style with 5 gilded cupolas by Rastrelli
in 1751. These buildings were burned down during
World War II and are under reconstruction, the
work proceeding in accordance with drawings, photographs, and other documents so that the reconstructed ensemble will resemble the original as
closely as possible. The grounds also suffered during the war when 25,000 trees were felled.

The Grand Palace stands on a terrace about 12
m (39 ft) high. The surrounding park and gardens
cover approximately 120 hectares (300 acres). From
the grounds in front of the palace there is a wonderful view of the Nizhny (Lower) Park that
stretches between the ridge of hills in the background and the shore of the Gulf of Finland. The
facade of the palace facing the sea towers over the
Grand Cascade, a great system of fountains that

descends in broad steps to the park below. The most famous of the 129 fountains now operative is directly in front of the palace facade, at the head of the Grand Cascade; this is the *Samson Fountain*, where Samson is portrayed tearing open the jaws of a lion from where a jet of water rises 20 m (66 ft) into the air. The lion represents Sweden defeated by Russia at the Battle of Poltava on St. Samson's Day in 1709. Other sights of interest include the *Chessboard Cascade*, and the *Zontik* (little umbrella) and *Dubok* (little oak) surprise fountains that shower any unsuspecting visitors who come near.

The *Hermitage* is a 2-storey pavilion built for Peter the Great. The walls of the dining room on the first floor are lined with Dutch paintings, and part of the table can sink to the floor below to be cleared and relaid. To the right of the Hermitage is a statue of Peter made by Antokolsky in 1883.

The small villa in Dutch style, built in the early 18th century, where Peter the Great lived while the Grand Palace was under construction, is known as *Mon Plaisir*. The stone wing of this miniature palace was built by Rastrelli and reconstructed by Quarenghi, and inside it is decorated with numerous paintings. The Dutch-style garden contains small flower beds and exotic trees. Marly is the name of the small 2-storey house in Louis XIV–style built in 1714 by Peter the Great.

The pavilions that stand on either side of the canal were designed by Voronikhin in about 1800.

The *Ladies-in-Waiting's Palace* was designed by Nikolai Benois. It now houses the *Nikolai Benois Museum*.

From Petrodvorets Intourist organises excursions to the Cottage Museum.

Lomonosov

40 km (25 miles) from Leningrad, beyond Petrodvorets. The palace is open in summer only; closed Tues. & the last Mon. of each month. In the 18th century, when Peter the Great had defeated the Swedes and regained the banks of the Neva and the southern shore of the Gulf of Finland, he was anxious that this boggy territory be developed as quickly as possible and, therefore, gave extensive properties to members of his retinue. The largest of all was presented to his close friend Alexander Menshikov who selected as the site of his summer palace a place just opposite Kotlin Island where the fortress of Kronstadt was being built under his supervision. His site was also quite near Petershof, Peter I's own summer residence that was nearing completion.

Oranienbaum was the name given to Menshikov's estate because of the bitter orange trees that were brought in to enhance the Lower Park around the palace. It was known as Oranienbaum until 1948. The construction of the palace began in 1710 under Fontana and Shedel (also responsible for Menshikov's town residence beside the Neva) and continued until 1725. Besides the palace and Lower Park, a picture gallery was also built, one of the first in Russia. When Menshikov fell victim to court intrigues in 1727, he was exiled and Or-

anienbaum reverted to the Royal Building Administration.

In 1746 Elizaveta Petrovna, daughter of Peter the Great, gave Oranienbaum to the future Tsar Peter III. Rastrelli reconstructed the Grand Palace and the Upper Park was laid out. Peter III's Palace was completed by Antonio Rinaldi in 1762 and he also built the entrance gate (restored 1952). Peter III's Palace is comparatively unspectacular and chiefly valued for its interior decoration. Most interesting are Fyodor Vlasov's lacquer paintings on wood, imitations of ancient Chinese paintings that were much in vogue at the time.

Catherine II then made Oranienbaum her summer residence and from 1762–68 Rinaldi was occupied in building her a *Chinese Palace*, so-called because again some of the interior was decorated in Chinese style. The 17 halls are lavishly decorated with stucco work and paintings, some of the canvases on the walls were by the Italians Serafino Barozzi and Stephano Torelli. Most of the ceilings were painted by the Venetian artists, Giovanni Batista Tiepolo and Jacomo Guarana. The exquisite parquet floors are particularly fine.

Beside the Chinese Palace, Rinaldi built the *Sliding Hill*, provided with low carts on little metal wheels. Hills of this kind were typically Russian structures; models were often sent abroad and, following their design, Russian Hills were constructed and enjoyed in other places. The colonnade and slopes were demolished but the 2-storey stone pavilion remains. Its walls are painted light blue and its columns, white. It stands on a lofty foundation and is crowned by a bell-shaped dome.

The vast Upper Park was carefully laid out at the same time as the construction of the Sliding Hill and Oranienbaum, which became the scene of parties, masquerades, and fireworks displays for the entertainment of the royal court and foreign diplomats serving there.

Oranienbaum had become a town by Catherine II's decree of 1780, and its coat-of-arms was appropriately an orange tree on a silver ground. The place had connections with many famous names. Mikhail Lomonosov had visited frequently while the Chinese Palace was being built and it was he who founded a stained-glass works in 1753 in the nearby village of Ust-Ruditsa; the glass was used for the decorative mosaics in the Chinese Palace. Portrait painter Orest Kiprensky lived here as a child between 1788 and 1793. Alexander Pushkin came in the spring of 1829 and rented a summer house here for his sister, Olga. Alexander Dumas once came as guest of writer Dmitri Grigorovich (1822–99). Nikolai Nekrasov lived and worked here from 1854 to 1858 and his frequent guests were Lev Tolstoy, critic Nikolai Dobrolyubov, Saltykov-Schedrin, Ivan Turgenev, and Alexei Tolstoy. Composer Modest Mussorgsky (1839–81) was another regular visitor and a number of 19th-century painters were attracted by the beautiful parks and lovely landscape around. Ilya Repin and Ivan Shishkin both lived and worked here in 1883.

The town of Lomonosov is now one of the

economic and cultural centres of Leningrad Region. The monument to Lomonosov was created by Glikman.

Gatchina

48 km (30 miles) south-west of Leningrad. The Gatchina estate was originally owned by Peter I's sister, Natalia; it changed hands before belonging to Count Orlov, for whom Rinaldi built a palace in 1776–82. The park with the White Lake in its centre was also laid out at that time.

The whole estate was subsequently purchased by Catherine II, and her son Paul who lived there turned the palace into a medieval castle with help from the architect Vincenzo Brenna. It acquired moats, drawbridges, battlements, and a parade ground in front. The castle was badly damaged in World War II, and has not been rebuilt.

The main entrance to the park is through *Admiralty Gate*. This gate with Corinthian columns was built in 1796 by Brenna. The private garden in formal French style with a statue of Flora in the centre was added at the end of the 18th century. The *Priory* with an octagonal tower and tapering spire was built by Lvov in 1797–8 on the shore of Black Lake. It was intended for a prior of the Knights of Malta, whose Order enjoyed Paul's special patronage.

Chesma Obelisk at the edge of the White Lake commemorates the victory of the Russian fleet at Chesma, as does the obelisk at Pushkin. It was designed by Rinaldi and is of many different shades of marble. At the end of the lake is the Island of Love with a *Temple of Venus* on it.

Pushkin

Komsomolskaya Street 7; 27 km (17 miles) south of Leningrad. Visitors can also reach Pushkin by train from Vitebsky Station in Leningrad. There are buses and taxis from the station to Yekaterininsky Palace, which is open 10–5; closed Tues. & last Mon. of each month.

Formerly Tsarskoye Selo (Tsar's Village), the place was called Detskoye Selo (Children's Village) after the revolution because the buildings were used as kindergartens, children's hospitals, sanatoria, and schools. In 1937 it was again renamed, this time after Alexander Pushkin on the occasion of the 100th anniversary of the poet's death.

The so-called *Egyptian Gates* mark the entrance to the village. They were designed by the English architect, Adam Menelaws, and built in 1828; Menelaws also built a ruined "chapel" and a Turkish-style elephant house for the zoo. By the Egyptian Gates stands a *monument to Pushkin* (1911) by Bernstam.

Yekaterininsky Palace was built during the reigns of Elizabeth (the youngest daughter of Peter the Great), and Catherine II. It takes its name from Catherine I, the wife of Peter the Great, who was given the village by her husband. The small 2-storey palace that was first built here in the reign of Peter was later incorporated into the main palace.

The palace was begun by the architects Kvasov and Chevakinsky, and completed by Rastrelli. With its azure facade over 300 m (328 yds) long and gold ornamentation and ornate pilasters and sculptures, it is one of the finest examples of Russian baroque architecture. It was badly burnt during World War II, but has since been restored in accordance with the original plans.

Part of the palace is now open as a museum. In a number of halls that have not yet been completely restored there is an exhibition relating the history of the palace, of its furniture and china. Other halls that have been completely restored and are open include the *Green Dining-room*, the *Light Blue Parlour*, and the *Chinese Light Blue Parlour*. The *Amber Room*, in which all the decorations were of amber, was completely gutted by the Nazi troops during the war, and the decorations have never been recovered. It is thought possible that the amber still lies under the ruins of Kaliningrad, then Konisberg. The *Hall of Paintings* contains 130 paintings, 114 of which were in the palace collection before World War II.

In the former Church Wing of the palace is the *Pushkin Museum*, which contains over 700 pages of the poet's manuscripts as well as a number of his personal belongings, rare books, a collection of portraits painted during his lifetime, and several portraits of his contemporaries.

Yekaterininsky Park covers 592 hectares (1,482 acres). The land was given to Catherine I by her husband, Peter the Great, and subsequently gardens, a hothouse, ponds, and a zoo were laid out. The gardens were developed in the course of 50 years and include many buildings of different styles. An obelisk, unveiled in 1771, commemorates the Russian victory over the Turks near the Danube. The *Orlov Column*, on an island in the middle of the lake, was erected in 1778 by Rinaldi to commemorate Prince Orlov's victory at Chesma; this was a sea battle where the Russians again beat the Turks.

Cameron's Gallery, built in 1779–93 by the Scottish architect Charles Cameron, is adorned with busts of Greek and Roman philosophers. The *Grotto* was designed by Rastrelli who, together with Chevakinsky, was also responsible for the *Concert Hall* on the island. The *Hermitage* was built in 1744 by Kvasov and completed in 1759 by Rastrelli. It was used as a place for relaxation by the imperial family. The fantastically carved facade is decorated with 64 columns and a mass of ornamentation. The ingenious cross-shaped layout of the building fits well into the surrounding gardens.

The *Agate Rooms*, a 2-storey building so named because of the interior, were fitted out by Cameron with jasper and marble to give the effect of agate, is being restored. The upper floor of the building is open in summer. Both the Agate Rooms and the Hermitage were used as stables by the Germans during World War II.

Also open is the *Upper Bath House* that was built in 1777–9 by Neyelov and used by the imperial family. The Lower Bath House, built at the same time, was used by courtiers. The *Marble Bridge* was designed in 1770–6, also by Neyelov, and built from Siberian marble which was carved in Siberia and transported here ready for erection.

Alexander I's Triumphal Arch was built by Stasov in 1817–21 in honour of the Russian victory of 1812.

Vecherny Zal (Evening Hall) near Yekaterininsky Palace was designed by Neyelov in 1796–1810.

The *Granite Terrace* was planned by Luigi Rusca in 1809.

The *bronze fountain*, "Girl with a Pitcher," was made by Sokolov in 1810. It was mentioned by Pushkin in one of his poems.

The *Alexandrovsky Palace* was built by Quarenghi in 1792–6 for Alexander I, grandson of Catherine II. Nicholas II lived here almost permanently after the 1905 revolution. The palace is not open to the public. In the Alexandrovsky Park are the Ruined Kitchen (built of real pieces of ancient ruins brought from Italy), many chinoiseries (including the Chinese village and the Chinese summerhouse) and the Grande Caprice built by Neyelov in 1770–3.

The *Lycee* is linked to the Yekaterininsky Palace by an arch over the road. Neyelov erected the building in 1791, and a school for the sons of nobles was opened here in 1811; Alexander Pushkin, who spent his schooldays here, was one of the first pupils. The school moved to Korovsky Prospect in Leningrad in 1843, after which time it was known as the Alexandrovsky Lycee. The garden was relaid under the direction of the architect Stasov at the beginning of the 19th century. The monument to Pushkin was made by Bakh in 1909. The Lycee building is open from 11–6, closed Tues.

By the Lycee is *Znamenskaya Church*, built in 1734–47 by the Moscow architect, Karl Blank, and the first stone building in the village.

Pavlovsk

Revolutsii Street 20; 35 km (22 miles) south of Leningrad and 3 km (2 miles) south-east of Pushkin. The entrance to the town on the road from Pushkin is marked by cast-iron gates designed by Rossi in 1826. Visitors to the palace, which is open from 10.30–5.30 (closed Fri. & first Mon. of each month), should leave their cars by the wooden bridge; it is a short walk across the bridge and up the drive to the palace itself.

This territory was originally the hunting grounds attached to the imperial estate of Tsarskoye Selo, 3 km (2 miles) away. In 1777 Catherine II gave the land, including 2 villages and their serfs, to her son Paul as a site for a country residence, who named it Pavlovskoye, Paul's Village.

The Scottish architect Charles Cameron, who was invited to Russia by Catherine II, was responsible for the original planning of Pavlovsk, which is one of the finest palaces in Russia. The Grand Palace was later enlarged and decorated inside by Voronikhin, Quarenghi, Brenna, and Rossi.

It now has 3 storeys and a central dome that rests on 64 columns. The palace was badly damaged during World War II, but it has since been restored according to the original plans. The *statue of Paul I* in the middle of the main courtyard was designed by Klodt in 1872.

All the downstairs rooms, approached through the Egyptian vestibule, were built for receptions and were never in daily use. 45 halls are open to the public at the time of writing, beautifully restored to the original designs. The ballroom, drawing room, billiard room, and dining room follow designs by Cameron. On display is a fine collection of paintings, furniture, and china. The collection of antique sculptures is one of the largest after the Hermitage in Leningrad. Many of these were bought by Catherine from the British collector, Lord Hamilton. All the furniture in the Greek Hall was carried here from St. Petersburg by soldiers during the reign of Paul I.

The 12 halls on the third floor were originally the small, cosy rooms used by the imperial family. Today, there is an exhibition of furnished interiors, faithfully reproducing the changing fashions in design in St. Petersburg through the years of the 19th century.

Besides the palace, Cameron was also responsible for the first plans of the surrounding park; with 600 hectares (1,500 acres) it is one of the largest landscaped parks in Europe. The river Slavyanka was dammed to form a lake, and trees were planted with special attention to their autumn colours. The park is intersected by avenues and winding paths that lead to pavilions and statues, and which constantly reveal new views of the beautifully landscaped estate. Unlike Petrodvorets, where the fountains and other objects of interest are so arranged that they can easily be seen from afar, the architectural sights of Pavlovsk are mostly cleverly concealed in the park in order to afford a series of surprises.

At the end of the 18th century the park was extended, mainly by the architect Brenna. The sections that were added under his direction were the Old Sylvia and the New Sylvia, to the north-west of the palace. In the New Sylvia (furthest from the palace) is the *Paul I Mausoleum*, a pavilion in the form of an ancient temple. It was never used as a burial place and its function is purely decorative. It was built in 1807–8 by the architect Thomas de Thomon with sculptures by Martos.

Adjoining the palace, between the lime avenue and the Slavyanka valley, is a section called the *Grand Circles*, which takes its name from two large circular stone terraces, also by Brenna. In the centre of each stand marble sculptures on granite pedestals. These statues, representing Justice and Peace, were carved in Italy by order of Peter the Great, long before the building of Pavlovsk. All the statues in the park were buried during World War II.

Apollo's Colonnade on the left bank of the Slavyanka was built by Cameron in 1780–3, and in the centre is a bronze copy of the Apollo Belvedere. Part of the colonnade collapsed during a flood in 1817, but it was decided to leave the fallen stones to create a more ancient effect. The *Pavillion of the Three Graces*, a stone terrace with 16 columns supporting the roof, is also by Cameron (1800–1) and the central statue was carved out of a solid block of marble by Trisconni. Cameron's *Temple of Friendship* on the bank of the river is a graceful domed rotunda in Doric style with 16 white columns, built in 1780–2.

There is a boating station and an open-air café in the park.

Repino

Formerly known as Kuokkala, this large village 44 km (27 miles) north of Leningrad is on Primorskoye Chaussee on the way to Zelenogorsk and stretches along the shore of the Gulf of Finland for 4 km (2.5 miles). It takes its name from that of artist Ilya Repin (1844–1930) who lived and worked here from 1900 until his death. He moved to Kuokkala in 1899 and the cosy, 2-storey house was built to his design. Repin was both the most accomplished of the 19th-century realists and the most prolific and versatile of Russian artists. He was skillful in expressing character and situation, and particularly in depicting dramatic incidents. Here he painted "Pushkin taking an exam at the Lycee," "Breaking up a Demonstration," "Zaporozhye Cossacks," and portraits of Tolstoy, Chaliapin, and the psychiatrist and neuropathologist Bekhterev. Among Repin's best known paintings are "Volga Boatsmen," "The Religious Procession in Kursk Province," "Ivan the Terrible with the Body of His Son," and "Zaporozhye Cossacks Drafting a Reply to the Turkish Sultan."

Penaty Estate, Open 10:30–5:30 in summer and 10–5 in winter; closed Tues. Repin called his estate Penaty, meaning Penates, the Roman gods of hearth and home. Gorky, Chaliapin, Mayakovsky, and Pavlov were among the prominent people to visit him here. The house was burnt down during the German retreat in 1944, but was restored in 1962 and opened as a museum. The house stands in a park, with beautiful avenues, pavilions, and lakes. One avenue is named after Pushkin while a glade encircled by tall pines is known as Homer Square. The wooden pavilion on the hill is the *Temple of Isis and Osiris*. At the end of Pushkin Avenue is the lacy structure of the 12 m (39 ft) *Tower of Scheherazade* from the top of which there is a fine view over the Gulf of Finland. Repin's grave is in the park.

Lenin also lived in Kuokalla in 1903–07 and it was from here that he went to London to participate in the 5th Bolshevik Party Congress.

Hotel, Pervaya Novaya Street 8, at the 164/47 km mark and on the left side of the road. Situated in wooded territory only 20 m (22 yds) from the sea; open from May to September with accommodation for 150.

Camping site, at the 168/43 km mark on Primorskoye Chaussee. 300 m (325 yds) to the left of the main road and in woodland not far from the sea. Furnished tents are provided for up to 300 foreign campers. There is a buffet, self-service kitchen, showers, and sports grounds.

Volna (wave) Restaurant, at Wonderful Beach. This restaurant will supply food directly to the motel.

Razliv

The village, opposite Sestroretsk across the river Sestra, and on the shore of the Razliv reservoir, was formed in 1716.

Shalash Museum, Open daily 10–6 in summer only. It was here, 4 km (2.5 miles) to the left of the main road, that Lenin hid from agents of the Provisional Government in the summer of 1917. He was secretly visited here by Dzerzhinsky, Stalin, Sverdlov, and Ordzhonikidze while he was living in a roughly built hut in the uninhabited area beside Lake Razliv. Now there is a museum here with a copy of the hut and various items such as an axe, saw, and shirt. The granite monument was built by Gegello in 1927 on the site of the hut.

Car park
Café
Souvenir shops

The *wall* behind the village of Razliv with the inscription "Lenin" and a monument were built to mark the centenary of Lenin's birth in 1970.

LENINSKIYE GORKI
See Moscow environs, p 362

LIPETSK Population—450,000
Lipetsk stands on either side of the upper course of the river Voronezh, at the point where the Lipovka flows into it.

It was first mentioned in the chronicles as a settlement in the 13th century. It became the capital of Lipetsk Principality and was then ruined by the Tatars in 1284. Earth walls are all that remain on the site of the original wooden fortress ("gorodische"), and a marble obelisk marks the archeological excavations.

In the 16th century there was mention of the village of Lipskoye or Lipovka.

When in the late 1690s Peter the Great decided to build his own fleet, Voronezh was chosen as the site for his shipyard. While visiting this area the tsar learned of the vast reserve of iron ore near the village of Lipskiye Malye Studenki. He had already established an anchor foundry and armament-assembly shop in the vicinity when, in 1703, he ordered the construction of a pig iron works on the banks of the river Lipovka. In 1709 the village was renamed Lipskiye Zheleznye Zavody (Lipsk Iron Works). Then additional factories were built by the river Voronezh, on the site of the present-day Central Park. A small palace was built for Peter, too, down beside the water, but it was burnt to the ground in 1806. Tens of thousands of labourers were sent to the Voronezh shipyard, and some were diverted to Lipetsk. The local workshops were soon able to produce naval guns as well as pistols, bombs, and other weapons.

The Empress Elizaveta presented the iron works

to Prince Petr Repnin in 1755, but the workers soon revolted against the bad treatment they received. The works were closed down in 1776 and were not reopened for more than a century.

While Peter the Great was in Lipetsk he ordered that a well should be dug so that the "iron water" could be used for cures. Thus, when the iron works lost its importance, new prosperity came with the opening of the spa, and in 1779 Lipetsk was proclaimed a town. For over a century invalids used to gather near the springs to cure themselves, but the official date of the founding of a real spa is 1805 for it was then that hotels and a bath house were built. Tsar Alexander I signed a decree upon the opening of the Lipetsk Mineral Waters state resort. At the beginning only water cures were practiced, but from 1871 mud was used too. Lipetsk mud has been compared in its mineral content to the ferruginous mineral mud of Franzensbad (now Frantiskovy Lazne in Czechoslovakia) and of Bad Libenstein in Germany. The spa was especially recommended for the treatment of women's diseases and was referred to as a "ladies' resort."

In 1885 the firm of Wagau & Co. built a distillery here, and after the revolution the ironworks were reconstructed and enlarged. In 1936 a new mill was built that produces pig iron, iron alloys, and cast-iron pipes using the nearby iron deposits. Apart from metallurgy, there are now machine-building, construction, chemical, and food industries. The tractor factory was built in 1944, the first caterpillar tractor being the Kirovets-35. One of these is mounted on a pedestal by the factory entrance gate.

The Lipetskiye Uzory factory produces painted souvenirs ranging from Tula samovars to wooden kitchen utensils and trays. They decorate these with flowers, fruit, or scenes from fairy tales using the brightest colours. These souvenirs exhibit in art shows and have recently become so popular in the United States that the factory has doubled its production.

Lipetsk has polytehnical, teacher training, and economics institutes.

The old part of the town is located on 2 terraced hills 46–61 m (150–200 ft) above sea level. They are divided by a deep ravine where the Lipovka flows into the river Voronezh. The spa is in the old part of the town, on the right bank of the Voronezh river. It is divided into 2 parts, on either side of the river Lipovka. The *Lower (Nizhny) Park*, which covers 25 hectares (63 acres), was laid out in 1805. Lipetsk Sanatorium is located in it. *Upper (Verkhny) Park* extends for 6 hectares (15 acres). *Komsomolsky* (formerly Peter's) *Pond* lies adjacent to the Lower Park. The bottom of the pond provides the curative mud.

If you stand in Revolutsii Square with the pond to your left, Resort Park and the spa itself are on the right, as is also the obelisk. The pond was built as a reservoir. From the square the way runs up to Lenin Square and the Nativity Cathedral where the museum is.

The former *Resort Centre (Kurzal)* in the Lower Park, opposite the Oktyabr Cinema, was built in 1890. A former resort hotel stands on the slope, on the right side. In the Lower Resort Park the drinking fountains (1870) still remain but they and the Kurzal (1890) are in a bad state of repair. There are new fountains for decoration and for drinking the waters. New 5- and 8-storey buildings have been put up for present patients.

There are many new houses along Lenin (formerly Nobles') and Gagarin streets. Artur Zegel Street is in the centre of the town. Among the new buildings is the impressive House of Soviets on the top of a hill on Lenin Square, reached from the lower part of the town by a long flight of steps. From the top of Lenin Square one can see the bridge and, across the river, over a panorama of the industrial area with its gigantic factories.

Uspenskaya Church, Saltykov-Schedrin Street. Built in the early 18th century.

Nativity (Khristorozhdestvensky) Cathedral, Lenin Square 4. Built in 1791–1842, this yellow church with a 5-storey belltower over the entrance now houses the local museum.

Preobrazhenskaya (Transfiguration) Church, Myasokombinat Area. Built in the 19th century and open for services.

Drevne-Uspenskaya Church, former Poroiskaya Pustyn.

Local Museum, in Nativity Cathedral, Lenin Square 4. Open 10–5; closed Wed. There is a hand-print in pig iron of Peter the Great here, and also an old metal plaque with an inscription referring to the resort.

Exhibition Hall, Lenin Street 9.

Plekhanov House-Museum, Plekhanov Street 36. Open 10–5; closed Mon. Georgy Plekhanov (1857–1918), the politician known as the "father of Russian social democracy," was born in the village of Gudalovka in this area before his parents moved to Lipetsk. He became active in revolutionary affairs at the age of 20 and soon had to emigrate to the West. Converted to Marxism in 1883, Plekhanov founded the Liberation of Labour Group and collaborated with Lenin, but became anti-Bolshevik when he returned to Russia in 1917. He was one of the leaders of the Socialist International and translated the works of both Marx and Engels into Russian. Plekhanov spent his youth in this house and there is a collection of his personal items, his library, and furniture from his study in Geneva. Both the house and an annex remain.

Gubin House, Lenin Street. This columned house belonged to Gubin who was the leader of the local nobles.

Peter the Great Obelisk, on Petrovsky Spusk (formerly Cathedral Hill). The monument was built by the merchant Paval Nebuchny. The bas-reliefs show the history of the town, including a representation of blacksmiths forging an arrow. The obelisk was cast in Tambov ironworks and was unveiled in 1839.

Guns Monument, in the town park. The three pig iron naval guns were mounted on a pedestal to

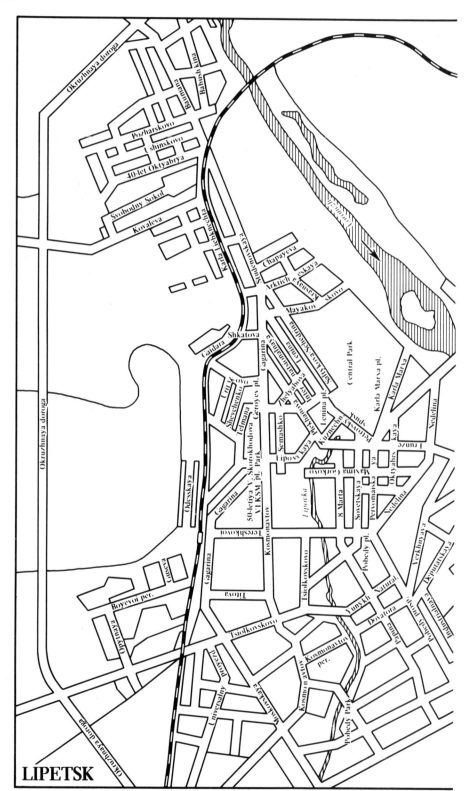

LIPETSK

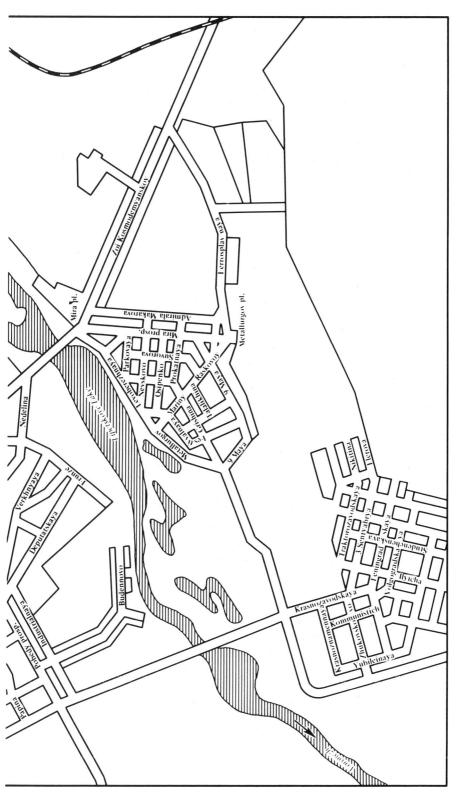

commemorate the first production of guns in 1710 by Peter the Great's ironworks.

Land and Freedom Monument, in the Central Park. This commemorates the 1879 meeting in Lipetsk of the Land and Freedom Populist revolutionary organisation. The architect of the monument was Polunin.

Monument to fighters establishing Soviet Power, Revolution Square. Sculpted by Grishko (1967).

Lenin Monument, Lenin Square, in front of the House of Soviets.

Skorokhodov Monument, Skorokhodov Park. Valentin Skorokhodov was a young communist who was shot during the collectivisation campaign.

World War II Obelisk, Heroes' Square, at the end of Kosmonavtov Street. The obelisk is 19 m (62 ft) high and there is an eternal flame beside it with a guard of honour.

Pioneers' Monument, Lenin Street. Children's figures framed by a giant concrete flame, commemorating the Young Pioneers who died in World War II. Sculpted by Grishko, designed by Polunin, and unveiled in 1972.

Pilots' Monument, 50-Years-of-Komsomol Square. A fighter plane commemorating the pilots of Lipetsk who lost their lives in World War II. Designed by Polunin and unveiled in 1969.

Tank Monument, Industrialnaya Street. Mounted on a concrete star to commemorate the tank army commanded by Marshal M. Katukov. Unveiled in 1978.

Tolstoy Drama Theatre, Teatralnaya Square 1
Puppet Theatre, Karl Marx Street 1
Philharmonia Concert Hall, Karl Marx Street 1
Zvyozdny Sports Palace, Tereshkovoy Street 13. Many competitions and ice-shows have taken place on the indoor rink here.

Metallurg Stadium, Pervomaiskaya Street
Zoo, Karl Marx Street, in Central Park
Lipetsk Hotel & Restaurant, Lenin Street 11; tel. 472-17
Metallurg Hotel, Prospect Mira 20
Tsentralnaya Hotel & Restaurant, Lenin Square 3; tel. 234-76
Turist Hotel & Restaurant, Karl Marx Square 1
Chaika Restaurant, Tereshkovoy Street 10a
Voskhod Restaurant, Geroyev Square 35a
Druzhba Restaurant, Plekhanova Square 1
GPO, Lenin Street 3
Department Store, Plekhanov Square

Ozyorki In this village is the estate that used to belong to the poet and Nobel Prize–winner, Ivan Bunin. He emigrated and died abroad. His home was opened as a *museum* in 1986.

LUTSK (Polish Luck)
Population—198,000
Lutsk, situated on the river Styr, was first mentioned in 1085, when it was one of the frontier fortresses of Kiev Rus and was known as Luchesk the Great. After the fall of Kiev Rus in the 12th century it belonged to the successive principalities of Volhynia, and was ruled for 357 years by the

princely Monomakh family of Kiev. Volhynia (Volyn) comprises an area that stretches eastwards from here to include Rovno and Zhitomir. Through the centuries it was successively Lithuanian, Polish, Russian, and Polish again until the occupation by Germany.

Lutsk itself suffered the Tatar invasion of 1240 and many fortifications were built at that time. The subsequent changes of Volhynian history were similarly important to the town. 100 years later the wife of Prince Lubart of Lithuania inherited Lutsk and so it became Lithuanian, remaining so until 12th March, 1569 when, by the Union of Lublin, the area passed to Poland. It was Prince Lubart who built the existing castle, which continued to bear the name of Lubart Castle even when the Prince became Orthodox and changed his name to Dmitri.

In 1429 a meeting of the monarchs of Europe was held in Lubart Castle to discuss the unification of the Eastern and Western churches and to establish joint measures to defend Europe against the Turks. The meeting lasted 70 days and was attended by Sigizmund of the Holy Roman Empire, King Jagaillo of Poland, Great Prince Vasili II (Tyomny) of Moscow, Great Prince Witovt of Lithuania, the kings of Denmark and Prussia, the Papal Nuncio, the Metropolitan Bishop of Moscow, 2 Tatar khans, and many others.

Magdeburg Law was given to Lutsk in 1432 and it became a sizeable centre for both crafts and trade. It was again attacked by the Tatars, being burned down in 1500–02, but was rebuilt and again rose to a position of considerable international economic importance. The 17th century saw the further growth here of Catholic influence. A Dominican monastery had been founded in 1393, but a Jesuit school opened in 1612. Among other religious orders the Carmelites and the Bernardines were well represented and some of their buildings have survived.

In 1706, during the Northern War, Lutsk was occupied by the Swedes for several months. After the Third Division of Poland in 1795 it became Russian, then Polish from 1919 till 1939, and then Russian again.

Today, among 50 industrial enterprises are a motor factory, machine-building, steel-smelting and ballbearing plants, garment and shoe factories, brick and tile works, dairy factories, a number of fruit canneries, and one of the largest sugar mills in the Ukraine. There is a teachers' training college here, an agricultural research centre, and a children's railway.

Lubart Castle, Krupskaya Street 1a. This is well preserved and still dominates the old town, in the eastern part of Lutsk. It was founded in 1327 at the confluence of the rivers Styr and Glushets and these served as a moat along the outer walls. Its irregular triangular form is emphasised by 3 Gothic towers, Nadvratnaya (over-the-gate), Styrova, and Wladiskaya. It is one of the oldest brick buildings in the Ukraine and although completed in 1383, it resembles 13th-century Russian architecture. The

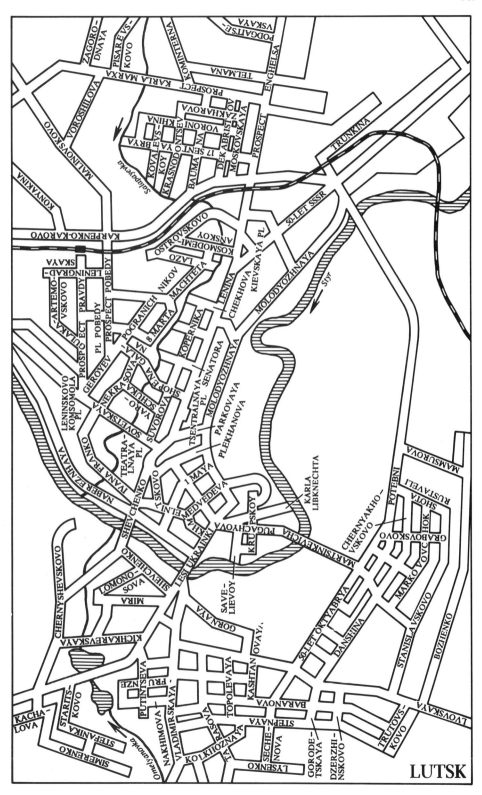

LUTSK

walls are 13 m (43 ft) high with apertures in the upper part for archers to use in the castle's defence. It was known as the Great or Upper Castle and was the site of the Bishop's Court. The walls surrounded the Cathedral of St. John the Divine, where Prince Lubart was buried in 1383; only the foundations remain now. Nadvratnaya Gate was built at the end of the 13th century. It now stands 27 m (81 ft) high, the final piece of reconstruction work adding the 5th storey. It was restored in 1970–77 to its 17th-century appearance. Styrova Tower is also 27 m (81 ft) tall. The 4th and 5th storeys were used by soldiers. Wladiskaya tower was built at the end of the 13th century. In 1987 the Ukraine's first bell tower for concert performances was built.

Inside the castle, between Nadvratnaya and Styrova towers, on the site of the Prince's residence, which was founded in the 13th century, restored many times, burned to the ground, and finally restored in 1963, is Volyn Art Museum with paintings by both Russian and foreign artists.

Beside the Upper Castle, in Pugachov Street, stands a smaller castle, the Lower or Small Castle, Prince Lubart's palace, built in the 14th–15th century; the defence wall and tower remain from those early days. In the 17th century it was decorated in early Renaissance style so that it resembles an Italian palazzo. A synagogue was built into the Lower Castle at the beginning of the 17th century and entrusted with the task of watching the crossing over the river Styr.

Lutsk Brotherhood Architectural Ensemble, Pugachov Street 2 and Herzen Street 5. The Monks' Cells (Bratskaya Corpus), built in the first half of the 17th century, was a printing house, a school, and an almshouse and hospital. The Brotherhood closed down in the 18th century, and the building passed into the hands of the Catholic Basilian Order. Now it is just a residential building.

St. Brigitte's Jesuit Monastery, Krupskaya Street 16, in the square in front of the castle. The building that remains stands on the site of a palace. Starting in 1612 it served as a college. It was rebuilt in 1624 and turned into a prison, and now it is a technical school. A monument to Pasha Savelyeva, a woman partisan who was burned alive in the prison yard in 1944, stands in the square; it was designed by V. Borisenko.

The Jesuit Church of SS. Peter and Paul, Krupskaya Street 6. Founded in 1610 and built in 1616–40 by D. Briano. It was reconstructed in classical style in 1781, but the belfry in front of it was built in 1536. The local Museum of Atheism was opened in the church in 1980.

Pokrovskaya (Intercession) Church, by the main road at Pugachov Street 12. Founded in 1538 and rebuilt in 1873, it was once the home of a famous icon, Our Lady of Volyn, which is now displayed in the Ukrainian Art Museum in Kiev. The belfry dates from 1876.

Roman Catholic Convent, to the right of Radyanska Street, the main street of Lutsk, linking the old and the new parts of the town. This was founded

in 1729 and under Polish rule, housed the Regional Court. Nearby is an Orthodox chapel and to the right stands Krestovozdvizhenskaya (Elevation of the Cross) Church, founded in 1647 and an example of the early transformation of wooden architecture into buildings of stone, and also demonstrating the way ancient Russian architecture was linked with that of the Renaissance. It is 30 m/yds long, 10 m/yds wide and the height of the interior of the central cupola is 25 m (75 ft). In 1702 the Ukrainian poet Danil Bratkovsky was buried in the crypt. The church was burned in 1802, rebuilt in 1890, and is now used as a planetarium.

Troitskaya (Trinity) Church, Krupskaya Street 19. Built in 1752 in baroque style, this once belonged to the fortified Bernardine Monastery. It was burned down in 1781, rebuilt, and taken over by the Russian Orthodox Church in 1977. Its belfry, at Krupskaya Street 7, was founded as a wooden structure in 1539. After the fire of 1781 it belonged to the Jesuit Monastery, and was restored in 1971.

Dominican Monastery, Karl Liebknecht Street 26. Founded in 1390, it was at first wooden, but was rebuilt in stone in the mid-18th century. It ceased being a monastery in 1847 and was turned into a military hospital. Now it belongs to the local artists' union.

Lutheran Church, built in 1910

Local Museum, Galen Street 2

Volyn Art Museum, Galen Street 2a. Open 10–6; closed Mon.

Volyn Museum of Atheism, Krupskaya Street 6, in the building of the Jesuit Church of SS Peter and Paul.

Planetarium, in the building of Krestovozdvizhenskaya (Elevation of the Cross) Church.

Lesya Ukrainka memorial plaque, Karl Liebknecht Street 35. The Ukrainian poetess, whose real name was Larisa Kosach, was born here in 1878 when the thoroughfare was known as Cathedral Street. The plaque was put up in 1953 to mark the 40th anniversary of her death.

Lenin Monument, Lenin Square, built by O. Oleinik.

Stepan Boiko bust, Tsentralnaya Square (opposite Radyanska Square). Stepan Boiko was a Ukrainian Communist who was tortured to death by the Polish police in 1930. The bust was designed by A. Neverov.

Shevchenko Music and Drama Theatre, Teatralnaya Square

Ukraina Hotel & Restaurant, Slovatskaya Street 2; tel. 43-351. Intourist office; tel. 44-758.

Teatralny Restaurant, Radyanska Street

Volyn Restaurant, Lenin Street

GPO, 1-Travnya Street 19 and Lenin Street 14

Gas Station, 17-Veresnya Street 157

Kolodyazhne Population—700
This is 70 km (43 miles) from Lutsk along the main road towards Brest. The name means "the village with wells" and indeed there were 2 deep wells in

the middle of the village where all passersby could quench their thirst. It was first mentioned in 1583 on the occasion of the death here of Prince Andrei Kurbsky at the end of the Livonia War. In 1558 Ivan the Terrible had invaded Livonia, domain of the Livonian Order of German Knights and today divided between Estonia and Latvia. The Knights turned for support to Poland, Lithuania, and Sweden, and in the course of a series of disastrous defeats Kurbsky, who served Ivan as a military leader and adviser, became fearful of persecution. In 1563 he gave his wife the choice that he should either remain with her and die or part from her forever, and then escaped to join the Lithuanian-Polish King Sigizmund August, who presented him with Kovel among other places. He served the king as leader of a military operation against Ivan the Terrible, which gave the Tsar every right to accuse him of being a traitor.

There followed an exchange of letters between the Prince and the Tsar of great historical interest. Kurbsky sent his first letter by the hand of his servant Vasily Shibanov. He delivered it to the Tsar and Ivan in fury pierced the messenger's foot with his iron-tipped staff of office. Blood poured from the wound but Shebanov stood unmoved and Ivan leaned heavily upon his staff as he ordered him to read the letter aloud. In it Prince Kurbsky accused the Tsar of all manner of atrocities and after the reading Shebanov was further tortured in an attempt to learn more of his master. Finally Ivan wrote to Kurbsky saying that he should be ashamed of himself as his own servant had remained faithful to him, even under torture, while he, the Prince, had betrayed his royal master because of unjustified fear.

After Kurbsky's death, the village of Kolodyazhne changed hands many times, becoming part of Russia upon the Third Division of Poland in 1795. From 1881 until 1907 the place was the home of the Ukrainian poetess Larisa Kosach, who is better known under the pseudonym Lesya Ukrainka. Her father, Peter Kosach, had purchased an estate on the north-west outskirts of the village and it was here that Lesya began her literary career.

There is a museum there now, 1 km from the main road, with a signpost indicating the way. Open 10–7. It is in 2 small houses known as the Grey House and the White House, but inside only the grand piano and a vase are original; during the war the trees were felled and the two houses demolished, and it was not until 1949 that everything was rebuilt and restored and ready for a second ceremonial opening.

A bronze bust of the poetess stands on a slab of red granite in the middle of the garden with Lesya's prophetic words:

People will come to me once more,
Many people from places far and near
Bringing both their joy and their sorrow here
And my heart will answer them just as
    before.

LVOV (Ukrainian: Lviv, Polish: Lwow, German: Lemberg) Population—790,000
The town of Lvov stands in the valley of the little river Poltva, a tributary of the Bug. Until 1985 it was thought to have been founded in 1256 by Prince Daniil Romanovich, who named it after his son, Lev, which is Russian for lion. As well as being featured on the coat-of arms of Lvov, lions were constantly used in the decorative metal- and stone-work of the town. Archaeological excavations near the Church of St. John the Baptist give evidence that the place was inhabited by the middle of the 12th century. Little is known about the early appearance of the town, but it is thought that the first walled fortress was built on the hill (Gora Zamkowa) under Prince Daniil Romanovich. At the foot of the hill, where Bogdan Khmelnitsky Street runs today, were a trading centre and the houses of nobles; the merchants' and craftsmen's houses stood along the banks of the Poltva.

From the beginning of the 14th century Lvov was an important centre on the Black Sea–Baltic trade route. Lvov also had trading connections with Cracow and Nuremberg, and many foreigners settled here. As well as Russians there were Poles, Armenians, Germans, Hungarians, Tatars, Greeks, Jews, Moldavians, Italians, and Saracens.

In 1387 Lvov was captured by Roman Catholic Poland and it remained part of that country until the First Partition of Poland in 1772, when it came under the Austro-Hungarian Empire. It was made the capital of the province of Galicia and grew considerably in commercial importance.

At the end of the First World War it was returned to Poland and in 1939, with the rest of Eastern Poland, it was incorporated into the Soviet Union.

Most of the Polish people have now been repatriated, so the greater part of the town's inhabitants are Ukrainians and the language spoken is Ukrainian.

The main industries of the town, beside the manufacture of buses, are connected with machine building, radios, and food products. There is also an interesting pottery factory; most of its products are sold in Moscow and Kiev, but you can visit the factory and purchase articles there through Intourist.

The old part of the town has narrow streets lined with houses, many of which date from the 16th century. *Market Square (Rynok)* and the streets leading off it have been restored, and designated a Historical-Architectural Reserve. The newest and largest building here is the *Rathaus*, standing in the centre. It was constructed in 1828–35 and is now used by the Town Council; the heraldic lions of Lvov can be seen over the main entrance. Of particular interest on Market Square are Nos. 4 and 6, which now house the Historical Museum. No. 4 is known as the *Black House* (Czarna Kamienica in Polish) and originally it belonged to an Italian merchant named Tomi de Alberti, and later to Marzin Anczowski, secretary to the Polish King, Jan Sobieski. It was built in 1577–84 in Renaissance style and its facade bears a strong resemblance to that of the Palazzo dei Diamenti in Ferrara. It is thought that the stone-work was rubbed with the juice of unripe nuts; as well as the black colour, this gave unusual resistance to the wear of time and weather. No. 6 was built by Pietro di Barbona in 1574–80 for a Greek merchant, Contantine Korniakt, who financed the building of several churches in Lvov. In the middle of the 17th century the house was bought by Jan Sobieski himself. In 1686 an "eternal peace treaty" was signed here between Poland and Russia in which Poland renounced its claims to Kiev.

On the other side of the Black House is another *16th-century house*, also built in Renaissance style. In 1637 the first post office in Lvov was opened here by the Italian owner Robert Bandinelli.

Above the main entrance of *No. 14* is a winged stone lion with a Latin inscription and the date of completion: 1600. The lion can be seen on the coat-of-arms of Venice for the house once belonged to the Venetian Consul, Massari. There are altogether 44 houses on Market Square dating from the 16th to 18th century, the latest being those on the northern side, almost all of which were built during the last half of the 18th century.

The old "Pharmacia," with its name inscribed on its glass door, was the first to be opened in Lvov over 500 years ago. Its owner was Vasil Rusin, and the building has changed little throughout the years. On the ceiling are little paintings of the four elements. There is a museum here as well, but the Pharmacia is still open as a shop.

The Lion Cafe has its walls painted with the sights of Lvov and scenes of daily life.

In the square are 4 different *fountains*, one at each corner of the Rathaus; these were designed at the end of the 18th century by Gartman Viver. They depict Poseidon, Amphitrite, Artemis, and Adonis.

There are a number of other interesting secular buildings in Lvov, many built by members of the Polish nobility.

The *Gunpowder Tower* (Baszia Prochowa), Podvalnaya Street 4, was built in 1554–56 and was 1 of 4 towers on the outer walls of the town. During times of peace it was used for storing grain. It is now the House of Architects.

In the same street is the *Town Arsenal* (Gorodskoi Arsenal), which was built in 1554 and was used as a prison in the 18th century. On the south wall is a coat-of-arms, which was taken from the demolished town walls in 1799.

The *Royal Arsenal* in Krivonosa Street was built in 1630 by Ladislas IV. The town archives are now kept here.

Count Potocki's Palace, Kopernik Street 15, was built in the 19th century and is now used by the Geological Institute.

Local Government Offices, Universitetskaya Street. These were built in 1877–81 by Hochberger, and have housed the University since 1918.

Polytechnical Institute, Mira Street. Built in 1872–77 by Zacharjewicz.

There is a wealth of cathedrals and churches in Lvov, some dating from the 14th century. Owing to the mixed population, Armenian and Greek churches were built as well as those for Roman Catholic and Russian Orthodox congregations.

St. Jura's Cathedral, Bodgan Khmelnitsky Street. This baroque Uniate cathedral was designed in 1744 by the Italian architect Bernard Merettini, and completed in 1770. The statue of St. Jura (George) on the facade is by Pinzel, who was also responsible for most of the other statues adorning the cathedral. In the bell tower is the oldest bell in the Ukraine, cast in 1341 for a church which was built here that same year. The cathedral was converted for Russian Orthodox use in the 20th century. Opposite is the former residence of the Uniate Archbishop. It was built in 1761 in the same baroque style, and is now occupied by the Lvov-Ternopol Episcopal Office.

St. Mary's Roman Catholic Cathedral, Rosa Luxemburg Street. The foundations for the cathedral, which is the only example of Gothic architecture remaining in Lvov, were laid in 1360 on the order of King Casimir III. The cathedral, which was completed in 1471, has been considerably altered through the centuries. It contains 18th-century frescoes and many decorative carvings and statues of the 17th and 18th centuries.

The tower was built in the late 16th century after the original one had been ruined by fire. In the 16th and 17th centuries a number of chapels were added, many of them in the graveyard of the cathedral. In 1765 an order was issued forbidding graveyards in the town centre and many of the chapels were destroyed. One of those remaining is the Boim Chapel, which was built in German Renaissance style in 1609 and which has a richly carved facade in sculptured stone. The Boim family was of Hungarian origin. One of the family was private secretary to the Polish King, Stephan Batori, and 14 members of the family were buried here. The chapel is open as a museum on Tues., Thurs. & Sat. 11–5.

Also nearby, on the northern wall of the cathedral, is the Campian Chapel. Campian was a ruthless pawnbroker who became Mayor of Lvov at the beginning of the 17th century. It was built in 1619 of red, pink, black, and white marbles in Renaissance style by the Italian architect, Paolo Romano.

The *Church of the Assumption* (Uspenskaya Tserkov), Russkaya Street. In 1527 the original church burned down. It was rebuilt but in 1571 the new church was similarly burned. Money was collected for the rebuilding, and it is recorded that Tsar Fyodor of Russia gave 200 sables, 200 martens, 50 gold coins, and 35 roubles because it was a stronghold of the Russian Orthodox Church in Poland.

The present building, one of the most beautiful churches in Lvov, was completed in 1629 by Paolo Romano. In the yard is a 66-m (217-ft) bell tower

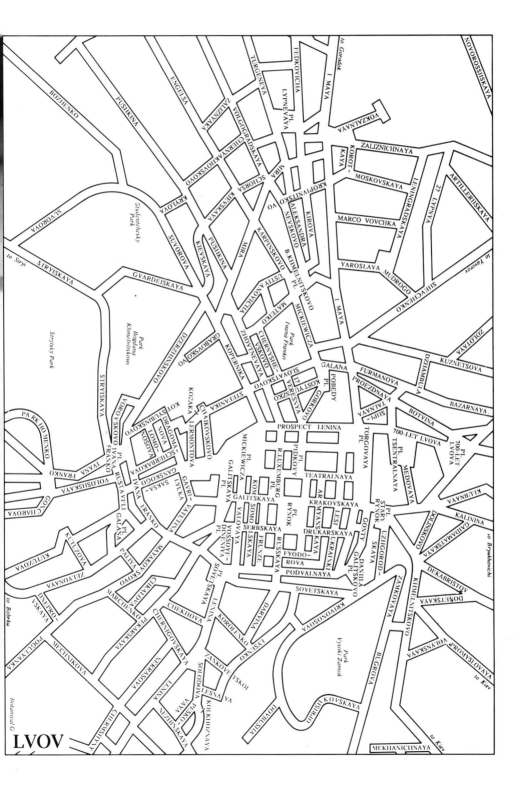

LVOV

dating from 1572–78, which is known as the *Korniakt Tower* (after the rich Greek merchant who financed its construction). In the tower is a bell called Kyril, which was cast locally in 1783 and which weighs nearly 5 tons.

On the outside walls of the church is a sculptured frieze of Biblical scenes. In the main dome are the carved stone coats-of-arms of Russia, Moldavia, and Poland. There are also 18th-century icons, and the altar dates from the same period.

The *Chapel of Three Saints* adjoining the cathedral was built in 1578–91 with money from the same Greek merchant, Korniakt. Inside are Ukrainian murals and icons dating from the 17th century.

St. Mary Magdalene's Roman Catholic Church, Mira Street 10. It was built at the beginning of the 17th century on the site of an earlier wooden church and rebuilt in 1784. The statues on the main facade and the decorative towers were added in the 18th century. Inside are some interesting 18th-century carvings and sculptures.

Church of St. Nicholas, Bogdan Khmelnitsky Street 28. Built in the 17th and 18th centuries on the foundations of a 13th-century church that had belonged to the local prince before it became the property of the Guild of Shoemakers. The cupola was added in 1880 after the original cupola was destroyed by fire in 1783.

Church of St. Onufre, Bogdan Khmelnitsky Street 14. Built in the 16th century on the site of a 13th-century church, and originally on the grounds of St. Onufre Monastery, which was destroyed by fire in the 16th century. It was rebuilt in the 17th and 18th centuries. Ivan Feodorov, the first Russian printer, is buried here. He produced his first book in 1564 in Moscow, and then fled, to continue his work in Lithuania and Poland. He died in 1583.

All of the above churches are open for services.

Armenian Cathedral, Armyanskaya Street 7, was built in 1363–70 and is thought to have been designed by a German architect from Silesia named Doring. This is doubted by many, however, who do not believe that a West European could have built a cathedral that is a blend of Gothic and Armenian architecture. The bell tower and the residence of the Armenian Archbishop date from the 16th century. The domed entrance of the cathedral, which is now 2 m (6 ft) lower in the ground than it was at the time of construction, is decorated with Byzantine mosaics and frescoes. In the cathedral courtyard is an 18th-century statue of St. Christopher.

Pyatnitskaya Church, Bogdan Khmelnitsky Street 63. Built in 1645 on the foundations of an earlier church from which there used to run an underground passage to the fortress on Gora Zamkowa. It contains a carved wooden iconostasis with over 70 icons by unknown masters dating from the 16th and 17th centuries.

Roman Catholic Church of Our Lady of the Snows (Matki Boskiej Snieznej), Snezhnaya Street. There was a Catholic church serving the German population of Lvov on this site at the end of the 13th century. Perhaps the present church was built in the 16th century from the materials of an earlier building; certainly, at the end of the 19th century it was rebuilt, and the interior was redecorated in rococo style. By the church is an 18th-century statue of the Virgin, and inside is a picture gallery, a branch of the Museum of Ukrainian Art.

Church of the Dominican Monastery, Stavropigiskaya Square. This impressive church in baroque style was founded in 1744, designed by Jean de Witte, and built by Urbanik, architect to the King of Poland. After a fire at the end of the 18th century it was reconstructed, then rebuilt again in the 19th century and again in 1956. The belfry dates from 1864 and the dome, decorated with 16 rococo urns, is a copy of that of St. Peter's in Rome. The facade, in baroque style, is flanked by 3 columns and there is a fine bay window over the entrance; the statues of saints were made by Fiesinger. Inside are some wooden 18th-century sculptures including those of SS. Peter, Paul, Luke, and John the Baptist around the altar. The figure above the arch leading to the altar is that of St. Augustine. On the left is a bas-relief made by the Danish sculptor, Bertil Thorvaldsen, in 1816 as a monument to Hrabina Dunin-Borkowska. There is also a monument immediately to the right of the entrance to the memory of the Polish artist Arthur Grottger (1837–67), made by Gadomski in 1880.

The building now houses a *Museum of Atheism* and in the centre hangs a Foucault pendulum of the type developed in Paris in 1851 to prove that the earth rotates on its axis. Attached to the church is a another museum displaying a wide range of articles from churches of many different denominations and also from local synagogues. Near the church are some 16th-century Gothic buildings belonging to the monastery that once stood here.

Benedictine Convent & Church, Vechevaya Square. The church and convent of the Benedectines were erected at the end of the 16th century by Paolo Romano. They were rebuilt after a fire in 1623.

Jesuit Monastery & Church, Teatralnaya Street 11/13. Work on the church began in 1613, 2 years after the foundation of the Jesuit college in Lvov. Inside are 18th-century woodcarvings, and frescoes dating from the 17th and 18th centuries. The monastery was built in baroque style in 1723–28.

Bernardines' Church, Vossoyedineniya Square. In the church are some frescoes and 18 wooden altars with decorative carving, all dating from the 18th century. The *Bernardine Monastery*, of which the church was a part, was built between 1600 and 1630. The remaining buildings are now used as workshops for art restoration.

St. Lazarus's Roman Catholic Church, Kopernik Street 27. This church was built in 1635–40. Near the church in Kopernik Street is a dried-up well guarded by two stone lions from the former Mayor's House.

St Casimir's Roman Catholic Church, Krivonosa Street 1. It was built in 1660 in baroque style and dedicated to Prince Casimir, the saintly son of King Casimir I of Poland and Lithuania (see Vilnius for his story). The building adjoining the church was constructed at the same time as an orphanage.

Church & Monastery of the Barefoot Carmelites, Radyanska Street 20. Both were founded in 1634 and enclosed in a thick defensive wall, the remains of which can still be seen. In the church are some 18th-century frescoes, and wooden sculptures dating from the 17th and 18th centuries.

Clarissa Roman Catholic Church, Lenin Street 2. Founded at the beginning of the 18th century.

St. Nicholas's Roman Catholic Church, Scherbakov Street 2, was beautifully designed in 1739–45 by the Italian architect, Placidi (1710–82), to blend with the surrounding buildings and landscape. It belonged to the Trinitarian Order until 1785, when it was converted for Russian Orthodox use. The interior is richly decorated, with carved wooden altars, statues, and a chair in the shape of a boat with a net. There are many paintings too, including a copy of Rembrandt's "Ecce Homo." In the chapel of St. Florian, to the left of the main altar, there is another altar, which was carved of black marble and alabaster in 1595. On either side of the crucifix are bas-reliefs of the Passion, with intriguing details of contemporary life and portraits of members of the Szolc-Wolfowicz family, who founded the chapel. The altar was originally in the Roman Catholic Cathedral and is ascribed to Herman van Gutte, a Dutch master who lived in Lvov.

St. Bridget's Roman Catholic Convent, Chapayev Street 24. This 17th-century convent was turned into a prison in 1792.

Wooden Church, Krivitskoi Street, was built in 1763 and brought here in 1920 from the Ukrainian village of Krivky as an example of folk architecture.

Historical Museum, Rynok 4/6. Open 11–6; closed Wed. The museum is housed in two of the oldest houses on Market Square (see above). The former throne room of No. 6 is now used for a display of present-day industry and the back of the house looks out on a pleasant galleried courtyard.

Ethnography & Craft Museum, Svobody (formerly Lenin Prospect) 15. Open 11–6; closed Mon. The building was constructed in 1874–91 by Zacharjewicz. The collection of timepieces here is one of the richest in the country; there are more than 300 clocks and watches of the 16th–20th centuries from many different countries.

Ukrainian Art Museum, Dragomanov Street 42, in the building of the Armenian church. Open 11–6; closed Fri. There is a good collection of 14th- to 18th-century icons here.

Picture Gallery, a branch of the Museum of Ukrainian Art, Snezhnaya Street, in the Roman Catholic Church of Our Lady of the Snows (Matki Boskiej Snieznej).

Art Gallery, Stefanik Street 3. Open 11–7; closed Mon. The collection of about 10,000 paintings includes works by Rubens, Titian, Goya, and Tintoretto and some Russian classics.

Lenin Museum, Svobody (formerly Lenin Prospect) 20. Open 10–7; closed Mon.

Natural History Museum, Franko Street 152. Open 10–6; closed Tues. The museum was founded by the Dzieduszyckis family in 1845.

Chemist's Shop Museum, built in 1735 and opened as a museum in 1986.

Galan Museum, Gvardeisky Steet 18. Open 10–6; closed Wed., Fri., & Sat. Yaroslav Galan was a Ukrainian political writer who was murdered in 1949 at the age of 47.

Open-air Museum of Wooden Architecture, Chernecha Hora, in a beautiful park in the suburbs of Lvov. Open 11–7; closed Mon. There are wooden houses and churches here and peasant cottages of the 18th and 19th centuries. The church with the belfry was built in 1863 and brought here, as were all the other buildings, from various parts of the Lvov region. Also included in the exhibit are living representatives of the region's wildlife—including elk, mountain deer, bears, foxes and also some rarer examples of animals familiar to the area.

Mickiewicz Monument, Mickiewicz Street, opposite the Intourist Hotel. The sculptors of the statue of the Polish poet Adam Mickiewicz were Tadeusz Popiel and Parashuk. It was unveiled in 1905.

Ivan Franko Monument, in front of the University. Ivan Franko (1856–1916) was a famous Ukrainian writer. This monument was unveiled in 1964.

Lenin Monument, Svobody (formerly Lenin Prospect). This monument by Merkurov was unveiled in 1952.

Kilinski Monument, by the pond in Streesky (formerly Kilinski) Park. Kilinski was a revolutionary cobbler of Warsaw and a hero of the Polish uprising of 1794. The monument by Markowski was erected in the 1890s.

Tank Monument, Lenin Street. The T-34 tank commemorates the Soviet Tank Corps that liberated Lvov in 1944.

Kholm Slavy (Hill of Glory), Leninsky Komsomol Prospect, near Lyczakow Cemetery and next to Lenin Park. Here, marking the graves of those who fell during World War I and II, is an architectural and sculptural complex, constructed in 1946–52. Since 1958 an eternal flame has been burning here. There are several statues, including one of a woman symbolising the Motherland.

Armed Forces Monument, at the entrance to the town from Stree. This massive structure includes an obelisk, bronze statues, and a stone bas-relief.

Franko Opera and Ballet Theatre, Svobody (formerly Lenin Prospect). The theatre was designed by Zygmunt Gorgolewski in a mixture of baroque and Renaissance styles and was built between 1897 and 1900. On top of the facade are bronze statues of Glory, Victory, and Love by Pyotr Wojtowicz. The theatre seats 1,100 and is very ornately decorated inside.

Zankowiecka Ukrainian Drama Theatre, Lesi

Ukrainki Street 1. The theatre was built in classical style in 1837–42 by Pikhl and Zaltsman.

Russian Drama Theatre, Pyervotravnaya Street 6

Gorky Youth Theatre, Gorky Street 11

Puppet Theatre, Galitsky Street

Circus, Pyervotravnaya Street

Summer Theatre, Khmelnitsky Park, Dzerzhinsky Street 43

Philharmonia Concert Hall, Tchaikovsky Street 7

Concert Hall, Franko Street 25. The Lvov choir is called "Trembita."

Stefanik Scientific Library, Stefanika Street. In 1677 a church stood on this site, but it was severely damaged by fire. The ruins were purchased in 1817 by Count Josef Maximilian Ossolinski, who had them restored and made into a library which was known as the Ossolineum. This building was designed by Nobile and Biema and erected in 1826–49.

Franko Park, Universitetskaya Street, opposite the main university building. The park dates from the 16th century. There is a restaurant here in summer.

Streesky Park, on the road leading to the town of Stree. Streesky (formerly Kilinski) Park is one of the most beautiful in Europe, and its 56 hectares (140 acres) also take their place among the richest arboreta in the Soviet Union. The park, which has a children's railway and permanent exhibition halls, was opened to the public in 1877. There is a cafe in the park.

Bogdan Khmelnitsky Park, Dzerzhinsky Street. In the park are a summer theatre seating 6,000, a restaurant, exhibition pavilions, and a monument to Lenin.

Prince's Hill (Gora Zamkowa). The remains of the 14th-century Vysoky Zamok (high castle) fortress, built by Casimir III on the site of an earlier wooden fortress, can be seen here. The fortress was in ruins by the end of the 18th century and a park was laid out here in 1835–39. There is also a stone monument to Maxim Krivonos, the Cossack colonel who seized the fortress in 1648.

Lenin Park, near Lyczakow Park and Cemetery

Lyczakow Cemetery, Mechnikov Street. In the 16th century this cemetery was used as a burial ground for those who died of epidemics. In 1786, when burials were no longer permitted on church premises, it became the municipal cemetery. It contains many monuments to the nobility. There is one to Ivan Franko, and also the graves of other Polish and Ukrainian writers and artists.

Botanical Gardens, Scherbakov Street

Hippodrome Racecourse, Streeskoye Chaussee

Spartak Swimming Pool, Instrumentalnaya Street 49

Komsomolskoye Lake, 3 km (2 miles) from Lvov on the road to Vinniki

Glinovnavaria Lake, 16 km (10 miles) from Lvov. This lake has a sandy beach.

Intourist Hotel & Restaurant, Mickiewicz Square 1; tel. 72-6751 Intourist office; tel. 72-6619

Dnestr Hotel & Restaurant, Mateiko Street 6; tel. 72-0783

Lvov Hotel & Restaurant, 700-Anniversary-of-Lvov Street; tel. 79-2271

Pervomaiskaya Hotel & Restaurant, Svobody (formerly Lenin Prospect) 21; tel. 79-9031

Ukraina Hotel & Restaurant, Mickiewicz Street 4; tel. 79-9921

Kiev Hotel, Chapayev Street 15; tel. 74-2105

Dnieper Hotel, Pyervotravnaya Street 45; tel. 74-2102

Varshavskaya Hotel, Vossoyedineniya Square 5; tel. 72-5964

Prikarpatskaya Hotel, Nalivaiko Street 6

Narodnaya Hotel & Restaurant, Kosciusko Street 1

Kolkhoznaya Hotel, 300-Letiya-Vossoyedineniya Square 14

Vysoky Zamok (high castle) Restaurant, tel. 72-2522. There is a beautiful view over the city from the restaurant. It puts on a floor show and stays open until 2 A.M. There is an entrance charge of 1.50 roubles and it is best to make a reservation.

Leto (summer) Restaurant, Gorky Street 17

Moskva Restaurant, Mickiewicz Square 7

GPO, Slovatsky Street 1

Kashtan Foreign Currency Shop, Rudanskova Street 3; tel. 74-1064

Gift Shop, Kopernik Street 1

Souvenirs, Galitskaya Street

Arts and Crafts, Mickiewicz Square, near the Intourist Hotel

Intourist organises excursions from Lvov into the Carpathian Mountains, to Rava Russkaya (q.v.) (near the Polish border, 67 km/42 miles to the north-west) and to the castle at Olesko, 75 km (46 miles) east of Lvov.

Olesko Population—2,500

The original wooden castle was first mentioned in 1327 but it was constructed much earlier than that, by Princes Andrei and Lev of Galicia, grandsons of the founder of Lvov. Its strategic position on a hill earned it the name of the Key to Volhynia. In 1366 it was taken from the Lithuanians together with the surrounding plain by King Casimir of Poland.

The cathedral was also founded at this time although it was later repeatedly reconstructed and enlarged. Olesko changed hands frequently but was under the Poles in 1432 when they occupied the castle and again in 1441, when the small town acquired Magdeburg Law. In the second half of the 15th century it lost its military importance and became the residence of a succession of noble families. In 1512 the Crimean Tatar khan Mengli Girei, whose camp lay between Olesko and Busk, ruined and devastated both Olesko and its castle.

In 1605 it was in the hands of Jan Danilovich, who built a new fortified palace on the site of the old wooden castle. In the 17th century Olesko again changed owners, and in 1629 Jan Sobieski (who later became King Jan III) was born in the castle.

10 years after that, in 1639, another Polish noble Michael Koribut-Wisniowieski was also born here. He likewise came to the Polish throne and so the castle came to be known as "The cradle of kings." In the 1680s Jan III decided to restore his birthplace from the ruins in which it lay and the castle was accordingly rebuilt and became a royal residence. Its present appearance owes much to the Polish builder, Severin Rzewuski, who died in 1754. A park was planted with exotic trees and fountains, and sculptures were introduced. Olesko's right to Magdeburg Law was reconfirmed in 1687. In 1711 the castle was occupied by the Russian army and in 1722 Olesko passed to Austria.

There was an attempt in 1890 to restore the castle and make it into a Jan III museum but a school was opened there instead.

As one enters Olesko from Lvov, Poland, and points west, the impressive cathedral stands where the main road curves round to the right. In its present form it dates from 1625 except for the octagonal defence tower, which was restored in 1960. Just before the cathedral is the left turn that leads along a causeway road to the castle.

Olesko Castle is now a museum, and contains an art gallery—open 11–5; closed Mon. The complex of white buildings with red-tiled roofs on the left opposite the entrance to Castle Hill is the *Capuchin monastery*, founded in 1730. A cloister adjoins the large baroque church and there is a surrounding wall. During World War II the territory of the monastery was used as a concentration camp for Jews and 900 were shot near the town in 1942.

The grounds of the castle now cover 15 hectares (35 acres). Several ponds follow the original line of the moat and the mediaeval earth walls are well defined. The formal gardens and sculpture are all in keeping with the period furniture, paintings, and church decorations on display inside the halls of the castle. The Gridnitsa Cafe is set in the castle walls, on the way up to the main gate.

Olesko's central thoroughfare is Lenin Street, lined with many new buildings. The town hall and merchants' houses can be seen on the former market square. In the centre are 2 gardens, one on the right with a bust of Lenin and the other on the left with a statue of Shevchenko.

Revolution Museum, with a bust of Nadezhda Krupskaya.

War Memorial, on the right on the way out of town; sculpted by Borisenko and unveiled in 1977 to commemorate those cavalrymen who fought here in 1920.

Summer Theatre

Hotel

Restaurant

Cafe, Lenin Street 47, on the left

GPO, on the left opposite the cathedral

MAGNITOGORSK Population—440,000
This city, a local cultural centre of the Chelyabinsk Region in the Urals, stands on both sides of the river Ural, about 113 km (70 miles) east of the watershed dividing Europe from Asia. It is one of the USSR's principal industrial centres with the country's largest iron and steel plant. This huge industry makes use of the iron ore deposits that have been worked here since the 18th century using coal from the Kuznetsk Basin and from Karaganda. Subsidiary industries include chemicals and engineering.

The area used to be used by the Bashkirs for cattle-raising. There was a small village on the site and they called the hills Eye-Derlui and Atach. When a Russian military post was established at Chelyabinsk, north-west of here, it was noticed that compass needles were strangely affected by Mt. Eye-Derlui. Digging proved that it was rich in iron ore. In 1747 an enterprising industrialist named Myasnikov began mining, and the ore was transported on sleighs about 113 km (70 miles) away to the town of Beloretsk where small blast furnaces produced up to 40 tons of iron a day. In 1753 Myasnikov and his partner, Tverdischev, were given the mountain by Tsarina Yelizaveta Petrovna. In a few years the mine and the smelting plant were sold to Vogau & Co., a Franco-Belgian metallurgical corporation. Most of the workers at that time were Bashkirs and Kirghiz.

In 1899 Dmitry Mendeleyev (1834–1907) stated that the deposits should be estimated as thousands of times larger than had previously been suspected, and that such a huge quantity of magnetic iron ore had never been seen before. In 1930, when Magnitogorsk was founded, Soviet geologist Alexander Fersman (1883–1945) wrote: ". . . the magnetic iron ore lies here at the very surface, which means it can be worked by opencast methods. So it is hardly surprising that the first lumps were found in 1742, but it has taken 200 years to transform these fabulous riches into a major project."

It was the distance of Magnitnaya Mountain from civilisation that had delayed the development. The nearest railway line, built in the 19th century, ran at a distance of 160–170 km (more than 100 miles) to the north. The old trade route from Orenburg to Irbit via Troitsk passed about 140 km (87 miles) away to the southeast. The nearest inhabited place was Magnitnaya village, a fortress 10 km (6 miles) from the mountain.

The first plan for the Magnitogorsk Metallurgical Kombinat was made in 1928 by Gipromez, a Leningrad projecting organisation. A contract for $2,500,000 in gold was signed with the McKee Company of Cleveland, Ohio, for the planning of the plant and the technical supervision of its construction.

Construction of the plant began on the left bank in 1929, and the town grew up around the mountain, renamed Magnitnaya Mountain; it is really a hill with four tops—Mayachnaya (or Biryuzovaya), Dalnaya, Uzyanka, and Yazhovka. The town was officially founded in July 1930. By September the population was already 30,000, by December, 60,000, and by the following March, 90,000. The first mine was commissioned in 1931. Building was in the hands of young enthusiasts and of forced labourers from the ranks of the peasants who had refused to join the collective farms. Technical advice came from American experts. The first pig-iron was produced in 1932 and that same year the original American contract was broken. The projecting of the rolling mill was given instead to the German firms Demag and Klein, while the detailed projecting of the coke plant was given to the American Koppers & Co. The blast furnace and mining departments were left to McKee while all the rest, including the open-hearth auxillary shops, went to Soviet organisations. The first steel was produced in 1933.

The town of Sotsgorod (socialist city) was built to house the builders and workers of the plant. It also stood as one of the symbols of the first 5-year plan, showing the transformation of old, pre-revolutionary, agrarian Russia into a modern, industrial nation. Many of the best and most experienced Soviet architects along with Fred Forbatt from Hungary and Ernst May from Germany worked on the design. There were plans for new buildings to follow the 8 major highways radiating for 25 km (16 miles) from the centre of the city. Another vast construction site grew here, like those of other young Soviet cities that were being built around dams, blast furnaces, and oilfields.

Dams were built on the Ural river to ensure a good water supply, but their reservoirs were insufficient, so the Verkhne-Ural reservoir was built, higher than the level of the city, its height allowing the generation of an extra 25 million kilowatts of energy annually for the city. The development of the Gazli gas deposits meant that cheap Central Asian gas could be pumped to Magnitogorsk as an additional source of fuel.

During World War II the Urals became a stronghold of Soviet resistance. An armament factory moved here lock, stock, and barrel from Leningrad complete with personnel, and went into production using Magnitogorsk steel. Construction work was resumed after the war.

Today Magnitogorsk is a modern town with broad, straight streets lined with apartment houses. Sotsgorod is now known as the Kirov district. The older part of Magnitogorsk is on the right bank of the river, and the new part is still growing on the left. Pride of place goes to Prospect Metallurgov, which runs between Sovietskaya and Oktyabrskaya squares. Magnitogorsk is encircled by a green belt of parks, orchards, and natural forest land.

Local Museum, Chaikovsky Street 41a

Ruchyov Museum, Lenin Prospect 69. Boris Ruchyov was a Soviet poet who participated in the building of Magnitogorsk.

Pushkin Monument, Pobedy Square. Sculptured by Merkurov in 1938.

Lenin Monument, Lenin Square. Made by Zaikov in 1967.

Kirov Monument, Mayakovsky Street. Unveiled in 1941.

Ordzhonikidze Monument, Ordzhonikidze Square. Made by Gilev in 1979.

Steelworker Monument, Privokzalnaya Square. Sculpted by Zelensky in 1970.

Pushkin Drama Theatre, Lenin Street 66

Buratino Puppet Theatre, Karl Marx Prospect 126

Circus, Gryaznov Street 55

Aziya (Asia) Hotel & Restaurant, Kirov Street 97

Turist Hotel, Karl Marx Prospect 139; tel. 40-544

Teatralnay Restaurant, Gagarin Street

Beryozka Restaurant, Karl Marx Prospect 57

Volna Restaurant, Pravdy Street 25

Ural Restaurant, Kirov Street 88

GPO, Lenin Street 32

Department Store, Metallurgov Prospect 20

MARGHILAN (also Murgnan, Marginon)
Population—125,000
(Intourist organises excursions here from Fergana, 12 km/7 miles away.)

Marghilan lies 12 km (7 miles) north of Fergana, at a height of 475 m (1,558 ft) above sea level. The maximum temperature is 28.9°C (84°F) and the minimum is −2.9°C (27°F). The town is crossed by the river Marghilan-sai and the South Fergana Canal. There are plans to join Marghilan to Fergana to make the third-largest urban complex in Uzbekistan (after Tashkent and Samarkand).

Although the exact date of Marghilan's foundation is unknown, it is certainly one of the oldest towns in Central Asia, probably dating from the 1st or even the 2nd century B.C. It stood on or near one of the great caravan routes and between the 10th and 12th century was an important trading centre. In the 13th century it was overrun by the Mongols but under Babur in the 16th century it was again a very important town in the Fergana Valley. Babur called it "a splendid town full of abundance." Ruins of the mediaeval fortress of Urda-Tagi remain and also some narrow streets with mud houses, and an ancient stone mosque.

In the 18th century Marghilan formed part of the Kokand Khanate and a high, gated wall was built around it in the 1840s as a defence against the attacks of the Emirs of Bukhara. In 1875 there were more than 250 mosques here. It was ruled by Sultan Murad-beg, uncle of the Khan of Kokand. During the Russian advance into Central Asia led by General Mikhail Skobelev, the local authorities tried to convert some Russian prisoners-of-war to Islam. They were brought to the central square and the interpreters tried in vain to persuade them to accept the new faith. Foma Danilov, officer of the 2nd Line Battalion was tortured; the skin of his back was cut into strips, his fingers were cut off one by one, and so on. But the martyr would not renounce his faith. Then the whole group was executed, and the tsar granted a pension to Danilov's widow. In 1875 Marghilan was taken by the Russians but among the conquered towns of Central

Asia it remained one of the more Asiatic, its total population of 47,000 in 1910 including no more than 150 Russians.

The poetess Uvaisa (1780–1846) was born in Marghilan.

Karl Marx Street is the main thoroughfare with the most important modern buildings on it. It runs into the centre from the railway station, 3 km (2 miles) outside. The centre of Marghilan is the point where Karl Marx and Kirov streets cross, on the site of the old fortress. Here also is the town's main bazaar. There is a legend that the grave of Alexander the Great is somewhere in the vicinity, though scientific sources doubt that the grave of Iskander-Pasha, which is what is probably referred to, is likely to be so old.

The town has been famous for its silk for hundreds of years, as well as for its pomegranates and apricots. The Institute of the Uzbek Silk Industry is here and also the largest silk mill in the country. The place is known for its decorative embroidery.

Mosque, Shevchenko Street 12

Yuldash Akhunbabayev Museum, on the right of Svoboda Square. Yuldash Akhunbabayev (1885–1943), the first president of Uzbekistan, came from Marghilan. This was opened as a memorial museum. Open 9–6.

Nurkhon Yuladashkhodzhayeva Monument, at the crossing of Kirov and Marx streets. Miss Yuldasheva was the first local actress.

Park, Krasina Street

Spartak Stadium, 26-Lyet-Oktyabrya Street

Marghilan Hotel & Restaurant, Akhunbabayev Square

Shark Restaurant, Marx Street 317

Cafe, Marx Street 150

GPO, Karl Marx Street

Department Store, Karl Marx Street 115

Hodja-Magyz Mausoleum, 4 km (2 miles) from Marghilan on the territory of the Frunze Collective Farm. It is about 200 years old (1986) and is still a place of pilgrimage for the local people.

MARI (Merv till 1937) Population—90,000 (Intourist organises day trips here by air from Ashkhabad.)

This is the largest built-up area in the Murghab oasis and is situated on either side of the Murghab river and the Karakum Canal, about 30 km (9 miles) west of the ruins of ancient Merv.

The region was a hub of civilisation in Central Asia from the 6th century B.C., when it was inhabited by an agricultural people. This oasis was one of the oldest to be developed by East Persian tribes after they conquered it in 512 B.C.. It was mentioned in the 4th century B.C., and was known as Marghiana to the Greeks and Romans. Antiochia Marghiana was among the most ancient cities in the world. Standing at the crossroads of Khorezm, Balkh, and Herat (the latter 2 now in Afghanistan), it suffered much from incursions from the west by the Greeks, Romans, and Arabs, from

the south by the Persians, and from the west by the Mongols. It was taken by Alexander the Great about 328 B.C., and stood upon the Silk Road, midway between Samarkand and Persia. The succeeding centuries of history are those of ancient Merv (see below).

During Russia's campaigns for control of the area, Turkmen resistance was overcome by the capture of Gok-Tepe fortress in 1881, but there was no further move for 3 years. Merv was then the centre of the only territory still beyond Russian influence. At this time only a small area of the Merv oasis remained under cultivation. To the east, the region around the ancient city lay desolate. The tribal chiefs and prominent citizens submitted to Russian authority of their own accord on 1st January, 1884.

The present town of Mari originated in 1884 on the site of the Koushut Khan Kala fortress, which had been built by the Tekke tribe in 1873. The fortress was surrounded by a reinforced clay wall of which there are remnants. (The place was called Merv then, but for clarity we use that name just for the ancient city.)

At the beginning of this century the right bank of the Murghab River was the traders' part of Mari and the site of the picturesque bazaars, while the left bank was the military part where the Russian troops were based. These two parts were joined by a bridge, and in general the town was cut by so many ditches with small bridges across them that it was like one large garden. Russians, Persians, Armenians, and Jews lived there and all in all there were about 60 nationalities. There were 3 Orthodox churches, an Armenian church, and 3 mosques. For many years Mari with its geographical position near the border remained a crucial point in international politics, and in 1918 when the Civil War spread all over Central Asia, the Persians thought nostalgically of Khorasan as stretching to the Murghab river. The Persian governor-general of Khorasan at that time was Ahmad Qavan, later to become prime minister; hearing that British troops might be entering Mari, he offered a British officer a valuable diamond ring if he would plant the Persian flag on the citadel, but his generosity was turned down.

Today the 2 parts of the town of Mari still face each other across the Murghab, joined by a bridge. The town was renamed in 1937, Mari being a derivation of Merv. Its main thoroughfare is Poltoratsky Street, called after the local revolutionary and Commissar who was shot near Mari by the White Guards during the Civil War. There is also a monument to his memory. Of the parks in the town the largest is Lenin Park, which follows the line of the river. At the entrance to the park is a bust of General Yakub Kuliev, the first Turkmen general to die during World War II.

Just as Merv stood at the meeting place of great highways, so Mari is a major junction. Through it runs the Krasnovodsk–Tashkent railway line with a southern branch running down to Kushka on the

316

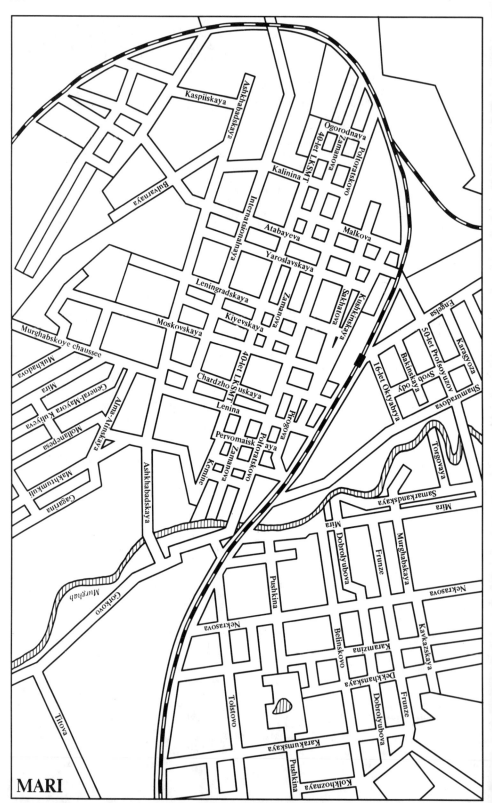

MARI

Afghan border. It is also an important road junction and the last port on the Karakum Canal.

Local industry is much concerned with cotton and with rug making. Ancient Merv was famous for its rugs. Each Turkmen girl, after having woven a few fine rugs for her dowry, usually wove some additional rugs for sale to merchants. On the international market these fine carpets would be sold as Bokhara or Merv carpets.

Other local products now include leather, pelts, textiles, and beer and there are fish and meat packing plants. The discovery of the Maiskoye gas deposit also added to Mari's industry. There are medical and pedagogical colleges here, a drama theatre, and several cinemas. The salt lake of Yazy-Kul has curative properties.

Pokrovskaya (Intercession) Church, Pushkin Street 8/10. Built in 1900 as a regimental church and known as the most southerly Orthodox church to be open for services in the Soviet Union.

Preobrazhenskaya (Transfiguration) Church, Nekrasov Street. Now used as the Officers' Club.

Local History Museum, Lenin Sreet 2. Open 9–6; closed Mon.

Poltoratsky Monument, Poltoratsky Street. Pavel Poltoratsky (1888–1918) was a Turkmen revolutionary and Commissar, shot by the White Guards not far from Mari in June 1918.

Obelisk, on the common grave of those who lost their lives during the Civil War.

Lenin Monument

Obelisk commemorating the border guards who died in 1925 in conflict with the Basmachi, members of an anti-communist resistance movement which was suppressed by 1924 except in the mountainous areas.

Kuliev Bust, at the entrance to Lenin Park.

Azalov Bust, Kluchniyar Azalov (1921–70) was a local hero who became a Hero of the Soviet Union.

Kurban Durdy Bust, Kurban Durdy was another local hero, proclaimed a Hero of the Soviet Union for his part in World War II.

Motherland Monument

War Memorial, Poltoratsky Street. The memorial and eternal flame commemorate those who lost their lives in World War II. By Atayev and unveiled in 1974.

Lenin Park, by the river

Drama Theatre

Intourist Hotel & Restaurant, Poltoratsky Street

Vostok Hotel & Restaurant, Poltoratasky Street; tel. 54-966

Gigant Restaurant, Pirogov Street

From Mari Intourist organises a trip (27 km/17 miles) along a modern highway, eastwards through the desert to ancient Merv, passing Bairam-Ali on the way.

Bairam-Ali Population—40,000

Bairam-Ali was constructed as the administrative centre of the Murghab Imperial Domain. It takes its name from one of the strongholds that formed part of the mighty city of ancient Merv.

In 1884, when Russia took possession of the area, the old irrigation system had long lain dry, but plans to reclaim the potentially fertile region were soon under way. The project for rebuilding Sultan-Bent Dam was approved in St. Petersburg and in 1887 Alexander III, following the Central Asian custom regarding the ownership of reclaimed desert territory, laid claim to "all uncultivated lands along the river Murghab which, by construction of the Sultan-Bent dam, it will be possible to irrigate without loss of other lands already irrigated by the waters of this river. . . ." The area was designated the Murghab Imperial Domain, and to start with covered 42 hectares (104 acres), although the total zone to be reclaimed covered 435 sq miles. As well as the old dams being rebuilt, a hydro-power station was constructed.

As the Domain's administrative centre, Bairam-Ali was designed as a model village with paved streets, a hospital, a post and telegraph office, a telephone exchange, electrically-lit houses for the employees, and a church. In the centre a small *palace* was built in Mauritanian style to be ready for the tsar, should he wish to visit his domain.

In 1892 two cotton-ginning plants were opened, and, as was the case with all the plants of the Murghab Imperial Domain, they were highly technologically equipped. An oil-processing plant was built and Bairma-Ali became the main processing and shipping centre for cotton. Murghab Imperial Domain was also the main centre for the valuable Tekin carpets. In 1915 Bairam-Ali became known as a resort for those with kidney ailments. It was given town status in 1931. There is a sanatorium in the building of the former imperial palace.

Former Mosque, 1905 Street, opposite the entrance to the sanatorium.

St Nicholas's Church, closed

Merv

Ancient Merv which is 27 km (17 miles) from Mari shows its centuries of history in the many archaeological sites upon its territory. It was a group of settlements surrounded by the ramparts of the fortress walls. The dark yellow hillocks are the ruins of old houses.

It was one of the officers in the army of Alexander the Great, Seleucus I Nicator, founder of the Seleucid kingdom, who established a Hellenic colony here. Merv subsequently belonged in turn to Parthia, the kingdom of Kushan, and again to Persia. It was called Mouru in ancient Persian texts and Margu in cuneiform inscriptions.

In the 4th century A.D. it came under Sassanid rule. In 420 the Nestorian episcopy in Merv was transformed into a metropoly and a building for conventions was erected surrounded by a vast garden that belonged to the archbishop. The Nestorian Christians stressed the independence of the divine and human natures of Christ and thus suggested that there were 2 persons loosely united by a spiritual union. During the 6th century A.D. most of the town's inhabitants were Nestorians. Famous for his charity and humanism, the 6th-century doctor Barzuye came from a wealthy family in Merv; he made a journey to India and was the translator of many legends, songs, and poems. In that period the outstanding singer Barbud or Pakhlabad ("pakhlav" means "a strong man"), who was the founder of the musical system of the Middle East, also lived in Merv.

The city was conquered by the Arabs in 651, and it was under Arab rule in that century that the city attained real prosperity and became one of the most beautiful centres of the ancient world, since it did not resist the Arab warriors and so was not devastated by them. The surrounding area where the Murghab River flows down from Afganistan was famed for its fertility long before the Arabs came. With its huge dam across the Murghab and its well-irrigated oasis, it then ranked among the wonders of the ancient world and even rivalled Baghdad as the greatest city of the Orient. It earned the description "one of the most glorious cities of Khorasan," and served as a base for Muslim expansion into Central Asia and later China.

Merv became renowned for its melons, cherries, and fine fabrics; special cotton clothes for the nobility bore the name of "marvi" or "mervi." In 832 the scholar Khabash lived in Merv and worked out astronomical tables. The popular oriental folk epic "Shakh Name" was compiled by the poet Masudi Mervesi (meaning "of Merv") in the 10th century.

In 1038 Merv was taken by the Seljuks, and under them attained the zenith of its glory. In the 11th–12th centuries it grew rapidly with its central part on the site of Sultan-Kala. It covered a territory of 4 sq. km (1.4 sq. mi) and was surrounded by a wall with many towers. Inside the citadel of Shakhriyar-Ark (which is literally "the ruler's fortress") a palace was built with 50 rooms; some remains of this have been preserved. The poet, mathemetician, and astronomer Omar Khayyam (1048?–1122) worked here in the Sultan's observatory. Handicrafts were developed, local china and pottery became especially renowned, Merv developed a monetary system of its own, and a school was started that specialised in the education of civil servants. Sultan Sandjar, who also built a dam, was the last ruler of the powerful Seljuk dynasty, for the city was taken in 1172 by Sultan Shakh and was thereafter ruled by the Shakhs of Khorezm. It was by now a cultural centre with fine libraries. Jakut ibn-Khamowi, the 13th-century geographer who lived in Merv, mentions that one library had as many as 12,000 books.

The mighty fortress was invincible, but its shah thought it best to yield to the threats of Genghis Khan with his army of 80,000. The great leader was enraged by the death of his grandson, Mutugen, at the walls of Merv, and in 1221 the gates

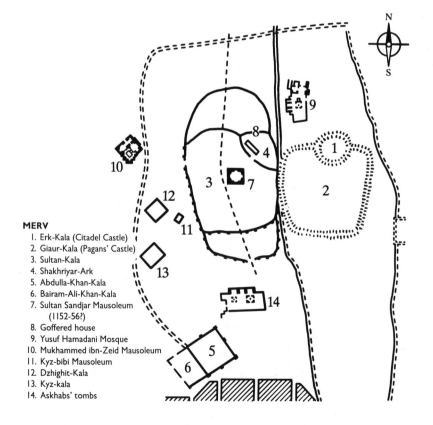

MERV

1. Erk-Kala (Citadel Castle)
2. Giaur-Kala (Pagans' Castle)
3. Sultan-Kala
4. Shakhriyar-Ark
5. Abdulla-Khan-Kala
6. Bairam-Ali-Khan-Kala
7. Sultan Sandjar Mausoleum (1152-56?)
8. Goffered house
9. Yusuf Hamadani Mosque
10. Mukhammed ibn-Zeid Mausoleum
11. Kyz-bibi Mausoleum
12. Dzhighit-Kala
13. Kyz-kala
14. Askhabs' tombs

MERV

of the city were opened to him. Both the dam and the city were destroyed. Arabian writers record that 1,300,000 people were slain on this occasion by the Mongols led by Genghis Khan's son, Tuli-Khan; never in the history of mankind was so much blood shed in a single night.

In 1381 Tamerlane conquered Merv and ruled it. Early in the 15th century the dam was restored by his son, Shakh-Rukh, and the town was rebuilt a little to the south of Giaur-Kala and Sultan-Kala, and named Abdulla-Khan-Kala. As the population increased it was necessary to extend the fortifications, so the south-western part, called Bairam-Ali Khan Kala, was surrounded by a new wall in the second half of the 15th century. Altogether the new town was much smaller than the Merv of the Seljuks (only 38 hectares/95 acres), but it was carefully planned with bath houses and caravansarais, and had a piped fresh water system. The Sardoba Reservoir is a brick-built structure that dates from this time. The irrigation system was maintained by no less than 12,000 workers. According to legend the sultan once abducted the beautiful daughter of the chief engineer in charge of the water works, and in revenge the angry father allowed the Persians to cut off the supply.

Merv was under Persian rule from 1510 to 1524, and Bukharan troops rode against it on many occasions. In 1593 it was taken by the Emir of Bukhara and Shakh Abbas I overran it in 1598. The Persians held it again from 1601 to 1742. Merv saw many rulers, Nadir Shakh, who ruled in the 1740s, one of the most prominent. It was he who, in anticipation of his march to India, fortified his northern border with a strong military unit, conquered Chardjou and took Bukhara without resorting to arms, ordered Merv to be rebuilt together with its dam, and encouraged many newcomers including professional soldiers, to settle the town. Bairam-Ali Khan, another outstanding ruler, perished in 1785. 10 years later Merv was again captured by Bukhara, but by then the ancient city was almost deserted and abandoned to the elements. It was proclaimed an archaeological site in 1923.

Erk-Kala (Citadel Castle), (1st millenium B.C.) was the citadel. It rises above the other settlements with a ramp leading to its southern entrance. This oval-shaped settlement covers a territory of 10 hectares (25 acres).

Giaur-Kala (Pagan's Castle), (3rd century B.C.–9th century A.D.) is a rectangular-shaped settlement covering a territory of 225 hectares (563 acres) adjoining the Erk-Kala. It was surrounded with a strong 100-towered wall 225 km (140 miles) long. The religious statues excavated demonstrate the complexity of the ideological life of that period. The main religion was Zoroastrianism (an ancient pre-Islamic religion founded in the 6th century B.C.), and temples have been excavated. In the northeastern part a Christian monastery was excavated, dating from the 5th century and erected on the ruins of an antique structure. It seems to have been a very modest building decorated simply with some scribbles of crosses on the walls. *Monuments of Buddhism* have been preserved in the southeastern part of the settlement; they date from the 3rd century and include a 13-m (43-foot) square platform with a central tower in the middle of it painted red. A staircase leads to the platform. There was a giant statue of Buddha in front of the platform (the head of the statue has been excavated). Another Buddhist temple stood outside the bounds of the settlement. An artisans' quarter was founded near the Christian monastery, and in the north was a sector where the potters lived and worked.

Sultan-Kala, 9th–10th century, flourished in the 11th–12th centuries under the Seljukids with the citadel of Shakhriyar-Ark. Here stands the *"fluted house,"* so-called because the walls are made of an entire row of half-columns. It is built of mud bricks and dates from the 11th century. It presumably served as an administrative building. Also here, originally as part of the centre of Merv along with the palace and a mosque, is the *Mausoleum of Sultan Sandjar* (who built the dam). He prepared this amazing piece of architecture in the 1140s, during his own lifetime. He called it "the House of Future Life," while the 14th-century historian Rashid-al-Din described it as "the largest edifice in the world." Certainly it was visible "from a distance of a day's journey away." Once it ranked with the Egyptian pyramids in majesty and fame. It stands 37 m (121 ft) high and measures 17 × 17 m (19 × 19 yd) inside. The walls are 5 m (16 ft) thick. The exterior is rather forbidding, with its reddish walls said to be saturated with the blood of Merv's 1,300,000 residents who were killed by Genghis Khan in 1221 (see above). The engineering of its cupola is unique. It is 25 m/82 ft in diameter and constructed as a double shell of brickwork. It was built by a Turkmen known as Muhammed ibn-Atsyz from Serahs 300 years before the same principle was first used in Europe, when Filippo Brunelleschi (1377–1446) completed his cathedral in Florence. The sultan was held prisoner for 3 years after a campaign against a Turkish tribe but escaped in 1156. When he died the following year, he was thus able to be buried in his mausoleum. The mausoleum was ruined during a Mongolian raid, but has been recently restored. In the dome it is said that there is a hole where the golden comb of the sultan's wife (or widow) was bricked up. It was stolen by robbers, although they were unable to demolish the building itself. There are the remains of frescoes inside the cupola. The tomb in the centre of the mausoleum probably belongs to the sultan. The stone that covers it was brought here from Baghdad.

During excavations the traces of ancient buildings adjoining the mausoleum were discovered. These were a mosque and an 11th-century palace of the Seljukids. The mosque was described as the world's largest since its cupola could be seen from as far as 30 km (19 miles) away, so it is believed to have been over 30 m (98 ft) high. Here one can also see the 15th-century *Askhabs' Tombs*, which are made of marble and which cover the graves of 2 7th-century Arab military commanders, Abu-Abdallah Bureida and Al-Khakam Al-Ghifari. The monuments are finely carved, and erected against the background of a 2-portalled structure faced with glazed brickwork.

The outskirts in the south are occupied by *Abdulla-Khan-Kala* and *Bairam-Ali-Khan-Kala*, which were both founded in the 15th century.

Kyz-Kala and *Dzhighit-Kala*, 2 feudal castles called locally "keshk," are in the western outskirts of the ancient town. They were built in the 6th–7th centuries on a raised platform and are rectangular-shaped with a row of semi-columns (earning them the nickname "accordions"). The former castle is the better preserved of the two.

Mukhammed ibn-Zeid Mausoleum, about 2.5 km (1.5 miles) distant from Sultan Sandjar Mausoleum. Ibn-Zeid is said to have been a direct descendant of the Prophet Ali. Although he lived in the 8th century, the mausoleum dates from 1112–13 and is also very interesting from an architectural point of view. It is a domed structure made of mud bricks and set off with fired bricks. Its interior is preserved with its ornamentation in cuneiform characters. Later a mosque was built on to it.

Yusuf Hamadani Mosque, south-east of Sultan Sandjar Mausoleum, and connected to it by an asphalt road. The mosque dates from the 16th century. Hodja Yusuf ibn Ayub was a dervish, born in Hamadan, who lived in Merv in the 12th century. The small mausoleum over his grave was reconstructed at the end of the 19th century. The mosque is open for services.

MARIUPOL Population—520,000

The town of Mariupol (Zhdanov from 1948 to 1989) grew out of a small 17th-century settlement situated in the lower reaches of the river Kalmius, near the sea fortress of Domakha.

In the middle of the 10th century this territory was part of Kiev Rus. The Cossacks started to settle here in the 16th century and built a stronghold, which from 1775 was known as Pavlovsk.

Mariupol became a town in 1779 when Suvorov, then in command of the Russian troops fighting in the Crimea against the Tatars, brought here from the Crimea about 30,000 Greek families. Besides the Greeks, the town was also populated by Russians fleeing serfdom in central Russia.

Mariupol developed as a major port in the south of Russia and as an industrial centre. Its development was greatly accelerated by the building in 1882 of a railway connecting it with the coal mines of the Don basin and the Azov region. The first industrial enterprises were set up in Mariupol at the end of the 19th century. In 1896 the French organised the Russian-French Nikopol-Marioupol joint-stock company, which purchased equipment in America and built a metallurgical plant near Mariupol. Next to it a Belgium joint-stock company built another metallurgical enterprise called Russian Providence. After the 1917 Revolution these were both nationalised.

In the 1930s one of the country's largest metallurgical enterprises, the Azovstal, was built here. Now there are other industrial plants in Mariupol—a welded pipe plant, a radiator plant, and a fish cannery, which produces the highest-quality smoked fillet of sturgeon and pressed caviar.

Mariupol is also a resort town on the Sea of Azov with 2 sanatoria and a holiday home.

Mariupol was the birthplace of an outstanding Russian landscape painter, Arkhip Kuindji (1842–1910). Most of his landscapes were inspired by the beautiful views of the South Ukrainian steppes, the Azov Region, and the Dnieper. Also born near Mariupol was the famous polar explorer, Georgi Sedov (1877–1914). He tried to sail through the thick polar ice to the North Pole aboard the "St. Foka." The third famous son of the town was Soviet statesman and Communist Party figure, Andrei Zhdanov (1896–1948), after whom it was renamed until his discreditation in 1989 for atrocities committed during the Stalin era as one of Stalin's close assistants.

Uspensky (Assumption) Cathedral
Art Gallery
Mazai Monument, Makar Mazai was a renowned steel smelter.

War Memorial, to the fighters for Soviet power.

War Memorial, commemorating Azov sailors who died in the Civil War and World War II.

War Memorial, to the victims of Nazism.

Balabus Monument, on the corner of Admiral Nakhimov Prospect and Portovaya Street. This was the place where the Young Pioneer Anatoli Balabus was killed.

MINSK

Minsk is the capital of Byelorussia (White Russia).

BYELORUSSIAN SOVIET SOCIALIST REPUBLIC

Byelorussia is one of the 15 Soviet Republics. It shares its western border with Poland. It is 207,600 sq. km (80,150 sq. miles) in area with a population of 10,200,000 (1984), of which a quarter lives in the towns. The people include Byelorussians (79.4%), Russians (11.9%), Poles (4.2%), and Jews (1.4%). The Byelorussians are closely related to the Great Russians and the Ukrainians, and they trace their origin from East Slav tribes such as the Krivichi and the Dregovichi. The language spoken is Byelorussian, which is closely akin to Russian and Ukrainian. Most of the inhabitants of the major cities speak Russian.

Until the 12th century the area was under the authority of the Kievan state; later the new principalities of Turov-Pinsk, Smolensk, and Volynia emerged, and these were incorporated in the 13th and 14th centuries into the Grand Duchy of Lithuania. Russian was the official language spoken until Lithuania's union with Poland in 1569. The whole of Byelorussia was taken over by Russia after the Polish partitions of 1772–95.

The first demands for autonomy occurred at the

beginning of the 20th century when the revolutionary Hromada (community) Party (later called the Socialist Hromada Party) was formed. This, however, gained little popular support. Strong Polish and Zionist movements were also active at that time. In 1918, during the German occupation, an independent Byelorussian Republic was proclaimed; in 1920 the country was temporarily occupied by Poles, who later partly withdrew while remaining in possession of the western part. In 1921 the Soviet Byelorussian Republic was formed, and it joined the Soviet Union in 1922. The size of the republic was increased in 1924–26 by the addition of adjacent territory to the east, and in 1939 by the inclusion of Western Byelorussia. It suffered a great deal during World War I, and even more in World War II.

Approximately 25% of the area of Byelorussia is covered with forests and about 10% with marshes. The climate is moderate continental.

Byelorussia's agricultural products are chiefly grain, potatoes, and dairy products. There is pig breeding too and Byelorussia is also the most important flax-growing area in the Soviet Union.

The republic's main industries are food production and light industry, wood processing, and engineering. The country also has large resources of peat (about 5,000,000,000 tons), which constitute the main source of fuel for its many power stations. Other mineral resources include lignite, potassium, and rock salt.

A few words of Byelorussian

Hello	dobraga zdarovya
I am a tourist	ya toorist
Please	kali laska
Thank you	dzyakooi
Yes	tuk
No	nye
Good	dobra
Bad	drena
I don't understand	ya nye razoome-yoo
I need an inter-preter	mnye patreben peravodchik
goodbye	da pabachenya

Minsk (in Byelorussian: Mensk) Population—1,590,000

The city is located in the centre of Byelorussia. Minsk stands on the river Svisloch, 20–30 m (22–33 yds) wide at this point, and unnavigable, and at the same time it is situated at the crossing of the important Moscow-Brest and Vilnius-Kiev railway lines. Its name comes from the word "menyat" (to change) and refers to its importance as a trading post.

The town is one of the oldest in Russia. Its first known mention dates from 1067, when it belonged to Prince Vseslav of Polotsk and stood on the ancient river trade route that linked the Black Sea to the Baltic, the river Svisloch being navigable at that time. From the beginning of its history Minsk has been ruined again and again. In 1084 it was utterly demolished, and according to an old chronicle, "not a single body nor a single beast" remained alive. Minsk was under Polish rule, and then under Kiev's, but in 1101 it became the capital of an independent principality. It was besieged for almost 2 months in 1116 by Prince Vladimir Monomach of Kiev, and in 1119 he seized it and annexed it to his own possessions. In the mid-12th century Minsk regained its independence and retained it until 1326 when it became subject to Lithuania. In 1499, when it had already risen to being an important commercial and cultural centre of that state, the autonomous municipal administration known as Magdeburg Law was introduced into the local city government. This gave a city a right to hold weekly bazaars and annual fairs and so encouraged economic growth and all forms of craftsmanship. It was granted to many townships now in Byelorussia and the Ukraine, and without exception proved a great stimulus to local development.

In 1505 Minsk was invaded and ruined by the Tatars. Later, in 1569, it formed a part of Poland after Lithuania's union with that country, and in June 1708 it was the mustering point for the army of Charles XII of Sweden as he prepared to march upon Moscow against Peter the Great.

It was not until 1793 that the region passed to Russia. In 1796 Minsk was proclaimed the provincial capital and then was again ruined, this time by Napoleon. In 1821–22 Nikita Muravyov and Alexander Bestuzhev-Marlinsky lived in Minsk. Muravyov wrote the first draft of his Constitution, which was therefore called the Minsk Variation. These two young men were involved in the first revolutionary movement of the 19th century; after the failure of a badly organised revolt in December 1825, the members became known as the Decembrists.

In 1835 Nicholas signed a decree which stated the few places in which Jews were allowed to live; Minsk was one of these, and until World War II the population was in fact half Jewish. Not only was Minsk devastated by wars and invasions many times in history but it was also ruined by recurrent fires; in 1881, half the city was burned to the ground. These catastrophes, however, did not halt its ever-increasing economy. Development was especially rapid after the completion in 1874 of the railway that followed the old trade routes. Minsk soon grew to be one of the centres of trade with the West.

On 1st January, 1919, the Byelorussian Soviet Republic was organised and Minsk was proclaimed its capital. During World War II the city was occupied by the Germans for 1,100 days and 80% of the houses were destroyed. Russians call Minsk "the town of partisans," for during the war, partisans killed many German officers in command of the region, including their leader, Commissar General Wilhelm Kube.

Minsk is unique among the capital cities of the Soviet Union for having been ruined over and over

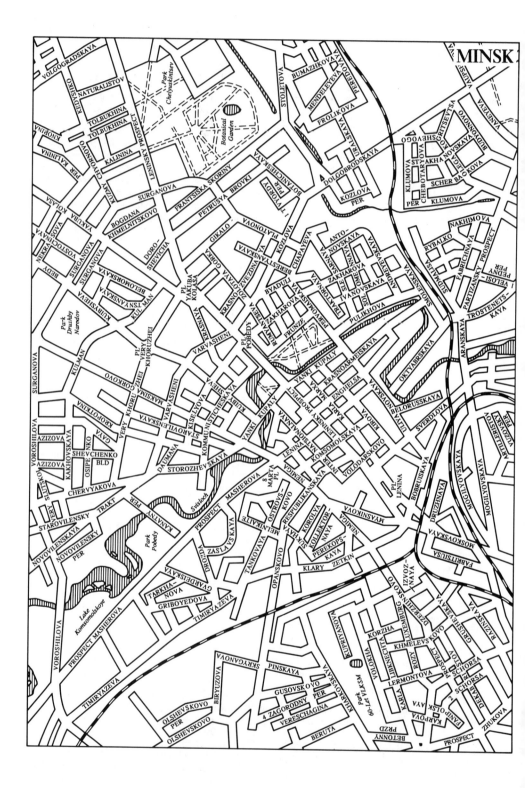

MINSK

again but still dominating the region. It is now a completely new town, rebuilt on the wartime ruins. As there were no outstanding valuable historical monuments, no attempt was made to try to restore the old parts of the town, as was done in Warsaw. The territory of Minsk, covering 9,000 hectares (22,500 acres) is about twice the size it was before the war. The central street of the town, *Leninsky Prospect*, called Zakharyevskaya Street before the revolution, crosses Minsk from north-east to south-west. As it was utterly destroyed during the war, it was widened from 14–19 m (15–21 yds) to 48 m (52 yds) when it was reconstructed. It is about 8 km (5 miles) long. The government buildings, theatres, museums, shops, hotels, and institutes are concentrated in the centre of town. Crossing the main prospect are the streets most worthy of note: Lenin Street and Engels Street. Like the other central throughfares, they are lined with 4- and 6-storey buildings. On the same prospect are Pobedy (victory) and Tsentralnaya squares, where the Minsk counterparts of the Moscow Red Square parades (which take place on the national holidays of 1st May and 7th November) are usually held. On Tsentralnaya Square is the *Trade Union Palace of Culture*, which has a Hall of Columns and a theatre, the stage of which is a replica of that of Moscow's Bolshoi Theatre. Close to the square is a big, old garden. When the central streets were rebuilt they were planted with 20- to 30-year-old trees, and this has helped to give them a more mellow look than they would otherwise have had.

The *Byelorussian Government House* is an 11-storey building on Lenin Square, designed in 1935 by Langbard. The *Byelorussian Academy of Sciences* was founded in 1922 and reorganised in 1929. Minsk is also a university town; Lenin University, which has 8 faculties, was opened in 1921. There are, besides, 12 different institutes and a total of about 35,000 students. The Polytechnical Institute is the second major educational establishment.

The Byelorussian Film Studio is in Minsk, and the capital of the republic is also one of the largest industrial centres of the Soviet Union. When it was reconstructed after the war, over 100 big industrial enterprises were built, and Minsk now produces 29% of all Byelorussian manufactures. These include lorries, tractors, motor-cycles, radios, watches, textiles, leather, and food products.

The population is now mainly Byelorussian, Jewish, and Russian.

There are in Byelorussia many burial mounds and barrows, most of which date from the 10th–12th centuries. In a field by the village of *Grushevsky*, near Minsk, excavations were made between 1945 and 1951. Here the old territory of a fortress (Zamchische) was discovered; part of the main street is discernible with traces of some houses and a 12th-century church.

Bernardine Convent, Bakunin Street 6. Built in the 17th century and situated in the oldest part of Minsk, this convent is now used to house the town archives.

Cathedral of the Holy Spirit, Bakunin Street 3.

This is one of the 2 churches open for religious services in Minsk, and it is where the Bishop officiates. Its twin towers are painted yellow and white and it stands high above the city. It was built in 1633 as a part of the Bernardine Monastery. Its most precious possession is a miracle-working icon of Our Lady; the age of the icon is uncertain, but according to a legend it was placed by Prince Vladimir in the Desyatinnaya Church in Kiev, where it remained for 500 years. Then, in the 15th century, when the town was suffering one of its periodic raids by the Tatars, it was thrown into the river Dnieper. In 1550 an unusual radiance was noticed by the inhabitants of Minsk in their own river Svisloch, and the icon was found and rescued.

St. Catherine's Church, sometimes called the "yellow church," Ostrovsky Street 4. Built in 1611 as a Roman Catholic church and at first known as the Church of SS. Peter and Paul, it has been fully restored and is now also used to house the city archives.

Voznesensky Monastery, Troitsky Hill. Founded in the 18th century and now used by part of Hospital No. 2.

Church of Mary Magdalene, Storozhevskoye Cemetery. Built in 1847, this now houses the Byelorussian cinema archives.

St. Alexander Nevsky Church, Chervonoarmeiskaya Street. This was built in 1898 in Byzantine style as a cemetery church in honour of those who fell in the Russo-Turkish War of 1877–78. Many other war heroes were subsequently buried here. Burials no longer take place although the church itself is open for services.

Church of SS. Helena and Simeon, Sovietskaya Street 15. Built in 1908 and known as the "red church," no service was ever held here because by the time it was completed, Catholic services were banned. It was damaged during World War II and is now used as Cinematography House.

Calvary Cemetery Gates, at the end of the Opansky Street. These gates were built in 1830 and are decorated with sculptures.

The Governor's House, Svobody Street. The Jesuits had a college in Minsk from 1650 until they were expelled in 1829. They used this building during the 18th century. Since 1932 it has belonged to Minsk Conservatoire.

Synagogue, Tsinskaya Street 109

Mason's Lodge, Muzykalny Pereulok 5. The 3-storey house was built in the 18th century; in the second part of the 18th century it was the meeting place for the Northern Torch Lodge. This was declared illegal in 1822, as were all Lodges in Russia.

House of Arts, Leninsky Prospect 26. This was formerly the Archbishop's Palace, built in 1913 with turrets topped by a strange mixture of Orthodox domes and Gothic spires. It was reconstructed in 1963.

World War II Museum, Lenin Prospect 25a. Also known as the Museum of History of the Great Patriotic War, this museum has 25 halls.

Byelorussian Art Museum, Lenin Street 20. Here are canvases by Aivazovsky, and also by

Shishkin and Repin, both of whom lived and worked in Byelorussia for some time. The Museum is open 11–7; closed Tues.

Museum of Old Byelorussian Art

Local History & Folklore Museum, Karl Marx Street 12. Open 11–7; closed Thurs.

Yanka Kupala Museum, Yanka Kupala Street 4. His real name being Ivan Lucevic (1882–1942), Kupala was one of the founders of Byelorussian literature and literary language.

His songs he began in that humble language
So bitterly scorned, the subject of laughter.
Let singer and song be judged by the masses—
See what he's thought up, Yanka Kupala.

—Trans. Walter May

Besides being a poet, he is also known for his translations of the works of Mickiewicz and Shevchenko into Byelorussian. Many of his manuscripts were lost when his house was burned in 1941 and the present museum stands upon the site. Open 10–5; closed Fri.

Yanka Kupala Monument, Kupala Park. Unveiled in 1972.

Yakub Kolas Museum, Lenin Prospect 66a. Yakub Kolas was the pseudonym of Kastus Mickevic (1882–1956), like Kupala a classic Byelorussian writer. He spent most of his life in Minsk and the 2-storey house which was built for him is now the building of the museum. Open 10–4.30; closed Tues.

Yakub Kolas Monument, Yakub Kolas Square, where the road forks left for Khatyn. The seated figure of Kolas, flanked by 2 statues on either side, was unveiled in 1972.

First Congress Museum, Lenin Prospect 31a. The building is a replica of that in which the Social democrats met in 1898; the original burned down. The Museum is open 10–6; closed Fri.

M. Bogdanovich Literary Museum

P. Brovka Literary Museum

The Minsk Lenin Library, Krasnoarmeiskaya Street 9. Built in constructivist style, this library has 2.5 million books on its shelves.

Byelorussian Exhibition of Economic Achievements, Kupala Street 27.

Lenin Monument, on Lenin Square in front of the Byelorussian Government House. The monument was designed by Matvei Manizer.

Dzerzhinsky Monument, Komsomolskaya Street. Unveiled in 1959.

War Memorial, Pobedy Square. This great obelisk was erected in memory of the soldiers and partisans who fell in World War II. It was built in 1954 by Zaborsky and Korol. It stands 38 m (125 ft) high, and on top is a model of the highest Soviet military award, the Order of Victory. At its foot burns an eternal flame.

Tank Monument, at the intersection of Karl Marx and Krasnoarmeiskaya streets.

Jewish Memorial, Rotamskaya Street. This monument is dedicated to the 5,000 Jews of Minsk who were killed here by the Nazis on 2nd March, 1942. Every year a memorial service is held here.

Bolshoi Theatre, Parizhskoy Kommuny Square 7. This opera house was built in 1935, and was designed by Langbard, who was also responsible for the Byelorussian Government House and the Council of Ministers building in Moscow. Besides opera and ballet, it also holds performances of the Byelorussian Capella Choir and the Byelorussian Folk Choir. The Puppet Theatre is located in the building.

Yanka Kupala Theatre, Engels Street 7. This was built in 1890 by Kozlovsky.

Gorky Russian Drama Theatre, Volodarsky Street 5. This was once a synagogue.

Youth Theatre, Engels Street 20

Puppet Theatre, Engels Street 20

Trade Union Palace of Culture, Lenin Prospect 25

Circus, Lenin Prospect 32

Philharmonia Concert Hall, Lenin Prospect 50

Conservatoire Concert Hall, Lenin Prospect 50

Dynamo Stadium, Kirov Street 8

The Spartak sports centre at Svobody Square 9 has an unusual history: A wooden chapel was replaced in 1656 by the building of a Jesuit monastery and their church was renamed the Mariinsky Cathedral in 1920. After suffering damage in World War II it was reconstructed for the Spartak Club.

Winter Swimming Baths, near Kolas Square

Gorky Park, Pervomaiskaya Street 17. This park was founded in 1880 as the Governor's garden and covers 26 hectares (65 acres). It contains fountains, a monument to Maxim Gorky, an exhibition hall, and an open-air theatre seating 1,800.

Chelyuskintsev Park, Lenin Prospect beside the main road to Moscow. This park was founded in a pine forest in 1930. It has an area of 45 hectares (112 acres) and contained an open-air stage, a cafe, and war graves decorated with the statue of a mourning woman. The children's railway 4.8 km (3 miles) long was completed in 1955 and is operated by schoolchildren.

Botanical Gardens, Lenin Prospect 80. The gardens cover 106 hectares (265 acres).

Victory Park, Zalivnaya Street. With a territory of 204 hectares (510 acres), this is Minsk's largest park. It has 2 boat-hire stations, a restaurant, and a billiard hall.

Yubileinaya (Intourist) Hotel & Restaurant, Masherova Prospect 19; tel. 29-8835. Intourist office; tel. 29-8018.

Planeta (Intourist) Hotel & Restaurant, Masherova Prospect 31; tel. 23-8416

Belarus Hotel & Restaurant, Kirov Street 13; tel. 22-5981

Minsk Hotel & Restaurant, Lenin Prospect 11; tel. 29-2326

Sputnik Hotel & Restaurant, Brilevskaya Street 2; tel. 25-8849

Tourist Hotel & Restaurant, Partisansky Prospect 81; tel. 45-4145

Sovietskaya Hotel-1, Komsomolskaya Street 13
Sovietskaya Hotel-2, Volodarskovo Street 6
Minsky (Intourist) Motel & Restaurant, Brestskoye Chaussee, 727 km; tel. 99-5105
Nieman Restaurant, Lenin Prospect 22. Called after the Lithuanian river Neamunas.
Cosmos Restaurant, Shevchenko Boulevard 26
Kammenny Tsvetok Restaurant, Tolbukhin Street 12
Naroch Restaurant, Respublicanskaya Street 26
Zhuravinka Restaurant, Kupala Street 25
Potsdam Restaurant, Lenin Street 2
Leto Restaurant, Pervomaiskaya Street 18
Paparats Kvetka Restaurant, Sverdlov Street 2
Raduga Restaurant, Kirov Street 1/13
Sosny Restaurant, Partisansky Prospect 70a
GPO, Lenin Prospect 10
Central Telegraph Office, Zakharova Street 26; tel 33-0752
German Consulate General, Sacharova Street 26; tel. 33-0752
Polish Consulate General, Omsky Pereulok 6; tel. 33-1313
Department Store, Lenin Prospect 21
Beryozka Foreign Currency Shop, Sverdlov Street 3
Podarki (gift) Shop, Kolas Street 32
Lyanok Linen Shop, Lenin Prospect 46
Minsk Sea, 16 km (10 miles) from town. This reservoir was completed in 1956; it is possible to bathe here.

Intourist organises boat trips on the reservoir, and also excursions from Minsk to Raubichi (22 km/14 miles from Minsk), Kurgan Slavy (Glory Hill), and to Khatyn (60 km/37 miles) to the north of Minsk, along Vitebskoye Chaussee, and to Vyazynka, where Yanka Kupala was born. Ivanets, where there is a museum commemorating Dzerzhinsky, is open to tourists from Poland.

Raubichi

Krestogorsk Catholic Church, now the home of the Byelorussian Folk Art Museum. Open 10–5; closed Mon. & Tues. Folk instrument concerts can also be arranged here.

The *Raubichi Sports Centre* opened in 1974 for the World Biathlon Championship. Beyond Raubichi and beside the main Minsk–Moscow road stands *Kurgan Slavy* (Glory Hill), a mighty war memorial marking the place where Nazi forces were surrounded during the liberation of Byelorussia in World War II. It was in July 1944 that 3 Byelorussian armies combined with 1 Baltic army to defeat the Nazis here and on 3rd July the Soviet Army drove the enemy out of the city of Minsk. 17 Nazi divisions were annihilated and 59 routed during the operation, recognised as an outstanding military achievement. Since then the day has remained of special significance to the Byelorussians. Glory Hill was designed by sculptors Bembel and Artsimovich and architects Stakhovich and Mitskevich. People heaped upon the mound earth from other hero cities, from the fortress of Brest, and from towns and villages that had distinguished

themselves during the war. The 4 bayonets crowning the Hill symbolise the united efforts of the 4 armies participating in the Byelorussian operation and the inscription reads: "Glory to the Soviet liberation army!" The memorial was completed in 1969.

Khatyn

The site of the village is kept as a memorial to the victims of Nazi occupation. The village was burned to the ground together with all its inhabitants by the Germans during World War II, as were 9,200 other Byelorussian villages. The only survivor was Iosif Kaminski, found lying beside the body of his son. He served as the model for the bronze sculpture by Gennady Slikhanov—a man carrying the lifeless body of a child. Behind the statue symbolic chimney stacks, each topped with bell, now mark the position of the peasants' cottages before the burning. The Khatyn Memorial, conceived as a place to commemorate all who perished in Byelorussia during the war, was opened in 1968. Urns with ashes from 136 Byelorussian villages that suffered a similar fate were brought here and beside the cemetery of the villages stands a Memorial Wall honouring those who died in Nazi concentration camps.

Vyazynka 45 km (28 miles) from Minsk. The Byelorussian poet Yanko Kupala was born here. A typical *house* has been turned into a branch of the Kupala Literary Museum in Minsk and furnished and equipped as his home would have been. Open 10-6, closed Mon.

Ivanets 59 km (37 miles) from Minsk. This village is not far from Dzerzhinovo, where Felix Dzerzhinsky (Polish: Dzierzynski) (1877–1926) was born into a Polish gentle family. He joined the Social Democratic Party of Poland and Lithuania, and was imprisoned and exiled to Siberia several times. After the 1917 Revolution, Dzerzhinsky became a member of the Central Committee of the Bolshevik Party, took an active part in its work and immediately established the Cheka (later GPU), of which he remained the chairman until his death. He was at the same time Minister of Transport and Chairman of the Supreme Council of National Economy. He supported Stalin in the party struggle for power that followed Lenin's death.

Dzerzhinsky Museum, in a 2-storey house. Founded in 1957 to celebrate the 80th anniversary of the revolutionary's birth. On display are family belongings, letters, and photographs. There is also a model of the house where the Dzerzhinsky family lived and which was burned during the enemy occupation in 1943.

MOSCOW Population—9,000,000

HISTORY AND
GENERAL INFORMATION

Moscow is by far the largest city in the Soviet Union. It is the capital of the Russian Federation as well as of the Soviet Union and the headquarters of the East European Economic Community, Comecon. As well as the seat of government, it is an important cultural and industrial centre with varied industries.

Originally a small defence post on the Moskva river, from which it takes its name, Moscow owes its importance largely to its geographical position. The policy of the early princes of Muscovy was to gain control of the main waterways with an outlet to the sea by conquering the neighbouring principalities. It became an important point on the Baltic–Volga–Caspian trade route, by which goods were transported from the south to the Baltic and thence to Europe. Today it is the main junction of all the road and rail arteries.

Moscow has always remained on the perimeter of Europe and its isolated position, supported by the descriptions of the winter in Russian novels, has led to the belief that it is much colder and more distant than it actually is. Its latitude of 57° is no further north than that of Copenhagen or Edinburgh and it is nearer to London than is Athens. The winter is certainly cold, with an average temperature of −10° C (14° F) in January, and odd days as cold as −30° C (−22° F), but the summer is usually hot with an average temperature in July of 19° C (66° F).

Various legends account for the name Moscow, but perhaps the most appealing explanation is that Moscow was founded by Japhet's sixth son, Mosokh. Mosokh's wife was called Kva and so the name Moskva was chosen. Mosokh and Kva had a son and daughter, whom they named Ya and Vuza. It is said that from these names the river Yauza, Moscow's second largest river, took its name.

Long ago Moscow was known as the sacred city of the Russians and the city of "white walls." In poetry and songs it was often referred to as "Matushka Moskva," Mother Moscow. During the last century it was sometimes referred to as "Brides' Fair" because of the society marriage market.

The official date for the founding of Moscow is accepted as 1147. It was in this year that Moscow was first mentioned in the Russian chronicles, when Prince Yuri Dolgoruky wrote to his friend, Prince Svyataslav, inviting him to Moscow to attend a banquet in honour of Prince Chernigov, saying, "Come to me, brother, in Moscow." 800 years later a statue was erected to Yuri Dolgoruky, whose name in Russian means "Yuri Longarm," and who was the Prince of Rostov-Suzdal and who founded Moscow as a southern border settlement. Prince Yuri, who undoubtedly played an important role in Russian history, had a certain amount of foreign blood, his mother being the daughter of the Swedish king, Ing. Prince Yuri Dolgoruky's Moscow estate consisted of a few wooden buildings and a church on a wooded hill at the confluence of the Moskva and Neglinnaya rivers, where the Borovitsky Gate of the Kremlin stands today.

A wooden fence was built around the settlement in 1146 but in 1238 the whole fortress was burned down by the Tatar hordes of Batu Khan. During the rule of the Golden Horde of the Tatars, Moscow actually grew in prosperity in spite of its vassal state.

The princes of Moscow acted as tax-collectors for the Tatars and even used Tatar soldiers in their campaigns against neighbouring principalities.

Ivan I, known as Ivan Kalita (Ivan Moneybag) for the way he accumulated treasure, became the first Grand Duke of Moscow in 1328. A few years earlier the Metropolitan of the Church had moved his seat to Moscow from the old church capital of Vladimir, which added to the already growing importance of Moscow. In 1395, when it seemed that nothing would halt Tamerlane's advance, the tsar commanded that the treasured icon of Our Lady of Vladimir be brought to Moscow. It had scarcely arrived when news was brought that Tamerlane had ordered a retreat, but the icon remained in the new capital. After the fall of Constantinople in 1453 a monk in Pskov wrote that "Two Romes have already fallen, but the third remains standing and a fourth there will not be," and Moscow became known as the Third Rome. This occurred during the reign of Ivan III (1462–1505), also known as Ivan the Great, who married Sophia, the niece of the last Byzantine emperor. Ivan thus considered himself the heir of the Byzantine emperors and adopted their arms of the double-headed eagle which remained the arms of the Russian state until 1917. During his reign the first stone and brick buildings of the Kremlin were built, including the walls and the cathedrals of the Assumption and Annunciation, which still stand today. They were built by foreign architects, mostly from northern Italy, who were all given the surname Friasine, meaning Franc, but with workmen and influences from the Russian towns of Vladimir, Pskov, and Novgorod. In this way the original form of Moscow architecture developed.

The prosperity of Moscow continued to grow but the city was periodically raided by the Tatars, who made their last attack in 1591 under Kara Girei. Territorial gains from nearby principalities, the final collapse of Novgorod in 1570, when Ivan the Terrible is said to have massacred 60,000 Novgorodians, and the opening of the trade route to Western Europe from the White Sea in the 16th century, all added to the importance of Moscow. In 1547, Ivan IV, known as "the Terrible" for his persecution of the "boyari" (barons), was crowned in Moscow with the royal diadem, and assumed the title of Tsar of all the Russias. During his reign the last of the other principalities fell and the kingdoms of Kazan and Astrakhan were conquered. The power of the tsar became absolute and Ivan the Terrible increased the crown lands by confiscation, as had Henry VIII of England.

The turn of the 17th century is known as the time of troubles in Russian history, but the growth of Moscow continued almost uninterrupted. When Ivan IV's son, Feodor I, died in 1598 he was succeeded by his brother-in-law, Boris Godunov, who died mysteriously in 1605. Boris Godunov had

MOSCOW

been opposed by two false Dmitris, both supported by the Poles, and both claiming to be Ivan's youngest son, who had died in 1591. At one point the Poles were threateningly near to the Kremlin but a meat merchant, Kosma Minim, and Prince Pozharsky, whose statue stands in Red Square, rose to the occasion. They and their followers, an army of volunteers, took comfort from the invincibility of the icon of Our Lady of Vladimir, which hung in the Kremlin's Uspensky Cathedral, and in 1612 the invaders were driven from the country. In the same year the first of the Romanovs, Mikhail, was elected tsar by the National Assembly in Moscow.

In 1712 St. Petersburg became the capital, but Moscow retained the status of Russia's second capital. Pushkin wrote:

And Moscow bowed to the new capital
As the Queen Dowager bows to the young
Queen . . .

Nevertheless, Moscow lost much of its former glory and an order of Peter the Great in 1714, which forbade any building from being built in stone except in St. Petersburg, reduced the status of Moscow still further. Even during this period, however, a few fine buildings were erected which, although of wood, were given the appearance of stone by stucco on the wood. Peter's successors mostly preferred the old capital and the reigns of Elizabeth (1741–61) and Catherine II (1762–96) were times of active building and many of the finest houses in Moscow appeared. The university, 2 large hospitals, and numerous mansions along the boulevards and in the fashionable district of the Arbat were built by the architects Bazhenov and Kazakov, and slightly later, by Ghilardi, Quarenghi, and Bovet. Several large estates, such as Arkhangelskoye, Kuskovo, and Ostankino, were built near Moscow, some by serf craftsmen.

The fire that ravaged Moscow for 3 days and nights in 1812 is well known. When the French troops under Napoleon were forced to evacuate the city, three quarters of the houses had been destroyed by fire but an order to blow up the Kremlin on departure was carried out only in part. Over a quarter of the 100,000 men who had entered Moscow with Napoleon had been taken prisoner or had died from hunger. The following year the reconstruction of the city began and was completed by a special commission for the reconstruction of Moscow set up by Alexander I in 1825. Most of the new building was in brick and whole new streets, such as Prechistenka and Vorovskovo, appeared. Several magnificent buildings were erected in Empire style, such as the manege and the Bolshoi Theatre by Bovet.

During the last half of the 19th century the population of Moscow grew rapidly, from 350,000 in 1863 to 1,039,000 in 1879. Moscow had been an important trade and craft centre since the middle ages and it was affected more than other Russian towns by industrialisation, specifically the industrial boom of the 1890s. By the eve of the Revolution Moscow was the financial, commercial, and industrial capital of Russia. The first Russian Revolution of 1905 was famous for its battles here, especially in the Presnaya region. It was of this that Vladimir Lenin wrote, "It trained the ranks of the fighters who were victorious in 1917."

By government decree on 16 November, 1917, Moscow was re-established as the capital of the country, and the government moved to the Kremlin in March 1918. It has been the seat of the government since then, except for the winter of 1941–42, when the government moved to Kuibyshev because of the threat of German invasion. Since the Revolution, reconstruction of the city has been carried out on a large scale. Many of the old buildings, including half of the churches, have been demolished and large new suburbs have been built. The first plan for the reconstruction of Moscow, drawn up in 1935, called for radical new building and alterations in the centre of the city. Tverskaya Street was widened and the Moskva Hotel and the Lenin Library built. During World War II the German army came dangerously close to Moscow but was stopped on the outskirts of the city in the winter of 1941–42. In 1965 Moscow was acclaimed a Hero City, sharing the honour with Odessa, Sevastopol, Volgograd, Kiev, Leningrad, Novorossisk, Kerch, and Brest Fortress. Moscow did not suffer much from the German air raids. Building work was held up by the war, but it later continued on an even grander scale. New avenues lined with vast buildings, such as Prospect Mira and Leninsky Prospect, were constructed and a few huge skyscrapers were built with a somewhat gothic appearance, such as the Ministry of Foreign Affairs and the new university.

The second plan, drawn up in 1951 and put into effect from 1954, called for fewer prestigious buildings with rich ornamentation and for more plain blocks of flats in an effort to solve the housing shortage. Building continues at an astounding rate, both in the suburbs and in the centre.

Moscow has developed outwards from the Kremlin in concentric circles that have been formed on the line of the old fortifications. The *Bulvarnoye Koltso* (boulevard ring) and *Sadovoye Koltso* (garden ring) serve as easily recognisable landmarks to the visitor. The Bulvarnoye Koltso, which has a line of trees and gardens down the middle, is the nearest to the centre and in fact forms a semi-circle on the northern banks of the river Moskva. The Sadovoye Koltso is a very wide busy street that intercepts all the main streets radiating from the centre.

The boundary of Moscow is marked by the circular bypass that lies at an average distance of 25 km (16 miles) from the city centre. This ring is 109 km (68 miles) long and crosses 14 main roads leading from the city. The territory within the bypass ring is 87,500 hectares (218,750 acres) and through it a number of new roads are being built to follow the concentric circle plan. The area of Greater Moscow (including the Green Belt) is 265,000 hectares (662,500 acres).

SEEING THE CITY

The centre of Moscow Red Square

(Krasnaya Ploschad) is the main square of the city, where demonstrations and military parades take place. Its name dates from the 17th century, the word "krasnaya" meaning "beautiful" in Old Russian. The square is 695 m (760 yds) long and 130 m (142 yds) wide. The best view of the square is obtained from the windows of the *Historical Museum*, which is on the northern side. To the south stands *St. Basil's Cathedral* with the *Minin and Pozharsky Monument* in front, to the west the *Kremlin* wall and the *Lenin Mausoleum*, and to the east *GUM*, pronounced "goom," the State Department Store.

Close to St. Basil's Cathedral is *Lobnoye Mesto*, a round platform of white stone that was constructed early in the 16th century. The Russian name for this platform, which is derived from the word for forehead, has come to mean "execution place." Executions were not carried out on the platform, however, but near it. The first historical mention of Lobnoye Mesto is when Ivan the Terrible used it to make a public confession of misdeeds to the assembled people. At that time it was a round brick structure with a roof supported by pillars and surrounded by a wooden fence. In 1786 it was faced with rough stone and the roof was removed. Until the reign of Peter the Great all edicts and decrees were read aloud here. The tsar used to present himself to his people here once a year and also presented the heir-apparant when the latter reached the age of 16. All religious processions stopped by the Lobnoye Mesto while the chief clergyman blessed the people from the platform.

The statue of Minin and Pozharsky (see above) by Ivan Martos in front of St. Basil's Cathedral was erected in 1818 from money collected by public donation. The 2 bas-relief ornaments on the pedestal of the monument depict episodes from the war of liberation. The monument originally stood in the middle of Red Square.

Two streets run out of Red Square to the east. They pass through the old part of Moscow called *Kitai-Gorod*. This name is thought to have been derived from the Mongol word "kitai," meaning fortification. In the 14th century Kitai-Gorod was surrounded by an earthen wall, but this was replaced in the 16th century by a fortified wall, remains of which can be seen from Teatralnaya Square, near the Metropole Hotel and from Kitaisky Proezd, which leads off Varvaka Street. In the 14th century Kitai Gorod was a busy district of small shops and markets, and later, banks and offices appeared here and the area became the financial and business centre of Moscow.

Nikolskaya Street runs from the north-east corner of Red Square into Kitai-Gorod. No. 9 in this street is the *Zaikono-Spassky (Behind-the-Icon-of-the-Redeemer) Monastery*, which was founded by Boris Godunov in 1600. It has been much altered and enlarged since then, but a few of the old chambers and the cathedral, which was built in 1661, are still standing. They can be seen from the courtyard of No. 7 in the same street. The Slavic-Greek-Latin Academy, the first higher-educational establishment in Russia, where Lomonosov, the famous 18th-century Russian scholar, studied, was housed here from its foundation in 1682 until 1814. No. 15, the *Institute of History and Archives*, was formerly the Synodal Printing Plant, which was built in 1814 by Bakarev. The facade is covered with intricate carvings in white stone and there is a sun dial above the portal. The Synodal Printing Plant was built on the site of the Tsar's Printer's Yard, the first printing plant in Russia, which was founded by Ivan Feodorov in 1563. The timber buildings were later destroyed by fire and only one now stands in the courtyard behind the institute.

Ilyinka Street runs out of Red Square at the other end of GUM and forms the main thoroughfare of Kitai-Gorod. Banks, offices and several ministries are situated here. Half way along the street on the right-hand side is the building of the former Moscow Stock Exchange, which was built in 1873–75 and which now houses the All-Union Chamber of Commerce.

Varvarka Street runs out of Red Square behind St. Basil's Cathedral, parallel to the 2 streets already mentioned. To the right is the large *Rossiya Hotel*, which was built by Chechulin and completed in 1967. It has accommodation for 6,000 and a number of restaurants, including one on the top floor with a very good view over the Kremlin. Beside the hotel stand a group of 16th- and 17th-century buildings of considerable historical and architectural worth. At the beginning of the street and at the top of the hill is *St. Barbara's Church*, built in 1514 by Alevisio Novi and rebuilt in 1796 by Kazakov. One of the oldest buildings here is known as the English hostelry. It was built in the 16th century by Russian craftsmen and in 1556 was granted by Ivan The Terrible to English merchants

to use as their Moscow base. Next comes the *Church of St. Maxim the Greek*, built in 1698 with its belfry added in 1829.

The *House of the Boyars Romanov* was built in 1565–67. This low house with thick walls and small windows was the birthplace of Mikhail Feodorovich Romanov, the first Romanov tsar, who is said to have been taught Greek and Latin by his English neighbours at an early age. In 1859 the house was reconstructed by Richter, who added stairways, galleries, and a small superstructure. The mansion now houses an exhibition of chattels of the 17th to 19th century. Behind stands the *Monastery of the Apparition*. The 5-domed cathedral was built in the late 17th century and the belfry, designed by Matvei Kazakov, was added in 1789. When the Romanov House was vacated by its owners, it was taken over for use as the residence of the abbot of the monastery. The cathedral with its magnificent accoustics is used occasionally now for concerts. At the bottom of the street, near Nogina Square, is *St. George's Church*, built in 1658, and now serving as an art exhibition hall. Down side of the Rossia Hotel, beside the river, is the 15th-century *Church of the Conception of St. Anne*. The *Church of All Saints* of Kulishki in Nogina Square was founded by Prince Dmitri Donskoy in 1380 to mark the victory over the Tatars at Kulikovo.

Revolution Square adjoins Red Square to the north. It is bounded by the Lenin Museum, a metro station, and the back of the Moskva Hotel. Adjoining Revolution Square is *Teatralnaya (Theatre) Square*. On the east side of Teatralnaya Square is the *Metropole Hotel*, which was built by Walcott in 1899–1903 in the fashionable art nouveau style of the period. It is decorated with a mural, "Dream Princess," which is a replica of the famous drawing by Vrubel of the same name. Above the second floor is a curious rebus inscription of intertwining letters that reads "The old story again—on completing a house you discover that you have learned something." The fountain in the centre of the square in front of the hotel was installed here in 1826–35 and is decorated with a sculptural group "Cupids at play" by Ivan Vitali. The other side of the square is surrounded by 3 theatres and a metro station.

To the north is the *Bolshoi Theatre*, built in 1824 by Bovet, to the east the *Maly Theatre* with a statue of the 19th-century Russian playwright Ostrovsky in front, and to the west the *Children's Theatre*. Facing the Bolshoi is a monument to Karl Marx by Kerbel unveiled in 1961.

Teatralny Proyezd runs downhill from Lubyanskaya Square to Teatralnaya Square. From there Okhotny Ryad (Hunters' Row) leads to Manezhnaya Square, and then Mokhovaya Street to the Lenin Library at the bottom of Vozdvizhenka Street. Passing Teatralnaya Square in this direction one sees the imposing building of the *Trade Unions House* on the right-hand side. It was built in 1784 for Prince Dolgorukov-Krymsky and later became the Nobles' Club. Inside it, the Hall of Columns, where concerts are now held, was at one time one of the largest and most fashionable ballrooms in Moscow. A little further down on the same side is the building of the *Council of Ministers*, which was built in 1932–35 by Langmann. Behind the building of the Council of Ministers is a small street, *Georgyevsky Pereulok*. It used to be one of the most fashionable residential streets in Moscow. No. 4 is a 16th-century mansion once belonging to the boyar Troyekurov and now housing musical archives. On the opposite side of Okhotny Ryad is the *Moskva Hotel*, which was built by Schusev in 1932–35. On the 15th floor is an open-air cafe, *Moscow Lights*, from which one can obtain a good view of the city. This part of the street was formerly a very busy market. On the right one passes the bottom of Tverskaya Street with the 22-storey *Intourist Hotel* dominating the scene. On the far side of Tverskaya Street, next to the *National Hotel*, is the head office of *Intourist*. It was built by Ivan Zholtovsky in 1934 in a style imitative of 16th-century Italian architecture and it once housed the American Embassy.

In front of the Intourist building is *Manege Square*. Before Mokhovaya Street was constructed in the 1930s this whole area was a mass of small shops and houses. On the far side of the square beneath the Kremlin wall is the *Alexandrovsky Garden*. The Neglinnaya river used to run here, forming a natural moat of which the stone bridge leading up to the *Trinity Tower* is a reminder. The garden was designed by Bovet in 1821–23 during the reign of Alexander I after whom it was named. The grotto "Ruins" near the *Middle Arsenal Tower* was also designed by Bovet. The *obelisk* beneath the wall was erected in 1913 in commemoration of the 300th anniversary of the House of Romanov (see p. 329). Near the Sobakin Tower is the *Grave of the Unknown Soldier*. The tomb, enclosed in red and black granite, was placed during the 25th anniversary of the Battle of Moscow (1941–42). The inscription reads: "Thy name is unknown, thine exploit immortal. To the fallen 1941–45." Beside the Intourist head office is the oldest building of the university (see p. 347). In the centre of the square is a small monument, which was erected in 1967 on the 50th anniversary of the revolution. The large building in the square is the *Manège*, which was built in 1817 by Augustin Betancourt and decorated by Bovet. When first built, it was considered an engineering feat because, despite its size of 167 × 47 m (183 × 16 yds), the roof was supported by the walls alone with no stanchions. Until the revolution it was an equestrian centre for officers of the Court. After the revolution it was used as a garage for government cars until it was restored in 1957. It is now the Central Exhibition Hall, where large art exhibitions are often held. Mokhovaya Street ends at the bottom of Vozdvizhenka Street with the Lenin Library and a metro station of that name on the corner. Between Mokhovaya Street and the Bulvarnoye Koltso are a number of small shopping streets which are an interesting contrast to the main streets such as Tver-

skaya Street and Vozdvizhenka Street. One of the busiest of these is *Kuznetsky Most (Blacksmith's Bridge)*. During the 14th and 15th centuries the blacksmiths from the Royal Arms Foundry lived here. Later aristocratic mansions were built here and when Catherine II (1762–96) issued an edict permitting trade outside the walls of Kitai-Gorod, Kuznetsky Most became a fashionable shopping street with a number of French shops.

Neglinnaya Street runs from Okhotny Ryad to the Bulvarnoye Koltso, intercepting Kuznetsky Most. It took its name from the Neglinnaya river, which was bricked over at the beginning of the 19th century and now runs under the street. No. 12, the State Bank of the USSR, was built in 1894 by Professor Bykovsky and rebuilt in 1930–31 by Zholtovsky.

The Bulvarnoye Koltso (Boulevard Ring)

The area between the Kremlin and present Boulevard Ring was known as the White Town during the 16th and 17th centuries. During the reign of Boris Godunov (1598–1605) this area was fortified with a brick wall and 28 towers and gates. Many of the squares that were made when the gates were removed still bear the names of the gates. The walls were demolished between 1750 and 1792 and the boulevards planted. The Boulevard Ring, although called a ring, does not in fact form a circle but ends on the northern bank of the Moskva.

Starting from the western end of the boulevard on the embankment, the ring leads to Kropotkinskaya Square. The Moscow *open-air swimming pool*, open all year, is on the right. On this site stood the *Cathedral of Our Saviour (Khram Spasitelya)*, which cost 14 million roubles to build during the last century. It was designed by the architect Konstantin Thon and was erected on the site of the Alexeevski Abbey in 1837–83 in commemoration of the liberation of Russia after the Napoleonic invasion.

From Kropotkinskaya Square, Gogolevsky (formerly Prechistensky—Immaculate Virgin) Boulevard leads up to Arbatskaya Square, where it crosses Novy Arbat Street. A monument to Gogol stands at the end of the boulevard. The small narrow streets to the left of the boulevard form the largest part of the old residential district of the nobles that remains. Sivtsev Vrazhek 40 was the 19th-century home of the writer, Sergei Aksakov; he was a friend of Gogol, who often visited him here. Many of the old houses in this area are now being demolished, but some fine examples of Russian architecture can be seen here as well as some old wooden houses. *The Praga Restaurant*, which stands at the end of Arbat Street, is famous for its small dome, said to be one of the finest in the city.

The next part of the ring is called Suvorovsky Boulevard after the Russian Field Marshal. No. 8 on the right-hand side is the *House of Journalists*, which was built in 1760. No. 7 on the opposite side is the house where Gogol died in 1852 and where he burned the second volume of his novel

"Dead Souls" 2 days before his death. A monument to the author by Nikolai Andreyev stands in the courtyard. No. 12a, known as *Lunin House*, was built in 1818–23 by Dementy Ghilardi in Russian empire style. The facade of the house is covered with inset sculptures of musical instruments in honour of the owner's wife, who was a well-known singer.

The junction with Herzen Street at the end of Suvorovsky Boulevard is known as *Nikitskie Vorota (gates)* after the old gate and tower that once stood here. On the corner to the right is the building of the Soviet news agency, TASS. The next section of the boulevard ring, Tverskoi Boulevard, was once the most-fashionable promenade in Moscow and is mentioned in a number of 19th-century Russian novels, including Tolstoy's "Anna Karenina." At the beginning of the boulevard is a *monument* to the botanist Timiryazev, showing him wearing a Cambridge University gown; the university awarded him an honorary doctorate. No. 25, built at the beginning of the 19th century, was the birth-place of Alexander Herzen, the revolutionary philosopher. A memorial stands in front of the house.

Tverskoi Boulevard leads to Pushkinskaya Square, where it crosses Tverskaya Street, so called because it leads to the town of Tver. A *monument to Pushkin*, erected in 1880, stands in the centre of the square. Admirers still bring tributes here on the anniversaries of the poet's birth and death, fulfilling his prophesy that:

My verses will be sung throughout all Russia's vastness,
My ashes will outlive and know no pale decay . . .

Behind the *Rossiya Cinema* on the far side of the square, Chekhov Street is to the left and Pushkin Street to the right. On the left of the square are the offices of the newspaper "Izvestia," which were designed in 1927 by Barkhin.

Strastnoi Boulevard starts behind the cinema and leads down to *Petrovskie Vorota (Gates)*, from where Petrovka Street on the right runs down to the Bolshoi Theatre. No. 25, built by Matvei Kazakov in the 1790s, is a good example of Russian classical architecture. Near the boulevard is the former *Petrovsky Abbey*, with a cathedral built in 1691. No. 15/29 Strastnoi Boulevard, now a hospital, is known as the *Gagarin House*. It was built by Matvei Kazakov and has the largest 12-column portico in Moscow. It was once the home of the tsar's chamberlain and in 1802–12 housed the English Club. It was damaged considerably during Napoleon's invasion but was later restored and slightly altered by Bovet. To the left of Strastnoi Boulevard is Karetnyi Ryad (Coachbuilder's Row) where the small but popular *Hermitage Garden* is situated.

The next square, Trubnaya Square, was formerly renowned for its bird market, which was transferred to B. Kalitnikovskaya Street. The Neglinnaya flows beneath the square, and the street to the right bears its name. Down this street on the right-hand side is the popular *Uzbekistan Restaurant*, which in summer has tables out in the garden.

Rozhdestvensky (Nativity) Boulevard, the steep hill which forms the next part of the boulevard ring, was once a real problem for horse-drawn trams. The walls of the old convent, founded in the 14th century, from which this part of the boulevard ring takes its name, can be seen on the right.

At Sretenskie Vorota the boulevard ring is crossed by *Sretenka Street*, another busy shopping street. The gardens in this part of the boulevard are always crowded with children and old people. In winter there is skating here and in summer it becomes an informal open-air club for playing chess and dominoes.

Myasnitskaya Street crosses the next square. To the right is the *Central Post Office* and, almost opposite, an unusual *tea and coffee shop*, built in 1890 in Chinese style. Nearby in Telegrafnyi Pereulok is the tower of the *Church of the Archangel Gabriel*. It was built in 1704–07 by Ivan Zarudnyi at the request of Alexander Menshikov, a favourite of Peter the Great and it has always been known as the *Menshikov Tower* after him. It is said that Menshikov ordered a tower to be built that would be taller than the Bell Tower of Ivan the Great in the Kremlin. It was originally topped with a flying archangel, but this was destroyed by lightning in 1723. A new vault and a cupola, topped this time with a cross, were added later and for a long time it was the second-tallest building in Moscow.

At the beginning of the next section of the boulevard ring, *Chistoprudnyi (clear pond) Boulevard*, is a *monument* to the writer Griboyedov. This is the widest part of the boulevard ring and has a *restaurant* and a *rectangular pond*.

From Pokrovskiye Vorota, Maroseika Street runs down on the right to *Staraya Ploschad (Old Square)*. In Chernyshevsky Street on the left of the boulevard ring is a rococo building erected in 1766, known as the *Chest-of-Drawers house* because of its abundant decoration.

The wide space along the boulevard was formerly a parade ground in front of the *Pokrovski Barracks*, which were built in the 1830s.

The last section of the boulevard ring, the *Yauzsky Boulevard*, is named after the river Yauza. The 22-storey block of flats at the end of the boulevard was built in 1953. The 32-storey tower is 173 m (568 ft) high.

One can return to the beginning of the boulevard ring near the Moscow swimming pool by going along the embankment of the Moskva. Opposite the Kremlin is a well-preserved merchant's house with iron gates that now houses the *British Embassy*. One of the best views of the Kremlin is from the *Bolshoi Kammeny (great stone) Bridge* that crosses the river at the far end of the Kremlin wall.

The Sadovoye Koltso (Garden Ring)

This, Moscow's widest street, was formed along the line of the old earthen wall that was pulled down at the beginning of the 19th century. The gardens in front of the small houses along the street gave it its name, the Russian word "sad" meaning garden. Trees were planted along the middle of the street in the last century, but these were removed and the gardens destroyed in the 1930s when the street was widened. The Sadovoye Ring forms an almost perfect circle with the *Bell Tower of Ivan the Great* as the central point. It is roughly 16 km (10 miles) in circumference.

Crossing the river by *Krymski Bridge*, a 700-m (766-yd) suspension bridge and one of the best designed bridges in Moscow, the Sadovoye Ring runs (going in a clockwise direction) under an overpass towards Zubovskaya Square. To the left is the beginning of Komsomolsky Prospect and to the right Ostozhenka Street that leads towards the Kremlin. The long white-washed buildings on the right were constructed by Stasov in 1832–35 as a food depot and, in spite of their utilitarian purpose, are among the finest examples of Russian classical architecture standing today. Next to them is the tall building of IAN (*Novosty Information Agency*) and the *Press Centre* that still cannot overshadow their beauty. The road to the left from Zubovskaya Square leads to Novodevichy Convent. To the right is *Prechistenka Street* with many nobles' houses of the last century still standing. The area between this part of the Sadovoye Ring and the inner Boulevard Ring was the old aristocratic district of Moscow, and the narrow winding streets with their quiet mansions retain the atmosphere of the old city.

Further along the Sadovoye Ring on the right is a green-painted house, *No. 18*. This was once the home of the millionaire Morozov. The 27-storey building on the right houses the *Ministries of Foreign Trade and Foreign Affairs*. It was designed by Gelfreikh and Minkus in 1951 and is 171 m (561 ft) high. The square in front is *Smolenskaya (formerly Sennaya—hay) Square*. To the right is *Arbat Street*, now often known as the Old Arbat, which is one of the busiest shopping streets in Moscow and now a pedestrian precinct. Much restoration work has been done to give it a 19th-century look. Pushkin spent several months living at No. 53 in 1831, and it is now a museum. Street musicians perform here while artists sell their works and passersby can sit for a portrait. Shops include a videotheque, an antique shop selling porcelain and crystal, and, on the left side at the far end, a shop with posters.

The Sadovoye Ring then passes under Novy Arbat Street. The large building on the left after the underpass is the *American Embassy*. The new Embassy building is some distance behind, nearer the river and not far from the MOES building. Here, too, is Moscow's unique *Humpbacked Bridge (Gorbaty Most)*, built in 1795 and restored in the 1980s. A monument near it is dedicated to the revolutionaries of 1905. Back on Sadovaya Ring,

next door to the old building of the American Embassy is the house where the famous singer Fyodor Chaliapin lived. The 22-storey block of flats on the same side was built by Posokhin and Mndoyants in 1954. It is 160 m (525 ft) high, comprises of 452 flats, and has a group of food shops on the ground floor. The square in front of the skyscraper is called *Vosstaniya (insurrection) Square* because of the heavy fighting that took place here during the revolutions of 1905 and 1917. It was formerly called Kudrinskaya Square after the village of Kudrino, which stood here in the 14th–17th centuries. The next section of the Ring still bears this name.

To the right of Sadovoye Ring is *Vorovskovo Street*, once one of the most fashionable streets in Moscow. At one time no shops were allowed in this part of the city, and even today it is relatively quiet. No. 52 Vorovskovo Street once belonged to Countess Sollogub and Leo Tolstoy is said to have based his description of the Rostovs' Moscow home in "War and Peace" upon it. It now houses the *Union of Soviet Writers* and a *monument to Tolstoy* stands in the courtyard. No. 25 was built by Ivan Ghilardi in the 1830s and now houses the *Maxim Gorky Museum*. A *monument* to the writer by Vera Mukhina stands in front of the building.

Leading down the hill on the far side of the skyscraper in Vosstaniya Square is *Barrikadnaya Street*, which takes its name from the barricades erected here during the 1905 revolution. On the right is a 2-storey building with a portico and classical colonnade. It was built in 1775 by Gigliardi, restored by his son after the fire of 1812, used as an almshouse for military officers and the widows and children of government officials and is still known as the *Widow's House*. Today it houses a medical institute.

On the right-hand side of the Sadovoye Ring past Vosstaniya Square is a small red house which is easily noticeable among the tall blocks. It was the home of Anton Chekhov during the 1880s and is now the *Chekhov Museum*. On the opposite side of the street is the *planetarium* with instruments on the grounds to observe planets and stars. *No. 15* is a mansion with a 4-columned portico, and is one of the few wooden buildings to have survived the fire of 1812. At one time No. 15 belonged to Princess Volkonskaya. On the left of Sadovoye Ring near the underpass and under Mayakovskaya Square is the *Peking Hotel*, easily recognised by its Chinese-style writing. On the opposite side is the *Satire Theatre* and the *Tchaikovsky Concert Hall*. In the middle of the square is a *statue* of the poet and playwright Vladimir Mayakovsky by Alexander Kibalnikov.

After the underpass, the Sadovoye Ring runs down to *Samotechnaya Square*. To the left is the Obraztsov Puppet Theatre. To the right is Tsvetnoi (flower) Boulevard, once a flower market, but today the location of the *circus* and *central market*. The boulevard to the left of the Sadovoye Ring leads to the *Soviet Army Theatre & Museum* located in a vast park. To the right stretches the modern *Olym-*

pisky Prospect, parallel to Prospect Mira, with the Olympic sports complex at the beginning of it. There is a stadium withi 45,000 seats, a swimming pool and the Olympic Penta Hotel. *Troitsy (Trinity) Church* which stands nearby was built at the beginning of the 17th century.

The next square on the Sadovoye Ring is *Sukharevskaya Square*. To the left Prospect Mira leads to the *Economic Achievements Exhibition* and *Ostankino Palace*. To the right is *Sretenka Street*, one of the oldest shopping streets. Further along the Sadovoye Ring on the left is an impressive hospital building. It was begun in 1794 by Nazarov for Count Sheremetiev, but when his wife died in 1803, he decided to put the building to public use. After alterations carried out under Quarenghi, it opened as a guest house in 1807 and later became a hospital. On the same side is a Corbusier–style building designed by the Russian architect Schusev in 1933 that now houses the *Department of Agriculture (Gosagroprom)*. To the right is Myasnitskaya Street with a genuine Le Corbusier building, the *Central Statistical Administration of the USSR*. It was built from 1929–36 with the assistance of the Russian architect Kolly, and in the original design had no ground floor, the space between the supporting piers being used for cars. A ground floor was added at a later date. There are few houses of interest in this street, the most notable being No. 42, which was designed by Matvei Kazakov. The modernistic Academician Sakharov Prospect, that crosses Sadovaya Ring was laid out at the beginning of the 1980s.

The next square on the Sadovoye Ring is *Lermontov Square*, which is still known by its old name of *Krasnye Vorota (Red Gate)*, and that is the name of the Metro station under the square. The monument to poet Mikhail Lermontov was unveiled in 1965. The 24-storey office block was built in 1952 by Dushkin and Mezentsev and is 133 m (436 ft) high. The road to the left leads through Komsomolskaya Square to *Sokolniki park*. The *Leningradskaya Hotel*, a 26-storey skyscraper 136 m (446 ft) high that stands in Komsomolskaya Square was built in 1953 by Polyakov and Boretsky. The department store on the square is the largest in Moscow. Here also are the 3 busiest railway stations in Moscow: Leningradsky, Yaroslavsky, and Kazansky. It is from Yaroslavsky Station that trains leave for Siberia and Vladivostok.

From *Lermontov Square* the Sadovoye Ring turns to the right towards Kursk Station. This part of the Ring is named Zemlyanoy Val Street and No. 47 was once Tchaikovsky's home. On the left is the *Naidyonov Estate*, a beautiful mansion built by Ghilardi in 1829–31 with extensive grounds leading down to the Yauza. It is now a sanatorium.

The Sadovoye Ring then crosses the Yauza, passes through a tunnel, over the Moskva and on through a district where petty merchants used to live.

The road going out to the left from Dobryninskaya Square, the next square on the Ring, is the *Varshavskoye Chaussee* that leads to the south, past the estates of Tsaritsino and Kolomenskoye.

At the next square on the Ring, *Oktyabrskaya Square*, the Ring itself goes through an underpass. On the square is the *Warsaw Hotel*, 2 hotels belonging to the *Academy of Sciences* and a number of government buildings. The grandiose *statue* of Lenin by Lev Kerbel was installed in 1986. On the left, after the underpass, is an impressive arch, the entrance to *Gorky Park*, which has, among other forms of entertainment, a *boating pond* and a *fun fair*. The Sadovoye Ring then crosses the Moskva again at Krymsky Bridge.

The Main Streets of Moscow

A brief description of the main streets, radiating from the centre of Moscow.

Tverskaya Street is considered by many to be the main street of Moscow and has a number of shops and other buildings that may be useful to the visitor. There are 5 *metro stations* on Tverskaya Street: Okhotny Ryad station at the bottom of Tverskaya Street, opposite the Kremlin; Mayakovsky Station at Mayakovsky Square, where Tverskaya Street crosses the Sadovoye Ring; Pushkinskaya and Tverskaya, close to the Izvestia newspaper building; and Byelorusskaya station at the end of 1-Tverskaya-Yamskaya Street.

Tverskaya Street was so called because it was the road that led to Tver on its way to St. Petersburg. It was reconstructed in the 1930s and now has little in common with the original street. Very few of the old buildings remained after reconstruction, during which the street was straightened and considerably widened to its present width of 40 m/yds.

On the left-hand side at the bottom of Tverskaya Street is the *National Hotel* and beside it the *Intourist Hotel* that was opened in 1970. The *café* of the National Hotel, which is situated on the ground floor and is approached from the Tverskaya Street entrance, is recommended to those wishing faster service than in a restaurant. The foreign currency cafeteria on the first floor of the Intourist hotel is even quicker. Slightly further up Tverskaya Street on the left is the *Central Telegraph Office*, designed by Rerberg in 1927. International telephone calls can be made from the office, which is entered from the side street. Opposite is *Proyezd Khudozhestvenny Teatra* with the *Moscow Arts Theatre* on the left.

Some of the small streets now join Tverskaya Street through arches in the large buildings that line it on both sides. On Sovietskaya Square is a *monument* to Yuri Dolgoruki, founder of Moscow. The *Aragvi Restaurant*, the popular Georgian restaurant, is on the right-hand side of the square as one faces the monument. The *City Hall* on the other side of Tverskaya Street was built in 1782 by Matvei Kazakov for the Governor-General of Moscow. In 1946, under the direction of architect Chechulin, the main edifice was moved back 11 m (12 yds) and 2 more storeys were added.

Further up Tverskaya Street on the right is the best *bakery* in Moscow, built in 1912, and formerly known as Philippov's. No. 14 on the same side is *Gastronom No. 1*, probably the only shop in Moscow that is still unofficially known by the name of its former owner, Yeliseyevsky. Its ornate decorations deserve a visit.

Tverskaya Street crosses the Boulevard Ring at Pushkinskaya Square. The garden with the *statue of Pushkin* was laid out on the site of the former Strastnoi Abbey, which was built in the 17th century and demolished at the end of the last century. At the end of the square is the *Rossiya Cinema* which has a seating capacity of 2,500 and is one of the largest cinemas in the country. Nearby on Chekhov Street to the left of the Rossiya Cinema is the *Church of the Nativity* which was built in the 17th century near the walls of Belyi Gorod (White Town). These old walls ran along the line of the present Boulevard Ring.

When Pushkin described Tatiana's arrival in Moscow in his poem "Eugene Onegin," he mentioned the lions on either side of the gates of No. 21 Tverskaya Street. The house was badly damaged during the 1812 fire and was then rebuilt in classical style by Adam Menelaws. It became the aristocratic English Club and has, since 1926, housed the Museum of the Revolution.

Mayakovsky Square with a *statue* of the poet, lies where Tverskaya Street crosses the Sadovoye Ring. This square contains the *Tchaikovsky Concert Hall* built in 1940 by Chechulin and Orlov.

At the end of 1-Tverskaya-Yamskaya Street in Byelorusskaya Square is a *monument* to the writer and playwright, Gorky, unveiled in 1951. On the left is the Byelorusski Station, the terminus for trains from Western Europe, which opened in 1870. Beyond the bridge is the beginning of Leningradsky Prospect.

Leningradsky Prospect, which starts from Byelorusski station, is the road leading to Sheremetievo international airport and towards Leningrad. Many new buildings were erected before World War II when it was developed as a residential area.

The *Sovietskaya Hotel & Restaurant* on the right was once known as Yar and was the best restaurant outside the city. It has now been partly reconstructed. The road to the left almost opposite the hotel leads to the race-course.

Further on is the *Dynamo Stadium*, which was built in the park of the Petrovsky Palace. The *Petrovsky Palace*, which looks like a battlemented fortress, was built in 1775–82 by Matvei Kazakov, and is one of the few remaining examples of Russian-gothic architecture. The imperial family often used it as the last staging point on their way to Moscow from St. Petersburg, and Napoleon stayed here for a few days after abandoning the Kremlin during the fire of 1812. It now houses the *Zhukovsky Air Force Academy*.

Further along on the left side of the Prospect is the *Central Air Terminal* and *Aeroflot Hotel*.

Near Sokol metro station is *All Saints' Church*, which was built in 1736, and is open for services.

The road to Leningrad bears right further on while the road through the underpass leads to Arkhangelskoye. Near the underpass is a 25-storey skyscraper, the offices of *Gidroproekt*, the organisation responsible for designing hydropower stations.

The Leningrad road now has the name Leningradskoye Chaussee and passes through the new residential area of Khimki-Khovrino. To the left is the Northern River Port from which one can take boat trips down the Moscow canal and the river Moskva.

Before one reaches Sheremetievo airport there is an unusual *monument* on the left of the road in the form of three crosses, resembling part of an anti-tank barricade. This is the spot the German army reached in World War II, when approaching Moscow.

Herzen Street runs from the Manège near the Kremlin, between the 2 old buildings of the university, to the Sadovoye Ring; it was formerly known as Bolshaya Nikitskaya. On the left is the *Moscow Conservatoire*, which was founded by Nikolai Rubinstein in 1866. The present building was erected in 1901 by Zagorsky. The *statue of Tchaikovsky* among the birch trees in front of the Conservatoire was designed by Vera Mukhina and erected in 1954. On the right-hand side of Herzen Street on Nikitskaya Square is the *Church of the Ascension*, built in the 1820s by Kazakov; the poet Alexander Pushkin was married here to Natalia Goncharova in 1831. In the small garden behind the church is a statue of the writer Alexei Tolstoy.

Vozdvizhenka Street runs from the Lenin Library, near the Trinity Tower of the Kremlin, westwards to the river Moskva, becoming Novy Arbat Street before leading into Kutuzovsky Prospect. A monument to Mikhail Kalinin (1875–1946), a prominent Soviet statesman, is on the right side. Vozdvizhenka Street still contains a few 18th century buildings. No. 5 on the left is known as *Golitsyn House;* it was mostly built in the 18th century but contains an older part dating from the reign of Ivan the Terrible. No. 7 is the former *Monastery of the Holy Cross.* No. 16 on the other side is an unusual building which stands out clearly on account of its Moorish style. It once belonged to the textile-king Morozov who is said to have wanted an ancient Spanish castle and who sent the architect, Mazarin, to Spain for ideas. Since 1959 it has been the *House of Friendship* where delegations from foreign Friendship Societies are entertained.

Arbat Square divides Vozdvizhenka Street from Novy Arbat Street. This was reconstructed in the 1960s when an underpass was built and a number of buildings demolished. Arbat is the old Tatar name for this area and is derived from the Eastern word "arbad" which means "beyond the city walls." When the walls of Byely Gorod (white town) were built, the name of Arbat was moved to the street running down to the left of the Praga Restaurant that still bears this name, and is now a popular pedestrian precinct.

On the left of Novy Arbat Street are four 25-storey office blocks with shops in front. The first shop is the largest *food store* in Moscow. Further along on the left side is a large *gift shop* and at the very end, the *Arbat Restaurant* which can seat 2,000. There are a number of shops on the right side of the street as well, including a very large *bookshop (Dom Knigi)*, which sells posters and post-cards on the first floor. Further along is a record shop and on the same side the *October Cinema*, one of the largest cinemas in Moscow, with a seating capacity of 3,000 in the 2 auditoriums. There are also a number of *cafés* on both sides of the street. Novy Arbat Street passes over the Sadovoye Ring and down to the Moskva. On the right are the headquarters of MOES, International Organisation of Economic Cooperation. The 30-storey building is constructed with materials from all the participating countries. A bit further to the right is a white building with a clock. It houses the government of the Russian Federation—the largest Union Republic of the USSR. Still farther to the right down the river are the grey buildings of Sovincentre built for the Moscow foreign business community. There are shops and restaurants that ept only foreign currency. To get there one should drive along the embankment and turn right.

Kutuzovsky Prospect starts from Kalinin Bridge at the end of Novy Arbat Street. The Prospect is named after the famous Russian field marshal who conducted the campaign against Napoleon.

On the right is the *Ukraina Hotel*, which has 1,025 rooms and is 32 storeys high. In the garden in front of the hotel is a *monument* to the Ukrainian poet Taras Shevchenko (1814–61).

New blocks of flats have replaced the old suburbs of Dorogomilovo. On the right side of the street is a *large shop*, *Malysh*, selling children's clothes, and on the left *two gift shops*, one dealing only in foreign currency. The part of the street by the underpass was mostly built before World War II. In Bolshaya Dorogomilovskaya Street, very close to the junction with Kutuzovsky Prospect by the underpass, is a food store accepting foreign currency only.

Where Kutuzovsky Prospect joins Bolshaya Dorogomilovskaya there is an *obelisk* dedicated to the 30th anniversary of the victory over Nazi Germany and the awarding of the city of Moscow the honorary title of Hero-City.

At the end of Kutuzovsky Prospect is the *Triumphal Arch* built in 1827–34 in celebration of the Russian victory in the 1812 war. It stood first at the end of 1-Tverskaya-Yamskaya Street, was demolished and eventually rebuilt here. (In fact it was down Kutuzovsky Prospect, then Smolensk Road, that Napoleon marched into Moscow and many people thought the old site, on the road along which the victorious Russian soldiers returned to Moscow, a more suitable one for the statue.) Beside the arch is the *Battle of Borodino Museum*, which was built in 1962 to display canvases of the battle painted by Roubaud (1856–1912). Nearby is Kutuzov's Hut Museum. It is situated in the peasant house where Kutuzov held the council of war at which he ordered the Russian troops to retreat from Moscow. On Poklonnaya Gora, the hill to the left

of the arch, is the Victory Memorial complex, dedicated to the victory in the 1941–45 war against Nazi Germany. The money for it was donated by private citizens, trade unions, and various other organisations.

To the right of Kutuzovsky Prospect is Fili-Mazilovo, a new residential district which has one important architectural monument, the *Church of the Intercession*. This church was built in 1693–94 by Lev Naryshkin, uncle of Peter the Great on his mother's side, and is a fine example of what is known as Naryshkin or Russian baroque.

Peter the Great is said to have visited the church a number of times and one of the icons reproduces his portrait as a young man.

Kutuzovsky Prospect eventually leads into the Moscow-Minsk road. The *Mozhaisky Motel and camping site* are situated on the corner where it crosses the circular bypass. Here also is the Mozhaisky Hotel that has a bar where foreign currency is accepted.

Volkhonka Street leads south-west from the centre, starting opposite the Borovitsky Tower of the Kremlin. It contains several old buildings, but none of particular merit. On the right is the *Pushkin Fine Arts Museum*, which was built in 1912 as a museum of plaster models and became the Museum of Fine Arts in 1924. Volkhonka Street ends in Kropotkinskaya Square with the *statue* of Engels at the far end. To the right and left is the Boulevard Ring and opposite, Prechistenka and Ostozhenka streets.

Prechistenka Street to the right was once a very fashionable street lined with aristocratic mansions, many of which are museums today. No. 12 on the right was built in 1814 by Afanasy Grigoryev in Empire style. It now houses the *Pushkin Museum*, not to be confused with the Pushkin Fine Arts Museum on Volkhonka Street which is also often called the Pushkin Museum. No. 11, almost opposite, was designed by the same architect and now houses the *Leo Tolstoy Museum*. No. 17 was the home of the poet Denis Davydov and No. 19 was built by Matvei Kazakov in 1790 for Prince Dolgoruky. It was badly damaged during the fire of 1812 and later restored. No. 21, which now belongs to the *Academy of Arts*, is a good example of early 19th-century Russian architecture. No. 22 further down on the right was built by Matvei Kazakov in the late 18th century and as the home of General Alexei Yermolov, active in the 1812 War, and later responsible for the construction of the Georgian Military Highway. It later became a police station where Alexander Herzen was held in 1834.

Ostozhenka Street passes overe the Sadovoye Ring into Komsomolsky Prospect. This in turn leads out to the new university building and the south-west residential areas. On the right is the brightly painted *Church of St. Nicholas*, built in 1682. On the same side are military barracks built from 1807–09. On the right before the bridge over the Moskva is a fair selling a wide variety of goods. The fair is especially crowded in the summer.

To the right of the bridge is the *Lenin Stadium*

where Moscow's main sporting events are held. In winter the tennis courts become popular skating rinks where skates can be rented. The bridge over the river is on 2 levels, the upper level for cars and the lower for the metro line. The *metro station*, Leninskiye Gory (Lenin Hills), is on the bridge itself and has glass walls overlooking the river. The area beyond the bridge is known as *Lenin (formerly Sparrow) Hills*. The best view of Moscow on a fine day is from the lookout point in front of the university. People also gather here on national festivals to watch firework displays over the city. There is a very steep ski jump down to the river where competitions are held in winter. Nearby is the small *Church of the Trinity*, built in 1811, which is open for services.

Beyond the river, Komsomolsky Prospect leads into *Prospect Vernadskovo*, named after the famous Russian scientist, academician Vladimir Vernadsky (1863–1945), mineralogist and geo-chemist. On the left is the new circus building which seats 3,000 and a Children's Music Theatre.

Leninsky Prospect, which leads out of Oktyabrskaya Square on the Sadovoye Ring, follows part of the old road to Kaluga. The *Kaluga Gate*, which stood on the site of the present square, was an important entrance in the earthen wall and the ambassadorial court of the Crimean Khan was situated here. Many armies retreated along this road, including that of Khan Kazy-Girei in 1591, the Polish interventionists in 1612, and the army of Napoleon in 1812.

At the beginning of Leninsky Prospect on the right-hand side are the buildings of the *Mining, Steel*, and *Oil Institutes*. On the left is the Children's Library. No. 8 is the Town Hospital that was built by Bovet in 1828–32. No. 10 is the former Prince Golitsyn hospital, designed by Kazakov in 1796–1802.

Beyond the hospital on the right is a side entrance to Gorky Park through the *Neskuchny Sad* that is now part of the main park. Neskuchny Sad, meaning "not boring" garden, was originally a botanical garden containing little-known foreign plants in the grounds of the Alexandrovsky Palace. The palace was first built in 1756 for the factory- and mine-owner Demidov. In 1830 the palace passed into the possession of Nicholas I. The sculptures "Seasons of the Year" on the gates are by Ivan Vitali. The palace park stretches down to the river and is one of the most pleasant spots in Moscow. The palace is now used by the *Academy of Sciences*, and this street is popularly known as the Prospect of Science because so many research institutes are located here.

The next turn to the left off Leninsky Prospect leads to Donskoi monastery.

A little further on, the older part of Leninsky Prospect ends at the crescent that was designed by Arkin. In 1940 this marked the city limits. The area beyond the site of the old Kaluga turnpike has been renamed *Gagarin Square* after the first Soviet cosmonaut and there is a large statue by Bondarenko to his memory.

The road to the right from the square leads to the university and the south-west part of the city. To the left of this road is the *Young Pioneers' Palace*, which stands on 54 hectares (135 acres) and which, amongst other amenities, has an observatory, auditoriums, a library, and various sports facilities.

A number of large shops and hotels have been built on the new part of Leninsky Prospect. Further down the Prospect are the hostels of the *Patrice Lumumba Friendship University* for foreign students. Further on, Leninsky Prospect runs into Kievskoye Chaussee that leads to Vnukovo airport.

Prospect Mira, which starts from the Sadovoye Ring at Kolkhoznaya Square, was once inhabited by middle-class merchants. It still has some old buildings but they are overshadowed by the huge apartment blocks. Prospect Mira follows the line of the old road from Kiev to Rostov Veliki and Suzdal.

Two houses of interest are *No. 14*, built at the end of the 18th century, and *No. 16*, built by Bazhenov in the 1770s. At *No. 28* is the oldest *Botanical Garden* in Moscow. Once known as the Apothecary's Garden, it was transferred here in 1706 by order of Peter I from its former site beside the Kremlin wall.

On the left side of Prospect Mira is the *Church of the Metropolitan Philip* that was built by Kazakov in 1777–88 in baroque style. Beyond the church is the Olympic sports complex.

Riga railway station, designed by Diderix in 1899, once marked the end of the city. Now another ring road cuts through in front of it, linking Leningradsky Prospect to Sokolniki. The whole region beyond the bridge was much altered during the late 1930s when the Agricultural Exhibition, now known as the *Exhibition of Economic Achievements*, was laid out. Since 1964 the soaring space-rocket monument by the main entrance to the exhibition has formed a landmark that is seen from far along the street. It stands on top of the *Memorial Museum of Cosmonautics* and nearby is an avenue lined with busts of the Soviet astronauts. The semicircular building to the right is the French-built *Cosmos Hotel*.

The turn to the left as one approaches the exhibition leads to Ostankino and the *television centre*; the tower is 537 m (1,762 ft) high. When gale force winds blow, it sways as much as 42 m (138 ft). At a level of 328 m (1,076 ft) is the revolving *Seventh Heaven Restaurant*.

To the right of Prospect Mira one can see an 18th-century *aqueduct* and *Tikhvinskaya Church*. Past the exhibition the Prospect becomes Yaroslavskloye Chaussee, which leads to Zagorsk and the town of Yaroslavl, on the Volga.

SEEING THE SIGHTS

The Kremlin

Before visiting the Kremlin, it is advisable to check the opening hours of the Armoury Museum at the

Intourist office. The cathedrals are open 10–6; closed Thurs.

Kremlin is a translation of the Russian word "kreml" or "kremnik," which means fortress. There are kremlins in a number of old Russian towns but none so well known as the Moscow Kremlin, which is often used as a synonym for the Soviet state and government.

The Kremlin stands on an irregular triangle of ground covering 28 hectares (69 acres) above the river Moskva. From the Kremlin an advancing enemy could be seen and a bell would be rung to warn those outside the walls of the fortress to seek protection inside. It used to be surrounded by water: the river Moskva on the south, the Neglinnaya (now bricked in) on the south-west, and a deep moat that was dug in the early 16th century along the east wall. The main entrances to the Kremlin, the Spassky, Nikolsky, Trinity, and Borovitsky gates, were all protected by drawbridges on the far side of which were portcullises.

The first wooden walls around the Kremlin were built in the 12th century under Prince Yuri Dolgoruky, the founder of Moscow.

At that time it was a much smaller fortress at the confluence of the rivers Moskva and Neglinnaya. In the 14th century, during the reign of Prince Ivan Kalita, the area of the Kremlin was considerably enlarged and surrounded by a strong oaken fence. During Ivan Kalita's time the first 2 stone buildings were erected—the *Cathedral of the Assumption (Uspensky Sobor)* and the *Cathedral of Archangel Michael (Arkhangelsky Sobor)*.

In 1367 the wooden fence was replaced by white limestone walls, which protected the Kremlin from the fires that constantly ravaged Moscow. But these walls soon crumbled and were replaced at the end of the 15th century with the battlemented brick walls that still stand. The circumference of the walls is over 2 km (1 mile) and in some places they are as high as 19 m (62 ft). They are from 3.6 to 4 m (12 to 13 ft) thick and are reinforced with 20 towers, 5 of which are also gates to the fortress. The towers were originally surmounted by battlements and each tower contained a firing platform. A platform for bowmen runs along the inside of the walls. The timber roofing that used to cover the platform was burnt down in the 18th century.

In the following description, those towers that since 1937 have been decorated with illuminated red stars in place of the tsarist double-headed eagle are marked with an asterisk*. The main gate to the Kremlin is that opposite St. Basil's Cathedral on Red Square. It is known as the *Spassky (Redeemer's) Gate** and was built in 1491 by Pietro Antonio Solario of Milan. The entrance is by a drawbridge over the moat. In 1625 the Scottish architect Christopher Galloway added the Gothic tower and steeple, and a clock was also installed. The present clock dates from 1851 and was made by the Butenop brothers. The chime of the largest bell in the tower clock is broadcast on Moscow Radio, like the broadcast of Big Ben on the BBC. The bell, which weighs over 2 tons, was cast in 1769 by Semyon

Mozhukin. Before the revolution there was an icon of the Redeemer above the gate, hence its name, and it was a strictly observed custom that anyone entering the Kremlin by this gate should bare their heads and enter on foot.

The next large tower (moving in an anti-clockwise direction) is the *Nikolsky Tower* near the *Historical Museum*. It was built in 1491 at the same time as the Spassky Tower, but was blown up in 1812 by Napoleon and rebuilt in 1820 by Bovet. It is named after the icon of St. Nicholas that used to hang over the gateway. The white stone decorations were added by Rossi at the beginning of the 19th century.

At the corner of the wall is the *Sobakina Tower* that was built quite solidly with walls 4 m (13 ft) thick; partly because it contained a secret well, important in time of siege, and also because it concealed a way out to the Neglinnaya that used to flow along the Kremlin wall. The *Trinity Gate** was built in 1495 and at 80 m (262 ft) is the highest of all the Kremlin towers. It is approached by a bridge over the Alexandrovsky Gardens, constructed in place of the Neglinnaya, from the Kutafia Tower. This was one of the first stone bridges in Moscow and was built in 1516. The mounds beside the wall further along the garden are the remains of earthworks constructed by Peter the Great in 1707 when Charles XII of Sweden planned to attack Moscow.

The next large tower is the *Borovitskaya (forest) Tower* which was built in 1490 by Pietro Antonio Solario, the upper half being added at the end of the 17th century. It was through its gate that Napoleon entered the Kremlin. At the corner nearest the Kamenny (stone) Bridge over the Moskva is the round *Water-Hoist Tower**, so named in 1663 when craftsmen found a way to raise water from the river and convey it along an aqueduct to the Kremlin palaces and gardens. It was built in 1488 by Antonio Friasin, blown up in 1812, and rebuilt by Bovet in 1817.

Along the river are 5 smaller towers. The first is the *Blagoveschenskaya (Annunciation) Tower*, named after a church that was attached to it. During the reign of Ivan the Terrible this tower was used as a prison. The next is the oldest of all and was built in 1480 by Antonio Friasin. It is called the *Tainitskaya Tower (Tower of Secrets)* because of a secret underground passage that led from here down to the river. It was partly demolished during the reign of Catherine II when plans were made to build a large palace on the site. The palace was never built and the present tower was built on the model of the old one in 1771–73. In 1930 the gates were bricked up but the outline can be seen from the road below.

Next come the *First and Second Nameless Towers* and then the *Petrovskaya Tower*, named after the Church of St. Peter the Metropolitan. The tower was destroyed and rebuilt several times. On the south-west corner is the *Beklemishev Tower*, which was built by the Italian Marco Ruffo in 1487. The next tower is the *Tower of SS. Constantin and*

Helen, which was attached to a church of the same name. The next is the *Nabatnaya (alarm) Tower*, which was so-called because it was here that a bell was rung in times of danger to warn the people to take refuge inside the Kremlin. During the rebellion of 1771, the insurgents rang the bell in order to summon the people of Moscow to the Kremlin. After the rebellion had been put down, Catherine II was so angry when the culprits could not be found that she ordered the clapper of the bell to be removed. In 1821 the bell was transferred to the Armoury where it can be seen today. The last tower is the *Tsar's Tower*, which was added in 1860. It is said to have been so named because Ivan the Terrible used to watch ceremonies in Red Square from a platform near the site of the present tower.

The central square of the Kremlin is *Cathedral Square* where the 3 principal cathedrals are situated.

The *Uspensky (Assumption) Cathedral* on the north side of the square is the largest of the Kremlin cathedrals. It was built in 1475–79 by the Italian architect Aristotle Fioravanti, who had spent many years in Russia studying the architecture of old Russian cities. The 5-domed cathedral was built in the style of the 12th-century Uspensky Cathedral in Vladimir and it became Russia's principal church. The tsars were crowned here and the cathedral served as the burial vault of the Moscow metropolitan bishops and patriarchs.

The walls of the cathedral are of white limestone and the drums beneath the domes and the vaulting are of brick. The exterior is divided into panels set off by columns and gables. On the west, south, and north facades is a belt of small arches and pilasters halfway up the walls.

The interior surprised visitors in the 15th century by its size and lightness. The Chronical of Nikon recorded that the cathedral "is amazing by virtue of its majesty and height, its lightness and spaciousness; such a church has never been seen before in all the land of Russia, save the Church at Vladimir."

The walls of the cathedral are covered in frescoes dating from the 16th to 19th centuries. These were considerably damaged by fires and were touched up in oils in the 19th century, but they have recently been restored. On the west wall is a mural of the Last Judgement and in the Chapel of Praise on the right side of the cathedral are some frescoes that are attributed to Dionisy.

The 5-tiered iconostasis, which was covered in embossed silver gilt at the end of the 19th century, includes some valuable icons of the 14th to 17th centuries. The icon of the Virgin of Vladimir is a copy of the 11th-century Byzantine icon that used to be in the cathedral but which is now in the Tretyakov Gallery. Originals still here, however, include the icon of St. George (early 12th-century Novgorodian school) and the icon of the Trinity (14th century).

Near the main entrance is the Tsar's Throne, which was carved in walnut in 1551 and which belonged to Ivan the Terrible. Known as the throne of Monomakh, it is covered in carvings and inscriptions depicting Vladimir Monomakh's Thracian campaign. In the south-east corner is a shrine encased in bronze openwork. It contains the relics of Patriarch Hermogen who was killed by the Polish invaders in 1612.

During the Napoleonic invasion the French soldiers turned the cathedral into a stable, using the icons as firewood. They took away with them as much as 288 kilograms (5.25 cwt) of various gold articles and 5,000 kilograms (5 tons) of silver, much of which was lost during the subsequent retreat and which has not yet been recovered. The central chandelier, however, is made of silver captured from the French troops.

The *Blagoveschensky (Annunciation) Cathedral* was designed as a chapel for Ivan III in early Moscow style in 1484–89. It was built on the foundations of a 14th-century stone church that had become unsafe. It had three cupolas at first, but, after a fire, was rebuilt in 1562–64 with additions by builders from Pskov. The vaults, galleries, 4 single-domed corner chapels, and 2 new domes were added. The domes and roof were covered in gilded copper and the 9-domed cathedral became known as the "Golden-domed." In 1572 a new porch and steps were added that are known as the *Steps of Ivan the Terrible*. The heavily ornamented portals on the west and north facades date from the 1560s and only that of the southern facade dates back to the 1480s when the cathedral itself was built.

The floor of the cathedral is of polished tiles of agate jasper and the walls are covered in frescoes dating from the 16th century. The pillars bear portraits of Greek philosophers and all the Moscow princes from Prince Daniel to Vasily III. The second and third tiers of the iconostasis include icons painted by Theophanes the Greek, Prokhor from Gorodets, and Andrei Rublyov. 6 of the icons in the third tier are attributed to Andrei Rublyov: "The Transfiguration," "The Entry into Jerusalem," "The Purification of the Blessed Virgin," "The Nativity," "The Epiphany," and "The Annunciation." Other works of art that can be seen in the south gallery include the 13th-century "Golden-Haired Christ," the 14th-century "Cloaked Christ," and the 16th-century "Our Lady of Vladimir."

A narrow staircase in the north wall leads up to the choir where female members of the tsar's family used to sit during services.

The *Arkhangelsky (Archangel Michael's) Cathedral* was built on the site of a 14th-century church in 1505–9 by an Italian architect from Milan, Alevisio Novi. 2 single-domed chapels, the Chapel of St. Var and the Chapel of St. John the Baptist, were added at the very end of the 16th century. The cathedral was designed in Russian style with only traces of Italian influence, particularly in the exterior. The north and south facades are divided into 3 sections, the east and west into 5. Each section is made to stand out by pilasters and is surmounted by gables or fluted niches. The

5 domes are painted silver. Originally only the central dome was gilded and the 4 outside ones covered in white iron. The decorative white limestone portals on the north and west facades show the Italian influence in the cathedral.

The walls inside the cathedral are covered in murals painted in 1652–66 by a large group of artists from several Russian towns. They depict scenes from every-day life and battle scenes as well as paintings of a religious and historical nature. On the south-west pillar is a portrait of Alexander Nevsky who defeated the Teutonic knights in 1242. The gilded carved wooden iconostasis is 13 m (43 ft) high, and contains icons dating mostly from the 15th to 17th centuries. The icon of the Archangel Michael is attributed to Andrei Rublyov.

From 1340 to 1700, first the smaller church that stood on the site and then the cathedral served as the burial vault of the grand princes of Moscow and the Russian tsars. There are portraits of many of the monarchs on the walls above the tombs. All the tsars from Ivan Kalita to Peter the Great, except for Boris Godunov whose body was exhumed in 1606, are buried here. The only tsar to be buried here later was Peter II, grandson of Peter the Great, who died in Moscow in 1730. The bronze encasements were added in 1903.

The *Bell-Tower of Ivan the Great*, which unites the various buildings of the Kremlin into a single architectural ensemble, is one of the most remarkable structures to be built in the 16th century. The lower part was built in 1532–43, and the belfry and cupola added in 1600 as famine relief work carried out under Boris Godunov. Below the cupola are 3 rows of Slavonic script that relate the circumstances under which the work was carried out.

The bell-tower is 81 m (266 ft) high and, when it was first built, served as a watch-tower from which all Moscow and the vicinity within a radium of 30 km (19 miles) could be observed. Inside the walls are 575 steps which lead in 3 stages up to the dome. There are 21 bells in the tower. They date from the 16th to 18th centuries and are each embossed with bas-reliefs and inscriptions relating the history of the bell, and when and by whom it was cast. The main bell, known as the *Bell of the Assumption*, weighs 63 tons.

In 1812 Napoleon, believing the cross on top of the dome to be pure gold, ordered it to be removed. However, it was found to be iron and those who had spread the rumour were shot.

At the foot of the Bell-tower of Ivan the Great is the *Tsar Kolokol (Tsar Bell)*, the largest bell in the world. It weighs over 200 tons and the fragment on the ground weighs 11.5 tons. It is 6 m (20 ft) high and 6.6 m (22 ft) in diameter. The bell was cast in 1733–35 in a special casting pit inside the Kremlin by Ivan Motorin and his son Mikhail. They used both new metal and an old broken bell dating from the reign of Boris Godunov. After its completion the bell remained in the casting pit, but during the Kremlin fire of 1737 several cracks appeared and a large piece was broken off. The damage is thought to have been caused by the un-

even cooling of the bell when cold water, used to extinguish the fire, fell on the bell. Almost a century later in 1836 the bell was raised from the casting pit and placed on the pedestal designed for it by Montferrand. The surface of the bell is decorated with bas-reliefs by Rastrelli representing Tsar Alexei and Tsaritsa Anna Ivanovna. There are also 5 icons on the bell and 2 inscriptions describing the history of its casting. The decorations are the work of Kobelov and Galkin.

Not far from the Tsar Bell is the *Tsar Cannon*, which has the largest calibre of any gun in the world. It was cast in 1586 by Andrek Chokhov at the Cannon Yard on the bank of the Neglinnaya where Teatralny Proyezd is today. It weighs 40 tons and is 5.3 m (17 ft) long with a calibre of 890 mm (35 ins) and a barrel 15 cm (10 in) thick. It used to stand outside the Kremlin in Kitai-Gorod where it covered the approaches to Spassky Gate and the ford across the Moskva. A special carriage was required to fire it, but the present carriage was cast in 1835 especially for display purposes. It is said to have been named after Tsar Feodor Ioanovich, the son of Ivan the Terrible, whose picture is carved on the barrel, but it is more likely that it was called the Tsar Cannon on account of its size.

Behind the Blagoveschensky (Annunciation) Cathedral is the *Church of the Twelve Apostles* and the *Patriarch's Palace*. The Patriarch's Palace consisted of the Church of the Twelve Apostles, the Krestovy Chamber, the personal chambers of the patriarch and the monks' cells. The present buildings were completed in 1656 for Patriarch Nikon, but the first stone chambers for the Metropolitan (later called Patriarch) were built in 1450. In 1473 they were completely destroyed by fire and rebuilt, only to be looted during the Polish invasion and then destroyed again by fire in 1626. The present church and 4-storey palace, which includes part of the older residence of Boris Godunov, were built by Okhlebib, Konstantinov, and Makayev in the Moscow style of the time, which was still heavily influenced by the architecture of Vladimir and Suzdal. The Krestovy Chamber in the Patriarch's Palace is a large hall where the patriarchs received tsars and foreign ambassadors and where church councils were held. The Church of the Twelve Apostles served as a private church of the patriarchs. It was first called the Church of St. Philip the Apostle, but it was given its present name in 1680 when it was rebuilt after a fire. The church and palace now house a museum of 17th-century applied arts. The exhibits were taken from the reserve of the State Armoury Museum and include books, domestic utensils, household linen, and clothing. In the church is a 17th-century carved wooden iconostasis, which was formerly in the Kremlin Monastery of the Ascension, demolished in the 1930s.

The *Church of the Deposition of the Robe (Tserkov Rizopolozheniya)* is a small, single-domed church standing between the Cathedral of the Assumption (Uspensky Sobor) and the Palace of Facets. It was built in 1484–86 by masons from Pskov on the site of an older church of the same name. This church served as a private chapel for the patriarch before the Church of the Twelve Apostles was built. The interior of the church is decorated with frescoes painted in 1644 by Osipov and Borisov, court painters who had also helped to paint the frescoes in the Cathedral of the Assumption. The silver chandelier was made in 1624 and the iconostasis was painted in 1627 by a group of icon painters under Nazary Istomin.

Behind the Church of the Deposition of the Robe one can see the 11 gilded domes of the *Upper Saviour's Church* (Verkhospasskaya Tserkov). The Upper Saviour's Church, which can be entered through the Great Kremlin Palace, was built in 1635–36 by Ogurtsov, Konstantinov, Sharutin, and Ushakov over the Tsarina's Golden Room in the Terem Palace. The church, which was used by the royal family, is also known as the Church behind the Golden Rail ("Tserkov za zolotoi reshotkoi") because of a railing around the terrace near the church that was cast in 1670 from copper coins; these had been withdrawn from circulation after the "Copper Revolt" of 1668 that broke out because of the debasing of copper coins. Inside the church are 17th-century frescoes and an 18th-century chased silver gate leading through the iconostasis to the altar. This church appears picturesque amongst the other more austere churches and cathedrals. The cupolas have long red brick drums that are decorated with blue and green tiles set by Osip Startsev after designs by the Elder Ippolit, a famous 17th-century carver. The copper roof of the church dates from the 18th-century.

The *Granovitaya Palata (Palace of Facets)* on the west side of Cathedral Square is the oldest public building in Moscow. Its name derives from the shape of the stone facings on the side looking onto Cathedral Square. It was built in 1473–91 by the Italian architects Marco Ruffo and Pietro Antonio. The ground-floor rooms were designed for administrative purposes and the upper floor as a single chamber for receptions. The chamber, 500 sq. m (5,380 sq ft) in area, has 4 cross vaults supported by a central pillar. The hall is lit by 4 large 19th-century chandeliers. The walls of the chamber were originally painted with religious frescoes. These were destroyed in a fire in 1682. Another fire ruined the decorations in 1696 and the present murals were painted in the 1880s by the Belousovs from the town of Palekh after the designs of 1683. The iron ribs of the vaulting are gilded and there are inscriptions in Slavonic lettering on the vaulting. Above the carved portal is a look-out room from which the tsarinas and their daughters watched the receptions as custom forbade any women to be present.

The *Grand Kremlin Palace* was built in 1838–49 by a team of architects under the supervision of Konstantin Thon on the site of an earlier palace built by Rastrelli in the 18th century. It was the residence of the imperial family during their visits to Moscow. It is now a government building where the Supreme Soviets of the USSR and of the Russian Federation meet, and where official receptions are held.

Although the palace appears to have 3 floors, it in fact has only 2, the upper floor having 2 tiers of windows. The grandest of the old halls is St. George's Hall named after the tsarist military order of St. George. Along the walls are marble plaques inscribed in gold with the names of officers and military units decorated with the Cross of St. George, the highest order in tsarist Russia. The 8 alcoves are fronted by 18 zinc columns supporting an allegorical figure of Victory, all the work of Ivan Vitali.

The doors in the centre of St. George's Hall lead into the Hall of St. Vladimir, named after the Order of St. Vladimir. One can then pass into the *Terem Palace (Palace of Chambers)*, which was built in 1635 by Ogurtsov, Konstantinov, and Ushakov. The palace contains the old private chambers of the tsar and was built on the site of still older chambers built for Vasily II and Ivan the Terrible. In the palace are the reception rooms, bedroom, and chapel room of the tsar. In the Throne Room, where the tsar worked and where very few boyars were admitted, stands the tsar's throne that was upholstered in velvet during the 19th century. The windows and entrances are decorated with fine carvings done in the 19th century by Kisilev.

The *Oruzheinaya Palata (Armoury)*, where the tsars' regalia and ambassadorial gifts are kept, is the oldest of all Russian museums. It is usually available to group excursions only and tickets are best obtained through Intourist. Open 9:30–5; closed Tues. Crown Jewels Exhibition open 9–6.

The museum exhibits are treasures of the tsars that were collected through the centuries. In the reign of Ivan III (1462–1505) there were already so many treasures that they had to be housed in a special building called the Treasure Court, which was built for this purpose between the Annunciation and Archangel cathedrals. Military weapons and armoury were also made in the same building, which gave the collection and the present building its name. Most of the treasures were made in the Kremlin workshops. The collection grew particularly large under Ivan the Terrible and, when Moscow was threatened by the Crimean Tatars under Devlet Girei, 450 sleds were needed to move the treasure to Novgorod. During the 16th and 17th centuries the treasure was augmented by gifts from foreign monarchs and ambassadors. During the reign of Peter the Great, the Kremlin craftsmen were moved to the new capital of St. Petersburg and work in the Kremlin workshops almost came to a halt. At the beginning of the 19th century the treasures were moved into the Imperial Palace Museum, which was housed in a building by Yegotov erected for this purpose opposite the Arsenal and Senate buildings. The collection was evacuated to Nizhny Novgorod during the Napoleonic invasion of 1812, but was moved back in the following year. In 1851 it was moved to the present building which had been built earlier in the same year by Kon-

stantin Thon. The facade of the building is decorated with carved white stone columns and ornate
window frames in the Russian style of the 17th
century. A white marble staircase with gilt banisters
leads up to the first floor where the tour of the
exhibits begins. The walls are lined with marble
bas-reliefs depicting Russian princes and tsars, the
work of the Russian sculptor Shubin.

Hall I: Weapons and Armour, 13th to 18th Centuries

Of special interest is the collection of helmets on
Stand 1. One of the earliest helmets is that of Yaroslav Vsevolodovich, the father of Alexander Nevsky. The helmet, which is covered in embossed
silver, was found on the site of a battle on the river
Koloksha that took place between Suzdal and Novgorod in 1216; the name of the owner is inscribed
on the front. Another 13th-century helmet, believed to be of Byzantine origin, is decorated with
images of the Virgin Mary, Christ, and John the
Baptist and is covered with a net of very fine silver.
Also on show here is the small helmet of the little
Prince Ivan, the son of Ivan the Terrible, who was
killed at the age of 28 by his father in an outburst
of anger. It bears an inscription saying that it was
made for the prince, who was then 4 years old, by
order of his father in 1557. On the same stand are
examples of Russian chain mail, the oldest type
being the "kolchuga," which was made from thousands of small iron rings linked together and weighing about 18 kg (40 lb). There are also some fine
breastplates on show, including those of the Tsars
Mikhail and Alexei, which are gilded and embossed. Some of the battle-axes and maces on show
were made in the 17th and 18th centuries but were
used only for ceremonial purposes since they were
already obsolete as battle arms. Some of the axes
made by Kremlin craftsmen in the 17th century
have blades covered in gold inlay.

On Stand 2 are Russian arquebuses and Dutch
and German muskets of the 16th and 17th centuries. The earliest arquebus in the collection dates
from the time of Ivan the Terrible and belonged
to the Boyar Belsky, Ivan's chief armourer.

On Stand 3 is a collection of ceremonial armour
and Russian and Oriental sabres. Of special interest
is the helmet of Tsar Mikhail Romanov, which has
a finely polished surface inlaid with gilt and decorated with diamonds, rubies, and emeralds.
Among the sabres on display are lavishly decorated
gold and silver sabres studded with precious stones
that were worn by the tsars on ceremonial occasions. Also here are the sabres of Minin and Pozharsky who headed the army that drove the Poles
out of Moscow in 1612. These sabres, made in
Egypt and Persia respectively, are outstanding in
their simplicity.

On Stand 4 is a collection of armour and weapons of the second half of the 17th century. The
breastplate in the centre was made in 1670 by Titov
and Vyatikin. The large quiver and bowcase set in
gold and gems were made in Constantinople and

given to Tsar Alexei in 1656 by Greek merchants.
Also here is Tsar Alexei's Oriental sabre with a hilt
and golden sheath. The heavy golden mace (1.2
kg/2 lb 8 oz), cast in pure gold with gold crests,
was presented to Tsar Alexei by Shah Abbas II of
Persia in 1658.

Stand 5 displays Russian arms of the reign of
Peter the Great and trophies from the Northern
War (1700–21). In the centre of the stand is a bas-
relief of Peter the Great hammered in pewter by
the architect Rastrelli who was responsible for many
of the imperial buildings in St. Petersburg. Among
the Swedish trophies from the war are a silver mace
bearing the crest of Gustavus Adolphus Vasa and
a Bible published in Stockholm in 1703 bearing
the monogram of Charles XII.

Stand 6 has a display of 16th-century pistols
and 15th- to 17th-century European suits of armour. In the centre is a suit of equestrian armour
cast by Kunz Lochner and presented to Tsar Feodor
by the Polish ambassador in 1584 as a gift from
King Stefan Batory of Poland. To the right of the
stand among the suits of armour are 3 that were
made for the royal children in the 17th century.
These were only worn on ceremonial occasions.

Hall II: Russian Gold and Silver, 12th to 17th Centuries

One of the earliest pieces of silver on display is a
12th-century chalice that was given to the Cathe-
dral of the Saviour in Transfiguration in Pereslavl-
Zalessky by Prince Yuri Dolgoruky, the founder of
Moscow. It is engraved with figures of the saints.
Another 12th-century cup here belonged to Prince
Vladimir Davydov of Chernigov, as is related on
the inscription beneath the rim. The fine work of
Kievan craftsmen is shown here on the so-called
Ryazan treasure that dates from the 12th or 13th
century and was discovered in Old Ryazan in 1822.
The treasure includes 2 heavy necklets decorated
with coloured enamel and filigree, a bracelet, rings,
earrings, and images of the saints. Novgorodian
work is represented by a 14th-century jasper chalice
in a silver filigree case studded with precious stones,
and 14th-century dippers in the shape of a sauce-
boat. Also on display are gold and silver dippers
that were used for drinking mead. These were made
by Moscow craftsmen in the 16th century and include one smelted out of a single nugget that belonged to Boris Godunov. The extremely
decorative gospel was given to the Cathedral of the
Assumption in 1571 by Ivan the Terrible. The gold
cover is picked out with enamel and precious stones
with pictures of Christ and the saints linked by
inscriptions in blackened gold. There is a large
collection of various drinking vessels on display.
Besides dippers there are "bratinas," tall round
bowls used as a toasting cup and for drinking beer
and kvas, "korchiks," small dippers on a saucer with
a goblet for strong drinks, and "endovas," low-
lipped vessels used for pouring drinks. One of the
finest "bratinas" is the silver-lidded one that was
made in Moscow in the first half of the 17th century

and belonged to the Tsarina Yevdokia Lukyanovna. There is one particularly fine "endova" on display that was made in 1644 in Moscow and belonged to the Boyar Streshnev. The articles on display dating from the second half of the 17th century are particularly lavish with bright enamel work studded with jewels. On view is a gold cup belonging to Tsar Alexei Mikhailovich that is covered in green enamel painted with bright flowers, the gold mounting for the icon of the Virgin of Vladimir studded with precious stones, including 2 emeralds weighing 100 carats each, and 2 gold-covered gospels with emerald-and-ruby-studded enamel.

Also on display in this hall are boxes, knives, forks, cups, and caskets, and a collection of Russian and foreign clocks and watches of the 16th to 18th centuries. The gilded copper watch in the form of a book belonged to Ivan the Terrible and the wooden watch was made in the 19th century by Russian craftsmen.

Hall III: Silver and Jewellery, 18th to 20th Centuries

At the beginning of the 18th century St. Petersburg, the new capital, became the centre of the Russian silver and gold trades. In the middle of the 18th century the predominant style was that of Russian baroque and rococo with lavish ornamentation and brightly painted enamel. One of the finest exhibits dating from this period is the pair of silver candlesticks made in St. Petersburg by Liebmann. They are mounted on tall cast stems with intricate ornamentation and scrollwork. Although the rococo style gave way to Russian classicism at the end of the century, the large silver beaker displayed in a separate case, which was made by Ratkov in Moscow in 1788, has rococo finish. Also on display is a collection of snuff-boxes made of gold, silver, mother-of-pearl, tortoise-shell, ivory, and porcelain. Many of them are decorated with precious stones and enamel portraits. The flat snuff-box bearing an enamel portrait of Peter the Great was made in 1727 by Andrei Osov, one of the first Russian miniaturists. Also here is a large, round, gold snuff-box with a plated bas-relief portrait of the Empress Elizabeth that is believed to have been made by Pozier, one of the most famous craftsmen of the last century. Further on is a collection of silver dating from 1770 to 1825, the period of Russian classicism. These articles are much plainer in decoration, such as the silver samovar shaped like a Grecian urn made by Unger and Eckert in 1801. On the same stand is a silver children's tea service made by Johann Blohm in St. Petersburg in 1784. In the centre of the stand is a oval gold dish, made by F. Sebastian in 1788, and presented to Catherine II by Prince Potyomkin. Further on are two small crowns woven out of silver laurel leaves that are said to be the crowns used during the ceremony of Pushkin's marriage to Natalia Goncharova in 1831.

The last section in this hall shows examples of the work of the famous jewellers' firms that flourished in Moscow and St. Petersburg after 1830. The Sazikov Jewellers is represented by a silver sculpture "Warrior on Watch" made in St. Petersburg in 1852. The work of Fabergé, probably the most famous of all Russian jewellers, is represented by a number of works. One of the most fascinating is a silver Easter egg, on the outside of which is engraved a map of the Trans-Siberian Railway. Inside is a gold clockwork model of a Trans-Siberian express with a platinum engine with a ruby headlamp. The carriages are inscribed with the usual inscriptions, such as "Smokers," "Ladies Only," and "Clerics," and have windows made of crystal. There is also a nephrite egg that contains a model of the Alexandrovsky Palace in Tsarskoye Selo (now Pushkin) near Leningrad. Another egg contains a gold model of the royal yacht, "Standard." The yacht is set in a sea of rock crystal and the crystal egg has 2 pear-shaped pearl pendants. Another fascinating exhibit is a vase of rock-crystal with a pansy decoration. If a button on the flower stem is pressed, the petals open revealing miniature portraits of the children of Nicholas II in frames of small diamonds.

Hall IV: Vestments

This hall contains vestments of silk, velvet, and brocade, woven and embroidered with gold and encrusted with jewels and pearls. They belonged to the imperial family, patriarchs, and metropolitan bishops. Before the 18th century no silk or brocades were made in Russia. Most of the articles on show in the first section of this hall were imported from Western Europe or from the Middle East.

The oldest vestment on display is the "sakkos" (robe) of Peter, the first Metropolitan of Moscow. It was made in 1332 of blue stain woven with gold stripes and crosses. Some of the robes, such as those of the Metropolitan Photius, are embroidered with portraits of the rulers of the time or with religious figures.

In the 17th and 18th centuries materials were particularly heavily embroidered with precious stones, pearls, and gold plates. One of the last vestments on display is a velvet cope that was presented to Metropolitan Platon of Moscow in 1770 by Catherine II. There are altogether 150,580 pearls on the cope.

Beyond the vestments are examples of Russian pictorial embroidery on altar cloths and other church articles. These date from the 15th century.

Hall V: Foreign Gold and Silver, 13th to 19th Centuries

Most of the items on display in this hall were gifts to the tsars from ambassadors on behalf of their country. The first exhibits are of Dutch silver made in Amsterdam in the 16th century. They are remarkable for their simplicity and limited decoration. Many of the articles are decorated with tulips, the most common motif on 17th-century Dutch silver.

The next section is a collection of English silver, mostly made in London in the 16th and 17th centuries. In 1553 Richard Chancellor was received in Moscow by Ivan the Terrible and was the first of a long succession of ambassadors to the Russian Court. The earliest item is a flat goblet, made in 1557, and thought to have been presented to Ivan the Terrible by the English merchant, Antony Jenkins. Other items of English silver on display are trays, cups, figured salt-cellars, wine flagons, pitchers, and chased livery pots.

Silver from Poland and Sweden is in the next section. Many of the gifts from Poland in the 17th century were made in Danzig, but a number of the items on show were made in Germany where they were brought by Polish tradesmen. The collection from Sweden is the largest of all and comprises about 200 items, all made in the 17th century. Some of these were made in Augsberg, such as the 2 oval basins that were gifts from Queen Christina to Tsar Alexei. The 2 globes, depicting the earthly and heavenly spheres and supported by the figures of Neptune and Atlas, were also made by German craftsmen and were brought to Moscow as gifts from Charles X. The work of Swedish silversmiths is represented by a number pieces including candlesticks, flasks, tumblers, filigree cups, and a water bowl in the shape of a silver swan.

The next stand is a display of gifts from Denmark, also mostly made by German craftsmen.

Further on are silver and gold vessels made by craftsmen in Nurenburg in the 15th to 17th centuries. There is a large collection of drinking-cups and goblets in various shapes, some in the form of a fruit or an animal.

At the end of the hall are some foreign dinner and tea services. The large silver service is only part of one consisting of over 3,000 pieces which was given by Catherine II in 1772 to Prince Orlov. It was ordered from Rottiers et Fils, but the order was so large that they were obliged to subcontract part of it. The Sèvres tea, coffee, and dessert services on show were presented to Alexander I by Napoleon when the Treaty of Tilsit was signed.

Hall VI: *Regalia of the Royal Family*

At the beginning of the hall on the left are the thrones of the tsars. The oldest throne on display is that of Ivan the Terrible that was made in Western Europe and is decorated with ivory carvings. The second throne was given to Boris Godunov by Shah Abbas of Persia. The throne is covered with thin plates of gold and studded with 2,200 precious stones and pearls. The third throne, of Iranian origin, was made in Moscow for Mikhail Romanov from a throne belonging to Ivan the Terrible. The next throne was presented to Tsar Alexei Romanov by a group of Armenian merchants. The throne, which was made in Persia, is decorated with 1,223 precious stones and 876 diamonds which have given it the name of the "Diamond Throne." The last throne is one that was used in the first years of the reign of Peter the Great when he shared power with his elder brother, Ivan, and his sister, Sophia, was regent. The 2 seats in front were used by the 2 tsars and the hidden seat behind by Sophia, who used to prompt the boys with the right answers to ambassadors' questions.

The oldest crown on display is the "Cap of Monomakh," which was made by craftsmen in the 13th or 14th centuries and is thought to have been given to the Grand Prince Vladimir Monomakh of Kiev by the Emperor of Byzantium. It is made of finely wrought gold lace smelted onto a strip of gold leaf, surmounted by a pearl-tipped gold cross and edged with a band of sable.

The Kazan Cap was made in Moscow for Ivan the Terrible to commemorate the capture of Kazan. Also on display is the regalia made in Moscow for the coronation of Tsar Mikhail Romanov, the regalia brought to Moscow from Greece for Tsar Alexei Romanov, and the diamond coronets made in Moscow between 1682 and 1689 for Peter the Great and his brother Ivan. Only 2 crowns made in the days when Russia was an empire are in the armoury; the crown of Anna Ivanovna, which is encrusted with numerous diamonds and a large ruby, and the crown of Catherine I.

The last section of this hall contains a display of Russian costumes from the 16th century. Until the end of the 17th century the most usual garment was a long loose caftan. There are a number on display, including one belonging to Peter the Great. From the end of the 17th century shorter, closer-fitting clothes were worn with short britches reaching just below the knee.

Beyond the men's garments is a display of accessories and jewellery. The earrings were worn by men in Russia until the reign of Peter the Great. At the end of the hall are a number of dresses, including coronation dresses, which belonged to the empresses and tsars' wives.

Hall VII & VIII: *Harnesses*

The harnesses in these 2 halls are extremely exotic. Most of them were made in Russia but some were gifts to the Russian court from foreign countries, particularly from Poland, which regularly sent saddles to the tsar.

The display begins with a collection of 16th and 17th-century German, Polish, and English harnesses. The oldest saddles here were gifts to Boris Godunov from the King of Poland. The German saddles were made in the second half of the 17th century and are decorated with embroidery.

Further on are a number of Persian harnesses that were mostly gifts from the Shah of Persia. A particularly exotic saddle is the one in a gold frame and covered in velvet, embroidered with gold threads and decorated with rubies, emeralds, and turquoises.

The oldest Russian saddle on display was made during the reign of Ivan the Terrible. It is covered with velvet, embroidered with golden 2-headed eagles. There are a number of childrens' saddles, no less ornate than those for adults, including one made in 1642 for the Tsarevich Alexei Mikhailovich.

Hall IX: Carriages

The oldest carriage is a 16th-century English one thought to have been a gift to Boris Godunov by Elizabeth I. The child's coach and closed sled were made at the end of the 17th century for Peter the Great when he was a child.

An unusual carriage is the one that Empress Elizabeth travelled in from St. Petersburg to Moscow for her coronation. It was drawn by 23 horses—1 pair and 7 trios. The most lavish of all, however, is the French carriage made in Paris in 1757 by Bourinhall. This one, with carved gilt wood made to represent sea foam and breaking waves, has panels painted by Francois Bouchet. It was presented to Empress Elizabeth by Count Razumovsky.

A new section of the museum has been opened to show the presents made to the Soviet Union by foreign countries.

The *Palace of Congresses* was completed in 1961 for the 22nd Soviet Communist Party Congress. It was designed by Mikhail Posokhin and built 15 m (49 ft) down into the ground, the height of a 5-storey house, so that it would not be higher than the rest of the Kremlin ensemble. It contains over 800 rooms and halls and the main auditorium has a seating capacity of 6,000. The acoustics in the auditorium are very good with 7,000 loudspeakers concealed in different parts of the hall. During congresses the speeches can be heard in 29 languages. The praesidium seats and the rostrum can be lowered to form an orchestra pit. Above the main auditorium is a banqueting hall seating 2,500. The Palace of Congresses is also used for concerts, ballet, and opera.

The Arsenal is the long, yellow building forming a quadrangle between the Trinity and Nikolsky towers. Work was started on the Arsenal under Peter the Great who planned it to store arms and ammunition. It was completed in 1736 but was badly damaged by fire the following year. It was later rebuilt under the direction of the engineer, Gerard. In 1812 the wall of the Arsenal near the Kremlin wall was blown up by Napoleon's troops and the whole building destroyed in the ensuing fire. It was rebuilt from 1816 to 1828, this time by Bovet. The final 2-storey structure that emerged can be seen to combine features of Petrine architecture and the baroque of the 1830s. Plans were made in the 19th century to open a museum of the 1812 war in the building. 875 cannon that were captured from the French army were placed along the south-east wall where they remain today, for the plans for the museum were never fulfilled.

The building of the *Council of Ministers* faces the south-east facade of the Arsenal. It was built by Matvei Kazakov in 1776–88 on a piece of land that had belonged to the Trubetskoi family and the Monastery of the Miracle. Before the revolution it was the Senate building and now houses the offices of the Council of Ministers. In the centre of the facade facing the Arsenal is an archway that leads into the courtyard. In the centre of the building is a large circular hall with a domed roof. Before the revolution the hall was known as the White Hall or the Catherine Hall and was used for meetings. It is now used for plenary meetings of the Central Committee of the Communist Party.

Churches and Cathedrals

St. Basil's Cathedral, Red Square. Open 9.30–5.30. closed Tues. & the first Mon. in the month.

The Cathedral of the Intercession (Pokrovsky Sobor) or St. Basil's as it is commonly called, was built in 1555–60 by order of Ivan the Terrible to commemorate the conquest of the Tatar City of Kazan on the Volga. Ivan the Terrible's first plan was for 8 churches to be built on Red Square, each church being dedicated to the saints on whose days he won his battles. A stone and 7 wooden churches were built in 1552, but Ivan the Terrible was dissatisfied and ordered them to be demolished. The task of building new churches was given to Barma and Postnik, two architects whom recent historical evidence has shown were probably the same person, Postnik Yakovlev, whose nickname was Barma. A new plan was drawn up, this time for one large cathedral surrounded by 7 subsidiary churches. 7 small churches would have spoilt the symmetry of the design so the architect(s) built 8.

The central cathedral, the dome of which is 46 m (151 ft) high, was named Pokrovsky Sobor (Cathedral of the Intercession) because the chief victory in the campaign fell on the day of the Intercession. The more popular name of St. Basil's was taken from a church built close to the cathedral in 1588, which was dedicated to the memory of a holy man named Basil, a Muscovite who had exercised a certain amount of influence over Ivan the Terrible.

Legend says that when the cathedral was completed Ivan ordered the eyes of the architects to be removed so that they could not build a similar cathedral elsewhere. It is known that when first completed the cathedral was painted in more subdued colours and that it was only in the 18th century that it was painted as it is now with all the details picked out in different colours. The exotic grandeur of the cathedral makes it one of the best and most striking examples of old Russian architecture.

The first room of the museum in the cathedral contains an exhibition relating the history of the building, the story of its construction and specimens of the materials used.

Among the more interesting sights in the cathedral are the iconostasis of the Trinity Church, the "Entry into Jerusalem" icon in the same church and the interior decoration of the Church of St. Alexander of Svir.

In the 16th century the crypt was used as the state treasury. In 1595 two nobles planned to rob it and started fires in different parts of the city in order to divert the attention of the city guard. Their plan failed and they were summarily executed.

In front of the cathedral is the monument to Minin and Pozharsky (see p. 328).

Novodevichy Monastyr (convent), Novodevichy Proyezd 1 (near the Sportivnaya metro station). Open 9–5.30; closed Tues. & first Mon. of each month.

Novodevichy Convent is one of the most interesting historical and architectural monuments in Moscow. It was founded in 1524 by Grand Prince Vasili Ioanovich to commemorate the union of Smolensk and Moscow. It formed a stronghold on the road to Smolensk and Lithuania and was enclosed by fortified walls with 12 towers.

Novodevichy was a convent for women of noble birth and many historical figures ended their lives here. When Tsar Feodor died in 1598, his widow, Irina, and her brother, Boris Godunov, came to the convent. Tsar Feodor had been almost imbecile for a number of years before his death and power had been in the hands of his brother-in-law, Boris, who realised that if he assumed power immediately he would be faced with opposition. His calculations proved right as he was soon entreated by the Patriarch and a number of nobles to leave the convent.

Peter the Great's elder sister, Princess Sophia, was banished to the convent in 1679 by her brother. In 1698 the Streltsy, whom she had supported in their revolt against the tsar, were hanged along the walls of the convent with their hands clasped in a begging posture. Sophia, who had become Sister Susanna in the convent, had her hair shorn and was banished to a tower where she died in 1704. Her sisters, Yekaterina, Maria, and Fedosia, also lived in the convent.

Peter the Great, unlike other Russian tsars, saw little good in monasteries and convents. At one time he turned the Novodevichy convent into a home for abandoned babies and he later issued an order that war veterans should be offered shelter in the convent.

Napoleon visited the monastery in 1812, but left it untouched until the last day of the French occupation when he ordered that it should be blown up. Barrels of gunpowder were set up in the convent, but a nun named Sara succeeded in extinguishing the fuses just in time and the convent remained undamaged.

The *Preobrazhenskaya Tserkov (Church of the Transfiguration)* is the first church the visitor sees when entering the convent through the main entrance. It was built in 1687–88 in Moscow baroque style over the gateway. The 7-tier iconostasis, which was painted in 1687 by Kremlin craftsmen, is of particular interest.

Nearby are the *Lopukhinskiye Palaty (Lopukhin Chambers)*, a 2-storey building erected in 1687–8 for the daughter of Tsar Alexei and sister of Peter the Great, Tsarevna Yekaterina. The first wife of Peter the Great, Evdokia Lopukhin, lived here from 1727 to 1731 and the building has been named after her ever since.

Smolensky Sobor (Smolensk Cathedral) was the main church of the convent. It was dedicated to Our Lady of Smolensk, which was an icon of the Virgin Mary brought to Kiev from Greece by the Greek Tsarevna Anna and then to the cathedral in Smolensk.

In 1398 the icon was moved to the Cathedral of the Annunciation in the Kremlin and, today, it can be seen in the Tretyakov Gallery.

The cathedral was built in 1524–25 by the architect Aleviz Fryazin. The side aisles and galleries were added at the end of the 17th century. The brick walls of the cathedral are set off by the architectural details in white stone. Of the three arched entrances with carved cornices, also of white stone, those on the west and north facades remain in their original form.

The interior of the cathedral is covered in 16th-century murals. The carved wooden iconostasis is worth special attention: it has 84 intricately carved columns and was the work of about 50 craftsmen under Konstantin Mikhailov in 1685. The icons date from the 16th and 17th centuries and were painted by the best Muscovite masters. The icon of Christ on the right-hand side of the first tier of the iconostasis and the icons on the doors of the sanctuary were painted by the famous 17th-century artist, Simeon Ushakov.

In the centre of the cathedral stands a large chalice that was made in 1685 and is decorated with brightly painted and embossed tulips and roses.

In the cathedral are the tombs of Princess Sophia, the first wife of Peter the Great, Evdokia Lopukhin, Tsarevna Anna, and the daughter of Ivan the Terrible.

The cathedral now houses a museum of Russian applied arts of the 16th and 17th centuries. The exhibits include embroidery, paintings, fabrics, woodwork, and metalwork. Exhibited along the south wall are the private possessions of Princess Sophia. There is also a large collection of 16th and 17th century books, beautifully illuminated and illustrated, bound in leather and decorated with gold, silver, and jewels.

The *Belfry* is situated near the east wall of the convent. This is contrary to Russian custom in which belfries were always built on the western side of the main buildings, but the site was chosen as it was thought that the belfry would be more striking on this side of the convent. It is indeed a fine example of the best architecture of the time and is considered by many to be superior to the Bell Tower of Ivan the Great in the Kremlin. The belfry, completed in 1690, is 72 m (236 ft) in height and consists of 5 octagonal tiers of varying width and height. Around the base of each tier is an open-arched gallery. The belfry, which was built of brick, is decorated with limestone details that makes it seem light in spite of its size.

Uspenskaya Tserkov (Church of the Assumption) was built in 1687 but was badly damaged in a fire in 1796 after which it was rebuilt and much altered. In place of the 5 cupolas only one was rebuilt. It is now open for religious services with particularly large crowds on feast days.

Trapeznaya Palata (Refectory). The refectory was built at the same time as the Church of the Assumption that adjoins it. It is a large hall with no supporting pillars which was the refectory for nuns and the hall where guests were entertained on feast days. After the fire of 1796 the refectory was rebuilt, but without the open galleries which formerly ran along the western facade of the building.

Near the refectory is the *Palata Iriny Godunovoy (The Chamber of Irina Godunov)*, sister of Boris Godunov, who came to live in the convent after the death of her husband, Tsar Feodor, in 1598. The building was completed in the same year and was then surmounted by a wooden chamber with a lavishly painted roof. The building was considerably altered at the end of the 18th century. It now houses the Arms Museum.

To the south of the convent, but still within the walls, is a cemetery with many famous graves. The writers Gogol and Chekhov are buried here, and also Stalin's wife Nadezhda Alliluyeva. Prominent statesmen, artists, and military officers are also buried here in the new part of the cemetery.

Novo-Spassky (Krutitsky) Monastery, 1-Krutitsky Pereulok 4/2, near Proletarskaya Metro station. Founded in 1272 in the Kremlin by Yuri Dolgoruki, and later moved to this site which was known as Krutisky, there was for many years little to remind one of the monastery's former grandeur and magnificent gardens. The Assumption Cathedral was built in 1685 and the richly decorated Teremok in 1694. Russia's foremost scientists assembled here in the 17th century to study geography, history, medicine, and astronomy and to translate foreign scientific works into Russian. Copernicus's works were first translated here under the capable supervision of Epiphany Slavinetsky. The monastery was closed in 1788 and mostly converted into army barracks. It is said that the walls were stained with the blood of Russians accused of starting the Moscow fires of 1812 and executed by Napoleonic soldiers. Alexander Herzen was imprisoned here for a year during which time he wrote his first literary works.

Danilov Monastery, Danilovsky Val 2, on the right bank of the river Moskva. Founded in 1282 by St. Daniel, Prince of Moscow. In 1330 the community was transferred to the Kremlin and the present site was neglected. Then in 1560 Ivan the Terrible had the Monastery restored to its original place. In 1872 the 600th anniversary of its foundation was celebrated, but after the Revolution the Monastery was closed. The belfry was demolished and the bells, among the finest in Moscow, disappeared—although the largest weighed almost 12 tons. They reappeared at Harvard University where they are today. For almost 60 years the monastery buildings were used as an orphanage. In 1983, in connection with the 1988 Millenium of the Baptism of Russ, it was returned to the Church. The walls and towers were restored, as was the Father

Superior's residence and other monastery buildings inside the walls, and the 45-m (148-ft) belfry was rebuilt. No new bells have been cast in Russia for half a century, and the 23 bells now hanging in the belfry were collected together from the Yaroslavl region and other parts of the country. After considerable reconstruction work, the *Spiritual and Administrative Centre of the Russian Orthodox Church* moved into the monastery grounds and the adjacent territory. The Department of External Church Relations is housed in a former monastic dormitory.

The following churches are among those open for services in Moscow: daily services at 10 and 6.

The *Cathedral of the Holy Fathers of the Seven Ecumenical Councils* was built in 1554–60 by the order of Ivan the Terrible. Trinity Church (1833) contained the relics of St. Daniel.

The *Patriarchal Cathedral of the Manifestation of Christ (often called Yelokhovskaya Cathedral)*, Spartakovskaya Street 15. The cathedral was built in 1835–45 and contains, among other treasures, the icons of Our Lady of Kazan and Our Lady of Tikhvin and a sacred relic, the shrine of St. Alexis, Metropolitan of Moscow in the 14th century, which was transferred here from the Assumption Cathedral in the Kremlin. It is the seat of His Holiness Pimen, Patriarch of Moscow and All Russia.

The *Church of the Ascension (Tserkov Vozneseniya)*, Sokolniki Square. This church was built in 1914, but it possesses many old icons, including the wonder-working icon of Our Lady of Iveria (Iveria was the old name for the country of Georgia).

Church of the Assumption, Novodevichy Convent (see p. 345)

The *Church of St. Nicholas in Khamovniki (Tserkov Svyatovo Nikolaya v Khamovnikakh)*. At the corner of Komsomolsky Prospect and Timur Frunze Street. This church was built in 1679 in the old weavers' district known as Khamovniki. The exterior is painted in white with bright decorations in red and green.

The *Church of the Consolation of All Who Sorrow*, Bolshaya Ordynka 20. This church was built in 1787 and contains the wonder-working icon "The Joy of All Afflicted." Its music is reputed to be the best in Moscow.

The *Church of John the Warrior* (Tserkov Ivana-Voina), Dimitrov Street 46. This church was built in 1709–13 on the order of Peter the Great in commemoration of the victory over the Swedes at the Battle of Poltava. It contains a finely carved iconostasis.

The *Church of the Deposition of the Robe (Tserkov Rizopolozheniya)*, Bryusovsky Pereulok 20. This church was built in 1683.

All Saints Church (Tserkov Vsekh Svyatykh), Leningradsky Prospect 73, near Sokol metro station. This church was built in 1736.

Church of St. Pimen (Tserkov Svyatovo Pimena), Novovorotnikovsky Pereulok 3. This very small church near the old Arbat was built in 1848.

Church of the Resurrection (Tserkov Voskreseniya), 2-Kadashevsky Pereulok 9. Not far from the Tretyakov Gallery. This church was built in the 17th century.

Trinity Church (Troitskaya Tserkov), Lenin Hills, in front of the university. This small church was built in 1811. It is not open every day.

The *Church of the Archangel Gabriel (Tserkov Arkhangela Gavriila)*, Telegrafny Pereulok 15a. The church was built in 1704–07 and is now used by the Greek Orthodox community in Moscow.

Uspenskaya Church, Volodarskovo Street 29, near Taganskaya Metro. Used by the local Bulgarian congregation.

Evangelical Christians' (Baptists') Meeting House, Maly Vuzovsky Pereulok 3. Meetings at 6 Tues., Thurs., and Sat.: 10 & 6 Sun.

Pokrovsky Old Believers' Cathedral, Rogozhsky Pereulok 29. 17th-century music.

Armenian Church, Malaya Dekabrskaya Street 27.

St. Louis's Roman Catholic Church, Markhlevsky Street 7. This church was designed by Ghilardi and was built in 1827–30.

Mosque, Vypolzov Pereulok 7. Daily services, the largest being on Fri. at 1 P.M.

Synagogue, Arkhipov Street 8. Daily services at 10 A.M. and 1 hour before sundown.

Moscow University

Moscow University was founded in 1755 by Russia's great scientist and encyclopaedist, Mikhail Lomonosov. It is now the largest univeristy in the country and has over 22,000 students attending its 14 faculties.

It is housed in many buildings in the city centre and since 1953 also in the large skyscraper on Lenin Hills. The main buildings in the centre are the 2 opposite the Alexandrovsky Gardens on either side of Herzen Street. The oldest building, on the right as one faces Herzen Street, was built by Matvei Kazakov in 1786–93. It was badly damaged in the 1812 fire, after which it was restored and altered by Gigliardi. Gigliardi was responsible for the facade with the 8-column colonnade and also for the semi-circular assembly hall that is adorned with Ionic columns and murals. The *monuments* to Alexander Herzen and Nikolai Ogaryov by Nikolai Andreyev in front of the building were erected in 1922.

The building on the other side of Herzen Street, still known as the "new" building, was built by Tyurin in 1836 in Classical style. Behind the "new" building is the *Church of the Apparition (Tserkov Znamenskaya)*, which was built at the end of the 17th century in Russian Baroque style. The monument to Mikhail Lomonosov in front of the university was made by Kozlovsky and erected in 1857.

The new building on Lenin Hills was designed by Rudnyev and built in 1949–53. It is used chiefly by the scientific departments of the university and for accommodation. The main building is 240 m (787 ft) high, including the spire, and the main facade is 450 m (492 yd) long. The whole university complex here, which is situated on a site of 166 hectares (415 acres), comprises 27 blocks and 10 ancillary buildings. To inspect all the premises here one would have to walk nearly 150 km (93 miles).

The monument to Lomonosov in front of the main facade was made by Tomsky and was unveiled in 1954.

Libraries

Lenin Library, Vozdvizhenka Street 3. With an overall stock of 25,000,000 books, this is the country's largest library, and it always received a copy of each book printed in the Soviet Union. The rare books and manuscripts section has a collection of early documents, and also many first editions and old manuscripts, both foreign (beginning with Gutenberg) and Russian, dating back to the time of Russia's first printer, Fedorov, in the 16th century. There are handwritten Slav and Russian manuscripts dating from the 11th century.

The library building was built in 1939–40 by Schuko and Gelfreikh. Along the facade are bronze relief portraits of famous writers and scientists.

Next to the new building in Vozdvizhenka Street is the magnificent old building of the library. It was built by Bazhenov in 1786, and is known as Pashkov House after its owner who was a descendant of an orderly of Peter the Great. It once housed a museum, which was bequeathed to the state by Count Rumyantsev.

Foreign Literature Lending Library, Ulyanovskaya Street 1. The library is housed in a new building completed in 1966. It was founded after the Revolution and has over 3 million books in 127 languages.

Art Galleries and Art and Architecture Museums

Tretyakov Gallery, Lavrushinsky Pereulok 10. *New Tretyakov Gallery*, Krymsky Val 10.

The Tretyakov Gallery consisted exclusively of Russian art from early religious works of the 10th century until the present day. It was the home of some of Russia's most famous icons, including those of Our Lady of Vladimir and Our Lady of Smolensk.

The foundation of the collection was laid by the art collectors Pavel and Sergei Tretyakov, after whom the gallery was named. Pavel Tretyakov began his collection with a number of lithographs and engravings and only later turned to paintings, in particular contemporary Russian art, and then to icons. His brother Sergei collected West European paintings and Russian sculpture. When Sergei died in 1892, he bequeathed his whole collection to Pavel, who in the same year gave the whole collection, then comprising 3,500 works of art, to the city of Moscow.

After the Revolution, the works of West European artists were transferred to the Pushkin Museum of Fine Arts. Since then the collection has grown and, although a new wing was built to accommodate works of the Soviet period, the present building, designed by Vasnetsov in 1898 to house the collection, is far too small. (The new gallery on the Krymsky Embankment opposite the main entrance to Gorky Park now houses recent acquisitions.)

In the forecourt is a copy of Yevgeny Vuchetich's sculpture "Swords into Ploughshares," presented to the United Nations by the Soviet Union.

Pushkin Fine Arts Museum, Volkhonka Street 12, near Kropotkinskaya Metro station. Open 9-7 (Sun. 10–6); closed Mon. & the last Tues. of the month. The museum, first known as Alexander III's museum, opened in 1912. The building was designed by Academician Klein and completed in the same year.

After the Hermitage in Leningrad this is the largest museum in the country. It was first planned, however, not as a museum of original works of art, but as an educational museum serving the needs of Moscow University. For this purpose, many copies of Egyptian, Greek, and Roman works of art were made under the direction of Professor Tsvetayev, the first director of the museum.

The museum collection was greatly enhanced by a number of donations, most notably those by the collector Golenischev of Ancient Egyptian Art and Ancient Coptic Art. In 1925 the collection of West European paintings that had belonged to Sergei Tretyakov was moved here from the Tretyakov Gallery, and also the renowned collection of French art that had belonged before the Revolution to 2 patrons of art, Morozov and Schukin.

In the first hall of the gallery is the collection of Ancient Egyptian Art dating from the 4th century B.C. to the 1st century A.D.

Hall 2 contains works of art dating from the 3rd century B.C. to the 7th century A.D. from Babylon, Assyria, Persia, et cetera.

Spanish and Italian art (Hall 28 and 29) is represented by such artists as Murillo, Jose de Ribera, Botticelli, Romano, and Fetti.

Hall 30 is devoted to Dutch art of the 17th century, including works by Ruisdael, Rembrandt, Steen, and Ostade. The next hall contains works by Flemish artists including Rubens and Van Dyck.

One of the most treasured sections is the collection of French paintings in Halls 27 to 22. Artists included here are Poussin (Hall 27), Watteau, and David (Hall 25), Delacroix, Rousseau, and Gericault (Hall 24), Cezanne, Courbet, Manet, Matisse, Gauguin, Van Gogh, Picasso, and Monet (Halls 23 and 22).

New Gallery, Marshala Shaposhnikova Street 4. Open 11–7; closed Mon. & the last Tues. of each month.

Andrei Rublyov Museum of Ancient Art, Pryamikov Square 10. Open 11–6; closed Wed. & Fri. The museum is inside the walls of the former *Spaso-Andronikov Monastery*, which was founded in 1360 by Bishop Alexei of Moscow as the fulfillment of a vow made during his return journey from Constantinople where he had been inducted;

when caught in a storm on the Black Sea, he vowed that if he escaped with his life, he would found a new monastery. It bears the name of Andronik, a pupil of Sergei Radonezhsky, who became the first abbot here. The monastery, which was originally made entirely of wood, was also a fortress on the road to Vladimir. The white stone walls and towers that stand today were built during the second half of the 17th century.

In the monastery is the oldest cathedral in Moscow, the *Spassky Cathedral*, which was built in 1420–27, but recent finds date parts of it to the 13th century. The cathedral was decorated by Andrei Rublyov, Russia's most famous icon painter, who was a monk in this monastery and who was buried here in 1430. Unfortunately, all the decorations were destroyed except for fragments of the murals, believed to be the work of Rublyov, which were found around windows that were once closed up.

The refectory building, built of brick with a high sloping roof, was erected in 1504. In 1691–94 the Arkhangelskaya (Archangel) Church was built onto the northern and eastern walls of the refectory.

The museum, which was opened in 1960, contains a number of icons dating from the 15th to 17th centuries. Most of the icons were found in churches and monasteries in old Russian towns and have been restored. The collection is being constantly enlarged.

Oriental Art Museum, Suvorov Boulevard 12a, in a mansion built by Gigliardi. Open 11–7; closed Mon. & the last Fri. in each month. The museum was opened in 1918 and comprised several private collections, including the Schukin collection, which had been taken over by the state. The collection has since been expanded and besides exhibits from India, China, and Japan, now has an interesting section of exhibits from the Soviet East.

The Chinese section includes stone bowls dating from the first millennium B.C., Chinese scrolls, wood and ivory carvings, and silk pictures.

Other exhibits of interest are the collection of miniature Japanese sculptures, Persian carpets, and Turkish gold-embroidered satin.

There is a branch of this museum at Obukha Street 16.

Literature Museum, Petrovka Street 28. Open 11–5.30; Wed & Fri. 2–8; closed Mon & the last day of the month. It is housed in the Naryshkin House of the *Vysoko-Petrovsky Monastery*. The monastery was founded by Dimitri Donskoy in the village of Vysoko to commemorate his victory over the Tatars of Kulikovo. The name Vysoko-Petrovsky was bestowed during rebuilding by Grand Prince Vasily Ivanovich. 3 additional churches and the Naryshkin House were built by Peter I at the end of the 17th century. The monastery is in a good state of preservation and forms one of the largest complexes of old Russian architecture in the centre of Moscow.

Folk Art Museum (Muzei Narodnovo Iskusstva), Stanislavsky Street 7. Open 10–5; closed

Mon. Samples of traditional lace and embroidery work, wood and bone carving, lacquer boxes, etc., can be seen in this museum. Periodically the work of students graduating from applied art courses are on display. The museum building was designed in 1870 in the style of 17th-century Russian architecture.

All Russia Decorative & Folk Art Museum, Delegatskaya Street 31. Open 11–7; closed Mon. & the last Fri. of each month.

Exhibition of Russian chattels of the 17th–19th centuries, Varvarka Street 10. The exhibition is housed in the House of the Boyars Romanov (see p. 329).

Simeon Ushakov Museum, Nikitnikov Pereulok 3 (off Razin Street). Open 10–6; Wed. & Thurs. 12–8; closed Tues. & the first Mon. of each month. The *Trinity Church in Nikitniki*, which is now open as the Simeon Ushakov Museum, was built in 1634 for Grigory Nikitnikov, a rich merchant and manufacturer. The church is notable for its murals on which Simeon Ushakov worked together with other Moscow artists. Many of them portray parables, which hitherto had been seldom used as motifs for church decorations and which are explicit of the more wordly attitude brought into the Church by such merchant patrons as Nikitnikov. Grigory Nikitnikov, together with his family, is portrayed in the mural on the southern wall of the church.

Schusev Architectural Museum, Vozdvizhenka Street 5. Open 11–7; closed Mon. & Fri. Academician Schusev (1873–1949) was a well-known Soviet architect who designed, among other things, the Lenin mausoleum. The museum covers the principal trends in Russian architecture from 1037 to the present day.

Donskoi Monastery, Donskaya Square 1. A branch of the Museum of Russian Architecture is housed in the cathedral of this monastery. Open 11–7; closed Mon., Fri. & the last Thurs. of every month.

The fortress-monastery was founded by Tsar Feodor in 1592 to commemorate Moscow's deliverance from the Crimean Khan, Kasi-Girei, in 1591. It is built on the camp site of the Russian troops who were sent to fight against the Crimean Khan as he approached Moscow.

The only building dating from the 16th century still standing is the small church of *Our Lady of the Don*, known as Maly Sobor (small cathedral) and containing the tomb of Patriarch Tikhon. It is open for services. The rest of the present-day buildings were erected between 1680 and 1730.

The stone walls with 12 towers were built at the end of the 17th century. The Great Cathedral (Bolshoi Sobor) was built in 1684–98. It has 5 domes and is a typical example of Moscow baroque containing a fine carved iconostasis that was made by Moscow craftsmen in 1693–98.

The museum is located in the cathedral. The display is very similar to that of the Schusev museum. In the former private church and chapel of the Princess Golitsyn that was built in 1809 are

Russian monumental sculptures of the 18th and 19th centuries.

The cemetery within the monastery walls contains many monuments to nobles, some of them the work of such renowned sculptors as Vitali and Martos.

Manege Exhibition Hall, Manezhnaya Square. Closed Tues.

Historical Museums

Lenin Mausoleum, Red Square, by the Kremlin walls. Open 10–1; Sun. 10–2 (in winter 10–3); closed Mon. & Fri. To avoid standing in the long queue, tourists should ask Intourist to arrange a special time for an accompanied visit.

The body of Vladimir Lenin (1870–1924), the founder of the Communist Party and the Soviet State, whose real name was Ulyanov, lies here. The body was evacuated in 1941, beyond the Urals to the Siberian city of Tyumen and brought back here at the end of the war. Stalin's body also lay in the mausoleum from his death in 1953 until 1961, when it was removed by popular demand and buried near the Kremlin wall among other Communist leaders, including Frunze, Kirov, Sverdlov, Dzerzhinsky, Brezhnev, Andropov, and Chernenko.

The building of the mausoleum was constructed in 1930 by Shchusev and is generally considered well-planned, harmonising with the older structures surrounding the square. It is made of red granite with black and grey labradorite. The present building replaced a wooden mausoleum which was erected after Lenin's death in 1924.

Steps lead up on both sides of the mausoleum to the roof where members of the government stand to watch parades and demonstrations in the square. 2 guards stand at the entrance to the mausoleum. Steps lead down to the underground vault where the embalmed body lies in a glass sarcophagus. A railing surrounds the sarcophagus and 4 guards stand nearby.

Lenin Museum, Revolution Square 2. Open 11–7; Fri., Sat. & Sun. 10–6; closed Mon. & the last Tues. of each month. The museum was opened in 1936 following a resolution by the Central Committee of the Soviet Communist Party.

It is housed in the Duma ("parliament") building that was constructed by Chichagov in pseudo-Russian style in 1890–92. It was built in red brick to blend with the earlier building of the Historical Museum alongside.

Over 7,000 exhibits are displayed in 22 halls of the museum. They cover the main periods of the life and work of the founder of the Soviet State, Vladimir Ilyich Lenin. Among the exhibits are some of Lenin's personal belongings such as a desk with secret drawers, a coat with bullet holes (the result of an attempt on his life in 1918), and his car. In one of the halls is a replica of his study in the Kremlin.

A newsreel of 1917–24, featuring Lenin, is shown. There are also numerous sculptures, paintings, carpets, carvings, and embroideries portraying the founder of the Communist Party.

Historical Museum, Red Square ½ (on north side). Open 10–6; closed Tues.—but now closed for restoration. The building was constructed in 1874–83 by the architect Sherwood and the engineer Semyonov under the influence of 17th-century Russian architecture. The museum was initiated by Moscow University and the first 11 halls were opened in 1883. It now has 300,000 exhibits and is the biggest repository of historical material and documents tracing the origin and history of the peoples of the Soviet Union from ancient times until the 1917 Revolution.

The first 7 halls carry the story up to the 1st century A.D. The painting "Stone Age" on the ceiling of the second hall is the work of the artist Vasnetsov and was commissioned for this hall in 1883–85.

Hall 9 contains many archaeological finds from Novgorod dating from the 9th to 15th centuries. There are models of old Novgorodian churches as well as a collection of icons from Novgorod and Pskov dating from the 14th and 15th centuries.

Hall 13 contains a number of interesting exhibits relating the development of central Russia in the 14th and 15th centuries. There are a number of icons, including the icon of "The Virgin Mary with Sergei Radonezh," which is attributed to the school of Andrei Rublyov. There are fragments of the wooden streets of Novgorod that are thought to have been relaid 32 times in the course of 700 years, and part of the bows of a rowing boat dating from the 12th century. The fresco is a contemporary reconstruction of the Moscow Kremlin during the 16th century.

Hall 15 contains a number of beautifully illustrated manuscripts and the first book to be published in Russia, the *Apostles* of 1564.

Hall 20 relates the history of the beginning of the 18th century when St. Petersburg was founded by Peter the Great. There are many documents regarding the reforms carried out by Peter and, in one of the showcases, garments belonging to the tsar.

Hall 23 chronicles the history of the second half of the 18th century, in particular the Peasant's Revolt of 1773–74. Above a portrait of Catherine II (1762–96) is one of the peasant leader, Pugachev, painted by an unknown artist in 1774. Also on display is the iron cage in which Pugachev was brought to Moscow after the revolt had been supressed.

Hall 28, the walls of which are covered with banners captured from the French army and of the Russian regiments, contains varied exhibits from the 1812 war. On the right of the hall is a marble bust of Napoleon by an unknown artist that was brought to Russia in order to be erected in the main square of Moscow. Also here is the field kitchen and sled that Napoleon used during the campaign.

The remaining halls illustrate the history of the 19th century, including the Crimean War and the abolition of serfdom.

Halls 38 and 39 are devoted to scientific, literary, and artistic developments.

The last hall, 40, contains documents relating to the 1917 Revolution and the personal belongings and arms of the revolutionaries who stormed the Winter Palace in St. Petersburg.

Revolution Museum, Tverskaya Street 21. Open 10–6, Wed. 12–8, Fri. 11-7; closed Mon. The museum is housed in the building of the former English Club. The 6-inch gun in the forecourt was used by revolutionary troops to fire on the Kremlin in October 1917.

The museum, which was opened in 1926, has 11 halls and the exhibits trace the history of the Revolution from 1915 until 1917 and also the evolution of socialism in the Soviet Union. Among the exhibits are battle-standards of the revolutionary troops, the horse-drawn machine-gun cart of the First Cavalry Army, texts of the first decrees of the Soviet Government and many photographs, paintings, and sculptures. Some of the halls display presents to the Soviet Union from foreign countries, including many given on the 50th anniversary of the Revolution.

Marx and Engels Museum, Marx Engels Street 5. Open Tues., Wed., Fri. 12–7; Thurs., Sat., Sun. 11–6; closed Mon. & the last day of each month. The museum exhibits chronicle the life and work of Marx and Engels and include manuscripts, letters, photographs, and early editions of their works. Also on display are a number of personal belongings of Marx, including the chair in which he died.

Soviet Armed Forces Museum, Kommuny Square 2. Open 10–5; Wed. & Thurs. 12–7; closed Mon. The museum is devoted to the history of the armed forces of the Soviet Union. It was completed in 1965.

The periods most fully represented in the museum are the years of the Civil War and of World War II. The display starts with the story of the workers' combatant groups of the 1905 revolution. While preparing for the armed uprising of 1917, the Bolshevik party established the "Red Guards," the core of the future Red Army. The appropriate decree was signed by Lenin on 28 January, 1918; the official celebration date is 23 February.

On display are hand-grenades, swords, and Maxim machine-guns (often the only weapons of the first Red Army units) and also some hand-made weapons used by the Siberian guerillas. The stands show personal belongings of some outstanding Red Army commanders, such as Chapayev, Frunze, and Budyonnyi. Among the exhibits of the years 1922 to 1939 are pictures of the first people to be awarded the title of Hero of the Soviet Union; these were pilots who rescued 100 members of the polar expedition on the icebreaker "Chelyuskin."

The remainder of the exhibits have to do with the conflicts with the Japanese (1937) and the Finns (1939–40), and the greater part of World War II. The display ends with exhibits demonstrating the present state of the Soviet Armed Forces and includes modern small arms, models of modern tanks, and a self-propelled rocket launcher. Outdoors, in the museum grounds, are an armoured train, some tanks, planes, and other large exhibits.

The museum used to be in the building next door, and was founded in the 18th century and rebuilt following Gigliardi's plans in 1802. In 1812 it was damaged by fire, and was again reconstructed in classical style by Gigliardi and Grigoryev and housed Catherine the Great's school for young ladies of noble birth. It is now the Soviet Army House.

Kutuzov's Hut Museum, Kutuzovsky Prospect 38. Open 10.30–7; closed Fri. Here in 1812 the Russian War Council, headed by Field-Marshal Mikhail Kutuzov, decided that it was necessary to retreat from Moscow in order to save the army. The painting by Kivshenko (1880) shows the council in session. In front of the hut is an obelisk, on which are inscribed the famous words of Field-Marshal Kutuzov: "The loss of Moscow is not yet the loss of Russia. For the good of our motherland I order a retreat."

Battle of Borodino Museum, Kutuzovsky Prospect 38, near Kutuzov's Hut and the Triumphal Arch (see p. 335). Open 9.30–8; closed Fri. & the last Thurs. of each month. The first building for the panorama was built at the beginning of this century, but it was damaged by fire and the present building was completed in 1962 to commemorate the 150th anniversary of the historic Battle of Borodino in August 1812, when Napoleon's Great Army suffered a serious defeat. The cylindrical building is 42 m (138 ft) in diameter.

The canvases of the panorama were painted in Munich by Roubaud (1865–1912), who came from Odessa and was also responsible for the Savastopol Panorama. They are 14 m (46 ft) high and the cylinder they form is 115 m (126 yd) in circumference.

Decembrists' Museum, Staraya Basmannaya Street 23. Open 10–7; closed Tues. This Empire-style mansion used to belong to the Muravyov-Apostol family, of which three brothers—Sergei, Matvei, and Ippolit—were Decembrists.

The Museum of History and Reconstruction of Moscow, Novaya Square 12, near Lubyanka Metro station. Open 10–6; Wed. & Fri. 2–9; closed Mon. & last day of each month.

The Museum is housed in the former Church of St. John the Baptist, built in 1825. It was founded in 1896 and by maps, photographs, engravings, lithographs, and models gives an outline of the history of Moscow's rise, telling the part it played in different periods of Russian history.

The reconstruction section deals with the modernization of the public services, building programmes, and plans of how the city will look in the future.

The display of presents received by the City of Moscow on the 800th anniversary of its foundation in 1947 is of interest.

Schusev Architectural Museum, Vozdvizhenka Street 5. Closed Mon. & Fri.

Literary, Theatrical, and Musical museums

Museum of Books, in Pashkov House (the old building of the Lenin Library).

Lev Tolstoy Museum, Prechistenka Street 11. Open 11–6; Wed. & Fri. 12–8; closed Mon. & the last Fri. of each month.

The museum is housed in the former Lopukhin mansion (see p. 000). It contains a very full collection of the writer's manuscripts covered with his corrections, as well as part of his personal library and a number of paintings and papers illustrating his life. Of interest are the 17 sketches Tolstoy intended to illustrate "Around the World in 80 Days" by Jules Verne. However, many people consider the museum to be less interesting than Tolstoy's Moscow home.

Tolstoy's Moscow Home, Lev Tolstoy Street 21. Open in summer 10–3; in winter 10–6; closed Mon. & the last Fri. of each month. 16 rooms of this house are preseved as they were during the time that Tolstoy lived here with his family from 1882 to 1909.

Chekhov's House, Sadovo-Kudrinskaya Street 6. Open 11–5.30; Wed. & Fri. 2–8.30; closed Mon. & the last day of each month.

Anton Chekhov lived here during the 1880s, and a brass plate reading DR. A. P. CHEKHOV can still be seen on the door.

Dostoyevsky Home, Dostoyevsky Street 2. Open 11–6; Wed. and Fri. 2–9; closed Mon., Tues. & the last day of the month.

Gorky's House, Kachalova Street 6/2. Open 12–7; Sat. & Sun. 10–5; closed Mon. & Tues. The house was built in the early 20th century by F. Shekhtel, architect of the Yaroslav Railway Terminal and the old Moscow Arts Theatre. It is renowned for its unique architectural design and is one of the outstanding monuments of the turn of the century. Maxim Gorky lived here from 1931 to 1936.

Gorky Museum, Vorovskovo Street 25a. Open 12–7; Sat. & Sun. 10–5; closed Mon. & Tues. The house in which the museum is situated was built in the 1820s by Ivan Gigliardi. The museum was opened in 1937 and contains books, letters, manuscripts, and photographs illustrating the writer's life. The monument to Gorky in front of the museum was designed by Vera Mukhina.

Lermontov Museum, Malaya Molchanovka Street 2. Open 11–6; Wed. & Fri. 2–9; closed Mon., Tues. and the last day of the month. This house was rented by Elizaveta Arseyenova, Lermontov's grandmother, in April 1840. He lived here for 2 years while studying at Moscow University.

Pushkin Museum, Prechistenka Street 12/2. Open 9–6; Wed. 12–8; closed Mon. & Tues. This mansion was built in 1814 (see p. 000). The exhibits include manuscripts, letters, first editions and paintings relating to the life and work of the poet.

Pushkin's House, Arbat 53. Open 12–7; Sat. & Sun. 11–6; closed Mon. & Tues.

Alexei Tolstoy Museum, Alexei Tolstoy Street. The writer Alexei Tolstoy (1883–1945) lived abroad as an emigre from 1918–1923.

Paustovsky Museum, Kuzminki Park. Konstantin Paustovsky (1892–1970) was a nature writer, known for his fine descriptions of the Russian countryside and wild life.

Bakhruschin Theatrical Museum, Bakhrushin Street 31/12. Near Paveletskaya metro station. Open 12–7; Wed. & Fri. 1–8; closed Tues. and the last Mon. of each month. This museum was founded in 1894 by the theatre-lover and collector whose name it now bears and is located in his house. The exhibits relate the history of Russian drama, opera, and ballet theatres from the 18th century to the present day. The exhibits include portraits of actors, manuscripts, playbills, programmes, personal belongings, and photographs.

Ostrovsky's Home, Ostrovsky Street 9, near Tretyakovskaya Metro station. Alexander Ostrovsky (1823–86) was a popular satirical playwright, regarded now as the founder of Russian drama.

Glinka Music Centre, Fadeyev Street 4. Open 11–7; Tues. & Thurs. 2–9; closed Mon. This is the national music museum. Different exhibitions are mounted here that include scores, letters, photographs, and recordings of many famous performers and composers besides Mikhail Glinka. Of special interest is the collection of musical instruments. The spacious museum building contains music rooms for individuals and for groups to hear works performed by Chaliapin, Caruso, and many others. There is also a hall seating 180.

Chaliapin's Home, Novinsky Boulevard 25.

Skryabin Museum, Vakhtangov Street 11. Open Mon., Thurs., Sun. 1–5; Tues., Fri., Sat. 3–7; closed Wed. The well-known Russian composer and pianist Alexander Skryabin (1871–1915) lived and died here.

Herzen Museum, Sivtsev Vrazhek 27. Open 11–4; Wed. & Fri. 2–9; closed Mon. and last day of each month. The museum is dedicated to the life and work of Alexander Herzen and is housed in his Moscow mansion. Herzen died in Paris in 1870 but spent 3 years of his life here.

Economic, Scientific, and Technical Museums and Exhibitions

The USSR Exhibition of Economic Achievements. This is located in the north-western part of Moscow, the main entrance being on Prospect Mira, on the way to Ostankino. Open 9:30 A.M.– 10 P.M.; Sat. & Sun. 9:30 A.M.–11 P.M. From 1st Sept. till 1st May pavilions open 10–6. The exhibition occupies a site of 216 hectares (553 acres) and includes about 80 large pavilions and many smaller structures. There is a 5-km circular road with various forms of public transport, including small buses, open-car trains, and motor-bike taxis.

There are pavilions built in the architectural styles of the different Soviet republics, and also many large pavilions devoted to different branches of agricultures, industry, and science. Among them are the pavilions "Atomic Energy," "Education," "Science," "Radio-Electronics," and "Machine Building," a domed pavilion where there is a display of Russian cars. One of the largest pavilions is the pavilion "Cosmos." In front of the pavilion there is a multi-stage rocket that is a replica of the one which launched Yuri Gagarin on the first manned space flight.

Also in the exhibition grounds are a circus, a circorama cinema, and an open-air theatre. There are many restaurants and cafés, but the best is probably the Zolotoi Kolos (Golden Ear) restaurant.

By the main entrance to the exhibition is a monument to commemorate Soviet space exploration. The monument, which is 90 m (295 ft) high, was erected in 1964 and there is a museum inside. In front of the monument is a statue of Konstantin Tsiolkovsky. A number of busts of leading scientists and cosmonauts line the avenue from the space monument to Prospect Mira.

In front of the North Gates entrance is a stainless steel statue "Worker and Farm-Woman" by Vera Mukhina, which was designed for the Paris Fair of 1937.

Korolyov's House, 6-Ostankinsky Pereulok 2/26 (not far from the Exhibition of Economic Achievements). Open 10–6; Wed. & Thurs. 11–8; closed Mon., Tues. & the last Fri. of each month. The museum is situated in the house where the founder of Soviet astronautics lived and worked from 1959 to 1966.

Polytechnical Museum, Novaya Square 3/4. Open 10–6; Tues., Thurs. & Sat. 1–9; closed Mon. & the last Thurs. of the month. This museum contains a large collection of technical and scientific exhibits, including some on space exploration. It also has a technical library. The building itself was constructed in Russian style in the 1870s from plans by Monighetti.

Natural History Museum, Herzen Street 6. Open 9–4; closed Sun.

Timiryazev Biological Museum, Malaya Gruzinskaya Street 15. Open 10–6; Wed., Fri. 12–8; closed Mon. The museum is named after Kliment Timiryazev (1843–1920), who championed Darwinism in Russia. His work as a botanist was chiefly concerned with photosynthesis. The exhibits of the museum illustrate plant and animal life, and the origins and development of life on Earth.

Darwin Museum, Malaya Pirogovskaya Street 1. Open 10–5; closed Sun.

Durov's Corner, Durov Street 4. Open 11–5; Thurs. 10–3; Sun. 10–5; closed Fri.

Durov's Corner is named after the famous Russian animal trainer and circus clown, Vladimir Durov (1863–1934). About 200 trained animals and birds are kept here. They can be seen in their cages and performing on the stage of the Animal Theatre (seating 120) on Sat. at 1 pm and on Sundays at 11, 1 and 3. More than 50 animals can be seen in the fairy tale production, "Terem-

Teremok." There is also a production called "The Story of How the Animals of Grandfather Durov's Corner Flew to the Moon."

Planetarium, Sadovaya-Kudrinskaya Street 5. Open 1–6; closed Tues.

Zoo, Bolshaya Gruzinskaya Street 1.

Botanical Garden, Academy of Sciences, Ostankino, Botanicheskaya Street 4. Open 1st April–1st Nov. 9 A.M.–8 P.M.; hothouses 10–5, in winter 10–4; hothouses closed Thurs. The botanical garden was opened in 1959 and occupies a site of 360 hectares (900 acres), which includes an attractive park and some forest land where you may encounter elk.

Botanical Garden of Moscow University, Prospect Mira 26. This botanical garden was founded in 1706 and was originally known as Apothecary Garden.

Parks and Recreation Facilities

Gorky Park, Krymsky Val 9. Near Oktyabrskaya and Park Kultury metro stations. Open from 9 to midnight. In the park there are amusements, sports grounds, a boating station, a chess club, a shooting gallery, a restaurant, cafés, a beer hall, and an open-air theatre seating 12,000. In winter many of the paths of the park are flooded and used for skating.

Sokolniki Park, Sokolniki metro station. Sokolniki Park is named after the falconers ("sokolniki") who used to live here and attend the tsars' hunting parties. For over 100 years it was a popular place to go for picnics, and the nobility used to drive their coaches along the avenues. It has become widely known for the American, Japanese, British, French, and other national fairs held here. Each country has added to the exhibition site's equipment and accommodation.

In the park are also an open-air theatre seating 5,000, an amusement park, a shooting gallery, bicycles for rent, restaurants, and cafés. In winter the park that covers an area of 612 hectares (1,530 acres) is a popular place to ski and one can rent skis here.

Izmailovo Park, Izmailovskaya metro station. Open 10 A.M.–11 P.M. The park covers 1,180 hectares (2,950 acres) and includes large stretches of pine forest. It was once the manor of the Romanov family and a favourite resort of the tsars.

Here, in a disused storehouse, Peter the Great found the old English boat that is now known as the "grandfather of the Russian fleet" and kept in a museum in Leningrad. There is an amusement park, an open-air theatre, and several cafés. Part of the park, called *Mir Skazok*, and covering an area of 3 hectares (8 acres), is specially laid out for children.

Hermitage Garden, Karetnyi Ryad 3. Open 10–10. This small garden has retained its popularity since the 1890s. During the summer season there are concerts and performances by variety and puppet theatres, and there are several cafés and a restaurant.

Sport

The 1980 Olympics made a significant improvement in Moscow's sport facilities, both for spectators and for participants. The *Lenin Stadium* and *Palace of Sports* at Luzhniki, near Komsomolsky Prospect and Leninskiye Gory metro station, is probably the most important centre. The complex was built in 1955–56 by Vlasov, Roshin, and other architects. Major national and international sports events are held here. The large arena can seat 103,000. There is also a Children's Sports Area and many different sections for swimming, tennis, basketball, and other sports.

Dynamo Stadium is Moscow's second-largest stadium and can seat 50,000. It is part of a large complex situated in Petrovsky park on Leningradsky Prospect and includes covered tennis courts and an indoor pool and room for 1,000 spectators. There are open-air facilities for basketball, volleyball, lawn tennis, and the Russian game of gorodki. There is an ice rink in the sports pavilion and the indoor soccer arena features a field of synthetic turf. The *Army Palace of Sports* and the *Young Pioneer Stadium* are nearby. Other important centres are the *Sokolniki Palace of Sports* in Maly Oleny Pereulok and the sport complexes in *Prospect Mira* and *Izmailovo*.

The *Moskva Open-Air Swimming Pool* opposite Kropotkinskaya metro station is open all year round and heated to a temperature of 28–30°C in winter when it is covered with a cloud of steam that protects bathers from the cold air. *Setun Swimming Pool and Gym* and the *Palace of Water Sports* in Mironovskaya Street are both well-equipped, and in the summer the beach at Serebryany Bor, the Dynamo Beach at Khimki, and the recreation area beside the Klyazma Reservoir are popular.

There is rowing on the Moskva river but the best place is *Krylatskoye Sports Complex*, which includes a cycle track and archery field. The rugged terrain in the vicinity is used for cross-country races and ski-jumping in the winter. Even the canal is used in winter because its frozen snow-covered surface is ideal for ski practice.

The *Hippodrome Racecourse* in Begovaya Street has meets on Wednesdays and on the weekends and riding classes are available both here and at *Sokolniki Park*. The racecourse was founded in 1883. Its gates are decorated with figures of people and horses by K. Klodt, grandson of the architect P. Klodt, and resemble the latter's famous sculptures on the Anichkov Bridge in Leningrad. There are about 500 horses in the stables, a totalisator or pari-mutuel, and a restaurant. The Olympic equestrian complex is to the south of the city, in Bitsy Park.

Transport

The Metro. Open 6 A.M.–1 P.M. The metro is the pride of the city. The 3 main lines crossing in the centre are linked by a circle line crossing them each in turn and forming a junction with 4 newer lines that serve the suburbs. This basic spider-web plan follows the layout of the city itself.

The metro works perfectly from a technical point of view; the escalators, air-conditioning, and the passenger tunnels are all well planned. During the rush hour trains leave the stations at intervals of 90 seconds and the maximum speed is 90 kph (60 mph).

The decor of each station is a separate work of art; some give the impression of a palace, with soft lights shining on the columns and intricate mosaics. Each line has its characteristic features; the noble simplicity of the Sokolniki-Yugo-Zapadnaya line is in contrast to the extravagant grandeur of the Circle Line. One of the most impressive stations is Mayakovskaya, named in honour of the poet Mayakovsky whose statute stands in the square above. Here the columns are of stainless steel and red marble from paintings by A. Deineka, a well-known artist in the Soviet Union. The first line of the metro was opened in 1935, and new construction is always in progress. The newer stations, however, are much plainer.

There is a standard fare of 15 kopeks. To enter the metro one must drop a 15-kopek piece into the turnstile on one's right hand side and wait for the yellow light to change.

The same 15-kopek fare is also used on buses, trolley-buses, and trams. On most routes the last run is made at 1 A.M.

Boat trips along the river operate from May or June until September or October depending on the weather.

Route 1: From the Kiev terminal (in front of Kievsky Station) eastwards to Novospassky Bridge. This route passes Novodevichy Convent, Lenin Hills, the stadium, and the Kremlin. The trip lasts 1 hour 20 minutes.

Route 2: From Kiev terminal westwards to Kuntsevo-Krylatskoye. This route goes to Fili-Kuntsevo Park and the river beach. The trip lasts 1 hour.

Monuments

Yuri Dolgoruky Statue, Sovietskaya Square. Prince Yuri Dolgoruky founded Moscow in 1147, and the foundation of this commemorative equestrian statue was laid to mark the 800th anniversary of the event. It is by Sergei Orlov.

Feodorov Monument, Teatralny Proyezd. Ivan Feodorov was the first Russian printer, and the date on the pedestal, 19 April 1563, is the day when the printing of the first Russian book was begun. The statue is by Sergei Volnukhin and was erected in 1909.

Lomonosov Monument, in front of the Old University building, Mokhovaya Street, and in the courtyard of the New University building on Lenin Hills. Mikhail Lomonosov (1711–65), was the scientist and encyclopaedist who founded Moscow University in 1755. The statue on Lenin Hills is by N. Tomsky and was erected in 1954.

Minin and Pozharsky Monument, on Red Square, in front of St. Basil's Cathedral (see p. 328).

Suvorov Monument, Kommuny Square. The bronze figure of Generalissimo Count Alexander Suvorov (1730–1800) stands on a granite pedestal and rises to 9 m (30 ft). It is by Oleg Komov and was unveiled in 1982. At the foot of the monument are guns that were trophies taken by the Russian army. Suvorov's military career spanned 50 years during which he participated in 20 military expeditions, and won each of the 63 battles he commanded.

Krylov Monument, by Patriarshyie Ponds. The monument to the fabler, Ivan Krylov (1769–1844), by Drevin was put up in 1976.

Griboyedov Monument, Kirovskiye Vorota, Chistoprudnyi Boulevard. Alexander Griboyedov (1798–1829) is famed for his single play, "Woe from Wit," which was rejected by the censor and only staged 2 years after he was murdered while serving as ambassador to Persia. The statue of him by N. Manuilov was erected in 1959.

Kutuzov Monument, Kutuzovsky Prospect, near the Triumphal Arch erected in honour of the 1812 victory. The equestrian statue of the Field-Marshal was designed by N. Tomsky and unveiled in 1973.

Pushkin Monument, in Pushkin Square. This statue by A. Opekushin was erected to the poet's memory by popular donations in 1880.

Lermontov Monument, Lermontov Square. This 5-m (16-ft) statue by Brodsky was unveiled in 1965 to commemorate the 150th anniversary of the poet's birth.

Gogol Statue, Arbatskaya Square. This statue of Nikolai Gogol (1809–52) by N. Tomsky was erected in 1952.

Dostoyevsky Monument, Dostoyevsky Street. This is the only outdoor statue of the great writer. It was designed by S. Merkurov and is among the best works of Russian sculpture of the turn of the century. It was first put up in Tsvetnoi Boulevard in 1918, but was moved here in 1936.

Herzen's Vow Monument, on the wooded slopes of Lenin Hills overlooking Moscow. This white stone monument was designed in 1978 by Schmakin and Ogayev to commemorate the 150th anniversary of the vow made by Alexander Herzen and Nikolai Ogaryov to devote the rest of their lives to fighting against the tsarist regime.

Shevchenko Monument, in front of the Ukraina Hotel, Naberezhnaya Shevchenko. Taras Shevchenko is the best known Ukrainian poet (1814–61) and this statue by Glitsuk, Sinkevich, and Fuzhenko was unveiled in 1964 to mark the 150th anniversary of his birth.

Ostrovsky Monument, Teatralnaya Square, in front of the Maly Theatre. Alexander N. Ostrovsky (1823–86) was a popular satirical playwright, and is regarded as the founder of Russian drama. The monument to him by Nikolai Andreyev was erected in 1929 in front of the theatre where his plays were, and still are, staged.

Pirogov Monument, Bolshaya Pirogovskaya

Street. This monument to Nikolai Pirogov, surgeon and scientist, by V. Sherwood, was erected in 1897.

Sechenov Monument, Bolshaya Pirogovskaya Street 2/6. Ivan Sechenov (1829–1905) is known as the father of Russian physiology; he was a professor of both St. Petersburg and Moscow universities. This statue, which was erected in 1958, is by Lev Kerbel.

Grenadiers of Plevna Monument, Ilyinskiye Vorota. This monument, designed by V. Sherwood, was erected in 1887. It was built with funds collected by the survivors of the grenadiers who fought at the Battle of Plevna (1887) during the liberation of Bulgaria from the Ottoman Empire.

Tchaikovsky Monument, Herzen Street, in front of the conservatoire. This seated statue of the composer was designed by Vera Mukhina and erected in 1954.

Timiryazev Monument, Nikitskiye Vorota. This monument to the naturalist and follower of Darwin was designed by Sergei Merkurov and erected in 1923.

Repin Monument, Repin (formerly Bolotnaya) Square. This statue of artist Ilya Repin was created by M. Manizer in 1958.

Lev Tolstoy Monument, Bolshaya Pirogovskaya Street. By Portyanko and unveiled in 1972.

Tsiolkovsky Monument, at the foot of the soaring rocket monument on Prospect Mira. Konstantin Tsiolkovsky (1857–1935) was a pioneer in the theory of space travel and rocketry.

Karl Marx Monument, Teatralnaya Square. This monument to the philosopher by Lev Kerbel was unveiled to mark the 22nd Soviet Communist Party Congress in 1961. The street in front of it was renamed Marx Prospect at the same time, but this was changed back in 1991.

Engels Monument, Prechistenka Street. This monument to Friedrich Engels, one of the founders of scientific communism, is by Kozlovsky and was unveiled in November 1976.

1905 Monument, 1905-Goda Street, opposite the Metro station. Commemorating the heroes of the December 1905 armed revolt.

Obelisk, in Alexandrovsky Gardens, beside the Kremlin Wall. This obelisk was erected in 1913 in commemoration of the 300th anniversary of the House of Romanov and was engraved with the names of the Russian tsars. After the Revolution these and the double-headed eagle were eradicated, and replaced with the names of Marx, Engels, Marat, Plekhanov, Spartacus, and other revolutionaries and philosophers.

Sverdlov Monument, Teatralnaya Square. Yakov Sverdlov (1885–1919) was the first Soviet chairman. The monument by Ambratsumyan was erected in 1978.

Lenin Monument, Sovietskaya Square in front of the Marxism-Leninism Institute. This statue by S. Merkurov was exhibited at the New York World's Fair in 1939 before it was erected here in 1940.

Lenin Statue, Oktyabrskaya Square. The bronze statue of Lenin on a pedestal of red granite and surrounded by figures of revolutionaries and soldiers was designed by Lev Kerbel.

Krupskaya Monument, Sretenskiye Vorota. Nadezhda Krupskaya (1869–1939) was Lenin's wife and a state and Party figure. The statue was designed byYekaterina Belashova.

Tombstones of the Soviet Union's outstanding leaders, beside the Kremlin wall, on Red Square. Here among the Soviet great lie Sverdlov, Frunze, Dzerzhinsky, Kalinin, Stalin, Brezhnev, Andropov, and Chernenko.

Vorovsky Monument, at the crossing of Kuznetsky Most and Bolshaya Lubyanka Street. The memorial to the literary critic and diplomat, who was assassinated in Switzerland in 1923, was erected in the year following his death by M. Kats.

Dzerzhinsky Monument, Lubyanskaya Square. This statue of Felix Dzerzhinsky (1877–1926), revolutionary and statesman, was designed by Yevgeni Vuchetich in 1958.

Gorky Statue, by the Byelorussy railway station. Designed by Ivan Shadr and made from his sketches by Mukhina, Zelenskaya, and Ivanova, the statue was unveiled on 10 June 1951.

Yesenin Monument, Yesenin Boulevard. This monument to the poet, Sergei Yesenin (1895–1925), was created in 1972 by Tsygal.

Mayakovsky Monument, Mayakovsky Square. This statue of Vladimir Mayakovsky (1893–1930), poet and playwright, ws designed by A. Kibalnikov and erected in 1958.

Worker and Farm-Woman Statue, at the entrance to the Exhibition of Economic Achievements. This gigantic statue created in 1937 by Vera Mukhina was on show at the Soviet Exhibition in Paris in that year.

Victory (Pobedy) Memorial, at the end of Kutuzovsky Prospect. The main avenue is 500 m/yd long and starts in Pobedy Square, just behind the Borodino Arch. It leads to a central monument, 72 m (236 ft) high and comprising a red granite banner above figures of a soldier, a sailor, an airman, a partisan, and a woman warrior, symbolising all who took part in the fighting. There is a bas-relief of Lenin on the banner, which is illuminated at night by a laser beam. Along the avenue are bronze steles with inscriptions about the main battles of each year of the war, and the 1,418 fountain jets represent the days the war lasted on Soviet soil.

Glory Monument, at the joining of Bolshaya Dorogomilovskaya Street and Kutuzovsky Prospect. This 40-m (131-ft) obelisk in the form of a bayonet is made of grey granite blocks of 4-6 cu m each and crowned with a golden star. The obelisk is dedicated to Moscow's award of the title of Hero-City. It was designed by A. Scherbakov and unveiled in May 1977.

Kalinin Statue, Vozdvizhenka Street. Mikhail Kalinin (1875–1946) served as Soviet president from 1922–46. The seated statue by Duzhev was unveiled in 1976.

Dimitrov Monument, Dimitrova Street.

Georgy Dimitrov (1882–1949) was a founder of the Bulgarian Communist Party and the first prime minister of the Bulgarian PR. The monument by Mekabishvili was unveiled in 1972.

Indira Gandhi Monument, Indira Gandhi Square.

Thalmann Monument, Ernst Thalmann Square. Ernst Thalmann (1886–1944) served as chairman of the German Communist Party from 1925–44 when he was shot as an antifascist. The sculpture by the Artamonov brothers was installed in 1986.

Practical Information

Theatres & Concert Halls

Bolshoi Theatre, Teatralnaya Square. This theatre was formerly known as the Great Imperial Theatre. It was built by Bovet in 1824 and restored after a fire in 1854 by Cavos. The statue of Phoebus in the Sun Chariot above the ionic portico is famous.

The theatre company is known all over the world for its incomparable ballet, and Russian and foreign operas are also in the repertoire. The orchestra, too, is one of the best in the country.

Maly (little) Theatre, Teatralnaya Square 1/6 (affiliated theatre, Bolshaya Ordynka Street 69). This theatre built by Bovet in 1824 and reconstructed by Thon in 1838–40, was formerly called the Little Imperial Theatre. It has been well known for many years for its staging of Russian classical plays, especially those by the satirist Ostrovsky, a statue of whom stands by the entrance. Plays by other Russian and Soviet playwrights as well as those translated from other languages are in the current repertoire.

The Moscow Arts Theatre (MKhAT), Proyezd Khudozhestvennovo Teatra 3. This theatre was founded in 1898 by the famous Russian actor and director Konstantin Stanislavsky (1863–1938) and director Vladimir Nemirovich-Danchenko (1858–1943). They staged Chekhov's and Gorky's plays here and it was here that Konstantin Stanislavsky developed his theories, based on the realistic traditions of the Russian theatre, which became known as the Stanislavsky method. After the production of Chekhov's "The Seagull," they chose the bird as their emblem and it now decorates the curtain, tickets, and programmes.

The Moscow Arts Theatre (MKhAT), New Building—Tverskoy Boulevard 24

Stanislavsky and Nemirovich-Danchenko Musical Theatre, Pushkinskaya Street 17. This theatre, which has a repertoire of classical and modern opera, operettas, and ballets, is named after the popular Russian directors.

Palace of Congresses, Kremlin, entrance for performances through the white-washed Kutafia Gate (by the Manege) which leads to the Trinity Gate (Troitskiye Vorota). Performances by the Bolshoi theatre and visiting companies are held here.

Operetta Theatre, Pushkinskaya Street 6

Children's Musical Theatre, Vernadskovo Prospect 5

Obraztsov Puppet Theatre, Sadovo-Kudrinskaya 3. Named after its founder and long-time director. The performances for adults are well worth seeing.

Moscow Puppet Theatre, Spartakovskaya Street 26

Central Children's Theatre, Teatralnaya Square 2

Central Soviet Army Drama Theatre, Kommuny Square 2. This theatre designed by Alabyan and Simbirtsev in 1934–38, is built in the shape of a huge, 5-pointed star.

Jewish Drama Theatre-Studio, Varshavskoye Chaussée 71

Lenin Komsomol Theatre, Chekhov Street 6

Mayakovsky Drama Theatre, Herzen Street 19

Moscow Drama Theatre, Malaya Bronnaya Street 2-4

Moscow Theatre of Drama and Comedy on Taganka, Zemlyanoy Val 76. This theatre is considered by many to be the most progressive and lively in Moscow.

Mossoviet Theatre, Bolshaya Sadovaya Street 16

Pushkin Drama Theatre, Tverskoi Boulevard 23

Romany Theatre, Leningradsky Prospect 32. This is the only gypsy theatre in the world, and many of the performances include gypsy songs and dances.

Satire Theatre, Bolshaya Sadovaya Street 18

Satirikon Theatre, Sheremetyevskaya Street 8

Sovremennik (Contemporary) Theatre, Chistoprudny Boulevard 19a

Vakhtangov Drama Theatre, Arbat Street 26. This theatre is named after Stanislavsky's pupil, Evgeny Vakhtangov (1883–1922).

Variety Theatre, Bersenevskaya Naberezhnaya 24

Yermolova Drama Theatre, Tverskaya Street 5. This theatre is named after one of the most famous Russian actresses, Maria Yermolova (1853–1928).

Yunovo Zritelya (Youth) Theatre, Per. Sadovskikh 10

Tchaikovsky Conservatoire, Herzen Street 13

Tchaikovsky Concert Hall, Mayakovsky Square 20

Rossiya Hotel Concert Hall, Moskvoretskaya Nab. 1

Oktyabr Cinema Concert Hall, Novy Arbat Street 42

Kolonny Zal (Hall of Columns), in the House of Trade Unions, Pushkinskaya Street 1/6

Circus, Tsvetnoi Boulevard 13 and Prospect Vernadskovo 7

Animal Theatre, Durov Street 4

Illusion Cinema, Kotelnicheskaya Nab. 1/15. Foreign-language films.

Hotels

Akademicheskaya Hotel-1, Leninsky Prospect 1; tel. 238 0902

Akademicheskaya Hotel-2, Donskaya Street 1; tel. 238 0508, 238 2550 (service bureau)

Aeroflot, Leningradsky Prospect 37; tel. 155 5624

Aerostar, Leningradsky Pr. 37, Kor. 9; tel 155 5989

Belgrade-1 (Intourist), Smolenskaya Square 5; tel 248 6734/7825

Belgrade-2 (Intourist), Opposite Belgrade-1; tel. 248 1643

Bucharest, Balchug Street 1; tel. 233 0029

Budapest, Petrovskiye Linii 2/18; tel. 924 8820

Cosmos (Intourist), Prospect Mira 150; tel. 217 0785, 217 0786

Intourist, Tverskaya Street 3-5; tel. 203 4008

Leningradskaya, Kalanchovskaya Street 21/40; tel. 975 3008 (enquiries)

Metropol (Intourist), Teatralny Proyezd 1; tel. 927 6002

Mezhdunarodnaya-1, Krasnopresnenskaya Nab. 12, tel. 253 2382, 253 7708 (reception), 253 2762

Mezhdunarodnaya-2, Krasnopresnenskaya Nab. 12; tel. 253 2378, 253 1391

Minsk, Tverskaya Street 22; tel. 299 1300/1215/1216 (service bureau), Rooms—2991 + Room no.

Mir, B. Devyatinsky Per. 9; tel. 252 9519

Moskva, Okhotny Ryad 7; tel. 292 1120, 292 6088 (service bureau)

Mozhaiskaya (Intourist), Mozhaiskoye Chaussee 165; tel. 447 3434, 447 3435

National (Intourist), Mokhovaya Street 14/1; tel. 203 5566 (service bureau), 203 6083 (enquiries)

Orlyonok, Kosygina Street 15; tel. 939 8853, 939 8844

Peking, Bolshaya Sadovaya Street 5; tel. 209 2135 (service bureau)

Pullman, Korovinskoye Chaussée 488 8020

Rossiya, Varvarka Street 6; tel. 298 5400/5531

Slavyanskaya, Berezhkorvskaya Nab. 2

Savoy (Intourist), Rozhdestvenka Street 3; tel. 929 8500

Sevastopol (Intourist), B. Ushunskaya Street 1a; tel. 318 2263

Solnechny, (Intourist) Motel, Varshavskoye Chaussee, 21 km; tel. 382 1465

Sovietskaya, Leningradsky Prospect 32; tel. 250 7255 (enquiries)

Soyuz-1, Levoberezhnaya Street 12; tel. 457 9004

Soyuz-2, 1-Krasnogvardeisky Proyezd 25b; tel. 250 3004

Sport, Leninsky Prospect 90/2; tel. 131 1191, 131 3515

Sputnik, Leninsky Prospect 38; tel. 938 7106

Tsentralnaya, Stoleshnikov Per. 18; tel. 229 8957/8589

Tsentralny Dom Turista, Leninsky Prospect 146; tel. 438 5510

Tourist, Selkhozyaistvennaya Street 17/2; tel. 187 6018 (service bureau)

Tourist Complex, Izmailovskoye Chaussee 69a; tel. 166 0109 (enquiries)

Ukraina, Kutuzovsky Prospect 2/1; tel. 243 3030 (enquiries), 243 2895 (service bureau)

Ural, Chernyshevskovo Street 40; tel. 297 4258

Varshava, Oktyabrskaya Square 1/2; tel. 238 1970 (switchboard)

Volga Korpus I, Skornyazhny Per. 10; tel. 280 7729

Volga Korpus II, B. Spasskaya Street 4; tel. 280 1364

Vostok, Gostinichny Proyezd 8; tel. 482 2597

Yaroslavskaya, Yaroslavskaya Street 8; tel. 283 1733

Yunost, Frunzensky Val 34; tel. 242 0353, 242 1980

Yuzhnaya, Leninsky Prospect 87; tel. 134 3065, 134 2089 (enquiries)

Zarya, Gostinichnaya Street 5; tel. 482 2347

Zolotoi Kolos, Yaroslavskaya Street 15; tel. 283 1694

Restaurants

Aragvi, Tverskaya Street 6; 229 3762. This restaurant specialises in Georgian cuisine. The following may be recommended:

Satsivi—in spicy sauce
Lobio—butter beans in spicy sauce
Kharcho—spiced meat soup
Osetrina na vertelye—spit-roasted sturgeon
Tsyplyata tabaka—roast spring chicken, flattened between hot stones
Shashlik (po-karsky or po-kavkazsky)—pieces of mutton roasted on a skewer
Koopaty— Georgian sausages

Arbat, Novy Arbat Street 26; 291-1445

Arkhangelskoye (country restaurant), 562 0328

Arlecchino (Italian), Druzhynnikovskaya Street 15; 205 7088

Atrium, Leninsky Pr. 44; 137 3008

Belgrade-1 (Yugoslavian), Smolenskaya Square 5 (near the Ruslan shop); 248-6713

Belgrade-2 (Yugoslavian), opposite Belgrade-1; 246 2696

Bombay (Indian), Rublyovskoye Chaussee 91; 141 5502

Bucharest (Rumanian), Balchug Street 1; 231 6239

Budapest, Petrovskiye Linii 2, in the Budapest Hotel; 221 4044. The restaurant has mainly Hungarian cuisine.

Business Club, Krasnopresnenskaya Nab. 12; 253 1792

Central, Tverskaya Street 3; 229 0241

Central House of Tourists, Leninsky Prospect 146; 434 7710, 434 3160

Continental, Krasnopresnenskaya Nab. 12; 253 1934

Delhi (Indian), Krasnaya Presnaya Street 23b; 252 1766

Dubrava, Cosmos Hotel, Prospect Mira 150; 217 0495

Dubrava, (50 km/31 miles) from Moscow along Kievskoye Chaussee

Galaktika, Prospect Mira 150; 217 1386

Glazour, Smolensky Bld 12/19; 248 4438

Havana (Cuban), Leninsky Prospect 88; 138 0091

Hermitage, Karetny Ryad 3; 299-1160

Intourist, Tverskaya Street 3–5; 203 9608

Iveria (Georgian), 45 km (28 miles) from Moscow along the Minskoye Chaussee; 593-4159. The menu is as at the Aravgi Restaurant.

Kropotkinskaya 36, Prechistenka Street 36; 201-7500

Late Night Bar, Tverskaya Street 3; 203 1345

Leningrad, Kalanchovskaya Street 21/40; 208 2008

Livian, Tverskaya Street 24; 299 8506. Their cuisine includes:

dovta—sour milk and meat soup
piti—thick mutton broth with potatoes, Caucasian peas, and herbs
pilaf—a choice of up to 23 different kinds of rice
golubtsy—meat balls wrapped in vine leaves

Maihua Café (Chinese), Rusakovskaya Street 2/1; 264-9574

Minsk, Tverskaya Street 22; 299 1100, 299 1248

Mir, B. Devyatinsky Per. 9; 290 9433

Moskva, Okhotny Ryad 7, in the Moskva Hotel; 292-6267

National, Tverskaya Street 1, in the National Hotel; 203 5550. The bar upstairs serves whisky and other drinks for payment in any convertible currency.

Peking (Chinese), Bolshaya Sadovaya Street 1/7, in the Peking Hotel; 209 1865

Pizza Hut, Kutuzovsky Prospect 17; 243 1727

Praga (Czech), Arbat Street 2; 290 6171. This restaurant has a pleasant open-air terrace on the roof.

Rossiya, Moskvoretskaya Nab. 1, in the Rossiya Hotel; 298 5474

Rus, Saltykovka Station, Krasnozvyozdnaya Street 12; 524 4202

Russian Hall, Tverskaya Street 3; 203 0150

Russkaya Chainaya (tea hall), Teatralny Proyezd 1; 225 6442

Russkaya Izba, 30 km (19 miles) from Moscow, in Ilyinskoye near Arkhangelskoye; 561 4244

Sakura (Japanese), Krasnopresnenskaya Nab. 12; 253 2894

Savoy, Rozhdestvenka Street 6, in the Savoy Hotel; 928 0450

Skazka, 41 km (25 miles) from Moscow along the Yaroslavskoye Chaussee; 584 3436, 44

Slavyansky Bazaar (Slav), Nikolskaya Street 13; 221 1872

Sovietsky, Leningradsky Prospect 32, in the Sovietskaya Hotel; 250 7459

Sofia, Tverskaya Street 21/1; 251 4950. This restaurant specialises in Bulgarian cuisine

Tsentralnaya, Tverskaya Street 10; 229 0241. All sorts of traditional Russian dishes are served here.

Ukraina, Kutuzovsky Prospect 2/1, in the Ukraine Hotel; 243 4732. Ukrainian cuisine is a speciality of the restaurant and includes:

Ukrainian borsch and vareniki—tiny dumplings filled with meat, fruit, vegetables, or cottage cheese.

Uzbekistan, Neglinnaya Street 29; 924 6053. This restaurant, which has some tables outside, is extremely popular. The Uzbek cuisine includes:

logman—meat and noodle soup
maniar—soup of minced meat, eggs, and dumplings
mastava—meat and rice soup
muntyi—large dumplings filled with meat
tkhum-dulma—Scotch eggs
shashlik—meat grilled on a skewer
pilaf

Varshava (Polish), Oktyabrskaya Square 2/1, in the Varshava Hotel; 238 1055. The name means Warsaw.

Villa Peredelkino; 435 1478/1211

Yakimanka (Uzbek), Bolshaya Polyanka Street 2/1

Zolotoy Zal (Golden Hall), Tverskaya Street 3; 203 1450

Zvyoznoye Nebo (Starry Sky), Tverskaya Street 3; 203 9608

44 Café, Leningradskoye Chaussée 44. Open round the clock.

Shops

Beryozka shops accepting hard currency

Gastronom (foreign currency only), Exhibition Complex, Krasnopresnenskaya Nab. 12. Open 10–2; 3–7

Department Store & Bar, B. Dorogomilovskaya Street 60. Open 10–2; 3–7

Hotel Mezhdunarodnaya-2, Krasnopresnenskaya Nab. 12

Hotel Rossiya, Varvarka Street 6.

Books & Prints (foreign currency only), Prechistenka Street 31. Open 9–8

Gift Shop, Furs, Kutuzovsky Prospect 9. Open 10–2; 3–7

Jewellery Salon, Grokholsky Per. 30. Open Mon.–Fri. 9–6

Vneshtorgbank Gold Shop (payment in foreign currency only), Pushkinskaya Street 9. Open Mon.–Fri. 10–5

Shops accepting roubles

GUM Department Store, Red Square 3. Open 8 A.M.–9 P.M.

TSUM Department Store, Petrovka Street 2. Open 7.30 A.M.–9 P.M.

Moskovsky Department Store, Komsomolskaya Square

Moskva Department Store, Leninsky Prospect 56. Open Mon.–Sat. 8 A.M.–9 P.M.

Detsky Mir Children's Department Store, Teatralny Proyezd 2. Open 8 A.M.–9 P.M.
Budapest, Kuzminki, Zelenodolskaya Street 40
Ganga, Smolenskaya Nab. 5
Leipzig, Akademika Vargi Street 8
Luxe, Olympic Village, Pelshe Street 4
Antique Shops, Tverskaya Street 46, Dimitrova Street 54 & Arbat 32
Art Galleries, Kutuzovsky Prospect 24, Smolenskaya Nab. 5 (old paintings), Petrovka Street 12 & Tverskaya Street 46b (graphics)
Jewellery, Beryozka, Tverskaya Street 32; Samotsvety, Arbat 35; Malakhitovaya Shkatulka (Malachite Box), Novy Arbat Street 24
Perfume & Cosmetics, Tverskaya Street 6, Petrovka Street 12 & Novy Arbat Street 44
Crystal & Glass, Tverskaya Street 15 & Myasnitskaya Street 8/2
Toys, Dom Igrushky, Dmitrova Street 28. Open 11–8; closed Sun.
Souvenirs, Tverskaya Street 4
Russian Souvenir, Kutuzovsky Prospect 9. Open Mon.–Sat. 11–8
Khudozhestvenny Salons (handicrafts), Ukrainsky Bld. 6 & Dmitrova Street 54
Markets, Central, Tsvetnoi Boulevard 15; Cheryomushkinsky Rynok, Lomonosov Prospect 1; Tishinsky Rynok, Bolshaya Gruzinskaya Street 50

Bank & Communications

USSR Bank for Foreign Economic Affairs, Krasnopresnenskaya Nab. 12
G.P.O., Myasnitskaya Street 26. Telegrams and poste restante deliveries around the clock, other transactions until 10 p.m.
Central Telegraph Office, Tverskaya Street 7; 924-4758. Open until 10 P.M. Entrance to the international telephone office around the corner at No. 10. Open 24 hours.
International Post Office, Varshavskoye Chaussee 37a; 114 4645. Open 9–9.
International Telephone Exchange, 8-194, 8-196 (on account); 333 4101 (booking a call from your hotel)
Aeroflot, 245 0002 (foreign enquiries); 155-0922 (enquiries for all airports)
Taxis (by phone), 927 0000/457 9005

Intourist, Visas

Intourist Head Office, Mokhovaya Street 16; 292 5230, 203 6962
UVIR (Soviet visa office, registration for foreigners), Chernyshevskovo Street 42; 207 0239.

Rent-a-Car

Hotel Cosmos, Leningradsky Prospect 150; tel. 215 6191
  Autosun, 280 3000/4310
  Europcar, 253 1369/2277
  Hertz, 448 6728
  InNIS, 927 1187
  Mosrent, 248 0251

Autoservice

Station No. 7 (specialising in Mercedez-Benz, Volkswagen, and BMW vehicles), 2-Selskokhozyaistvenny Proyezd 6; 181 2169, 181 1374
Car Breakdown, Varshavskoye Chaussée 87; 119 8000, 119 8108
Emergency Service Station, Novoryazansky Per. 13 (day & night); 267 0113

Four "Country" Estates

Apart from the out-of-town trips organised by Intourist, there are 4 venerable estates that used to be in the country but which have now become part of the urban spread. They are open as museums and well worth visiting.

Ostankino Palace Museum, 1-Ostankinskaya Street 5. Open 10–5 (summer); 10–3 (winter); closed Tues. & Wed.

When Count Sheremetiev inherited the Ostankino estate through his marriage with Princess Cherkasskaya in 1743 it was already one of the richest estates in Russia, having 210,000 serfs and an annual income of 1,500,000 roubles.

The palace, which is wooden although it appears to be built of stone, was built in 1792–97 by the serf architects Arguno, Mironov, and Dikushin under the supervision of Quarenghi, Camporesi, Nazarov, and Blank, all prominent architects of the time. The interior decoration was also the work of serfs and is particularly notable for the intricate wood carving around the doors and ceiling cornices. The parquet flooring is beautifully finished and every room has a different design, executed in various costly materials such as amaranth, rosewood, and ivory.

There is a fine collection of 17th- and 18th-century paintings, engravings, rare carvings, crystal, porcelain, and fans.

In the 18th century the theatre in the centre of the palace was particularly renowned and its company included about 200 actors, singers, dancers, and musicians. The state is very large in comparison with the auditorium and could hold the whole company at once. At the end of a performance the armchairs in the auditorium could be removed in a matter of minutes by a special device, thus turning the theatre into a ballroom. It also had very advanced lighting, scenic and sound effects, all designed by serfs. The most popular of all the actors was a serf-actress, Parasha Kovalyova, who had been taken into the company as a girl. She came from a blacksmith's family and was unusually beautiful and had great talent. Count Sheremetiev fell in love with her and later married her. One of the streets in Ostankino bears her name.

The existing park and lands were replanned when the palace was built. The palace was so grand and striking in contrast to the shabby peasant huts of the nearby village that on one occasion when many guests were invited, the huts were hidden by huge screens on the top of which burning torches were placed.

On the left of the main entrance to the palace is the Trinity Church, which was built in 1683 by the serf-architect Pavel Potekhin.

There is a café behind the palace, and two places where boats can be rented.

Kolomenskoye, Kashirskoye Chaussee. Open 11–5; Wed. & Thurs. in summer 1–8; closed Mon. & Tues. Kolomenskoye was once the favourite summer residence of the Grand-Dukes of Moscow and later of the Russian tsars. Situated on a hill overlooking the river Moskva, the first historical record of Kolomenskoye was in 1339 when it was mentioned as the estate of Ivan Kalita. In the second half of the 17th century a large wooden palace was built and Peter the Great spent some of his childhood here. The palace was demolished in 1767 by Catherine II because it was in a state of decay. (There is a model of it in the museum.)

One of the earliest buildings still standing is the *Church of the Ascension*, built in old Russian "tent" style in 1532. At the time of its construction it was the tallest church in Russia. Hector Berlioz, the French composer, wrote after a visit to Russia in the 1840s, "Nothing has impressed me more than this relic of ancient Russian architecture in the village of Kolomenskoye."

The *Kazan Church*, with 5 onion-shaped domes, was built in 1660. It is open for services in the mornings. The picturesque Dyakovskaya Church, built in the 16th century, served as the prototype for St. Basil's Cathedral in Moscow's Red Square.

Of the original royal estate only the *Main Gate*, the *Clock Tower* and the *Water Tower* are now standing.

The museum is housed in the former domestic quarters of the estate. There are exhibitions of Russian wood-carvings, metalwork, ceramics, and displays illustrating the peasant war waged by Ivan Bolotnikov in 1606–07 and the "Copper Mutiny" of 1662, so-called because of the tsar's decision that copper coins be accepted for the value of silver.

In the park are a number of wooden buildings from different parts of Russia, including the *log cabin* in which Peter the Great lived in Archangelsk (1702), a *prison tower* from Bratsk in Siberia (1631), a *defence tower* from the White Sea (1690), and a 17th-century *mead brewery* from the village of Preobrazhenskoye near Moscow.

There is an open-air *cafe* in the park in summer.

Kuskovo Palace Museum, about 10 km (6 miles) from the centre of Moscow along the Ryazanskoye Chaussee. Open in summer 11–6; in winter 10–4; closed Mon., Tues. & the last Wed. of each month.

First mentioned in 1510, the present architectural ensemble of Kuskovo dates from the 18th century when it was the summer residence of the Sheremetiev family, one of the oldest Russian noble families whose members were statesmen and soldiers.

The palace was built in 1769–75 by the Moscow architect Karl Blank in place of a smaller 2-storey house. It was built in early Russian classical style, but is unusual for its walls of pine logs faced with painted boards. It contains about 800 objets d'art, including one of the best collections of 18th-century Russian art in the country. The rooms of most interest are the White Hall, the dining room, the children's room, the crimson drawing room with a large stove covered with coloured tiles, the oak-panelled study, the main bedroom, and the ballroom. The 140 sq. m. of the ballroom ceiling were painted by the French artist Lagren. Sr.

In front of the palace is a small square flanked by a *church* built in 1737 and a *belfry* built in 1792 by the serf-architects Mironov and Dikushin.

The park was laid out in French style under the direction of Andrei Vogt, a landscape gardener, and Yuri Kologrivov. The park that has been preserved is much smaller than the original one, which included a zoo and was surrounded by woods.

There are an number of interesting buildings in the park. Near the palace is the *kitchen building*, which was built by the serf-architect Argunov. Argunov was also responsible for the *grotto* and the *greenhouse*. The grotto was built in 1755–61 and is faced with seashells. Beyond the grotto and behind the pond is the *menagerie*, reconstructed from old etchings and drawings; the pens spread out in a fan-shape running back to the semi-circle of 5 buildings housing the animals and birds. The greenhouse was built in 1761–65 and included a 2-storey concert hall in the centre.

The *Dutch house* was built in 1749. The interior is decorated with pink-and-blue Delft tiles.

The *Italian house* was built in 1754–55 by Kologrivov in the style of a 17th-century Italian villa.

The *Hermitage* was built by Karl Blank in 1765. The statue on the cupola is of the goddess Flora. The table in the dining room on the first floor was lowered to the ground floor after each course to be cleared and reset, thereby avoiding the need for servants to be present throughout the meal.

Also known as the State Museum of Ceramics, Kuskovo houses one of the best collections of Russian porcelain. There is also china, majolica, and glass, and a considerable number of the exhibits are of Chinese, French, Dutch, and English origin.

Tsaritsyno, about 20 km (12 miles) from the centre of town, along the Kashirskoye Chaussee, passing Kolomenskoye and the way to Domodedovo airport.

The palace of Tsaritsyno, where Catherine II intended to live as a "simple country woman," was never completed. Work began on the palace in 1775 under Bazhenov. 10 years later it was nearly completed but Catherine was not satisfied with it and ordered that it be pulled down. It is said that she did this only to punish Bazhenov for his association with Nikolai Novikov, the eminent educator who had earned Catherine's disapproval. When work on the palace resumed under Kazakov, it was again built in the Russian Gothic style that Bazhenov had designed. The war with Turkey and subsequent financial difficulties prevented its completion during Catherine's reign and work was stopped on her death in 1796.

Besides the half-ruined palace, one can see the *Entrance Bridge* and some *pavilions* scattered in the park. The most remarkable are the round Temple of Ceres, the Milovida Pavilion, and the Ruined Tower.

Tsaritsyno is situated in one of the most beautiful spots in Moscow, in hilly country intersected by ravines. In the English-style park there are numerous lakes and ponds. Boats can be hired and there is a *café*.

Intourist's recommended trips in the environs of Moscow described below include Arkhangelskoye, Krasnogorsk, Dubosekovo, and Leninskiye Gorki. Listed under their own names are Abramtsevo, Borodino, Istra, Klin, Pereslavl-Zalessky, Podolsk, Rostov Veliky, Vladimir and Suzdal, Yasnaya Polyana, and Zagorsk.

Arkhangelskoye

16 km (10 miles) from Moscow. Motorists should leave Moscow by Leningradsky Prospect, then pass under the tunnel onto Volokolamskoye Chaussée, and then fork left to Petrovo-Dalnoye Chaussée. The museum is open from 11–5; closed Mon. & Tues.

The park of Arkhangelskoye, overlooking the Moskva, is one of the most pleasant spots near Moscow and, together with the exterior of the palace, merits a visit even when the museum is closed.

The main complex of the estate was built at the end of the 18th century for Prince Golitsyn by the French architect, Chevalier de Huerne. In 1810 it was bought by Prince Yusupov, one of the richest Russian landlords and a descendant of the Tatar Khans. He was the director of the Imperial Theatre and Hermitage Museum and he used his frequent trips abroad, during which he bought works for the Imperial family, to build up his own collection. There are in the palace many pictures by old European masters, including Hubert Robert, Van Dyck, and Roslin, and also tapestries and numerous marble sculptures. A number of portraits of the royal family hang in the study. Also on display are examples of fabrics, china, and glassware that were made on the estate.

The park was laid out in French style and the avenues are lined with numerous statues and monuments. There is also a monument to Pushkin who visited Arkhangelskoye a number of times. In the western part of the park is a small pavilion known as the Temple to the Memory of Catherine the Great, here depicted as Themis, goddess of justice.

The two buildings at the end of the park were built in 1934–37 as a sanatorium. There is a delightful view over the river Moskva from the balustraded terrace at the end of the park between the buildings of the sanatorium.

On the eastern side of the park is a *colonade*, an *arched storehouse*, and the grandoise Holy Gates leading to the *Church of St. Michael the Archangel*. Built in 1667, this is the oldest structure on the

estate and the one from which the name of Arkhangelskoye comes.

The *Serf Theatre*, on the right side of the main road a little beyond the main entrance, was built in 1817 by the serf-architect Ivanov. It is now sometimes open as a museum. The well-preserved stage decorations are the work of the Italian artist, Gonzaga. At the beginning of the 19th century the company was one of the largest and best known companies of serf actors.

There is a *restaurant* opposite the main entrance to the park.

Krasnogorsk (see Moscow environs)
Population—80,000
(Intourist organises excurions here from Moscow.)

Znamenskoye-Gubailovo Estate. The name of the estate was compounded from the village of Gubailovo, known since 1620, and the name of the local church, Znamenskaya, built in 1683 and demolished early in the 19th century. At the end of the 18th century the estate of Znamenskoye-Gubailovo belonged to Prince Vasily Dolgorukov-Krymsky (1722–82), Governor-General of Moscow. In 1854 a wool mill was built here which was mechanised by 1870. In May 1917, before the October Revolution later in the year, the estate was seized by the local peasants on the grounds that "the palaces of landlords and princes should serve the purposes of cultural enlightenment of the peasants."

In 1927 15 cooperative houses were built near the estate and the new village was named Krasnaya Gorka, hence the name of the town, Krasnogorsk. There are several industrial enterprises in Krasnogorsk, among them one of the Soviet Union's largest optical engineering plants, where Zenith cameras are manufactured. Town status was granted in 1940.

The estate stands in its landscaped park, with a cascade of ponds, to the right of the main highway by the Gorsoviet bus stop. Gorsoviet means town hall and this is on the left of the road. *Znamenskaya Church*, built in 1910 in pseudo-Russian style in place of the original Znamenskaya Church, is now the local travel office with a large car park in front, and immediately behind the church is a small, early 20th-century *chapel* with some of its iridescent glazed tiles still in place. Further behind the church and to the left, is the estate's main *mansion*, which served as partisan headquarters during World War II. It is now the local House of Young Pioneers with a *statue* of Lenin in front, and its 2 annexes house the law courts and legal offices.

There is a *stadium* for 1,500 spectators and, near the town, the small river Banka has been damned to form a large lake, adding to the popularity of the recreation area.

Zorky Restaurant, Oktyabrskaya Street; tel. 562-6344.

Dubosekovo
138 km (86 miles) from Moscow in a north-westerly direction. The excursion takes 8 hours.

This was the site of heavy fighting during the German advance upon Moscow in the autumn of 1941. On 16th November 20 enemy tanks approached the position held by General Panfilov. 4 hours later 14 of them had been destroyed, but another 30 were sent in to replace them. Army Commissar Klochkov-Deyev's pathetic words to the Soviet troops were: "Russia is immense but there is nowhere for us to retreat. Moscow is behind us." And he thereupon tied the last bundle of grenades around himself and threw himself under an oncoming tank. The soldiers barred the way to Volokolamskoye Chaussee for a whole day in unequal battle.

The *memorial* is in the form of 6 monumental figures standing on the hillside.

Dubosekovo Cafe, to the right of the road.

Leninskiye Gorki, (see Moscow environs)

34 km (21 miles) from Moscow. The Lenin museum is open 10–5; closed Tues. & the last day of each month.

The house was built in 1830 and stands in a park of 70 hectares (175 acres), which has old oak trees and a number of ponds. Just before the Revolution the estate belonged to Mayor Reinbolt of Moscow. Lenin and his family lived here from time to time from September 1918 until his death here on 21st January, 1924.

Many of the rooms in the museum have been kept as they were during Lenin's lifetime. In the garage are old motor cars, including Lenin's 1916 Rolls-Royce which was adapted in the Putilovsky plant in Leningrad for use in heavy snow by the addition of caterpillar wheels and skis. The motor was started in 1985 and the car driven 8 m/yds; it was then given a thorough overhaul and is now maintained in perfect condition.

MTSKHETA

(Intourist organises excursions here from Tbilisi, 70 km/43 miles there and back.)

Mtskheta is an ancient capital of Georgia. It is situated at the confluence of the Aragvi and Kura rivers, 3 km (2 miles) to the right of the main road coming from Tbilisi. Historic trade routes from the countries of the Mediterranean ran via Mtskheta to the North Caucasus. Mtskheta is often mentioned in the works of the ancient writers Strabo, Pliny, and Plutarch. On the right bank of the Kura, on the slopes of Mount Kartli, the mythological father of the Georgian people, Kartlos, is said to have been buried. He is reputed to have been a direct descendant of Japhet, and it was his son, Mtskhetos, who founded this town and gave it its name. Mtskheta became the cradle of Georgian culture, and until the 5th century it was the capital of the kingdom of Iberia, where both its religious and political life was concentrated. It was also the residence of the Patriarchs.

On Mount Kartli, which is a holy mountain, stood the shrine of an idol called Armaz, the Georgian version of the Persian Ormuzd, god of compassion and life. On the mountain-side east of Mtskheta, above the left bank of the Aragvi was the shrine of another idol, Zaden; these two were the most important gods worshipped in pagan Georgia. On the other hills around Mtskheta were shrines to lesser gods, with names and characters derived from the gods of the various peoples upon whom Georgia had depended at different times. At the entrance to the town, for example, stood a statue of Aphrodite. Armaz and Zaden, however, were the most highly esteemed, being the gods who spread the sun's rays and in general protected the country from all harm. They were the gods of fertility too, and were sometimes offered human sacrifices. Armaz Monastery was so called because it was founded on the site of the pagan temple; now only a bell tower remains among the ruins.

The centre of the town was at the point where the two rivers converge; a fortress and the tsar's palace were built, and the rest of the town spread further up the river valleys. From the 3rd century B.C. the citizens of Mtskheta were advanced culturally, and during the town's early history they had military and trade connections with Greece, Rome, and Parthia.

Owing to the fact that there is a great number of ancient monuments in Mtskheta, it has been recently turned into a museum city by the government of Georgia. The existence here of the Armaz-Tsikhe acropolis, Dzhavari Church, Samtavro convent, and Sveti-Tskhoveli Cathedral explains why Mtskheta has long been a tourist attraction.

Sveti Tskhoveli Cathedral, open 10–6 (till 7 in summer).

This cathedral, down to the right of the road, was dedicated to the Twelve Apostles but was also known as the Church of the Pillar of Life. As legend has it, a local Jew named Elioz (Eliazar) was summoned to Jerusalem to participate in the trial of Christ. He was present at the crucifixion and when lots were drawn for Christ's robe, it was Elioz who won it and brought it back to Mtskheta. There he was met by his daughter (or, according to other legends, his sister), Sidonia, herself a secret Christian. When she learned that Jesus had been crucified, she fell down dead, clutching the robe. None could wrench it from her grasp—it was as though it had grown onto her flesh, and all the city was witness to the strange occurrence. That night during the earthquake a crevasse opened and Sidonia was buried together with the robe. Later a cedar tree grew on the spot.

About 250 years after this there lived in Jerusalem a certain Nina, daughter of a Roman general. She had been born in Cappadocia, but when she was 12 her parents took her to Jerusalem. There she was taught by an old woman named Nianphora, who told her that after the Crucifixion Christ's Robe had been taken to pagan Iberia (the old name of Georgia). Inspired by this story, Nina prayed constantly to the Virgin asking to be able to go to the place where the Robe had been taken, and finally she was told by the Virgin in a dream that she could go to Iberia and that Christ Himself would help her.

Simply clad, and carrying a cross of vine branches tied with her own hair, Nina set off on the long, difficult journey. Her way led through lands inhabited by fire-worshippers and other pagans and finally to Mtskheta, where she arrived in 314 A.D. At the moment of her arrival King Mirian and a crowd of followers were about to go to Mount Kartli to offer the usual human sacrifice of the blood of newborn babes and of young girls to Armaz, but Nina prayed, and a in a violent electric storm the idol was overturned. She erected a cross on the slope of the mountain and then went down to begin her missionary work in the city. Even King Mirian himself came to the door of her hut to hear the Gospel. He had been blinded by the lightning, but Nina restored his sight. After 10 years her sermons and her holy life fully persuaded the King, his wife and children, and with them the whole population of the town, to be baptised.

The pagan temples and idols were destroyed. According to the Georgian chronicles, King Mirian said of his former religion, "I am the thirty-sixth King, and the first Christian King of Georgia. My fathers sacrificed children to idols; the Mountains of Armaz and Zaden deserve to be destroyed by fire." In the year 328 King Mirian had the great cedar tree chopped down, and beneath it, still held in Sidonia's hands, he and Nina found the Robe of Christ.

Apart from curing the king's blindness, among her other miracles Nina cured the Queen of sickness. From Mtskheta she travelled on to Kakhetia (see Telavi), where she founded a convent. It was there that she died in 338, and she was buried there. After her death Nina was canonised and is today, like Queen Tamar, remembered as one of the Georgian greats.

Mirian built a wooden cathedral over the spot where the tree had stood, and this was rebuilt in stone in the 5th century. There are places in the floor covered with glass where the old foundation can be seen. The wooden cathedral was replaced in 1010–29, when an outstanding Georgian architect named Arsukidze built a great stone cathedral here. At the end of the 14th century during the invasion of Tamerlane, this was badly damaged and robbed upon Tamerlane's personal orders.

The present building of Sveti Tskoveli Cathedral is a perfect example of the high architectural standards of 15th-century Georgian architecture. The great, crenellated fortress wall with batteries and towers that surrounds the cathedral was built in the 18th century. The cathedral itself was erected in 1440 during the reign of Alexander I of Georgia, and under the supervision of Patriarch Melchisadek. The upper dome was restored in the 17th century, and in the 19th century, some small outbuildings were pulled down and most of the frescoes were whitewashed. The fragments that remain of the original frescoes are worthy of mention. The interior decorations still to be seen date from the 16th and 17th centuries, while the iconostasis is 19th-century work. On the southern wall is a 17th-century fresco illustrating the words of Psalm 150,

"Let every thing that hath breath praise the Lord." The site of the legendary cedar tree is still marked by a *stone column* reputed to ooze holy oil. The column, which stands in the southern part of the cathedral, was decorated by Grigory Guldzhavarishvili in the 17th century with themes from the history of early Christianity in Georgia, and was originally embellished with gold and silver.

The facade of the cathedral is decorated with ornamental carving and reliefs. Over the arch of the northern facade there is a hand holding a set square, and this inscription: "The hand of the servant of the Lord, Arsukidze."

Christ's Robe was kept in Mtskheta until the 17th century, when Shah Abbas captured the town and sent the Robe as a gift to the Russian Tsar Mikhail Fedorovich, who in turn placed it with great ceremony in the Uspensky Cathedral in the Moscow Kremlin.

The coronation of the Georgian kings took place in this building and near the altar are royal tombs including those of Vakhtang Gorgasali, Destroyer of the Persians, Erekle II, who 200 years ago united Georgia with Russia, and Georgi XII, Georgia's last king. In 1795 it was the tombs that saved the cathedral; the Persians had captured Mtsketa, but the Khan of Nakhitchevan refused to permit the desecration of the resting place of so many brave kings. In the southern corner of the central aisle is the Patriarch's stone throne decorated with 17th- and 18th-century frescoes. Also inside the cathedral is a small chapel, a copy of the Chapel of Christ's Sepulchre in Jerusalem. The stone font is that in which King Mirian is said to have been baptised.

For many years Sveti-Tskhoveli was the residence of the Georgian Patriarchs. Now there is a small theological seminary attached to the cathedral; it has 30 students. Services are held in the cathedral between 10 A.M. and noon on Saturdays and Sundays and on all Church feast days. There is a museum in the cathedral precincts. Now beside the walls of ancient Sveti Tskhoveli, the Tbilisi Opera and Ballet Theatre stages some of its best productions, the operas "Daisi" and "Abessalom and Etheri" by Zakhari Palrashvili.

Samtavra Convent. The main church is dedicated to St. Nina, Enlightener of Georgia, who was buried there, and it is similar in form to the Cathedral of the Twelve Apostles. It was built at the beginning of the 11th century in mediaeval Georgian baroque style, on the site of a 4th-century church erected by King Mirian. Its name comes from "mtavara," meaning "ruler." The grave of King Mirian and that of his wife, Queen Nina, are still in the cathedral, but the sepulchres date from the 19th century and are of little historic interest.

Beside the cathedral to the north-west is a 3-storeyed, *16th-century bell tower* and the small and ancient *Chapel of St. Nina* on the place where the saint's hut once stood. The site is surrounded by walls. The cathedral was restored at the same time as the rest of the convent in 1903. There are now 7 nuns in the convent.

An ancient *cemetery* was found in 1871 beside

the highway near Samtavra Convent. It had been used from the Iron Age until the 11th century, and during the excavations some coins of the time of Caesar Augustus were found. The upper row of graves are in the form of stone boxes.

Dzhavari (Cross) Church. Up on the hill on the other side of the Aragvi River are the ruins of a church built in 585–604, the name meaning "cross." It was designed to catch the attention, and from many points can be seen dominating the town. When Christianity was adopted in the 4th century, a cross was erected here as a symbol of the religious victory. The present church was built to enclose the older one completely. The ascetic simplicity and logic of the architectural design, the facades with reliefs and ornaments, and the high-quality masonry put this church among the best examples of mediaeval Georgian architecture.

During its 1,400 years of existence Dzhavari Church was damaged only once—in the 10th century, when it was set on fire by invading Arabs. The eastern and southern facades are lavishly decorated with reliefs, including images of patrons and people who gave money for, and organised, the building. There is a legend that this church and the Sveti Tskhoveli Cathedral were linked by an iron chain, and that the monks used to leave their cells on the hilltop and climb down for services in the cathedral, but when faith grew weaker among the people the chain broke and was lost.

Dzhavari has served as the prototype of many other churches. It was described in Lermontov's poem "Mtsiri." Today concerts of Georgian folk music are arranged here for Soviet and foreign tourists.

Mount Zedazeni, 3 km (2 miles) north-east of Mtskheta. Here, on the top of the mountain are the ruins of *Zedazeni fortress* dating from 109 B.C., and the monastery of Ioann of Zedazeni, which was built in the 7th century. The mountain is 1,350 m (4,430 ft) above sea level and is locally called "the staircase to the skies." It is said that once upon a time a mythical God who guarded Mtskheta lived here. At sundown he used to kneel by the river to drink water. Two big cavities on the rock near the river are said to have been made by his knees. During the reign of the Iberia's fourth King, Parnaoze (112–99 B.C.) a statue of Jupiter was erected on Mount Zedazeni. Prior to the spread of Christianity in Georgia (circa A.D. 337), various sacrifices, including human ones, were offered to this idol. After the adoption of Christianity, it was thrown down from the mountain into the abyss. Until the 11th century this fortress, defending the approaches to the Kingdom of Kakhetia, was considered impregnable. A garrison of up to 6,000 people could be kept inside the fortress where there were many springs of pure water. Behind the fortress walls large wine vessels dug into the ground were found, which testifies to the long centuries of wine-making in Georgia. In 1101 the fortress was taken by David the Builder, who was then able to capture Kakhetia and start storming Tbilisi, which had for over 400 years been occupied by foreign invaders. On the western wall of the ruins of Zadazeni fortress there is a plaque with an inscription: "1841. M. Lermontov," and some verses from his poem "Demon."

About 150 m (160 yds) from the fortress stands the *Monastery of Ioann of Zadeny.* The story of its foundation is this: About two centuries after the adoption of Christianity in Georgia, a group of monks known as the Thirteen Holy Fathers of Syria and headed by Ioann came to teach the Gospel to the Georgians. Ioann chose Mount Zadeni for his residence, while the other monks spread around the country. Georgian historians believe that the Syrian monks were in fact not Syrians at all but Georgians, since straight after their arrival they began preaching in Georgian. Their stay in Syria is explained by the close cultural ties that existed between Georgia and the Orient in the 5th–7th centuries.

The area around the Zedazeni fortress and monastery is state-protected and all hunting is prohibited. One of the main attractions is the flower pavilion, which supplies Tbilisi with fresh flowers all year round. 20th May is the monastery's holiday when festivities take place. Tourists can spend a night in Zedazeni to see the sunrise, which is really beautiful here. There is a house inside the monastery that provides accommodation for tourists, or they are given tents and camping equipment.

Today Mtskheta is famous for the garden of one of the inhabitants, who was named Mamulanshvili. He lived to be 100 and it is his daughter who looks after his very rich collection of plants and flowers.

MUKACHEVO (Hungarian Minkacs)
Population—90,000

Intourist organises excursions here from Uzhgorod, 45 km (28 miles) away.

The town stands on the Latoritsa River and is bypassed by the highway. It is the second-largest town in Soviet Transcarpathia. Archaeological finds date the earliest settlement on the site from the Stone Age. In the "Gesta Hungarorum" (Hungarian Chronicles of the 12th century) it is mentioned that the town was known in the 9th century. It gains much importance from its position on the Veretsky Pass. In the 10th and 11th centuries it was part of Russia under the rule of Kiev but then it became Hungarian. During the Tatar invasion of 1241–42 Mukachevo was burned to the ground.

Prince Fedor Koryatovich of Podolia owned the town between 1396 and 1414, and he is credited with encouraging the development of local arts and crafts and with fostering trade. He also built a castle here. After his death, Mukachevo was a prize, jealously guarded both by the Transylvanian princely family of the Rakoczis and by the Habsburgs of Austria; it continued to change hands between them until the 20th century.

In 1919, under the Treaty of St. Germain, Mukachevo was incorporated into Czechoslovakia. Then in 1939, after the Munich Treaty, it was occupied by German and Hungarian forces until

MOSCOW–The ornate Znamenskaya Church at Dubrovitsi, near Moscow, was built by the Golitsyn family and consecrated in 1704.

MOSCOW–From Bolshoy Kamenny Bridge the cathedrals and the Great Kremlin Palace make a great background for the Water-Hoist Tower. It was founded in 1490 but rebuilt after Napoleon's destruction of the city in 1812.

MOSCOW–Pushkin Square; poetry is recited beside the poet's statue, and fresh flowers brought in tribute to his memory.

MOSCOW–The Spassky Tower entrance to the Kremlin from Red Square.

MOSCOW–Novo-Devichy Convent: Preobrazhenskaya Church was built over the entrance gate in 1687.

MOSCOW–Panorama from the top of Cosmos Hotel. In the foreground is the round building of the Metro station, behind that the soaring Space Monument while to the right is Ostankino Television Tower.

OREL–The main building of the Turgenev family estate of Spasskoye-Lutovinovo, near Orel.

OLESKO–Aerial view of Olesko Castle Museum.

POLTAVA–Local museum, 1906.

NOVOCHERKASSK–Voznesensky (Ascension) Cathedral.

PSKOV–Pechory Monastery (4 views): the towers and outside walls of the monastery follow the folds in the hillside. Inside the walls a group of churches stands above the caves.

1944, when the Soviet Army moved in. It has since been part of the Soviet Union.

The town's population is multinational—Ukrainians, Russians, Jews, Hungarians, Czechs, and Bulgarians have all made their home there.

Local industry: machine-tools, furniture, skis, tourism.

Polanok Castle, on a lofty hill, 68 m (233 ft) high, to the south of the town; as one approaches Mukachevo, the castle seems to be floating above it. The road to the castle is along Karl Marx Street, turning left at the end, then right and up the rather bumpy hill road. The ancient stronghold was built at the crossroad of important trade and military routes. Archaeological excavations on the site have yielded rich trophies dating from the Stone, Bronze, and Iron Ages. The main buildings were constructed at the end of the 14th and the beginning of the 15th century under Prince Fedor Koryatovich, as mentioned above; King Sigizmund of Hungary had given him Mukachevo as a present. 3 round towers date from that time but subsequent owners further enlarged and reinforced the castle. The Middle and Lower Castles were built in the 17th century and are reached by a bridge. It was in 1633 that Yuri Rakoczi ordered the excavation of a moat 12 m (40 ft) wide and 6 m (20 ft) deep, which was filled from the river Latoritsa. When construction was completed, a Latin inscription went up on the eastern wall of the Lower Castle saying: "If the arts of war and nature and God are on my side, I fear no cannon, and if the stars are favourable I shall stand for centuries."

After the death of Yuri Rakoczi, his widow continued his work and built the third floor of the Middle Castle; another stone plaque bears witness:

"The most famous and illustrious Princess of Transylvania, Her Highness Susannah Lorantvi saw to the building of this part of the Fortress in 1657."

The rocky hill upon which the castle stands is of volcanic origin and its slopes were once covered with fertile soil. Many fierce battles were fought for possession of Polanok. Princess Ilona Zrioni of Hungary was besieged here for 2½ years between 1685 and 1688 before the castle was finally taken by Austrian troops. In 1703–11 it was her son, Ferenz Rakoczi II, who led the Hungarian uprising and then made the castle his headquarters. Coins have been found that were minted in 1705 and that bear the transcription CM standing for Castrum Munkacs. Peter the Great of Russia sent his ambassadors here and the coat-of-arms of the Rakoczi family still remains above the Old Fortress gates.

In 1773 the Austrians, by order of Maria Theresa, turned the castle into a prison with an awesome torture-chamber. Between 1821 and 1823 Alexander Ipsillanti, a fighter for Greek independence, was held here, and in 1847 it was visited by the Hungarian poet, Szandor Petefi, who wrote of its masters:

You raised the walls of Munkacs
so no flame of thought
Might melt slaves' chains,
but be stamped out in dungeons dark.

After 1897 there were military barracks in the castle. It was restored after World War II and now houses both an agricultural school and the local museum; the latter is in the armoury, built in the Middle Castle in 1624.

In the river valley are the remains of a 17th–18th century fortress.

St. Martin's Chapel, Mira Street 51. Built in Gothic style in the 14th century, this is the oldest example of stone architecture in Transcarpathia. From the 16th century it served as the altar of a Roman Catholic Church, but the latter fell to ruin at the beginning of the 20th century, and the chapel stands in the yard of a church built in 1904. There are interesting stone carvings around the windows of the chapel and the stained-glass is also very fine. The chapel was restored in 1969 and is now an exhibition hall.

Convent on Chernechya Gora (monk's hill). In the 11th century Anastasia, daughter of Prince Yaroslav the Wise of Kiev, came here to be married to King Andrei I of Hungary, and with her were a number of monks who were the first to inhabit this site. In the second part of the 16th century a monastery and a convent were built here, but both were destroyed in the ensuing wars. The present baroque structure dates from 1766–72. It is used by the Russian Orthodox Church and services are held regularly. The library has a collection of valuable books.

Trinity Church, Dukhnovicha Street 11. This church, built in 1795, has a belfry like the turret of a castle.

The White Palace, Mira Street 28. This was built in the second half of the 17th century as the town residence of the Rakoczi family. When the town was once again taken over by the Habsburgs in 1711, the palace became the property of the Austrian Emperor. Then in 1728, when Mukachevo was presented to Count Schonborn of Wurzburg, the palace became his residence. In 1748 it was enlarged by an architect called Neimann and now it houses a school.

The centre of old Mukachevo used to be the market square. It is where Lenin, Mira, and Dukhnovicha streets are today. In the 1930s Kirov Street was built up with groups of houses in contemporary style; that on the corner of Kirov and Gorky streets is the attractive building of the former commercial school.

Lenin Monument, Mira Square. There is also a *War Memorial* on this square and the building (1904) of the City Council, which was once the town hall.

Liberation Monument (1979), in the town park.

Mukachevo Civil Guards' Monument, in the park, on the bank of the river Latoritsa. This was built in 1901 in honour of the Guards who took part in the Hungarian Revolution of 1848–49.

Munkacsy House, Mira Street 15. Mihaly Lib (1844–1900) was a famous Hungarian painter who was born in a house which stood on this site. He was made an honorary citizen of Mukachevo in 1880 and took the name Munkacsy. The original house burned down in 1925 and this one was built in 1941. The memorial plaque was put up in 1969.

Russian Drama Theatre, Mira Street
Park, On the left bank of the river Latoritsa. The park has an open-air swimming pool.
Zirka Hotel, Mira Street 20; tel. 24-37
Zvezda Restaurant, Karl Marx Street 2
Latoritsa Restaurant & Cafe, Mira Street 2, on the right just over the bridge on the way into town.
Krasnaya Gorka Restaurant
Ukraina Cafe, Mira Street
GPO, Lenin Street 9
Souvenir Shop, Mira Street 24

MURMANSK Population—468,000

"Murman" in the local Saami language means "the edge of the earth," which is a true description of the place if one looks at the map. Another theory as to the origin of the name is that it comes from "normann" meaning "Norwegian," although the Kola Peninsula has been in Russian hands since 1478. Until 1917 Murmansk was known as Romanov-na-Murmane, Romanov after the imperial family.

Murmansk is located on the east side of the Kola Gulf of the Barents Sea, 50 km (31 miles) from the open sea. It is so far north that there are 9 months of winter and the polar night lasts for 52 days, from 26 November until 16 January. During this time about 80 powerful floodlights are used to light the port area, the railway station, building sites, and factory yards, and all the children receive sunlamp treatment. In winter the temperature may fall to − 50°C, but in spite of its position its average January temperature is only − 12°C and while Russia's southern ports in the Caspian and Azov seas are covered with ice in winter, Murmansk remains ice-free all year round. The relatively mild winter is explained by the North Cape Stream, the last branch of the Gulf Stream, which warms all this part of the coast. The town is known as the venue of the last of the country's winter competitions each year; at the end of March and the beginning of April is the Festival of the North, which includes reindeer racing. In summer Murmansk may be as warm as 35°C (95°F) and the midnight sun shines from 17 May until 27 July.

The town stretches 20 km (12 miles) in a narrow line along the coast. It stands upon what was once part of the sea bed, worn out of the rocks by ancient glacial action. Murmansk is bounded in the north by the river Rosta and in the south by the old settlement of Kola (see below). The stony hills, called the "stone sack," which prevent it spreading further inland, keep its width to about 1–5 km (up to 3 miles) from the sea.

In the 16th century the request of the King of Denmark to begin trading with the Kola area was

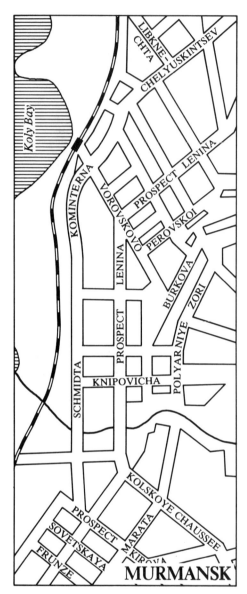

MURMANSK

turned down because the Russians considered the place inconvenient.

During World War I the Russians' need for a port that would remain open all the year round led them, under British instigation and with British assistance, to build the port. It was constructed in September 1915, and in the following year, when Russia was still cut off from her allies because her usual southern route through the Black Sea was blocked, it was decided to build a railway up from Petrozavodsk to the Kola Peninsula. The line runs through 965 km (600 miles) of marshland and dense forest and was completed with great difficulty by the end of 1916. The first buildings in Murmansk were brought from England. The Russians were surprised by their semi-circular iron roofs and called them "trunks," referring to the traditional rounded shape of Russian trunks and chests. Thus it was that the town's first important role was handling supplies from the allies.

After the 1917 Revolution, in March 1918, Royal Marines under Rear-Admiral Thomas W. Kemp landed here from the battleship "Glory." The Admiralty also sent the cruiser "Cochrane," the French their heavy cruiser "Admiral Aube," and the Americans their cruiser "Olympia." They were forced to leave the area in February 1920. The pretext for the occupation had been "the defence of the Murmansk region from the power of the German coalition."

The varying size of the local population reflects the state of well-being of the town. There were 30,000 inhabitants in 1917 but in 1920 this had dropped to 19,000. However by 1938 the figure had soared to a booming 300,000. It was in that year that the Norwegian writer, Nordahl Grieg, wrote of his visit: "In Murmansk I noticed 2 huge buildings under construction in this newly built town between the Arctic Ocean and the snowy mountains. One was a power station, the other a theatre; the hammer blows sounded in unison. This is the way the world of the future is built."

During World War II Murmansk was again an important transit point for incoming supplies. The battle front was only 80 km (50 miles) away from the town, and in 1941 Murmansk was almost entirely ruined by German bombing. The border however held firm and this was the only section of the country's western frontier that the Nazi forces were unable to cross. Murmansk was awarded the title of Hero-City of the Soviet Union in 1985 to mark the 40th anniversary of VE-Day.

The town's importance as a trading port is considerable; it stands fifth in the USSR for cargo turnover. The Soviet Union's largest atomic-powered ice-breaker, the "Arctica," is based here, and Murmansk is the western terminus of the Northern Sea Route to Vladivostok. Besides the cargo vessels, the local fishing fleet numbers about 1,500 boats, and there is a special fishing harbour. Cod, haddock, turbot, wolf-fish, flat fish, and eel make up the greater proportion of the catch, and sharks are also caught for medical and technical purposes. It is the Soviet Union's most important fishing port and the local fish processing plant is one of the largest in Europe.

Nothing at all is left now of the old wooden Murmansk. Today's town is the largest inside the Arctic Circle. The main thoroughfare is Lenin Prospect; as the popular Soviet lyric writer Stepan Schipachov described it:

A spacious street and straight—
This way it leads to Moscow;
That, to the Arctic sea.
(Trans. J. M. Louis)

With the administrative buildings and the best shops, it is also the busiest street in Murmansk. It is divided into 2 parts by Pyat Uglov (5 corners) Square, an architectural device reminiscent of Leningrad, and ends at the Gun Monument. Karl Marx Street runs from the gulf to the hill. The town is laid out on 3 terraces: first the industrial zone and the bay, then the centre, and thirdly the Northern Region, where the living quarters are. There is an observation point near the Panorama Restaurant in the Northern Region which has an excellent view over the town and the port. The port was subjected to 97 air raids during the war and was completely ruined. Allied ships came in and anchored under the protection of an overhanging cliff that can be seen from this point. 100,000 people, a third of the population of Murmansk, now live in the Northern Region, where there is no industry at all. The buildings are mostly from 9 to 14 storeys high, in an area where but 30 years ago people used to go gathering golden cloudberries.

There is a pedagogical institute in Murmansk and a marine school as well as the Polar Institute of Fishery and Oceanology. The town has also a large ship-building industry.

A highway is under construction between Murmansk and Leningrad, and there are border crossings to Finland and Norway (see below).

St. Nicholas's Church, This church with 5 cupolas and a belfry over the west door is in the traditional style found in many Russian towns. What is unusual is that it was completed in 1988. It has excellent accoustics, holds a congregation of 2,500, and was built with local help and support by workers from the Carpathians at a cost of 580,000 roubles collected by the local parishoners. Still to be finished is the rectory, baptistry, bakery, and an almshouse.

Local Museum, Lenin Prospect 90. Open 11-6; closed Fri. It consists of 3 sections, the picture gallery on the ground floor, the natural history of the Kola Peninsula on the second floor, and the history of Murmansk section on the third floor. In the latter is an interesting display of wartime maps and plans showing the German advance and attack.

Polar Institute of Fishery and Oceanology Museum, Knipovicha Street 6. Open 10–5; closed Sat. & Sun. Tells the story of research in the White and Barents Seas.

Ethnographical Museum, Open 10–5; closed Mon. Illustrates the way of life of the indigenous peoples of the Arctic coast.

House of Soviets, Lenin Prospect.

Regional Library, Perovskoy Street

New Library, Profsoyuznaya Street, near the Sever Hotel. This was built in 1970 and holds a million books.

1918–20 Intervention Victims' Monument, in a garden on Leningradskaya Street in the centre of the town. The monument was designed by Savchenko in 1927 in the constructivist style of the time and is in the shape of a captain's bridge.

Obelisk, commemorating the 30th anniversary of the foundation of Murmansk port, unveiled in 1945.

Lenin Monument, Lenin Prospect. Nikolai

Tomsky was the sculptor and the statue was unveiled in 1940.

Anatoly Bredov Monument, Lenin Prospect, in front of the House of Soviets. Bredov was a local docker who died at the Northern Front at Pechenega, near Murmansk, in October 1944. Rather than surrender he blew himself up together with the advancing Germans, and was posthumously proclaimed a Hero of the Soviet Union. The monument, made jointly by Tatrovich and other sculptors, was unveiled in 1958.

The Gun Monument, Kolskoye Chaussee, at the end of Lenin Prospect. This stands to the memory of the 6th Artillery Battery which, until it was annihilated in September 1941, bravely withstood the attacks of the approaching Germans in the valley of the Western Litsa River. The monument was unveiled in 1959.

Memorial Complex, on the hilltop. Here is the gigantic statue of a woman, and also the town's eternal flame, transferred from the Gun Monument at the end of Leninsky Prospect.

Drama Theatre, Lenin Prospect 49. This was built in 1963 and has seats for 800.

Puppet Theatre, Perovskoy Street 21a

International Seamen's Club, Karl Marx Street 1

Trud Stadium, Sport Square. This stadium seats 15,000.

Winter Swimming Pool, part of the sports complex in the centre of town, which also includes football and hockey stadiums. The pool holds 3,600 cu m (127,132 cu ft) has seats for an audience of 840, and was opened in 1966. It is one of the largest indoor pools in the country.

Garden, Leningradskaya Street. This is one of the most popular parks in the town. It has a good view over the gulf.

Arctica Hotel & Restaurant, Lenin Square 22; tel. 55-159. Has accommodation for 1,000.

Severnaya (north) (Intourist) Hotel & Restaurant, Profsoyuznaya Street 20; tel. 55-040. There is an Intourist office in the hotel; tel. 54-372.

69th Parallel Hotel, Sopka Varnichanaya Street

Polyarnye Zori Hotel & Restaurant, Knipovich Street 17; tel. 50-282

Dary Morya (ocean's gifts) Fish Restaurant, Lenin Prospect 26/9

Vstrecha (meeting) Restaurant, Oskoldovtsev Street 28

Panorama Restaurant, Northern Region. There is an excellent view from here. Nearby is a monument that was built to commemorate the town's wartime defenders.

Yunost (youth) Cafe, Lenin Prospect 50/7

Uyut (cozy) Cafe, Kominterna Street 15

Sport Cafe, Karl Marx Street 40

Theatre Cafe, Teatralny Boulevard

Bank, Profsoyuznaya Street 11

GPO & Telegraph Office, Leningradskaya Street 27

Ingosstrakh Insurance Office, Pushkin Street 7

Rubin Gift Shop, Vorovskovo Street 4, opposite the railway station.

Beryozka Foreign Currency Shop, Lenin Prospect 80

Department Store, Lenin Prospect 33

Children's World Department Store, Lenin Prospect

Bookshop, Burkova Street 43

Souvenirs, Lenin Prospect 34

Jewellers, Vorovskovo Street 4/22

Neptune Fishmonger's, Lenin Prospect 28. Most unusual and worth seeing, this splendid shop stocks fish from the 7 seas, from wherever the Murmansk fishing fleet lets down its nets.

Intourist organises visits to a fishing vessel, salmon fishing on the river Tuloma, and motorboat trips on the sea, as well as excursions from Murmansk to Kola (see below).

There is a motor road open to *Finland* for Scandinavian tourists, leading through the town of Padun and along the valley of the river Lotta (dolina Lotta) to Ivalo in Finland.

A railway runs from Murmansk to Nikel and it is only a short drive across the Soviet-Norwegian border to Kirkenes. This crossing is only for Scandinavians and Russians and 2 days' notice of a planned crossing is required.

Both Ivalo and Kirkenes are linked by regular transport service with Helsinki and Oslo respectively. The telephone number of the Tourist Office in Kirkenes is 917-82.

Kola Population—10,000
(Intourist organises excursions here from Murmansk.)

Kola is located at the mouth of the river Kola on the Kola Gulf 12 km (7 miles) south of Murmansk.

It was founded in 1264 and has been known for its importance as a trading port with foreign countries since the 16th century.

The remains of the original earth wall and the moat can still be seen, and there are still many old houses which belonged to local merchants. There is an interesting 19th-century wooden church that is now used as a school workshop, and the gun that is proudly pointed out to visitors was used in 1854 when British battleships sailed in close to the town. Since the foundation of Murmansk, Kola has lost much of its former importance and soon it will merge entirely with its growing neighbour.

The town produces furniture, plaster-of-Paris, and food products.

By the main road is a *church*, now closed.

The *wooden cross*, opposite the Volna Cinema, bears an inscription saying that it was erected "in the summer of 1635, on the 12th day of June, to be revered of all Christian folk."

NAKHODKA Population—165,000
The name of this new port means "find" or "godsend." The bay in which it is located was discovered by Russian explorers in 1859 when after 2 stormy

days their corvette "Amerika" put in at a quiet bay. It is one of the most perfect bays on far eastern Russian territory, and opens on the Sea of Japan.

It was decided before World War II to build a port here, but it was only at the end of the war that construction began. It has been a town since 1950 and lying 69 km (43 miles) east of Vladivostok it is, after Vladivostok, the second-most important port in the area. Since 1958 Vladivostok has been closed to foreigners, and Nakhodka serves as the transit point for travellers going to Japan, with which it is connected by regular sailings. One of its advantages over Vladivostok is that the Sea of Japan near Amerika Gulf never freezes over and near the port the ice is weaker than it is at Vladivostok.

The town is picturesquely situated in the amphitheatre of the shore of Amerika Gulf and now stretches 19 km (12 miles) around the bay. Intensive construction is in progress following a recently approved 20-year plan. The town around the Gulf is divided into 3 regions: north, central, and south.

The railway station, called locally Tikho-okeanskaya (Pacific), is in the centre of town, close to the port, and terminates a branch line from the Trans-Siberian Railway. Vostochny Port is the container terminal. The container facilities now run from the Baltic to the Pacific, shortening the freight route and the costs involved.

Apart from its importance as a transport centre, Nakhodka has a ship-repairing yard and a considerable fishing industry. There is a club for foreign sailors here, a branch of the Far Eastern Polytechnical Institute, and a naval school.

Local Museum, Vladivostokskaya Street 6. Open 10–7; closed Tues.

History of Nakhodka Museum, Open 11–7; Sat. & Sun. 12–8; closed Mon.

Revolution Museum, Lenin Street

Stadium

Vostok (east) Hotel & Restaurant (Intourist), Central Square; tel. 65-02

Nakhodka Hotel, Shkolnaya Street 3

Intourist Office, Nakhodkinsky Street 11; tel. 57-344

Japanese Consulate General, Lunacharskovo Street 9; tel. 56-371

Korean Consulate General, Vladivostockskaya Street 1; tel. 55-310

Beryozka Foreign Currency Shop, Lenin Street 17. Open 11–8; closed Sun. There is another similar shop at the Sea Terminal.

Book Shop, Nakhodkinsky Prospect 50

Department Store, Nakhodkinsky Prospect

Excursions include picnics and fishing near the village of Vasilievka (25 km/16 miles from Nakhodka).

NALCHIK is the capital of the Kabardino-Balkarian Autonomous Republic.

THE KABARDINO-BALKARIAN AUTONOMOUS REPUBLIC

The Kabardino-Balkarian ASSR, part of the Russian Federation, occupies the central (northern) part of the Caucasus and the Kabardinian valley. Its territory is 12,500 sq km (4,800 sq miles). In the south it is divided from Georgia by the Greater Caucasus with some of its summits over 5,000 m (16,000 ft) about sea level. Parallel to this (to the north) stretch 3 other mountain ridges, all of which are cut through by deep and narrow mountain gorges. The mountains occupy almost half the Republic's territory while its other half is taken by the Kabardinian valley, the bread basket of Kabardino-Balkaria.

The Kabardino-Balkarian mountains represent almost all known geological epochs and are rich in different kinds of minerals.

The Republic's population of 700,000 consists mainly of Kabardins and Russians and about 100,000 Balkars. The Kabardins, who were Christians and whose language is akin to other Caucasian tongues, came here in the 12th and 13th centuries. Since that time the lower part of Kabardino-Balkaria has been called Kabarda. Local legend connects this name with that of Prince Kabarda Tambiyev. The Kabardins were grain growers and cattle breeders, but became widely known as horse breeders and riders. Kabarda-bred horses were renowned through the Caucasus and the whole of Russia. The Kabarda women are skilful in gold and silver embroidery.

The Balkars, whose language is like Turkish, settled in the mountain gorges of Cherk, Khulam, Bezengi, Chegem, and Baksan. Their main occupations, besides grain growing, were processing wool and manufacturing felt rugs, weaving, tanning, and working iron. Being neighbours, the Kabardins and the Balkars maintained close and friendly ties and conducted brisk trade and barter among themselves as well as with their Caucasian and Russian neighbours. In the 13th and 14th centuries they fought against the Tatars and Mongols, and in the 1390s they suffered from devastating raids by Tamerlane. In the 16th century they fought against the Turks and the Crimean Tatars. Divided into several principalities, Kabarda could hardly defend itself against the invaders. In 1552 the Tatar capital of Kazan fell to Ivan the Terrible, and the Kabardinian prince Temryuk Idarov sent envoys to Moscovy requesting that the Kabardins be accepted into the Russian state. In 1557 Kabarda voluntarily joined Russia, the first of the Caucasian peoples to do so. Some time later, the Balkars followed suit. In 1561 Ivan the Terrible built a church for the Kabardins and, perhaps in order to strengthen ties with Kabardino-Balkaria, married Temryuk's daughter, Kuchenei, who took the name of Maria when she was baptised. She died in 1569.

In 1567 the region's first Russian fortress, called Terki, was built on the Terek river and Russian troops were sent there in 1714–22. But it was not until the Russian victory in the 1768–74 Russo-

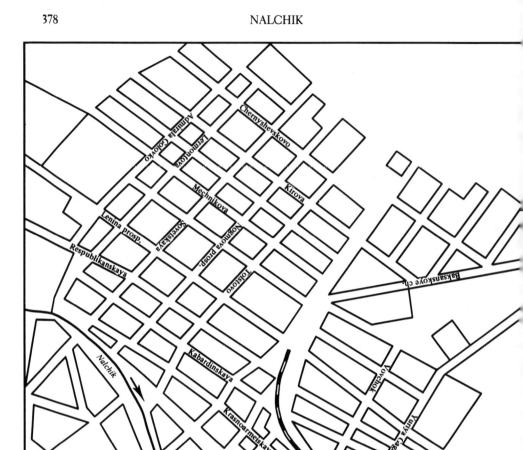

NALCHIK

to Ordzhonikidze

Turkish War that Kabarda's fate was finally decided. According to the Kuchuk-Kainarji Peace Treaty of 1774, the Turks had to recognise Kabarda as part of Russia. At the turn of the 19th century many Russian fortresses and strongholds were built in Kabarda, Kamennomostskaya, Nalchik, Baksan, and other places.

In December 1936 Kabardino-Balkaria became an autonomous republic. In 1942 the republic was the scene of fierce fighting. The Balkars, a Turkish group, were accused of collaboration with the Germans during World War II and resettled in 1943 (just as it was with the Karachai people, of the Karachai-Cherkess Autonomous Region, as mentioned under Kislovodsk). In 1957 they were permitted to come back and the republic once again became known as Kabardino-Balkaria.

The main branches of industry here are machine building, electrical instrument making, and mining. Among its sports the most highly developed is riding, which has long standing traditions in Kabardino-Balkaria. The republic is a tourist, mountaineering, and skiing centre.

Nalchik Population—235,000
(Intourist organises excursions here from Pyatigorsk, Kislovodsk, and Terskol.)

Nalchik, the capital of the Kabardino-Balkarian Autonomous Republic, lies on the left bank of the mountain river Nalchik, but the road goes over the Shalushka at the entrance to the town. Nalchik stands at a height of 554 m (1817 ft) above sea level. Its name, meaning "horseshoe" in Kabardinian, refers to the shape of the mountains around, for it is in the foothills of the northern spur of the Black Mountain. It is famous for its picturesque environs and for its view of the Caucasus Mountains. One of the local mineral waters, Nartan, takes its name from a nearby mountain.

During the Caucasian War of 1822, a Russian

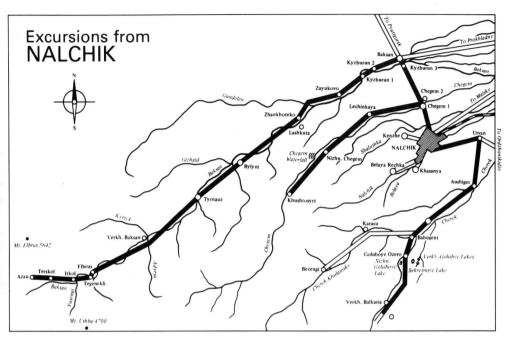

Excursions from NALCHIK

fortress was founded here on the site of a former village. By the end of the 19th century it was a Cossack settlement and the number of its inhabitants had already increased considerably. In 1863 the fortress ceased to exist but the settlement that had formed around it became the district centre of Nalchik with the river Nalchik flowing through its eastern part. Only in 1921, after the Revolution, did it become a town and a regional centre of the Kabardinians and Balkars, and in 1936 it was made the capital of the Republic. Nalchik is a major administrative and cultural centre. In 1957 the republic's university was opened here. Nalchik is also the central point for tourists and mountaineers going to the central Caucasus.

Local Museum, Gorky Street 52. Open 10-5:30; closed Mon. Some of the items on display are 4,000 years old.

Fine Arts Museum, Lenin Prospect 35. Open 11-7; closed Fri.

Marco Vovchok House Museum, in Dolinsk, 3 km (2 miles) south-west of town. Marco Vovchok (1834–1907), was the pseudonym of a Ukrainian writer, Maria Vilinskaya-Markovich, who lived here for the last year of her life. Here are preserved her own furniture, her piano, and beautiful lace shawls besides literary mementos. Open 9-5; closed Tues. Her grave and that of her husband, Lobach-Zhuzhenko, are in the garden, near the museum.

Semyon Stolpnik Church, Pyatigorskaya Street 7. Open for services.

Sunnite Mosque, in Volny Aul, in the Moslem cemetery; go along Profsoyuznaya Street and then turn left. Built in red brick in 1928; open for services.

Synagogue, Rabochaya Street 16. This was used by the Tati, the local Mountain Jews. There used to be a community of more than 1,000, but many have emigrated. An early morning market is held near the synagogue.

Statue of Lenin, Sovietov Square, made by A. Posyado and unveiled in 1957.

Unification Monument, Lenin Prospect. This statue of a woman in national dress by M. Listopad and S. Makhtin was unveiled in 1957 to mark the 400th anniversary of Kabardino-Balkaria's union with Russia.

Kazanokov Monument, Svoboda Square. Jabagi Kazanokov (1686–1750) was a local philosopher.

2 busts, of *Bekmurza Pachev* (1854-1936), a Kabardinian poet, and of *Kyazim Mechiyev* (Balkar poet), in the park

Sergei Kirov Monument, Respublikanskaya Street.

Maxim Gorky Monument, Gorkovo Street

Kalmykov Statue, Lermontov & Respublikanskaya streets. Betal Kalmykov (1893–1940) was a local statesman and Party activist.

Marco Vovchok Monument, Marco Vovchok was a Ukrainian writer who lived here. Her house is now a museum (see above).

Obelisk to the Civil War heroes

Monument to Civil War Victims, near the Nart Hotel, at the place of the execution in 1923; there is an eternal flame.

Monument to Komsomol heroes, Baisultanova Street. These young people were killed during the Civil War and World War II.

Stone Cavalryman with his Horse, at the entrance to the town. To the Soldiers of the 115th Cavalry Unit.

Monument to Tankmen, also at the entrance to the town. Commemorating those who liberated Nalchik in 1943.

War Memorial, in the main square; the eternal flame was lit in 1965.

Monument to Victims of Fascism, Gorky Street, opposite the museum. In memory of the citizens of Nalchik who lost their lives.

Monument to the 50th anniversary of the Komsomol

Shogentsukov Drama Theatre, in the park, built in national style. Ali Shogentsukov (1900–41) was one of the founders of Kabardin poetry.

Russian Drama Theatre, 400-Year Square

Musical Theatre, 400-Year Square

There are 2 parts to the town park. Part of it is in the town itself, and part begins immediately outside the town on the way up to Dolinsk, and continues for 3 km (2 miles). There is a collection of trees from the Caucasus, Europe, and America and the avenue of pines and the rose gardens are especially worthy of note. The town park has a chair-lift to the top of Mt. Kizilovka, from which there is a good view.

Botanical Garden, between Dolinsk and the river Belaga

Spartak Stadium, Respublikanskaya Street

Hippodrome Racecourse, Baksanskoye Chaussee

Nalchik Hotel & Dolinsky Restaurant, Lermontov Street 4, tel. 23-133

Nart Hotel & Restaurant, Lermontov Street 2, tel. 27-026

Sokol Hotel & Restaurant

Intourist Office, Pushkin Street 56; tel. 55-534

Kavkaz Restaurant, Kabardinskaya Street 17

Dorozhny Restaurant, Osetinskaya Street 132

Elbrus Restaurant, in the park

Bereg Restaurant, in the park

Sosruko Restaurant, at the upper station of the chair-lift to Mt. Malaya Kizilovka; Sosruko is a Kabardinian epic hero.

G P O, Respublikanskaya Street 5

Bank, Golovko Street 2

Bookshop, Lenin Prospect 46

Service Station, Gagarin Street 143

Camping Site, 20 km (12 miles) along the road to Ordzhonikdze, in the village of Urvan.

Popular short excursions from Nalchik are those to *Mount Nartan* (1,008 m/3,300 ft) and *Mount Sarai* (1,329 m/4,700 ft). 42 km (26 miles) away (towards Pyatigorsk) are the *Chegem Waterfalls*; the trip there takes 3 hours, with lunch at the *Vodopady (waterfalls) Restaurant*. 56 km (35 miles) away (towards Vladikavkaz and via Urvan) is the Cherek Ravine and the Golubiye Ozyora (blue lakes). Longer is the excusion up to Elbrus from Nalchik (142 km/88 miles), following the road that runs southwards from Baksan into the mountains. It goes through Lashkuty, Bylym, and Tyrnauz and lunch is provided at the *Adyr-Su Restaurant*. The Golubiye Ozyora and Elbrus trips can also be made from Kislovodsk, but Nalchik is nearer.

Dolinsk is 3 km (2 miles) southwest of Nalchik.

The road there follows the valley of the river Nalchik upstream, and runs through the upper part of the town park. Dolinsk is a satellite town of Nalchik, where many sanatoria are located. There is also a swimming pool and the building of the Geophysical Institute of the Academy of Sciences.

Dolinsk Restaurant

Urvan (see Nalchik)

This little village, formerly known as Misostovo, stands on the banks of the river Urvan.

Urvan burial mounds dating from 2nd millennia B.C. *Remains of an ancient settlement* of the 4th–13th centuries.

World War II Memorial

Urvan Restaurant

Urvanskiye Dubki (Urvan oaks) is a hunting reserve that is part of Nalchik forest reserve. Occupying an area of 800 hectares (2,000 acres), this is one of the largest reserves in the northern Caucasus. Here wild boars, wild goats, foxes, jackals, wild cats, racoons, pheasants, and many varieties of birds are found.

Take a right turn in Urvan. The beginning of the road up to Golubiye Ozyora (blue lakes), 39 km (24 miles) up the valley of the river Cherek, runs through Nalchik forest reserve. Pass the villages of AUSHIGER and SOVIETSKOYE, cross the Cherek Bezengisky river, and take the left fork.

The road to Elbrus:

Tyrnauz (see Nalchik) Population—20,000

The town is situated 1,700 m (5,580 ft) above sea level. Until 1955 it was known as Nizhny Baksan. It owes its present name to the Tyrny-Auz mountain ridge, which means "Gorge of the Winds" in Balkar. High up in the mountains is a molybdenum quarry. The workers are taken up there by a ropeway, though there is a road leading to it through the mountains.

Tyrnauz has tungsten-molybdenum mills, one of the leading enterprises in Kabardino-Balkaria. It took 4 years to build. The mills were damaged during World War II but were restored by 1945.

Tungsten was discovered here in 1934. A young geologist, Boris Orlov, and his wife, Vera Flyorova, were looking for gold, antimony, and arsenic. They found an unknown metal which had been taken by other geologists for lead or tin; analysis proved it to be tungsten.

World War II Memorial

Memorial to Vera Flyorova, the geologist who discovered molybdenum in the area and died a tragic death. A nearby mountain summit is called Vera Peak.

Elbrus Hotel & Restaurant

Elbrus (off the road, see Nalchik)

The village is situated at the confluence of the rivers Baksan and Irik, which run noisily down from the glacier. From here two roads lead off, one to the beautiful valley of the Irik, with a Narzan spring at the beginning of it, and the other to the picturesque Adyl-Su valley, where several Alpine camps are situated. Here there are also Narzan springs, and at the top of the valley is *Shkheldinsky Glacier*.

Obelisk, in the village. To those killed in 1941-1945.

Sokol (Intourist) Winter Sports Centre, tel. 267. The usual service bureau facilities are provided by the Itkol Hotel in Terskol, a little further up.

Andyrchi tourist camp, on the outskirts of the village.

In the village there is also a small scientific centre for the study of avalanches and mud-streams.

Itkol (see Nalchik)
The name means "dog's spur" in Balkar. This place is 2,000 m (6,560 ft) above sea level. From it opens up a unique view from Baksan Gorge to Elbrus; the whole of the mountain can be seen, from its foothills up to its large glaciers and the very summit. (See Pyatigorsk for more about Mt. Elbrus, including legends and mountaineering stories.)

Yunost Young Pioneers' camp and a *Ukrainian alpinists' camp*.

The slopes of Mount Cheget, situated south-west of Itkol, are excellent for mountain-skiing, and equipped with cable-cars. It is said that the Cheget ski runs equal those of Switzerland, Italy, and France in their layout and complexity. In May the south-facing slopes are bright with yellow azaleas.

Cheget Hotel & Restaurant

Terskol (see Nalchik)
The village and tourist centre is situated at a height of 2,100 m (6,890 ft). From here, along a winding path, the ascent to Elbrus begins.

Obelisk, World War II Memorial, at the foot of the mountain. Heavy fighting took place here in August 1942–January 1943 against German Alpine units, among them men from the Edelweiss Division. The Germans were not able to get through the Pass to the Black Sea.

The *observatory* here belongs to the Ukrainian Academy of Sciences. The East German telescope which was installed in 1983 has a mirror 2 m (over 6 ft) in diameter.

Itkol Hotel, to the right of the road, tel. 51-261. It has a variety of sports facilities, and from here Intourist organises skiing at Cheget, trips to Yusengi, Chegetsky, Irik-Chat, Adin-Su and Adyr-Su ravines, to Donguz-Orun Pass, and to Elbrus with the Adyl-Su Ravine and Shkheldinsky Glacier (see above). There are also excursions down to Nalchik, Pyatigorsk, and Kislovodsk (all described under their own names).

Intourist Office - tel. 51-104

NAMANGAN Population—308,000
Namangan is the major town of Namanganskaya Region in the northern part of the Fergana Valley. It stands on the Namangan-sai River 396 m (1,300 ft) above sea level and has an extreme continental climate.

Its name comes from the Tadjik "naman-kan,"

literally "salt mine," as they say there used to be a salt lake here and salt was excavated.

In the 9th century the capital of Fergana Valley was the town of Akhsy (Akhisekent) on the right bank of the Syr-Darya. It was a sizable town, ruled in the 15th century along with the rest of the province of Fergana by Sultan Umar-Shaikh, father of the great Babur. In 1620 Akhisekent was devasted by a terrible earthquake and those who remained alive resettled in Namangan 15–20 km (9–12 miles) from the ruined town, and influenced it greatly by bringing their handicrafts and trade. A second story tells how Namangan was founded in 1582 by Abdulla-Khan, ruler of Bukhara. As legend has it, he took many prisoners while warring with Persia and settled them on the site of present-day Namangan. The newcomers were given the girls of a gypsy tribe known as Aga as wives.

In 1664–84 Divan-i-Mashrab (b. 1640) lived in Namangan. He was a Muslim mystic, and a famous poet and a man of wit and cynicism.

The town suffered greatly from lack of water. According to legend, in olden times hermits lived where Namangan now stands. They needed good water and once one of the hermits said to another "Follow a stick and go to the north; God will help you to bring water from over there." The water followed the trace of the stick and did come to the place where the hermits used to live. As they say, it was God's providence to lay out the canal and in 1819–21 the canal of Yangi-aryk was laid out in Namangan, adding to the town's prosperity. It was built by the inhabitants, and each house was represented by one worker. The day when the canal was first opened became a great holiday. 10 years later the canal was enlarged.

Handicrafts were very well developed in the town, and its jewelry and silk were renowned. At the end of the 18th century it became part of the powerful Kokand Khanate. The last ruler of the Khanate was Khudzhiyar Khan, and when in 1875 an uprising broke out against him, he escaped to Tashkent. Russian troops, which were advancing successfully into Central Asia, attacked Namangan, and led by Governor-General Kaufmann, took it at the end of 1875. In February 1876 the Kokand Khanate was abolished and joined to Russia as the Ferganskaya Oblast. Namangan became a regional centre. It was a typical town divided into the Russian part, with 60 houses and all sorts of administrative buildings, and the local part, with mud-houses and 331 mosques.

By the turn of the century the population had reached 75,000, and 20 cotton gins were functioning. In 1912 the town was linked by railway with Kokand. Due to great influx of cotton merchants in the autumn, some hotels bearing such great names as "France" and "Grand Hotel" were built.

Modern industry is represented by light and food branches as well as machine-building, and the chemical industry developed mostly during World War II, when some factories were evacuated here from Moscow, Leningrad, and other major cities. The construction of the Great Namangan

Canal, 140 km (87 miles) long, contributed to the town's growth.

Khodzhamin Kabra Mausoleum was erected at the end of the 18th century by Mukhammad Ibragim bini Abduraim. This is a domed burial structure that is incrustated by carved terracotta and dark-green, glazed tiles—a decoration that was replaced in the 16th century by multicoloured facing. In the 19th century a complex of buildings consisting of the Azis-Khodzha Ishan mosque and khudzhaïs (dwellings) sprang up around it.

Mulla Kirghiz Medressah

Atavalikhon Mosque

Local Museum, Roza Luxemburg Street 70

50th Anniversary of the Uzbek SSR Monument

Ali Sher Nawai Drama Theatre, Sovetskaya Street 4. The theatre was founded by the prominent local poet, Hamza Hakim-zade Niyazi in 1932.

Summer Branch of Drama Theatre, Margilanskaya Street 1

Pushkin Park was laid out as the garden for the district chief in 1884. Since 1938 it bears the name of Russia's favorite poet. It is situated in the centre of the city, and 12 streets lead to it. It covers an area of 14 hectares (35 acres).

Namangan Hotel & Restaurant, Lenin Square; tel. 62-154

Vostok Restaurant, Kommunisticheskaya Street 58

GPO, Kommunisticheskaya Street

NESVIZH (Polish: Nieswicz)

Between Baranovichi and Stolbtsy a right turn leads to Nesvizh which lies 20 km (12 miles) off the main road.

The name of Nieswicz (meaning invisible) is said to have been that of a very high mountain that once stood on the site of the present town. The town was first mentioned in 1223 when it belonged to the Lithuanians. In 1513 it became the property of Prince Nikolai Radziwill, who had rejected Catholicism for Calvinism. At the height of the reformation movement in Nesvizh a printing works was organised here, which played an important role in the development of Byelorussian culture. In 1562 a catechism by the Byelorussian educator Simeon Budny, and a Byelorussian translation of the Bible were published here.

Prince Nikolai was succeeded by his son, known as Nikolai the Orphan, who disapproved of his father's decision and returned to the Catholic fold. All the non-conformist books were destroyed and the printing works were given to the Jesuits. The new landlord built a beautiful castle in 1584, and in 1593 Bernardoni, an Italian architect, built a Jesuit basilica, which was Poland's first baroque church. The town's Bernardine convent was founded by Nikolai the Orphan in 1598.

In the 17th century the castle was a real treasury of ancient arms made of gold and silver. There were also rich archives containing rare historical documents and letters from the monarchs of Europe. There was even a genuine copy of Pope Urban VI's bull on the establishment of unitarian churches in Western Russia.

Other old buildings include the 17th-century *town hall* and the *Slutskaya Brama* (Polish: Brama Slucka) *Gate* (1760).

Printing works, built by Simeon Budny in the 16th century.

Farny Catholic Church, 1583

Radziwill Castle, 1593

Bernardine Convent, 1598

Town Hall (Rathaus), 17th century

House at the Market Place, 1721

Slutskaya Brama Gate, 1760

Old Park, laid out in 1878

NOVGOROD Population—230,000

The name Novgorod means "new town" in Russian, but it is actually one of the oldest towns in Russia, and was founded over 1,100 years ago by the Ilmen Slavs.

The town is situated on either side of the river Volkhov, which until recently was spanned by a single bridge. The 2 parts of the city have retained their mediaeval names of Sophia Side, after the Cathedral of St. Sophia in the Kremlin, and Market Side, the side of the town which was occupied by the important merchant class. The town stands on a hill and the surrounding lowlands are flooded in spring.

Novgorod played an important role in Russian history until the end of the 15th century when it lost its independence. An early chronicler writes that the northern Slavs, having combined forces and successfully driven out invaders, were overtaken by internal strife so great that in 862 Slavonic legates went beyond the sea to the Norse Rus and said: "Our land is great and fruitful, but there is no order in it. Come and reign and rule over us." Three brothers came with their armed followers and the eldest, Rurik, settled in Novgorod. Russia is supposed to have been named after Rurik's tribe. It is considered more likely, however, that the Norse settlers in Novgorod were merchants who were exploiting the trade routes to the south.

In 882 Prince Oleg with his Novgorodian army conquered Kiev and transferred his government there. Novgorod, now governed by a viceroy, continued to grow, and was given special concessionary privileges by the Princess of Kiev. Christianity was accepted in Novgorod in 990, scarcely later than in Kiev, and by the 12th century it was virtually independent of Kiev, which it long outlived as an important trading centre. Largely on account of its postion on the trade route between the Baltic and Black Seas, Novgorod became known as "Lord Novgorod the Great" and its power was expressed in the saying "Who can resist God and Lord Novgorod the Great?" Novgorod also had the advantage over other Russian towns of not suffering the full weight of the Mongol invasion, although the town did pay tribute to the invaders.

The sphere of trade covered by Novgorod was extremely wide. Silks and spices, many of which were shipped on to Europe, came in from the south

NOVGOROD

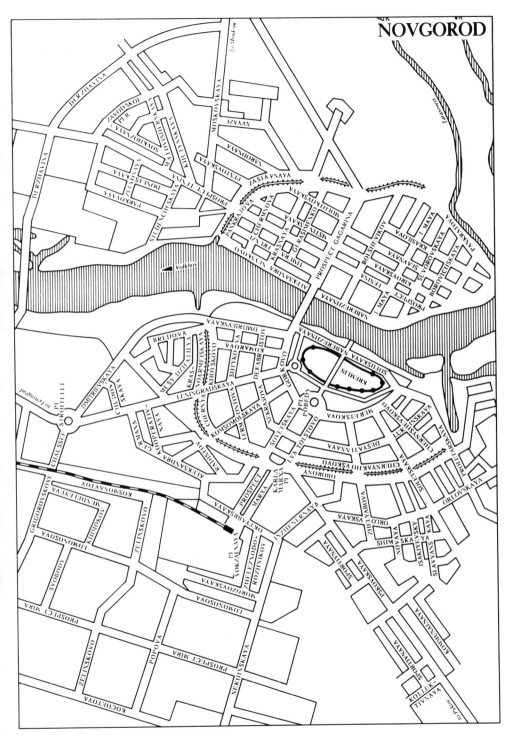

and the east, and furs and precious metals were sent out to the east and to Europe. In the 11th century there was a group of German merchants in Novgorod and, in the last years of its independence, it was the easternmost member of the Hanseatic League.

Novgorod was also the only Russian town where there was any real form of democratic power. Novgorod's veche (a popular assembly of citizens that used to govern in most Russian towns) was extremely powerful and the Prince of Novgorod was little more than a military leader. His rights were strictly limited by a number of treaties and neither he nor his family were allowed to purchase land within city domain. On more than one occasion the ruling prince was removed at the will of the veche. There is an old Novgorodian saying: "If the prince is bad, into the mud with him."

Between 1100 and 1150 there are supposed to have been 230 churches in Novgorod. There were numerous struggles among the principalities of Novgorod, Suzdal, and Moscow, and in 1170 Novgorod is said to have been saved by a miracle. Andrei Bogolyubsky, Prince of Suzdal, was besieging the town when Archbishop John had a vision, advising him to take the Znamenskaya Icon of Our Lady from the cathedral, carry it in procession around the city wall and then hang it on the gate. This done, although arrows flew "thick as rain" into the icon, it remained unharmed and real tears ran down the Virgin's face, so upsetting the attacking army that it fled. The Novogorod victory was so complete that, according to the chronicler, one could buy 3 Suzdalians for a single sheep. The event is commemorated by a famous icon, "The Battle between Novgorod and Suzdal," which can be seen in the Kremlin Museum.

In 1471, in a battle near Lake Ilmen, the armies of Novgorod were defeated by the combined forces of Ivan III of Moscow and the Tatars. Growing rivalry between the 2 principalities and a religious dispute involving allegations that the Novgorodians were defecting from the true Orthodox faith to a latinised form of Christianity gave rise to the battle. The woman, Martha, who led the anti-Moscow faction in Novgorod is described in a Moscow chronicle of the time as a person wanting "to seduce the whole people, to turn them from the right way, and to join Latinism."

After this date the prosperity of Novgorod steadily declined and suffered a final blow in 1570 when Ivan the Terrible is said to have butchered 60,000 citizens in order to suppress a plot against his life. For 6 weeks there were tortures, murders, robberies, and fires and, according to an old chronicle, every day hundreds of Novgorodians were thrown into the Volkhov together with their wives and children. The river was choked with dead corpses and since then, the legend runs, it has never frozen at this point.

By the middle of the 17th century the population that had once totalled 400,000 had fallen to about 2,000. It is written that after the Swedish war of 1627 there were only 850 people left alive in the town. The foundation of St. Petersburg at the beginning of the 18th century and a succession of fires completed the ruin of Novgorod.

65 out of the 66 most-valuable monuments here were damaged during World War II, but 40 churches and part of the 12th-century earth wall of the town still remain. Massive building work has been carried on since the war and the ancient name of Novgorod seems most appropriate for the present-day town. Many of the historical monuments have also been restored and no tall buildings or trees are allowed near the main historical buildings. Archaeological excavations are still in progress on Proletarskaya Street.

The 3 main thoroughfares of the town are Sadovaya (garden), Leningradskaya, and Gorky streets. They are all intersected by the main Leningrad–Moscow road. In Pobeda (victory) Square, on Gorky Street, are the buildings of the Palace of Soviets and the Communist Party School, and also a monument to Lenin.

The town's industries are mainly concerned with timber (particularly matches), ship repairing, and food. It is also the centre of an important agricultural area.

The Kremlin. The first Kremlin was built on this site in 864 by Rurik. It was known as the Detinets, a name given to the fortress in many towns at that time. Since then it has been repeatedly reconstructed in accordance with the defensive needs of the town.

The wall, which has 9 towers, is 1,386 m (1,516 yds) in circumference, between 8.5 and 10.6 m (28–35 ft) high and between 2.7 and 3.3 m (9–11 ft) thick. The wall and most of the towers were built between 1484 and 1490 on the site of an earlier wall that had fallen into disrepair.

The main church in the Kremlin is Sofiiski Sobor (St. Sophia's Cathedral). Open 10-6; closed Wed. & the last Mon. of each month. It was built in 1045–50. An earlier cathedral, built entirely of oak with 13 domes, was destroyed by the fire in 1045. The present cathedral was built on the order of Prince Vladimir and was intended to imitate the famous St. Sophia's Cathedral in Kiev. The design was simplified in many ways, however, with 3 apses instead of 5, frescoes instead of mosaics, and stone-and-brick work instead of marble. In addition, a new feature was the emphasis laid upon the apses, which, in subsequent Novgorodian architecture, became the most important feature. At the beginning of the 12th century galleries were built onto the northern, southern, and eastern facades of the cathedral, thus enclosing within the walls the spiral staircase and tower that originaly projected at the southern end of the west facade.

The central dome of the cathedral is a gigantic copy of the helmet of an ancient Russian warrior, topped by a cross and bronze dove. According to legend, Novgorod will stand until the dove flies away.

At the west entrance are the Sigtuna or Korsun doors, thought to have been made by Master Riquinius of Magdeburg in 1152–54 for the Bishop of Plotzk and captured in 1187 from the ancient Scandinavian capital of Sigtuna, where they served as town gates. They are about 3.5 m (11 ft) high, and are made of oak overlaid by 48 plates of bronze. 3 of these plates portray scenes from the Old Testament, 23 portray scenes from the New Testament, and 22 are of allegorical or mythological subjects. The inscriptions are partly in Slavonic and partly in Latin, but it is thought that the Latin inscriptions were added at the beginning of the 15th century.

The interior of the cathedral was not decorated until 1109, almost 60 years after completion of the building, because life was too unsettled in Novgorod at that time to allow continuous work on the cathedral. The original frescoes can be seen in only a few places because the cathedral was redecorated with oil murals in the 1830s. Work was stopped by Nicholas I, who occasionally passed through Novgorod on his way from St. Petersburg to Moscow, but the painting was resumed in the 1890s. The best frescoes that are left from the 12th century are in the southern part of the cathedral where there is a life-size one depicting the Byzantine emperor Constantine and his mother Helen. The one in the drum of the main cupola was unfortunately almost completely destroyed during World War II and can only be seen in parts. It was painted in the 12th century and, so the legend says, was the first portrayal of Christ with His hand raised in blessing. The day after the fresco was completed, the artists found that the hand was in a clenched position. They repainted the hand 3 times, only to find that whatever they did the hand remained clenched. On the fourth day they heard a voice saying, "Painters, painters! Do not draw me with a hand of blessing, but with a clenched fist for I hold Novgorod the Great in my hand and when it is open, the town will fall." And so indeed it happened; in 1941 the main cupola of the cathedral was holed by a bomb, the fresco was destroyed, and the old town of Novgorod was ruined.

The 11th-century mosaics that were originally behind the altar are now in the Kremlin museum. Fragments of the mosaics, thought to have been made by Byzantine craftsmen, can be seen in the main apse of the cathedral.

The iconostasis dates from the 16th century and is richly ornamented with silver and gold. Before it stand the painted and gilded thrones, also dating from the 16th century, of the Metropolitan and Tsar. There are a number of tombs in the cathedral, including the silver sarcophagus of John of Novgorod, who died in 1186. Also of interest are the "golosniki" (earthenware jars) built into the walls at certain points in order to improve the acoustics.

Sofiiskaya zvonnitsa (the St. Sophia Belfry) is situated near the wall of the Kremlin. The present building dates from the 15th to 17th century, and was restored and slightly altered during the 19th century. The first historical mention of the belfry here was in a chronicle of 1473 that states that together with the Kremlin wall it fell into the river during a flood.

Behind the cathedral is *Vladychny Dvor, the archbishop's court*. The 3-storey *Granovitaya Palata (Palace of Facets)* was built in 1433 at the order of Archbishop Yefimy and was one of the first secular structures to be of stone instead of wood. It was intended for important receptions and meetings and in the last years of the town's independence it was used by the boyars' council. The main hall is roofed with low arches supported by a central column. The palace used to be much larger, covering the whole area from the clock tower to the 2-storey Nikitsky Building, which now houses the offices and the museum library. The *Applied Art Museum* inside the Palace of Facets contains icons and other articles of value from local churches and monasteries. Open 10-6; closed Tues. & the last Fri. of each month.

Next to the Palace of Facets is the *Church of Sergi of Radonezh*, which was built in 1563 by Archbishop Iona in the same style as many of the gate churches in the Moscow Kremlin. Contrary to custom, it was dedicated to a Moscow saint instead of a local saint, as the Archbishop was an advocate of union with Moscow. The interior of the church was formerly covered in frescoes. The church as it looked at the time of building can be seen on one of the frescoes.

Next to the church is the *clocktower* (chasozvon), which was built in 1673 on the site of a 15th-century watchtower. There used to be a grammar school inside it but now an exhibition is held here. The clock was the second of its kind to be installed in Russia. The Nikitsky building is named after Archbishop Nikita and it was built in the 17th century on the foundations of a 12th-century wooden building.

In front of the Palace of Facets is the *grave* of the Russian poet Gavriil Derzhavin (1743–1816). Derzhavin lived near Novgorod and was buried in the grounds of the Khutinsky Monastery, 6 km (4 miles) outside the town. This was destroyed during World War II, and the coffins of Derzhavin and his wife were later moved to their present resting place.

Returning to the Sophia belfry, a little further along the wall is the tiny *Church of Andrei Stratilat*, which is reputed to have been built in one day in the 17th century.

Near this church in the centre of the Kremlin is the *Historical Museum & Art Gallery*, housed in a former office block built in 1783 and reconstructed in 1809. The two lions guarding the entrance were brought here from the estate of Count Alexei Arakcheyev (1769–1834), favourite and War Minister of Alexander I. The lion on the left has his tail well polished from the touches of passersby; it is said that to touch him brings luck in love. The museum was founded in 1863. It has over 80,000 exhibits in its 35 halls, mostly from the churches of the Kremlin, Novgorod, and the surrounding area. There are over 550 icons, the oldest being an 11th century icon of SS. Peter and Paul, which is thought to have been painted by a travelling Greek artist. There are also many icons dating from the 12th to 15th centuries, when there was a flourishing school of icon painting in Novgorod marked by strong images and vivid colours. Many of the icons depict local saints. Also in the museum are manuscripts dating from the 10th century and a collection of private letters written on birchbark dating from the 11th century. Open 10–6; closed Tues. & the last Thurs. of each month.

The Picture Gallery contains Russian paintings of the 18th to the early 20th century, with works by Levitsky, Aivazovsky, and other well-known artists. The portraitists include Venetsianov, Bryullov, Kramskoi, and Serov. There is also a fine collection of miniatures.

In front of the museum is a *monument* commemorating Russia's 1,000th anniversary. It was designed in 1862 by the sculptor Mikyeshin. On the imperial orb stands a figure of Russia, watched by her guardian angel, who leans upon a cross. The 6 statues surrounding this centre-piece represent the 6 major periods in Russian history: the times of Rurik, St. Vladimir, Ivan III, Dmitri Donskoi, Peter the Great, and Mikhail Romanov.

Also in the Kremlin is a *war memorial* with an eternal flame commemorating those who fell during the liberation of the town in January 1944 after it had been held for 29 months by the German army.

Novgorod is renowned for its numerous churches, some dating from the 12th century. Many of these are situated across the river from the Kremlin on the Market (Torg) Side.

Opposite the Kremlin on the bank of the river is a group of old buildings on a site known as *Yaroslavov Dvor* (Yaroslav's Court). The first mention of Yaroslavov Dvor was in a chronicle of 1113 and it is thought that this is where the Prince of Yaroslavl resided until the end of the 14th century. The main building in this complex is *St. Nicholas's Cathedral*, which was founded in 1113 and is the oldest church open for services in Novgorod. In fact it was elevated to the status of cathedral because of this.

The principal icon, a circular one depicting St. Nicholas, is now in the museum in the Kremlin. According to the legend, Prince Mstislav of Novgorod became fatally paralysed and sent ambassadors to Kiev to fetch this icon, which he believed could cure him. On the return journey, their ship was wrecked but the icon was found floating in the river Volkhov. Prince Mstislav recovered his health and in gratitude built a church to house the icon. The church was designed with 5 cupolas and 3 aisles in the style of Kievan churches of the same period. The present roof was added much later and so was the wooden staircase leading to the choir. Inside the church are fragments of the original 12th-century frescoes. The Church of St. Nicholas was a princely church, the priests being subordinated to the Prince of Novgorod rather than to the Archbishop. When Archbishop Nifont refused to

marry Prince Svyatoslav to a Novgorodian girl for political reasons the prince was married in this church by his own priest.

The *Church of St. Prokopiy* nearby was built in 1529 in the Moscow style.

The *Church of Zhon Mironosets* (the Myrrhbearing Women), also near the Cathedral of St. Nicholas, was built in 1510.

To the northwest of St. Nicholas's Cathedral is an old 3-storey building with 2 entrance arches and an octagonal tower. It is commonly known as the Vechevaya Tower (from "veche," the assembly of citizens that used to govern the town). The assembly used to hold its meetings here in the tower, and it is an interesting example of early civil architecture.

On the other side of Yaroslavov Dvor are 2 churches, built in the 14th century. The nearest is the *Church of St. Michael* on Mikhailov Street. It was founded in 1300, but was rebuilt in 1454 and again in the 19th century. *Uspenskaya (Assumption) Church* on Birkov Pereulok was founded in 1362 and although rebuilt in 1466 and again in the 17th century, it has retained its original appearance to a great degree.

The southern part of the Torg (Market) Side used to be known as Slovensky Kholm (Slav Hill). There are a number of old churches here. One of the earliest is *Ilyinskaya (St. Elijah's) Church* in Krasilova Street. It was built in 1198–1202 and rebuilt in the 15th century. Only the lower part of the walls date from the 12th century.

In the same street is the *Church of SS. Peter and Paul*, which was built in 1367. It was restored in the 1950s and the old portals on the northern and southern facades deserve attention.

Nearby in Krasilova Street is the *Church of the Apostle Philip*, which was built in 1383–84 and rebuilt in 1526.

At the junction of Krasilova and Pervomaiskaya streets are 2 churches. The oldest one of the two is the *Spasopreobrazhenskaya (Transfiguration) Church*, which was built in 1374. Inside the church are frescoes dating from the 14th century and attributed to the well-known icon painter, Theophanes the Greek.

Znamenski Sobor on Pervomaiskaya Street was built in 1682–88 in the Moscow style. The tympans are decorated with colourful frescoes.

There are a number of churches in Lenin Prospect. The oldest of all is the *Uspenskaya (Assumption) Church*, which was founded by Prince Vsevolov shortly before he was driven out of Novgorod, and which was built in 1135–44. It was considerably altered in the 15th century.

Of more interest is the *Church of Dmitri Solunsky*, which was built in 1381–82. The upper part of the southern and eastern facades is decorated with intricate stone work.

There are 2 churches of minor interest in Lenin Prospect, the *Church of St. Clement*, founded in 1386, and the *Church of Nikita the Martyr* (Tserkov Nikity Muchenika), founded in 1557.

One of the most outstanding churches of the

Market Side is the *Church of Feodor Stratilat* on Feodorovsky Ruchei Street. The church was built in 1360–61 and is now open as a museum. Apart from the frescoes, which are believed to have been painted shortly after the church was completed, there is a display of wrought ironwork. Open 10–5; closed Wed.

Another church renowned for its frescoes is the *Nativity* in Rozhdestvenskoye Kladbische (Nativity Cemetery), built in 1381–82.

In the northern part of the Torg Side are the remaining buildings of the Antoniev Monastery, which was founded at the beginning of the 12th century by a monk, Antonio Romano, from Rome. The principal church of the monastery was the Rozhdestva Bogoroditsy (*Nativity of the Virgin*) *Cathedral*, built in 1117–19. It was considerably altered in later centuries, however, when the large onion-domes were added. Inside the cathedral are fragments of murals dating from the 12th century. It is now a museum. Open 10–6.

Below is the list of some of the other churches remaining in the Torg Side of the town.

Church of St. Ioan, Herzen Street. This church was built in 1127–30 and rebuilt in 1453.

Church of St. George, Pervomaiskaya Street. This church was built in the 13th century.

Church of Paraskeva Pyatnitsa. This church was founded in 1207 by a guild of Novgorodian merchants who traded abroad. It was rebuilt in 1345.

Church of St. John the Divine (Tserkov Ioana Bogoslova), by the river Volkhov. This church was founded in 1536 on the site of an earlier church.

Church of St. George, Pervomaiskaya Street, 17th-century.

In Herzen Street on this side of the river, is a small *imperial palace*, which was used by the tsars on their journeys from St. Petersburg to Moscow. It was built in the 18th century and is thought to have been designed by Matvei Kazakov. It is now a House of Culture.

There are also many churches on the Sophia Side, so many that it is impossible here to describe them all fully. One of the oldest is *Blagoveschenskaya* (*Annunciation*) *Church* on the way to the Yuriev Monastery. This was built in the 12th century and it belonged to the Arkazha monastery, the remains of which can be seen not far from the church. The church was rebuilt in the 16th century and only the lower part of the walls dates from the 12th century. Fragments of the original frescoes of 1189 can be seen near the altar.

Another 12th-century church which can be seen in this part of the town is the *Church of SS. Peter and Paul* in St. Peter's Cemetery (Petrovskoye Kladbische). It was founded in 1185 and, unlike many 12th-century churches, still retains its original appearance.

An interesting 13th-century church is that of *Feodora Stratilata* in Kolomenskaya Street. It was built in 1292–94 and rebuilt in 1682. The murals inside the church are well preserved.

Troitskaya (*Trinity*) *Church* on Proletarskaya Street was founded in 1365, but was radically reconstructed in the 19th century.

Just off Proletarskaya Street is the *Church of St. Ioan*, which was founded in 1421. Nearby is *Uvereniya Fomy* (*the Conviction of St. Thomas*) *Church*, founded in 1463. An earlier church stood on this site and until recently it was thought that the present building contained elements of the older one. Recent research, however, has shown that the original church was completely ruined in the 15th century before the present one was constructed.

A good example of 15th-century Novgorodian architecture is the *Church of SS. Peter and Paul* in Zverninskaya Street. It was founded in 1406. At one time there were over 20 monasteries in Novgorod. The churches of 2 of these can be seen on the Sophia Side. The *Zverinov Monastery* was first mentioned in a chronicle of 1148, when a wooden church in the monastery was hit by lightning. The name Zverinov comes from the Russian word "zver" meaning wild animal. In the 9th to 12th century there was a forest here that was one of the most popular hunting grounds of the Princes of Novgorod.

In 1339 the *Pokrov* (*Intercession*) *Church*, which can be seen today, was built on the site of the wooden church destroyed by lightning. It was repeatedly rebuilt in the ensuing centuries and almost eclipsed from view in the 19th century when a large church was built beside it.

Near the Pokrov Church is that of *St. Simon*, built in 1467 with a large, onion-shaped dome. The frescoes inside date from the 15th century and are well preserved.

The *Dukhov* (*Holy Spirit*) *Monastery* was founded in the 12th century. The principal church of the monastery, the Church of the Holy Spirit, has unfortunately not survived. Of most interest here is the *Church of the Trinity*, which was built in 1557.

Yuriev Monastery can be reached by driving along Proletarskaya Street from the Kremlin, past the White Tower; it stands on the other side of Lake Myachino beside the Volkhov River. It can also be reached by boat. It is possible to drive right into the monastery compound by passing the main entrance gate and going through another gateway a little further on. The principal church of the monastery was *Georgiyevsky Sobor* (*the Cathedral of St. George*). It was founded in 1119 by Prince Vsevolod and is considered the best architectural monument in Novgorod after St. Sophia's Cathedral, which it was intended to surpass in grandeur. It was designed by a Russian architect named Piotr, who is thought to have also been responsible for the Cathedral of St. Nicholas.

The cathedral was restored during the 1930s when additional structures were removed from the facades, thereby returning to the cathedral its severe and impressive lines. Unfortunately the original frescoes were almost all removed during the 1840s, but fragments have been found during recent restoration work. Of particular merit are the figures of saints in the tower of the cathedral and the portrayals of sinners in hell at the entrance to the second floor. Open 10–6 daily in summer; closed Wed. in winter.

Also within the monastery walls is *Vozdvizhenskaya (Elevation of the Cross) Church* (1828), which has five blue domes.

Vitoslavitsy Open-air Museum of Wooden Buildings, in the park opposite Yuriev Monastery. The collection on a territory of 30 hectares (75 acres) has been growing since 1960 and now consists of churches, houses, and peasants' huts of artistic or historical value from all parts of the Novgorod region. Particularly interesting is the 17th-century *Uspenskaya (Assumption) Church,* which was brought here in 1965 from the village of Kuritskaya on the shore of Lake Ilmen. The church from Peredki stands 30 m (98 ft) high and now contains an art gallery. An inscription on one of its bells tells that it was specially cast for the church in 1539. The Ryshevo House was built at the end of the 18th century and is furnished with a variety of household objects dating from the turn of the century. The museum is open 10–6 daily in the summer; closed Wed. in winter.

Novgorod Museum, in the Kremlin and in the Granovitaya Palata of the Kremlin (see above).

Lenin Monument, Pobeda Square (formerly called Sophia Square) near the Kremlin. The bronze statue of Lenin was designed by Merkurov and erected in 1956 on an earlier pedestal, constructed by Osipov in 1926.

War Memorial, by the river in the form of an equestrian statue.

Drama Theatre and Concert Hall, in the Kremlin

Kremlin Park

Park of the 30th Anniversary of the October Revolution, in the Antonev region of the Torg Side. The Dynamo Sport Stadium, which can seat 30,000, is in the park.

Intourist Hotel & Restaurant, Dmitriyevskaya Street 16, tel. 75–089. Intourist office; tel. 74–235

Volkhov Hotel & Restaurant, Nekrasova Street 24, tel. 92–498

Sadko Hotel & Restaurant, Yuri Gagarin Prospect 16, tel. 95–170

Ilmen Hotel, Alexander Nevsky Embankment 23/1, tel. 73–117

Rossia Hotel & Restaurant, Alexander Nevsky Embankment

Detinets Restaurant, in the Pokrovskaya Tower of the Kremlin. Traditional Russian dishes and old style decor.

Bathing Beach, below the Kremlin wall

Beryozka Foreign Currency Shop, L. Tolstoy Street 5

Russky Souvenir, Leningradskaya Street 6

Service Station, Leningradskaya Street 92, on the main road into the town from Leningrad, tel. 10–73. Open 8–4.

Novgordsky Camping Site, near the village of SAVINO, 11 km (7 miles) south of Novgorod, 219 m (200 yards) to the left of the main road. Tel. 724 48. There are furnished tents on the grounds

of 2 hectares (5 acres), and a buffet, self-service kitchen, and post office. The site is on the banks of the Vishersky Canal with a bathing beach and fishing; campers are warned that the mosquitos may be a nuisance.

Khutonsky Monastery, Leave Novgorod along Leninsky Prospect and go as far as Khuton. The red-brick monastery buildings stand on a slight rise some distance to the left of the road. It was built in the 16th–17th centuries. Spaso-Preobrazhesky Cathedral was built in 1515, the refectory, the western block of monks' cells, and the bishop's palace date from the 17th century, and the southern block of cells from the 16th–17th centuries. The refectory church is dedicated to St. Varlaam Khutinsky, who was known as Alexei Mikhailovich before he took holy orders. There is a 3-storey bell tower over the entrance gate, and parts of the surrounding wall still stand. Reconstruction work is under way.

Just outside the monastery, to the right of the entrance gate, a *memorial* marked "229" shows the site of the military grave belonging to members of the 229th Artillery Division who lost their lives here during World War II.

Intourist organises boat trips on the river Volkhov, and excursions to Staraya Russa (q.v.) by road or by hydrofoil over Lake Ilmen, and to Seltso.

Seltso (see Novgorod)

This village stands on the river Nereditsa, 5 km (3 miles) from the centre of Novgorod. The trip there is made by boat in summer only.

Spasa na Nereditse Church. Open, as a museum, 10–6. The fragments of 12th-century frescoes inside are a fine example of the Novgorodian style of that time.

NOVOCHERKASSK Population—190,000

(Intourist organises excursions here from Rostov-on-Don, 40 km/25 miles away.)

The town stands on a high hill dominating the rivers Tuzlov and Aksai, two of the many meandering waterways in the lower part of the Don Valley. It was founded by the Don Cossack Ataman Matvei Platov in 1805. Platov (1751–1818) was a general famous for his warring against Napoleon. During the retreat of the French, he led a Cossack regiment, recaptured Smolensk, and seized Danzig (1813) and Namur (1814). He went to London in 1814 in the retinue of Tsar Alexander I and was presented with a sword, in exchange for which he left his uniform behind.

Soon Platov's settlement became a Cossack centre and Russian stronghold on the river Don. In 1837 the new town was visited by Tsar Nicholas I, who was satisfied with the construction work and the site chosen and ordered that the town "be at this very place." Development was stimulated by the laying of the nearby railway line in 1870. Also, during its early years the town received financial support and considerable privileges from the government.

There are buildings that remain from those times, including the Cossack headquarters, some 19th-century barracks, and a number of attractive small houses once owned by rich Cossacks.

After the revolution of 1917, Novocherkassk became the stronghold of the counterrevolution under Ataman Krasnov and the site of the Don Krug (Cossack parliament). This was due partly to its history, since it was the Cossack capital and had long been the centre of the political life of the Don Cossacks loyal to the Tsar. Krasnov negotiated a provisional agreement with the Germans, but he had too many enemies for his Don regime to survive. As the Red forces steadily advanced upon Novocherkassk and Rostov, the Don Krug passed a vote of no confidence in their military leaders, forcing Krasnov's resignation. In 1919 the Red Army defeated the White Guards, and in 1920 Novocherkassk became Soviet.

With the end of the civil war Novocherkassk regained its importance as a cultural centre. The first higher educational establishment—the Don Polytechnic Institute—had opened in 1907. In 1916 the Don Veterinary College was founded on the basis of the Warsaw Veterinary College evacuated here.

In the 1930s Novocherkassk became a major industrial centre of the southern European part of the Soviet Union. After the Second World War one of Russia's largest locomotive engine plants was built here. It manufactures VL (for Vladimir Lenin) locomotives and the more modern N-81 model. It boasts three research institutes, five establishments of higher education, and eight specialised secondary schools.

Voznesensky ("*Ascension*") *Cathedral*, Yermak Square. The cathedral was designed by Zlobin and Yashenko in Byzantine style and is one of the best examples of its kind in Russia. It was built between 1891 and 1905 and is 74.5 m (244 ft) high, 77 m (84 yds) long, and 62 m (203 ft) wide, while the diameter of the dome measures over 21 m (69 ft). It can hold a congregation of 5,000 and was formerly the Don Cossack army's cathedral. Pictures of army life decorate the choir stalls. The cathedral is open for services.

St. Michael's Cathedral, by the former Zapadensky market

St. Constantine's Church, Krylov (formerly Sennaya) Street

St. George's Church

History of the Don Cossacks Museum, Sovietskaya Street 38. Open 10–5.30; closed Mon. Here is an interesting collection of banners and the sword presented on 8 July 1814, to Hetman Platov with the following inscription on the blade:

A common council holden in the chamber of the City of London on Wednesday the . . . day of June MDCCCXIV decided unanimously that a sword of the value of two hundred guineas be presented to the Hetman Count Platoff in testimony of the high value this court holds of the consummate skill, brilliant talents and dauntless bravery displayed by him during the protracted conflicts in which he has been engaged for securing the liberties, the repose and the happiness of Europe.

The sword was presented to Platov by England's national hero, the Duke of Wellington.

The museum also contains a 17th-century English clock captured from the Turkish fortress of Azov in 1695. Local excavations of the burial mounds near Novocherkassk in 1864 brought to light much-prized gold items worked by the Sarmats in the 2nd century B.C. Most of the collection is now in the Hermitage Museum in Leningrad, but some originals and a number of copies can be seen here. There are also works by Nikolai Dubovsky (1859–1918), a native-born artist who bequeathed some of his works to the town.

Near the Don Cossacks Museum is the *Hauptwachter*, the *Guards' House* (built in 1853), and also the old wooden building of the *Posting Inn*, which was used by Pushkin (1820) and Lermontov (1840).

Ataman Palace, beside Lenin Garden. Built in 1863, it now serves as the town hall and the local party headquarters.

Grekov Museum, Grekov Street 124; open 11–5; closed Mon., Wed., and Fri. This museum is the former home of Mitrofan Grekov (1882–1934), a well-known Soviet artist who painted military pictures and battle scenes.

Krylov Museum, Krylov Street. Ivan Krylov (1861–1936) was a landscape painter, born 70 km from Novocherkassk. He lived and worked here for part of his life. Many of his paintings are of Moscow, but some are of Paris and Venice. One of his best pictures, "Steppe," recieved a gold medal in Paris in 1913; it is in the History of the Don Cossacks Museum.

Yermak Monument, Yermak Square. The monument by Mekeshin and Beklemishev was unveiled in 1904. The various inscriptions read, "To the Don Ataman Yermak Timofeyevich, Conqueror of Siberia, in memory of three hundred years of the Don Army from grateful descendants, (1570–1870)"; "He lost his life in the waters of Irtysh on 5 August, 1584"; "Russia, History and the Church pay tribute to Yermak's undying memory" (Karamzin, Russian historian); and "To Yermak from the Cossacks, 1904." The Siberian campaign lasted from 1581 to 1584.

Baklanov's Tombstone, Yermak Square. Yakov Baklanov (1809–73) was a Cossack general and a writer.

The *two triumphal arches* of Novocherkassk, one of which is in Herzen Street on the way in from the north, were erected in 1817 in memory of the visit of Alexander. They also mark the triumphal return of Ataman Matvei Platov and his Cossacks from Paris after the defeat of Napoleon. There is a personal memorial to the popular Russian folk hero, Cossack Stepan Razin, who in 1670–71 was the leader of one of the largest peasant revolts. He was executed in Moscow.

Monument to Matvei Platov, founder of Novocherkassk; by Klodt

Podtelkov and Krivoshilikov Monument, Revolution Square. These fighters for Soviet power are commemorated by a statue in the square at the entrance to the town from the north.

Lenin Statue, in the square next to the Don Cossack Museum

Drama Theatre, Karl Marx Street 16. The famous Russian actress Vera Komissarzhevskaya (1864–1910) began her career in Novocherkassk. This drama theatre, opened in 1965, was named after her.

Park, Karl Marx Street 7

Trud Stadium, Podtelkov Street

Novocherkassk Hotel and Restaurant, Platov Prospect, on the right side on the way out of town toward Rostov

Hotel, Podtelkov Street 90

Yuzhny Restaurant, Moskovskaya Street 1

Druzhba ("Friendship") Restaurant, near the entrance to the town, approaching from Moscow

Krepost Yermaka Restaurant, on the road leading out of Novocherkassk for Shakhty

Bank, Moskovskaya Street 9

Telegraph Office, Podtelkov Street 102

NOVOROSSIISK Population—186,000 (Intourist organises excursions here from Krasnodar, 141 km/88 miles away.)

Novorossiisk Bay is large, deep, and sheltered from the west. Long ago there was a Greek town called Bata on this spot at the mouth of the river Tsemes. During the 13th and 14th centuries it was held by the Genoese, but in the 16th century the Turks took it and in 1722 built a fortress called Sundzhuk-Kale. The Russians first took the fortress in 1808, and it belonged to Russia continuously from 1829. In 1838, when the Black Sea fleet under Vice Admiral Mikhail Lazarev (1788–1851) docked here, a temporary fortification called Tsemesskaya was built, and soon it was renamed Novorossiisk. Tsemes Bay, from which the fortress derived its first name, is deep enough for oceangoing vessels to dock. The Genoese called it Calo Limena ("Beautiful Bay"), and it has been used as a port since 1848.

Northeast winds blow into Novorossiisk from the mountains. These winds, known here as "bora," sometimes blow at gale force for days on end during the winter. Novorossiisk itself is sometimes called the Sea-Gate of the Kuban.

On the 31 March, 1855, during the Sevastopol campaign, Novorossiisk was bombarded by the joint Anglo-French fleet and the fortress was blown up and deserted, as were many other small fortresses in this region. Near the port is the black building of an old 9-storey grain elevator, the tallest in Europe and the second tallest in the world. Novorossiisk was the country's second-largest grain exporting port and 4,000 workers were employed in the docks. The elevator was built in 1894 by an engineer named Kerbedz and was at that time the largest in the world. It is no longer used, but a modern, green one stands next to it.

During the first Russian revolution of 1905 a Novorossiisk Republic was in existence for two weeks.

The port played an active part in both world wars. During the civil war and the time of British intervention Novorossiisk was a supply base containing large stores of material and munitions. On 18 June 1918, the Russian Black Sea fleet was sunk in Tsemes Bay because the Germans had cornered it there and Kaiser Wilhelm II demanded that it be handed over to them. They went down with their flags signalling: "Sinking. I do not surrender!" To commemorate the event, there stands a memorial that says: "In Tsemes Bay which lies before you, in 1918, by order of Vladimir Lenin, the Black Sea Fleet was sunk so as not to surrender to the German imperialists." A total of 11 naval vessels and 6 merchant ships were sunk. Later all but two were raised. In March 1920 the port became the evacuation base for the White Army retreating from the Kuban area. More than a million pounds sterling's worth of stores were left behind.

In 1942 Novorossiisk became an important bridgehead in the battle for the Caucasus. Most of the port was held by the Germans, but on the west coast of Tsemes Bay, at the foot of Mt. Koldun ("Sorcerer"), one can see a small cape. This is the Myskhako Peninsula, now more often called Malaya Zemlya ("Small Land"), where in 1943 a small Soviet landing party held out against the enemy for 225 days (4 February-16 September), defending the city and preparing a bridgehead for the future Soviet army offensive. The fiercest fighting took place in Death Valley, below Mt. Koldun, where an average of 1,250 kg (1.2 tons) of bombs and shells fell upon each of the embattled defenders. The late President Leonid Brezhnev was among the forces on Malaya Zemlya and there is a *memorial stele* there now. Most of the peninsula is now known as Malaya Zemlya Memorial Park; a zig-zag road links the various monuments. As its focal point stands the *Gallery of Combat Glory,* inside a concrete structure designed by Malaya Zemlya veteran Vladimir Tsigal, an academician, symbolizing a ship coming in to the shore at the very place where the 1943 landing was made. This was opened in 1982, as the third part of Novorossiisk's memorial complex, the others being the *Seamen's Memorial* and the *Frontline Railway Carriage* (see the listing below). Malaya Zemlya is near the town, on the way to the airport and well indicated. In 1973 Novorossiisk was awarded the title of Hero-City.

The Sugar-Loaf Mountain of the Markhotsky Range yields high-quality marl lime from which cement is made locally. This source was first exploited in 1879 and the first cement factory was completed in 1882. Now local industries also include oil production, fruit growing, fish curing, rolling-stock repairing, flour milling, and slate quarrying. The Soviet Union's first Pepsi-Cola factory operates in Novorossiisk. The contract between Pepsico and V/O Soyuzplodoimport was signed on barter terms: the Soviet Union buys the patented concentrated Pepsi-Cola syrup in exchange for Sto-lichnaya Vodka and Sovetskoye Shampanskoye (Soviet champagne). The factory puts out 50,000 litres a day.

The main thoroughfare of Novorossiisk is *So-vietov Street* (formerly Serebryakovskaya Street). A few old houses have survived here and have been carefully restored. The large and impressive green one at Sovietov Street 40 used to be the town hall; built in 1909, it now houses the Young Pioneers' Palace, some shops, and a gallery. Further on, the road goes along Mira Embankment, which follows the line of the bay.

The city has a naval engineering school and technical schools. Of late the port of Novorossiisk has become the home of the Soviet tanker fleet.

Assumption Church, Vidov Street 26. This church dates from the end of the 19th century.

Local Museum, Sovietov Street 58. Open 10–5 daily.

Tanker Fleet Museum, at the Sea Terminal

Cement Industry Museum, by the old cement factory, along the road near the chemist's ("ap-teka"). Open 10–6; closed Mon. This museum, which shows the development of the cement in-dustry in Russia, is the only one of its kind. In 1879 Professor Josef Kucera from Prague identified the kind of marl necessary to produce Portland-type cement. Using French and German capital, the first factory was opened in 1882. Most of the equipment was British, supplied by Babcock and Wilcox Ltd. of London and Glasgow. Foreign workers were invited to take jobs here, and it was for them that the *Lutheran church* was built on nearby Sudostalskaya Street, along Sukhumi Chaussee. Part of the museum is kept as a me-morial to the writer Fyodor Gladkov (1883–1958), who lived here while writing his novel *Cement* in the 1920s.

Gagarin Planetarium, in Lenin Park

War Memorial, Heroes-of-World-War-II Square. Here beside the sea are war graves, and between two tombs with monuments to heroes of the Soviet Union Tsaezar Kunikov and Nikolai Sipyagin burns an eternal flame. A tape-recording of "Novorossiisk Chimes," by Dmitri Shostako-vich, is played each hour between 6 A.M. and 1 P.M. and schoolchildren form a guard of honour. Another *monument* is dedicated to the Seamen of the Revolution and an *obelisk* commemorates the 20th anniversary of the liberation of the town from the White Guards.

On the Cape of Love the *Fishermen's Monu-ment* commemorates twelve fishermen who died in a storm in 1953.

Defenders' Monument, Svoboda ("Freedom") Square. The 13-m (43-ft) high monument com-memorating the liberation of Novorossiisk from the Germans in 1943 depicts a soldier, a sailor, and a partisan, symbolizing the unity of the armed forces with the civilians; the sculptors were Nikolai Ti-moshin and Ivan Shamagun, and the monument was unveiled in 1961.

Monument to the Hero-Sailors of the Black Sea, at the port

Frontline Railway Carriage, on the grounds of the October Cement Factory. The remains of this shot-through railway carriage are all that is left of a carriage that formed part of the battlefront that was held for a year in World War II.

Obelisk with Sculptured Group, on the road out of town. The soldiers and civilians shot here in 1943 are commemorated.

Drama Theatre, Letny Sad ("Summer Gar-den"), Sovietov Street 35

Planetarium, Sovietov Street 53

Foreign Seamen's Club, Portovaya Street 8, in the port

Trud Stadium, Sovietov Street 55. Seats 10,000.

Chernomorets ("Black Sea Sailor") Hotel and Restaurant, Sovietov Street 42; tel. 523–34

Brigantina Hotel and Restaurant, Anapskoye Chaussee 18

Novorossiisk Hotel and Restaurant, Isayeva Street 2

Khizhina Lesnika ("Forester's Hut") Restau-rant, Anapskoye Chaussee 23

Mayak ("Lighthouse") Restaurant, at the port

Lada Restaurant, Engels Street 47

Yuzhny ("South") Restaurant, Frunze Park

GPO, Sovietov Street 36

Gift Shop, Sovietov Street 36

Bank, Sovietov Street 47

Beyond the town in the direction of Sochi, driv-ing beside the sea and over the bridge, one passes the elevators and then, along the chaussee, a *tank monument* commemorating a heroic tank crew. Behind the tank monument stand the ruins of the cement workers' Palace of Culture, kept as a mon-ument. It is said that the building was completed and there were plans to hold a ceremonial opening on 22 June 1941, but that was the very day that Germany invaded the Soviet Union. So it was never opened, and was burned down during the 1942–43 fighting. In front of it are military graves.

On the other side of the road is the bullet-ridden railway carriage and "The Hands," a *monument* of four clenched fists with machine guns. The in-scription there records that it was near the cement factories that the Germans were halted in October 1942.

12 km (7 miles) along the main road toward Sochi there is another *memorial*, this time of a sunken ship.

Intourist organises visits to the vineyards of Abrau-Durso, which lies 17 km (11 miles) from Novorossiisk and 14 km (8.5 miles) from the main road leading in from Krasnodar.

Abrau-Durso Population—4,000

This is a small village surrounded by mountains with Lake Abrau lying 84 m (276 ft) above sea level. The lake is rich in fish, especially carp, and owes its name, which means "slope" or "fall" in Cherkes-sian, to the steepness of its shores. The little river

NOVOSIBIRSK (Akademgorok)

1. Presidium of the Siberian Academy of Sciences
2. Hydrodynamics Institute
3. Economics & Industrial Engineering Institute
4. Chemical Kinetics & Combustion Institute
5. Mechanics Institute
6. Semiconductor Physics Institute
7. Nuclear Physics Institute
8. Organic Chemistry Institute
9. Catalysis Institute
10. Inorganic Chemistry Institute
11. Thermal Physics Institute
12. Multi-User Computing Centre
13. Cytology & Genetics Institute
14. Mathematics Institute
15. Geology & Geophysics Institute
16. Automation & Electrometry Institute
17. History, Philology & Philosophy Institute
18. Novosibirsk University
19. Scientific Library
20. Physics, Maths & Chemistry Boarding School
21. Botanical Garden
22. Scientists' House
23. Geological-Mineralogical Museum
24. Young Technicians' Club
25. Academia House of Culture
26. Kaleidoscope Kindergarten
27. University Hostel

NOVOSIBIRSK

Durso derives from four separate springs, and its name means "Four Waters."

Both the climate and the soil here resemble those of the champagne country of France. In November 1870 the area became an imperial estate. Tsar Alexander II agreed to import vine stock from abroad and in 1872 the agronomist Geiduk brought 20,000 Riesling-type vines from Germany, while others came from Austria and France. Some French wine makers were employed here to start with and the enterprise was supervised by Prince Lev Golitsyn (1845–1915), himself an authority on the subject. From 1896 the production of sparkling white wines developed rapidly, and today, from vineyards that cover 1,100 hectares (2,750 acres), more than 2 million bottles of Soviet champagne are made annually. The production process and subsequent storage of this and other high-quality, prizewinning wines are greatly facilitated by the tunnels and caves that have been dug into the rocky mountains.

Museum and Wine-tasting Hall, up on the hill; tel. 97–2116. Open 9–6; closed Sat. It is best to arrange a visit here through the Intourist office in Novorossiisk.

World War II Memorial, on the top of the hill near the museum

NOVOSIBIRSK is the largest city in Siberia.

SIBERIA

Area: 10,000,000 sq km, larger than either China or the United States. Population: approximately 25,500,000, which is small for such an area, averaging about 10 to 15 persons per square mile. The people are 94 percent Russian and the others include a wide variety of indigenous nationalities. There are Buryats, of Mongol origin, in the Buryat Autonomous Republic, whose capital is Ulan Ude, the Yakuts of the Yakut Autonomous Republic, whose capital is Yakuts, and many others belonging to Turkic-speaking, Finno-Ugrian, and Tungus groups.

Siberia is the largest part of the Soviet Union in area and one of the most important economically. It stretches from the Arctic Ocean to the Mongolian steppes and from the Urals almost to the Pacific. Its mineral resources include coal, iron ore, gold, diamonds, and various nonferrous metals. Also of great value are the timber resources and power of the mighty rivers—the Ob, Yenisei, and Lena—and their tributaries.

There are several theories as to the origin of the name "Siberia." One is that it derives from the Russian word "syever," meaning "north," and this is quite in line with the impressions of Siberia gathered by the first travellers from Russia. These were people from Novgorod who reached the river Ob at the end of the 11th century. The main attraction for the Russians at that time were the furs, and when the grand princes of Moscow imposed taxes on the inhabitants of the Ob region, they were paid in sable, mink, and other valuable furs.

The conquest of Siberia received new impetus after Ivan IV (the Terrible) defeated the Kazan Tatars. However, even then the movement into Siberia was strongest in the east and the north, while in the southern regions the Russians met with staunch resistance from the nomadic Tatars under the leadership of Khan Cochoum. The way to the southern part of the Ob basin was opened only after a campaign against the Tatars was won by the Russians under the leadership of the Cossack Yermak, who died during the fighting.

At the end of the 16th century the first Russian towns were built in Siberia and in the course of about half a century the vast new continent was more or less colonised by Russians. The second period of colonisation started during the first half of the 18th century, when the first attempts were made to utilise Siberia's mineral resources. Nevertheless, the country's main use was as a place to which undesirable elements of society could be exiled and also as empty territory ready for the resettlement of surplus population from the European part of the country. In 1891–1900 the Trans-Siberian Railway was built, crossing the whole of Asia.

Since the late 1920s a great deal of research has been done regarding the utilisation of the immense wealth locked in the forests, steppes, and mountains of the country. The great rivers Ob, Yenisei, and Angara, which were of enormous service as communication routes during the colonisation period, now constitute the source of electrical power and a whole network of hydroelectric stations has been established, among them those at Bratsk and Kransnoyarsk, which are the largest in the world.

The fertile soil of southern Siberia was used during the virgin lands campaign at the end of the 1950s, and today such cities as Novosibirsk, Irkutsk, and Vladivostok have become important scientific centres, with Novosibirsk having its own branch of the Soviet Academy of Sciences.

Novosibirsk Population—1,440,000
In 1893 the village of Gusevka was founded during the construction of the Great Siberian Railway, and ten years later it already was granted town status and known as Novonikolayevsk, after an engineer. It grew quickly, for it was a transit point for settlers going into the Altai area or further on into Siberia. Along the banks of the rivers Ob and Kamenka wooden houses sprang up like mushrooms, and at the point where the railway crossed the Ob both trade and transport encouraged the growth of the town. The old bridge is a great iron construction, like a Meccano toy with seven enormous rectangles. The engineer responsible, Nikolai Belelyubsky (1845–1922), was bribed to build a fine bridge in Tomsk, but instead he took the money and used it for this fine bridge. Opened in 1897, it is one of the engineering highlights of the Trans-Siberian. In spite of the bridge, the opposite sides of the river really were united only in 1956; before that the river Ob had served as the border between the two time zones, so there was an hours' time difference

as well as the distance between the left and right banks.

The city itself is the Russian Federation's third largest, after Moscow and Leningrad. Most of it lies on the right side of the river Ob and its tributaries, the Kamenka and the Yeltsovka, but new blocks of flats are going up on the left side, too, in the industrial part of the city known as the Kirov Region, formerly the village of Krivoschekovo.

Local industry took on its first real importance during the early five-year plans of the 1930s, and during World War II industrial plant evacuations from the European part of Russia increased local industry ten times over. Now the city is one of the country's biggest machine-building centres, but there is also considerable metallurgy as well as chemical, food, and light industries.

Since the Academy of Sciences opened its Siberian branch here in 1943 Novosibirsk has been the educational centre of Siberia. It has 16 higher educational establishments. It is also a vital railway junction where the Trans-Siberian joins the lines to the Altai and Kuzbas areas, and it is an important river port. The most recent railway construction is the city's underground line, which also goes under the river; the first seven stations were opened in 1985.

The main thoroughfare is Krasny ("Red") Prospect, which crosses the city from the mouth of the Kamenka to the airport. It serves as a shopping street and has administrative and office buildings, too. The most outstanding are the buildings of the Regional and City Executive Committees and also the banks and theatres, some of them built in constructivist style, popular here in the early 1930s. The Academy of Sciences and the drama theatre are both on Lenin Street. From Sovietov Square, which joins Krasny Prospect, there is a good panoramic view from the high bank of the Ob across the river to the Kirov Region on the left bank.

The *Cathedral of St. Alexander Nevsky*, built in the Byzantine style, is considered the original source of all Russian Orthodox architecture. It was designed by Solovyov, who followed the blueprints of the New Church of Our Lady in St. Petersburg. The interior decoration by the Pankryshev icon-painting workshop of Tomsk is disappointing, but because there is a film studio inside at present it is not open to the public anyway. The cathedral was completed in 1889. It was a landmark on the route to the east, and it welcomed new settlers. Its dedication was in honour of Tsar Alexander III, the Peacemaker. It is still the largest church on the Trans-Siberian route.

Below the cathedral are both the Trans-Siberian and the Turksib railways. Above the cathedral Krasny (formerly Novonikolayevsky) Prospect runs into the centre of the city. To the right is the 100-flat Residential House built by Kryachkov in the French neoclassical style developed by August Perret. This was among his projects to be awarded a gold medal and Grand Prix diploma at the 1937 Paris World Fair. Further on are art nouveau buildings. The former high school building (1910–12

by Kryachkov) was for many years the largest on the street; it was reconstructed in the late 1920s. The second largest was Kryachkov's city trade building on Yarmarochnaya ("Market") Square, which now houses the local museum. Other impressive buildings are Stevedores' House on Fabrichnaya Street, built in 1934–38 by Osipov, and his Renaissance-style Generals' House.

Novosibirsk sometimes has been compared to an American city for the way its population increased. In 1897 there were 7,800 inhabitants, 20 years later 69,800, in 1937 400,000, and now there are over 1.5 million. It was renamed Novosibirsk in 1926, and between 1927–29 alone nearly 5,000 buildings went up in the town. In spite of the rapid construction, there are still plenty of old wooden houses. Those with the finest carved decorations are protected by the state. Good examples are at Gorky Street 16, Irkutskaya Street 74, Lenin Street 11, Saltykov-Schedrin Street 5 and 120, Chaplygin Street 7 and 25, Kolvyanskaya Street 5, Oktyabrskaya Street 15, Bolshevistkaya Street 29, and Inskaya Street 19.

Tourists to Novosibirsk are proudly shown many different things that are record breakers: the *railway station*, which was built in the 1930s and is the largest on the Trans-Siberian route, the circular, domed-roofed *Opera House*, which is bigger even than Moscow's Bolshoi Theatre, and one of the country's largest airports. The railway station building is a mixture of classical and constructivist style, and it is unusual in that instead of being abstract in design, it is really in the shape of a gigantic railroad engine; looking at it from the town side, the main entrance is the driver's cabin, with the arch representing the big wheel, and the tower on the right-hand side is the funnel, while smaller arches are the little wheels.

In the Sovietsky Region of the city on the river Ob is a hydropower station built in 1950–59 with a total output of 400,000 kilowatts. The Novosibirsk Reservoir is 1,070 sq km in area, 200 km (124 miles) long, and 17 km (11 miles) across at its widest point.

Vozneseniya ("Ascension") Cathedral, Sovietskaya Street 91. This wooden building dates from 1902. It is open for services.

Rozhdestva Bogoriditsy ("Nativity of the Virgin") Church, Pestel Street 10/12. This is an Old Believers' church and is open for services.

Baptists' Prayer House and Baptistry, Open for services.

Local Museum, Vokzalny Magistral 11. Open 10–6; closed Mon. and the last Tues. in each month. The natural history section is especially interesting. It includes the skulls of a mammoth and woolly rhinoceroses that were found when new foundations were being laid in Novosibirsk. The mammoth was discovered under Kalinin Square in 1936 and one of the rhinos in Kalinin Street in 1950.

Exhibition Hall, Sverdlova Street 10

Art Gallery, Sverdlova Street 9. Open 11–6; closed Tues. The 60 canvases of works by Nikolai

Roerich is the largest collection in the Soviet Union. He loved Siberia and the Altai region very much and wanted his paintings to hang in the first gallery to be opened in Siberia, which happened to be this one. His mountain landscapes are particularly fine. Also in the gallery is a slide show of Siberia with a musical accompaniment.

Planetarium, Michurina Street 12

Kirov's House Museum, Lenin Street 35. Sergei Kirov (Kostrikov, 1886–1934), a well-known Bolshevik, lived in this wooden house in an apartment that belonged to Alexandr Petukhov for a few months in 1908 when he was working in the town. The museum was opened in 1947.

Shopmen's House, Chaplygin (formerly Asinkritovskaya) Street 65. This two-storey wooden house was the headquarters of the Board of the Social-Democratic Shopmen's Society. There is a memorial plaque on the facade.

Dusya Kovalchuk's House, Lenin Street 82. This small wooden house with a memorial plaque is hard to find among the tall new buildings. It belonged to a young woman revolutionary called Dusya Kovalchuk, and from 1910–19 it was used secretly by the Bolsheviks for meetings and as a printshop. Kovalchuk was tortured and killed by Kolchak counterintelligence in 1919.

Glinka Monument, Sovietskaya Street, at the corner of Schetkina Street, by the Glinka Conservatoire

Monument to Revolutionaries, in Revolutionary Heroes' Garden, next to the Youth Theatre. 104 Soviet soldiers who had been killed by Kolchak's army in December 1919 were buried here on 22 January 1920. A monument in the shape of a hand holding a burning torch by V. Sibiryakov and Kudryavtsev was put up over the common grave on 7 November 1922. In 1927 the partisan commander Pyotr Schetinkin (1885–1927) was killed in Ulan-Bator and buried here; his gravestone was added in 1934. On 9 January 1942, Adrien Legin (1846–1942), one of the last heroes of the Paris Commune of 1871, died in Novosibirsk. He had been a member of the French Communist party since 1922 and had lived in the Soviet Union since 1928. He was reinterred in the square in 1946, and a memorial stele by M. Menshikov was erected in 1957. In 1971 his mortal remains were returned to France and buried by the wall of the Commune near the Pere Lachaise Cemetery. A 40-m (131-ft) pictorial panel by A. Chernobrovtsev was unveiled here in 1960. In 1957 marble busts by M. Menshikov were created to honour renowned Siberian Civil War heroes—Pyotr Schetinkin, Vasili Romanov, Alexandr Petukhov, and Fyodor Serebrennikov. Four other busts, including one of Dusya Kovalchuk, were added in 1977.

Siberian Guards' Obelisk, in the garden in front of No. 28 Sibiryakov-Gvardeitsev Street. The obelisk was completed in six weeks. The inscription on the grey stele below the guards insignia reads, "The heroic feats of the dead and the deeds of the living are one."

Lenin Monument, Lenin Square. Built by I. Brodsky and unveiled on the 5th of November, 1970. To the left of the statue of Lenin stand three smaller ones, of a worker, a soldier, and a peasant, each 6.5m (21 ft) high and weighing 10 tons, while figures of a young couple stand to the right.

Dzerzhinsky Monument, in Dzerzhinsky Garden, on Dzerzhinsky Prospect

Glory Monument, in Slavy Garden, between Stanislavksy and Rimsky-Korsakov streets. Dedicated to Siberian World War II heroes and unveiled on 6 November 1967, the ensemble, designed by Yermishin, Pirogov, and Zakharov, is encircled by a thick hedge, and five concrete paths lead to Solemn Square. Across this are 5 10-m (33-ft) concrete steles decorated with bas-reliefs and quotations. The back of the central stele bears a sculptured figure of a grieving mother overlooking Sorrow and Grief Square, while those on either side carry the names inscribed in steel lettering of 33,000 Novosibirsk residents who died during the war. An eternal flame burns in a great bowl at the statue's feet and a schoolchildren's guard-of-honour keeps regular watch. Coins thrown into the bowl go toward the maintainance of the memorial and, as in other Soviet cities, it has become a tradition for newlyweds to lay their wedding bouquets here.

Zayeltsovskoye Memorial Cemetery, Zayeltsovskoye was a military cemetery where soldiers and officers of World War II who died in local hospitals of their war wounds were buried. There are 1,279 graves here and it was decided to make it a city memorial in 1977. Gavrilov was responsible for the reconstruction, and now each grave is covered with an iron slab bearing the name and dates of the deceased. The centrepiece is a 4-m (13-ft) statue of a wounded soldier by Valeria Semyonova.

Pokryshkin Bust, Sibiryakov-Gvardeitsev Square. Air Marshal Alexander Pokryshkin, thrice Hero of the Soviet Union, was born here in 1913. A fighter pilot during World War II, he made 560 operational flights, took part in 156 air engagements, and shot down 59 enemy planes. The bust was unveiled on 6 November 1949.

Bogatkov Monument, in the garden at the crossing of Boris Bogatkov and Kirov Streets. Boris Bogatkov is known as a soldier-poet. The monument by Menshikov was unveiled on 2 July 1977.

Barbashev Bust, Pyotr Barbashev, Hero of the Soviet Union, was born here. The monument, constructed with money earned by the pupils of School No. 171, was sculpted by Valeria Semyonova and unveiled on 19 October 1968.

Opera and Ballet Theatre, Krasny Prospect 38. The building was designed in 1931 by the architect A. Grinberg and it was intended to be the largest opera house in the world. A number of other architects took part in the work before it was completed. The opening took place on 12 May, 1945, with a performance of Glinka's *Ivan Susanin* as part of the victory celebrations marking the end of the Second World War in Europe. The theatre seats 2,000 and has a cupola 35 m (115 ft) high. The attached concert hall seats 800. The repertoire of the Novosibirsk Chamber Choir includes old church music. The bas-relief "Soviet Art," which decorates the main entrance, was sculptured by Stein.

Mikhail Glinka Conservatoire, This was constructed in the 1920s by Kryachkov for the trading organisation, Sibdalgostorg. There is an organ in the concert hall.

Krasny Fakel ("Red Torch") Drama Theatre, Lenin Street 19. This building was constructed as the Commercial Club in 1912–14 by Kryachkov and later reconstructed by Osipov. In 1918 it was renamed the House of the Revolution and was the headquarters of the local Soviet. In 1920 it was renamed the Workers' Palace. The Siberian State Musical Drama Theatre was opened here in 1922, the first performance being *The Mermaid*, by Dargomyzhsky. It has been called the Krasny Fakel since 1 November, 1932.

Regional Drama Theatre, Kotovskovo Street 8
Musical Comedy Theatre, Michurina Street 12
Youth Theatre, Krasny Prospect 34. Commonly known as TYUZ, this imaginative modern building is designed like a sailing boat, with windows like portholes and a high, triangular roof like a sail. Across the nearby ravine stands a tall Communist party building.

Youth Theatre, Zhertv Revolutsii ("Victims of the Revolution") Square. Immediately after Lenin's death in January 1924 the workers of Novonikolayevsk decided to build a house in his memory. A million postcards and stamps were sold as "bricks" to subscribers to finance Lenin House. The first idea was to follow the lines of Tatlin's III International Monument, but another plan was accepted and work went ahead under the guidance of Burlakov, Zagrivko, and Kuptsov. The opening ceremony took place on 21 January, 1925, the first anniversary of the leader's death. It was in Lenin House on 3–9 December, 1925, at the first session of the Siberian Territorial Soviet, that it was decided to change the name of the city from Novonikolayevsk to Novosibirsk. Lenin House was reconstructed in 1944 by Teitel and then housed the Youth Theatre.

Puppet Theatre, Titov Street 25
Circus, Chelyuskintsev Street 21. Built in 1969, it seats 2,300.
Zoo, Gogol Street 47. The new zoo will make good use of the natural ravines in the city.
Spartak Stadium, Michurin Street 14
Botanical Garden, by the Academy of Sciences
Central Park, Michurin Street 12
Kirov Park, in Kirov Region
Zayeltsevsky Park, 2nd Yeltsova Street
Bathing beach, on the left bank of the river Ob, near the railway bridge. Other popular recreation areas are *Bugrinskaya Grove* on the left bank and *Zayeltsoveky Grove* on the right bank of the river. The warmest time of Novosibirsk's rather short summer is July, with an average temperature of 18 to 20°C (64 to 69°F).
Siberia Hotel and Restaurant, Krasny Prospect 26

Novosibirsk Hotel and Restaurant, opposite the railway station. Opening soon.
Tsentralnaya Hotel, Building 1, Lenin Street 1; tel. 22 4626
Tsentralnaya Hotel, Building 2, Lenin Street 3; tel. 22 0313. Intourist office, tel. 22 5281. There is a Beryozka foreign currency shop here as well as at Tolmachevo Airport.
Oktyabrskaya Hotel
Ob Hotel, Dobrolyubova Street 2
Tsentralny Restaurant, Krasny Prospect 23
Snezhinka ("Snowflake") Cafe, Lenin Street 6
Aeroplane Children's Cafe
GPO and Telegraph, Sovietskaya Street 33. The building was erected in 1914–16 by Kryachkov as a trade arcade belonging to the Morozov textile mills. A strike committee was located here in 1918, and in 1922 it became the post office. Its present appearance dates from reconstruction in 1927. A memorial plaque reads, "A meeting of the strikers of Novonikolayevsk was held here in August 1918."
Bank, Krasny Prospect 25, at the corner of Kommunisticheskaya Street. This red-brick building dates from 1903–04.
Beryozka Foreign Currency Shop, Chelyuskintsev Street 18/1
Department Store, Dmitrova Prospect 5
Book Shop, Krasny Prospect 9
Souvenirs, Ordzhonikidze Street 27
Market, Trolleynaya Street. 30 percent of the families in Novosibirsk have their own place in the country and their own gardens. This is the main source of the market produce.
Taxi Rank, 298 982
History and Architecture Museum. This open-air museum displays examples of old architecture gathered from all over Siberia. Among the most interesting exhibits are the two towers from the Uilsky settlement in the north of the Tyumen region. The northern and southern towers of the Uilsky settlement are the oldest surviving Russian buildings in Siberia. It took three months to transport them to the museum.

Also interesting is the *Zashiverskaya Church* (1700) from Yakutia and a Buddhist temple from the Buryat Autonomous Republic.

Intourist organises boat trips on the river Ob and excursions to Academgorodok, 26 km (16 miles) from Novosibirsk city centre.

Academgorodok Population—60,000

This stands on the bank of the Ob Sea, the reservoir that was formed after the completion of the hydro-power station.

Its name means "Academy Town." It was decided in June 1957 that a scientific centre should be built in Siberia. Three academicians, Mikhail Lavrentiev, Sergei Khristianovich, and the mathematician Sergei Sobolev, were the initiators of the scheme because they pointed out that scientific development of Siberia was lagging behind the current demand. In fact, there was practically no sci-

AKADEMGORODOK

NOVOSIBIRSK (Akademgorok)

1. Presidium of the Siberian Academy of Sciences
2. Hydrodynamics Institute
3. Economics & Industrial Engineering Institute
4. Chemical Kinetics & Combustion Institute
5. Mechanics Institute
6. Semiconductor Physics Institute
7. Nuclear Physics Institute
8. Organic Chemistry Institute
9. Catalysis Institute
10. Inorganic Chemistry Institute
11. Thermal Physics Institute
12. Multi-User Computing Centre
13. Cytology & Genetics Institute
14. Mathematics Institute
15. Geology & Geophysics Institute
16. Automation & Electrometry Institute
17. History, Philology & Philosophy Institute
18. Novosibirsk University
19. Scientific Library
20. Physics, Maths & Chemistry Boarding School
21. Botanical Garden
22. Scientists' House
23. Geological-Mineralogical Museum
24. Young Technicians' Club
25. Academia House of Culture
26. Kaleidoscope Kindergarten
27. University Hostel

most important scientific centres of the Soviet Union. Now it has a complex of research institutes belonging to SOAN, the Siberian Department of the Academy of Sciences, about eighteen in all, and a university. Most of these are sited either on Prospect Nauka or on Universitetsky Prospect, which runs down at right angles from it toward the Omsk Sea. The university opened in 1959. The students benefit from the facilities in the institutes, their practical work forms part of real scientific research, and 60 percent of the university teaching staff are professional scientists. A boarding school built among the trees near the university is run in close association with it. Here 500 senior school-children, selected by competitions throughout the eastern parts of the country and by an entrance exam that requires individual thinking, follow a special two-year course of physics, mathematics, and chemistry. The teaching is up to university level and many pupils go straight to university from this school. Among the other schools in the town are some that specialize in either English or French.

There are five more institutes in Novosibirsk, and others at the branches of SOAN in Irkutsk, Ulan Ude, Yakutsk, Tomsk, and Krasnoyarsk are affiliated. A typical feature that they have in common is their broad use of mathematical methods in tackling the various problems they set out to solve. Besides being interconnected through their SOAN affiliation, the scientists of each institute have their work linked through Academgorodok with the country's current plan for industrial development, so that new scientific methods may be incorporated into industrial production without delay.

Academgorodok has become a mecca for scientists from all over the world who come to attend congresses here.

When the town was being built, efforts were made to save as many of the existing trees as possible, so there are generous stretches of birch and bracken among the buildings. The local inhabitants have found that blocks of 4 and 5 storeys are the warmest in winter, but there are a number of separate 2-storey houses, too. All of the flats are fully equipped with modern conveniences.

Geological Museum, in the building of the Institute of Geology and Geophysics, Universitetsky Prospect. Tours are by special arrangement. The spectacular purple stone, discovered near the river Chara in 1960 and accordingly named charoite, is worth a detour. It polishes to reveal beautiful silky lines. So far it has not been found anywhere else.

House of Scientists, This acts as a club and a theatre to which visiting theatre companies come from Novosibirsk. There is an exhibition hall with regularly changing exhibits, a conference hall, a shopping centre, and a cinema.

Botanical Garden, Voyevodskovo Street, down beside the Omsk Sea

Bathing Beach, down Morskoy Prospect to the sandy shore of the Omsk Sea

entific research work going on beyond the Urals. Lavrentiev found a good site for his dream city quite near Novosibirsk and many young scientists from Moscow and Leningrad moved into Golden Valley, as the first settlers called their new home. They even made up a song about it:

Moscow farewell! With Siberia round
We live as one happy family,
And our new home deserves its name—
We call it Golden Valley.

Lavrentiev Street bears the name of the founder.
Academgorodok grew fast to become one of the

Heated Swimming Pool
Academy of Sciences Hotel, This is a 7-storey building.
Intourist Hotel constructed by Polish builders in 1988
Zolotaya Dolina Restaurant, Ilicha Street 10, by the Academy of Sciences Hotel
Shopping Centre, Tsvetnoy Prospect 2
Academkniga Bookshop, Morskoy Prospect 22

Vaskhnil

On the left bank of the Ob, opposite Academgorodok, is the second academic township, Vaskhnil. It specializes in agricultural research. Workers here have developed low-growing, frost-resistant apple trees, such as Stelyushiya and Sibirskaya, and a quick-ripening strain of tomatoes to take advantage of the short, hot summer.

The ten institutes and the greenhouses behind them are linked by 1 km of glazed galleries to obviate chilly walks outside from one building to another in winter. 4 hectares (10 acres) of territory nearby is fenced off by the biologists as an insect reserve.

Beyond Vaskhnil is the site for yet a third scientific centre, this one devoted to medicine.

NUREK

See Dushanbe, p. 119.

ODESSA Population—1,115,000

Odessa is the Ukraine's third-largest city. Situated 30 km (19 miles) north of the mouth of the river Dniester, the central part of the city stands on a plateau divided by three ravines: Quarantine, Military, and Water Ravine. The city now covers them all. Odessa's coat-of-arms is of St. George and the dragon above a four-fluked anchor.

The city has many flattering epithets: "Capital of the south," "Southern Palmyra," "Little Paris," and "Little Vienna." It is also frequently referred to as Mother Odessa in song, and the city is an unfailing source of jokes; thanks to the local Jewish humour that gives a special Odessa flavour to the way Russian and Ukrainian are spoken here.

In the Middle Ages the settlement and port of Kotsubievo sprang up on this site. It flourished because of its proximity to the mouths of the Dniester, Danube, Dnieper, and South Bug, rivers that brought goods from the steppes and the northern regions. It was important chiefly for exporting grain, mainly through Italian merchants. The city was destroyed by the Tatars and then rebuilt under the name of Hadjibei, and it regained its importance as a trading centre. The Tatars were then succeeded by the Turks, who in 1764 built a fortress called Yuni-Dunia ("New Light"). In 1789, during the third Russo-Turkish war, Russian troops led by the Neapolitan de Ribas captured the fortress and the town together with the entire region between the rivers Dniester and Bug. By the Iasi Peace Treaty of 1791, the captured area finally was declared to be Russian. Alexander Suvorov built a new fortress in 1792–93, and the foundations of

the present naval port were laid in 1794 under the supervision of Vice Admiral Osip de Ribas and on the order of Catherine the Great. The following year the town was given its present name of Odessa, after the ancient Greek settlement of Odessos, then believed to have been located on one of the estuaries ("limany") near the river Bug, although subsequent research placed Odessos much farther south, where the Bulgarian resort of Varna is today.

At this point the history of Duke Richelieu becomes interwoven with that of the city of Odessa. Duke Richelieu Armand Emmanuel du Plessis (1766–1822), a descendant of the famous cardinal of the time of Louis XIII, came to Russia at the beginning of the French Revolution and remained a devoted follower of Louis XIV. At the end of her reign Catherine the Great put him in command of her Cuirassier Regiment. He fell from favour under Paul I and went to Vienna. However, when the throne passed to Alexander I in 1801, the new tsar gave an order that the privileges given to Odessa by Catherine the Great be returned for a period of 25 years, and in 1803 the tsar recalled Richelieu and made him mayor of Odessa and governor of the surrounding region of Novorossia, with great independence of action and local power. Through him one-fifth of all of the Odessa customs duty was paid in to the town treasury; as a result banks, theatres, and institutes were built and street lighting was installed, and under his guidance the town grew five times larger.

In 1803 some German colonists settled near Odessa to farm, and their successors lived there in the villages until the Second World War.

When Louis XVIII became king of France in 1814 he offered Richelieu a high government post. The latter accepted, leaving his country house and his pension to the city of Odessa. The city was neglected after his departure and its development slowed down considerably, but Richelieu fully intended to go back again. On learning of his death in 1822 Alexander I told the French ambassador, "I mourn Duke Richelieu as a real friend who always spoke me the truth. His merits will be eternally commemorated by the gratitude of all honest Russian people."

From 1816 Count Langeron was mayor of Odessa. The new city grew rapidly because of the speed of building, the privileges afforded to the population, and the establishment of a porto franco in 1822. In 1854 the city was bombarded by the Anglo-French fleet for 12 hours but was successfully defended. As its development continued, it gradually acquired its European aspect. By 1881 it had risen to be Russia's greatest port through its turnover, which still consisted largely of grain. Its industrial growth also was considerable, and by 1900 it ranked third after Moscow and St. Petersburg in the number of its industrial concerns.

In 1875 the first Marxist working organisation, the South Russian Union of Workers, was formed; this was the first revolutionary political organisation in Russia. During the 1905 revolution the workers of the city were joined by the mutineers of the

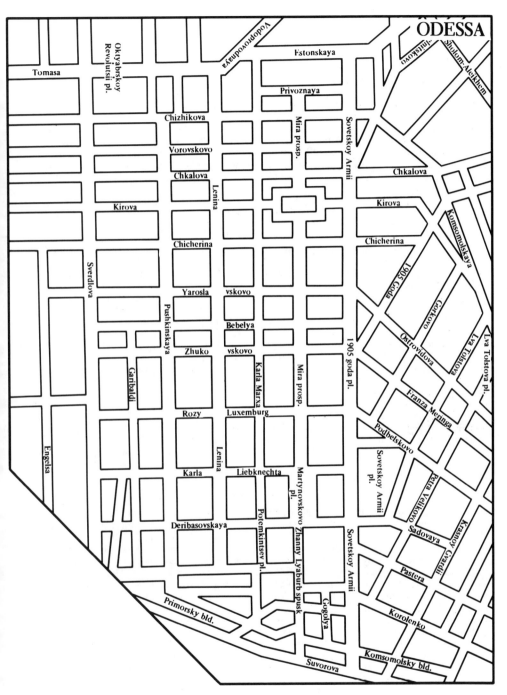

Prince Potyomkin Tavrichesky, a battleship of the Black Sea fleet. After the suppression of the uprising the pogroms began, and as a result more than 13 percent of the total population of 600,000 (including many of Jewish origin) left the city. Odessa suffered greatly during the civil war of 1917–20, when it changed hands several times. The war dragged on especially long in the south because of the Austro-German intervention in 1918 and that of France and England in 1920. A third of the city's houses were destroyed and the population decreased considerably; it was not until after the famine of 1921–22, when at last renewed sea traffic brought back trade with foreign countries, that the city began to revive.

In 1941 Odessa endured a 69-day siege by Nazi troops and suffered heavy damage. After World War II it was given the title of Hero-City.

Many famous personalities are connected with the town. Pushkin and Gogol were here, as was the Polish poet Adam Mickiewicz. Sholom Aleikhem Street (formerly Myasoyedovskaya Street) is named after the popular Yiddish writer who lived here while working for local newspapers. Other Yiddish literary figures include Mendele-Moiher Sporim. Maxim Gorky worked here as a docker in 1896. Modern writers are represented by Isaak Babel, Eduard Bagritski, and the humorists Ilya Ilf and Evgeny Petrov, among others. Odessa also is known as the cradle of the cubo-futurist movement in Russian art, led by Mikhail Larionov, Natalia Goncharova, and the Burlyuk brothers, all of whom lived and worked here and arranged the extraordinarily rich Exhibition of International Art here in 1910–11. Besides many of their own works, those of Tatlin and also 53 Kandinskys were on view.

Today Odessa boasts 16 colleges and 23 technical training centres with more than 85,000 students, making it the fifth-largest educational centre of the Soviet Union. Among its institutes is the world famous Ophthalmic Diseases Institute, for many years headed by Professor Filatov (1875–1956).

Just as in all seaside towns, the Marine (*Primorsky*) *Boulevard*, formerly called Nikolayevsky, is the most popular place for a promenade. It is only 450 m (492 yds) long, just a couple of blocks, but the 15 houses with a larger building at either end, designed in 1822 by French architects, are worthy rivals to those in St. Petersburg. Leading up from the sea are the *Potyomkin Stairs*, best seen from the bottom, for they were especially designed to give an illusion of greater height than they really have. They were built by Boffo in 1837–41 in 10 flights, first of all being finished in limestone brought here from Trieste, but this was later replaced by granite. The optical illusion of height was achieved by the steps at the top being narrower than those at the bottom. The first step is 21 m (23 yds) wide and the top one (the 192nd step) no more than 12.5 m (14 yds). From the top just the landings are visible and from the bottom only the risers can be seen. First known as the Richelieu Stairs, they

later were renamed after the battleship that took part in the uprising of 1905. There is an escalator beside the stairs.

At the top is a *statue of Duke Richelieu*. This figure of the Duke, shown wearing a Roman toga, was cast in Paris in 1828 by Ivan Martos, Dean of the St. Petersburg Academy of Art. Part of the pedestal was broken by a cannonball during the Anglo-French bombardment, and was restored with an artificial cannonball remaining for all to see. Inside the biggest stone of the pedestal were placed the most important medals and coins minted during the reigns of Louis XVI, Catherine II, Paul I, Alexander I, and Louis XVIII, all of whom Richelieu had served, as well as a medal of Napoleon I and a bronze medal cast in Paris to commemorate the great man's death. A little ways inland from the statue is Potyomkin Square, with a *monument to the sailors who participated in the 1905 uprising*. This used to be Catherine Square; a *statue of Empress Catherine II* is in the centre. Karl Marx Street, which runs out of the square to the south, was called Yekaterininskaya. Back on the boulevard, at the far right-hand end, is *Prince Vorontsov's Palace*, built for him by Boffo in classical style in 1826–27 while he was governor-general. It became the Palace of Pioneers in 1936. On the far left is Seamen's Palace, another building by Boffo. Here also stands a *bust of Pushkin*. It was sculpted by Polonsky and below is the dedication: "To Pushkin from the citizens of Odessa." The dates 1820–24 engraved on the upper part of the pedestal indicate the years when Pushkin lived in exile in Odessa. The monument, financed by private donations, was unveiled in 1888. Beside the bust is one of the cannons used in the Crimean War. It came from the English frigate *Tiger*, weighs 40 tons, and was brought up from the bottom of the sea. Behind the bust is the *Duma*, which Boffo completed in 1834, now used as the town hall. It is decorated with statues of Mercury and Ceres, and the large clock on the main facade has figures of Day and Night. The town hall stands on the side of Kommunarov Square; here also are the *Archeological Museum* and an evening school, which occupies the old building of the *English Club*, designed by the French architect Thomas Thomon.

The modern building of the passenger port is a recent addition to this old part of the town, and another is the spectacular bridge spanning the ravine that divides Primorsky Boulevard and Komsomolsky Boulevard. Gogol Street runs inland from Komsomolsky Boulevard, so called because the writer, Nikolai Gogol, lived here at No. 11 in 1850–51. No. 2 is known as the Shah's Palace; in 1909 Mohammad Ali Shah of Iran rented it when he found asylum in Odessa after being deposed. No. 1 is an interesting example of art nouveau style.

The city's main street is Deribasovskaya, after Admiral Osip de Ribas. There have been repeated attempts to rename it after the German socialist Ferdinand Lassalle (1825–64), but, just as it happened with Nevsky Prospect in Leningrad, the use of the old name persisted and is now officially accepted. Perhaps its early popularity was due to the fact that Odessa's first garden was laid out there. No. 16 was the building of the Lycee Richelieu, founded in 1817 in memory of the mayor who at that time still had hopes of returning. No. 16 formed the nucleus of the university. Plaques on the wall bear witness to the fact that both Mendeleyev and Mickiewicz lived and worked here. Deribasovskaya was also one of the first trading streets, and the shopping arcade at No. 33 known as *Passage* was built at the end of the last century. It is well worth going inside to admire the very lovely plasterwork. No. 24 was the office of the governor-general.

Prospect Mira (formerly Alexandrovsky), leading out of Deribasovskaya, is the widest street in the city, with a boulevard down the centre. It was planned as Odessa's Champs Elysees. Parallel to it runs Soviet Army Street, formerly known as Preobrazhenskaya ("Transfiguration"), after the old cathedral. No. 24 was first occupied by Odessa University in 1865; it still belongs to the university, but the main building is now at No. 2 Peter-the-Great Street and there are other branches in other parts of the city. It is known as Mechnikov University, after the biologist Ilya Mechnikov (1845–1916), who lived at Pasteur Street 36 and whose work brought fame to the university. Later, in 1865, the art school opened at Nos. 14–16 *Soviet Army Street*, one of the main shopping streets. At the beginning of the street is a *bust of Marshal Rodion Malinovsky*, a native of the city and commander of the liberation army in April 1944. The unusual numbering of the houses (the left side has even numbers instead of odd) is said to be due to a wealthy and superstitious homeowner who managed to get all of the numbers changed to avoid his being No. 13. Beyond Soviet Army Street is *Sadovaya Street*, which has souvenir shops and, at No. 10, one of the grandest post offices in the country.

Pushkin Street, also parallel to Prospect Mira but lying to the east of it, used to be called Italianskaya until 1880 because of the number of emigrants, visitors, and businessmen from Italy who settled and prospered here.

> The tongue of golden Italy
> Rings out along the laughing street

wrote Pushkin in *Eugene Onegin*, but to commemorate his stay here at No. 13 (a hotel in 1812), a plaque was put up on the house and the street was renamed after him. No. 13 is now the *Pushkin Literary Museum* and a number of local newspapers have their offices on the street. No. 9 is the *Museum of Western and Oriental Art*. No. 15 is the *Krasnaya Hotel*, the oldest in the city, and No. 17 the *Philharmonia Concert Hall*, designed by Yuri Bernardazzi in 1899 in Florentine Gothic style as the stock exchange. It is one of the best pieces of architecture in Odessa. Inside, the ceiling by Karazin is painted to symbolise trade and in-

dustry. Further down the street is No. 47, where revolutionaries in 1880 planned to blow up the carriage of Tsar Alexander II; they were to dig a tunnel under the road where he would pass.

At the far end of Pushkin is *October Revolution Square*, where parades and demonstrations take place. Special guests of the city each have been asked to plant a tree here. Around the square are the modern buildings of the party and regional executive committees, and there is a *monument to Lenin* as well as another *monument marking the grave of 177 soldiers who died during the civil war*.

The suburbs of *Moldavanka* and *Vorontsovka* in the west, *Melnitsy* in the southwest, and *Peresip* in the north are now integral parts of the city.

Uspensky ("Assumption") Cathedral, Sovetskoy Armii Street. This five-domed cathedral was built in 1855–69. Its facade is a mixture of Russian and Byzantine styles. The bell tower is 47 m (154 ft) high. A memorial plaque tells that during the German occupation of World War II a certain Georgi Dubakin raised a red flag on the top of the cathedral. Services take place in the cathedral, which has a miracle-working icon of Our Lady of Kasperovka. The icon formerly was kept in *Preobrazhenskaya Cathedral* during the winter months, but after Easter, during Holy Week, it would be taken with great ceremony back to the village of Kasperovka.

Ilya Proroka ("Elijah the Prophet") Church, Pushkin Street 79. This church, built in the second part of the 19th century, also is open for services.

Morozlivskaya Church, Komsomolskaya (formerly Portofranco) Street 18

St. Peter's Roman Catholic Church, Khalturin Street 5. Services take place in Polish and Russian. There is a mosaic of St. Peter over the entrance door.

Kirche, the Lutheran Church, Ostrovidova Street. Closed.

Troitsky Greek Orthodox Church, Karl Marx Street. Open for services.

There are other late-19th and early-20th century churches in Odessa, but they are of little historic interest and mostly are closed.

Andreyevsky Monastery, near the railway station. This monastery now houses the tramworkers' club.

St. Pantheleimon Monastery, at the end of Pushkin Street, opposite the railway station. This monastery bore the same name as the Russian Orthodox monastery at Mt. Athos, to which it once belonged. Now the Odessa Planetarium is housed here.

Synagogue, Lesnaya Street 5. This building is 70 years old. Other synagogues at Pushkin Street 20 and Chkalov Street 73 no longer serve their original purpose.

Odessa Fortress, in Shevchenko (formerly Alexandrovsky) Park. The old tower and wall remain from the military fortress built by Suvorov in 1793.

Catacombs, There are many entrances and exits, but the majority are on the slopes of Mt. Shevakhovo. Most of the caves were formed early in the 19th century when the sandstone was quarried to build up the growing city, and later they were used by smugglers. Numerous revolutionaries hid in the caves during the civil war of 1917–20, and an underground printing shop also was hidden in them. During World War II the catacombs were a headquarters for partisans. The tunnels run for a total of more than 800 km (497 miles). In some places they are very narrow and in others several metres wide; even now, new corners are still being discovered with the remains of soldiers and their munitions in them.

Archaeological Museum, Lastochkina Street 4. Open 10–6. This museum, dating from 1825, shows the history of the people living on the northern shore of the Black Sea from ancient times until the 13th century. It also has one of the largest collections of ancient Egyptian relics in the Soviet Union as well as material from the ancient Greek settlements on the Black Sea.

Historical-Ethnographical Museum, Khalturin Street 4. Open 9–5.30; closed Fri. This museum is divided into two parts: the historical section at Khalturin Street 4, in the former Commercial Club, and the geological and natural history departments, at Lastochkina Street 24.

Merchant Marine Museum, Lastochkina Street 6, in the building of the old English Club, with a lighthouse outside. Open 10–5; closed Tues. Many of the exhibits, such as those concerning the old trading vessels, are of great historical interest. The story of the development of the whaling industry is also well displayed.

Museum of Western and Oriental Art, Pushkin Street 9. Open 10–6; closed Wed. This 2-storey building was erected in 1856 by the architect Otton for a merchant named Abaza. It contains 18 halls, with the exhibits falling into 3 groups: antiques, mostly copies; Western European art, including original works by Rubens, Rembrandt, Veronese, and Murillo; and oriental art, Persian miniatures, and handicrafts from China, India, and Japan.

Picture Gallery, Korolenko Street 5a. Open 10.30–5; closed Tues. Russian artists of the 18th and 19th centuries, Soviet art, and graphics are displayed here. The 19th-century classical-style building was once the home of Count Potocki. The gallery was opened in 1889.

Vorontsov Monument, Sovetskoi Armii Square. This bronze statue was cast in 1863 in Munich by Brugger. Prince Nikolai Vorontsov is shown on a pedestal of Crimean porphyry decorated with bas-reliefs of battles. He was governor of Novorssiisk and fought against Napoleon at the Battle of Craonne in 1814.

Grigory Vakulinchuk Monument, Tamozhnaya Square, near the port. This monument commemorates one of the organisers of the mutiny on the battleship *Potyomkin* who was killed by an officer and whose funeral became the excuse for a mass demonstration. The monument, his bust on a pedestal of red granite, stands 6 m (20 ft) high. It was unveiled in 1958.

Potyomkin Uprising Monument, Karl Marx Square. The monument by Bogdanov commemorates the uprising of 1905 and was unveiled in 1965.

Kotovsky Monument, Kotovsky Street

Obelisk to the Unknown Seaman, Shevchenko Park, near the remains of Suvorov's fortress. An eternal flame burns beside the obelisk. This is one of the numerous monuments being erected in a 60 km (37 mile) semicircle, the Belt of Glory, around Odessa to commemorate the defence of the city in 1941. It does in fact follow the main line of defence.

"Saved Childhood" Monument, This monument by Tokarev was unveiled in 1987.

Opera House, Lenin Street 1. This was designed in 1884–87 by Fellner and Hellmer, two Viennese architects who immediately afterward built the Italian renaissance–style Deutsche Volkstheater in Vienna. On the elaborate facade of the Odessa Opera House are busts of Glinka, Gogol, Griboyedov, and Pushkin.

The interior is in Louis XVI style, and the ceiling of the auditorium is decorated with scenes from Shakespeare's "Midsummer Night's Dream," "As You Like It," "Hamlet," and "A Winter's Tale," all painted by the artist Teffler from Vienna. The theatre seats about 1,600. It was damaged by fire in 1925 and then restored. It suffered again with the rest of the city during World War II. The companies of the Paris Opera and of La Scala of Milan both have been heard here, as have such famous singers as Enrico Caruso and Chaliapin. Sarah Bernhardt and Anna Pavlova both performed here, and Tchaikovsky, Rubinstein, Glazunov, and Rimsky-Korsakov all conducted here in their day.

October Revolution Ukrainian Drama Theatre, Pasteur Street 15

Ivanov Drama Theatre, Karl Liebknecht Street 18

Musical Comedy Theatre, Chizhykov Street 3

Ostrovsky Youth Theatre, Tchaikovsky Pereulok 12

Puppet Theatre, Pasteur Street 62. The Gothic-style building (1896) was formerly a Lutheran Church.

Philharmonia Concert Hall, Rosa Luxemburg Street 15

Nezhdanova Conservatoire, Ostrovidova Street 63. David Oistrakh, Emil Gilels, and many other eminent Soviet musicians graduated from this conservatoire.

Intourist Concert Hall, Rosa Luxemburg Street 14. Open May to Sept. Intourist office, tel. 22–3143.

Circus, Podbelsky Street 25. This circus is one of the best in the Soviet Union.

Shevchenko Park, Engels Street 1. Formerly Alexandrovsky Park and now named after the famous 19th-century Ukrainian poet, this 90-hectare (225-acre) park has an excellent view of the Black Sea and has its own bathing beach, *Komsomolsky Beach*. There is a *monument to Bogdan Khmelnitsky*, who united the Ukraine and Russia in 1654. Also in the park are the *Avangard Stadium*, which can seat 40,000 and is one of the largest in the Ukraine, an *open-air theatre, boat hire stations*, and the University *observatory* and *planetarium*.

Pobeda ("Victory") Park, Perekopskaya Pobeda Street. This park was formerly called Dukovsky Gardens. There is a swimming pool here and a permanent local *Economic Achievements Exhibition*.

Charles Darwin Garden, near the Opera House. This garden was once known as Palais-Royale.

Zoo, near Ilyicha Park. Open daily.

Hippodrome Racecourse, Bolshoi Fontan, Chetvyortaya Stantsiya

Odessa Hotel and Restaurant, Primorsky Boulevard 11. Formerly the London Hotel, this is now run by Intourist.

Chyornoye Morye ("Black Sea") Hotel and Restaurant, Lenin Street 59; tel. 24–2025

Krasnaya Hotel and Restaurant, Pushkin Street 15, at the corner of Kondratenko Street; tel. 22–7220. Previously called the Bristol Hotel, this is also an Intourist hotel.

Bolshaya Moskovskaya Hotel, Deribasovskaya Street 29

Spartak Hotel, Deribasovskaya Street 25

Passage Hotel, Sovetskoi Armii Street 34; tel. 22–4849

Tsentralnaya Hotel, Sovetskoi Armii Street 40

Arcadia Hotel, Shevchenko Prospect 24; tel. 29–6001

Delfin Camping Site, Kotovsky Road 298, near Luzanovka Beach; tel. 55–0066. The *Delfin Restaurant* is here.

Chernoye Morye ("Black Sea") Motel, near Zolotoi Beach

Bratislava (Slovak) Restaurant, Deribasovskaya Street 13

Zarya Cafe, Lenin Street 53, in a synagogue building

Zolotoi Telyonok ("Golden Calf") Cafe, Sovetskoi Armii Street

Gambrinus Beer Cellar, Deribasovskaya Street, where it is crossed by Zhukova Street

Bank, Lenin Street, at the corner of Deribasovskaya Street

GPO, Gorky Street 12

Central Telegraph Office, Sadovaya Street 3

Bulgarian Consulate General, Posmitnovo Street 9; tel. 66–2015

Indian Consulate General, Kirov Street 31; tel. 22–4333

Department Store, Pushkin Street 75/73

Podarki ("Gift") Shop, Deribasovskaya Street 33

Gift Shop, Sadovaya Street 19

Kashtan Foreign Currency Shop (Souvenirs), Pushkin Street 33

Beryozka Souvenir Shop, Deribasovskaya Street 17

Souvenir Shop, Deribasovskaya Street 16

Odessa's estuaries are former river mouths that have become separated from the sea by sandbanks; through evaporation they have turned into saline-bitter lakes of varying degrees of salt concentration.

The water contains more magnesium, lime, iodine, and bromine than does seawater, and the mud is rich in sulphur, which is efficacious in the cure of rheumatic, nervous, and skin diseases. Besides these natural assets the sea itself is very shallow and is quickly warmed by the sun. There are over 30 sanatoria and 15 rest homes in this part of the Black Sea coast.

Lermontovsky Resort

Lermontovsky Resort is located southwest of the centre but within the city boundaries of Lermontovsky Pereulok. It stands on a high plateau from which a 220-m (240-yd) slope with terraces leads down to the sea. There is a large park and sanatoria for rheumatics.

Beyond Shevchenko Park and the Komsomolsky Beach the western resort region begins. Langeron, near Shevchenko Park, was named after Count Langeron, who took the place of Richelieu as mayor of Odessa in 1816. There is a good bathing beach, and behind it, on Chernomorskaya Street, are many sanatoria.

After Otrada comes *Arcadia*, a park that runs along the seashore. This is the most popular place near Odessa and the most picturesque. Some parts of this region, along the shore, are known as Malyi Fontan ("Minor Fountain"), Srednyi Fontan ("Middle Fountain"), and Bolshoi Fontan ("Major Fountain")—but these names have nothing to do with fountains. They simply indicate Odessa's problem with its freshwater supply in the 19th century; there were artesian wells ("fontany") here. The Malyi Fontan region lies between 1st and 7th Stantsiaya, Srednyi Fontan between 7th and 9th, and Bolshoi between 10th and 16th. *Golden Beach*, the beach at Bolshoi Fontan, is exceptionally good.

There is a summer theatre, a restaurant, and many sanatoria in what were formerly private villas. Near Primoriye Sanatorium are the medicinal baths. Here also is one of the entrances to the catacombs.

Uspensky Monastery, Mayachny Pereulok 6, Bolshoi Fontan. The monastery was founded in 1824 and today 40 monks live there while 50 students attend the seminary. There are vineyards on the grounds, and the patriarch usually spends the summer here. St. Nicholas's Church was built in the 1840s, the Uspenskaya Church in 1892.

Chernomorka and the Beaches Beyond

Chernomorka is 18 km (11 miles) southwest of Odessa. The name of this resort means "Black Sea"; it was formerly the German settlement of Lustdorf. The beach of quartz sand is one of the best in the Odessa region and there are many sanatoria here, including a special one for children suffering from ossicle tuberculosis. There is a cafe in the resort.

Malodolinsky was also at one time a German colony, known as Klein Libental. The liman here is 10 km (6 miles) long and 1 km (0.6 mile) wide.

The road from Odessa to the eastern resorts leads through the seaside suburb of Peresip to Shevakhovo on Mt. Shevakhovo. It is 11 km (7 miles)

from the centre of the city. Here, too, is Luza-
novka, which has two parks, Verkhny and Nizhny.
The beach is wide and sandy; at a distance of 5 km
(3 miles) the sea is not more than 2 m (6.5 ft) deep.
There is a large children's sanatorium called
Ukrainian Artek at this point.

Ilyichevsk

Leave Odessa by the Ovidiopol Road, passing Ve-
likodolinskoye. Odessa's new cargo port lies to the
left of the main road. They way to it runs parallel
with the local railway line.

Most of the activity of Odessa's lively port has
been transferred to the newly built facilities here.
Its name is taken from that of Lenin, from his
patronymic Ilyich. Construction began in 1957;
and it is to become the largest port in the Soviet
Union. From here a railway ferry plies to the Bulgarian port of Varna. The way to Belgorod-Dnestrovsky passes Ilyichevsk, so a visit there could be
combined with the longer trip.

Neptune Restaurant
Frigate Restaurant

Kuyalnitsky Resort

13 km (8 miles) north of Odessa. Formerly known
as Andreyevsky, after Dr. Andreyev, who founded
the first medical establishment here in 1833, Kuyalnitsky stands beside Kuyalnitsky Liman. This is
30 km (19 miles) long, up to 2 to 3 km (1 to 2
miles) wide, and 2.2 m (7 ft) deep. It is divided
from the sea by a 2 km (1 mile) wide sandbank and
has the most concentrated salt solution of any of
the Odessa limans (4.5 to 27 percent). There is a
summer theatre and a restaurant as well as sanatoria, mudbaths, and a mineral spring used for
bathing and drinking.

Nerubaiskoye

In this village to the northwest of Odessa and 2 km
(1 mile) to the right of the main road is the *Partisan
Glory Museum*, partly at ground level and partly
70 steps below ground, where there are workshops,
a hospital, and a kitchen, among other things.
Open 9–6 daily. Further on in the same direction,
near the village of Kholodnaya Balka, 21 km (13
miles) northwest of Odessa, is Hadjibeyevsky
Liman, 34 km (21 miles) long, 2.5 km (1.5 miles)
wide, and, in the southern section, 10.5 to 14 m
(34 to 46 ft) deep. The salt solution is weaker than
that of many of the other limans (2.5 to 12 percent).
There are a park, beach, cafe, and mudbaths on
the liman.

Intourist organises a variety of boat trips, including
those on the catamaran *Khadzhbei* and yachting.
A catamaran goes to Ilyichevsk (see above), and
there are day trips from Odessa toBelgorod-Dnes-
trovsky (q.v.) (105 km/65 miles) and to Kishinyov
and Kherson (q.v.). Boat trips also go to Yalta
(q.v.), with visits to Livadia and Alupka and two
nights on board.

ODZUN

See Erevan Environs, p. 138

OGRE

See Riga, p. 447

OKTEMBERYAN

See Erevan Environs, p. 131

OLESKO

See Lvov, p. 312

OREL Pronounced "Ahr-yol" and meaning "eagle"
Population—340,000

The town stands at the confluence of the rivers Oka
and Orlik. The Oka here is quite small as it flows
northward toward Kaluga. Orel was founded in
1566 in the reign of Ivan the Terrible; it was a
border fortress of the Muscovite State against the
Crimean Tatars. It was said that once, when a
group of Tatar invaders was in these parts, an eagle
fell like a stone onto the Khan who led them. After
a short fight between them, the eagle, pouring
blood, rose into the air and then folded its wings
and plunged down into the river. The Khan, however, also was wounded, and he fled with all of his
men far from the Oka Valley. Ivan the Terrible
heard this legend and decided to name the new
fortress after the eagle.

Orel was an especially important border fortress
because it was on the main route by which the
Tatars came north to attack Moscow. It was ruined
by the Poles at the beginning of the 17th century
and in the 1660s was devastated again by the Tatars;
in 1673, after a tremendous fire, it was transferred
to a new site known as Yamskaya Hill. It played
a useful role in the extension of Russia's do-
minion further south, and after that, life became
more peaceful in Orel. The fortress remained
until 1702.

The present layout of the town dates from 1779,
when Orel became the district capital and, according to new plans, was divided into three parts,
each part containing a certain area in which it was
forbidden to build. Thus originated the three main
squares: Komsomolskaya (formerly Kromskaya),
Promyshlennaya (formerly Vozdvizhenskaya), and
Polesskaya. Near Lenin (formerly Market) Square
arcades and shops were built in 1843, but little
remains of them. There was next to no industry in
the town and just sufficient tradespeople to serve
the predominantly noble population. It is on record
that in 1853 the number of townsfolk of noble birth
was 19,398 out of a total population of 32,000. In
the 1860s the town served as a place of exile for
Polish insurgents, and later a central prison was
built to accommodate prisoners on their way to
Siberia. On 7 June 1884, there was another devastating fire, but there was still little industry to
suffer; the town's principal trade was the traditional
grain, hemp, eggs, and poultry.

Orel was the scene of much fighting in 1943 and was largely destroyed. When it was liberated on 5 August 1943, a salute was fired in Moscow; this was the first of such salutes that afterward heralded the liberation of each of the larger cities and towns.

Orel now stretches 11 km (7 miles) from north to south. From Lenin Square the main Moscow-Simferopol road runs along Moskovskaya and Komsomolskaya streets, which are the busiest in town. Most of the buildings here are of postwar construction.

The quiet Normandy-Neman Street is named after the French squadron that fought with the Russians for Orel in the Second World War.

Lenin Street is among the oldest in Orel, with many prerevolutionary houses, and Dzerzhinsky Street, which leads into the town from the south, is still lined with many solid, respectable houses where merchants lived with their families during the last century. The *governor-general's residence*, standing in front of the park and opposite St. Michael's Church, now houses a technical college. The *Youth Theatre* is in the old building of the Girls' High School and the 18th-century seminary building at Studencheskaya Street 2 is now the *Railway Workers' College*. The two long buildings on either side of Moskovskaya Street just before the first large bridge are the shopping arcades. The old *town hall building*, which dates from 1779, is in Moskovskaya Street. There is a pedagogical institute in the town, and the local House of Soviets stands on Lenin Square.

Orel is an important railway junction. Its industries include the manufacture of machinery for agriculture, road building, and the textile, footwear, and food industries. Leather, food products, clocks, and watches also are produced.

St. Nikita's Cathedral, Rabochy Pereulok 18, at the top of the hill over the bridge. This yellow-and-white painted church with five small domes and a tall spire to its belfry was built in 1775 and is open for services. Other churches similarly open are *Afanassiyevskaya*, just behind Nikitsky and originally part of Rozhdestvensky Convent, *Nikolskaya* (painted blue and standing way across the Oka), *Vsekhsvyatskaya*, *Vvedenskaya*, *Voznesenskaya* in Kazansky Pereulok, and *Predtechenskaya* at Troitskoye Cemetery. It was in Orel, enquiring when a particular church was founded, that we were given the gentle reply, "God alone knows—but it's not important for His people!"

Epiphany Church (*Bogoyavleniye-na-Ryadu*), Moskovskaya Street 1/3. This church was built in Naryshkin baroque style in the 17th century.

Church of St. Michael the Archangel, Sacco and Vanzetti Pereulok, on the bank of the Orlik beside the bridge. The church was built in 1801 in Russian classical style.

Church of Vasili Veliki, Karl Liebknecht Street. This church is near St. Michael's, on the same side of the river but a bit further upstream. It is now very dilapidated and serves as a sports club.

Nikola-na-Peskakh ("*Church of St. Nicholas-on-the-Sand*"), at the crossing of Normandy-Nieman (formerly 1-Parkovaya) Street and Gagarin Street. Formerly known as Ilyinskaya, this five-domed church and its belfry were built in 1790 and have not been restored.

Smolenskaya Church, Normandy-Nieman Street. This five-domed brick church is very large and is visible from the "Nest of the Gentry" (see the Writers' Museum below), but it is of 19th-century construction and architecturally of little interest. It serves as a bakery.

St. Catherine the Martyr (*Yekaterina Velikomuchenitsa*) *Church*, to the left of the road on the way into town from the south

Many of the streets of Orel are named after writers and poets who were born or lived here. Among them are Ivan Turgenev, Leonid Andreyev, Nobel Prize–winner Ivan Bunin, Timofei Granovsky, Nikolai Leskov, Afanasy Fet, Mikhail Prishvin, and others whose names mean much to any admirer of Russian literature. The Writers' Museum is in a hilly part of the town, and the surrounding region is known as the "Nest of the Gentry." Many old houses typical of the homes of Russian nobles have survived. Leskov, talking about the importance of Orel in Russian literature, said that his birthplace, "with its shallow waters, nourished for the motherland more Russian writers than any other Russian town." Local enthusiasts used to call Orel the literary capital of Russia.

Turgenev Museum and Museum of Local Writers, Part I, Turgenev Street 11. Open 9–6; closed Fri. and the last Mon. of the month. These museums are located in two houses which belonged to landlord Trubitsyn and to Vice-Governor Galakhov. Turgenev never lived here, although he was born in Orel. Among the exhibits is a Remington typewriter that belonged to Leonid Andreyev and articles of furniture that belonged to Turgenev's friend, the French singer Pauline Viardot-Garcia (1821–1910), and a drawing by her own hand dating from the 1850s.

Granovsky Museum and Museum of Local Writers, Part II, 7-Noyabrya Street 24. Open 9–6; closed Fri. and the last Mon. of the month. The building was the home of historian and writer Professor Timofei Granovsky (1813–55), and the museum is dedicated specifically to him and to literary critic and thinker Dmitri Pisarev (1841–68).

Leskov Museum, Oktyabrskaya Street 9. Open 9–6; closed Fri. and the last Mon. of the month. Nikolai Leskov (1831–95) was an outstanding Russian writer who devoted many of his works to descriptions of the scenery and life in old Orel and the vicinity. English readers know too little of Leskov and he deserves wider popularity. His Aunt Polly married an Englishman and followed the Quaker way of life. She proved a lasting influence on her nephew's early years. After several secretarial jobs, Leskov entered the employ of an Englishman named Scott, a Nonconformist who held the position of chief steward of the estates of a rich no-

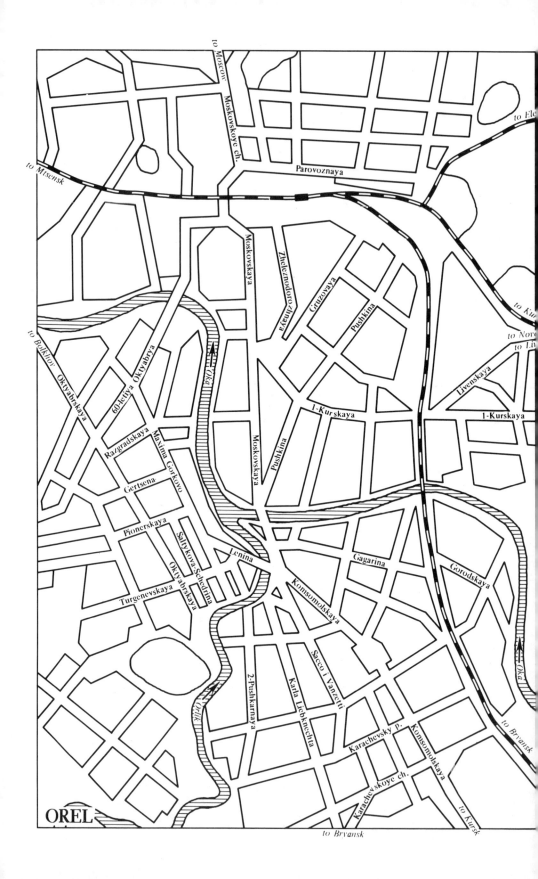

bleman. It was Scott who first appreciated Leskov's common sense, keen observation, and knowledge of people as shown in the business reports his young assistant was required to write. Leskov worked as a journalist before turning to fiction. "The Tale of the Left-Handed Smith and the Steel Flea" is perhaps a good story to start with. Emperor Alexander I is presented with a lifesize flea made of steel by an English smith. The renowned smiths of Tula take up the challenge to go one better, and they achieve this by shoeing the flea in gold. The rather gruesome story "A Lady Macbeth of the Mtsensk District" was used by Dmitry Shostakovich as the basis of his opera of the same name (it also is known as "Katerina Izmailova"). The museum is in the house where Leskov lived as a child from 1831–39. Inside is a reconstruction of his study in St. Petersburg, with his desk and bookcases and much documentary material, contemporary photographs, old street scenes, and so on. From Leskov's house, Oktyabrskaya (formerly Nobles') Street leads down to a balustrade and a small pavilion overlooking a graceful bend on the river. Here, too, is a *bust* of Turgenev under the birch trees.

Kalinnikov Museum, Moskovskaya Street 1/3, with the entrance from Gagarin Street. Open 10.30–6; closed Tues. Vasily Kalinnikov (1866–1900) was a Russian composer.

Rusanov House-Museum, Rusanov Street 3. Open 10–5; closed Mon. and Fri. Vladimir Rusanov (1875–1912) was born in Orel and is famous as a polar explorer who vanished on his last expedition to Spitzbergen and Novaya Zemlya. Here are displayed documents, books, and photographs about his life.

Local Museum, Moskovskaya Street 1/3. Open 10–6; closed Mon. and the last Thurs. of the month.

World War II Museum, Normandy-Neman Street 1. Open 10–6; closed Mon. and Tues. The museum contains a diorama showing the great battle that took place in the vicinity in the summer of 1943. The museum was opened in 1985 to mark the 40th anniversary of VE day.

Normandy-Neman Museum, Fomina Street 8. The museum was created by local schoolchildren.

Picture Gallery, Saltykov-Schedrin Street 33. Open 9–6; closed Thurs.

Orel Memorial, on the site of the former fortress, on a small spit at the confluence of the Oka and Orlik rivers. This stone column and two figures were constructed to commemorate the 400th anniversary of the foundation of Orel.

Turgenev Monument, near Leskov's House in the "Nest of the Gentry" park area on the high left bank of the river Oka. The 2.7-m (9-ft) bronze figure by Bessarabsky is mounted on a 3-m (10-ft) pedestal of granite. It was unveiled in November 1968 to mark the 150th anniversary of Turgenev's birth.

Civil War Memorial, on the left, just across the bridge from St. Michael's Church. The statue is of a soldier wearing the traditional cavalry cap and holding his rifle high above his head in triumph.

General Yermolov's Grave, Troitskaya Church. General Yermolov was a hero of the 1812 war but was exiled to Orel and died there. His memorial plaque is installed in the church wall.

Lenin Monument, Lenin Square, in front of the House of Soviets. The sculpture by Tomsky was unveiled in 1949.

Maxim Gorky Memorial Plaque, at the crossing of Turgenev and Gorky streets.

Polikarpov Statue, in the garden on Moskovskaya Street. Nikolai Polikarpov (1892–1944), an aeroplane designer, was born in Orel. His Po-2 fighter was very popular during World War II and he headed the group that later designed the Stormovik. The statue shows him seated with a model plane in his hand.

Medvedev Monument, Moskovskaya Street. Mikhail Medvedev (1897–1919) was a civil war hero.

Tank Monument Tankistov Garden, on Mostovaya Street. A tank marks the grave of those who fell here in World War II; an eternal flame burns here.

Komsomol Monument, This monument commemorates those members of the Komsomol movement who lost their lives in the Second World War.

Guriev Monument, Guriev Square. Major General Guriev was killed during the liberation of Orel in 1943. The monument, sculpted by Vuchetich, was unveiled in 1954.

War Memorial, Komsomolskaya Street. The figure of a soldier supports his wounded comrade.

Fighter Plane Monument, on the left of the main road leading into the town

Metal Worker Monument, on the way north, on the left of the road. Behind the monument is a new residential region.

Turgenev Drama Theatre, Lenin Square, near the Rossia Hotel. Founded in 1815, this is one of the oldest theatre companies in the country. It was organised as a theatre of serf-actors by Count Mikhail Kamensky on his estate 12 km (7 miles) from Orel. The count was a real tyrant and used to sit in his box with a book in front of him in which he wrote down each mistake the actors made. Nearby hung an assortment of whips, and during the interval he would select one of these and go backstage to beat those who had displeased him. Their cries could even be heard by the audience. The count was eventually murdered by his own serfs, but in the meantime the company thrived, and in 1817 it is recorded that during 6 months 82 productions were staged, including 18 operas, 15 dramas, 41 comedies, 6 ballets and 2 tragedies. The playwrights included Shakespeare, Schiller, Beaumarchais, and the Russian classics, and there were also works by local serfs. Productions were extremely lavish, with costumes of silk and velvet. The theatre is described in the writings of Leskov. The new, white building designed by Rozanov was completed in 1980. The main auditorium has 800 seats but there is an additional hall for 250 on the ground floor that is used for recitals and concerts.

Youth Theatre, Karl Marx Square 2

Puppet Theatre, Kooperativny Pereulok 5

Philharmonia Concert Hall, Lenin Street 23

Park, Guriev Square, beside the river Orlik. There is a summer theatre here.

Children's Park, in the centre of town, where the Orlik and the Oka meet and where the fortress once stood

The region beside the river Tson, a tributary of the Oka, called *Botanika*, 5 km (3 miles) from the town centre, is one of the most beautiful in the area. The Orel Exhibition of Economic Achievements and a fruit-farming research station are here.

Lenin Stadium, Turgenev Street 55

Hippodrome, near Troitskoye Kladbische (cemetery).

Rossia Hotel and Restaurant (Intourist), Gorky Street 37; tel. 74–550. Intourist office, tel. 67–463.

Orel Hotel and Restaurant, Pushkin Street 5; tel. 50–589

Shipka (Intourist) Motel, Moskovskoye Chaussee 175, to the left of the main road leading toward Moscow; tel. 30–704. There is a hotel here, a restaurant, and service station.

Zelyonaya Dubrava ("Green Oaks") Camping Site, 3 km (2 miles) south of Orel, 300 m/yds to the left of the main road when approached from the town. There is a telephone, hot showers, a car wash, and a repair ramp. 300 m/yds from the camping site are places on the river Tson for fishing and bathing. This camping site has a buffet (open till 10 P.M.) and a self-service kitchen.

Oka Restaurant, Lenin Street 16

Orlik Restaurant, Komsomolskaya Street 228

Tson Restaurant, a little out of town to the south along Krymskoye Chaussee, on the way to Zelyonaya Dubrava Camping Site

Druzhba ("Friendship") Restaurant

Druzhba Cafe, Moskovskaya Street

GPO and Telegraph Office, Gorky Street 43

Bank, Teatralnaya Square. The bank is in an interestingly decorated building dated 1860.

Department Store and Souvenirs, Moskovskaya Street 5

Souvenirs, Lenin Street 10

Podarki (Gifts), Karl Marx Square 1/3

Jeweller's, Lenin Street 32

Filling Stations, by the main road as it enters, and again on the left as it leaves the town.

Repair Station, at the Shipka Motel, just north of Orel

Intourist organises excursions from Orel to Spasskoye-Lutovinovo, Turgenev's home, 65 km (40 miles) north of the town.

Spasskoye-Lutovinovo (Turgenev's Home)

Spasskoye-Lutovinovo lies 6 km (4 miles) off the main road north of Orel, past Mtsensk. The left turn is at the 1091/308 km mark and a signpost points the way.

The *Turgenev family estate* is now a branch of the Orel Museum. Open 8–5; closed Tues. and the last Mon. of the month. Ivan Turgenev (1818–

1883) was exiled here in 1852–53 by the order of Nicholas I for writing a questionable obituary on the death of Nikolai Gogol.

Lutovinov was Turgenev's mother's family name and the small *Church of the Transfiguration (Spaso-Preobrazheniye)*, on the right by the entrance to the estate, was founded in 1809 and built by his great-uncle Ivan Lutovinov. The estate's name then derived from it.

Although after 1855 Turgenev spent many years abroad, mostly in Germany and France, this place, where his family had moved when he was three years old, was nevertheless his favourite. In a letter written in France to a Russian friend he said: "When you are next to Spasskoye give my regards to the house, the grounds and my young oak tree, to my homeland." Turgenev's oak tree is still there.

The main part of the house was burned down in 1906, but in 1976 it was rebuilt and the side wings and other buildings that had remained were restored to their appearance of 1881 when Turgenev was last here. The reconstruction owes much to the use of the original plans and the old drawings and other documents, including Turgenev's letter to Flaubert, in which he describes the place clearly. Some of the original furniture has been found, among the pieces a grand piano. Its last owner was a retired officer living in Siberia and he quite accidentally discovered the barely readable inscription "Turgenev" on the mahogany surface. Other interesting items of furniture displayed in the eight halls now open include a grandfather clock and a kneehole desk, both made in England. The 400-year old icon was a gift to the Turgenev family from Ivan the Terrible. Some of the author's works, including the novel "Rudin," were written here, and "Fathers and Sons" and "A Nest of the Gentry" were completed here as well. William Rollston was the first to translate Turgenev into English; he also translated Saltykov-Schedrin and Krylov. Turgenev brought Rollston here to show him more of Russia and organised a demonstration of folk song and dance on the lawn in front of the house.

The park was laid out in 1808. Some of the avenues were planted in the figure "XIX," signifying that it originated in the 19th century. The longest avenue is of lime trees, and it forms the "I" of the number. The undergrowth is cut back every five years to maintain the original appearance of the avenues.

Along the avenues there are wooden boards with quotations from Turgenev's works, for he is known in Russia as one of the most competent of nature writers. A path through the woods leads to a pond, called Savinsky Prud after Maria Savina (1854–1915), an actress who took part in Turgenev's plays. On the further bank the ghost of Uncle Lutovinov is said to keep up a vain search for a small plant, the properties of which will help him return from the grave.

Mausoleum, opposite the entrance on the estate, outside. This was built at the same time as the church, and beside it on the green is the tomb-

(SPASSKOYE-LUTOVINOVO)

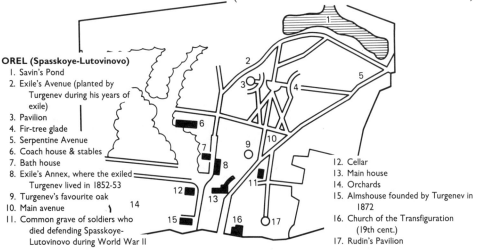

OREL (Spasskoye-Lutovinovo)
1. Savin's Pond
2. Exile's Avenue (planted by Turgenev during his years of exile)
3. Pavilion
4. Fir-tree glade
5. Serpentine Avenue
6. Coach house & stables
7. Bath house
8. Exile's Annex, where the exiled Turgenev lived in 1852-53
9. Turgenev's favourite oak
10. Main avenue
11. Common grave of soldiers who died defending Spasskoye-Lutovinovo during World War II
12. Cellar
13. Main house
14. Orchards
15. Almshouse founded by Turgenev in 1872
16. Church of the Transfiguration (19th cent.)
17. Rudin's Pavilion

stone of Nicholas Erren, a Frenchman from Nancy who held the post of family tutor and died on 13 July, 1793.

Dubok Cafe, near the mausoleum

ORSHA Population—125,000

At the 571/483 km mark and a little to the right of the main Minsk-Moscow road, this ancient Byelorussian town on the Leningrad-Kiev highway spans the Dnieper where the river Orshitsa flows into it.

Orsha was first mentioned in 1067, and in 1359 it was taken by Prince Olgerd and became Lithuanian. Although it was captured by the Russians by storm in 1502, the subsequent peace treaty returned it to Lithuania. The fortress was reinforced to serve as a boarder point between Lithuania and Poland. Its position between the frequently warring states meant that its development constantly was interrupted. In 1623 the *Bogoyavlensky Monastery* was founded and in 1631 the *Uspensky Convent;* both were known as the *Kuteinsky Monasteries,* after the little river Kuteinka above which they stand. Bogoyavlensky Monastery was Byelorussia's most important printing centre in the 17th century. After the first division of Poland in 1772, Orsha became part of Russia. It was almost completely burnt down during the invasion by the French in 1812, but in the mid-19th century a new period of development began.

During World War II the local partisans were headed by Konstantin Zaslonov (1911–42), posthumously declared a Hero of the Soviet Union. He organised railwaymen into paralysing movement at this large railway junction but died during fighting between the partisans and a German punitive expedition. A *monument* was erected over his grave and a memorial museum was opened in 1948.

Local industry includes machine building,

metal processing, building materials, light and food industries.

Katyusha Monument, This monument is dedicated to the Stalin-organ multiple rocket launchers that were first used near Orsha on 14 July, 1941.

War Memorial, by the main road at the 563/493 km mark where it crosses the Leningrad-Kiev highway

OSHAKAN
See Erevan Environs, p. 132.

PAIDE
See Tallinn, p. 533.

PALANGA
(Intourist organises excursions here from Vilnius and Klaipeda.)

Palanga is now the largest and best-known Lithuanian seaside resort, and its popularity is growing. Famous for its dunes, Palanga is 25 km (16 miles) from Klaipeda, 242 km (150 miles) from Kaunas, and 348 km (216 miles) from Vilnius. One of the explanations of its name is that it comes from the Lithuanian word "palange," which means "windowsill." The fishermen's cottages stood so close to the shore that sometimes the waves reached the sills.

The river Ronze flows into the Baltic Sea here and divides Palanga; the resort is on the left bank and the town on the right. The beach is 200 m/yds wide and stretches for several miles. The seabed here is sandy and flat, sloping very gradually, and there is amber to be found.

In 1589 British merchants were permitted to build a proper harbour here. The place was mentioned as well established in 1611, and for a long time it was the only Lithuanian port. As such it was very important, rivalling even Riga. The stone breakwaters and the port were destroyed in 1701 by the Swedish army and were never rebuilt, but even today, when the sea is still, the remains of the port can be seen.

Palanga has been known as a resort since the 18th century. In 1824 Count M. Tyszkiewicz of Poland sailed here with the idea of making the place really fashionable. Most of the villas belonged to his family, as did the restaurant, the bathhouse, and other buildings. The count's own palace was built in 1879 by French architect E. Andre, who also was responsible for laying out a special park around it. The palace is still in the centre of the park. It was restored in 1957 and now houses the Amber Museum.

Between the world wars the president of Lithuania had a summer residence in Palanga.

It is a local tradition to go out onto the breakwater to watch the sunset—the "sun's farewell," as they call it.

Amber Museum, Vytautas Street 140. This is located in the palace built by E. Andre for Count Tyszkiewicz. There are about a thousand specimens of natural amber here as well as many articles made of amber by local craftsmen. Perhaps most interesting of all are the chunks of amber containing insects that became stuck in the resin of prehistoric pine trees 4 million years ago and were fossilised together with the resin.

Occasional "night serenades" are organised with chamber music concerts on the verandah of the Amber Museum.

Jurate and Kastytis Statue, in the seaside garden, by Gaigalaite. This statue illustrates a favourite local legend explaining the origin of the amber: Once upon a time a handsome young fisherman of Palanga named Kastytis sailed out to sea and was far from home when night fell. On the bed of the Baltic, in an amber castle, lived the goddess Jurate, daughter of the lord of the sea, and when she saw Kastytis she fell in love with him. He forgot his home and his mother awaiting his return, gazed long at the eyes clear as water and the skin whiter than foam, and kissed Jurate. Perkunas, god of thunder and lightning, was so angry at this violation of the laws of behaviour between gods and mortals that he summoned his thunder and lightning to drive Kastytis to the shore so that there the waves of the Baltic should kiss him to death. Now the moaning of the wind is said to be the crying of Jurate and the amber tossed up on the beaches to come from her castle, ruined by Perkunas.

Lenin Monument, in front of the town hall, by Vutechich

Palanga Park was laid out by the same French architect, E. Andre, who designed the count's palace. He was assisted by the Belgian dendrologist B de Cologne. They planted 300 different species of trees and bushes, some imported from different parts of the world, so that it became a real botanical garden. There are two picturesque ponds connected by canals and decorated with bridges. Also, here used to be a statue of Christ by the well-known Danish sculptor Bertel Thorwaldsen, but it was broken sometime after the Second World War. The park covers about 70 hectares (185 acres) and is still one of the principal attractions of the resort.

Hotel, Basanavicus Street 9

Jura Restaurant, Bacanavicus Street 3

GPO, Vytautas Street 29

One of the most popular excursions is the walk to the top of *Birute Hill*, once the site of pagan sacrifices but cleared by the Jesuits in the 16th century. They built a chapel here instead. The area was a stronghold of paganism even as late as the 16th century, when the rest of the country had already long been Christian and the people had become devoted Catholics.

PALEKH

See Ivanovo, p. 173.

PANEVEZYS Population—126,000

(Intourist organises excursions here from Vilnius.)

Panevezys, the fifth-largest city of Lithuania, is situated 142 km (88 miles) northwest of Vilnius on either side of the river Nevezys.

It was founded in September 1503 by King Alexander Jagelon of Poland (1460–1506); he had become Prince of Lithuania in 1492 and King of Poland in 1501. He donated the territory of the Panevez estate on the right bank of the Nevezys to the parish of Ramigolas. It is this part of Panevezys that is known as the Old Town today. The other part of the town on the left bank of the river appeared later as the commercial and craft centre.

The river Nevezys was navigable until the 18th century and Panevezys grew fast, being particularly well known for its grain milling industry. It was at that time part of the Upite district, and in 1568 the district law courts were transferred from Upite to Panevezys. (Today Upite is only a small settlement.) Panevezys was destroyed by the army of Charles XII of Sweden in 1704 and became a town only in 1811. It was again destroyed in 1812 by Napoleon's retreating army. The railway reached the town in 1873.

The local sugar and soap factories have been modernised, and now, besides the brewery, the town's industry includes the Ekranas Cathode-ray Tubes Plant as well as factories making cables, truck compressors, electric equipment, computing blocks, and glass. The linen mill is the largest of any in the Baltic countries.

Local Museum, Republikos Street 3. Besides local history, there is a good collection of insects and butterflies in the natural history section.

Branch of the Local Museum, Kranto Street 21. This 17th-century house formerly was used to store the district archives.

Andrus Domasavicus Museum, A Domasavicus Street 28. Andrus Domasavicus (1865–1935) was a doctor who in 1919 became the first commissar of the People's Health System of Lithuania.

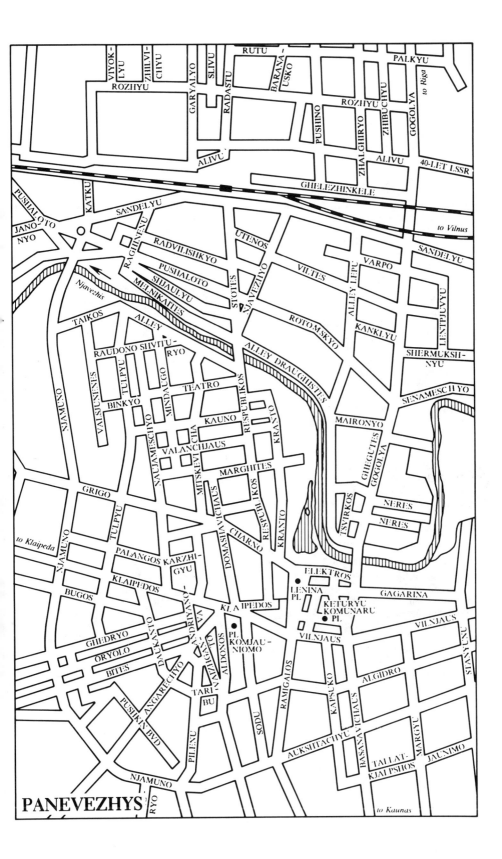

PANEVEZHYS

Memorial Stone, Gogom Street. This is a memorial commemorating the rebels of 1863.

Lenin Monument, Lenin (formerly Market) Square

Petkevicaite-Bite Bust, Gabriele Petkevicaite-Bite (1861–1943) was an authoress.

Song of Liberty Monument, This monument was sculpted by Dimzlis to commemorate the 30th anniversary of the liberation.

Eternal Flame, Adriyanova Street. On the fraternal grave of those who died in World War II.

Earth-Mother-Peace Monument, This monument was sculpted by Kiselis.

Drama Theatre, Lenin Square. The theatre company was founded in 1940 and was rehoused in the present building in 1968. It is among the leading theatres in the Soviet Union, and a number of the actors are also widely known as film stars.

Zalgiris Sports Hall

Skaistakalne Park

Nevezys Hotel and Restaurant, Lenin Square 2. This was the first 14-storey building to be constructed in the town.

Rambinas Hotel, Respublikos Street 34

Upite Hotel, Respublikos Street 36

Biculis Restaurant, Rotomske Street 27

Sjaklica Restaurant, Lenin Square 1

Daile Souvenir Shop, Lenin Square 7. Local souvenirs include nutcrackers in the shape of a devil's head, and candlesticks.

Sipsena Souvenir Shop, Lenin Square 24

Bookshop, Respublikos Street 21

PARNU Pronounced "Pyar-noo"
Population—55,000
German: Pernau; Russian: Pernov
(Intourist organises day and overnight trips here from Tallinn.)
Parnu, 125 km (78 miles) south of Tallinn, is Estonia's second-most-important seaport and one of its best resorts. It stands on both banks of the river Parnu, where it flows into Parnu Bay on the northern arm of the Gulf of Riga. Old Parnu lies on the right bank of the river and New Parnu, which runs on into the resort area, is on the left. The two parts are joined by a bridge, and the parts on the left bank stand on a narrow strip of land 1 to 2 km (1 mile) wide between the Gulf of Riga and the river. The river Parnu flows parallel to the coast for about 5 km (3 miles) and then turns southwest to the sea, cutting the town in two. Parnu Beach is 1.5 km (1 mile) long and consists of coarse, clean sand. It is very level and slopes gradually to the sea. The bathing season lasts from mid-June until September, when the temperature of the water is between 17 and 20°C (63 and 70°F).

There are fish canneries here, and local textile work includes flax.

Although the town is shown as a settlement on an Arab map dating back to the 12th century, the first written documentation is dated 1251, when Heinrich, Bishop of Saare Maa, declared that the existing church would become a cathedral and the town a bishop's seat.

Because of its favourable situation it soon became a flourishing trading port and, in the 14th century, joined the Hanseatic League. Owing to wars and epidemics between 1483 and 1533 the town was almost entirely devastated four times. It was occupied during the course of the 16th century by the Swedes, the Poles, and the Teutonic Knights in turn. It was again held by the Swedes from 1617. Just as Charles XII was entering the town in 1700 at the head of a strong army, a messenger dashed up to bring him the news that Peter the Great had laid siege to the town of Narva. The Swedish king struck his horse in anger and ordered an advance to the east. His horse then cast a shoe, but it was instantly picked up and nailed to the wall of the most handsome house in the street, that belonging to a merchant named Moor. The Swedes held Parnu until 1710, when it was taken by the Russians. The Swedes built a fortress in the 1670s, but of all the old fortifications only *Punane Torn* ("Red Tower") in Hommiku Street remains, together with parts of the town walls, which run from Tallinn Gates to the Venus Bastion near the river, and part of the fortress moat. The remains of another bastion, the Mercury Bastion, which collapsed in the 19th century, is now known as *Munamagi* ("Egg Hill"). During Swedish rule there was a Swedish University here called Academia Gustavo-Carolina.

The town became known as a resort in 1838, when an old tavern by the beach was turned into the first bathhouse. It contained six bathrooms and four apartments. The idea was taken up immediately, and each year the mudbaths and the excellent beach attracted more and more people. In 1863 stone breakwaters 2.5 km (1.5 miles) long were built, and today they are one of the most popular places to walk.

In 1882 the *Marine Park* was planted; in fact, none of the trees in the town were growing here naturally.

Before the First World War the resort enjoyed international popularity, with especially large numbers of visitors from Finland and Sweden. Fashionable hotels were built there in the mid-1930s—the Ranna, now the *Estonia Sanatorium*, and the Vasa Hotel, now the *Soprus Sanatorium*—as well as a new house for mudbaths, restaurants, and other public buildings.

Among the few old buildings of interest are the *Old Barn* (1763), at Vana Street 3, near the Old Parnu Bridge, and the *former town hall* (1788), also in Vana Street in the centre of Parnu.

St. Elizabeth's Church, Kingissep Street, near the Parnu Hotel. The church was built in 1740.

Lutheran Church, Hommiku Street. This is open for services.

Estonian Orthodox Church, Apa Street. Open for services.

St. Catherine's Church (Russian Orthodox), Vee Street. Built in 1765–68, it remains open for services.

Local Museum, Kalevi Street 53. Open 11–5; closed Mon. and Tues.

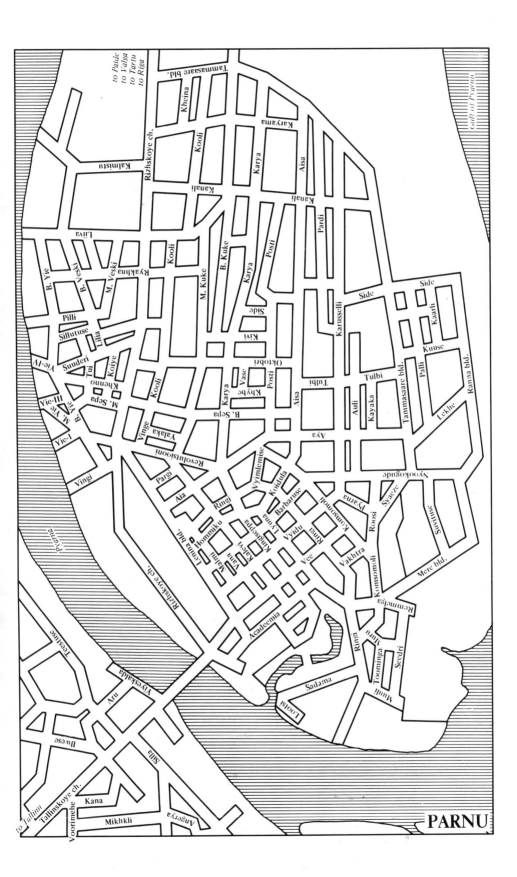

PARNU

Lydia Koidula Memorial Museum, Silla Street 37. Open 11–5; closed Mon. and Tues. Lydia Koidula (1843–86) was a famous Estonian poetess and playwright. This museum is in her parents' home and everything is kept as it was in their day.

Lydia Koidula Monument, Koidula Street, in a pleasantly planted garden with a pool and fountains near the Parnu Hotel. This bronze sculpture of the poetess was cast by Adamson in Italy and was unveiled in 1929.

Jacobson Monument, near the central square. The monument commemorating August Jacobson is by Soans and was unveiled in 1973.

Koidula Drama Theatre, in the House of Culture, Vee Street. The company was founded in 1911 and its new home was completed in 1967.

The *Resort Club*, by the shore, has a concert hall and a cinema. Nearby is a shell-shaped open-air song theatre.

Kalev Stadium, Ranna Puiestee 2

Tennis Court, Ringi Street

Indoor Swimming Pool, Silla Street 3

Parnu Hotel and Restaurant, Kalevi Street 44; tel. 421–45

Voit Hotel and Restaurant, Kingissepp Street 25; tel. 431–45

Sputnik Motel

Rannahoone Restaurant, Rannapuiestee 3; tel. 40–222. This restaurant is one of the largest in the country.

Zolotoy Lev ("Golden Lion") Restaurant

Postipoiss Restaurant, Vee Street 12

Snack Bar, Lastepargi Square

Snack Bar, Kahlevi Street

Perona Bar, Kahlevi Street 41

Bank, Kalevi Street 28

GPO, Vee Street

Taxi, tel. 41–240

PASANAURI
See Georgian Military Highway, p. 155.

PAVLOVSK
See Leningrad Environs, p. 299.

PECHORY MONASTERY
See Pskov, p. 430.

PENATY
See Repino, Leningrad Environs, p. 300.

PENDZHIKENT Pronounced "Pyan-ji-kent"
Population—16,000

Pendzhikent lies 70 km (43 miles) to the east of Samarkand. (Intourist organises excursions here from Samarkand.) The history of Pendzhikent goes back to that of Sogdiana, an ancient kingdom that occupied the valleys of the Zeravshan and the Kashka-Darya. The capital was Afrosiab (the old name for Samarkand), and during the waning years of the kingdom, Pendzhikent flourished further upriver to the east. The town, which formerly was known as Rudak, stands on the left bank of the Zeravshan at a height of 1,000 m (3,281 ft) above sea level.

It was founded at the end of the 5th century, and it was then that the walls and towers appeared. By the 7th century the town and its suburbs had spread to cover nearly 20 hectares (50 acres) and the population is thought to have numbered 7,000. "Pendzhikent" means "Five Settlements."

The town ran its own mint, and, thanks to coins found on the site, it has been possible to date the period of its heyday as the 7th century A.D. In 712 A.D. the town was taken by the Arabs, as was Samarkand, capital of Sogdiana. The last ruler of Pendzhikent, Divashtich, rose against the Arabs in 721–722 but had to retreat to his castle of Abargar on Mug Mountain, 50 km (31 miles) further east. Subsequently the town was completely sacked and burned by the Arabs under Sulaiman-ibn-Abusori. Divashtich was betrayed, captured, and executed. After the decisive battle, which took place 5 km (3 miles) east of Abargar near the village of Qum, Pendzhikent lost its importance as the capital of a princedom, and in the 770s it ceased to exist entirely. It revived again later, but only as a small country town.

In 1932 at Abargar, not far from the village of Qum, 81 documents from the archives of Divashtich were found, buried in a basket, by a local shepherd. Most of them are written in Sogdian and hard to decipher, but others are in Chinese and a Turkic language, and one in Arabic gives the prince's name and that of the castle, and it is from these that the story of Pendzhikent has been drawn. Archaeologists from Leningrad and Tadzhikistan began digging here in 1936. They located the centre and worked on three other parts, but so far only a quarter of the whole area has been excavated. One remnant of the ancient past is the holiday that is celebrated on 21 March in Tadzhikistan and Uzbekistan, the date of New Year's Day in Sogdiana.

Gorodische (ancient Pendzhikent). The ancient capital of Divashtich is located in the southern suburbs of the modern town, by the beautiful Kainar Spring which still supplies the town with excellent water. Pendzhikent was mentioned as a small town in the 10th century. Archaeologists have found that it consisted of a fortified citadel called "Kukhandiza" (the usual word for a ruler's castle in central Asia), a town ("Shakhristan") surrounded by towered fortress walls, suburbs known as "Rabad," and a necropolis, where ossuaries were discovered. Regarding the latter, rather than burying the dead, they fed their flesh to animals, then put the bones in the ossuaries.

The living quarters of Shakhristan were studied carefully and special attention paid to the reception halls, whose ceilings were supported on four columns. More than 50 of these have been discovered, the walls and ceilings being covered with multicoloured tempera murals very similar to artwork of India and Persia. Two Sogdian temples also were found, and under the buildings ran a water supply system in two different sizes of ceramic pipes.

The mediaeval town of Pendzhikent lay on the left bank of the Zeravshan at some distance to the east of the present town.

The teachers' training college was opened in 1930, and there are medical and technical schools here as well. Local industry includes a wine factory, a cannery, and brick works.

Rudaki Historical Museum, in town. Open daily, 9–6. The most valuable finds from ancient Pendzhikent are on display in the Hermitage Museum in Leningrad, but there are some here, too, including frescoes in which the people portrayed seem very Japanese-looking. The museum was opened in 1958. Its facade was decorated by Gremyachinskaya, a woman artist from Leningrad, with carved panels following the designs of the murals of ancient Pendzhikent. The museum bears the name of the locally born Abu Abdollah Jafar ebn Mohammad Rudaki (859–940), father of Persian poetry and hence of Tajik classical literature. A talented singer and instrumentalist, he served as court poet to the Samanid ruler Nasr II (914–943) but fell out of favour in 937, was blinded and expelled, and ended his life in poverty.

Olim Dodkhobek Medresseh-Mosque, on a hill in the centre of town, near the market. Built in the 18th and 19th centuries.

Lenin Statue, in the central square

Theatre

Pendzhikent Hotel, Mirny Street

Druzhba Restaurant, in the centre

Intourist Office, Lenin Street 25; tel. 3131

Komsomol Lake, on the outskirts of Pendzhikent

Hadja Muhamed Bashor Mausoleum, in the village of Faizabad, 24 km (15 miles) from Pendzhikent. Founded in the 11th and 12th centuries, it is a square building with annexes. The carved "mihrab" ("prayer-niche") inside is exceptionally valuable and very beautiful. The carved portal was added to the northeastern side in the 14th century, and its mediaeval decorations make it a real masterpiece. It was fully restored in 1967.

Rudaki Mausoleum, in the village of Pandzhrud ("Five Streams"), 60 km (37 miles) from Pendzhikent. The mausoleum was built in the village where Abu-Abdullo Rudaki was born.

The Road to Pendzhikent from Samarkand

The distance to Pendzhikent by road from Samarkand is 53 km (33 miles). The road follows up the valley of the river Zeravshan, passing through the villages of Pulimugob, Chumchukli, Lenin Inli, Madaniat, and Kurgancha. The Zeravshan is the third-largest river of the area. It runs for 700 km (435 miles), rising at a height of 3,500 m (11,483 ft) in the Zeravshan Mountains. Its name means "Gold Bearer," for the local people have panned its waters from ancient times to extract the gold dust. Like the peoples of the southwestern Caucasus (Land of the Golden Fleece), they used lambskins to trap the tiny particles. The waters are still spoken of as golden, but now it is because of their value in irrigation and in providing electric power.

The first part of the valley is entirely given over to vineyards. The vines here are untied in the autumn and covered with earth to protect them from the cold.

The next villages are Kutirbulok and Saroosiye. The western end of the valley opens out into the Djartepinsk Steppe. The best crops here are fruit and grapes. Specially sweet grapes are used to make dessert wines and brandy. The other most-important industry is the manufacture of silk. It was introduced 1,600 years ago from China by itinerant monks who carried the silkworms with them inside the bamboo canes they used as walking sticks. All of the roads here are lined with mulberry trees.

Beyond the village of Ilpak is the 3,000-year-old Dargon Canal mentioned by Ptolomy and marked by Alexander the Great on his map. This is one of the five largest canals and part of one of the world's oldest irrigation systems.

Past the villages of Ustokhona and Zhartepa at the 37 km mark from Samarkand a sign marks the republican boundary between Uzbekistan and Tadzhikistan. From this point the road runs downhill. Near the village of Sarazm the most ancient settlement in all of central Asia was found. Archeologists date it back to the 3rd century B.C. Beautifully decorated ceramics were discovered here as well as articles of bronze and stone. There was evidence that the inhabitants traded with people in Kazakhstan, southern Siberia, on the shores of the Persian Gulf and in the valley of the Indus.

From Sarazm it is 16 km (10 miles) through Chimkurgan to Pendzhikent. The snowcapped Zeravshan Mountains come into view in front, and to the left rise the mountains of Turkestan. The local fauna includes cobras and porcupines.

PERESLAVL-ZALESSKY Population—35,000

(Intourist organises excursions here from Moscow via Zagorsk and from Yaroslavl. It is 176 km/109 miles from Moscow and 130 km/81 miles from Yaroslavl.)

The town was established at the mouth of the river Trubezh in 1152 by Yuri Dolgoruky, also founder of Moscow (in 1147). Alexander Nevsky was born here in 1220. In 1302 the Pereslavsky princedom was united with Moscow and became a great trading centre, flourishing especially in the 16th and 17th centuries. Most of the surrounding lands belonged to the monasteries, which then numbered more than 50. The English traveller Anthony Fletcher listed Pereslavl as one of the 16 greatest towns in Russia.

In 1688 Peter the Great, exploring as a boy, found an English boat in Moscow. He began his boatbuilding and marine exercises there on Beloye Ozero in Kosino, a little to the east of Moscow, but there was not really enough room to sail. He went instead to Plescheyevo Lake at Pereslavl. The name "Plescheyevo" comes from the word "pleskat" ("to splash"). On its southeastern shore is Alexandrov Hill, where it is said locally that the "khoromy" ("house") of Alexander Nevsky stood. Here also is an enormous stone, the Blue Stone,

416

PERSLAVAL-ZALESSKY

which was worshipped by the people who lived here before the Slavs came. And here Peter organised a shipyard, studied navigation, and, within a few months, built other vessels which formed the basis of the future Russian navy. The first parade of the fleet took place in 1692, and Peter's relatives, foreign ambassadors, clergy, and a regiment of soldiers from Moscow came to the opening ceremony. Peter went on to build sizable ships in Archangel, Voronezh, and the Baltic. When he passed through Pereslavl in 1722 on his way to his Persian campaign he found Botik in a sad state and decreed that it be tidied up and care taken of the boats (as is inscribed on the monument in the museum yard). They were looked after for another 60 years, but in 1783 87 of them were destroyed by a fire.

Botik Museum, near the village of Veskovo, 3 km (2 miles) from Pereslavl. Open 10–4; closed Tues. After the fire, money was collected and in 1803 this museum was opened by Prince Ivan Dolgoruky. It was formerly part of the Botik estate, which, with the neighbouring village, belonged to a group of nobles from Vladimir. There is now a *wooden palace*, a *dance hall*, some of Peters' *naval guns*, and a *museum* with relics of the flotilla. Only one of Peter's ships, the *Fortune*, remains; the rest perished in the fire of 1783. In 1850 the grand-dukes Nikolai and Mikhail Nikolaevich visited Botik and laid the foundation of the *monument*, which was designed by Campioni. It was completed two years later, at the same time as the pink-and-white triumphal arch at the entrance, behind the trees, was built. From Botik there is a good view across the lake to Nikitsky Monastery (see below).

Veskovo Village Church is dedicated to St. Egor the Martyr.

Veskovo's earthen-walled *kremlin* was founded in 1152–57; the wall is 2.5 km (1.5 miles) long and the oldest part of the town is still surrounded by it. The main road into the town is Kardovskovo Street. There are a number of old houses still, as, for example, that of the Temerin family, built in the second half of the 18th century on Rostov Street. The photographic film factory, built in 1931, was the first of its kind in the country. There is also a lace factory.

Goritsky Monastery, Kardovsky Street, reached before entering the town on the way from Moscow; an arrow pointing to the left shows the way to the white-walled monastery. Open 10–4; closed Tues. A wooden monastery was founded here in 1337–1340, but nothing remains of it; the present complex dates from the 18th century. The Holy Gates were built in the 17th century. The *Uspensky Sobor* ("Cathedral of the Assumption") dates from 1757, as does also its iconostasis, which was carved by Yakov Zhukov of Moscow. The bell tower was put up at the same time but the refectory is older; Peter the Great lived in it when he stayed here in 1689. The length of the surrounding wall is 800 m (875 yds). Both the *Local Museum* and the *Picture Gallery* are housed in this monastery; the gallery contains mainly the works of Academician Dmitri Kardovsky (1866–1943), who was born in this re-

gion. The Tsar Gates from Vvedenskaya Church were exhibited in 1867 in Paris, where they won a medal. The plaster mask of Peter the Great was taken from the living tsar in 1719 by Rastrelli. Falconet's original model for the "Bronze Horseman" is also in the museum. In front of the entrance gate stands a *tank monument*.

Transfiguration Cathedral. Open 10–4; closed Tues. This cathedral was built in 1152 and restored in 1894. At the beginning of the 13th century it was the burial place of local princes. The frescoes were painted at the time of the restoration and so are of little historical interest.

Convent of St. Nicholas. This convent was founded in 1392, and its principal church was built between 1690 and 1721.

Fyodorovsky Convent, on the right of the main road on the way into the town. This convent was founded in 1551. The *Cathedral of St. Theodore Stratilat* was built in 1557 by order of Ivan the Terrible; it is thought to commemorate the birth of his son Fyodor. The *Vvedenskaya Church* (1710), the *Kazan Hospital Church* (1714), a *bell tower* (1705), and restored buildings of the monks' cells are also here. Fyodorovsky Convent is now a tourist centre with a cafeteria.

Danilov Monastery, Bolshaya Krestyanskaya Street. This monastery was founded in 1508, and its Trinity Cathedral with 17th-century frescoes was built in 1532. Other buildings include *All Saints' Church* (1687) and a two-storey *refectory* (1695) incorporating the little *Pokhvali* ("Glory of Our Lady") *Church*. The monks' cells date from 1696 and there is a gate-church over the entrance. There was a German prisoner-of-war camp here during World War II. The monastery is due to be restored but is closed at present.

Many of the other churches around the town are all that now remain of the surrounding monasteries.

Smolenskaya Church, Hilovaya Street. This church was built between 1697 and 1705.

Novi-Vladimirsky Cathedral. This cathedral was built in 1745 together with the nearby Peter and Paul Church.

Simeonovskaya Church, Rostovskaya Street, to the right of the main road on the way out of town to the north. This church was built in the style of Rastrelli in 1771.

Sorokosvyatskaya ("Forty Saints") *Church*, Rybnaya Sloboda ("Fish Quarter"). This church was built in 1775.

Pokrovskaya ("Intercession") *Church*, Pleshcheyevskaya Street 11. Built in the 18th century, this is the only church in Pereslavl at which services are still held.

Alexander Nevsky Church, Nagornaya Sloboda ("Village on the Hill"). This church was built in 1746.

Church of the Metropolitan Peter, Sadovaya Street 5. This church was built in 1585 and restored in 1889 and in 1957.

Museum of Enamels, on the bank of the river Ishna

Museum of Ancient Wooden Architecture, on the bank of the river Ishna

Hotel and Restaurant, Rostovskaya Street 7 (a new hotel is under construction in the centre of the town)

Service Station

Filling Station, on the right on the way into the town from the south

Nikitsky Monastery, in the Nikitskaya Sloboda, on the way out of the town to the left of the road to Yaroslavl. A local monk by the name of Nikita came here in 1170 to live out his ascetic life. He followed the tradition of the pillar-saints such as St. Simeon Stylites, who in the early years of Christianity vowed to remain isolated from the world on the top of a pillar. Nikita, in addition, wore heavy iron chains for penance, and these led to his cruel death. One day in 1186 he was visited by brigands pretending to seek his blessing. Thinking that his chains, which shone from constant wear, were of silver, they killed him there and then. St. Nikita's bones and chains were preserved in the monastery. The stone buildings were founded in 1561 upon the order of Ivan the Terrible, and he was present at the consecration of *St. Nikita's Cathedral* in 1574, when the revered remains of the saint were placed in the crypt. Close to the cathedral is *Blagoveschenskaya* ("Annunciation") *Church*, with a huge 17th-century refectory and a bell tower built in 1668. The monastery entrance is through the *Archangel Gabriel gate-church*.

Nikitsky Monastery is a good example of the monastery-fortresses of the time of Ivan the Terrible. It was under siege from the Polish army in 1611 and the walls and towers suffered some damage, but this was repaired in 1643. Peter the Great stayed here at the Abbot's House in 1688. Much of the monastery has been restored.

PETRODVORETS

See Leningrad Environs, p. 296.

PETROVSKOYE

See Pskov, p. 431.

PETROZAVODSK is the capital of the Karelian Autonomous Republic.

KARELIA

Karelia is in the northwest of the European part of the Soviet Union, bordered by Finland in the west, the Murmansk region in the north, the White Sea in the northeast, and Lake Ladoga in the south.

It covers 172,000 sq km (66,550 sq miles), more than half of which is forested with pine, spruce, and birch. The broad, flat, and very swampy plain was carved up and polished by the ice age, and there are as many as 11,000 rivers and 60,000 lakes in the area. The largest of these are Ladoga, Onega, and Vygozero, the latter having been enlarged during the construction in 1931–33 of the 227-km (141-mile) White Sea–Baltic Canal. Its timber reserves are unusual for the presence of the valuable Karelian birch, which can be worked to resemble

fine marble and has long been used for decorative boxes and furniture. The mineral wealth includes clay, mica, granite, marble, and iron ore, the latter having been worked since the first century A.D. The local climate is influenced by both the Arctic and the Atlantic, and the average temperatures are −14°C (7°F) in winter and 16°C (61°F) in summer.

Eastern Karelia belonged to the principality of Novgorod from the 12th century, and in 1227 Prince Yaroslavl of Novgorod enforced Christian baptism. Part of western Karelia belonged to Sweden, and by the Treaty of Oreshek in 1323 part of the Novgorodian territory near Vyborg (now Viipuri) passed over to Sweden, too. The Russian Orthodox monasteries, especially that on the Solovetsky Archipelago in the White Sea, were important colonists of Karelia, and by the time Novgorod lost its sovereignty in 1478, Karelia became part of the state of Moscow. It became an increasingly important source of fish, salt, iron, and furs.

At the beginning of the 17th century Tsar Vasili Shuisky (1606–10) sought help from Sweden in defending his domains against the Poles and gave Sweden additional Karelian territory in exchange. As the Swedes moved in, many of the Karelians migrated to Tver and the surrounding area. The subsequent development of the ironworks are described under Petrozavodsk, below.

The Kirov Railway was built across Karelia in 1916 to link Petrograd and Murmansk. During the civil war a special Karelian Regiment, 4,000 strong, fought against the new Soviet state for independence, and Finnish troops made successive attempts to unite Karelia with Finland. The provisional Karelian Workers' Commune was formed in 1920, and from this it became the Karelian Autonomous SSR in 1923.

Following the Soviet-Finnish Winter War of 1939–40, the border was redrawn, definitely in the favour of the Soviet Union. From 1940 to 1956 the area was the Karelo-Finnish SSR, and since then it has been the Karelian Autonomous SSR again.

Local industries are still mining, metallurgy, and timber working, the metallurgy being concentrated in Petrozavodsk and Vyartsilya. Quarrying for building stone includes granite on the eastern shore of Lake Onega and marble near Sortavala (q.v.) at the northern end of Lake Ladoga.

The population of 760,000 is 63 percent Russian and 23 percent Karelian, with smaller numbers of Finns and Veps.

Petrozavodsk Population—270,000

Petrozavodsk stands on the shore of Lake Onega, 306 km (190 miles) northeast of Leningrad. The region had been known in the 16th century for its iron ore and metal industry, and in 1703 Peter the Great ordered that a cannon foundry be built here. Some skilled workers were brought from England and even the coal was imported. Present-day Karl Marx Prospect was known as English Street, indicating that this was where the foreign specialists lived. In 1774 the *Alexandrovsky Zavod* ("*Iron-works*") was founded, so called after Catherine the Great's grandson, who became Tsar Alexander I. The foundries produced sea cannon, bombs, steam engines, and looms as well as artistic ironwork for decorating the streets, bridges, and buildings of St. Petersburg. The standard of work was of the highest quality, and those responsible for examining the finished products declared that the local guns were very often superior to those of English make. The foundry is now a tractor factory; it stands away from Marx Prospect, beyond the park.

In 1777 Petrozavodsk became a town. Its coat of arms showed three hammers against a green-and-gold striped background. The first governor was poet Gavriil Derzhavin (1743–1816), whose poetry praised the beauties of the north in general and Kivach waterfall in particular in "The Cascade." The inhabitants of St. Petersburg considered Petrozavodsk to really be out in the wild. They sometimes called it "Siberia-near-the-capital" because it was a place of exile for those who had committed minor offences.

Lenin Square, formerly known as Round Place, is the oldest in the town. The 2-storey, semicircular buildings made a pleasing ensemble. They were erected by Nazarov in 1775, in late Classic style. They housed offices and storehouses, and one was the governor's residence. Some were reconstructed in 1839.

The central square of the town is *Kirov Square*, where theatres and a *monument* have been erected on the sites of demolished churches. The building

of the *Russian Drama Theatre* was designed in 1953–55 by Brodsky, and the friezes on the sides and the sculptured group "Friendship" on the pediment are by Sergei Konenkov. The *Finnish Drama Theatre*'s modern building occupies the west side of the square.

Little of old Petrozavodsk has survived. Kuusinen University was founded in 1940, and there is a Teachers' College with six faculties. Many of the town's original buildings were wooden and Petrozavodsk suffered severely during World War II. There are still some merchants' houses (of no particular architectural interest) in the central part, and on Kirov and Herzen streets can be seen Lutheran churches, now closed. There is much construction work in progress.

Krestovozdvizhensky ("*Raising of the Cross*") *Cathedral*, Volkhovskaya Street. The cathedral dates back to the 1880s.

Local Museum, Uritsky Prospect 32. Open 11–6; closed Fri. Founded in 1871, the exhibits tell of the history of Karelia and its natural history, including items from the 18th-century ironworks.

Fine Arts Museum, Karl Marx Prospect 8. Open 11–6; closed Thurs. The building, which used to be a school, dates from 1789; artist Vasili Polenov was among the pupils from 1861 to 1863. His paintings, and those of many others, especially those who depicted northern landscapes, hang here. Also included are fine local wood carvings and embroidery based on a collection founded in 1871. Among its other exhibits is an excellent collection of ancient icons (15th to 18th century).

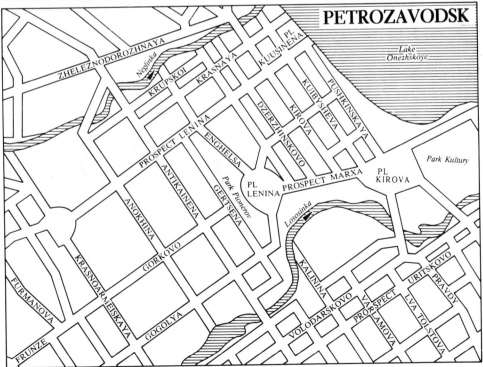

Artists' Exhibition Hall, Marx Prospect 14

Museum of Decorative and Applied Folk Art, Engels Street 5. Open 10–6; closed Mon. Here are a wide variety of wooden articles; examples of embroidery, especially with pearls; metalwork; ceramics; and toys.

Peter the Great Statue, Zavodskaya Square, by the quay. The bronze figure by Ivan Schroder originally stood in Round Place and was unveiled in 1873 to celebrate the centenary of the foundation of the Alexandrovsky Ironworks. The inscription reads: "To Emperor Peter the Great, founder of Petrozavodsk," and the statue points toward the river Lososinka, where the foundry was built.

Pushkin Monument, near the library at Pushkin Street 5. By Gavriil Shults, the monument was unveiled in 1966.

Cannon Monument, Kirov Square. Cast in 1862 and placed here, on the site of the first anchor and wire workshops, in 1974, this monument marks the 200th anniversary of the foundation of Alexandrovsky Ironworks.

Marx and Engels Monument, Kuibyshev Street. This monument of two seated figures is by Belostoksky, Friedman, and Osipenko and was unveiled in 1960.

Lenin Monument, Lenin Square. This is an early work by sculptor Matvei Manizer and the only statue of Lenin that he carved in granite. It was unveiled in 1933 amd restored in 1946. It stands 11 m (36 ft) high, including the pedestal, and uses 14 blocks of local grey granite weighing 140 tons.

Kirov Monument, Kirov Square. Sergei Kirov (1886–1934) did much to help the development of these northern regions. This monument, also by Manizer, was unveiled in 1936.

Anokhin's Bust, Lenin Prospect/Anokhin Street. Peter Anokhin (1891–1922) was a local revolutionary. The bronze bust by Afanaseyev was unveiled in 1968.

Shotman's Bust, Kirov Street. Alexander Shotman (1880–1939) was an associate of Lenin's who became Karelia's first president. The bust was sculpted by Gennadi Lankinen.

Common Grave, at the corner of Karl Marx Prospect and Komsomolskaya Street. An obelisk marks the graves of those who fell during the civil war and World War II. Another impressive memorial, on Lenin Square, is that of the *Tomb of the Unknown Soldier*, where there is also an eternal flame (1969).

Kuusinen Statue, Kuusinen Square. Otto Kuusinen (1881–1964) was a founding member of the Finnish Communist party and a Soviet party leader and statesman. He was influential in editing the Finnish *Kalevala* folk epic as well as in having Lenin's works translated into Finnish. The granite statue by Boris Dyuzhev was unveiled in 1973.

Finnish Drama Theatre, Karl Marx Prospect 19. The theatre company was founded in 1932 and moved here after the reconstruction of the building in 1965. The building was formerly the Nobles' Club (1912).

Music and Russian Drama Theatre, Kirov Square. The theatre was built in 1955.

Puppet Theatre, Karl Marx Prospect 19

Philharmonia Concert Hall, Gogol Street 6

Pohjola ("North": "Severnaya" in Russian) *Hotel and Restaurant*, Lenin Prospect 21; tel. 76–354. The local Intourist office is here, tel. 76–306. The hotel restaurant was designed in 1948 by Gutin.

Karelia Hotel and Restaurant, Gyulling Embankment 2; tel. 58–897.

Severny Restaurant, Engels Street 6

Petrovsky Restaurant, Komsomolskaya Street 1

Kalevala Restaurant, Pyervomaisky Prospect 2

Kivach Restaurant, Lenin Prospect 52

GPO Dzerzhinsky Street 5. This building was constructed in 1950 by Lev Andreyev.

Karelia Department Store, Kirov Street 2. Open 11–8; closed Sun.

Podarki Gift Shop, Lenin Prospect 17

Book Shops, Engels Street 13 and Karl Marx Prospect 14

From Petrozavodsk, Intourist organises excursions to the spa of Martsialnye Vody, Kivach Nature Reserve, and the Island of Kizhi (q.v.), 80 minutes away by hydrofoil. The ancient wooden buildings there have a magic all their own, and seeing them is certainly an experience that should not be missed by anyone visiting Karelia.

Martsialnye Vody

Martsialnye Vody ("Waters of Mars") is 60 km (37 miles) from Petrozavodsk. Open daily 9–6; in winter, 9–4.

After his visit to Europe, Peter the Great wanted to have a spa of his own, and this spring, discovered in 1714, immediately attracted his attention. The mineral water was very rich in iron and was appropriately named after Mars, god of war and iron; thus the first Russian resort, the Waters of Mars, came into being.

Palaces were built in the vicinity, but nothing of these has remained. What can be seen, however, is the *wooden church* (1719–21), dedicated to the Apostle Peter, that was built according to Peter's plans. There is also a giant candlestick inside made by the tsar. The icon of the Saviour is unusual in that Christ is holding a ship's wheel, has a halo in the form of a compass, and has features that bear a strong resemblance to Peter the Great's.

In 1730, after Peter I's death, the resort was abandoned, and the palace buildings were dismantled in 1782. A wooden *pavilion* was built over the spring in 1833, and in 1946 a historical reserve was opened here to include the pavilion, the church, and a wooden house, built in 1830, which served as a museum. The spa was revived in 1964 when a sanatorium was built here.

Museum, opposite the church. Open 11–2; in summer, 11–5. One can sample the mineral water in a pavilion near the museum. The pavilion was built to commemorate the visit of Tsar Alexander II in 1858.

Kivach Nature Reserve

It is easy to go on to Kivach after visiting Martsialnye Vody. Kivach is 85 km (53 miles) from Petrozavodsk.

On its way down to Lake Onega, the river Suna forms about 50 waterfalls. Those of Por-Porog and Girvas are well known, but Kivach, the largest waterfall in Europe, is the most famous of all. Governor Derzhavin of Petrozavodsk sang of its beauty in his poem "The Cascade":

A hill of diamonds pours down
In a four-stepped cliff precipitate.
In the deep abyss pearl and silver
Boil below in seething mounds;
Spray shimmers in a hill of blue,
The roar flies far through distant woods . . .
O waterfall! All, all is drowned
In your crater's fathomless darkness!
Do the pines crash before the gales?
You splinter them in pieces;
Can thunder crack the mighty boulders?
You grind them into sand.
Thunder on, O waterfall,
As wonderful as you are precious!
(Trans. J. M. Louis)

Kivach is 27 km (17 miles) from the mouth of the Suna. The river rises near the Finnish border and flows 290 km (180 miles) through 22 lakes before it reaches the Kondopoga Bay of Lake Onega. It is rightly called the "Mother of Waterfalls." At Kivach it drops 10.7 m (35 ft). The best time to see it is in May or early June, when the river is full. There is a local legend about its origin which goes as follows:

The lovely sisters Suna and Shuya, rising from one of the same spring, flowed side by side for many miles, never tiring of each other's company. When they reached the rocks and bogs of the forests, they decided to rest awhile. Kindhearted Suna, who always let her younger sister take the easiest path, fell fast asleep and in the meantime the ungrateful Shuya ran far ahead. When she awoke, Suna rushed angrily after Shuya, hoping to catch up to her, but great rocks stood in her way. She threw herself against the boulders and began to force them apart. When at last she had broken through, she leapt down in three gigantic strides—and so the waterfall was formed.

The area surrounding the fall is a nature reserve of 10,500 hectares (26,250 acres), 12 km (7 miles) from north to south and 14 km (9 miles) from east to west. The reserve was organised in 1931 and its area was increased in 1975. Some of the pine trees here are over 350 years old.

Natural History Museum

PIRCUPIS

See Vilnius, p. 616.

PIROGOVO

See Vinnitsa, p. 619.

PITSUNDA

See Sukhumi, p. 513.

PODOLSK Population—210,000

(Intourist organises excursions here from Moscow, 38 km/24 miles away.)

Podolsk is on the river Pakhra, 43 km (27 miles) from the centre of Moscow. The villages that stood on the site of the present-day town were known from the 15th century.

The town's name comes from "Podol" ("dolina" means "valley"), and it was under this name that the first mention of the place was made in 1627, when it belonged to Moscow's Danilov Monastery. The first stone building here was a church built in 1728 from local limestone. The town grew rapidly, thanks to the construction of a highway from Moscow via Brest-Litovsk to Warsaw; since it became a town in 1781, the upper half of its coat of arms has carried gules Moscow's St. George and the Dragon while the lower half is azure crossed pickaxes, signifying the large marble and limestone quarries in the vicinity. It was Podolsk limestone that went into the building of Moscow's Kremlin.

A cement works was founded in the 19th century and a Singer sewing machine factory was built in 1904; both of these have been enlarged and are in operation today. During the civil war, Podolsk helped to supply the Red Army with arms and munitions as well as repairing the locomotives, which were vitally important at the time. Being so close to the capital, during the last fifty years Podolsk has turned into a vast industrial suburb. Its factories produce concrete and machinery, locomotives, bicycles, and batteries, but it is still known in the country at large for the local sewing machine factory, which now produces close to 1.5 million sewing machines annually.

Among the changes in street names is Fevralskaya for Dumskaya (from "duma," "town council"). Reminders of the past include the town's old houses, such as the trading arcades (1819–32—built at the same time as Troitsky Cathedral, described below) and the posting station, today usually referred to as the "Peasant's House," which stands at the fork of the Serpukhov and Warsaw chaussees; it was at this posting station that writer Nikolai Gogol stayed when he visited Podolsk.

Troitsky ("Trinity") Cathedral, Karl Marx Street 3, stands back on the right from Lenin Prospect, on Revolution Prospect, just visible as one drives up the hill. The cathedral dates from 1820–26 and is in the architectural style favoured by Osip Bove (who designed the Bolshoi Theatre in Moscow).

Local Museum, Revolutsii Prospect (formerly

Bronnitskaya Street), in a white building close beside the cathedral. Open 10–5; closed Mon.

Lenin Museum, Lenin (formerly Serpukhov) Prospect 47, on the left as one enters the town from Moscow. Members of Lenin's family, the Ulyanovs, his mother Maria and his sisters Maria and Anna, moved here from Moscow in 1898. Lenin was then living in exile in Shushenskoye in Siberia. After the first three members of the family had settled in, Lenin's younger brother, Dmitri, was expelled from St. Petersburg, accused of spreading revolutionary propaganda, and came to join them. They lived here for some time at the turn of the century, in the two houses belonging to a local schoolteacher, Miss Kedrova. The museum occupies both Kedrova Houses. The one on the left contains a display of photographic and documentary material, and the one on the right is furnished as it was in 1900, when Lenin stayed here in the summer of that year for ten days after his three years of Siberian exile. The little room with a balcony that he used is upstairs. The museum dates from 1937. Open 10–6; closed Tues. and the last day of the month.

Podolsk Revolutionaries' Monument, in front of the railway station. This monument was constructed in granite and metal by local workers in 1969.

War Memorial and Eternal Flame, Revolution Prospect

Talalikhin Park, Rabochaya Street. There is a *bust* of the fighter pilot here and an *amusement park*. Lieutenant Victor Talalikhin (1918–41) rammed a German bomber on 7 August, 1941, and was made a Hero of the Soviet Union. The remains of the bomber lie to the west of Podolsk by Warsaw Chaussée, where there is another commemorative monument. Talalikhin died in an air battle in October 1941. The remains of a small *chapel* stand in the corner of the park by the fun fair.

Podmoskoviye Hotel

Podolsk Restaurant, Revolyutsii Prospect 31

Cafeteria

GPO, Lenin Prospect 109

Souvenir Shop, opposite Podolsk Restaurant, at Revolyutsii Prospect 31

Ivanovskoye

To reach the estate of Ivanovskoye, 2 km (1 mile) from Podolsk, leave town from Lenin Square, taking the right fork along Varshavskoye Chaussee; turn right by the *war memorial* (built by the local machine-building factory to the memory of the military cadets of Podolsk) and drive straight on to the end of the road.

Ivanovskoye used to belong to the ancient noble family of the Veliaminovs, who occupied major posts at the court of the princes of Moscow. This property belonged to Ivan Veliaminov whose name it bears. In the 15th century Ivan Veliaminov betrayed his prince and challenged the Tatars to march on Moscow. However, Prince Dmitri (later surnamed Donskoy for his victory over the Tatars

in the Battle of Kulikovo in 1380) defeated them. Veliaminov was captured and executed, and his estates, including Ivanovskoye, were confiscated.

At the beginning of the 19th century Ivanovskoye was bought by Count Fyodor Tolstoy, who built the palatial, 3-storey house with a 6-columned portico, impressive wings on either side, and a private theatre. Eventually it passed to the count's son-in-law, Count Alexei Zakrevsky, who was mayor of Moscow. The buildings have been restored recently and some are used by a club.

Dubrovitsi

To reach Dubrovitsi, return to the war memorial outside Podolsk and turn to the right along Varshavskoye Chaussée. Take the first right turn, at the 40 km mark. Follow this road around a big left curve and take the next turn to the right.

Belonging first to the Morozov family, in 1656 Dubrovitsi was added to the properties belonging to Prince Boris Golitsyn, one of Peter the Great's tutors. The prince was disappointed with the way serf-architect Vladimir Belozerov had built the church at his main estate, Marfino, and he decided to construct a really splendid edifice at Dubrovitsi. The site overlooks the point where the river Desna flows into the Pakhra. It is said that an architect and nearly 100 builders and craftsmen were brought from Italy in 1690 and that they worked here for 14 years. However, modern descriptions of the *Znamenskaya Church* deny the "Italian story" and speak of it being in Naryshkin style, after the Naryshkin family, relatives of the tsar, who liked to see Western elements in Russian architecture. Indeed, the pompous decoration is reminiscent of the baroque style of southern Germany, and the bas-reliefs and statues of saints (originally accompanied by Latin inscriptions and later replaced by the Russian translations) have the somewhat heavy proportions characteristic of German Catholic style. The church was consecrated in the presence of the family by the Metropolitan Bishop Stefan Yavorsky in 1704.

The existing *mansion*, known for its rich interior decoration, was built beside the church in the mid-18th century. In 1782 the estate was sold to Catherine II's favourite, Prince Potyomkin-Tavrichesky, and after his death Catherine presented it to another favourite, Prince Dmitriyev-Mamonov (1790–1863). This gentleman suffered from persecution mania and lived at Dubrovitsi like a hermit, seeing no one, not even his servants. As he bore a certain likeness to Peter I, he thought that he was the tsar's illegitimate son and feared that he would be poisoned.

The estate passed once again into the hands of the Golitsyn family in the mid-19th century. From 1848 to 1850 the house was partially redecorated and the church restored by architect F. Richter. Prince Sergei Golitsyn, to whom the estate belonged right up to the 1917 revolution, furnished the house anew, bringing some furniture from Rome and other things, including family portraits, bronze, china, and two large marble vases for the garden in front of the house, from his other estate at Kuzminki, now part of the city of Moscow. Beside the mansion a formal park of lime trees was laid out. The main building now houses an animal-breeding research institute.

The red-brick church with two domes, visible to the left across the river and fields as one approaches Dubrovitsi, is the *Church of Elijah the Prophet* (1753) in the village of *Lemeshevo*, which also belonged to the Golitsyns. Its architecture is unusual and the limestone ornamentation is akin to that at Dubrovitsi. The chapels were added to either side at the beginning of the 20th century and are in keeping with the original design. Beside the church is a tombstone marking the *grave of Yelizaveta Golitsyna*, who died at the beginning of this century.

PODVOLOCHINSK Polish: Podwoloczyska
Population—9,000

Podvolochinsk is a district centre.

From time immemorial a trade route crossed the river Zbruch at this point. The two villages that grew up on either side of the river were Volochinsk on the left bank and Podvolochinsk on the right. Podvolochinsk was first mentioned in 1463. In 1648 the villagers took part in the peasants' revolt led by the Ukrainian Bogdan Khmelnitsky, and in 1653 the village was devastated by the Tatars. It was raided by the Tatars again in the late 17th century, and its economy was slow to recover. It was seized by Austria in 1772, so becoming part of the Austro-Hungarian Empire. The construction of the road linking it with Ternopol in 1786 hastened its development, and, except for five years of Russian rule between 1810 and 1815, it remained within the Austro-Hungarian Empire until that collapsed in 1918.

The Ukrainian poet Ivan Franko visited Podvolochinsk in 1883, 1897, and 1916. At the beginning of the century Podvolochinsk was one of the points through which Lenin's newspaper, *Iskra* "Spark," and other illegal literature was smuggled into Russia.

In 1920 Podvolochinsk again became part of Poland, and until 1939 it remained a Polish frontier town on the Russian border. Across the bridge over the Zbruch stood the Soviet border station and customs point of Volochinsk (Polish: "Woloczyska"). In 1939 Podvolochinsk was taken into the western Ukraine and so became Soviet.

At present it is a major railway junction. The local Selkhoztekhnika Association services the district's agricultural machinery. There is also a plastics factory, a dairy, a bakery, a car repair works, and a fruit- and berry-wine factory. The surrounding farmland grows grain, sugarbeet, and cattle.

Church, Lenin Street. Open for services.

Zbruch Hotel

POLTAVA Population—315,000

First mentioned in 1174, this town was known until 1430 as Ltava, then Oltava, and finally Poltava.

The Poltava Motel lies just to the left of the main road, and beyond it a left turn leads along Frunze Street into the centre of town. The oldest part of Poltava is to the right, the battle memorial is in the middle, and out on the far left is the road that leads to the battlefield.

Poltava is picturesquely situated on three hills and a plateau on the right bank of the river Vorksla. It is one of the oldest settlements in the Ukraine, known since the 7th century. In the 12th century, although well fortified, it was ruined several times by the Tatars. It was under Lithuanian rule until 1430 and was the headquarters of the Poltava Cossack Regiment until 1654, when, with the rest of the Ukraine, it was united with Russia.

Today Poltava is famous mainly for having been besieged for three months in 1709 by the Swedish army under Charles XII before Peter the Great, with General Prince Alexander Menshikov, won his victory at the battle of Poltava on June 27. The defenders of the town were so resolute that when someone suggested in church that it was time to surrender, he was taken outside and stoned to death. As it happened, events on the day of the battle were influenced by a series of factors that combined to turn the luck of the famous Swedish army. Perhaps most important was the festering of the bullet wound King Charles had received in his left foot ten days earlier while inspecting his troops on his 27th birthday. Field Marshal Carl Gustav Rehnskiold, in charge of the Swedish cavalry, had to take supreme command of the army in Charles's stead, and this regardless of the fact that he and Count Adam Ludwig Lewenhaupt, who was in charge of the infantry, were not on speaking terms. Also, as a cavalry officer Rehnskiold was inclined to belittle the advantages of heavy artillery, which meant that when, after preliminary manoeuvres, the two armies were drawn up in readiness for battle, the weary Swedes, with no artillery, faced the main Russian army, well rested, straight from its base camp, and supported by 70 cannon. The story of the battle, which so clearly reflected the clash of character of the principal participants, is superbly told by Robert K. Massie in *Peter the Great*. The battle concluded the great Northern War and established the position of Russia in Europe. There had been 30,000 men in the Swedish army and 42,000 in the Russian army; 9,234 Swedes and 1,344 Russians lost their lives. Charles XII narrowly escaped being taken prisoner; his wound meant that he had to be carried, but his stretcher was shot to bits. He returned to the saddle, only to have his horse shot out from under him. A certain John Giertta, who also survived the battle, dismounted for the king, but in the end Charles had to be carried on a chair of crossed spears. When the Swedes fled, he was carried off, too, and only because the tsar and his generals were so delighted with their victory no attempt was made to pursue the retreating Swedes.

In 1787 Catherine the Great visited the battlefield, which is near the town, and soldiers demonstrated the manoeuvres of the two armies for her. She was much impressed and very moved by what

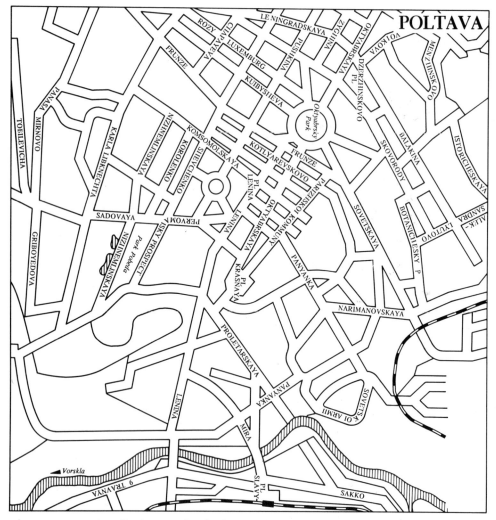

POLTAVA

she saw, commenting, "Look upon what the fate of nations depends. A single day and a few hours decided their fate." The manoeuvres were repeated 30 years later for the benefit of Alexander I.

In 1808 a group of 54 German families moved to Poltava to establish various factories. Their houses formed a German colony where Skovoroda, Balakina, and Boulevard streets are today. It is recorded, however, that the mud in the unpaved streets of the town was so deep that ladies had to use oxcarts to go to a ball.

Before World War II Poltava had a large Jewish population.

The most important part of the town is the circular place known as *October Park* where the *Column of Glory* stands. This monument, designed in the shape of an enormous gun barrel by Thomon, is 11 m (36 ft) high and made of pig iron. It is surmounted by a bronze eagle turning toward the battlefield. It was unveiled in 1811. Nine Russian and nine Swedish guns are set into the base

of the monument. The eagle was gilded in 1953. The buildings around the square include the governor's office (a three-storey square-looking building on the corner), the old post office, the House of Nobles (with a six-columned portico that has seven arches below it), and regional administrative offices. A little further on, the Institute of Construction Engineering is in the former School for the Daughters of Gentlemen. The art nouveau building in Ukrainian-Russian style was formerly the Land Bank.

Poltava is now an important educational and industrial centre and boasts one of the largest chemical machine-building factories in Europe. Local industry produces knitwear, footwear, food products, string, glass, bricks, china, and accordions. There is also a metal-processing factory.

Spassky Church ("Church of Our Saviour"), at the crossing of Parizhskoi Kommuny and Dzerzhinsky streets. This church was originally part of the nearby Monastery of the Elevation of the Cross, which was overrun by the Tatars in 1695. The wooden church was brought here in 1705–6. It was here that the townspeople vowed to defend Poltava from the enemy, and it is said that Peter came here to give thanks for his victory over the Swedes. The church stood for 100 years until, in 1811, it was partially demolished because it was unsafe. A single side chapel was left to serve as a church. Then in 1845 the St. Petersburg architect Konstantin Thon, who had just finished rebuilding the Kharkov cathedral, was commissioned by the townsfolk to build an outer shell to protect the wooden building. The church still is open for services.

Trinity Church, Zhovtneva Street

Krestovozdvizhensky ("Elevation of the Cross") Monastery, Sverdlova Street 2-A. The monastery was founded in 1650 by a certain local, Colonel Pushkov, to mark his victory over the Poles in that place. The belfry of 1786 shows Italian influence.

St. Macarius Church, Lyalya Ubikovka Street 13, which lies off Frunze Street, to the left when one first makes the turn toward the town. This little brick church, painted blue and green, was built in the 19th century and now serves as Poltava's main church.

There are a number of other churches in Poltava but they are of no particular architectural interest.

Local Museum, Lenin Square 2. Open 11–7; closed Wed. and the last day of the month. The museum was built in 1906 in national style and decorated with the coats of arms of the towns of the region. Inside the museum the decor is continued as on the outside: pale blue, green, and yellow tiles and murals in curly plant designs (like the school building in Lubny, back on the main road toward Kiev). There is plenty of folk craft, woodwork, pottery, and so forth, plus a large collection of painted Easter eggs of the 19th and 20th centuries.

Art Gallery, Dzerzhinsky Street 11. Open 10–6; closed Mon. The collection includes western European art of the 15th through the 19th centuries as well as the work of local artists. The handicraft section is of special interest.

Korolenko Literary Museum, Korolenko Street 1. Open 11–7; closed Mon. Vladimir Korolenko (1853–1921) was brought up as a Pole but with the rest of the family declared himself a Russian after the Polish uprising in 1863. He was exiled to Siberia, and his best work is probably "Makar's Dream," which has a Siberian setting but was published in 1885 after his return to European Russia. He lived in this house for 18 years. His grave is nearby, in Peremoga Park, marked by a monument of black granite.

Kotlyarevsky Museum, 1-Travnevy Prospect 18. Open 10–6; closed Mon. Ivan Kotlyarevsky (1769–1838) was a classical Ukrainian writer, and, in fact, his parody of the Aeneid counts as the starting point of modern Ukrainian literature.

Kotlyarevsky's House, Chervona ("Red") Square 3. Open 9–5; closed Mon. and Tues. The house was rebuilt following a drawing made by Shevchenko to commemorate the 200th anniversary of the birth of Ivan Kotlyarevsky.

Panas Mirny Museum, Panas Mirny Street 56. Open 10–6; closed Fri. The classical Ukrainian writer Panas Mirny (1849–1920), whose real name was Rudchenko, lived here from 1903–20.

Kelin Monument, 1-Travnevy Prospect. This monument was erected to Colonel Kelin, commander of Poltava fortress, in commemoration of the 230th anniversary of the Battle of Poltava; the bronze lion and the Poltava coat of arms were stolen during World War II and had to be recast.

Peter the Great Monument, near Spasskaya Church, on the site of the house where Peter the Great rested after the battle. On the side of the pediment is a bas-relief of a lion asleep, and the monument is topped by a sword, a shield, and a warrior's helmet.

Kotlyarevsky Monument, Kotlyarevsky Boulevard. Sculpted by Posen and Shirshov using money collected by subscription from all parts of the Ukraine, this monument was unveiled in 1903. The granite pedestal is decorated with bronze hautreliefs of scenes taken from Kotlyarevsky's works.

Gogol Monument, Lenin and Gogol streets. This monument was made in 1915 by Posen.

Lenin Monument, in Lenin Square. This monument stands 9 m (30 ft) high and was made in 1960 by Kerbel.

Taras Shevchenko Monument, Petrovsky Park. The monument was designed by Kavaleridze in 1926.

World War II Memorial, Kotlyarevsky Park. The eternal flame by an unknown soldier's tomb and the 22-m (72-ft) granite obelisk commemorate those who fell in World War II. 3,411 citizens of Poltava were killed here, in this very park.

Lieutenant General Zigin's Monument, Zigin Square. This statue of Lieutenant General Alexei Zigin (1896–1943) by Kerbel is one of a number of World War II memorials, obelisks, stellae, and plaques in Poltava.

Gogol Theatre, Zhovtneva Street 23

Concert Hall, Zhovtneva Street 21

Puppet Theatre, Zhovtneva Street 16

Kiev Hotel and Restaurant, Leningradskaya Street 2; tel. 22-533

Poltava Hotel and Restaurant, Zhovtneva Street 19

Teatralny Hotel and Restaurant, Zhovtneva Street 26; tel. 72-678.

Poltava Motel, Sovnarkomovskaya Street 1; tel. 30-024. The local Intourist office is here, tel. 30-041.

Poltava Restaurant, Lenin Street 16

GPO, Zhovtneva Street 13

Kashtan Foreign Currency Shop, by the Poltava Motel

Art Salon, Zhovtneva Street 27. Items of folk art are on sale here.

Gifts, Gogol Street 20

Ukrainian Souvenirs, Zhovtneva Street 25

Poltava Battlefield, Road 561 from Poltava.

Leave the town along Zhovtneva Street, then bear right along Road 561.

Chapel, Zinkivska Street 34, on the right on the way to the battlefield. The chapel was built in art nouveau style, possibly in 1906.

Poltava Battle Museum, 7 km (4.5 miles) out of town, to the right of the main road. Open 10–6; closed Mon. and the last day of the month. Inside are some of Peter the Great's clothes, a model of the battlefield, a panorama, Russian and Swedish battle flags, documents, and equipment. Just outside stands an imposing *statue of Peter the Great*. On a hill opposite the museum a 7.5-m (25-ft) *granite cross* unveiled in 1894 marks the Russian soldiers' grave.

St. Samson's Church, behind the hill across from the Poltava Battle Museum. Built of red brick and completed and consecrated in 1909, this church was dedicated to St. Samson because the battle was fought on St. Samson's Day. A plaque bears part of Peter the Great's stirring address to his troops before the battle: "Soldiers, the hour has struck which will decide the fate of the motherland. You must not think of yourselves as armed and drawn up to fight for Peter, but for the motherland. . . . And of Peter it should be known that he does not value his own life, but only that Russia should live on in felicity and glory for your well being."

Troyanda Cafe
About 500 m/yds from the battle museum is the reddish-grey granite Russian *memorial* to the Swedish soldiers who fell in the battle. It is topped with a cross and was unveiled in 1909 to commemorate the 200th anniversary of the battle. A second *monument* to the Swedish soldiers, a 6-m (20-ft) obelisk of granite brought from Sweden and unveiled on the same date, is 3 km (2 miles) from the battle museum; turn to the right on the main road from the museum and pass a chicken farm. After the sign marking the end of Poltava, a turn to the right leads to the monument.

Intourist organises horseback riding at the Lenin Stud Farm, in the Chutovsky region.

PORONAISK
See Yuzhno-Sakhalinsk, p. 676.

PSKOV Population—205,000
Pskov is an ancient Russian city situated southwest of Leningrad. Its fortress-centre stands above the river Velikaya at the point where the little river Pskova flows into it. It is not known when it was founded, but it was first mentioned in Russian chronicles in 903. In spite of this, one legend says that it was founded by Princess Olga in 957. Excavations show that Slav settlements have existed here since the 6th century, which means that Pskov is one of Russia's oldest cities.

Originally Pskov was an outpost of Novgorod the Great, and there is an old saying referring to the two rivers upon which the towns stand: "Soul on the Volkhov—heart on the Velikaya." After the

11th century Pskov became more and more important as a Russo-German trading centre. Its political organisation was similar to that of Novgorod, an aristocratic merchant republic in which the work of the elected prince was concerned mainly with defence and justice. In all administrative, economic, and other respects the city was run by two commissioners who presided over the gospoda ("council of nobles") elected by the people's forum.

From the beginning of the 13th century the city waged an almost unceasing struggle against the Teutonic Knights. Invariably the Germans were beaten off. Only once, in 1240, did they manage to seize Pskov for a short time, and that was only because one of the city commissioners had opened the gates for them. In 1242, after Alexander Nevsky, Prince of Novgorod, destroyed the military strength of the Teutonic Order in the Chudskoye Lake ice battle, the Germans were driven out of Pskov.

It was in 1266 that Prince Dovmont, a Lithuanian, came with his whole family and a small private party to seek refuge in Pskov. He became a Christian, taking the name of Timofei when he was baptised, and was the first to be chosen prince of any Russian town without being a descendent of St. Vladimir. He had a long list of military victories to his credit, including that over the Germans in a battle near Pskov's river Velikaya in 1299. He ruled for 33 years, a period that was the best in Pskov's long history. His sword, in the shape of a cross, measured 1.65 m (3 ft 6 in) in length and weighed 106 kg (235 lb). It was kept in Troitsky Cathedral, in front of the alter, and in later years, even in 1480, when the town was besieged by Germans, the prince reappeared in dreams to help the townsfolk and urge them to defend their homes. The first church to be dedicated to St. Dovmont was built in 1574.

In 1348 Novgorod officially recognised Pskov's independence, and it respected this for more than a hundred years. When Novgorod fell to the position of a province of the Moscow State in 1478, Pskov lost much of its independence. All the same, it still was powerful, simply because of its size. In the Middle Ages it ranked among the largest towns of Europe; a German traveller in the 16th century counted 41,000 homes here and compared it to the city of Rome.

The last princes of Pskov were appointed by the rulers of Moscow. In 1510 Vasily III ordered the arrest of the leaders of the city's nobility who opposed Moscow's rule, had the Forum Bell removed, and sent two governors to the city. To cement the union, the prince of Moscow exiled 300 influential families from the town and settled Muscovites in their stead. The nobles of Pskov did not submit easily to Moscow's domination and there were several uprisings, the last being ruthlessly suppressed by Ivan the Terrible. Rimsky-Korsakov based his opera *The Maid of Pskov* on the story of this last uprising.

In 1581–82, during the Livonian War, when Ivan the Terrible was trying to secure Russian ac-

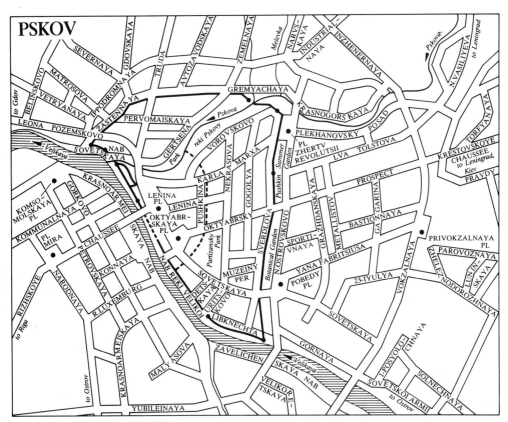

cess to the Baltic, the Poles besieged Pskov. They were utterly defeated, although, under their king, Stefan Batory, their army ranked among the best in Europe. In 1615 the same fate met the Swedish army under Gustav Adolph.

In the 18th century Pskov became a provincial centre. It was here, on 15 March, 1917, that Nicholas II formally abdicated, in his train at the Pskov railway station, and it was near Pskov that in 1918 the first battle of the newly formed Red Army was fought against the Germans.

During World War II Pskov was occupied by the Germans and reduced to ruins, but its recovery was good. The traditional industry of flax processing was augmented by machine-building factories and branches of the textile and food industries. The ancient churches suffered particularly in the war, but there has been much restoration and there are many good examples of this venerable city's traditional church architecture. The different architectural styles that developed in Kiev, in Vladimir-Suzdal, in Novgorod, and in Pskov were much influenced by the materials used. Kiev continued in the Byzantine tradition of bricks and mortar, Vladimir-Suzdal used the magnificent white stone available locally, and the northern cities used what stone they could find and set it in thick mortar, smoothing out the surface, plastering it over, and painting it. Brick was used for pilasters and

cornices, often very effectively. Building in the north, however, had always been of wood, and the forms and decorations of the new stone buildings retained many characteristics of wood structure.

Pskov's churches demonstrate a "coarsening" of the characteristics of Novgorod architecture. The columns supporting the piers inside are very square, the walls are thick, and the detail is more rude. The idea of a church porch originated in Pskov in the 12th century. Ivan III summoned Pskov architects to restore the Annunciation Cathedral in the Moscow Kremlin, and they also helped in the construction of the monastery at Zagorsk. Old-fashioned ideas were an important aid in emphasizing the continuity of the princely line and also of Moscow's supremacy. Besides, the Pskov architects' skill in roofing was well known.

A good way to see Pskov is to walk from the 16th-century *Church of St. Anastasia the Roman* on Oktyabrsky Prospect (formerly Trupekhovskaya Street), down Nekrasova (formerly Bolshaya) Street, passing *New Voznesenskaya Church* (1467) on the right, until you come to the prerevolutionary part of the local museum, on the left, at No. 7, in Pogankin House.

Pogankin House consists of a 2-storey building with deep cellars, a single-storey house with smaller cellars, and a third house without cellars. These are all united into a single massive building reminiscent of a small fortress. The house was built by one of the leading Pskov merchants, Pogankin, who was the manager of the Pskov Mint in the middle of the 17th century. During World War II the place was badly damaged by the Germans, but it has since been reconstructed and adapted to house the pre-revolutionary part of the local museum. Among the exhibits is Dovmont's sword (see Troitsky Cathedral, below), weapons, 13th- to 17th-century jewellery, icons, old manuscripts, and books.

From the museum, walk down to the river, where St. George-from-Vzov stands to the left, in Liebknechta Street. This church was built in 1494 and has well-preserved slit windows, typical of most of the churches in Pskov because they also had to serve as military fortifications.

The buildings across the river to the left and at the mouth of the little river Mirozh belong to Mirozhsky Monastery. This is the oldest monastery in Pskov, founded in 1156 by Nifont, archbishop of Novgorod and Pskov, who was trying to make Pskov a stronghold of Christianity. It was not, however, very strongly built from a military point of view, and from the time of its foundation in the middle of the 12th century it was devastated repeatedly by Germans, Poles, and Swedes as they tried vainly to breach the sturdy walls of Pskov. Mirozhsky, however, had an inner strength, for it was a great cultural centre; some think that the copy of "The Lay of Igor's Host," which has come down to our day, was made here. The finest of the buildings to survive is Spaso-Preobrazhensky Cathedral. Founded in 1156, it is the oldest building in Pskov. In architectural style it is like a Greek church, and the use of a row of narrow bricks alternating with a row of big blocks of limestone is reminiscent of the churches of Novgorod. But it is not only for its walls that it deserves a visit. In 1858 the interior, which for hundreds of years was plastered, was accidentally found to be decorated with wonderful 12th-century frescoes. By the end of the 19th century all of the plaster had been removed, and the frescoes, perhaps without equal, recently have been restored. The most interesting are those of the annunciation, nativity, assumption, and entombment. Judging by their design, they may well be Greek, but their execution is Russian in style. St. Stephen's Gate-Church was built at the end of the 17th century and dedicated to an archdeacon. The monastery bell tower is over another gate. The present monastery walls date from the 18th and 19th centuries.

A little downstream from the monastery, on the other side of the Mirozha, is the Church of St. Climenti. It stands by the river's edge, was built in the 16th century, and has a 17th-century cross on the roof. It was named after the pope and belonged to the Mirozhsky Monastery. Of special interest is the small Church of Nikolai Kamenogradsky ("St. Nicholas by the Stone Wall"), built in the 15th century and formerly also belonging to Mirozhsky Monastery. Its arched roof was built without any pillars, and it is the only church of this type in Pskov.

On the town side of the river again, one can follow the embankment along under the old walls of the town right up to the kremlin.

The kremlin, or "krom" (Nekrasov Street 7), is open 12–7; closed Mon. and the last Tuesday of each month. The entrance is on the south side, next to the October Cinema on Lenin (formerly Market) Square. The stronghold is entered through a series of archways, the first from the riverbank into Sredny Gorod ("Middle Town"), past the Governor's House (1693–95) with 19th century windows, and the second from Sredny Gorod into Dovmont Gorod, (Dovmont's Town) where excavations show the foundations of a number of churches. In the 15th and 16th centuries there were 18 of them here, but they were destroyed in the 18th and 19th centuries. Part of the old wall of Dovmont Gorod and the Vasiliyevskaya Tower have been rebuilt. They give one an idea of the size and shape of the original structures. The last archway leads into the inner stronghold of the kremlin.

We have no historical evidence as to what ancient Pskov looked like. It is known that in the 13th century the kremlin (called "detinets") was built of oak. Oaken walls also surrounded the part of the city closest to the kremlin. In the 14th and 15th centuries the oaken walls were replaced by limestone ones that surrounded the whole of Sredny Gorod. The emergency stock of gunpowder, cannonballs, and food was kept in the northern part of the kremlin. The market place was kept inside the inner city and there was a rule according to which no foreigner on pain of death could enter the kremlin of the inner city and see the defences. Foreign merchants had to trade with the inhabitants of Pskov in a specially designated place.

In the centre of the kremlin stands Troitsky ("Trinity") Cathedral. It has always been the sacred heart of the town, just as St. Sofia's is for Novgorod. According to legend, the first cathedral in this place was built in the 10th century. The building that survives is the fourth and was built between 1682 and 1699. Its appearance was much altered in 1894–95, when it was plastered over and redecorated in pseudo-Byzantine style. Built on Trinity Hill, 72 m (236 ft) high to the top of the cross, the building can be seen at a distance of 30 to 35 km (19 to 22 miles) from Pskov. It has five domes and is entered by a wide, covered flight of steps. Inside the cathedral is St. Olga's Cross, made in 1623 to replace an older one that had been burnt in 1509. It is said that the original was put up by St. Olga to mark the site for building Pskov after she had a vision of the future greatness and glory of the town. The cross with its pedestal measures 5 arshin high. Here also is the tomb of the first prince of Pskov (d. 1138) and the oaken tomb of Prince Dovmont (d. 1299), the most capable and honoured prince in the history of the city. Dovmont's sword, with which later princes were girt at their coronation in the cathedral, used to be kept here; it is now in the local museum (see below). The vaults below the cathedral contain the tombs of the princes of Pskov.

The open place in front of the church served as the people's forum. The belfry was built in the 17th century and reconstructed in the 19th century. From the south the kremlin was protected by a strong wall with two towers. The wall was called "Persy," the old Russian word for "breasts." Reconstructed in the 1860s, the wall's original shape was not preserved.

Outside the kremlin again is the square that was the site of the old market place and that was surrounded with trading arcades until they were destroyed along with most of Pskov's buildings during World War II. Now there is the impressive building of the *Teachers' Training College* and the *Trade Unions' House of Culture*. From here Sovietskaya Street runs down to the bridge over the little river Pskov, leading to the Zapskoviye region.

There is a good view of the kremlin from Zavelichiye, on the other side of the river Velikaya, and also from Soviet Army Bridge.

Walking along Oktyabrsky Prospect one passes the belfry-gateway of the *Church of the Archangels Michael and Gabriel*. This was built in 1338, but its appearance was much changed during the reconstructions of 1699 and 1819. It was last reconstructed in 1947–49. Further along, close to the street, on the right, is the 14th-century church of *St. Nikolai-na-Usokhiye*, rebuilt in 1537. Standing further back is a church formerly dedicated to Odigitria and founded in 1537; it was rebuilt in 1866 and called *Vvedenskaya* ("*Presentation of the Virgin*") *Church*. It stands on the site of the Pechersky Podvorye ("Pechersk Monastery compound"). On higher ground to the left is *St. Vasili-na-Gorke* ("*on-the-Hill*") (1413), close to which once stood a tower where Pskov's alarm bell hung.

On Sovietskaya Street are two examples of *17th-century houses*, which once belonged to the Menshikov and Sutotsky families. Another example of 17th-century civil architecture is the building called *Solodyezhnya*, the "Malt House," on Gogol Street, and in Kalinin Street the *Church of Joachim and Anna* (15th century) is a fine specimen of the Pskov style of church architecture.

Zavelichye is the part of the town across the river Velikaya, on its left bank. *Uspeniya-u-Paroma* ("*Assumption-by-the-Ferry*") *Church* is the first one you come to after crossing the bridge; locally it is known as *Paromenskaya Church*. It was built in 1521 on the site of an older church but in its present form dates from the 17th and 18th centuries.

Further downstream on the Velikaya from the Paromenskaya Church, at the end of Gorky Street, is *Ivanovsky Cathedral* (the Cathedral of John the Baptist, dating from the end of the 12th century or the 13th century), which is all that is left of the Ivanovsky Convent, founded in 1240 by Princess Efrosinia, an aunt of Prince Dovmont, and first mentioned in the chronicles in 1243. This convent served for centuries as the burial place for the princesses of Pskov. The cathedral was rebuilt several times after the 15th century, burned down during World War II, and restored to its original appearance in 1949–50.

In the Zapskoviye region, lying across the little river Pskova which flows by the northeastern walls of the kremlin, are the following churches: *Cosma and Damian* (1464), on Leon Pozemsky Street (housing a workshop for the blind who make musical instruments); the *Church of the Epiphany* (1489), beside the river, an outstanding piece of Pskov architecture with an interesting four-arched belfry; the *Resurrection Church* (1532); and *Varlaamy Khutinsky Church* (1495), which is open for services. Also in the Zapskoviye region is another example of 17th-century civil architecture, the house of the merchant Postnikov, consisting of two buildings with deep cellars and secret vaults, called *the Sack* because of its shape. From 1482 to 1525 this part of the city was surrounded by walls with several towers, of which the *Varlaamova Tower* and the *Gremyachaya Tower* remain. They played an important role in the defence of the city from the Poles and, later, the Swedes.

Pogankin House Local Museum, Nekrasovskaya Street 7. Open 12–7; closed Mon. There are historical and Soviet departments and a picture gallery on the second floor. Here are "Two," by Petrov-Vodkin (1917), pictures by B. Grigoryev, Bakst, Benois, and Levitan, and "Self-Portrait," by L. Pasternak (the poet's father). The museum is housed in the former art school, the picture gallery in its auditorium. On the ground floor of the museum is a diorama depicting the capture of the city. On the second floor there is an exhibition of silver and church items made locally. On display also is a bowl ("kovsh") presented to Peter the Great by Empress Elizabeth and a bowl presented to Sergei Pogankin by Pskov merchants in 1689.

Vlasyevskaya Tower. Open 12–5; closed Fri.

Lenin Museum, Lenin Street 3. Open 11–6; closed Wed. Lenin lived here in 1900. The museum is in the room that he used.

Lenin's House, Iskra Pereulok 5. Open 11–6; closed Wed.

1581 Memorial, Near the fortress wall, next to the Grave of the Unknown Soldier and the eternal flame. This monument with a cross commemorates the victory of Pskov over the army of Stephan Batory.

"Pushkin and a Peasant Woman" Statue, Pushkin Garden, in the centre of town, facing Letnyi Sad. The bronze statue, which was unveiled in 1983, is of the poet with his beloved nanny, Arina Rodionovna. It is by Konstantinov and Butenko.

Liberators' Memorial, Martyrs of the Revolution Square, near 50-Years of October Bridge, in the northeastern part of the city

Lenin Monument, Lenin Square, in front of the House of Soviets. Sculpted by Arapov, the monument was unveiled in 1960.

Kirov Monument, Nekrasov Street, near the House of Soviets. This monument was sculpted by Tomsky and unveiled in 1937.

War Memorial, by Krestovskoye and Leningradskoye Highway. This memorial is in the shape of a bayonet and honours the Soviet army.

Grave of the Unknown Soldier and Eternal Flame, near the fortress wall

Obelisk, on the way out of town to the south

Pushkin Drama Theatre, Pushkin Street 13. Formerly this building was called the Pushkin People's House.

Concert Hall, Liebknecht Street 2

Racecourse, Zapskoviye, Ippodromnaya Street

Trud ("Labour") Stadium

Pushkin Garden

Rizhskaya Hotel and Riga Restaurant, Rizhskoye Prospect 25; tel. 32-397. The local Intourist office is here, tel. 24-254.

Oktyabrsky Hotel and Restaurant, Oktyabrsky Prospect 36; tel. 99-400

Turist Hotel and Restaurant, Krasnoznamenskaya Street 4, near the Soviet Army Bridge

Kolos Hotel, Krasnykh Partizanov Street 6

Aurora Restaurant, Oktyabrsky Prospect 36

Rus Restaurant

Chebureki Caucasian Restaurant, Oktyabrskaya Prospect 10

GPO, Oktyabrskaya Square

Telegraph Office, Sovietskaya Street 20

Bank, Oktyabrskaya Square

Department Store, Sovietskaya Street 13, Oktyabrskaya Square

Souvenirs, Oktyabrsky Prospect 18

Gift Shop, Sovietskaya Street 53/15

Snetogorsky Monastery, 5 km (3 miles) from Pskov. This monastery was founded in the 13th century. The *Cathedral of the Nativity of the Virgin* was built in 1312.

Intourist organises excursions from Pskov via Izborsk (32 km/20 miles) to Pechory (52 km/32 miles), and to Pushkinskiye Gory (130 km/81 miles).

Izborsk

Izborsk is a small village on the way to Pechory Monastery. Below it lies Gorodischenskoye Lake and the river Smolka. Izborsk was founded in the 8th or 9th century, first mentioned in chronicles of 862, and being older than Pskov there are many stories about its history.

At one time the village was called "Slovensk," after the prince who founded a "great town." Then his son Izbor inherited it and the name was changed to Izborsk. Later it became dependant on Pskov, and being nearer to the border, it bore the brunt of countless attacks, withstood sieges, and was burnt and ruined. In the 18th century, after Russia gained her access to the sea, Izborsk lost its strategical importance and gradually declined until it was only a small town and then no more than a village.

There is now a plaster of paris factory here. The region specialises in growing flax.

The *fortress* that remains was built on Zheravi Hill in 1330 but has been reconstructed several times over the years. Six of the original *early-15th-century* towers remain, varying in height from 13 to 19 m (43 to 62 ft).

St. Nicholas Church, inside the walls of the fortress. This church dates from the early 14th century. In the same way that Pskov was considered the home of the Holy Trinity, Izborsk was the home of St. Nicholas.

SS. Sergi and Nikander Church. The church dates from the 17th century.

Gorodischenskaya Church. This church was built in the 17th century.

St. Sergius Radonezhsky Church. This church dates from the 18th century.

Local Museum, in the SS. Sergi and Nikander Church.

Pechory Monastery

Long ago hermits lived in the caves in the hill here. In 1470 some hunters heard their singing and found the caves. They called the place Svyataya ("Holy") Hill. Only one of the hermits, Mark, is known by name. Possibly they were monks who had fled here from Kiev.

In 1473 a priest, Ioann, settled here with his family, because they had been persecuted by the Germans in their hometown of Yuriev (now Tartu). When his wife Vasa died, Ioann buried her in the caves, but the legends say that the following day he found that her coffin had leapt out of the ground. Afraid that he had not recited the funeral service properly, he repeated the ceremony and buried her again. But the same thing happened again, so he left her simple wooden coffin unburied and today it rests in an alcove on the right at the entrance to the caves. Vasa came to be considered the guardian of the caves and the earthly mother of the monastery. It is said that on one occasion intruders tried to force the coffin open but, as the lid was raised, flames shot out. The monks still show the scorch marks that remain.

After Vasa's death, Ioann became a monk, taking the name of Iona. He excavated an underground church dedicated to the Assumption of the Virgin. When he died he was buried near the tomb of the hermit Mark and that of a monk called Lazar who had died at age 91 after sealing himself into his cell. His food and water had been passed through to him daily and he had worn an iron harness and cross weighing 12.5 kg (28 lb).

There have always been monks living in this way, and there still are today. The temperature of the caves is always 5°C (41°F) in both summer and winter. The monks estimate that it takes about twenty years for the body to get so used to the underground climate that it will not decay after death. The passages of the caves stretch for perhaps 300 m (328 yds), and about 10,000 people are buried here. The *Fraternal Sepulchre* holds 400 coffins, and many individuals have their own memorial plaques on the walls. Some of these belong to nobles who gave money to found a family vault.

The monastery grew gradually. Many of the fortifications date from 1519 and the walls with their towers from 1565. It was robbed several times and damaged, and in the 16th and 17th centuries, because of its strategical position, it was besieged by the Poles and partly destroyed by the Swedes and the Lithuanians. In 1701 Peter the Great surrounded the monastery with an earthen wall and a moat, and two years later a Swedish siege failed.

The entrance to the monastery is through the *Holy Gate*, and the first church down the slope is dedicated to St. Nicholas (1654). The *Church of the Annunciation* (Blagoveschenskaya) (1540) is the red and white one in the centre of the grounds and *St. Lazar's* (18th century) is the yellow church across the courtyard. The *Pokrova Church* (1759) stands high above the caves. The *Church of the Archangel Michael* (1827), commemorating the liberation of Pskov from Napoleon, is up by the wall; it is large and white, with three imposing porticos and a broad green dome. Inside are impressive 19th-century decorations and plaques of honour. The monastery's *bell tower* (1521) now has 13 bells instead of the original 18.

In the underground *Assumption Cathedral* (1473), the woodwork of the iconostasis is in a baroque style called Yelizavetinkoye baroque, after the Empress Elizabeth, who preferred her baroque to have a little more symmetry than was customary at the time. The figure on one of the icons, on the left as you enter, bears a strong resemblance to her. Most of the icons in the iconostasis are 17th century. In this cathedral is the *tomb of St. Cornelius*, who was head of the monastery for 42 years in the 16th century. He was responsible for reinforcing the surrounding walls. Legend has it that Ivan the Terrible was angered by this show of independence and ordered that Cornelius be beheaded. When the deed was done, the tsar repented of his hasty demand and he himself carried the body into the cathedral in which it now lies. Then in retribution he made rich presents to the monastery, including that of a golden cross weighing 3.6 kg (8 lb).

Here also is a wonder-working icon, hung with pale-blue satin and embroidery. When it is carried out with all of its decorations of silver and silver gilt, it weighs more than a quarter of a ton. The lamp in front of it is decorated with inscriptions of prayers, and words of prayer even form the fringe of letters hanging from it. The icon was painted in 1521 by a monk named Alexei Maly, and it is said that it helped to save Pskov from the army of the Polish king Stephan Batory in 1581 and from Napoleon in 1812. The Virgin is said to be guardian of the whole Pskov area. Another underground church is the *Church of the Resurrection*, which was excavated in the 1930s.

Today about 80 monks live in the monastery. Three-quarters of these are over 80 years of age. Their lives are calm and ordered and they live long. They have 10 cows, 50 chickens, and 8 bee hives, and they care for their apple orchards and vegetable garden. Their fish is bought locally.

Just outside the Holy Gates is the long, dark-blue building of *St. Barbara's Church*, which is used for Russian Orthodox services in the Estonian language. Near it is the white *Church of the Forty Martyrs*, and between these two stands the little *Chapel of St. Alexander Nevsky*, both built in the 19th century.

Rus Restaurant
Eating House, Oktyabrskaya Street

Pushkinskiye Gory

Pushkinskiye Gory is 130 km (80 miles) from Pskov. Near it is Mikhailovskoye, which was the estate of the Pushkin family to which the Russian poet Alexander Pushkin (1799–1837) belonged. It was given to the poet's great-grandfather, Abram Hannibal, by Empress Elizaveta in 1742.

Alexander Pushkin came here frequently and spent two years here (1824–26) when he was exiled from the capital for his dissident poetry. It proved a prolific period; he wrote more than 100 significant works here. The estate was destroyed by the Germans during World War II and re-created after the war. Inside the house everything is as it was during the poet's lifetime. Some of Pushkin's personal belongings as well as those of his close friends or relatives are displayed here.

Near the main house is a small cottage that belonged to Pushkin's nurse, Arina Rodionovna, whom he mentions affectionately in many of his works. The surrounding park has matured beautifully.

Other places in the vicinity are associated with Pushkin's life, including the villages of *Petrovskoye* and *Trigorskoye* and *Svyatogorsky Monastery*—all 3 to 4 km (about 2 miles) from Mikhailovskoye. In Petrovskoye the house of Pushkin's grandfather, Hannibal, has been restored as a museum (closed Mon., the last Tues. of the month, and all of April and November). Trigorskoye was the home of the Osipov-Wulff family, with whom Pushkin was very friendly. But the most interesting of these three places is probably the monastery, which was founded in 1569 on the order of Ivan the Terrible.

Until the end of the 17th century it officially was listed among Russia's 30 principal monasteries. A legend tells how the tsar's order followed reports of miraculous deeds performed by a shepherd boy who lived in these parts and had visions of holy icons with extraordinary healing powers. Historians, more prosaically, point out that the founding of the monastery coincided with a terrible epidemic. The main gates and parts of the wall date back to the 16th century. *Svyatogorsky Cathedral*, inside the monastery, also was built in 1569, but it has two annexes that were added at the end of the 18th century. The cathedral is 23.5 m by 13.5 m (77 ft by 44 ft) in area and 9 m (29 ft) high. Its austere style is typical of the old architecture of the Pskov region. The top of the cathedral was badly damaged during World War II and later was restored. The belfry, built in 1821, is 37 m (121 ft) high. There are two exhibits inside the cathedral, one about the building itself, including some of the icons, and the other about Pushkin. The poet

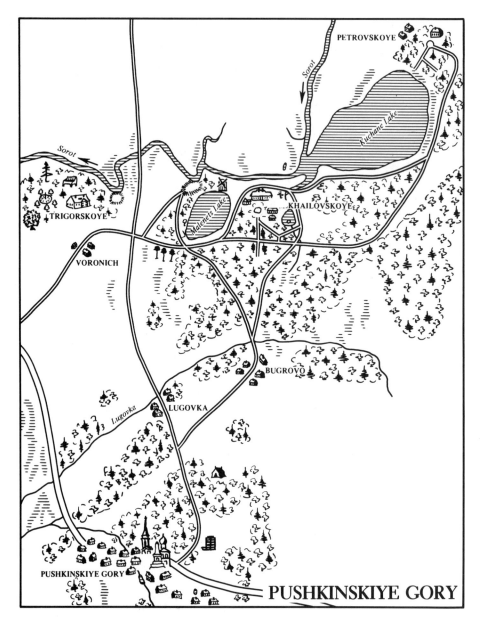

PETROVSKOYE

Sorot

Kuchane Lake

Sorot

TRIGORSKOYE

KHAILOVSKOYE

Malenets Lake

VORONICH

BUGROVO

Lugovka

LUGOVKA

PUSHKINSKIYE GORY

PUSHKINSKIYE GORY

was fatally wounded at a duel in St. Petersburg on 8 February, 1837. To avoid publicity his body was brought secretly to Svyatogorsky Monastery and buried in the family grave.

Druzhba ("Friendship") Hotel and Lukomorye Restaurant, in Pushkinskiye Gory

PUSHKIN

See Leningrad Environs, p. 298.

PUSHKINO

See Kishinyov, p. 235.

PUSHKINSKIYE GORY

See Pskov, p. 431.

PYATIGORSK

Intourist uses this spa as its centre in the Mineralniye Vody region, which includes Lermontov, Essentuki (q.v.), and Zheleznovodsk (q.v.). It also organises trips here from Kislovodsk, Terskol, and Stavropol.

MINERALNYE VODY

There are over a hundred mineral springs in the Caucasus, but the most important are the group

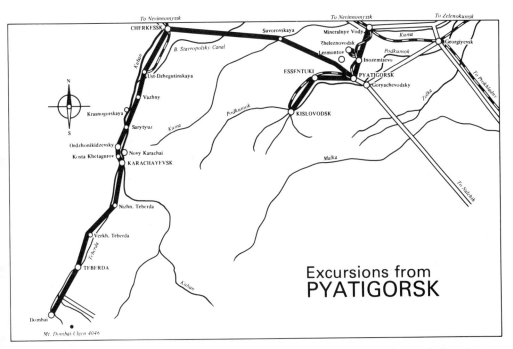

Excursions from
PYATIGORSK

known as the Caucasian Mineralnye Vody ("Mineral Springs"), known as "Minvody" for short. Here, within a radius of about 20 km (12 miles), are all sorts of spa cures, comparable to those available throughout the length and breadth of Germany and France. Some of the waters are even unique to the Caucasus.

The territory is in steppeland not far from Mt. Elbrus. On the same latitude as Genoa, Italy, it lies considerably further south than Yalta. But because it is separated from the warm Black Sea by the main Caucasian mountain range, it has a continental climate, but the summers are cooler here than in the southern part of the steppes.

Hermann Abich (1806–86), an explorer who was one of the first to study the geology of the Caucasus, called this region the "cliff archipelago." It has now been confirmed that when the low-lying steppeland to the north of the Caucasus was under the sea, the isolated mountains here were indeed islands.

The first Russian records of the people living in the Pyatigorye ("Five Hills") region date from the middle of the 16th century, but it was not until the 1774 peace treaty with Turkey that the region finally passed to Russia.

Russia had been searching for health resorts of her own since the time of Peter the Great, and in 1773 an Academy of Sciences expedition confirmed the healing qualities of the Pyatigorye mineral springs. It was noticed that wounded soldiers recovered much quicker when they used the springs. The first Russian residents of Pyatigorye were retired soldiers who stayed on after their cures, and in fact all of the main buildings of the future spas were built by soldiers.

Only in 1803, by the decree of Alexander I, was Caucasian mineral water proclaimed to be of national importance. Two resident doctors were then appointed; the present spas really date from then. In 1810 Dr. Friedrich Haaz (1780–1853), a German physician working for the Russians, discovered the first mineral springs at Zheleznovodsk and Essentuki quite by chance, because local people reported that in some places their horses drank especially greedily. Pyatigorsk was proclaimed a town in 1830.

Now more than 70 springs have been developed in this region, yielding up to 6,000,000 litres (1,300,000 gallons) a day of 12 different types of water; Pyatigorsk is famous for its hot carbonic hydrogen sulphide springs, and it takes first place among the spas because of its great variety of waters. Pyatigorsk alone has 34 springs yielding up to 2,000,000 litres (450,000 gallons) of water a day.

In spite of the different qualities of the waters from the various springs, all the towns in the vicinity are known collectively as the spas of the Northern Caucasus and all share the same emblem which is depicted everywhere, an eagle with spread wings, perching on a mountain peak. The emblem probably reflects a legend that Simurg, an old king of the birds, who with one eye views the past and with the other penetrates the future, lives on top of Mt. Elbrus. When he flies, the flapping of his wings makes the earth tremble. When he moans the birds become silent, the flowers fade and the mountains cover themselves with clouds. There are statues of this eagle in the hilly parks that rise above each spa.

Minvody Population—64,000

The town of Minvody is situated in the valley of the Kuma River. It is a large transport junction of the Stavropol area, and its railway station and airport serve as gates to the Caucasian spas of the Mineralnye Vody region. A new 31-km (19-mile) highway links it to Essentuki, bypassing the other spas.

At first it was only a tiny railway station near the village of Sultanovsky, which had been founded in 1876 and named after Prince Sultan Takhtamysh Girei. Soon a large glass factory belonging to the Malyshev brothers was built 3 km (2 miles) from the station, which is now the Adzhiyevsky village. Sultanovsky was once called Illarionovsky, after the Caucasian governor-general Illarion Vorontsov-Dashkov. In 1920 the village became the town of Mineralnye Vody (the same as the railway station). At present Minvody is developing industrially, with a gelatine factory, a dairy, building materials enterprises, and a meat factory.

Pokrovskaya Church, Svobody Street

Museum, Lenin Street 41. Open 9–5; closed Sun. and Mon.

War Memorial, on 30-Years-of-Victory Square. There is an eternal flame on the left, and beyond the square Mt. Zmeika forms an impressive background to the memorial.

Aeroplane Monument, by 22-Party-Congress Street, a dual carriageway

Tank Monument, 50-letiya-Oktyabrya Street, on the left

Lenin Statue, 22-Party-Congress Street

Lenin Bust, Lenin Street

Kavkaz Hotel and Restaurant, Karl Marx Prospect 53

Beryozka Cafe, 50-letiya-Oktyabrya Street

Tourist Cafe

GPO, 22-Party-Congress Street 28

Bank, Lenin Street 55

Filling Station, on the left of the main road on the way into town

Railway Station, at the end of 22-Party-Congress Street

Minvody Airport, on the left after leaving Kangly and just before Minvody (the town)

Pyatigorsk Population—129,000

In 1780 Konstantinovskaya fortress was founded at the foot of Beshtau (Turkish for "Five Hills") Mountain on the left bank of the Podkumok River. In 1823, on the initiative of Professor Nelyubin, one of the discoverers of the Caucasian mineral waters, the village was called Goryachevodsk ("Hot Waters"). In 1830, however, it was decided to call the town Pyatigorsk ("Warm Sulphur Springs") "as a tribute of respect to Beshtau Mountain to whose foothills the town is adjoined." The spa lies 550 m (1,800 ft) above sea level.

The five Beshtau peaks are: Lysaya Gora ("Bald Mountain") (758 m/2,415 ft); Mashuk, after a beautiful girl of that name (994 m/3,250 ft); Zmeika ("Snake"), where it is said that a big snake named Poloz used to kill people until Russian soldiers shot it; Beshtau; and Zheleznaya Gora ("Iron Mountain") (854 m/2,806 ft), whose name was derived from a legend about old Elbrus cutting the iron helmet of his son Arslan in two pieces. All of these are of volcanic origin and, with the exception of Beshtau, have a layer of limestone over lava. Other mountains in the vicinity are Razvalka (930 m/3,051 ft), which because of its silhouette was first called the Sleeping Lion, then got its present name of Razvalka ("Falling to Pieces") because its top broke into several mountain rocks; Byk ("Bull") (821 m/3,693 ft); Verblyud ("Camel") (902 m/2,959 ft); and Goryachaya ("Hot").

Pyatigorsk is located on the southern and southwestern slopes of Mt. Mashuk. It has about 50 springs, which can be divided into four types: carbonic-acid-hydrogen sulphate, carbonic acid, salt-and-alkaline, and radon. Their temperatures range from 14 to 60°C (57 to 140°F). The majority of the springs are at the foot of the mountain, but another part of the resort, Proval, is on a terrace on the southern slope of the mountain.

The waters are particularly valuable in the cure of digestive, metabolic, nervous, skin, and gynecological diseases. Pyatigorsk's industry is first linked to the spas. There is a meat-packing factory, a dairy, a bakery, a wine-producing factory, a brewery, and a sweet factory as well as a footwear and garment factory. There is also an agricultural machinery repair plant.

There are pedagogical and pharmaceutical colleges in Pyatigorsk and also a Research Institute of Balneology and Physiotherapy.

Pyatigorsk was visited by many outstanding Russians—writers, poets, and composers. Pushkin was here twice, in 1820 and 1829, when he visted Zheleznovodsk. But Pyatigorsk is connected first and foremost with the name of the Russian poet Mikhail Lermontov (1814–41), who was killed in a duel at the foothills of Mashuk in 1841. Lermontov was a guards officer of Scottish ancestry, famous for his novels and poems, which earned him his position as the greatest Russian Romantic. There are many mementos of Lermontov in Pyatigorsk, which is the setting of one of his most famous stories, "Princess Mary," a part of his novel *A Hero of Our Time*.

In the story he conveys with such realism the atmosphere of an early-19th-century Russian spa that having once read it, it is difficult to think of Pyatigorsk in any other way. Michael Pereira, in his book *Across the Caucasus*, writes: "Walking through Pyatigorsk streets with their pleasant trees and rather tumble-down houses one would not be in the least surprised to bump into Pechorin, or Grushnitsky, Princess Mary herself. Indeed, one is rather surprised when one doesn't bump into them. One feels they ought to be there."

The *Lermontov Baths*, formerly called the Nikolayevsky Baths, are fed by the Alexandro-Yermolovsky spring. The temperature of the water is 42°C (107°F) and it contains natron-chloric, bicarbonic lime, sulphuric natron, free carbonic acid, and sulphuric hydrogen. The bathhouse was built in 1831 and is the oldest of its kind in Russia.

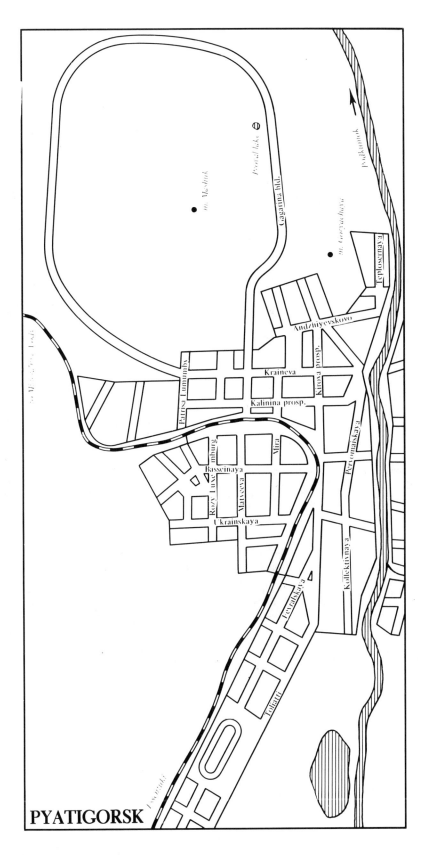

435

PYATIGORSK

Proval ("Gap") is a great grotto, 41 m (135 ft) deep, on the slopes of Mashuk. It was washed out many years ago by a subterranean sulphuric stream. Later a hole appeared in the roof of the grotto, and lakes, one of them 11 m (36 ft) deep, were formed. It has a warm sulphur spring and the water is blue in colour from the sulphuric combination. As legend has it, it originated from the beautiful Mashuk's heart when jealous old Elbrus cut it in half in a fit of rage. The lakes in the grotto are the hot blood of Mashuk's innocent heart, which was not red but blue. More recently, when Russians first settled here, they were instructed to live peaceably with the Tatars and use no weapon against them. The Tatars knew this and took advantage of it, but when the Russians' patience could stand no more, they are said to have thrown their enemies into the lake, leaving no trace of their misdeeds. A local legend says that Lermontov was cured of rheumatism by swimming in Proval Lake.

In the past it was one of the sights that visiting society went to see, and in 1837 a suspension bridge was erected, wide enough for six couples to dance a quadrille upon, but the bridge lasted only four years. The grotto is entered by a 45-m (50-yd) gallery. Open 11–6 or during daylight hours. There are interesting private houses in the Proval area as well.

On the road to Proval from the town is an imposing *stone monument* by the architect Svetlitsky to four Soviet commissars shot here in 1918.

A pleasant walk starts from Proval and leads around Mt. Mashuk, passing the site of Lermontov's duel and ending near the Tyoply ("Warm") Narzan spring. There is a *cable car* service from the centre of Pyatigorsk to Mt. Mashuk.

The duel in question took place at the foot of Mt. Mashuk, 4 km (2.5 miles) from the centre of Pyatigorsk. Lermontov was challenged by a certain Major Martynov, an old school friend of his. The latter was something of a dandy and liked to get himself up in full Caucasian dress, complete with daggers and other accoutrements. In this splendid but, for a Russian officer, absurd costume, Martynov once appeared at a soiree, and when Lermontov saw him come into the room he said mockingly, "Here comes our brave mountaineer!" Martynov at once called him out.

When they met early the next morning, July 15, at the appointed place, Lermontov explained that he had never intended to insult Martynov and that what he had said had been meant as a joke; he said that if Martynov would not be offended, he was ready to ask his pardon, not only there but at any other place he chose. Martynov replied, "Shoot! Shoot!" Lermontov was to fire first and he fired into the air, but Martynov came closer and shot him through the heart, so he died instantly.

Lermontov had been opposed to the tsar and was sent to the Caucasus as punishment for his verses, especially those devoted to the death of Alexander Pushkin, who also was killed in a duel in 1837. "Butchers of freedom, genius and glory" was how he described the members of the government in the offensive poem, referring to the poet's death. His novel *A Hero of Our Time* also met with official disapproval. When Nicholas I learned of Lermontov's fate he said: "A dog's death befits a dog," and Martynov, instead of being sentenced to hard labour (the punishment for duelling at the time), was simply ordered to seek religious absolution. Lermontov's death was understood by many Russians to have been murder planned by the authorities. Lermontov was buried in Pyatigorsk; later his body was transferred to the family crypt at Tarkhany in the Penza region and he was buried next to his mother.

Lermontov Museum, Lermontov Street 4. Open 10–5; closed Mon. and Tues. and the last day of the month.

Lermontov's House, Lermontovskaya Street 18. The writer lived here for two months, and after the duel his body was brought back here.

Lermontov's Statue, Lermontov Garden, Andzhievsky Street. This bronze statue by Alexander Opekushin was unveiled in 1889. The terrace in front of it commands a fine view of the mountains, with the snowcapped summit of the twin-peaked Elbrus (white breasts) 97 km (60 miles) distant as the crow flies.

Lermontov's Grotto, opposite the Akademicheskaya Gallery in the park. This cave was discovered in 1829. Inside it a stone bench was carved out. Lermontov had often visited this grotto in 1837, and he described it in *A Hero of Our Time*. In 1858 the grotto was lined with stone and an icon fence was installed. A marble sign marks the entrance.

Lermontov Monument, on the site of the duel. The monument, which takes the form of a bust of the poet surrounded by griffons atop four stone posts connected by chains, was designed by Mikhail Mikeshin and unveiled in 1915.

Church, on the hilltop at the end of Andzhievsky Street. This church was built at the end of the 19th century.

Local Museum, Sacco-and-Vancetti Street 2. Open 10–5; closed Wed. There are natural history and art sections at this museum, which was founded in 1905.

Central Library, Oktyabrskaya Street 6. This building used to be the Hermitage Hotel.

Akademicheskaya Gallery, on top of Goryachaya Mountain, with a good view of Pyatigorsk. Formerly known as Elizavetinskaya Gallery, this has long been one of the principal baths of the spa. It was built in 1851 of white Mashuk stone by the English architect Upton, who also was responsible for the fortifications of Sebastopol in 1847–49.

Restoratsia, Kirov Street. This was built in 1829 as the town's first hotel. Pushkin, Lermontov, Tolstoy, and others stayed here in their time. Restoratsia was built in the Ionic style by two Italian architects, the brothers Iosif and Giovanni Bernardazzi, in 1825. In Lermontov's time Restoratsia was a very grand restaurant with frequent balls and dances. Lermontov attended these and in his *A Hero of Our Time* he describes Restoratsia and two balls held there. This is now part of the State Balneological Research Institute.

Eolova Arfa ("Aeolean Harp"), this monument also was built by the Bernardazzi brothers in 1930–31 and devoted to Aeolus, the Greek god of the winds. Originally there was a wooden column with two harps; when the wind blew, a weather vane plucked the strings and made music. This was replaced by the present small pavilion in ancient Greek style which has the best view over the town and surrounding region. It stands on the spot where, in Lermontov's time, Cossack guards kept watch to protect patients from unexpected attack by the local mountain tribesmen.

Mikhailovskaya Gallery, Proval Street 2. This, too, was built by Upton in 1848.

Obelisk, on the top of Mt. Mashuk. The obelisk commemorates the topographer and mountain climber Alexander Pastukhov, who climbed the western cone of Elbrus in 1890 and the eastern cone in 1896. He was the first to draw a map of Elbrus.

Mt. Elbrus (its native name is Mingy-Tau, or "Mountain of Thousands") is an extinct volcano with two peaks, eastern and western with a saddle between them. As the former reaches 5,621 m (18,441 ft) and the latter 5,642 m (18,510 ft), Elbrus is the highest mountain in both the Caucasus and Europe. The huge mountain mass is coated in ice up to 100 m (330 ft) thick. The first man to climb Elbrus was supposed to be the locally born Kilar Kashirov, who reached the summit in 1839. In 1868 the Britons Douglas Freshfield, Thomas Moore, and Tucker climbed the eastern slope. The best point to see the mountain is from Bermamutskaya Skala, 34 km (21 miles) from Kislovodsk; from there it can be viewed in its entirety. Intourist also runs excursions to the resort of Elbrus from Nalchik (q.v.).

Kirov Monument, Kirov Square, opposite the railway station. This monument to the revolutionary and statesman is by Kondratyev.

Bust of Andzhievsky, in the park on Kirov Prospect. Shotskikh made this bust in memory of the first local party chairman; Georgi Andzhievsky was executed by the White Guards in 1919.

Diana Grotto, in Tsvetnik ("Flower Garden"). This big artificial cave named after the Roman goddess of hunting was excavated in 1830–31. Even on the hottest day it is cool inside. It was designed, like Restoratsia, by the Bernardazzi brothers. In 1841, on Lermontov's initiative and a week before his tragic death, a big ball was organised in the grotto that was described later by the participants.

Stone eagles, the emblem of the Mineralny Vody spas, stand in all the spas of the region. The Pyatigorsk Eagle was built on Goryachaya Mountain by the local architect Shotskikh.

Musical Comedy Theatre, Kirov Street 17

Philharmonia Concert Hall, in Lermontov Gallery, Tsvetnik Park. The gallery, like the Pushkin Gallery, was brought from the Nizhny-Novgorod (now Gorky) Fair, but in 1899.

Open-air Theatre, Dunayevsky Street 5

Kirov Park, Dunayevsky Street 5. Here is the *planetarium*, an *open-air theatre*, *amusement grounds*, a *dance floor*, and a *boat hiring* station.

Hippodrome Racecourse, Kursovaya Street 219. Open from 2 May until October; racing on Sat. at 4 and Sun. at noon. There is a totalisator and a *restaurant*.

Mashuk Hotel and Druzhba ("Friendship") Restaurant, Kirov Prospect 25; tel. 57-260. The hotel, built in 1908, formerly was known as the Bristol.

Pyatigorsk Hotel and Restaurant, Krainev Street 41a; tel. 52-470

Intourist Hotel, Lenin Street

Intourist Office, Kirov Prospect 21; tel. 57-360

Tsentralnaya Restaurant, Kirov Street 27a. The restaurant serves Caucasian cuisine.

Druzhba Restaurant, Caucasian cuisine

Mashuk Restaurant, Kirov Street 60

Lesnaya Polyana ("Forest Glade") Restaurant, at the site of Lermontov's duel

Rybachy Kuren ("Fisherman's Hut"), on the banks of the reservoir

Proval Cafe, in the Proval area

GPO, Kirov Street 52

Bank, Kirov Street 25

Beryozka Foreign Currency Shop, Kirov Street 26

Department Store, Mira Street 3

Souvenirs, Kirov Street 26

Bookshop, Kirov Street 48

Jeweller's, Dzerzhinsky Street 42

Volna (Intourist) Motel and Camping Site, by the reservoir, Ogorodnaya Street 39, tel. 50-528

Motel, Kalinin Street 2, Belaya Romashka ("White Daisy") region. The motel stands on the right side of the road coming into town from Mineralnye Vody. There is also a *cafe*, a *garage*, and a *service station*. The name of the region comes from prerevolutionary times. Charity campaigns were conducted to help tuberculosis sufferers. Donors had an artificial white daisy pinned to their lapels and collection day was called White Daisy Day; the name of the region came from this.

Camping Site, beside the motel at Kalinin Street 2, Belaya Romashka region

Tambukanskoye Lake is about 11 km (7 miles) along the main Ordzhonikidze road from Pyatigorsk. This curative mud lake was first described by Guldenstedt in 1773 under the name of Tambi, which probably comes from the name of an old Kabardin tribal chief, Murzabek Tambiyev, who in the 18th century won the battle against the Crimean-Turkish invaders on the banks of the Podkumok River. The road passes by the shores of this lake, the mud of which is used for curative mud baths at the spas.

From Pyatigorsk, foreign tourists can take excursions in Intourist cars or coaches to Teberda and Dombai, but these are described under Kislovodsk because the distance up the mountain road from there is shorter. In July and August the brave can train for a week in Teberda, go by bus to Sev-erny Priyut, and then make the 31-km (19-mile) walk, not too fast, over the top of the mountains to Yuzhny Priyut, from where a bus takes them to Sukhumi. Luggage goes by plane to await your arrival. The trip to Elbrus can be made more easily from Nalchik. There are excursions to Kislovodsk (including Medovyi Vodopad and Kum-Bashi), Es-sentuki, Zheleznovodsk, Nalchik (including Go-lubiye Ozyora), and Stavropol; these are all described under their respective names.

RAUBICHI
See Minsk, p. 325.

RAVA RUSSKAYA Rawa Ruska in Ukrainian and Polish, Population—8,000
(Intourist organises excursions up here, near the Polish border, from Lvov, 67 km/42 miles away to the southeast.)

Rava Russkaya was founded in 1455 by Prince Vladislav Mazovetsky. It stands by the river Rata, a tributary on the left side of the river Bug. The first part of the name of the place came from a local village, and the second, most likely, came from the name of Galicia, which in those days was called Russian.

In the 16th century the town received a number of privileges. Crafts and commerce developed here because the town stood on an east-west trade route. In 1622 it was granted the privilege of holding an annual fair.

The soldiers of Bogdan of Moldavia damaged it badly in 1509, and it suffered from fire and chol-era in the 16th and 17th centuries.

The town was a place of important meetings. In 1698 King August II of Poland met Peter I here, and after three days of talks they agreed to act to-gether against the Swedes. It was also here that in 1704 Charles XII of Sweden met with the Polish noble Stanislaus Leszczynski (later proclaimed King Stanislaus I of Poland) to plan their war against Peter I. Finally, in 1716 it was here that talks were held between Leszczynski and August II.

After the first division of Poland in 1772 Rava Russkaya passed into Austrian hands, but the sur-rounding area was left to various Polish nobles.

The opening of the railway in 1887 gave a new boost to the town's economy, and it became an important railway junction. A limited local indus-try developed to include a factory that impregnated railway sleepers, a ceramic and brick works, and different branches of the food industry. All are still operating.

Being close to the border, the town was one of the first to be attacked by the Germans when they turned on Russia on 22 June, 1941, but the small force of border guards could not hold out against the Nazi army for long. The Germans opened their Stalag-325 concentration camp here for prisoners of war, which included a number of Frenchmen. 18,000 Jews were confined to the local ghetto; most of them perished.

The Roman Catholic and Orthodox churches, two monasteries, and synagogue were all put to secular use after World War II.

Museum of Military Glory, in the local board-ing school. The school also takes an active part in caring for the graves of the World War II dead.

RAZLIV
See Leningrad Environs, p. 300.

REPETEK
See Chardzhou, p. 98.

REPINO
See Leningrad Environs, p. 300.

RIGA is the capital of Latvia.

LATVIA
Area—64,000 sq km. Population—2,681,000, of which 53.7 percent are Latvian, 32.8 percent Rus-sian, 4.5 percent Belorussian, 2.7 percent Ukrain-ian, 2.5 percent Polish, and 1.5 percent Lithuanian.

Latvia is situated in western USSR, on the east-ern coast of the Baltic Sea. The Latvians trace their origin from several Baltic tribes—the Latgali, the Zemgali, and the Livi, who were akin to the East Slavonic tribes. In the 12th century these tribes and the lands they occupied attracted the attention of both German landlords and the Teutonic Knights. After the failure of the Crusades, the con-quest of the country began under the guise of con-verting "pagan tribes" to Christianity.

In 1196 the pope proclaimed the Northern Cru-sade against the Livs. In 1201 the Livonian bishop (Livonia was the name under which these lands were known at the time) founded the fortress of Riga, which became the main stronghold of the German invasion.

After a bloody struggle that continued until the end of the 13th century the archbishop of Riga became sovereign of the Baltic provinces. The Order of the Brethren of the Sword (or the Livonian Order) proved to be the strongest force, and by the end of the 14th century all real power in the area belonged to the grand master of that order.

In 1558 Ivan the Terrible, in his efforts to gain access to the Baltic Sea, declared war on the Li-vonian Order and, having reached Riga, soon de-feated the knights. Poland, Sweden, and Denmark claimed the area as well, and Russia had to with-draw. Western Livonia went to Denmark and the central part, with the newly formed Duchy of Kur-land, went to Poland. After the 1598–1642 war between Poland and Sweden the whole of northern Livonia, with the exception of Courland, was taken by Sweden.

In 1721, after the Russo-Swedish War, the Swedish possessions in Livonia went to Russia, and by the end of the 18th century all of Livonia (as well as the other Baltic provinces) was taken over by Russia as a result of the partitions of Poland, and it remained part of the Russian empire until the 1917 revolution, when it became a Soviet republic. But this was short-lived and from 1919 until 1934 Latvia was an independent republic. In 1934 the prime minister, Ulmanis, set up a dictatorial nationalist regime that existed until 1940, when Soviet troops entered the country. Now, along with the other Baltic republics, it seeks independence from Moscow.

Foreign visitors may go to Riga, the capital of Latvia, and to the seaside resorts that lie along the coast to the southwest of it.

The following national dishes are well worth trying:

zamieku Brokastis—"peasant's breakfast," a large omelette

maizes zupe ar putukrejumu—"corn soup with whipped cream"

skabe putra—"sour milk"

biezpiens ar kartupeliem, krejumi—"cottage cheese with potatoes, sour cream, and butter"

Unlike Russian, the Latvian language uses the Latin alphabet. To avoid confusion please remember that in the public lavatories "V" stands for "Gentlemen" and "S" for "Ladies." Here are a few words of Latvian:

hello	sveiki
I am a tourist	es esmoo turists
please	ludzu
thank you	paldies
yes	ya
no	ne
good	labi
bad	slikti
I don't understand	es nesaprotu
I need an interpreter	man vajag tulku
good-bye	sveiki (as for "hello")

RIGA Population—915,000

Latvia's capital city lies beside the river Daugava (the Western Dvina), not far from its mouth in Riga Bay. Its name was taken from that of a stream called Ridzene or Rige, meaning "pure."

In the 12th century German merchants began to trade with the tribes that lived by the Western Dvina River. Riga was founded in 1201 by Bishop Albert of Bremen, who came here with the Teutonic Knights and established a trading station on the right bank of the river, where Old Riga now stands.

In 1223 Riga was given municipal rights. The Baltic coast was at the time inhabited by the Livi, the Kursi, the Zemgali, and other tribes. Bishop Albert set himself the task of bringing Christianity to the area. He established the Order of the Brethren of the Sword. The citizens of Riga, which quickly was becoming an important trading centre, soon joined in serious rivalry with both the bishop

and the order. Then Riga joined the Hanseatic League in 1282. Sometimes the burghers had an upper hand in their quarrels, but finally in 1330 Riga had to submit to the supremacy of the order. In 1561 Riga became a merchant city-state.

In 1582 after the Russo-Polish War, Riga fell under Polish domination, and during the 17th century it frequently changed hands between the Poles and the Swedes. During the Russo-Swedish War at the beginning of the 18th century the Russian army seized Riga (1710), and as a result of the war the Baltic countries, including Riga, became part of the Russian empire.

After the 1917 revolution in Russia and the disintegration of the Russian empire, Riga became the capital of the Latvian Republic in 1918, of the Latvian Soviet Socialist Republic in 1940 and of Latvia in 1990.

Riga is an important industrial centre, producing electrical and radio goods, road vehicles, agricultural equipment, and chemicals. There also are woodworking, light, and food industries. The city is also a scientific and cultural centre, with the Latvian Academy of Sciences (which has 14 affiliated research institutes), a university (founded in 1861 as the Polytechnical Institute), and a wide assortment of colleges, technical schools, and trade schools.

Lenin Street, formerly Brivibas ("Freedom") Street, is the principal thoroughfare. In it stands the *Freedom Monument*, which was erected in 1935. Zale was the sculptor and Stalbergs the architect, and the inscription "Tevsemei un Brivibai" means "Fatherland and Freedom." Further on, where Kirov Street crosses Lenin Street, stands a *statue of Lenin* erected in 1950. The sculptors were Ingal and Bogolyubov, and the architect was again Stalbergs. The best shops and the most popular cafes are along this street.

The most interesting part of the city is *Old Riga*, a small region covering an area of about 35 hectares (87 acres) that lies just around the corner from the Riga Hotel. The oldest section is that lying between Kaleij, Daugavas, and Lenin streets. Old Riga suffered heavily during World War II, when several historic buildings, including the 14th-century House of the Blackhead and the 13th-century Rathaus, were burnt down.

The *city walls* were erected in 1201 and were rebuilt several times. They used to be 11 m (36 ft) high and as much as 2m (7 ft) thick. Remains of the walls can be seen from Troksna, Minsterejas, and Janeseta streets. Several of the original 24 towers have survived to the present day. One of them is the *Powder Tower* (once called the "Sand Tower") on Smilsu Street. It took its first name from the sand dunes nearby but was renamed when it was turned into a gunpowder depot. It was first mentioned in 1330 and was one of the largest in the town, being 25.5 m (84 ft) high, 14.3 m (47 ft) in diameter, and having walls 3 m (10 ft) thick. In the 14th and 15th centuries it served as a dungeon and torture chamber. It was badly damaged in 1621, when the Swedes besieged the city, and at

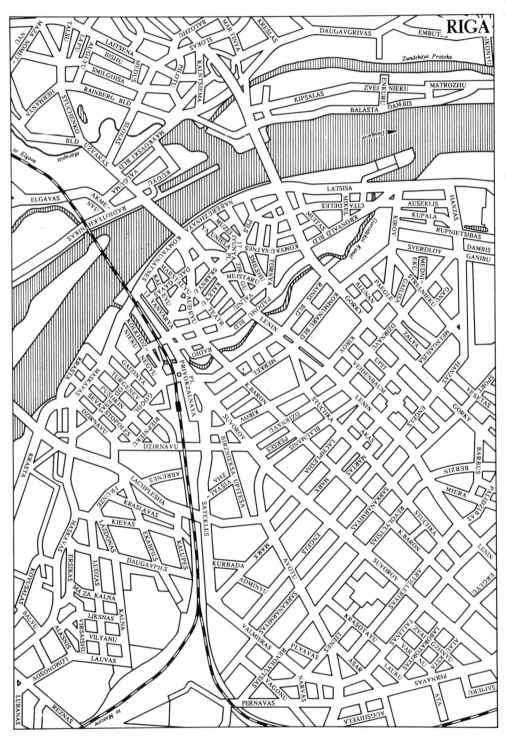

the end of the 19th century it was reconstructed, although the outward appearance was little changed. It now forms part of the Museum of the Revolution (see below).

Riga Castle, Pioneriu Square 3. The castle was built in 1330 and was the Livonian Order's stronghold in Riga. In the 15th century the townspeople ruined it during their conflicts with the order, but when the order subsequently regained its powerful position the burghers had to rebuild the castle for the knights in 1515. From the middle of the 16th century it was the residence of the governors of Livonia and later it was that of the president. In the 18th century a new building was added to it, and the White Hall was constructed at the beginning of the 19th century.

The tower with the spire is a 20th-century addition. Now the castle houses the *Palace of Pioneers* and three museums, the Latvian History Museum, the Janis Rainis Literary Museum, and the Foreign Fine Art Museum (see below).

Mater Dolorosa Church, Pils Street 5, next to the castle. This is a Roman Catholic church.

St. Saviour's Church, a little further along the embankment from Mater Dolorosa, and facing the river. This was built as the English Church in Riga, but is now closed.

Domkirk and Monastery, Dom Square. Open 2–6; Sun., 10–2; closed Wed. and Sat. Formerly the Cathedral of Our Lady, the Domkirk ("Doma Basnica") was founded in 1211, when Bishop Albert first consecrated the site. The brick church was designed as the seat of the archbishop of Livonia and Prussia. Since the second half of the 15th century it has been converted, restored, and reconstructed several times. It bears evidence of the Romanesque, Gothic, Renaissance, and baroque periods of architecture. It is 87 m (95 yds) long, 43 m (47 yds) wide, and 90 m (295 ft) high. It is a magnificent example of mediaeval architecture, although, unfortunately, the architect is unknown. But the name "Dom" derives from the Latin "Domus Dei," meaning "House of God." The floor and walls are lined with numerous tombstones and memorials with epitaphs. In a niche in the northern wall is the tomb of the first Baltic Christian missionary, Meinhard, who died in 1196. His tomb was uncovered in 1883 and his body found to have become mummified. The pulpit dates from 1641, and there is a statue of the order's grandmaster, Walter von Plettenberg. In the centre of the cathedral is a chair made in 1641 in Renaissance style and remade in Gothic style at the beginning of the 19th century. It is ornamented with fine wooden figures and is attributed to a prominent sculptor from Jelgava, Tobias Heincs.

The organ is one of the largest in the world. It was made in 1883–84 and has 6,768 pipes ranging from 13 mm to 10 m (half an inch to 33 ft) in length. It was restored in 1984 by the Flentrop, a Dutch company that specialises in restoring ancient organs. The balcony of the organ also has been restored. Visitors are advised not to miss the opportunity of attending a concert in the Domkirk.

There are seats for 1,500, and when the cathedral is full the echo lasts five seconds, which is considered ideal for the music of Bach, Beethoven, and Handel.

Construction of the monastery began in the 13th century. It was on the southern side of the cathedral and was U-shaped. On the ground floor there was a parlour to receive guests. The monks' cells were on the first floor. The monastery was connected with the cathedral by a gallery, one of the largest of its kind in Europe.

The cloisters, with Romanesque columns, Gothic arcades, and a tonsorium, now house the *Historical and Navigation Museum*. This was founded in 1773, when for the first time a collection of rare objects belonging to the town doctor, Nikolai Himzels, was put on display.

The Reformation reached the Baltic countries in the middle of the 16th century and the cathedral was sold to the Lutherans by the last archbishop of Riga for 18,000 Riga marks. The Domkirk is no longer used for services. This is not the first time the building has been put to secular use; in 1681 it was converted into a wine store.

Peter I's Mansion, 11-November Embankment, on the way down to the river from Domkirk. Peter the Great lived in this house in 1711. It had belonged to a rich merchant, but Peter was offered it as a gift from the city and he was glad to accept. He was fond of the house, especially the garden terrace on the first floor, for which he was said to have ordered trees and flowers from abroad.

The next group of buildings are all in the oldest section of Old Riga, where they stand at no great distance from one another.

Warehouse, formerly St. George's Church, Skarnu Street 10. The Church was built by the Order of the Brethren of the Sword at the beginning of the 13th century and served as both chapel and hall. In 1297 it was damaged during the city uprising against the order and subsequently was rebuilt. In the second half of the 17th century it was turned into a warehouse. The huge roof of the building is covered with old tiles.

Convent of Ekk, Skarnu Street 22. The building was put up in 1435 out of city funds as a guesthouse for visitors. At the end of the 16th century it was rebuilt, and N. Ekk, then mayor of Riga, established a "convent" here, a home for poor widows. The mediaeval heating system is preserved; it includes a huge, pyramidlike pipe with room enough in the bottom for a small kitchen.

St. John's Church, Skarnu Street 24. This church, which at one time belonged to the Dominicans, was built at the beginning of the 13th century and consists of two parts, the higher in Gothic style and the lower in Renaissance style. It was rebuilt in the 16th century and decorated with star-studded vaults. A richly ornamented baroque altar was added in the 18th century and the small pseudo-Gothic tower was built in 1849.

St. Peter's Church, Veerigas Square. Founded in the 13th century and built with money donated by the townspeople, this church was first mentioned in the chronicles in 1209 and happily escaped the fire of 1215. In 1352 Riga's first clock was installed on the church, and soon a lookout post was established in the tower to give warning of enemy invasion or the outbreak of fire anywhere in the town. The main building of the church was rebuilt in the 15th century. It is 80 m (87 yds) long, 35 m (38 yds) wide, and 123 m (404 ft) high. The tower is open 9–8; closed Mon.

The spire is one of the best examples of Gothic style. It collapsed in the 17th century but was reconstructed in 1690 by an architect from Strasburg named Bindensu, who built a new one on a wooden frame. However, it was severely damaged during the Northern War, and in 1721 both the steeple and the frame were struck by lightning and badly burnt. They later were restored by special order of Peter the Great, who had taken part in the fire fighting. The new steeple was 130 m (427 ft) high. In 1746 an architect by the name of Vilberns began reconstructing the steeple, basing his work on ancient drawings. On the day of the inauguration of the newly built tower, he climbed it, sipped a glass of wine, and threw it down, saying that the spire would last as many years as there were pieces of the broken glass. But the glass fell into a heap of straw and was safe. Nevertheless, the admirable spire lasted till the summer of 1941, when it caught fire after a Nazi bombardment. It was reconstructed in 1970, and the architect in charge, his work completed, also dashed a glass to the ground.

House of Reutern, Marstalu Street 2/4. Built in 1684–85 for a rich merchant named Johann von Reutern, it is elaborately decorated with reliefs and garlands cut in stone.

Reformed Church, Marstalu Street 10. Members of the Reformed Church appeared in Riga in the 16th century, but they were granted a legal parish here only in 1721. This church was built between 1727 and 1733. In 1805 the interior was divided into two floors, the ground floor being used for storage and the first floor for religious services. The wooden turret on the facade is about 35 m (115 ft) high, and the church itself is one of the largest in Riga.

House of Dannenstern, Marstalu Street 21. Built in 1696, this house is typical of that of any rich Riga merchant.

There are as many as 24 *medieval warehouses* in Old Riga, the most characteristic of them being the ones at 7 and 11 Sakarnas Gvardes Street (behind the Reformed Church) and at 10 and 11/17 Vecpilsetas Street. The one at 11 Sakarnas Gvardes Street still has the hoisting mechanism intact.

The *Guildhalls*, Amatu Street 3 and 6. The Virgin's Guildhall at No. 6 Amatu Street was formerly known as the Great Guildhall. Its present form dates from 1854–59, when the architects Beine and Schel designed it in Anglo-Gothic style to preserve its original appearance. In fact, it embraces two much older constructions. The first is the Munster Hut, founded in 1330 and used as a meeting hall by the merchants of Riga. It can now

be seen as a crossvaulted, divided room painted in mediaeval character with the coats of arms of the 46 member cities of the Hanseatic League. 12 cross-vaults rest on 6 octangular columns. The chandeliers date from the 17th and 18th centuries and the oak minstrels' gallery from 1644. In the centre of the hall is a display of gifts presented to the Riga Philharmonic Society, which uses this hall for concerts.

In the past the main hall was used for wedding parties. It is recorded that the "floor had to be covered over with hay to protect it from pouring beer." The Bride's Room ("Brantkammer") is the second oldest part of the building. It was built in 1521 and now contains a collection of national instruments. The beautiful sandstone chimneypiece dates from 1633 and the chandelier from 1649.

St. John's Guildhall, or the Small Guildhall, stands at No. 2 Amatu Street. It was built in 1864–66 by Felsko and was the meeting hall of the town's craftsmen. Appropriately, it is now the House of Culture of the Riga Trade Unions. St. John was the patron saint of the guild and his statue can be seen on the outside, under the Gothic tower. Of special interest inside is the Hall of the Elders, or Upper Hall, which is decorated with oak. There are painted views of St. Petersburg, Lubeck, Riga, Moscow, Hamburg, Bremen, and Rostock, although the latter two are now hidden by the stage. The stained glass windows that were installed in 1888 depict the presidents of the guild in mediaeval costume. Permission to see the hall can easily be obtained from the door keeper.

St. Jacob's Church, Vestures Square. This church was built in 1226, and its altar and interior are well preserved. The spire was erected in 1756 and is now the only authentic Gothic one in Riga, although all of the churches had them in the Middle Ages. During the Reformation the church was Lutheran, at the end of the 16th century it belonged to the Jesuits, and from 1621 till 1922 it was Lutheran again. It is open for services.

Three Brothers' House, 17, 19, and 21/23 Maza Pils Street, beside St. Jacob's Church. No. 17 was built in the 15th century and is the oldest surviving dwelling in Latvia. It is typical of houses of that time. Since 1687 it has been used as a bakery. No. 19 was built in 1646 by a merchant. The ground and first floors were lived in and the top floor used for storage. Only the outer appearance of 21/23 is preserved.

Armoury, Torna Street 1, on the other side of St. Jacob's Church. The Armoury was built in 1828–32 using part of the old city walls and the Maiden Tower. Now it is used as a storehouse.

Swedish Gate, Torna Street 11. Built in the city wall in 1698 during the Swedish occupation, the Swedish Gate stood near the semicircular Yurgen Tower. Later on several houses were put up and the whole complex came to be known as the Swedish Gate. It now belongs to the Latvian Architects' Union.

SS. Peter and Paul Church, in the citadel district. This church was built in 1776–86 by order of Catherine II to replace the Swedish Citadel Church. The plan of the church forms a cross, and the stone towers were built without a trace of wood. Services are held here.

Jesus Church, on the crossing of Sevastopol and Odessa streets, beyond the market and the skyscraper. This is one of the few historic buildings outside the bounds of Old Riga. It was built in 1818–22 on the site of earlier wooden churches, the first of which was founded in 1638, and is the largest wooden structure in Latvia. The building is octagonal with a flat wooden cupola resting on 16 pairs of columns, following the plan of the Roman Pantheon. There are four symmetrical wings to the main body of the building and the tower is 12 m (40 ft) high.

Voznesenia ("Ascension") Church (Russian Orthodox), Meness Street 2. This church is open for services, as are the synagogue and the churches listed below, with the exception of the Nativity Cathedral and the old St. Gertrude Church.

St. Joseph's Church (Roman Catholic), Embutes Street 12/14

Baptists' Church, Hospitalu Street 32

All Saints' Church, Klusais Street 10. Founded in 1812, the church was reconstructed in 1870–83.

St. Alexander Nevsky Church (Russian Orthodox), Lenin Street 56. This church was built in 1820–25 following the plan of the Pantheon.

Old St. Gertrude Church, Gertrūdes Street 78. This church was built in Gothic style in 1867 by Felko.

Cathedral of the Nativity of Christ the Saviour, Lenin Street, in the centre of the city. The architect Flug designed the building in neo-Byzantine style in 1876–84.

New St. Gertrude Church, Lenin Street 112. Built in 1903–6, this church has a side tower and is in new Greek style.

Ivanovskaya Church, close to the former cemetery

Uspenskaya ("Assumption") Old Believers' Church, Grebeščikova Street. Also known as the Grebenschikov Church, this was founded in the 1760s, but the belfry and the present building date from 1905. It is open for services and is very unusual and interesting to visit.

St. Francis Catholic Church, Klusais Street 16. Closed.

Troitsky-Sergievsky Convent, Krisjana Barona Street 126. Forty nuns live here. Their cathedral is the *Trinity Cathedral*, built in Russian style with five domes in 1892–93. Near the cathedral is the small wooden *St. Sergei's Church*, where among other relics are some belonging to St. Andrew and some pieces of the cross of Christ and His sepulchre.

Synagogue, Peitavas Street 6/8

History of Old Riga Museum, Palasta Street 4, in the building of the Domkirk Monastery. The museum has existed since 1773 and has departments of archaeology, history, navigation, and politics. It covers the history of Riga from ancient times to the present day. Included are 16th-century guns and ammunition, parts of the decor from the destroyed House of the Blackheads, and a minor coat of arms (a stone carving of 1777) from the town gateway. Open 11–5; Wed. and Sat., 1–7; closed Mon., Tues., and the third Friday of each month.

Latvian History Museum, Pionieru Square 3, in the castle. The museum was founded in 1869 and has a large collection of arms starting from the 16th century. Open 11–5; Wed. and Fri., 1–7; closed Mon., Tues., and the last Fri. of the month.

Domkirk Museum, Dom Square; entrance is from Palasta Street. Since 1962 this building has been open as a branch of the History of Riga Museum. Open 2–6; Sun., 10–2; closed Tues., Wed., Sat., and the first Mon. of each month.

Foreign Fine Art Museum, Pionieru Square 3, in the castle. Some of the collections date from 1783, but this museum was founded in 1920. It contains Dutch and German paintings, French engravings, antique sculpture, china, and, among other things, an Egyptian mummy. Open 11–5; Fri. 1–7; closed Mon.

Latvian and Russian Art Museum, Gorky Street 10a. Once the Fine Art Museum, the building was designed by Neumann in 1905 in 18th-century southern German baroque style. The four Ionic columns hold a portico with figures, including that of Pallas Athene. The collection of Latvian and Russian paintings dates from 1905. Open 12–6; Mon., Wed., and Fri., 1–7; closed Tues. and the last Thurs. of each month.

Museum of the Revolution, Smilsu Street 20. Formerly the Military Museum, built in 1938, the present layout was opened in 1940. Part of it is in the adjoining Powder Tower. Open 10–5; Tues. and Thurs., 12–7; closed Fri. and the last Mon. of each month.

Natural History Museum, Krisjanis Barona Street 4. Among the different sections are those devoted to zoology, anthropology, geology, and botany. Founded in 1846, the earliest collections date from the 18th century. Open 10–5; Tues. and Thurs., 1–8; closed Mon.

Janis Rainis Literary Museum, Pionieru Square 3, in the castle. When it was founded in 1951 the museum was entirely devoted to the Latvian poet, but now there is also material on display on other Latvian authors and an exhibit illustrating the history of the theatre in Latvia. Open 11–5; Wed., 1–7; closed Sun.

Paul Stradius Museum of History of Medicine, Leona Paegles Street 1. This unqiue museum, based on academician Stradius's collection, was opened in 1958. Open 12–6; closed Mon. and Tues.

Smilgis Theatre Museum, Smilgja Street 37/39. Open 11–6; closed Mon. and Tues.

Upit Museum, Lenin Street 38. Open 11–6; closed Mon. Andrei Upit (1877–1970) was a writer.

Krisjanis Baron Museum, Krisjanis Barona Street 3. Open 11–5; closed Mon., Wed., and Fri. Krisjanis Baron (1885–1923) was a Latvian writer.

Zander Museum, Zander Street. Friedrich Zander (1887–1933) was an inventor who wrote much about space rocket technology.

Lenin Museum, Cesu Street 17. This museum opened in 1961 in the flat where Lenin stayed in April 1900. Open 10–5; Tues, 12–7; closed Fri.

Vilis Lacis Museum, Stokholmas Street 33. Open 11–6; closed Mon. Vilis Lacis (1904–66) was a Soviet statesman and writer.

Telephone Network Museum. This museum was founded in 1982 to commemorate the 100th anniversary of the first telephone station in Riga, the largest in western Europe in its day.

Fire Fighting Museum, Hanzas Street 5. Opened in 1980, this demonstrates the history of fire fighting in Latvia. Open 10–5; closed Mon., Tues., and the last Fri. of each month.

Latvia Exhibition Hall. Closed Mon.

Open-air Latvian Ethnographical Museum, Brivdabas Street 21, 12 km (7 miles) from Riga, beside Lake Yugla. The buildings stand in an area of pinewood covering 90 hectares (225 acres). The collection was founded in 1924, making it the oldest museum of its kind in the country. The 46 buildings, which were brought here from various parts of Latvia, vary from 80 to 400 years in age. The wide variety of utensils, tools, and farming and fishing equipment furnishing the buildings number more than 4,000 items, and in addition the museum attendants wear national dress. Apart from houses and farm buildings there is an old *Lutheran church* (1704) from Usma and a *warehouse* (1697) from the port of Piepaja. Concerts are organised here in summer. Open daily from May till October; closed on the last day of each month. It can be reached by a number 1 bus.

Latvian Exhibition of Economic Achievements. Closed Tues.

Johann Gottfrid von Herder Monument, near the Domkirk. The bust in memory of the poet and city librarian Johann Gottfrid von Herder (1744–1803) was designed by Schaller in 1864. Von Herder was one of the 18th-century German humanists who played an important role in the evolution of national culture. He lived in Riga from 1764 till 1769 and taught history, geography, and German culture in the Dom School. Simultaneously he worked in the town library and was the pastor of two small churches in Riga. He collected Latvian folk songs, which he later included in his book on Latvian folklore.

Stucka Monument, in front of the castle. Peteris Stucka (1865–1932) was a great Latvian revolutionary and Lenin's comrade-in-arms. He also was one of the creators of Soviet jurisprudence. The sculptor was E. Melderis and the monument was unveiled in 1962.

Opera and Ballet Theatre, Basteja Boulevard 3. The building was constructed in 1863.

Upit Latvian Drama Theatre, Kronvald Boulevard 2. Named after the writer (see Upit Museum, above).

Raines Latvian Drama Theatre, Lenin Street 75

Russian Drama Theatre, Kalku Street 16
Youth Theatre, Lacplesa Street 37
Musical Comedy Theatre, Lenin Street 96
Puppet Theatre, Krisjanis Barona Street 16/18
Circus, Merkela Street 4. This is one of the largest circus buildings in the Soviet Union. It was opened in 1872.

Domkirk Concert Hall, Dom Square; entrance is from Palasta Street. There are organ music concerts daily in summer except Mon.; from September concerts take place on Wed., Sat., and Sun.

Riga Philharmonic Concert Hall, Amatu Street 6, in the Great Guildhall. Closed Mon.

Conservatoire Concert Hall, Krisjanis Barona Street 1

The large pinewood beside Lake Kiserzers is called *Mezaparks*. It can be reached by tram, trolleybus, or river-bus from the center of the city. The Riga Park of Culture and Recreation is in Mezaparks. There is a *cinema* there, some *restaurants*, and a large *open-air concert platform* where annual song festivals are held; the tradition of the festivals goes back to 1873. There is room for an audience of 30,000 and for 10,000 singers. An *exhibition of the national economy* has also been opened in the park, and there is a *Children's Railway* with three stations.

Riga Zoo is to the right of the park entrance. It was founded in 1912 and has about 3,000 animals.

The Warriors' Cemetery in Mezaparks was laid out in 1923 and attractively decorated with fountains, sculptured groups, and landscaping.

Nearby is *Rainis's Cemetery*, where a birch avenue leads to the grave of the Latvian poet. The monument of polished red granite was designed by K. Zemdega. War victims and prominent people from the realms of art, literature, and politics are buried here.

The oldest park in Riga is the *Viestura Garden* at the far end of Aneskla Street. It was laid out in 1721 by order of Peter the Great. An elm that he planted still stands here, with a memorial stone beside it. Also in the garden is *Alexander's Triumphal Gate*, erected in 1818 by the merchants of Riga to commemorate the victory over Napoleon. Until 1923 the garden was called the Tsar's Garden.

Vermanes Park, in the centre of Riga, bounded by Kirov, Markela, Krisjanis Barona, and Terbatas streets. It was founded in 1816–17.

Arkadijas Park, in the Pardaugavas district. This park opened at the end of the 19th century.

University Botanical Garden, Kaudavas Street 2. The garden dates from 1922 and has a rich collection of tropical and subtropical plants.

Hippodrome Racecourse, Tomsona Street 30 and Grotonas Street 6

Yacht Club, Mezaparks, Bernudarza Street 19

Latvia (Intourist) Hotel and Restaurant, Kirov Street 55; tel. 21 2503. Intourist office, tel. 21 2889.

Riga Hotel and Aspazijas Restaurant, Boulevard 2; tel. 21 2503 This new hotel across the river is usually reserved for tourist groups.

Tourist Hotel and Restaurant

Daugava Hotel and Restaurant, Kugu Street 24; *tel.* 61 2112

Metropols Hotel, Restaurant, Cafe. Aspazijas Boulevard 16; tel. 21 6184

Astorija Restaurant, Audeju Street 16, on the top floor of the department store

Rostock Restaurant, Terbatas Stucka Street

Tallinn Restaurant, Gorky Street 27/29

Staburags Restaurant, Suvorov Street 55

Maskava Restaurant, Kirov Street 53

Kaukazs Restaurant, Merkela Street 8. This restaurant serves Caucasian cuisine.

Lira Restaurant, Dzirnavu Street 45/47

Pribaltika Restaurant, Merkela Street 13

Daugava Restaurant, Terbatas Street 7, but the entrance is from Dzirnavu Street

Baltija Restaurant, Melnsila Street 22

Cosmos Restaurant, Vienbas Allee 51, on the other side of river Dvina

Sports Restaurant, in Mezaparks, Kokneses Prospect 35

Fish Restaurant, Suvorov Street 55

Shashlik Bar, Suvorov Street 46

Astoria Café, Valnu Street 18

Confectioner's and Cafe, Kirov Street 55

Flora Café Lenin Street 35

Luna Café, Valnu Street 9

Daugava Café, Lenin Street 25

Nica Café, Lenin Street 70

Peter Tornis Café, Beside St. Peter's Church

Vidzeme Café, Lenin Street 83

Sigulda Café, Gorky Street 25

Pancake Kitchen, Blaumana Street 8

Latvian Society for Cultural Relations with For-eign Countries, Leona Paegles Street 2; tel. 21 607

GPO, Lenin Street 21

Central Telegraph Office, Lenin Street 33

Bank, Gorky Street 2a

Dzintarkrasts ("Amber") Foreign Currency Shop, Lenin Street 39. Open 9–6; closed Sun.

Souvenir Foreign Currency Shop, Valnu Street, next to the Riga Canal

Sakta, Lenin Street 32. Sakta has national arts and crafts and souvenirs of amber, leather, and wood. Open 10–7; closed Sun.

Maksla Art Salons, Lenin Street 52 and 84. Open 10–7; closed Sat. and Sun.

Dailrade, I. Sudmalya Street 20. Open 10–7; closed Sat. and Sun.

Souvenirs and Jewellery, Lenin Street 40

Paintings and Sculptures, Padomju Boule-vard 20

Jewellery, Lenin Street 15 and Suvorov Street 11

Photographic Equipment, Suvorov Street

Photo Processing, Kirov Street 69 and 77

Central Bookshop, Teatra Street 11

Foreign Books, Basteja Boulevard 24

Central Market, Negu Street 7

Central Department Store, Audeju Street 16

Taxi Ranks, by the railway station, Vermanes Park, Agenskalne Market, and at the crossing of Lenin and Matīsa streets

*   *   *

Intourist organises excursions southwest from Riga to the centres of the Jurmala seaside resort region and inland to Salaspils, Ogre, Bauska (with Rundale Palace not too far away), Ligatne and Gauja Park, Sigulda, and Cesis. Trips can be made by hydrofoil on the sea and on the river Daugava. Longer day trips follow the coastline north of Riga for 100 km (62 miles), stopping at Saulkrasti and Ainazhi.

Riga has been a famous seaside resort for many years. Sand dunes topped with pine trees stretch for over 16 km (10 miles) along the coast of Riga Bay from Lielupe to Kemeri and they are paralleled by a wide sandy beach. The climate is temperate and the sea averages 18 or 20°C (64 to 68°F) during the summer. The place has been used for summer holidays since the end of the 18th century but it was only at the end of the 19th century that it acquired its real popularity as a resort. As if to emphasize how far away the holiday makers were from their city of Riga, the first settlements were given names such as Australia, America, and even Edinburgh.

Since 1939 the area has been administered as a single resort region known as Jurmala, but as it in fact consists of a series of coastal villages, they are listed here in turn as they lie westward from Riga. Jurmala can be reached from Riga by electric train, bus, river-bus, or taxi.

Lielupe

Lielupe is 15 km (9 miles) from Riga, at the mouth of the river Lielupe. Nearby is *High Dune,* the highest point along this part of the coast with a wide view over the sea. The Daugava Yacht Club is on the river Lielupe.

Bulduri (Bilderlingshof)

19 km (12 miles) from Riga is Bulduri. The new *railway station building* is the best in Jurmala. *Bulduri Horticultural College* (founded in 1911) on Viestura Street has many lime trees on its 83-hectare (207-acre) grounds.

Intourist Hotel and Jurmala Restaurant, Buld-uru Street 52

Dzintari and Majori (Edinburgh and Majorenhof)

22 km (14 miles) from Riga are Dzintari and Ma-jori, Jurmala's cultural and social centres.

In 1925 the only building on the Edinburgh beach was the *Pavilion,* which provided supper with good musical accompaniment. Now there is a *concert hall* for 700 with a garden and an *open-air theatre* seating 3,000, right beside the shore at Turaidas Street 1.

Juras Perle Restaurant, on the beach front at Jurmala. This is the best restaurant in the region.

Dzintars Restaurant (Formerly Lido), Turaidas Street 6/8

The following are items of interest in Majori:

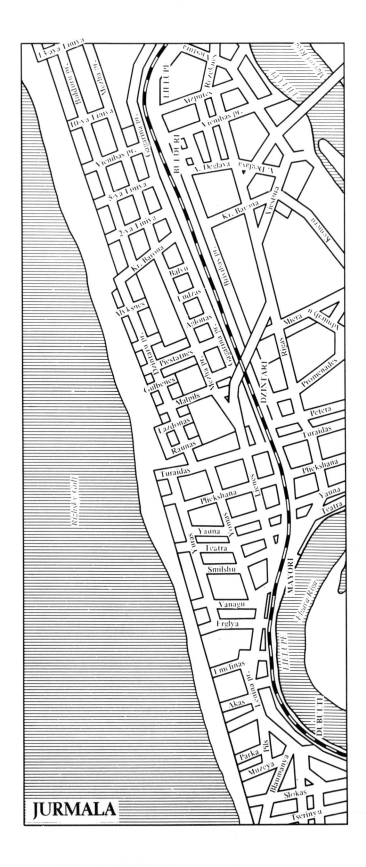

JURMALA

Roman Catholic Church, Pilsonu Street 32. This is a wooden church where services are held in Latvian and Polish.

Russian Orthodox Church

History Museum, Jomas Street 43. This is a branch of the Jurmala History and Art Museum.

Dzintaris Exhibition Hall, Turaidas Street 11

Janis Rainis's Cottage, Alexandra Street 7. Here is a small museum dedicated to the Latvian poet (1865–1929).

Majori Hotel and Restaurant, Jomas Street 29. This is one of Jurmala's smallest buildings.

Jurmala Restaurant is one of the best eating places on the coast.

There is a statue of Lacplesis in Majori. Lacplesis the Bear-Slayer is a legendary giant-hero of Latvia. He is reputed to have been able to break a bear's jaws with his fist and even to harness bears to the plough. His great strength was sometimes a hindrance, because in spite of his good intentions to be of service to his people and his country, he frequently broke the man-made tools he had been given to use. The giant met his match in a terrible duel with a three-headed ogre, as fierce a fight as any described in Beowulf. While the struggle was on, the ogre's mother travelled the seven seas to learn from the inhabitants of the underworld just where Lacplesis's weakness lay. The ogre had already lost two of his heads when he was told to strike off Lacplesis's ears. The writhing pair fell into the river Daugava and were carried out to sea.

Dubulti (Dubbeln)

Dubulti, 28 km (17 miles) from Riga, is the oldest settlement near the sea in this area. A 4-km (2-mile) birch avenue leads to Jaundubulti.

Lutheran Church, Muzeia Street 13. Built in 1909 in art nouveau style, this church now houses the Jurmala History and Art Museum. Open 12–5; closed Tues.

Jaundubulti

Jaundubulti is famous for its natural parkland and its pine groves on the dunes.

Pumpuri, Melluzi, Asari (formerly Assern), and Vaivari are quiet seaside places with an abundance of locally grown fruit and vegetables.

Kemeri (formerly Kemmern)

40 km (25 miles) from Riga, Kemeri is the largest and best-organised unit of the Baltic resort region. The curative qualities of the local mineral water and mud have been known since the end of the 18th century. Early in the 19th century a forester by the name of Ans Kemer built some wooden huts with primitive baths here. Now 20,000 patients a year can be accommodated, but still the place bears its founder's name.

Sanatorium 1 is called the White Palace. It is a building in classical style with Corinthian columns. There is another former spa building that was opened in 1909.

Lutheran and Orthodox Church

In the Warriors' Cemetery lie those who fell during both world wars.

Hotel, Tukuma Street 19. This hotel was built in 1936 by Laube.

Restaurant, Tukuma Street 23

Salaspils

18 m (11 miles) east of Riga is Salaspils, first mentioned in 1186. During the German occupation a concentration camp was set up in the nearby woods. More than 100,000 people were murdered here—Czech, Polish, Austrian, Dutch, Belgian, and French as well as Soviet citizens. Some 47,000 were prisoners of war, and of the civilian victims, most of whom were Jewish, 7,000 were children. The gallows stood in a glade surrounded by pine trees planted by the camp inmates themselves. A sculptural memorial ensemble has now been built here and an annual commemoration day is organised.

Also in Salaspils is the Physics Institute and the atomic reactor of the Latvian Academy of Sciences. One of the attractions of the place is the Botanical Garden, which covers 130 hectares (325 acres).

Ogre

Ogre is a health resort 57 m (187 ft) above sea level and 38 km (24 miles) inland from Riga on the river Ogre, a tributary of the Daugava. The river was once called the Vogene, or Voga. There is a legend telling how it got its present name:

There once was a village called Maziye Staldaty where Latvian serfs lived, among them a young girl called Martha. She was as quick as she was beautiful, and the landlord wanted to make her his housemaid. In horror Martha ran away to the village of Aluksne where she took refuge in the pastor's house. Pastor Gluke brought her up, educated her and brought her out in the local society. After the Northern War (1700–21) began, she found herself at the Emperor's Court and became the wife of Peter the Great, the Empress Catherine I. But Martha longed for her native village and wanted to find it. She remembered there was a river nearby which was abundant with eels (in Russia "ugri"). In search of such a river the royal cooks reached Maziye Staldaty and the local people who heard the word "ugri" from them called their place Ogre to commemorate Catherine I.

At the confluence with the Daugava River the Ogre divides in two, forming an island. To the north of the station there is a range of pine-covered hills called Vilkukalny (Wolves' Hills), because allegedly when the first summer cottages were under construction, the builders heard wolves howling. Another range of hills is called Ziliyekalny ("Blue Hills"), perhaps because of the blue flowers that grow here. Some say they seem blue due to the smoke of the devil's own pipe. In the vicinity are deposits of gypsum, tufa, and dolomite. In the 9th century at the confluence of the Ogre and the Daugava, on Konteskali Hill, there stood an ancient castle. Another castle measuring 60 m by 25 m (66 yds by 27 yds) stood on Ziliyekalny; the traces of an ancient settlement with ramparts and fortifications can be seen.

In the 12th to 16th centuries the territory of present-day Ogre belonged to the archbishop of Riga. In the course of the Livonian Wars that took place all through the 13th to 16th centuries the area was ransacked and badly damaged. Later Ogre changed hands between Poland and Sweden.

In the middle of the 19th century on the site of present-day Ogre there was a group of villages, and after Riga was connected by rail with Daugavpils in 1861, Ogre became a popular country resort and amusement ground. The authorities of the Riga-Daugavpils railway rented forestland in Ogre and built pavilions and a restaurant here. They laid out paths and started to organise regular amusement trips to Ogre. In 1875 the townspeople began building summer cottages for themselves here, and by 1914 there were more than 300 of them. Thus Ogre turned into a country retreat for the cream of society.

Modern Ogre is one of the major centres of Latvia, an important railroad junction, and a popular health resort. There are three sanatoria here as well as the largest knitted-goods factory in the Baltic countries. It lies on either bank of the river Ogre. The left bank is built up with summer cottages and is called Parogre, and the area that stretches 2 km (1 mile) from the railroad station in the direction of Riga is called Yaunogre.

Tourists enjoy the picturesque landscapes, the river bathing, and the sports grounds here. Ogre differs from other Latvian resorts by its dry climate and numerous sunny days. The place is never foggy and is recommended for cardiac patients.

War Memorial, by the road to Taurkalne. The monument here marks the fraternal grave of 196 Soviet soldiers.

Pie Zelta Liepas Café

Bauska (Rundale Palace)

Bauska is an agricultural centre 50 km (31 miles) from Riga at the confluence of two rivers, the Memele and the Mushe, which together form the Liyelupe. On the main road it stands at the 376/411 km mark.

The place was founded in 1443 by the Livonian Knights, to whom the area belonged at that time. From 1561 to 1795 it was part of the duchy of Courland (Kurland or Kurzeme) under the suzerainty of the king of Poland. Most memorable of the dukes must be Duke James of Courland, godson of James I of England, who enjoyed his title for forty years (1642–82). He became an active participant in the civil wars in England. He lent 6 warships, quantities of grain, gunpowder, and arms that in 1649 were valued at a total of £74,584, but this was never repaid. His income came partly from his ambitious colonial policies. While the strong maritime powers of England, Holland, Spain, and France ruled the waves, the duke's own ships carried the flag of Courland across the oceans of the world, trading, pearl fishing, acquiring colonies in Africa and America, and even joining in the lucrative slave trade. He held the island of Tobago, and when threatened by the Dutch he obtained protection from Charles II of England on the condition that Courland and England should share the monopoly of "any Merchandise or products of the said Island." He purchased the Island of St. Andrew in the mouth of the river Gambia and built Ft. James on it, garrisoned by soldiers from Courland, but the English took it from him in 1660. Duke James protested in London, but, as the King of Sweden commented, he was "too poor for a king, too rich for a duke." He did, however, do his best to continue trading until he died at the age of 72.

Bauska was given the privileges of a town in 1609. The present-day Riga-Panevezys-Vilnius highway that crosses Bauska used to be an important trade and military route. This small town witnessed many historical events during the Northern War: the Polish troops retreated here in 1702 and the Russians passed through it on their way to Riga in 1709 after the battle in Poltava. Peter the Great visited Bauska in 1710. After 1795, in connection with the third partition of Poland, Bauska passed to Russia along with the surrounding territory. In 1812 the town was taken by Napoleon's Marshal McDonald.

The local *castle* was last to be built by the Livonian Knights; the oldest part dates from 1443–56 and the other half from the 16th century. The imposing towers, with walls 4 m (13 ft) thick, are made of small blocks of stone, like cobblestones. The castle is now under reconstruction and is to be a museum.

For a long time Bauska preserved the features of a mediaeval town, and there are still many *old houses* with red-tiled roofs. The centre could well be the set for a musical. The houses are of all kinds: —wooden, plastered, shuttered, half-timbered, of decorative brick, with art nouveau woodwork, and with log cabin walls below and half-timbered upper storeys. There is a woollen mill and a food-processing plant in the town. Uzvaras Street is the main street.

Lutheran Church of the Holy Spirit, at the end of Andrei Upisa Street. It was built in 1591–94, the tower being added in 1614 and the spire and cock weather vane in 1623. Inside the church are tombstones of the 16th to 18th centuries, and the bishop's throne is 17th or 18th century. The roccoco organ was installed in the 18th century and the painting of the crucifixion was done by Julius Doering (1818–98) in 1860.

St. George's Russian Orthodox Church was built of red brick by Bauman for a congregation of 200 in 1879–81.

Roman Catholic Church, at the end of Andrei Upisa Street

Museum, Padomju Street 6. Open 10–6; closed Mon.

Lenin Statue. A seated figure of the leader was executed in granite.

Hotel, by the bus station on the way out of town toward Vilnius

Pilskalns Restaurant, on the right on the way out of town toward Rundale Palace (see below)

GPO, by the bus station on the way out of town toward Vilnius

Sights in the vicinity of Bauska include:

Kauminosky Palace, 5 km (3 miles) away

Pludonis's House-Museum, 7 km (4 miles) from Bauska. V. Pludonis was a poet.

Victims of Fascism Monument, 9 km (6 miles) away

Mezhotnensky Palace and Kurgan, 11 and 12 km (7 miles) away

Rundale Palace is at Jelgava, 7.3 km (5 miles) from Bauska (77 km/48 miles altogether from Riga). Open 11–6; closed Mon. and Tues. The road there is the A-217. It crosses the river Musa and passes a *statue of Lenin,* and then a left turn is signposted RUNDALIS PILS 1.2 KM.

The Latvian word "Rundale" derives from the German "Ruhetal," "Valley of Rest." The palace was built by Bartholomeo Francesco Rastrelli, the descendant of a famous family of Florentine artists, who was born in Paris in 1700. His father had been invited to work at the court of the Russian tsar, and he taught Francesco himself.

One of the German favourites of Empress Anna Ioanovna was the unpopular Duke Iohann Biron of Courland. The period during which he lorded over the imperial court in St. Petersburg, tyrannizing and exploiting his Russian subordinates, has gone down in Russian history as a time of terror. When the empress died in 1740, he even enjoyed the regency for a short while. Biron ordered Rastrelli to build a palace in Rundale on the ruins of a 15th-century castle. The first stone was laid by Rastrelli in May 1736, and then builders came from St. Petersburg and Riga. All in all, 1,500 workers were engaged, and by the end of 1737 the outside of the palace was completed. Rastrelli kept to the western European tradition in his grouping of the rooms. The first floor was reserved for administration and for the household, and Biron's residence was on the second floor. Guest rooms were in the right wing and reception rooms in the left. By this time Duke Biron had become the duke of Courland, as the local area was called, and he ordered Rastrelli to build one more palace—in nearby Mittau (now Jelgava), so Rastrelli was occupied with the construction of two palaces at once.

When Anna Ioanovna died, Biron was exiled and Rastrelli stopped work; he resumed it only in 1764, when the duke returned. Work on the Rundale palace proceeded with a number of foreigners, including other Italians, to help with the decoration. The sculptor Johann Michael Graff from Berlin was chiefly responsible for the stucco ornamentation. The ironwork of the entrance gates bears Biron's initials—E.J., for Ernst-Johann.

Biron resided in the palace with his courtiers until his death in 1772; his successors, however, did not like it, and the palace was left empty for a long time. In 1795 Catherine II presented it to her favourite, Count Zubov, and it flourished until the war of 1812, when it was partially destroyed. After the war it fell into decay. In 1915–17 it suffered from the Germans and in 1918 from the White Guards under Colonel Bermonte.

In 1972 restoration work began on the palace and is still in progress. Part of it now houses the Fine Arts Museum. The main building is rectangular, with two wings enclosing the principal cobbled courtyard. It is painted yellow and white while the service buildings, including the stables and coach houses at the entrance, are red and white. House martins build their mud nests under every available cornice. As regards decorative style, the outside is most like Rastrelli's Vorontsov Palace, built in St. Petersburg in 1750. The strength and weight of the exterior hides the lightness and dynamic splendour of the interior, the late baroque and roccoco styles in complete harmony. Tourists are shown its finely painted and sculptured halls, the Golden, Marble, White, and Pink halls among them. There are 140 rooms in the palace altogether. The park that surrounds it is also a masterpiece.

Rundale Cafe

Sigulda Population—7,000
German: Segewold

On the way to Sigulda is a good restaurant, the *Senite* ("Mushroom") Restaurant.

Sigulda is situated 52 km (32 miles) northeast of Riga on the road to Pskov and Novgorod. Russian soldiers marched along here on their way home from Paris at the end of the Napoleonic War, and the area around Sigulda is renowned for its beautiful scenery, which has led it to be known as Livlandische Schweiz ("Livonian Switzerland").

Sigulda was founded in 1207, when the area around the town was divided between the Teutonic Order (also known as the Brethren of the Cross) and the archbishop of Riga. The land on the left bank of the river Gauja went to the archbishop of Riga and that on the right to the Teutonic Knights. Stone castles were built on both banks of the river, the remains of which can be seen today.

However, the area around Sigulda passed through many hands, both before and after the foundation of the town. Recent archeological excavations have revealed weapons and other articles dating from the beginning of the second millennium B.C., when the area was inhabited by Finn and Ugor tribes.

In the 16th century Sigulda was captured in turn by the Russian, Polish, and Swedish armies. After the Northern War (1700–1721) Sigulda and the surrounding country came under Russian power. Only a third of the population remained after the war and the ensuing plague, but the town soon grew as people moved here from other parts of Latvia. After the Russian revolution of 1917 Soviet power was established here until 1920, when Latvia became an independent country.

There are the ruins of a number of castles in Sigulda. They are mostly at the tops of hills, but

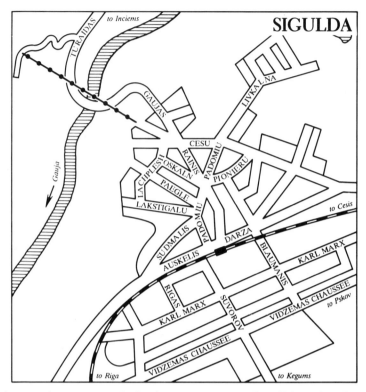

funicular railways and a suspension bridge has made them more easily accessible. At the end of Livkalna Street are the *Satezel Ruins* of the ancient town that stood here long before the foundation of Sigulda. A castle was built here later. Nearby is *Peter's Cave*, so named because a baby named Peter was born here during the Northern War.

The path from here to the top of the hill, known as Artists' Mountains, gives a good view of Sigulda and the river Gauja. The path leads on to a *cemetery* with a *monument* to those killed during the 1905 revolution.

The white 18th-century *Lutheran church* is open for services, and in front of it is a pond with swans.

Steps lead down to the ruins of *Sigulda Castle*, which was built by the Teutonic Order in 1207– 26. It was destroyed on several occasions and was not restored after the Northern War. Over the gate is the inscription "Omne Trinum Perfectum," and in the inner courtyard is a platform used for song and dance festivals. In the outer courtyard is the *"new" castle*, which was built in 1878–81 (although the gates are inscribed 1867). This once belonged to Prince Kropotkin, but it is now a sanatorium. In front of the sanatorium is a *monument* to the Latvian linguist Atis Kronvald (1837–75).

At the end of Turaida Street on the other side of the river is the Gutman Ala (Cave of Gutman). The cave is about 14 m (46 ft) deep, 9 m (30 ft) in height, and 18.8 m (21 yds) long, making it the largest in the Soviet Union. There are some in-

scriptions on the wall dating from the 16th century. The cave is said to be named after a man named Gutman who lived here and healed sick people with water from a spring inside the cave. Water from the spring also is reputed to bring back lost love. There is a tradition that a girl unsure of her lover's feelings drinks the water. According to another legend, a girl known as Turaida's Rose—because of her remarkable beauty—was killed in the cave by a Polish nobleman who had sent her a letter in the name of her fiancé. When Turaida's Rose saw that she had been tricked, she still refused to marry the nobleman and told him that the scarf she was wearing was a magic scarf that would protect her from any attack. She challenged the nobleman to strike her with his sword and was thus killed. Her grave is at the top of the hill near the cave and dates back to 1600–1620. 263 steps lead up the hill to where an old lime tree stands and a marble plaque on the tree reads: HERE LIES TURAIDA'S ROSE. The attractive wooden Lutheran church that stands nearby, known as *Turaida's Baznica*, was built in 1750. There is now a museum inside the church, with some paintings and carved wooden pews. Open 10– 5; closed Tues.

On the same hill are the remains of *Turai (Treyden) Castle*, which was built in 1214 for the Archbishop of Riga. It later belonged to Baron Stael von Holstein. The castle was destroyed by a fire in 1776 and only the main tower remains. A model of the original castle is on display in the local museum. The main tower has been restored to its original height of 35 m (115 ft), and the walls are 3 m (10 ft) thick. It is possible to climb up to the top. The grounds of the castle are now the site of archeological excavations.

Local Museum, in a red-brick building near the ruins of Turai Castle. Open 10–5.

The path down the hill from the church leads to the ruins of the *Castle of Krimuld*, which was built in 1255–73 and was used as a residence for foreign dignitaries. It was destroyed at the beginning of the 17th century. Nearby is a children's tuberculosis sanatorium housed in the former von Liven estate, which later served as a Red Cross hospital. The church, stables, and coach house of the estate still remain.

Sigulda Restaurant, in the local department store, opposite the church

Turaida Café

Gauja National Park

The Gauja River is fast flowing and winds its way through a deep valley. It has so many convolutions that although it is only 90 km (56 miles) as the crow flies from its source to its mouth, it is fully 461 km (286 miles) long. Gauja National Park was organised in 1973. It covers 90,000 hectares (225,000 acres), and in it stands Sejas Oak, estimated to be between 600 and 800 years old. In general it is a popular holiday place, with its beautiful scenery and the remains of castles of the 13th and 14th centuries.

Ligatne

This small town stands on the river of the same name, a tributary of the left side of the Gauja, a little further upstream than Sigulda. It lies within the bounds of Gauja National Park and is known throughout Latvia for its paper mill. Paper was first produced here in the 18th century. A mill was built in 1815–16, and after its reconstruction in 1858 it is still in excellent working order and produces top-quality writing paper.

Ligatne Research Park is part of the national park, and work is carried out with the local flora and fauna. There is a small collection of tame wild animals, and at Lieltimani are facilities for horseback riding.

Saulkrasty

This village stands right on the edge of the Gulf of Riga on the rivers Peterupe and Kisupe. The sea bathing is very good and there are many summer holiday camps for children here.

Church, on the right side of the road. This church is open for services.

Varava Restaurant, on the main road

Shashlik Bar, by the road

Cafeteria, on the right of the road

Post Office, by the main road

Ainazi Population—1,200
(Ainazhi)
The name "Ainazi" means "Wet Place." The remains of a large port can be seen; it used to be

second only to Riga in size. Its pride was the Navigation School, founded in 1864 by Krisjan Valdemars, an official of the Imperial Society for the Promotion of the Russian Merchant Fleet. The school was closed in 1915, but during the 50 years of its existence over 1,000 merchant sea captains graduated here. Often these captains would decide to retire here, and some of their impressive wooden houses are still to be seen.

Also here is the border railway station between Estonia and Latvia. Near the road is a partly ruined customs house and some stone farm buildings dating from the turn of the century. Ainazi was proclaimed a town in 1926.

St. Arseni's Church, at the turn to Valmiere. This Orthodox church built in 1894–95 is now only a museum. The granite-and-brick priest's house behind it serves as the local savings bank.

Navigation School Museum, Namu Parvalde Street, behind No. 21a, in the former school building. Open 10–4; closed Mon. and Tues.

World War II Memorial, beside the church. The memorial is made of granite and was built in 1944.

Eating House, by the main road

Shopping Centre, to the right of the road

RITSA, LAKE

See Sukhumi Environs, p. 512.

ROSTOV-ON-DON Population—1,020,000

The story of this area really begins with that of Tanais, nearer the mouth of the Don (see below). Peter the Great used the river as a border with the lands held by the Turks, and the fortress of St. Anne was founded in 1730 beside the Don to strengthen the Russian position. Traders were among the new settlers and the place was called Bogaty Kolodez ("Rich Spring").

Rostov-on-Don was established in 1749 by the order of Elizaveta Petrovna and was then known as Temernik, from the name of the little tributary of the Don on which it stood. It was an important place for trading in the Sea of Azov and in the Black and Mediterranean seas, and so a customs house was established; that year counts as the date of the foundation of Rostov. The fortress of St. Anne was declared strategically worthless in 1761, but the Empress Elizaveta ordered the construction of a new fortress, to be named after St. Dmitri Rostovsky, metropolitan bishop of Rostov the Great, who had died in 1709. Rostov the Great, also known as Rostov Yaroslavsky, is an ancient Russian town northeast of Moscow. The young port on the Don took its name from that of the fortress.

In 1779 more than 12,000 Armenians, as well as many Greeks, were transferred here from the Crimea after the Russo-Turkish War of 1768–74, the Russian idea being to diminish the profits accruing to the Crimean khan, and it was they who founded the independent township of Nakhichevan to the east of the fortress. The name (meaning "First Hut") was taken from that of the ancient Armenian capital on the Araks ruined by the Tatars

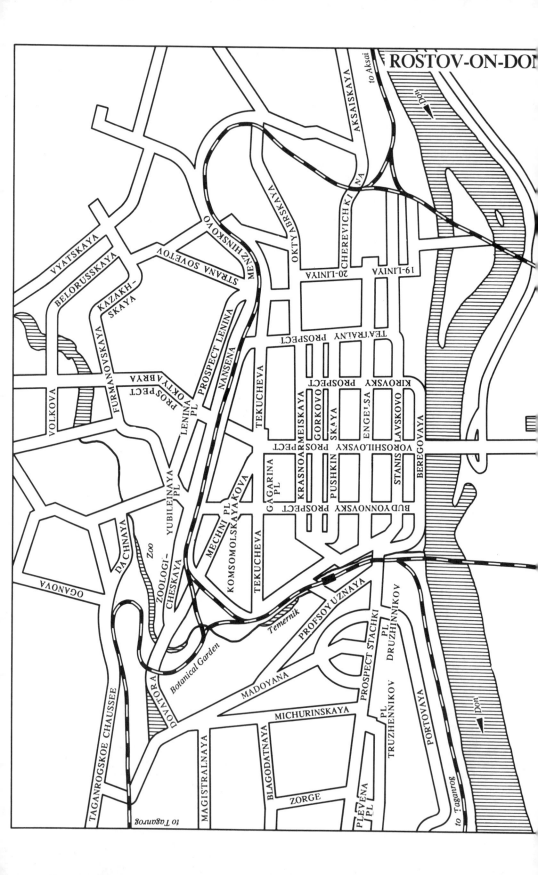

ROSTOV-ON-DON

in the 13th century. By imperial decree Nakhichevan was granted independence, freedom from certain taxes, and other privileges, and there was even a border line between it and Rostov, running for a kilometre near today's Theatre Square. Nakhichevan was absorbed by the growing Rostov in 1928.

Important foreign trade began to develop in Rostov, and the settlement, now a large economic centre, was declared a town in 1797. Among others, Sidney, James and Co., an English company, was established here in 1778. Rostov became the regional centre in 1806 and was given its new coat of arms—azure a fortress with captured weapons above. When Alexander I approved the town plans in 1811, (na-Donu), or "on-Don," was added to the name to distinguish it from Rostov the Great. When the garrison was transferred in 1835, the second fortress fell into disuse and later was demolished.

At this point Rostov-on-Don became a centre of the grain trade, and this was when its population really began to grow. There had been 1,700 inhabitants at the beginning of the 19th century, by the 1850s there were more than 10,000, and by 1914 there were 258,000. In 1836 the customs offices, which had been closed at the end of the 18th century, were reopened, the town became an international port, second only in importance in the south to Odessa, and the volume of freight was the third greatest in Russia. Much of it was handled by the Greek firm Ralli and the English firm William Ems. Regular navigational services opened along the Don in the 1840s with the first steamer, the *Donets*, built in England. Goods destined for shipment to Turkey, Greece, Italy, and even England sailed down the Don, and foreign merchants encouraged Rostov's growth. A French firm laid down the municipal water mains and a Belgian dredging company saw to the improvement of the waterways.

Rostov expanded rapidly as the region's industrial and agricultural potential began to develop, overtaking the Urals in the output of both coal and metal. The railway link with Moscow was completed in 1871 and that with Vladikavkaz in 1875, and at the turn of the century the Societe Anonyme Belge built the first tramway between Rostov and Nakhichevan. Planning was inadequate, however. Rostov looked shabby beside the elegance of Nakhichevan and the city's standard of hygiene failed to rise with its rapid growth. At the turn of the century Rostov took third place (after Calcutta and Shanghai) for the number of local deaths from cholera, and it had the highest crime rate in Russia. The town itself reflected the tendency. Gradually more of the municipal budget was spent on urban improvement, and Rostov was rich, but this did not prevent it from running into serious debt in 1913.

Rostov played its part in Russian revolutionary history; 30,000 workers went on strike in 1902. During the civil war it was one of the White Generals' strongholds, and the Germans occupied the city for some time in 1918. They also held it twice during the Second World War.

In Russian the city is often called the "Gate to the Caucasus" and it is the unofficial capital of the Don area. It stands at the meeting place of roads running from the Ukraine, the Volga region, Siberia, and the northern Caucasus and Transcaucasia. It is 46 km (29 miles) from where the river Don flows into the Sea of Azov, and it spreads for more than 25 km (16 miles) along the high right bank of the river. Since the completion of the Volga-Don Canal its port has grown in economic importance, for it is now connected with five seas. The canal links the Don with the Volga near Volgograd (formerly Stalingrad) and is 100 km (62 miles) long. The first attempt at such a canal was made by the Turks in 1569, and from the time of Peter the Great onward there were repeated plans to build it; it was finally constructed between 1947 and 1952.

Today Rostov is the administrative and economic centre of a region of 100,000 sq km (38,600 sq miles), equal to the combined territories of Belgium, Holland, and Denmark, and is one of the granaries of Russia. There are 20 project organisations here, making plans for factories in the Caucasus and other parts of Russia. The university was founded in 1869 in Warsaw and was transferred to Rostov in 1915. There are now six faculties, and the main building is at Engels Street 105 with a statue of Lomonosov by Aleschenko in the garden in front of it. Nearby is the modern building of the Solnyshko Department Store. Besides the university there are many institutes, including that of agricultural machinery; machinery of this sort has been produced here in Rostov since 1898 and this institute has 10,000 students. Rostov's main industrial development dates from 1846; it now has tobacco, food, footwear, textile, aircraft, and shipbuilding industries. The wine-making factories offer a selection of table wines. One of the Soviet Union's most famous is a local sparkling red wine; often called red champagne here, its real name is Tsimlyanskoye Igristoye. One of the largest Soviet factories to produce agricultural machinery, the Rostselmash factory, was built in 1930 and produced its first combine harvesters in 1931. Rostov now produces 86 percent of Russia's combines and 70 percent of her cultivators and seeding machines. One of the newest colleges is a factory-institute where students who work at Rostselmash attend lectures. Rostov's 25 libraries contain more than 2,000,000 books.

A number of Soviet writers have lived and worked here, among them Alexander Fadeyev and Vera Panova. The author of "And Quiet Flows the Don," Mikhail Sholokhov, certainly lived beside the river, but his village of Veshenskaya is a long way upstream and about 200 km (125 miles) from Rostov.

Engels Street (formerly Bolshaya Sadovaya Street) begins at Temernitsky Bridge, near the railway station. It is the main street and most of the buildings of interest are to be found along its 3-km (2-mile) length. The 11-storey block of flats at the beginning of the street was completed in 1958. Many of the large prerevolutionary buildings also were built as flats, not always in the best of taste. One merchant-landlord, Cherikov, argued with his architect about the decoration of a 6-storey block. He wanted two large columns on the facade, but the architect said that they would spoil the proportions of the Renaissance-style house. Cherikov replied, "Who is paying you, the Renaissance or me?" The columns were put up. The building at the corner of Semashko Prospect was designed by Pomerantsev in 1899. It was damaged in both world wars but was restored twice and is still used as an administrative building. The crossing of Engels Street and Budyonnovsky Prospect is known as the architectural entrance to the town because it has one of the most impressive architectural ensembles of Rostov. Nearby is *Gorky Park*, behind which can be seen the western facade of the *Town Hall* (1896–99).

Engels Street runs next to Dom Sovetov Square. The *House of Soviets* was built between 1929 and 1941. It was partly burned down during the war, but it has been reconstructed. In the square is a fountain, dating from 1917, with two stone lions by the sculptor Vaide. Nearby stands the huge building of the *bank* (1910).

Engels Street ends in Teatralnaya Square, which was once at the edge of the town and had a sign saying BORDER, meaning the border with the Armenian town of Nakhichevan. Now it is the biggest square in Rostov and the place where sports parades and public festivals are held. In the 1930s some houses, and also *Gorky Theatre* (1930–35), built by the architects Schuko and Gelfreich, were designed in the constructivist style much in favour immediately after the revolution, when all forms deriving from the past were cast aside. This style was soon to be officially condemned and these buildings are among the last of their kind. Gorky Theatre is unusual in that it has two halls in one building; the main auditorium seats 1,200 and the smaller concert hall seats 550. The building is situated on a hill, and its white forehead, which can be seen for miles around, forms part of the silhouette of the city. It was damaged during World War II and reconstructed in 1963.

Further east begins the part of Rostov originally known as Nakhichevan. The continuation of Engels Street is called Pervaya Sovietskaya Street. It ends in Karl Marx Street, where a *monument* to the philosopher was unveiled in 1935. There used to be a monument here to Catherine II, put up by grateful Armenians in commemoration of her decree that encouraged them to settle here, but it was subsequently removed. In *Frunze Garden*, opposite a *war memorial* dedicated to all those who perished in World War II, there is an *eternal flame*. Running parallel to the full length of the north side of Engels Street is Pushkin Street. The promenade on the river embankment was built in 1949; steps

lead down to it from Budyonnovsky Prospect. Across the river are an attractive woods and one of the best river beaches in the south of Russia.

New blocks of flats and whole new residential areas are springing up throughout the town and around it. Among other impressive new buildings is the *Rostselmash Palace of Culture* (Selmashevsky Prospect 3), built in 1961. There is a theatre of opera and ballet here for the use of amateur groups.

Cathedral of the Nativity of the Virgin, Stanislavsky Street 58. The cathedral is open for services.

Synagogue, Gazetnyi Pereulok

Also in Rostov are churches of the Old Believers and the Baptists, and six other Russian Orthodox churches.

Local History Museum, Engels Street 79. Open 10–5; closed Mon. The stone idols worshipped by nomads in the 11th and 12th centuries are of interest. Upstairs are doors carved in Scythian style, and among the treasures is a beautiful diadem decorated with trees and tiny leaves. The *Rostov Planetarium* is located in the same building.

Fine Art Museum, Pushkin Street 115. Open 10–5.30; closed Tues. Here are paintings by Repin and other Russian and Soviet realists. The building used to be a lawyer's private house.

Children's Art Gallery, Chekhov Street 60. Open 10–6; closed Tues.

Nalbandyan Memorial Complex and Museum of the History and Culture of the Don Armenians, in Nakhichevan. The cathedral (1783–92) was once the main building of the Armenian Surb-Khach Monastery. It was designed by Starov in classical style. The monastery was the cultural centre of the whole of Rostov, not only Nakhichevan, and the town's first printing press was set up here. Open 10–5:30; closed Mon. In front of the cathedral are the *graves* of Rafael Patkanyan (also known as Gamar-Katipa) (1830–92), a classical Armenian writer, and the Socialist poet Mikael Nalbandyan (1829–66), who was born in Nakhichevan. Both tombs are by Andreas Ter-Marukyan, from Paris, and were built with donations collected in 1901–2. There are also two *busts*, of Patkanyan on the right and Nalbandyan on the left.

Revolution and Labour Museum, Gusev Street 2

International Friendship Museum, in the western residential neighbourhood

People's Friendship House, Engels Street 60

The following are among the considerable number of monuments and busts in the city.

Stepan Razin Monument, on the river embankment. The monument is by Sergei Konenkov.

Pushkin Statue, at the crossing of Pushkin and Karl Marx streets. The 4-m (13-ft) statue by Schultz was unveiled in 1959.

Karl Marx Monument, Marx Square. This was sculpted by M. Altschuller in 1959.

Monument to the Rostov Strikers of 1902, Stachki Prospect. In 1902 local workers struck for

3 weeks and some of them were killed. The monument by A. Sknarin was unveiled in 1975.

Gorky's Statue, on the embankment. Maxim Gorky worked here as a docker in 1891. The 3.5-m (12-ft) statue was unveiled in 1961.

Budyonny's Bust, Budyonny Prospect. Marshal Semyon Budyonny was a hero of the civil war, and this tribute to him by Vuchetich was unveiled in 1966.

1st Cavalry Army Monument, Sovietov Square. This civil war monument was sculpted by Vuchetich in 1972.

Sedov Monument, Novo-Bulvarnaya Street. Georgi Sedov (1877–1914) was a sailor and Arctic explorer who died while on an expedition. The sculptor of the monument was N. Avedikov.

Revolution Monument, Gorky Park. This monument is by V. Dubrovik and was unveiled in 1979.

Lenin Monument, at the entrance to Gorky Park. This statue by Neroda was unveiled in 1929.

Lenin Monument, Lenin Prospect. Unveiled in 1963.

Kirov Monument, Kirov Street. By Vilenski, unveiled in 1939.

World War II Victims' Memorial Complex, Zmiyevskaya Balka. This memorial is by N. Avedikov and was unveiled in 1975 to commemorate the 30th anniversary of VE day.

Liberators of Rostov Memorial, in Frunze Park. There is an eternal flame here.

Obelisk, Komsomol Square. This 15-m (49-ft) stele commemorates the young people who fought for the Don. It was put up in 1967.

Pleven Memorial Complex, Pleven Square. This monument to Bulgarian-Soviet friendship is by D. Tsonkov.

Gorky Theatre, Teatralnaya Square 1

Musical Comedy Theatre, Serafimovich Street 88

Youth Theatre, Svobody Square 3

Puppet Theatre, Universitetsky Prospect 46

Philharmonia Concert Halls, Engels Street 170

Circus, Budyonnovsky Prospect 45. Completed in 1957, this is the largest permanent circus building in the Soviet Union.

Open-air Theatre ("Zelenyi Teatr"), Oktyabrskoy Revolyutsii Park. Built in 1962, it seats 3,000.

Gorky Park, Engels Street 45

May Day Garden, Engels Street 129

Zoo, Zoologicheskaya Street 3

Botanical Garden, Zheleznodorozhny Rayon

Ulyanovoy Park, Oktyabrskaya Street. Here is the Rostov Exhibition of Agricultural and Industrial Achievements. There is also a children's railway.

Sport Palace, Khaltyrkinsky Per. 3

Rostselmash Stadium, Oktyabrskaya Street. There is room for 33,000 spectators. At the entrance is a monument commemorating the launching of the first Soviet sputnik.

Dynamo Stadium, Tekuchev Street

Hippodrome Racecourse, Maluginoy Street 233

Bathing Beach, from the centre of Rostov, where the main road to the Caucasus crosses the Don. After the bridge, turn left to the beach on the riverbank.

Intourist Hotel and Restaurant, Engels Street 115; tel. 65-9066. Intourist office, tel. 65-9000. There is a Beryozka foreign currency shop in the hotel.

Petrovsky Prichal Tourist Complex, 3 km (2 miles) from town, on the left bank of the Don; tel. 65-9066. Accommodations are in separate cottages, and the facilities include a sauna and Russian bathhouse, bathing, and tennis.

Rostov Hotel and Restaurant, Budyonnovsky Prospect 59; tel. 39-1818

Moskovskaya Hotel and Restaurant, Engels Street 62; tel. 38-8700

Tourist Hotel and Restaurant, Oktyabrya Prospect 19; tel. 32-4309

Camping Site, Restaurant, and Turist Cafe, Novocherkasskoye Chaussee, 12 km (7 miles) from the centre of town; tel. 52-0586

Frigate Restaurant, Petrovsky Prichal, 3 km (2 miles) out of town. This building is built in the shape of a ship of Peter the Great's time.

Tsentralny Restaurant, Engels Street 76

Volgodon Restaurant, Beregovaya Street 31

Teatralny ("Theatre") Restaurant, Oktyabrskoi Revolyutsii Park

GPO, Podbelskovo Street 24

Telegraph Office, Serafimovicha Street 62

Telephones, Semashko Street 34

Bank, Sokolova Street 26

Department Stores, Engels Street 46, 65, and 103 (children's)

Foreign Languages Book Shops, Pushkin Street 199 and Engels Street 84

Podarki (Gifts), Engels Street 60

Art Salon, Engels Street 128

Market, Oborony Street

Filling station, Novo-cherkasskoye Chaussée

Intourist organises boat trips on the river Don and a number of excursions. It is 40 km (25 miles) to Starocherkasskaya Stanitsa (see below) and to Novocherkassk, 42 km (26 miles) to Azov, and 75 km (47 miles) to Taganrog, all listed under their own names. Tanais is 30 km (19 miles) from Rostov-on-Don along the road to Taganrog; the way is described below.

Starocherkasskaya Stanitsa

Founded about 1570, Starocherkasskaya Stanitsa is the oldest Cossack settlement. Formerly known as Cherkassk, it was named after the Cossack Avgust Cherkas. Between 1644 and 1805 it was the capital of the Don Cossacks. The town was well fortified with earthen walls and wooden towers in which 80 guns were mounted.

It is well known in Russian history for its capture in 1670 by the Cossack and peasant leader Stepan Razin, and again in 1708 by Kondrat Bulavin. Peter the Great came here several times, and on one occasion he noticed a naked Cossack with a rifle riding on a barrel. It was explained to him that a Cossack can drink away everything except his rifle, and the tsar was so delighted by this that he approved as the design for the Cossack army a naked Cossack on a barrel holding a rifle.

St. Ephraim's Convent in Cherkassk was one of the richest in Russia.

Ataman Platov found a better place for the administrative centre and the capital was transferred to Novocherkassk in 1805. Cherkassk lost its importance and was given its present-day name. The prominent Russian artist Surikov came here in 1893, looking for Cossack models for his painting "The Conquest of Siberia by Yermak."

Today one can visit the nine-domed *Voskresensky (Resurrection) Cathedral* (1706–19), which is now a branch of the Novocherkassk museum. Some interesting fortified houses of the 18th century also remain.

The town is often flooded in the spring and the people use small boats to get about. It still keeps its old name of Cossack Venice. The road to Starocherkasskaya is very bad, and visitors are recommended to get there by boat.

Chaltyr

The majority of the population in Chaltyr are Armenian, the signs are written in Armenian, and the Armenian language is spoken.

Armenian Church, on the right of the road. It is open for services.

Lenin Monument
Chaltyr Cafe
GPO, beside the main road

Tanais

To reach Tanais leave Rostov in a northwesterly direction along Taganrogskoye Chaussée. Tanais, which is now an archaeological museum-reservation, was the ancient Greek name for the Don and also for the town at the river mouth. It was founded by Greeks from the Bosporus in the 3rd century B.C. at the estuary where the river Tanais used to flow into the Sea of Azov. The capital of the Bosporus kingdom was Panticapaeum, now the town of Kerch. A Christian church built here during the 1st century A.D. is said to date from St. Andrew's missionary visit; the site was excavated in 1957–59. For more than six centuries Tanais was a large economic and cultural centre in the Azov and Don basin. The Greek geographer Strabon called it "the largest barbaric market place." Greek merchants brought wine, oil, cloth, and pottery and exchanged them here for slaves, fish, skins, wool, and grain. It was the most distant Greek settlement and their outpost in these nomadic lands. The town developed in close contact with the nomadic tribes and acquired traces of two different cultures, Hellenic and Scythian. It perished in a gigantic fire in A.D. 375. Scientists assume that the nomadic tribes of the Black Sea basin united to destroy it.

Excavations of the fortress and part of the residential area have shown that the fire was a surprise, as the inhabitants appear to have left their town in a hurry and quite unprepared. Probably the invaders captured the town and then started a fire, which would have spread very quickly, since the houses were thatched roofed. Tanais is often called the "Pompei of the Don."

In A.D. 534 Emperor Justinian built a *church* in Tanais dedicated to St. John the Baptist. It was one of the many churches he built but one of the few to remain intact. In the 7th century the gospels and psalms were translated from Greek into Slavonic by Bishop John of Gothia (in Greek, Phonagoria), who lived and worked at the mouth of the river Don.

Kievan Rus expanded as far as this in the 9th and 10th centuries, and from the 13th century the Tatars held it. The Russians called it Dikoye Polye ("Wild Field"). When the Genoese came to colonise the northern shores of the Black Sea, they built a Mauritanian-style chapel onto St. John's Church, and services continued to be held there from the date of its consecration until very recently without a break. However, in the 14th century, when the Russian metropolitan bishop Pimen passed here on his way to Constantinople, he and members of his party were surprised to find the area so wild and deserted. Russian colonization really began from the time of Peter the Great, when the river Temernik served as Russia's border with Turkey.

In 1959 the territory of Tanais was proclaimed a state reservation. The *archaeological museum*, opened in 1961, tells of the town's history and of the surrounding lands. A good collection of Greek amphoras, vessels, artistic items of bronze, glass, and women's jewellery is on display. Especially interesting are marble plates with inscriptions, the oldest of which dates from A.D. 224. Open May to October, 9–5; closed Tues.

ROSTOV VELIKY (Rostov Yaroslavsky)
Population—40,000
(Intourist organises excursions here from Moscow 225 km/140 miles away.)

This town was named Rostov Veliky ("the Great") to distinguish it from the town of Rostov-on-Don. Founded before the days of Rurik, it is one of the most ancient towns in Russia. It is situated on Lake Nero and was first mentioned in the chronicles in 862. It was named after Prince Rosta. The local merchants traded with Scandinavia in amber and silver coins from the Arabian east, exchanging them for honey, fur, and grain. Christianity officially was accepted in 989, when the local inhabitants were baptised by being divided into groups of about 10 or 15 and forced to immerse themselves in the lake. Priests from Byzantium sailed around on rafts and boats and gave one Christian name to each group. Paganism, however, did not die out completely for some years. It is thought that the origin of Rostov's coat of arms—a silver deer with golden horn and hoofs on a red field—is that the deer was held sacred here in pagan times.

Rostov was first called the "Capital of the North." Then in the 12th century it received the title of "Great," because its territory and population were no less than those of ancient Kiev and Novgorod. As it grew wealthier, the number of its churches increased until it was said:

The devil went to Rostov
But the crosses scared him off!

In 1207 Rostov became the capital of a separate princedom, which, like other parts of Russia, was under Tatar rule in the 13th and 14th centuries. It came into the possession of Moscow under Dmitri Donskoy in 1474. At the end of the 16th century it grew in importance as a town on the trade route between Moscow and the White Sea. In the 17th century it was invaded by Poles and Lithuanians; it was ruined and sacked by them, and among the rich booty was a golden sepulchre weighing 100 kg, stolen from the Uspensky Sobor and presented to a Polish lady.

The layout of the centre is very straightforward, with the *kremlin* in the middle and then the *earthen walls*. These were built in 1631–33 and the remains are still to be seen. Beyond the walls, where the moat would have been, comes a ring of green gardens and then Sverdlov Street.

Local industry includes the production of chicory coffee, food (especially treacle), linen, and painted enamelware. This enamelware has been manufactured here in the Rostov Finift Factory since the 18th century. The technique came from Byzantium during the days of Kiev Rus and was first practiced in Kiev, Ryazan, and Vladimir. The colours are produced by the oxidization of a variety of metals: iron, for instance, gives yellow, orangered, and brown; copper gives green and blue; tin a nontransparent white; and gold with tin a cold ruby red and shades of pink. During the years of political instability the art was little practiced, but it was revived at the turn of the 15th century, first in the northwestern part of the country and then gradually spreading eastward until it reached Moscow by the 16th century. In France and England portrait miniatures were in vogue, and when in 1620 to 1930 the innovation was made of using painted enamel for these, Charles I of England and the French kings were among those to commission renowned artists to work in the new medium. They were much favoured in Russia, too, and a number of portraits of Peter the Great and his contemporaries are still in existence. Later Rostov became the centre of painted enamel production. Enamels, particularly those with religious motifs, became popular as souvenirs, but as mass production began, so their high quality was lost. By the 1870s the annual output of little pendants reached 2,500,000.

The *Kremlin*, until the mid-19th century called *Rostov Metropolia*, is surrounded by a wall with 11 towers, 2 of them square gate-towers and the others round. Its territory is a rough rectangle covering 2 hectares (5 acres), and it differs from other Russian kremlins and monasteries in that it has no main cathedral dominating the other buildings. Its churches are good examples of Russian 17th-century architecture and were built under the aegis of Metropolitan Ion Sisoyevich between 1667 and 1691. The wall (2 m/7 ft thick and 10 to 12 m/33 to 39 ft high) and towers were built not for military defence but simply to guard the metropolitan's palace. When the ecclesiastical centre moved to Yaroslavl, little more building of interest took place here.

Of the kremlin's two gate-churches, the *Church of the Resurrection* (1670) in the north wall has five domes and gates known as the Holy Gates; its southern door is decorated with allegorical paintings. The *Church of St. John the Divine* (1683) is in the west wall. Above the choir stalls are some interesting canopies. Both gate-churches contain well-preserved murals and old frescoes restored in 1954, and both have holes in the west walls that held empty jars to improve the acoustics.

The *Church of the Smolensk Mother of God*, built in 1693, is painted in brightly coloured triangles.

The *Church of the Redeemer* also has pot holes in the walls; its iconostasis has been replaced by a screen with 5 arches.

Among the secular buildings is the *Metropolitan's Palace* (1672–80) and a series of halls. The *Byelaya Palata* ("White Palace") was built in 1675 to accommodate important visitors; it was restored by the Imperial Moscow Archeological Society and first opened as a musum in 1883. The *Krasnaya Palata* ("Red Palace"), to the right of the main entrance just inside the kremlin, was built especially for Ivan the Terrible's visits and later used by Peter the Great and Catherine; it is now a hotel run by the Sputnik Youth Organisation. The Samuilovsky Block houses the *Rostov Museum* (see below).

In the centre of the courtyard is a square pond.

In the 19th century the kremlin was in such a sorry state that the town administration decided to sell it for 28,000 roubles. Fortunately, no one could afford such a price, so the ancient fortress was saved from demolition. It was damaged by a hurricane in 1953 but has since been restored.

Uspensky ("Assumption") *Cathedral*, outside the kremlin. This cathedral was founded in 1214 and consecrated in 1230. It was built on the lines of Moscow's Uspensky Cathedral, but its present appearance dates from the 15th to 16th centuries. To the left of the Holy Door is the wonder-working icon of the Vladimir Virgin, painted in the 11th century. The 4-domed belfry of the cathedral (1620–82) is 32 m (35 yds) long and 17 m (56 ft) high. It has four arched openings and the 13 bells play 4 tunes; the melodies were written by A. Izrailev in the 19th century. Stasov, Mussorgsky, and Berlioz came to listen to the chimes. The bells were cast in Rostov in the 17th century by Frol Terentiev, Filipp, and Kipriyan. The heaviest, the Sisoi Bell, weighs 32,000 kg (about 32 tons).

ROSTOV-VELIKI

Church of St. Gregory, near the kremlin. This church was built in 1670. It has a stone iconostasis and 17th-century frescoes, which suffered badly in a fire in 1730 but were restored in the 19th century.

Saviour-in-the-Market-Place Church, Sovietsky Per. 6. This church was built in 1690 and now houses the town library.

Church of the Ascension, Karl Marx Street, to the northeast of the kremlin. Built in 1566, this is a typical Moscow-style church. The people of Rostov usually call this the Church of Isidore the Blessed. It has 5 domes and there is an interesting stone engraved with the builders' names. The belfry dates from the 19th century.

Abraham (Avraam) Monastery, Zhelyabovskaya Street, over the level crossing in the eastern suburbs of the town. A temple of Veles, the pagan god of cattle, stood here on the bank of Lake Nero. Avraam, the enlightener of the area of Rostov, founded a monastery here at the end of the 11th century, making it the oldest monastery in Russia. The entrance is through the *Nikolskaya Gate-Church* (1655–91), whose towers on either side are round. Within its walls is the five-domed *Epiphany Cathedral* (1553), which has 18th-century frescoes, two small adjoining chapels, and a tall, square, 19th-century belfry. *Vvedenskaya Church* (1650) is classical in style with porticoes. All of these buildings are now sadly neglected.

Nearby is *Kikin's Rolma Linen Mill* (1878). The red and white house on the right by the turn to Abraham Monastery was the mill's administrative building.

Spaso-Yakovlevsky ("Jacob") Monastery, Engels Street 44, in the western suburbs of the town, on the banks of the lake. Founded in 1389 by St. Jacob ("Yakov"), bishop of Rostov, the existing buildings date from the 17th to 19th centuries and the original wall with four Gothic corner towers is still standing. At the entrance is a bell tower of the 18th century and two other gates. Inside is the *Zachatyevsky ("Immaculate Conception") Cathedral* (1691) and, under the same roof, *St. Jacob's Church* (1721–25), rebuilt to include a refectory by Countess Orlov-Chesmensky in 1836. This is a rather complicated piece of architecture, with the later construction added onto the northern and western sides of the earlier church. *St. Dmitri's Church* (1794–1802), designed in classical Russian style, was built by Count Sheremetiev; on the walls are bas-reliefs illustrating the Nativity and the Massacre of the Innocents. The cells by the walls date from 1776 and 1786, and the abbot's house is from 1786–95.

Close to the monastery in Kirov Street is the *Church of the Transfiguration-on-the-Sands (Preobrazheniye-na-Peskakh)*; this was built in 1603 as the cathedral of a now-vanished 13th-century monastery. Its frescoes are 19th century. The solid building to the right of the approach road used to be a hotel belonging to Spaso-Yakovlevsky Monastery.

Rozhdestvensky Convent, Sovietskaya Square 10, at the corner of 2-Proyezd of Tolstoy Embankment. Founded in the 14th century by Archbishop Fyodor of Rostov, nephew of Sergei Radonezhsky, it was run as a convent from 1764. The 17th-century *Cathedral of the Nativity of the Virgin* is now used as a bank and archive building. The church just outside the bounds of the convent is *St. Nicholas's*.

Services are now conducted in two churches: *St. John's Church* (1761), on Dekabristov Street, where there are 14th- to 16th-century icons, and *St. Nicholas-in-the-Field*, on Gogol Street, which was built in 1830 and has a two-storey belfry behind it. Inside are icons of the 15th and 16th centuries.

Traders' Row was built to serve as small shops in 1830. The architect was Melnikov and his design was then used for the building in Sverdlov Street known as the *Customs Yard* (1830–33). There are private houses of the 18th and 19th centuries along Lenin and Proletarskaya streets, and on Krasnoarmeiskaya Street are *Emelyanov House* and *Serebryanikov House*.

Local Museum, in the Samuilovsky Block in the kremlin, in the former Church School. Open 9–5; closed Wed. This museum was established in 1883, when the kremlin first was restored. Downstairs it contains an excellent collection of icons, beautifully restored and presented. Upstairs is a display of Rostov enamels and of china from many different factories. There is an interesting collection of presents made to the monasteries. Other examples of applied art include some fine metalwork and woodcarving of the 16th to 20th centuries. There is also a small prison cell called the Stone Sack.

Carriage Museum, in Konny Dvor (stables). Here one can hire a carriage to go on a sightseeing tour of the town and out to Lake Nero. The lake is one of the main attractions of Rostov Veliky; there are boating stations.

Loom Museum and Russky Lyon ("Russian Flax") Shop, Slavyanskaya Street

World War II Memorial, by the earthen wall, between the Rostov Hotel and the kremlin

Rostov Hotel and Restaurant, Sverdlov Street 64

Beryozka Restaurant

Along the kremlin walls are shops and workshops producing and selling lace and other handiwork.

Park, beside the lake. Boats can be hired here.

Belfry, on the left on the way out of town. The belfry is under restoration. No church remains.

Kosmodemianskaya Church, go along Proletarskaya Street and then right onto Perovsky Pereulok, just on the right on the way out to the north. This red-brick, single-domed church with its tent-style belfry over the entrance was built in 1775.

Looking back one can see the churches of Rostov Veliky beyond the hilltop.

There are some more churches and remains of monasteries around the town. *Belogostitsky-Georgievsky Monastery* stands on the left bank of the river Vexa. It was founded in the 15th century by Archbishop Grigori of Rostov long before building began in the Rostov Kremlin. There were four churches: *Blagoveschenskaya* (1657), *Mikhail Ar-khistratig* (1658), *Kazanskaya* (1867), and *Efraim Sirin* (1878). Under the apses of Blagoveschenskaya Church were buried Mikhail Tyomkin and his relatives, who had done much to finance the construction of the two older churches. The monastery is now in a state of dilapidation.

Also of interest is *Borisoglebsky Monastery*, 24 km (15 miles) west of Rostov.

Borisoglebsk Population—6,000

The town of Borisoglebsk is 20 km (12 miles) from Rostov Veliky on the road to Uglich. It stands on the river Ustye. At the entrance to the town are some interesting houses in art nouveau style.

Borisoglebsk Monastery is further on, to the left of the road. Tickets are sold to the right of the entrance. Open 10–5; closed Tues. The monastery was founded in 1363 with the help of Sergi of Radonezh by the Novgorod monks Pavel and Fyodor. By the 16th century it had grown into a fortress against military threats from the west. In 1606–7 Nicolas de Melo, a Spaniard, was held prisoner in the monastery, accused of being an "agent of the Catholic church." His letters have survived, complaining that he was fed only once in three days and was tortured. He was, however, finally released.

Around the monastery are strong walls with 12 towers and 2 entrance gates, the main way in being from Sovietskaya Street under the *Sretenskaya Gate-Church* (1680). The circumference around the top of the walls is 1.5 km (0.9 mile) and it is possible to walk all around, starting from the Sretenskaya Gate-Church. Inside, the oldest churches are the *SS Boris and Gleb Cathedral* of 1522–24, which has a classical entrance built on, the single-domed *Church of the Annunciation* (1527), and the 5-domed *St. Sergius-over-the-Gate* (1545). There is also a 16th-century refectory, a 17th-century bell tower with decorative tiles and 3 domes, the abbot's house, the kitchen, and the treasury. The exterior of the cathedral is decorated with remarkable tiles and the interior with 16th-century frescoes. There are some more 16th-century frescoes on the St. Sergius Gate-Church.

Museum, in the Sretenskaya Gate-Church. The exhibits here illustrate the history of the monastery and there are some good ceramics.

Restaurant, on the main road, Transportnaya Street 29

Near Borisoglebsk is the village of *Voschazh-nikovo*, where the Sheremetiev family had an estate in the time of Peter the Great.

ROVNO Population—228,000
Polish: Rowne

Rovno is 321 km (200 miles) from Kiev. It lies among gardens and parks beside the small river Ustya, which divides the town into two parts. Local legend gives an explanation for the origin of the town's name: when it belonged to the Ostrogski family they are said to have possessed 99 towns and

then purchased this place so that they could claim to have exactly 100 towns. The Russian word for 100 is "rovno." Certainly in the old documents Rovno was known as "Rovensk" or "Rovnoye" and can be so found on Mercator's 1554 map of Europe.

The site was inhabited during the Bronze Age and a Roman shield and some coins of the second century A.D. were found here in 1877. It was first mentioned in writing in 1282 in connection with a battle between Prince Chorny of Cracow and the Lithuanian prince Vitan, when it was described as a trading point. The castle was built in the 15th century, and at the end of the century Rovno was granted the Magdeburg Law, which permitted the holding of fairs. Between 1518 and 1521 it was in the hands of the Ostrogski family (see above). It passed to Poland after the signing of the Union of Lublin in 1569 but suffered particularly from the Tatars during the 16th century.

A Roman Catholic church was built here in 1606 and the town had three gates leading out to the roads to Dubno, Kievan, and Ostrog, which is why on the old coat of arms, one strong tower with three gates are depicted. In 1667 the population was stricken by plague and then the fire of 1691 ruined the whole of the central part of the town. In 1706 Rovno was taken by the Swedish army and held by the Swedes for about a year.

The town became the setting of the brilliant court of the Lubomirski family in 1723 and so remained for 150 years. Prince Stanislaw Lubomirski possessed 31 other towns and 738 villages besides. In 1738 they built a new palace in place of the castle, which had been burned down in the great fire of 1691. The palace stood on Castle Island, which, among a number of other islands, was known locally as Venice. In 1765 the architect Toucher redesigned it in rococo style, but at the end of the century, under Auguste Bourguignon, it was reconstructed again in classical style and decorated with frescoes by two Italian artists, Villiani and Carmaroni. Originally it was reached by a drawbridge. A contemporary said that Prince Lubomirski lived in Rovno just like a king in a small country of his own; he wrote the laws for his subjects and the military regulations for his private army (which was the largest maintained by any Polish lord). A good example of the family's grand style is that when the prince complained that there was nowhere nearby where he could go coursing, just to please him a thousand cartloads of young trees were brought in and planted, a hill was created, and a variety of animals, including hares, were introduced into the new forest. A park was laid out near the palace and a theatre was built. Most of the buildings of Rovno, apart from the town hall, were of wood, and the palace burned down in 1927. The wooden Uspenskaya ("Assumption") Church of 1756 has managed to survive. It has a single cupola.

In 1793 Rovno passed to Russia. The construction of the Kiev-Brest highway in 1857 was of great importance to local economic development as it

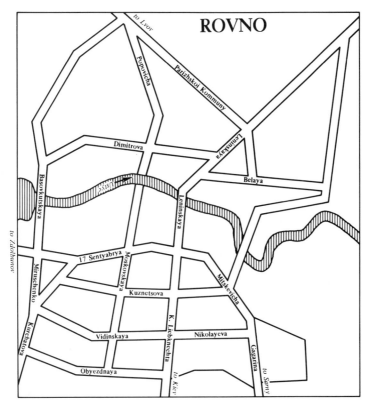

ROVNO

ran through the town. Balzac stayed here in 1847.

There are still old people in Rovno who remember the excitement in 1912 when 15,000 gathered to watch Louis Bleriot and the Russian pilot Alexander Vasiliev take off in a monoplane, circle the town 3 times, and land in the town square after a 12-minute flight.

In 1921 Rovno became Polish again and remained so until 1939, in which year it also was proclaimed the provincial capital.

During the Second World War this area was a centre of underground resistance and partisan activity. A number of books have been written and films made about the exciting military operations that took place here, but perhaps the best known is that of the story of an engineer called Nikolai Kuznetsov who came here from Tyumen, beyond the Urals. He took the disguise of a German officer, went by the name of Paul Ziebert, and organised the assassinations of General Hansgel and Alfred Funk, the senior judge of the SS. Then his group succeeded in capturing General von Ilgen, chief of the Special Armed Forces in the Ukraine. Kuznetsov was posthumously made Hero of the Soviet Union.

Rovno's main street is Lenin Street, where there is a *bookshop* and a *jeweller's*. It runs through a square named after Kuznetsov. Lenin Square is the town's grandest; the *statue of Lenin* is by Bronsky. The town centres around *Theatre Square*, where there is the *Ostrovsky Music and Drama Theatre*,

seating 800, and the Rovno Hotel with the Vesna Cafe and Ukraina Restaurant. Parallel to Lenin Street is Shkolnaya Street, a typical part of old Rovno where a number of synagogues have been rebuilt and are now used as houses. Zamkovaya Street leads off to one side, and here No. 8 and No. 10, both now serving as the gymnasium, were synagogues. There is a teachers' training college in Rovno and it is also the home of the Ukrainian Institute of Water Transport. Food products and high-voltage electric apparatus are both manufactured here, and the linen mill is among the largest in Europe. The railway junction is also of importance.

Uspensky ("Assumption") Cathedral, Shevchenko Street. This cathedral was built in 1756.

SS. Peter and Paul Roman Catholic Church, Lenin Street. Built in the 1890s, it now houses the Globus Cinema.

Voskresenskaya ("Resurrection") Cathedral, Lenin Street 38. Built in 1894, it is now the *Atheism Museum*.

Local Museum, Kalinin Street 19. Open 12–6; closed Wed. This is in the building of a former school, which was built in classical style in 1835. Among the exhibits is a round seal which was found recently during the excavations of an 11th- to 13th-century settlement near Drogobuzh. It bears the image of St. David on the right and a cross on the left and belonged to Prince David, son of Prince Igor, who owned Drogobuzh in 1084–1112. Korolenko studied in the school here, and during the war the building served as the Nazi headquarters of Erick Koch, who was responsible for the Ukraine.

Nikolai Kuznetsov Museum, Partisan Street 55. Open 11–7; closed Mon. This little house, which belonged to Evdokia Dovger, was in fact one of Kuznetsov's four secret hideouts.

Komsomol Glory Museum, Krasnoarmeiskaya Street 25. Open 10–6; closed Wed.

Nikolai Kuznetsov Monument (1961), at the entrance to the local museum.

Bronze Bust and Grave of Dundic, in Shevchenko Park. Oleko Dundic (1893–1920) was a Serb who died during the civil war. Of him Voroshilov said: "Red Dundic! Who can forget him? Who can be compared with this literally fairy-tale hero in valour, courage, kindness and friendly warmth? He was a lion with the heart of a child."

Bogomolov Monument, Pershovotravnya Street. Bogomolov was a hero of the civil war.

Victims of Fascism Monument, Bili Street, on the site of a former concentration camp where 82,500 lost their lives. The 12-m (40-foot) monument, whose sculptors were Prozhenko and Richkov, was built in 1969.

World War II Memorial and Eternal Flame, at the end of Parizhskoy Kommuny Street (the road in from Lvov), by the cemetery on the right. This memorial was unveiled in 1975.

Military Grave, in the park. Here is also a *monument* to those who liberated Rovno from the Germans in 1944.

Monument to the Victors over Fascism, Peremoghi Square. This monument was unveiled in 1972.

A cascade of *waterfalls* with fountains can be found on Lenin Street. This was built in place of a tank trap.

Vanguard Stadium. Seats 20,000.

Rovno Hotel and Restaurant, Lenin Square 2; tel. 23-02

Mir Hotel and Restaurant, Mickiewicz Street 32; tel. 21-335. Intourist office, tel. 22-183.

Ukraina Restaurant, Lenin Street 156

Goryn Restaurant, on the left, just before leaving the town

Art Salon, Kommunisticheskaya Street 25

Children's Railway, Lenin Street

Beside Basivkutsky Lake there is a popular *recreation area* with a *boating station* and other facilities. The lake is 1.4 km (0.8 mile) long and 400 m (440 yds) across.

Petrol Stations, Popovicha Street, Kikvidze Street, Vidinskaya Street, and on the right on the way out of town toward Kiev

RUMSISKES

See Vilnius, p. 617.

RUNDALE

See Bauska, Riga, p. 448.

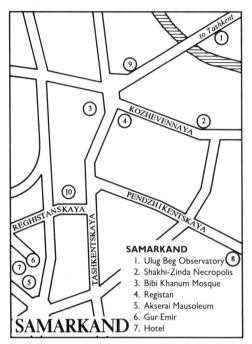

SAMARKAND
1. Ulug Beg Observatory
2. Shakhi-Zinda Necropolis
3. Bibi Khanum Mosque
4. Registan
5. Akserai Mausoleum
6. Gur Emir
7. Hotel

SAAREMAA

See Kuressaare, p. 257.

SALASPILS

See Riga, p. 447.

SAMARKAND Population—366,000

Samarkand is situated 700 m (2,300 ft) above sea level in the fertile valley of the river Zeravshan, which is 11 km (7 miles) from the centre of the town. The climate is extreme, the temperature sometimes falling below zero in January and rising up to 40°C (104°F) in July, but the town is considered more healthy than other central Asian towns because of a cold wind from the Hissar range of mountains to the south.

In the 4th century B.C. Samarkand was known as Maracanda and was the capital of Sogdiana. Even then it was renowned for its beauty, and Alexander the Great wrote after his capture of Maracanda in 329 B.C. that "everything I have heard about the beauty of Maracanda is true, except that it is more beautiful than I could imagine." Alexander's stay in Maracanda is well recorded, as it was here that he murdered his favourite general Clitus during a banquet.

Samarkand began to prosper from the 2nd century A.D., as it was an important town on the Great Silk Road from China and the East to the ports of Syria and thence to Europe. It was overrun many times, though, and its periods of prosperity were interspersed with deep depressions. At the beginning of the 8th century the whole of this part of central Asia was conquered by the Arabs, who brought Islam with them. However, the great power of the area was not so much the Arabs as it was the Chinese, who were petitioned by the local princes for help—and by the Arabs who feared Chinese intervention and looked upon Turkestan as a province wrested from the Chinese emperors. Direct Arab rule lasted only until 750, after which date Samarkand became part of the territory of the Samanid dynasty of Persia. Under the Samanids, Samarkand was a famous seat of Arabic civilisation, and Islam was firmly established.

In 1221 Samarkand was seized and pillaged by Genghis Khan. It is said that the soldiers looted the city for three days and nights, after which the population was reduced to a third. The soldiers destroyed the main water pipe, so the town was without water. It is said that more than 1,000 citizens who gathered in a mosque were burnt by the Mongol invaders; this story seems to be true, as in 1905 a Russian archaeologist, V. Vyatkin, found the remains of a mosque and traces of a fire on this spot.

The city remained under Mongol rule until 1369, when it was captured by Tamerlane (1333–1405), the Tatar conqueror who ruled a vast area, from Yelets in Russia to Kuch in Sinkiang and from Izmir to Delhi. He made it his capital, and his name is the most famous to be associated with its long history. He called himself the "Scourge of God and Lord of All the Earth," and he planned to make his Samarkand the capital of the world. He gave small villages near Samarkand the names of the greatest cities of the world—Baghdad, Damascus, and Cairo, for instance—with the idea that compared with Samarkand, these cities were only poor villages. He built many fine monuments in Samarkand and decorated them with booty from his plundering raids, but none of these were palaces; he always preferred to camp with his retinue in one of the magnificent gardens that surrounded the city. During Tamerlane's reign Samarkand became the most important cultural and economic centre of Asia. Tamerlane, who also was known both as "Timur the Lame" and simply as "Timur," became a legendary figure and is the eponym of Marlowe's play *Tamerlane*.

When Tamerlane died in 1405 at the age of 70, Samarkand continued to flourish under his grandson, Ulug Beg, the famous astronomer who also was known as the "Great Enlightener." Ulug Beg continued biulding splendid monuments, and during this time Samarkand was also a famous seat of learning. It remained in the hands of Tamerlane's descendents, including Babur, who was no more than 14 years old when he marched on Samarkand from his capital of Fergana in 1497. He lost it again after three months, and in 1500 power

passed to the Shaibanids. Babur took it from Shaibani Khan that very year, but as before, it was only for a short spell. Although Bukhara was the Shaibanid capital, some remarkable edifices were put up in Samarkand at this time as well.

By the beginning of the 18th century the countries of western Europe were obtaining their goods from the East by sea. Samarkand, together with other towns on the caravan route, gradually slipped into oblivion. In 1784 it fell under the rule of the emir of Bukhara, and in 1868 it was captured by the Russians under General Kaufmann. A new Russian quarter was built to the west of the old town and Samarkand was slightly helped economically by the opening of the Transcaspian Railway in 1896. From 1924 to 1930 it was the capital of the Uzbek Soviet Socialist Republic, but in 1930 Tashkent was made the capital.

Today Samarkand is an important centre for fruit, cotton, wine, and sheepskin. Recent construction includes both a new airport and a new railway station.

The *Registan*, in Registanskaya Street, was the old trading centre of Samarkand. The name "Registan" means "Sandy Place," after a spring that flowed here and washed sand onto the surrounding ground. The square is enclosed on all but the southern side by three "medressehs." A medresseh is a Mohammedan college, and the basic plan of all three is similar: a large portal leading onto an enclosed courtyard around which were the rooms of the college and a mosque. All three have been restored and are in good condition. In the evenings when the weather is good there are son et lumiere performances in the square.

The *Ulug Beg Medresseh and Mosque*, on the west side of the square, were built in 1417–20 by Ulug Beg and are the oldest buildings in the square. The medresseh was exceptional for the 15th century, as the syllabus included astronomy and mathematics as well as theology. Ulug Beg, who ruled Samarkand after Tamerlane's death in 1405, was renowned as "the prince of astronomers" and is said to have taught in the medresseh himself. There is no evidence for this, but it is known that many of the clergy considered astronomy blasphemy and that they plotted together with Ulug Beg's son to assassinate him in 1449. The medresseh was damaged considerably in the 18th century, and later the 4 minarets leaned at a dangerous angle. In 1932 the northeast minaret, which was the most precarious of the 4, was straightened.

The *Shir-Dar Medresseh and Mosque*, on the east side of the square, were built between 1619 and 1636 by Yalangyushbee, the military governor of Samarkand under the Astrakhan khanate. The proportions of the medresseh are the same as those of the Ulug Beg medresseh opposite, of which it is clearly a copy. During Ulug Beg's rule a "khanaka," a religious rest house for travellers, had been built on this site, but it fell into ruins by the beginning of the 17th century. The portal of the medresseh is 24 m (79 ft) high. The tympanum over the main arch is decorated with a colorful design of a lion chasing a doe, from which the building takes its name—"Shir-Dar" means "Lion-Bearing," although in fact it looks more like a tiger.

The *Tillah-Kari Medresseh and Mosque*, on the northern side of the square, also were built by Yalangyushbee in 1647. The name means "Covered with Gold" and probably was given because of the elaborate guilding on the inside walls of the mosque. The medresseh was obviously planned to unify the square. The southern facade is much longer than was usual for a building of comparable height, and this gives the square an enclosed appearance.

The *Chorsu*, a few yards to the northeast of the Shir-Dar Medresseh, was built at the beginning of the 19th century, when Samarkand was under the rule of the emir of Bukhara. The sextagonal building with a cupola was built as a trading centre; its bricks were taken from the ruins of the Bibi Khanum Mosque.

About 500 m/yds north of the Registan along Tashkentskaya Street is the *Bibi Khanum Mosque*, built from 1399 to 1404. For many years there were only the grandiose ruins to see, but now the edifice is being entirely rebuilt. According to legend the mosque was built by Tamerlane's wife Bibi Khanum, daughter of the emperor of China, while Tamerlane was on a campaign in India. There is no historical evidence of Bibi Khanum's existence and it is much more likely that Tamerlane himself built the mosque when he returned from his victorious campaign in India, during which he captured Delhi. The legend says that Bibi Khanum was very beautiful, and in order to be remembered by future generations as Tamerlane's favourite wife, she asked the best craftsmen to build a mosque that would surpass all oriental architecture in size and grandeur. The craftsmen doubted their ability, but when they saw the piles of gold that were to cover the cost, they began to work. The building rose quickly and was completed except for the portal when the work slowed down. The architect had fallen in love with the beautiful Bibi Khanum and he knew that once the mosque was completed, he would never see her again. He laid down the condition that if the mosque were to be completed before Tamerlane's return, she must allow him to kiss her. She tried to persuade him to kiss one of her ladies-in-waiting instead, but the architect was adamant. Just as he was about to kiss her, she covered her face with her hands, but even so, the heat of the kiss burnt her cheek and left a mark. When Tamerlane returned, she was unable to conceal the story behind her burnt cheek, and Tamerlane immediately ordered the guards to find the culprit. They were unable to find him and were told by one of his pupils that he had made wings for himself and flown down from the top of one of the minarets.

The mosque measures 101 m by 140 m (110 yds by 153 yds). It was one of the largest in the Moslem world, and of all of the cathedrals of Europe, only that of Milan was larger. The height of the main mosque was 36 m (118 ft), and the cupola

was 20 m (66 ft) in diameter. The main portal was 34 m (112 ft) high. It is said that it was originally slightly lower, but that Tamerlane was dissatisfied with it and ordered it to be rebuilt. The building techniques of the time were not sufficiently advanced for such a building, and extra-strong mortar had to be used in order to make it sound. Heavy mortar is more susceptible to earthquakes than normal mortar, however, and the mosque began to collapse on the heads of worshippers during services, but as it was a holy building it could not be demolished in any way. It gradually fell into ruins and the earthquake of 1897 damaged it irrevocably. Reconstruction work is in progress on the outer walls and the four minarets. A fragment of the original Arabic on the tiles reads: "Ask Allah His forgiveness before you die."

Between the main mosque and the entrance arch there were a number of *small mosques*, parts of 2 of which stand today. The grey marble *Koran desk* in the courtyard originally stood inside the mosque where it was placed by Ulug Beg. It consists of 2 huge wedge-shaped stones lying on a pedestal 2.5 m long and 2 m wide (8 ft by 7 ft). There is a legend that a childless woman who crawls under the desk will bear children.

Opposite the Bibi Khanum Mosque is the *mausoleum of Bibi Khanum*. This also is attributed to Bibi Khanum, who is said to be buried here, but historians consider that it was built by Tamerlane in honour of his mother-in-law, Sarai Mulk-Khanum. There was also a medresseh here, but it was destroyed in the 17th century. Only the ruins of the mausoleum, an octagonal building with a cross-shaped interior, stand today.

The largest group of monuments in Samarkand is the *Necropolis of Shakhi-Zinda*, open daily, 9–6. It is situated in the northeast part of the town, to the left of Kozhevennaya Street and just over 1 km (half a mile) from the Bibi Khanum Mosque. On the left of the main road, just opposite the right turn that leads to Shakhi-Zinda, stands *Khazret-Khizr Mosque*, which is under restoration. Mausoleums were first built at Shakhi-Zinda in the 10th century, but they were almost totally destroyed during the Mongol invasion. The mausoleums one can see today were all built during the 14th and 15th centuries.

Shakhi-Zinda, which means "Shrine of the Living King," takes its name from the grave of Kussam-ibn-Abbas, a Moslem saint and cousin of the prophet Mohammed who is reputed to have brought the Islamic faith to Samarkand in the 7th century. The legend says that during a sermon in Samarkand, Kussam-ibn-Abbas lifted his head off his shoulders and, carrying it under his arm, climbed down a well leading to an underground garden, where he continues to live to this day. Other reports say that he died in battle and, according to some historians, he died not in Samarkand but in Merv. Nevertheless, *Kussam's tomb* in Samarkand attracted visitors as far back as the 15th century and is considered the most holy place in Samarkand. The mausoleum of Kussam is situated at the far end of Shakhi-Zinda from the main entrance arch and is approached through a beautifully carved walnut door with the date 1404–05 carved on the bottom. Kussam's tomb has 4 tiers and is covered with elaborate, brightly coloured tiles and much gilt. On the 2 lower tiers is written the quotation from the Koran: "Those who were killed on the way of Allah are not to be considered dead; indeed they are alive . . ." It was perhaps this quotation that gave rise to the legend of the living king. Beside the mausoleum is a *small mosque* that is thought to be the oldest building in Samarkand. It is separated from the mausoleum by a carved wooden fence. The mausoleum is not dated, but it is thought that it was built soon after the mosque—that is, in the first half of the 14th century. From the accounts of travellers in the 14th century it is clear that the mausoleum of Kussam was much more elaborate then than it is now, and it is thought that there was another mausoleum on this site before the present one was built.

The *entrance arch* to Shakhi-Zinda has an inscription on the west wall saying that it was built by Ulug Beg in 1434–35. On the left of the arch is a *mosque*, built at the same time as the arch, and a *souvenir shop*. To the right there are some *service rooms* leading to a *small medresseh* (1812–13). This arch itself gives into a passage, on both sides of which are buildings of some size in varying states of preservation. In many of the mausolea there are good mosaics and decorated majolica.

The *summer mosque* on the left with a painted wooden porch ("aivan") was built in 1911. Further on on the same side is the *mausoleum* with the two highest turquoise-coloured cupolas. It is thought to contain the grave of Kazyzade Rumi, a 15th-century astronomer and Ulug Beg's teacher and friend. The *tomb* is under the smaller cupola, while the larger covers a prayer room. It was all restored in 1950–52.

The flight of *brick steps* was built in the 18th century over the remains of the town wall. It is said that women should count the steps on their way up, and recount them on the way down. If the numbers differ, it shows that they have sinned and should do penance with more prayers. There are in fact 36 steps, and they lead up to a small domed *archway* built in the 18th century that opens onto a very narrow passage, along the beginning of which is a group of colourful mausolea built in the second half of the 14th century, when Tamerlane made Samarkand his capital. The first one on the right is the *Tuglu-Tekin mausoleum*, built in 1376 in honour of the mother of Emir Hussein, one of Tamerlane's military commanders. The second one on the right is that of *Shirin-Bika-Aka*, Tamerlane's sister. She died in 1385 and the mausoleum is of the 14th–15th century, built on the remains of the old town wall. The decorations inside show birds, trees, and rivulets. The first mausoleum on the left after coming through the arch is known as the *Emir Zadeh* ("Emir's Son") *mausoleum*, although the real name of the person buried here is unknown. The inscription over the

portal gives only the date of his death, 1386, but the mausoleum was built a little later. The second one on the left is the *mausoleum of the Shadi-Mulk-Aka*, daughter of Tamerlane's eldest sister, Kutlug-Turkan-Aka, who probably was buried here also. This mausoleum is in a very good state of preservation and the interior is worth seeing for the majolica work. It was the first mausoleum to be built here during Tamerlane's rule.

Passing other less-interesting monuments, toward the end of the passage is a third *archway* leading on the left to the *mausoleum of Tuman-Aka*, the wife of Tamerlane who was responsible for building the lodging house for travellers that stands beside it. Tamerlane stayed here on his return from India. At the end of the passage is a small square, on the far side of which stood the *mausoleum of Hoja Akhmade*, which was built at the beginning of the 14th century. Only the portal remains. To the right of the square is an *unknown mausoleum* that mistakenly was attributed to Tamerlane's wife but was built before Tamerlane's rule in 1366. The cupola and interior are covered with coloured terra-cotta. There is no mosaic in these earlier mausolea, as this appeared only during Tamerlane's time.

To the right of the little archway over the passage is a 16th-century *mosque* with a minaret leading to the revered *shrine of Kussam-ibn-Abbas*.

The *Gur Emir* is in Akhunbabayeva Street, which goes southwest from the top of Gorky (formerly Abramovsky) Boulevard where it runs into Registanskaya Street. Tamerlane started building this large mausoleum for his grandson, Mohammed Sultan, who died in Iran on his way to meet Tamerlane. Tamerlane died a year later in 1405 and was buried here himself. The mausoleum was then given the name of "Gur Emir," which means "Grave of the King." The tombs of other members of Tamerlane's family were placed here later, including those of his two sons, Shakhrukh and Miranshakh, and that of Ulug Beg. Tamerlane died before the building was completed but it was finished under Ulug Beg. The building suffered much from earthquakes and a fire, but it has been well restored and the interior has been beautifully regilded.

The blue dome of the mausoleum is 33.5 m (110 ft) high, with decorative tiles on the drum. A little window on the right side looks down into the crypt. The mausoleum is entered by a large portal that was completed in Tamerlane's lifetime and is the best-preserved part of the building. It is decorated with bright mosaic that stands out against the almost plain walls of the facade. The inner chamber of the mausoleum is 22 m (72 ft) high. In the centre of the chamber is the tombstone of Tamerlane. It consists of two blocks of dark-green nephrite fitted into each other; they are the largest pieces of nephrite known. The tombstone is 2 m long, 45 cm wide, and 35 cm high (6 ft 6 in by 1 ft 6 in by 1 ft 2 in). The Arabic inscription on the tombstone claims that Tamerlane and Genghis Khan were descendants of the same ancestor, the son of a virgin named Alankuva who conceived from light that came through a door. There are 8 other tombstones in the chamber, all made of grey marble or alabaster. That of Tamerlane's teacher is situated in a niche opposite the entrance. Those in the centre of the chamber around Tamerlane's tombstone belong to members of his family. Except for the tombstone in the niche, they are all surrounded by marble railings. The lower part of the wall of the chamber is decorated with octagonal blocks of alabaster, above which is a band of jasper on which the genealogy and deeds of Tamerlane are written.

The actual graves, which are in a crypt below, were opened in 1941. The skeletons were examined, and it was clear that Tamerlane had been lame and that Ulug Beg had been murdered. The skeletons were replaced in the graves together with an account of the investigations that was sealed in a glass tube and set in marble.

In the courtyard of the mausoleum is the *Kok-Tash Stone*. This piece of dark-grey marble, 3.5 m (11 ft) long with arabesques on the sides, was the coronation stone of the emirs of Bukhara.

53 m (58 yds) southeast of Gur Emir are the ruins of the *Ak-Serai mausoleum*. Little is known about this, but historians judge it to have been built in the latter half of the 15th century, as the interior decoration is very similar in style to that of another monument of that period, the Irshat-khana. It is thought that it probably served as a family tomb for the male descendants of the Timurides. Although in ruins, some restoration work has been done, and there is a very beautiful fresco inside.

A little to the north of the Gur Emir is the *mausoleum of Ruh-Abad*. It contains the grave of Burkha-eddin Sagardee, a 14th-century mystic, and therefore was given the name "Ruh-Abad," which means the "Abode of the Spirit." The date of the mausoleum is not known, but it is thought to belong to the latter half of the 15th century.

The *Ulug Beg Observatory* is situated about 3 km (2 miles) from the centre of Samarkand, on the right of the road to Tashkent. It was built in 1449 by Ulug Beg but was destroyed soon after his assassination the following year. The stones of which it was built were taken away for use on other construction, and the exact location of the observatory was not known until it was discovered in 1909 by the Russian archaeologist V. Vyatkin. During excavations in 1909 remains of the outer wall as well as part of a large sextant, the astronomer's principal instrument, were found. From later excavations it was ascertained that the observatory was a large, circular three-storey building. Low walls have been built to mark the ground plan of the observatory. The observations made by Ulug Beg at the observatory were very advanced for the time and surprisingly accurate, such as his calculation that the stellar year is 365 days, 6 hours, 10 minutes, and 8 seconds—only 62 seconds more than the present estimation. In 1914 the sextant was covered by an arched roof, and an entrance arch was built. A

marble monument to Ulug Beg was erected on the site of the observatory in 1949. Vyatkin was buried there and there is also a museum. Open daily, 9–5.

Not far from the observatory of Ulug Beg is the *mausoleum of Chupan-Ata*, which commands a very good view over the town and beyond to the Hissar Mountains. It is thought to belong to the period of Ulug Beg and is remarkable for its simplicity and fine proportions. Although a mausoleum in style, no graves or crypts were found here during excavations, giving the building an air of mystery.

To the northeast of the present town is *Afrasiab*, the ancient site of Maracanda. There is a legend that the true founders of Maracanda were the emperors of Kaikaous and Afrasiab, who lived c. 4000 B.C., and that Afrasiab takes its name from the latter, but few believe this legend today. Maracanda was situated on a plateau 5 km (3 miles) in circumference and high above the Zeravshan River. After the Mongol invasion in the 13th century the plateau was deserted except for the extreme northern part, which was inhabited until the 15th century. The ancient ramparts and approaches to the town from below are still recognizable. The first excavations here were carried out in 1874, and since then many items, including Graeco-Bactrian coins, plain and enamelled tiles, cooking utensils, tools, frescoes, terra-cotta figurines, and jewellery, have been found. A large collection of these can be seen in the *History of Samarkand Museum*. In 1885 remains of the wall of the ancient town were found. Later the remains of dwellings, other buildings, and also the mound on which the citadel stood, were discovered. Excavations made in 1965 revealed 6th- and 7th-century frescoes, and probably further work will tell more about ancient Sogdiana.

On the opposite side of the road from Afrosiab is the *Archaeological Institute*.

Below Afrasiab on the left bank of the Zeravshan there is a large brick archway, which is all that now stands of a large dam and sluice for regulating the river. It is known as the *Bridge of Tamerlane* but actually was built at the very beginning of the 16th century by Shaibani Khan.

In Tashkent Street, in the courtyard of the former Shaibani-Khanum Medresseh, is the *Shaibani-Khanum Monument*, which is a block of grey marble 6.5 m long, 5.5 m wide, and over 2 m high (21 ft by 18 ft by 7 ft). It is covered by 30 tombstones decorated with inscriptions and designs of the Shaibanid rulers of Bukhara of the first half of the 16th century.

Only the ruins of the *Ishrat-Kana mausoleum* remain. The name, which means "House of Amusement," is rather a misnomer, as it is in fact a mausoleum and mosque. It was given this name on account of the elaborate interior decorations and architectural design. It was built from 1451 to 1469, apparently at the wish of the wife of Abu-Sanda in memory of their little daughter.

The *mausoleum of Abdi-Darun* is situated in an old cemetery in southeastern Samarkand. It was built in 1633 by Nadir-Divanbegi.

Tamerlane's Summer Palace, near Samarkand. It is being excavated and is to be restored and opened to tourists.

The single-storey building of the old *Grand Hotel* stands at Karl Marx Street 42.

The *Namazbogh Mosque* is in Kairnanskaya Street and the *Abdidarun Mosque* in Aini Street, but the main one open for worship is the *Hodja Akhror*, in the village of Ulug-Beg, just outside the town, 4.5 km (3 miles) from the centre.

Georgievsky Cathedral, in what used to be the governor's park on Kommunisticheskaya Street, is painted violet and has been converted for use as a sports hall, as has another church on Engels Street.

Pokrovsky ("Intercession") Cathedral, at the crossing of Vozvrazhiye and Sovietskaya streets. This was built in 1902 with a tent-roofed belfry. It is now the Russian Orthodox cathedral and is open for services.

Synagogue, Khudzhunskaya Street. This was built in the 15th century or earlier by Jews from Bukhara.

Local Museum, Sovietskaya Street, in a house that used to belong to a merchant called Kalantarov. Open 9–5; closed Thurs.

Samarkand Museum, Afrasiab Place. Open 9–5; closed Thurs.

Culture and Art Museum, Sovietskaya Street 47. The final section of the museum contains many items of interest illustrative of the old life of Samarkand. Open 9–5; closed Wed.

Uzbek Art Museum, in a square building by the Registan.

Anti-Religious Museum, at the foot of the hill

Town Hall, Volkova Street. This interesting building with oriental-style domes used to be the governor's house.

University, Gorky Boulevard 15. 7,000 students study here. One of the faculties of the university is housed in a two-storey brick building near the Samarkand Hotel that used to be a girls' school.

Karakul Institute, Karl Marx Street. This institute breeds sheep for research and has a good collection of samples of famous skins, including gold, bronze, platinum, and white.

War Memorial, Bortsov Revolutsii Square, next to Gorky Park. On 6 November 1962, an eternal flame was lit here to burn in memory of the victims of the civil war.

Babayev Monument, in front of the Opera and Ballet Theatre.

Khamid Alimdjan Uzbek Drama Theatre, Gorky Park; tel. 3-2513

Opera and Ballet Theatre, Registanskaya Street, opposite the hotel. This modern building designed by Balayev seats 1,000 and was completed in 1964.

Russian Drama Theatre, Ikramova Street

Puppet Theatre, Lenin Street

Concert Hall, Lenin Street 58

Son et Lumière, Registan Square, in the old city. This is the only show of its kind in the Soviet Union. The 45-minute performance covers Samarkand's 2,500 years of history. The narration is in Russian and Uzbek, but French, English, and Arabic translations are planned.

Summer Concert Hall, Gorky Park

Gorky Park, Sovietskaya Street; there is an amusement ground here and a dance floor.

Hippodrome Racecourse. There is no tote at this racecourse.

Dynamo Stadium, Karl Marx Street

Spartak Stadium

Samarkand (Intourist) Hotel and Restaurant, Gorky Boulevard 1; tel. 58-812. Intourist office, tel. 51-652. There is a souvenir kiosk in the hotel with pottery and lengths of silk for sale.

Registan Hotel and Restaurant, Karl Marx Street, at the corner of Lenin Street

Tourist Hotel and Restaurant

Nadir Divanbegi Medresseh. This building is under restoration, and there are plans to turn it into another hotel.

Shark Restaurant, Kozhevennaya Street

Yubileiny Restaurant, behind the Registan

Cafe, Lenin Street

Ice-cream Parlour, opposite the Registan

GPO, Kommunisticheskaya Street, Pochtovaya Street

Central Telegraph Office, Pochtovaya Street

Bank, in the original old bank building, resembling a mosque in style, opposite Georgievsky Cathedral in Kommunisticheskaya Street

Beryozka Foreign Currency Shop, Lenin Street

Shopping Centres, Lenin Street and Tashkentskaya Street

Department Stores, Lenin Street, Karl Marx Street, and Registan Square.

Souvenir Shop, Tashkentskaya Street near the Bibi Khanum Mosque. Look for local pottery—dishes, vases, and curious little monster ornaments.

Market, at the crossing of Pochtovaya and Kommunisticheskaya streets

Taxi Ranks, near the Samarkand Hotel, the railway station, and Registan Square.

Intourist organises day trips from Samarkand to Pendzhikent (q.v.), Shahr-i Sabz (q.v.), and Aman-Kutan.

Aman-Kutan

Aman-Kutan is located in a ravine to the west of Samarkand where there are marble quarries. It is a picturesque place with a rapid mountain brook ("sai" in Uzbek), groves of acacia, oak, and pine, and plantations of walnut trees.

In 1947–51 an archeological expedition from Samarkand University discovered a cave that had been used by humans in the paleolithic period.

SANAHIN

See Erevan Environs, p. 139.

SARDARAPAT
See Oktemberyan, Erevan Environs, p. 131.

SATAPLIA
See Tskhaltubo, p. 576.

SAULKRASTY
See Riga, p. 451.

SAYANO-SHUSHENSKAYA GES
See Abakan, p. 32.

SELTSO
See Novgorod, p. 388.

SEMYONOV-BASHI
See Dombai, p. 240.

SEVAN
See Erevan Environs, p. 135.

SEVAN, LAKE
See Erevan Environs, p. 135.

SEVERNY PRIYUT
See Kislovodsk, p. 240.

SHAHR-I SABZ Population—30,000
Russian: Shakhrisabz
(Intourist organises excursions here from Samarkand, 80 km/50 miles away. The road runs through Zadargomsky Steppe, now agricultural land predominantly under wheat, maize, and fodder crops. The parallel terraces on the hill slopes date from prehistoric times. The name of the village Aman-Kutan on the way to Shahr-i Sabz, means "Aman's Fold," and the same shepherd must have given his name to the spring to the left of the road, which is known as Aman Bulag. In a valley also to the left of the road is the place where Intourist organises picnic parties with barbecued shashlik. The trees here include juniper, walnut, and poplar and the area is popular as a cool summer resort. There are a number of sanatoria here as well as Pioneer camps.)

Takhta-Karacha Pass (1,700 m/5,577 ft above sea level) was opened in 1966. It can be dangerous, with ice or fog (or both) in winter. The spring on the left on the way down is Rakhat Bulag.

Minchinar Restaurant, on the left, just below the pass

In the past Shahr-i Sabz was also called "Shaar" in Russian, and "Shakhrisabz" or "Sharshauz." Actually the place is made up of the twin cities of Shakhr and Kitab. They are 650 m (2,133 ft) above sea level and 87 km (54 miles) from Samarkand in the fertile and well-irrigated valley of the river Kashka-Darya where its two tributaries, the Aksu and the Tankhaz, flow into it. The village of Oktyabrskaya is also part of the town. The climate here is mild and the average July temperature is 28°C (82°F), which is not very hot compared with other places in the region. The geographical position of the town is very convenient, since it stands on the

Great Uzbekistan Road (formerly the Great Silk Route), which connects the Kashka-Darya with Samarkand.

The town of Kitab is relatively young. It was founded in the middle of the 18th century, while ancient Shakhr witnessed the invasion of kings Darius and Cyrus of Persia (6th to 5th centuries B.C.), and Alexander the Great also held it for a short period as part of his Graeco-Baktrian empire (3rd to 2nd centuries B.C.). In historical sources it is referred to as "Tsishi" and "Kesh." In the 7th century A.D. Kesh was known for its trade. Silver and lead were mined nearby. Soon it was seized by the Arabs and became one of the centres of rebellion against them. The rebellion was headed by Khashim-ibn-Hakim ("Mukanna") from Merv in Khorassan, who was considered a prophet among the local people. His nickname, Mukanna, means "Covered by a Cloth," because he is said to have covered his face with green silk. Mukanna and his disciples hid from the Arabs in a fortress in Mt. Ciyam near the Severtsev Glacier, the source of the river Aksu, and it was there that he committed suicide rather than be taken prisoner. The English poet Sir Thomas More dedicated his poem "The Veiled Prophet of Khorassan" to him. In the 13th century the town suffered great damage from the Mongol hordes.

It was perhaps Tamerlane (also known as "Timur"; "Tamerlane" means "Iron Lame Man") who played the most important role in the history of the town, since he was born in 1336 in Khodja Ilgar, a small village nearby. Tamerlane belonged to the noble Barlas family, whose family burial place was in Shahr-i Sabz. Among the graves were those of Tamerlane's grandfather, father, and other relatives as well as that of Sheikh Shamsetdin Kulala, the spiritual instructor of Tamerlane and his father, Emir Taragai. He even wanted to make his native town the capital of his kingdom. Samarkand became the capital, but Kesh was a flourishing city of that period. Soon it was renamed Shahr-i Sabz, meaning "Garden Town." It was a well-developed town as well. Scientists from many countries came to work and live here and it was even called the "cupola of science and morals." It was surrounded by a wall with round towers and a moat. The wall had four gates facing north, south, east, and west, and four main streets led from them, crossing in the centre of the city. A precious carved holy gate moulded from seven noble metals and brought from the conquered Herat (now in Afghanistan) was set into the Northern Gate. Many houses and temples were erected in Tamerlane's reign, for example, Ak-Sarai Palace, allegedly built on the place where Tamerlane was born.

During the time of the Bukhara emirate, Shahr-i Sabz remained a typical feudal town, and it was third in importance after Samarkand and Bukhara. The inhabitants were mostly artisans and merchants. In the 1820s the "bek" ("ruler") of Shahr-i Sabz declared himself independent from the khan of the emirate. During the Russian advance to central Asia in the 1860s the bek gave shelter to anti-

Russian rebels. The town continued to grow, and at the end of the 19th century the population had risen to 30,000.

Now it is an important industrial centre. The Shahr-i Sabz Cotton Gin was built in 1924 on the site of an older one dating from 1916. The Kitab Wine Factory was built in 1927; its wine has won many medals at home and abroad. The place also is renowned for the embroidered skullcaps produced by the Khudzhum Factory, which also manufactures picturesque national garments, carpets, and scarves. Also here is the Karabair Stud Farm. The only altitude laboratory in the Soviet Union was founded in Kitab in 1930. Its scientists, together with 4 other laboratories, in Italy, Japan, and 2 in the United States, follow a unified programme of work to research the movement of the North Pole. The laboratory, which used to be in Chardzhou, on the same altitude of 39° 8′, was demolished by an earthquake in 1919. In spite of this evidence of progress, part of the charm of Shahr-i Sabz lies in its rural Muslim atmosphere. It is worth taking time as the locals do to sip tea in a chaikhana (tea house) and watch the world go by.

The road from Samarkand goes through Kitab first. It follows Magistralnaya Street, passing a caravanserai that is now used as a furniture shop, a *Detsky Mir children's shop*, and the *local theatre*. It makes a right turn and then a left before running into Shahr-i Sabz.

On the northeast side of the city are the imposing ruins of the palace known as *Ak-Sarai* ("White Palace"). The construction of this palace is connected with Tamerlane's 1379 triumphant raid on Khorezm (a state in the south of modern central Asia, surrounding modern Urgench). Tamerlane celebrated his victories by constructing new buildings. This time skillful builders were brought from the conquered towns and put to work, and construction began in spring 1380. An Andalusian traveller and envoy of Granada at Tamerlane's court, Grande Rui Gonsalez Clavijo, visited the construction site in 1404 when the palace was not yet completed. So the work took more than 20 years. There are many legends connected with it. One of these tells how the chief architect decided to test Tamerlane to see whether he had the courage to surrender his wealth for the building of the palace; he prepared the clay for the first bricks out of the gold dust of Tamerlane's treasury. However, the ruler was not worried by this fact, and so the work began. When the brick skeleton of the edifice was ready, the builder suddenly disappeared, leaving a chain attached to the central arch that did not reach the ground by the height of a full-grown man. Construction ceased. Two years later the builder returned secretly, examined the chain, saw that the building had not sunk, and then told Tamerlane he was ready to begin the incrustation of the palace. When the palace was completed, its splendour amazed contemporaries. Tamerlane did not want anything like it to be built again and accordingly, so it is said, had the architect, together with

a servant, tied to an eagle. The servant was ordered to cut the ropes when the eagle was high in the sky, and so the architect fell to his death.

Historical sources describe Ak-Sarai as a complex of dwellings and public buildings in a vast yard. In the centre of the yard was the main domed building for the sessions of the "divan" (the council of state), and on the sides were smaller halls for the counsellors' sessions. The central arch, with a span of 22.5 m (74 ft), was the largest in central Asia. The height of the pillars was about 40 m (131 ft) and that of the portal about 50 m (164 ft). It is unusual in that instead of facing westward toward Mecca, the building faces northward in the direction of Samarkand.

De Clavijo, the Andalusian envoy at Tamerlane's court who visited Shahr-i Sabz in 1404, left an enthusiastic description of how Ak-Sarai looked inside with its numerous halls decorated in gold, glazed tiles, and remarkable carvings. One of the palace's wonders was a pool (locally called "hawuz") on its roof, from which the water cascaded into a beautiful garden. The water came through a lead pipe from Takhta-Karacha Pass.

Nowadays only two pillars, encrusted in azure tiles and measuring 38 m (125 ft) high, are left of the remarkable palace. The tiling includes the inscription "Timur is the shadow of Allah," or so it should have read on both sides of the great arch, but either 1 of the columns was a bit smaller than the other or else the writing turned out bigger, because on 1 side it reads "Timur is a shadow." Tamerlane was justly offended at the slight and had the artist responsible thrown to his death from the top of a minaret.

Near the columns, to the left and the right are the mosaic floors that belonged to the guard houses. The central arch fell down about 200 years ago but the 4-storey palace was mostly devastated by Emir Abdullakhan II of Bukhara in the second half of the 16th century during the wars for the Sheibanid throne. As legend has it, when the emir's army was approaching Shahr-i Sabz, the walls and the dome of Ak-Sarai appeared on the horizon in the desert. The emir decided that the city was quite near and galloped ahead accompanied by a runner. It was a long journey. The runner fell dead and soon the emir's horse collapsed, too, but although Ak-Sarai became bigger and bigger and soon covered half the sky, the city of Shahr-i Sabz was still not to be seen. So later, when the emir and his warriors at last reached the walls of the town, the angry emir ordered Ak-Sarai to be destroyed for causing his mistake.

In the centre of Shahr-i Sabz, down Lenin Street from the hotel and to the left, in Rabochaya ("Workers") Street, rises one of the most interesting architectural monuments in the Middle East, Dorus-siadat ("Seat of Power and Might"), which consists of the tall building of a mausoleum with a blue, cone-shaped dome and an underground crypt that stands almost 40 m (44 yds) to the side. Tamerlane envisaged this as a dynastic sepulchre for himself and his descendants. Dorus-siadat was a big building, 70 m by 50 m (230 ft by 164 ft). The main western facade carried a portal entrance with an arch spanning 20 m (66 ft) and the pillars housing mausolea. It was built in between 1380 and 1404, additional structures being added in the 19th century and at the beginning of the 20th.

In his description De Clavijo also mentions the crypt that was being built in Shahr-i Sabz in 1404 for Tamerlane. This has remained intact, although Tamerlane was buried in a mausoleum in Samarkand that originally had been intended for his grandson, Muhammad-Sultan. The stone sarcophagus of Dorus-siadat was used for the burial of other people.

The crypt is small and cross-shaped and lined with marble. The basic structure is 3.5 m (11 ft) square, and the architecture is marked by splendour and stylistic reserve. The inscriptions in the drop-shaped medallions carved in the pendentives and niches carry no historical information; they are merely excerpts from prayers and the Koran. In 1376 Tamerlane's eldest and best-beloved son Djekhangir ("Subjugator of the Universe") died in Samarkand. His body was brought to Shahr-i Sabz for interment in the Barlas family burial place. In 1394 another of Tamerlane's sons, Omar-sheikh, who had perished on a combat march, also was buried here. Later on some other people were interred in *Djekhangir's mausoleum*, which adjoins the *Khazreti-Imam Mosque*. In full accordance with descriptions by ancient authors, it was a tall structure. Its total height including the dome is 27 m (89 ft), with a square hall 6.3 m (20 ft) square. The walls of the hall have wide, shallow niches. The interior had murals painted on the plasterwork. Under the pendentives there has survived a fragment from an Arabic saying: "Wise men act with lofty intentions, fools await with lofty intentions."

The Djekhangir mausoleum mostly was spared during the devastating activity of Abdullakhan II in the second half of the 16th century, thanks to the intercession of the clergy, because it stood next to the alleged tomb of Imam Muhammad Sheibani, also known as Khazreti Imam, who had lived in Iraq at the end of the 8th century and died in Reya. As legend has it, the remains of the imam were brought on Tamerlane's orders to Shahr-i Sabz. In fact, the false burial place was one of the many holy places in the Muslim world. In the 18th century the cult of Khazreti Imam was transferred to the Djekhangir mausoleum and the entire complex and the mausoleum became a kind of bulwark of the Muslim priesthood. In the 1860s, upon the order of the ruler of Kokand, a district mosque was erected nearby and the yard was closed from the north by the residential cells of the medresseh. In 1868 Emir Muzaffar presented the mausoleum with a precious carved door, but there is a strong suspicion that it was this emir who had uncovered Tamerlane's crypt and robbed it. In 1904 a new entrance was added to the complex, and in 1914 the cells were rebuilt and the mosque reconstructed into a closed building with a dome and terrace.

The territory of Dorus-siadat was virtually covered by graves. The crypt was lost for many years until a little girl playing in a garden fell in through the roof.

Dorut-tilavat ensemble (meaning "the receptacle of those who honour the Koran") is to the southeast of Dorus-siadat. There are the remains of two *mausolea* and, opposite them, a *mosque*, which is open for services. The foundation of this complex dates back to 1370, when Sheikh Shamseddin Kulala Fakhuri died. This sheikh was the spiritual instructor of Tamerlane and his father, Taragai. So after the sheiks's death Tamerlane gave orders that he should be buried near the main mosque of Shahr-i Sabz. A domed mausoleum was constructed "by the pir's feet" in 1374 and Taragai's mortal remains were transferred here from his former resting place. The walls of the square building remain, with part of the splendid marble tomb and the carved entrance door.

Now the remains of the tomb form a kind of entrance to the second mausoleum, *Gumbazi Seiidan*, which is scientifically known as the magbarat (burial vault) of Ulug Beg's descendents. It was built in 1437–38 and there are some marble sepulchres with blue and white ornamentation that were brought here from the nearby cemetery. The tombs carry the inscriptions of the names of the Saiids from Therezm, hence the name of the mausoleum of Gumbazi ("Cupola") Seiidan. One of the tombs has been particularly worn with the touches of those who sought a cure for smallpox. The mausoleum is a building of gracious proportions with a blue cupola. The interior is magnificently painted, but unfortunately the paintings are badly preserved.

Kok Gumbez ("Blue Cupola") Mosque was erected in 1435 by Tamerlane's grandson, Ulug Beg, most probably on the site of the former main mosque of Shahr-i Sabz. The blue cupola has not survived; it collapsed during an earthquake and now only its drum and the inner dome can be seen. The Dorut-tilavat ensemble is united by a small yard with three venerable plane trees. At the turn of the century new cells belonging to the Shamseddin Kulyalya Medresseh were constructed on ancient foundations.

Charsu Trade Cupola, over the former crossroad of the main town streets, was built in the 15th and 16th centuries. It is a five-domed, square brick edifice with each side measuring 21 m (23 yds). The domes are brown. In central Asia, besides this one only Samarkand and Bukhara have retained such traditional markets in the form of a roofed arcade with a dome of 14 m (46 ft). Small shops are inside.

The *mediaeval bathhouse* (still in use) in the centre of the city probably was built in the 18th century, but in Uzbekistan some think it is about 700 years old. It has salubrious qualities. It is a classic mediaeval bathhouse, rectangular in shape and with three sections—for hot, cold, and warm bathing. A network of heating flues run under the marble-covered floor. There are places of interest of later origin in Shahr-i Sabz as well, the *Malik-Azhdara hanaka* (religious house) and *Kazy-Guzar* · district mosque among them.

Monument, Lenin Square. This monument is to the memory of soldiers killed in 1923, during the civil war.

Lenin Statue, to the left of the road in Kitab

World War II Memorial, on the left in Kitab

Shahr-i Sabz Hotel and Restaurant, Gagarin Street 26; tel. 33-861. Here is an Intourist office, tel. 38-60.

Ok Suv Restaurant, on the left in Kitab

Bakhor Restaurant, Gagarin Street 88

Tourist Restaurant, in Kitab, to the left of the main road

There is another good *restaurant* a little out of town, decorated in national style and serving Uzbek dishes.

Dustlik Stadium

GPO, Leninism Street 18a

Intourist organises picnic excursions to the settlement of Miraki, 30 km (19 miles) away.

SHAKHTINSK
See Karaganda, p. 180.

SHEKI Population—60,000
Sheki stands 380 km (236 miles) inland from Baku at a height of 675 to 850 m above sea level (the unusual figure is due to its reconstruction after the flood; see below) at the foot of the southern slopes of the Caucasus Mountains. It is about 2,500 years old, one of the oldest towns of Azerbaijan, and took its name from that of the Saki tribe, which once lived in these parts. Sheki developed as a trading centre on the road to Daghestan, to the north where it crossed the east-west route linking the Caspian and Black seas. It served as the capital of the khanate of Sheki and was resited at Nukha in 1772, but the old name of Sheki was restored in 1968. The mountain river Kish flows to the west of the town and part of Sheki is on the banks of the Kish-chai.

In 1743 Hadji Chelyabi (who reigned from 1742 to 1754) fortified himself in a fortress on a piece of high ground 4 km to the northeast of Sheki town centre, and proclaiming himself khan of Sheki. The following year the Persians came in force, but he refused to surrender. The Persian Shah Nadir was furious and asked how these people could behave with such impudence. He received the reply: "Gyalyarsyan-gyoryarsyan" (meaning "Come and see"). He came, failed to take the fortress, and went away again. But legend has it that this is the origin of the unusual name of the fortress, called *Gyalyarsyan-gyoryarsyan* to this day. There is a road leading to it, and there is a good view from the walls.

Hadji Chelyabi then founded the new fortress at Nukha in the northeastern part of the present-day town, and the khanate became independent of Persia in 1747. Agakishi Bek, the next khan, ruled from 1754 to 1757. The construction of the fortress was completed in 1755, and in 1762 an elaborately decorated palace was built within the fortress walls. The old town of Sheki lay spread in the valley of the Kish at some distance below the fortress, and in 1772, when Hussein Khan Mushtag (1757–79) was khan, tragedy struck in the form of a devastating flood when the river burst its bank and rose to sweep away almost every building. Rather than rebuild the town of Sheki, the population moved to the east to Nukha and up into the ravine through which flowed the Gurjan-chai River. Here, around the fortress, they built their new town, which they logically called Nukha. The next khan was Hadji Abdul Kadir (1779–83).

Shah Muhamed-Hasan-Khan, who ruled the khanate from 1784 to 1804, still acknowledged his vassalage to the larger state. In 1795 Agha-Mohammad Khan of Persia gave orders that Muhamed-Hasan be blinded, but the latter nevertheless clung to his post. The khanate was ceded to Russia in 1805, and in 1807 Selim Khan, the last of the house of Chelyabi, emigrated to Persia, whereupon the tsarist government appointed Djafar Kuli-Khan as khan of Nukha in his place. He was succeeded in 1816 by his son Ismail-Khan, but he was to be the last of the khans. He died in 1819 and the khanate was abolished in 1820, the place subsequently being governed by a military commander.

Although the oldest part of the town is in the ravine, the newer part has spread westward down the valley again, and in 1968 the old name of Sheki was restored. Today Sheki is unusual for an oriental town in that the new building after the flood was planned and because so much was constructed at the same time, there is a degree of architectural cohesion seldom to be found in towns of comparable age and history. The town is criss-crossed by wide streets where used to stand the caravanserai, with names such as Isfahan, Armenian, and Tabriz, indicating where the majority of the merchants came from. The old street names, named after the potters, weavers, tanners, and so on, show the areas in which these trades were practiced. The business centre was near the caravanserai and ran along the right bank of the Gurjan-chai River. Marked by their small domes are a number of *bathhouses* dating from those early days, and the two caravanserai that remain are two-story constructions, built around their courtyards and with wide gates leading inside. They look like small fortresses and are known as the *Verkhny* and *Nizhny Caravanserai* (meaning "Upper" and "Lower"). All of this area is now designated a historic reserve.

From the earliest times the manufacture of silk has been of vital importance to the local economy. The art had been learnt from the Chinese and is still the most important item of local industry. The *Lenin Silk Mill* is the largest in the country. There are a number of smaller silk and other textile mills besides, and in 1981 a large dye works was built.

The new *fortress* now stands right in the town. The total length of the surrounding walls is 1,300 m (1,422 yds) and their thickness is 2.20 m (7 ft). Because the walls follow the complicated contours of the site, they appear shorter in length, and some people even believed that the twists and turns in the walls corresponded to the Arabic spelling of Muhamed Hasan-Khan's name. Parts of the fortress have been reconstructed and the height of the walls was increased at the beginning of the 17th century, at the time of the Caucasian wars.

Inside the fortress walls stands the 2-storey *palace* built in 1762 as a formal summer residence by Abbasgulu, an architect from Shemakha. The two plane trees in front of it are already 400 years old. The palace is now open as a museum. The facade is 32 m (35 yds) in length, plastered and painted in patterns of green, beige, apricot, and grey like a gigantic carpet. The two balconies on the facade were of special significance: that on the left, toward the western end of the building, was known as the *Balcony of Mercy*; the khan would appear upon it dressed in a light-coloured robe to pardon supplicants. That on the right was the *Balcony of Wrath*, and from there, clad in red, he would deal out punishments as he deemed fit. The ceilings of the balconies are of mirror mosaic, which must have added to their effectiveness. The doors and windows are all made of wood and coloured-glass mosaic. In the finest parts of the work as many as 14,000 pieces are used to decorate a square metre/yard, but it is said that the intricate design was completed without using glue or nails. Some of the doors bear designs that are copies of Persian miniatures, and there are fireplaces made to look like ancient helmets. There is a legend that when the khan asked his architect whether he could build another palace as magnificent as this and was told that indeed he could build an even better one, to prevent any such occurrence the khan ordered that he be beheaded. Alexandre Dumas (père) was lavish in his praise of the beautiful building when he wrote up his travel notes; indeed, an ode written at the time of its opening compared its rooms to heaven itself.

The palace stands in a garden and most of the designs used to decorate the building are plant-and-flower motifs. The murals and painted ceilings inside date from 1902 to 1904, when there was a plan that the palace should be used as a summer residence by the governor of the Caucasus. Two artists from Shemakha, Abas-Kuli and Kurban-Ali, renewed the paintings following the original lines. There are scenes of battle and hunting that are especially interesting. It is open daily, 10–6, except on the 30th of each month.

The *khan's mosque* also stands inside the fortress. There are two other *mosques* in Sheki that number among the town's older buildings. Both date from the 17th and 18th centuries.

Djuma Mosque, up a side road just above the Upper Caravanserai. It has a wrought-iron entrance gate. There are *shahs' tombs* in the little backyard and four giant plane trees. The mosque now serves as a reading room. The building opposite is a silk mill.

Geleilyn Mosque and Minaret, reached by walking further up from Akhundov's House (see below).

Mosque, up the hill from the hotel at Sheki Street 57, to the left.

Mosque, outside the fortress walls, about 150 m/yds to the west.

Armenian Church, Lenin Street. There are the remains of a church only.

Shekikhanov House, behind House No. 16, at the top of the hill. It can be reached by turning left below the caravanserai and then walking up the hill. This was built for the khan's relatives at the same time as the palace, and although it is very dilapidated, it is a good example of the civil architecture of the period. There are a number of good murals inside.

Akhundov's House, Akhundov Street, up to the left of the fortress. Mirza Fetkh-Ali Akhundov (1812–78) was a philosopher and writer who earned the name "the Moslem Molière." Russian educated, he has strongly influenced modern Azerbaijan literature. This little house, where he spent his youth, has two rooms and a verandah, typical of those in these parts. Beside it is a musum with documentary material about the writer. Open daily, 10–6, except on the 30th of the month.

Aliyev House, on the main road up the hill, opposite the Upper Caravanserai. Aliyev was a millionaire who owned textile mills. In 1922 he emigrated to Turkey. His house is now a boarding school.

Efendiev Local Museum, Sheki Street, in the barracks building on the left inside the fortress, above the entrance gate. Here are costumes, musical instruments, and a collection of old money. Open daily, 10–6, except on the 30th of the month.

Museum of Military Glory, in Narodny Park, up on the hill near the *World War II memorial*. The memorial is designed in a twisted shape to represent a flag. Open daily, 10–6, except on the 30th of each month.

Museum of Revolutionary Glory, also up on the hilltop

Art Gallery, in the fortress, below the Efendiev Local Museum

Akhundov Monument, in front of the entrance to the fortress

Monument. This monument, which has a stepped column, commemorates Communists who were shot here in the 1930s.

Welcome Statue, at the turn from the main road toward Sheki. The shiny metal statue of a welcoming lady stands beside a double arch.

Lower Caravanserai, further on up the hill, facing the river. This is to be turned into a shopping centre with demonstrations of carpet weaving and the manufacture of exotic sweets.

Upper Caravanserai, still further up the hill, facing the river. This was built by a Greek merchant. It is to be an Intourist hotel with accommodations for 150 guests.

Fortress Walls, up a cobbled road, which leads to the entrance arch. The walls date from the 18th century. Inside is a *Russian Orthodox church* built in 1828.

Palace, inside the fortress walls.

Gyal Palace, 7 to 8 km (4 to 5 miles) away, in another fortress still higher up

Sabit Rachman Drama Theatre, Lenin Street, next to the post office. Sabit Rachman (1910–70) was an Azerbaijani playwright.

Sheki Intourist Hotel and Restaurant, Sheki Street 8; tel. 24-88.

Intourist Office, Lenin Street 18a; tel. 31-72.

Soyug Bulag Restaurant

Iyeddi Gyozal Restaurant

Saadat Restaurant, 120 m (394 ft) above the city centre, on the top of the hill behind the stadium and the curly World War II memorial. Also here on the hilltop, next to each other, are the Museum of Military Glory and the Museum of Revolutionary Glory.

GPO, Lenin Street

Bank, Lenin Street

Trout Farm, in the *Markhal recreation area*, 9 km (6 miles) from the centre of town

Beyond Sheki the main road runs up toward the Kakhetia region of Georgia.

Zakataly

Located on the right bank of the river Talachai, 543 m (1,781 ft) above sea level. Eastward, between Zakataly and Sheki, was the scene of battle in 65 B.C., when the Roman army under Pompey advanced against Mithradates VI to extend the bounds of the empire to include the states lying to the south of the Caucasus. At that time this area was known as Albania.

Later the village here belonged to the Dzhvari

Lezghins, who terrorized the surrounding peoples with their barbarous raids. To maintain order in the area the fortress of Novye Zakataly was founded here on the right bank of the Talachai in 1830. It proved its worth in 1853–54, when Imam Shamil (1797–1871), a political and religious leader who organised resistance to the Russian army, made 12 attempts to capture it. (Shamil was an Avar from Daghestan, the Avars being one of the Muslim peoples of the Caucasus.) The insurgents' camp was 25 km (16 miles) north of their own, at a place now called Mt. Shamil, and the stones that were used to sharpen their arms can still be seen there. Today it is the Zakataly fortress that is best known as *Shamil's Fortress*. It is at the end of Mira Street. A flight of stone steps in the centre of the town leads up to the ruins of the 19th-century stronghold.

In 1905, following the mutiny of the crew of the battleship *Potyomkin* at Odessa, the seamen from the battleship were exiled to this fortress.

Today the town is surrounded by plantations of rice, tobacco, tea, and roses. Local industry includes the processing of nuts, fruit, and tea, and there is lumbering in the nearby forests.

Church, just off the central square. It is closed.

Local Museum, in the fortress. This is connected with the local nature reserve and has a complete collection of stuffed local animals.

Shevchenko Memorial Complex, Gadzhibekova Street. This includes a bas-relief of the Ukrainian writer Taras Shevchenko.

Demeshko Monument, in Lenin Park. Stepan Demeshko was a sailor from the battleship *Potyomkin*, famed for the revolt that took place on board in 1905.

Lenin Monuments, in Lenin Park and in the

ZAKATALY

garden at the crossing of Kommunisticheskaya and Seville Kazievoy streets

War Memorial, Tbilissky Prospect. This memorial commemorates the soldiers who fell in the battles of World War II.

Hotel, in the centre of town

Gyulustan Restaurant, Komsomolskaya Street, near the station

Shimshak Restaurant, Tbilissky Prospect

Department Store, Nizami Street

Market, Budapest Street

Zakataly Airport, below the town, to the right of the 43/121 km mark.

Zakataly Forest Reserve, to the north of the town. This was founded in 1930 and includes a scientific research station. The most highly valued local animals are the Daghestan goats (Capra caucasica), some of which weigh as much as 100 kg (220 lb). They were hunted for their horns almost to a point of extinction. Also here are the Caucasian chamois and the Caucasian deer.

Shamil's Camp, up in Mt. Shamil

SHEMAKHA
See Baku, p. 63.

SHEPETOVKA
See Khmelnitsky, p. 215.

SHEVCHENKOVO
See Cherkassy, p. 101.

SHUSHENSKOYE
See Abakan, p. 32.

SIBERIA
See Novosibirsk, p. 393.

SIGNAKHI
See Telavi, Kakhetia, p. 553.

SIGULDA
See Riga, p. 449.

SIMFEROPOL is the capital of the Crimean Peninsula, now part of the Ukrainian SSR.

THE CRIMEA

The Crimean Peninsula is saved from being an island only by the 8-km (5-mile) wide Perekop Isthmus that links it to the mainland. The shallow sea of Azov bounds it to the east and the Black Sea to the south and west. It has long been regarded as the Riviera of the Soviet Union, and many have written about the beauty of the precipitous cliffs and subtropical vegetation of its southern shore. An additional attraction is the amazing variety of architecture, some comparatively modern and some extremely ancient. Of the ruined castles of the Crimea, Adam Mickiewicz wrote in the last century:

These castles heaped in sheltered piles once graced

And guarded you, Crimea, thankless land!
Today like giant skulls set high they stand
And shelter reptiles, or men more debased.
Upon that tower a coat-of-arms is traced,
And letters, some dead hero's name, whose hand
Scourged armies. Now he sleeps forgotten and
The grapevine holds him, like a worm embraced.

Here Greeks have chiseled Attic ornament,
Italians cast the Mongols into chains
And pilgrims chanted slowly, Mecca bent:
Today the black-winged vulture alone reigns,
Where mourning banners flutter to the plains.

Immediately behind the coast rise the Crimean Mountains, 50 km (31 miles) in length. Although the range drops sharply seaward, to the north it slopes gradually and runs down into the steppeland that makes up three-quarters of the area of the Crimea. The central plain becomes very dry in summer, but the mountains provide good pasture then.

In antiquity the Crimea was inhabited by Cimmerians, Taurians, and Scythians, who grew corn on the inland steppes. In the 6th century B.C. Greek colonies began to grow up at various points along the coast, but the eastern region of the peninsula fell into Roman hands and by the 4th century A.D. was a part of the East Roman Empire. The colonies subsequently changed hands between Rome and Byzantium and from the 13th century they belonged to Venice and Genoa.

The Turks conquered the southern part of the Crimea in 1475 and held the area till 1783, when Catherine the Great forced the last khan to abdicate and made the Crimea a Russian province. It was then that the majority of Tatars emigrated to Turkey. At the end of the 18th century as many as 300,000 left, and by the time the Crimea had been ruled by Russia for a whole century only 60,000 remained. The Crimea was the site of hostilities that are still remembered, such as the Crimean War of 1853–1856 between Russia, on the one side, and Britain, France, and Turkey on the other, when the Allies landed here.

The Crimea witnessed many a battle during the civil war. Anti-Bolshevik forces under General Pyotr Wrangel were unexpectedly acknowledged de facto as the government of southern Russia by France and the United States in August 1920. In October the French high commissioner, Comte de Martel, and General Brousseau were sent to Sebastopol to find out what help was required. In the same month the Red Army began its advance on the last position of the White Army in Crimea. On 14 November 1920, 145,693 men left the Crimea in Russian and French ships. Wrangel declined an offer to surrender and so ended the civil war. The

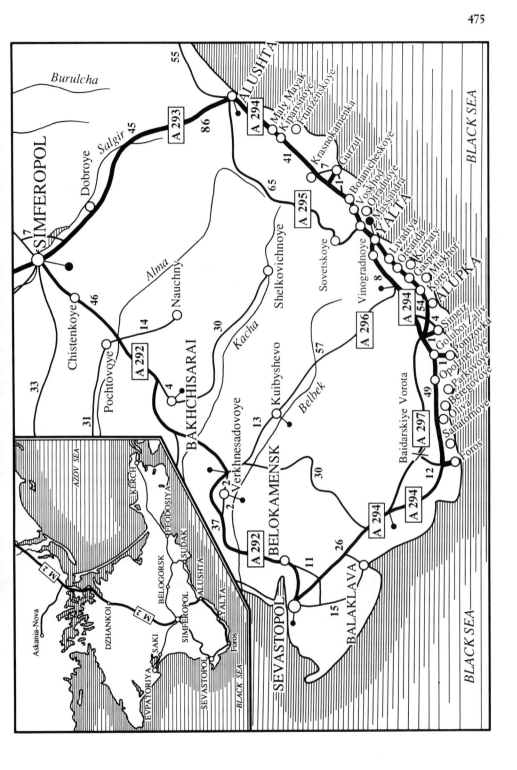

Crimean (Tatar) Autonomous Republic was established in 1921.

In 1945, however, all of the Tatars living in the Crimea, then numbering about 200,000, were deported along with some Caucasian minorities to Asiatic Russia for alleged cooperation with the Germans during World War II. After the deportation the Crimean Autonomous Republic was dissolved, and in 1954 it became part of the Ukraine. Many of the old Tatar place names were changed but there are still plenty left. There was an idea among the Russian Jews to have this peninsula for the Jews, instead of the existing Jewish autonomous area of Birobidjan in the Soviet Far East.

Although they were allowed to return to Europe in 1967, the Crimean Tatars were not permitted to resettle in the Crimea until 1988, following prolonged protests in Moscow. Even so, the Tatar Autonomous Republic was not to be restored.

Simferopol Population—345,000

Simferopol is the capital of Crimea. It is situated in the steppe on the river Salgir, with the mountain Chatyr-Dag (1.5 km/4,921 ft) forming its background. From the north the city is open to the winds, while from the south it is surrounded by mountains, consequently it is not as hot in summer as it is in Yalta on the southern coast, but it has more sunny days.

The place was inhabited as far back as the Stone Age, and at the beginning of the 1st millennium B.C., here roamed the savage tribes of the Taurians, hence the Crimea's old name, Taurida. In the 7th century B.C. the Scythians came, and on the site of present day Simferopol stood their capital, Neapolis, repeatedly mentioned by ancient writers. Neapolis reached its apogee in the 2nd century B.C. during the reign of King Skilur. It was surrounded by strong walls and entered by two subsidiary gateways besides the main gates in the middle of the southern wall.

In 1827 some marble slabs with inscriptions and pictures were noticed on a passing cart. A bas-relief depicted a horseman in a Scythian hat and there was a Greek inscription addressed to Zeus and Athens from a certain Posidei. The slabs had come from a quarry in the steppe where subsequently Roman coins and stelae were found. One of the latter carried a text about King Skilur and his son Palak. There is a story by a Greek writer, Polien, of the 2nd century B.C. that tells how the Scythians in the time of Skilur and Palak harassed Khersones. The townspeople asked for help from King Medosakk of the Sarmatians, who already had begun to threaten the Scythians from the east. In fact, however, it was Medosakk's wife Amaga, a real Amazon by nature, who came to the rescue. In the course of a single day she galloped 222 km (138 miles) at the head of 120 horsemen, captured Neapolis, killed King Skilur, passed his crown to his son, and returned the territory that the Scythians had seized to Kherosones. Polien is the only historical source of this story.

In 1945–46 while they were working on the town, archaeologists found the remains of a coffin thought to have belonged to a queen. To the west of the main gates there was also a stone mausoleum that had never been robbed and held 1,300 golden objects plus other treasures. In later excavations a sepulchre supposed to be that of Skilur was discovered.

The *ruins of Neapolis* may be seen in the southeastern part of the city. Some of the finds from the ancient city are held in the *Local Museum*.

In the Middle Ages the Greeks formed a settlement on the ruins of Neapolis and then the Tatars, who seized the Crimea in the 14th century, named the place Kermenchik ("Little Fortress"). At the beginning of the 16th century the Tatar town of Ak-Mechet ("White Mosque") stood here and became the residence of Kalghi-sultan, second in importance only to the Crimean khan.

In 1771, during the Russo-Turkish War (1768–74), Ak-Mechet was taken by the Russian troops and in 1783 the last Crimean khan abdicated, having agreed to become a Russian subject. The Crimea and the Taman Peninsula were transformed into a new administrative unit—the Taurian province. Following the proposition of Empress Catherine II, the new town of Simferopol (the name meaning "Collective-Town" in Greek) was made its capital. It was granted a coat of arms depicting a beehive with three bees below an inscription: "Healthful." The construction of Simferopol began in 1785 beside the Tatar Ak-Mechet, but work soon ceased. Emperor Paul I, whose reign began in 1796, abolished the Taurian province, the town again took the name of Ak-Mechet, and life came to a standstill. However, at the beginning of the 19th century the town (Simferopol again) slowly was being built. It was divided into two parts, the Asian part, with narrow crooked streets populated mainly by Tatars, and the European part. A fragment of the old town remains still. The European part on the left bank of Salgir had many social and administrative buildings. At the end of the 1880s the new town on the right bank began to be built up with rich private mansions.

During the Crimean War (1854–56) Simferopol became the ultimate point before soldiers were sent to the front line, and it also became a huge hospital. The famous Russian surgeon Pirogov and the chemist Mendeleyev both worked in the hospitals at Simferopol. As a young officer Leo Tolstoy also came here. In 1888 Chekhov stopped in Simferopol on his way to Yalta. He wrote in his notebook: "Beyond Simferopol the mountains begin and with them—beauty."

A Russian traveller at the turn of the century wrote: "This town is always passed in transit. Some stop here but not for long. From it and through it roads lead to all parts of the Crimea. It seems impossible to choose a more appropriate place for 'standing at the crossroads' than Simferopol." And today it is just the same. Air travellers continue their way to Yalta by car or trolleybus.

The main materials used in building houses

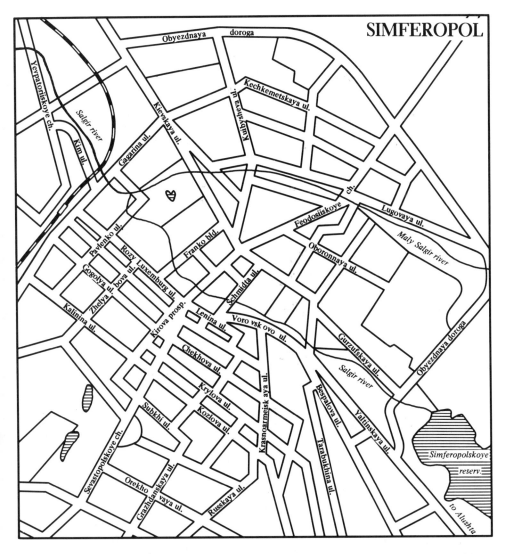

here are limestone and greenish blue diorite, which is harder than granite, for facing.

The industries are mainly connected with food and tobacco, using regionally grown produce. In 1914 a Belgian company introduced a tramway. Two years later an unusual development for these parts was the construction of the Anatra Aeroplane Plant, named after the Odessa enthusiast, Arthur Anatra. As a subsidiary of the Hispana-Suisa automobile company, the plant began to assemble biplanes, but in 1918 the whole enterprise was taken out of the country.

At present there are also machine-building and electrical goods factories, footwear and canned-goods industries. The Krasnaya Rosa ("Red Rose") firm is well known for its oils used in perfumery. There is Frunze University in the city and medical and agricultural colleges.

The city's main highway, Kirov Prospect (for- merly Salgirskaya Street), traverses Simferopol from the southwest to the northeast. Among the new buildings is the *House of Soviets*, which faces the former central square, Fontannaya. On the eastern side of the square stands a columned building, the *House of Trade Unions*. There is a new *theatre* and *department store*.

The present Karl Marx Street formerly was called Yekaterininskaya (in honour of Catherine II) and was the main street. It is adjoined by little, old streets, now mainly reserved for pedestrian use only, where some interesting buildings remain.

Lenin Boulevard runs for about 1 km (0.6 miles) from the railway station to the centre of the town, and a *monument to Lenin* stands on it. During the summer season some of the central streets, includ- ing Pushkin Street and its surrounding bystreets, also are closed to traffic and used only by pedes- trians.

The *Regional Library*, containing more than 500,000 books, is situated on Gorky Street in the mansion of the former Dvoryanskoye Sobranie. In 1855–56 a hospital functioned here. On the same street, the impressive *Shevchenko Cinema* building was built in 1915 as the Bayan Cinema. Across the street at No. 4 is the *bank*, built in 1913.

Pushkin Street, which crosses Karl Marx Street, is an old trading thoroughfare. The inscription on No. 7, "Semirdjiev's Photography," shows that it was built for a photographer. No. 11 merits attention for its art nouveau style; it used to be a café and shop. At the corner of Karl Marx Street is the local fruit processing plant, or *Krymconservtrest*, built in the 1920s, with the figure of a Tatar girl; the architect was Belozersky.

In Gogol Street at No. 14, formerly the premises of the Regional Courthouse, is the *Regional Party Committee*. In the adjoining street, Geroyev Adjimushkaya, stands the building of the former theological seminary, now the Photon Construction Bureau. In front of it is an *obelisk to the victims of the 1918–20 civil war*. At the corner stands *Trekh Svyatiteley Church*, built in 1873 but now closed.

Zhukovsky Street is named after the poet Vasily Zhukovsky, who lived here in 1837 in house No. 13. In this street stands an interesting building in the constructivist style of the 1930s, the *Tourist Club*, at No. 5.

Holy Trinity Cathedral, Odesskaya Street. This was built in 1868 as a Greek church.

Church of SS. Peter and Paul, Oktyabrskaya Street 7. This church now serves as a warehouse.

Kebir Djami Mosque, Kurchatov Street 4, but not visible from the road. This was built in 1508, was reconstructed in 1740, and is now used as a book-binding workshop.

Karaim Kenass, Parkhomenko Street 6. This large temple was built in 1911 for use by the Karaite Jews (see Chufut-Kale, below) and now houses the editorial office of the local radio station.

Local Museum, Pushkin Street 18. Open 10–6; closed Wed. and the last day of the month. The museum contains the *Taurica Library* (named after the old name for the Crimea), which has some 50,000 books on the Crimea. The Neapolis excavations are also a part of the museum. These are to be found just off the main Alushta road, near the town; a signpost saying "1 km" points the way. The remains of the old defence walls are here, together with some houses, a mausoleum, and tombs with frescoes.

Picture Gallery, Karl Liebknecht Street 35. Open 10–4; closed Fri. and the last day of the month.

Art Exhibition Hall, Karl Marx Street 15

Obelisk, at the crossing of Zhukovsky and Liebknecht streets. On one side of this 18-m (59-ft) monument is written: "In commemoration of the liberation of the Crimea from Turkish invaders by Russian troops in 1771." And on the other: "Here in 1771 were the headquarters of General Dolgoruky, commander of the Russian Army." The bas-relief depicts General Dolgoruky and his family's crest. When the monument was unveiled in 1842 an inscription read "To Prince Vasily Dolgoruky from his grandson," but the present inscriptions were made recently. Around the monument stand 18th-century cannon.

Bronze Bust of Suvorov, on the bank of the Salgir River ("Spusk Suvorova") on the site of a Russian military camp that was under the command of the famous leader. He was in charge of a military detachment in Simferopol in 1777, and the redoubt that was built here later formed the beginning of the town that marked its 200th anniversary in 1985.

Trenev Monument, Trenev Garden, at the corner of Gogol Street and Kirov Prospect. The writer Konstantin Trenev (1876–1945) taught Russian language and literature and lived in the Crimea for 40 years. The monument, unveiled in 1958, was sculpted by Balashov.

Tomb of the Unknown Soldier and Eternal Flame, Gagarin Park, Kiev Street

Tank Monument, Young Pioneers' Garden. This monument on a high platform stands to those who were killed in 1944 during the liberation of the Crimea.

Gorky Russian Drama Theatre, Pushkin Street 15. Formerly the Nobility Theatre, it was built in 1911 by the architect Beketov.

Ukrainian Drama and Musical Comedy Theatre, Sovietskaya Square

Circus, Gorky Street 3

Philharmonia Concert Hall, Pushkin Street 9

Gagarin Park

Children's Park, Kirov Street 81

Moskva Hotel & Restaurant, Kievskaya Street 1; tel. 32-012

Ukraina (Intourist) Hotel and Restaurant, Rosa Luxembourg Street 9; tel. 94 4472. Intourist office, tel. 94 4477.

Airport Hotel and Restaurant, at the airport

Kechkemet Restaurant, Gagarin Street 26

Selena Restaurant, Kievskaya Street 90

Okean Restaurant, Kirov Prospect 27

Astoria Restaurant, Karl Marx Street 16

Simferopol Restaurant, Karl Marx Street 2

Souvenirs, Karl Marx Street 7

Crimea Department Store, Kechkemetskaya Street 1

Art Salon, Kirov Street 25. Open 10–8; closed Sun.

Syurpriz, Karl Marx Street 14. Open 10–7; closed Sun.

Gorizont, Karl Marx Street 17. Open 10–7; closed Sun. This store sells cameras and gramophone records.

Solntse v Bokale (Wines), Kirov Prospect 4. Open 9–7; closed Sun.

Telegraph Office, Rosa Luxembourg Street 11

GPO, Karl Marx Street 17

On the outskirts of Simferopol at a place named Dubki stands a *Monument to the Victims of Fascism*, dedicated to the 22,652 people killed in local concentration camps.

*   *   *

Intourist organises excursions from Simferopol to Bakhchisarai (q.v.), 40 km (25 miles) away. A longer trip (110 km/68 miles) goes down to the seacoast, visiting *Nikitsky Botanical Garden* (closed Tues. and the 4th Thurs. of the month), Livadia, and Alupka (see Yalta and its environs).

SKOVORODINOVKA
See Kharkov, p. 204.

SLAVYANOGORSK
(Intourist organises excursions here from Donetsk, about 175 km/108 miles away.)

The area used to be known as Svyatiye Gory ("Holy Hills"). It was best known for its monastery, but there was also a village here called Bannoye. This grew as the local resort facilities expanded, and in 1964 it was granted the status of a town and renamed Slavyanogorsk (meaning "Slav Hills").

Much of the approach road runs along a raised causeway. The *Zhuravushka ("Little Crane") Restaurant* stands to the left and there is another restaurant to the left of the crossroads at the end of the approach. Turn right over the bridge across the Seversky Donets to reach the monastery, now the *Slavyanogorsk Historical-Architectural Museum Preserve.*

Slavyanogorsk is the home of *Svyatogorsky ("Holy Hills") Uspensky Monastery*, which is believed to have been founded in the 1240s by Kievan monks who fled here after Kiev was devastated by Batyi Khan. It is, however, more likely to have been founded in the 14th century. It is situated on the steep right bank of the river on 5 chalk hilltops that used to serve as a stronghold for Russian settlers. At first the monks lived in cells carved out of the cliffs. The Holy Hills (today known as the *Artyom Hills*) were first mentioned in Russian sources of 1541, the cathedral in 1624. All was devastated by the Tatars in 1679 and 1737, and in 1787 it was relegated to the status of a parish church. It revived only in 1844 on the request of the landowning Potyomkin family—they had donated money and land—and the buildings that can be seen now are of the mid-19th century. The monastery grew to have 8 churches. The cathedral church is that of the *Assumption of the Virgin*, built in 1850–68. There were more than 500 souls, three schools, a library, and various workshops here.

On the top of *Favour Hill* is the former *church of St. Nicholas* (1846), reached by a flight of 511 steps called the *Kyrill and Methodius Steps*.

The hills rise 120 m (394 ft) above river level. Anton Chekhov, who was here in May 1887, wrote to his sister Maria, "The place is unusually beautiful and original; the monastery is on the bank of the river Donets, at the foot of a huge white cliff on which crowd and tower one above the other gardens, oaks, and century-old pines. It seems that the trees are so crowded on the cliff that some sort of force pushes them up higher and higher. . . . The cuckoos and nightingales are never silent, singing day and night." Since 1975 the area has been a national park, sometimes called the Donets

Switzerland. The chalk hills indicate that there was a seabed here about 170 million years ago. A rare species of pine grows on the chalk, reminiscent of the Italian Pinas. Most of the chalk pines were lost during the civil war and World War II and only a limited number remain, so it is listed with other endangered species in the Red Book of the USSR. The pine is unusual for its short needles. It stands 28 m (92 ft) in height and some trees are up to 100 years old.

On the top of the hills are the remains of fortifications and caves and secret tunnels. On the hilltop is a 27-m (89-ft) *monument to Artyom*. This was the party name of Fyodor Sergeyev (1883–1921), revolutionary, party activist, and statesman. He took part in the 1905, 1907, and 1917 revolutions, and in 1918 he was chairman of the Council of People's Commissars of the Krivorozhsk-Donetsk Region. He died in 1921 in an accident while trying out an experimental propeller-driven railway wagon. The monument was erected in 1927 by Kavaleridze after a competition in which artists were asked to create a monument that would challenge the beauty of the monastery and the Holy Hills. Near it are other monuments—an *obelisk to Major General N. Batyuk*, who died here in 1943, the military *graves of World War II soldiers*, and the charred trunk of an oak, known as Lieutenant Vladimir Kamyshev's oak, where he maintained an observation point.

The *Artyom Cardiological Sanatorium* now occupies the monastery buildings and grounds. Slavyanogorsk itself is a resort town with a number of other sanatoria as well. The pure air is a valuable factor in the curative properties of the place.

Restaurant, on Artyom Hill

Near Slavyanogorsk, on the left bank of the river, is an oak grove; the trees are 200 to 300 years old and cover 300 hectares (750 acres).

SMOLENSK Population—344,000
Once known as the "Key and Gate of Russia," Smolensk is attractively situated on either side of the river Dnieper. It was first mentioned in a document of 863 and was the chief town of the large Slav tribe known as the Krivichi. It stood on the ancient north-south trade route, linking the Baltic lands with Byzantium and running, as it was said in Russian, "from the Vikings to the Greeks." Emperor Konstantine Porphyrogentus described how each spring many boats came down the Dnieper, heading for the markets of Byzantium. Smolensk maintained extensive links with many distant lands and entertained a variety of foreign guests. Archaeological excavations in Smolensk have brought to light all kinds of articles of trade and coins of Arabian, Persian, and Byzantine origin.

Near Smolensk are the hills that form the watershed between the basins of the Volga, the Dnieper, and the western Dvina. In 882 Prince Oleg conquered Smolensk on his victorious way from Novgorod to Kiev and made it a part of the principality of Kiev, but after 1054 it continually changed hands and was attacked in turn by Tatars, Muscovites, Lithuanians, and Poles.

The town became independent in the early 12th century and flourished under the rule of Prince Rostislav, grandson of Prince Vladimir Monomakh. Trade agreements were made in 1229 between Smolensk and a number of towns in Scandinavia and western Europe. A terrible epidemic of plague and cholera was recorded in 1388 as having left no more than 10 survivors. Smolensk was captured by the Lithuanians in 1395 and lost in 1401, but a large Lithuanian army led by Prince Vitovt besieged the town for 2 months in 1404 until it fell, and it remained in Lithuanian hands for 110 years. In 1654, after the third war with Poland, Smolensk was retaken by the Russians and in 1667, according to the Truce of Abdrusovo, the town, together with Kiev and part of the Ukraine lying to the east of the Dnieper, was formally turned over to Russia by the Poles.

It was northward to Smolensk that Peter the Great marched in September 1708 to stage a triumphal procession after his victory against Charles XII of Sweden at the Battle of Lesnaya; while cannon thundered, his troops paraded through, followed by columns of Swedish prisoners. In 1709, in recognition of its strategic importance, Peter proclaimed Smolensk a provincial capital and it was granted its coat of arms—a black gun with a golden carriage on a silver field surmounted by a bird of paradise.

It was to Smolensk in 1780 that Catherine the Great came to meet Emperor Josef II of Austria. Napoleon was in town twice during his Russian campaign of 1812; he thought of using it as a source of provisions for his soldiers and advanced against it on 4 August. However, when it fell after a 2-day battle, most of it had been burnt by the retreating Russians and there were the barest supplies to be found. On 28 October, when his Grande Armée was already in retreat, he returned and spent 4 futile days attempting to rally his troops. Then he retreated with his own trusted soldiers and left Marshal Ney to fight a rearguard action and to blow up the kremlin that had been spared by the Russians in August. Accordingly gunpowder was placed under all of the towers and fires were lit in many places; 8 were destroyed but the rest were saved. At that time only 600 people remained alive in the town, but it quickly recovered and grew into a small industrial centre, becoming especially active when the railways were opened.

Smolensk suffered greatly in World War II, being one of the first Russian cities to be bombed. It was awarded the title of Hero-City of the Soviet Union in 1985, to mark the 40th anniversary of VE day.

The old kremlin, which was known as Detinets, is enclosed by a wall 5 km (3 miles) in length and lies amid trees on the steeply sloping left bank of the river. The walls date from 1596–1602, when they were built by Boris Godunov on the order of Tsar Fyodor Ioanovich from plans by Fyodor Kon. They are 5.5 m (18 ft) thick and 15.2 m (50 ft)

high and originally boasted 38 towers, of which only 16 remain today. Once the walls were known as the "precious necklace of Russia." Parts of them are to be seen in many places in the centre of the town; some towers are enclosed by the *Park of Culture* and the *Garden of the Heroes of the Patriotic War*.

Gromovaya Tower. Open 10–6; closed Mon. and Fri.

Earth Fortress of King's Bastion. Part of this great 15th-century earthen wall is also in the town park near the Spartak Stadium. It dates back to the wars against the Poles. After capturing Smolensk in 1611 King Sigismund III of Poland hoped to hold the town by reinforcing it with this mighty bastion. It was heavily damaged during the fighting in 1654, but being a border town, Smolensk was kept battle-ready. Thus, on the eve of the outbreak of the Northern War (1700–1721) Peter I ordered the reinforcement of the earthen wall. It is believed that in the 18th century the Ukrainian heroes Kochubei and Iskra, who informed Peter I of the treason of Hetman Mazepa, languished in one of the dungeons here. In August 1812 the King's Bastion once again served to defend Smolensk; it was here that Napoleon made a concentrated attack on the Russian armies. The battle raged for a whole day and the French suffered great losses. The park was laid out in 1874.

Reconstruction work is now taking place in Smolensk, and the old houses in the streets leading to Smirnov Square in the centre of the town are interspersed with new buildings. Beside the old and the new, there are a number of buildings in the constructivist style of the early 1930s. Perhaps the most spectacular street is Oktyabrskoy Revolutsii, particularly at the point where it is crossed by Dzerzhinsky Street. One of the biggest buildings is the postwar *House of Soviets*, on Karl Marx Square. In the southwest part of the town are the modern Ryadovka and Popovka residential regions.

Smolensk has four colleges, including those for medicine and teachers' training, and the various local industries include machine building, woodwork, clothes manufacture, and diamond cutting at the Kristall Factory.

Uspensky ("Assumption") Cathedral, Soborny Dvor 5, on a hill to the south of the bridge over the Dnieper, which motorists cross on their way into town. By driving up Bolshaya Sovietskaya Street one reaches the cathedral straight away. The huge 5-domed building dominates the whole town. When Napoleon walked into it he was so struck by its splendour that he took off his hat and set a guard to protect the building from his own men. The gilding of the iconostasis was only done in 1820 and the murals still later, so Napoleon was not so much dazzled as simply overawed by the majestic proportions of the cathedral. The original cathedral on this hill was founded in 1101 by Vladimir Monomakh, but 500 years later it was destroyed by the Poles, when all of the people who had sought sanctuary inside it also perished. King Sigismund is said to have built a Catholic church in its place, but in

SMOLENSK

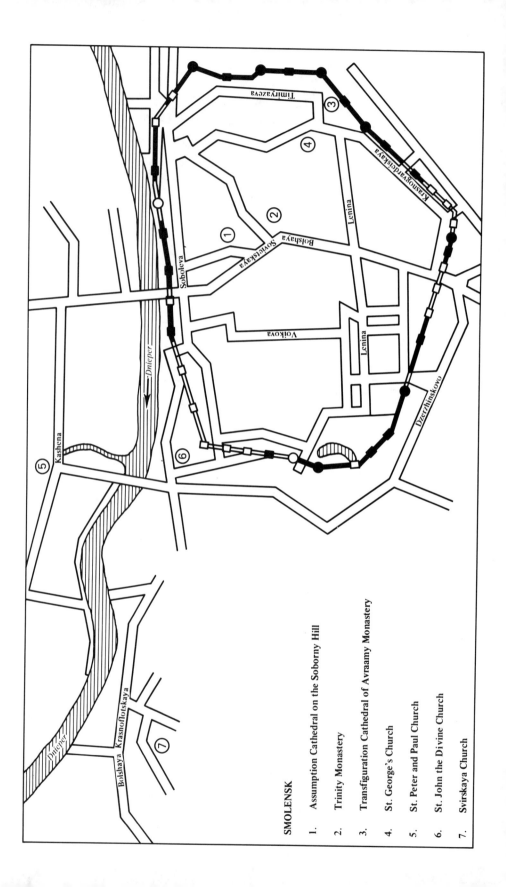

SMOLENSK

1. Assumption Cathedral on the Soborny Hill
2. Trinity Monastery
3. Transfiguration Cathedral of Avraamy Monastery
4. St. George's Church
5. St. Peter and Paul Church
6. St. John the Divine Church
7. Svirskaya Church

1677, at the end of the Polish period of Smolensk's history, this was dismantled as being out of keeping with the Orthodox faith. Tsar Alexei Mikhailovich provided Archbishop Simeon of Smolensk with plans, money, and master builder Alexei Korolkov to create a fit monument to the heroic defence of Smolensk against the Poles in 1609–11. The plans resembled those of the great Moscow cathedrals, but it is twice the size of the kremlin's Uspensky Cathedral. Work on it stopped completely when the east wall collapsed in 1679, but it was started again in 1712 under the architect Gotfrid Schedel and the building was consecrated in 1740.

The cathedral is in use today. It stands 69.7 m (229 ft) high and is 53 m (58 yds) long and 36 m (39 yds) wide; the central dome is built of wood and is decorated. The iconostasis of gilded lime wood stands 10 m (33 ft) high; it was carved by Sila Mikhailov with the help of three assistants, and the icons were painted by twelve artists working under the Ukrainian Trusitsky. Both teams took 10 years to complete the project. The principal treasure is a wonder-working icon of the Virgin, said to have been painted by St. Luke for Theophilus, ruler of Syria. Afterward the icon went to Jerusalem and Constantinople, and it came to Russia in 1046 when the Emperor Constantine gave it to his daughter Anna upon her marriage to Prince Vsevolod of Chernigov. In her turn, Princess Anna gave it to her son Vladimir Monomakh of Smolensk on his wedding day. It was placed in the cathedral in 1103; the original was stolen in 1923 and the present one is a 16th-century copy, equally revered and standing upon a stone platform. Other valuable icons are those of Our Lady of Vladimir, brought to Smolensk in 1445, and Our Lady of Jerusalem, painted probably as early as the 12th century. Also to be seen here is a shroud, dated 1561, embroidered with a picture of the Entombment. This formerly belonged to the Uspensky ("Assumption") Cathedral in Moscow's kremlin, but it was stolen by Napoleon in 1812 and recaptured in Smolensk, where it remained.

From the cathedral yard an impressive sweep of *steps* founded in 1766 leads down to the street. These were originally baroque in decoration, but in 1784 they were redesigned by Mikhail Slepnyov in classical style. The cathedral's belfry near the top of the steps was built in the 17th century and reconstructed in St. Petersburg baroque style in 1767. On the other side of the steps is *Bogoyavleniya* ("Epiphany") Cathedral, also built by Mikhail Slepnyov in 1784, very small in comparison with the larger summer building but warmly heated in winter. Nearby is the 2-storey ecclesiastical courthouse; this and the other buildings in the complex now house the bishop's offices, archives, and the town's natural history museum.

Also on Soborny Hill is *St. John the Baptist's Church*, built on the eastern slope in 1703, and the *Church of the Annunciation*, built in 1774 and restored after being damaged in World War II.

Further up Bolshaya Sovietskaya, at No. 11, the street cuts through the precincts on *Troitsky* ("Trinity") Monastery. This explains why the belfry (1738–40) stands on the right of the street while the cathedral to which it belongs stands on the left. *Troitsky Cathedral* originally was built with Lithuanian brickwork as part of a Dominican monastery to stand above the little river Klovka. In 1674, on the order of Tsar Alexei Mikhailovich, it was reconstructed as an Orthodox monastery, and until 1740 it served as the residence of the bishops of Smolensk. In the first half of the 18th century it was fundamentally rebuilt according to plans by Ivan Kalinik, who gave it its present baroque appearance. Beside it is *Anno-Zachatievskaya Church* (1767), but these buildings are all that remain of the monastery now. First there was an ecclesiastical school on this site, but Tsar Alexei Mikhailovich converted it to a monastery. Until the 19th century it served as the prelate's residence and then was used as the church burial place; the three first bishops of Smolensk were buried here. From this point a surprising number of churches can be seen in the spreading panorama of Smolensk.

Where Lenin Street crosses Bolshaya Sovietskaya stands the former *Europa Hotel*, and then it leads to the right toward Lenin Square and Glinka Garden, which is known locally by its old name of "Bloniye." Here, too, are the impressive buildings of the House of Soviets, the drama theatre, and the Rossia Hotel. The children's hospital at Glinka Street 4 was rebuilt in the 1890s from the von Engelhard family mansion, and the music school at Oktyabrskoy Revolutsii Street 8 was formerly the governor's residence.

To get a good general impression of Smolensk and take in the most important of the churches, go back to Bolshaya Sovietskaya Street and go on up it, turning left to follow the line of the city walls down Krasnogvardeiskaya and Timiryazeva streets. Beside the road on the right is *Spaso-Preobrazhenskaya* ("Transfiguration") Church, formerly part of the monastery of the same name on the far side of the Klovka River and then converted into a Jesuit church by the Poles. Their seminary building still stands beside it. The church was used as a prison by the French in 1812. Also here are the remains of the *Spaso-Avramiev Monastery*. This was founded by Bishop Ignati of Smolensk in the 13th century when he dedicated a church to St. Ignati Bogonosets, later changing its name to *Rizopolozhenskaya* ("Deposition of the Robe") Church. The monastery became famous when the learned Father Avraam, who kept the rich library there, drew crowds to hear his sermons and prayed successfully for rain in time of drought. The abbott was envious and banished him to another monastery for a number of years. After 1610 Avraam Monastery was demolished by the Dominicans and rebuilt to be used as a religious school until 1634. In 1658 it was reconverted again to Russian Orthodox use. *Transfiguration Cathedral* was built in 1753 with a ground-floor church dedicated to Holy Father Avraam of Smolensk.

At the bottom of the hill turn left along Soboleva Embankment by the Dnieper, passing the impressive *Dniprovsky Gate* (1793–1814), which now houses the puppet theatre and the concert hall.

Turn right to cross the bridge and reach the ancient lower part of the town, the "posad," where the craftsmen and merchants lived and worked. On the right of Kolkhoznaya Street on the other side of the river is a group of churches. *Nizhne-Nikolskaya Church* is a gate-church surmounted by a belfry and the small *Nizhne-Nikolayevskaya Chapel*, now serving as a souvenir shop. From Kolkhoznaya Square turn along Cachin Street to find the red-brick building of the *Church of SS. Peter and Paul*, which has been newly restored, standing back on the right, not far from the railway station. Dating from 1146, the time of Prince Rostislav, grandson of Vladimir Monomakh, this is the oldest church, and indeed the oldest building, in Smolensk. It was built in Kievan style but was changed and reconstructed many times, then restored to its original form in 1962–64. Beside it to the west are other buildings of the 17th and 18th centuries that also belonged to *St. Barbara's Monastery*. These include *St. Barbara's Church* (badly damaged by fire in 1812), a bishop's palace, and a belfry with decorative staircases.

Next drive straight down to the river and cross to the left bank by the second bridge, turning off to see *Ioanna Bogoslova* ("St. John the Divine") *Church* on the left, in Bolshaya Krasnoflotskaya Street. Built in 1160–80 and drastically reconstructed in 1770, the church is in Kievan style and similar to that of SS. Peter and Paul, which it faces across the Dnieper. From here drive westward beside the river along Malaya Krasnoflotskaya Street to find *Svirskaya Church*, also known as St. Michael the Archangel's, standing high on the left above the little river Smyadinka, which flows here into the Dnieper. It was built in 1180–97 as a court cathedral by Prince David Rostislavovich, whose tomb is inside. It is believed to have been designed by Pyotr Milonezh, an architect who worked for the princes of Smolensk and who was compared by a Kievan chronicler to Veseleil, architect of the Temple of Solomon in Jerusalem. The belfry is of a later date. The church itself was heavily damaged in World War II. Its name, Svirskaya, is due to its location at the place where the roads from the north ("svirsk") converged outside Smolensk.

Voznesenskaya ("Ascension") *Church*, Konenkov Street 9a. *Voznesensky Convent* was founded under Vasili III in 1515, and Peter I's mother, Natalia Naryshkina, spent several years here as a young girl. On Peter's order in 1694–1696 a brick church was built here in place of the original wooden one. It is believed that the blueprints were drawn by Peter himself, while the architect was Gura Vakhromeyev. Between the years 1610 and 1660, during Smolensk's Polish period, the convent was run by Jesuits. Behind and adjoining the main building is the tiny white single-domed *St. Catherine's Church*, designed by Matvei Kazakov in 1765. Heavily damaged during World War II, the main church was restored to its original form in 1969. The convent's *Akhirskaya Gate-Church*

(1830) also was restored then. The convent now houses the Konenkov Museum's Exhibition Hall.

Roman Catholic Church, Uritsky Street. This imposing red-brick church in Gothic style with twin spires now houses the city archives. It was built in 1894.

Local History Museum, Lenin Street 8. This is one of the oldest museums in the country. The most interesting exhibits here come from the ancient barrows, of which there are 2,000 at Gnezdovo near Smolensk. The barrows mostly date from the 10th century; scientific excavation began in 1869. Also interesting are 13th-century messages written on birchbark about trade between Smolensk and Novgorod.

Natural History Museum, Soborny Dvor 7, beside Uspensky Cathedral

Art Gallery, Krupskaya Street 7. Open 10–7; closed Fri. This collection is housed in a building specially designed in 1905 for the Museum of Ancient Russia by the well-known Russian artist Sergei Malyutin. In 1911 Princess Maria Tenisheva of Talashkino, art connoisseur and patron, presented the museum to the town of Smolensk. There is a good collection of 17th-century icons, and on the 2nd floor are examples of west European and Russian art, including a portrait by Konstantin Korovin of the princess wearing a hat and another of her painted by Valentin Serov in St. Petersburg in 1898. Also here is the Merlinskaya Shawl, named after Merlina, who owned the workshop where it was made in the 1830s; the embroidery on the finest linen is done with thread finer than human hair, but the secret of how it was done was lost with Merlina's death.

Konenkov Museum of Sculpture and Applied Art, in the monastery at Mayakovsky Street 7. The famous Russian sculptor Sergei Konenkov was born in 1874 in the village of Karakovichi, near Smolensk. He spent most of his life abroad, in Paris and the United States, and returned to Russia only after the Second World War. As well as works by other artists, there are 45 of Konenkov's postwar works here, among them projects for monuments to Tolstoy, Gorky, and the soprano Antonina Nezhdanova, and 3 of his whimsical chairs, the swan, the mapleleaf, and the fairytale. Shortly before his death in 1971 Konenkov wrote to the city of Smolensk: "I present my art to the dear people of Smolensk."

Lenin Museum, Lenin Street 15. Lenin visited Smolensk in 1900.

Military Museum, in Pamyat Geroyam Square

Smolensk Lenin Museum, Bolshaya Sovietskaya Street 19, in an 18th-century building. Open 10–6; closed Mon.

Planetarium, Boikova Street 9

House of Nobles, Glinka Street 3, opposite Bloniye. This impressive 3-storey columned building in late classical style was designed in 1825 by architect Melnikov of St. Petersburg. Mikhail Glinka was feted here in 1848, the occasion being commemorated on a plaque, and the house saw concerts by many outstanding Russian musicians—

Glinka, Chaliapin, Sobinov, Nezhdanova, Rakhmaninov. Today it is used by the Smolensk Medical Institute. A second plaque is a reminder that during the civil war, in 1918, the establishment of the Soviet Republic of Belorussia was proclaimed here.

1812 Monument, in the centre of the Park of Culture. This huge cast-iron monument resembling a steeple and commemorating the defenders of Smolensk against the French attack of 4–5 August 1812, was designed by Antoni Adamini, cast in St. Petersburg, and unveiled on 5 November 1841, on the 29th anniversary of the liberation of Smolensk from the French. It weighs over 6.5 tons and stands 26 m (85 ft), high, and the 2 guns on either side were captured from the Grande Armée.

Sophia Regiment Monument, on the 17th-century earthen wall in the Park of Culture. The Sophia Regiment was one of those engaged in the defence of Smolensk in 1812 and distinguished by its gallantry. The monument was designed 100 years later by Private Boris Tsapenko, also of this regiment, and unveiled in 1912.

Monument with Eagles, Kutuzov Garden. This interesting symbolic monument was founded in 1912 and unveiled in September 1913. It was designed by Lieutenant-Colonel Engineer Shutzmann and shows an eyrie high on a rock, guarded by a pair of eagles. One of these prevents an ancient Gaul from attacking the nest with his sword while the other prepares to attack the marauder from behind. The great rock symbolizes Russia, and the two eagles the 1st and 2nd Russian armies. On the eastern side of the monument is a plaque saying: "From Grateful Russia to the Heroes of 1812."

Kutuzov Monument. In the central walk of the *Garden of the Heroes of the Patriotic War* is a bust to Field Marshal Mikhail Kutuzov by Maria Strakhovskaya. It was erected with money collected in the Smolensk region and unveiled on 26 August 1912, the 100th anniversary of the Battle of Borodino. In 1954 a statue of Prince Kutuzov-Smolensky by Georgi Motovilov was unveiled in Bolshaya Sovietskaya Street. The title of prince of Smolensk was awarded to Kutuzov after the rout of the French army near the city.

Glinka Monument, in the Glinka Garden ("Blonie"). Composer Mikhail Glinka was born in Novospasskoye, 150 km (93 miles) from Smolensk in 1804. Later he was befriended and taught by John Field (1782–1837), a remarkable player and composer and one of the earliest of the purely piano virtuosos, who had come to Russia from Dublin in 1903. Glinka is honoured every year by the *Glinka Musical Festival*, which takes place in Smolensk during the first ten days of June. This bronze statue by von Bock was unveiled in 1885. It was erected with money donated by the citizens of Smolensk and with funds raised from concerts organised by such outstanding cultural figures as Vladimir Stasov and composer Arthur Rubinstein. The phrases of music included in the iron fence designed by Bogomolov that surrounds the statue come from the scores of *Ivan Susanin, Ruslan and Lyudmila*, and other works by Glinka.

Lenin Monument, in Lenin Square. This was designed by Professor Lev Kerbel of Smolensk and unveiled in 1967 on the 50th anniversary of the October Revolution.

Grieving Mother Monument, Ryadovsky Park, in the southwestern suburbs of Smolensk. Here are the common graves of 3,000 World War II victims, most of them partisans. The sculptor of the woman's figure was A. Sergeyev, and near the monument is the *Hill of Immortality*. There are many other common graves in the town, marked either by an obelisk or by an unpretentious monument. The ashes of a number of officers were immured in a wall in the War Heroes' Garden on October Revolution Street; there is also an eternal flame there.

Bayonet Obelisk, Frunze Street. Designed by Kovalenko in the shape of a bayonet and standing 19 m (62 ft) high, this stands in memory of the divisions that died defending the town in July 1941.

Kurilenko's Statue, Kurilenko Garden. Vladimir Kurilenko (1924–42) served as a young partisan and succeeded in blowing up a railway line and derailing a German troop train. He was posthumously awarded the title of Hero of the Soviet Union. The sculptor Konstantin Pasternak portrays him holding a hand grenade.

Tank Monument, on the left of the main road where it enters the town from Demidovskoye Chaussée

Gagarin Monument. This monument was unveiled in 1973.

Drama Theatre, Lenin Square; tel. 319-86. The theatre was built in 1936 by Ilyinskaya. The Smolensk Theatre Company is one of the oldest in Russia, having given its first performance in 1803.

Puppet Theatre, Sobolev Street 1; tel. 204-47

Philharmonia Concert Hall, Sobolev Street 1

Spartak Stadium, Dzerzhinsky Street. It has a seating capacity of 12,000.

Tsentralny Park, in the city centre. Founded in 1874, this park contains a variety of *monuments* and *memorials*.

Tsentralny Hotel, Lenin Square 2/1; tel. 336-04. There is a *Beryozka foreign currency shop* in the hotel.

Smolensk Hotel and Dnieper Restaurant, Glinka Street 11/30; tel. 995-66

Rossia Hotel and Tsentralny Restaurant, Karl Marx Street 2/1

Tourist Hotel, Dzerzhinsky Street 25

Phoenix (Intourist) Motel and Restaurant, 15 km (9 miles) from town on the main road coming from Brest, at the 384 km mark; tel. 214-88. There is another *Beryozka foreign currency shop* here. Intourist office, tel. 21-565.

Khvoinaya Camping Site, at Lipuny, 0.5 km to the left of the main road coming from Brest, at the 384 km mark, a little before the *filling station*; tel. 349-06. Situated in woodland beside the *Phoenix (Intourist) Motel and Restaurant*, the site has a *cafe*, a kitchen, showers, a *shop*, a *post office*, and *telephones*.

Zarya Restaurant, Konenkov Street 2/12

Smolensk Restaurant, Nikolayev Street 30
Vityaz Restaurant, Kutuzov Street 2
Delfin Cafe, on the right on the way out of town
Zarya Cafe, Kommuny Street 2/2
Otdykh Cafe, Glinka Garden
Sputnik Cafe, Nikolayev Street
GPO, Oktyabrskoy Revolutsii Street 6
Department Store, Gagarin Prospect 1
Beryozka Souvenir Shop, in the Tsentralny Hotel, Lenin Square 2/1
Souvenirs, Bolshaya Sovietskaya Street
Souvenirs of Smolensk, Lenin Street 11/1
Tsentralny Book Shop, Bolshaya Sovietskaya Street 36

Intourist organises excursions to Flyonovo (Talashkino), 18 km (11 miles) from Smolensk to see the *Teremok Museum*, which belonged to Princess Tenisheva.

Talashkino

Talashkino estate stands on the river Sozh. In 1893 it was purchased for Princess Maria Tenisheva (1867–1927). The princess was an artist of no small talent and also was possessed of a singing voice that pleased both Rubinstein and Tchaikovsky. In 1884–85 she took singing lessons in Paris and became interested in mediaeval methods of enamel work. At Talashkino she first reorganised the school, which had been founded by the previous owner. Soon she bought the adjoining estate of Flyonovo and transferred the school there. It was not long before woodcarving, musical instruments, ceramics, and embroidery workshops were opened, the princess proving her own capabilities as an artist and designer. As at Abramtsevo, north of Moscow, a number of contemporary artists, including Repin, Vasnetsov, Vrubel, Polenov, and Serov, participated in the creative work undertaken here, and each contributed to whatever project was in hand. *Teremok* is the name of the wooden house designed by Sergei Malyutin and decorated with ornate carving in the florid tradition of Russian peasant art.

At nearby Flyonovo stands the simple brick *church* designed by the princess at the end of the 19th century and completed in 1903, just in time for her own husband's burial. In 1905 the princess left for Paris, taking many of her most precious possessions with her, as she feared for their safety during the time of political turmoil that followed the first Russian revolution. They were successfully shown at the Musée des Arts Decoratifs between May and October 1907 as the exhibition "Objets d'Art Russe Anciens Faisant Partie des Collections de la Princesse Marie Tenichev," which later was transferred to Prague. In Paris she continued her research into enamel work and it was upon this subject that she was to write her thesis for Moscow University in 1916. It was not until her return to Talashkino in 1908 that work began on the exotic murals and mosaics that distinguish the little church today. Over the entrance is a large mosaic of Christ. Nikolai Roerich and Vladimir Frolov

finished their task in 1914 and the cupola was gilded by Fabergé.

Teremok is now a museum containing 2,000 different items of folk art. It is a branch of the Smolensk Art Gallery. Open 10–6; closed Mon.

Novospasskoye

The village of Novospasskoye is 150 km (93 miles) from Smolensk on the way to Yelnya. It is where the composer of Mikhail Glinka was born in 1804.
Glinka Museum. Open 10–6; closed Mon.

GREATER SOCHI RESORT REGION

The village of Vishnyovka, 12 km (7 miles) south of Tuapse, marks the northern end of the Greater Sochi resort region.

Makopse

Makopse, which is off the main road, is a seaside resort. A *World War II Memorial* is located by the Smena Sanatorium and tea plantations are in the vicinity.
Makopse Boarding House, at the 199 km mark
Druzhba Boarding House, a little off the main road, at the 203 km mark

Ashe Population—1,000

This place is named after the river Ashe, upon which it stands; and the name "Ashe" means "Weapons" in the local Adygei language.

The imposing cliff overhanging the river is known as Old Men's Cliff because it is said that in times long ago each young Adygei man was expected, when his father became old and sick and a burden to the community, to hurl him to his death from this cliff down into the sea. The old people knew their fate and submitted to it without a sound. There is a legend that once upon a time there lived here an old man called Takir. He was already 90 years of age and his son hoped that he would die a natural death so they might avoid the ordeal of the cliff. It so happened, however, that their village was surrounded by enemies and it became hard to feed extra mouths. Accordingly, Takir's son took his father upon his shoulders and set off toward the cliff, but his eyes were blinded by tears and he stumbled and fell with the old man. Takir laughed in sympathy and told his son how the same thing had happened when he was carrying his own father to the cliff. He said that instead of killing his father he had hidden him in a cave and cared for him, bringing him food in secret. His devotion had seemed well rewarded, for that very year had brought the villagers victory over their enemies. Takir's son was much impressed by this story and accordingly hid the old man in a cave, too. In due course, when the village was next attacked, Takir emerged from his hiding place and led the exhausted villagers through a secret pass in the cliff about which he alone knew. It led to a sheltered valley where they rested and regained their strength, and from it they were able to return to the fray and defeat their attackers.

Later on the villagers blocked the way to the

cliff with a mighty boulder and no one ever climbed the stoney path to the top of Old Men's Cliff again, but the cliff and the cave are still there for all to see.

Kavkaz Boarding House
Mayak Cafe, at the 208 km mark
Zvezdochka Cafe
GPO, by the main road

Lazarevskoye

Lazarevskoye stands at the mouth of the river Psezuapsye, which has a good bathing beach of sand and shingle where the water gets deep quickly. The bathing season lasts from June to October, but it is best in the autumn, when the temperature of the water rises to 22°C (72°F).

A *fortress* was founded here in 1835 and named after Admiral Mikhail Lazarev (1788–1851). Lazarev had served as a volunteer in England until 1808, but by 1833 he had risen to the command of the Black Sea fleet. He was responsible for landing parties establishing themselves on this part of the Black Sea coast, and it was here that his victory over two Turkish warships earned his brig, the *Mercury,* the flag of St. George. The construction of the fortress was no easy matter, for all of the necessary equipment had to be brought in by sea and it was sometimes unloaded under fire from the local inhabitants. Lazarev's command lasted until 1845 but the fortress stood until 1954, when, along with other similar fortresses on the coast, it was abandoned and blown up.

The present village of Lazarevskoye grew from a small Greek village into which Russian settlers moved at the end of the 1880s. There are still many Greeks among the population. Since the beginning of the 20th century tea has been cultivated in this region, which was in fact the first place in Russia to grow it. Now there are many tea farms in the neighbourhood. Cork oaks also are grown commercially and Lazarevskoye mineral water is bottled here.

Nativity of the Virgin Church, Shevchenko Street 1. This was built in 1904 as a Greek Orthodox church.

Lazarev's Bust, near the railway station and the ruined fortress walls. There is also an ancient gun by the sea.

Odoyevsky's Bust, Alexander Odoyevsky (1802– 39) was a poet, officer, and member of the Decembrist Northern Society who was exiled to Chita in 1827 and sentenced to 15 years hard labour for his active participation in the 1825 St. Petersburg revolt. In 1837 he was sent here as an ordinary soldier. He died of malaria in Lazarevskoye Fort on 15 August 1839. The monument was unveiled in 1952.

Lenin Monument
World War II Memorial, Kalarash Street
Biryuza Hotel and Restaurant, Pobeda Street
Volna ("Wave") Holiday Home, for young foreign visitors
Chernomorskaya Restaurant, Pobeda Street 168
Kuren Restaurant, 2 km (1 mile) from the ma'n

road, following the valley of the little river Arsha; the turn, which is by the 215/532 km mark, is signposted

Priboi Restaurant, Pobeda Street 2, at the motel
Chaika Motel and Service and Filling Station, Pobeda Street 2. On the left of the main road are small bungalows and on the right is the car park, service station, and *restaurant.* 150 m (160 yds) from the motel is a *buffet.* The filling station is open 7 A.M.–6 P.M.

Zelenaya Dubrava Camping Site, Sochinskoye Chaussee 2a, on the right of the main road toward the sea; this turning is the first on the right after the bridge over the river Pszeuapsye, and the camping site is at the mouth of the river, near the sea. There is a *buffet, shop, self-service kitchen,* and other facilities.

The *Mamedovo Gorge* is near Lazarevskoye. There are small waterfalls here and some ancient tombs in the shape of old sea chests. Other waterfalls in the vicinity are called Lesnaya Skazka ("Forest Tale") and Slyozy Laury ("Laura's Tears"), and two other picturesque ravines are called Box Gorge and Svirsky Gorge.

It is 79 km (49 miles) from Lazarevskoye to Sochi.

At the 253/494 km mark is the *Tourist Cafe.*

The next villages are Soloniki, Katkova Schel, and Chemitokvadze, the latter standing by the river of the same name.

Golovinka

This village at the mouth of river Shakhe took its name from *Golovinskoye Fortress,* built here in 1822, of which some ruins remain. The surrounding territory is worked by a forestry organisation.

World War II Memorial

Loo Population—5,000

The name, pronounced like "law," comes from that of a local tribe. An ancient burial mound has been discovered here, and 1.5 km (1 mile) from the main road, on the grounds of the *Magadan Boarding House,* are the ruins of an 11th-12th century *church.* There are two children's sanatoria in Loo. The roads are not good.

Gorizont ("Horizon") Cafe

Uch Dere

The name "Uch Dere" means "Three Gorges" in the Adygei language. One of the country's first tuberculosis sanatoria was built here. From this point runs a stretch of forest mainly composed of ash, beech, hornbeam, and hazel.

Dagomys

(Intourist organises excursions here from the town of Sochi.)

There used to be an imperial estate here and the park was laid out in 1900. The park covers the western slopes of Mt. Armyanka, where many rare trees flourish in the Mediterranean climate. There

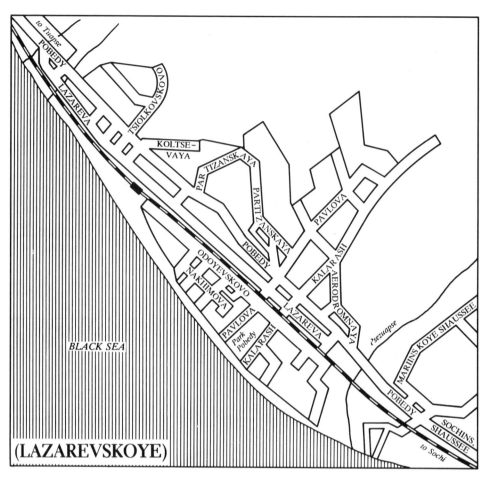

BLACK SEA

(LAZAREVSKOYE)

is a large tea factory in Dagomys and furniture is also manufactured in the town.

Dagomys (Intourist) Hotel, in the park, Leningradskaya Street 7, tel. 32 2994. Yugoslavs were responsible for the construction of this 27-storey hotel, which is part of a comprehensive tourist complex catering to 2,500 guests and includes a *camping site, restaurants*, a *skittle alley*, a *sauna*, a *concert hall*, and a variety of *sports facilities*.

The *clinic* is a branch of the local medical service and provides comprehensive treatment, including diagnosis, to those wishing to take advantage of a wide range of traditional spa treatments, including baths, massage, and inhalation.

Olympiskaya (Intourist) Hotel, Leningradskaya Street 7, tel. 32 2294. This is also part of the tourist complex.

Meridian (Intourist) Motel, on the right side of the main road, Leningradskaya Street 7, tel. 32-2987. This is part of the tourist complex. The grounds are wooded, with nut trees, crab apple, and wild pear growing. There are two hotel buildings, a *cafeteria, sports grounds, reading and tele-vision rooms*, and a fully equipped and covered carpark and *carwash*.

Dagomys Camping Site, near the motel. Motorboats leave for Sochi from here.

The following *restaurants* belong to the tourist complex: Rubin, Agat, Saturn, Olymp, Druzhba, Dubrava, and Kavkazskaya Kukhnya. There are also a variety of *bars*.

Solokh Aul

Solokh Aul is reached by making a 25-km (15.5-mile) side trip inland and along a picturesque mountain road from Dagomys, passing the village of Volkovka on the Dagomys River and some tea plantations. Intourist organises excursions from Sochi to visit the plantations.

It was here that Krasnodar tea, the most northerly type of tea to grow anywhere, was first planted and picked by a Russian settler named Koshman in 1901. He brought it here from Chakva, near Batumi, further down the coast toward the Turkish border, and according to his wish he was buried here, on his plantation.

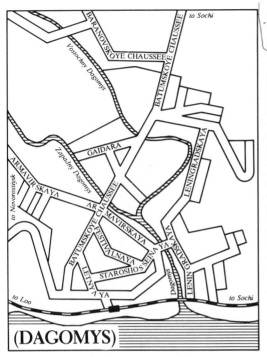

(DAGOMYS)

Beyond Dagomys on the main road to Sochi are two restaurants, *Lesnaya Polyana* ("Forest Glade") and *Ogni Sochi* ("Sochi Lights").

Sochi Population—340,000
Local archaeological finds prove Sochi's ancient history. Greek and Roman merchants came here to trade, and in the 8th, 9th, and 10th centuries Christian communities built churches in the vicinity. Ruins of a Christian church have been excavated on Mt. Akhun near Sochi as well as in Khosta and other places nearby. In the Middle Ages the Genoese trading centre of Mami stood by the river Shakhe (now the Mamaika).

Up to 1829 the Black Sea coast of the Caucasus was under the Turks, and it only became Russian as the result of protracted wars. The native people here were the Ubykhs, a very warlike tribe that taught their sons to use arms from earliest childhood. They had their own military tactics: they never hid themselves in any stronghold but preferred to engage the enemy in open battle. Ubykh mothers, instead of mourning for their fallen sons, took great pride in their military gallantry. The Ubykhs undertook dangerous marches over the snowy mountain passes to make surprise attacks on their enemies. At the beginning of the 19th century about 40,000 Ubykhs lived in the territory of the present Greater Sochi, between the Shakhe and the Khosta rivers. The little river here was called Sochipsy and there was a small Ubykh landing place at its mouth. Despite their bellicose nature these people were good fruit growers. The care of

orchards was part of their religion; they maintained that nobody planting less than 50 fruit trees would go to heaven. And so it was that their land was covered with orchards. That was also the reason why the Ubykhs fought so fiercely to defend their native region. In 1837 Russian troops entered Sukhumi, Gagra, and Adler, but the cape upon which Sochi stands was still in the hands of the Ubykhs. In 1838 Nicholas I visited the southeastern coast of the Black Sea and ordered his troops to take the cape. The battle lasted for 3 hours and the Russians seized a small area, where Sochi's lighthouse stands today. A fortress called Alexandria, after Nicholas I's wife Alexandra, was founded, but later it was renamed Navaginskoye. In 1840 it held out against a local uprising and siege. The heroine of the occasion was the commander's wife, Mme. Posypkina, who even under fire walked with her parasol along the earthen wall to encourage the men. Afterward the commander was promoted and Mme. Posypkina received a costly necklace as a personal gift from Tsaritsa Alexandra.

In 1854, during the Crimean War, Navaginskoye Fortress was blown up and its garrison evacuated. The Russians did not come back to this area until 10 years later, when, after a battle near the river Godlikh, the Ubykhs and other mountain tribes acknowledged their defeat. In 1864 they informed the tsar that they would cease their resistance and lay down their arms if he would permit them to live on their native soil. However, the tsarist command refused these demands and all of the Ubykhs left these parts and emigrated to Turkey. At this time Navaginskoye Fortress was renamed once again, this time to Dakhovsky, after the Dakhovsky Regiment that won the battle against the Ubykhs. In 1874 the military post became a village, which gradually developed into a resort. It was first called Sochi in 1896, after the name "Shashe," which is what the Ubykhs called themselves.

Sochi is the largest resort on the northeastern coast of the Black Sea. It stretches along the shore for 30.5 km (19 miles) and lies between the Mamaika and Kudepsta rivers. Its climate is as good as that of Nice, San Remo, and other popular places in Europe, and it has more hours of sunshine per day than Davos. The average summer temperature is 23°C (73°F) and the temperature of the sea rises from 18°C (64°F) in mid-June to 29°C (84°F) later in the summer and early autumn. The bathing season lasts 5 months. Autumn lasts from October till December and spring begins in March. The best time of the year is late summer, known in these parts as the "velvet season."

Sochi's curative properties were recognized as far back as 1872, when a certain German, Grabbe, who two years later was elected a member of the town council, built a *villa* called Vera, which became the first civil building in Sochi. It can be seen even now below the ruins of the warehouse of Dakhovsky Fortress. In 1909 Sochi became known as the Caucasian Riviera, and a fashionable hotel opened under that very name right on the

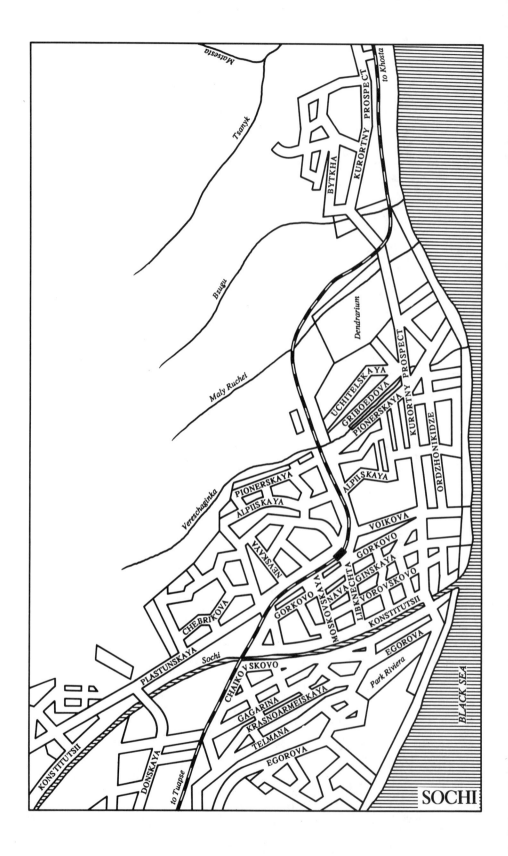

SOCHI

sea front. Its 4 buildings (which can still be seen, now housing the Caucasian Riviera Sanatorium) had a total of 360 rooms, a concert hall, a casino, and a restaurant. Sochi really dates as a health resort from that time. Professor Edouard Martel (1859–1938), a speleologist visiting from France in those early years, said that it was hard to imagine any place more like Cannes, because of its blue sea, beaches of fine sand, and verdant hills rising to snowy mountain peaks on the far horizon. The opening of the railway line in 1925 led to Sochi's speedier growth, and since 1933, when it was decided to turn it into a resort of national importance, millions of rubles have been spent on it and the best Soviet architects, including Ivan Zholtovsky and Alexei Schusev, have been employed in local construction. The harbour building by Karo Alabyan was completed in 1955; its spire is 37 m (122 ft) high.

Sochi has 230 resort establishments, including 58 palatial sanatoria, 6 resort polyclinics, 19 boarding houses, 8 rest homes, 14 tourist stations, 27 recreation bases, 55 Young Pioneer camps, and 12 camping sites. In order to turn Sochi into a winter resort as well, special transparent screens have been designed and installed on the beach to keep off the wind and the cold while letting through the ultraviolet rays, so it is possible to sunbathe even on cold winter days. There are 20 seawater swimming pools in Sochi, all heated in winter.

At present over 3 million holidaymakers come to this area annually and more sanatoria are under construction. Since 1958 the *Chaika* ("Seagull") *Sanatorium* has accepted visitors from abroad; it has a funicular railway connecting it with the beach, as have the *Lazurny Bereg* ("Azure Coast") and the *Ordzhonikidze* sanatoria. The Ordzhonikidze Sanatorium is among the largest and most splendid. It was built between 1935 and 1941 by Kuznetsov in Italian Renaissance style with a flight of white marble steps leading up to it; part of the interior has decorations in traditional Russian style by artists from the villages of Palekh and Mstera. The *Metallurg* ("Steel Worker"), *Sochi*, and *Rossia* sanatoria are among those with heated seawater swimming pools to attract winter visitors. The Sochi and *Dzerzhinsky* sanatoria are linked with the beach by tall lift-towers, and the *Novye Sochi Sanatorium* has a lift, built in 1961, going down inside the cliff for 35 m (115 ft). From here a 112-m (123-yd) tunnel leads to the beach.

Since 1961 the territory around the town has been known as Greater Sochi; it includes about 160 km (100 miles) of coastline, running from Vesyoloye to Shapse (near Tuapse).

The Sochi *Experimental Station of Subtropical and Southern Fruit Crops* lies up the valley of the Bzugu River. It was first organised in 1894, when it dealt chiefly with garden crops, but now tea, vines, and other fruits are studied here.

Cathedral of the Archangel Michael, Mayachnaya Street 14. The cathedral was built in 1852 and is open for services.

Ruins of Mamai-Kale, a 16th-century fortress
Ruins of Dakhovsky (Navaginskoye) Fortress, not far from the lighthouse
Exhibition Hall, Kurortny Prospect 51. Open 9–7; closed Mon. and the 1st day of the month. Included here are sections on the natural history of the Caucasus and the Black Sea.
Ostrovsky Museum, Korchagin Street 4. The museum is located in a new building completed in 1957 and in his house. Literary section: open 10–6; closed Wed. and the last Tues. of the month. House museum: open 10–6; closed Wed. and Sat. and the last Tues. of the month. Nikolai Ostrovsky (1904–36) served in the civil war and then at the age of 20 became paralysed, blind, and bedridden. He moved to Sochi in 1924 and wrote "How the Steel was Tempered" and the greater part of "Born of the Storm," now standard literature for Soviet youth. A street is named after him, as are a school and a library.
Ostrovsky Monument, on the main road
Statue of Lenin
Cannon and Anchor, Primorskaya Naberezhnaya. On the seashore and near the Pushkin Library is a cannon on a concrete pediment; this has long been one of the sights of Sochi, although it was in disgrace for some time after having participated in revolutionary activities in 1905. In front of it stands an anchor weighing 2,800 kg (nearly 3 tons) that was made in the Urals in 1719. This came from the naval frigate *Penderaklia*, which sank nearby in the 1840s with, so it was said, a considerable sum of gold on board. At the beginning of the 20th century divers raised the ship with its anchor but found no trace of the gold.
Theatre, Teatralnaya Street 2. Built in 1937 by architect K. Chernopyatov, it seats 1,100.
Summer Theatre, Frunze Park
Open-air Theatre, Riviera Park, Chernomorskaya Square. Built in 1937, it is open only in summer.
Circus, Deputatskaya Street 8. This seats 1,180 people.

During the summer season many guest performers, companies, and exhibitions come to Sochi.
Central Stadium, Bzugu Street 2
Yachting Centre, Bzugu Street 40
Dendrarium, Kurortny Prospect. Open 10–6. The Dendrarium covers an area of 16 hectares (40 acres) and is divided in two by Kurortny Prospect. It was founded at the end of the 19th century and belonged to the wealthy publisher of "St. Petersburg Gazette," a local resident by the name of S. Khudekov. Here he built his villa, Nadezhda, and planted his garden with a rich variety of specimens, many imported from abroad. The grounds have expanded to contain as many as 2,500 different shrubs and trees, including subtropicals, from all over the world, and it is really worth a visit. The upper part, connected with the lower by cable car, is the most decorative, with a pavilion, sculptures, and fountains, while the lower part is more natural,

with bamboo groves and magnolias. A *botanical museum* is housed in the villa. There are plans to extend the territory to 60 hectares (150 acres).

Riviera Park, Fabricius Street 2/28. This covers 10 hectares (25 acres) and contains 100 different species of trees and bushes from all parts of the world, including the subtropics. There are a number of cafes here, a dance floor, and an open-air variety stage. Here also is *Friendship Glade*, where a number of visiting celebrities have planted an avenue of magnolias; the Friendship Tree is a citrus on which 147 grafts have been made by visitors from different countries.

There are three *public swimming pools* in Sochi as well as a *boat-hiring station, tennis courts*, and as many as 400 *sports grounds*.

Other parks include Frunze Park and those belonging to the sanatoria.

Intourist-Camelia Hotel Complex and the Camelia and Intourist Restaurants, Kurortny Prospect 91, 7 km (4 miles) from the centre of town; tel. 99 0292. There is a *Beryozka shop* in the hotel that accepts foreign currency and the hotel has its own *bathing beach*. Intourist office, tel. 99 0290. The Intourist organisation also rents accommodations for foreign visitors at the Chaika, Kirov, Lazurny Bereg, Zarya, and Caucasian Riviera sanatoria.

Zhemchuzhina ("Pearl") Intourist Hotel and the Khrustalny, Zhemchug, and Vecherny Restaurants, Chernomorskaya Street 3, 2 km (1 mile) from the centre of town; tel. 93 4355. A 19-storey building with accommodations for more than 2,000, this hotel belongs to Intourist. The hotel has a number of *bars*, 2 *swimming pools*, 1 for adults and the other for children, and a *Beryozka foreign currency shop*.

Leningrad Hotel, 2-Morskoy Pereulok; tel. 92 3368

Moskva Hotel and the Russky Zal, Evropeisky, and Molodyozhny Restaurants, Kurortny Prospect 18, tel. 92-36-17.

Sochi-Magnolia Hotel and Magnolia Restaurant, Kurortny Prospect 50; tel. 99 5554. Intourist office, tel. 99 5527.

Kavkaz Hotel and Restaurant, Kurortny Prospect 72; tel. 92 3048. Intourist office, tel. 92-3566.

Primorskaya Hotel and Restaurant, Primorskaya Street 21/1; tel. 7-97-43; service bureau 9-91. The hotel faces the sea.

Yuzhnaya ("South") Hotel, Teatralnaya Street 8; tel. 21-69. Intourist office, tel. 28-29.

Kuban Hotel, Gagarin Street 5

Svetlana Boarding House, Kurortny Prospect 75, 3 km (2 miles) from the centre of Sochi; tel. 92 1314. Intourist office, tel. 92 5633.

Zarya Sanatorium, Kurortny Prospect 108; tel. 96 0460. Intourist office, tel. 96 0424.

Chaika ("Seagull") Sanatorium, Kurortny Prospect 98

Additional Intourist accommodations are provided out of town at Dagomys and Adler.

Akhun Restaurant, on the slopes of Mt. Bolshoi Akhun

Dieticheski ("Dietetic") Restaurant, Voikov Street 10

Goluboy ("Light Blue") Restaurant, Voikov Street 8

Gorka ("Hill") Restaurant, Voikov Street 22

Novye Sochi Restaurant, Vinogradnaya Street

Primorye ("Seaside") Restaurant, Chernomorskaya Street 10

Svetlana Restaurant, Pushkinskaya Street 10

GPO, Voikov Street 14

Bank, Ordzhonikidze Street 2

Long Distance Telephone Exchange, Parkovaya Street 15

Sochi Information Bureau, Gorky Street 3; tel. 20-52

Savings Bank, Voikov Street

Shopping Centre. This shopping centre is in a building that is a reproduction of the trading arcades typical of Russian towns in the 17th to 19th centuries.

Souvenirs, Pushkin Street 9

Gifts, Gorky Street 40

Holidaymakers' Needs, Kooperativnaya Street 6

Bookshops, Navaginskaya Street 17 and Voikov Street 5 and 16

Chemist's, Kurortny Prospect 24

Art Shop, Bulvarnaya Street, opposite Morskoi Vokzal

Jeweller's, Kurortny Prospect 26

Market, Kirpichnaya Street 30

Taxi by Phone, tel. 25-29

Adler Airport, 36 km (22 miles) out of town; tel. 33-11

Sputnik International Youth Camp, at the foot of Mt. Akhun

Filling Station No. 2, Kurortny Prospect, Primorye. Diesel oil also is supplied, and there is round-the-clock service.

Lenin Sanatorium, 3 km (2 miles) from the Rheumatics Institute. The walk leads through a wooded park and across mountain streams and gorges with good views.

Bikhta Hill (305 m/1,000 ft), 6.5 km (4 miles) from the Voroshilov Sanatorium. There is a good view of Sochi from this hill. The *Old Mill Restaurant* is here.

Green Grove Boarding House. At 120 m (394 ft) above sea level this boarding house has a beautiful *garden, dance floor, eating house, club*, small *shops*, and an elevator to the beach.

Agur Ravine. The road begins 8 km (5 miles) south of Sochi, runs through forested country, and ends where there is a carpark. From here a path with pleasant views leads on across a small bridge over the river Agur to a little lake. Although it is 7 m (23 ft) deep, the bottom is clearly visible. The 27-m (89-ft) *waterfall* of the Agur is nearby, and a path leads up to a 2nd waterfall.

Mt. Akhun. Near the turning to the Agur Waterfalls is another turning, from which a good road leads to Mt. Akhun (663 m/2,175 ft). It is 22 km (14 miles) from the centre of Sochi to the mountain, and Intourist organises walks. 3 km (2 miles) up this mountain road are the ruins of a 13th-

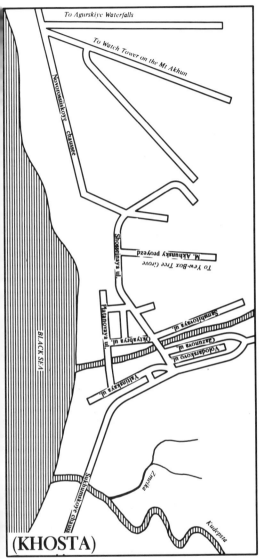

To Agurskiye Waterfalls

To Watch Tower on the Mt Akhun

Novorossiiskoye chausse

BLACK SEA

Shosseinaya ul.

M. Akhunsky proyezd

To Yew-Box Tree Grove

Samshitovaya ul.

Oktyabrya ul.

Platanovaya ul.

Gazunaya ul.

Volodarskovo ul.

Yaltinskaya ul.

Sukhumskoye chausse

Zmeika

Kudepsta

(KHOSTA)

---

of which are described under Sukhumi, the capital of Abkhazia.

Matsesta

Although there were always plenty of legends about the wonder-working waters of Matsesta, there was never any historical record of the place until the first literary reference, found in the diary of an English traveller named Bell who visited the Caucasus in 1837. 35 years later A. Vereschagin, a Russian agronomist, visited the valley of the Matsesta River and saw hydrogen sulphide springs gushing from an outlet in the rock. It was discovered that this water flows from a lake at the bottom of a great cave. Its temperature is 38°C (100°F), which is not too hot at all, but it is called "fire-water" because it causes the skin to redden. It has nearly three times the highest sulphur content ever found in a natural spring. New wells have been sunk to a depth of 1,524 m (5,000 ft) and the source is inexhaustible.

The water is recommended for treating circulatory, muscular, nervous, gynecological, and skin diseases. Intourist's courses of treatment last 26 days.

The avenue that leads from the main road toward the bathhouses has been known as Cheltenham Avenue, ever since Matsesta and the English spa became sister towns.

Restaurant, in the building of the saltwater baths

Orlinye Skaly ("Eagle Rocks"), 377 m (1,237 ft) above sea level and within walking distance from Matsesta. The path leads through the orchards of Matsesta Valley and then climbs steeply through the woods above the town. The pits beside the trail are the remains of natural limestone caves. From the top there is a fine panorama of the Bolshoi Akhun and the Caucasus Mountains, and below, at the foot of a precipice, is the Agur with its first waterfall and little lake.

At the 435/312 km mark is *Filling Station No. 3,* which has round-the-clock service; tel. 56-83.

From Matsesta the main highway takes you directly to Adler, passing through a tunnel.

Khosta

Off the main road, below the highway, is Khosta. The name comes from "kho," meaning "be careful," and "sta," meaning "river," in Abkhazian. The legend of the origin of the name tells that there once lived an outlaw in the ravine who used to scare people passing by. On Italian maps of the 13th to 15th centuries the Genoese settlement of Casto is shown instead of the present-day Khosta. From 1901 to 1903 fertile plots of land were given to people on the condition that within three years they clear the ground where necessary and begin to build.

The little river Khostinka runs out of a deep ravine. Khosta is surrounded by mountains on three sides and lies on the edge of a small bay with a good *beach* of mixed sand and shingle, better than the beaches at Sochi. The mountains protect

century *church. Akhun Restaurant* is on the mountain, and a lookout tower, 30 m (98 ft) high and built by Vorobyov in 1936, commands a good view of the snow-covered Caucasian peaks, Sochi, and the whole region around. From near the tower a path runs down the mountain to the Agur Ravine and the waterfalls.

Intourist organises boat and helicopter trips from Sochi. There are also a number of excursions, including northwestward to Dagomys Tea Plantation (20 km/12 miles) (see above) and southeastward to Khosta Box and Yew Grove (20 km/12 miles) (see below), and to Pitsunda (80 km/50 miles), Lake Ritsa (125 km/78 miles), Novy Afon Caves (140 km/87 miles), and Sukhumi (150 km/93 miles), all the resort from the northwesterly winds, so it is always calm and warm here, the temperature being 1 to 2 degrees higher than in Sochi.

Khosta is famous for its *marine park*, founded in 1930, and near this, 3 km (2 miles) inland from the sea, are 300 hectares (750 acres) of *woods* of box and yew. There are many ancient trees, 700 and 800 years old; 1 is more than 1,000 years old. In the middle of the trees are the *ruins* of a 12th-century fortress, supposedly Genoese. Intourist organises excursions here from Sochi.

Caucasian State Reservation Museum
Civil War Monument with an Eternal Flame, at the entrance to the town
World War II Memorial, on the way to the box woods
Khosta Hotel, Yaltinskaya Street 14; tel. 95 0240
Khosta Restaurant, Kiparisovaya Street 5
Volna ("Wave") Restaurant
Cork Oak Plantations and Caves
Valley of the White Rocks

Adler

These lands belonged to Ared-bei and the landing stage here was called "Artlar," hence the name "Adler" (meaning "Eagle" in German). According to the Adrianopol Peace Treaty of 1829, Turkey lost all rights to the lands along the coast. On June 20, 1837, Russian troops landed at the mouth of the river Mzymta ("Fierce" in Georgian), by the Cape of the Holy Spirit, which rises 1,990 m (6,529 ft) above sea level. Among the Russian soldiers killed in the ensuing battle was Alexander Bestuzhev-Marlinsky (1797–1837), a poet-Decembrist who had been exiled to the Caucasus after completing a hard labour sentence in Siberia. In the 2nd half of the 19th century the indigenous population, Djigets, were encouraged to leave, and the majority went to Turkey. In the 1880s the new settlers, mostly from the Ukraine, started to grow tobacco for export and to fish. The whole area at that time was a hotbed of malaria.

The winter here is colder than in Sochi, which is 23 km (14 miles) to the northwest, and the summer is hotter but has less rain. Tea and tobacco, citrus fruits, plums, olives, and vines are grown; fruit trees and violets begin to flower in the middle of January. There are some sandy patches on the wide shingle beach.

In the northwestern suburbs of Adler is a large tea factory, and across the bridge over the Mzymta is a poultry farm that supplies all of the resorts in this region. On the left bank of the Mzymta, south of Adler, is the *Yuzhnye Kultury Horticultural Research Station*. A good park with attractive ponds was laid out here in 1910. It has a rose garden and an avenue leading down to the sea. The territory of the research station covers 20 hectares (50 acres) and includes 800 kinds of subtropical plants.

As recently as 1968 a new beauty spot appeared near Adler. Huge rocks, the largest weighing about 100 tons, were dislodged by the force of wind and water and fell with tremendous crashes into the river. The local seismic station registered 4-point earth tremors at the time. The rocks settled to form a natural dam, and the lake that built up behind it is 2 km (1.2 miles) long and 300 m (328 yds) wide. The water is 19 m (62 ft) deep in places.

One of Adler's suburbs is being developed as a new resort to accommodate another 5,000 visitors. Adler is the southernmost point of the Russian federation and its airport serves Sochi.

Fortress, by the sea. These are the remains of a fortress built here in 1837.

Russian Soldiers' Monument, on the boulevard. This monument commemorates the Russian soldiers who fell in the Russo-Turkish War.

Bestuzhev-Marlinsky Bust, in the park. The Russian poet-Decembrist Alexander Bestuzhev-Marlinsky was among the Russian soldiers killed upon landing here in 1837.

Lenin Monument

Priboy-Gorizont Hotel and Gorizont Restaurant, Prosvescheniya Street 24; tel. 44-0803. Intourist office, tel. 44-1677.

Motel, Pervomaiskaya Street 41, in the centre of Adler and 10 minutes' walk from the sea. This motel has *shops*, a *cafe*, and a fully equipped carpark. The *filling and service stations* are both open 7 A.M.–6 P.M.

Fregat Boarding House, Kurortny Gorodok, Building No. 15; tel. 45-0032. Intourist office, tel. 45-0120.

Cosmos Restaurant, Lenin Street

Camping Site, on the road going southward from Adler to Gagra, turn right toward the sea at the village of Vesyoloye, 10 km (6 miles) from Adler. The camping site is in a eucalyptus grove on the territory of the local state farm and close to the edge of the sea.

The way to Krasnaya Polyana: Soon after leaving Adler, where there stands a *statue* of a man holding a little girl in his arms, a left turn leads up into the mountains. It is about 60 km (37 miles) to Krasnaya Polyana, where the territory of the Caucaus State Reservation begins. The very spectacular road leading there, through the villages of Moldavka, Kazachy Brod, Kamenka, and Golitsyno, was built in 1897–99 by engineer V. K. Konstantinov.

Moldavka Population—7,000
Moldavka is the first village on the road to Krasnaya Polyana. Its name derives from the word "Moldavia," since its first settlers were Moldavians. Most of the present-day population are Greeks and Armenians.

Kazachy Brod Population—1,700
At the 14-km mark is the village Kazachy Brod. "Brod" means "ford," so this is the Cossack Ford over the river Mzymta.

Golitsyno Population—1,000
Golitsyno is at the 21-km mark. Most of the population here, too, are Greeks and Armenians. In Lesnoye, a few kilometres off the main road, is the

Greek *Church of St. George.* Also here are Kudep-tskiye and Vorontsovskiye *stalactite caves,* at the source of the river Kudepsta.

Chkalovsky

At the 24-km mark and halfway to Krasnaya Po-lyana is Chkalovsky. People come here to drink the water from the local spring.

Krasnaya Skala

Krasnaya Skala ("Red Cliff") is at the 31-km mark. Here are the *ruins* of the Holy Trinity Monastery, which was founded in 1902 by Father Markian. The monks used to extend their hospitality to trav-ellers making their way up to Krasnaya Polyana. There was a beautiful iconostasis here of carved boxwood.

The most impressive part of the road is beyond the village of Monastyrka, at the 33-km mark. In Akhtau Gorge the road begins to look more dan-gerous; a steep precipice drops down to the river Mzymta, roaring at the bottom of the gorge, and an enormous cliff hangs overhead. It seems as if even a small fall of stone could cause a disaster. This place is called "Carry us through, O Lord!" Two crowbars can be seen above, wedged into the cleft. It is said locally that they were left by two construction workers who fell down the precipice, but in fact they were left by a Greek supervisor who wanted to commemorate the construction workers' labours. Next, at the 33-km mark, the road runs through a tunnel 100 m (109 yds) long. On the right of the tunnel one can see a cornice that tes-tifies the attempts of the road builders to smooth off the outline of the cliff. There used to be an icon at the entrance to the tunnel, and candles were lit in front of it. One of these set fire to the icon and it burned. Now a sooty niche is all that is left.

Also at the entrance to the tunnel, on the right side, is the *grave* of a road builder named Kiselyov. The *obelisk* with a star on the top, which stands just before the tunnel, commemorates Red Army soldiers who were executed here and thrown into the abyss in September 1920. Krasnaya Polyana was occupied after the 1917 revolution by Denikin's counterrevolutionary army; it changed hands sev-eral times, and this is just one of the incidents of the fighting in this area. The soldiers, who had tried to break through to the Black Sea, were ex-ecuted by General Khvostikov of the White Guards, but one of them, Kyril Gusev, escaped to tell the tale. The sculptor of the obelisk was A. I. Kolobov.

On the other side of the tunnel a second *obelisk* commemorates partisans who died during the civil war. The stone slabs that can be seen down in the river at this point, with the Mzymta roaring among them, remain from an avalanche that occurred on 18 January 1968. A piece of rock said to weigh around a million tons fell into the river and blocked it so that a lake about 15 m (49 ft) deep appeared.

However, it was shortlived, for the Mzymta wore the rock away.

Kepsha Population—300

There is a sawmill and a *cafeteria* in the village of Kepsha.

It is worth making a 1-km detour to the *Progress Trout Farm,* whose *restaurant* is open during the season.

At the 37-km mark the stream that gushes out from the rocks on the left of the road forms a *wa-terfall* known as Maiden's Tears.

On the slope of a small hill there is another 19th-century *monument,* this one to construction workers who died during the building of the road.

Along the road one can see the remains of Turk-ish and Greek *cemeteries.*

Medvezhy Ugol

At the 38-km mark is Medvezhy Ugol (Bear's Haunt), a small settlement marked by the sculpture of a bear.

A few hundred metres from the road there are a number of mineral springs (Chvizhensky Nar-zan).

Approaching Krasnaya Polyana the road by-passes a hydropower station and the Greek Bridge over the river Beshenka ("Mad").

Krasnaya Polyana

Krasnaya Polyana nestles in the hills. The average annual temperature here is 21°C (70°F). Krasnaya Polyana (red glade) is 6 km (3.7 miles) long and 1 km (a half mile) wide, covering 400 hectares (1,000 acres). It is situated 60 km (37 miles) from Adler at the point where the valleys of two rivers, the Mzymta and the Beshenka, join, and it is the be-ginning of the *Caucasus State Reservation,* which stretches on to cover 100,000 hectares (250,000 acres) and has about 1,400 different kinds of trees and plants and 60 species of mammals, including deer, boar, leopards, bears, and a herd of more than 100 bison.

Krasnaya Polyana has been inhabited since pre-historic times, both on account of its good geo-graphical position and because it is near routes leading to passes over the mountains. Both Stone Age and Bronze Age *burial mounds* have been found here and the *ruins* of the fortress in the vicinity date back to the reign of Mithridates the Great of Pontus. The natural wealth of the area includes furs, game, honey, wax, and precious woods, and these drew expeditions from Byzan-tium, Greece, Rome, and Genoa.

Until the middle of the 19th century Krasnaya Polyana was inhabited by members of various mountain tribes, such as the Cherkess, the last in the whole Caucasus area to hold out against the Russians. In 1864 4 Russian detachments led by Grand-Prince Mikhail Romanov attacked the vil-lage of Kbaade along the rivers Psou, Mzymta, Sochi, and Laba and scored a decisive victory. A thanksgiving service was held by the 25,000 sol-diers, and afterward a manifesto was read announcing the end of the war in the Caucasus. Following this, most of the Cherkess moved to Turkey. The village of Kbaade (meaning "Red Glade" in the Cherkess language, referring to the russet-coloured ferns and bracken in autumn) was renamed Romanovsk in honour of the imperial family. The place, however, remained desolate until 1878, when about 40 Greek families moved here from Stavropol Province. It was they who first used the name Krasnaya Polyana (the Russian for "Red Glade"). Some years later a group of Estonian peasants settled close to the village, too.

In 1898 a special state commission visited Krasnaya Polyana and found it suitable for development as a mountain resort, since it was healthier than places along the coast infected with malaria. A sign was put up on the road into the village reading: THE TOWN OF ROMANOVSK. For a long time Romanovsk was badly organised and hardly resembled a town. It consisted of 50 to 60 buildings stretching along a single street. Schools and 2 churches were built here for Russian and Greek families. But few of the new residents wanted to live here, as supplies were irregular, there was no medical help, and in the winter it often was isolated by snowdrifts. There were, however, many who liked living here in the summer to escape the heat on the coast, but the 2 small hotels could not meet the demand for accommodations. An imperial hunting lodge with 50 rooms was built and the area was proclaimed an imperial hunting reserve. It is said locally that in 1909 hunters came here from Britain for aurochs.

After the 1917 revolution Krasnaya Polyana was held by Denikin's army; they made it their stronghold from which they wanted to find an outlet to the sea.

The first tourist base, Gorny Vozdukh ("Mountain Air"), was set up here in a summer cottage belonging to the Russian tenor Leonid Sobinov (1872–1934). The cottage, built in 1914–15, was burned down during World War II.

The mountains surrounding Krasnaya Polyana are Mt. Achishko (2,365 m/7,759 ft), which in Cherkess means "Wet Bag," it being the most humid place in the Caucasus; Mt. Aibga (2,380 m/7,808 ft); and Mt. Shoogoos (3,245 m/10,646 ft). It is possible to walk to Mt. Achishko, to Lake Kardyvach, and through the Kutakheku Pass to Lake Ritsa, a distance of 24 km (15 miles).

Two cableways (3.5 km/2 miles long) lead up to Mt. Aibga. About 2 km (1 mile) further into the mountains along the road from Krasnaya Polyana is *Krasnaya Polyana Restaurant and Bar*. There is an observation point here with a wonderful view of the mountains; it looks like Switzerland. This is the site of the imperial hunting lodge mentioned above, which is now used as a sanatorium. Here also is the *Nature Museum*, with stuffed bison and aurochs. Krasnaya Polyana also has an *Intourist hunting lodge*. In the centre of the settlement is a modern school built in 1972 that accommodates 600 pupils from the nearby villages and has a well-organised *museum of local lore*. There is an *apiary* near Krasnaya Polyana.

War Memorial Obelisk, Pochtovya Street
GPO, Pochtovaya Street
Cafeteria and Bar, Komsomolskaya Street.
Back again on the main coastal road as it leads out of Adler is the *Kosmos Restaurant*.
Filling Station, at the 428/319-km mark
Shashlik Bar, at the 419/328-km mark

Veseloye

The name of this village means "Merry." It is 10 km (6 miles) from Adler but still part of Greater Sochi.
Camping Site, turn right toward the sea. The camping site is in a eucalyptus grove on the territory of the local state farm and close to the edge of the sea.
Druzhba Restaurant
Veseloye is the last point on the way south in the territory of Krasnodar. After crossing the natural border, the river Psou, the road enters Abkhazia, which is described under Sukhumi, its capital. Here, at the border, watches must be put ahead 1 hour.

Intourist organises excursions from Sochi further south, to Gagra, Pitsunda, Lake Ritsa, Novy Afon, and Sukhumi, but these are all described under Sukhumi, the capital of Abkhazia.

SOKOLOVO
See Kharkov, p. 203.

SORTAVALA Population—25,000
(Serdobyl from 1783 till 1918)
Sortavala spreads around the amphitheatre formed by one of the big gulfs on the northern shore of Lake Ladoga (Ladozhskoye). It stands on a huge granite rock, and many of its streets make use of the natural granite and need no other paving.

Lake Ladoga ("Laatokka" in Finnish) is the largest lake in Europe. It is 208 km (129 miles) long and 126 km (78 miles) wide with an average depth of 91 m (300 ft). It is fed principally by the Saimaa lake system and empties its waters by the river Neva through Leningrad into the Gulf of Finland.

Sortavala was founded in 1617 and received commercial privileges in 1646, since which time it prospered by trading with settlements around the Baltic coast. The town was almost entirely destroyed by fire in 1705 and took until 1875 to recover from the damage done at that time. From the turn of the century it was known as an important educational centre of the northeastern part of Finland. Sortavala and Valaam, along with other places in the area, were part of Finland when the latter became independent of Russia after the 1917 revolution. The administration of the Greek Orthodox Church in Finland used to be here, and there was an Orthodox cathedral and several church schools.

After the Winter War, by the Treaty of Moscow

signed between Finland and Russia on 13 March 1940, Finland ceded this region to the Soviet Union. Following the German attack on the USSR in June 1941, the Finnish parliament proclaimed that all territories ceded to the Soviet Union under the Treaty of Moscow be rejoined to Finland. The displaced Finnish population returned and the Soviet-Finnish front remained quiet until June 1944. In September 1944 Finland signed a new treaty in Moscow whereby she had to withdraw from East Karelia and pay reparations. So the reconquered territory, including the whole of Lake Ladoga, was returned to Russia and once more its population became refugees.

Now there are agricultural, commercial, and medical schools in Sortavala, and it is the second-largest town in the Karelian Autonomous Republic (after Petrozavodsk). There is a wharf, and besides fishing, local industry includes a textile mill, clothing, and furniture factories, a printing works, and branches of the food industry.

Most of the important houses and offices here are on the oldest street, Karelskaya (formerly Kariankatu) Street, or in the vicinity. In the upper part of the town is *Vakkasalmi Park*, from which there is a fine view over the lake. The grey granite quarry in the suburbs has been used since the 18th century. Stone was sent from here to face the buildings of St. Petersburg. The Atlantids guarding the entrance to the *Hermitage Palace* are carved from Sortavala granite. Thanks to the clean air of the surrounding countryside, the picturesque landscape, and the favourable climatic conditions, there are a number of sanatoria and holiday centres nearby.

Shemeikka Statue, in Vainamoinen Garden on Theatre Square. Petri Shemeikka (d. 1915) was a Karelian hunter who settled in Sortavala and lived here until his death. He was best known for singing the ancient sagas, such as the Finnish *Kalevala*, and for telling fairy tales. Many of these heroic epics were collected by Dr. Elias Lonnrot while he was practicing medicine among the peoples of the northwestern frontier region. The statue by Finnish sculptor Alpo Sailo shows the bearded Shemeikka seated on a bearskin and playing a zitherlike national instrument called a "kantele."

War Memorial. This memorial bears the inscription "He who falls fighting for freedom never dies!"

Seurahuone Hotel

Kuhavuori Tower

Valaam

The Valaam Archipelago consists of 1 large island and 50 small ones. The largest, Valaam Island, is 23 km by 9 km (14 miles by 6 miles) with an area of 27.8 sq km (11 sq miles). The total area of all of the islands is 36 sq km (14 sq miles). They are composed of granite and diabase, and although not naturally fertile, Valaam is an island of pine trees. The gardens there and the oak and cedar woods were the result of the monks' labours over the years. Seals live in the waters around the island.

The islands were 1st inhabited in the 10th century, when it is said that 2 Greek monks from Mt. Athos, Herman and Sergius, founded the monastery in 992, making it the most northwesterly outpost of the Greek Church in Europe. The monastery is said to have been destroyed for the 1st time in 1163. However, it is more likely that the Transfiguration Monastery was founded here in 1329 to serve also as a fortress. Missionaries worked from here among the Karelian population, and the monks even went to the Aleutian Islands and to Alaska. The monastery was destroyed more than once by the Swedes. It is said that King Magnus II Eriksson of Sweden (Magnus VII Eriksson of Norway), a persecutor of Orthodoxy, was buried here. In 1371 he prepared to land with a great army and destroy the monastery, but his ships were caught in a storm and all of his soldiers drowned. The king clung to a piece of floating wreckage for 3 days, and when he was rescued by the monks he took monastic vows and the name of Grigory, but he died three days later. He was buried beside the cathedral, and his story is inscribed on his tombstone. However, the story is historically inaccurate.

The monastery was destroyed again by the Swedes in 1578 and 1580 and razed to the ground in 1611. From the end of the 17th century and until the end of the Northern War (1700–1721) the island was populated mainly by Swedish colonists. The main cathedral was restored on the order of Peter the Great in 1719, and the monastery served as both an economical and a political centre for the surrounding area. Tchaikovsky visited here in the summer of 1866, and the part of his 1st Symphony titled "Winter Dreams" was based on his impressions of the Valaam landscape and Lake Ladoga. Many Russian painters came here as well, including Shishkin, Roerich, and Kuindji.

In 1911 the Holy Synod decided to create a collection of historical relics in Valaam Monastery. By 1918, when the territory became Finnish, there were only half the previous number of monks. The collection was moved to Kuopio, Finland, where there is an ecclesiastical seminary. It included the gilded, forged-silver sarcophagus made in 1824 for the remains of the founding fathers, the Greek monks Herman and Sergei. Its cover was made in 1896 and it measures 227.5 cm by 135 cm by 92.5 cm (7 ft by 4 ft by 3 ft). (In 1969 the Orthodox Church Museum was built in Kuopio to house the collection.)

In 1938 there were 182 monks on Valaam. There was a hotel with accommodations for 200 visitors. There was also a candle factory, a forge, a photographic workshop, and a boat-building yard. The monks engaged in fishery, agriculture, and horticulture. They grew 60 different kinds of apples.

In 1940 Valaam was taken back into the Soviet Union and the monastery was closed. Some of the monks went to other monasteries and others founded New Valaam Monastery in the centre of Finland. A naval college was opened on Valaam Island.

Valaam Monastery is situated on the shore of Monastyrskaya Bay. Monastery buildings, mostly of the 19th or early 20th century, can still be seen. There used to be as many as 23 churches and 19 chapels on Valaam and the surrounding islands. A flight of 62 granite steps leads up to the *Holy Gates of SS Peter and Paul*. The small *Tsar Chapel* of granite and marble that stands on the right is a memorial to the visit of Alexander II in 1858. Opposite the chapel is an *obelisk* commemorating visits made by Peter the Great and other Russian tsars.

The present *Preobrazhensky Cathedral* was built in 1887 and 1892 on the site of earlier cathedrals. It is in Byzantine style with 5 gilded cupolas. Its walls are covered in frescoes (copies of the religious paintings of Gustave Dore, popular at the end of the 19th century), and above the altar is a copy of Leonardo da Vinci's "Last Supper." The cathedral belfry stands 70 m (230 ft) high and has a 16-ton bell.

Other buildings include the *Church of the Assumption of the Virgin* and 3 *hermitages*, known as the White, the Yellow, and the Red hermitages, 3 to 4 km (2 miles) from the rest of the monastery. An attractive road leads to the White Hermitage, where inside a fence there stands a white church designed by St. Petersburg architect Gornostayev plus 8 small buildings for the monks. 150 m/yds from here was a stone chapel that only the monks were permitted to approach. The Yellow and Red hermitages are further on, with the Red Hermitage standing on a hill.

There used to be 12 hermitages on other islands. *Nikolsky Hermitage*, built in 1853, is on Nikolsky Island.

Holy Island lies 8 km (5 miles) to the east of Valaam Island.

SOSNOVKA

See Cherkassy, p. 99.

SPASSKOYE-LUTOVINOVO

See Orel, p. 408.

STARAYA RUSSA Population—40,000

(Intourist organises day trips here from Novgorod, which is 100 km/62 miles to the north by road. In summer and good weather the excursion goes via Lake Ilmen in a hovercraft; the distance by water is 74 km/46 miles.)

Lake Ilmen is shallow, about 4 m (13 ft) deep, but it is 45 km (28 miles) long and 35 km (22 miles) wide and used to be known as the Slov Sea. It is still referred to as the "Lake with the Golden Bottom" because of its rich mud, which is a valuable fertilizer. Its greatest pride, however, is in the 40 different species of fish in its waters; in mediaeval times it supplied fish to the court.

Korostyn

On the way to Staraya Russa both the hovercraft and the road pass the village of Korostyn, where an *imperial coaching palace* overlooks the lake. It

was designed by Stasov in the 1820s for Alexander I, who frequently visited his military colonies. The ground floor is built of stone and the upper floor of wood, as are the Doric columns decorating the facade. The balustrade of the loggia on the 1st floor is of pig iron, but the building is badly in need of restoration.

In 1471 a battle took place near the village, by which Novgorod lost her independence. The Moscow army overpowered 40,000 Novgorodians, killing 12,000 of them and taking many prisoners. The prisoners had their noses and ears cut off and were then sent home. Great Prince Ivan III of Moscow came to the village in 1471, and the 4 leaders of the Novgorodians were brought before him, accused, and immediately beheaded. As a final gesture Ivan commanded that the tongue of Vasili Seleznyov-Guba, who had spoken to him especially rudely, should be cut out and thrown to the dogs. Finally a treaty was signed with Novgorod confirming its dependence, and this led to its incorporation into the princedom of Moscow in 1478.

In the village was a crown garden that grew fruit to be sent to Moscow. The place has been known for its fruit for the past 500 years.

There is a *war memorial* to the left of the road through the village, and the green-domed *Uspensky Church*, in the cemetery to the right, was built in the 18th century and is open for services.

In Russian chronicles Staraya Russa is 1st mentioned in 1167, when the saltworks belonged to the prince of Kiev. Its origin, however, dates back to the 9th century, when it served as an important trading post between the Baltic and the Volga on the international river route by which Scandinavian metalwork and Russian furs were carried down to Byzantium and the East. In 1120 this route was described as the Russian route, linking Staraya Russa with Kiev Rus. Even now excavations in the streets reveal the remains of wooden pavements and the foundations of houses of those times.

One of the versions of a legend connected with the town's foundation tells of two brothers, Sloven and Rus, the chiefs of Slav tribes, who wandered in search of good lands. They moved northward from the shores of the Black Sea and after many years came to the shores of a great lake, which they called Ilmen, after their sister. The elder brother founded the town of Slovensk Veliky, while the younger founded Rusa and named the rivers Polist and Porusya, on which it stands, in honour of his wife and daughter.

Both towns soon were destroyed by the Ugro-Finnish tribes that came from the Urals. The people of Slovensk moved away from the ruins and built Novgorod ("New Town"), but Rusa was rebuilt and called Staraya ("Old"). There are a number of pagan burial mounds in the vicinity, and huge boulders with notches carved into them. Here, as in many places in the north, are place names with the root "rus" or "ros," and it is a local tradition that this is the real Russian homeland.

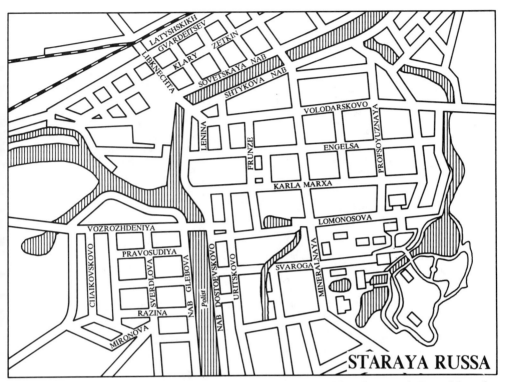

STARAYA RUSSA

This is not quite true, however. The Russians originally lived near the Dnieper, on the banks of the river Kurland, and it was from that that their name derived. The chronicle bears witness to this, too, describing how "the Slavs, which are now called Rus," came to the lands of the north where Novgorod and Pskov stand today. Staraya Russa probably was given its name at the same time.

The town grew fast, mainly due to the saltworks that developed here. From the 13th century it was part of the Novgorod republic, the most powerful Russian state of that period. By the 16th century it was the 4th-largest town in Russia (after Moscow, Pskov, and Novgorod) and was so rich that in 1591 Giles Fletcher, English ambassador to the court of Muscovy, wrote that Staraya Russa paid more in customs dues "by salt and other commodities" than any other town or city in the whole realm, and even half as much again as Moscow, the capital and trade centre of Russia.

At the beginning of the 17th century, when the area was laid waste by the Polish-Lithuanian wars, only 38 souls remained alive in Staraya Russa. It was seized by the Swedish army under Feldherrn Pontus de la Gardie in 1611 and agreed to recognize Prince Philip, son of Charles XI of Sweden, as its own sovereign. The Swedes built a small fortress at the confluence of the Polist and Pererytitsa, where the Voskresensky Cathedral stands today. Staraya Russa was returned to Russia in 1617 in accordance with the Treaty of Stolbovsk between Russia and Sweden and through the mediation of

English ambassador John Merrick. Toward the end of the 17th century the town gradually showed signs of recovery. It was visited by Peter the Great in 1693 and he decreed that the dilapidated saltworks should be restored. Salt was increasingly in demand with the foundation 10 years later and the subsequent growth of St. Petersburg, and Staraya Russa's economy burgeoned accordingly. Peter visited the town once again in 1724 and commanded that a canal be dug linking the river Polist to the saltworks; traces of the canal can still be seen.

Staraya Russa grew steadily, but a terrible fire at the end of the 18th century almost totally destroyed it. The rebuilding followed a regular plan, and most of the new houses were built of stone. The saltworks, too, were reconstructed, and the pipes through which the salt solution flowed are still in place. It was at this time that Staraya Russa was granted its 1st coat of arms—the upper part reproduced elements of the arms of Novgorod—a red-cushioned golden throne supporting a crossed sword and sceptre on a silver field, and with a triple candlestick rising from the back and a bear on either side; the lower part had a stove and pan for drying salt.

In 1824, as part of Alexander I's military reform, a military colony was established nearby. When the exceptionally hot, dry summer of 1831 helped spread an outbreak of cholera from the south, the colonists in Staraya Russa panicked and accused the local officers of poisoning them. 12 regiments were involved in a mutiny and a number of officers and some German chemists were lynched. The army was called in from St. Petersburg and 3,000 people were arrested. 2,667 sentences were passed; 138 men were flogged to death and hundreds were branded and sent to Siberia.

Staraya Russa was developed as a spa after the visit of Dr. Friedrich Haaz and Dr. G. Rausch in 1815. (It was Dr. Haaz who had discovered the Caucasian mineral springs 5 years earlier.) Soldiers were the 1st patients; the 1st spa building was opened in 1834. Minister Muravyov ordered that a new artesian well be drilled in 1913. The fountain that resulted still works, and indeed, it is one of the highest in Europe, rising 10 m (33 ft). It is housed in a glass pavilion. Conveniently situated between the two capitals, the resort became very popular, with a fine hotel and casino, and during the season its entertainment included a theatre where the country's finest actors and actresses performed. A plaque on the wall of the hotel and casino building tells how its list of famous patients has included the writer Nikolai Dobrolyubov in 1858, Mendeleyev in 1882, and Maxim Gorky in 1904. While he was here Gorky wrote to his little son, "I live in a town where there is no bookshop. Fountains of very salty water spring out from under the ground. There are lots of bandy-legged children, women with no legs at all and in general all kinds of cripples. It is not at all nice to look at them."

The 1st steamboat service between Novgorod and Staraya Russa opened in 1858.

From 1941 to 1944 the town was under enemy occupation and was almost completely destroyed. Upon liberation in February 1944 there were only 2 wooden buildings left intact and 1 of brick, including a school and the post office. All the rest were no more than empty shells.

There were a number of monasteries around the town and in the town itself, but they were devastated by the Swedes in the 17th century and later were closed or so impoverished that they survived only as parish churches. The general destruction during the Second World War was the final blow.

The way into town from Novgorod follows Karl Liebknecht Street, which runs from the railway station to the centre. All of the buildings there are postwar. A few old houses were restored, such as the red 2-storey *Grushenki House* in Karamazov Street and a dark-green and white house at the corner of Karl Liebknecht and Klara Tsetkin streets belonging to the merchant Tokaryov. On Volodarsovo Street in the former House of Nobles there is now a knitting factory. There are other old houses along the embankment of the river Polist, near Zhivoi Most. That name means "Live Bridge"; there was a ferry at this point until the end of the 18th century, and then a pontoon bridge was built on rafts, which gave it its present name. Even when the stone foundations of the bridge were built in 1830, the old name remained. Among the old houses on the embankment is one of the 1830s in classical style with columns.

Staraya Russa is now a fairly large industrial centre, with a cheese factory, among other food industries, and a plant producing building materials. There is also a chemical machine-building plant and a textile mill. The spa has been revived. The original hotel and casino building is now Block 1 of the resort complex. The waters are used in treating motor diseases and digestive and nervous complaints. Staraya Russa's coat of arms has been modified to show Muravyov's fountain above, with 2 bears below stirring a boiling cauldron of salt.

Spaso-Preobrazhensky Monastery, at the crossing of Timur Frunze and Volodarskovo streets, most easily found by asking for "Sportivnaya Shkola," the sports school that is located nearby in a converted church. The monastery was founded in 1192 by St. Martiry, archbishop of Novgorod. *Spaso-Preobrazhensky Cathedral* is the largest part of the complex. It was rebuilt in the 15th century; after being devastated by the Swedes it was again rebuilt at the end of the 17th century. It was destroyed in World War II and has now been rebuilt according to the 17th-century plans on the lower parts of the old walls with their great boulders which date from the 12th century. Fragments of the early frescoes dating back to the 15th to 17th centuries have survived. The cathedral now houses the local museum, which has some particularly interesting old documents written on birchbark.

The other monastery buildings were built when the Swedes were driven out. The single-domed *Rozhdestva Khristova Church* (1620) adjoins the cathedral on its northern wall. It is connected with it by a covered gallery that served as the foundation for the octagonal *bell tower* (1720s), which stands at the northwest corner of the cathedral. The *Literary Museum*, which is in the church, now includes an interesting collection of old postcards of the town.

Sreteniya Refectory Church (1630), nearby. It now houses the art gallery. Its lower chapel served as the monastery prison until 1826.

Troitskaya Church, at the crossing of Timur Frunze and Karl Marx streets, 1 block away from the monastery. This was built in 1680 on the site of an earlier church. It was reconstructed by Thon and then was restored in 1980. It is to serve as an exhibition hall.

Nikolskaya Church, near the spa, at the corner of Svaroga and Krasnykh Komandirov (formerly Dmitrievskaya) streets; follow the bank of the river Malashka from Troitskaya Church. This was founded in 1371 right in the centre of town by the market square. Only the lower part survived; the rest was ruined by the Swedes in 1614. It was rebuilt in 1710 and was fully restored once more in 1961. It is a 5-domed edifice and decorated with elaborate brickwork. The bell tower is of the 19th century.

Georgievskaya Church, Uritskovo Street 22. Opposite Nikolskaya Church but on the other side of the Malashka. This was built in 1410 and reconstructed in 1740. The original stone walls are only the lower 2.5 m (8 ft). The iconostasis dates from the 18th century. It is open for services.

Church of St. Mina the Martyr, a little further down Uritskovo Street, not far from Dostoyevsky's house. This church was founded in the 1430s, devastated in 1614, and restored in 1751. Only partially restored again since World War II, it is still without its dome.

Voskresensky Cathedral, Vozrozhdeniya Street, across the river Pererytitsa and right at the confluence of that river with the Polist. This is a 5-domed cathedral built in 1692–96 and rebuilt following a project by Stasov in 1830. The bell tower dates from 1801. Both were rebuilt in 1956–60. The cathedral is now the *Museum of the Northwestern Front* (see below). Open 10–6; closed Tues.

Two other churches, *Nikolskaya* (15th century) and *Varlaam* (end of the 19th century) stand 3 km from the centre of the town, where the river Snezh flows into the Polist. Both were badly damaged during World War II and have yet to be restored.

Local Museum, in Spaso-Preobrazhensky Monastery, Volodarskovo Street. The exhibits here include many mediaeval archaeological finds of great interest, among them documents written on birch-bark and perfectly preserved.

Art Gallery, in Sreteniya Church, Preobrazhensky Monastery, Volodarskovo Street. Open 10–6; closed Tues. and the last Thurs. of the month. The gallery was opened in 1974. Upstairs there are many works by the local artist Vasili Svarog (1883–1946) and his pupils, the most prominent of whom was Nikolai Tomsky, the late president of the Academy of Arts, who donated 200 canvases to the collection. Svarog's real name was Korochkin; he took his pseudonym from the name of the ancient god of fire of the pagan Slavs. His watercolours are particularly fine, especially his interiors and still lifes.

Dostoyevsky's House, Dostoyevsky Embankment 42. Open 10–6; closed Mon. The house was built by a retired officer, Lieutenant Colonel Alexander Gribbe, in the mid-19th century. Fyodor Dostoyevsky summered here with his family from 1873 to 1875, renting the upper floor. In 1876 he bought the house to use for summer holidays, and it was here that he worked on *The Brothers Karamazov*, besides other books, dictating the novel to his wife Anna, who took it down in shorthand. Dostoyevsky took Staraya Russa as his model for the town where the action of the novel takes place. After his death in 1881, Anna, who was then only 35, kept the house, opened a school that bore Dostoyevsky's name, and took care of the publication of his books. Later she moved to Yalta, where she died and was buried. Andrei Dostoyevsky (1908–68), the writer's grandson, did much to prepare the way for the opening of the museum. He also followed his grandmother's wish that she be buried beside her husband in the Alexander Nevsky Cemetery in Leningrad. This was done in 1967, and Alexander was buried there, too, the following year. The museum was opened on May 4, 1981, to mark the 160th anniversary of the writer's birth. The spacious and comfortable flat appears as it did when Dostoyevsky lived here. His original posses-

sions include his top hat and white gloves, the harmonium by Hinkel, and all of the tableware in the dining room. Downstairs is a museum of war mementoes, also put together by Alexander Dostoyevsky.

Museum of the Northwestern Front, Voskresensky Cathedral, Vozrozhdeniya Street, across the river Pererytitsa and right at the confluence of that river with the Polist. Documentary materials are displayed in the gallery surrounding the main building, while the centre serves as a *war memorial* with commemorative plaques and military flags. Open 10–6; closed Tues.

Eagle Monument, Mineralnaya Street. The bronze eagle was placed on its obelisk in front of the barracks where the Vilmanstrand regiment was quartered. (Vilmanstrand was the former name of the Finnish town of Lappeenranta.) The inscription reads: "To the brave men of Vilmanstrand, who gave their lives in the Russo-Japanese War of 1904–1905. The 86th Vilmanstrand Infantry Regiment." The barracks were destroyed during World War II and the Starorusspribor Factory stands in their place.

Lenin Monument, by the bridge over the river Pererytitsa. This monument is by Tomsky.

Glory Memorial, in the town garden. An eternal flame burns by the grave of those who fell in World War II. Other *war memorials* are the tank and the fighter plane that have been set up at the two entrances to the town.

Frunze's Bust, in a garden near the fighter plane memorial. Timur Frunze (1923–42) was a Hero of the Soviet Union and a fighter pilot who was shot down in the vicinity of the town.

Theatre. A number of leading Russian actors played here. The theatre opened in 1866 and was damaged in the Second World War, but it has been restored.

Polist Hotel and Restaurant, Engels Street 20; tel. 219-47

Ilmen Restaurant, Mineralnaya Street 43a; tel. 217-59

Bank, Lenin Street 6

Bookshop, Timur Frunze Street 12

STAROCHERKASSKAYA STANITSA
See Rostov-on-Don, p. 455.

STAVROPOL Population—318,000
(Intourist organises excursions here from Kislovodsk.)

Known as Voroshilovsk from 1935–43, Stavropol is situated to the east of the main road to the Caucasus.

The Stavropol region lies in the steppeland to the north of the Caucasus Mountains. In the past it was crossed by hordes of nomads migrating to the west with their herds. The city of Stavropol occupies a raised part of the Stavropol Plateau in the northwest of the region and is on the rivers Tashla and Mutnyanka.

Stavropol was founded in 1777 as one of the fortresses on the Azov-Mozdok defence line and

STAVROPOL

was at first simply known as Fortification 8. Its present name, derived from the Greek for "Crosstown," was given later. According to legend, a cross was found when the foundations for the fortress were being laid at the place where Komsomolskaya Gorka park is today.

The site for the fortress was selected by General Suvorov. A stone wall 1 m (3 ft) thick and 2 m (7 ft) high was built to enclose an area of 10 hectares (25 acres). It ran for 1,630 m (more than a mile) and stood on Cathedral Hill, now Komsomolskaya Gorka, linked by a wide flight of granite steps to Marx Prospect. At first it was occupied solely by the army, but in 1780 the 1st civilian settlers moved in from the central part of Russia. Then in 1808–10 about 50 Armenian merchants and their families arrived and the town gained considerably in economic importance. The garrison was transferred in the 1820s, but until the end of the fighting in the Caucasus, Stavropol remained the residence of the military commander and the military headquarters and supply centre of the whole area, including the Azov-Mozdok line and the parts by the Black Sea. In 1822 it also was declared the civil administrative centre of the region. In 1842 the seat of the bishop of the Caucasus was transferred here and in 1847 it became the centre of Stavropol Province. Its all-around importance accounts for the number of notables that passed through it; anyone visiting the Caucasus would have been bound to come this way.

After the departure of the garrison, what is now the oldest part of the town flourished in the territory of the old fortress and outside its walls. The original street names, like Armenian Street and Jewish Lane, as well as the style of a few old buildings, indicate where people of different nationalities had their homes. Some of the fortress walls were used to form integral parts of houses, as, for example, the building of the former St. Alexandra's School for the Daughters of Gentlemen near Pionerskaya Street.

In the 1870s the town became a marketing centre for sheep and other livestock, but in 1875 the Rostov-Vladikavkaz railway line was built bypassing Stavropol, and when, toward the end of the 19th century, there was no further military action in the area, the army offices were closed. With the loss of its advantageous position the town's economy suffered considerably.

It now has well-developed food and light industries and an important gas pipeline. Its higher-educational establishments include colleges for agriculture, medicine, and foreign languages.

Stavropol is well planned, with a rectangular pattern of streets and tall buildings in the centre, although most of the houses are only 1 or 2 storeys. Among those of the 1st half of the 19th century to have survived are the former town hall on Prospect Marx and, nearby, the Regional Treasury. And in Pushkin Street is the Teachers' Training College.

St. Andrew's Cathedral, Dzerzhinsky Street 155. Built in the 19th century, it remains open for services.

Uspenskaya ("Assumption") Church, Yarmarochnaya Street. This church also was built in the 19th century and is open for services.

Mosque, Morozova Street 12. This 19th-century building is now used to house archives.

Prave Local Museum, Dzerzhinsky Street 135. Open 10–6; closed Mon. This museum was founded in 1904 and named after the founder's wife, Maria Prave. Now it has a collection of 100,000 items, with pride of place given to a mammoth's skeleton.

Fine Arts Museum, Dzerzhinsky Street 115. Open 10–6; closed Sat.

Khetagurov Museum, Pushkin Street. Kosta Khetagurov (1859–1906) was an Ossetian writer and is revered as the Ossetian Leonardo da Vinci (see Ordzhonikidze).

Stavropol Monument, Komsomolskaya Gorka. This commemorates the founding of the town.

Lopatin Monument, Komsomolskaya Gorka. Herman Lopatin (1845–1918) went to school in Stavropol. He was a revolutionary and a personal friend of Karl Marx, so he was ideally suited to be the 1st to translate Marx's *Das Kapital* into Russian.

Lenin Monument, Lenin Street

Khetagurov's Bust, Marx Prospect

Liberation Monument, Oktyabrskoy Revolyutsii Prospect. This monument commemorates the 50th anniversary of the liberation of Stavropol from the White Guards.

Eternal Flame, Komsomolskaya Gorka

Apanasenko Monument, Komsomolskaya Gorka. General Iosif Apanasenko (1890–1943) commanded a Caucasian division during the Second World War.

Lermontov Drama Theatre, Lenin Square 1. The theatre was founded in 1845 and was among the most popular in the country with plays by Shakespeare, Schiller, and Gogol in its repertoire and the participation of Russia's leading actors. Its original building is now the *House of Officers* in Oktyabrskoy Revolyutsii Prospect.

Philharmonia Concert Hall, Marx Prospect 51

Circus, Ordzhonikidze Square 1. The building seats 1,810.

Open-air Theatre, Lenkomsomol Park

Pobeda Park. This park spreads over 224 hectares (560 acres).

Lenkomsomol Park, Oktyabrskoy Revolyutsii Prospect 22. There is an *open-air theatre* here.

Botanical Garden, in the southeastern suburbs of the town

Kavkaz Hotel and Restaurant, Kominterna Street 1; tel. 323-66

Stavropol Hotel and Restaurant, Karl Marx Prospect 34; tel. 376-14

Gorka Restaurant, Suvorova Street 1

Kolos Restaurant, Dzerzhinsky Street 100

Elbrus Restaurant, Karl Marx Prospect 56

Lesnaya Polyana Restaurant

Niva Restaurant

Intourist Office, Bulkin Street 2; tel. 99 0290

Bank, Lenin Street 286

Department Store and Souvenirs, Karl Marx Prospect 131
Bookshop, Lenin Square
Souvenirs, Oktyabrskoy Revolyutsii Prospect 26
Fialka ("Violet") Souvenir Shop, Karl Marx Prospect 26
Almaz Souvenir Shop, Lenin Street 237

From Stavropol, Intourist organises excursions to local farms, the Strizhament Forest Reserve (20 km/12 miles), and Nevinnomyssk (65 km/40 miles) and day trips to the resorts of the North Caucasian spa area of Minvody (200 km/124 miles and listed under their separate names: Essentuki, Kislovodsk, and Pyatigorsk) and to the high mountain resort of Teberda (245 km/152 miles) (see Kislovodsk for a description).

The black earth of the Stavropol region is some of the richest in Russia. Many farms here grow grain and sunflowers, while further east, where it is hotter and drier, cotton is the principal crop. Quantities of sheep also are raised, merinos for wool and other breeds for their meat. Intourist organises trips to a number of different farms, often including an invitation to lunch. Depending on the distance from Stavropol the excursions may take anywhere from 3 to 7 hours.

Strizhament Forest Reserve, in the mountains, 20 km (12 miles) from Stavropol. Intourist arranges excursions to the reserve on request. The slopes are well forested and the reserve includes the highest point in the area, 831 m (2,726 ft) above sea level. Of particular interest to botanists are the beech woods, where the undergrowth includes giant ferns 2 to 3 m (7 to 10 ft) high and also a collection of the region's flora that has a number of survivals of prehistoric species. The *Stone Chaos* is as its name implies an impressive heap of limestone rocks.

The name of the reserve, which sounds very strange in Russian, comes from the fortress that was built on the top of the mountain in 1784. At that time it was fashionable to use foreign military terminology, and the fortress was known as "Retrenchement"—hence Strizhament.

Nevinnomyssk Population—101,000
Nevinnomyssk lies on both sides of the river Kuban at the point where it is joined by the river Bolshoi Zelenchug and is dammed to form the beginning of the Nevinnomyssk Canal. The town is situated at the tip of a great upland that runs down from Mt. Elbrus far out into the North Caucasian Steppe, just like a cape of land running out into the sea. A Cossack village was founded here in 1825. There is a local story of how enemies took advantage of the Cossacks' absence to attack the village and kill all of the women and children, "pouring their innocent blood." So it was that the place became known as the "Cape of the Innocents"—"Nevinnomyssk."

Today the town appears very new, clean, and green. It is divided into the old and the new towns, on either side of the railway line—the new part lying to the north and the old to the south. Most of the town lies to the right of the main highway. Mira Boulevard is a whole street of green gardens; Gagarin Street is lined with poplars.

Nevinnomyssk has a tyre factory, one of the largest nitrogen fertilizer plants in the country, and a wool-washing factory. The town is rapidly expanding—its outskirts stretch beyond the Nevinnomyssk Canal.

Museum of Local Lore
Statue of Gorky, Mendeleyev Street
Kochubey's Bust, Engels Street, in the old town. Ivan Kochubey was a civil war cavalry hero under whose command the Reds fought the White Guards near the town.
World War II Monument, Gagarin Street
Timofei Podgorny Monument, Timofei Podgorny was a Hero of the Soviet Union.
Youth Monument, at the crossing of Mendeleyev Street and Mira Boulevard. This monument is in the form of a letter from the young people of 1975 to those of 2025.
Kuban Hotel and Restaurant, Mendeleyeva Street 14
GPO, Engels Street 77, in the old town
Bank, Gagarin Street 114
Market, by Gagarin Street
Filling Station, by the turning from the main road

STRIZHAMENT FOREST RESERVE
See left column, this page

SUKHUMI is the capital of Abkhazia.

ABKHAZIAN AUTONOMOUS SOVIET SOCIALIST REPUBLIC

The small republic of Abkhazia has a population of 503,000 (1977) and covers an area of 8,600 sq km (3,300 sq miles). The people are Abkhazians, Georgians, and Russians, the Abkhazians being the indigenous population. Long ago they called their land "Apsny," meaning the "Land of the Soul." Most of its territory is mountainous and is known as the Abkhazian Alps. A great number of rivers and rivulets flow from the ice caps of the mountains. The main Caucasian Ridge becomes gradually lower in these parts and the Gagra Ridge branches off here, forming a watershed between the turbulent mountain rivers of the Psou and the Bzyb. The highest Abkhazian peaks are Dombai-Ulgen, the Gwandra (3,983 m/13,067 ft), Belaya Kaya (3,913 m/12,837 ft), Ertsakhu, and Marukha. The roads crossing the Abkhazian Alps used to connect the villages in the river valleys with the North Caucasus; many of these roads have now become popular tourist routes. The climate here is wonderful. Abkhazia has about 215 sunny days every year. Snow is rare and even the winter temperature is 7°C (45°F). Mimosa begins to flower in January, while March and April see the fruit trees blossoming. Though small in area, Abkhazia has several climatic zones. The humid subtropical zone stretches along the coast up to 400 m (1,312 ft) above sea level. Higher up the climate becomes more moderate, and at 2,000–2,800 m (6,600–9,200 ft) the Alpine zone begins. Along the coastal zone tobacco, tea, and citrus fruits are grown, while coal and honey come from higher up in the mountains.

Abkhazia belonged in turn to Colchis, Pontus, Rome, and Byzantium before gaining its independence in 756. Christianity had begun to spread here in the 5th century. In 982, after the death of Tsar Feodosy the Blind of Abkhazia and during the reign of the Georgian tsar Bagrat III, Abkhazia became a part of Georgia, but later it regained its independence until taken by Turkey in 1578. Russia ruled it from 1810 and following local uprisings many Abkhazians emigrated to Turkey, especially after 1864, when the Caucasus was finally subjugated by Russia. In 1921 Abkhazia became a Soviet Republic.

Apart from the well-developed coal industry and the growing of tea, Abkhazia is a land of health resorts. The Abkhazian Black Sea coast is to have a network of new sanatoria, rest homes, camping sites, and motels. There is a camping site for foreign tourists by the river Gumista just north of Sukhumi.

Sukhumi Population—121,000
(Abkhazian Akua)
Sukhumi is the capital of the Abkhazian Autonomous Soviet Socialist Republic.

Sukhumi Bay lies between the rivers Gumista and Kelasuri, while the town itself is crossed by the river Besleti. Behind the town stands Sukhumi Hill, 201 m (659 ft) high. There is no other place on the Black Sea coast with so much sunshine and warmth as Sukhumi; from April till November there are sea breezes during the day and a light wind from the mountains at night. Citrus trees, bananas and other palms, and eucalyptus trees grow in the parks and streets of the town. "The Sukhumi Valley is a corner of Spain and Sicily dropped at the foot of Old Man Caucasus," wrote Russian travellers in the 19th century. In fact, it lies on the same latitude as Nice and has an average annual temperature of 15°C (50°F) and about 270 sunny days during the year. It is at its best in autumn, winter, and spring.

Sukhumi is one of the world's most ancient towns. Its history covers more than 25 centuries. The remains of a Stone Age settlement was discovered here in 1934. 2,600 years ago Greek merchants from Miletus founded a great trading colony here. The legend that grew based on this history is the story of Jason and the Golden Fleece.

Once upon a time a fabulous ram, a gift from the god Hermes, carried two children through the air to safety from the wrath of their stepmother. When the ram alighted in Colchis it was sacrificed in gratitude to Zeus and its golden fleece was presented to King Aeetes of Colchis. He hung it from a tree and set a wide-awake dragon to guard it.

Back in Greece, Jason, rightful heir to a throne that had been seized by his uncle Pelias, claimed his share of the kingdom and was told that his demand would be met when he brought back the fabulous Golden Fleece. Athene helped him build a ship with 50 oars which he called the *Argo*, and he rounded up a crew of heroes to man it, including Orpheus and the Dioscuri brothers, Castor and Pollux. After many adventures the argonauts reached Colchis and King Aeetes agreed to let them have the Golden Fleece, but only when Jason had managed to plough a field using two wild bulls that breathed fire and to sow it with dragons' teeth. This seemingly impossible task was handled deftly by Medea, daughter of King Aeetes and a skilled magician who had fallen in love with Jason. When Aeetes failed to keep his word, Medea helped to deal with the dragon under the tree after Orpheus had lulled it to sleep with his music, and then she fled with Jason and his crew and the precious Golden Fleece.

Castor and Pollux's name of "Dioscuri" comes from "Dios Kouros," meaning "Sons of Zeus," and it is said that the brothers founded a rich and flourishing town in Colchis that was called Dioscuria after them. According to Strabo, ships flying flags of different countries called on Dioscuria and trade here was conducted with the help of interpreters. In the 2nd century B.C. Dioscuria minted its own coins. A little way out to sea and buried beneath 5.5 m (18 ft) of mud and fine silt, the ruins of this town have laid hidden for 1,500 years. There is a theory that Dioscuria was the victim of either the lowering of the coast or a gigantic landslide. The town is supposed to have been robbed and ruined by Pompey's Roman legions in 65 A.D., but an acropolis, contemporary to the Parthenon, still stands under the water. The site is under investigation, and exhibits, including an ancient marble tombstone dating from the 5th–4th century B.C., have begun to come into the local museum.

At the end of the 1st century B.C. Dioscuria, like all of the Black Sea coast, fell under the influence of the Romans. In the 2nd century B.C., by order of Emperor Hadrian, the Romans built a military stronghold here and called it Sebastopolis, while the Georgians spoke of it as Tukhomi.

At the end of the 5th century the stronghold fell under Byzantine rule and underwent considerable reconstruction. In the 7th to 13th centuries many residential and administrative houses were built in Sebastopolis and it became one of the largest towns along the coast. In the 13th century, during the Genoese and Venetian trade expansion, Sebastopolis became the residence of the governor of the Caucasian trading colonies belonging to the Italian republics. In 1455 it became Turkish and was called Su-Khum-Kale ("Water-Sand Fortress"). It was annexed to Russia in 1810, but it was held by the Turks again in both 1855 and 1877. It previously had been one of the chief slave markets on the Black Sea.

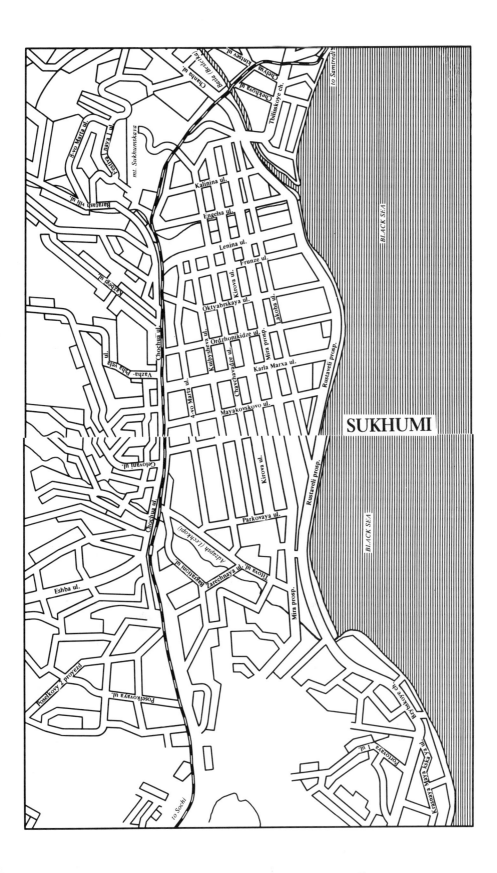

For a long time Sukhumi was just a small provincial town. However, its exotic nature attracted the attention of travellers, who described this "wild area" and its inhabitants. In the 19th century Sukhumi was visited by many outstanding people—Decembrist writer Alexander Bestuzhev-Marlinsky, then later the writers Chekhov and Gorky, the Georgian poets and statesmen Chavchavadze and Tsereteli, and the Russian artists Aivazozsky, Repin, Vasnetsov, and Vereschagin.

Local industry now deals with tobacco, sweets, and food products. The Soviet Union's first industrial installation for obtaining extracts from spices is here. Sukhumi is also the site of a unique educational establishment, the Georgian Institute for Subtropical Economy, which is attended by about 5,000 students, including many foreigners. Sukhumi has a number of technical secondary schools, a teacher's training college, and several research institutes. It is a major resort town.

Sukhumi Fortress, by the sea. This fortress possibly was founded by the Romans at the beginning of the 2nd century and was called Sebastopolis, as was the rest of the settlement. In 1578 the Turks built a new fortress on the remains of the old one. There was a slave market outside the walls. In the 19th and 20th centuries it was used as a prison by the tsarist government. One of its towers now houses the *Dioscuria Restaurant*, where national dishes are served. The *lighthouse* was built in Paris in 1861 and brought here by sea to be reassembled in Sukhumi Bay, where it still works.

King Bagrat's Castle, Chelyuskintsev Street. Built in the 10th–11th centuries, in the time of Bagrat III (965–1014), only the ruins remain, but the entrance gateway shows traces of underground tunnels.

Besletsky Most ("Venetian Bridge"), 6 km (4 miles) to the northeast of Sukhumi along Besletsky Chaussée. The legend is that the 13.3-m (44-ft) bridge was hastily built sometime in the 10th to 12th centuries at a time when invaders threatened the coast. It is said that the mountain people had stone and sand for their construction but lacked a source of lime. They appealed to all who cherished freedom to bring an egg—and in a single day collected 40,000 eggs. They built the bridge that very night, and it is so perfectly engineered that it can still carry 7 to 8 tons. The bridge remained of considerable military importance, as the *ruins* of a nearby defence tower show. 300 m/yds from the bridge on the left bank of river Besletsi are the *ruins* of an old church. The bridge itself is 13 m (14 yds) long and varies in width from 5 to 7 m (16 to 23 ft); it has not yet been established whether it is really of Venetian or local construction.

Blagoveschensky ("Annunciation") Cathedral, Leselidze Street 59. The cathedral was built at the end of the 19th century and was formerly a Greek church.

Monkey Colony, Baratashvili Street 5A. Founded in 1927, this research enterprise, run under the auspices of the USSR Academy of Sciences, is situated on the slopes of Mount Trapetsiya. There are more than 2,000 monkeys in the colony and they have reached the 9th generation. The inmates are mostly baboons and macaque monkeys. They thrive out of doors in this southern climate and eat locally grown fruit; they each have a daily allocation of 70 to 80 kopecks' worth. These monkeys are used for medical experiments. In 1948, after 9 years of experiments on cancer, artificial sarcoma were induced. The scientists at the colony work in 8 laboratories.

Local Museum, Lenin Street 22. Open 10–5; closed Mon.

Gulia's House Museum, Chavchavadze Street 47. Open 10–5; closed Mon. Dimitri Gulia (1874–1960), an Abkhazian writer, poet, and ethnographer, was the founder of Abkhazian literature. He lived here from 1912. Today films are shown about him and poetry readings are held.

Simonov Museum, to the south of Sukhumi, in the village of Gulripsh. Konstantin Simonov, the Soviet writer, spent his holidays here. The museum was opened in his house in 1986.

Shota Rustaveli Monument, in Rustaveli Park. Merabishvili created this monument to the Georgian poet. It was unveiled in 1939.

Gulia Monument, Lenin Street 18. Rukhadze made this monument of Dmitri Gulia, unveiled in 1962.

Tsereteli Monument, Shota Rustaveli Prospect, which is the esplanade at the same time. Akaki Tsereteli (1840–1915) was a writer and playwright. The monument by Razmadze was unveiled in 1961.

Lenin Monument, in front of Government House. This monument by Asatiani and Georgadze was unveiled in 1959.

Chanba Monument, Pushkin Street 1. Samson Chanba was a local writer. Gogoberidze was responsible for this monument, unveiled in 1959.

Eshba Monument, Lenin Street, in front of the town hall. Efraim Eshba was a local political figure and the monument was made by Marina Eshba, his daughter.

Lakoba Monument, at the entrance to the Botanical Garden. Nestor Lakoba was another local political figure.

War Memorial and Eternal Flame, between the Dioscuria Restaurant and the hotel. This is dedicated to an unknown soldier.

Chanba Drama Theatre, Pushkin Street 1. Built in 1952 in Georgian style, this theatre is decorated with stone carving, a waterfall in a grotto, and gryphon fountains. On the facade are busts of Georgian representatives of the arts.

Konstantin Gamsakhurdiya Georgian Drama Theatre, Lenin Street 10

Abkhazian Philharmonic Society, Kirov Street 46. This was built in 1949 by Sergo Tsintsabadze. Here one can hear the 30-man choir of centenarians. Their repertory consists of folk songs, legends, and ballads that have been passed on from 1 generation to another.

Summer Theatre, Kirov Street, in the park

Republican Stadium, Kirov Street

Botanical Garden, Chavchavadze Street 20. Open daily, 10–5. The gardens were founded in 1840 on the initiative of General Nikolai Rayevsky, friend of Pushkin. It was devastated by the Turks in 1878 and restored in 1894. There are 4 ponds for water plants, and many of them, including the Blue Waterlily, the Water Poppy, and the giant Victoria Regia, with leaves 2.5 m (8 ft) in diameter, are subtropical. The Indian Lotus also is grown in the open, and papaya, and the greenhouses contain many rare tropical plants and cacti. The gardens are used by a botanical research institute.

Dendrarium, Tbiliskoye Chaussee. Open 10–5.

Ordzhonikidze Park, Ordzhonikidze Street

Trudovoy Slavy Park, near Frunze Street

Shota Rustaveli Park, Teatralnaya Street. There is a *bust* of Shota Rustaveli, and the many palm trees include Blue Palms.

Sukhumi Hill Park. A road leads up to the carpark at the top. The *Amza ("Moon") Restaurant*, from which there is a good view, is reached by a wide flight of steps.

The best bathing beaches are 1 km/mile from town and reached by either car or motorboat. The Intourist beach has sand and shingle.

Abkhazia Hotel (Intourist) and Restaurant, Frunze Street 2; tel. 25-201. Designed by Schuko, it was built in 1937. Intourist office, tel. 23-313.

Tbilisi Hotel, Dzhguburia Street 2; tel. 26-027

Ritsa Hotel, Rustaveli Prospect 34

Gumista Camping Site, by the main road, 9 km (6 miles) north of Sukhumi; tel. 98-137

Aragvi Restaurant, Mir Prospect 67

Dioscuria Restaurant, Rustaveli Prospect, in the ruined fortress on the esplanade

Ritsa Restaurant, Lenin Street 2

Kavkaz Restaurant, Frunze Street 2

Psou Restaurant, Tbilisskoye Chaussee 15

Amza ("Moon") Restaurant, on the top of Sukhumi Hill

Amra ("Sun") Restaurant, Rustaveli Prospect, by the sea

GPO, Mira Prospect 92

Bank, Lenin Street 14

Department Store, Mira Prospect 52

Souvenirs, Mira Prospect 94

Abralash Book Shop, Mira Prospect 62

Art Salon, Frunze Street 22

Foreign Currency Shop, Rustaveli Prospect 60. Open 9–6; closed Sun.

Philately Shop, Rustaveli Prospect 60. This shop is for stamp collectors.

Market, Kirov Street

Filling Stations, beside the road, both on the way into town and on the way out

Sinop Motel, 1 km/mile from Sukhumi along Tbilisskoye Chaussee, near the road, among tropical and subtropical trees. This motel has a *cafeteria*, *carwash*, and *service station*. 100 m/yds from the exit gate is the *Medicinal Beach*, with a carpark, a *cafe*, and a *shop*.

*   *   *

Intourist runs a number of excursions from Sukhumi. Those to Novy Afon, Lake Ritsa, Pitsunda, and Gagra are to the north, following the coastal road. There are even day trips from here to Sochi (q.v.), 320 km (199 miles) there and back. The excursion to Khobi follows the road to the south.

Novy Afon

It is 28 km (17 miles) in a northwesterly direction to Novy Afon from Sukhumi. Novy Afon is situated near the sea on the river Psyrtskha, which runs through a picturesque gorge between the Afonskaya and Iverskaya hills. The bathing season here lasts 6 or 7 months.

The place has been inhabited from time immemorial. In the 3rd millennia B.C. a settlement appeared on the southern slope of Iverskaya Hill. Each generation left architectural monuments that perished in successive wars. But even the remaining ruins tell much of the talents and industriousness of the previous inhabitants of these parts.

The ancient Greek colony and citadel here was called Nycopsia or Anacopia (meaning "Twisty"), while the name of Novy Afon was given it only when the monastery was founded here in 1875.

Anacopia knew Roman domination and the remains of their construction can be seen on *Iverskaya Hill* (350 m/1,150 ft). In the 5th century Anacopia became the seat of a bishop, and in the late 6th century it was the residence of the Byzantine rulers of Abkhazia. Anacopia stayed under Byzantine rule for many years, until in the 7th century it became the residence of the rulers of Abkhazia, who held their tenure under Byzantium. In 756 Leon I was chosen as king and Abkhazia became a separate kingdom, with Anacopia as its capital.

From the 7th century the stronghold was encircled by a wall, except on its northern side, where a steep cliff dropped down sheer to the sea, rendering it inaccessible to any enemy. This did not make it completely impregnable, however; once upon a time it was taken by the enemy, but only due to cunning and treachery, as described in this Abkhazian legend:

It happened long ago, in the time of Tsar Bagrat IV. Bagrat's nephew, Dmitri, envied him his crown. Dmitri, through his mother, the Ossetian princess Aida, entered into agreement with the Byzantines and under cover of night they captured the fortress. But they only stayed for a single day; fearing his uncle's anger, Dmitri fled to Byzantium together with his mother. 5, or maybe 10, years later, a rumour spread that Princess Aida wished to return home and would bring rich presents for her brother-in-law, since she had become the wife of a very wealthy merchant. When the people of sacred Apsna (Abkhazia) saw dozens of ships loaded with presents, their hearts overflowed with joy. Aida was met with all ceremony and for a whole day celebrations and riding competitions were held. That night, when the sun had set beyond the

510

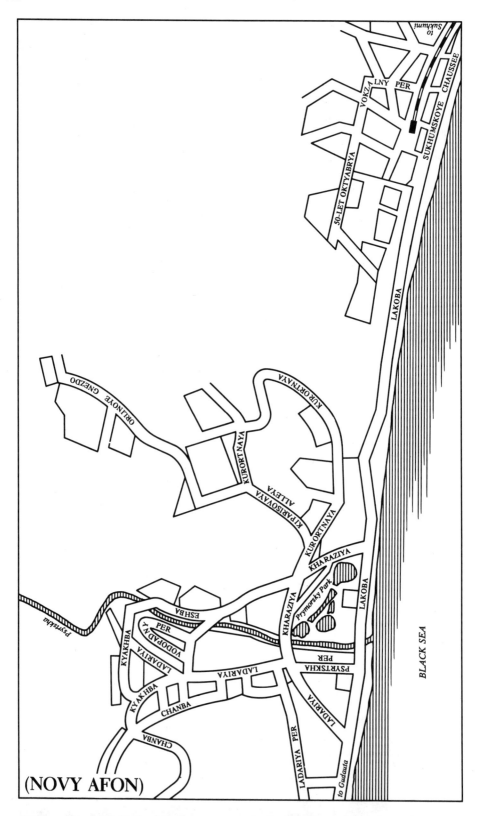

(NOVY AFON)

western sea, the princess ordered all the presents to be taken into the fortress. Hundreds of carts followed the road up from the sea to the fortress and each cart carried two huge cases. All of these were stored in the tall tower that crowned the northwest of the fortress. The princess promised that all of the presents would be shown to the people first thing in the morning, and everyone went peacefully home in anticipation of the treat in store. Night fell and the whole fortress and all around slept. Only Aida and her loyal servants stayed awake, preparing to carry out Dmitri's plan. Under cover of darkness they broke into the tall tower and opened all of the cases. Each one contained two uniformed soldiers, who lost no time in slaughtering their victims. In an hour everything was over and the fortress passed into Byzantine hands.

On the hilltop are 3 *Roman towers* remaining from Aspar Fortress, supposedly built in the time of Trajan. On the slope of the hill is a Byzantine wall with a tower and on the hilltop there are the *ruins* of an 8th-century Christian church that was restored in the 11th-12th century and contains ancient sepulchres with Byzantine decorations. The *remains* of a 13th-century Genoese tower stand in the grounds of the Primorski Sanatorium down by the sea; another walk leads to *Armyanskaya Ravine* and to *Spusk Hill* (800 m/2,625 ft), where there is a 2-storey house known as the Swallow's Nest.

The name "Novy Afon" means "New Athos," for the monks of Mt. Athos founded a large *monastery* here in 1875. The imposing *cathedral* dedicated to the martyr Pantheleimon was built here in 1900 by Nikolai Nikonov. The cathedral is in Byzantine style and is designed to take a congregation of 3,000. The height of the main dome is 40 m (131 ft) and the length and width of the building are 50 m (55 yds) and 32 m (35 yds), respectively. The frescoes were completed in 1914 by a Moscow painter, A. Serebryakov. Since 1959 the cathedral has been open as a branch of the State Abkhazian National Museum. Open 11–5. Also in the monastery complex is the 9th-century *Church of Simon the Canaanite* (one of the saints most venerated in Novy Afon), founded on the ruins of a 4th-century temple and reconstructed in 1882. Simon the Canaanite was the apostle who came here with St. Andrew in 55 A.D. According to legend, they brought Christianity to Abkhazia. The church now contains a library, and the monastery is also the home of the country's only *Museum of Tourism*. Of the 3 other churches the most interesting is the *Iberian Chapel*, from which there is an excellent view of the surrounding countryside. At the end of the ravine of the river Psyrtskha (4 km/2.5 miles) is the *Monk's Cave*.

Originally there were 720 monks in the community, and Novy Afon was one of the richest monasteries in Russia, being granted 14,000 hectares (36,000 acres) at the time of its foundation. After the revolution the monastery was shut down,

and in 1924 most of the buildings were turned into sanatoria. The monks' orchards and gardens became the *Abkhazia Farm*, which owns the largest olive grove on the coast (65 hectares/162 acres), also planted by the monks.

Novy Afon's attractive *park* is situated in the centre of the resort by the sea. It was laid out by the monastery in the 19th century. The monks dug the ponds, which are now rich with carp. An avenue of pyramidal cypresses leads to V*odopad* ("*Waterfall*") *Sanatorium* in the grounds of which stands a well-preserved 9th–10th century *church* that used to be a burial place for the Abkhazian clergy.

Not far from the church is Novy Afon hydroelectric station, built as one of Russia's first electric power stations in 1902; it was reconstructed in 1935. The 10-m (33-ft) waterfall is fed by the river Psyrtskha. Goluboye Ozero ("Blue Lake") formed after the construction of the station.

Novo-Afonskiye, or Iverskiye, Caves, Chanba Street 16. Open 9–7.30; closed Mon. A miniature electric railway runs into the heart of the caves, long known locally as the Bottomless Pit. Stalactites, stalagmites, and glassy lakes abound, but summer visitors are advised to take a jacket as the underground temperature is only about 12°C (54°F). The acoustic qualities enable choral concerts to be held in one of the halls.

The tour round Novy Afon Caves starts with the *Abkhazia Hall*. This is a gigantic stone bag, 30 m (98 ft) in height with a floor of 4,570 sq m (49,190 sq ft). The next, *Georgian Speleologists' Hall*, is between 25 and 50 m (82 to 164 ft) high and its floor area is 10,635 sq m (114,478 sq ft). This is the largest hall among all caves so far studied in the Soviet Union.

Leading from its northern end is *Clay Corridor*, its name due to the clay deposits found here. A steep climb brings one to *Canyon Hall* and the dry part of the caves, which abounds in stalactites and stalagmites. The last part of the caves is *Tbilisi Hall*, with a large stone waterfall. This is especially beautiful when it is raining outside and water penetrates through the earth and trickles down it.

The excursion lasts an hour and a half and covers 1.5 km (1 mile), not too long considering that these underground sights are 1.5 million years old.

Psytskha Restaurant, in the town centre

Restaurant Adzharia, Sukhumskoye Chaussee, near Swan Lake

Cafe, by the caves

Motel, at the 27-km mark, among cypresses and by an olive grove. At the motel are the *Gemo Restaurant* and a *cafe*.

A *historical-architectural reserve* is being organised on Iverskaya Hill. A cableway will lead to the top of the hill, where various panels will retell the military events and everyday life of ancient Anacopia. On the slope of Mt. Afon is to be a *tourist centre*, decorated following the theme of the Abkhazian epic about the Nartes, a legendary people who lived here in the 2d millennia B.C. A Nart family consisted of a mother, a hundred brothers, and one sister. After marriage all of them settled near their mother's home in small houses called "amharas." The main building of this tourist centre will be the mother's house and it will be surrounded by small "amharas" with accommodations for 2. There will be a *sports centre* next to the Nart village. Novy Afon is to be one of the largest tourist centres in the Soviet Union, able to cater to over a million Soviet and foreign tourists annually.

Lake Ritsa

This beauty spot is 95 km (59 miles) from Sukhumi. The way to Lake Ritsa climbs high into the mountains, 39 km (24 miles) inland from Bzyb on the main coastal road. The mountain lake, known as the Gem of the Caucasus, can be visited from May to November, but in winter the valley is blocked with snow.

There are many beehives in the vicinity, the Bzyb River gorge providing excellent conditions for beekeeping. Apiculture, a most profitable branch of the local economy, has been practiced in Abkhazia since times immemorial. The old Greek writers and geographers Xenophon (4th century B.C.) and Strabon (1st century B.C.) noted how highly developed apiculture was among the ancestors of the present-day Abkhazians. Abkhazian honey and beeswax were in great demand abroad.

There is also a factory producing prefabricated building parts for use in the growing coastal resort town of Pitsunda.

Down a smooth cliff near the road there runs a little stream that forms a beautiful waterfall called Maiden's Tears. The legend about it tells that once upon a time a family lived here. The only daughter, the beautiful Amra, tended her sheep and goats along the rocky banks of the river Bzyb and sang songs to her beloved Adgur, who lived high up in the mountains. The girl's beauty and her sweet songs evoked the jealousy of a water nymph who lived in the Bzyb. One day this nymph came out of the water, climbed the cliff, and wanted to throw Amra down into the river. Amra's bitter tears ran down the cliff face into the Bzyb. The angry god of the river turned the water nymph to stone, but Amra's tears still pour down the cliff.

A little further on is a second cliff with a stream known as Man's Tears—and a continuation of the story. When Adgur, who was hunting in the mountains, suddenly felt a pain in his heart, he realized that his sweetheart was in danger, but he was unable to come to her rescue. The manly hunter's tears, few and far between, fell down to the cliff, and they still ooze from the rocks.

To the left of the road are the *ruins* of a 10th- to 12th-century fortress and an 8th-century Christian church.

5 km (3 miles) further on is the village of Shota Rustaveli, and a little further, on the left, stand the *ruins* of the 13th-century Hasanta-Abaa watchtower that barred the road to enemies coming down into the Bzyb River gorge from the high mountain passes.

At the 14-km mark lies *Goluboye Ozero* ("Blue Lake"), called "Adzia-vitsva" in Abkhazian. The lake, supplied by underwater springs, really is blue. It is over 70 m (230 ft) deep and its temperature is never higher than 7 to 12°C (45 to 54°F). After Blue Lake the road follows the valley of the river Geggi; the river is yellow on one side and steel blue on the other because the waters of the Geggi and the river Upshara flow, hardly mixing, along a single riverbed (just as the Black and White Aragvi rivers do in the southern Caucasus). The steep slopes of the gorge are covered with thick forests that caught the eye of timber dealers. In 1893 a Belgian joint-stock company negotiated for the right to cut this precious timber. The surveying was begun, but the 1917 revolution interrupted the work and saved the trees. The road zig-zags up through the narrow *Upsharsky Ravine* (25 m/27 yd wide), where the cliffs rise to over 400 m (1,300 ft) on either side. After the last climb, Mt. *Atsetuk* (2,455 m/8,050 ft) and Mt. *Agepsta* (3,261 m/ 10,670 ft) can be seen from the road, their summits covered with snow.

Lake Ritsa lies 925 m (3,035 ft) above sea level. It is 2.6 km (1.5 miles) long, 1 km (0.6 miles) wide, and 115 m (377 ft) deep. The water is cold, the temperature never rising above 15°C (59°F). The lake appeared a few hundred years ago after a great landslide from Mt. Pshegishkha ("Table Mountain") dammed the river Lashipse. The story attached to its formation is as follows:

Nobody, not even the 1,000-year-old boxwood nor the river Bzyb, remember how Lake Ritsa appeared. But to a shepherd who climbed high up into the mountains to find a good pasture for his sheep, the singing, chattering stream told the story. The shepherd told the tale to his children, and so it was passed down from generation to generation.

Once upon a time there were three brothers, hunters who lived in the mountains beside a gentle stream. Their names were Atsetuk, Agepsta, and Pshegishkha. Every evening their lovely sister Ritsa cooked for them in the high mountain valley that they had made their home. One day they were very late in returning, but Ritsa sang happily to herself and to the stars while she waited. Her song was heard by the bandit brothers Geggi and Upshara, and the latter rushed away on horseback to seek the owner of the sweet voice. On seeing her, he was filled with passion and seized her fiercely, despite her cries for help. Her plight was seen by the mountain eagle, who flew off to tell her brothers. They all ran back as fast as they could, without letting Upshara know of their approach. Pshegishkha threw his shield at the intruder but missed him, and the shield blocked the stream and caused the water to rise, quickly forming a lake. Ritsa was so filled with shame that she plunged into the lake, and the waters instantly turned as clear as teardrops. In dismay her three brothers pursued Upshara, caught him, and threw him into the lake, too, where he would have drowned but for the bubbling and seething of the water, which cast him over the shield-dam. He rushed madly down to join his brother Geggi, tearing down trees and boulders on his way. Ritsa's three brothers turned to stone and still watch over the sparkling waters of the lake.

Ritsa Hotel and Restaurant
Shashlik Bar, across the lake, by motorboat
Motel. The building of this motel is interesting. It was built in the style used by the boyars (the Russian aristocrats) up until the 17th century.
Cafeteria
Filling and Service Stations
From the lake, beside which Stalin had a country house, the road runs for 16 km (10 miles) along the valley of the river Lishipse until this joins the Avadhara, 1,600 m (5,250 ft) above sea level. Here, in the Avadhara Valley, are mineral springs that, in their physico-chemical composition and curative properties, resemble those of Borzhomi and of Vichy in France. A new spa called Avadhara is developing here.

Pitsunda

The resort of Pitsunda is almost halfway between Sukhumi (73 km/45 miles) and Sochi (69 km/43 miles). It lies at a distance of 13 km (8 miles) to the left of the main road, by the sea.
Service Station, at the turning to Pitsunda.

Alakhadzy is the first village on the way to Pitsunda and the centre of the large Sergo Ordzhonikidze farm, which spreads far along the coast and is mostly engaged in tobacco and vine growing.

The road then passes eucalyptus groves and for a few miles goes along the Monk's Avenue, planted as a penance by monks of the local monastery. Further on the road passes the Gagra poultry farm that supplies all of the resorts of Abkhazia. The poultry farm has a small *restaurant* with good, fresh food. At the 4/9-km mark the road goes through a large dairy farm, behind which lies *Lake Inkit*. This is 1.5 km (1 mile) long, 500 m/yds wide, and 5 m (16 ft) deep and is the largest of the 3 lakes in this region. It has good fishing and nutria are bred successfully on its shores.

An area of 200 hectares (500 acres) runs for 7 km (4 miles) beside the sea and is covered by ancient flora of the Tertiary period. Here stand tall new buildings of sanatoria belonging to the Writers' Union, *Pravda* newspaper, and cinematography workers. There are also a number of houses used by government leaders, where high-level international meetings have taken place from time to time. To the southeast of Pitsunda is a box grove with some trees reaching 12 m (39 ft) high. Entrance to Pitsunda proper is restricted; a special pass may be required.

Pitsunda lies on the same latitude as Nice and has a bathing season of 4 to 5 months. Swimming is good between May and October, and as this is a period when storms are rare, many trips can be made by sea as well as by road to other places along the coast. Tourist ships tie up at piers near the shopping centre. Special buses go daily to Lake Ritsa (50 km/31 miles away in the mountains; see above). A path of multicoloured slabs has been laid along the beach. On either side are magnolias, oleanders, cypresses, palms, and Pitsunda lilies. The pines, the good harbour, and the average of 216 sunny days each year make this a very pleasant place.

The local pines were named Pitsunda pines by Christian Steven, founder of the Nikitsky Botanical Garden in the Crimea. This tree is salt and drought resistant and can survive in polluted air. It is found only in two places in the world, here in Pitsunda and in Dzhankot (see above).

In 700 B.C. Greeks from Miletus had built, among other towns and settlements, the "great and rich town of Pitiunt." Excavations of this Greek colony are in progress. The name "Pitsunda" comes from "Pitus," the Greek for "pine." The particular pines that grow here are Pinus Pithysa, which in the past were felled for shipbuilding because they were straight and made strong masts. The Georgian name for Pitsunda is "Bichvinta" ("Pine Grove").

In 100 B.C. Pitiunt, with other towns nearby, fell into the hands of Mithradates the Great of Pontus and was known as one of the richest towns of Colchis. Later Pitsunda came under Roman rule. The Romans turned it into a military stronghold and from it lorded over all of the local tribes. After the Romans, the next to come were the Persians. In 55 A.D. St. Andrew and Simon the Canaanite visited Pitsunda on their missionary travels; St. Andrew was buried here.

Pitsunda became the residence of Bishop Stratophil, who was a participant of the first Nicaea Ecumenical Council, in 325. It is believed that it was here that the first Abkhazian baptisms took place for another, Abkhazian, name for this town is "Ldzaa," which means a "Baptising Place." It was Justinian I who finally converted the local inhabitants to Christianity in the 6th century and who, in 551, built the large cathedral in Byzantine style and dedicated it (like that in Constantinople) to St. Sophia. A local legend says that within it is the grave of St. John Chrysostom, who died here in exile in the 5th century.

Simultaneously with the construction of the cathedral, the laying out of an aqueduct was begun. The Abkhazians have a rather sinister legend about both constructions. The builders of the cathedral and those of the aqueduct argued as to who would be first to finish his work. The price of losing the dispute was very high: the loser must jump down from the roof of the cathedral. Work began, but when water started flowing out of the pipes of the aqueduct, the cathedral builders had only got as far as the base of the dome. The architect threw himself down from the roof to his death. It is said that the place from which he jumped is marked by a little hollow in the roof.

The cathedral played an important part in local

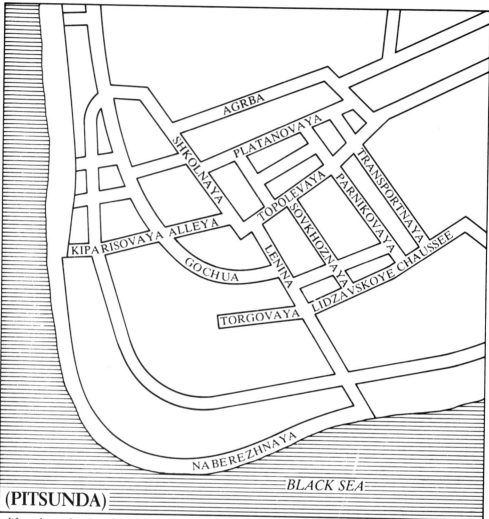

(PITSUNDA)

BLACK SEA

life and was for about 100 years the seat of the Abkhazian patriarchs, until under the Turks in the 15th century Pitsunda lost its former glory. The following legend belongs to the time of Turkish rule.

Once upon a time, when Pitsunda was besieged by the enemy, all of her men were killed in an unequal battle. Women, old folk, and children hid in a tower in the centre of the village. The enemy burned down all of the houses and asked them to surrender. Those in the tower had no more food or water, since the enemy had blocked the aqueduct from the river Bzyb to the tower. Then the elders convened a council and decided to die rather than surrender. Mothers began throwing their children down upon the enemy spears and then jumped down themselves. All of a sudden a flock of huge mountain eagles descended upon the tower and started catching up the children, women, and old peo-

ple and taking them to safety. Later those rescued by the eagles came back to Pitsunda and it was built anew from the ruins.

In 1882 Pitsunda became part of Novy Afon Monastery and monks built their cells here. Among the ruins of the monastery is a surrounding wall built in the 17th century from the ruins of Pitiunt.

St. Sophia's Cathedral was rebuilt in 1869 and reconsecrated to the Assumption of the Virgin Mary. The acoustics of the cathedral are such that the voices of a few singers sound like a full choir. In 1972 the East German firm Schukke built an organ with 4,000 pipes especially for this cathedral. Professor C. Kestner of Leipzig, who plays the very organ that Bach used to play, gave the opening concert. The building is now open as a museum. Open 11–5.30, closed Mon.

There are *14-storey boarding houses* in the town instead of the usual sanatoria. They cater to 10,000 holidaymakers and serve as a model for the planning of other resorts. The boardinghouses have *air-conditioned double rooms*. On each floor are lounges with television and observation platforms. Lifts transport guests to the roof in a matter of seconds. On the roofs are solaria and cafés, and from here there are breathtaking views of the Black Sea and the snowcapped Caucasus Mountains. The pediments of the Apsny ("Abkhazia"), Amra ("Sun"), Iveria (ancient name for "Georgia"), Zolotoye Runo ("Golden Fleece"), Kolkhetia, and Mayak ("Beacon") boarding houses are decorated with emblems explaining their names.

Intourist Office. Tel. 2045.

There is an *open-air cinema* seating 1,000 in the centre of the resort, as well as a *stadium*, a *boating station*, a *sports ground*, and an *open-air swimming pool* with heated seawater. All technical services use electricity to minimize pollution.

A big but is the existence of underwater canyons that endanger the resort of Pitsunda. They are constantly eating away at the coastline; *Shark Canyon* is the biggest and most aggressive. Scientists are busy considering various solutions of saving this popular resort.

Medea Statue, by Merab Berdzenishvili

The *Apsny, Bzyb, Iveria, Zolotoye Runo, and Mayak boarding houses* provide accommodations here; tel. 2045. There are *cafeterias* nearby and *souvenir kiosks* in Apsny and Iveria.

Pitsunda Restaurant, at the entrance to the town

Inkit Restaurant, on the left side of the road before entering Pitsunda

GPO, Lenin Street 87

Pitsunda Motel, close to the sea on Pitsunda Cape. Leave the main road by an asphalt road signposted to the cape and running toward the sea. The Motel is 12 km (7 miles) away, at the end of a cypress avenue. There is a *sports ground* by the motel.

Filling Station, at the 384/363-km mark, back on the main road

Service Station, on the left before entering Pitsunda. Here are carwashing facilities and a guarded carpark.

Gagra

The resort of Gagra 140 km (87 miles) from Sukhumi. It is located on a narrow coastal strip, and at this point the mountains, which are of porous limestone and full of gorges and caves, come down very close to the sea. Some of the peaks rise to 2,750 m (9,020 ft). Gagra is the warmest place on the eastern coast of the Black Sea; roses bloom in winter and the trees are nearly always green. From May till November the sea is between 16 and 23°C (61 and 73°F). The beach is of shingle with some sandy places. Thanks to the climate, experiments are being made with the cultivation of cacao. In the last 20 years more than several hundred trees have been planted.

Gagra has a long history and has almost always been known as a fortified place. In the 2d century

B.C. it was the site of the Greek colony of Triglith. After the Greeks came the Romans, who founded here a fortress called Nitica, while the place became a prison and a place of exile for, among others, early Christians who were extradited by the Roman emperors, particularly Diocletian. In the 4th and 5th centuries Abaata Fortress was built, the *ruins* of which still can be seen, closing off Zhoekvara Gorge. According to the 6th-century Byzantine historian Procopius of Caesarea, the fortress was built by the local Abzghi tribe against foreign invaders. In his book *The Gothic War* Procopius describes this place, under the name of "Trachea," as very difficult to traverse. The name "Gagra" first appeared on the map compiled by Pietro Visconti in 1308 (now kept in the St. Marco Library in Venice). On this map Gagra is called "Kakara," while on other Italian maps it was called "Khakary." At that time Gagra was a Genoese colony.

The present name derives from that of one of the oldest Abkhazian families, Gagaa.

Gagra was under Turkish rule, as was most of the Black Sea coast, for almost 300 years. The population was taken into captivity and the town's fortunes declined. With lack of careful tilling, the land became boggy and malarial. Even after the 1830s, when Gagra was taken by the Russians, it remained an unpleasant place. Alexander Bestuzhev-Marlinsky, the Decembrist poet exiled here by Nicholas I, wrote in one of his letters, "Gagra is a coffin for the Russian garrison."

The fortress was very often subject to raids by the northwestern Caucasian tribes. To prevent these, a stone watchtower was built in 1841 by order of General Nikolai Muravyov. This tower is known in literature as Bestuzhev-Marlinsky Tower. Lieutenant Colonel Konstantin Danzas took part in its construction; he had been a close friend of Alexander Pushkin, acting as his second in the fateful duel, and later serving in the Gagra regiment. Gagra Fortress, devastated and rebuilt many times, was abandoned by the Russian troops during the Russo-Turkish War of 1877–78 but stood till the end of the 19th century. Because there was a small church in the fortress, the monks of Novy-Afon Monastery asked the tsar for permission to bring Gagra under their jurisdiction.

The town of Gagra began to revive at the beginning of the 1890s with the construction of the Novorossiisk-Batumi highway. However, it began to develop as a resort in 1901 when Prince Alexander Oldenburgsky, who was married to a niece of the tsar, decided to popularize it. By order of Nicholas II he founded here a climatic station that was solemnly inaugurated in the presence of high tsarist officials. The prince ordered a hotel building to be prefabricated of pine in Norway, and he brought it here, where it was assembled without a single nail. He also built a palace for himself, which is now the Chaika ("Seagull") holiday home. To impart an exotic appearance to the place the prince ordered ponds to be dug, and these were stocked with black and white swans. Parrots and monkeys also were introduced. According to Prince

516

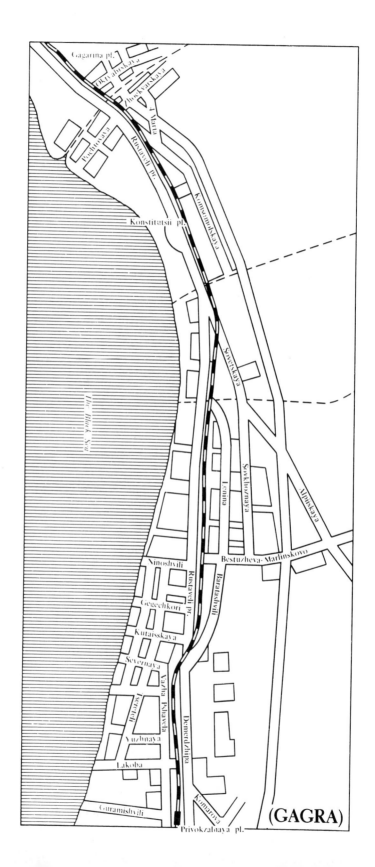

(GAGRA)

Oldenburgsky's plan, Gagra was to become a Russian Nice. However, nothing came of his idea, as almost everybody who arrived for treatment was primarily concerned not to catch malaria, which still abounded.

Today Gagra is a flourishing Black Sea resort. It has 30 sanatoria, mostly located on the steep slopes of the mountains. Paths, avenues, and steps link them to *Marine Park*, which runs for 3 km (2 miles) beside the sea and covers 14 hectares (35 acres). Many of the trees and shrubs are subtropical and there are *statues* and *fountains*, and the lake in the park still has its black and white swans. At the eastern end of the park is a semicircular *colonnade* and a carpark. Gagra's plantation of cork oak was transplanted from somewhere in Africa in the 1st half of the 19th century. The trees have now reached a height of 30 m (98 ft). In the southern part of the park is a summer theatre where guest performances are held and where, in 1929, Vladimir Mayakovsky gave a recital of his poems. To the west of the park the little river Gagripsh runs into the sea.

Abkhazian Weapons Exhibition, in the remains of the 6th–7th-century church in the grounds of the Zhoekvara Sanatorium. On display are different types of arms, from the old Abkhazian national variety to the firearms of the 19th century. The exhibition was organised in 1971.

Rustaveli Bust, near Gagripsh Restaurant

World War II Memorial

Abkhazia Hotel and Restaurant

Gagripsh ("Beauty of Gagra") Hotel, Rustaveli Prospect

Gagripsh Restaurant. This is in the building of the hotel that Prince Alexander Oldenburgsky had built in Norway and brought here. Before the revolution the hall of the restaurant was used as a theatre, where Fyodor Chaliapin and other outstanding Russian and foreign singers performed.

Ritsa Cafe

Bank and GPO, Rustaveli Prospect

Kholodnaya Rechka ("Cold River") Motel, inland from the main road, 8 km (5 miles) from Gagra. It has a *cinema*, baths, showers, a *shop*, a *post office*, and an *international telephone call box*. There is also an open carpark, a garage, a *service station*, a *carwash*, and a *filling station*. The motel is near the sea and has its own *beach*, and it is only 70 km (43 miles) from here to Lake Ritsa.

Repair Station, by the main road on the way into Gagra from the south

There are many pleasant walks in the vicinity. The *Tsikhera Ravine* is 3 km (2 miles) away. At the beginning of it there is a 2-storey cave that in the 19th century was inhabited by monks who called it the Euphratus Cave, after St. Euphratus, a 5th-century evangelist of these parts. Another cave higher up in the gorge, at 350 m (1,150 ft) above sea level, is adorned by stalactites. It is about 8 km (5 miles) to the picturesque *ravine of the river Zhoekvara*, which is lined by cliffs and has 2 waterfalls; by the road are the *ruins* of the Bestuzhev-Marlinsky watchtower. Another walk of about 10 km (6 miles) leads to a grotto with a spring in the ravine of the river Gagripsh; the path runs through beech woods and has a good view of the sea.

Khobi

Khobi is 132 km (82 miles) from Sukhumi and stands inland, to the south, on the river Khobi.

Khobi Restaurant, Lenin Street 82, to the right of the main road. Opposite is the main square with modern buildings.

3 km (2 miles) from Khobi are the *ruins* of a 13th-century monastery, including a church, a belfry, and a palace.

SURAKHANY

See Apsheron, Baku, p. 61

SUZDAL

(Intourist organises excursions here from Moscow 230 km/143 miles away.)

Suzdal is situated on the river Kamenka, just 35 km (22 miles) north of Vladimir. Vladimir was once its younger rival but is now superior in most things except the wealth of ancient architecture Suzdal still possesses. There are more than 50 examples of church and secular architecture dating from the mid-12th to the mid-18th century. The town's coat of arms, a falcon in a prince's crown, bears witness to the grandeur of its past; only the red part of the background shows its connection with Vladimir, while all of the other townships in the region repeat the crowned lion of Vladimir above their own particular symbol.

The town was 1st mentioned in chronicles of 1024 and there are several theories concerning the origin of its name. It was once "Suzhdal," indicating that perhaps it was here that the princes meted judgment. Until the middle of the 11th century it was, however, nothing more than a small settlement. Several of the streets even today have names derived from the names of the old Slavic gods—Yarunova Street and Kupala Street among them.

As early as 990 Prince Vladimir of Kiev came to Suzdal and established a missionary bishop here who later built a church. From 1096 onward Suzdal is always mentioned in the chronicles as being a town. Its heart was the kremlin, fortified with earthen walls, of which traces still remain. At the very end of the 11th century builders from Kiev constructed Suzdal's first stone church here.

Prince Yuri Dolgoruky (who later founded Moscow) decided in 1125 to make Suzdal his capital, but after his death, his son Andrei Bogolubsky moved to Vladimir in the vain hope of escaping the hostility of the nobles. This was the beginning of the rivalry between the two neighbouring towns that gradually led to Vladimir's superiority.

In 1238 Suzdal was seized and burnt by the Tatars, but it soon was rebuilt and in 1328, when the seat of the grand princes was transferred to Moscow, Suzdal became the centre of the political struggle against Moscow's domination. It held this position until Grand Prince Vasili annexed it to

Moscow at the end of the 14th century. Although it lost its former political and economic importance, the town was still one of the major religious centres of northern Russia. At the end of the 16th century local builders restored and added to the existing buildings, especially the kremlin, the town walls, and the monasteries, but their work was damaged by the invading Poles and then again by the Tatars as well as by recurrent fires, notably that of 1644. At the end of the 17th century more building work was undertaken, including the Archbishop's Palace.

From that time Suzdal's religious importance dwindled little by little, and now the town is nothing more than the centre of a small food-producing district of little importance. Architectural restoration is progressing on a large scale, but one needs to remember that between 1238 until the beginning of the 16th century no stone buildings were constructed in Suzdal, so no architecture of that time remains.

It is suggested that visitors to Suzdal turn right from the main road coming in from Vladimir before they get into the centre of the town. 5 km (3 miles) further on is the little village of *Kideksha*, standing on the high bank of the Nerl. Inside a walled enclosure stands the *Church of Boris and Gleb*, built in 1152 for Prince Yuri Dolgoruky, who had a small palace here, too. It is open as a museum; closed Tues. and the last Fri. of the month. This was the 1st of all of the limestone edifices to be constructed in this region. It should not prove hard to find the villager in charge of the key to the church, inside of which are the remains of some frescoes as well as plans and pictures illustrating the history of the place. Yuri Dolgoruky's son Boris and his daughter-in-law Maria were buried here. The limestone church was somewhat spoiled by reconstruction in the 16th and 17th centuries. Beside it stands *St. Stephen's Church* and belfry (1870), the design of which is typical of a stone church following the characteristics of wooden architecture.

The *Vasilievsky Monastery* stands a little to the south of the Kideksha Road. It was founded at the beginning of the 13th century and run as a monastery until 1899. The *cathedral* was built in 1668 and the other stone buildings, including the smaller, 2-storey *Sretenskaya ("Purification of the Virgin") Church*, a belfry, and the white walls surrounding them, all date from the 17th and 18th centuries.

Znamenskaya Church (1749) stands beside the road leading into Suzdal from Vladimir and the south, and the elegant white church to the right of the same road on a hill is *Kosmo-damianovskaya Church* (1725).

The best view of the town is obtained from the west side. The main street is still lined with small houses typical of a Russian provincial town of the last century.

The *kremlin* lies beside the Kamenka River, southwest of the central square, surrounded by well-preserved 11th-century earthen walls. Once they were 10 m (33 ft) high and 1,400 m (1,530 yds) in length; on top of the earthen walls are wooden walls and towers. The kremlin was surrounded on 3 sides by the waters of the river and along the 4th, the eastern side, ran a moat 8.5 m (28 ft) deep and 35 m (38 yds) wide.

Inside the kremlin walls the blue-domed *Rozhdestvensky ("Nativity of the Virgin") Cathedral* commands immediate attention, but it is wisest to keep to the rule of visiting the local museum before setting off on a sightseeing tour. The *Suzdal Local Museum* is housed in the obtuse-angled building of the Archbishop's Palace, built in the 16th–17th century in the western part of the kremlin. It is open 10–5; closed Tues. and the last Fri. of the month.

In the museum is a portrait of Solomonia, the wife whom Vasili III divorced, in violation of church law, having accused her of barrenness (although surviving chronicles describe Solomonia as an energetic woman in the prime of life and accuse Vasili of sterility). Nevertheless, with the consent of the Moscow Metropolitan Danil, a shrewd and unscrupulous politician, Vasili obtained his divorce. He sent Solomonia to the Pokrovsky Convent in Suzdal (described below) and married a noble girl of Polish origin named Elena Glinskaya. Later, news reached Moscow that Solomonia had given birth to a son whom she had named Georgi. An inquiry was ordered, and as the child was in obvious danger, Solomonia found trustworthy people to care for him, spread rumours of his death, and staged a fake burial.

Historians regarded all of this as a folk legend, but in 1934 in the crypt under the Pokrovsky Cathedral a small 16th-century limestone tomb was discovered beside the tomb of Solomonia, who died in 1542. There was, however, no skeleton, nor any bones at all under the stone, only a bundle of rags stuffed into a tiny, expensive silk shirt embroidered with pearls. It is hardly surprising that the son born to Vasili III by Elena, no less a person than Ivan the Terrible, saw to it that evidence of the findings of the inquiry should disappear. The small shirt and the little limestone tomb are both in the museum.

This museum also contains much of interest concerning the history of Suzdal and its ancient architecture. There is an exhibit showing the type of decorations to be found on the Church of Boris and Gleb (Kidesksha, 1152), the Pokrovsky Church on the Nerl (Bogolyubovo, 1165), the Dmitrievsky Cathedral (Vladimir, 1194–97), and the Rozhdestvesnky Cathedral (here in Suzdal, 1222–25), and demonstrating how in the course of 75 years the ornamental stonework gradually changed from a simple frieze to an intricate tapestry of stone. The evolution was brought to a sudden halt by the Tatar invasions that began in 1240.

The art section of the museum is reached by passing through the gateway on the left of the Archbishop's Palace and going on to where a porch and stairway lead up to the floor above. Here are some of the best examples of "basma": thin sheets of gold

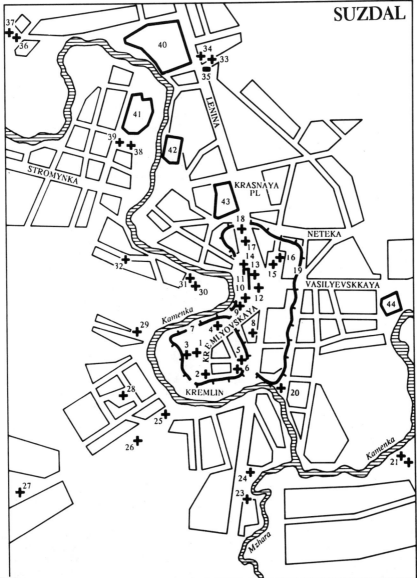

SUZDAL

1. Rozhdestvensky Cathedral
2. Archbishops' Palace; local museum
3. Nikolskaya Wooden Church
4. Uspenskaya Church
5. Nikolskaya Church
6. Nativity Church
7. Earthen walls of Kremlin
8. Pretechenskaya Church
9. Pyatnitskaya Church
10. Vkhodoierusalimskaya Church
11. Traders' Row
12. Voskresenskaya Church
13. Kazanskaya Church
14. Krestovaya Church
15. Tsarevokonstantinovskaya Church
16. Skorbyashenskaya Church

17. St Antipi's Church
18. Lazarevskaya Church
19. Earthen town wall
20. Kosmodamianovskaya Church
21. Archangel Michael's Church (early 18th cent.)
22. Church of SS Flora & Laura (1803)
23. Znamenskaya Church
24. Rizpolozhenskaya Church
25. Preobrazhenskaya Church
26. Voskresenskaya Church
27. Ivanovskaya Church (1747)
28. Borisoglebskaya Church
29. Ilinskaya Church
30. Church of the Nativity of John the Baptist (1703)

31. Bogoyavlenskaya Church
32. Tikhvinskaya Church
33. Smolenskaya Church
34. Semionovskaya Church
35. Tailor's house
36. Bogolyubskaya Church (1698)
37. SS Kosma & Damian's Church (1696)
38. Petropavlovskaya Church
39. Nikolskaya Church
40. Spaso-Efimevsky Monastery
41. Pokrovsky Convent
42. Alexandrovsky Monastery
43. Rizhpolozhensky Convent
44. Vasilievsky Monastery

or silver were beaten onto moulds and then cut out for use as icon frames or buttons. There are also embroideries here, items of metalwork, icons, silver and gold lace, pottery, and decorative tiles. The modern crafts section of the museum is interesting, too.

A museum guide will open the doors of the *Rozhdestvensky Cathedral* and point out the items of greatest interest. Open 10–5; closed Tues., last Thurs. of the month, and in wet weather. This is the oldest church in Suzdal, built in 1222–25 on the site of a brick church that Vladimir Monomakh had built. It was added to in the 16th century. Here princes and eminent clergy were buried and the tombs of Fyodor (1023) and Ioann (1372), the 1st and 6th bishops of Suzdal, are here. Generally speaking, the lower part is 13th and the upper part 16th century; the building was restored in 1964. Some small fragments of frescoes painted in 1230 remain, but there are more of the 17th century. The south and west doors of the cathedral are especially interesting. The west doors, known as the Korsunskiye Gates, have scenes from the New Testament depicted in gold on copper that has darkened with age. This type of decoration, called damascene work, was much used in Byzantium. Some of the icons inside the cathedral date from the 17th century, and standing on the floor is the 17th-century King of the Lanterns, which used to be filled with lighted candles and carried in religious processions.

The octagonal belfry to the south of the cathedral was built in 1635. Besides the numbers on the old clock face there are Slavonic letters to tell the time—A for 1, B for 2, and so on.

Other churches on the territory of the kremlin are the 17th-century *Uspenskaya ("Assumption") Church*, the *Nikolskaya Church* (1720–39) with its bell tower and, close beside it, a *church* for use in summer only and dedicated to the same saint. Also here is the wooden *Nikolskaya Church*, built in 1766 and brought here in 1960 from the village of Glotovo, near Yuriev-Polskoy.

Voskresenskaya Church (1732) stands in the centre of Sovietskaya Square (formerly Trade Square). It is a whitewashed brick cube with a single dome, typical of local church architecture of the 18th century. It houses the *Wood-carving Exhibition*, open in summer, 10–5; closed Tues. and the last Fri. of the month. The belfry has attractive tiles.

Kazanskaya Church (1739) is also on the square and at present is the only one among so many that is open for services.

Between Voskresenskaya Church and the river Kamenka is the 18th-century *Traders' Row*. This is a good example of the arcades of small shops that used to be rented out to merchants for the storage and sale of their wares, and it has been tastefully restored to house a variety of shops. On the bank of the river, standing side by side in the manner Colin Thubron happily describes as an architectural marriage of different buildings for summer and winter use, are 2 very small churches, the *Vkhodoierusalimskaya* (1686) and the *Pyatnitskaya* (1772). South of the square is another pair, *Predtechenskaya Church* (1720) and nearby *Krestovaya Church* (1765). On the northeast side of the square is a third pair, the *Skorbyashenskaya Church* (1750), which was used in winter, and the *Tsarevokonstantinovskaya Church* (1707), a summer church, the small classical rotunda of which was added at a later date. Going north up the main road, Lenin Street, is *Lazarevskaya Church* (1667).

Further on up Lenin Street, on the left in the highest part of the town, stands *Rizopolozhesnki Convent*, founded in 1207, before the Tatar invasion. There is a story told about its early years:

The 15-year-old daughter of Prince Mikhail of Chernigov, himself later murdered by the Tatars, entered this convent under the name of Evfrosiniya when her fiancé died on the eve of their wedding. In 1238, during the 10th year of her sojourn in the convent, the Tatars, who already had invaded Russia came right up to its walls. By some miracle they left it standing and it was popularly believed that her prayers were responsible. She was canonised at the end of the 14th century.

The wooden walls were replaced by stone ones in the 17th century and the *Holy Gates* were constructed in 1688. The 60-m (197-ft) belfry that dominates the town was built into the eastern part of the wall in 1813–19 to commemorate the victory over Napoleon.

The *Alexandrovsky Monastery* stands a little back from the main road, again on the left-hand side, but nearer the river, on its high left bank. It was founded in 1240 by Alexander Nevsky and was once known as the Great Monastery. Now only a small section of its white walls remains. Inside is *Voznesenskaya ("Ascension") Church* and its red belfry, both built in 1695. The gates, built at the beginning of the 18th century, were restored in 1947. The monks left the monastery in 1764 but the church remained open to the public.

Instead of continuing up Lenin Street it is possible to go down to the river past the Alexandrovsky Monastery walls and across it to *Pokrovsky Convent*. The latter, however, is a pleasant place to rest when one has finished the walk through Suzdal, so perhaps it is advisable to go straight on to the little town's largest monastery complex.

The *Spaso-Efimievsky Monastery* stands right above the high bank of the Kamenka and dominates the surrounding territory. It contains museums and exhibitions, and it is closed Mon. and the last Thurs. of the month. The monastery was founded in 1352, and the high stone walls (over 1 km/0.6 mile) long and 12 mighty towers make it look like a fortress; indeed, it served as such for centuries. In 1445 the Russians who were defending the monastery from the Tatars were all killed in a bloody battle and the Tatars captured Grand Prince Vasili Tyomni (the Blind).

The present-day brick walls replaced the wooden ones in the 17th century. They are 6 m (20 ft) thick. On the northern, eastern, and southern sides they stand 8.5 m (28 ft) high and on the western side 7.5 m (25 ft). Of the greatest interest is the massive entrance tower protecting the Holy Gates on the southern side. Its height of 23 m (75 ft) made it a good watchtower. The stone carving gives an impression of lacework. Near the entrance is the *Blagoveschenskaya ("Annunciation") Gate-Church* (17th century). The monastery now houses the *Museum of Applied Art* and the *Rare Books Museum*, open 10–5; closed Mon. and the last Thurs. of the month.

The most important building in the ensemble is the *Spaso-Preobrazheniya ("Transfiguration") Cathedral*, which was founded in 1594 on the site of an older church. It has 5 main domes and the outside decoration of half-columns echoes Vladimir-Suzdal architecture of the 12th and 13th centuries. The south and west outside walls were decorated with frescoes, which is unusual in Russian church architecture. It is on record that they were painted in 1689 by Nikitin and Savin from Kostroma, and the frescoes on the inside walls were painted by artists from Vologda at the same time. The bell tower probably was finished in the 1530s, but arches were added in 1599 and 1691. The bells were replaced after many years of silence in 1984. Beside the east wall of the cathedral, facing the bell tower, is the tomb of Prince Pozharsky, who drove the Poles from Moscow in 1612; his mausoleum has been removed, but there is a monument to his memory by Z. Azgur outside the main entrance gate saying "Dmitri Mikhailovich 1578–1642."

The prison is open as a museum. It was built in 1764 and a 2d one was constructed inside the *Uspenskaya ("Assumption") Refectory Church* (1525) by the order of Catherine II in 1766. Most of the prisoners were those who had committed crimes against the church. More recently the German Field Marshal von Paulus was held here for some time after his capture in Stalingrad in 1943. Adjoining the Uspenskaya Church is the *Archimandrite's Palace* (17th century). The 2-storey residential block in the northeast part of the territory is from the 18th and 19th century and *Nikolskaya Church* was built in 1669. Another museum housed in the monastery is the *Rare Books Museum*, open 10–5 but closed Tues.

Outside the monastery, near the entrance, is *Smolenskaya Church* (1707), which has an elegant belfry. Beside it is the 17th-century stone-built *Tailor's House*, a unique structure because such houses were invariably built of wood. It is open as a museum 10–5; closed Tues. and the last Fri. of the month.

The whitewashed *Pokrovsky ("Intercession") Convent* (1364) stands across the Kamenka on the low right bank, opposite the Spaso-Efimievsky Monastery. The present-day walls and towers were built in the 18th century, except for the 2 17th-century towers that remain in the north wall. The convent is open as a museum 10–5; closed Tues. and the last Fri. of the month.

Pokrovsky Convent is known in Russian history as the place of exile of many Russian ladies of noble birth, including the wives of Vasili III and Ivan the Terrible and Peter the Great's first wife, Evdokia. The story of Solomonia, wife of Vasili III has been told above (see Local Museum). She was buried in 1542 in the crypt under the Pokrovsky Cathedral and it was here in 1934 that the small 16th-century limestone tomb said to be that of her son was discovered.

Inside the convent walls is the 3-domed *Pokrovsky Cathedral*, which was built in 1518 on the site of a wooden church and restored in 1963. It is surrounded by an arcade on 3 sides. The lower part of the octagonal belfry was built in 1515 but the upper part was reconstructed in the 17th century. The refectory building dates from 1518, too, as do the 3-domed *Blagoveschenskaya ("Annunciation") Gate-Church* in the south wall and the *Zachatievskaya ("Immaculate Conception") Church*, both of which were built by Vasili III. The refectory operates as the *Pokrovsky Restaurant*. The Blagoveschenskaya Church is interesting for the way in which the church's and fortress's architecture are smoothly blended. Inside the main gates, by the wall on the left, is a single-storey 17th-century building that served as the monastery's administrative offices; in its cellars were punishment cells.

The *Tikhvinskaya Church* was built in the late 17th century and it is unusual in that it is without apses. Today it is used as a bakery. Also nearby are the *Petropavlovskaya Church* (1694) and *Nikolskaya Church* (1712). The many other churches on this side, the low bank of the river, include the *Bogoyavlenskaya ("Epiphany") Church* (1755), the *Ilinskaya Church* (1788), the 17th-century *Borisoglebskaya Church*, and the *Spasskaya Church*, whose dome is in a state of dilapidation.

Further along on this side of the river and overlooked by the kremlin is the *Museum of Wooden Architecture*, which has a collection of buildings that has been moved here recently. Open 10–5 in summer; closed Tues. and the last Fri. of the month. The *Preobrazhenskaya ("Transfiguration") Church* (1756) was brought here from Kozlyatyevo in 1967 and *Voskresenskaya ("Resurrection") Church* (1766) was brought from Potakino. There is also a *house* with *outbuildings* and 2 *windmills*.

Suzdal Hotel and Restaurant, in the Tourist Complex, 4 km (2 miles) from the centre of the town; tel. 217-57. The complex has a *swimming pool*, a *sauna*, 5 *bars*, and a *shuttle bus* service to the centre of town.

Suzdal Motel, in the Tourist Complex

Pokrovsky Monastery Hotel, in the Tourist Complex

Pokrovsky Restaurant, in the old refectory building of the monastery

Trapeznaya Restaurant, in the kremlin, on the ground floor of the Archbishop's Palace. Closed Mon.

Pogrebok Restaurant, Kremlyovskaya Street (that leading from the kremlin to Torgoviye Ryady). Open 11–7; closed Mon.

Sokol Restaurant, Lenin Street

Tea Room, Lenin Street

Beryozka Foreign Currency Shop, in the shopping arcades

Suzdalskaya Lavka Souvenir Shop, Lebedeva Street 3. This shop is very near the kremlin and is easily identified by its Swiss-style window shutters. Open 9–5.

A *bus station* and a *taxi rank* are located in Lenin Street near the old hotel.

SVIYAZHSK

See Kazan, p. 194.

SVOBODA

See Kursk, p. 264.

TAJIKISTAN

See Dushanbe, p. 114.

TAGANROG Population—291,000

(Intourist organises excursions here from Rostov-on-Don, 75 km/47 miles away.)

Taganrog is situated to the west of Rostov-on-Don on a cape protruding into the Sea of Azov. In the 13th to 15th centuries the Italian colony of Porto-Pisana stood on the site. The town's history is very much like that of Rostov and Azov. In 1698, 2 years after the capture of Azov, Peter the Great founded Trinity Fortress on this cape, which was called Tagany Rog ("Tagany Horn") and which later gave its name to the town of Taganrog. Peter ordered the construction of the first real naval base in Russian history and subsequently organised from here his first naval manoeuvres, which culminated in a mock sea battle of the kind he had watched when he was in Holland.

The fortress, however, had to be demolished according to the Pruth Treaty of 1712 with Turkey, but it was restored in 1738. In the same year a port was opened near the fortress, and due to its favourable geographical position it became one of the major ports in the southern Russian seas. In 1739 the fortress was captured again by the Turks. It became Russian again only 30 years later, this time forever.

Azov province was founded in 1775 and included the town of Taganrog. Until the 2d half of the 19th century Taganrog was a major port at which hundreds of foreign ships called every year. They brought citrus fruits and other foods from southern countries and took cargoes of grain, fat, hides, and skins from Russia.

Taganrog was bombarded by the Allies in 1855. Its importance diminished with the development of Odessa and with the construction of a railway line to Rostov. It became an insignificant provincial town with practically no industry. It was under German occupation in 1918 and again from 1941 to 1943.

There is a historical mystery connected with the death of Tsar Alexander I in Taganrog in 1825. Alexander I came to Taganrog with his wife, Empress Elizaveta Alexeyevna, whom the doctors had advised to live in the southern climate because of her poor health. 2 months later, in November 1825, Alexander I suddenly died here. It is said that Alexander I, the conqueror of Napoleon, was a man given to mysticism. After his death his body was brought back in a sealed coffin, in accordance with his dying wish, and for seven days it rested in St. Petersburg's Kazan Cathedral. It was opened only once, at night, so that the body could be viewed by his mother, who noted in her diary her son's unusual appearance. No one else was permitted to view it, and this breach of tradition gave rise to rumours that the body in the sealed coffin brought from Taganrog was not that of the late tsar but of a servant, a gamewarden by the name of Markov, who had a striking physical resemblance to the tsar and died in Taganrog 1 day before him. A year later a new holy man appeared among the Russian colonists in the Tobolsk region, calling himself Fedor Kuzmich. He bore a strong resemblance to the tsar, both in his distinct military bearing and his physical appearance. The mystery about this holy man and the tsar's death in Taganrog has yet to be solved.

The town is connected with the names of many outstanding people in Russian history, such as the explorer Vitus Bering (1680–1741) and Admiral Fedor Ushakov (1743–1818) both of whom sailed from Taganrog, artists Arkhip Kuindji (1842–1910) and Konstantin Savitsky (1844–1905), and sculptor Ivan Martos (1750–1825), who was responsible for the monument to Minin and Pozharsky in Moscow's Red Square. In 1833 Taganrog was visited by Italian revolutionary Giuseppe Garibaldi (1807–82). In one of the town's numerous bars for sailors, owned by one Johann Ardizeri, Garibaldi met Kuneo, an active member of the revolutionary organisation Young Italy. Garibaldi was so excited by Kuneo's speech that he immediately joined the organisation, and it was in Taganrog that he vowed to give his life for the freedom and independence of his country. During his short stay Garibaldi went to the local steps and to the home for invalid foreign sailors built by Greek merchant Gerasim Depaldo.

The town also was visited by surgeon Nikolai Pirogov. Russian writer Anton Chekhov was born here in 1860 and spent 19 years of his life in the town. From 1890 till 1893 Lieutenant Pyotr Schmidt (1864–1906) lived and worked here; Lieutenant Schmidt was chosen as commander by the crew of the cruiser *Ochakov* (570 men) that mutinied and took part in the Sevastopol uprising in 1905 during the first Russian revolution.

At present Taganrog's industry includes the production of iron, steel, steel sheets and pipes, high-pressure boilers, combine harvesters, machine

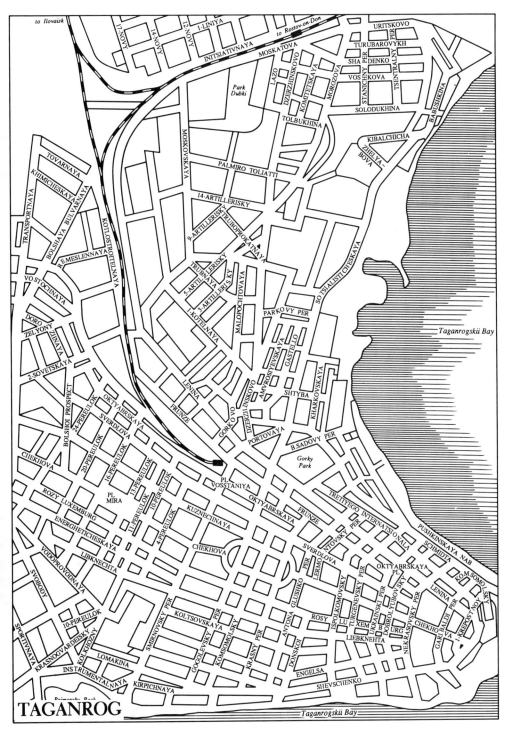

TAGANROG

tools, and aircraft. There are also ship-repair yards, leather working, and other branches of light industry.

Local Museum, 3-International (formerly Grecheskaya) Street. The museum opened in 1909 with the participation of Anton Chekhov in the former mansion of a wealthy merchant named Alferaki. It contains an interesting exhibition about the construction of the port by Peter the Great and a number of early maps and prints.

Art Gallery, Sverdlov (formerly Monastyrskaya) Street 56. Open 11–5; closed Mon. Paintings by Aivazovsky, Levitan, Kuindji, Vereschagin, Saryan, and other prominent artists are on display.

Chekhov's House Museum, at the corner of Sverdlov Street and Gogolevsky Pereulok. Open 11–5; closed Mon. Chekhov was born in this 2-storey red-brick house. In a letter dated 1902 Chekhov wrote, "I was born in the Bolotovs' house (so my mother asserts) or in the Gnutovs', in a small annex in Politseiskaya Street. This house probably exists no more. . . ." Luckily he was wrong. The house was built in the 19th century and the 3 rooms re-create the atmosphere of Chekhov's childhood. Chekhov's father had a shop here and the painted sign by the door set into the corner of the building reads: TEA, COFFEE, SUGAR AND OTHER COLONIAL GOODS. The shop was excellently situated for business, just east of the trading arcades. Behind the shop, high gates led into a goods yard. Politseiskaya Street was renamed in Chekhov's honour in 1904, following his death.

Chekhov Literary Museum, Oktyabrskaya Street 9, in the building of the school Chekhov attended. The museum collection was founded in 1935 from the Chekhov Room at the Local Museum. The Taganrog Chekhov Literary Museum is the country's largest to the memory of the great writer. On display are hundreds of memorial books, photographs, autographs, documents, and other materials.

Popov's House, 3-International Street 40. Popov was the town's governor. Many important visitors stayed here, including Tsar Alexander I and the empress. Pushkin was here in 1820 on his way to the Caucasus with the family of General Nikolai Raevsky, hero of the war of 1812. Poet Vasily Zhukovsky and painter Ivan Aivazovsky also stayed here in 1837 and 1895, respectively.

Ippolit Tchaikovsky's House, 3-International Street 56. Ippolit Tchaikovsky was brother of the famous composer. Pyotr Tchaikovsky visited his brother here in 1886, 1888, and 1890. At present it houses the music department of the Chekhov Library.

Schmidt's House, 3-International Street 102. This is where Lieutenant Pyotr Schmidt, commander of the cruiser *Ochakov* uprising, lived with his family from 1890 to 1893.

Stone Staircase, 3-International Street. This staircase was built in 1823.

Former Trade Arcades, Chekhov (formerly Politseiskaya) Street 98. Built in 1840, these are typical of 19th-century buildings of this type.

Art Nouveau House, at the corner of Frunze and Gogol streets. Built by architect Shekhtel, it is to be opened as a museum.

Monument to Peter the Great, Komsomolsky Boulevard, at the tip of the horn. On the initiative of Anton Chekhov, this monument was built in commemoration of the founding of Taganrog on the steep shore of the cape. Peter the Great is portrayed here in the uniform of an officer of the Preobrazhensky regiment, looking out over the sea with the port below. The statue is mounted on a grey granite pedestal and altogether is 8.8 m (29 ft) high; the height of the statue alone is 3.4 m (11 ft). The monument was built in 1903 according to the design of the renowned Russian sculptor Mark Antokolsky (1843–1902). It was erected by public subscription and bears the inscription: "To the founder of the town of Taganrog—Peter I. 1682–1725." It stands in a garden with a cobbled square laid out like the plan of the fortifications of a fortress.

Giuseppe Garibaldi Obelisk, Pushkin Naberezhnaya. This obelisk was built by B. Yakovenko in 1961. On one of the sides of the 5-m (16-ft) obelisk is a bas-relief portrait of Garibaldi with the inscription: "In 1833, while in Taganrog, Giuseppe Garibaldi pledged loyalty to the cause of liberation and reunification of his Motherland— Italy. Under the leadership of the national hero Giuseppe Garibaldi, the country was liberated and reunited."

Monument to Anton Chekhov, Chekhov Square. It was sculpted by I. Rukavishnikov and unveiled in 1960 on the occasion of the centenary of Chekhov's birth.

Lenin Monument, Oktyabrskaya Square. It was built by N. Tomsky and A. Zavarzin and unveiled in 1970.

Monument to Komsomol Partisans, Spartakovsky Pereulok. Built by V. M. and V. P. Grachevs to the memory of those who lost their lives during World War II, the monument was unveiled in 1973.

Monument to Seamen, Sea Terminal (Portovaya) Square. This was built by P. Bondarenko and V. Grudev in 1975 to commemorate those who fell during the battle for Taganrog in World War II.

World War II Memorial, Lenin (formerly Petrovskaya) Street

Glory Memorial, at the entrance to Taganrog on the Sambek Hills on the Mius River. Dedicated to the liberators of Taganrog in World War II, it was opened on the eve of the 35th anniversary of VE day.

Chekhov Drama Theatre, Lenin Street 90. On its facade it has a memorial plaque reading: "Taganrog Drama Theatre was visited by Anton Chekhov; by decree of the Soviet Government it was given the name of the Chekhov Drama Theatre in 1944."

House of Culture, B. Bulvarnaya Street 12

Central Gorky Park is 1 of the oldest parks in the southern part of the country.

Sports Palace with Swimming Pool, B. Bulvar-
naya Street
   Torpedo Stadium, Instrumentalnaya Street 12
   Sports Palace, Lenin Street 216
   Sports Palace with Sadko Swimming Pool,
Mezhevaya Street
   Taganrog Hotel and Restaurant, Dzerzhinsky
Street 161
   Tsentralnaya Hotel, Lenin Street 64
   Temirinda Hotel, Portovaya Street 3
   Kolos Hotel, Gogol Pereulok 29
   Volna ("Wave") Restaurant, Lenin Street 64
   Staraya Krepost ("Old Fortress") Cafe, Lenin
Street 86
   Russian Tea Cafe, Lenin Street 81
   Tagany Rog ("Tagany Horn") Cafe, Vtoraya
Liniya Street
   Department Store, Lenin Street 91
   Aeroflot Agency, Lenin Street 83
   Filling and Service Stations
   Taganrog Beach

TALLINN is the capital of the Estonian Republic.

ESTONIAN REPUBLIC
(Eesti in Estonian)
   Area: 47,559 sq km (18,364 sq miles) of which
4167 sq km (1609 sq miles) is made up of 818
islands, and 2328 sq km (899 sq miles) of the country's 1512 lakes. Estonia is larger than Denmark,
Holland or Switzerland.
   Population: 1,573,000 of which 64.7% are Estonians and 27.9% Russians, besides smaller proportions of Ukrainians and Belorussians.
   Estonia is in the extreme northwest of the
USSR, on the coast of the Baltic Sea. It is bounded
in the east by Lake Peipsi and by Russia, and in
the south by Latvia. Its principal cities are Tallinn
(the capital), Narva and Tartu.
   In the early days of its history this land was
inhabited by Finnish-speaking tribes which established close economic ties with the neighbouring
territories. From the end of the 12th century the
Teutonic Knights and Scandinavian nobles tried to
conquer the area, under the pretext of converting
the local tribes to Christianity. After a long and
bloody struggle the Teutonic Knights seized southern and central Estonia while Denmark took the
northern part of the country.
   In the second half of the 16th century Estonia
became the field of contest between Russia, Poland, and Sweden, who were fighting for the Baltic
provinces. The result was that Poland gained southern Estonia. During the next 50 years Poland and
Sweden fought for possession of the whole country.
In 1721, after the Russo-Swedish War, the whole
of Estonia was included in the Russian Empire.
   During the First World War, Estonia was occupied by German troops but it was freed in 1919
and remained a parliamentary republic until 1934
when a dictatorship was established by President
Pats. He was turned out of office in 1940 and Estonia was proclaimed a Soviet Republic and joined
the USSR. In March 1990 the newly elected Su-

preme Soviet announced that Soviet power had
been unlawfully established in Estonia, and
dropped the words "Soviet" and "Socialist" from
the name of the Republic.
   Estonians use the Latin Alphabet. Here are a
few useful words:

Hello	Tere or Tervist!
I am a tourist	Olen tourist
Please	Palum
Thank you	Tanan
Yes	Ja
No	Ei
Good	Hea
Bad	Halb
I don't understand	Ma ei saa are
I need an interpreter	Ma vajan tolki
Goodbye	Nagemiseni or Head aega

The following are among the favourite Estonian
dishes:

Hapukapsa supp—sauerkraut soup
Seapraad—pork with sauerkraut
Seajalad—pig's trotters
Mulgikapsad sealihaga—cabbage with pork
Mannakreen piimaga—semolina pudding

Tallinn Population—485,000
Formerly German Reval; Russian Revel
   Capital of the Estonian Republic
   The name of the city comes from "taani linn"
meaning "Danish Castle," but Tallinn is only one
of the city's three names. The Revele were a local
tribe and for many years it was known as Revel,
although some believe the town's name to have
come from the Danish word "revel" which means
"reefs" and would have signified the treacherous
nature of the submerged rocks in the bay. As an
alternative name, in 1154 Revel appeared on a map
by the Arabian geographer Idris as Koluvan, from
the name of Kalev, an Estonian folk hero, reputed
to be the guardian of the stronghold.
   The first settlement of all was made on Toompea
(called Vyshgorod in Russian), the 49 m (161 ft)
limestone hill in the centre of the present city.
Legend has it that Toompea was built by Linda,
Kalev's mother, as a burial mound over the grave
of her son; she is said to have carried the stones
here in her apron. *Tonismagi Hill* is 30 m (98 ft)
high.
   The average temperature in July is 20.7°C
(69°F) and in January −9.9°C (14°F). The bathing
season lasts from mid-June until the end of August.
   It was in the first centuries A.D. that the Estonians, a people of Finno-Ugric stock, moved into
this area. Their central stronghold was called Lin-
danissa. Early in the 13th century they were united

under a single chieftain but were attacked by the Danes and the German knights.

King Waldemar II of Denmark founded Revel "in the country of Revelers" in 1219 on the site of the ancient fortress and after a battle on June 15 of that year. It is recorded that at a critical point in the encounter his weary soldiers were inspired by the appearance of a red flag with a white cross which floated down from the heavens and which has ever since been the national flag of Denmark. The Danish castle was founded in Toompea in the autumn of 1219, but Revel was besieged by the Estonians between 1221 and 1223 and came under the Order of the Teutonic Knights in 1227. They occupied the fortress on Toompea and added to it until Revel again fell to the Danes in 1238. In 1248 Revel attained "Lübeck Law" and it remained in force until the 19th century; it meant that in spite of different conquerors and masters, Estonian law suits could always be taken to the Lübeck court for final jurisdiction.

From 1284 when Revel became a member of the Hanseatic League, the town's trading importance grew rapidly. It even controlled the trade of the great inland centre of Novgorod. The Estonians again besieged the city in 1343. They were led by the Estonian Knights of St. George, but were entirely vanquished at the Battle of Revel. Three years later the Danish king Waldemar IV sold Revel with the rest of his share of Estonia to the Teutonic Knights, who held it until the area fell to Sweden in 1561. There were Russian attacks on Revel in 1560, 1570 and 1577, but it remained in Swedish hands until the Great Northern War at the beginning of the 18th century and finally fell to Peter the Great in 1710. The city suffered the usual run of triumph and tragedy throughout its medieval history. There are records of the terrible fire of 1433, of Revel rising to the foremost place in the Hanseatic League in 1496, and of the plagues of 1591 and 1657. It was under Russian rule from 1786, and the economic importance of its port led it into trouble in the 19th century; Nelson was in Revel in 1801, and the harbour was blockaded by the British Fleet under Admiral Napier during the Crimean War (1853–56).

In 1902 Tsar Nicholas II established himself at sea near Tallinn to meet Emperor Wilhelm II of Germany, and once again in 1908 he followed the same procedure and used the imperial yacht, Standart, to welcome King Edward VII of Great Britain and, a few months later, President Armand Fallieres of France.

Estonian independence was proclaimed on 24th February, 1918, but it lasted a single day. On the 25th the Germans moved in and were in occupation for eight months. It seemed likely that the Red Army would take over, but they were prevented from doing so by the Estonians themselves with the help from Britain, Finland and Scandinavia. Parliament met in April 1919, and the following year the country was at peace with Russia.

Tallinn remained the capital of independent Estonia until 1940.

In Tallinn are an *Art Institute and Conservatoire*, founded in 1919, the *Vilde Pedagogical Institute*, the *Polytechnical Institute* (1936) and the *Academy of Sciences* (1946). Local industries include the manufacture of textiles, electrical and mechanical equipment, and food products. Estonian shipbuilding has a long history and the *Tallinn Experimental Sports Shipyard* was where the Finn and 470-class hulls were built for the 1980 Olympics. The yard was resited on the Kopli Peninsula, around the coast to the west of Pirita. Most of the workers here are themselves yachtsmen and it was they who devised the Olympic yacht, yet to be included in an Olympic programme but which is nevertheless very popular for training. The city keeps growing, just like other cities, but the Estonians are in no hurry to finish their construction projects. There is a legend that when Tallinn is completely built, Jarvenana, the little old man who lives at the bottom of Lake Ulemiste which serves as the city's water supply, will pull out the plug and Tallinn will be inundated.

About two-thirds of the original length of the old town walls remain, as do 18 of the original 25 towers, and the ruins of 6 more can be seen. The northwest side of the wall is particularly well preserved and starting from Nooruse Street the first three towers are open to the public, their names are *Kostritorn*, *Saunatorn (bath house tower)*, and *Kuldjalatorn (golden leg tower)*. The average height of the wall is 15 m (49 ft) and its thickness varies between 2.25 and 3 m (7 and 10 ft). The towers are extremely varied and many bear attractive names which suit their particular character. *Kiek in de kok (peep-into-the-kitchen)* (46 m/151 ft high) was built in 1475 on the slopes of Harju Hill. It is 5 storeys high and has 2 vaulted cellars. Once it afforded an excellent view over the most thickly populated part of the town; it is said that one could even look down the wide chimneys, hence its strange name. The little museum inside is open 10.30–6; closed Mon.

Stout Margaret together with another, thinner tower guards *Rannavarava*, the ancient Sea Gate, founded in 1510; the coat-of-arms above the arch bears the date 1529 which is when the construction was finished. *Viru Gate* (15th century) stands at the end of Viru Street, the main gate is no longer there, and these two towers stood on either side of the outer archway. *Bremer Tower* stands in Venne Street. The 2 gates on the *Short- and Long-Toompea* were put up about 1380; the former has a thick oaken door. In places parts of the old *Maiden's Wall* remain. This used to divide the "toom" from the lower part of the town. Its name recalls the legend that it was a warrior-maiden who brought the stones for the construction of the wall, coming secretly, under cover of night. (Perhaps the story springs from the same source as that of Kalev's mother, Linda, bringing stones in her apron for Toompea.)

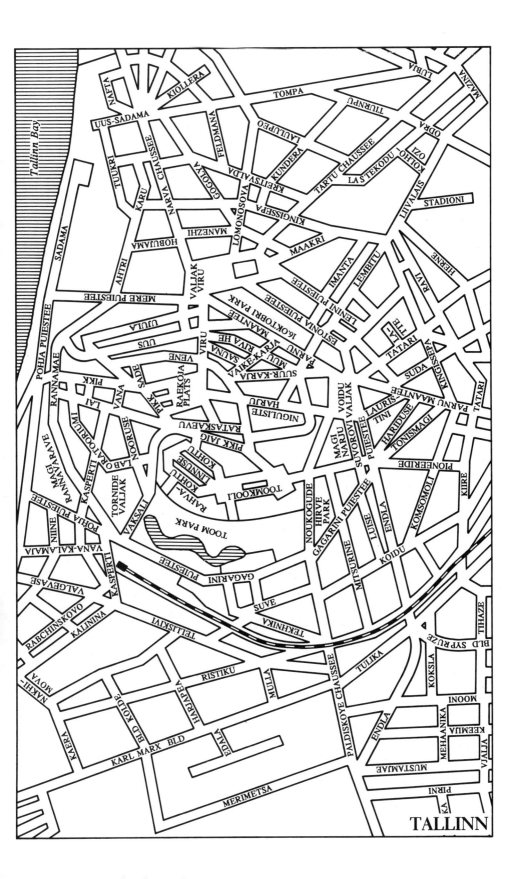

TALLINN

The Dom has always lived a life a little apart from that of the bustling streets below. It has its own administration which it even retained after 1346 when the city passed to the Teutonic Knights.

Dom Castle and the *Long Hermann watchtower* were already standing in 1227, but now only the western part remains. The rebuilding dates from 1780; Long Hermann is the only remaining one of the four corner towers. It is 47 m (154 ft) high and there are another 30 m (98 ft) of stonework underground. Its height is emphasised by the 30-m (98-ft) ravine which falls away below. The Castle housed, in succession, the Danish Governor, the Commander of the Teutonic Order, Swedish and Russian Governors-General, Russian commissioners and German generals. Finally it was used as Estonian government offices. Some of the old rooms were once used as a prison but they were burned down in 1917.

Domkirk, Kirku Street, Toompea. This church was built in 1232 but it suffered many fires and much reconstruction. It was finally rebuilt after the fire of 1684. One of its bells bears an inscription in German which points to the building's fiery past. "The heat of the fire melted me as the whole of Toompea burnt down. One year later I was cast in this shape and called Maria's Bell." There are several interesting tombs to be seen. One of marble near the altar, by Arend Passer from Holland, marks the grave of Swedish General Pontus de la Gardie, who was of French origin, and his wife, Princess Sophia, daughter of King Johann III of Sweden and sister of King Gustav Vasa; the bas-relief shows the siege of Narva in 1585 where de la Gardie was leading the Swedes and where he himself was drowned in the Narva river. The sarcophagus in white Italian marble in the form of a miniature Greek temple of Admiral Samuel Greig (1736–88) was designed by Giacomo Quarenghi and Martos. Greig came to Russia from Scotland in 1764 and served gallantly in the Russian Navy, notably against the Turks (1770) and the Swedes (1788). Another great seaman buried here is the Estonian-born Admiral Adam Johann von Krusenstern (1770–1846) who was the first Russian to sail around the world (1803–6). From the end of the 18th century it was forbidden for burials to take place in the Domkirk, but von Krusenstern was laid to rest here by special order of Nicholas I. The carved, wooden altarpiece was made in 1696, and the painting of the Crucifixion by Eduard von Gebhardt (1838–1925) from Dusseldorf was installed in the 19th century. The church is now used by the Lutherans and is open for services.

The *Nobility House* stands in the centre of Toompea. The oldest part, in Kohtu Street, was rebuilt after the fire of 1684, and the main part, opposite the Domkirk, was built in 1840. The Assembly Hall is decorated with noble coats-of-arms and with portraits and busts of Russian tsars.

Also commanding a fine position of Toompea is *St. Alexander Nevsky's Russian Orthodox Cathedral*. It was constructed during the reign of Alexander III, between 1894–1900. It measures 43 m (47 yds) long and 26 m (28 yds) wide and the steps leading up on three sides are of Finnish granite. The domes were once gilded and of the 11 bells the largest weighs about 17.5 tons. The mosaics inside are the only ones of their kind in Estonia. The Cathedral is open for religious services. In 1934 it was recorded that by far the greater proportion of the population was Lutheran, but that more than 10% were Russian Orthodox; there were besides a very small number of Jews and even fewer Roman Catholics. Today the Domkirk and St. Alexander Nevsky's Cathedral are among 17 churches and meeting houses open for worship.

Kalinin's Statue is one of the later additions to Toompea; it is by Kaasik and was unveiled in 1950.

The best view of the city is from the top of *Patkuli Trepp*.

A walk from the *town hall* down Pikk Street to the *Sea Gate* takes one past a good selection of the sights of the old town. The *town hall* (1371–74) stands in the centre of the large market square, laid out in 1288 and used as a market place until 1896. In style the town hall is a solid and gloomy Gothic building with a Renaissance tower resembling a minaret added in 1629 and surmounted by a special weathervane known as *Old Thomas*. This depicts an ancient warrior of the town and is a copy made in 1952 of a vane of 1530 now in the town hall museum. The citizens of Tallinn are very fond of Old Thomas, and from being their guardian he has come to be regarded almost as mascot.

The town hall is open as a museum during the summer months. Open 11–6; closed Mon. & Tues. Inside the town hall there are vaulted ceilings in the rooms of all three storeys. The tapestries on the walls were made in Netherlands in 1547 and are marked with the arms of Tallinn. In the museum are paintings and friezes, as well as some fine examples of carved furniture of the 15th and 16th centuries including a bench depicting Tristan and Isolda (15th century) and a beautiful frieze with hunting scenes in the main hall, carved by a local 17th-century master, Elert Thiele, and presented to the city in 1697 by Charles XI of Sweden. This is the only mediaeval Gothic-style town hall surviving in the Baltic Countries. It was restored in 1959–60.

Also in the market square is the old *Weighing House*. Its steeply gabled roof is tiled and the side walls are decorated with busts of German rulers.

On the southern side of the market square is the *Old Pharmacy*. The house itself was built in 1461 but the pharmacy business was founded earlier in 1422.

The first building of especial interest in Pikk Street (Pikk Tanav) is No. 17, the *Great Guild* (1405–10) in Gothic style. It stands on the left as one prepares to walk down the street. Once it was used for weddings, trials, religious services, plays and concerts. The central pillars are decorated with inscriptions and with the figures of animals.

On the right is the *Church of the Holy Spirit*, at Puha Vaimu Street 4; "Vaimu" means "spirit." The church, built at the end of the 14th century, is one of the oldest in the town. It was built in Gothic style but the baroque spire is 17th century. On the corner of the church facing Pikk Street is the oldest clock in Tallinn, with carvings of 1684, and in the tower housing Estonia's oldest bell (1433) with the inscription: "I chime just as accurately for all, for maid and servant, for mistress and master, and for that I am beyond reproach." The church is now used for worship by the Lutherans. Its original altar has been transferred to *St. Nicholas's Church*, at Rataskaevu Street 11/13, which serves as a museum.

A little further down on the right side is *St. Kanuti-Guild*, a large building in Roman style. The zinc statues represent King Canute and Martin Luther, and the medallions on the facade bear the coats-of-arms of the old city. Inside, the lofty hall on the ground floor is decorated with paintings, as are some of the other rooms.

St. Olai-Guild is at Pikk Street 24. It was built in the 15th century and has a Gothic-style hall.

Next door to St. Olai-Guild is the *Blackheads' Club*. The Blackheads were a corporation of bachelor merchants, founded in the 14th century, with St. Mauritius as their patron saint. His head, represented by that of a Moor, was part of their coat-of-arms and it was from this that they derived their strange name. The Blackheads were the oldest of a number of similar corporations in the Baltic States. The facade of the club was rebuilt in 1591 and is decorated with limestone bas-reliefs. Over the door are the coats-of-arms of Bruges, Novgorod, London, and Bergen, the four most important cities of the Hanseatic League. Higher up on the facade are two "blackheads" and, above them, figures of Jesus Christ, Justice and Peace. Inside the building is a museum where paintings, arms and plates are on display.

Further down Pikk Street, but this time on the left, stands *St. Olaf's Church*, in Lai Street. Officially it was named after King Olaf II of Norway who, at the age of 19 and in the year before his coronation, had led the successful attack on London in 1014; he toppled London Bridge into the Thames by lashing ropes around the piles and rowing his dragonheaded ships downstream "as hard as they might." Canonised after his death in 1030, this fearless warrior was the last Western saint to be accepted by the Eastern Church. In spite, however, of its official dedication, the story of this church is linked with another, local, Olaf. He was an architect who was called in by the citizens of Tallinn, so it is said, to help them build a new and marvellous church to beautify their city. When the edifice was almost completed, he fell to his death from the roof, and as he lay on the ground a toad and a serpent crept out of his mouth. He was buried where he fell, and a stone plaque illustrates the story. A wooden church was first mentioned as being on this site in 1288, restored in 1329, and the spire was struck by lightning six times during the 17th and 18th centuries. In 1625 the fire that resulted from the lightning was so severe that the bells melted with the heat. It was again restored in

1628 and the spire was built in Gothic style. The church is now 58 m (63 yds) long, 28 m (31 yds) wide and 28 m (92 ft) high. The steeple rises to 140 m (459 ft) and was again struck by lightning in 1931. Beside the church stands the *Bremen Chapel of St. Mary* built between 1502–14 by Hans Pavels. The work was financed by a donation from the merchant, Poulsen. A memorial to him dated 1513 decorates the wall facing the street. There is also a curious memorial depicting a skeleton with a toad on his chest and a serpent round the skull, perhaps linked to the legend of the architect. The church is used by the Baptist and Methodist communities of Tallinn.

Pikk Street ends with the *Sea Gate*, guarded on the right side by the formidable figure of *Stout Margaret*, 24 m (26 yds) in diameter and the largest of all the towers in the town wall, constructed between 1510 and 1529 during the reign of Queen Margaret of Denmark, mother of Erik VI. The walls are 4 m (13 ft) thick at the base and the tower itself is 4 storeys high. It was used as a barracks at the end of the 19th century and after 1905 it served as a prison until 1917. It was restored in 1937.

St. Nicholas's Church, Nicholas Street, is also a museum. The church was built between 1316 and 1350 and dedicated to the saint among whose other responsibilities are the seamen of the world, which explains his popularity in this ancient port. In the early 16th century it was saved from the ravages of the iconoclasts by a quick-thinking warden who poured molten lead into the locks. After 1524 it belonged to the Lutherans. The building measures 48 m (52 yds) long and 28 m (31 yds) wide. Its steeple was rebuilt in 1898, but was badly damaged during Second World War. The oldest dated memorial slab on the stone floor is from 1330. The St. Anthony Chapel now houses the altarpiece from the Church of the Holy Spirit which was made in Lübeck in 1483 by Berent Notken, a professional woodcarver and painter. Also from Lübeck is the 15th century painting, "Dance Macabre," a copy of which used to be in St. Mary's. Lübeck was destroyed during the war, and for some time it was believed that the original had perished and that the painting in Tallinn was the copy, instead of the other way about. There is a second large altarpiece, by Herman Rode of Lübeck, which was commissioned by the Blackheads. It is 6 m (20 ft) long and 3.5 m (11 ft) high and when the inner covers are closed there appear 16 scenes from the lives of St. Nicholas and St. Victor, the last scene of all showing the earliest known picture of Lübeck. Another altarpiece with scenes of the Passion was made in Bruges in the late 15th century. The chandelier in front of the main altar was made in north Germany in 1519. On the wall is a memorial to a Tallinn merchant called Bugislaus von Rosen who died in 1651 and whose loans largely financed Sweden's part in the Thirty Years' War. It was he who donated the 17th century carved wooden pulpit to the church; on its door are his coat-of-arms and those of his two wives. There are also some interesting carved wooden pews in the church. St. Nicholas's was also famous for a number of years for a more gruesome sight, the mummified body of Duke Charles de Croix. This Belgian nobleman sought adventure and joined the Russian army where he rose to be given the rank of field marshal by Peter the Great. He was in command at the outbreak of the Great Northern War, but was taken prisoner by the Swedes in 1700 and confined to Tallinn. His gambling and heavy drinking led him into such debts that when he was released he had to leave the town to avoid his creditors. He died suddenly in 1702, but his creditors still pursued him, saying that he should not receive proper burial until his debts were paid. Meanwhile his body was laid in the crypt of St. Nicholas's, and there it remained until, at the beginning of the 19th century, it was discovered that it had turned into a mummy, probably because of the sandy nature of the ground there, but many suspected it was because of the vast quantities of alcohol he had consumed in the last years of his life. The mummy was on view to the public for several years and it was only given due burial under the floor of the Klodt Chapel, beside St. Nicholas's, 117 years after the Duke's death.

Since 1980 concerts of organ music have been given in the church.

In Vene Street 12–18, not far from the town hall, are the remains of the *Dominican Monastery* (13th century or late 14th century). Its principal church was St. Catherine and part of its cloisters were converted into the Roman Catholic Church of SS. Peter and Paul in 1840. Open April–October only 11–5; closed Mon.

Further along Vene Street just before it runs into Pikk Street, is the Russian Orthodox *St. Nicholas's Church*. Its existence is first mentioned in documents of 1422. It was rebuilt, again in Novgorod style, in 1825. The chandelier was received as a gift from Boris Godunov in 1599.

Kazanskaya Church, Kazan Street. Founded in 1749 and still used for Russian Orthodox services.

Rootsi-Mikhli Church, Ruutli (knights) Street 9. This church with no steeple used to be the almshouse chapel and a part of the city hospital. It was given to the Swedes in 1733 but is now disused. There is a round Roman Catholic font with the statues of the apostles and also a memorial slab mentioning the plague of 1602.

Issanda-Moutmise Church, S. Kloostri Street 14

Preobrazhensky (Transfiguration) Cathedral, at the Sustern Gates, Nooruse Street. This Russian Orthodox Church, open for religious services, stands on the site of the ancient Convent of St. Michael which belonged to the Cistercian Order. The original cathedral was turned into a Lutheran church for the local Swedish garrison, but in 1716 Prince Menshikov ordered that it be handed over to the Russian Orthodox Church. It was soon after this that the spectacular iconostasis of carved woodwork was specially made by Zarudny, the master also responsible for the iconostasis in the cathedral of SS. Peter and Paul in St. Petersburg. This ca-

thedral was rebuilt in 1828 using money donated by Nicholas I.

Simeoni Church, Simeoni Street 5

Kopli Church, Kopli, Vene-Balti Tehas 73

St. John's Church, Vabaduce (liberty) Square. This bears a strong resemblance to St. Nicholas's Church except that the steeple is not as tall. It was constructed in limestone in 1867 and is now used by the Lutherans.

St. Charles's Church, Kaarli Avenue. This church with two steeples was built in Roman style without pillars and with large windows in 1870. It was named after King Charles XI of Sweden. Inside is a fresco of Christ by the Estonian professor, Koehler. The acoustics are good and there is an excellent organ.

The *Boys' High School*, Kloostri Street. This school was founded in 1630 by Gustavus Adolphus.

City Museum, Vene Street 17. Open 10.30–6; closed Tues.

Town Hall Museum, Raekoja Square 4/6. Open April–October 11–6; closed Mon. & Tues.

Historical Museum, Pikk Street 18. This museum was founded in 1864 and now belongs to the Estonian Academy of Sciences. Open 11–6; closed Wed. (There is a branch of the museum in Marienburg Palace, in Peoples' Friendship Park.)

Kiek-in-de-Kok Tower, contains a collection of ancient arms. Open 10.30–6; closed Mon.

Rabochi Podval (workers' cellar) Museum, Estonia Boulevard 8. Open 12–6; closed Sun.

Art Museum, in Kadriorg Palace, Kadriorg Park (see p. 532). Open 11–6; closed Tues. Here are examples of Estonian art from the 19th century to the present day as well as works by Russian and European artists—17,000 pictures in all.

Museum of Applied Art, Lai Street 17. This was opened in 1980. Open 11–6; closed Mon. & Tues.

Theatrical and Musical Museum, Muurivahe Street 12. Open 10–6; closed Tues.

Niguliste Museum–Concert Hall, Rateskaevu Street 11/13. The building is that of the 13–18th century Baptist church. Open 11–6; closed Mon. & Tues.

State Maritime Museum, Pikk Street 70. Open 10–6; closed Mon. & Tues. The museum has a rich collection of articles which show how Peter the Great founded the Russian navy. It also has on display the famous 16th-century gun emplacement Pax Margarete and articles dating back to the Northern War in which Russian sailors took part.

Baltic Fleet Museum, Narvskoye Chaussee 44. Open 10–5.30; closed Fri. & Sat.

Museum of the History of the Estonian Fire-Fighting Service

House of Arts, Voidu (victory) Square 8. Temporary Exhibitions are held here. Open 12–7; closed Tues.

Peter the Great's House, Myaekalda Street 2, Kadriorg Park. Peter the Great lived here during the construction of the harbour and Kadriorg Palace. Open from May till October 9.30–7.30; closed Tues.

Vilde's House, Koidula Street 34, Kadriorg. Edward Vilde (1865–1933) was a well known Estonian writer; he spent his last years in this house. Open 11–6; Sat. 11–5; closed Tues.

Tammsaare's House, Koidula Street 12a. Anton (Hanzen) Tammsaare (1878–1940) was an Estonian writer. Various art exhibitions are held here. Open 10–5.30; closed Fri. & Sat.

Adamson-Eric Museum, Lukhike-Jalg Street 3. Open 11–6; closed Tues. Adamson-Eric (1902–68) was an Estonian painter.

Natural History Museum, Lai Street 29, in a 15th-century house. Open 10–6; closed Tues.

Health Museum, Tyuve Street 25. Open 10–4; closed Sun. & Mon.

Wooden Buildings Museum (Estonian State Park-Museum)—Rocca-al-Mare, Vabaohumuuseumitee Road 12 to the west of Tallinn, 3 km (2 miles) from the centre. Here stand barns, farmhouses, a watermill and windmills, all of wood, and some stone buildings too. There is also an inn and on Sundays during the summer displays of folksong and dance are arranged here for the tourists. Open June–August 10–7, September & October 10–6 and November–May 10–5.

Estonian Exhibition of Economic Achievements, Pirita Tee 28. Open 11–6; closed Mon.

Linda Statue, on the slope of Tommpea known as Linda's Hill; the site was chosen by the sculptor, August Weizenburg. Linda, who is said to have turned to stone, was the mother of Kalev, Estonia's national hero. This statue was unveiled in 1920 having been cast from the original marble made in 1880.

Monument to the Victims of the Russian Revolution of 1905, in 16-October Park. Commemorating the 90 who died during a mass meeting here. More than 40,000 people attended their funeral. Made by Paluteder and unveiled in 1959.

Memorial Complex, in Peoples' Friendship Park, east of the city, a bit further along from the Song Stage, on the Maarjamagi Plateau; the obelisk serves as a good landmark. Open 10–5. This stands in memory of those who lost their lives while Soviet power was being established in Estonia. The Complex was executed by a group of Estonian architects and sculptors led by Allan Murdmaa. It is laid out in the form of a cross lying parallel to the coastline. It is reached by a long, straight walk up a gentle slope. The "Dying Seagulls" sculpture represents violent death as an introduction to the rest of the Complex. Other units included in it so far are, to the left, a 35-m (115-ft) obelisk in memory of the 1918 Ice Cruise of the Baltic Fleet (first from Tallinn to sanctuary in Helsinki and then to Kronstadt), an eternal flame protected by hands carved into the stone surround and an archway bridged by a flame of bronze. Beyond the arch is a Garden of Remembrance with the grave of the 19-year-old Hero of the Soviet Union, sailor Evgeni Nikonov, and the tree where he was burned alive by the Germans on 19 August, 1941. His monument was designed by Erika Haggi and Heikki Karro in 1960. Also here is a monument to 36 other sailors, of the minelayers Spartak and Avtroil who were shot on Naissaar Island on 3–5 February, 1919, by the White Guards. The memorials to Nikonov and the sailors were here long before the construction of the Memorial Complex was begun, but the choice of site was partly made because of their existence here. The right arm of the cross leading inland to higher ground has yet to be completed.

Below the Memorial Complex, beside the sea and built out into it, is the Olympic Regatta site.

Kingisepp Monument, on the slopes of Harju Hill, sculpted by Roos and unveiled in 1951. Victor Kingisepp (d. 1922) was a leading Estonian communist; the town formerly known as Yamberg on the road from Leningrad has borne his name since 1922.

Lenin Monument, Lenin Boulevard. Sculpted by Tomsky and unveiled in 1950.

Kalinin Monument, in Tower Square (Tornide valjak). Mikhail Kalinin was exiled to Tallinn for his revolutionary activities, and lived here from 1901–04.

Estonian State Opera House, Estonia Boulevard 4. This white building near the Viru Hotel has held chess and wrestling matches besides the more traditional opera, ballet and concert programmes.

Kingisepp Drama Theatre, Parnu Chaussee 5

Russian Drama Theatre, Voidu Square 5

Youth Theatre, Salme Street 12

Puppet Theatre, Lai Street 1. This theatre was founded in 1952.

Philharmonic Society, Estonia Boulevard 4

Concert Hall, Merepuieste Chaussee. Built to seat an audience of 6000.

Dominican Monastery, Vene Street 12. Sometimes used for plays and concerts.

Open air Concerts, Town Hall Square

Circus, Lenin Boulevard 6. The circus operates during the summer only.

Yacht Club, Pirita. The Gulf of Tallinn was selected for the 1980 Olympic Regatta for its natural assets. It is deep and wide, sheltered from the sea waves by Aegna Island to the north and Baissar Island to the west but with a low shoreline that does not cut off the winds from inland. The Olympic harbour at the mouth of the little river Pirita is protected by breakwaters jutting far out into the sea. The pier has room for 650 yachts. Pirita has long served as the Tallinners' main recreation area and there is a hotel, cafes, bars, a restaurant, shopping centre, gyms and a swimming pool. A wide motor road along the shore links Pirita with the centre of Tallinn.

The Palace of Culture and Sports, Mere Boulevard 11. Seats 6,000; there is a covered skating rink near the main hall.

Komsomol Stadium, Staadioni Street 3

Dynamo Stadium, Koidula Street 38

Kalev Sports Hall, Liyvalaia Street 12

Kalev Tennis Stadium, Herne Street 28

Kalev Ice Hockey Stadium, Suvorov Boulevard 2

Kalev Cycle Track, Pirita, Rummu Tee 3

Hippodrome Racecourse, Padlisky Chaussee 50

Motor Cycle Racetrack, Pirita

Zoo, Maekalda Street 45, Kadriorg. Open in summer 10–8; winter 10–5.

Peoples' Friendship Park, covers a territory of 72 hectares (180 acres) to the north of the Narva highway. Within its bounds are the Song Stage, the Exhibition of Economic Achievements, a flower garden belonging to the Pirita State Farm, Marienburg Palace (containing a branch of the local History Museum) and park and the Memorial Complex.

Botanical Garden, at Pirita

Viru (Intourist) Hotel & Restaurant, Viru Square 4; tel. 65 2070. Intourist office; tel. 65 0770.

Tallinn (Intourist) Hotel, Gagarin Boulevard 27; tel. 44 1504

Olympia Hotel & Restaurant, Kingisepp Street 33; tel. 60 1768

Kungla Hotel, Kreutzwaldi Street 23; tel 42 2506, 42 7020

Palace Hotel & Restaurant, Voidu Square 3; tel. 48–116

Europea Hotel & Restaurant, Viru Street 24; tel. 44–049

Kopli Hotel & Restaurant, Kalinin Street 2A; tel. 42–761

Balti Hotel, Vaksali Lane; tel. 44–047

Hotel, at the crossing of Lauteri and Kingisepp Streets. Built on the same scale as the Viru Hotel and with a cafe-restaurant and a bar with room for 200 guests.

Hotel, at the Olympic Regatta site, Pirita

Kloostreemetsa Camping Site, 8 km (5 miles) from Tallinn, Kloostreemetsa tee 56; tel. 23 8686. Room for 150 cars.

In the restaurants in Tallinn, music and dancing begin at 8 P.M. and the establishments are open until midnight.

Nord Restaurant, Rataskaevu Street 3/5

Vana Toomas Restaurant, Raekoja Square 8. Estonian cuisine.

Pirita Restaurant, Pirita Beach

Kevad Restaurant, Lomonosov Street 2

Gloria Restaurant, Muurivahe Street 2

Kyannu Kukk Restaurant, Vilde Tee 75

Viru Restaurant, Viru Street

Snack Bar, Viru Street

To make room for the more serious eating places, cafes are not usually listed, but they are such a part of Tallinn life and so varied in character that they deserve a mention and a visit. Journalists and artists each have their favourite haunt, while young people go to the Pegasus and the older folk to the Karika Bar and the Tallinn. The Moscow and Energia are sure to be lively and crowded while the tiny Gnome Cafe (Vana-Turg Street 6) has, by contrast, no more than five tables. Perhaps the most unusual is the Kihnu Jonn, a schooner moored near the yacht club.

Pegasus Café, Harju Street 1; tel. 44 0807

Karika Bar, Niguliste Street 3; tel. 44 1780

Tallinn Café-Music Hall, Harju Street 6; tel. 449–204

Moscow Café, Voidu valjak 10; tel. 44 3818

Energia Café, Lenin Boulevard 4; tel 44 4131

Tuljak Café, Pirita Tee 28

Neitsitorn Café, Nyukogude Street 1

Majasmokk Café, Pikk Street 16

Gnom Café, Vana-turg Street 6

Café, At a height of 170 m (558 ft) up the 314 m (1030 ft) TV tower.

GPO, Viru Square; this and all other post offices remain closed on Monday until 2 P.M.

Telegraph Office, Vene Street 9

The building of the *Estonian Bank* was designed by Eliel Saarinen (1873–1950).

Turist Foreign Currency Shops, Tartu Chaussee 17, Raekoja Square 4, Gagarin Square 31, Narva Chaussee 6. Open 9–1; 2–7

Department Store, Ujula Street 7, Lomonosov Street 2

Souvenir Shops, Viru Street 6, Myundi Street 3, Pikk Street 9

Art Salon, Voidu Square 6

Heli (gramophone records) Ratushnaya Square 16. Open 10–8, Sat. 10–5.

Bookshops, Harju Street 1, Pjarnu Chaussee 10, Viru Street 23

Taxi Ranks, Balti Railway Station, Town Hall Square, (Raekoja Plats), Voidu Square and Central Market

Kadriorg (Catherine Dale) lies on the eastern side of Tallinn. The palace and park were laid out in 1718 by Peter the Great for his consort. The baroque-style building contains some beautiful painted ceilings and interesting fireplaces. The architect was an Italian by the name of Michetti. Once there were fountains and statues to beautify the park but the Empress Anna had them transferred to Petrodvorets (see Leningrad).

Kreutzwald Monument, in Kadriorg, near the Swan Pond. Friedrich Reihold Kreutzwald (1803–82) was the most popular Estonian poet, regarded as the founder of the nation's literature. He collected folk songs and proverbs but he was especially famous for rewriting the ancient epic, "Kalevipoeg," which was performed in modern dress in 1861. The sculptures by Saks and Taniloo were unveiled in 1958.

Peter the Great's House, is where Peter I lived while the palace was under construction. Nearby is a Dutch-style bath house.

Song Stage, Peoples' Friendship Park. The Estonians are famous for their choirs. Up to 30,000 people participate here, and the auditorium can take 100,000. The tradition of a song festival originated in Tartu in 1869, but Tallinn's first open air song festival took place in 1880, so the 100th anniversary in 1980 was planned to include a double celebration with a repeat performance at the time of the Olympic regatta.

Rusalka Monument, by the edge of the sea at Kadriorg. The monument, a figure of an angel holding a cross, by the Estonian artist, Adamson,

was put up to commemorate the sailors of the Rusalka (mermaid), a Russian battleship which sank
in the Gulf of Finland in 1893. The bronze statue
stands 16 m (52 ft) high on a pediment of Finnish
granite. It was unveiled in 1902.

Nikonov Monument, by the seashore. Yevgeni
Nikonov was a seaman who was captured by the
Germans in 1941, tied to a tree, and burned alive.
He was declared a Hero of the Soviet Union. The
monument that marks his grave is by Haggi and
was unveiled in 1960. The ash-tree, against which
he died, has been transplanted to his grave.

Another monument here beside the sea is an
obelisk (architect Port, sculptor Tolli) which was
unveiled in 1960. It commemorates the 1918 ice-
crossing when most of the Russian Baltic Fleet
made the dangerous midwinter journey of 300 km
(186 miles) through the ice from Tallinn to Kronstadt to avoid capture by the German army.

Marienburg Palace, in Peoples' Friendship
Park, by the seashore behind Kadriorg. The gate
pillars are surmounted by cast iron eagles and inside
is an attractive tower. Steps lead down to the sea
from the stone pavilion by the gates. Inside the
palace is a branch of the local History Museum.

Kose Forest, further on to the northeast. Here,
near the mouth of Pirita Brook, are the ruins of
St. Bridget's Abbey. In the 14th century a Swedish
woman by the name of Brigitta (Pirita in Estonian)
was widowed, took the veil, and founded a new
religious order with the centre in Vadstenas in
Southern Sweden. Brigitta was the author of some
mystical "Revelations." The order spread until
there were more than 70 abbeys in different parts
of Europe. This one was of the duplic or mixta
type which served both monks and nuns of the
order. It was built in 1407–36 and the monks lived
on the ground floor and the nuns above. It was
ruined in 1577 during the Russo-Livonian War.
The cathedral church was 56 m (61 yds) long and
24 m (26 yds) in width. Part of it has been restored
and concerts of mediaeval and renaissance music
are given here. In the southwest corner is an old
staircase which used to belong to the belfry and
there is an excellent view from the top of the wall.

The village of *Pirita* took on a new lease of life
with the preparations for the 1980 Olympics. The
sandy beaches stretch for 2 km (1 mile) and there
are other good beaches at the nearby resorts of
Vaana-Joesuus, Rannamoisas, Keila-Joal and
Kloogal. 60 km (37 miles) to the east of Tallinn,
is the Merivalja residential district.

Agricultural Exhibition, Pirita Tee 12 & 24;
open 12–7

Pirita Restaurant, by the sea

Nomme, on the opposite side of Tallinn, 7 km
(4 miles) to the south

Mustamae, further on in the same direction.
There is an excellent view from the highest point
of the castle here.

Intourist organises day and overnight trips from
Tallinn to Parnu and Viljandi, day trips to Paide,
Tartu (all q.v.) and to Vandra (see below) and trips
by air to Kingisepp (q.v.) on the island of Saaremaa.

There is also an 8-hour excursion to the Jakobsen
Museum 160 km (99 miles) from Tallinn.

Vandra Population—3,000
The settlement of Vandra is 35 km (22 miles) northeast of Parnu on the Paide road.

The first written mention of Vandra dates from
1515. A small place around a farmstead (myza) had
grown into a large settlement by the end of the 19th
century. The last owners of Myza Vandra were the
von Ditmars. Local peasants broke into the house
in 1905 and now only the park remains.

Vandravskaya Church, 1787. The tower was
added in 1885.

19th-century Inn, This was originally a barn.

Schoolhouse, built in art nouveau style in 1914.
It has two storeys.

Ludig's House, Kingisepp Street 68. The composer and choir master, Mikhail Ludig (1880–
1958) lived here from 1939–1958.

Café

Jakobsen's Estate, 160 km (99 miles) from Tallinn. In Kurgya, on the road between Parnu and
Viljandi, but closer to the latter. If coming form
Parnu, pass Riyuza and then turn right, to the south
of the main Viljandi road.

Carl Robert Jakobsen (1841–82) was a journalist, writer and one of the most prominent figures
in the Estonian national movement. He was also
far ahead of his time in his ideas about conservation. The museum is in the houses on the left bank
of the river Parnu, in a park which was planted out
by Jakobsen himself. The living quarters were never
completed for the family's use, and in 1877–82
they lived in the bath house. A direct route leads
through the woods to Viljandi. This path was the
one Jakobsen took when he needed to go to town,
where he was in charge of the newspaper "Sakala";
the trees have been painted to show the way. The
main building was only completed after the revolution, and the museum was opened in 1950.

Jakobsen is buried in his family tomb, in the
local cemetery on the right bank of the river Parnu
near the road. His grave is marked by his bust, the
boulder was placed nearby in 1882 by his friends
and the stone slab was donated by the Linda Society.

TARTU Population—112,000
(Tarpatu, Yuriev, Dorpat)
Intourist organises day trips here from Tallinn, 187
km (116 miles) away.

The town was founded in 1030 by Prince Yaroslav the Wise (Yuri) of Kiev, and called Yuriev
after him. It grew up beside the river Emajogi on
the site of an old Estonian settlement, Tarpatu,
which dated back perhaps as far as the 5th century
B.C. The name Tarpatu may be linked with the
word "tavras" (wild ox) or perhaps with Taara, a
god of Estonian mythology. The present name of
Tartu derives from that of Tarpatu. Yuriev was
ruled by the Kievan princes until 1212 when the

Teutons took it over and later it became the seat of the Livonian bishops.

Situated strategically between warring Russia, Sweden, and Poland, Tartu was seldom left in peace. It is on record that the town was destroyed by the Germans in 1212 but was soon rebuilt. It was captured by them again in 1215 and all the inhabitants were then baptised. Christian Tartu took SS. Peter and Paul as its patrons and its coat-of-arms still bears their crossed key and sword motif. Advancing and retreating armies continually burnt and ravaged the town until in 1710 Russia, under Peter the Great, finally established control over the region. From 1918 Estonian rule lasted until 1940, then from 1941–44 the town was under German occupation.

Wars apart, Tartu also suffered badly from fires, and after the Great Fire of 1775 only two houses remained standing, Voimala Street 12 and Ulikooli Street 40. The latter is where Peter I stayed in 1704, after taking Tartu from the Swedes. Tradition has it that he attended a wedding party there. Trees were planted following the lines of the old fortifications after the Great Fire.

Tartu once served as an important economic centre. It was a member of the Hanseatic League and even now ranks as Estonia's second city, but its chief claim to fame has long been its university. Founded in 1632 by King Gustav II of Sweden, the university was transferred to the town of Parnu. It reopened in Tartu in 1802 and grew and pros-

pered until, in the 19th century, it ranked among the very best European centres of learning. During World War II Tartu University was evacuated to the city of Voronezh and was influential in the foundation of Voronezh University. Today there are seven faculties and a student population of 4,000. Ulikooli, the name of the main street, means "university." The university is justly proud of its laboratories, museums, and particularly of its library of two million books, where there is a copy of Thomas More's "Utopia" printed in 1516. There is also a fine collection of 8,000 graphics which include works by Dürer and Rembrandt. Most of the library is housed in the *Cathedral of SS. Peter and Paul* on *Toome Hill*. The cathedral was in ruins and was reconstructed when the University was reopened in 1802. Part of the cathedral dates from the 13th century and so it is probably the oldest building in Tartu.

There is a legend attached to the cathedral. When it was founded, the building made no progress because the stones that the masons laid during the day were pulled down again during the night. Someone suggested that the only way to combat the problem was to immure a beautiful virgin in the walls of the cathedral. The girl who was chosen was told only that she would be the keeper of the keys, and when she realised what the job entailed, she pleaded and cried to no avail. It is said that the unfortunate maiden is allowed out once a year, some say on New Year's Eve and some say on

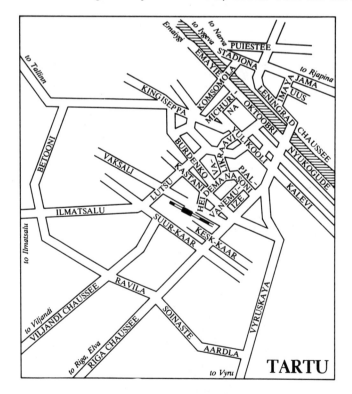

TARTU

midsummer night, to look for another woman around whose neck she can hang the cord upon which the keys are threaded.

Other stories about the cathedral tell of hidden treasure and underground passages and a hall where ravens meet once in a hundred years; whoever overhears their talk will become immensely wise.

Among the other notable buildings on Toome Hill, most of them used by the medical or scientific members of the university community, are the *observatory* and the *Old Anatomical Theatre*. The observatory was built in 1807 and in 1824 the largest refracting telescope in the world at the time was presented by Alexander I and installed there. The observatory was in use until 1963. The central part of the Old Anatomical Theatre, the rotunda, was completed in 1805 but in 1825 and 1856 the wings and then the annexes were added.

The *Powder Cellar* was built into the slope of Toome Hill at the end of the 18th century in such a way that it has only one external wall. The main room is about 30 m × 11 m (98 × 36 ft) and is surrounded by a corridor. The ceiling is vaulted and there is an efficient ventilating system. The cellar served as a gunpowder store until 1809 and then as a store for beer. At the end of the 19th century the university installed a pendulum here to record earth tremors but after World War I the building was neglected and reverted to a storehouse.

Also on Toome Hill are the busts of a number of scientists associated with the University, and at the foot of the hill is a *monument* to "persons of several nationalities . . ." marking the new resting place of those who had been buried in an ancient graveyard which was discovered on the site chosen for the university. The *park* on the hill was laid out in 1802 on the initiative of the first university rector, Georg Parrot. It was considered to be English in style and one of the decorative bridges, although dedicated to Parrot, is still known as *Angel's Bridge*, the name supposedly being a corruption of "English Bridge." However there is also a *Devil's Bridge* not far away, and a tradition for students to sing from the bridges is still observed.

Historically, Toome Hill has probably seen more of interest than any other part of Tartu. It is thought to have been the site of heathen temples and sacrificial altars. Certainly early Christian churches were almost always founded in places which had been held sacred by the ancient Estonians and May Day celebrations took place here until 1874. The hill was also a natural site for a fortress, although nothing now remains of the castle that stood where the observatory building is today.

There are other buildings of interest to be seen on Ulikooli Street. Nos. 13 and 15 are 18th-century houses, No. 16 was formerly a medical clinic and No. 18 is the main building of the university. The house opposite the entrance to the university was built in 1775–80. Nearby is *St. John's Church* (St. Ioanni Kirik), founded in 1330. Partially ruined since 1944, there still remain lavish decorations of rare terracotta sculpture. Notable are the 15 figures of the Judgement Day over the main entrance. It is planned to restore the church completely.

The *Town Hall* (1782–89), Ratushnaya Square. The architect of this structure was masterbuilder J. Walter from Germany who took 17th-century Dutch buildings for his models. Of interest are the two clocks; the student body was of such importance that the university asked for one to be installed so that it would be visible to the students from Toome Hill. Ratushnaya Square was built up by rich merchants at the end of the 18th and the beginning of the 19th centuries and today only the southern side is new.

Uspensky Church (1776–83), city centre. This church stands on the site of a Jacobite Monastery. There was a wooden church here before the Great Fire.

St. Peter's Church (1882–84), Leningrad Chaussee

Yurievskaya Church, Leningradskaya Chaussee 101. This is a Russian Orthodox church with services in Estonian.

Russian Orthodox church, Abovjani Street

St. Ioanni Kirik, Ulikooli Street

Catholic Church, beside the road on the way into the city from Tallinn

Local Museum, Oru Street 2

Art Museum, Valikraavi Street 2

Ethnological Museum, Burdenko Street 22

Luts's House, This was the home of the writer, Oskar Luts.

Starkopf's House, This was the home of the sculptor, A. Starkopf, and in the garden is an open air sculpture exhibition.

Powder Cellar (Pyssikohu Kelder), Late Street 28

The Falling House, Ratushnaya Square. This house stands 6 degrees out of the vertical. It belonged to the widow and descendents of the Russian Commander-in-Chief Barclay de Tolly (1761–1818) in 1819–79, and then a pharmacy was opened in it.

Botanical Garden, Michurin Street 38–40 (open May to September).

People's Monument, Toome Hill. This is Tartu's oldest monument.

Barclay de Tolly Monument, in a small square not far from the town hall. The Russian Commander-in-Chief (1761–1818) lived in Tartu on Ratushnaya Square, and owned an estate at Jogeveste not far from Tartu, where all that remains is his mausoleum. The monument by Demut-Malinovsky and Schedrin was unveiled in 1849.

Kreutzwald's Bust, on the right bank of the river Emajogi. Friedrich Kreutzwald (1803–82) was a physician who is now better known for his literary work. He compiled Estonian folklore, including the national epic of Kalevipoeg, and did much to form the Estonian literary language. Saks and Hirv were the designers of this monument which was unveiled in 1952, the year of the university jubilee.

Pirogov's Bust, on the slope of Toome Hill,

behind the town hall. Nikolai Pirogov (1810–81), a surgeon of international repute, was a graduate of the university here. He pioneered the use of ether anaesthesia in field conditions and was among the first to employ women as professional nurses. Raudsepp and Molder designed the monument, also unveiled in 1952.

Lenin Monument, in front of the Agricultural Academy in Lenin Square.

World War II Memorial, Raadi Park. The figure of a soldier, erected in 1945, marks a common grave.

Burdenko's Bust, N. Burdenko (1876–1946).

Victims of Fascism Monument, 2 km (1 mile) along the Riga Highway, a white stone wall with a bas-relief marks the site of an antitank trench where 12,000 people were massacred.

Liiv Memorial, A bas-relief portrait of the Estonian poet J. Liiv has been carved on a granite boulder.

Vanemuine Theatre (the Big House), Vanemuine Street 6, in the Concert Hall.

Drama Theatre (the Little House), Vanemuine Street 45. The theatre company was founded in 1870 but this building was completed in 1967.

Concert Hall (the Big House of Vanemuine Theatre), Vanemuine Street 6

Eduard Vilde People's Theatre

Park Hotel, Vallikraavi Street 23; tel. 33–663

Tartu Hotel & Restaurant, Turu Street 2; tel. 33–041

Kaseke Restaurant, Tahe Street 19

Kaunas Restaurant, Leningradsky Chaussee 2, on the bank of the river

Volga Restaurant, Kingissepp Street 10

Tarvas Restaurant, Riia Street 2

Pyussirohu Kelder Cafe, Lyatte Street 28

GPO, 21st-June Street 19

Department Store, Riia Street 2

Bookshops, Ulikooli Street 1 & 11; Ratushnaya Square 16

Souvenirs, Ratushnaya Square 4

Art Shop, Ratushnaya Square 8

Taxis, Ratushnaya Square, at the crossing of Pargi and Tahe Streets, and by the railway station; tel. 33–867

TASHKENT is the capital of Uzbekistan.

UZBEKISTAN

Area: 500,000 sq km, Population 19,906,000. People of more than 100 different nationalities live here, but the majority (over 68.7%) are Uzbeks, who derive from a group of Moslem, Turkic-speaking, nomadic tribes of mixed Turkic, Mongol and Iranian origin. The population also includes 10.8% Russians, 4.2% Tatars, 4% Kazakhs, 3.9% Tajiks and 1.1% Koreans.

Uzbekistan is the largest republic in Soviet Central Asia and it is also economically the most advanced. It lies in the southeast part of the country, between the two great rivers, the Amu-Darya and the Syr-Darya, and borders Afghanistan and Pakistan. Also adjoining it are the Soviet Republics of Kazakhstan, Kirghizstan, Tajikistan, and Turkmenia.

Archaeologists have found traces of the very earliest civilisations here. There is a camp of primitive man in the Samarkand region dating back over 100,000 years. The skull and bones of a Neanderthal man were discovered in the south of Uzbekistan together with remarkable rock drawings. Once the fire-worshipping Sogdians and Baktrians lived near present-day Tashkent and Khorezm, and as long ago as the third millennium B.C. the inhabitants of the lower reaches of the Amu-Darya made pottery and built houses large enough for more than a hundred people each.

For centuries the country suffered countless wars and conquests. In the 6th century B.C. Cyrus the Great, founder of the Persian Empire, conquered Central Asia, but the Persian Empire fell to Alexander the Great in 300 B.C. In the 6th century A.D. the whole of Central Asia was held by the Turks, but they were driven out by the Arabs in the 7th–8th centuries only to return in the 10th century.

It was then that the territories of Central Asia became known as Turkestan and the name remained in use until the 1920s. The region flourished under Tamerlane who created a huge empire with Samarkand as its capital. The time of his rule was a golden age of architecture, science, and the arts. The emergence of the Uzbek nation is attributed to the 16th century.

In 1868 the Kokand and Bukhara Khanates recognised their dependency on the Russian Empire and submitted to Russian authority. Soviet power arrived in November 1917, but was immediately followed by a period of civil war. The Uzbek Soviet Republic was finally set up in October 1924.

Uzbekistan is now the Soviet Union's primary cotton producer. In world cotton production the republic stands next to the United States and China. It also holds leading places in manufacturing silk and cotton fabrics, different machinery and mineral fertilisers, and its natural gas reserves are immense. Although three-fifths of the country is desert, extensive irrigation has made it an important region for commercial fruit- and vine-growing. The markets of Tashkent, Samarkand, Ferghana and other Uzbek towns display mountains of grapes, melons, and other fruit. Over a thousand varieties of melon alone are grown. The famous Astrakhan pelts also come from Uzbekistan and are now produced in a wide range of shades and colours.

The climate here is continental with extreme variations between summer and winter temperatures. The sky is clear and sunny for more than 250 days a year and in summer the temperature is often 42°C. (108°F.). Thermez, a town in the south of the republic, sometimes records more than 50°C. (122°F.), which is the maximum for the

Soviet Union. In winter the temperature occasionally drops to −25°C. (−13°F.).

The Uzbeks value their national traditions, and although many people wear European dress, the old costumes are often to be seen. Both men and women wear long, tunic-like shirts and broad trousers, with colourful robes as outer garments. They both wear skullcaps, but the men sometimes put on turbans. The women do their thick, black hair in 2 plaits, while young girls may have as many as 40 thin braids.

The Uzbeks are famous for their public spirit and for their respect for the elderly. Children are brought up to be quiet and polite and would never raise their voices when speaking to an adult. A typical Uzbek would automatically remove a stone from the path so that others would not stumble over it.

An old and very popular tradition is a competition of wit and quick thinking. Such an occasion may draw crowds numbering thousands. They assemble around a platform on which two men, the competitors, stand facing each other. One of them begins with a witty remark about the other and it must be immediately parried by his opponent. The two go on to the delight of the onlookers until one of them fails to answer promptly or cleverly enough, when the crowd announces him the loser. At present the most popular form of this "battle of wits" is called "payr"; the opponents have to keep to one particular topic, chosen beforehand.

The sights of Central Asia, and of the cities of Uzbekistan in particular, include a wide variety of examples of Moslem architecture. There are mosques and minarets and Moslem seminaries called "medressehs" built around a square or rectangular courtyard. Other architectural terms that are most frequently encountered include "pishtak" (large portal), "chortak" (small gateway), "gurkhona" (mausoleum containing a sepulchre), and "ziaret-khona" (a prayer room, often to be found adjoining the gur-khona).

The written language of the Uzbeks is very poetic but it has changed alphabets three times in its history. Arabic letters were used from the 8th century until 1929 when Latin letters were introduced, and in 1940 the Russian alphabet was adopted.

Here are a few more words of the Uzbek language:

hello	salaam aleikhem
I am a tourist	men saiarkhatchiman
please	markhamat
thank you	rakhmat
yes	shundei
no	yok
good	yasha
bad	yomon
I don't understand	men tushumaiman
please fetch me an interpreter	on-ne chakharin
good-bye	haiyere
how do you do?	akhwallar halei

Tashkent Population—2,075,000

The city which is the capital of Uzbekistan was originally called Chach-Kent, which means "stone town" or "fortress" in the Tajik language.

Tashkent stands in the valley of the Chirchik, whose old name, Parak (rushing), indicates its behaviour, as its waters pour down from the Chatkalski Mountains. The weather is spring-like in February, but the colours then are still grey and brown until the grass begins to sprout. In general the climate is very warm, especially between April and October. The average July temperature is 43°C (109°F) and the surface temperature of the ground may rise as high as 74°C (166°F). In spite of the heat, Tashkent ranks as one of the Soviet Union's greenest cities.

The city covers an area of 160 sq km, and is the third largest in the Soviet Union after Moscow and Leningrad. Its inhabitants are mostly either Uzbek or Russian, and visitors are often surprised at the way Europe and Asia mingle here. In many places modern buildings are still surrounded by mud houses. Tashkent is however more interesting as a new city than as an old one, and for those who have the opportunity of going on to Bukhara and Samarkand, the few ancient monuments here are of comparatively little importance.

Tashkent's earliest historical reference is in a Chinese chronicle of 2nd–1st century B.C.; it then formed part of ancient Khorezm. From the 7th–11th century A.D. Tashkent was ruled by the Arabs, from then until 1363 by the Khorezmians, until 1500 by the Mongols, until 1814 by the Uzbeks and the Kirghiz-Kaisaks, and between 1814 and 1840 and then again between 1846 and 1863 by the Kokandians. In 1865 Tashkent was taken from the Bukharians by the Russians.

Like most of the cities of Central Asia, Tashkent is divided into the old and the new towns. Beginning in 1865 (following the union of Turkestan with Russia) the left bank of the Ankhor Canal was used for building houses for Russian administrative offices. They were single-storey like the Uzbek houses, but nevertheless the Ankhor and the Bozsu Canals became the geographical boundary and the social border of the city.

The new town grew rapidly, planned by Russian architects who made no attempt to change the older part. In 1866 the Tashkent slave market was closed and slaves were granted their freedom. The following year the town became the administrative centre of the Turkestan Region and was the seat of the Governor-General. The Russians mainly consisted of ex-servicemen and their families, but Governor-General von Kaufman encouraged newcomers to move in on a three-year provisional contract before deciding to settle permanently.

Tashkent soon became the principal centre for Russian trade with Central Asia and the construction of the railway in 1898 stimulated the development of local industry. The building at Gogol Street 101 was constructed as a stock exchange at the beginning of the century and was so used until

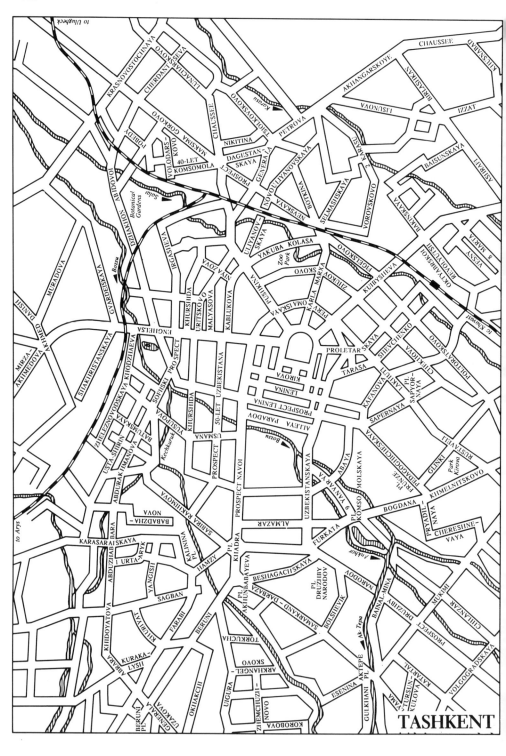

TASHKENT

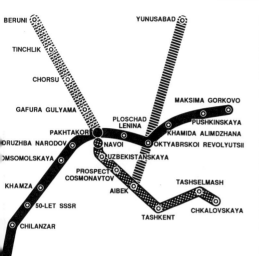

BERUNI
TINCHLIK
CHORSU
GAFURA GULYAMA
PAKHTAKOR
ORUZHBA NARODOV
OMSOMOLSKAYA
KHAMZA
PROSPECT COSMONAVTOV
50-LET SSSR
CHILANZAR
SABIRA RAKHIMOVA

YUNUSABAD
MAKSIMA GORKOVO
PLOSCHAD LENINA
PUSHKINSKAYA
KHAMIDA ALIMDZHANA
NAVOI
OKTYABRSKOI REVOLYUTSII
UZBEKISTANSKAYA
AIBEK
TASHSELMASH
CHKALOVSKAYA
TASHKENT

TASHKENT (Metro)

1915 when it was turned into the Winter Theatre; it later served as the local Art Museum. It was the railway workers who led the strikes and demonstrations of 1905–07. The 1916 revolt was instigated by the Bolsheviks and the Moslem nationalists. After the 1917 revolution Tashkent was the capital of the Turkestan Republic until 1924, and in 1930 the capital of Uzbekistan was transferred here from Samarkand.

The city is now a stop-over for flights between Europe and the Far East.

Local industry is mainly concerned with the production of textiles, agricultural machinery, and food products. American cotton was planted here experimentally in 1878 and it has become one of Uzbekistan's principal forms of agriculture. Under construction is one of the largest power stations fuelled by natural gas; the gas is piped from Bukhara.

The Uzbek Academy of Sciences, formed in 1943, is centered here and there are 28 research institutes carrying out important work in physics, cybernetics, heliotechnique and other branches of science. Lenin University, founded in 1919, has 11 faculties with over 4,000 students and is the largest of the city's 16 higher educational establishments.

Tashkent is located in a seismic area and earthquakes have been recorded in its history. The 6-point (Richter scale) quake of April 26, 1966, was the worst ever suffered. Over 1,000 tremors were recorded in a period of several months. 35% of the homes were destroyed and 78,000 families made homeless. In addition 2,100 public buildings that housed offices, shops, and schools were either destroyed or badly damaged. In spite of the widespread damage there were no more than 19 deaths and only 156 injured. When the quake began it was too early for factories and schools to be occupied, and the weather was warm enough that many people were sleeping in the open air. A third helpful

factor was that the tremors began gradually so that people had time to get out if they were inside their homes. Rebuilding began almost immediately after the disaster. Help and construction material came from all parts of the Soviet Union and as a result Tashkent quickly changed its appearance and whole new regions sprang up.

A tour of the city may be conveniently started from *Teatralnaya (theatre) Square*. (Our description keeps aboveground, but there is a 2-line underground railway system to link the further points very conveniently. The below-ground stations are impressive with fine decorated columns.) Teatralnaya Square used to be the noisiest market place and was known as the Drunken Bazaar. Its importance as a shopping centre was revived after the earthquake for that was where the main department store was built.

The *Opera and Ballet Theatre* after which the square was renamed was built in 1947 by Schusev and can seat almost 1,500. The six foyers are interesting, for each is decorated in the traditional style of one of the six cities whose names they bear—Tashkent, Bukhara, Samarkand, Khiva, Fergana and Termez. Opposite the theatre is the *Tashkent Hotel* and on the north side of the square is a big publishing house where about 40 newspapers and magazines are printed. Moscow "Pravda" and "Izvestia" are received by photo-telegraph and appear on the streets earlier than they do in Moscow because of the time difference. Nearby is the Central Trade Union Club, called the *Palace of Labour*.

Pravdy Vostoka Street leads from the square to another hotel, the *Shark* (east), which bears a memorial plaque saying that during the civil war it housed the headquarters of the Turkestan military front. Mikhail Frunze, the Red Army organiser, was in command here. A little distance from the hotel is the *Sverdlov Concert Hall*. At the crossing of Pravdy Vostoka and Proletarskaya Streets is the *City Council Building* and opposite, on Proletarskaya Street is *Gorky Children's Park*. Nearby stands the *clocktower* built by Mukhamedshin in 1947 to commemorate the victory in World War II.

At Proletarskaya Street 12 stands a *constructivist-style building* which was designed as a public kitchen. Appropriately it is in the shape of a casserole; it is round and there is a small handle on the top of its "lid". It later served as a museum.

Also in Proletarskaya Street, in the *Kafanova Garden*, is the common grave of 14 Turkestan commissars, the first Soviet ministers in Tashkent, who were killed during a counter-revolutionary uprising in 1919. An obelisk stands on the grave. Close by are buried the first Uzbek President, Yuldash Akhunbabayev, the first Uzbek general, Sabir Rakhimov, and the poet, Khamid Alimdjan, one of the founders of Tashkent University. The garden and the street leading to the railway station are named after Kafanov, a leading Uzbek communist, who is also buried here. In *Vokzalnaya (railway station) Square* there is another monument to the 14 commissars. Sculptured in Ukrainian granite, it stands 12 m (39 ft) high and has an eternal flame burning near it. It was unveiled in 1962.

Minguryuk, Proletarskaya Street. Here are the remains of an ancient town. The 7th–8th century fortress of Tashkent which used to stand on Ak-Tepe Hill, Unus Adab Street, has been completely demolished to make room for new buildings.

Revolutsii Square and Garden is at the beginning of Proletarskaya Street and links 5 other streets, Karl Marx, Engels, Pushkin, Leningradskaya and Kuibyshev. The *Karl Marx Monument* was unveiled in 1968 to mark the 150th anniversary of his birth. The bronze head was made in Moscow and the granite foundation was brought from the Ukraine. On the outside of the curve that bounds the garden stands the modern *Uzbekistan Hotel*.

Karl Marx Street is one of Tashkent's main thoroughfares and, with the department store and other shops, is also one of the busiest. It runs right through Revolution Garden to cross Kirov and Lenin Streets. Where it crosses Lenin Street there is an old garden with a yellow-and-white *palace* with two lions guarding one entrance and two deer the other. It used to belong to Grand-Prince Nikolai Konstantinovich. The Prince was born in 1850, a cousin of Nicholas II, and he came to Tashkent in 1881. It was then that this palace was built for him, as a winter residence following a plan by Geintselman based on the outline of the double-headed eagle (also used for the former Russian Embassy in Tokyo). In fact he only used it for receptions and to house his art collection. Besides paintings, drawings and portraits of the imperial family, he had guns, embroidery and items of Chinese and Japanese art. In spite of his background, the Prince was an unexpectedly progressive person; he even took part in the demonstrations in 1917. When he died that same year (of natural causes), he bequeathed everything he possessed, including the 552 items in his collection, to Tashkent University. When the collection was first opened to the public, it proved immensely popular. The palace was restored in 1983 and now houses the *Museum of Antiques and Jewellery*, a branch of the Art Museum. Many of the Grand-Prince's belongings and some of the furniture from the palace are in the museum, while his collection of paintings occupy two halls in the *Art Museum*. Opposite the palace is *St. George's Church* which was built at the same time, and the *Puppet Theatre*.

Marx Street ends in *Lenin Square* (formerly known as Cathedral Square) where stands the building of the *Uzbek Supreme Soviet* (the local parliament), built in 1940 by Polupanov. The square is used for parades, and the pedestal of the *Lenin monument*, decorated with red granite and black labradorite, is used as a tribune by members of the government and important visitors during festivities. The *Council of Ministers* and the *Uzbek Komsomol* buildings are at the end of the square. The *Ali Shir Navoi Library* which stands nearby was founded in 1870, has over 2,000,000 books and is the largest library in Central Asia. Nawai

Prospect is the main street of the old town. It is lined by the dignified buildings of the *Central Telegraph Office*, the *Ministry of Culture* and other administrative organisations and by some of the University buildings. The *Vatan (Motherland) Cinema* is an interesting structure which was built in 1939 by Timofeyev. Its 6 columns resemble the decorations of mosques in Khiva and Bukhara, but the carving is upon concrete instead of wood. Another unusual building on Navoi Prospect is the *Palace of Arts*. It has the city's largest hall for stage performances and films. It is also used for all gala meetings on important occasions. A broad avenue leads from the Palace to the *Pakhtakor (Cottonworker) Stadium* which, after reconstruction, seats 100,000. The largest building in the street is the *Press House*. Here are the headquarters of the Ministry of Culture, the Press and Cinematography Committees, and the editorial offices of a number of newspapers. The local television studios and tower are nearby. Further on, the *Khamza Drama Theatre* is considered to be one of the most attractive new buildings in the street.

Running from Navoi Prospect to Uzbekistan Street is a wide space called *Alleya Paradov* (Parades Avenue). It was inaugurated with the first parade on 7 November 1967, to mark the 50th anniversary of the Soviet state. Alleya Paradov at its Navoi Prospect end comes almost right up to *Ankhor Canal* which, before the reconstruction of the city, used to divide the old and the new parts of Tashkent.

Kukeldash Medresseh, Chorsu-Navoi Street, near the market, and a good place from which to explore the old town. The medresseh was built in the 16th century as a Moslem theological college. It stood just inside the walls of Tashkent, beside the trade route leading into the town from Samarkand. It has been reconstructed several times. Kukeldash was a local ruler, religious enlightener and poet. He was also, however, greedy and fierce. There is another building that bears his name in Bukhara. This one that dominates the area here is now a museum. Near it on the square stands the Djuma mosque. The square used to be an execution place and it is said that unfaithful wives were sewn into sacks and then thrown down from the top of the building.

The *Khast-Imam Ensemble*, up Khamza Street, about 2 km (1 mile) to the north of Kukeldash Medresseh. Here is the *Masar Qaffal Shashi*, a domed brick mausoleum to Abubakr-Ismail-Qaffal, one of the first local Islamic prophets who died in 976. The mausoleum was built in 1541 by the architect, Gulyam Husein, in an old cemetery. There is a disused mosque standing near the mausoleum.

Barak-Khan Medresseh, Khamza Street 103. Barak-Khan, a relative of Tamerlane, ruled in the 16th century and built this medresseh in the centre of the old city of Tashkent in the 1550s by linking two mausolea dating from the 1530s. Single-storey cells (khudzhr) surrounded the courtyard and 100–

120 students studied here. Locally, it is the best architectural monument of its time still standing. Here also is the mausoleum of the Tashkent Shei-banid dynasty (16th–17th centuries). The medres-seh's excellent present state is due to reconstruction in 1904–05 and rebuilding after the earthquake of 1966. A garden has been planted inside and the inscription over the gate reads: "Let there arise from among you a band of people inviting to all that is good, enjoining what is right and forbidding what is wrong; these are the ones who will attain felicity." The medresseh is now the residence of the Mufti of Central Asia and Kazakhstan, and since 1940 it has been the headquarters of the Muslim Admin-istration Board of this area. (The Soviet Union's other Muslim centres are in Baku, Makhachkala and Ufa.) To the right of Barak-Khan Medresseh is a working medresseh with 40 students.

Namezgokh Mosque, across the road from the medresseh. This was built in the 1880s and is open for services. In the courtyard of the mosque is the Mufti's library containing 2,000 unique books, some very old and some relatively new. Of especial interest is the 800-year-old Koran which has had marginal notes added by each reader. Permission may be granted to visit the library, but remember that shoes should be removed at the entrance just as they should on entering a mosque.

Sheikh An-Takhur Cemetery, Nawai Street. One of the ways into this area, which is now en-closed by a new house, is opposite the Estrada Theatre and the television tower. Walk up the steps and through a small garden where "shashlik" (char-coal-grilled skewers of meat) and tea are on sale. The place was used as a cemetery for over six cen-turies and, together with others which were en-gulfed by the growing city, was closed at the end of the last century. In 1924 the territory was re-planned and built up with new houses, but some of the ancient buildings were preserved. Most im-pressive of all is the *Mausoleum of Unus-Khan* who once ruled Tashkent; it has interesting carved-stone columns inside. It was built at the end of the 15th century as was the medresseh which stands near it.

The *Mausoleum of Sheikh An-Takhur*, whose name the cemetery bears, stands to the right of the *Mechanics Institute*. The mausoleum was built in accordance with a 16th-century design. The 15th-century *Kaldirgach-Bia Mausoleum* with a pyra-mid-shaped roof was reconstructed in 1911–12. The *Zengi-Ata Mausoleum and Mosque* were built by order of Tamerlane. They have been re-constructed several times, but the carved wooden doors of the 15th century are of interest.

Abdul-Kasymsheikh Medresseh, Druzhba Na-rodov Square. Built in the 16th century, there is a whole architectural complex here including a mosque and baths. Originally having but one floor, a second storey was added in 1864. It was renovated in 1983 and is now used as offices for Tashkent's Bureau of Ancient Monuments.

Sheikh Zein-ad-Din Mausoleum and Mosque, Viloyat Street, in an old park which was formerly a cemetery. These date from the 16th century. There is an underground crypt (hor-hana) where people went to pray; many people gathered here, especially on religious holidays.

The central street of the new Chilanzar region is named after astronaut Gagarin as is a new *garden* there. The blocks of flats here are designed to ac-commodate 100,000 people.

Uspensky (Assumption) Cathedral, Gospital-naya Street 91. This was built in the 1890s as a hospital church dedicated to St Pantheleimon but was rebuilt in 1957, and is open for services.

St. George's Church, opposite the palace. This church was built in the 1880s.

Alexander Nevsky Church, in a local cemetery
Our Lady of All Sorrows Chapel
All Saints' Baptist Chapel
Roman Catholic Church, Zhukovsky Street
Lutheran Church, down Karl Marx Street and across the bridge. This was built at the end of the 19th century.

Synagogues, Chempiona Street 101 and Karl Marx Street

Rakat (new) Mosque, Pryadilnaya Street. The mosque is practically new, having been built at the end of the 1950s, and is one of the city's 15 mosques still in use, including the Barak-khan (see above).

Art Museum, Proletarskaya Street 16. The col-lection displayed here now was founded in 1918 on the basis of the collection which belonged to Grand-Prince Nikolai Konstantinovich; this now occupies two halls of the twenty, which together contain carpets, embroidery, woodcarving, and Western, Oriental, Russian, and Soviet art (mostly in reproduction) including the works of local artists. Open 10:30–6; closed Tues.

Artists' Exhibition Hall, Lenin Prospect 40

Museum of Antiques and Jewellery, a branch of the Arts Museum, Karl Marx Street 3, where it is crossed by Lenin Street. In the palace which used to belong to Grand-Prince Nikolai Konstantino-vich. The interior decoration of the palace is dis-appointing until one reaches two rooms which are richly painted in local style. A third room decorated in lacelike, white carved plaster on mirrors dates from the restoration of the building in 1983. The Grand-Prince had the spiral staircase brought from Paris. The museum contains many of the Grand-Prince's belongings including his collection of por-celain and some of his furniture. There are also gold-embroidered robes; in the first room, known as the Bukhara Room, are very large robes which belonged to the Emir of Bukhara, who needed them large so that he could wear several, one on top of the other, to demonstrate his affluence. The good display of Uzbek jewellery includes a number of the tiara head dresses aptly known as "golden brows." Much use was made of turquoise and coral, the latter being valued for supposedly drawing all kinds of sickness out of the wearer.

Downstairs in the cellar is a collection of much

older gold treasures which date from the 5th, 6th and 10th centuries B.C. and were dug up locally. Especially interesting are the gold items of the 1st century A.D. which were found in 1972, squashed into a jar which accounts for their being bent. The silver jewellry was mostly made by Bukhara craftsmen in the 19th century. Some of the pieces make use of delicate pastel-coloured stones, rose quartz and aquamarine with pearls. Open 10:30–5:30; closed Thurs.

Applied Art Museum, Shpilkov Street 15, in what was once Count Polovtsev's house. Open 10–6; closed Mon.

Carpet and Tapestry Museum, Pravda Vostoka Street 16, on Dzerzhinsky Square, in the old building of the National Hotel.

A curly design symbolising ram's horns is a favorite ornament in Uzbek carpet design. A pomegranate pattern is typical of carpets from Khiva, while the sharp contrast of navy blue and red is favoured in Fergana. The very woolly carpets known as "dzhul-khyrs" (bearskins) are used as floor coverings. The embroidered wall-coverings are called "suzany," and very often household objects are hidden among the flowers, or the flower petals themselves may resemble fish, parrots, butterflies or even coffee pots and vases. Many embroideries were left unfinished on purpose, so that a mother's work could be completed by her daughter later on. The larger pieces were divided up for group work. The embroidered skullcaps (tubeteiki) vary from one region to another and even between villages. In addition there are different designs for boys and girls, and others for married women, so traditionally the local headgear told much about its wearer. The ribbed ones are stiffened with padded sticks inside. Open 10:30–6; closed Tues.

Aibek History of the Peoples of Uzbekistan Museum, Kuibysheva Street 15. Here there are over 3,000 examples of local applied art. Open 10–6; closed Mon.

Reconstruction Museum, at the crossing of Lenin Prospect and 50-Let USSR Street. This blue-roofed building tells the story of the rebuilding of Tashkent after the earthquake of 1966.

Lenin Museum, Lenin Prospect 30. Open 10–6; closed Mon.

Natural History Museum, Sagban Street 16

Ulug-Beg Planetarium, Hamza Street 6

Exhibition of Economic Achievements, in Pobeda Park

Navoi Monument, Navoi Street. Nizamaddin Ali Shir Navoi (1441–1501) was the poet who is now celebrated as the founder of Uzbek literature. The *Literary Museum* nearby was opened in 1967. It has some rare manuscripts.

Biruni Monument, Biruni Street. Abu Reikhan Muhammed ibn Ahmed al-Biruni (973–1048), a scientist versed in mathematics, astronomy, history, geography and mineralogy, with especially valuable writings on India.

Gogol Statue, near Pushkin Street. Nikolai Gogol (1809–1852) was the author of "The Inspector General," among other works.

Lenin Monument, Lenin Square. Unveiled in 1935.

Frunze Monument, Frunze Square. Mikhail Frunze (1885–1925) was a leading Bolshevik, and the Red Army commander who did most to establish a Soviet power in Central Asia.

Bust of Kuibyshev, near Pushkin Street. Valerian Kuibyshev (1888–1935) was a leading Bolshevik who helped to establish Soviet power in Central Asia.

Gorky Monument, Gorky Square

Akhunbabayev Monument, Akhunbabayev Square. Yuldast Akhunbabayev (1885–1943) was the first Uzbek president.

Kalinin Statue, in a garden near Khamza Street. Mikhail Kalinin (1875–1946) was president of the USSR for eight years.

Soviet People's Friendship Monument, on Soviet People's Friendship Square. This was unveiled on 26 May 1982 and is dedicated to the Shamakhmudov familly who adopted 15 war orphans; these included children of different Soviet nationalities and a little German too.

50th Anniversary Stele

Earthquake Monument, The figures of a mother and father stand brave and firm, protecting their child, before a cracked stone cube which bears the time and date of the earthquake that so damaged Tashkent on 26 April 1966. The panels behind the statues symbolise the various construction teams that came to help rebuild the city.

Shastri Monument, by the special Indian language school

Kasibeg Monument, Cosmonavtov Prospect. Kasibeg was a spaceman.

Indira Gandhi Monument, sculpted by Anvar Akhmedov

Navoi Opera & Ballet Theatre, Kirov Street 28

Khamza Uzbek Drama Theatre, Navoi Prospect 34

Russian Drama Theatre, Prospect Navoi

Gorky Russian Drama Theatre, Karl Marx Street 28

Mukimi Musical Theatre, Almazar Street 189

Youth Theatre, Kalin Square, in the old Khamza Theatre building

Sverdlov Concert Hall, Pravda Vostoka Street 10

Conservatoire, Pushkin Street 31

Puppet Theatre, Kosmonavtov Prospect 11

Circus, Khadra Square, off Navoi Prospect

The *Molodaya Gvardia Cinema* building used to be the Court Theatre. It was built in 1910 and decorated with sabres.

Zoo, Alimdzhana Street 23

Botanical Garden, Karamurtskaya Street

Hippodrome Racecourse, Ak-Ui Street 30, on the edge of town on the road to Samarkand. Both flat racing and trotting take place.

Pakhtakor Stadium, Sotsializma Street 23

Mitrofanov Water Sports Centre, Pervomaiskaya Street 76

Komsomol Lake Park, Almazar Street 188. In this park boats can be hired. The bathing beach is the most popular in the city.

Pobeda (Victory) Forest Park, Shevli Street 6. There is also a bathing beach here.

Tashkent has 16 other parks and 27 smaller public gardens. They all seem to illustrate the Uzbek saying: "Before chopping down one tree, plant three or four young ones."

Uzbekistan Hotel & Restaurant, Karl Marx Street 45; tel. 33 3959. Intourist office: tel. 33 7786.

Tashkent (Intourist) Hotel & Restaurant, Lenin Street 50. When ringing a number in the town, hotel residents should dial 9 before the number they wish to engage.

Moskva Hotel, at the end of Navoi Prospect, near Kukeldash Medresseh. This 23-storey skyscraper accommodating 1,200 guests is the tallest building in Tashkent.

Rossia Hotel & Restaurant, Rustaveli Street. Built in 1967.

Shark (eastern) Hotel & Restaurant, Pravda Vostoka Street 16

Zaravshan Hotel & Restaurant, Akhunbabayeva Street 15a

Pushkinskaya Hotel, Pushkin Street 18

Bakhor (spring) Restaurant, Kuibysheva Street 15

Gulistan Restaurant, at the crossing of Kalinin Square and Khamza Street, seats 800

Anchor Tea Room, Tukayeva Street 33

GPO, Krylova Street 4

Bank, Kirov Street. The Renaissance-style building dates from 1915.

Central Telegraph Office, Navoi Street.

Local Society for Cultural Relations with Foreign Countries, Akhunbabayeva Street 1

Afghan Consulate General, Gogol Street 73; tel. 33 9180

Indian Consulate General, A. Tolstoy Street 5; tel. 33 0697

Mongolian Consulate General, Gogol Street; tel. 33 8313

Interesting purchases which can be made locally include small, embroidered skull-caps called "tubeteiki," a "khalat" (a quilted men's coat with a silk scarf for a belt that could be used as a dressing gown or housecoat for men or women), and lengths of gaudy, ziz-zag striped silk material.

Beryozka (foreign currency) Shop, Pyervomayskaya Street

Central Department Store, Rashidov Prospect 17

Department store where there is a souvenir department, Karl Marx Street 35.

Souvenir Kiosk, in the Tashkent Hotel

Art Salon & Handicrafts, Karl Marx Street 47

Bookshop, Karl Marx Street 31

Antique and secondhand goods, Karl Marx Street 25

Children's World, children's department store, Rustaveli Street 43.

Embroidery, carpets, etc., Karl Marx Street 20

Jeweller's, Kirov Street 29 & Navoi Street 1a

Almaz (diamond), Mukimi Street 1. Open 10–7; closed Sun.

Florist's, Revolutsii Garden 1

Tobacconist's, Karl Marx Street 26

Gramophone Records, Druzhby Narodov Prospect 4

Paintings, Karl Marx Street 25

Wine, Karl Marx Street 26

Alaiski Market, Engels Street

Oktyabrsky Market, at the end of Navoi Street in the old town. A new, domed market building is under construction.

Taxi Ranks, in the square near the Tashkent Hotel, in Pushkin Square and in Engels Street, near the market.

Intourist organises a number of excursions inside the city including those to an arts and crafts factory and to see the manufacture of folk instruments. Excursions outside Tashkent are usually connected with local agriculture and with opportunities to swim. Tashkent Sea, is located 50 m (31 miles) from Tashkent.

Chirchik, 30 km (19 miles) northeast of Tashkent; founded just before World War II and now boasting a population of over 60,000. Here can be found an electro-chemical works and the hydropower station on River Chirchik. There are collective farms nearby. Agricultural machinery and building materials are produced, as well as foods.

St. George's Church

From here tourists are taken to one of two recreation areas; Ak-Tash is 75 km (47 miles) from Tashkent, and Chimgan 95 km (59 miles).

(Bostandyk, Mojikent, Brichmolla, Chimgan, Ak-Tash and Khumson are all located in the resort area which supplies Tashkent, Chirchik and Angren with agricultural produce. Until 1956, this region was part of Kazakhstan.)

Yangi-Yul, 35 km (22 miles) southwest of Tashkent. This is the centre of the local cotton-growing area with a cotton gin.

Angren, 115 km (71 miles) from Tashkent; founded during World War II-population 55,000. This is the centre of a coal-mining area. There are also a hydropower station, building materials, and food industries.

Almalyk, founded in 1949, population over 50,000. There are large deposits of copper ore here and the town, which has copper, lead, and zinc refineries, is growing fast.

Begovat, also founded during the Second World War and now with a population of over 40,000. Here is a hydropower station, and food and building materials are produced. Here also is the only metallurgical plant in Uzbekistan.

Samarkand A longer journey takes one all the way to Samarkand (q.v.). It is a three-hour drive, most of it along a dual carriageway. The road out of Tashkent passes *Trudovy Reservy Stadium*. To start with, the highway runs through rolling agricultural country with orchards. After crossing the Syr-darya river the *Chkhra Restaurant* with a gaily painted dome stands to the left. There are vineyards and paddyfields, all dependent upon irrigation from the ubiquitous canals. In many places these are on legs above ground, and then water is channelled into a pipe which passes under the road and up again on the other side. There are herds of cattle and horses, flocks of sheep and a variety of wild birds of prey to be seen.

Dzizhak is 5 km (3 miles) to the right of the main road, and there is a *restaurant* just above a *monument* with a statue of a woman. Beyond Dzizhak the terrain becomes more hilly and stoney, with good grazing for sheep and goats, and pleasant spots for human picnics. The road finally passes between the two towering cliffs known as *Tamerlane's Gate.*

The *Myzobulak Restaurant* is in the village of Mylla-Bulak and a clock sign marks the place for one hour's time change between the two time zones before reaching Krasnogvardeisk. In Oktyabr there is the *Mekhr Restaurant* on the right. The road crosses the *Mirzaaryk Canal* and the *river Zarafan*, and climbs some more hills before running down into Samarkand.

TBILISI is the capital of Georgia.

GEORGIA

The Georgian Republic occupies an area of 180,500 sq km (69,700 sq miles) and has a population of 5,449,000 (1988). 68.8% are Georgians, but there are also Armenians (9%), Russians (7.4%) and Azerbaijanis (5.1%), with smaller proportions of Ossetians and Abkhazians. Georgia is one of the oldest countries in the USSR. A Georgian kingdom of Iberia was known to exist as early as the 3rd century B.C. The Georgians, known for their generous hospitality, when seated at their lavish tables enjoy telling their guests the following story. When God was creating the world He got so caught up in the work that He forgot to choose a place for Himself. Taking a good look He discovered a tiny little corner that had sea, mountains, vineyards and orange groves—in other words, a real paradise. So He decided to leave it just as it was for His own use. Besides the country's natural beauty it has also over 3,000 examples of ancient architecture, many of which have been carefully restored while others are protected to prevent further deterioration.

Christianity came here in 318, and has, since 337, been the official religion of the country. The natural wealth of the area and its strategic position drew the attention of various invaders. It suffered conquest and domination by Romans, Byzantines, Persians, Arabs, Mongols, Seljouk Turks, the Ottoman Empire, and finally the Persians again. There were times when the country was united and when it included, together with vassal territories, the whole of Transcaucasia and neighbouring areas. At the end of the 18th century Western Georgia was under Turkish domination and Eastern

Georgia under Persian rule. The King of Eastern Georgia sought Russian protection and then in 1800 his successor ceded his country to Russia, being helpless against the Persian threat.

In 1921 a Soviet Republic was established in Georgia, but from 1922 to 1936 it was a part of the Transcaucasian Soviet Federal Republic. Then it was the Georgian Soviet Socialist Republic until 1991.

The present Republic consists of Georgia proper, the Ajar Autonomous Republic (the population of which is mainly Moslem), the Abkhazian Autonomous Republic, and the South Ossetian Autonomous Region.

Climatically the country can be divided into two zones: Western Georgia (the Abkhazian and Ajar Autonomous Republics, Imeretia and Mingrelia) with a Mediterranean climate and subtropical vegetation, and Eastern Georgia (South Ossetian Autonomous Region and Kakhetia) with a dry, continental climate.

Georgia has the best manganese in the world, and its other mineral resources are coal, iron ore, oil, natural gas and stone. The country's industry includes engineering, metallurgy, oil extraction and refining, manganese- and coal-mining, light and food industries. Agriculture is mainly concerned with tobacco, tea, maize, wheat, citrus and other fruit, vines, silk, and sheep, pig and poultry breeding.

Georgia's principal towns are Tbilisi (capital), Batumi, Sukhumi, Kutaisi and Poti.

Georgian churches deserve a special word of introduction. The acceptance of Christianity from Byzantium led to the Georgian Orthodox Church's adoption of Byzantine forms of church architecture. By the 10th–12th centuries a more complex type of church, with three to five elongated aisles and a decorated facade, had evolved. Later still the characteristic Georgian tower developed, drum-shaped and crowned by a many-faceted conical dome. The height of the cone sometimes equalled the width of the drum, but the more recently constructed churches tend to have taller cones.

The interior of the churches have very simple frescoes in imitation of Byzantine style, and there is usually little statuary, although there may be some very attractive decorative stone work (patterned reliefs and borders). The head of the Georgian Orthodox Church is the Katolikos Patriarch.

Useful expressions in Georgian:

Hello	gamardzhobut
how do you do	rogor brdzandebit
I am a tourist	me tooristvar
please	getakhvat
thank you	madlobt
yes	ki
no	ara
good	kargyet
I don't understand	ar mesmis kartuli
good-bye	nakhvamdis

Georgian dishes popular far beyond national boundaries, are shashlik and chicken tabaka. Others you may enjoy are:

suluguni—mild, flat cheese
khachapuri—cheese-filled bread
lobio—beans in walnut sauce
chicken satsivi—chicken in walnut sauce
chakhokhbili—chicken stewed with tomatoes
Tsinandali—good white wine
Mukuzani—good red wine

Tbilisi Population—1,260,000

Tbilisi is the capital of Georgia. It is located in the eastern part of the country and in the central part of the Caucasian isthmus. It is 350 km (217 miles) by rail from the Black Sea and 550 km (342 miles) from the Caspian. The highest part of the town lies 91 m (299 ft) above the rest of Tbilisi, and altogether it covers over 6,000 hectares (15,000 acres), twice as much territory as in 1921, prior to the establishment of Soviet power in Georgia. On the west side of the town is Mt. Mtatsminda (Holy Mountain or Mount David) (727 m/2,385 ft), to the east lies the Makhat Range (650 m/2,133 ft) and to the south the Sololax (488 m/1,601 ft). Mount David is said to have been named after King David the Builder who recaptured Tbilisi from the Muslims, but was known for his generosity towards his victims. King David claimed descent from the Biblical David the Psalmist, and the royal Georgian coat-of-arms appropriately bore a harp and sling.

The river Kura, the longest river in the Caucasus, rises in Turkey and flows through Tbilisi to the Caspian sea. From ancient times the site of Tbilisi has been a trading point between Europe and India.

The climate is continental with an average annual temperature of 12.7°C (55°F). The summer is long, dry and hot with an average temperature of 24.5°C (76°F), but it may rise to more than 40°C (104°F). The winter is mild with little snow; the average winter temperature is 1–3°C (34°F) but if there is a north wind it may drop to −15°C (5°F). Autumn is considered the best season of the year, and in general the climate must be a healthy one, for in Georgia there are over 20,000 people who are over 90, and more than 600 of them live in Tbilisi.

The name Tbilisi came from the Georgian word "tbili" meaning "warm" and now it is understood to mean "the town of the warm springs." The Georgians, however, have long called it simply Kalaki, meaning "town" because it is the biggest built-up area in Georgia. A legend chronicled by Leonti Mraveli says that long ago the Georgian King Vakhtang Gorgasali (452–502) was hunting in the place where Tbilisi now stands, and he wounded a deer. While it was bleeding to death, the beast fell into a warm, sulphur spring where its wound was washed. It was cured and rushed from the spring and ran off to the forest. The king examined the spring, found its waters warm and curative, and ordered that a settlement be made on that spot. There is a monument to him here, in Tbilisi, commemorating his discovery.

The first written mention of Tbilisi as a fortress-town was made in 368, and in the 5th century, under King Vakhtang Gorgasali it became the capital of Georgia instead of Mtskheta. During its history it was pillaged by enemies 40 times, and during the space of 1,400 years was entirely devastated 29 times. Especially severe were the attacks by the Mongols at the end of the 13th century and those made at the end of the 18th century by Persian Shah Aga-Mohammed. Khazars, Huns, Persians, Byzantines, Arabs, Mongols, Turks, and numerous tribes from the mountains have all forced their way inside its walls. Each time it was rebuilt. Tbilisi showed the influence of its new masters, and that of the Persians was especially strong.

Georgia has had contact with Russia since the 15th century. As the Georgians held the Orthodox faith in common with the Russians, it was to them that they appealed for help in moments of crisis. Ivan the Terrible sent his Cossacks as reinforcements in the 16th century, and Russo-Georgian relations were even closer in the 17th and 18th centuries when Peter the Great and King Vakhtang established a military alliance. In 1736 Georgia was divided between Turkey and Persia, the Turks dominating West Georgia and the Persians East Georgia and Tbilisi. After that the Georgian kings were appointed by the Persian shahs, but the Georgians frequently revolted and sought the protection of the Russian tsars. In the second half of the 18th century the Georgian King Erekle II came to power, and in 1783, to save his country from military disaster from Persia and Turkey, signed an agreement passing supreme power to Russia. The last king, Georgi XII, passed practically all power to Russia after the massacres and seizure of Tbilisi by the Persians under Shah Aga-Mohammed in 1795. This warlike leader was a eunuch and was renowned for his ferocity; his men would take babies from their mothers and try to cut them in half in a single blow to test the sharpness of their swords. After their attack on Tbilisi nothing remained of the town except two caravanserais and a few houses.

In the second quarter of the 19th century many new houses appeared in Tbilisi, especially in the central part of the town. The architecture shows elements of Russian classicism combined with the old Georgian style; for instance, on the traditional flat roofs appeared a second floor with balconies and carved columns. With its ancient culture and natural beauty Georgia attracted Russian intellectuals as visitors. These included the playwright Alexander Griboyedov, Pushkin, Lermontov and Tolstoy. In 1851 Tolstoy wrote "Tiflis is a very civilised town, closely imitating Petersburg and doing it rather well. The high society is select and fairly large and there is Russian theatre and Italian

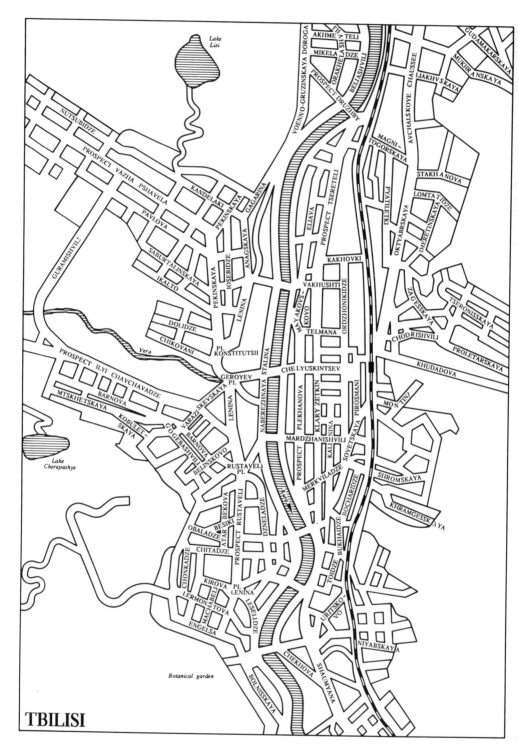

TBILISI

opera." Tchaikovsky, Chaliapin, Chekhov, Rubinstein and Gorky all visited it with pleasure.

The first *funicular railway*, 501 m (548 yds) in length, was built on Mount David in 1905. It ends with a three-storey building, the top floor of which is used as a *restaurant*. Tbilisi's largest *park* is at the top of Mount David. The old *Asian quarters* of Tbilisi are not very extensive but their narrow streets and lanes form a labyrinth fascinating to tourists. The section known as *Maidan* may be reached by walking from Lenin Square along Leselidze Street. One of the old *caravanserai buildings* (now used as a depot) stands at the end of Sionskaya Street, to the south-east of Sioni Cathedral. There are other similar buildings still in existence in Tbilisi. Among the new buildings in the area is the fine *registry office* (Dom Ritual), on the left bank of the river, opposite *Sioni Cathedral*.

The *palace* at Rustaveli Prospect 6 was built in 1807 and reconstructed in 1865. Before the revolution it was the residence of the Governor of the Caucasus, and until 1941, when the new government building was put up nearby, it was the seat of the Georgian government. Now it is a Palace of Young Pioneers, the Soviet equivalent of the Boy Scouts' and the Girl Guides' Associations. Chavchavadze Street 33 is the building of the former

seminary, and was erected in 1905; now it is used by the Agricultural Institute. The new *Government Building*, Rustaveli Prospect 8, was built between 1938 and 1953 by architects Kokorin and Lazhava; it is 5 storeys high and has an unusual covered courtyard. The *Georgian State Museum* was designed by Severov and built between the establishment of Soviet rule in 1921 and the outbreak of the Second World War. A *university* and 12 *institutes* are among Tbilisi's educational establishments and there are 19 *museums*. An *underground railway* was constructed in 1966 and new housing is going up on all sides. An imaginative redevelopment of Maidan, the site of the old bazaar, has led to the laying out of Shaumyan Square with a *memorial* to the leader of the Baku Commissars, shot in 1918. A number of *balconied houses* have been restored nearby to create a photogenic corner of old Tbilisi. There is a *garden* here and a *cafe* and the buildings which have taken on a new lease of life include Princess Davidyan's *18th-century palace* and the *Priest's House* beside *St. Karapet's Church* where there is a *museum*. In Khetagurov Street another *Armenian church*, with decoration in red brick, has also been restored along with the adjoining priest's house. *Daryalsky Church*, by the old fortress wall and with its belfry topped by a thin

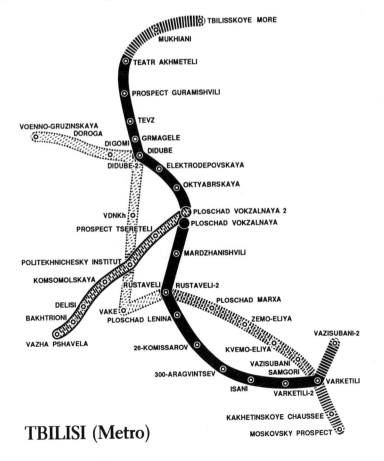

TBILISI (Metro)

spire, is Armenian too. In the valley below, the nearest church is *Sioni Cathedral* (see below). Further away to the left with the black roof is the *Armenian Convent* at Engels Street 19, while even more distant and further left is an *Armenian church* dedicated to Our Lady. Saburtalo on the city's northern outskirts is probably the best looking of the new residential areas. The main road in from Mtskheta runs through it.

The reservoir known as the *Sea of Tbilisi* was completed in 1951. There is a *bathing beach* there, and a regular bus route connects it with the city.

The town's greatest wealth has always been in its warm *sulphur springs*, but for many centuries only the Moslems used them. Most are to be found in the Maidan sector on the banks of the river Kura. Those on the right bank are similar to the springs of Bataglia and those on the left resemble the waters of Ems and Baden. The waters come from Mtabori Hill and emerge from thermal cracks in the bituminous layers. Their temperatures fluctuate from 47.5°C (117.5°F) to 24°C (75°F). The old *bathhouses*, similar to the caravanserai in architecture, are mostly to be found in the old town in the Legvis Khevi Ravine. The oldest is the *Erekle Bath*, on the corner of Nabbaya and Akhundova Streets. It was long a bone of contention between the kings and the clergy until King David gave it to Sioni Cathedral in 1549. Opposite this bathhouse is another dating from the 17th century, known as the *Sumbatovskaya Bath*, and of similar date is *Bebutovskaya Bath* on the southern side of Akhundov Street. Further on from this is *Kazyonnaya Bath* which in the 18th century belonged to Tamara, daughter of King Georgi XII. The *Seidabadskaya Bath* in Mesnikov Street was built in 1840. There are several others, but these have been restored and are the best and the most interesting. They are crowded at the weekends, but certainly worth a visit; there are Turkish baths with traditional massage and separate baths for men and women.

Sioni or Assumption Cathedral, Sionskaya Street 4. The original cathedral was built between 575 and 639, during the reigns of the Georgian Kings Guram and Ardanas. After the death of Queen Tamar it fell into decay. As legend has it, Sultan Gelal Eddin tore down the dome in 1226. The local Metropolitan Bishop, Saginshvili, rebuilt the dome and redecorated the whole church. It suffered badly in 1795 during the invasion of Aga-Mohammed Khan when the wooden iconostasis was burned down. In 1811 it became the seat of the Georgian Exarchs. The present belfry on the other side of the street was built in 1816 to replace one of the old ones which had been destroyed by the Persians. The cathedral was repeatedly restored, and in 1853–4 it was repainted by the Russian artist Prince Grigory Gagarin in Byzantine style, as a result of which the old frescoes were lost. The stone iconostasis was built at the same time, and in 1882 the paintings in the dome were restored. There is another belfry built in 1425 and restored in 1939. St. Nina's Cross, interwoven with vines and her own hair, was brought to the Sioni Cathdral from

Mtskheta and can be seen here, on the left, behind a carved, cross-shaped window with frescoes of St. Nina above it. Among the cathedral's other treasures are 2 cherished icons, "St. Nina" and "Our Lady of Sioni," the latter to the right of the iconostasis. Prince Pavel Tsitsianov, murdered during the capture of Baku in 1806, is buried here. Here are also the graves of King Guram and King Ardanas, the builders of the cathedral. Alexander Griboyedov and Princess Nina Chavchavadze were married here in 1822.

Unchiskhati Church, Shavteli Street 5/7. This church standing beside the river Kura is named after the 11th-century icon which was brought here in the 17th century from the village of Unchi in south western Georgia. Now the icon hangs in the Art Museum. The church itself was founded in the 6th–7th centuries and reconstructed several times, extensively in 1675 when new gateways and a bell-tower over them were added upon the orders of Catholicos Dementi. The external form of the basilica was spoiled by the 19th-century Russian-style reconstruction of the dome.

St. David's Church, Mtsminda Mountain. The building of the first church on this site is ascribed to St. David, one of the 13 Syrian church fathers who came to Georgia to preach Christianity (see p. 545), and who lived here on the mountain. Another church was founded here in 1542, restored several times and completely rebuilt, including the dome, at the end of the last century. In a grotto by the church is the tomb of Alexander Griboyedov, author of the Russian play "Woe from Wit," who was killed in Teheran on January 30, 1829. Nearby is the tomb of his widow, Princess Nina Chavchavadze, who died in 1857. Since 1829 it has been known as the pantheon of prominent Georgian public figures and writers, including Nicoloz Baratashvili, Akaki Tsereteli, Vazha Pshavela, and Ilya Chavchavadze. There is a second pantheon of public figures and writers in the Didubei district of Tbilisi. On the summit of Mtatsminda there used to be an observatory, built by the Arabs under whom Tbilisi rose to be one of the most important towns in the Caucasus.

Didubei Pantheon, Tsereteli Prospect 38, in the Didubei district of Tbilisi. Founded in 1939 as a resting place for Georgian writers, artists, actors, and scientists who are buried in the cemetery. In the Church of Our Lady of Didubei is a miracle-working icon of the Virgin. Open 12–7, closed Mon.

Kvashvetskaya Church, Geordzhadze Street 2, just off Rustaveli Street. Kva means "stone" and shva means "to give birth"; as the legend runs, the church was so called because long ago the daughter of a Tbilisi noble was expecting an illegitimate child and was advised to accuse St. David of being the father. He was summoned to court and touching her with his staff asked, "Who is the father of this child?" From within her a voice proclaimed the name of the real father, and thereupon the girl began to labour. She brought forth a stone which was used as the foundation of a new church. The present building was erected between 1904 and 1910.

Dzhavaris Mama Church, Lesilidze Street. The name means Holy Cross; the church was built in the 15th century and reconstructed in the first half of the 18th century.

Metekhi Chapel crowning the cliff above a bend in the river Kura, and well viewed across the river from Lesilidze Street. This chapel is a good example of the efforts of an architect to harmonise a building with the landscape. It is designed with regard to its silhouette and placed so that it can be seen from many points in the town. The first chapel on the site dated back to the time of King Vakhtang Gorgasali, and one of the most honoured Georgian saints, St. Shushanika, who was tortured to death in 544 by her Mohammedan husband for her Christian faith, was buried there. The existing chapel was founded in 1278–83 and reconstructed several times. It was for many years the chapel of the Georgian Exarchs. A new dome was built at the beginning of the 18th century but in the 1820s the chapel was turned into a prison. The 3 buildings near it also formed part of the prison but the rest was demolished in 1937. The round tower of red brick is Rusadan Palace, where the royal wives once lived. Now it houses the Metekhi Youth Theatre.

Lurdzhi Monastery, near Kirov Park. The name means "blue," referring to the blue glazed tiles which decorate it. The basilica dates from the 12th century although the dome is of more recent construction. On the southern wall is an ancient inscription about Vasily who founded the monastery.

St. George's Church, Rustaveli Prospect, odd numbered side. This church is run half as a Russian Orthodox Church and half as Georgian.

St. Nicholas's Church, reconstructed in 1982 as a concert hall for folk music.

St. George's Armenian Church, Krasilnaya Street, just below the castle. Open for services. The Armenian church opposite which is closed used to belong to the Armenian seminary.

Kirochnaya Church, Mardzhaniashvili Street 38. A small Russian Orthodox church.

St. John the Baptist's Church, Vazha Pshavela Prospect 21. This Russian Orthodox church was built in 1901 and is open for services.

Greek Church, Grecheskaya Street 47. Closed.

1st Synagogue, Leselidze Street 47. Services in Georgian.

2nd Synagogue, Leselidze Street 32. Services here are in Russian. There are also synagogues in Gori, Surami, Sukhumi, and Sivinvali.

Mosque, Botanicheskaya Street

Shuris Tsikhe, Komsomolskaya Alleya, Narikala. The ruins of the "rival fortress," also known as Sololaksky Citadel, can be seen above the old part of the town on Sololaksky Hill. The oldest fortress in the town, it is supposed to have been founded by the Persians in 368 to counterbalance the power of nearby Mtskheta. It was reconstructed by King Erekle and several other times during its history, and was newly rebuilt in the 17th century.

In the earthquake of 1827 it was severely damaged but some parts were again restored in 1909.

Sachino (noble) Palace, Avlabari. Formerly the castle of Queen Darya, wife of King Erekle II, the palace was built in 1776 and partly rebuilt in the 19th century. The chapel also survives. Nearby in Avlabari, at Matekhskaya Street 18, stands a typical example of an *old Tbilisi house.*

Academy of Art. This was built in 1857–58, and was at that time the most beautiful building in Tbilisi. Balls and banquets were held here and the parquet floors, marbles and carved decorations are still well preserved.

Town Hall, Lenin Square. The Town Hall was erected in the 1880s in Moorish style.

Dzhanashiya Georgian State Museum, Rustaveli Prospect 3. Open 10–5, closed Mon. Originally the Caucasian Museum founded in 1852, this museum was renamed after the Georgian historian, Academician Simon Dzhanashiya (1900–47). It contains much of interest, especially in the ethnographical section on the top floor. In the basement is a collection of fine gold work which can only be visited with a guide. It shows the development of jewellery-making from the 3rd millennium B.C. with especially valuable examples dating from the 2nd century A.D. which were found in burial sites near Mtskheta.

Georgian Art Gallery, Rustaveli Prospect 11. Open 11–5; closed Mon. The building was originally that of the Khram Slavy (temple of glory), built in the 1880s to commemorate the victories of the Russian Army in the Caucasus.

Georgian Art Museum, Ketskhoveli Street 1. Open 11–6, closed Mon. There is an excellent collection of icons, frescoes and china, and among the Georgian paintings worthy of note are those by the primitivist Niko Pirosmanishvili (Pirosmani, 1862–1918).

The unique gold items in the museum include those of the 5th century B.C. from Akhalgoriysky Monastery (up in the Caucausus Mountains, not far from Ananauri) and a cross which belonged to Queen Tamar, great granddaughter of King David the Builder. The cross is decorated with 4 polished emeralds, 5 large rubies and 6 pear-shaped pearls. It was left, together with other treasures, by Tamar to the Khobsky Monastery, but everything was taken to Europe by the Georgian Mensheviks when they emigrated in 1921. The French Commercial Bank in Marseilles was paid for a single year for keeping the treasures, and after 12 more years had passed the bank claimed them to cover the costs. Stalin learned of this in 1944 and ordered the Soviet Ambassador to France to negotiate the return of the treasures. General de Gaulle assisted personally and 3 special aircraft brought the gold back to Tbilisi on 5 April 1945.

Dating from the 1830s, this building once housed the Ecclesiastical Seminary and on the outside wall by the entrance is a plaque saying that J. Stalin lived and studied here from 1 September 1894 to 29 May 1899.

Ethnographic Museum, Komsomolskaya Alleya

11. Open 10–6; closed Mon. This collection was founded on that of the old Municipal Museum.

Georgian Literary Museum, Georgiashvili Street 8

Lenin Museum, Rustaveli Prospect 29. Open 11–7; closed Mon. The museum is located in the large building of the Marxism-Leninism Institute, designed by Academician Schusev in 1938.

Avlabarsky Underground Print Shop, Kaspiskaya Street 7. Open 9–5; closed Mon.

Friendship Museum, Lenin Square 5/7. Open 10–5; closed Mon. Describes the links between Georgia and the other Soviet republics during and after World War II.

Georgian Folk-Architecture Museum, Chachavadze Prospect, near Pobeda Park. Open 9–6; closed Mon. This is an open-air collection of various buildings from all corners of Georgia.

Chavchavadze's House, Ordzhonikidze Street 22. Open 10–6; closed Mon. Alexander Chavchavadze (1786–1846) was an outstanding Georgian romantic poet who translated both Russian and French poetry.

Museum of Children's Toys, Rustaveli Street 6

Marx Library, Ketskhoveli Street 5. The library was founded in 1846. On the facade of the building, only completed in 1913, ancient Georgian architectural motifs were used in decoration. The carving was executed by the Agladze brothers.

New Funicular Railway, entrance from Rustaveli Street up a spiral staircase. This overhead railway is 906 m (991 yds) long and rises to a height of 287 m (942 ft). It can carry 30 people at a time.

"Friendship of the Peoples" and *"Happiness of the Peoples,"* at the entrance to Tbilisi. These two monuments, by Zurab Tsereteli, were unveiled for the 200th anniversary of the Treaty of Georgievsk, uniting the Russians and the Georgians. The Soviet poet Andrei Voznesensky, who is an architect by training, helped create the monuments.

Vakhtang Gorgasali Statue, overlooking the Kura, just below Metekhi Church. This fine equestrian statue is of King Vakhtang, founder of Tbilisi.

Shota Rustaveli Monument, Rustaveli Square. Designed by Merabishvili and unveiled in 1942 to commemorate the 750th anniversary of Rustaveli's poem "The Knight in the Panther's Skin."

Obelisk, Vakhtang Gorgasali Street. This commemorates 300 warriors who lost their lives in 1795 as they covered the retreat of the Georgian army from the Persians.

Pushkin Monument, Pushkin Square. This monument was designed by Hodorovich in 1892.

Gurdzhi Monument, in the old town. Etim Gurdzhi was a minstrel and the sculptor of his monument was Mikatadze.

Bagration Equestrian Statue, on the Kura embankment. General Prince Pyotr Bagration (1765–1812), well-known for his heroic leadership in the 1812 war against Napoleon. The 6-m (20-ft) statue by Merab Merabishvili and Nodar Mgaloblishvili was cast in Leningrad.

Griboyedov's Grave, on St. David's Mount, by the church. The Russian writer and diplomat,

Alexander Griboyedov (d. 1829), was killed while serving as Ambassador to Persia. His tomb is of black marble with a bronze crucifix and a mourning female figure on it. To the left is a monument to his wife, Princess Nina Chavchavadze, who was left a widow at the age of 16 and who never remarried although she lived on until 1857 when she was 64. A statue of Griboyedov by Merabishvili (1961) stands beside the river Kura on the northeastern embankment.

Kamo Monument. This monument was erected in 1957 in memory of the revolutionary Semyon Ter-Petrosyan (1882–1922), who used Kamo as his Party name. It was designed by Okropirdze.

Lenin Monument, Lenin Square. By sculptor Topuridze, the 18.5 m (61 ft) monument was unveiled in 1956.

Ordzhonikidze Monument, Guramishvili Street. Sculpted by Merabishvili.

General Leselidze Bust, Lesilidze Street. Konstantin Lesilidze (1903–44) was a World War II hero.

Symbol of Georgia Statue, Komsomolskaya Avenue. The 16-m (52-ft) figure of a woman holding out a sword for her enemies and a bowl to her friends was designed by Amashukeli and unveiled in 1958 to commemorate the 1,500th anniversary of the founding of Tbilisi. The statue is known locally as Kartlis Deda.

"Granny, Iliko, Illarion and Me," in the children's village. This bronze group of characters is from a favourite children's book by Nodar Dumbadze.

Paliashvili Opera House, Rustaveli Prospect 25. The company was founded in 1851 and the Moorish-style building was completed at the end of the 19th century. The grave of Zakhari Paliashvili, who was a composer of Georgian national music, is in the theatre garden.

Mardzhanishvili Theatre, Mardzhanishvili Street 8. The theatre bears the name of a well-known Georgian stage director, Kote Mardzhanishvili (1872–1933), whose grave is in the garden of the Paliashvili Opera House.

Rustaveli Theatre, Rustaveli Prospect 19. The company was established in 1920 on the basis of the old Georgian Theatre. The Rustaveli Georgian Theatre Institute is to be found in the same building.

Griboyedov Russian Drama Theatre, Rustaveli Prospect 2. The building dates from the 1850s and was originally constructed as a caravanserai.

Shaumyan Armenian Drama Theatre, Shaumyan Street 8. This theatre was opened in 1936.

Georgian Youth Theatre, Rustaveli Prospect 37. The Georgian Puppet Theatre is at the same address.

Georgian State Philharmonic Society, Concert hall, Plekhanov Prospect 123. This is the home of the State Symphony Orchestra, the Capella Choir, the national dance ensemble (which has earned high praise during its tours abroad, and is well worth seeing), and a string quartet.

Vano Sadzhishvili Tbilisi Conservatoire, Griboyedov Street 8. The conservatoire is named after the lyrical tenor, Vano Saradzhishvili (1897–1942), "nightingale of Georgia," who now lies buried in the garden of the Paliashvili Opera House.

Concert Hall, Melikishvili Street 1

Abashidze Musical Comedy Theatre, Plekhanov Prospect 182

Circus, Heroes' Square. The building was completed in 1940.

Mount Mtatsminda. The park, which lies 362 m (1,188 ft) above the town, was opened in 1935. It is reached by two funicular railways.

Ordzhonikidze Park, Plekhanov Prospect 180/182. The park was laid out on the base of the old Mushtaid Garden, named after the onetime head of the Persian clergy in Tbilisi. There is a children's railway here.

Khudadovsky Park, Khudadovskaya Street 1. The park was planted in 1893.

Kirov Park, Lenin Street 37. The park was opened in 1933 and there is a monument to Kirov in it.

Kommunarov Garden, Rustaveli Prospect 13. This was formerly the Alexandrov Garden, founded in 1859. There is a monument to Gogol designed by Hodorovich in 1903, and other monuments to Georgian revolutionaries.

Vakei Park, Chavchavadze Prospect. The park covers 120 hectares (300 acres) and contains the Burevestnik Stadium which can hold 35,000 people. "Burevestnik" is the Russian name for the stormy petrel or Mother Carey's chickens.

Park of Physical Culture & Sport. Patrice Lumumba Naberezhnaya 1. There is an open-air swimming pool.

Palace of Sport, Ordzhonokidze Square 1. There are seats for 10,000 people.

Heated Swimming Pool, Chavchavadze Prospect

Zoo, Heroes' Square. Opened in 1927, the grounds cover 20 hectares (50 acres).

Botanical Gardens, Botanicheskaya Street 1. These gardens were founded in 1845, based on the old garden of Tbilisi fortress.

Iveria Hotel & Restaurant, Inashvili Street 4, tel. 93–0595. Both this hotel and the Adzharia have small *foriegn currency shops*.

Adzharia Hotel, Constitution Square 1; tel. 36–2716. There is a post and telegraph office in this 22-storey building.

Tbilisi Hotel & Restaurant, Rustaveli Prospect 13, tel. 99–7866. This hotel was built in 1915.

Intourist Hotel & Restaurant, Rustaveli Prospect 7. This was formerly the Orient Hotel, built in the 1880s.

Abkhazia Hotel & Restaurant, Vazha Pshavela Prospect 25

Georgia Hotel & Restaurant, Melikishvili Street 12

Sakartvelo Hotel & Restaurant, Melikishvili Street 113

Rustavi Hotel, Plekhanov Prospect 103

Ushba Motel & Restaurant, 4 km (2 miles) out of town on the way to Mtskheta; tel. 51–4922. There is a filling station here.

Intourist Office, Rustaveli Prospect 15; tel. 99–7089.

Aragvi Restaurant, Pushkin Street 29

Darial Restaurant, Rustaveli Prospect 22

Dynamo Restaurant, Dynamo Stadium, Brdzola Street 2

Isani Restaurant, Meshkishvili Street 3

Samgori Restaurant, Nekrasov Street 10

Funicular Restaurant, in Mt. David Park

Nad Kuroy (above-the-Kura) Restaurant, Ordzhonikidze Park, Plekhanov Prospect

Kazbek Restaurant, Elbazvidze Spusk 1

Sulkhino Restaurant, Sherozia Street 2

Gemo (taste) Restaurant, Lenin Street

Tsikari (twilight) Cafe, Melikishvili Street

GPO, Plekhanov Prospect 44

Central Telephone & Telegraph Office, Rustaveli Prospect 12

Bank, Kirov Street 3/5

Tsitsinatela (Foreign Currency) Shop, Rustaveli Street 23. Open 9–6; closed Sun. In the cellar is a good choice of wine.

Art Salon, Rustaveli Street 19, next to the Tbilisi Hotel. Handicrafts are on sale here.

Georgian Tea Shop, Rustaveli Street 20

Department Store, Mardzhinishvili Street 5

Filling Station, on the right embankment of the Kura

Repair Station, Saburtalinskaya Street and Plekhanov Prospect

Airport, To find it by car, from Maidan Metro station go eastwards, then follow the tramlines, turn left, under the railway bridge and follow the sign to Telavi and the airport. Once on Telavi Motorway look for a right turn to the airport.

Camping Site, at the entrance to the town by the 196/11 km mark.

Visitors may play tennis, go tea-tasting, visit a bakery or take boat trips on the Kura, but there are a variety of longer journeys too. Intourist organises *excursions* from the Georgian capital along the Georigan Military Highway passing Pasanauri, Inner Kartli, Krestovy Pass and Kazbegi. Separate trips to Mtskheta, to Gori (and Uplis-tsikhe), to Borzhomi and to Telavi. There is an *overnight trip* to Vladikaukaz via the Highway, and a two-day trip to Bakuriani. Each place is described under its own name except for those on the Georgian Military Highway which come in their order along the route (listed under "Georgian") starting from the south.

TELAVI

Intourist organises excursions to Telavi from Tbilisi, 140 km (67 miles) away.

Telavi is the capital of Kakhetia, and usually we describe republics or regions when we write about their capital. However, as foreigners are only able to reach Telavi by road from Tbilisi so it seems logical to put Kakhetia at the beginning of the journey through the region.

KAKHETIA

Kakhetia is rightly considered to be the pearl of Georgia. It is certainly a most beautiful part of the world. The basins of the rivers Iori and Alzani form the republic's largest agricultural region, growing grapes and other fruit, wheat, sunflowers, and tobacco.

Viniculture and the art of winemaking go back to the 2nd and 3rd millennia B.C., and it is mentioned in the 1st century B.C. writings of the Greek historian Strabo. Its antiquity is further proved by the fact that it is from the Georgian word "gvino" that "wine", "vin" and "wein" are derived, and that Virtis vinifera, the species of vine from which most of the world's wine is made, probably originated in the Caucasus. Autumn is the best time of the year to visit Kakhetia, to see the grape harvest and the folk festivals that accompany it.

Even in the centuries B.C. this area was part of the kingdom of Iberia and was called Kiziki or Kambechovani (Georgian for "buffalo" due to there being plenty of buffaloes in this region). Since those times this was "the area of abundance, wine and bread. It seems as if the mountains are spread with butter, so fertile is nature here and so abundant the harvest," wrote the Georgian poet Titsian Tabidze.

In the early centuries A.D. the town of Khornabudzhi was the administrative centre of Kiziki, and after the introduction of Christianity, the archbishop had his residence there. During the Arab rule of the 7th–9th centuries Kiziki (Kambechovani) was included with the rest of Kakhetia in the Princedom of Geret, and at the beginning of the 11th century King Bagrat III joined Geret-Kakhetia to the kingdom of Georgia. This unification was completed by David the Builder in 1104. The rulers of Khornabudzhi were highly esteemed at the court of Queen Tamar for their brave part in struggles with Georgia's enemies.

Throughout the 13th century Georgia was devastated by the raids of Shakh Dzhelal-ed-din of Khorezm, and later by the Mongols, so that Khornabudzhi became dilapidated, although it did not entirely lose its former importance. In 1586 I. D. Rusin arrived at the court of King Alexander II of Kakhetia as the representative of Tsar Feodor Ivanovich of Russia. In the 16th–17th centuries Kakhetia suffered greatly due to the invasions from Turkey and Persia, especially from the Persian Shah Abbas II. Kakhetia lost two-thirds of its population; Abbas II forced about 100,000 prisoners to move to Persia, and the famous gardens and vineyards were levelled.

Kiziki recovered in the 18th century during the reign of Erekle II, locally called "small kakhetinets," who loved Kiziki deeply, as he was born here and spent his childhood here. It was here at the age of 15 that he led an army of local warriors to defeat the Lezghinian troops, and here later that he reinforced the fortress at Signakhi as a stronghold against the Lezghis' raids.

After Georgia was united with Russia according to the Treaty of Georgievsk of 1783 the local people suffered greatly from Russian colonial policy. The Kakhetian rebellion of 1812 was fiercely suppressed and another large anti-Russian uprising occurred in Signakhi in 1878. Soviet power was proclaimed in Signakhi in February 1921.

For the road into Kakhetia from Tbilisi, leave the Georgian capital by Shaumyan Street in the left-bank part of the city, and follow the signs pointing to the airport and Telavi; then turn left, under the bridge and right.

Diesel oil is available to the right of the road leading to the airport.

Kakhetinskoye Chaussée crosses river Lochini and also the Tbilisi Ring Road which is under construction. It goes over the vast Iorskoye Plateau, through Badiauri, across the southern spurs of the Gombor Ridge, whence the snow-capped peaks of the Caucasus are visible, and into the Alzani river valley where there are many ancient mounments.

Sartichale

World War II Memorial, on the right in the form of a black obelisk.

Shashlik Bar, on the right.

Filling Station, beyond the village on the left of the road.

The road crosses the river Iori. There is an oil well on the right and plenty of rigs about in general.

After crossing the Patardzeulis Khavi, there is another *World War II memorial* on the left. It was unveiled in 1975 and is unusual for its bas-relief of Stalin and quotation of his words, and is dramatic in its use of dead trees and bells. Behind the memorial lies the village of Patardzeulis. This village has a country atmosphere with sheep, pigs, geese and vineyards. Behind the village and to the left are the remains of Ninotsminda.

Ninotsminda Fortress

On the far right, at the foot of the hillside, there is an 18th century *fortress* of brown stone with the *ruins* of a 5th–6th century church inside its walls. This was built as a cathedral dedicated to St. Nina, Illuminatrix of Kartli and Kakhetia, who first brought Christianity to Georgia. Her origins are obscure, but there are many legends about her. Some think that before coming to the Caucasus she had been a slave in one of the Anatolian provinces of the Byzantine Empire.

The cathedral was renovated in the 11th–12th century, and again between 1650 and 1671. The four-storey stone tower of the fortress was added to the walls in the 16th century; its arched upper floor served the dual purpose of belfry and lookout post. The exterior decoration of the tower is unusual in that it combines huge Christian crosses with Islamic art forms. Facing the southern facade of the church was the two-storey palace of Archbishop Savva Tusishvili, built between 1774 and 1777. All the buildings in the complex suffered from the earthquake of 1823.

The road crosses the Tvaltkhevi river just before reaching Sagaredzho.

Sagaredzho

This is a district centre, 50 km (31 miles) from Tbilisi and lying a little to the left of the new main road; Lenin Street leads right into the town. There are factories for processing grapes and for producing bricks and lime.

Petropavlovskaya Church, up to the left of the main road, up Rustaveli Street. Built of grey stone in 1690–1712 and decorated with beautiful carvings.

Stone Obelisk, just beyond the town, at the 55 km mark. This commemorates the 20th anniversary of VE-Day.

Garedzhi Restaurant, Lenin Street 7, in the centre of the town

Filling Station, on the left of the main road

Service Station, on the way into town

Upon leaving Sagaredzho the road passes through the Gsiv-Gomborsky Range, which is thickly covered with trees and undergrowth. Then it descends into the Alazani valley.

Tokhliauri

The *ruins* of Manavi stand on a hilltop to the left.

There is a stone *church* on the lower slopes on the left.

Up on the left, above the road, is a *war memorial* in the form of two columns with swords and a shield hanging on them.

The road crosses the river Chailuri.

The dramatic scenery in these parts lends itself to filmmaking and on the right a castle under construction.

Ninotsminda (formerly Bogdanovka)

Here the main road follows the railway line.

Restaurant, on the right at the 83/76 km mark.

The road crosses the river Lakbiskhevi, and then a right turn branches off the main road and leads after 15 km (9 miles) to Signakhi. A little further on, the road swings around again and there is a good view of the snow-capped mountains ahead.

Tractor Monument, to the right of the road.

The road then twists up into the hills.

Nukriani

In this small village also known as Bodba, 2 km (1 mile) before Signakhi, is *St. Nina Bodbinsky Convent*. (Take the turninig where a sign indicates "Hospital—1 km" to the right.) The foundation of the convent in the 4th century is linked with the first period of Christianity in Georgia, and in particular with Nina, the zealous advocate of Christianity who is considered a saint in Georgia.

According to one legend Nina was among 37 sisters who escaped from pagan Rome to Jerusalem, where they accepted Christianity before moving to Armenia. King Tiridat of Armenia fell in love with one of the sisters and proposed to her, but the beauty rejected the heathen's offer, and after a series of trials and tribulations, she was executed along with the rest of the sisters. Nina was the only one to survive, because she had moved to nearby Iberia (Georgia). Nina travelled to Mtskheta (q.v.), settled

there and preached until she had converted King Mirian and all his people to Christianity.

Later she moved to Kakhetia where she converted Queen Sodzha and erected a Christian Church in Bodba (Nukriani). She died in 338 and was buried near the church, and a few years later a convent was established there.

Bodbinsky Church and Convent were very dear to the Georgian kings; Vakhtang Gorgasali (452–502) and David IV (1089) were among those who made tributes. It was run as a college from the 16th century, and had certain privileges over other religious centres. The archibishop had the right to anoint the kings of Kakhetia, among whom were David the Builder, Levan III, Alexander II and Teimuraz I. During royal receptions the Archbishop of Bodba sat next to the king. He also led the army of Kiziki in battle and was both a political and a public figure.

All the original buildings collapsed in one of the series of earthquakes that troubled the region so that now the oldest buildings are of 18th-century construction. The belfry was built to commemorate the union of Georgia and Russia in 1783. In the 1820s the church was renovated and painted by Ioann Makashvili, Archbishop of Signakhi and Kiziki, and there were monks in residence. In 1889 a teachers' training school for women was opened there, and also the workshop where icons and vestments for clergy were made. More restoration work was undertaken in the 1890s and a three-storey building was erected for priests and monks. The *Church of St. Nicholas* was founded in 1897 to replace the earlier churches. It contains the tomb of St. Nina. At the beginning of the 20th century the convent was attached to *Khirsko-Stefan Monastery*, 8 km (5 miles) away. The convent was reopened in 1957 and there are a few nuns in residence. The school and workshops are still in operation and St. Nicholas's Church is open for services.

Museum, open daily 10–5. There are old photographs of churches in the vicinity and a map showing 12th-century canals in the valley.

In the convent grounds are the burial places of prominent people and members of their families, including Feofilakt, the first archbishop (ekzarkh) of Georgia.

Signakhi Hotel, up above the road on the right.

Filling Station on the right.

Signakhi Population—60,000

This picturesque and ancient town stands at a height of 790 m (2,592 ft) above sea level on hilly terrain, hidden in the valleys of the rivers Alazani and Iori. At the 98 km mark, on the main Tbilisi-Telavi road, a side road branches off to it. It was founded by Armenians who sought refuge from the Persians, and its surrounding walls enclose an area of 40 hectares (100 acres). They stretch for an enormous length and have towers and gates. Signakhi's projecting buttress of rock juts out over the wide, flat valley of the Alazani, a smooth, fertile plain 48 km (30 miles) wide. The town is all built at different levels and divided by steep walls, and winding streets link the various parts. There are still many ancient buildings including a number of churches.

The name of Signakhi derives from the Turkish word for "refuge" or, according to other sources, from the Turkish word "signi" meaning "deer." From the very earliest times this was "the area of abundance, wine and bread. It seems as if the mountains are spread with butter, so fertile is nature here and so abundant the harvest." So wrote the Georgian poet Titsian Tabidze about Signakhi.

The real foundation of the town of Signakhi is credited to Erekle II, although the place had long been inhabited and the fortress of Signakhi (see below) already stood. But on Erekle's order the fortress was fundamentally restored and made a stronghold against the Lezghis' raids.

After Georgia was united to Russia according to the Treaty of Georgievsk of 1783 the local people suffered greatly from Russian colonial policy. Signakhi was granted town status in 1801, but the Kakhetian rebellion of 1812 was fiercely suppressed. Another large anti-Russian uprising occurred in Signakhi in 1878. Soviet power was proclaimed in Signakhi in February 1921.

At present Signakhi is a well-developed agricultural centre mainly concerned with dairy products, sheep, poultry and bees. Signakhi is particularly renowned for its vineyards. The "Tibiani," "Khirsa" and other vines have won many awards both in the Soviet Union and abroad. The area has been irrigated by the Alazan Canal since 1930.

Signakhi Fortress. All through Signakhi's history, its fortress played an important role in defending the town, and the foundation of the town is closely connected with the fortress which is presumed to have been built in the 12th–13th centuries and reconstructed by Erekle II who came to the throne of Kakhetia in 1744. It was he who reinforced the walls and added towers to the fortress because of his policy of giving priority to the defence of Kiziki against the Lezghis, Turks and other invaders.

The fortress is roughly triangular and covers a territory of 40 hectares (100 acres); the total length of the walls fortified with 23 towers is 3.5 km (2 miles). Each tower was built by the inhabitants of the nearby villages and was named accordingly. There were six entrances to the fortress, also bearing the names of the nearby villages (Magaroisky, Bodbisky, etc.).

The fortress has a double wall. The thickness of the lower one is 1.5 m (5 ft) and of the upper one 70–80 cm (2–2.5 ft). The space between the walls formed a corridor for the defending soldiers. To climb this corridor there were flights of stone staircases on the sides of the towers. The fortress is of limestone, and brick was also used in small quantities. Inside the fortress stood *St. Stephan's Church*.

Armenian Church, 1-Chelyuskintsev Pereulok

Armenian Church, inside the monastery walls; under restoration

Fortress, built by Erekle II in the 17th century as a defence against the Lezghis. It is of triangular form, with turrets, and is in a good state of preservation.

The *Local Museum* was founded in 1951, and attached to it is the *Georgian Applied Art Museum,* founded in 1961.

Irodion Evdoshvili's Home Museum

Varno Saradzhishvili Monument. The great opera singer was born in Signakhi in 1879; the monument was unveiled in 1967.

Lenin Statue, in the square with a war memorial just opposite

World War II Victims Monument, in front of Kiziki Hotel. Unveiled in 1968.

Folk Theatre, in the local Palace of Culture

Mir Hotel

Kiziki Hotel & Restaurant

From Signakhi the road twists down hairpin turns through the trees to the plain below and into *Anaga.* There is a fine view of the mountains across the valley to the right. The road next goes through *Bakurtsikhe, Kolagi and Vedzhini* and rejoins the main Tbilisi-Telavi road just 10 km (6 miles) before Gurdzhaani.

Gurdzhaani Population—10,000

This town is the administrative centre of the best developed vine growing district in Georgia. Among other well known brands of wine, Gurdzhaani, Mukuzani and Akhashini are produced here.

Dormition of the Virgin Church. This is 1.5 km (1 mile) off the main road. Turn up to the left, up Kvela-Tsminda Street. A good road leads to the top, and then a gravel road runs down for 100 m/yds. The church is all that remains of Kvela-Tsminda (All Saints) Monastery. Dating from the 8th–9th centuries, this ancient church has two domes, and low drums with tiny windows in it. It is very similar to the church at Dzveli Shuamta on the other side of Telavi.

Park, up on the hill and linked to the town by a cable car service. Here there is an *open air theatre, sports grounds* and *restaurants.*

Hotel & Restaurant

Service Station

Akhtala Spa, 1.5 km from Gurdzhaani. This is a resort where one can be treated with the local medicinal mud.

Our road goes through Akhasheni, and crosses the Chernis Khevi river.

Mukuzani

The Mukuzani State Farm lies to the left of the road. Mukuzani wine can compete with the finest wines of Burgundy.

The road next goes through Vazisubani, Shashiani and Kalauri.

Shroma
Amidasturi Church, 6th–7th century
  Palaty Palace Building, in ruins
There are a number of *ancient churches* at
Vachnadziani near the village. They were built at
different periods.

(Near Gurdzhaani the Kakhetinskoye Highway
divides with a branch to the right leading through
Tsnori-Lagodekhi and then on to Azerbaijan.) We
cross the Shromis Khevi, pass Akura, cross the
Vantis, pass Vanta, Busheti, and Khodasheni.

Tsinandali
145 km (90 miles) from Tbilisi and on the bank of
the river Kasiskhevi.

In the 19th century the estate belonged to the
Georgian poet and statesman, Prince Alexander
Chavchavadze (1784–1846), a son of the first Geor-
gian Ambassador to St. Petersburg. His daughter,
Nina, married the Russian playwright, Alexander
Griboyedov (1795–1829).

In its time, Tsinandali was a cultural centre
visited by many outstanding Russian and Georgian
literary figures, including Pushkin, Lermontov,
Odoyevsky and the Decembrist Bestuzhev brothers.

In July 1854 it was devastated by the Lezghis
who swept down upon Kakhetia from Daghestan.
A Muslim sect known as the Murids had originated
in Bukhara in 1823, and now, led by the Imam
Shamyl, it was the Murids whose aim it was to
drive the Christian Russians out of the Caucasus.
They captured three beautiful princesses, of the
Chavchavadze and Orbeliani families. Princess
Chavchavadze was carrying her tiny baby and refused to let it go. Her captor gripped her by her
right hand but she held the baby in her left until
she had no more strength and the infant fell to the
ground to be trampled to death by the horses. The
captives were held at Veden for nine months, until
the Imam Shamyl freed them in exchange for the
life of his son who was serving as an officer with
the Vladimir Lancers. The Murids were defeated
in the end, and by 1856 the sect had ceased to
exist.

Tsinandali is famous for its vineyards, and wine
has been produced here for hundreds of years. The
most famous brands now are perhaps Tsinandali
and Teliani. The latter, which is made from the
juice of Cabernet grapes, is considered one of the
best of its type in the Soviet Union.
Saparisi Church, 10th–11th century.
  Chavchavadze Museum. Prince Alexander
Chavchavadze (1786–1846) made this house his
home, and it is now open as a museum. Open 10–
6; closed Mon. The entrance is at the right side of
the house. The entrance to the park is through a
pair of wrought-iron gates, and the park, which
covers an area of 11 hectares (27 acres), has a dis-
tinctly English look about it. It is planted with a
wide variety of trees including pines, cedars and
limes, as well as cypress, ginko, magnolia, box, yew,
laurel, palm, catalpa and a bamboo grove. The
outbuildings and the stables beyond the park now

serve as wine cellars where Tsinandali wine is produced and kept.
  Church ruins, on the river bank. Nina Chavchavadze and Alexander Griboyedov were married
in 1822 in the Sioni Cathedral in Tbilisi, but they
attended services together here, too.

We cross the Dolauris Khevis, and pass a tower
on the left and then go through Nasamkhrali.
There is a *filling and service station* on the right
on the way into Telavi.

Telavi Population—25,000
Situated 568 m (1,864 ft) above sea level and 155
km (96 miles) from Tbilisi, Telavi is a hillside town
built on a slope and spreading into the flat valley
below. It follows the undulations of the slope, so
Batonis-tsikhe Fortress juts out, then there is a
creek, then on a prominence stands the *main
church*, then another creek and then, up behind
the Armenian church, stands the *citadel (Dzveli
Galovani)* with the remains of a church inside the
walls.

High up above, on another rocky prominence
is a scroll-shaped *World War II memorial* with an
eternal flame, *Shashlik Restaurant No. 3*, and a
fine view across the valley of the Alazani to the
mountains, snowcapped in autumn.

Telavi was once the residence of the local rulers. Now it is the administrative and cultural centre
of Kakhetia, and has a horticultural and viticultural
experimental station as well as a pedagogical institute. Its industry is mainly concerned with the production of consumer goods, bricks, other building
materials and food.

According to the "Vakhushta Geography," Telavi was founded here on the foothills of Mt. Tsivi
in the upper reaches of the Alazani in the 9th
century by Kirik I of Kakhetia. The first mention
made in the Georgian chronicles, however, dates
from the 13th century. King Archil of Kakhetia
made it his residence in 1664, and it was here in
1798 that King Erekle II of Georgia, familiarly
known as "the little Kakhetian," died.
  Batonis-tsikhe Fortress, in the centre of the
town. Now in ruins, there still remain parts of the
round towers and high walls which were built in
the 17th–18th centuries. At that time the fortress
served as a royal residence both for the Kakhetian
and the Georgian kings, notably Erekle II who was
born here in 1720 and died here in 1798.

Within the walls stands the royal palace,
undergoing restoration, and two churches, the
larger of which was built in 1758 and now serves
as a museum. The tiny, old *basilica of St. Ketevan*
was built at the same time as the fortress. From the
lower corner of the walls there is a fine view across
the valley to the left where Alaverdi is visible, a
large white church.
  Gorichvari (Cross-on-the-Mountain) Fortress,
Chavchavadze Street 10; go along 1st-May Street,
beyond the red-brick Armenian church, with old,
balconied houses lining the road. There is now a
sewing factory inside the fortress, up on the right,

and previously there was a tourist centre. *Tsveli-Golovani Church* inside the walls has a decorative belfry. It used to be the Church of Our Lady, 16th–17th century.

Many Telavi walls are built of round stones and boulders, worn smooth by the waters of the river valley. These are set in rows, sometimes slanting, herringbone fashion.

Dzveli Galavani Citadel, dating from 8th–11th centuries, commands a wide view over the surrounding area. Its name means "old fortress."

Church of Our Lady, Pyervomaiskaya Street 8. This large, 11th-century brick church is now closed.

Transfiguration Church, Tsereteli Street 8, up to the right from the main street, past the fortress. This white church is said to have been built in the 5th or 6th century, and is open for services.

Ethnographical & Historical Museum, in a wing of the palace

Art Gallery, inside the fortress, down the hill towards the main gate, and on the left

Erekle II Statue, in front of the hotel. An equestrian statue.

Ilya Chavchavadze's Bust, by the fortress, on the way up from the street

Lenin Monument, Svoboda Square

Victory Monument, in Pobeda Park. Unveiled in 1970.

War Memorial, on the hilltop overlooking Telavi. In the form of a scroll with the figures of three men.

Vazha Pshavela Theatre, Svoboda Square. The theatre was opened in 1981 and it encloses the building of a little, old church.

Kakhetia Hotel & Restaurant, Nadikvari Street 13, near the fortress; tel. 3406. The local Intourist office is here; tel. 31–610.

Telavi Restaurant, Rustaveli Prospect 2

Shashlik Restaurant No. 3, on the top of the hill, by the war memorial

GPO, Lenin Street

Bank, Rustaveli Street

Filling & Service Station, on the right on the way into Telavi

From Telavi, Intourist organises trips to Tsinandali (see above), Ikalto, Dzveli Shuamta, Alaverdi, Gremi and Kvareli.

The road onwards passes Vardis Urbani, crosses the Turdos Khevi and goes through Ruispiri where there is an old tower to the right of the road and a white church away in the valley to the right.

Ikalto Monastery, 6 km (4 miles) from Telavi, to the left of the main road and signposted "Ikalto Academy." The side road goes up the valley of the river Ikal to a churchyard planted with box and with a good view across the valley to the mountains which in autumn will already be topped with snow. Here are the ruins of the academy buildings; open-air lectures are given here in the summer.

Founded in the 6th century by St. Zenon, one

of the 13 holy fathers of Syria (see Mtskheta), Ikalto served as a fortress as well as a monastery. Its importance a centre of culture grew and during the 12th century, at the time of David the Builder, the academy was founded here where the poet, Shota Rustaveli, is said to have studied. There were so many churches in the vicinity that the Georgians talked of the "sixty minus one churches of Ikalto." Three have survived which date back to the 6th–9th centuries.

Transfiguration Church, 8th–9th century and the main building of the complex. It contains the tomb of St. Zenon.

Refectory

Academy, now in ruins.

Return to the main road by the same route.

Akhali-Shuamta and **Dzveli-Shamta,** 7 km (4 miles) from Telavi. Turn left at the sign saying "Tbilisi—96 km." Cross the river Shushanas Khevi, pass a spring on the left and then take a left turn up hill where there is a sign saying "Shuamta." We would recommend now leaving Akhali-Shuamta for later, and following the sign "St. Shuamta." Drive on for 3 km (2 miles) up a road which climbs with hairpin bends through beechwoods to the older establishment which stands down a slope to the left.

Dzveli-Shuamta is on a spur of the forested mountains. In fact "shua-mta" means "in the midst of the mountains" while "dzaveli" means "old." Of this ancient settlement there remain a 5th-century *basilica* and two other tiny, domed *churches* dating from the 7th century, all well preserved. They have white tufa at the corners and stone infilling, while the arches are of brick. The church in front of the northern facade of the basilica was originally undecorated inside, but the vault surfaces were painted in the 11th–12th centuries. The third church is a *sepulchral chapel* with a crypt beneath it.

Returning down the same road, there is a fine view over the buildings of *Akhali-Shuamta*, similarly sited and with "akhali" meaning "new." The convent was founded in 1519 and as it grew and prospered, so Dzveli-Shuamta fell into decay. The Akhali-Shuamta complex includes the *Nativity of the Virgin Church*, built with big cross patterns in the brickwork by Queen Tinatin, wife of King Levan II of Kakhetia. The queen died in the convent in 1534 and her tomb is here with a marble plaque to her memory on the left. There are some fragments of frescoes inside the church; one to the right of the entrance shows the queen with her husband and their eldest son, Alexander. Among the other tombs are some belonging to the Chavchavadze family. Other convent buildings include a small, domed chapel, a multi-storeyed belfry and "open-air structures." The local people used to seek refuge within the convent walls during the raids of the Lezghis. The convent was operational until 1932.

Return to the main road and continue through Akmeta, over the Ikaltos Khevi, through Atskuri and Khodasheni where we turn right, and drive 9 km (6 miles) out into the flat river valley, passing Ozhio and Kogoto, to Alaverdi.

Alaverdi, 25 km (16 miles) to the north of Telavi, on a spreading plain called Alvan or Alon in Georgian. The geographer, Vakhusht, says that the name of the place was Alon-gverdi, meaning "Alon-slope" but that later it came to be known as Alaverdi.

The first church on this site, on the banks of the Alazani, was founded by a monk called Iosif and dedicated to St. George, the patron saint of Georgia. Iosif was one of 13 Georgian monks who lived in monasteries in Syria, but who suffered from religious persecution in the mid-6th century, and returned home to become the founders of the monastic life in Georgia. They are usually referred to as the Syrian Fathers. Joseph arrived here in 572.

The *cathedral* is one of Kakhetia's most precious monuments. It is 54 m (59 yds) long, 29 m (32 yds) wide and its height of 68 m (223 ft) makes it certainly the tallest cathedral in the whole of Georgia. It is almost completely bare of decoration, as are all the churches of Kakhetia, and owes its grandeur to its fine proportions and the beauty of the stone which was used in its construction. It was long thought to have been built by Kirik I of Kakhetia (893–918) on the site of the 6th-century Church of St. George, but it is most likely to have been constructed at the beginning of the 11th century by King Bagrat III "in the shape of gigantic cross." Bagrat III in 1008 had been the first to become king of a united Eastern and Western Georgia. The cathedral appears to have had much in common with his church in Kutaisi and with Sveti-Tskhoveli in Mskheta. It was badly damaged in the second half of the 15th century, but rebuilt of brick between 1476 and 1495 by Queen Nestan-Darejan, King Alexander and Queen Anna. In the 16th century it became a metropolitan see, and subsequently the religious centre of Kakhetia. It was again ruined in 1615, this time by the soldiers of Shah Abbas I of Persia (1587–1629). During an earthquake in the 17th or 18th century the original stone dome collapsed and the wooden one was constructed in its place.

The present massive, white cathedral was built early in the 18th century, and also dedicated to St. George. In 1742 it suffered another severe earthquake. The wife of King Teimuraz II was responsible for the restoration work after the earthquake, and it was then that the facades were coated with mortar and whitewashed. The task was completed by her son, Erekle II (1744–98). It was rededicated to the Holy Cross and stands still, surrounded by its great fortified walls. Inside, the marble tomb on the left belongs to St. Iosif who died in 597. Others are of some of the bishops of Alaverdi and of Queen Ketevani of Kakhetia who was tortured to death in 1624 by Shah Abbas of Persia because of her faith, and later canonised. Also here is a *parchment copy of the gospels*, made in the 11th century. There are still *frescoes* on the walls, in spite of the earth-

quakes. Those in the southern part of the cathedral were painted at the beginning of the 16th century, while those in the northern and western parts date from the 16th–17th centuries. The porch, built onto the western side of the cathedral, dates from the middle of the 18th century.

There were a number of buildings on the cathedral territory. Among those remaining are, to the west of the cathedral, the *refectory*, the *reception rooms* and the *residence of the bishop*, built in the 16th–17th centuries. The lower part of the *belfry* by the refectory was built in the 16th–17th centuries, and the upper part in the 19th century. In the northern part of the cathedral territory are wine cellars, and to the northwest of the cathedral are the *ruins* of what is usually called Shah Abbas's palace, but which may have been a mosque. By the western wall are the ruins of the monastery bath house.

To reach Gremi and Kvareli from Telavi, go down into the valley and cross the river Alazani, taking the road towards the Azerbaijani border. The mountains opposite will be snow-covered from late November onwards, but as they face south it all melts in the summer.

Gremi Population—2,000

This is the old capital of Kakhetia and lies 16 km (10 miles) from Telavi on the main road which runs to the northeast, towards the border with Azerbaijan. It overlooks the river Intsoba (or Gremistskhali).

The *fortress* stands on a hilltop to the left of the main road. Excavations have revealed 4th-century tiles and 10th-century water pipes, and a small 11th-century church stood here. Gremi was proclaimed the capital in 1466, and so remained for nearly a century. During the reign of King Levan II of Kakhetia (1520–74), when the Georgian kingdom had disintegrated and the separate parts were struggling for existence against the armies of Persia and the Ottoman Turks, this royal fortress protected the surrounding districts and was the centre of local resistance. New building was undertaken, including the construction of a tall belfry which also served as a watchtower.

The place was long known as the Hill of the Archangels Michael and Gabriel. It was so called after the *Cathedral of the Archangels Michael and Gabriel (Mtavar Angelozi)*, brick built in 1565, following the lines of the church at Akhali-Shuamta near Telavi (see above) which had been completed in 1550 and where King Levan's queen, Tinatin, was buried. Inside the cathedral over the western entrance it is written that it was built in 1565 by King Levan. He was himself buried here, and following tradition, his portrait is on the wall to the right of the entrance; he holds a model of the church in his hand. Other frescoes decorating the interior walls are of the Archangels. They were painted by Georgian and Greek artists and were completed in 1577.

Also inside the fortress is the *King's Palace*, older than the cathedral, and the domed *Uspen-*

skaya (Assumption) Church with its strategically tall belfry. In 1615 the fortress was all but destroyed by Shah Abbas, and although the castle churches are almost intact there is little left of the living quarters. There are just the foundations of residential houses and of bath houses. The foremost buttress of the fortress contains a secret spiral staircase leading right down to the town and to river level. Built onto the southeastern wall of the fortress is a wine-cellar with a stone vat and wine jars embedded in the ground just outside the cellar. The fortress serves as a *museum* containing archeological finds, and is open daily 9–6.

Matarsi Chapel (Tarsa-Galavani) stands to the left, in the western part of the territory. Over the western door it is written in Georgian, Armenian and Persian that the church was built in 1595 by Matarsi, King Alexander's scribe.

There are other towers in the vicinity. The red-brick ruins up on the hill behind the fortress belonged to the 13th-century *Trinity Church.*

Church of Our Lady, by the bridge, on the left of the road from the fortress into Gremi.

In Gremi itself are the remains of a *covered market* and a *caravanserai.*

The villagers are now mostly occupied with viticulture and wine-making.

Snack Bar, below the castle

After leaving Gremi the road crosses River Intsoba and goes through **Eniseli** where there are the *remains* of *Mepis-Gakhti Palace.* It then crosses the Chelti. **Nekressi** is 3 km (2 miles) left of the main road, towards the mountains, and 1 km walk uphill. Nekressi dates back to the beginning of Christianity in the 4th century when the smallest of the three surviving churches was built. The *Nekressi monastery* was founded 200 years later by one of the Syrian fathers named Aviv. Besides the churches, there are also the *ruins* of an episcopal palace, and the fortifications which were built in the 16th–17th centuries and must have served as a fine lookout point over the Alazani valley.

Kvareli

Here are the headquarters of a vine-growing state farm, as well as an experimental tobacco-growing station. The wine manufacturing plant has caused the town to become known for the production of the rich, red Kinzmarauli wine. Brandy is also produced here, and essential oils.

Turn left to reach the town centre, along an avenue with vines growing down the middle. Chavchavadze Street is the main thoroughfare, and Mardzhanishvili Street runs parallel to it.

Galavani Fortress, 18th century

White Church, to the left of Chavchavadze Street, down Rustaveli Street. This was the Chavchavadze family church and was built in the 19th century.

Chavchavadze Museum, Chavchavadze Street. Ilya Chavchavadze, an outstanding 19th-century Georgian writer and public figure, was born here. The new building is of an eye-catching design, but unfortunately the photographic display inside is disappointing.

Chavchavadze Estate. The little tiled house belonged to the poet's parents, and on the terrace is a statue of Chavchavadze with Stalin as a school-boy, when he brought his own poetry for approval. Chavchavadze said, "You won't be a great poet, but you'll be a statesman." The white house in the centre is the one in which Chavchavadze was born, and where he lived.

Mardzhanishvili's House. This was the home of the theatre producer Konstantin Mardzhanishvili (1872–1933).

Watermill, by the road

Wine cellars, to the left, in a rock-hewn tunnel up in the hillside.

Lenin Statue, in the square

Stadium, behind the wall and gateway remaining from a fortress.

Kvareli Restaurant, Chavchavadze Street

Cafe, Chavchavadze Street 140

Filling station, on the right on the way out of town.

In the vicinity are a number of old churches, including the 6th-century *Dube* and the *Sameba Church* (10th–11th centuries).

TERNOPOL Population—205,000

Ternopol is a regional centre of the Western Ukraine. It stands on the river Seret and people have been known to live here since the 10th century. At the time of the Tatar invasions of the 13th and 14th centuries the village was entirely devastated and the ruins were soon hidden by a thick growth of blackthorn. "Ternovoye Polye" means "field of blackthorn" and this is the origin of the name of the town.

The Polish baron, Jan Tarnawski, was ordered by his king, Sigizmund, to build a fortress by the river. In 1540 a strong castle was accordingly constructed with walls 4.5 m thick and with formidably deep moats and dungeons. Part of the castle remains to this day. It is on Svobody Square, near the Ternopol Hotel, but it is now known as the Palace of Sports.

During the 16th, 17th and 18th centuries Ternopol remained an undistinguished town of merchants and craftsmen which failed to reach any great degree of prosperity. In 1772 it was incorporated, together with the surrounding region, into Austria, but by the end of the 18th century it was in Russian hands again. Growing unemployment and poverty led many people to emigrate; between 1900 and 1914 thousands left the area, many of them to North America.

After the Russian revolution and the years of civil war Ternopol returned to Poland and so remained until 1939 when it was incorporated into the Soviet Ukraine.

The Germans occupied the town in 1941, at the outbreak of war with the Soviet Union, and held it until 1944. During this period about 23,000 of the inhabitants were shot and a further 42,000 deported to Germany. When the Soviet army regained the area in 1944, they had to fight for the town literally building by building. The fighting went on for forty days and little of old Ternopol survived. 85 per cent of the town was levelled to the ground and for a number of years the townspeople that remained dug themselves into the ground for shelter while branches of the local administration had its headquarters in neighbouring towns.

Present-day Ternopol was rebuilt according to the original town plan. Noteworthy among the new buildings are the Ternopol Hotel, the post office, the Music and Drama Theatre and the Regional Council Building. Of old Ternopol there remains the castle, some Roman Catholic churches, and several small residential houses on Karl Marx Boulevard which have been carefully restored and are now used as town offices. On Lenin Street there are a number of pleasant 2-storey houses which date from the end of the last century.

Ternopol has electrical equipment factory, a machine-building plant, a polytechnical school, a medical institute with 2,300 students and pedagogical and financial institutes.

16th century castle, Suvorov Street, near Ternopol Hotel.

Rozhdestva (Nativity) Church, built in 1602, this is the town's oldest church and is open for services. In 1653 a meeting of townspeople held here decided against union with Turkey.

SS. Peter and Paul Dominican Church, near the monastery. This was built in 1749 in late Baroque style. It was reconstructed in 1959 to house the local museum.

Nadstavnaya Church, the church above the lake

Local Museum, Bugaichenko Street 3. Open 11–7; closed Mon. & Wed.

Art Gallery, Svobody Square 3. Open 11–6; closed Wed.

Music and Drama Theatre, Karl Marx Street 6

Philharmonic Concert Hall, Ostrovsky Street 9. The Ukrainian poet and writer, Ivan Franko, read his works there in 1911.

Pushkin Monument, Teatralnaya Square

Taras Shevchenko Monument, Shevchenko Park. The famous Ukrainian author and artist visited Ternopol in 1846.

Lenin Monument, Svobody Square; unveiled in 1967

Karl Marx bust, Karl Marx Square

World War II Memorial, Lenin Street. The obelisk is 20 m high.

Tank Monument, Peremogi (victory) Square; erected in 1969 on the 25th anniversary of the liberation of Ternopol from the Germans.

The Tomb of the Unknown Soldier, Slavy (glory) Park, which was formerly called the Old Garden. The tomb and the eternal flame also date from 1969, marking the 25th anniversary of the town's liberation.

Fighter plane monument, eastern residential district

Ukraina Hotel, Karl Marx Street 27; tel 246–47

Ternopol (Intourist) Hotel & Restaurant, Suvorov Street 12; tel. 22–537; Intourist office—tel. 28–066

Khutor (village) Restaurant, Shevchenko Park. Ukrainian cuisine.

Bank, Shevchenko Street 6

GPO, Krasnoarmeiskaya Street 3

Kashtan foreign currency shop, Suvorov Street 8

Beryozka Gift Shop, Lenin Street 32

Kobzar Bookshop, Karl Marx Street 37

Market, Myaskovsky Street 4

Komsomolskoye Ozero (lake) is also known as the Ternopol Sea. It covers 400 hectares (1,000 acres) just outside the town. Intourist organises *motorboat trips* here.

TIRASPOL Population—185,000

(Intourist organises *excursions* here from Kishinyov.)

On the river Dniester which has every right to be called an ancient river. It was mentioned by the Greek historian Herodotus (484–420 B.C.) when the Greeks named the Dniester Tiras after their mythical hero Tiresias. With "polis" meaning "city" in Greek, this explains how Tiraspol got its name of "the city on the Dniester."

Before 1791, when the Ochakov area was united with Russia, there was a Moldavian fishing village here called Sukleya. In 1792 Generalissimo Alexander Suvorov (1730–1800) founded a fortress here, opposite the Turkish fortress of Bendery, to guard the frontier of the Russian Empire. It also served as a trade centre on the way to Odessa from Kishinyov, but had no more industry than local craftsmanship, a vodka distillery, a tobacco factory and three steampowered timber plants. Some of the small houses built then by merchants remain today. Between 1929 and 1940, where Kishinyov and other parts of Moldavia belonged to Rumania, Tiraspol was the capital of the country. Now it is Moldavia's second town, both in size and importance.

The main thoroughfare is 25-October Street which leads down to the newly built Constitution Square. Many of the streets are lined with cherry trees, covered with blossoms in the spring and heavy with ripe cherries late in June. The Shevchenko Teachers' Training College was the first higher educational establishment to be opened in Moldavia. Of greatest industrial importance is the Kirov foundry's machine building plant. Other local products include generators, transformers, motors for washing machines, automatic control stations for underwater pumps, mining equipment, packing cases, glass jars, furniture and clothing. The local wine factory and distillery produces more than 30 different wines and 8 kinds of brandy.

Srednyaya (middle) Fortress, outside the town. Built in 1792, the fortress was so called because it stood in the middle of a line of three other fortifications which Generalissimo Alexander Suvorov helped to design. Now only the ruins remain.

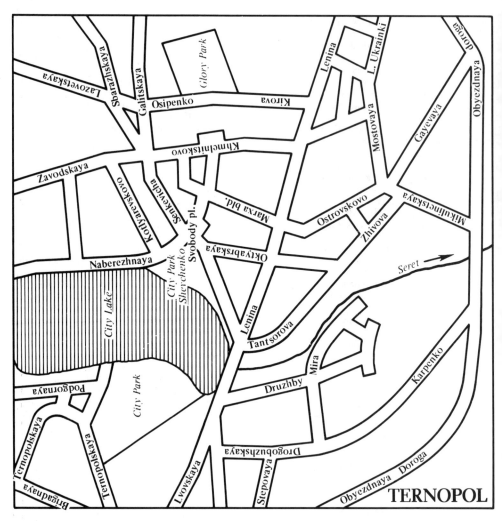

TERNOPOL

Local Museum, 25-October Street 44. Open 11–7; closed Wed.

Pokrova (Intercession of the Virgin) Church, Lunacharskovo Street 29. This belongs to the Old Believers and is open for services.

Kotovsky Regimental Museum, Kommunisticheskaya Street 34. The headquarters of Kotovsky's regiments was organised here on 12 February, 1920, after the liberation of Tiraspol from the White Guard during the Civil War. The regiment, numbering about 600, took prisoner 6 generals, 1,100 officers and 10,000 enlisted men as well as capturing various arms.

Picture Gallery, Pravda Street 4; tel. 2-11-06. Open 11–7; closed Wed.

Suvorov Equestrian Statue, Constitution Square, on the left of the main road. The Pioneer Palace is also on this square.

Shevchenko Monument, 25-October Street

Lenin Bust, Soviet Constitution Square, in front of the House of Soviets

Kotovsky Monument, Pobeda Park

War Memorial, Pravda Street, dedicated to the heroes of World War II

Victory Obelisk, at the end of the 25-October Street, erected in 1969 in gratitude to the liberators who freed Tiraspol in 1944.

Tank Monument, on the banks of the Dniester. This tank fought its way from the Volga to Budapest where it suffered damage. It was later delivered to Tiraspol and set up as a monument to the memory of 15 officers of a World War II tank regiment. There is another *tank monument* on 25-October Street which is decorated with the scarves of Young Pioneers.

Fighter Plane Monument, to the right of the road on the way out of town

Gagarin Bust, in a square on 25-October Street

Paleontological Monument, Kalkatova Balka. Animal bones were found here.

Russian Drama Theatre, 25-October Street 130; tel. 3-22-48

SOCHI–The seafront showing the spire of the port building.

TELAVI–Deep in Kakhetia, with the snow-capped Caucasus Mountains in the background, stands the ancient stronghold of Gremi. The Cathedral of the Archangels and Uspenskaya Church still stand among the ruined walls.

SAMARKAND–Inside Ulug-Beg's observatory. Although this large sextant was built in 1428, its site was unknown until it was discovered by archaeologists in 1909.

TBILSI–A panoramic view of the Georgian capital. In the background is the funicular railway running up to the park and television tower on the top of Mount David.

TBLISI–Monument to the Georgian poet, Nikoloz Baratashvili (1817–45). The sculptor was Boris Tsibadz.

SUKHUMI–A popular Black Sea resort.

TALLINN–An amateur Estonian folk instrument orchestra; musicians in national dress, as well as singers and dancers, come to Tallinn from all over the republic to take part in traditional musical festivals.

TALLINN–The Old Town in the centre of the Estonian capital. The tall, green spire on the left belongs to St. Olai's, the smaller one to the Church of the Holy Spirit and the spire to the right, to the Town Hall.

VOLGOGRAD–A city rebuilt and renamed since the devastation of the Battle of Stalingrad.

UZHGOROD–Looking down from the castle onto the collection of wooden buildings which make up the Fold Architecture Museum. These roofs belong to the Church of the Archangel Michael, built in 1777 and brought here from the village of Shelestovo.

ZAGORSK–The Church of the Holy Spirit, the top of which used to serve as the monastery-fortress's watch-tower.

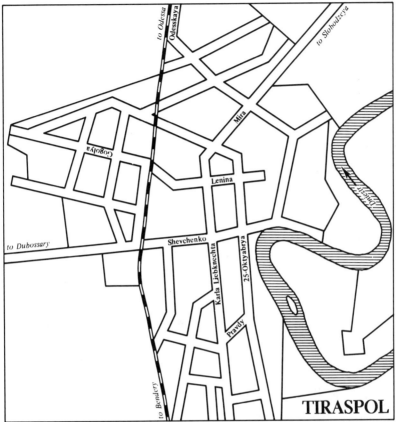

TIRASPOL

Kirov Park
Pobeda Park, Mir Street
Town Bathing Beach & Boat Hire Station
Druzhba (friendship) Hotel and Restaurant,
25-October Street 118, opposite the House of Soviets; tel. 3-42-66
Aist (stork) Hotel, Naberezhny Pereulok 3
Dniester Restaurant, Shevchenko Street 14.
Closed 4–5 p.m.
Souvenir Shop, 25-October Street. Open 8–6;
tel. 3-60-14
Shashlik Bar, on the embankment
Borodino Cafe, 25-October Street
Souvenirs, 25-October Street 104, 87 and 74
Moldova Souvenir Shop, Sverdlov Street 45
GPO, 25-October Street
Service Station, Odessa Road; tel. 49-18
Filling Station, Energetikov Street 14 (round the clock service), and on the left of the road out of town.

TOGLIATTI Population—630,000 (till 1964 Stavropol-on-Volga)
(Visited by tourists on Volga river cruises.)

Togliatti stands beside the Volga in the region of the Zhiguli Mountains. The average temperature in winter is −10°C (14°F) and in summer, +20°C (68°F).

Before Stavropol was founded, the surrounding lands served as a buffer, defending Russia from the invasions of nomads. There were many attempts at subjugating the Volga steppe tribes before they bowed to Russian rule. Some of the Kalmyks adopted Christianity and were encouraged to make their homes in the vast territory of the Volga steppes. One of their leaders named Peter went to St. Petersburg to ask for permission to build a fortress that would serve as a centre for the baptised Kalmyks, and so Stavropol, "the city of the cross," was founded as a fortress in 1737. His wife, the Kalmyk Princess Anna Taishina, lived in the fortress, and many Kalmyks transferred here from the lower reaches of the Volga.

In the second half of the 18th century, Stavropol already had a population of 9,000, and in 1780 it was given its coat-of-arms. During the Pugachev uprising of 1773–75, the Kalmyks fought in Pugachev's army under Derbentov, and Stavropol was taken on January 19–20. After the quelling of the uprising, 37 percent of the Kalmyk population was killed.

As time went by, the fertile lands around the town began to attract the attention of the Tsarist government, and in 1842 a decree was issued concerning the evacuation of the Kalmyks to the Orenburg steppes. Thus it became a Russian town but remained typically provincial, with a diminishing population. At the beginning of the 20th century there were only 6,000 people living there.

In 1948 the population of the town was 12,000, the main industry being small fish and food factories. In 1949 a state geological expedition began working here, exploring the bed of the Volga for the best site for a dam. In due course it was decided to build the Lenin-Volga hydropower station, at that time the largest in the world. But with the erection of the dam Stavropol would have been flooded, so it was decided to resite the town. While life in the old town came gradually to a halt, a new one was under construction some distance upstream. Old buildings were taken apart and moved to the new site; a total of 2,540 houses were brought there. The new place was very beautiful, situated on the banks of the newly formed Kuibyshev reservoir and surrounded by dense forests. The power station was commissioned in 1958, powered by the Zhiguli Reservoir. The Kuibyshev hydro power station was commissioned in the same year.

The town became a large river port, while the railroad connected it with Kuibyshev and other cities. In 1964 Stavropol was given the name of Togliatti, in honour of the late Italian communist leader.

The city's third birth grew rapidly after the construction of the Volga car plant—one of the largest in the country. Now other vehicles are produced there too, the most popular Soviet passenger cars, the Zhiguli (known in the West as the Lada) and the Niva. The Zhiguli was designed as the adaptation of a Fiat, and many Italians came to help create the modern plant. The Zhiguli Motor Works has 408 conveyer belts with an overall length of 315 km (196 miles). A new car leaves the Works every 22 seconds. The Works is situated in a district of its own and next to it is a car-testing track. The settlements are linked by a dual carriageway.

New houses of a better design sprang up in new regions, but there are still some old ones behind the new buildings that line Lenin Street. Togliatti is a city of experimental planning where, along with multi-storey buildings, architects resort to small houses and tree-planting, separating the residential part of the city from the industrial enterprises. It is still in a state of growth with new enterprises under construction, and it is a city of young people, the average age being only 28. It is also a city of mixed nationalities as representatives of 82 peoples of the Soviet Union have made it their home. The planning has created many parks and public gardens; in one of them, in the centre of the city on Svobody Square, stands a World War II memorial.

A bridge connects the town with Zhigulyovsk, a town on the right bank of the Volga that grew up after the construction of the hydropower station was completed. There is a small local oilfield.

Local Museum, Lenin Boulevard. Open 11–6; closed Mon. In the museum there is a photograph showing Stavropol in 1951, and another picture taken from the same point in 1955 after the flooding, showing a bell tower sticking up through the water. The bell tower was later destroyed.

Lenin Monument, Gagarin Street, at the end of Lenin Street

World War II Memorial, Svobody Square. Unveiled in 1958.

House of Culture, on Svobody Square, near the hotel

Volga Hotel and Restaurant, Gagarin Street 14; tel. 2660-381

Zhiguli Hotel and Restaurant, tel. 2660-246

Intourist Office, Zhilina Street 24; tel. 22-2097

GPO, Nira Street 67

Beryozka Foreign Currency Shop, Leningradskaya Street 23

Department Store, Karl Marx Street

Book Shop, Lenin Boulevard

TORZHOK Population—55,000

(Intourist organises excursions here from Kalinin)

This very picturesque old Russian town lying on either side of the river Tvertsa is in fact by-passed by the main road, but the turning to it is signposted.

Torzhok was built at the crossing of the river and road routes leading into Russia from the west and long retained its strategic importance. The place was first mentioned in 1015, and by 1139 it was a valued colony of Novgorod. It served as a trade centre between Novgorod and Suzdal, and its name actually comes from the word "torg" meaning "trade." In 1238 it held out against the attacks of the Tatars, and some historians think that it was this resistance that saved Novgorod.

A local legend tells how in 1405 the last Prince of Smolensk, Yuri, while exiled in Torzhok, fell in love with Juliana, wife of Prince Simeon of Vyazma. When he found that his love was unrequited, he killed the unfortunate husband but was himself wounded by the Russian Lucretia, who then fled. Prince Yuri pursued her, put her to the sword and had her body thrown into the Tvertsa. Too late, he repented of his evil deeds and spent the rest of his days doing penance in a hermitage in Ryazan.

Torzhok grew to cover 26 small hills and during its history changed hands continually between Novgorod and Suzdal, sometimes even being divided between them. It suffered in turn from attacks by the Lithuanians, the Tatars and the Poles and was completely devastated by the latter in 1607.

After the subsequent rebuilding, Eric Palmqvist attempted to draw up one of the first plans of the town. He was a military engineer, accredited in 1673 to the Swedish Embassy for the purpose of collecting information about Russian fortresses. However, as a foreigner he was not allowed to go inside and was only able to depict the eleven towers in the surrounding wall from the outside. In 1742 there was such a terrible fire that even the ancient walls collapsed. From this time the wooden houses and churches began to be replaced by stone buildings. The impressive shopping arcades on 9-January Square date from 1764 and there are a number of houses of the same period including that which now serves as the town hall. Torzhok was heavily bombed during World War II.

Since the 18th century the town has been known for its lace and for its gold and silver embroidery on velvet and morocco leather. The finely decorated slippers and boots were especially popular and are commemorated in an old Russian song:

"Bring me from Torzhok a treat
Two soft boots for my two feet!"

Today the work is carried on at the 8-March Factory which runs its own training school. Among other items of production they specialise in dress uniforms for the services.

Alexey von Jawlensky (1864–1941) was born in Torzhok. He joined the Russian Imperial Guard, but in 1889 he chose instead to study painting under Repin. Seven years later he moved to Munich and thereafter worked in association with Kandinsky, Matisse and Paul Klee until in 1929 he became crippled with arthritis.

Torzhok is now an industrial centre. It has machine-building, timber-processing, footwear and garment industries. It is the site of the world's only flax research institute and of the Soviet Union's largest printer's ink factory.

Borisoglebsky Monastery is one of the oldest in Russia. It stands near the old town but is separated from it by a ravine. It was founded in 1038 by Boyar Efrem, who was in charge of the stables of Prince Vladimir of Kiev, in memory of the prince's sons, Boris and Gleb, who were treacherously murdered by their adopted brother, Prince Svyatopolk, nicknamed the Cursed.

Vvedenskaya Church (Presentation of the Virgin) is the oldest building within the monastery walls. It was erected in 1620 and shows nice architectural restraint. Borisoglebsky Cathedral was founded on the site of an earlier cathedral in 1785. The foundation ceremony was a great occasion as the money for the new cathedral had been donated by Catherine II, and she was there in person with her court. Nikolai Lvov was the architect and the icons were painted by Borovikovsky. The work took 11 years and the cathedral was consecrated in 1796. The classical-style *belfry* and *gate-church* are also ascribed to Lvov, the project having been drawn up by him and put into effect in 1804, after his death, by a local architect called Ananyin.

There were at one time about 30 churches in Torzhok. Many of them were destroyed during the war, and most of the remainder are closed or are being used for various secular purposes.

Underground prisons and some interesting architectural details are preserved among the relics of the town's fortifications.

Voznesenskaya (Ascension) Church, in the old town cemetery high above the river. It was built in 1653 and is the only wooden church to have survived in Torzhok.

Troitskaya (Trinity) Church, Respublikansky Pereulok, on the hill. Services are held in this church which dates from 1562.

Voskresensky (Resurrection) Convent, on the left bank of the river. This was founded at the beginning of the 17th century. Confined within its walls were local landladies who had been unnecessarily cruel to their servants and those who were accused of witchcraft. The two 19th-century *churches* are dedicated to the *Resurrection* and to *St. John the Baptist*. The grave of Anne Kern, subject of one of Pushkin's greatest poems, is by the wall of the church; it has become a place of pilgrimage for admirers of Pushkin's work.

Preobrazhensky (Transfiguration) Cathedral, built in 1822 by Carlo Rossi, is among the largest and most impressive churches in Torzhok. It has five cupolas, and the classical porticos are of the Doric order. It is said that the tomb of Princess Juliana, of the legend related above, is down in the crypt. The cathedral is now used as a bakery. The church and belfry standing next to it date from 1842 and are being rebuilt. *St. Clement's Church* and *belfry* also belong to the 19th century.

St. Michael's Church, Rzhevskaya Street. Open for services.

Local Museum, Lunacharsky Street. The museum is located in what was originally built in 1763 as a small imperial palace, but which was later converted into the Governor's House.

Putevoi Dvorets (coaching palace), Revolutsii (formerly Palace) Square 6a. Built in the 18th century for Catherine II.

Pushkin Monument, in Pushkin Square, sculpted by Rukavishnikov.

Lenin Monument, in Revolutsii Square.

Hotel, Tverskaya Naberezhnaya 26; tel. 52-141. The town was famous for its "Pozharskiye kotlyety," chicken rissoles which were named after the owner of the hotel, Fedukhin-Pozharsky. It is said that a Frenchman once stayed overnight in the Torzhok hotel. When the time came for him to pay, it transpired that he had no money at all, so he paid for his bread and board with a recipe then unknown in Russia. From that time Pozharskiye kotlyety have been a speciality of Torzhok. It is known that the poet Pushkin enjoyed them when he stayed here or he would never have written the lines we translate:

"Pozharsky of Torzhok
Will dine you quite the best;
Sample his fried rissoles
And go your way refreshed."

TSELINOGRAD Population—277,000 (till 1961 Akmolinsk)

Tselinograd is the regional centre of the Tselinogradskaya region of Kazakhskaya SSR which was founded in 1824 as the stronghold of Ak-Mola (White Graves) on the right bank of the River Ishim, a tributary of the Irtysh. It is 1320 km (820 miles) from the Kazakh capital of Alma-Ata in the north of the Republic. It is situated 347 m (1,138 ft) above sea level and has a climate of an extreme continental type.

The fortress proper was founded on July 1, 1830, by Lt. Col. Fyodor Shubin.

Tselinograd was a Russian defence fortification on the route from Central Asia to Siberia. Craftsmen and retired soldiers were the first settlers. In 1838 the place was burned down by the local sultan, Kenesari Qasim-uli, and to strengthen the settlement in 1845 Tsar Nicholas I ordered that hundreds of Cossack families be transferred here from western parts of the country. In 1862 the fort and settlement acquired town status and was renamed Akmolinsk. The town's coat-of-arms depicts a fortress in the centre of a wreath entwined with laurels. In 1868 it became the centre of the Steppe Region. Thanks to its favourable geographical position, the town grew into an important trade centre, and regular spring fairs were held there. Russian rural colonisation of the Kazakh plain began in 1890–92, spurred on by the bad harvest and famine in central Russia. By the turn of this century Russian settlers made up 40 per cent of the population.

Russian and Ukrainian settlers moved in the thousands until 1916. The town looked more like a large village, with almost no trees and it was built up with small wooden or mud houses. There were two large churches and two mosques in the town. During the Civil War the town's industry was ruined and its population considerably decreased. In 1929 the first railroad connected Akmolinsk with Karaganda and other major Kazakh centres, and in 10 years time with Siberia.

During World War II many industrial enterprises were evacuated to Tselinograd and served as a basis for the town's future industrial growth. When in 1954 the campaign for the development of the virgin lands began, Akmolinsk became the centre of the enormous Tselinny Territory, and on March 20, 1961, it was renamed Tselinograd, meaning "town of the virgin lands." It was then that people came from Moscow and Leningrad to help with the construction work.

The town is now a railway junction, and its industry is engaged in processing local raw materials and servicing agricultural machines. It has also developed food industry and the manufacturing of gas equipment. There are four agricultural establishments in the town, including an agricultural institute and a teacher's training college.

The town follows a rectangular plan and consists of several parts; the old town with the remains of the *fortress*, the *Cossack village*, the *Tatar settlement* and the *market* area. The main streets are Mira and Pobedy Prospects. The No. 4 Polyclinic is housed in one of the old mansions, and the Raduga shop is in a former commercial centre. Among the new buildings is a fine registry office. In the southwestern part of town there are good beaches on both sides of the Ishim.

Mosque, near the market

SS. Konstantin & Helena Church, Budyonny Street 12

German Church, Kuibysheva Street 101

Catholic Church, Akulsky Pereulok 2-2a

Baptist Church, Leningradsky Prospect 2

Local Museum, Oktyabrskaya Street 57. Open 11–6, closed Mon. The two-storey house used to belong to the merchant Kubrin.

Civil War Memorial, in the central square. Founded on May 1, 1920, when the body of a partisan was buried here and a wooden memorial was put up. Other warriors were buried here in 1921. The present memorial by Kolotilina was built in 1972. There is an Eternal Flame here.

Lenin Monument, Lenin Square. By Novikov and Bildyushkin, and unveiled in 1975.

Seifullin Monument, Saken Seifullin (1894–1939) was a poet and statesman. The monument was built by Yuri Bushtruk.

First Virgin Land Farmers Monument, at the beginning of Tselinnikov Prospect. The statue is of farmers with a tractor.

Youth Palace, Tselinnikov Prospect 40

Tselinnikov Palace, Mira Street 1

Russian Drama Theatre, Komsomolskaya Street

Hippodrome Racecourse, Student Prospect

Ishim Hotel (Intourist) and Restaurant, Mira Street 8; tel. 27-686

Moskva Hotel and Restaurant, Mira Street 10; tel. 23-672

Tourist Hotel and Restaurant, Tselinnikov Prospect

Zolotaya Niva Restaurant, Tselinnikov Prospect

From Tselinograd Intourist organises a variety of agricultural *excursions*, taking in grain-growing, poultry and mixed farming.

TSKHALTUBO

Intourist organises overnight excursions here from Kobuleti in Ajaria on the Black Sea coast.

Tskhaltubo lies 12 km (7 miles) to the northwest of Kutaisi, Georgia's second largest city. The name of this spa means "warm water." The first mention of Tskhaltubo dates back to the 12th century. It is said locally that once upon a time an old shepherd stopped to rest beside an unknown stream. He bathed his feet as he sat there, and enjoyed the surprising warmth of the water. When at last he got up to continue on his way, he was amazed that all the aches and tiredness to which he had long been accustomed had gone from his legs. He returned as quickly as he could to his village to tell his story, and the fame of the water soon spread far and wide. There is also a legend that the brave warriors of Queen Tamar healed their wounds in the curative waters of Tskhaltubo. These may only be legends but the collections of discarded crutches and walking sticks left behind by patients that have been cured at the various sanatoria here are proof of the water's powers.

In the olden days Tskhaltubo was a royal

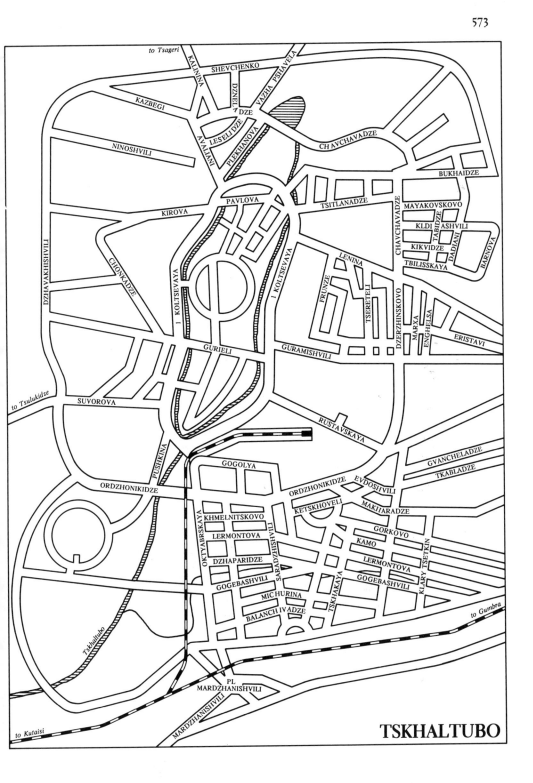

TSKHALTUBO

bathing place and many came to benefit from the water. Some thought that the longer they spent in the water, the quicker their cure, and they settled down for the night, comfortably warm and tied to a low-hanging tree so they would not drown or drift downstream while they slept.

Although the place had been known for centuries, it only became a proper spa in the 1920s. It is only 70 km (42 miles) from the Black Sea coast, and is located in the picturesque valley of the Tskhaltubo River, surrounded by hills and mountains, and protected by them from the wind. The river now flows through two channels which meet again near the railway station and then it flows into the Tubis Tskhali. The river is dammed not far from its source and forms a reservoir of 5 hectares (12.5 acres). Visitors come here all year round, but the best time is October and November, though the winter is mild. The water maintains a steady temperature of 33–35°C (92–96°F) summer and winter because the river is fed by many warm springs which flow straight into it. The chemical content of the water is also constant; it contains radon and nitrogen and is slightly radioactive (from 3 to 30 Mache Units) and is recommended for the cure of rheumatism, metabolic disorders, gynaecological diseases and diseases of the circulatory and nervous systems. Clinical data show the extraordinarily wide range of curative properties of this pearl of Georgian health resorts. There are 15 sanatoria with first-class therapeutic laboratories and balneological institutions, and 9 bath houses. Since 1965 Intourist has organised special courses of treatment lasting 20 days at Tskhaltubo.

Theatre

Park of 800 hectares (2,000 acres) where there are about 100 specimens of subtropical flora.

All parts of the resort including the railway station are linked by the Circular Road; within this are parks with palms and springs. Oktyabrskaya Street leads out from the Circular Road towards Kutaisi, passing tea plantations.

Local Museum, Koltsevaya Street 25; open daily 10–6

Speleology Museum, beneath Mount Sataplia, in a karst cave

Tskhaltubo Motel, Hotel and Restaurant, Pushkin Street 4; tel. 32-47, 93-558. Intourist office: TEL. 93-333

Shakhtyor Sanatorium, 1-Koltsevaya Street 33, tel. 2395

Tskhaltubo Restaurant, Circular Road

Cafes

GPO, Circular Road

Sataplia Department Store, in the centre

Intourist organises *excursions* from Tskhaltubo to Terzhola (35 km/22 miles), to the town of Kutaisi (12 km/7 miles), and from there to Geguti, Rioni Power Station, Sataplia and Motsametra (all about 5 km/3.5 miles from Kutaisi, but in different directions) and also to Ghelati (24 km/15 miles), and with special permission, to Nikortsminda (90 km/56 miles).

Terzhola

The large village of Terzhola lies 35 km (22 miles) from Tskhaltubo.

Navenakhevi Caves. Here there are fine stalagmites and stalactites of the most varied shades and colours.

Kadiashvili's House and Museum. David Kadiashvili (1862–1931) was a satirical writer who also served in Batumi as a colonel in the infantry. He was buried in Tbilisi. There is an asphalt road to the house and the museum is open 10–6.

Intourist also organises visits to the local *wine factory* which specialises in sparkling wines.

There are farms and vineyards by the road and it is a good opportunity to get a glimpse of more natural country life than that on either side of the main road.

Kutaisi Population—235,000

Kutaisi is located on either side of the river Rioni at the place where it leaves its ravine to flow over the Plateau of Colchis. There is an excellent panoramic view from the height of the right bank where the remains of one of the world's most ancient cities can still be seen. Some archeologists are of the opinion that it was not Nakalakheli but Kutaisi that was really the town of Ea or Kitea, residence of the legendary King Aeetes of Colchis (who owned the Golden Fleece and whose daughter was Medea—see Sukhumi). With its great age of more than 3,000 years, it is 5 centuries older than Rome itself and the classical geographers wrote of its importance. To start with, the town was in the colony of Miletus, and then in the 6th century B.C. it became the capital of the ancient empire of Colchis. It stood in the most beautiful and fertile part of the country, on the crossroads of 3 important trade routes—1 from Iveria (the old name of Georgia), 1 from the south and 1 from the Black Sea coast. Later it became the capital of Imeretia and the residence of the king.

At the beginning of the 6th century Imeretia was, for about forty years, the battlefield of the forces of Emperor Justinian and Shah Hozroi of Persia. In the mid-6th century, in the time of the Eastern Roman Empire, its territory was known as Lazica. It was then nominally a dependency of the Greek Emperors, and the fortress was called Ukimirioni. In the first part of the 7th century Lazica was devastated by the Arabs. Leon I deserves credit for building up Kutaisi and its fortress, but the area really only recovered when it was united with the rest of Georgia by Bagrat III (975–1014). Tbilisi at the time remained in enemy hands, and so Kutaisi became the political and administrative centre and the capital of the whole of Georgia. It retained its position until 1122 when Tbilisi was finally recaptured. David the Builder transferred the capital from Kutaisi to Tbilisi and at the same time founded Kutaisi's Ghelati Monastery. Bagrat III, Bagrat IV, David the Builder and the famous Queen Tamar each did much to rebuild the country, and a great deal of their construction remains to be seen. Kutaisi has suffered greatly, but the ruins of towers, churches, bridges and chapels in the Kutaisi region mostly belong to this time.

In 1510 the Turks burned the town and the monastery too, and again they siezed Kutaisi fortress in 1666. Only in 1770 did Russian and Imeretian forces under Solomon I liberate Kutaisi from the Turks who had held it for 102 years. Kutaisi became an important trade centre. In 1804 the last king, Solomon II, signed an act of subservience to Russia; he abdicated in 1810 and Imeretia belonged entirely to Russia and became the seat of the governor. After 1840 trade increased rapidly and industry began to develop. In the middle of the 19th century it was the centre of the revolutionary movement in the southern Caucasus.

Today Kutaisi is Georgia's second largest city and a sizeable industrial centre. There is a big agricultural and mining machine building plant, and factories producing footwear, furniture, leather and canned foods, while numerous lorries on Soviet highways bear the trade mark of the Kutaisi factory. There is the Tsulukidze State Pedagogical Institute here, an agricultural institute and the Balanchivadze Musical School. Kutaisi's beauty and heroic past have inspired generations of Georgian writers, and many outstanding Georgian actors have performed in the State Drama Theatre.

The city and environs possess numerous relics of the past. Part of the ruined walls of *Kutaisi fortress* can be seen on the high right bank of the Rioni. The road up to the top starts from *Tsepnoy (chain) Bridge*. Here, in the old town, is a most impressive and ancient *cathedral* built by Bagrat III in 1003. King Bagrat paid particular attention to its construction, which was intended to symbolise the unification of Georgia, since he himself was the first king of United Georgia. It was built in the shape of a cross, and for 700 years visitors marvelled at its splendour. It was partly ruined in 1691 during the Turkish attack and was damaged again in the war of 1770. Recent restoration work has prevented further dilapidation.

St. George's Church, Asatiani Street. This church, built in 1890, is not far from the cathedral; it is open for services.

At *Mtsvanekvavila*, not far from the fortress but on the left bank of the river, is a well-preserved *17th-century tower* and a number of *churches*, mostly dating from the 17th to 20th centuries. Among them, however, are the remains of a church built in 1013. Since 1956 the *cemetery* here has been reorganised as a burial place (pantheon) for prominent people.

Tsulukidze Garden, on the left bank of the Rioni, was the garden of Alexander III of Imeretia (1674–1710). Palatial buildings stood here, but only one has survived. It is famous for its hall called *Okros Chardakhi* (golden tent), which was built in the 17th century and was completely reconstructed in the 1830s. It was used for receiving ambassadors, holding feasts and other important occasions. In the garden is a great plane tree, its trunk 10.6 m (35 ft) in circumference. According to tradition, the Imeretian kings conducted trials and executed justice beneath its branches.

Also in the garden bearing his name is a *monument* to the revolutionary, Alexander Tsulukidze (1876–1905) by Tvavadze and Merabishvili which was unveiled in 1935.

SS. Peter and Paul Cathedral, Kommunarov Street 26. The cathedral is open for services.

Tavar-Angelogis (Archangel) Church, Tkibuli Street. This was built in the 16th century.

Roman Catholic Church, Tehlmann Street. The building has now been put to secular use, but its very existence points to the fact that the foreign colony here must have been of considerable size.

Synagogues, Shaumyan Street. These are located in the old quarter of the town which has long been inhabited by Jews. The synagogues stand close to each other. They were built about 150 years ago and are in good condition.

Berdzenishvili History & Ethnography Museum, Tbilisi Street 1. Open 10–6; closed Mon. In the museum's rich collection are 10th–13th century icons; some of them are of gold and silver and came from Ghelati Monastery, as did many manuscript books. There are 700 manuscripts dating from the 11th to the 19th centuries, including an 11th-century copy of the gospels. Other items include armour and old musical instruments.

Georgian Art Museum, Rustaveli Prospect 8. Open 10–6; closed Mon. & Tues.

Tsulukidze Museum, Tsulukidze Street 21. Open 10–6; closed Mon. Kutaisi was the birthplace of Alexander Tsulukidze (1876–1905), a Georgian revolutionary. The museum is located in the house that used to be his home. The monument to him that stands in the museum courtyard is by Nikoladze.

Lenin Museum, Lenin Square. The 6.4 m (21 ft) bronze figure by Merabishvili was unveiled in 1958.

1905 Revolution Obelisk, Town Garden. This was unveiled in 1955 to mark the 50th anniversary of the 1905 revolution. It stands on the place where demonstrators clashed with the Cossacks.

Kikvidze Monument, Avtozavodskaya Street. Vasili Kikvidze (1895–1919) was a hero of the Civil War. Unveiled in 1959, the 2.5 m (8 ft) bronze figure is by Mizandari and Nikoladze.

Military Glory Memorial, Avtozavodskaya Street. The complex, with an eternal flame and an arch standing 50 m (164 ft) high, was designed by Berdzenishvili and Kalandarshvili and unveiled in 1981.

Meskhishvili Drama Theatre, Rustaveli Square. The theatre was founded in 1861.

Paliashvili Opera and Ballet Theatre, 1905-Revolution Street 19

Puppet Theatre, 1905-Revolution Street 11
Concert Hall, Pushkin Street 12
Open-air Theatre, in the park
Park, on the banks of the Rioni
Central Stadium, Engels Street
Tbilisi Hotel & Restaurant, Tsulukidze Street, tel. 26-29

Kutaisi Hotel and Restaurant, Rustaveli Street 5, tel. 42-47

Ghelati Restaurant, on the left of the main road, at the 204/46 km mark

Imeretia Restaurant, Rustaveli Street 15

Tskhalitsitela (red river) Cafe, beside the road, on the way out of town

GPO, Kirov Street 64

Bank, Pushkin Street 18

Department Store, Paliashvili Street 18

Podarochny (gifts), Rustaveli Square

Jeweller's, near the market

Market, Paliashvili Pereulok 2. The market is an interesting place as people from the most distant parts of the Caucasus gather here.

Filling Station, Kvitiri Village

Service Station, Gori Street 155

Geguti

To the south of Kutaisi, near Rioni railway station, are the ruins of Geguti Palace, which was built during the reign of Georgi III (1156–84) as a winter and hunting palace. It had 21 rooms. Excavations have been going on here since 1953.

Rioni Power Station

5 km (3 miles) from the town. The Rioni was dammed here in 1934, and the very attractive reservoir is known locally as Kutaisi Sea. The power station has a capacity of 50,000 kilowatts. Two more power stations were completed in 1956 in the nearby village of Gumati, and they have a joint capacity of 66,500 kilowatts.

Sataplia

This lies 6 km (3 1/2 miles) to the southwest of Kutaisi and is accessible by road. The name means "honey-bearing" and refers to the wild bees that nest in the hills there. Sataplia is a reservation of 500 hectares (1,250 acres), famed since 1933 when a local scientist, Peter Chabukiani, found traces of dinosaurs here. There is a huge *karst cave*, about 600 m (650 yds) long, with stalactites and stalagmites; another, with an open arch, is called *Jason's Grotto*. In 1914, some tools belonging to Paleolithic Man were found in the Sakazhia Cave.

Motsametra (martyr) Monastery, 6 km (3 1/2 miles) to the east of Kutaisi, standing upon a cliff above the right bank of the Tskhalitsitela (red river). The road is not very good, but one can get there by train and it is only two stops from Kutaisi.

The story of the monastery's foundation tells how in the middle of the 8th century there were in the royal house of Mkheidze two princely brothers called David and Constantine. They ruled this territory and were famed for their nobility and courage. When they were attacked by the Arabs they and their army defeated the vanguard of the invaders, but later fell before the main force. The Arab emir, surprised by their youth, bravery and uncommon beauty, offered them their freedom and honour if they would accept the Muslim faith.

This they refused to do, and so they were tortured and then, with heavy stones around their necks, they were thrown into the Rioni. The river cast the bodies up upon the shore where they were found by a peasant. He laid the brothers on his bullock cart and then gave the bullocks freedom to wander. The beasts made their way up the hills to where the monastery now stands. The princes were buried there, and in 1040 the monastery itself was founded, while the sacred remains were objects of pilgrimage to the faithful.

Ghelati

24 km (15 miles) from Tskhaltubo. The way from Tskhaltubo to Ghelati, Tkibuli and Nikortsminda:

Take the direct road (12 km/7 miles) into Kutaisi, and from there follow the Ossetian Military Highway 7 km (4 miles) to Ghelati, the nearest point of especial interest. Further on the highway passes through Tkibuli to Nikortsminda, the latter a distance of 90 km (56 miles) from the Intourist hotel in Tskhaltubo. No special permission is needed to visit Ghelati, but foreign tourists should check with Intourist in Tskhaltubo before setting out on the full journey to Nikortsminda.

From Kutaisi the Ossetian Military Highway leads up into the mountains. It was built for transport purposes, linking Kutaisi with Vladikavkaz on the northern side of the Caucasus Mountains. It was completed in 1888 but is today only used by tourists hiking over the pass.

Ghelati Monastery was founded in 1106 on the left bank of the Tskhaltsitela river by King David II of Georgia (1089–1125), often referred to as David the Builder, and the founder of the powerful united state of Georgia. He built the monastery in gratitude for his first victories and he was later canonised by the Georgian Church. From the day of its foundation King David and his successors always cared for the monastery and donated many gifts of gold, silver and rare manuscripts, so much so that at one time it was the richest in the Caucasus. The monastery complex is a good example of Byzantine and Georgian architecture of the Georgian Golden Age, although much has crumbled away owing to the softness of the sandstone blocks used in the construction. Inside the thick walls are three churches, the main one dedicated to the Nativity of the Virgin. It is from this that the monastery itself takes its name, the Georgian word genati having been changed to Ghelati. Other buildings include the bell tower and the refectory which until the 16th century was the Academy hall.

King David was well versed in both Christian and Islamic culture. Besides founding Ghelati, he assisted other Georgian monasteries, both in Georgia and abroad. When the monastery was founded, King David invited scholars from Georgia and other countries to come and join the brotherhood, and he endowed it well. The Academy soon became a centre of learning and art; histories, philosophy and scientific works were written here, and almost all the important literature in the world at that time was translated into Georgian. The outstanding

Gelat. General plan of the monastery built after 1106
1. Academy, 12th century, 13th–14th century;
2. Cathedral consecrated to the Dormition of the Virgin, 12th and 13th–14th centuries;
3. St. George church, 13th and 16th centuries;
4. The two-storey church of St. Nicholas, 13th–14th century. Belfry, second half of the 13th century

Gelat. General plan of the monastery built after 1106
1. Academy, 12th century, 13th–14th century;
2. Cathedral consecrated to the Dormition of the Virgin, 12th and 13th–14th centuries;
3. St. George church, 13th and 16th centuries;
4. The two-storey church of St. Nicholas, 13th–14th century. Belfry, second half of the 13th century

Georgian philosophers and thinkers, Ioan Petritsi and Arseni Ikaltoeli, lived and worked here.

The mosaics and the work in precious metals created here were noted for their beauty. Even in the time of David the Builder, the Academy was called the New Athens and the New Jerusalem. The Academy school was run along the lines of similar schools in Byzantium, and geometry, arithmetic, music, rhetoric, philosophy and astronomy were taught. The monastery was sacked and burned by the Turks in 1510, but was soon rebuilt and restored and became the residence of the Patriarch of Western Georgia. The Academy, however, did not survive, and the Academy hall was rebuilt as a refectory. In 1759, the monastery was again pillaged, this time by the Lezghins, and the cathedral was burned down once more. However, it was rebuilt and the monastery tradition continued until Ghelati was closed in 1923.

Construction of the *Nativity of the Virgin Church* took nineteen years (1106–25). It was consecrated in 1126 by order of King David's son, Demetre. It is built in the shape of a cross and measures 29.2 m (32 yds) long, 20.2 m (22 yds) wide and 36.3 m (119 ft) high. The 13th–17th century frescoes inside the cathedral show the saints and portraits of various Georgian kings including, on the north wall, one painted in the 16th century which is the only surviving portrait of David the Builder himself; he is depicted as a giant dressed as a king with a crown and carrying a model of the church in his left hand. At the corner of the apse is a large 13th-century mosaic of the Virgin and the Archangels Gabriel and Michael. Ghelati Monastery was the burial place of both the Georgian and the Imeretian kings. It is believed that the famous Queen Tamar who ruled from 1184 to 1212 lies buried on the right side of the cathedral. On the left are King Bagrat IV, Solomon I and others.

David the Builder's grave is in the 2-storey building, a combined chapel and entrance gate, which stands to the south of the main church. His tomb is covered with a stone slab bearing the inscription in Georgian: "This is my resting place for all eternity. And I would not wish for anything more." The slab of stone was set in the floor so that all who passed might tread it underfoot; it is said that this was David's own wish and a sign of his humility. Another of his epitaphs reads, "There was a time when seven kings were guests at my feasts; and I was so mighty that I swept the Persians, the Turks and the Arabs away from my borders and let the fish of one sea into another—but being so mighty still I lie here with my hands folded upon my chest."

St. George's Church stands to the east of the main church and measures 11 m (12 yds) long, 5.5 m (6 yds) wide and 21.4 m (70 ft) high. Built in the 13th century, it was damaged in 1510, when the main church was burned by the Turks, but Bagrat III restored them both, and he and his consort are buried here. The frescoes are of the 16th and 17th centuries and Bagrat III's portrait is on the south wall.

St. Nicholas's Church is to the west of the main church. It was built in the 14th century and has two storeys. It is 8.5 m (9 yds) long and 6.5 m (7 yds) wide. The bell tower dates from the 12th–14th centuries and there is a spring under it. To the west of St. Nicholas's are the ruins of the Academy building founded in the 12th century. It is roofless, but inside the 10 m (33 ft) walls the stone benches remain. The other buildings in the compound are of the 19th and 20th centuries. Outside the monastery walls, near the eastern entrance, is a church over a spring; it was rebuilt in 1903. To the northeast are the ruins of the Sokhasteri (hermitage).

Ghelati Monastery is open 10–6; closed Tues.

Upon leaving Ghelati there is a *World War II memorial* by the road, and then follows a series of villages—*Orpiri, Chkepi, Buyeti, Khrestili* and *Satsiri*—on the way to Tkibuli.

Tkibuli Population—25,000 (1963)

Located in a ravine through which the Tkibula river flows and known as a village from the middle ages. Its name comes from "tke" meaning forest. Up to the west rises the rocky mountain where Prometheus is said to have been chained, if not in the cave at the foot of Mt. Ertsakha near Mokvi (see above).

Coal was discovered in the area in 1845 and the town's development dates from this time. Local coal was tried on a naval vessel and its quality proclaimed to equal that of Newcastle. A French company opened the mines, and by 1885 a railway line linked them with the Black Sea port of Poti. Mendeleyev was all in favour of their exploitation saying, "In Tkibuli the thickness of the coal layers reaches 7 sazhen (49 ft or 15 m). There is already a railway line and conditions are incomparable. It is a fine, rich layer of coal which reaches the surface slightly sloping—and the sea is nearby." In fact the mines yield a kind of brown coal, while a good quality coking coal comes from the Tkvarcheli mines in Abkhazia.

Tkibuli was proclaimed a town in 1939 and now it is a modern place. To the southwest spreads Tkibuli Sea, a reservoir supplying the local hydropower station. There is a coal cleaning factory and a tea factory.

Lenin Monument, on the main square

Nikortsminda

Standing on a little plateau and towering over the village of Sinathle, the *Church of St. Nicholas* was built in 1010–14 during the reign of Bagrat III. It is well preserved and famed for its carvings. An unusual feature is that although the exterior is in the shape of a cross, the interior is based on a hexagonal plan (as is also the cathedral of Kumurdo, built in 964, in the south of Georgia, near Khertvissi, probably in honour of the mother of Bagrat III). The hexagon represented the concept of God and the Holy Trinity and was symbolic of Georgia's military triumphs over Islam. The carved bas-reliefs are executed in lively style and the figures' movements are emphasised by the enlarged size of the hands. The variety of styles in the execution is hardly surprising since a number of different artists worked on the facade together. The porticos were added after the completion of the central part of the church, and the antechambers in front of the southern entrance were used by womenfolk.

Inside, the frescoes date from the 16th–17th centuries, and include Prince Tsulukidze's family portraits.

TURKESTAN (Azret, Yassy) Population— 72,000

(Intourist organises 2-hour excursions here from Chimkent.)

Turkestan, one of the cultural centres of Southern Kazakhstan, is 165 km (103 miles) from Chimkent. It is situated 254 m (833 ft) above sea level, was first mentioned in the historical chronicles of the 10–13th centuries as Yassy. In the 16th–17th centuries it was the capital of the Kazakh Khanate and had extensive ties with the northern regions of Kazakhstan and Central Asia. The town was also a religious centre because of the Hodja Akhmet Yassavi Mausoleum-Mosque which was an object of pilgrimage for Islamic nomads. It is one of the very few such religious monuments on the territory of Kazakhstan, the rest being ordinary tombs and burial places. This is explained by the fact that the Kazakhs were never zealous followers of Islam, which was forced upon them by their conquerors.

The Kazakhs believed that after death people turn into a holy spirit or "Aruakh," who can be good or evil depending on the attitude of people to his memory. Hence the earthly well-being of people is dependent on the good or evil will of Aruakhs. This is why ancestral tombs were so highly revered and monuments constructed over them, and

mosques were mostly built in Southern Kazakhstan where the population was nomadic.

By the time of the Russian advance into central Asia in the 1860s, the town was encircled by a mud wall with towers, the ruins of which can still be seen. As a result of incessant feudal wars that entailed plundering and killing the local population, the town lost its former importance. Turkestan was one of the first native towns to which the Russians came on their way to Central Asia. It was captured by Colonel Nikolai Verevkin in 1864 after a short siege. At the turn of the century it was divided, like most of the large towns, into a Russian section and a native one. When the Russians moved there, the native town was surrounded by a high wall, and inside there was a famous mosque.

Local industry is concerned with cotton ginning, chemicals and food products.

Khazaret Hodja Yassavi Mausoleum-Mosque, open as a museum 10–6; closed Tues. The mausoleum-mosque was built over the tomb of one of the active advocates of Islam, Hodja Akhmet Yassavi, a son of Ibrakhim-shekh ben Makhmudsheikh-ben Iftikar-sheikh. Akhmet Yassavi died in 1166. He is the author of the religious book of wisdom, "Divan and Hikmet." He was an advocate of Sufism (Suphism), the central tenet of which is poverty. With his sermons on poverty, he succeeded in converting a part of the Kazakh population to Islam. After his death he was proclaimed a saint and thousands of pilgrims visited his grave. His wife and son were buried nearby. The building of the mosque over his grave was begun in 1397 on the order of Tamerlane and was completed around 1405. By building this mosque, Tamerlane, flattering the feelings of the nomadic peoples towards their saint, wanted to use the spiritual unity of newly converted Moslems in his own interests. The mosque was built of firebricks with its sides measuring 62.5 m and 47 m (215 × 154 ft) respectively, and covering 330 sq m (3,552 sq ft). The central hall, or kazanlyk, had no special function, but was used for prayers on special holy days. It is domed with the largest cupola in Central Asia; it is 18 m (59 ft) in diameter. Its doors bear the words: "A gift to Allah from a ruler searching for the doors to obedience." Around the kazanlyk are different structures that traditionally go together, a *mausoleum*, a *mosque*, a *medresseh* and a *palace*. The palace was a khan's residence for 250 years.

The walls of the mausoleum as well as the vaults of the interior and the cupola are lined with white, light blue and dark blue tiles that form an intricate oriental ornamentation. In the centre of the kazanlyk stood a huge pot called Tai-kazan, made in 1399 of an alloy of seven metals, and with ten loops around its edge. It measures 2.42 m (8 ft) in diametre, stands 1.62 m (5 ft) high, holds 3,000 litres (793 gallons) and weighs about 2 tons. It still bears the name of its maker, Abd-Al-Aziz. Since 1936 it has been on display in the Leningrad Hermitage Museum.

Behind the kazanlyk is *Kabyrkhana*, the *mausoleum of Hodja Akhmet Yassavi* with a small square hall called the Zirat-khana in front of it that served as a place of worship. Visitors were not allowed inside the mausoleum and could look at the saint's grave only through the open door. On the tomb, made of light green marble, stood Aisha-Tash, a huge polished stone. In the northwestern corner was a small mosque where the followers of the saint performed the principal service every Friday. In the northeastern corner is the Askhana, a kitchen where ritual foods were cooked, including khalim, a porridge of boiled grain and mutton. Opposite is Kitabkhana, the library. To the south of Kabyrkhana is the unfinished Shlibdikhana, a hall for rituals.

In one of the rooms of the mosque were once great candlesticks called Chirag-Khany, brought here as trophies by Tamerlane. Like the Tai-kazan pot, they are now on display in the Hermitage Museum in Leningrad. The mosque was built by the architects from Iran, Shiraz and Tabriz. Numerous ornaments of multicoloured tiles have interwoven quotations from the Koran in Arabic. According to legend thousands of local people were engaged in its construction. The bricks for the mosque were manufactured in the town of Sauran and were passed from hand to hand along the 30-km (19-mile) route between that town and Turkestan.

Burials next to the mosque were supposed to relieve the deceased of all their earthly sins and promised them paradise. Nearby is the 15th-century *mausoleum* of Ulug-beg's daughter, Rabiga-Sultan-begim, and the 11th–12th century *Aulie Kunchuk-ata Mausoleum* with an underground mosque. The 16th-century *Esim-khan Mausoleum* is under restoration.

Archaeological Museum, in the 1878 mosque near the Yassavi Mausoleum-Mosque

New Mosque, by the road on the way into the town

Oriental Bath, 15th–16th century; open as a museum

From Turkestan, tourists are taken to Kentau (30 km/19 miles further on). This new town lies in the desert region, lunch is organised here and the whole Intourist excursion from Chimkent takes 10 hours.

Kentau Population—40,000
Kentau is on the slopes of the Karatau mountain range, about 30 km (19 miles) northeast of Turkestan. It was founded in 1955 when two villages, Kantagi and Mirgalimsai were joined.

Ore is mined here and there are factories producing tractors, excavators and electrical transformers.

Local Museum, Panfilova Street. Open 10–6; closed Mon.

Museum, in Achpolimetal Factory, Mira Street. The factory produces lead ore for Chimkent's lead factory.

Lenin Monument, 50-Years-of-October Street
Monument of the country's first mining machine
Sorrowing Mother Memorial

Gornyak (Miner) Hotel, 50-Years-of-October Street
Cosmos Restaurant

Otrar
50 km (31 miles) from Turkestan, near the Timur railroad station, are the ruins of the mediaeval town of Otrar, once the largest town in Kazakhstan and Central Asia, formerly an agricultural oasis in the middle reaches of the Syr-Darya. At present this is a huge hill up to 20 m (66 ft) high with slopes covered with multicoloured, broken tiles.

The place is famous for the fact that Tamerlane died here on February 19, 1405. The town is connected with the historical events of 1218 that led to the conflict between the Shakh of Khorezm and Genghiz Khan whose army stormed Otrar and completely devastated it. The story runs as follows: Genghiz Khan sent his envoys with rich presents to Shakh Mokhammed of Khorezm to establish good neighbourly relations with Bukhara. The caravan was stopped by Inal-Khan, one of the Shakh's governors in Otrar, all the goods were taken and Genghiz Khan's envoys killed. The enraged Genghiz Khan came to Otrar with his large Mongol army and after a 5-month siege captured it, killing most of its residents. Inal Khan was taken alive. He was brought before Genghiz Khan and the latter ordered that molten silver be poured into Inal Khan's ears as punishment for the death of his envoys. Genghiz Khan's troops sent after the escaped Khan Mokhammed of Khorezm, marched through Persia, the Caucasus and southern Russia where they joined the Polovtsi and gained a resounding victory over the Russians in the battle by the river Kalka in 1223. With the formation of the Mongol Empire, Otrar became one of the major trade centres; for the next two centuries, however, it is hardly mentioned in the historical chronicles. Then it was subject to numerous raids by the Kirghiz, the Vossacs and the Kalmyks, its irrigation canals dried up, the population decreased sharply and it ceased to exist as a town.

No architectural monuments are preserved except for a *mosque* built in the 19th century on the site of the ancient mausoleum of Aryslan-Bob who is said to have been a teacher of Haji Akhmet Yassavy. Of interest in this mosque are two wooden columns still preserved from the ancient mausoleum.

TVER (Known as Kalinin from 1931–90)
Population—451,000
An old song tells of "Tver, wonderful, charming and dear to my heart." Tver, supposedly derived from the old Russian word "tverd," meaning "stronghold," was the name of this ancient town until it was renamed Kalinin in 1931. Mikhail Kalinin (1875–1946) was born in this region. An Old Bolshevik, he played an important role in establishing Soviet power in Central Asia and was Soviet president until 1946. The town became Tver again in 1990.

A Novgorodian trading post originally stood

here on the bank of the river Volga, at its confluence with the rivers Tvertsa and T'maka. The town was really founded by Grand-Prince Vsevolod of Vladimir in 1134–81. The main part of the town lay at that time on the left bank of the Volga, and it was not until 1240 that Grand-Prince Yaroslav Vsevolodovich built the wooden Kremlin fortress on the right bank. The Kremlin stood on the place where the Khimik Stadium is today.

In 1246 Tver separated from the Vladimir principality and became independent, its first ruler being Yaroslav, brother of Alexander Nevsky. In 1327, when the Kremlin had become large and well fortified, Tver organised the biggest uprising against the Tatars in the whole of Russia at that time. The local Tatar chief, Chol Khan, was torn to pieces in the battle. This action cost most of the local population their lives because Khan Uzbek gave 50,000 soldiers to Moscow's ruler, Ivan Kalita, and ordered Tver's largest church bell back to Moscow, the greatest possible humiliation in those times.

Tver survived nevertheless, and in the 14th and 15th centuries was well known for the expertise of its local craftsmen. The townsmen not only built their own churches but sent their craftsmen to build churches in other towns as well. They made bells and armaments, and at the beginning of the 15th century the local artillery was among the strongest in Russia. Tver minted her own coins, and her craftsmen were famous for their jewellery and fine metal work.

The town was represented at the Conference of Churches in Florence in 1439, when the question of interchurch unity was being discussed, and decided not to submit to the authority of Rome. After Novgorod was joined to Moscow in 1478, Tver was surrounded by Moscow's territory and had no choice but to yield to Moscow when Ivan III came with his army in 1485. Ivan Mikhailovich, the last prince of Tver, fled to Lithuania. It is hard now to believe that Tver was ever the rival of Moscow and had fought her for nearly 200 years for control of the surrounding territory.

When Ivan IV passed through Tver on his campaign against Novgorod in 1569, he sent Malyuta Skuratov, a trusted member of his bodyguard, to the Metropolitan Philip (then exiled from Moscow to a monastery in Tver) to ask a blessing before his journey north to punish the citizens of Novgorod. The priest said that he felt able to bless those with good intentions only; Skuratov was frightened to bring such a reply to the tsar and accordingly strangled the old man with his own hands before reporting that he had not found him alive. Ivan the Terrible then lived up to his name and delivered Tver's inhabitants up to the brutality of his soldiers. Over 90,000 people were murdered. Afterwards he set a Christian Tatar, Simeon Bulatovich, to rule over those who remained alive.

Tver was ruined by the Poles during the Time of Troubles, and in 1763 there was a disastrous fire that demolished most of the buildings. Catherine the Great sent architects to rebuilt the town, among them the famous Matvei Kazakov (1738–1813). As a result Tver became a well-planned town, a "provincial Petersburg," and Catherine the Great herself wrote in a letter, "The town of Tver, after Petersburg, is the most beautiful in the empire." In the 18th century and the first part of the 19th, it was the biggest town on the way from Petersburg to Moscow, and the court used to stop here, thus encouraging a certain degree of sophistication. This was very evident between 1809 and 1813, a time of real prosperity and growth for the town, when Prince Georgi Oldenburgsky (married to Catherine, Alexander I's favourite sister) was governor-general. In 1860–62 the post of vice-governor was held by the famous Russian satirist Mikhail Saltykov-Schedrin, who had published his "Provincial Sketches" 4 years earlier. Fyodor Dostoyevsky lived here also for some time after his return from exile.

Following the 18th-century plan of the town, there are still 3 main streets radiating from the centre. The central street used to be Millionnaya Street, where the rich people lived, which is now a shopping street. It is still the main Leningrad–Moscow road but is now called *Sovietskaya Street*. Along it are 3 squares, *Pushkinskaya*, *Pochtovaya* ("post office") and *Lenin*. The latter, formerly Fountain Square, is the most interesting in the town; it contains the town hall (1770–80), the *House of Nobles* (1766–70), now the local Party headquarters, and a school built in 1786 which is now the *Youth Theatre*. In the centre of Tver is *Sovietskaya Square*, where demonstrations and parades take place.

Tver is in the middle of a flax-growing region and is also an industrial centre, especially concerned with light industry. There is a cotton mill over a hundred years old, and much of its production is exported. The town also produces rolling stock and textile machinery, and there is a large printing works. There are pedagogical, medical, and peat research institutes, several technical colleges, and a Suvorov Military Academy. A new part of the town is now under construction on the left bank of the river Volga. After World War II, when much reconstruction had to be done in the old parts of the town, most of the houses in the centre had 2 or 3 storeys added, but the 18th-century style was preserved.

Beloy Troitsy (White Trinity) Church, Engels Street. Founded in 1563–64 by a local townsman, this is the oldest building in Tver. There is a plaque on the wall saying the church was built in the time of Ivan the Terrible. Some of the icons in the iconostasis date from the 17th century. High up in the building there were secret rooms, and it is said that the blood of those killed there long stained the pillars and walls of the church below. This is probably true because it could have trickled through the ventilation holes. The church is open for services.

Spaso-Preobrazhensky (Transfiguration) Cathedral. Built by Archbishop Sergius in 1689–96. Originally there was a wooden church dedicated to SS. Kosma and Damian on this site, but this was

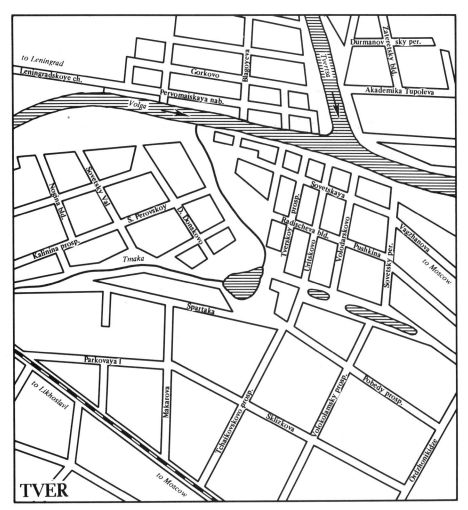

TVER

replaced by two other Transfiguration Cathedrals before the existing one, following the layout of the Uspensky (Assumption) Cathedral in the Moscow Kremlin, was constructed. Like the Moscow cathedral, it has 5 domes. The *belltower* standing near it was built between 1739 and 1758.

Rozhdestvensky (Nativity) Convent, Proletarsky Pereulok, on the banks of the river T'maka. This is known to have been in existence already in the 16th century, because a deed was granted to Abbess Euphemia by Ivan the Terrible. It was not until 1756 that the first of the wooden buildings was replaced by a stone structure, and the oldest building in the complex now is a church of 1770. The tower beside the road once guarded a corner of the surrounding walls. The impressive classical-style church in the centre of the square formed by the other buildings is Tikhvinskaya (Our Lady of Tikhvin), founded in 1810 but only completed in 1820 after serious setbacks.

Rozhdestvenskaya (Nativity) Church stands beyond the convent, nearer the river, and is best viewed from the bridge. It is impressively large and was designed in "modern" style in 1912, its dome resembling the helmet of an ancient warrior. Behind the church is a Young Pioneer House in constructivist style.

Ilya Proroka (Elijah the Prophet) Church, by the Volga on Pervomaiskaya Naberezhnaya. Constructed in 1689 on the site of the wooden church of SS. Constantine and Helen.

Voznesenskaya (Ascension) Church was built in 1813.

Tver Region Restoration Workshop, beside the stadium along Donskaya Street. This is housed in another church, which has itself been fully restored.

Putevoy Dvorets, Sovietskaya Street 3. This was built in 1763–75 by Matvei Kazakov as a coaching palace for Catherine the Great, on the same spot where the old Archbishop's Palace had been destroyed by fire. Dvorets was partly reconstructed by Rossi in 1809. The central façade is reminiscent of Leningrad's Winter Palace but is simpler in design. The palace used to contain a church dedicated to St. Catherine. The Grand Duchess Ekaterina Petrovna lived here when her husband, Prince Georgi Oldenburgsky, was governor-general. Her brother, Tsar Alexander I, often visited her here, and it was in this building that he listened to historian Karamzin reading the first chapter of his "History of State of Russia." The local museum and picture gallery are both housed in the palace.

Local Museum, Revolution Square 3, in the left wing of Putevoy Dvorets. Open 11–6; closed Mon. and Tues.

Picture Gallery, with the Local Museum in Putevoy Dvorets. There is a good collection of icons here.

Old Tver Museum, Nakhimov Street 3/21. Open 11–6; closed Mon. and Tues. The building is Arefiyev's 18th-century merchant house, reconstructed to show everyday life in old Tver and containing many varied examples of arts and crafts.

Saltykov-Schedrin House Museum, Saltykov-Schedrin Street 11/37. Open 11–6; closed Mon. and Tues. Mikhail Saltykov-Schedrin (1826–89) was an influential satirical writer who was born in the province of Tver and in 1860 became vice-governor. He lived in this house from 1860–62.

Chaikin Komsomol Museum, Saltykov-Schedrin Square. Open 11–6; closed Sun. and Mon.

Industrial Exhibition, Sovietskaya Street 38. Open 10–5:30; closed Sun. and Mon.

There is a group of *old houses* built by Matvei Kazakov on Pervomaiskaya Naberezhnaya, near the church of Elijah the Prophet and by the building of the theological college, now used as a technical college. There are many *bridges* over the Volga to Tver. The newest was completed in 1956.

Nikitin Monument, on the bank of the river Volga. Afanasi Nikitin was a great traveller and merchant who went to India via Persia between 1466 and 1473, 30 years before Vasco da Gama. He spent 3 years there and died in Smolensk on his way back home to Tver. He wrote a book of his travels called "The Crossing of Three Seas." His 8-m (26-ft) statue designed by Orlov and Zakharov rests on a red granite pedestal with a Russian ship's figurehead. It stands on the left bank near the jetty, supposedly on the spot where he first set sail. It was unveiled in 1955.

Krylov Monument. Ivan Krylov (1769–1844) was a writer of fables who spent his childhood and adolescence in Tver. The monument by Shaposhnikov was unveiled in 1959 and stands 7 m (23 ft) high. Around it are 8 separate bas-reliefs illustrating his fables.

Saltykov-Schedrin Monument, in a garden on Pravda Street

Obelisk, in the garden in front of Putevoy Dvorets. This obelisk commemorates those who fell during the revolution.

Lenin Monument, Lenin Square. This statue by Kenig was unveiled in 1959; near it are the graves of those who fell during the Second World War.

Kalinin Statue, in front of Putevoy Dvorets

Peace Monument, Mira ("peace") Square. This sculptured group in the town's newest square was unveiled in 1959.

Theatre, Svobodny Pereulok 43/18

Puppet Theatre, Pobedy Prospect 9

Youth Theatre, Sovietskaya Street 44. This building was formerly a school, built in 1786

Concert Hall, Teatralnaya Square 1

Circus, Tverskaya Square 2a

Central Stadium, Krasnoflotskaya Naberezhnaya. Seats 20,000 spectators.

Khimik ("chemist's") Stadium, Revolutsii Square. The stadium, which can hold 11,000 people, is where Tver's Kremlin once stood.

Tsentralnaya Hotel and Restaurant, Pravda Street 33/8; tel. 381–57

Seliger Hotel and Restaurant, Sovietskaya Street 52; tel. 307–53

Tver (Intourist) Motel and Restaurant, Leningradskoye Chaussée 130; tel. 55–692. Intourist office: tel. 55–768.

Tver Camping Site, Leningradskoye Chaussée 130; tel. 596–96

Rossia Restaurant, Stepan Razin Naberezhnaya 10/11

Volga Restaurant, Pravda Street 60/37

Berezovaya Roscha Hotel and Café, on the way out of town

Orel Restaurant, Naberezhnaya Stepana Razina

Vostok Café, at the end of Sovietskaya Street. This building has a minaret and looks very like a mosque.

Bank, Sovietskaya Street 56/35

GPO, Sovietskaya Street 56/35

Beryozka (foreign-currency) Shop, Tverskoy Prospect 18

Central Market, Kommuny Square

Department Stores, Sovietskaya Street 84 and Uritsky Street 35

Souvenirs, Sovietskaya Street 31

(Intourist organises excursions from here northwest to Torzhok and southeast to Klin, where Tchaikovsky lived. Both are listed under their own headings.

UFA is the capital of Bashkorstan.

BASHKORSTAN

Bashkiria is an autonomous republic within the Russian Federation. It is situated in the southern part of the Ural Mountains and the adjacent lowland to the west and is crossed by the river Belaya, a tributary of the Kama. It is 143,000 sq km (55,450 sq miles) in area and is rich in oil, iron ore and nonferrous metal deposits. The vast forest reserves are also of great value and include a great many lime trees which are a prime source of the excellent local honey.

The names Bashkirs and Bashkorstan appear in written chronicles from the 10th century. The Bashkirs (who call themselves Bashkort) are a Turkic-speaking people who have been known since the 9th century when they were nomadic and partly spoke a Ugrian language related to Hungarian. Originally animists and shamanists, the Bashkirs had their first contact with Islam in 1152 and the religion was firmly established by 1326. In the 12th–14th centuries they suffered greatly from the Mongol-Tatars. After the disintegration of the Golden Horde in the middle of the 15th century, the Bashkir territory was divided between the Nogai Horde and the Kazan and Siberian khanates.

In 1552, after the conquest of Kazan by Ivan the Terrible, the Bashkirs recognised the overlordship of Muscovy. Each Bashkir family had to pay an annual tribute of "90 kopeks worth of honey, 80 kopeks worth of fox pelts and 40 kopeks worth of marten skins," but accepted the Russian rules on the condition that they were to remain masters of their own lands. Bashkirian horsemen became worthy defenders of Russia's eastern border, and in the 16th century they also participated in the Li-

vonian War and in Crimean expeditions. Russian colonisation in their part of the world did not proceed smoothly, however, and Russia's first trouble with the Bashkirs occurred in 1584. All the same, loyal soldiers still continued to serve the tsar, and at the beginning of the 17th century they helped fight the Poles and the Swedes. Back in Bashkorstan there was a serious revolt in 1645, Seitovskoe led another in 1662 which dragged on for ten years, and Aldaro-Kusyumovsky another in 1707. In general the unrest continued throughout the 17th and 18th centuries and included an uprising under their national hero, Salavat Yulayev (born 1752), who was a folk poet as well as a soldier and whose name has become a legend. He was very popular among the Bashkirs and other peoples of the Urals and, although only 20 years old, led them to take part in Pugachov's peasant revolt of 1773–75. (Emelyan Pugachov (1726–75) was a Cossack who led his bands with the help of Ivan Chika.) Yulayev earned the respect and trust of Pugachov, and was promoted by him to the rank of colonel. Together they besieged Ufa, but the town stood firm. 28,000 Bashkirs were killed and 396 of their villages were burnt. In 1774 Yulayev (then 22) and his father were both captured and sentenced to life imprisonment in the Baltic countries by Catherine the Great. It is said that when he was much older he and some friends managed to make their escape by boat from the fortress where they were held, but that they were drowned at sea.

By 1794, in spite of the dissention on the home front, the fine performance by the cavalry Bashkirs led to a decision by the Senate that all Bashkirs should be classed as Cossacks. They were obliged to serve on the Russian borders, but in return received all kinds of privileges including exemption from tax. Sometimes there would be groups of brothers fighting side by side, and sometimes their wives would join them, and even whole families might earn military decorations. In 1798 a special irregular army of Bashkirs was organised to defend the border known as the Orenburg Line. Their equipment included bows and arrows as well as spears, and when they were in Germany and France as part of the Russian Army in 1813–15, the people there were quite frightened by their appearance. The French called them "cupids," and Goethe was given a bow and arrows, after which he practiced archery in his garden.

During the 18th century it became increasingly popular to travel to Bashkorstan to drink "kumys," the fermented mare's milk that was credited with a variety of cures. Kumys is still popular, and has earned such names as "live water" and "Bashkir champagne." The mares are milked every two hours, coming voluntarily without any sign of protest. Most give between 8 and 10 litres a day, but some produce more than 20 litres. There were attempts in the 19th century to produce kumys in England from Bashkirian mares, but lacking the natural grasses, the result was but a poor substitute for the real thing.

Lev Tolstoy was in Ufa in 1862 when he came

to drink mare's milk for a cure. He purchased some property and thought of moving from Yasnaya Polyana and settling here. During the 1872–73 famine in the Urals he was among those who organised help for the hungry. Chekhov was another enthusiast for the drink.

A nationalist Bashkir government was formed in Orenburg in 1917 at the time of the Russian Revolution, but in 1919 it joined the Bolsheviks and on March 23, 1919, Lenin signed a decree on the organisation of the Bashkir Autonomous Republic. This was the first autonomous republic to be formed. It changed hands during the fighting of the Civil War, and until 1920 the capital was Sterlitamak, but then it was changed to Ufa. In 1922 it became the Bashkirian Autonomous SSR, and for a while its districts were known as cantons, like Switzerland.

As part of the Volga economic area, Bashkorstan has developed both agriculturally and industrially. The republic's rich mineral resources provide many raw materials for its expanding industries. Explorers claimed to have found gold in the region, and at the end of the 18th century some excavation was carried on, but the mineral was in fact pyrites. In the course of the digging oil was struck, but not for the first time. It had been discovered long before, and permission for the construction of an oil refinery had been given as early as 1754, but nothing came of it at the time. Prospecting only began in earnest in the 1930s, and oil was struck in May 1932. By 1944 Bashkorstan had overtaken Baku as the most important area for oil extraction in the country, and earned the name of the Second Baku. Later Tatarstan, which adjoins Bashkorstan, took the lead as far as oil extraction was concerned, but Bashkorstan did the most refining. Now it has been far surpassed by gas and oil fields in the Tyumen region. The centre of the Bashkorstan oilfields is near Oktyabrsky and Tuimazy, near the Ufa-Ulyanovsk railway line. Today people speak of the triumvirate of oil, oil refining and chemistry, and the town is best known for its highly-developed chemical industry based on its oil and gas deposits. Two of the most important pipelines start from the borders of Bashkorstan and Tatarstan; one is the Druzhba pipeline which goes westwards to Europe and the other runs eastwards to Siberia.

In the Belaya Valley agriculture is most important, while stockbreeding predominates in the Urals. The area is famous for its own breed of horses, known as Bashkirtsy, and the traditional occupation of apiculture is widespread.

The population includes Bashkirs, Russians, Tatars, Ukrainians, Chuvash, Mari and Mordvinians. Bashkirs only make up 22.1% of the total and live primarily in the eastern part of the Republic. Besides Muslims, there are also here adherents to the Eastern Orthodox rite.

Cultural progress has led to the establishment of several institutes of higher education, over 1,700 libraries and a number of theatres, several of which perform in the Bashkir language.

Ufa Population—1,090,000
The city is situated on the right bank of the Belaya river, just below the point where it is joined by the Ufa. The two rivers form a loop around an easily defensible site and the ancient town of Tura-Tau once stood here; it was later renamed Kazan-Tau. A little further downstream on the opposite side of the Belaya, another tributary, the Dyoma, flows in.

The ruins of older fortifications dating from the first centuries A.D. can be seen 3 km from Ufa. They were excavated in 1911 and are called *Chortovo Gorodische (Devil's Town)*.

Old manuscripts record how Prince Ufimsky ("of Ufa") was sent by Khan Megmet-Amin of Kazan to Moscow for talks with Ivan III. A local legend tells how the last ruler of old Ufa was Khan Tyurya-Babatu-Klyusov who had to move over to the shores of the river Dyoma because his people were being molested by a dragon. When he heard of the fall of the Kazan khanate he himself went south to the Kuban. Apparently the dragon went away too, because it was never heard of again as a threat to the people of Ufa.

After the conquest of Kazan, the Bashkirs appealed to Ivan the Great for protection from the Kirghiz incursions, and in 1574 this site was chosen for a fortress. Construction was in the hands of the noble Ivan Nogoi. The stronghold served a double purpose because it was also designed to protect the trade route from Kazan across the Urals to Tyumen. It derived importance from the trade and was proclaimed a town in 1586. Its coat-of-arms was argent a running marten. It was, however, regarded by Murza Urus of the Nogai, the Kirghiz Khan Ak-Nazar, Prince Ablai of Siberia and Murza Tevekkel as a challenge to their authority in the area. They claimed that the tsar was intruding into their territories and together launched an attack upon Ufa, but they were defeated and both Ablai and Tevkel were taken prisoner. There were further attacks upon the town by insurgent Bashkirs, and by 1664 it was so dilapidated that Tsar Alexei Mikhailovich ordered that it should be rebuilt.

In 1708 Peter the Great decreed that Ufa should become part of the province of Kazan, but it regained its independence in 1728 and was directly responsible to the Senate. A wall was built around the town in 1732, and the town itself was largely rebuilt again at that time. It had, however, already earned the name of the Devil's Inkpot for its dirty streets, and people said that until you had visited Ufa, you didn't know what real dirt was.

The institution of the Mufti of Ufa, or the Mufti of Orenburg which was the original title, took place under Catherine the Great in 1784. The Directorate of the Sunni Muslims of European Russia and Siberia has its seat in Ufa today and is still headed by the Mufti.

The railway reached Ufa in 1879 and, together with the development of river shipping, greatly helped the growth of the town. In 1773 the population numbered but 2,313, while by 1897 it was already about 50,000.

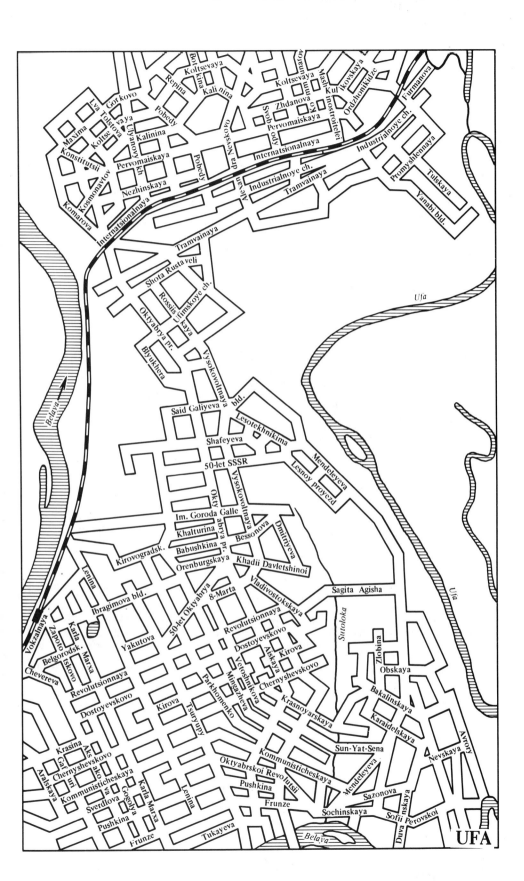

UFA

The Revolutionary Committee proclaimed the transfer to Soviet power on 8 November 1917. During the Civil War, in 1919, there was heavy fighting near Ufa beside the river Belaya between Admiral Kolchak's army and units of the Red Army led by the Civil War heroes, Frunze and Chapayev. The capture of Ufa that year is considered Chapayev's greatest military feat. Ufa was declared the capital of the Bashkir ASSR in 1922.

The popular writer, Maxim Gorky, visited Ufa on many occasions and described it: "The town was somehow very low. It really seemed to be sitting down instead of standing on the ground."

During World War II a number of foreign Communist leaders were evacuated here from Moscow, including Dolores Ibarruri of Spain, Gheorghi Dmitrov of Bulgaria and Wilhelm Pik of Germany.

Present-day Ufa stretches for almost 40 km (25 miles) along the river Belaya and is divided into the old and new parts of the town. In Old Ufa, where the small river Sutoloka flows into the Belaya, a monument now stands on the site of the kremlin and of the 16th-century Troitskaya Church in the tower of which the Bashkir national heroes, Salavat Yulayev and Chika Zarubin, were imprisoned. This was the last part of the kremlin and it was demolished when the square was reconstructed. In its place stands *Friendship Monument*, dedicated to the 400th anniversary of the voluntary union of Bashkorstan with Russia. The old town is on the slope up behind the square to the east. There are still a number of attractive old mansions standing, some of the wooden ones being decorated with fine woodcarving. The woodcarving skills are said to have been brought to Ufa by craftsmen from Vyatsk (Kirov). From the square, Frunze (formerly Ilinskaya) and October Revolution Streets lead to New Ufa. Lenin Street with shops and hotels is one of the main thoroughfares. On Soviet Square are the House of Government and the House of Industry. The 10-km (6-mile) October Prospect links Old Ufa with the new industrial region.

Ufa has sizeable engineering industries manufacturing power and mining machinery, electrical apparatus, telephones and typewriters. There is also a range of timber-processing industries making furniture, prefabricated houses and matches, and there are various enterprises belonging to the food and light industries. Ufa is a major crossroad of railways, roads and oil and gas pipelines with the river Belaya. It is an important cultural centre with a university, institutes of petroleum, aviation, teacher training, medicine, agriculture and art and with many scientific establishments.

Ufa was the birthplace of the 19th-century Russian writer, Sergei Aksakov (1791–1859) and also of the artist Mikhail Nesterov (1862–1942).

Sergievskaya Church, Kommunisticheskaya Street

Pokrovskaya Church

Mosque, Tukayevsky Street, by the river; built in 1830 with a thin minaret and roofed by a cupola. (There used to be five other mosques as well.)

Agricultural Institute, Karl Marx Street. This is in the former seminary building, the best example of 19th-century architecture in Ufa.

Medical Institute, Frunze Street; in the building of the boys' grammar school, built in classical style in the 19th century

Aviation College, Lenin Street; formerly the Commercial College

Governor's House, at the crossing of Tukayevsky and Sovietskaya Streets; built in classical style.

Trading Arcades, standing in the middle of the market square bounded by Frunze and Tukayevsky Streets; built in the 19th century

Library, built in the first half of the 19th century as the Nobles' Assembly Building.

Provincial Government Building, at the crossing of Frunze and Tsyurupy Streets; built in the second half of the 19th century

Muslim Administrative Building

City Council Offices, Kommunisticheskaya Street; built at the end of the 19th century for the same purpose

Art nouveau house, at the crossing of Pushkin and Karl Marx Streets

House of Scientists, Karl Marx Street; in an old mansion

Old mansion, Sotsialisticheskaya Street; set in a fine garden

Regional Party Building, formerly the Peasants' Bank

Local Museum of Bashkorstan, Oktyabrskoy Revolutsii Street 10

Nesterov Bashkir Art Gallery, Gogol Street 27; in an old mansion with fine plasterwork ceilings inside

Lenin Museum, Kirov Street. Ufa was the first town where Lenin stayed in February 1900 on his way back from exile in Siberia. Since his wife, Nadezhda Krupskaya, had to stay in Ufa for an additional year of exile, Lenin visited the town again for 2 weeks in June of that year before he went abroad. Besides visiting his wife, he also used the opportunity to meet the local social democrats. This was the house where Krupskaya lived and the memorial plaque is inscribed: "Vladimir Lenin stayed here in 1900." He spent about three weeks in Ufa altogether. In 1900 this was on the very edge of the town, and now the surrounding area has been designated as a memorial zone, and log houses of the period are being restored and others brought in.

Gafuri's House, Gogol Street 28. Mazhit Gafuri (Gabdulmazhit Gafurov, 1880–1934) was a local poet and the founder of Bashkir literature. His house is open as a museum.

Planetarium

Hippodrome, Mendeleyev Street

Friendship Monument, Pyervomaisky Square. This was erected to mark the 400th anniversary of the incorporation of Bashkorstan into Russia. It stands 35 m (115 ft) high and was built by Baburin and Levitskaya.

Yulayev Monument, Gafuri Street, between the buildings of the university and the telecentre. This equestrian statue of the national hero, Salavat Yu-layev, stands 10 m (33 ft) high and was sculpted by A. Tavasiyev. It is said to be the largest equestrian statue in the world.

Aksakov Bust, Pushkin Street. Sergei Aksakov (1791–1859) was a 19th-century Russian writer who was born in Ufa. In his "Chronicles of a Russian family" and "The Childhood Years of Bagrov the Grandson," he draws upon his own family background and describes conditions in Bashkorstan at the beginning of the 19th century.

Gafuri Monument, Frunze Street

Eternal Flame and War Memorial, Lenin Street. This is dedicated to those who fell during the Civil War.

War Memorial, 50-Lyet-Oktyabrya Street; commemorating revolutionaries and soldiers of the Civil War. This group of three warriors is by Kuznetsov.

Lenin Monuments, in the garden in Lenin Square and on Kommunisticheskaya Street. (One of them is by Ivan Mendelevich.)

Mayakovsky Monument, in Mayakovsky Square; commemorating the poet Vladimir Mayakovsky.

Matrosov and Gubaidulin Monument, in Pobeda Park (formerly Ushakovsky Garden). A Matrosov (1924–43) was born in Ufa. He blocked an enemy machine-gun embrasure with his body during fighting near Pskov during the Second World War, and his action was later repeated by another soldier called Gubaidulin. They were both awarded the title of Hero of the Soviet Union for their courage. The monument which was unveiled in 1983 is by Kerbel and Lyubimov.

Obelisk, 50-Lyet-Oktyabrya Street. This marks the common grave of World War II soldiers who died of their wounds in the hospitals of Ufa.

Bashkir State Opera and Ballet Theatre, Lenin Street 5. Designed by Rudavsky and founded in 1908 as a memorial to the writer, Sergei Aksakov (who was born in Ufa), and formerly known as the Sergei Aksakov People's House.

Gafuri Bashkir Drama Theatre, Frunze Street 34

Russian Drama Theatre, Gogol Street 58

Circus, Prospekt Oktybrya 71

Puppet Theatre, Prospekt Oktyabrya 158

Bashkiria Hotel and Restaurant, Lenin Street 25/59; tel. 22 0831

Tourist Hotel and Restaurant, Sorge Street 11

Rossia Hotel and Restaurant, Prospekt Oktyabrya 81

GPO, Lenin Street 28

Ufa Department Store, Prospekt Oktyabrya 31

Souvenirs, Lenin Street 31/30

House of Books, Prospekt Oktyabrya 129

Chishma

40 km (25 miles) from Ufa. Here on the bank of river Dyoma and near Lake Akziarat is the *mausoleum* (locally called "the white grave") of the Nogai missionary Imam Kraji-Husein-Bek (1090–1166). He was sent here from the town of Turkestan

(q.v.) in Central Asia by a holy man called Akhmet Yassavi (d. 1166), an advocate of Sufism, the central tenet of which is poverty. He died here aged 76 and his grave is not only holy for the Bashkirs but also for other Muslim peoples. The mausoleum was founded by Tamerlane.

Keshene or *Tura-khan Palace* is another local mausoleum. It stands on a hilltop near the village of Nizhniye Tirme. Both these structures are small and stocky and roofed with a cupola.

UGLICH (pronounced "ooglich") Population—30,000

Uglich is one of the oldest Russian cities. According to legend it was founded in 937, but the first written records date from 1149. The name Uglich is believed to be derived from the word "ugol" (angle), because of the sharp turn made by the river Volga just where the town stands.

In 1207 chronicles recorded Uglich as being part of the Rostov Princedom, but in 1218 it became the centre of an autonomous princedom. It was razed to the ground in 1237 and again in 1284 by the invading Tatars, but in 1375 Ivan Kalita purchased it back from the Tatars and brought it into the domain of the Grand Princes of Moscow.

In the middle of the 15th century Dimitri Shemyaka of Uglich challenged the rights of his cousin, Vasili II, Grand Prince of Moscow. Vasili was captured, blinded, and banished to Uglich while Dimitri took his place in Moscow. Dimitri was soon betrayed however and his cousin ruled again as Vasili Tyomny (the blind).

Ivan the Terrible presented Uglich to his newborn son, also called Dimitri, and in 1584, after Ivan's death, it was to Uglich that 2-year-old Dimitri and his mother, Maria, were banished by Tsar Fyodor, his step-brother. 7 years later Dimitri was found dead in the palace courtyard with his throat cut and the news was tolled out on the big bell of Spassky Church. The event gave rise to serious unrest, and it was believed that the Prince's death had been arranged by Boris Godunov, Fyodor's right-hand man. In fact the tragedy may have been a pure accident, as all little boys like playing with knives and this particular little boy was an epileptic. At the time, however, anti-Moscow feelings ran so high that much blood was shed and many citizens of Uglich were exiled before Godunov felt there was no longer a threat of disturbance. Later, a number of pretenders to the throne took the name of Dimitri, denying that the young prince had ever been killed.

Uglich was much fought over during the Time of Troubles, and changed hands between the Russians and the Poles several times until the Polish defeat in 1612. In 1619 Tsar Mikhail Romanov hoped to revive the town by bringing in several thousand new inhabitants from other places, but by the middle of the century fewer than 3000 lived there. Uglich nevertheless became a district centre, under the jurisdiction of St. Petersburg, until 1727 when the district was included in the Province of Moscow.

In 1784 it is recorded that the town was re-planned with straight streets; this planning has survived, but up till the beginning of this century the town was of little economic, cultural, or political significance. In 1911 the population was about 10,000, only a quarter of what it had been before Godunov's massacres, nearly 300 years before. It has tripled now, and its most important industries are metal-working and machine-building. There is also a watch factory. The local dairy farming is also reflected in the town's Institute of Butter- and Cheese-making and Uglich is one of the country's major cheese-producing centres.

Nothing remains of the ancient wooden Kremlin which stood in the centre of Uglich, but in its place stands the Palace of the Princes of Uglich, originally built in 1480 by Andrei Bolshoi, the brother of Ivan III. It is usually known as *Prince Dimitri's Palace*, after its last occupant. The 3-storey structure is square and built of large red bricks. The ground floor consists of 2 rooms, and was probably used for domestic purposes. It appears to be sunken, as the level of the ground around the palace has already risen by some 1.5 m (5 ft). An outside staircase leads to the next floor which has 3 rooms. The top floor has a single spacious room, probably used as a throne room and for ceremonial receptions and gatherings.

In 1892 *Uglich Museum* was opened in the palace. Now the museum has a collection of about 16,000 exhibits of the 16th–19th centuries. Among them are manufacturing and agricultural tools, badges of the artisan's guilds, and armaments. Of special interest is the *bell* which rang from the belfry of Spaso-Preobrazhensky (Transfiguration) Cathedral on the day of Prince Dimitri's death, causing unrest in the town. After an investigation was carried out, the bell, upon the orders of Boris Godunov, was pulled down, whipped, and exiled to Siberia after its "tongue" had been removed. When it reached its destination, it was registered as "the first inanimate exile from Uglich." It was only 1892, 300 years later and after numerous requests by the people of Uglich, that a special commission was sent to Tobolsk to bring the bell back.

Close to the Palace, on the spot where Prince Dimitri had been found dead, a wooden chapel was built at the beginning of the 17th century. In 1630 a wooden church was built here and, in 1692, a stone one. This church came to be known as the *Church of Prince-Dimitri-on-the-Blood*. It is small in size and is characteristic of the decorative architecture of the second half of the 17th century. The decorative style is emphasised by the coloured tiles on the facades. Some late 18th-century frescoes may be seen inside the church; those on the western wall give a full account of the happenings connected with the death of Prince Dimitri in 1591. The frescoes in the refectory are mainly biblical, illustrating the story of the creation. The realistic treatment of Adam and Eve is rare for Russian Orthodox paintings of the period.

Spaso-Preobrazhensky (Transfiguration) Cathedral is the largest building on the Kremlin territory.

It was built at the beginning of the 18th century to replace a church pulled down by the order of Peter the Great. It occupies a dominant position with its 5 domes visible from every part of the town. The span of the central vault is 14 m (15 yds). The decorations were painted at the beginning of the 19th century. In front of the eastern wall is a huge iconostasis; the 2 lower rows contain the oldest, though not the best preserved, icons. The Church of Prince-Dimitri-on-the-Blood is part of Uglich Museum.

The *belfry* to the south of the cathedral and close to the Palace was built in 1730. Its highly bulky structure has an unexpectedly light and elegant spire.

Kazansky Church on Kommuny Square was built in 1778 in place of an old wooden church. It played an important part as a focal point at the end of one of the main streets. Only the lower part has been preserved.

Voskresensky (Resurrection) Monastery and the *Church of the Nativity of John the Baptist* (1689) are picturesquely situated on Sovietskaya Square, by the Volga. They are fine examples of 17th-century Russian church architecture. The monastery was built in 1674–77 by the order of, and under the supervision of, Iona, Metropolitan of Rostov Veliki. The monastery buildings have much in common with similar buildings in Rostov. Here, for the first time in Uglich, green tiles were used with pictures of battles and daily life, animals, and emblems. The largest building here is the *Voskresensky Cathedral* with 5 cupolas. Even the rich decor cannot detract from the pure lines of this building. The other buildings are the *belfry*, the *Church of Odeghitria*, and the *refectory*. The small fragments of frescoes preserved in the Church of Odeghitria and in the cathedral give an impression of the quality of the original decoration of the monastery. In 1764 the monastery was closed and the churches turned into parish churches. Though some restoration has been done recently, the structures are still much in need of attention.

The *Church of the Nativity of John the Baptist* was built before the monastery. It attracts attention by the contrast between the light, well-proportioned belfry and the squat, heavy porch with massive columns.

Alekseyevsky Monastery, at Krestyanskaya Street 27, was founded in 1371 by Aleksei, Metropolitan of all Russia, upon the orders of Dmitri Donskoy, Grand Prince of Moscow. It was planned to guard Uglich from the Yaroslavl side. In 1609 Polish troops approaching Uglich besieged the monastery, where about 500 citizens had taken refuge. Infuriated by their staunch defence, the Poles burnt down the wooden structure, killing everybody inside and burying some people alive.

The monastery was rebuilt after the Time of Troubles, and in 1628 the *Uspenskaya Divnaya Church (Wonderful Church of the Assumption)* was erected. It is a masterpiece of old Russian architecture. A characteristic feature is its three octagonal spires topped with onion-shaped cupolas.

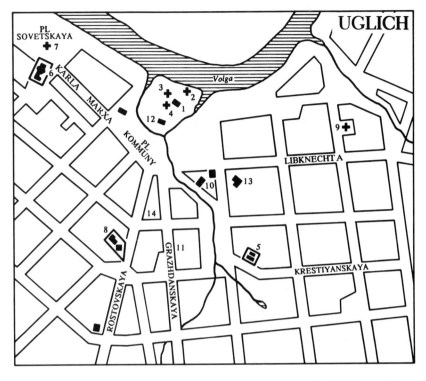

UGLICH

UGLICH
1. Prince Dmitri's Palace
2. Church of Prince Dmitri-on-the-Blood
3. Spaso-Preobrazhensky Cathedral
4. Belfry

5. Alekseyevsky Monastery
6. Voskresensky Monastery
7. Church of the Nativity of John the Baptist
8. Bogoyavlensky Monastery
9. Korsunskaya Church

10. Mekhov-Voronin's House (18th cent.)
11. Kazimirov's House (18th cent.)
12. Town Council (1815)
13. Ovsyannikov's House (18th cent.)
14. Kalashnikov's House (18th cent.)

The ground plan is quite simple. The refectory adjoins a small church hall on the first floor. At various times the vaults of the crypt served as a prison. Uspenskaya Church is one of the best examples of old Russian architecture of the 16th and early 17th century.

When *Bogoyavlensky (Epiphany) Monastery*, at Rostovskaya Street 22, was originally founded, it was housed in the northwestern part of the kremlin, but in 1661 it was transferred to new buildings by the road leading to Rostov. The earliest stone structures date from the end of the 17th century. In 1853 the huge *Bogoyavlensky Cathedral* was built. Its most interesting feature is the cost of construction—60,000 silver roubles—an enormous sum for that time. *Smolenskaya Church* (1700) and *Fyodorovskaya Church* (1818) are also in Bogoyavlensky Monastery.

Other churches, less interesting from the architectural and historical point of view include:
Pyatnitskaya Church (1764), Sovietskaya Square.

SS. *Flor and Lavr Church*, Ostrovskovo Street 1a. This church, built in 1762, stands on the site of the mews of the Prince of Uglich.

A number of old houses also remain in the town. There is *Mekhov-Voronin's House* at Kamenskaya Street 4, which some experts think dates from the 17th century. It follows the usual plan with the ground floor occupied by household implements and storage rooms, while the living quarters and accommodation for guests occupy the upper floor. Of interest are the carved wooden banisters and the decorative tiled stove. *Kalashnikov's House* at Pervomaiskaya Street 13/10 is an 18th-century stone house and *Kasatkin House* at Nekrasova Street 13, decorated with elaborated wood carving, was built at the beginning of the last century.

Museum, in the Kremlin. Open 10–5; closed Wed.

Trud (labour) Stadium, Liebknecht Street 54
Hotel, Liebknecht Street 16
Uglich Restaurant, Rostovskaya Street 2
Volga Cafe, Liebknecht Street 54
Bank, Liebknecht Street 23
GPO, Liebknecht Street 18

ULAN-UDE is the capital of the Buryat Autonomous Republic or Buryatia.

BURYATIA

The Buryats are a Mongolian-speaking people. They have been known since 1207. When the Russians arrived in the area in the 17th century, they were ruled by several clans headed by local princes.

The Buryat language and customs are akin to those of the Mongolians. The majority embrace either the Buddhist faith or Christianity. During the reign of Catherine the Great, Buryatia was one of the areas to which Old Believers were exiled. Apart from Russians, there were also foreign missionaries in Buryatia. Two English missionaries, A. D. Stallybrass and Edward Swan, lived among the Buryats from 1818 until 1841, and it was they who translated the Old Testament into Mongolian. A decree on Lamaist clergy was signed by Tsar Nicholas I in 1853. Before the revolution there were 36 Buddhist monasteries staffed by 16,000 lamas for Buddhists in the Transbaikal area. The exact number of Buddhists in the Soviet Union now is not known, although official sources vary between 50,000 and 100,000. The majority reside in the Buryat, Kalmyk and Tuvinian Autonomous Republics. The Buddhists' centre and the residence of the Chairman of the Ecclesiastical Board of the Soviet Buddhists is the *Ivolgin Monastery*, 40 km (25 miles) south of Ulan-Ude.

In 1970, when the Buddhist Movement for Peace was organised in the Mongolian capital of Ulan-Bator, the first Peace Congress was held at Ivolgin Monastery. Since then similar congresses have been held more or less regularly.

In the 1820s local self-government was introduced in the form of the Twelve Steppe Dumas to which they elected their own representatives. During the Civil War a theocratic Buryat state was proclaimed for a short time. The Steppe Dumas remained in nominal operation until the 1917 Revolution. After the Civil War and the restoration of Soviet power, the Far Eastern Republic was organised in March 1920 as a buffer state with Verkhneudinsk as its capital. This was recognised by Moscow almost immediately, and when the Japanese had to "leave the country and Vladivostok" in 1922 a Maritime Province was incorporated into the Far Eastern Republic, and the Republic itself in turn was dissolved and joined the Soviet Union. In 1923 the Buryat Autonomous Republic was established, until 1958 called the Buryat-Mongol Autonomous Republic.

Ulan-Ude Population—350,000

Ulan-Ude is the first large city to the east of Lake Baikal and all trains bound for the Soviet Far East pass through it. It is situated on either bank of the river Uda and along the right bank of the wide Selenga of which the Uda is a tributary. The Selenga drains the whole of the central part of Mongolia and flows past Ulan-Ude to empty into Lake Baikal. The city stands on the slopes of the Ulan-Burgasy, the Khamar-Daban and the Tsagan-Daban ranges. The climate here is continental with cold winters and a short, hot summer. The average summer temperature is 18.5°C (65.3°F) and in winter −22°C (−8°F).

Some people believe that the name Uda derives from that of the Usu (Uduit) Merkit tribe which lived here in the 12th century along the banks of the Orkhon and Selenga rivers. Others are of the opinion that it comes from the Mongol word for "noon," and connect it with the legend which says that some Mongolian army or nomads reached this river one day in time for their midday break for lunch as "ude" means midday. Still others think it comes from the Selkup word "ut" meaning water or the Samodi word for hand.

Russian explorers first appeared in these parts in 1649, but at that time their winter camp was shortlived. In 1666 the Cossacks founded a winter camp called Udinskoye for the purpose of collecting the fur tribute from the local Buryat tribes. It was devastated by the Mongols but the favourable position on the established trade routes to Mongolia, China and points east persuaded the Moscow government to reconstruct it as a stronghold. This was done in the winter of 1668–69 upon the order of Fyodor Golovin, the Tsar's envoy here. The fortress was encircled by wooden walls with embrasures, its garrison was reinforced by another 200 guardsmen and Cossacks, and its name was changed to Verkhneudinsk.

In 1691 it became the town of Verkhneudinsk. Following the construction of the Siberian trade route and the Kyakhta China tea route, and the development of Russia's commercial ties with Mongolia and China, Verkhneudinsk lost its military significance and became a lively Russian trade centre in the east. The population grew rapidly and new settlers built their houses outside the walls of the fortress. The town was thus divided into two parts: the fortress within the wall with the powder cellar, artillery storehouse and the guardhouse, and the outskirts (sloboda) with food stores, shops, administrative buildings, barracks, wine cellars, a market place, private houses and churches.

From 1768 the largest annual Trans-Baikal fair was held here. It was important for the Buryat cattle-breeders and hunters to sell their produce. From 1780 the fairs were held twice a year and attracted merchants and industrialists from different places all over Russia. They played an important role in Buryat economic development. In 1783 Verkhneudinsk became an administrative centre of the Trans-Baikal Region and on 26th October, 1790, it was given its own coat-of-arms, with Mercury's staff and a cornucopia symbolising both the trade profits and the wealth of the area.

Among the new settlers were many Cossacks and also peasants, resettled from other parts of the country. Verkhneudinsk was at the same time a place of exile for political prisoners and church dissenters. All these varied people helped Siberia to become the most international region of the whole of Russia. The first exile here was A. Muravyev who arrived in Verkhneudinsk in 1827. He was one of the founders of the first clandestine societies, the Union of Salvation and the Union of

Prosperity (Soyuz Spaseniya and Soyuz Blagoden-stviya). Nikolai and Mikhail Bestuzhev were exiled in Seleginsk, further up the river Selenga in a southwesterly direction from Verkhneudinsk, where they started teaching the Buryats to read and write. They visited Verkhneudinsk on more than one occasion.

A Russian traveller who was in Verkhneudinsk in the early 19th century wrote that the place was well built and had beautiful wide streets, and that a straight road led from their right to the Chinese border.

At the end of the century an English visitor wrote: "Verkhneudinsk is a cheerful-looking little town, with the Uda river bounding one side of it, and the pine forest every other. It has a population of about five thousand, whose white dwellings are overlooked by the towers of three or four churches. The streets are very wide, but they have no pavement of any kind, and making one's way along them is like walking on some sandy shore above the water-line." The predominantly wooden-built town had suffered much damage in the great fire of 1878, and at this time there were no more than nine stone or brick buildings.

The construction of the Trans-Siberian Railway was of great importance to the Trans-Baikal Region. The first train arrived in Verkhneudinsk on August 15, 1899, and the citizens were ordered to decorate their houses by day and to illuminate them at night. The town became the major junction of the West Trans-Baikal area and a period of rapid growth began. New construction included a railway depot, a large marshalling yard, an electric powerstation, and timber and glass factories. The population rose to 20,000 in 1914.

In 1918 Verkhneudinsk was occupied by the rebellious Czech Legion, the ex-prisoner-of-war troops who were assisting the counterrevolutionaries as they made their way westward in an attempt to leave Siberia. American and Japanese forces also held it for short periods at that time. After the Civil War it became the capital first of the Far Eastern Republic and then of the Buryat Autonomous Republic. In 1934 it was renamed Ulan-Ude ("red Uda" in Buryat).

Ulan-Ude is the home of the Buryat branch of SOAN, the Siberian Department of the Academy of Sciences. The research here is mostly concerned with local problems, particularly those related to the exploitation of the natural resources of Buryatia and Mongolia. The institutes include those of natural science, geology, biology and economics. The Institute of Social Sciences specialises in oriental ethnography. Its library has more than 6,000 volumes and it has a department devoted to the study of writings on Indo-Tibetan medicine.

Among the city's varied industries is the manufacture of engines and glass as well as timber and light industries. There is also a meat-processing plant, one of the largest in the country, which mostly handles meat from Mongolia.

In its layout the town is picturesquely shaped like an amphitheatre. It consists of three districts—Sovietsky, Zheleznodorozhny and Oktyabrsky, which are divided by the rivers and the railway line. Lenin (formerly Bolshaya) and Kirov Streets are pedestrian precincts. Lenin Street is the main street of the city. Starting from Pioneers (Pionerskaya) Square it runs in a northwesterly direction crossing the central part of Ulan-Ude. It links the two largest squares—Revolutionary (formerly Market) Square and Sovietov (formerly Nagornaya) Square, the latter being the city's most important. In 1931 the House of Soviets was built here in constructivist style and was the biggest building in the town. Now there are state and party offices in new buildings around the square, and there is an enormous head of Lenin in the centre. This is the square that is used for parades and demonstrations.

Our Lady of Odigitria Cathedral, Lenin Street, near Revolutsii Square; built in 1745 and now housing a museum

Troitskaya (trinity) Church

Among the city's oldest buildings are the following:

Former Primary School, Kommunisticheskaya Street; built in 1806 and now used by the Institute of Advanced Teachers' Training

Trade and Bolshiye Gostinye Arcade, Revolyutsii Square. The construction of the Gostinye Arcade began in 1804 and lasted until 1856, but it was never completed. The Trade Arcade opposite was built in the 1830s. The large, decorated stone arcade in Russian classical style and the small wooden one now house a polyclinic.

Verkhneudinsk High School (Ghimnazia), Lenin Street; built in the early 19th century and now a kindergarten

Merchant's Mansion, Lenin Street; built in the late 19th century and now a House of Young Pioneers

Girls' School, Kuibysheva Street; built in 19th century and now a Young Technicians' Centre

Town Hospital, Kuibysheva Street; built in 1880 and now a police station

Gorky Library, Lenin Street 21; founded in 1881

Residential House, Lenin Street 23; built in 1889 and now the Erdem ("science" in Buryat) Cinema

Kurbatov's House, Lenin Street 27; built in Russian classical style in the late 19th century. A second floor was added in 1957, and it now houses the Regional Trade Union Council.

Russian-Asian Bank, at the corner of Lenin and Kalandarishvili Streets; now the central chemist's shop

Rosenburg's House, at the corner of the Sukhe-Bator and Lenin Streets. Built in art-nouveau style at the end of the last century, it was the tallest building in the town. In 1904 the Vladivostok Institute of Oriental Languages was transferred here due to the Russo-Japanese War. It is now an Institute of Culture.

Vtorov's Wholesale Storehouse, Kommunisticheskaya Street; built in the 19th century. In 1918–

20 it served as the residence of the commander-in-chief of the American troops. Now it is the East Siberian Institute of Technical Engineering.

The most interesting wooden houses, richly ornamented with woodcarving and dating from the turn of the century, can be found on Nekrasov, Kommunisticheskaya, Sovietskaya, Pervomaiskaya, Sverdlov and Smolina Streets.

M. Khangalov Local Museum and Oriental Art Museum, Profsoyuznaya Street 29; open 10–5. The house was built in 1902, and a large annex was added in 1983.

Local Museum, Lenin Street 4

Art Gallery, Lenin Street 19; open 10–5

Sampilov Applied Art Museum, named after the artist, Ts Sampilov

Natural History Museum, Lenin Street 46

Geological Museum, Lenin Street 59

Decembrists' Museum, in the village of Novo-Selenginskaya

Namsarayev's Flat Museum, Hotsa Namsarayev (1889–1959) was the founder of Buryat Soviet literature

Sampilov Flat Museum, Schmidt Street 18

New Gorky Library, Erbanov Street

Trans-Baikal Region Ethnographical Museum, in Verkhnyaya Bereznovka, behind the racecourse, 10 km (6 miles) out of town. Opened in 1973, this covers a territory of 40 hectares (100 acres) and includes wooden houses and other buildings of the area brought here from different regions. There are exhibits illustrating the customs and culture of the local peoples—Russians, Buryats and Evenks.

1905–07 Revolution Memorial, Gagarin Street

Civil War Memorials, in the Park of Rest and Recreation and in Partizanskaya Street, the latter dedicated to soldiers killed while capturing Verkhneudinsk in 1920

Fighters for Communism Monument, Revolutsii Square, in front of a department store and shopping arcades. This was built by Kotov in the shape of a parallelepiped. It was unveiled in 1920 and bears words from the Internationale on the northern part. Another inscription saying to whom the monument is dedicated is written in Mongolian, Korean and Chinese.

Serov Monument, Serov Street, in front of the Natural History Museum. Vasily Serov (1878–1918) was a professional revolutionary, and one of the organisers of Soviet power in the Trans-Baikal area.

Lenin Monument, in a garden on Lenin Street and in Sovietov Square

Erbanov's Bust, in front of the Agricultural Technical School. Mikhei Erbanov (1889–1938) was a local revolutionary and statesman.

T-34 Tank Monument, Pobedy Prospect

Opera and Ballet Theatre, Sovietov Square

Khosha Namsarayev Buryat Drama Theatre, Pobedy Prospect

Russian Drama Theatre, Lenin Street 46. Built in 1914 as a public club, it was transformed into the Lenin People's House in 1921. Then it was used consecutively as a theatre for musical productions, drama and then opera and ballet.

Puppet Theatre, Pushkin Street 3

Hippodrome Racecourse, near the brickworks at Verkhnyaya Berezovka, 10 km (6 miles) out of town

Sovietov Hotel Annex, Erbyankov Street 18; tel. 25–85, 37–18

Intourist Hotel Annex, Lenin Street

Baikal Restaurant, Erbykov Street

GPO, Lenin Street 61

Bank, Lenin Street 28

Department Store, Revolyutsii Square

Bookshop, Kuibysheva Street 28

Ancient Hun Settlement, 15 km (9 miles) southwest of Ulan-Ude along the road towards Kyakhta. This site excavated by Academician Okladnikov dates from the 2nd–1st centuries B.C.

Buddhist Monastery, 27 km (17 miles) along the Kyakhta route near the village of Shishkino. This is a functioning monastery, and in addition to the faithful here it also serves those in the Tuva Republic on the Mongolian border.

ULYANOVSK Population—625,000

Known as Simbirsk until 1924, Ulyanovsk stands on a high hill on the Volga-Sviyaga watershed, on the right bank of the river Volga with the river Sviyaga flowing through the town. The average temperature is −14°C (7°F) in winter, 22°C (71.6°F) in summer. The old Chuvash name of Simbirsk means "hill of the winds," but some contend that the name has another source—a Bulgar tsar once ruled here and his name was Sinbir. Lenin was born here in 1870, and lived here for 17 years; after his death in 1924 the town was renamed after his family name, Ulyanov. It is the centre of the Ulyanovsk Region.

When the town was founded in 1648 it was first called Sinbirsk after the ancient settlement of Sinbir, 30 km (19 miles) further down the Volga. It served as the first fortress on the Russian line of defence against the Nogai Tatars. To the southwest a continuous earthwall was built, fortified with a stockade and occasional wooden towers. The wall was intended as a barrier against "the thieving people" and also to facilitate the collection of taxes on goods being carried in and out of Russia.

Some 20 years after its foundation, Simbirsk was the centre of one of the bloodiest peasant uprisings in Russian history, led by the Cossack leader, Stepan Razin. Simbirsk held out against the rebels for a month until the arrival of government troops. By the end of the 17th century Simbirsk had lost its military importance and become a peaceful country town. After the Pugachev uprising of 1773, Catherine the Great awarded Simbirsk the coat-of-arms of a coronet on a pole because, unlike most of the towns along the Volga, it had remained loyal to the throne. The name "venets" (coronet) belongs to the hilly part of the town which stands 140–170 m (460–560 ft) above the Volga.

In 1796 Simbirsk was made the capital of a province of the same name. At the beginning of the 19th century exiles sent there included the Georgian princess, Tamar, who spent 10 years in Simbirsk after a plot to regain Georgian independence had failed. In 1864 a fire broke out and continued for 10 days, destroying three-quarters of the town.

Simbirsk was often referred to as the birthplace of poets. The names of many prominent Russian writers, scientists, and statesmen have been connected with the town, including Karamzin, the 18th-century historian, and Goncharov, author of "Oblomov," after whom the main street is named.

Among the town's more impressive old buildings is the *Palace of Books* on Karl Marx Street. This was formerly the House of Nobles, built in 1847, but now it is a library which was formed by merging the Karamzin and Goncharov Memorial Libraries. The first collection was founded in 1848 and contains 2,100 expensive volumes which the historian Karamzin himself presented to the town, and the second collection dates from 1891. Lenin Square is where the *House of Councils* stands, the home of the local municipal offices.

Ulyanovsk has grown in importance. It boasts 3 institutes and a House of Technicians, and its position as both a railway junction and a river port have encouraged the development of industry. There is a large automobile factory, machine tools are made here, and there are leather, food, and timber industries.

Its chief claim to fame, however, are its associations with Lenin, whose real name was Vladimir (Volodya) Ulyanov and who was born here in 1870 soon after his parents and elder brother and sister moved here from Nizhny-Novgorod. His father, Ilya Nikolayevich Ulyanov, had been appointed inspector of public schools in Simbirsk Province. Their first home, where Volodya was born, was in Streletskaya Street (now Ulyanov Street) but they moved house several times before they finally settled at 68 *Lenin Street* where the *museum* now is. From 1876–8 they lived at 28 Tolstoy Street. When he was old enough Volodya followed his brother Alexander (Sasha) to the local grammar school, the headmaster of which was Fedor Kerensky. It was Kerensky's son, Alexander, born in 1881, who grew up to head the Provisional Government which was overthrown by Lenin's October Revolution in 1917.

The *Lenin Memorial Complex* was opened in April 1970, to commemorate the 100th anniversary of Lenin's birth. The chief architect was Boris Mezantsev from Moscow. The complex includes the top of Venets Hill and the semicircular area formed by Goncharov Boulevard and the Volga Embankment, and incorporates Lenin Square, Lenin Street, Sovietskaya Street, and Ulyanov Street, all places connected with Lenin's youth. In addition there are some impressive buildings which were specially erected.

The *Memorial Centre* is a huge quadrangle with sides 100 m/yds long. The building stands upon 8-m (26-ft) columns and so one is able to see into the quadrangle from outside. Within it stands the house where the Ulyanov family lived from 1869 to 1875, and where Lenin was born. Open 10–6; closed Thurs.

The Centre houses a branch of the *Lenin Museum* on the first floor. Open daily 10–6. There is also a *House of Political Education* with study rooms, a lecture hall and a combined cinema and concert hall which seats 1400. Also in the Centre is the white marble *October Hall* with a 6-m (19-ft) statue of Lenin.

From the Centre a wide flight of steps leads down to the Volga, and nearby stands the *Venets Hotel*, the study block of the *Pedagogical Institute*, and in Sovietskaya Street, overlooking Karamzin Garden, *Lenin School No. 1*, formerly Simbirsk Grammar School. Open 10–5; closed Sun. It was founded at the beginning of the 19th century and the outside has been altered but it was here that Lenin studied from 1879 till 1887. It is still run as a regular school, but next to the assembly hall is the classroom where Lenin worked when he was in the 7th form (1885–86). This is kept as a memorial room to him and his desk stands in its place near the window. In April 1970, 100 young trees were planted to mark the centenary; one more is added each year.

Lenin's House Museum, Lenin Street 68, quite near the school, in the house where the Ulyanov family lived from 1878–87. Open 10–6; closed Tues. It contains a portrait room, a drawing room with a piano, the inspector's study, his wife's room with her knitting basket and her library of books in French, English, and German as well as Russian, and the dining room which was the largest room in the house. The children's rooms were in the attic. Sasha, who was 4 years Volodya's senior, had a strong influence upon his brother. His chemical equipment is in place in his room as a tribute to his love of the subject. He left school with a gold medal and was awarded another at St. Petersburg University for his scientific research work. Gradually he became involved in student revolutionary activities which led to his execution in May 1887, when he was 21, for the attempted assassination of Alexander III. Volodya's room, above the staircase, is the smallest in the house. It contains an iron bedstead, a table, two chairs, a bookshelf, a large map, and the boy's school-leaving certificate. On the table are the books Lenin received at school as annual prizes. There is a croquet lawn outside the house.

Close to the river at the beginning of Goncharov Boulevard is a *Pioneer Palace* with workshops, studios, and gymnasia to cater for 2,000 children at a time. There is also a hotel for young visitors. An old wooden house has been left just as it was when a group of Simbirsk revolutionaries used to gather there at the time of the first Russian Revolution in 1905. They had contact with Lenin through his younger brother Dmitri.

St. Nicholas's Church (20th century), Verkhnyaya Polevaya Street.

Goncharov Local Museum, Novy Venets Boulevard 3/4, facing the river. Open 10–5:30; closed

ULYANOVSK

Mon. Donations came from all over Russia in 1914 to commemorate the centenary of the birth of Ivan Goncharov, the Russian novelist and editor. The museum bearing his name houses all sorts of exhibits including those of the Provincial Ethnographic Museum.

Plastov Picture Gallery, named after A. Plastov.

Art Museum, Novy Venets Boulevard 3/4, facing the river. Open 10–5:30; closed Mon. Besides a variety of paintings and some icons, there is a special room devoted to Goncharov himself, showing family portraits and a number of watercolours he painted in Japan.

Goncharov Literary Museum, Goncharov Street 30. Open 10–5:30; closed Mon. On display are the personal and family effects and furniture of Ivan Goncharov (1814–91), the Russian novelist and editor. There are also rare 18th–19th century books.

Education Museum, in the building where the first women's school was opened by Ilya Ulyanov. Opened in 1986.

Lenin Gallery, L. Tolstoy Street 55. Open 9:30–5:30; closed Tues. This contains a large collection of paintings of Lenin by many different artists.

Karamzin Monument, in Karamzin Garden. Nikolai Karamzin (1766–1826) was a historian who wrote "The History of the Russian State," the first comprehensive work on the subject. The inscription on the monument reads: "To N.P. Karamzin, an historian of the State. By Order of Emperor Nicholas I, 1844." Local nobles were responsible for carrying out the imperial order. The bronze figure of Clio, muse of history, lays Karamzin's book upon an altar. The statue, by Galdberg, was cast by Klodt. The pedestal is decorated with two brass bas-reliefs showing episodes from Karamzin's life and in a niche in the front wall of the pedestal is a bust of Karamzin by Ramazonov and Klimchenko.

Gai Monument, Gai Prospect. G. Gai was a Civil War hero, and the sculptor was Nazaryan.

Bust of Goncharov, in a garden near the Palace of Books, on Karl Marx Street. This bust of the novelist by Vetrov was unveiled in 1948.

Goncharov's Birthplace, Goncharov Boulevard 16. The house is marked by a black marble plaque and a bas-relief by Mikeshin, unveiled in 1907.

Ilya Ulyanov Monument, in a garden on 12-Sentyabrya Street. The bust of Lenin's father was sculpted in pink granite by Manizer in 1957. Below him, at the corner of the pedestal, stands the bronze figure of a peasant boy with a staff in one hand and an open book in the other, symbolising Ulyanov's work as an educationalist. Ilya Ulyanov's grave is nearby, in a cemetery on Liebknecht Street.

Civil War Memorial, Novy Venets Boulevard, near the Volga. The white obelisk marks the grave of soldiers killed in Simbirsk in 1918. The architect was Voltsev and the unveiling took place in 1927.

Karl Marx Monument, at the crossing of Kommunisticheskaya and Ulyanov Street. The 2-m (7-ft) figure in black granite stands on a pedestal of grey granite, 1.8 m (6 ft) high. It was designed and executed by Schuko, Merkurov, and Antonov and unveiled in 1921.

Lenin Monument, Lenin Square. The statue in granite by Manizer stands 14.5 m (48 ft) high and was unveiled in 1940.

Lenin as a Schoolboy, in front of the railway station. This statue by Tsigal was unveiled in 1954.

Drama Theatre, Sovietskaya Street 8. Built in 1879 and reconstructed in 1970.

Puppet Theatre, Goncharov Street 10

Philharmonia Concert Hall, Lenin Square 5

Concert Hall, in the Lenin Memorial Complex

Sverdlov Park, Plekhanov Street 12

Regional Economic Exhibition, Narimanov Road, in a forested park

Spartak Stadium

Venets Hotel and Restaurant, Sovietskaya Street 15; tel. 94–595. There is a Beryozka foreign currency shop here, an *art salon* and the local *Intourist office*; tel. 94–816.

Volga Hotel and Restaurant, Goncharov Boulevard 3; tel. 14–577

Rossia Hotel and Restaurant, Karl Marx Street 23; tel. 17–862

Sovietskaya Hotel and Moskva Restaurant, Sovietskaya Street 6

Bank, Goncharov Street 42/1

GPO, Goncharov Street 9/58

Beryozka (foreign currency) Shop, in the Venets Hotel

Department Store, Goncharov Street 21

Book Shop, Goncharov Street 24

Souvenirs, Goncharov Street 36 and Lenin Street 28a

Gifts, Goncharov Street 17

Intourist organises *boat trips* on the reservoir and a number of *excursions*.

Vinnovskaya Grove, a little way out of town, to the south along the Volga. This was formerly known as Kindyakovskaya Grove and is a popular recreation spot. Goncharov described it in his novel "Obryv" ("The Precipice") and to commemorate the centenary of his birth a rotunda was built here with an obelisk and a bas-relief of the writer.

Bathing Beach, on Paltsensky Island 30 km (19 miles) up the Volga. One can get to this very pleasant beach by boat from Olyanovsk.

Lenin Hydropower Station, 150 km (93 miles) down the river, reached by hydrofoil.

UMAN Population—70,000

(Intourist organises excursions here from both Kiev and Cherkassy. The road passes through country which is mainly steppeland with some forest areas. It is an industrial and agricultural region; its production has chiefly to do with food and the food machinery industries, chemicals, coal and consumer goods. The agriculture is mostly grain, sugar beet, beef and dairy cattle and melons.)

The town of Uman stands beside the river Umanka in a hilly locality on the eastern branch of the Avratin Hills, and is a little to the west of the Odessa-Kiev Motorway. It is first mentioned in 1616, its name deriving from that of the river. The Cossacks built one of their strongest fortresses here in 1650.

From 1726 it belonged to Count Potocski's family. They owned a total of 400,000 serfs, hundreds of villages and 70 other small towns, but Uman was judged to be one of the best in the western Ukraine. There were regular fairs, some of which lasted for two weeks at a time, and the Roman Catholic church was very active here, both a monastery and a school being founded in Uman in 1765.

Shortly after this, in 1768, the religious intolerance of the local peasants vented its wrath upon the Polish and Jewish inhabitants of the town. During the Uman Massacre 18,000 townsfolk lost their lives and Uman itself was razed to the ground. Subsequently the insurgents were brutally punished, beheading and quartering being the more usual forms of execution.

Uman is a holy place for the Braclav Hasidim (Hasidic Jews from nearby Braclav—pronounced "Bratslav"), as their Rabbi Nahman is buried here.

Sofievka Park (see map) was laid out in 1802 by Count Felix Potocki, but following the family's participation in the Polish uprising of 1831 it was confiscated by the state along with all other Potocki property. Uman had already earned the descriptive title of "Kiev in miniature," and by the turn of the century it had grown into an important industrial centre.

Uman now lies to the left of the main road and near the turning are the *Dorozhnaya Hotel* and the *Tourist Restaurant*, both on the left, and a *service station* on the right.

The town's main square is named after Lenin, whose monument appropriately stands there. Next to the monument is another, of granite, bearing the text of two cables which were sent to the town by Lenin in 1922 and 1923. The square is surrounded by administrative buildings.

The Potocki house is now used by the Gorky Agricultural Institute and in Uman is also the Tychina Pedagogical Institute. Pavlo Tychina (b. 1891) was a Ukrainian poet. There is a flour mill and a brickworks in the town and local industry includes more than thirty different enterprises altogether which manufacture machinery, ready-made clothing, vitamins, butter and other food products.

Uspensky (Assumption) Cathedral, Leningradskaya Iskra Street 79. Built in 1812 and formerly known as St. Nicholas's Church, it was rededicated as Uman Cathedral when the original Uspensky Cathedral, near the market place, was closed; this one is open for services.

Old Uspensky Cathedral, at the end of Lenin Street, near the market place. Built in Byzantine style in 1907 and now closed. The market itself is housed in part of the old shopping arcade and in the 18th-century town hall building.

St. Michael's Church, Artyom Street; closed

St. Alexander Nevsky's Church, originally built as a military church, then used as a concert hall; now the Chernyakhovsky Cinema

St. Basil's Monastery, Radyanska Street. This was built in 1766 and until it was closed it ran a school for 400 pupils.

Local Museum, Zhovtneva Street 31. Open 10–7; closed Wed.

Iskra Museum, Leninskaya Iskra Street 128. Open 10–7; closed Tues. and Wed. This is one of the places where the revolutionary newspaper was printed, literally in an underground printshop.

Kotovsky's Home, Smidovicha Pereulok 6. Open 10–7; closed Tues. and Wed.

Picture Gallery, Kolomenskaya Street 2. Open 10–7; Closed Thurs. It is housed in the building of the Roman Catholic *Uspenskaya (Assumption) Church*, built in 1825 and used as the church of the Polish cemetery until it was closed in 1935.

Volkonsky Monument, erected in 1975 to the 150th anniversary of the Decembrist uprising. Sergei Volkonsky was here on military service, and the grey granite monument bears the dates 1819–1826 (those being the years of his activity here with the movement) and also the bas-relief portraits of five members of the movement.

Lenin Monument, Lenin Square

Kotovsky Monument, in a garden on Radyanska Street near the old cathedral

Kalinin's Bust, in Budyonny Park

Obelisk of Glory, in Geroyev (heroes') Park in the centre of the town, commemorating those who fell during World War II. It stands beside a common grave and an eternal flame.

Piontovsky and Urbalis Monument, next to the obelisk. This monument marks the grave of two heroes of the Civil War.

Ivan Chernaykhovsky Monument, Karl Marx Street. This bust is dedicated to the memory of General Chernyakhovsky who was born in this area and who died in the Second World War.

Kotovsky Garden. There is a monument here to the soldiers who established Soviet power in Uman.

Kalinin Park

Budyonny Park

Sofievka Park. The park and gardens date from the 18th century. Sofievka was formerly a country house, built by Count Felix Potocki for his wife, Sofia de Felice, in 1802. It is on record that Potocki purchased his wife from a major in the Polish army for 2 million zloty; she had been a Turkish slave.

The park covers 150 hectares (375 acres) and contains 520 different species of trees, shrubs and other plants. At the main entrance to the park is an iron gate with two classical-style guard towers. The main avenue is lined with horse chestnuts and ends with the *Flora Pavilion* in Doric style. Pools and waterfalls were made using the water of the little river Kamenka. There is 23 m (75 ft) in difference between the height of the Upper and the Lower Pools. The area between the two pools is called the Champs Elysées and, among other artificial structures, it contains the Caucasian Mount. In the Upper Pool is the artificial Isle of

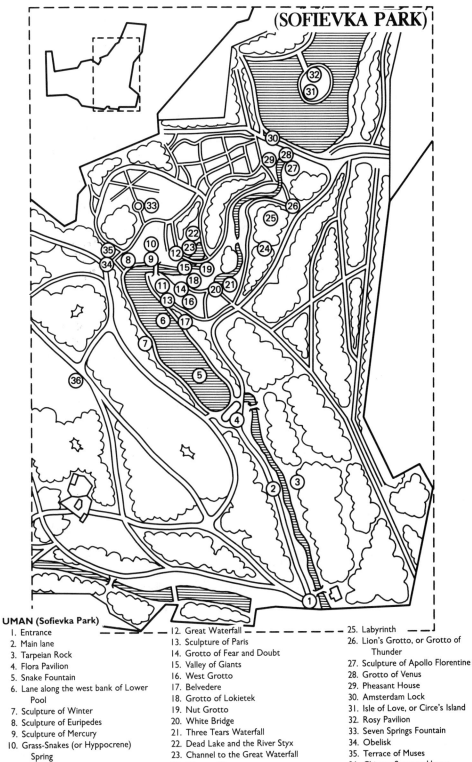

(SOFIEVKA PARK)

UMAN (Sofievka Park)

1. Entrance
2. Main lane
3. Tarpeian Rock
4. Flora Pavilion
5. Snake Fountain
6. Lane along the west bank of Lower Pool
7. Sculpture of Winter
8. Sculpture of Euripedes
9. Sculpture of Mercury
10. Grass-Snakes (or Hyppocrene) Spring
11. Meeting Square
12. Great Waterfall
13. Sculpture of Paris
14. Grotto of Fear and Doubt
15. Valley of Giants
16. West Grotto
17. Belvedere
18. Grotto of Lokietek
19. Nut Grotto
20. White Bridge
21. Three Tears Waterfall
22. Dead Lake and the River Styx
23. Channel to the Great Waterfall
24. Champs Elysees
25. Labyrinth
26. Lion's Grotto, or Grotto of Thunder
27. Sculpture of Apollo Florentine
28. Grotto of Venus
29. Pheasant House
30. Amsterdam Lock
31. Isle of Love, or Circe's Island
32. Rosy Pavilion
33. Seven Springs Fountain
34. Obelisk
35. Terrace of Muses
36. Chinese Summer House

Love with a small pavilion, and in the centre of the Lower Pool is the Belvedere Cliff whose side view resembles a human profile. In the western part of the Pool stands the Cliff of Death, weighing over 200 tons. It is said that during the work, it fell down and crushed many serfs, killing 300 outright. There is also the so-called Dead Lake, surrounded by a granite embankment and well-grown trees. From this flows an underground river, the Styx, through a 234-m long (245-yd) granite tunnel, leading to an open wooden canal, the Amsterdam Lock. The river sometimes dries up through lack of water. There is another fountain called the Seven Springs, and the farther end of the Lower Pool joins the Valley of the Giants, filled with great disordered rocks. In this valley are the Three Tears Waterfall and the Columns of Mourning. In the park there are many grottoes, dedicated to Fear, Doubt, Diana and Venus among others, and a part of the park is known as the English Park. It is open daily 8 A.M.–10 P.M.

Uman Hotel and Restaurant, Lenin Square 21/32; tel. 23–45

Druzhba (friendship) Restaurant, by the entrance to Sofievka Park

Cafeterias, Lenin Square and Radyanska Street 13, to the left down the street from the hotel. Breakfasts are provided at the latter.

GPO, Lenin Square

Telegraph Office, Engels Street 8

Bank, Kolomenskaya Street 16

Department Store, Radyanska Street, at the corner of Lenin Square

Filling Station, at the 203 km milestone, on the right side of the main motorway (round the clock service) and just to the south, beyond the turning to Uman

Repair Station, at the 203 km milestone, on the left side of the main motorway; open 8–4

URGENCH (Novo-urgench until 1929)
Population—130,000
Modern Urgench lies in an oasis squeezed from two sides by the deserts Kara-Kum and Kyzyl-Kum and open to the Aral Sea on the third. It is on the Shavat Canal, in the valley of the river Amu-Darya.

Here lay Khorezm, the ancient seat of Central Asia civilisation. The capital of Khorezm was also called Urgench, but it was a city which sprang up more than 2,000 years ago on the left bank of the Amu-Darya. Today it is known as the district centre of Kunya-Urgench (Old Urgench).

In the first centuries A.D. it was mentioned as "jue-ghan," in the Middle Ages the city was called Gurganj, which means "city of cities." However a legend gives another interpretation of this name: it is said that long ago, before Urgench even came into existence, there was a small settlement where the inhabitants lived in constant fear and seldom left their homes. The huge Ajarho dragons demanded of them a terrible contribution; every day a young girl was led beyond the walls to be devoured by them, and every family waited in terror for their turn. At last came the turn of Chur-Jamal (Chur

meaning lovely), the daughter of Mahmud Gaznevi, the ruler of the town. She was bound hand and foot and brought to the tomb of a saint near the town. And here she was found by two wandering heroes to whom she told her tale of woe. When one of the youths heard the description of the fire-breathing dragon, three metres (18 feet) long, he ran away in fear. But Khorazm, the second one, remained, fought and defeated the dragons, and learned the secret of the treasure they were guarding. Khorazm found the treasure, returned to town and married Chur-Jamal. On the site where the treasure had been buried a city was built which in honour of the girl, Chur, and the dragons' treasure (gandji) was named Churgandji.

In the 7th century the city belonged to a nomadic tribe called the Kanguians. At that period Urgench existed as a place where trading took place between the people of the steppe and the settled citizens. In 712 Khorezm was seized by the Arabs, who called Churgandji Djurdjaniya. From then on there were two rulers in Urgench—the local khorezm-shah and the emir, who represented the Arab caliph. It lay at the crossroads to Mongolia and China, Bulgaria and Persia; there was a trade in meat, leather, wool, cattle and slaves in exchange for the goods of more developed countries: woollen cloth, garments, glassware, metalware and jewelry. Mamun ibn Muhammed, the last emir of ancient Khorezm, captured new provinces in 995, but Urgench retained its status of capital and flourished even more. Towards the 11th century Urgench was a large cultural city, the centre of caravan trade, and it remained so till the end of the 13th century when it was destroyed by Genghis Khan, who besieged it for six months, and then, using the forces of his three sons, took it in April 1221 and destroyed it. Muslim sources give evidence of Urgench being razed from the face of the earth and flooded by the waters from the dam, and all the inhabitants being killed.

However, the traces of destruction soon disappeared. Khorezm became one of the wealthiest and most cultured provinces of the Golden Horde, and Urgench not only healed its wounds but became an even busier trade centre than before. More caravans passed through it, travelling from Russia and Europe to Mongolia, China and Persia.

The rule of Kutlug Timur and his wife Turabek-Khanum (1321–1360) in Urgench was the most brilliant in the city's history, marked by the construction of numerous palaces and living quarters. But at the end of the 14th century another calamity befell Urgench, this time fatal. Its wealth attracted Tamerlane, the most prominent statesman and military commander of Central Asia. Between 1372 and 1380 he made five devastating raids on Khorezm and all the material and cultural wealth of Khorezm was carried off to Samarkand while the territory of Urgench was ploughed up as a barley field. Urgench never recovered; her political life moved to Samarkand, Khiva became the capital of Khorezm, and the caravans followed other routes that bypassed Urgench.

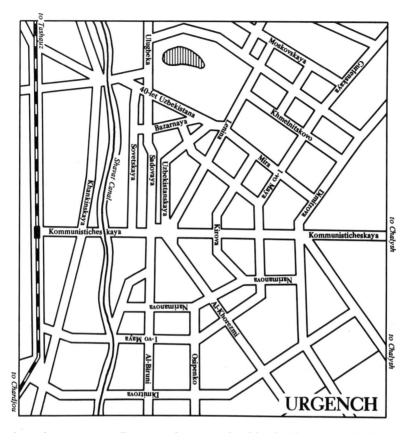

URGENCH

It was doomed to remain a small town standing on the fringe of the ruins of the former Urgench. In 1558 Anthony Jenkinson, traveller and trader from London, was passing through Urgench. He wrote: "Urgench is located on a plain and is surrounded by earth ramparts 4 miles long. The town's structures are also earthen but they are half destroyed and built without any order. There is a long street in the town under a canopy which serves as a market place. The town has greatly suffered from internecine wars, so there are only a few merchants left and very poor at that, so I could hardly sell four pieces of serge."

In 1645–46 a small fortress was built not far from the ancient capital and it was named New Urgench. To avoid any confusion, the old capital of Khorezm is now called Kunya Urgench meaning "old Urgench." Before the annexation of Central Asia to Russia in 1873, Novo-Urgench remained a small settlement, but at the turn of the century the Russians built a cotton-ginning plant and a creamery, set up the offices of three freight companies and opened a branch of the Russo-Asian Bank.

Russia carried all her purchases of agricultural goods from Central Asia through Novo-Urgench along the Amu-Darya River. Many years passed before the town started to grow. It consisted mainly of twisty, narrow streets, each leading to a dead end and lined with one-storey buildings. In 1938 Urgench became the administrative centre of the Khorezm district. The construction of a railway, a gas pipeline and high-voltage lines speeded up its progress.

Now it has grown to cover 12 sq km and is a centre of light and food industries, including silk spinning and seed oil extraction. There is a teachers' training college here and an economics institute.

Picture Gallery, Uzbekistanskaya Street 9. Open 10–7; closed Mon.

Avaz Utar Statue, Avaz Utar Square. Avaz Utar was a poet.

Razmi Statue, in a new square with modern buildings around it

Civil War Memorial, in front of the Picture Gallery on Uzbekistanskaya Street. There is an eternal flame here.

World War II Memorial, on the right of the main road to Khiva

Agakhi Musical Drama Theatre, Mira Street 11. Agakhi (1809–74) was a local writer, poet and translator. The theatre was opened in 1933.

Park, covers a territory of 33 hectares (82.5 acres) and is a popular recreation area with its Komsomolskoye Lake in the centre.

Lenin Monument, Lenin Square

Khorezm Hotel, at the airport

Khorezm Hotel and Restaurant, Al Biruni Street 2, tel. 65–408. There is a foreign currency shop in the hotel. Intourist office; tel. 65–666

GPO, Kommunistichesakaya Street, in a new building with a clock tower.

Market

From Urgench, Intourist organises excursions to Khiva (q.v.) and to the Nariman Collective Farm which grows cotton. Visits can also be made to the Kyzyl Kum ("red sand") desert and to the banks of the Amur Darya.

UZHGOROD is the most important town of the region of Transcarpathia.

TRANSCARPATHIA (Russian: Zakarpatiye)

The name means "beyond the Carpathians." 1,185,000 people live here, 80% of them Ukrainian but there are also Russians, Hungarians, Jews, Rumanians and Slovaks. Their occupations are timber and woodworking, winemaking and horticulture, and only 28% of them live in the towns.

For nearly 1000 years, from the time when, at the beginning of the 11th century, the Hungarians took it from the state of Kiev Rus, Transcarpathia was outside Russia. In the 16th century it was attacked by the Turks. Their insane cruelty to the Protestants provoked the revolt of General Istvan Bocskay in 1606, and his effort did much to increase the hold of the Calvinists and the Lutherans upon Transylvania. The area now known as Transcarpathia was then divided in two, with Uzhgorod under the rule of Habsburgs, and Mukachevo belonging to Transylvania. During the 17th century the Uniate Church, also known as the Ruthenian Catholic Church, an Eastern Catholic church of the Slavo-Byzantine rite, in communion with Rome since the Union (hence Uniate) of Uzhgorod of 1646, became established in the region. Early in the 18th century the whole Carpathian country, together with Hungary, was under Austrian rule. Count Schonborn was the most influential landlord in the area. The Hungarian revolution of 1848–49 also affected Transcarpathia, and in the mid-19th century Austria stimulated the building of factories there. Ruthenian (deriving from the Latin name for Russia) nationalism was also encouraged under the Habsburgs for a brief period. After the fall of the Austro-Hungarian Empire, Transcarpathia passed to Czechoslovakia as the province of Ruthenia.

After the Treaty of Trianon in 1920, when Uzhgorod became the centre of a part of Czechoslovakia called Podkarpatska Rus, there were various attempts made to establish Ruthenian autonomy and the language was used in schools, but when independence was finally achieved with the fall of Czechoslovakia to Germany in March 1939, it lasted for no more than a day after which the ill-fated Carpatho-Ukraine was annexed by Hungary. After World War II, in June 1945, the Soviet Union and Czechoslovakia signed an agreement by which Ruthenia was ceded to the USSR, and in the following year it was united with the Ukrainian Republic.

Uzhgorod Population—117,000 (Ukrainian and Czech: Uzhgorod; Hungarian: Ungvar)

The town is situated in the foothills of the Carpathian Mountains, on either side of the river Uzh (meaning "grass snake," so Uzhgorod is "grass snake town"). The surrounding area is a vinegrowing region and the ancient coat-of-arms of the town bears a vine with two golden bunches of grapes. Uzhgorod is the largest town in Transcarpathia.

Uzhgorod, known in the chronicles since the 9th century, is one of the oldest Slavonic towns, its troubled history one with that of the rest of Transcarpathia and with the rise and fall of Transylvania. As in most mediaeval towns, the older and more interesting parts are close to the castle. However, the oldest civilian building in the town is a baroque-style 16th–17th century *palace-estate* in the Radvanka suburbs; the famous Hungarian poet, Istvan Gyongyosi (1629–1704) was born here. In Radyanska Square is Zhupanat, the town's first important administrative building, dating from the 18th–19th centuries when many Jewish and German families settled here. The impressive white, 6-storey building known as *Narodnaya Rada* was built by Antonin Krupka, a Czech architect, in 1934–36 and now houses the local executive committee. Also Czech-built are some of the houses built between the wars on the embankment of the river and around Lenin Square. Radyanska Square and Teatralnaya Square along with Suvorov (formerly Velikomostnaya) Street are usually full of people, particularly in the evening. After World War II local time was changed from Central European to Moscow time, but even now people keep late hours and, when they make a date, often need to make sure whether they are talking about local time or Moscow time.

At the turn of the century one of the main branches of industry was furniture manufacture; the Mundus factory had been established in 1886 and a rival concern was the Begun factory. Food products were also manufactured. Since the early 1960s Soviet oil from the Volga-Caspian area has flowed through the Druzhba pipeline to refineries in Eastern Europe. Now there is a gas pipeline as well as an electric power grid, all passing near the town. Local industry: machine building, gas equipment, light industry, furniture and food products.

There are *mineral springs* of the carbonic acid type in front of the main university building in Gorky Park, and in Podgarsky and Protsky Streets.

Castle, Kremlivska Street 33. Open 10–6; closed Mon. It is known that a fortress was founded upon this site by the Romans in the 5th century A.D., and chronicles tell how it was subsequently taken over by the Hungarians. However, the oldest parts of the existing castle date from the end of the 9th century, and the Slav Prince Latorets resided here until he died in 903 in battle against the invading Hungarians, whereupon a nearby river was

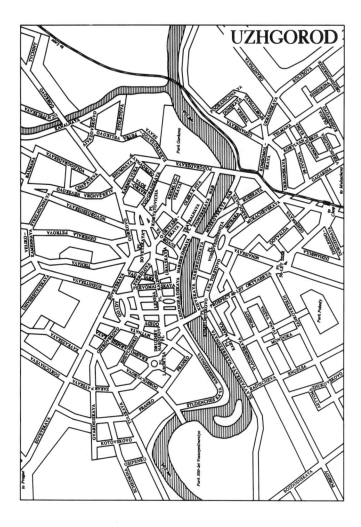

named after him. In 1290 the last king of the Arpad dynasty presented the town to his vassal, Amadei, but it was not long in his hands. In 1317 the Hungarian king, Charles Robert of Anjou, defeated all opposition and distributed the territory to his commanders, members of the Druget family who had come to Hungary from France but were really of Italian origin. Jan Druget was given Uzhgorod and it was the Drugets who invited builders from France and Italy to reconstruct the fortress here and who held it for the next 350 years.

It is from those early times that the legend of the castle's haunting comes. Once there was a secret passage leading down from the castle to the bottom of the hill, and during one of the numerous sieges in the history of the stronghold, the daughter of its master recognised her own beloved down below among the attacking forces. Frantic to find out how he happened to be there, she sent a message on an arrow shot from the castle walls asking him to meet her at the end of the passage at a certain time. Her letter was intercepted and she was caught on the way and accused of treason for disclosing the passage. Treason was punishable by death and so the young man was killed and the poor maiden was bricked up, alive, in the wall of the castle. She is said to emerge from her tomb at midnight and, dressed in white and with her hair dishevelled, search vainly around the castle for her sweetheart, returning with piteous sobs before dawn lightens the sky.

The Druget family were devoted Catholics, and it was due to them that monks of the Order of St. Paul opened a school here and later the Jesuits were made welcome. The date 1598 engraved over the entrance gate is that of one of the reconstructions of the castle. Much of the rebuilding that took place during the 16th century had been necessitated by the increasing use of gunpowder in contemporary warfare. After the death of Valentin Druget, the last of the line, it passed to Count Nicholas Berceni who was in charge of the rebel forces. In the 17th century it was seized several times during local disturbances. It was in the Roman Catholic chapel in the park that the Union of Uzhgorod was signed in 1646, marking the foundation of Uniate Church (see Transcarpathia, above).

The present castle has a 16th-century facade. Reconstruction was done principally to suit the requirements of new military techniques. The second date of 1653 engraved on the northern wall commemorates further structural changes. In 1703 the castle was captured by rebellious peasants led by Ivan Betzel at a time when many townspeople took arms against the Habsburgs under Ferenz Rakoczi II in the 1703–11 War of Independence. Rakoczi was himself resident in the castle by 1707 and conducted diplomatic negotiations there. The local garrison surrendered to the Austrian Army in 1711 but was granted an amnesty by the Treaty of Szatmar. Later in the 18th century the castle lost its military importance, and when the upper storey of the main castle building was burned down in 1728, it was rebuilt. In 1775 it was presented to the Uniate

Bishop of Mukachevo. Soon after that a seminary was opened in the castle and was only closed in 1944.

The castle, under reconstruction again, is quadrilateral in form and surrounded by a wall enclosing an area of 3 hectares (7.5 acres). There are extensive dungeons and cellars under the castle and from the top of the eastern tower there is a good view of the valley of the Uzh, while in fine weather the ruins of Nevitskoye Castle (see below) are visible to the northeast from the lookout platform in the southern wall. Immediately below the platform are the wooden buildings of the *Folk Architectural Museum*. The statue of Hercules engaged in his second labour, killing Cerberus, which stands in the castle yard opposite the entrance, was cast in Uzhgorod in 1842 by Kinne and is one of the exhibits of the local art museum. Another statue in the castle grounds is that of the mythical Turul bird of Hungary. Originally the castle had a moat on three sides while the fourth was naturally protected by a steep hill. The local museum and the art gallery are both housed inside the castle and the *Folk Architecture Museum*, looking like a small village, is also on the territory of the Castle Hill.

Russian Orthodox Cathedral, Kremlivska Street 9, on the way to the castle. This was built in 1644, originally as part of a Jesuit monastery; it was rebuilt in the 18th century as a Uniate church. Open for services.

Roman Catholic Church, Zhovtneva Street. Open for services.

St. Paul's Church (Russian Orthodox), Moskovskaya Naberezhnaya. This church was built in 1932 to commemorate the Russian soldiers who fell in the Carpathians in World War I, but now houses the Atheism Museum.

Calvinist Church, Radyanska Street. Built in 1796 and open for services.

The church at Gorky Street 48 is used as a gymnasium.

Vasilian Monastery, Velikaya Street. This 5-storey structure was built in 1912.

Main Building of the University, Gorky Square. The University was founded in 1945. Its other buildings are in Lenin Square and Zhovtneva Street.

University Library, This building was originally founded in 1644 as the residence of the Uniate Bishops of Transcarpathia; it was reconstructed in 1848 in baroque style and encloses an interesting old sundial.

Town Council Building, This was built in 1809 in baroque style and is now used as newspaper offices.

Local Museum, Kremlivska Street 33, occupying 30 halls inside the castle. Open 10–6; closed Mon. There are sections on natural history and local handicrafts in the museum, and a model of the castle as it appeared in the 17th century.

Picture Gallery, Kremlivska Street 33, inside the castle. Open 10–6; closed Mon. Opened in 1948, this gallery now contains the works of Russian and Ukrainian artists.

Art Museum, Radyanska Square 3. Open 10–6; closed Mon. There are 2,000 paintings and sculptures in the collection.

Handicraft Exhibition Hall, Kremlivska Street 33

Folk Architecture Museum, Kremlivska Street 33a, through the wooden arch just beyond the exhibition hall. Open 10–6; closed Tues. The wooden buildings are set out next to the castle on the slopes of the hill where the seminary garden used to be. The mature fruit and walnut trees add greatly to the charm of the place. A collection of peasant huts with a smithy and a well in the form of a crane have been imaginatively set out on 3.5 hectares (9 acres) to resemble an 18th–19th century village; well-tended flowers and cabbage patches complete the picture. The *Church of Michael the Archangel* came from the village of Shelestovo, near Mukachevo, and was built in 1777. It is an outstanding example of folk architecture and especially interesting for the way the two styles of baroque and ancient Russian are used together. It is typical of the most popular type of church building in this area during the 16th and 17th centuries. Some of the icons from the church are now in the Uzhgorod picture gallery, among them those of the Archangel Michael, St. Nicholas and Our Lady Odigitria.

Zoological Museum, Zhovtneva Street 54. Open 9–3; closed Mon.

Natural History Museum (Nature House), in a 4-storey building in Ukrainian style

The *Pyramid Memorial*, Karl Marx Square, and the *Monument*, Leningradskaya Naberezhnaya. These two memorials were built in memory of those who fell in World War I.

Fenzik Monument, This monument is in memory of a local poet E. Fenzik (1844–1903).

Heroes' Cemetery, Geroyev Street

Ukrainian Drama Theatre, Teatralnaya Square 8. This theatre dates from 1907.

Musical Comedy and Drama Theatre, Teatralnaya Square 8

Philharmonia Concert Hall, Teatralnaya Square 10. This hall was formerly a synagogue; the Transcarpathian Folk Choir sings here and an organ has been installed.

Spartak Swimming Pool, Roscha Gogolya Street, in Gorky Park

Uzhgorod Avangard Stadium, This stadium can seat 10,000.

Gorky Park, on the right bank of the River Uzh, on the north side of Castle Hill. The park contains playgrounds, an open-air stage, sports pavilions, a library, a dance floor, a pets' corner and a children's railway, the Small Carpathian Railway, opened in 1947 and running for 1200 m (0.7 miles) along the river bank.

Botanical Garden, Zhovtneva Street 60. Here there are more than 3000 species of plants including many that are only to be seen in this region. Tropical and subtropical plants can be seen in the hothouses.

Zakarpatye (Intourist) Hotel & the Zakarpatye,

Russky Zal, Ukrainsky Zal, Vengersky Zal and Cheshsky Zal Restaurants, 50-letiya-SSSR Square 5, southwest of the castle, across the river; tel 97–140 (reception), 36-370 (service bureau). This modern, 14-storey structure belongs to Intourist. Intourist office; tel. 36-210.

Verkhovina Hotel & Restaurant, Teatralnaya Square 5; tel. 34-046

Kiev Hotel & Restaurant, Koryatovicha Street 1; tel. 34-096. Part of the restaurant is in the open air.

Uzhgorod Hotel & Restaurant, Khmelnitsky Square 2; tel. 35-060

Druzhba (friendship) Hotel & Restaurant, Vysokaya Street 12; tel. 33-232

Edelweiss Restaurant, Zhovtneva Street 24

Skala Restaurant, Radyanska Street 32

Winetasting Shop, Suvorov Street 13

GPO, Geroyev Cosmosa Square 4

Gift Shop, Suvorov Street 10

Kashtan (for foreign currency), Tolstova Street 46. Open 10–7; Sat. 10–3.

Ukraina Department Store, 40-Let-Oktyabrya Prospect 48

Kobzar Book Shop, Koryatovicha Square 1

Mriya (Dream) Jeweller's, Zhovtneva Street 18

Umelets Folk Handicrafts, Suvorov Street 13

Transcarpathian Souvenir, Teatralnaya Square 11

Filling Station, Radyanska Street 157 and at the 199/10 km mark on the Mukachevo road, on the right just out of Uzhgorod.

Goryany

In this village, quite near the town, is *St. Nicholas's Church*, built in the 12th–13th century and the oldest in the area. It is popularly known as the rotunda because of its shape. Some *frescoes* painted in the 1370s have survived, the "Flight into Egypt" being especially worthy of note.

Intourist organises several *trips* out of Uzhgorod. Nevitskoye is 15 km (9 miles) away, the town of Mukachevo (q.v.) is 45 km (30 miles) and the scenic trip up to Veretsky Pass in the Carpathian Mountains is 120 km (75 miles) one way.

Nevitskoye (Hungarian–Nyevickei)

Population—1,000

To make the side trip to Nevitskoye leave town along Gorky Street following the signs to Perichin. The road turns along the valley of the Uzh. There is a small church with a spire on the right at the 31 km mark, and in Onokovtsi (Hungarian: Felsodomonya) a church and the Dubki Restaurant stand to the left.

Nevitskoye Castle is 12 km (7 miles) from Uzhgorod. It can be seen up among the trees on the hillside to the right overlooking the river; it can only be reached on foot.

The castle was first mentioned in historical documents in 1317 although it was founded earlier, before the Hungarian tribes came here. Local legend says that its name comes from "nevesta" meaning "bride." It is also told that it was built by a princess. She required such large quantities of milk and eggs to strengthen the walls that the local villagers went hungry. They cursed her and the hexagonal tower is also called *Pogany (evil) Tower.*

The history of the castle here was one with that of Uzhgorod Castle. It was stormed in 1322 during the local rebellion and was devastated in 1644 by Gyorgy Rakoczi II of Transylvania. There is conservation and restoration work in progress upon it now.

War Memorial, dedicated to the volunteers who fought in the Second World War.

Hotel

Verkhovina Camping Site

Restaurant, Shashlik bar and cafe, below the castle.

To travel to Veretsky Pass use the road that follows the valley of the river Latoritsa and passes through the village of Chinadeyevo. After 1387 it belonged to the Perenyev family and the *castle* that was their home still stands; it was used as a prison during the Second World War by the Germans.

Just outside Chinadeyevo, in a park lying to the left of the road to Lvov, stands the *Carpati Sanatorium,* housed in the mediaeval-style red-roofed *castle* which the Schonborns built in 1890.

Beside the road, and 11 km (7 miles) before reaching Svalyava, is the *Solnechnoye Zakarpatiye Sanatorium.* It provides treatment for diseases of the liver and the digestive organs, using water from the local mineral springs.

On the right side of the road leading to Svalyava from Chinadeyevo there is a *spring* where one may sample the local mineral water.

Svalyava

The village lies 2 km (1 mile) to the right of the main road. Its name derives from the Slav word for salt; mines here supplied all the surrounding area. There are many mineral springs in the vicinity and their waters are used by the local sanatoria (of which the largest is the Polyana) and also by factories which bottle them for sale.

Polyana

In this village are a number of mineral springs, the most well known being Luzhanskaya, Polyana Kvasova (between 1842 and 1911 it was named the best mineral water in Central Europe 21 times at international contests) and Polyana Kupel. The latter two were first mentioned in 1463. The *Polyana Sanatorium* makes use of these waters in curing diseases of the digestive organs. This was the first sanatorium to be opened in this district after the Second World War.

Nizhniye Vorota

This village is to the right of the main road. It stands 450 m (1,476 ft) above sea level, beside the river Latoritsa at its confluence with the Zavodka. Its name means "lower gates" and it is not far from here to the main Carpathian Mountain range and

to the Veretsky Pass, 845 m (2,772 ft) above sea level. Here the first few *log cabin-type houses* are to be seen. The experimental agricultural station carries out research in mountain farming.

First historical mention was made of the place in the 12th century. In 1433 it belonged to the noble Bilkei family and in 1600 it was devastated by the Crimean Tatars.

From the 18th century on, it was part of the Ugorskoye kingdom, being presented to the Schonborn family by the Austrian emperor in 1728. In 1732 it acquired the right to hold fairs. In the second half of the century it is recorded that many villagers were employed in running a postal service for their landlord from his residence to the Austrian capital; it took 12 days to make the journey one way.

St. Peter's Russian Orthodox Church, built in the 18th century

Roman Catholic Church, on the main street

Obelisk, commemorating Russian soldiers killed during World War II.

Monument, in the centre of the village. This memorial stands to the memory of local Communists killed here in 1945.

Beskid Restaurant, opposite the Roman Catholic Church on the main street

Post office

From Nizhniye Vorota the road continues to climb up the valley of the Latoritsa, passing the villages of Tishev, Belasovitsa and finally Laterka where there is a good *lookout point* with a little church in the valley to the right. Veretsky Pass is at a height of 4,200 m (13,779 ft), and on the other side there are gentians to be seen growing by the road on the slope down to the valley of the river Stree. Away across the river to the left the silvery roofs of a church come into view; it looks more like a squat pagoda than a church.

VILJANDI (German: Fellin)

(Day trips are organised to Viljandi from Tallinn (147 km/91 miles), but it is also possible to stay the night.)

This typical south Estonian town stands on the northwestern shore of Lake Viljandi, which covers an area of 150 hectares (450 acres) and contains 16 different species of fish. Viljandi is very picturesque and is rich in legends and memories of the past. One of the legends about the lake says that once upon a time a church stood beside the water, but it fell right in when seven brothers entered it at the same time. Another says that the lake is the home of a water nymph who seeks victims every year. The terrain is divided by Viljandi Valley and the valley of the Valuoja and Uueveski Springs.

The word "viljandi" in Estonian means "crop" because the place used to be the bread basket of the country, but the history of the town is mirrored in that of Estonia. Long ago there was an Est settlement here and the first mention of the place dates back to 1211. In 1224 it was invaded by the Teutonic knights (the Knights of the Sword), and it was they who built the castle on Lossimaëd (Castle Hills) surrounded by high stone walls. The ruins of part of the western wall and a vast basement remain in the park, and there is another local legend that they are haunted. It is said that Furstenburg, the penultimate Master of the Knights of the Sword, was once put in chains, and that now he makes his rounds every night, crying out in a loud voice, just as the sentry used to do.

The settlement which grew up around the castle was called Fellin and first mentioned as a town in 1283. It became extremely well fortified, and after it joined the Hanseatic League it became one of the most important political and commercial centres of Estonia. The local horses were much sought after and the blacksmiths highly esteemed. Also valued were Viljandi's woollen blankets and jewellery of silver and bronze. The castle was ruined in the Livonian War of 1558–1583.

From 1481 Viljandi suffered much from changing hands between the Russians, the Poles and the Swedes. By 1682 there remained no more than 55 families, living in 43 houses. During the Northern War of 1700–21 between Russia and Sweden, Viljandi was joined to Russia with the rest of Estonia. By this time the fortress had been ruined and the town had lost its strategic importance.

In 1744 the Empress Elizabeth presented one of her ladies-in-waiting, Maria Choglokova, with lands in Viljandi, and also their local fishing rights.

In 1765 and 1770 the town was so damaged by fires that people were not allowed to smoke their pipes in the streets or even in the courtyards for many years afterwards. Householders were obliged to roof their homes with tiles, build proper chimneys and replace the wooden pavements in front of their houses with stone. In 1783 Catherine II proclaimed Viljandi a district centre, and in 1789 Maria Choglokova's properties were returned to the town. A local school was opened in 1804 and a hospital in 1827. By 1840 the population numbered 1,670 and by 1881 3,385. Just as in the villages round about, the traditional Estonian love of music led in Viljandi to the formation in 1869 of the male voice choir and a brass band. The Koit (Dawn) Society staged Lidya Koidula's "Etaki Mulk" in 1873, with actresses taking the female roles, in contrast to traditional practice. Song festivals were organised in 1892, 1894, 1896 and 1897. The town began to develop rapidly, and was one of the first in Estonia to have piped water (1911), a sewage system, street lighting and paved roads.

By the late 19th century Viljandi had become a prominent centre of the Estonian national movement. The match factory founded in 1890 is still the only one in Estonia. Other large enterprises included the steam-powered mill, a brewery and a copper foundry. Agricultural products were still very important commercially, especially flax. It was upon the initiative of local landowners that the narrow-gauge Viljandi Railway was opened in 1897.

The population had risen to 13,018 by 1939

and important buildings dating from that time include a hotel, another hospital, the town hall, a primary school, an old people's home and a bank.

Viljandi was taken by the Nazis on 9 July 1942, and one of the largest prisoner-of-war camps in Estonia was opened where 27,000 lost their lives. Upon their retreat in September 1944 they destroyed the railway station, burned the boys' school and blew up a munitions dump which started other fires.

Soviet power was established in 1944, and postwar restoration was completed by 1950. Light and dairy industries began to develop in addition to the linen mill. There is now also a fur factory, and food products, textiles, matches and furniture are made here today. The town has grown with the development of the residential districts of Uueveski, Paalalinn and Männimäe.

In the centre the twisting, narrow streets are reminders of Viljandi's mediaeval origin. Parts of the town are located upon three hills, West Hill, Cherry Hill and Kissing Hill, from all three of which there are good views upon Lake Viljandi. Kingisepp (formerly Lossi/Castle) Street leads right into the castle from the town, across bridges and causeways which have been replaced to link the three earth walls.

The *town hall* dates from the beginning of the 18th century and was one of the first stone buildings in the town; it was a single-storey private house, but the tower was added when the magistracy took it over. It was completely rebuilt in 1931 and now houses local administrative offices. The house at Kingisepp Street 11 dates back to the second half of the 18th century, and there is an 18th-century barn in the courtyard. Kingisepp Street 13 was built at the end of the 18th century as were the house at No. 19 and also the house in early classical style at the corner of Tallinn and Jakobsen Streets, designed as an almshouse for spinsters of noble birth. The classical-style house at the corner of Tallinn and Posti Streets (Tallinn Street 16) was built in the 1830s and adjoining it is a wooden building where the first public concerts were held. The Sewing Factory at Posti Street 11 was German-built of wood in classical style in 1843 as a casino.

Tomp Square, formerly Market Square, is named after Jan Tomp (1894–1924), an Estonian revolutionary. The cobbled square has been grassed over and laid out as a park, the fountain in place of the original well depicts a boy being sculpted by August Vomm. Around the square are a number of interesting buildings. No. 3 dates from the 18th century. No. 5 was built in 1768 as the District Law Court, but has been used by different schools since 1790. No. 12 was a Chemist's Shop, built in 1780 and now houses the *local museum*. The building at No. 8, now used as a political college, was formerly the Grand Hotel built in 1911.

The Agricultural Technical College is on the former estate of Count Fers.

Castle Ruins, in the park. Founded in 1221 (the part known as Willi's Cellar), construction by the Teutonic Knights began seriously in 1224. In its heyday this was one of the strongest fortresses in Livonia. In 1300 it was rebuilt as a convent which was richly decorated with carvings inside. The stronghold had then five towers, one of which was known as Long Herman, and the three earth walls in front of it gave it added protection. There were deep moats with drawbridges between the earth walls. The framework of the castle well which went down to a depth of 26 m (85 ft) can still be seen on Well Hill. The castle was further strengthened in the 16th century.

Jaani Kirik, in the southwestern part of the town, by the entrance to the park. This white church is all that remains of the Franciscan Monastery. It dates from the 14th–15th centuries.

Lutheran Church, overlooking one of the main roads out of town. Built in red brick in 1866.

Local Museum, Tomp Square 12, in the building of the Old Chemist's Shop (1780). The museum was founded in 1878 as the Ditmar-Museum, and is now the largest local museum in Estonia. Its collection includes mediaeval stone carvings. It moved into this building in 1941.

Warriors' Monument, at the end of Viydu Boulevard, on the high slope of the Uuaveskin River, by August Vomm, marking the common grave of those who perished during World War II.

Memorial Monument, at the foot of Khantaugu Hill. Here are two common graves of the 58 people who were shot without trial as victims of the 1905 revolution. The monument is by Eskel.

Obelisk, at the beginning of Rizhskoye Chaussée. The obelisk with a bronze bas-relief stands by the common grave of 16,000 victims who died in Viljandi concentration camp during World War II.

Memorial Monument, in the park to the south of the castle. This commemorates the victims of the 1905 revolution and also the 30,000 people who died in the local concentration camp during World War II.

Koehler's Statue, in a garden on Kingisepp Street. Johann Koehler (1826–99) was an artist.

Ugala Drama Theatre, Jakobsen Street 18. Estonia's oldest theatre, opened in 1920 and professional since 1926.

Puppet Theatre, founded in 1955

Open-air Theatre, in the park

Lossipark (Castle Hills). The surroundings of the castle have been landscaped into an exceptionally beautiful natural park, much favoured by birds and squirrels for their nests. Full use has been made of the slopes of the ancient moats and the nearby hills. In 1931 a 50 m/yd suspension bridge was thrown over a former moat to connect the park with the castle; the bridge was brought here from Tarvastu, not far from Viljandi. There is a good view from the castle keep over the lake. The trees are mostly elms, and are especially lovely in the autumn. Philosophers' Avenue has a romance of its own. In the western part of the park is the festival site, known as Singing Field. Nearby are limestone gravestones with skeletons of prehistoric fish.

Trepimyagi Steps were built at the beginning of the century to link Viljandi with the lake. 158 steps in 5 flights lead down to the lake shore. Near the hills is a water tower built in 1911, the symbol of the town.

Dendrarium, Koidu Street. Founded in 1921 and based on the garden of the photographer I. Riet who had a collection of rare trees.

House of Sports, Vaksali Street 4

Viljandi Hotel & Vikare Restaurant, Tartu Street 11; tel. 53-852. This was formerly known as the Eve Hotel.

Viljandi Hotel Annex, Vyayketru 4

Vikerkaap Restaurant

Viljandi Café, Kingisepp Street 31

GPO, Tallinn Street 11

Filling Station, Tallinn Street 11

Kapp Museum, in a village just outside Viljandi, Tallinn Street 30. Open 10–5; closed Tues. & Wed. This is dedicated to the three composers, Wilhelm, Eugene and Artur Kapp.

Carl Robert Jakobsen worked here as a leader of the Estonian national movement in the 1880s; he founded the "Sakala" newspaper in Viljandi. His estate is nearby at Kurgya, a little along the road towards Parnu, and Intourist organises excursions to the museum there from Tallinn (q.v. for a fuller description).

VILNIUS is the capital of the Lithuania.

LITHUANIA (Lithuanian: Lietuva)

Area: 65,000 sq km. Population: 3,690,000 (1989), of which 80% are Lithuanians, 8.9% Russians, 7.3% Poles and 1.7% Belorussians.

Lithuania lies on the coast of the Baltic Sea in the north-west of the USSR. It is the most southerly of the three Baltic republics. Its principal cities are Vilnius (the capital), Klaipeda, and Kaunas.

The Lithuanians are one of the most ancient peoples of Europe. Their language is the only living one that is closely allied to Sanskrit.

The Lithuanian state dates from the beginning of the 13th century. From its foundation this state had to fight for its independence against the Teutonic Knights, but at the same time it expanded to the east and south at the expense of declining Kievan Russia. One of the most outstanding Dukes of this period was Gediminas (1316–41) who conquered many Russian principalities to the southeast and established his capital in Vilnius. In 1386 the pagan Grand-Duke Jogaila (in Polish, Jagello) married Queen Jadvyga of Poland and was himself elected King of Poland, thus uniting the two countries. Jogaila was baptised at the age of 35, and subsequently began, somewhat unsuccessfully, the baptism of Lithuania.

By the middle of the 15th century the Grand Duchy of Lithuania stretched from the Black Sea in the south almost to Moscow in the east. At that time the majority of its population were Orthodox Russians, but it was in 1474 that young Prince Casimir (1458–84), grandson of Jogaila, first visited Vilnius after a hunting trip with his father, King Casimir of Poland and Lithuania. He came again for Christmas in 1476, and then increasingly frequently until he took up residence and participated in administrative work. He was extremely religious, but always a champion of the poor and needy, distributing his possessions and caring for the sick. As a loyal Catholic he forbade the construction of new Orthodox churches. Perhaps because of this he was almost assassinated in 1481. He spent two years in Cracow, living ascetically, and at the time of his return to Vilnius was already suffering from the tuberculosis from which he was to die at the age of 25. He was buried by his father in the Blessed Virgin Chapel of the Cathedral in Vilnius, and following a series of miracles attributed to him, was canonised in 1521. In 1569 Lithuania and Poland were united in the Polish Commonwealth, and the Jesuits encouraged devotion to the princely saint which was largely responsible for the spread of Catholicism in Lithuania.

In 1795, after the third partition of Poland, most of Lithuania was included into the Russian Empire. Over a hundred years ago, at a time when it was forbidden to use the Lithuanian language, Vincas Kudirka (author of the national anthem) wrote:

Nor print nor writ they allow us;
They want Lithuania dark and dull.

During World War I the country was occupied by the Germans and after the 1917 Revolution it seceded from Russia and became, in 1919, a parliamentary republic which in 1926 was turned into a dictatorship under President Smetona. In 1919 Vilnius University was restored for the first time since its closure by Russian authorities in 1832. However as Vilnius had already been seized by Poland, the university only opened in 1922 and when it did so it was in the provisional capital of Kaunas.

In 1940 the newly elected parliament proclaimed Lithuania a Soviet Republic which was incorporated into the USSR two months later. By 1989 the red, yellow and green flag of Lithuania was flying here once more, and in 1990 the Supreme Soviet of the Lithuanian Republic announced the intention to leave the USSR and to strive for full sovereignty.

Here are a few words of Lithuanian:

hello	lobas (pr. labas)
I am a tourist	as turistas (ush tooristas)
please	prasau (prashaoo)
thank you	dekoju (dekoyoo)
yes	taip (to rhyme with "ape")
no	ne
good	gerai
bad	blogai
I don't understand	as nesuprantu (ush nesooprantoo)
I need an interpreter	man reikalingas vertejas (mun . . . verteyas)
good-bye	viso gero (visa gero)

Vilnius Population—582,000
(former Wilno, Vilna)
The capital of Lithuania stands at the confluence of the little river Vilneles (Vilnois) and the Neries (Vilijos) and is surrounded by attractive, hilly country.

Archaeologists have found that there have been settlements here since the 5th or 8th century A.D. There are in existence some documents belonging to the Order of Teutonic Knights which mention that in the time of Duke Mindaugas (in the middle of the 13th century), Vilnius was already the centre of the Lithuanian State, but the majority of chronicles state that the city was founded by Gediminas, Grand-Duke of Lithuania (1316–41).

Legend has it that Gediminas spent a day hunting in the hills here. While resting he dreamed of a gigantic iron wolf standing on the hill where he lay, howling "like a hundred wolves." The High Priest (Christianity did not reach Lithuania until nearly the end of the 14th century) explained the dream as an omen sent by the gods which meant that Gediminas should build his capital city on the place where he rested. Accordingly, two castles were built, one in the valley and another on the hill.

A more practical reason for establishing the fortified city in this place was the necessity of blocking the way to the country of the Teutonic Knights and also of establishing a secure and efficient trading route both eastwards and westwards.

Old Vilnius consisted of two parts, the Grand-Duke's court and the castles belonging to his courtiers, and the city proper. In 1387, the city was granted Magdeburg city rights, but the importance of Vilnius as a political centre considerably decreased after 1569 when Poland and Lithuania merged into one state, Rzecz Pospolita, following the Union of Lublin. The Grand-Dukes of Lithuania, who were at the same time Kings of Poland, ceased to reside in Vilnius, and spent most of their time in Warsaw. The "golden freedom" of the nobility which characterised the Polish state took the place of law and order and no one was safe from the persecutions and insults of his superiors.

Vilnius suffered a great deal during the 17th-century Russo-Polish wars over the Ukraine and Belorussia. During the Northern War between Russia and Sweden at the beginning of the 18th century, Vilnius fell to Sweden on several occasions, but after the last partition of Poland it became part of the Russian Empire. In 1812 it was seized by Napoleon.

In 1831 and 1863 anti-Russian rebellions in Poland and Lithuania both had their effects on the life of Vilnius. In 1832 Vilnius University was closed, and in 1863 an underground committee directed the uprising in Lithuania from Vilnius.

608

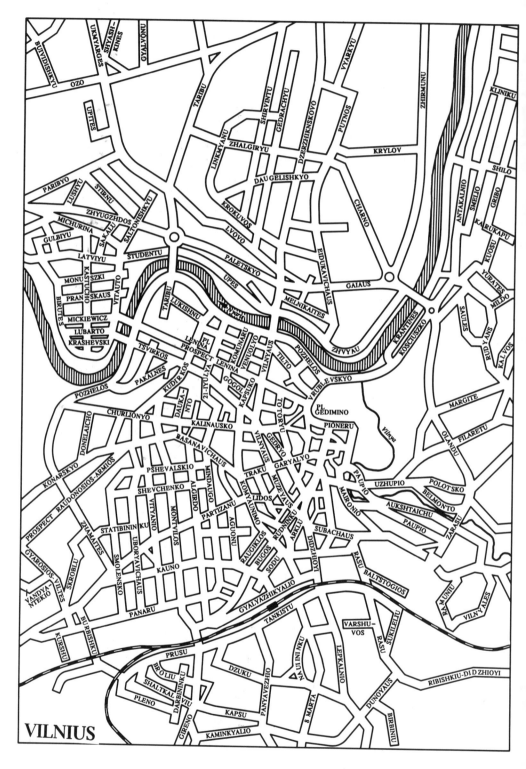

VILNIUS

The leaders of the uprising, Zigmont Sierakauskas and Kastus Kalinauskas, were hanged in Lukiskiai (now Lenin Square).

After the Revolution of 1917 the Soviets, in cooperation with Poland, assigned the sovereignty of the city to Lithuania, although they did not themselves evacuate it until suffering one more defeat at the hands of Poland. The League of Nations proposed that there should be a plebiscite within the district.

An important role in the history of Vilnius belongs to Marshal Joseph Pilsudsky, the greatest modern hero of Polish nationalism, known as the Great Deliverer. He was born in 1867 near Vilnius and spent his boyhood here. He asked that his heart be interred by the side of his mother in Vilnius, and now in Rossa Cemetery there is a slab of polished black marble, reachable by a staircase. It lies over the combined grave of the mother and her son's heart, while his body rests in Cracow. In 1920 the Polish General, Zeligowski, a Lithuanian Pole himself, seized Vilnius with the secret approval of Pilsudsky; he then formed the small state of Central Lithuania which was avowedly in favour of union with Poland. A year or so later an election was held in Central Lithuania; the result was a clear majority for incorporation into the Polish Republic. Against protests by the Lithuanian government, Poland thus assumed control of the territory of Vilnius.

The Lithuanians proved irreconcilable and refused even to have diplomatic relations with the Poles. For eighteen years the border was closed, the roads barred and no direct postal service was carried on between Lithuania and Poland. During this period Vilnius was still known for its annual fairs, for being the centre of the flax market and for trade in furs, leather and timber. It was also notable for the unusual variety of religions among its citizens: Catholics, Protestant reformists, Lutherans, Russian Orthodox, Old Believers, Orthodox Jews, Caraite Jews and Muslims of Tatar origin. The years of resentment finally reached a dramatic climax in 1938, when the Polish Marhsal Rydz-Smigly assembled more than 50,000 troops along the Lithuanian frontier with an ultimatum to open the border. In the face of this military threat, Lithuania, with an army of only 22,000, thought it wise to comply with the wishes of the Polish government. In 1939, after the Soviet-Lithuanian Treaty, Vilnius once more became the capital of Lithuania. Speaking at a mass demonstration President Smetona of Lithuania proclaimed: "As a result of an agreement with the great Soviet Union, which is friendly towards us, we have received Vilna Province." On October 12, 1939, "The Times" published the following cable from its Riga correspondent: "The acquisition of Vilna, the name of which has in the course of 20 years become sacred for the Lithuanians, like that of Mecca for the Moslems or Jerusalem for the Jews, has produced unexampled enthusiasm today." In 1940, as a result of the Molotov-Ribbentrop pact, Lithuania was incorporated into the USSR as a Soviet Republic.

Pre-war Vilnius hardly had time to put on the visible trappings of a capital city. It had never been known for its cleanliness and comfort. Just as happened during previous wars, it suffered greatly during the Second World War, but afterwards the dirt and squalor gave way to a rebuilding that replaced wooden construction with brick, single-storey houses with taller ones and unpaved roads with asphalt. The bridges over the river had to be reconstructed. Trolley buses were introduced in 1956. Today the city has become industrialised and modern, its products including computers, machine tools, electric meters and equipment, drills, farming machinery, building materials and a variety of foods. Its university is the oldest in the whole country, and there are a number of other higher educational establishments. The Lithuanian Academy of Sciences has its headquarters here as do 10 scientific research institutes.

The Old Town runs uphill southwards from the castle and the cathedral by the river. Here the picturesque old buildings of architectural value are being rebuilt and restored to provide comfortable accommodation while retaining their old appearance. To the east, beyond the river Vilnia, is the Antakalnis region, and to the west is the newer part of the centre, built at the turn of the century, with Gedimino Prospect as its main thoroughfare. Contemporary buildings on the river bank include the *Opera and Ballet Theatre*, while those across the river are dominated by the tall *Lietva Hotel*.

Vilnius Castle, more usually known as Gedymin's Castle, stands on Gedymin's Hill, overlooking the city. The name of Gedyminas (Grand Prince of Lithuania and founder of the Lithuanian Empire) was given to the castle, although in his time the fortress was only built of wood. There is a story about the castle's foundation:

Gedyminas asked the pagan priestesses what should be done in order that the castle should never be taken by enemies. They advised him to find a mother willing to sacrifice her son. As it happened a number of mothers volunteered, but one succeeded in bringing her 18-year-old son to the construction site before the others, and ordered him into the pit where a huge rock was to be thrown as the castle's foundation stone. The young man did not resist; he just begged the Grand-Duke to allow him to put three questions to the priestesses before he died. The questions were: What is the lightest thing on earth, what is the sweetest thing on earth, and what is the hardest thing on earth? The priestesses replied: "The lightest thing is a feather, the sweetest thing is honey, and the hardest is iron." "No," said the youth, "you're wrong. The lightest thing on earth is a child in its mother's arms, the sweetest is mother's milk, and the hardest is the heart of a mother who, without a single tear, sends her only son to his death." The Grand-Duke was pleased with these words and spared the youth his life.

A stone castle was built here in 1420 by Grand-Duke Vyatautus, but it was badly damaged in the Russo-Polish War of 1654–61 and was never rebuilt. Best preserved is the octagonal Western Tower. The castle was last used for military purposes in 1705–8 when Peter the Great stored food and munitions here. The flagstaff rising from the centre of the flat roof of the tower carried the Lithuanian standard.

Of the Lower Castle which stood at the foot of the hill, on the southern side, nothing remains but the tower which was converted into the cathedral belfry. It dates back to the 13th century and is said to stand on the site of a pagan shrine to Perkunas. The round part was built in the 14th century as one of the defence towers of the outer wall of the Lower Castle in Gedyminas's time.

The *Roman Catholic Cathedral* was itself founded in 1387 by Grand-Duke Jogaila, Gedymin's grandson, after his marriage to Polish Queen Jadvyga and the subsequent introduction of Christianity to Lithuania, and was dedicated to St. Stanislaus. It is the city's finest building, and unusual in that although it was first of Gothic design, it was reconstructed in Greek style, six massive Doric columns forming its portico. It is unusual, too, in having been founded by a pagan prince. Jogaila renounced his heathen ways and founded this Christian church on the site of a former sanctuary of Perkunas, the pagan god of light (whose name is still used for swearing in Lithuanian). From the tower the Chief Priest announced the will of the gods to the people. Grass snakes were kept in the cellar because they were considered holy by the Lithuanians.

The cathedral has been restored and reconstructed several times. Between 1777 and 1801 it was fully reconstructed by the prominent Lithuanian architect, Laurinas Stuoka-Gucevicius. He managed to preserve several baroque parts of the old Cathedral, such as the St. Casimir Chapel with Italian frescoes by Palloni, although his building is in Renaissance style. 6 sculptures by the Italian artist, Riggi, stand at the main facade, representing Abraham, Moses and the four Evangelists. The sculptor's autograph is carved at the foot of the Moses statue. Also on the facade is a sculptured group showing Noah and his family sacrificing a lamb after the flood. The sculptures on the southern side are of the Grand-Dukes of Lithuania and on the nothern side of some of the apostles and some Jesuits. The two sculptures by the altar are also by Riggi. There are interesting tombstones and memorial tablets on which the biographies of those they commemorate are carved. Workmen uncovered the graves of King Sigismund (II) Augustus, who came to the throne in 1548, and those of his two queens. He was the last of the Jogailas whose dynasty lasted for almost two centuries. He refused to renounce the throne for the woman he loved, yet love triumphed in the end, and it was in the chapel of St. Stanislaus that his marriage took place. Although the main edifice has long since been completely remodelled, this chapel was untouched because an inscription which was uncovered prophesied that ill luck would follow anyone who dared to touch it. At the beginning of the 20th century, the river, swollen with rain, overflowed its banks and completely inundated the lower city. The stream undermined the cathedral's ancient timber foundations until the whole fabric of the edifice was threatened. With funds donated partly by American Catholics, a new concrete underpinning was made capable of withstanding the ravages of time and tempest.

From 1953 till 1989 the city's Picture Gallery was housed inside the cathedral. The remains of St. Casimir were transferred to the Church of SS. Peter and Paul, but were returned when the cathedral was reopened for worship. The 19th-century organ, which is the largest in Lithuania, was restored in 1969 by craftsmen from East Germany.

Of the belfry, the upper (fifth) storey of the tower was erected in the 16th century specifically as a belfry, but it was frequently restored in the 18th–19th centuries. It is 57 m (187 ft) high, and its chiming clock was made at the end of the 17th century. The bigger bell was cast in 1673 by a Dutchman called Delamars and the smaller one, which chimes every quarter of an hour, was made in 1758 by a German, Merk. Its clock mechanism was last restored in 1803. The locals set their clocks by its chimes. In 1967 17 bells of different dimensions were hung in the tower and they chime during festivals and are also used by the local radio for a midday time signal.

Ruins of the City Wall and Tower, at the end of Boksto Street. Very little remains of the city wall which was erected at the beginning of the 16th century. The area encircled by the wall totalled 120 hectares (300 acres), and the wall itself was 2.9 km (1.8 miles) long, 12 m (39 ft) high, and up to 3 m (almost 10 ft) thick.

There are some *15th–17th century houses* in Didzioji (Main) Street. No. 12 and No. 14 have interesting Gothic decoration and No. 4 and No. 6 have typical 16th–17th century attic storeys. A walk up Didzioji Street and Austros-Vrata at the top, with a diversion to the right to the university, takes in a great many of the sights of old Vilnius. Vilnius Street leads up from the cathedral to the main building of the university.

Pyatnitskaya (Pentecost) Church (Russian Orthodox), at the crossing of Didzioji and Boksto Streets. This is "the first stone chapel of the true God to be erected in the Lithuanian capital and land." It was built in 1345 in place of a pagan temple upon the order of Maria, Russian-born wife of Grand-Duke Olgherd. It was reconstructed several times because of fires; the most recent reconstruction took place in 1865. It was in this church in 1705 that Peter the Great gave thanks for his victory of Charles XII of Sweden, presenting the church with a captured Swedish banner. At the same time he had an Ethiopian negro called Hannibal baptised here. Hannibal took the name of Abraham, rose to become a full general in the Russian army, and is chiefly remembered for being the great-grandfather of Alexander Pushkin, the Russian poet. The church is now used as the Small Picture Gallery.

University, Dolgandasa Square, not far from Didzioji Street, on the right on the way up. The university was founded in 1579 by Stephen Batory as a Jesuit institution called Academia et Universitas Vilnensis, and by 1586 it had already 700 students enrolled in its two faculties of philosophy and theology. The law faculty was opened in 1644 and the medical faculty in 1781. The Nobel prize winner Milosz was once a student here as was also the Polish poet, Adam Mickiewicz. The University was closed by the Russian government in 1832, and permitted to reopen in 1919, but as Vilnius was then in Polish hands, the reopening in fact took place in the provisional capital of Kaunas, and then only in 1922. It was at that time renamed in honour of the revolutionary and political figure, Vincas Kapsukas. After World War II it returned to its proper home in Vilnius.

The central building of the university is a complex structure which has existed since the 16th century but which was rebuilt and reconstructed several times since then. The University Library, which occupies the middle part of the building, has a good collection of old manuscripts and books. The oldest example dates back to 1467; it was printed in Strasburg. Vilnius is itself an ancient printing centre. The first books in Lithuanian and the Slav languages appeared here in the 16th century. Now the library collection numbers more than 3,000,000 items. It was founded by Wilno Bishop Albinius in 1570, together with King Sigizmund August. It was augmented by the collection of Lelewel, a famous Polish historian, brought from Paris. By Lelewel's will his library was loaned to the City of Paris with a provision for its return to Vilnius when that city achieved freedom. Now the collection has returned to its place of origin.

In the buildings on the south side are the Hall of Columns (built in 1817) and the Graduation Hall. The Observatory (1782) is also interesting. In 1944, when the Germans were leaving the city, they set fire to the University buildings but these were saved by the efforts of people living nearby.

St. John's Church (Roman Catholic), Didzioji Street, on the right, a little beyond the University. Founded in 1388 in the presence of King Jogaila, the very next year after the foundation of the cathedral. Work, however, proceeded slowly and the building was only completed in 1426, and it was consecrated in 1427. It is in Gothic style, and was enlarged and redecorated in 1571. The Jesuits took it over when they arrived in Vilnius in the second half of the 16th century. Subsequently it belonged to the University. It was damaged by fire, and during the restoration some late-baroque elements were added. Now the Museum of the History of the University is housed here.

Governor-General's Palace, Dolgandasa Square, near the University and Didzioji Street. In the 14th century this was the site of the Bishop's Palace. It suffered several fires and was rebuilt. At the end of the 18th century and the beginning of the 19th, the palace was among the finest buildings in the city. Napoleon stayed here in June–July 1812 after

the French entered Vilnius. At the end of the Franco-Russian War of 1812 it was used as Field Marshal Kutuzov's residence. In 1820–32 the palace was wholly rebuilt in Empire style following a project by Stasov and other architects. In the 1930s the building carried the name of the Palace of the Republic, and it was the residence of Marshal Pilsudsky on his frequent visits to Vilnius, which as the home of his youth had many endearing associations.

St. Nicholas's (Mikalojaus) Church, Didzioji Street 12. Founded by King Vytautas the Great, this is probably the oldest structure in the city. It was built in 1416 in Gothic style with some elements which are characteristic of Lithuanian national architecture. It was restored in the 16th century by the Jesuits, but following the long Russian regime of the 18th century it was converted into an Orthodox church in 1840. The new iconostasis that was subsequently installed earned a gold medal at the World Exhibition in Paris in 1867. It can easily be identified from a distance as its spire is decorated with gilded ridges. Open for services.

St. Casimir's Church (Roman Catholic), Didzioji Street 74. This church is easily recognised by its dome in the form of the crown of St. Casimir. The plan of the building, which dates from the beginning of the 17th century, is in the form of a cross. It is in early baroque style and the facade was rebuilt in the 19th century. The dome is 17 m (19 yd) in diameter and 40 m (131 ft) high. The monastery buildings beside it are now used as a school. The church is open for services.

Opposite St. Casimir's at Didzioji 35 is the art nouveau *Astoria Hotel*, built in 1901.

Roman Catholic Missionary Church, Subaciaus Street (to the left off Didzioji Street beyond St. Casimir's). In 1685 Catholic priests were invited to Vilnius to help the spread of Roman Catholicism. They began the construction of this church in baroque style in 1695 and it was completed in 1730. The prominent Vilnius architect, L. Stupka-Gucericuius, studied at the seminary here.

The Gate of the Basilian Monastery stands to the right at Didzioji Street 49. It was built in 1761 in Rococo style and the wrought-iron railing in the upper part of the gate is the work of local craftsmen. Through the gate are the Church of the Trinity and another 18th-century building that used to belong to the monastery. It used to house a seminary when it was the property of the Orthodox Church, but then it was taken over by the Uniates and has stood empty since the 1930s.

At Ausros-Vartu 6 is the building of the Archbishop's Chambers where there is now in the basement the excellent Medininkai Restaurant.

The Monastery of the Holy Spirit (Russian Orthodox), standing back on the left of Ausros-Vartu at No. 8, was first built of wood by Orthodox monks in 1593–97, but was rebuilt in stone in 1633. The monastery flourished after Troitsky Monastery opposite was taken over by the Uniate Church. In the crypt are relics of the Holy Martyrs of Vilna, Anthony, Ioann and Eustaphy. They were three courtiers of a Grand-Duke, who secretly practised Christianity while the country was still pagan. Eustaphy had his legs broken up to the knees and was scalped, after which they were all hanged. One of the priors of the monastery was Melety Smotritsky, author of the first Russian grammar book. The church was rebuilt in 1873 and was roofed with eastern-style cupolas. The monastery is now run as a joint cloister for 10 brothers and 16 sisters, and the church is open for services.

The Church of St. Theresa (Roman Catholic) is next to the monastery, on the left of the street and facing down it. It was built in 1635–50 by the Vice-Chancellor of Lithuania, Sefan Cristofer Pac. Imported materials such as Swedish granite and white marble were used. It used to be part of a Barefoot Carmelite monastery. The Rococo decoration is 18th-century too. The church was badly damaged during the Napoleonic occupation of 1812, when French troops were quartered here and it was used for storage. It was completely restored in 1857. The building is 106 m (116 yds) long and 15 m (16 yds) wide, and is open for services.

Medinsky Gate (Ausras Gate, the Gate of Dawn or Ostra Brama), Ausros-Vratu, at the top of Didzioji Street. This is the only gate of the Old City remaining. It is called the Pointed Gate and in Polish, Osztra Vrata, probably because of the Gothic features of its appearance after the reconstruction of 1498. When approaching the gate from the outside, one can see a bas-relief of the coat-of-arms of the Grand Duchy of Lithuania held by two griffins. Above the gate is a small chapel built by the Carmelites in 1826 to replace the earlier wooden chapel which was burned down.

The icon of the Virgin in the chapel called Our Lady of Vilnius is believed to be part of the loot taken by Grand-Duke Olgherd during a raid on Khersones (in the Crimea) in 1363. It was kept in Troitsky Monastery and then mounted over the gate in the city wall, facing outwards. When the walls were rebuilt in 1498, the icon was hung over the new, pointed gateway. It went to the Uniates when Troitsky Monastery became their property, but when St. Theresa's was built, it passed to the Barefoot Carmelites, and it was they who turned it round, to face the city, looking down the street, as it hangs today.

The icon is considered to be miracle-working and a constant stream of people come here to pray, some climbing the stone staircase on their knees before "The Queen of the Polish Crown" as it was called. A painting on wood, and similar in technique to the art of an earlier period of Christianity, perhaps of the Siennese school, it was probably painted long years before it was installed here. An inscription on the chapel wall reads: "Mater misericordiae! Sub tuum praesidium confugimus!" The icon is about 2 m (6 ft) high and 1.5 m (5 ft) wide. It is visible through a large window from the street below. The way up to the chapel is through a door on the left of the street.

Prechistensky (Immaculate Conception) or Uspensky (Assumption) Russian Orthodox Cathedral, Maironio Street. It was founded in the 14th century and built to follow the plan of St. Sophia's in Kiev, but rebuilt several times. The present-day building, with a conical dome like those typical of Armenian churches, dates from 1868, during the reign of Tsar Alexander II. Open for services.

The Dominican Church of the Holy Spirit, at the crossing of Garelias and Giedris Streets. Originally founded in 1441, this church was burned down in 1655 and rebuilt in 1688. It was given to the Dominican order and they had a seminary here. The church was reconstructed in late baroque style in the 18th century. The interior is richly decorated with reliefs, sculptures, frescoes, and other ornaments of both wood and metal. The main cupola is also painted with frescoes. The organ was built in 1776 by Casparini. The church has huge underground vaults, constructed on two floors. Here many parts of human bodies were mummified naturally due to the dryness of the place. The entrance to the vaults was sealed in 1849. The church was converted to serve as a prison in the first half of the 19th century. It is now open for services which are held in Polish.

St. Katherine's Church (Roman Catholic), Vilniaus Street. Built in 1622 in baroque style, and later part of a Benedictine convent complex. After a fire it was reconstructed according to a project by the architect Jonas Kristupas Gliaubicas of Vilnius. Near the church is a chapel decorated with a leaf-pattern ornament. During the occupation by French troops in 1811 the convent served as a hospital and the church was an apothecary's store room. It is now to be a concert hall.

St. Anne's Church (Roman Catholic), Maironio Street. This is one of the most interesting Gothic-style buildings in Lithuania. Originally built in 1392–96, it was dedicated in honour of Princess Anna, the wife of Grand-Duke Vyatautus, but the first written record of it mentions its rebuilding after the town fire of 1501. In 1563 the vaults collapsed and the church was finally reconstructed in 1581, the most important date in its history. Neither the name of its architect nor of its builders are known. This church caught Napoleon's fancy and brought forth the exclamation that it was so beautiful that he would like to take it down and move it to Paris.

The yellow bricks, painted red, of which it is constructed are of 33 different shapes and the building is 22 m (24 yds) long and 10 m (11 yds) wide. The facade has three towers separated by pinnacles. Its decorations form rectangles and arcs and on a sunny day there is an interesting play of light and shade on its surface. The belfry to the right of the church was designed by the architect, Chagin, who tried unsuccessfully to imitate the Gothic style of the church itself. The Catholic services here used to be conducted in German. The church is open for services.

The Bernardines' Church of SS. Francis of Assisi and Bernard of Sienna, close behind St. Anne's. This church, founded in 1469, belonged to a monastery. It was rebuilt in 1550 and 1677 (having suffered from the fighting of 1655), and although Gothic in style, it is at the same time a fine example of the 15th–16th century religious architecture of the fortress type. The baroque features were added after the reconstruction of 1677.

St. Michael the Archangel's (Mikolas) Church, opposite St. Anne's and the Bernardines' Church. This is the only Renaissance-style church in Vilnius. It was founded in 1594 by Chancellor Leon Sapieha beside his family residence which he then had converted into a Bernardine convent. Of especial interest in the church are the vaults decorated with geometric figures and stone rosettes. The tomb of coloured marble belonging to Sapieha was placed in position in 1632, and the church served as their family mausoleum. The exterior of the church is best observed from the side facing Svietimo Street. Open for services.

SS. Peter and Paul's Church, at the end of Kosciusko and the beginning of Antakalnio Streets, in the Antakalnis ("on the hill") region of Vilnius. Open for services, and as a museum 10–6; Sun. 3–6; closed to tourists on church holidays. This church was one of the twelve houses of worship built by one citizen to bring spiritual uplift to the town. He was Hetman Mikhail Pac. A rich and pious member of the nobility, he dedicated much of his wealth to the service of the church. Standing on the site of a pagan temple of Milda, goddess of love, this is the most famous baroque structure in Vilnius. It was built in 1668–74 and the decoration continued until 1684, but was never completed. At various times different Italian architects took part in the construction and decoration of the church, including Di Luca and Giovanni Maria Galli from Rome, and Pietro Peretti from Milan. The exterior is quite simple. It is a baroque-style building surrounded by a stone wall intended for defence purposes. There is an astonishing contrast between the exterior and the interior of the church. Inside, every corner of the walls and ceiling is decorated with sculpture, bas-relief figures and elaborate ornaments. There are well over 2,000 sculptured and bas-relief figures, most of which were created by 200 craftsmen working under Peretti and Galli, but they were unable fully to finish their project and 120 years later another group of artists undertook the completion of the decoration. The Italians Beretti and Piano supervised the work until they realised that they could not equal Peretti and Galli's standards and so gave up the task. Recent research has shown that the strong but easily worked material from which the statues were made is composed of egg white, lime and marble dust.

The tomb of Hetman Pac, who founded the church and died in 1682, is on the right of the porch on the way in. Just inside the entrance door on the right stands the figure of Death while on the left is a statue of St. Christopher symbolising Life. Death is depicted scythe in hand, trampling royal and papal crowns and bishops' mitres. Near him stand two big Turkish war drums made of copper, captured in 1673. From 1953, when Vilnius's Roman Catholic Cathedral was desecrated,

the silver sepulchre of St. Casimir was also housed in this church, but it went back to the cathedral when it was reopened in 1989.

The whole interior of the church is divided into small chapels, each with specific decorations. Most of the sculptures depict mythological, historical or biblical scenes. Some of them tell the history of Vilnius and Lithuania and the themes of others were taken from the city life of the period when they were made. One of the most beautiful figures in the church is the statue of Mary Magdalene in the St. Ursula Chapel (the Chapel of Eleven Thousand Marys) on the right side.

The frescoes on the vaults were painted by Martino de Alto Monte from Rome. The big crystal chandelier in the shape of a ship was hung before the altar in 1803. On either side of an archway in one of the left side chapels are the simple faces of two Lithuanian girls, in delightful contrast to the predominantly classical features of the other statues.

Znamenskaya Church (Russian Orthodox), Vytautas Street, overlooking the river and the bridge at the end of Gedimino Prospect, in the region known as Zverinas. Built in 1903 in Byzantine style with the characteristic horizontal striped brickwork. Open for services.

Church of Grigori Blazhenny, Kretingos Street. In a bad state of repair.

Church of the Immaculate Conception (Roman Catholic), Michurin Street 17, Zverinas Region. Built in 1914 and restored in 1976. Open for services.

Church of St. James and St. Philip, Lenin Square, behind the statue of Lenin. Founded in 1655 as a wooden cemetery church, it was burned down, and in 1690 new stone foundations were laid. Building was only finished in 1727 when it took on its present form. It then became part of a monastery. Many of Napoleon's French soldiers were buried here after they died during their return from Moscow and Smolensk. Napoleon was so appalled by the local mud that he described it as a fifth, and previously unknown, element.

Russian Orthodox Church of SS. Konstantine & Helena, Basanaviciaus Street. Open for services.

St. Efrosinia's Church (Russian Orthodox), a small cemetery church. Founded in 1838 and named in honour of Princess Efrosinia of Polotsk. It was later reconstructed and is open for services.

St. Raphael's Church (Roman Catholic), on the right bank of the Neris, opposite the castle. This was built in baroque style in 1703 by the Jesuits, and was part of a "Pyari" Monastery. But the monastery was closed at the beginning of the 19th century and the buildings were used as military barracks.

Synagogue, Pylimo Street 39

Synagogue, Linbarto Street 6. Unusual in that it has an onion dome.

Other old buildings include the remains of four 17th-century *nobles' palaces*. There are the park gates and a section of the old walls with beautiful windows of the *Sapeiha Palace*; the stucco mouldings are by the same artists as were employed to create the sculptures in the Church of SS. Peter and Paul. The *Sluszka Palace* was built by Dominic Sluszka on an artificial bank in the river Neris, having ordered that part of the river should be filled in with earth taken from a neighbouring hill. Peter the Great stayed here as a guest in 1705, and at the end of the 18th century it housed a brewery, then barracks and finally a prison. It is best viewed from the river. The *Pac Palace* at Didzioji Street 43 and the *Katkiewicz Palace* at Didzioji Street 50 are both much changed due to being reconstructed several times.

Local Museum, Traku Street 2. Open 11–5; closed Tues. and the last Monday of each month. Material shows the history of Vilnius.

Gediminas Castle, T. Vrublevskovo Street 1. Open 11–5; closed Tues.

Historical-Ethnographical Museum, Vrublyov-skovo Street 1. Open 11–7; closed Tues.

Art Museum, Didzioji Street 55. Open 12–6; closed Mon. This is in the former town hall. The magistrature was here from the 15th century, and in 1781 the town hall tower collapsed and damaged the rest of the building. The best project for the restoration was one by Laurinas Stuoka-Gucevicius, who had already designed the classical building of the cathedral, and the work was done between 1785 and 1799. In 1845 it was converted into a theatre. Now the gallery contains 16 paintings by the Italian, Viliani, and other paintings of the Italian schools of the late- and post-Renaissance periods, Flemish, German, and Dutch paintings of the 16th–18th centuries which are of no special significance, and works by Lithuanian artists from the 16th to the beginning of the 20th century.

Small Picture Gallery, in Pyatnitskaya Church, at the crossing of Didzioji and Boksto Streets. The Lithuanian, Polish and West European paintings of the 18th–19th centuries include portraits, landscapes, miniatures and scenes of daily life. In the apse is a bronze bust of Lady Hamilton by Faure de Brousses.

Museum of Folk Art, Rudninku Street 22/2. Housed in the 17th-century All Saints' Church. Open 12–6; closed Mon. The area to the right of Runinki Street was the city's Jewish quarter.

Exhibition Halls, Vokieciu Street 2, near the Art Museum. This building of glass and concrete was completed in 1967. There is an art salon on the ground floor and a shop selling artists' materials, and on the first floor are three exhibition halls, the largest of which is 1000 sq m. There is also an open-air sculpture exhibition here. Open daily 11–8.

Theatre & Music Museum, Traku Street. Open 12–6; closed Mon. Photographs of theatrical production, protraits of famous actors and sketches for decor and costumes.

Revolution Museum, Studentu Street 8. Open 11–6; closed Tues. and the last Monday of each month.

I-Lithuanian Communist Party Congress Mu-

seum, Cvirka Pereulok 9. Open 11–6, closed Tues. and the last day of each month.

The Pushkin Literary Museum, Subaciaus Street 124. Open 11–6:30; closed Tuesday. The museum is in a wooden building set among oak trees on a wooded hill a little way out of town. The bust of Pushkin was unveiled in 1949. Just below the museum is a small *Russian Orthodox chapel* (1903) and an unusual *monument* to the memory of a pet dog.

Adam Mickiewicz Museum, Pilies Lane 11, where the Polish poet lived in 1822. The museum was founded here after his death in 1855, but damaged during the Second World War and reopened in 1955.

Felix Dzerzhinsky's Home Museum, Paupe Street 26. Open 11–6; closed Tues.

Exhibition of Economic Achievements, Kosmonavtu Street 5. Open 11–7; closed Mon.

Planetarium, Basanaviciaus Street 15, on the corner of Pylimo Street.

Guardian of Vilnius. This little figure stands in a niche at the beginning of Traku Street.

Stanislav Monivszko Monument, in a small garden near St. Katherine's Church. The monument by Bazulkevitch to the prominent Polish composer (1819–1872) was unveiled in 1922.

Kapsukas Statue, in front of the Art Museum. Vincas Mickecicius-Kapsukas (1880–1935), a writer and outstanding revolutionary who headed the local government in 1918, at which time this building was the Town Hall.

Zemaite (pr. Zhemaite) Monument, in a small garden, was unveiled in 1970 to commemorate Julija Zhemaite (1845–1921), a classical Lithuanian writer.

Lenin Statue, Lenin Square. Behind the monument by Tomsky stands the Church of St. James and St. Philip.

Salomeya Neris Monument, in front of the school named after the outstanding Lithuanian poetess (1904–1945).

Cvirka Statue, at the crossing of Cvirkos and Pylimo Streets, in a small garden, which also bears the name of the writer, Petrs Cvirka (1909–1947).

Chernyakhovsky Statue, in Chernyakhovsky Square, at the crossing of Gedimino Prospect and Vilniaus Street. The monument by Tomsky was unveiled in 1950 to commemorate General Ivan Chernyakhovsky who in the summer of 1944 freed Vilnius from the Nazis. Twice decorated as a Hero of the Soviet Union, he died in battle in 1945 in Prussia, and his bronze statue here stands on the gun turret of a tank.

Military Cemetery, Karyu Kapu Street 11. Open 9–6. Here are memorials to Lithuanian soldiers who lost their lives in World War II, and to eminent public figures.

Opera and Ballet Theatre, Venuolis Street 1. This modern building of stone and glass is outlined in black.

Lithuanian Drama Theatre, Gedimino Prospect 6

Russian Drama Theatre, Kapsukas Street 4
Youth Theatre, Arkliu Street 5
Lele Puppet Theatre, Arkliu Street 5
Philharmonia Concert Hall, Didzioji Street 69.
Built as the City Hall in the early 20th century. It
was here that Soviet power was proclaimed in 1918.
The building is now under reconstruction with Pol-
ish help until 1993.
Central Park, B. Radvilaites Street 8
Zoo, Zverinas Street
Zalgirio Spartak Stadium, Eidukeviciaus
Street 3
Jaunimo Stadium, Lentipiuvie Street 19
Darbo Reserve Stadium, Vingis Park
Lietuva (Intourist) Hotel & Restaurants, Luk-
merges Street 20; tel. 73 6016/13. Intourist office;
tel. 73 2215.
Guintaras Hotel & Restaurant, Sodu Street 14,
tel. 63 4496
Neringa Hotel & Restaurant, Gedimino Pros-
pect 23, tel. 61 0516
Turistas Hotel & Restaurant, Totoriu Street 14
Vilnius Hotel & Restaurant, Gedimino Pros-
pect 20; tel. 62 4157
Astoria Hotel & Restaurant, Didzioji Street 35,
opposite St. Casimir's; tel. 66 2711
Narutis Hotel, Didzioji Street 24; tel. 23-880
Zvaigzde Hotel, Pylimo Street 63; tel. 20-926
Dainava Restaurant, Venuolio Street 4. This
one and the next two have bars with floor shows.
Erfurtas Restaurant, Architectu Street 19
Saltinelis Restaurant, Zirmunu Street 106
Medininkai Restaurant, Ausros-Vartu 6
Sianasis Rusis Restaurant, Gedrio Street 16
Zirmunai Restaurant, Zirmunu Street 67
Literary Svetain (Authors' Club) Café, Gedi-
mino Prospect 1
Ruta Café, Gedimino Prospect 22
Snaige (snowflake) Ice-cream Parlour, Vilniaus
Street 9/2
Lokys Café, Antolsky Street 8. A very popular
café in a restored 15th-century cellar. Many other
old buildings in the neighbourhood are also being
restored.
Kregzdute Café, Antakalinio Street 51
Saulute Café, Kestucio Street 35
Tauras Café, Petrs Cvirkos Street 30/8
Bank, Gedimino Prospect 6
GPO, Gedimino Prospect 9
Foreign Currency Shop, Konarskio Street 17
Department Store, Gedimino Prospect 18
Dovana Souvenir Shop, Antokolskio Street 6
Souvenirs, Gedimino Prospect 1 & 5, Vokieciu
Street 2
Books, Gedimino Prospect 13; *East European
publications*, Gedimino Prospect 4; *books on art*,
Gedimino Prospect 62.
Art Salon, Stikliu Street 2
Folk Art, Gedimino Prospect 1
Central Market, at the crossing of Basanavi-
ciaus and Pylimo Streets
Collective Farm Market, Eidukeviciaus Street
Taxi Ranks, railway station, Katedros Square,

Gogol Street 2, Didzioji Street and Kosciusko
Street 34

Verkiai Palace, 9 km from Vilnius, beside the
river Neris; leave town along Kalvariju Street. It
can also be reached by river boat. In 1387, when
Lithuania became Christian, King Jagaila gave
Verkiai to the Bishops of Vilnius as a summer residence. At the end of the 18th century it passed
into the hands of the Masalski family and the young
Laurynas Stuoka-Gucevicius (later architect of Vilnius cathedral and the town hall) designed in classical style a whole complex of palace, smaller
residences and various farm buildings. Water was
laid on, a park laid out and a theatre and hot houses
were built. The main building was destroyed in the
middle of the 19th century, and the rest suffered
badly from the two world wars.
   Among the remining parts of the estate are the
western wing of the palace, now used as the Lithuanian Palace of Sciences, the Little Palace with
a round hall domed in glass, stables, hothouses and
servants' quarters. The halls in the Palace furnished
in styles of the 16th–19th centuries display items
belonging to the Art Museum.

Intourist organises excursions from Vilnius to
Trakai (25 km/16 miles), Pircupis (pr. Pirchupis)
(44 km/27 miles), Elektrenai (50 km/31 miles),
Rumsiskes (80 km/50 miles) and Druskininkai (135
km/84 miles), and also to Kaunas (100 km/62
miles), Panevezys, Klaipeda and Palanga, each
listed under their own name.

Trakai

To reach this village leave Vilnius via Savanoriu
Prospect which leads out to the southwest, following the signs to Trakai. Where the road forks off
to the right the small Church of the Heart of Jesus
stands in a cemetery back from the road on the
right. It is about 300 years old but has a new story
attached to it, dating from World War II. A group
of Soviet soldiers were sheltering in it when a German bomb fell but remained unexploded, hanging
from the cross above the church. As they came out
and realised what had happened, their commanding officer said: "Now we can be sure that God
exists!"
   Trakai is a small town lying 28 km (17 miles)
west of Vilnius. It can be reached by rail and by a
good road. It is situated in an area which has inspired many Lithuanian poets and which is now
one of the most popular recreation areas near the
Lithuanian capital.
   The town is located on a long, narrow strip of
land which separates the three lakes of Galve, To-
toriskes and Bernadinai and there are about 30
other smaller lakes in the vicinity. Trakai was
founded in the 14th century by Duke Gediminas
and was his capital for some time. Then it was the
seat of one of his seven sons, Kestutis, who later
built a new castle by Lake Galve in New Trakai,
abandoning his father's less strongly fortified castle

in Old Trakai. Prince Vytautas, son of Kestutis, built in his turn a new castle on an island in Lake Galve. It was completed at the beginning of the 15th century. In 1477 the young Prince Casimir stayed here with his father, King Casimir of Poland and Lithuania, and his younger brother on one of his first visits to Lithuania. He was also here in 1484, when he was very ill and weak, shortly before his death. In the 16th century the town lost its importance and the castles were turned into prisons.

The ruins of the first castle are down on the shore of Lake Bernadinai, to the right of the road. Vytautas Castle, Melnikaite Street 22, stands on its island in Lake Galve a little further on. There is a museum inside the main building, open daily 11–6, in summer 9 A.M.–9 P.M. Restoration work was begun in 1939, but was interrupted by the Second World War. It was completed under B. Paskevicius in 1951–59. The rebuilding was done with bricks specially made in unusual shapes to regain the original appearance. The reception hall (21 m long by 9 m wide) can be visited as can a number of rooms and towers. There are very few mediaeval castles on Soviet territory and Trakai attracts tourists from far away.

The palace beside the lake which is now used as a tourist base was built in the 19th century and belonged to Count Tyszkiewicz.

The main thoroughfare of Trakai is Vytau Street. As one enters from Vilnius there is a Russian Orthodox church (1864) to the right of the road. Higher up and further back is St. Mary's Roman Catholic Church. Although it has an 18th-century appearance, it was founded in 1409 and later a Bernardine monastery stood on the same site, some ruins of which remain. In the town itself is the Roman Catholic Vytautas Church and by the gates of the town park are the ruins of a Dominican monastery and a church.

Karaim Temple, Melnikaite Street 30

Karaim Museum, open 11–6; closed Tuesday. The Karaites were Jews from the Crimea who settled in Trakai in the 15th century and whose descendants still live here. (The largest community is that of 10,000 near Tel-Aviv.) The polemical literature that accumulated in both Hebrew and Aramaic during the controversies between Karaites and other Jewish communities is mostly preserved in the public library in Leningrad.

Galve Hotel & Restaurant, to the left of the main road, by the main square with St. John's Column in the centre.

There is a boat-hiring station by the lake.

Panerai

To reach Panerai take the left turn at the cross roads where the church in Trakai stands, to reach the museum and memorial here. This is the site of a Nazi death factory where 100,000 lost their lives between 1941–44. 70,000 of the victims came from Vilnius, about a third of the city's population. They were mostly Jews but there were considerable numbers of non-Jews too, including young children

from orphanages, the aged and the sick, patients and staff of hospitals, Soviet prisoners of war, partisans and party members. Six large pits had been prepared here in the sandy ground under the pine trees to house fuel storage tanks and the bodies of the murdered were burnt in these pits. There is a small museum and a granite memorial.

Pircupis (pr. Pirchupis)

44 km (27 miles) from Vilnius on the road to Grodno are the twin villages of Syanasis (Old) Pircupis and Neuyasus (New) Pircupis, otherwise called Pircupai (pr. Pirchupai). The surrounding countryside was sandy and boggy, and the local harvests were very small. Traditionally the villagers relied heavily on the mushrooms, berries and whatever else they could gather in the forests for their sustenance. After Lithuania became part of the Soviet Union in 1940, the Pircupis Collective Farm was organised and mechanised. The Old village survived World War II, while the New was entirely burnt to the ground by the Nazis. This occurred on June 3, 1944, just 40 days before the area was liberated, and 119 people, children included, were burnt alive.

On the right side of the road there is an imposing monument, depicting a mourning mother, and known as the Mother of Pircupis. The 5.5-m (18-ft) statue sculpted by Gediminas Yakubonis was unveiled in 1960, and won a Lenin Prize in 1963. Behind the monument is a wall with the victims' names engraved on it. The monument is erected on the spot from which the Nazis started to encircle the village. The wooden village has been restored on its own site, but there are now two tombs—one over the fraternal grave and the other on the threshing-floor where the people were burned.

A path across the field to the Varensky Region leads to the Museum, which was opened in the old school building in 1959. The museum tells about the tragedy of Pircupis and about the life of the present-day village. Open 9–7, closed Tues.

Elektrenai Population—10,000

50 km (31 miles) from Vilnius, halfway along the road to Kaunas. The town is in fact bypassed by the main road and lies to the left of it. The top of the circus building and the big wheel of the fun fair can be seen from the road. Bus trips here organised by Intourist take 4–5 hours.

In 1960 this spot was but a rough meadow near Lake Anyksciai. Now it is a new, modern town with much of its architecture executed in pre-cast concrete. It serves as a good example of the work of local architects who have designed the streamlined shops and public buildings. The Palace of Culture can seat 500 people, and also in the town is a branch of the Kaunas Polytechnical Institute.

Elektrenai stands beside the lake which formed after several lakes were dammed because of the construction of the Lenin thermal power station. This runs on natural gas from the Ukraine. The eighth and final power unit was completed in 1972, bringing the total capacity of the largest Lithuanian thermal power station up to 1,800,000 kilowatts.

Rumsiskes

On the Vilnius-Kaunas Highway, 23 km (14 miles) from Kaunas and 80 km (50 miles) from Vilnius, is a turn to the village of Rumsiskes which stands not far from the main road near Kaunas Reservoir. The excursion from Vilnius takes 7 hours. The village was transferred in 1958 to this undulating valley from that of the river Neman when it was to be flooded to make the reservoir. Now it is part of an open-air museum of 18th–20th century wooden architecture, covering a territory of 175 hectares (437 acres) and showing the life of Lithuanian peasants. Open daily 10–7; closed the first Monday of each month. Apart from farm buildings and windmills there are workshops to be seen including the clog maker's, a bakery and a pottery.

The territory is divided to show the ethnographical regions of the country. Long ago there were several large tribes living here, the Zemaiciai, the Aukstaiciai and the Juotvingiai (Suduviai). Typical farm buildings have been brought here from all the four zones: Zemaitija (Samogitia), Aukstaitija, Dzukija (southeastern Lithuania) and Suduva. Even today the people from the different parts tend to show distinctive character traits, and these are reflected in the everyday objects they use. The west Lithuanians, the Zemaiciai (Samogitians) are sedate, reserved and persistent. Most of the Aukstaiciai, especially the southwestern group called the Suvalkieciai, are very economical, neat and orderly in their thinking and behaviour. The Druzkai, in southeast Lithuania, which is the least fertile part of the country, are very cheerful, hospitable and friendly.

Zemaitija (Samogitia) has always been known for the skill of its wood carvers, particularly the "dievdirbiai" (god-makers) who carved the statuettes of the saints used to decorate churches, chapels and wayside crosses. The skirts of the Zemaiciai women are mostly striped lengthways while those of the Aukstaiciai are checked. The Dzukai people make great use of ribbons and sashes in enormous variety. Swaddling clothes are bound with them, brides are decked with them and coffins are lowered into the grave with them.

A folk song and dance group gives concerts here on Sat. and Sun. There is a buffet at the entrance. Motorists are advised to go to the main entrance for tickets and then return to the car entrance. The buildings stand in groups at a fair distance from each other, and the full tour on foot is impossible if time is limited.

Druskininkai

The spa lies in the extreme south of Lithuania, 150 km (93 miles) from Vilnius. "Druska" means "salt" and its name comes from its saline springs. It is located on the right bank of river Nemunas, into which flows the rapid rivulet, Ratnychele. The town was founded in the 14th century when a pro-

tecting castle was built. It was declared a resort by a special decree in 1794 but it really counts its days from 1837 when it was fully recognised by the public.

It was here, on August 22, 1891, that the late sculptor Jacques Lipchitz, was born. His real name was Chaim Jacob Lipchitz and he was the son of a wealthy building contractor. After attending school in Bialystok where he began to draw and model, he went to study engineering in Vilna (Vilnius), because his father was opposed to his artistic inclinations. His mother sent him to Paris in 1909 without his father's knowledge, and his artistic training began in earnest. It was interrupted in 1912 when he had to return to Russia for military service, but he had had tuberculosis and was discharged as unfit. He then left Russia, never to return. Lipchitz eventually took French citizenship, but nevertheless chose for his bride a Russian poetess, Berthe Kirtrosser. He left occupied France during the war and lived the rest of his life in the United States.

Now Druskininkai is one of the biggest year-round resorts in Lithuania. People are attracted here by the pine forest and the excellent beaches along the river Nemunas. There are modern sanatoria and mud baths. The spa is recommended for the treatment of diseases of the joints, the nervous system, the heart and the circulatory system.

Kirov Street runs through the town from the railway station to Melnikaites Street by the entrance to the park. There are mineral water and mud bath establishments here and also a statue of Maryte Melnikaite by Autinis; she was a partisan during the last war, and was made a Heroine of the Soviet Union.

21-July Street (Liepos 21) is the shopping centre of the resort and has a covered market.

Shkoplairni Catholic Church, in the centre. It is built of red brick in pseudo-Gothic style and surrounded by gardens.

Skorbyaschei Bogoroditsy Virgin Church, Russian Orthodox

Ciurlionis Memorial Museum, Ciurlionis Street 41. Open 12–6; closed Mon. The Lithuanian painter and composer, Mikalojus K. Ciurlionis (1875–1911), spent his childhood here. He was born into the family of a church organist, seven of whose nine children were musical. Prince Oginsky took the 12-year-old boy into his orchestra and Ciurlionis played and studied for several years. At the same time he painted landscapes and composed music. He graduated from Warsaw Conservertoire and tried to express colours by the means of music. His personal possessions and documents are on display here.

Lake Druskouis is in the town and there is a boating station there.

Turistas Hotel & Café, Kirov Street 41, on the central square

Ratnychele Restaurant

Ruta Lunchroom

Market, at the entrance to the town, on the left.

The environs of Druskininkai are very picturesque with small lakes among the dense pine woods. The valley of Raigardas, which inspired Ciurlionis in his painting and music, is especially beautiful. Raigardas has been made a national park because of its unique landscape, and is also known as the site of the "sunken town." A local legend says that the rich town of Raigardas stood here before it disappeared under the earth.

VINNITSA Population—374,000

The town probably derives its name from the old Slavic word, "vyeno," meaning "ransom" or "transferred property." It stands on the Yuzhny (south) Bug and was first mentioned as a Lithuanian fortress in 1363.

It became Polish in 1569 following the Treaty of Lublin, and from 1598 it served as the centre of the Braclav military district. It was granted the Magdeburg Charter in 1640. In 1648 it was besieged and taken by the Cossacks under Krivonos, and subsequently, commanded by Bogdan Khmelnitsky, played an important role in the 1648–54 war against the Poles, passing back to Poland in 1667 in accordance with the Treaty of Andrusov. In 1793 it went to Russia, along with the rest of the Right Bank Ukraine. Soviet power was established in November 1917.

The town's first castle, built to protect it from the Turks and the Tatars, stood on the river's high left bank, opposite the old town and surrounded by a stone wall, "muri," the remains of which can be seen near Lenin Street 15, where the town archives are now kept.

During World War II 40% of the town was destroyed. The occupation lasted for 970 days and during this time many citizens suffered torture and a total of 42,000 lost their lives. Hitler and Goering stayed in Vinnitsa for a short time in June 1942. Little is now left of the old buildings in the town centre. Kozitsky Street is interesting because one can see there the changing architectural styles of the century. No. 18 is in the Constructivist style of the 1930s and there are others in Empire style. No. 16 is an old water tower which is kept as a historical monument.

The main thoroughfare is Lenin Street, and the central department store and the Yuzhny Bug Hotel are on Gagarin Square. Among the more impressive of the new buildings is the Lyalya Ratushnaya Pioneer Palace, built in 1969 with facilities, including a swimming pool, for 3,000 children. During the War Lyalya Ratushnaya left her studies at Moscow University to serve with the resistance for four years; she was killed on the eve of the liberation of Vinnitsa from the enemy.

The Pirogov Regional Hospital was opened in 1914 and now has beds for 600 patients, and the Pirogov Medical Institute for 2,500 students was built in 1931. There is also a pedagogical institute in Vinnitsa. The town is noted for its food processing and light industry; it has electrotechnical and fertiliser factories, and in the surrounding region sugar-beet is both grown and refined.

Vinnitsa celebrated the 600th anniversary of its foundation in 1972.

Dominican Monastery, Lenin Street. This monastery was built in 1634, but was converted into a Russian Orthodox church in 1774. It is now used as a sports club.

Muri Jesuit Monastery, built in the 17th–18th century. It originally consisted of a fortified monastery-house but now only the ruins remain.

Capuchin Monastery, Lenin Street. This monastery was founded in 1760 and one building now serves as a lecture hall.

St. George's Church, in the old part of the city; one turns down from the main road just past the Lenin monument and the church is across the bridge, on the other side of the river. It was built, without nails, in 1726.

Local Museum, Lenin Street 11a. Open 10–5; closed Mon. The museum is in a new building, next to the Dominican Monastery building. Paintings by Italian, Dutch and other European artists of the 16th–19th centuries are on display here as well as more recent Russian and Ukrainian works. There is also a model kremlin made entirely of sugar.

Museum of Decorative & Applied Art, in St. Nicholas's Church (1746), Mayakovskovo Street 6. Open 10–5; closed Mon.

Kotsyubinsky's House, Bevza Street 17. Open 10–5; closed Wed. Mikhail Kotsyubinsky (1864–1913), Ukrainian writer and teacher, and friend of Maxim Gorky, was born in this house and lived here as a child. The museum was organised in 1927.

Pirogov Monument

Kotsyubinsky Monument

Lenin Monument, Lenin Street, in front of the large new building housing the town's administrative offices. Sculpted by Kovalyov and unveiled in 1972.

In *Kozitsky Children's Park*, there is an obelisk commemorating World War II, an eternal flame, and a monument to those who fell during the 1917–19 Civil War. Another *monument* of granite on the left bank of the river commemorates the victory of the Cossack Colonel Ivan Bogun over the Poles in 1651. It was unveiled in 1954.

Space Exploration monument, in front of the entrance to Gorky Park, in the centre of the town. This monument is in the form of an arch and a rocket.

War Memorial, along the Kiev highway

Air Force Pilots' Monument, on the right of the road leading into town from Khmelnitsky. This monument is a fighter plane on a pedestal.

Sadovsky Musical and Drama Theatre, Dzerzhinsky Street 13

Puppet Theatre, Lev Tolstoy Street 6a

Philharmonia Concert Hall, Lenin Street 64

Gorky Park, Liebknecht Street 1

Zhovtnevaya (October) Hotel (Intourist) & Restaurant, Pirogov Street 2; tel. 26-540. Intourist office; tel. 27-785

Yuzhny Bug Hotel (Intourist) & Restaurant, Gagarin Square; tel. 24-655, 23-876.

Ukraina Hotel & Restaurant, Lenin Street

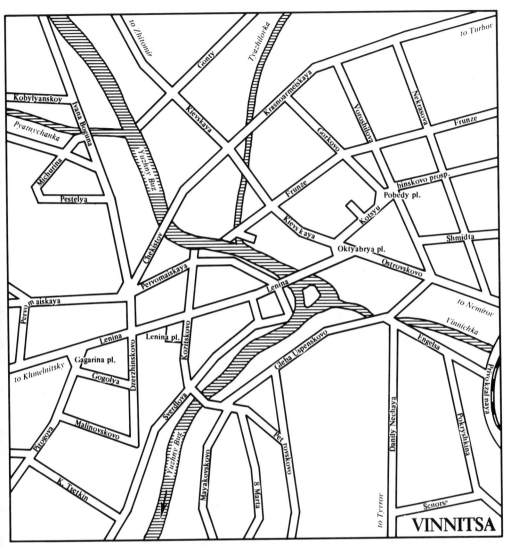

GPO, Kozitsky Street, where it crosses Lenin Street

Department Store, Gagarin Square 10

Surprise Souvenir Shop, Lenin Street 39

Gift Shop, Kozitsky Street 61

Filling Station, Franz Mering Street 43, on the right approaching Vinnitsa from Khmelnitsky.

Service Station, Kievskaya Street 26, on the left on the way into town from Khmelnitsky.

Camping Site. There are two camping sites, one on the left approaching the town from the west but better is that on the road to Zhitomir, at Kolo-Mikhailovka, on the right 10 km (6 miles) north of Vinnitsa. This is one of the best of its kind in the Soviet Union, pleasantly situated in a pine-wood, with good service and a cafe.

Intourist organises *boat trips* on the Youzhny Boug between May and September. Out-of-town excursions can be arranged to Pirogovo (5 km/3 miles), Voronovitsa (24 km/15 miles), Nemirov (45 km/28 miles), to visit the *museums* of the Ukrainian authoress Marko Vovchok and the Russian poet Nekrasov and also the fine *park*, Tulchin (83 km/ 52 miles), Timanovka (95 km/59 miles) and Mo-gilyov-Podolsky (154 km/96 miles), all described below, and to Khmelnitsky (listed under its own name).

Pirogovo

Formerly Vyshnya. This is on the outskirts of the town. 1 km (0.6 miles) from the main road is the *Pirogov Museum*, organised in 1947 and open 10–5; closed Mon. The museum is in the house occupied by the Russian surgeon from 1866 until his death in 1881. Nikolai Pirogov (1810–81) was accepted as a medical student at Moscow University when he was only 14 and he qualified at 18. From there he went on to Tartu University where, at 22, he took his Ph.D. and where, four years later, he became professor of surgery. He acquired world fame when in 1841, and upon the basis of 15 years' work, his "Surgical Anatomy" with an accompanying surgical atlas was published in St. Petersburg. In 1847, during the Caucasian War, he became the first doctor in the world to use ether as an anaesthetic during operations in the field.

1 km (0.6 miles) from the house is *Pokrovskaya Church* which was built in 1882 over Pirogov's glass tomb; this is now in the crypt. The surgeon's body was embalmed by a pupil of his, Dr. Vyvodtsev, and was then dressed for burial in the uniform of an army doctor. Pirogov's son, also called Nikolai, was buried in the same crypt and there is a gravestone set in the floor to mark the spot.

Voronovitsa

In the village, 18 km (11 miles) from Vinnitsa, is the 17th-century *house* where Alexander Mozhaisky (1825–90) lived from 1869–76. He was the Russian inventor who is credited in Russia with having constructed in 1881 the first full-size aeroplane. It was tested in 1882–85 and there are indications that once it even left the ground. It possessed all the essential parts of modern planes: body, wings, motor and undercarriage. There is now a school in the house.

Nemirov Population—11,000

This district centre is 45 km (28 miles) to the southwest of Vinnitsa on the road to Uman, and it is where foreign tourists turn right to reach the other places described below.

Nemirov was founded at the end of the 14th century. It was under Polish rule from 1569 until the Turks seized it in 1672. The Poles took it back in 1699 and held it until 1793 when with the Second Division of Poland it passed to Russia. It was from here that the Russian general Alexander Suvorov set out to besiege Warsaw in 1794.

Local Museum

Roman Catholic Church (1801)

Trinity Church (1881)

School, built in 1838 by F. Mekhovich

Rest House, in a 19th-century park. The main building used to be a princely palace.

Marko Vovchok Literary Museum, Marko Vovchok was the pseudonym of the Ukrainian authoress, Maria Vilinskaya-Markovich (1834–1907). She lived here from 1855 to 1858.

Nekrasov Literary Museum, the Russian poet, Nikolai Nekrasov (1821–77), was born in Nemirov.

Nekrasov Monument, by Skoblikov, V. Zhigulin and A. Kreichi; unveiled in 1971.

Marko Vovchok Monument, by P. Movchun and A. Gaiduchenya; unveiled in 1975.

Lenin Monument, by V. Borisenko and A. Ignaschev; unveiled in 1978.

Nemirovskoye Gorodische, 3 km (2 miles) from Nemirov in the valley of the river Mirka is the site of one of the largest Scythian settlements in the Ukraine. The earth walls and moats date from the 7–6th centuries B.C., and the local people appropriately called it Bolshiye Valy (big banks).

Tulchin Population—16,000

This town lies 80 km (50 miles) southeast of Vinnitsa. It is reached by taking the Uman road as far as Nemirov and then bearing right, through Bratslav.

The town grew up around the fortress of Nestervar (meaning "fortress beyond the Dniester" in Hungarian). The fortress was built in 1607–1609 but was demolished and the rough stones that can be seen in some of the buildings of the town were taken from the ruins. When the Turks occupied the town in 1672 they called it Turchin which was later easily changed to Tulchin. It remained in Turkish hands until 1699 and then it was Polish until 1793 when it was united with Russia. In the same year it was granted its coat-of-arms of a shield and fortress on a gold ground.

Uspenskaya (Assumption) Church, Pestel Street

Dominican Monastery, built in the 18th century when Tulchin belonged to the Polish Count Potocki. He asked English architects to design a building following the lines of St. Peter's in Rome. It has been restored several times and is now used as a sports school, a technical school and a computer station.

Suvorov Museum, Gagarin Street 1, in the 18th century house where Alexander Suvorov (1730–1800) lived in 1796–97. The generalissimo was in Tulchin when he received the order of Emperor Paul I that he retire. He put on all his orders and medals when he came out to bid his soldiers farewell and after the ceremony he unpinned them all, saying that he would only put them on again when he was with his men once more. Taras Shevchenko depicted this incident in his painting "Suvorov Bidding Farewell to the Garrison in Tulchin," a copy of which is hanging in the museum. It was here that Suvorov wrote most of his famous book, "The Art of Victory." The museum was opened in 1947.

Decembrists' Museum, Pestel Street 24. This house was the home of Pavel Pestel from 1818 to 1825. Pestel was the leader of the Southern Society, a secret society of officers who planned to dethrone the tsar. The museum was opened in 1975 to commemorate the 150th anniversary of the December revolt.

Pushin's House, 50-letiya-USSR Street, where the poet stayed in 1821 and 1822.

Palace of Culture, Lenin Street 85. The bronze monument here is of the Ukrainian composer, Nikolai Leontovich. The building of the girls' school where he taught is at Leontovich Street 10, and is now a boarding school. The monument was designed by Ignashenko, sculpted by Kalchenko and unveiled in 1969.

Memorial Arch, built in 1954 to commemorate the 300th anniversary of the reunification of the Ukraine and Russia.

Suvorov's Bust, at the entrance to the Suvorov Museum. There is also an *obelisk* to his memory in Tulchin and a *monument* which is a copy of that which was unveiled in Izmail in 1945. A box was put into the pediment containing Suvorov's banner, some Russian coins and a copy of "The Art of Victory." The monument was designed by Edwards and unveiled in 1954.

War Memorial, dedicated to those who lost their lives in the Civil War.

Lenin Monument, in the centre of the town on Lenin Street, the main street

   GPO

Timanovka

Suvorov Museum, in another house where the great general worked on his book, "The Art of Victory."

Here also are three wells which were dug by Suvorov's men. They are marked by an inscription reading: "Suvorov's Wells, dug by Russian soldiers in 1729 and repaired by the grateful descendants in 1949."

Mogilyov-Podolsky Population—35,000

Mogilyov-Podolsky is 154 km (96 miles) southwest of Vinnitsa, on the left bank of the river Dneste in the valley of the Dekla and the Nemiya, near the Ukrainian-Moldavian border.

The town was founded at the end of the 16th century and named after the Moldavian noble, Mikhail Mogila. It was an important place on the trade route from the Ukraine to Moldavia and Turkey. It was Polish until 1648 when it became the headquarters of the Mogilyov Cossack regiment that fought hard against the Poles in 1648–54. It belonged to Bratslav military district in 1649, and according to the Treaty of Andrusov in 1667 it was returned to Poland. From 1672 to 1699 it was in Turkish hands, but was then again returned to Poland until 1793 when, with the rest of the Right Bank Ukraine, it became Russian. It had been granted the Magdeburg Charter in 1743. Soviet power was announced on 24th December, 1917 but the town was occupied by the Austro-German army in 1918. There was a rebellion here and in 1923 the town was renamed Mogilyov-Podolsky.

   Local Museum
   Mogilyov Castle ruins (17th century)
   St. Nicholas's Church (1757)
   18th-century Church
   Cathedral (19th century)
   Nikolai Gogol Monument, unveiled in 1872
   Lenin Monument

In the suburbs at Lyadova is an 11th-century Rock Monastery, at Ozakintsy, the ruins of a fortress, and in Kukavka a 19th-century church designed by V. Tropinin which is now open as a museum.

VITEBSK Population—350,000

My own town, there, by the Dvina!
Look upon it, friends, both long and well
For at midday as at night time
My dearest Vitebsk is beautiful.

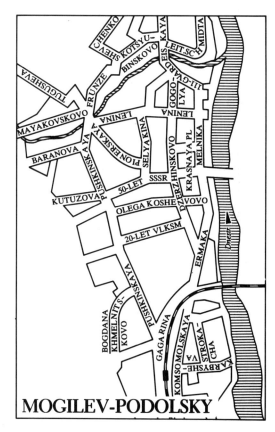

MOGILEV-PODOLSKY

Vitebsk is the third largest town of Byelorussia, 90 km (56 miles) northwest of Smolensk.

It was built at the confluence of the rivers Zapadnaya Dvina and Virba, from the latter of which comes the name of the town. It was said to have been founded by Saint Olga; she was Princess of Kiev, the widow of Prince Igor and the first Russian woman to have become a Christian.

Vitebsk was first mentioned in 974. In ancient times it was a trading centre with merchants coming here from Kiev, Smolensk, Novgorod and the Baltic. Up to the 12th century the town belonged in turn to Smolensk and Polotsk, but later it became a small independent principality. Grand-Duke Olgerd of Lithuania married Princess Maria of Vitebsk, and subsequently in 1320 the Princedom of Vitebsk was united with Lithuania. Its position on the frontier made it a bone of contention between Poland and Russia. In 1667 Poland became the owner of Vitebsk. Peter the Great was here several times including 1701 and 1705, in which year he ordered the town to be burnt to the ground because he knew that the citizens had been holding secret talks with King Stanislav Leschinski of Poland.

Vitebsk finally fell to Russia at the first partition of Poland (1772). In 1796 it became the centre of the Byelorussian Province, and in 1802 the centre of Vitebsk Province. On 16 July 1812 Napoleon entered the town.

The railway line from Riga that runs through Vitebsk was opened in 1866. Local trams were introduced in 1898 by a Belgian-French company and right up to the time of the revolution Vitebsk was the only Byelorussian town with a tramway system. The prewar population of the town was 180,000 but upon liberation in 1944 there were but 180 inhabitants to be found. There is little left of old Vitebsk today as 93% of the town was destroyed by the Nazis during World War II.

The 18th-century *Governor's Palace* at Sovietskaya Street 18 had a wing built on to the side in the 19th century. During the war of 1812, Napoleon lived here for two weeks together with members of his staff, including the marshals Joachim Murat, King of Naples, and Louis-Alexandre Bertier, Prince of Wagram. The building was restored after the Second World War and now houses administrative offices. The two-storey, 19th-century building at Pushkin Street 2 houses the local Communist Committee, while the Komsomol Committee uses Lenin Street 32, built by Kaminsky in 1879–82. The District Council at Gogol Street 6 is in the building of a former girls' convent school, built in 1899–1902 by Pavlovsky and Vinogradov. The former Officers' Club at Mayakovsky Street 1 was built at the beginning of the 20th century. In 1886 the Peasants' Landbank was at Lenin Street 18, but in 1917 it moved into the art nouveau style building at 1-Dovatora Street 7/11 designed by Tarasov; the Veterinary Institute has been here since 1924. The carpet factory is in the Dvina Factory, built by Belgians in 1899. There are also some examples of constructivist style buildings which include the House of Culture at No. 2 Engels Street which was built in 1928–32 by Vasiliev. No. 25 Gorky Street (1927–28) was designed by Vyshelessky and No. 34 Suvorova Street (1928–32) by Vukolov.

Victory Square covers 16.7 hectares (42 acres) and is among the largest town squares in the Soviet Union.

Right up until the war the town had a large Jewish population. It was in Vitebsk that Marc Chagall (1887–1985) was born. The painter, graphic artist and designer is famous for his dreamlike paintings based on personal experience or using symbolic imagery. The son of Zachar Shagal, a poor herring merchant, the boy was named Moses by his parents. There were eight other children in the family besides himself and their upbringing was profoundly Jewish. He attended the local Jewish elementary school, the cheder, and later went to the local Russian public school. His school drawing lessons were followed by a study of painting under a local realist, Jehuda Pen. In 1906 he left for St. Petersburg, enrolled at the Zvantseva School of Art where Leon Bakst taught him for a short while, but long enough to inspire him to go to Paris in 1910. That was the time when artists from all over the world were being drawn there, among them Picasso and Modigliani and, like Chagall also from Russia, Jacques Lipschitz.

After a successful exhibition in Berlin, Chagall returned to Vitebsk in 1914 and the following year he and his childhood sweetheart, Bella Rozenburg, were married. In 1918 he became Commissar of Art in Vitebsk, designed theatrical scenery for political satires, was responsible for decorating the town to celebrate the first anniversary of the revolution, and founded the Vitebsk Art Institute. His use of green cows and goats proved unpopular, and although he had insisted that El Lissistsky and Malevich should join his art school at Pravdy Street 3, it was Malevich who took over Chagall's post and in 1920 Chagall left Vitebsk for ever. He went to Moscow and worked on decorations for the Jewish Theatre and the prestigious Stanislavsky Theatre, but there were political difficulties and in 1922 he returned to Berlin and finally settled in Paris in 1923, the same year that his art school in Vitebsk closed. Never, however, did he completely abandon his childhood memories, and many of the pictures executed in Paris could just as well have been created in his native Vitebsk.

Church of the Annunciation (Blagoveschenskaya), 1000-lyet Vitebska Square. This 12th-century church was rebuilt several times, but now only ruins remain. The walls were of a construction unusual in Russia; a row of narrow, Byzantine bricks alternated with a row of large, limestone blocks.

Church of the Resurrection (1772), Town Hall Square

St. Barbara's Roman Catholic Church, Leningrad Street 25. Built in 1785 and restored at the end of the 19th century.

Greek Catholic Basilian Monastery, Politekhnicheskaya Street 2. Built in 1785 by the Italian architect Fontani. In 1857 a seminary was opened here, but now it serves as a technical school.

Local Museum, Lenin Street 34. Open 11–6; closed Mon. The building was formerly that of the Town Hall, built in late baroque style in 1775. The clock was installed in the tower at the end of the 18th century and the third floor was added in 1911.

Branch of the Local Museum, Komissara Krylova Street 7. Open 11–6; closed Mon. In 1804 there was an elementary school here, then from 1808 till 1876 it was a boys' grammar school. It served as a prison during the German occupation in World War II.

Exhibition Hall, Moskovsky Prospect 5. Open 12–8; closed Mon. & Tues.

Tram Museum, 5-Frunze Street 7

Shmyryov Museum, Chekov Street 4. Open 11–5; Mon. & Fri. 1–7; Wed. 11–3; closed Tues. Minai Shmyryov (1891–1964) was a partisan commander.

Victory Obelisk. This commemorates the war of 1812.

Lenin Monument, Lenin Square. The 9-m (30-ft) statue by Arapova and Alexeyenko was unveiled in 1956.

Memorial to the dead of World War II, next to Smolensk Market

Liberators' Memorial, Victory Square. The memorial, sculpted by Pechkin and Markov, includes an eternal flame.

Victims of Nazism Monument. The 14-m (46-ft) stele by Belsky was unveiled in 1964.

Underground Fighters' Monument, Krasnobrigadnaya Street. The rectangular stele was designed by Pavlichyuk in 1967.

Masherov Bust, Zamkovaya Street. Pyotr Masherov (1918–1980) was a party leader.

Yakub Kolas Drama Theatre, Zamkovaya Street 2. Yakub Kolas (1882–1956) was a Byelorussian author.

Philharmonic Hall, Engels Street 2

Central Park

Vitebsk Hotel & Restaurant, Zamkovaya Street 5; tel. 63-642

Dvina Hotel, Ilinskovo Street 41/18

Sportivnaya Hotel, Lazo Street 50

Sovietskaya Hotel, Suvorov Street 17/21; tel. 62-456

Avrora Restaurant, Lenin Street 59, tel. 64-253

Frankfurt-na-Odere Restaurant, Zhestkova Street 8/1, tel. 50-189, 50-149

Department Store, Zamkovaya Street 19

Globus Bookshop, Zamkovaya Street 21/30

Zdravnevo. The artist Repin lived here for eight years. In the 1920s there was an art school on his estate where his daughter, Tatiana, taught.

VLADIKAVKAZ (formerly Ordzhonikidze) is the capital of the North Ossetian Autonomous Republic.

(Intourist organises overnight excursions here from the Georgian capital of Tbilisi via the Georgian Military Highway, a journey of 210 km/130 miles.)

NORTH OSSETIAN AUTONOMOUS REPUBLIC

This republic has a territory of 8,000 sq km (3,100 sq miles).

The majority of the Ossetians refer to themselves as Irons. However, those who inhabit the Urukh Valley in the western part of the territory are known as Digors. There is a slight difference in their dialects but they are both a mixture of Caucasian and Persian whose predecessors were called the Alani. There is a theory that the Catalonians in Spain are related to the people here—"Cata" stands for "false" or "pseudo" plus "Alan" makes "Catalan." This is similar to the relation thought to exist between the Georgians and the Basques. Certainly in both cases there are some words in their languages that really do correspond. The Alani lived here in the plains at the beginning of the 1st century A.D., then moved in the 4th century, following a devastating attack from the Huns, to the valleys of the rivers Terek and Kuban, and there built up a powerful state that maintained connections with Rome and Byzantium in the 7th and 8th centuries. They were good warriors, and they adopted Christianity in the 9th century, through both Byzantium and Georgia. When Genghis Khan overran the country in the 12th century, most of the Alani were killed and the remainder driven up into the mountains. Here they were divided by the mountains into four separate groups, while a fifth group moved over the mountains to their present home in Georgia. Some Ossis (the Georgian word for Ossetians) were reconverted to Islam, but all the same, the old pagan traditions died hard, including that of having a family god. Today only a minority are Moslems, although most of them still prefer not to eat pork. The population is now mainly Russian and Ossetian, but there are also Armenians, Georgians, Persians, and other minorities. In fact, the Ossetians form a tiny pocket of extreme interest to ethnologists; their language (which belongs to the northeastern group of Iranian languages) and customs, their traditional courage, their hospitality, and their fearlessness in the face of death are among the attributes that have been found to prove them to be the sole survivors of the legendary Scythian and Sarmatian peoples. They are known for their skilful wood and stone work and also for their metal engraving and embroidery. Some of the houses in the mountain villages still have national architectural features, as, for example, the watchtowers that were so necessary for defence in the past.

This all refers to North Ossetia, but there is a southern republic, too, with quite separate administration. The language is the same in both, but the southern group has lost the Ossetian customs and adopted those of the Georgians. Each has relatives in the opposite group's territory and they visit each other all the time.

When the Kuchuk-Kainarji Peace Treaty was signed between Russia and Turkey in 1774, Ossetia joined Russia, becoming the Vladikavkaz region.

Vladikavkaz Population—300,000

Vladikavkaz is the capital of the North Ossetian Autonomous Republic. Today the population is mainly Russian and Ossetian; minorities include Armenians, Georgians, and Persians.

The first settlements appeared here in the 3rd to 2nd millennia B.C., and the present town is surrounded by burial mounds dating from the 7th to 4th centuries B.C. Gold and silver ornaments as well as objects of bronze have been excavated here. The town is guarded by the cliffs of the Table Mountain (3,009 m/9,870 ft) whose silhouette from the side resembles the sleeping princess in this local legend:

Long ago the Cyclops lived in caves in the thick forests. Each year one came down to the kingdom that lay to the north of where Table Mountain now stands and demanded that the most beautiful seventeen-year-old girl be given him to eat. The people found out that the spell would be broken if the loveliest girl would sacrifice herself voluntarily. At last came the princess's turn to be devoured. Her father locked her away, but she learned of the trouble and escaped. She rushed forward to sacrifice herself to the Cyclops. There was a howl, a flash, and a cloud of smoke, and when the air cleared, the people saw that the princess had turned into a mountain—but the monster had gone.

The princess's suitor, a brave shepherd called Kazbek, heard the sound and looked down from the hills upon the scene. He could not sacrifice himself as his beloved had done, but he turned immediately into the mountain now called Kazbek.

The Ossetian town of Dedyakov (Tetyakov) which had grown up on this spot was destroyed by the Arabs in 1277. An Arabian writer, Masoudi, recalls that there was already a stronghold here.

In the second part of the 18th century the area became especially important because of Russian trade with the Caucasus and Persia and, later, because of its position on the Georgian Military Highway leading south through the mountains to Tbilisi. The existing village of Dzauga grew larger, expanding on either side of the Terek; a fortress was built here in 1784 to subdue the mountain people, but in fact it never was used. It was surrounded by a 1.5-m (5-ft) rampart and a moat 5 m (17 ft) wide. Catherine the Great donated funds in 1785 for the construction of an Orthodox church within the fortress—"to tame the Kumyks and other local peoples." However, the local people themselves took the fortress in 1788. The first of a series of restorations was made in 1803 and the last in the 1830s.

The fortress was visited by many Russian writers. Alexander Griboyedov (who wrote the classic play *Woe from Wit*) first passed by in 1818 on his way to taking up his position as Russian ambassador to Persia, and he often repeated the journey. Mikhail Lermontov described it in the "Maxim Maximych," part of his novel *A Hero of Our Time.* In 1829 Alexander Pushkin stayed at the fortress inn (since demolished) and subsequently described it in his "Journey to Erzrum." His diary entry reads, "The Ossetian people is the poorest tribe of all inhabiting the Caucasus"—in spite of the fact that the commandant had given such a splendid dinner in his honour that he felt obliged to chalk up some grateful lines on the door as he left. Lev Tolstoy stayed here, too.

In 1860 the place was proclaimed the town of Vladikavkaz ("Mistress of the Caucasus") but was renamed in 1931 in honour of Ordzhonikidze. Grigory ("Sergo") Ordzhonikidze (1886–1937) was a prominent Communist, a Georgian who concerned himself with the political life of the whole of Caucasus. When he was posthumously held in disgrace from 1944–54, the town was again known by its ancient name of Dzaudzhikau, but the name was changed back to Ordzhonikidze when the revolutionary was rehabilitated; until reverting to Vladikavkaz in 1990.

During World War II the German army was as close as 6 km (4 miles) from the town. Vladikavkaz's main thoroughfare is *Mir Prospect* (formerly Nesterovsky, so called in 1844 after Nesterov, the commander of the fortress). It runs for 1 km (0.6 mile) and is lined with many of the original old houses and with an avenue of fine lime trees. There are shops, hotels, and restaurants here and it is a favourite place for taking the air.

Tseretelli Street (formerly Fortress Street) retains the same appearance it had when Vladikavkaz fortress was founded. It was here that the commandant lived and that the inns were situated. A *monument* was set up on the site of the inn in 1949, and the *governor-general's house*, where Pushkin stayed, is in Pushkin Square and serves as a military hospital. There is a *bust of Pushkin* in the square and, opposite him, another of the Bulgarian revolutionary Georgi Dimitrov. Several fragments of the old fortress can be seen in Titova Street, in 1905 Street, and on the grounds of School No. 1 on Ossetian Hill. Solyani Pereulok is where the salt warehouses used to be; the mountain people were issued salt by the urban administration.

Nonferrous metallurgy based on zinc and silver is the most important section of the local industry, but also well developed are the machine and instrument building and food and timber processing industries; there is a rolling-stock repair station and factories producing tractor, car, and electric equipment, while the local mineral water known as Karmadon ("Hot Water") is bottled. Before the revolution considerable Belgian capital was invested here, and it was a Belgian company that installed the first horse-drawn trams. Khetagurov North-Ossetian University was opened in 1969; the other educational establishments include mining, medical, teacher's training, art, and agricultural colleges. Not far away are hunting reserves where bears can be found. It is planned to extend the local hunting facilities and to organise fishing on Lake Bekan.

St. George's Church, Armyansky Pereulok 1. This Armenian church was built in 1843 and is open for services.

Armenian Church, Bayeva Street 15

Ossetian Church, Kosta Khetagurov Street

Russian Orthodox Church, Dzerzhinsky Street

Local Museum, Prospect Mira 11. Open 10–6; closed Mon.

Makharbek Tuganov Art Museum, Prospect Mira 12. Open 10–6; closed Wed. Makharbek Tuganov (1881–1952) was a local artist. This interesting mansion, with some of its art nouveau decor well preserved, was built in 1909 by a rich merchant called Oganov for his French wife, but she is said not to have been very pleased with it in spite of all his trouble. Inside there are some works by the Russian realists Repin and Levitan.

Khetagurov Museum of Ossetian Literature, Muzeiny Pereulok 3. Open 10–5.30; closed Mon. This building, which dates from 1902–6, used to house the Cossack Military Museum, founded in 1897.

Kosta Khetagurov Museum, Voikov Street 20. Open 10–6; closed Thurs. Kosta Khetagurov (1859–1906) was called the Leonardo da Vinci of the Ossetian people. He was poet, artist, writer, and playwright and is venerated as the founder of the Ossetian literary language. The museum illustrates the development of this literature. It is housed in a 19th-century Ossetian church, and in the churchyard outside is Khetagurov Grove where stands a black marble bust of the poet by Sanokoyev. Nearby is the *grave of Arsen Kotsoyev* (1872–1944), another Ossetian writer, who also worked as a translator.

Khetagurov's House, Butyrina Street 19. Open 10–5.30; closed Mon.

Kirov and Ordzhonikidze Museum, Kirov Street 50. Open 10–6; closed Thurs. These were both well known Bolshevik revolutionaries.

Pliyev Museum, Borodinskaya Street 7. Open 10–6; closed Thurs. General Issa Pliyev (1902–79) was twice acclaimed Hero of the Soviet Union during World War II.

Planetarium, at the bridge over the Terek, Katsoyev Street 64, near Vladikavkaz Hotel. Open 10–6; closed Tues. The building in which the planetarium is housed is one of the most impressive in Vladikavkaz. It is the *Mukhtarov Dzhuma Mosque*, a Sunnite mosque built in 1906–8 with money donated by a Baku oil magnate named Mukhtarov in honour of his Ossetian wife. (The "Dzhuma" part of the mosque's name comes from the Arabic word for Friday.) It was designed as a small-scale copy of the mosques built in St. Petersburg and Kazan. Some of the motifs of its architecture and decor were taken from Egyptian architecture of the 10th, 11th, and 12th centuries. The mosque, which is the largest in the North Caucasus, was closed in 1928 and a Foucauld pendulum was installed, but over 300 inscriptions from the Koran still adorn the walls.

Natural History Museum, Lenin Street 19. Open 9–5.30; closed Tues.

Pushkin Bust, in Pushkin Garden, Tsereteli Street. The inscription reads, "The Caucasus admitted us to its sanctuary fortress inn where Pushkin stayed in 1829." The monument was set up in 1949.

Decorative Panel, in the middle of Pushkin Garden. A medallion shows Pushkin's profile, and the panel illustrates his journey along the Georgian Military Highway. It was designed by Alexander Zharsky after Pushkin's sketches made in 1829 in Kobi aul ("village").

Kosta Khetagurov Statue, Karl Marx Square. The 13-m (43-ft) statue by Tavasiyev was unveiled in 1949.

Grey Marble Obelisk, Geroyev Square, at the entrance to the town. This is in memory of the Chinese soldiers who died here during the civil war in 1918. Sanakoyev was the sculptor and the obelisk was unveiled in 1960.

Granite Obelisk, on the left of Tbilisskoye Chaussee on the way out of town toward the south. This obelisk is in memory of 17,000 Red Army soldiers who fell in 1919 during the civil war. The obelisk by Dziova and Poluyektov stands 24 m (79 ft) high and was unveiled in 1957. There is an eternal flame. On the right of the road is the funicular railway leading up to Lysaya Gora (see below).

Lenin Statue, Lenin Square. This statue by Azgur stands 12 m (39 ft) high and was unveiled in 1957.

Ordzhonikidze Statue, in Svoboda Square. Svoboda Square is the local place for ceremonial parades and has a tribune for dignitaries to take the salute.

War Memorial, Pobeda Square. This memorial commemorates the defenders of the town who lost their lives in World War II.

Pliyev Bust, in a garden on Mir Prospect. The bust commemorates General Issa Pliyev, born here in 1902.

Theatre, Naberezhnaya 18. The theatre was founded in 1935, but the building was not completed until 1958.

Russian Drama Theatre, Lenin Square 2. The theatre company was founded in 1896, the building in 1972.

North Ossetian Drama Theatre, Karl Marx Street 77

Musical Theatre, Naberezhnaya 18

Shabi Puppet Theatre, Titov Street. "Shabi" means "child."

Concert Hall, Sovietov Street 34. This red-brick Gothic building was formerly a Lutheran church.

Kosta Khetagurov Park, Mir Prospect 7. The park is pleasantly situated beside the Terek. There are artificial lakes with islands linked by miniature bridges.

Spartak Stadium, Shmulevich Street

Riding School, Pushkinskaya Street 2

Racecourse, Beslan, 17 km (11 miles) along the main road toward Nalchik

Intourist Hotel and Restaurant, Prospect Mira 19; tel. 34-626. Intourist office, tel. 32-612.

Vladikavkaz (Intourist) Hotel and Restaurant, Kotsoyev Street 75; tel. 57-162. A 10-storey Intourist hotel.

Terek Hotel, Mir Prospect 56

Kavkaz Hotel and Restaurant, Vatutin Street 50

Daryal Motel & Restaurant, Moskovskoye Chaussee 11, 7 km (4 miles) from the centre of town, where the turn to Vladikavkaz joins the bypass; tel. 59-287. Behind the motel there stretches a hunting reserve with boar and bear. Hunting licences are available for foreigners.

Terek Restaurant, Prospect Mira 32

Nar Restaurant, Khetagurov Park. National food is served here. The most popular are all sorts of pies, "ualibah," with cheese; "fidchin," served very hot with a meat filling (one has to be careful not to let the delicious gravy leak out through the bottom); "kartofchin," with potatoes; "sakharadzhin," with beet tops and cheese; and "lyavzha,"

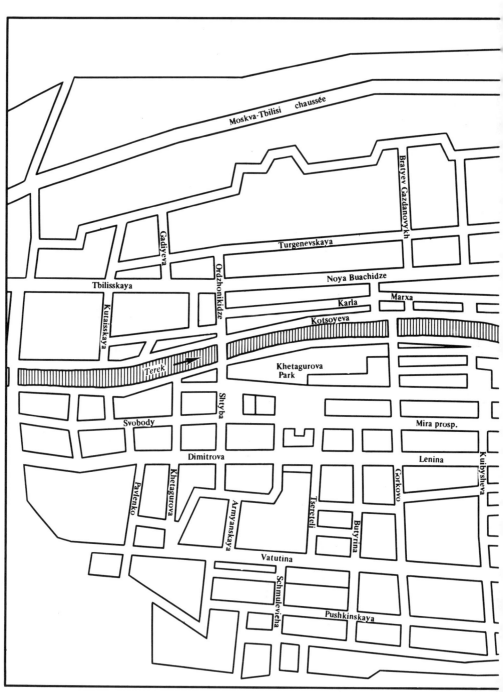

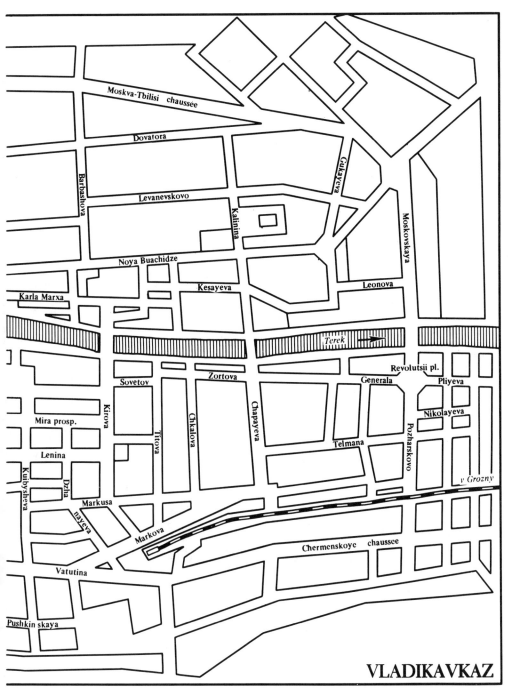

VLADIKAVKAZ

chicken sauce with sour cream and "tsakhton," a sour cream sauce with garlic. The national drink is beer; the Ossetians are the only Caucasian people to have a long tradition of brewing beer.

Kaban Restaurant, at the beginning of Kaban Gorge, on the banks of the mountain river Gizeldon, 12 km (7 miles) from town. Built in national style, this restaurant has a good selection of national dishes on the menu.

GPO, Gorky Street 14
Bank, Kuibyshev Street 4
Znaniye and Druzhba—Bookshops, Prospect Mira 12
Art Salon, Prospect Mira 10
Jeweller's, Prospect Mira 26
Fatima—Souvenirs, Prospect Mira 16
Souvenirs, Prospect Mira 33

Intourist organises a number of trips out of Vladikavkaz. Those that lead up into the mountains in the direction of Alagir pass through valleys noticeably more lush with vegetation than those further eastward, which receive less rain.

Lisaya Gora is reached by cable car from Tbiliskoye Chaussee, 4 km (2.5 miles) from town and 2 km (1 mile) from the Daryal Motel. The cable car system has three stations—at Tbiliskoye Chaussee, where the *Balta Cafe* is, at Moskovskaya Doroga, and at Lisaya Gora, where there is another *restaurant* and a fine view over the main Caucasian massif.

Beslan Stud Farm is on the main road, 20 km (12 miles) before reaching Vladikavkaz from Nalchik.

Kazbegi village is on the Georgian Military Highway, 40 km (25 miles) away. The route there and the village are described under "Georgian Military Highway" as an excursion up from Tbilisi in the south.

The routes to Dargavs, Kurtalinsk Gorge, and Tsei are described in the following pages.

Dargavs, the City of the Dead (from the 11th to the 14th century), is 50 km (31 miles) from Vladikavkaz. This is also the way to Karmadon Sanatorium; the excursion here takes about 6 hours.

Gizel

The name is supposed to come from the Turkish "guzel," meaning "beautiful." Here the road crosses the Giseldon River.

An *obelisk* marks the grave of World War II defenders of Vladikavkaz.

Barbashov Monument. In November 1942 Pyotr Barbashov threw himself in front of enemy guns, and for his selfless courage he was posthumously declared a Hero of the Soviet Union. The 12-m (39-ft) statue is of a soldier dashing forward uphill, with his cloak flying out behind him.

Further up the valley of the Gizeldon a road branches off to the left to follow its tributary, the Genaldon, up to the spa of Karmadon, where the mineral water comes from.

Karmadon

The Spa Karmadon is in Genaldonskoye Gorge, 35 km (22 miles) from Vladikavkaz. This spa dates from 1863 when it is said that Tepsariko Tsarakhov, a local hunter, who was chasing a deer, suddenly saw his quarry fall through the ice. When he came up to the spot, he saw a warm mineral spring welling up from the ground.

The village was founded in 1909. "Karmadon" means "Warm Water," and the waters, similar to those of Kislovodsk and Davos, are good for sufferers of cardiovascular diseases, rheumatism, and kidney and liver ailments. There are more than 70 springs here with temperatures ranging from 15° to 60°C (59 to 140°F). A second spa, New Karmadon, has grown up where there are more springs, 9 km (6 miles) away.

Koban

Back again on the left bank of the Gizeldon, this mountain village is the oldest in the area. In the 19th century during excavation work, Bronze Age items were found, and a villager called Khabosh Kanukov made a collection which he later donated to the museum in Tbilisi. The place gave its name to the Koban culture and the Bronze Age burial mounds attracted archaeologists from many countries, including, in 1880, Wierhof from Germany and Chantre from France. The graves were found to have been made in eight distinct layers over a territory of 2 hectares (5 acres). The Koban culture is dated from the 4th to the 3rd millenia B.C. until the 2nd to 1st century B.C. Of particular interest here are the special axes, which are long, narrow, and curved, as well as a variety of ornaments, including wide, plated belts and many ceramic pieces with linear and animal decorations. The people had been hunters and primitive herdsmen, and examples of their possessions are now in museums in Vladikavkaz and Leningrad as well as in Austria, Germany, France, and the United States.

Now most of the Koban villagers work at the local hydropower station, which was built in 1932. The waters of the Gizeldon flow through a 2 km (1 mile) tunnel before falling 300 m (980 ft) into the turbines of the power station.

Up on a cliff just outside Koban is an ancient defence and guard tower where a fire used to be lit to signal approaching danger.

Dargavs

The name "Dargavs" means "Long Pass." There are 95 stone *mausoleums* here, built in the 14th to 19th centuries like little houses with curious, stepped tiled roofs, their doors well above ground level. The Ossetians buried their dead in stone tombs because of the shortage of good arable land. It was an old Ossetian saying that every piece of good land big enough for a cow to stand on is worth a cow. So the villages were built only on poor ground, and nearby would grow a second settlement, for the dead. Each house of the living in the village had its corresponding mausoleum in the "City of the Dead," and each mausoleum had its own character, just as the ordinary houses had. Beside the bodies, dressed in their best, were placed the things their owners might need—knives, bayonets, axes, and tobacco for the men, and needles, beads, and mirrors for the women. The bodies were laid on wooden shelves, and a very special system of ventilation ensured that instead of decomposing, the corpses gradually became mummified. Some bodies were buried in ordinary graves and during excavation work, bows and arrows, cloth of gold, and other items were discovered and taken to local museums.

Here, too, is the *defence tower* of the princely Mamsurov family, which dates from the 15th to 17th centuries and stands 15 m (49 ft) high. In this area there are a number of other ruined towers where villages used to be. The towers of the mountainous parts of Northern Ossetia are major architectural monuments. They differ in height and form. The lower ones were built for defence or as places of refuge, while the taller, isolated ones were lookout posts. The refuge towers usually had high stone walls around them, while the defence towers reached a height of 20 to 25 m (66 to 82 ft) and usually were sited so that it would be almost impossible for an enemy to take them. Lookout towers were erected mostly at the entrances to the gorges or at other important strategical points. Like the mausoleums, the entrances of these towers are all some distance above the ground.

Kurtalinsk Gorge is 60 km (37 miles) from Vladikavkaz. The full excursion takes about 6 hours. Here are several mediaeval sepulchres and defence towers, and the road goes right up to the glacier source of the river Fiagdon.

The beginning of the excursion follows the same route as that to Dargavs (see above) as far as Gizel.

Dzuarikau
At the crossroad of Kurtalinsk Gorge a *schist pyramid* has been split off the rock and dedicated to Lenin by the local inhabitants.

A *monument* commemorates the 7 Gazdanov brothers of Dzuarikau who lost their lives at the front during World War II.

At the entrance to the gorge of the Fiagdon is another local hydropower station. "Fiagdon" means "Rushing Water," and it is a very apt name. The gorge runs up into the mountains in a southwesterly direction.

Tagardon
Tagardon, on the left bank of the Fiagdon, has a small timber mill.

Gusyra
4 km (2.5 miles) beyond the village of Gusyra the gorge narrows and there are 5 postlike *tsyrty* ("tombstones"), which stand in memory of 5 brothers. One day these young men were cutting hay, but they were so busy that they didn't notice a snake falling into their soup kettle, and after their meal

they all died of poison. On the posts are carvings of everyday items, such as hats, boots, and arms. Such monuments are quite common in this part of Ossetia. They are usually situated by the grave or near the place where the person died. On some of them are inscriptions in Arabic or Russian.

9 km (5.5 miles) from Gusyra the road goes over Forest Pass (Kadargavan) and then descends to the river again.

Dzivgis
At Dzivgis, on the left bank of the river, the walls of an ancient fortress support the cliff and there is a big cave inside. The area around Dzivgis is rich in archeological monuments; there are a number of *mausoleums*, known as "dzappaz," and some more *tsyrts*. Near the village is a *17th-century church*. It has a bell with 1683 written in Georgian. After Dzivgiz the road runs through a valley that is 1,200 to 1,400 m (3,900 to 4,600 ft) above sea level.

Dallagkau
Here, on a small hillock, stands a riderless, stone horse, in memory of all of the riders who perished in the battles of World War II; there are many names engraved on the *monument* behind the horse.

To the left (eastward) runs Hanigkom Gorge, at the entrance of which are the ruins of some towers, all that is left of the village of Uallagsykh.

To the south of Dallagkau, on the right bank of the Fiagdon River, the small villages of Barzikau, Lats, and Hidikus are situated at a distance of 2 to 3 km (1 to 2 miles) from each other. On the opposite bank are Guli, Tsimiti, Urikau, Kadat, and Kharidzhin. Near each of them are *ancient monuments*, such as towers, burial mounds, tsyrts, and the typical Ossetian tombs with their stepped stone roofs.

Lats
Nearby is a cemetery called *Narts' Cemetery*. According to local legends, the Narts were the ancestors of the Ossetians. They are said to have been attributed with all possible good qualities—bravery, skill, wisdom, and great physical strength. The cemetery consists of underground stone vaults. It was said that the Narts buried their dead here. Depressions in the stones are said to have been left from the touch of the giants' fingers. In the middle of Lats is a semicircle of stones with depressions that look as though they were meant for sitting on, like chairs. The largest is called the *Chair of Uruzmag*, the oldest of the Narts, and the whole place is called "nyhas," or the "Narts' meeting place." Lats is in the centre of Kurtalinsk Gorge. Nearby, in the spurs of Mt. Kariu-Hoh, large deposits of nonferrous metals have been found.

Kharisdzhin
The most interesting part of the gorge begins from this village. The mountain river Tsaziukomdon, a tributary of the Fiagdon, flows in from the left. 5

km (3 miles) away from Kharisdzhin on a small hillock are the remains of an old defence wall that used to close off the entrance to the gorge. The width of the wall reaches a maximum of 6 m (20 ft), while its highest part is 3.5 m (11 ft).

About 13 km (8 miles) from Lats, at the bottom of the valley by the Fiagdon, are gloomy old towers of the abandoned villages of Gutiatikau and Andiatikau, and about 3 km (2 miles) further on are the ruins of the village of Bugulovykh, which is situated at 2,000 to 2,500 m (6,600 to 8,200 ft) above sea level. 2 km (1 mile) beyond these ruins a tower of the abandoned village of Kalotykau is to be seen on the left bank of the river, and after another 2 km (1 mile) is the Suar carbonic alkaline spring. Here the enormous cone of Mt. Teple-Khoh rises from the depths of the gorge. From its slopes a glacier sprawls in a semicircle. The glacier is quite unusual and extremely beautiful. It does not have a single tongue but is sliced through in many places by the jagged rocks. It feeds numerous streams that in confluence become the Fiagdon River.

Tsei

This is a full 100 km (62 miles) from Vladikavkaz; the Intourist trip there takes 10 hours.

The road is the same as that to Kurtalinsk Gorge (see above) as far as Dzuarikau. Then it leads to Alagir and thereafter follows the northern section of the Ossetian Military Highway. At Tsei is the *Shrine of Rekom* and a little further on is the village of Nar, Khetagurov's birthplace.

Alagir Population—15,000

To the south rises the tablelike peak of Mt. Kariu-Hoh (3,434 m/11,266 ft).

Northern Ossetia is rich in nonferrous and polymetallic ores. The first deposit to be worked was that known as Sadon, and it was already in use at the beginning of the 5th century. A survey was made in the mid-1700s, but it was a hundred years before the first zinc factory was built here in the Ardon River Valley. In 1850 about 380 families of serfs were brought here from the Urals and Lugansk (in the Ukraine, just north of Rostov-on-Don), and it was their settlement that grew into the village of Alagir.

The Sadon silver, lead, and zinc mines in the Alagir Gorge were for some time known as Alagir and were run by the Belgians until 1918. In the middle of the 19th century a special carriage brought a 12 kg (26 lb) bar of silver from Alagir to St. Petersburg. The Tsar ordered it to be made into two silver chalices, one for the church in Petrodvorets and the other for St. Isaac's Cathedral. Both vessels bore an inscription saying that they were made of silver melted at the Alagir plant on 21 May, 1853. The Alagir silver mines were exhausted by the end of the 19th century. The other mines are among the oldest in the Caucasus and at 2,000 m (6,600 ft) are, with the Mizur ore-concentrating plant, among the highest-located workings in the USSR. The factory that remains was built with the idea of being able to fight back against the local mountain tribes and was fortified with cannon.

Today Alagir, situated on a branch of the main railway line, is one of the greater industrial centres of Northern Ossetia; besides the Elektrozink plant, which was built in 1932 and is still one of the country's largest metallurgical works, it has canneries and a timber mill.

In 1853 the Russian architect Prince Grigory Gagarin (1810–93) designed *Voznesensky ("Ascension") Cathedral* surrounded by a defence wall with 5 8-m (26-ft) towers and three gates. It was designed and built as a fortress church and, apart from its religious purpose, also was to serve for defence, which accounts for the wall. It was built on the lines of the Moscow Kremlin, with its height reaching 2.1 m (7 ft). The murals were painted in the 1880s by the Ossetian poet and painter Kosta Khetagurov. During World War II the cathedral was damaged by German shells. The murals suffered especially badly, but in 1959 they were restored by artists from Moscow. The cathedral is now a branch of the Ossetian State Museum.

Alagir is famous for its pears, which keep well. It also is known as a resort town. After travelling 3 or 4 km (2 miles or so) into the gorge, one notices the sharp smell of sulphuric gas. There is a group of mineral springs, five on the right bank of the Ardon and three on the left. Their sulphurous water is piped to the spa of Tamisk.

Ossetian Military Highway. Alagir marks the start of the northern end of the Ossetian Military Highway. The construction of this road was begun in 1858 and it was opened to wheeled transport in 1888. It stretches 244 km (152 miles), from Alagir right over the Caucasus Mountains to Kutaisi, connecting northern Ossetia with western Georgia.

Tamisk

Tamisk is located in a small, isolated depression protected by hills from the cold, northern winds. It is valued not only for its balneology but also for its climate.

Mizur

This is the largest village in the Sadon industrial area. A village of miners, Mizur is also in the Alagirskoye Gorge, enclosed in the valley by the towering mountains and with a local hydropower station. The valley is scarred by the numerous workings. Lead and zinc ore is transported to the local ore-concentrating plant (built in 1928) by a chain of special trolleys on a suspended ropeway; it is then sent for smelting to the metallurgical works in Vladikavkaz. The deposits at Sadon, which are a little further along the main road off to the right, are almost exhausted, and new mines are being developed higher up in Verkhny Zgid and at Buron, beyond Nuzal.

Nuzal

The village of Nuzal was the birthplace of David Soslan, husband and consort of Queen Tamar of Georgia, whom he married in 1189. It is believed

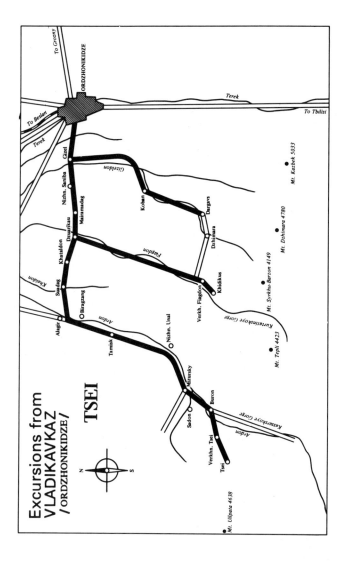

that he was buried in a *local chapel*. The 12th-century building, which measures no more than 6 m by 2 m (20 ft by 8 ft) and stands 5 m (15 ft) high is in the traditional Ossetian style, with its stone walls curving inward to form the roof. Soslan, an Ossetian nobleman and descendant of King Bagrat IV, was Queen Tamar's second husband. His coffin was discovered by archaeologists in 1946. The frescoes decorating the chapel include those of St. George, St. Eustace, and members of the Tsarazonov family, who are said to have founded this chapel. The style of the frescoes reflects elements of Georgian ecclesiastical painting of the 11th to 13th centuries with an admixture of Ossetian motifs.

Buron

Buron is a mining village where new mines are being opened.

Verkhni Tsei and Rekom

The *Shrine of Rekom*, near the Tsei rest home, is in a picturesque glade encircled by a pine forest and mountains at a height of 1,800 m (5,900 ft) above sea level.

Rekom would be more correctly spelt Irkom, since "Ir" is the name by which the Ossetians call themselves and "kom" is Ossetian for "gorge." Rekom, Ossetia's most venerated sanctuary, is now dedicated to St. George, who, with the coming of Christianity, took over from Uastardzhi, the god of hunters in Ossetian. There is a legend that St. George decided to build a church for the Ossetians. On the other side of the mountains there was a forest of trees that never rotted, so St. George ordered oxen to carry logs over the river opposite Rekom. The logs loaded themselves, and the oxen went along without being driven. Having unloaded the logs in Rekom, they returned by the same route and the sanctuary built itself without being touched by human hand.

The site is prehistoric, and while it belonged to Uastardzhi, animal sacrifices were performed here, which accounts for the skulls and antlers of deer, sheep, and Capra Caucasica ("Caucasian goat") piled beside the walls. These were contributed by hunters, and it was customary to bring the antlers or horns of the first-killed deer or Caucasian goat of the season to the chapel. It is not unusual for a Christian church to have been built on the site of a pagan temple. The Ossetians kept the pagan feasts as well as Christian holidays. A big festival, something like the original Olympic games, used to take place near Rekom.

The building itself, standing inside a dry stone wall, must be very old indeed. It is wooden and was constructed without a single nail. It is believed to have been built in the 15th and 16th centuries, but it may date from the time of the spreading of Christianity in northern Ossetia in the 10th century and may have been built by Georgian missionaries. During excavations several coins were found under the floor; many of these were Arabian and Khwarazmian dating back to the 12th century. It was restored in 1936 and again in 1960.

From Tsei it is necessary to return to the main road and then follow the Ardon Valley up to Zaramag. Here a rough road leads up to the left to Nar.

Nar

Nar consists of separate groups of cottages on the mountain slopes, while in the centre of a hollow, watered by the Zakka and the Zrug, is a cliffed spur of Mt. Pse that is called Khetadji Kuldin by the locals. On the top are a number of ancient houses and towers all squashed together as though struggling for a hold on the rocks. The name means "Khetag's Spur," and from Khetag comes Khetagurov; members of the Khetagurov family lived here as long ago as the 14th century.

> Still, the dead raven's wings . . .
> The storm fiercely roars . . .
> To black scree, trancelike, clings
> Lost Nar with locked doors.

The house where Kosta Khetagurov was born in 1859 is now a *museum*. It was rebuilt and all of the surroundings were restored; even his cradle is inside. He lived here till 1868, when the family moved to Vladikavkaz. Near the house is a granite *monument* in the form of an obelisk with a bas-relief of the poet and an inscription saying that he was born here.

VLADIMIR Population—350,000

Intourist organises excursions here from Moscow on the way to Suzdal which is 230 km (143 miles) from the capital, and from Suzdal itself. The Russian Winter festival takes place here and in Suzdal annually between December 25 and January 5.

At the 184 km mark, on the right on the way into the city, there is a *service station*.

This ancient city stands on the left bank of the river Klyasma.

According to the chronicles, Prince Vladimir Monomakh who later became Grand-Prince of Kiev, founded this city bearing his name in 1108. It was then designed to serve as a frontier fortress guarding the northeast of his domain. The original fortress was built of earth and wood and had a wall 2.5 km (1.5 miles) in circumference.

Vladimir's heir, Yuri Dolgoruky, founder of Moscow, turned his attention to these lands only during the last years of his reign when he understood that the Kievan state was losing its economic and political influence. Vladimir owed its rise and subsequent period of glory to Dolgoruky's son, Andrei Bogolubsky (god-fearing). He realised that in order to unite all the lands of Russia, the grand-princes would have to centralize and consolidate their power, but to achieve this the seat of power should be transferred from Kiev further up, to the northeast. Dolgoruky opposed his son's decision to go north, fearing that without him he would be unable to defend his throne. Nevertheless, in 1158 Andrei Bogolubsky, with his family and household, left the south secretly at dead of night under the protection and guidance of a holy icon which was said to have been brought from Constantinople and to have been painted by St. Luke himself. Later, under the name of Our Lady of Vladimir, it became the most revered object in northern Russia.

Having chosen Vladimir for his capital and settled there, Andrei strengthened its defences and welcomed architects, icon-painters, jewellers, and other craftsmen to beautify it. Dolgoruky died in 1157 and Andrei became Grand-Prince of Kiev. He wished to remain in Vladimir, but in order to hold his title he marched against his opponents in Kiev in 1169, defeated them, and appointed a governor of his own. He himself was killed by the nobles in 1174 because they could no longer tolerate his autocratic government. He was succeeded by his brother, Vsevolod III, who managed, with the help of the citizens, to suppress the nobles. During his rule (1176–1212) the Rostov-Suzdal princedom with Vladimir as its capital reached the peak of its political power.

In 1237 the Tatars under Baty-Khan (Ghengis Khan's grandson) invaded Russia. Vladimir, like dozens of other Russian cities before and afterwards, suffered heavy damage, and she never regained her status as a major city because the Princes of Moscow received the title of Grand-Prince from the Tatars, and Moscow accordingly became the political centre of the lands of Russia. In spite of this for the next 200 years the nominal seniority among Russian cities belonged to Vladimir. It had as its coat-of-arms gules a crowned lion rampant and it was here, in the Uspensky (Assumption) Cathedral, that the grand-princes were crowned, and it was here that the Russian princes held council.

Between the 15th and the 17th centuries Vladimir's importance was mainly due to her position as a centre of trade and transport. It has now a new, industrial appearance and produces tractors, electrical machinery, and chemicals. There are also food and light industries.

III-International Street, the city's main thoroughfare, follows the route of the pre-revolutionary Vladimirka Road along which exiles and prisoners were sent to Siberia, usually on foot.

Zolotiye Vorota (the Golden Gates) (1158–64) stand in the centre of the city today. The arch is a unique example of ancient Russian defence architecture and was built to serve as a powerful tower, guarding the western part of Vladimir. It was also used as the ceremonial entrance gate to the city. While building his capital, Prince Andrei Bogolubsky tried to copy the architecture of the southern capital of Kiev as much as possible. The Golden Gate of Vladimir was built to resemble the Golden Gate of Kiev, which has recently been rebuilt.

It is said that when the tower was finished, crowds came to wonder at the beauty of its construction. However, the mortar was still damp and the gates fell, trapping twelve people beneath their mighty weight. Prince Andrei prayed to the Virgin, accusing himself of the death of innocent souls, and the general surprise was great when the gates were lifted to reveal all twelve safe and sound.

During the Tatar invasion of 1238 the gate was badly damaged, but it was reconstructed in the 15th century. It was the custom that on the principal religious holidays processions would wend their way from the Archbishop's Palace to the Uspensky Cathedral and from there to the Golden Gate, and costly embroideries were hung on cords along the route. The originals, which perished in the great fire of 1183, were of cloth-of-gold and pearl. There are now no traces of the other four gates of ancient Vladimir.

In the 18th century, in the course of general reconstruction, the church surmounting the gate was rebuilt, and the side walls had to be reinforced when the adjoining town walls were pulled down. The gate itself is a gigantic cube pierced by a high arch. There is a second, lower, arch inside where, on the east side, can be seen the upper pair of the huge iron loops upon which the gate hung; the lower ones are below ground level now. The gates themselves were plated with sheets of gilded copper, hence the name.

The building now forms part of the *Local Museum* and houses the section dealing with military history. Open 10–5; closed Mon. and the last Thursday of each month.

The Uspensky (Assumption) Cathedral (1160), III-International Street 56. Open for services. This was the most important building in Prince Andrei's new capital and the one upon which he chose to bestow "a tithe of the income from trade." It was so richly decorated that it was compared with the Temple of Solomon and for centuries it served as Russia's principal cathedral. The original outer walls were frescoed and had gilded half-columns. It was here that all the princes of Vladimir and of Moscow were crowned until the time of Ivan III (1440). In the first quarter of the 14th century the cathedral was the seat of the Metropolitan Bishop of All Russia.

Exquisite proportions, faultless masonry and beautifully finished architectural details made the cathedral a masterpiece of ancient Russian architecture. The best architects of Russia and Europe were summoned by Prince Andrei to Vladimir to contribute to the work and there is some evidence that Frederik Barbarossa may have sent builders to work on the project. When at the end of the 15th century the Italian architect, Aristotle Fioravente, was building the Uspensky Cathedral in Moscow's Kremlin for Ivan III, he chose the cathedral at Vladimir as a model.

In 1185–89, after the terrible fire, Prince Andrei's brother, Vsevolod III, erected a 2-storey gallery around 3 sides of the structure as the old limestone walls had been irreparably calcined. At the same time, the east end of the cathedral was enlarged. Thus the original building was encased and the old walls were pierced with arches so large

VLADIMIR

that what was left simply formed pillars inside the body of the new structure. The cathedral was given 4 additional cupolas and had room for a congregation of 4,000. In 1238 it suffered at the hands of the Tatars who set it on fire together with the people who were seeking sanctuary within its walls. With time the frescoes gradually became dilapidated, and in 1408 Andrei Rublyev and Daniel Chornei came from Moscow to replace the earlier decorations and to paint the iconostasis. In 1411 the Tatars again attacked, ransacked the cathedral, and again set fire to it. They carried off the original flooring of copper plates framed with ceramic tiles.

Reconstruction began in the 18th century, the baroque iconostasis was installed in 1774, and work continued until the end of the 19th century. Since the 1917 revolution the building has been constantly in the hands of artists and architects. The 12th- and 13th-century frescoes, including fragments of the 12th-century "Last Judgement" on the western wall, have recently been restored. Those by Andrei Rublyev (c. 1360–1430) are in the centre, under the choir gallery. Particularly noteworthy is his depiction of heaven and the saints being summoned by St. Peter. There are other frescoes by this great master on the altar pillars. The Uspensky Cathedral was the burial place of the princes of Vladimir, including Andrei Bogolubsky and Vsevolod III. It was here that the ceremonies of accession of princes Alexander Nevsky and Dmitri Donskoy took place and that the first chronicles of Vladimir were compiled. The tomb on the left of the Holy Gates is that of Prince Georgi, grandson of Vladimir Monomakh.

Beside the Uspensky Cathedral stands a 3-storeyed *belfry* with a pointed golden spire. It was built in 1810 to replace a 16th-century belfry which had been destroyed by lightning. The building linking it to the cathedral dates from 1862.

The *Dmitrievsky Cathedral* (1194–97) stands close to the Uspensky. It was once enclosed by the courtyard of Vsevolod III's palace and was used for his private services. The tsar built it in honour of his patron saint and his newborn son, Dmitri, and when it was finished he enriched it with relics of St. Dmitri specially brought here from Salonika. It is one of the best finished structures of ancient Vladimir and almost two-thirds of the total wall area is richly decorated with bas-reliefs of fantastic creatures, trees, and human figures including King David, a series depicting the labours of Hercules, and one figure that is thought to be Vsevolod himself holding his little son. Inside the church are some 12th-century frescoes by Byzantine and Russian painters. The monument and grave to the right of the door inside the cathedral belong to Count Roman Vorontsov (1717–83), the first governor of Vladimir.

In 1834 Nicholas I ordered that the church be restored to its "original appearance" and although literal adherence to his command meant the loss of some valuable frescoes, the cathedral's purity of line is now unspoiled. It is the most beautiful build-ing in Vladimir and indeed among the loveliest in the country. Certainly it is the best example of ancient white-stone construction where carved decorations play an important role. Now the cathedral is part of the Local Museum where materials on the architecture of Vladimir are exhibited. In winter the key may be obtained from the Local Museum.

The white battlemented walls of *Rozhdestvensky (Nativity) Monastery* (1191–96) stand to the east of Dmitrievsky Cathedral. Until the middle of the 16th century this was Russia's most important monastery. Many future bishops served here in their early years and it was here that the oldest existing Russian chronicle, the Lavrentyevskaya, was kept. Prince Alexander Nevsky (1220–63), who defeated the Swedes and the Teutonic Knights in 1240 and 1242, was buried here and his remains were transferred to St. Petersburg in 1724 at the instigation of Peter the Great. His battle against the Swedes took place near the river Neva, and it was then that he earned his surname, Nevsky. In 1744 the monastery was closed and in 1864 the main church was dismantled stone by stone and a full-sized replica of it was later made by local architects.

Nikolskaya Church, just outside the monastery wall, was built in the 18th century and now serves as a *planetarium*.

In Vladimirsky Spusk, to the northwest of Vladimir, stands the *Uspenskaya (Assumption) Convent Church* (1200–2), built of small bricks instead of the usual limestone as the cathedral church of the Convent of the Assumption (and now the only building of it remaining), founded by Maria Shvarnovo, wife of Vsevolod III. It was later called Knyagynin, meaning "princess's," and ever afterwards the convent was used as the burial place of the princesses of Vladimir. The whole building and the frescoes too were restored after World War II. On the southwestern side are paintings of the princesses, depicted as saints. The church is now used as the headquarters of the organisation in charge of the restoration of ancient buildings in and around Vladimir.

The baroque church with the attractive belfry standing nearby is *Nikitskaya Church*. It was built between 1762 and 1765, added to in the 19th century, and restored in 1970.

Uspenskaya (Assumption) Church (1644–49), Frunze Street. This church has five cupolas and a belfry and is surrounded by other, smaller buildings. It was built with the donations of rich merchants and is notable for its interesting brickwork.

Spasskaya (or Spasopreobrazhenskaya) Church, Sovietskaya Street, up the hill, not far from the Golden Gate. Spasskaya Church was built in 1778 on the site of a church of 1164. In the same street is *Georgievskaya Church* which was built in 1784 on the site of a limestone cathedral of 1129 which Yuri Dolgoruky dedicated to St. Yuri (the Russian name for St. George). It now houses a radio club.

The red brick church by the Golden Gate was
built at the beginning of this century and was used
by the Old Believers, a large sect which was opposed to reforms being introduced into the Russian
Orthodox Church in the 17th century, and accordingly became separated.

Local Museum, III-International Street 64.
Open 10–5; closed Mon. and the last Thursday of
each month. Among the exhibits is the white sepulchre of Alexander Nevsky whose mortal remains
were transferred from Vladimir to St. Petersburg
in 1724. Also here are the Gospel and a piece of
a winter coat which belonged to Prince Pozharsky
who drove the Poles out of Moscow and who was
buried in Suzdal. There is a rich collection of old
manuscripts and books, rare old Russian paintings,
and weapons.

Picture Gallery, in the park.

Planetarium, III-International Street, in the
18th-century Nikolskaya Church near the corner
of Rozhdestvesnky Monastery.

Old Vladimir Museum, Open 10–5; closed
Mon. and the last Thursday of each month. This
is devoted to the life of a provincial town in the
19th century.

Local Industrial Exhibition, Oktyabrsky Prospect 47. Open 10–5; closed Mon. and the last
Thursday of each month.

Museum of Crystal and lacquered Miniatures,
Open 11–7; closed Mon. and the last Thursday of
each month.

Watches & Time Museum, Pushkin 1. Open
12–7; closed Mon.

Exhibition of Economic Achievements, Mira
Street. Open May–October.

In front of the baroque Nikitskaya Chruch is a
garden where there is a *bust of the writer Gogol*,
painted blue. Near the Golden Gate is a *bust of P.
Lebedyev-Polyansky* (1881–1948), literary critic.
There is also a *monument to Mikhail Frunze*.

Lunacharsky Drama Theatre, Moskvy Street 4

Taneyev Concert Hall, Lenin Prospect 1

Vladimir Hotel & Restaurant, III-International
Street 74; tel. 26-14 or 30-42. Intourist office; tel.
24-262.

Klyasma Hotel & Restaurant, Lenin Street 2;
tel. 22-72

Zarya Hotel & Restaurant

Traktir Restaurant, Sovietov Street 2. Russian
cuisine.

U Zolotykh Vorot, III-International Street 11.
Decorated with the coats of arms of the towns of
Vladimir region.

Russkaya Derevnya, Moskovskoye Chaussée
5a. Built in old Russian style.

Dieticheskaya Restaurant, Frunze Street 88

Café, III-International Street 6

GPO, Podbyelskovo Street 2

Long-distance telephone calls office, III-International Street 24

Central Bookshop, III-International Street 34

Souvenirs, Moskovskaya Street 10a, in the trading arcade.

Bogolyubovo

This village lies 10 km (6 miles) from Vladimir,
further to the east, at the 174 km mark along the
main road to Gorky.

Its history goes back to 1158 when Prince Andrei Bogolubsky secretly left Kiev and went north.
According to the legend, his horses stopped where
Bogolyubovo is now and would go no further. Later
the Virgin appeared to the prince in a dream and
asked him to build a church here. Accordingly he
founded the *Rozhdestvenskaya (Nativity of the Virgin) Church* and subsequently built his new "city
of stone" called Bogolyubovo, his own surname,
although whether he was named after the city or
the city after him is not clear. Apart from the legend, the reason for building the city was Andrei
Bogolubsky's desire to create a stronghold of autocratic power against the rebellious nobles. Certainly it was worthy of being a royal residence. Of
the decoration of the church alone the chronicler
wrote, "It was hard to look at all the gold."

The chronicle says that Prince Andrei "hath
built himself that city of stone" but until recently
scientists thought that the chronicler had exagger-
ated and that the actual city was built of wood with
only the towers of stone. After the prince's assassination the city of Bogolyubovo lost its status of royal
residence and gradually fell into oblivion. The Tatar
invasion and numerous fires left little standing. It
was only in 1954 that the words of the chronicler
were proved to be true. Excavations revealed the
foundations of 12th-century limestone walls.

Rozhdestvenskaya Church survived the earlier
period of destruction but it suffered in the 17th
century when an ignorant priest ordered that the
windows be made wider; as a result in 1722 the
building collapsed. Architects think that the church
which was restored in the 18th century on the old
foundations closely resembles the original structure. It stands well to the left of the big cathedral
which now dominates the territory.

Beside Rozhdestvenskaya Church and adjoin-
ing it is an entrance gate and a staircase tower where
Prince Andrei was assassinated and which are all
that remain of his 12th-century palace; these are
interesting as they are unique examples of early
Russian secular architecture. The story of Prince
Andrei's death was painted on the inside walls.
Legend has it that the assassins of the prince, who
was later canonized by the Russian Orthodox
Church, were put into tarred coffins. These are
still supposed to be floating in the swamps near
Bogolyubovo and it is said that the weeping and
wailing of the evil-doers can still be heard at night.
These buildings are open as a museum, 10–4,
closed Mon.

The *Uspensky (Assumption) Cathedral* (1866)
is the largest construction on the territory. The
belfry at the gate was built between 1820 and 1840.
On the opposite side of the big cathedral is a *16th–
17th century refectory*, now used as a bank. The
holy well dates from the foundation of Bogolyubovo, but the existing stonework is 18th-century.

Less than a mile southeast of Bogolyubovo is *Pokrovskaya (Intercession) Church* on the river Nerl. To get there, turn right from the main road about 200 m/yds before reaching the churches. A path leads under a railway bridge and across the fields, making a pleasant walk in summer, although in winter the snow is likely to be deep. Open 10–5; Tues. 10–4; Sat. & Sun. in summer only 10–6; closed Mon. and the last Thursday of each month. The little white church is the loveliest of all that have survived from the days of Vladimir's greatness, and stands in the meadows, reflected in the slowly moving waters of the Nerl. The perfectly proportioned, faultlessly finished structure was built in 1165 in memory of Prince Andrei's son, Izyaslav, who was killed in a victorious campaign against the Kama Bulgars.

The site of the church is usually flooded in the spring, so the builders put the limestone foundation into a 2 m (6 ft 6 in) trench and on this erected 4 m (13 ft) walls which they filled and covered with earth, forming a hill. The hill was then paved with limestone in which special drainage holes were made.

On this 6 m (20 ft) foundation they proceeded to erect the church walls. The foundations of the 150 m (492 ft) Leningradskaya Hotel in Moscow are not so deep as those of this 20 m (66 ft) church.

The church is well preserved with the exception of the frescoes, the last traces of which disappeared 100 years ago. At the end of the 18th century the Bishop of Vladimir gave permission to the peasants of the village of Novoye to pull down the church and use the stone to build a church in their own village. When the first worker climbed the cupola to take down the cross, particles of gold paint from the cross got into his eyes and he cried out that he had been blinded. When he was helped to the ground, he regained his sight and what appeared to be a miracle saved the church from destruction.

VOLGOGRAD (Known as Tsarytsin until 1925, then as Stalingrad until 1961)
Population—999,000
The city stretches along the right bank of the river Volga for more than 70 km (43 miles) and its width varies from 2 to 10 km (1–6 miles). The architects describe it as a ribbon-city because of the way it has grown. The Volga bank is cut by deep ravines which divide the city into sections. It was originally the lack of rain combined with the strong, dry winds blowing from the nearby steppes in the heat of summer that forced people to settle close to the water.

The old Tsarytsin coat of arms, a design with two fish, can be seen on the facade of the 2-storey, red brick building of the Trud Sports Club (formerly the fire station) at Kommunisticheskaya Street 5. The new coat of arms, adopted in 1968, has red battlements and the golden star medal awarded to heroes on the upper half; the lower part, which has a blue background, bears a golden cogwheel and a sheaf of wheat symbolising the pow-

erful industry of the city and the fruitful soil upon which it stands.

Tsarytsin was founded in 1589 as a fortress on Russia's southern boundary, guarding the country against the Tatar nomads which were the survivors of the Golden Horde. Its name was derived from the Tatar words "sary-chin" which mean "yellow sand." Its fortifications were increased and its importance grew during the reign of Peter the Great (1682–1725) and later it was the centre of several popular uprisings. There was the Stepan Razin uprising in 1670, the Cossack uprising under Bulavin in 1708, and in 1774 the peasant revolt led by Yemelyan Pugachov who designated himself Emperor Peter III and who was subsequently quartered.

By the mid-19th century Tsarytsin was of considerable commercial importance, particularly as far as the transport of oil from Baku was concerned. During the Civil War (1918–20) it saw much fierce fighting because all the food supplies for Moscow and Petrograd from the south passed through it. The "defence of Tsarytsin" against the Whites was an important step towards the establishment of Soviet power.

The biggest tractor plant in Russia was built here in the 1930s, and by 1941 the city had a population of 445,000 and was one of the Volga Basin's biggest industrial centres. Then during World War II the city once again became the scene of fighting and it was at the Battle of Stalingrad that the Germans suffered one of their most significant defeats.

When the Germans turned their attention to Stalingrad in the summer of 1942, they intended to cut off the Red Army's supply of Caucasian oil and to reach Moscow from the southeast. This was after they had attacked from the west in December 1941 and failed. Hitler declared in November 1942 that Stalingrad was "of decisive importance" to him, just before the turning point in the battle, which lasted from July 1942 to February 1943. The course of the battle can be roughly divided into four periods:

1) 17 July–19 November—German advance followed by fierce street fighting.

2) 19 November–30 November—the pincer-like Soviet advance from the northeast and the south split the German forces in two.

3) December 1942—German attempts to relieve their encircled troops were rebuffed.

4) 10 January–2 February 1943—the encircled German troops were defeated and destroyed.

During the street fighting in November neither side was willing to give up a single house, staircase, or even a room. The defence of Pavlov House for two months by a handful of soldiers under Sergeant Pavlov has become a legend. Among the prominent Soviet military leaders who distinguished themselves in the Battle of Stalingrad were Marshals Voronov, Rokossovsky and Chuikov. Nikita Khrushchev was a member of the Military Council of the Stalingrad Front during the battle.

As a result of the fourth period of the battle (as

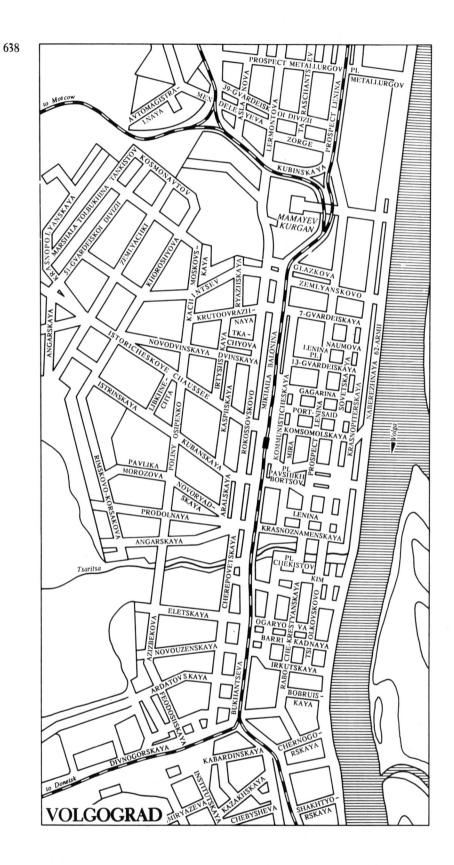

VOLGOGRAD

described above), a German grouping of 22 divisions (330,000 men) under Field Marshal von Paulus was taken with 6000 guns, 1312 mortars, and 744 aircraft.

In the course of the battle the city of Stalingrad was utterly destroyed. There had been 48,190 houses in the city, most of them built of wood. During the German attack the enemy dropped nearly a million bombs on Stalingrad, not counting land bombardment. (By comparison, about 50,000 were dropped on London during the blitz.) Out of the 48,190 houses, 41,685 were burned or otherwise destroyed. But housing was only one of the many problems the city authorities had to solve. According to official statistics they had to bury, between February and April 1943, 147,200 German dead and 47,700 Russians. People aged between 18 and 60 were all mobilised to collect and bury the corpses.

There was a suggestion that a new city be founded nearby and the ruins left as they were as a gigantic war memorial, but it was more sensibly decided to reconstruct the city where it stood. Immediately after the Germans were defeated the work of reconstruction was decreed a matter of prime importance to the state, and so the stupendous task was undertaken. Even the clearing of the site was no easy matter when it is realised that it took 800 railway trucks of rubble and dust to clear the territory of the tractor plant alone. Bricks from the ruins were used again, scattered doors and window frames collected and iron hammered into shape.

Today Volgograd is the administrative and economic centre of the Lower Volga Region and is also the major transport centre of this area. It has over 150 industrial enterprises, including one of the country's biggest tractor plants, a metallurgical plant and machine-building factories. Volgograd region now ranks sixth in the Soviet Union's oil producing areas. The city also has five research institutes.

Down by the Volga, Central Quay now serves as a promenade and a river-bus station. The *monument* on the embankment is to Victor Kholzunov (1905–39), a test pilot and hero of the Soviet Union who was killed in 1939. The embankment with 100 steps of grey granite and a monumental colonnade was built in 1952 on the completion of the Volga-Don Canal (properly known as the Lenin Canal). It makes an impressive entrance to the city from the river. On the lower terrace of the embankment there is a *children's railway*, and on the upper terrace is the 7-m (23-ft) *Victory Fountain.*

The heart of Volgograd is *Pavshikh Bortsov* (Fallen Fighters) Square. Before the revolution it was called Alexander Square and was the trading centre of the city. Now it is the venue of demonstrations, parades and meetings and is also revered as a shrine. Where the boulevard leads out of the square towards the river, a common grave is situated. A *monument* has been erected to those who fought against the White Guards in 1919 and against the Nazis in 1942–3. Here too is the grave

of Ruben Ibarruri, son of Dolores Ibarruri, Secretary General of the Spanish Communist Party, who died during the Battle of Stalingrad while serving in the Soviet Army.

The building of the *Gorky Drama Theatre*, on one side of the square, housed the City Soviet in 1917–18. On the northern side of the square a new department store stands on the site of the old store which von Paulus used as his headquarters before his capture.

The *railway station* nearby was built in 1954 in place of the one destroyed during the war.

A 9-m (30-ft) *monument to Lenin* stands on a red granite pedestal in the square bearing his name; it was designed by Vuchetich with a semicircular colonnade by Zakharov and was unveiled in 1960. Nearby is *Pavlov House* (see p. 637) which is reached by going through the colonnade. The ruins of the flour mill not far from Pavlov House are preserved as a *war memorial*. Between the two a *museum* commemorating the defence of Stalingrad was opened in May 1985 to mark the 40th anniversary of VE-Day.

Battle of Stalingrad Panorama, Marshal Chuikov Street 17. Open 9–8; closed Mon. The foundations of the circular building were laid in 1968 on the occasion of the 25th anniversary of the battle. 16 stone slabs bear the names of all the divisions which took part. Inside, the panorama shows the moment on January 26, 1943, when the two pincer-arms of the Soviet forces met, cutting off the German army under von Paulus. It was painted by a team from the Grekov military art studio.

To the north of the central part of the city stands *Mamayev Kurgan*, dominating the whole area and being the place where the fighting was most fierce (see below). A flight of triumphal steps lead up to it from Lenin Prospect, the city's main street. In many places near Lenin Prospect one can see the gun turrets of T-34 tanks mounted on small pedestals marking the line of defence of the 62nd Army. The prospect is one of the longest in the world; it runs for nearly 70 km (43 miles) and was built on the site of the most terrible ruins. Among the very few old houses that survived here is No. 2, a red brick mansion and now the *House of Architects*. Along the street are government, party, and trade union buildings as well as apartment houses. The part between Krasnoznamenskaya and Lenin Squares has been planted as an avenue which makes it most attractive.

Mamayev Kurgan was named, according to legend, after the Tatar Khan Mamai who once made his camp on the hill. It stands 102 m (335 ft) high. During the Battle of Stalingrad the fight for the possession of this vantage point lasted more than 4 months. The surface was left absolutely riddled with bullets and shells. Pieces of shrapnel can still be found here, which is hardly surprising when it is estimated that there were 500–1,250 shells and bullets in every square metre. In the spring of 1943 no grass grew at all on the hill.

The memorial complex which has been built here and which starts with the flight of steps up from Lenin Prospect, was designed by the sculptor Evgeni Vuchetich and the architect Belopolski, but there were, besides, many others assisting in the work. The sculptural groups on the steps depict various scenes of the battle, and halfway up is a platform with a circular pool. A stone plaque on one side is engraved with the words: "A steely wind hit them in the face, but still they went forward, and again a feeling of superstitious fear seized the enemy—Were these really people going in to attack? Were they mortals?" Here, in the Hall of Military Glory, a round building, burns an eternal flame. 32 mosaic plaques carry the names of the fallen. The 12-m (39-ft) statue of a soldier with a machine gun and a hand grenade is called "Stand to the Last Man." The ruined walls symbolise the ruined city and here and there are inscriptions such as "Not a Step Back," and "Beyond the Volga is No Place for Us"; these slogans were to be seen in many parts of the city during the fighting. The main sculpture on the top of the hill, that of a woman with an uplifted sword, can be seen from all parts of the city. She symbolises the Motherland calling upon her sons to rise in her defence. The statue is 51 m (167 ft) high and, with the pedestal, 72 m (236 ft).

Kazansky Cathedral, Lipetskaya Street 10. Built in 1903 and restored in 1948.

Local Museum, Lenin Prospect 38; entrance from the courtyard. The museum has five halls and the exhibits include items excavated in Serai-Berka, a 13th–14th century settlement 80 km (50 miles) from Volgograd. Here there are also a cap and a stick which belonged to Peter the Great and some documents dating from the time of the Revolution and others pertaining to World War II. Open 11–6; closed Tues.

The Defence of the City Museum, Gogol Street 3. Open 11–6; closed Tues. The building served as the headquarters during the defence of the city in 1917–18. The exhibits tell of the establishment of Soviet power in Tsarytsin, but most belong to the 1942–43 defence. There is a printing block left behind by the Germans; it has been prepared to print leaflets announcing "The Fall of Stalingrad." There are German flags, medals, a model of the ruined city, and a sword sent by King George VI in 1944 which bears the inscription: "To the steel-hearted citizens of Stalingrad—the gift of King George VI in token of the homage of the British people." There is also a shield which was presented by Emperor Haile Selassie of Ethiopia, a copy of a scroll sent by Franklin D. Roosevelt, a tea set from Iran, a chess table from Luxembourg, and a tablecloth from Coventry with 830 embroidered signatures.

Art Museum, Lenin Prospect 21. Open 11–6; closed Wed. The antique section of the museum is represented by copies. The pride of the West European section are two small sculptures by Rodin, "Jealousy" and "The Kiss," which were presented in 1947 by Lady Westmacott. The Russian section includes a portrait of Catherine II by Antropov and in the Soviet section is Dostoyevsky sculpted by Konenkov. The museum has over 3000 works.

Planetarium, Gagarin Street 14. This planetarium was a gift from the German Democratic Republic and the main auditorium seats over 500. Open 9–9.

Dzerzhinsky Monument, Dzerzhinsky Square, in front of the tractor factory. This was unveiled in 1935.

Chekhist's Monument, in the garden on the right bank of the river Tsaritsa, near Astrakhan Bridge. This statue of a soldier with a sword raised is dedicated to the members of the security forces who fell between August 1942 and February 1943, defending the city. The 5-m (16-ft) sculpture is mounted on a 17-m (56-ft) pedestal. The project was by Kaimshidi and was unveiled in 1952.

Efremov's Bust, at the corner of Lenin Prospect and Alleya Geroyev (Heroes' Avenue). The airforce pilot, Captain Vasili Efremov, was twice made a Hero of the Soviet Union.

A 24-m (79-ft) granite *obelisk* dedicated to those who fell in 1919 stands in front of a fraternal grave decorated with a 4-m (13-ft) bronze wreath. It was designed by Shalayev in 1958.

Gorky Drama Theatre, Pavshikh Bortsov (Fallen Heroes) Square.

Musical Comedy Theatre, Krasnopiterskaya Street 40. Before the 1917 Revolution the building was a club and in 1918 it was occupied by the Communist Party Committee. It was badly damaged during World War II and was reconstructed and then rebuilt in 1960.

Youth Theatre, Raboche-Krestyanskaya Street

Puppet Theatre, Lenin Prospect 15

Philharmonia Concert Hall, 62-Army Embankment 1

Circus, Krasnokazarmennaya Street 15

The *Volga Stadium* can seat 40,000.

City Garden, Kommunisticheskaya Street

Bathing Beach, on Golodny (hungry) Island, in the middle of the Volga, facing the city. It is reached by boat.

Volgograd Hotel & Restaurant, Mira Street 12; tel. 36 1722

Intourist Hotel & Restaurant, Mira Street 14; tel. 36 1468. Intourist office; tel. 36 4552.

Leto (summer) Restaurant, in the City Garden

Mayak (lighthouse) Restaurant on the Volga embankment. There is an excellent view from this restaurant and it is easily identified by its spire surmounted by a sailing ship.

Molodyozhnoye (youth) Café, Lenin Prospect 10

GPO, Pavshikh Bortsov Square

Bank, Lenin Prospect

Beryozka Foreign Currency Shop, Alleya Geroyev 2. Open 9–6; closed Sun.

Department Store, Pavshikh Bortsov Square. Open 10–8.

Art Salon, Sovietskaya Street 8

Souvenirs, Lenin Prospect 15

Podarki Gift Shop, Alleya Geroyev, where it crosses Krasnopiterskaya Street

Market, Sovietskaya Street

The *Volga Hydropower Station* is one of the largest in the world. It started working in 1959 and since 1961 has been operating at its full capacity of 2,575,000 kilowatts. Not far from it is the largest aluminium plant in Europe.

Intourist organises *boat trips* from Volgograd, along the river to the hydropower station at Volzhsky, and by motorboat or hovercraft along the Volga-Don Canal.

Volzhsky Population—230,000

Volzhsky lies 30 km from the centre of Volgograd, on the left bank of the river Volga, 2 km from the hydropower station, and with the river Akhtuba forming its western boundary.

The site was first settled in 1951 by those working at the hydropower station. It received town status in 1954.

Volzhsky was planned as a single architectural ensemble and was built by one construction organisation which enabled them to put up parts of the town in large, completed sections. Most of the houses are heated from a central plant. The main streets were planned to run from northwest to southeast to protect the houses from the frequent winds. Many 15-year-old trees were transplanted to form boulevards and a park. Lenin Prospect is the main thoroughfare. It is 40 m/yd wide and leads to the central square which is surrounded by impressive buildings with columns, the *Palace of Culture*, which seats 830 people, a hotel, shops, and administrative buildings.

The growing industry of the town includes ball-bearing and synthetic rubber factories, and one of the country's largest chemical plants is under construction.

At the *Sport Complex*, on the high and low terraces by the River Akhtuba, there is a stadium for 10,000 and an indoor swimming pool.

Local Museum

Volga Restaurant, Lenin Prospect 15

The *Volga-Don Canal* connects the Volga and the Don rivers and so makes Volgograd a port of five seas: the Caspian, the Black, the Azov, the Baltic and the White. It is 101 km (63 miles) long and was opened in 1952. The main source of water for the canal is the Tsimlyansky Sea, an inland stretch of water 360 km (224 miles) long, 38 km (24 miles) wide and 30 m (98 ft) deep. It holds 24,000,000,000 cu m.

First attempts to build the canal were made by Peter the Great at the end of the 17th century. Now it is finished it has 15 locks and is decorated with sculptural groups commemorating the events of the Civil and Second World Wars. At the opening from the Volgograd end stands a *lighthouse* with rostral columns in honour of the sailors of the Volga flotilla who fought here in 1918–19 and in 1942–43. Between the 9th and 10th locks is a *Monument to the Heroes of the Civil War* with busts of several of them. By the 13th lock is a *monument* devoted to the encirclement of the German forces by Soviet troops during the Battle of Stalingrad. On the towers of the 15th lock stand *Equestrian Statues of Cossacks*.

VORONEZH Population—890,000

Voronezh is situated on the bank of the river Voronezh, 12 km (7 miles) from the point where it joins the Don. Its name comes from "voron" (raven) and its ancient coat-of-arms shows a raven perched upon a gun.

Archeologists have found that Slav tribes have inhabited this region for the past 1000 years and the area is mentioned in chronicles of 1177. In 1586 a fortress was built here as a link in the chain of defences called the Belgorod Line, across the Don Steppes, which was designed to stop Tatar raids.

> Your town stood as Russia's shield
> 'Gainst the nomadic Eastern horde.
> —KONSTANTIN GUSYEV

The fortress guarding the southeastern border of the Moscow State stood on the high right bank of the river, and beyond it stretches "the wild field," the limitless steppe.

Voronezh was important as the point where prisoners of war were exchanged, as the place where foreign ambassadors were greeted as they travelled up the river Don, and also where they took their leave when their missions were accomplished. Its situation beside the waterway leading 800 km (500 miles) to the Black Sea and the Sea of Azov led to the town's rapid growth and by the 17th century it had become the centre for trade with the south. Bishop Mitrophan, who died in 1703 and was later canonised, was influential in its development, and so was Peter the Great who first visited Voronezh in 1694 and was struck by its strategic location. The following year, when he had failed to take the Turkish fortress of Azov, Peter proclaimed, "Any potentate who has infantry only is one-handed; he who has also a fleet has two hands," and Voronezh forthwith became his shipyard. Shipbuilders came from far and near to construct seaworthy vessels. Among the conscripted unskilled labour were 27,828 men from the surrounding area, while skilled carpenters and experienced shipbuilders came from as far away as Arkhangelsk, where Peter had spent two summers and where he kept his three ocean-going vessels. Shipbuilding was also going on in Moscow and Pereyaslavl, and from there prefabricated parts were brought by sledge to Voronezh for assembly. The new fleet was built in record time and in 1696 Peter, as captain (and builder) of the "Principium," led his fleet to capture Azov.

Veronezh lies in the black earth region which has long been Russia's breadbasket. Consequently most of the town's trade was at first in grain, but later the exports of wool and fat increased considerably. Voronezh was also celebrated for its cattle and particularly for its horses; Russian Trotters originated here.

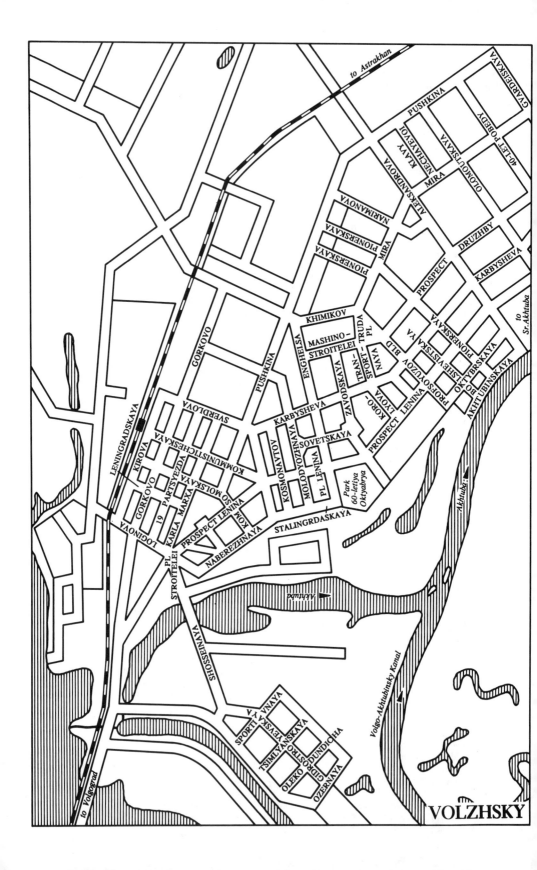

VOLZHSKY

After his victory Peter himself travelled to Holland and to England to study the shipbuilding profession, and invited shipwrights to Voronezh from both countries. The shipyards were now to build the fleet for the new naval base at Taganrog. Foreigners who settled in the town brought their own architectural styles with them. There were wide-roofed Swiss houses with balconies, narrow-windowed English cottages, and the Dutch houses with their pointed gables, although built of wood, were painted over to resemble brick. Open fire-places caused a great sensation and indeed a local historian described the new buildings as a "real miracle." Voronezh was one of the first Russian towns to conform to Peter's innovations and re-forms during his campaign to modernise his country, including such recommendations as that those of noble birth discard traditional dress and adopt French fashions. Most of the buildings put up in Peter's time were destroyed in a great fire in 1748, including a palace, the Admiralty and the houses which belonged to foreigners. Only the Admiralty Church remained intact.

At the end of the 19th century the town's industry began to catch up with its flourishing trade. New factories were built on the left bank of the river, including a synthetic rubber plant. During the 1905 Revolution, local workers rebelled and in the civil war which followed the 1917 revolution the town changed hands several times. The local Jews suffered much from the pogroms.

Voronezh was a front-line town during the Second World War. The German army occupied the right bank of the river but were unable to cross it. "Pravda" newspaper wrote in December 1942 that the Germans had "bumped their head on Voronezh." The battle for the town went on for 200 days, but although it was heavily bombed it was never taken. The town lost 95 percent of its industry, and out of 18,000 buildings, only 10 per cent survived the war. After the liberation the place was like one enormous minefield; only Stalingrad and Sevastopol were riddled with more mines than Voronezh. All the same, rebuilding had to go ahead, even on a minefield. During the first 4 months a further 58,000 unexploded mines were detected among the rubble.

After the war many old buildings were reconstructed to preserve the town's original appearance. The main street is Revolyutsii Prospect, formerly Great Nobles' Street, which ran for more than 2 km (1.5 miles), parallel to the river. No. 22 in this street is the building of the *Governor's House* which was constructed in 1725. Nearby is *Petrovsky Garden* with a statue of Peter the Great by Gavrilov; it was put up in 1956 in place of another statue of Peter which had been erected in 1860 but which was destroyed during the war. There is a pleasant fountain behind the statue.

On Victory Square there is a *War Memorial Complex* consisting of two steles, sculptured figures of soldiers and civilians and a granite wall inscribed with the names of the army units which fought here on the Voronezh front. An eternal flame completes the Complex, and illuminates the figures in a dramatic way at night.

During the early 1930s a number of buildings in Constructivist style were put up along Revolyutsii Prospect, the *House of Books, Communications House,* and the offices of the *Southeastern Railway.* They, too, were badly damaged but have been restored. The Railway offices were built 1928–32 by Troitsky, and reconstructed by him in 1952. Its 13-storey tower stands 70 m (230 ft) high and dominates the centre of the town. In *Lenin (formerly Old Horse) Square* is a monument to the founder by Nikolai Tomsky which was restored in 1950. Parades and demonstrations take place here. The big *House of Soviets* (1959) was designed by Mironov. At the southern end of the street is the *House of Trade,* built in 1934 by Popov-Shaman and popularly known as the Smoothing Iron because of its shape.

Another important square is *Chernyakhovsky Square,* in front of the railway station. General Ivan Chernyakhovsky, Hero of the Soviet Union, was an army commander whose soldiers fought for Voronezh during World War II. Plekhanovsky (formerly Bolshaya Moskovskaya) Street starts from University Square and crosses the centre of the town from southeast to northwest. Among the new buildings there are some old ones which have been restored, such as No. 3, and No. 29 where the *Local Museum* is.

Voronezh has ten higher educational establishments, including the university which was opened in 1918 when Dorpat University and the Agricultural Institute (founded in 1913) were both evacuated here from Tartu in Estonia. Now there are 13,000 university students, including a number of foreigners, studying in 13 different faculties. The building of the Glinka Agricultural Institute is in baroque style, designed by Dietrich. The other institutes include those for medicine, polytechnics, civil engineering, lumbering, pedagogy and art, while among the research institutes are those specialising in the black earth region and in sugar production.

On an island in the river on Stepan Razin Street stands what is grandly known as *Peter the Great's Arsenal,* built in the 1740s as one of the workshops of a broadcloth factory. It survived all the disasters that have befallen the town, and now houses an exhibit about World War II. The bas-relief above the portico depicts guns and cannon balls to suit its name.

On the left bank is the newer part of Voronezh, founded in 1928. It is an industrial area, now stretching along the river for over 16 km (10 miles). One of its main thoroughfares is Heroes-of-the-Stratosphere Street.

Local industry produces equipment for agriculture and the food industry, construction machinery such as excavators, chemical products (especially synthetic rubber), tyres and food products. The aviation factory was built in 1932. The first Tupolev plane was built here in 1934. More recently the Russian Concorde, TU–144, was built

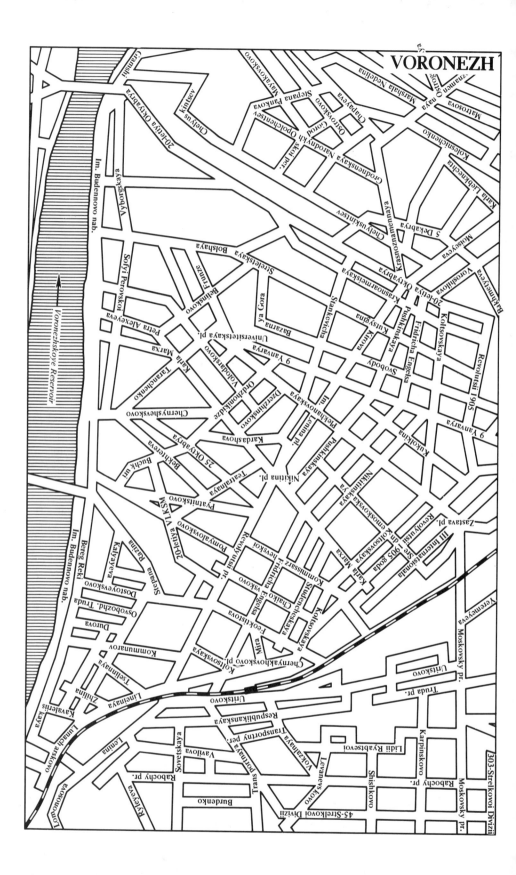

here, as well as the IL–86 airbus. The atomic power station that stands on the banks of the river Don 50 km (31 miles) from the town was built in the 1960s. The first turbine was commissioned in 1964 and its output is 1.5 million kilowatts. The town is divided into the right and left banks by the reservoir which was formed in 1972, and the opposite banks are linked by three bridges. The reservoir is 35 km (22 miles) long, 2–3 km (1–2 miles) wide and 3 m (10 ft) deep. It is known locally as Voronezh Sea. The hydropower station is on the river Voronezh, near the village of Shilovo.

Uspenskaya Church, on the right riverbank. This five-domed church was built in 1694, and subsequently called the Admiralty Cathedral by Peter the Great. It is now under restoration, and is to house the Naval Museum. The bell tower was built in 1808.

St. Nicholas's Church (1712–49), Taranchenko Street. This church was built in the style of Moscow churches; it is open for services.

Pokrovsky Cathedral (1792), Bekhtereva Street. Open for services.

Alexeyev Church, Osvobozhdeniye Truda Street. Although this church was built in the 19th century, its belfry was built in 1674 and is the oldest architectural monument in the town. It was badly damaged during the war. It used to belong to the Alexeyev Monastery, founded in 1700 as Akatov Pustyn (hermitage).

Blagoveschensky-Mitrophanovsky Monastery, New Moscow Street. Founded in 1836 and partly designed by Giacomo Quarenghi, this complex of churches and other buildings catered to more than 40,000 pilgrims annually before the Revolution. It was mined during World War II.

Vvedenskaya Church, Osvobozhdeniye Truda Street

Ilyinskaya Church, now housing state archives

Local Museum, Plekhanovskaya Street 29. Founded in 1894.

Nikitin Museum, Nikitinskaya Street 23. Ivan Nikitin (1824–61) was a very popular poet. The museum was founded in 1924 and the stone building in which it is housed is a replica built in 1955 of the wooden house in which the poet lived and died.

Durov House Museum, Anatoly Durov (1865–1916) was a famous Russian circus clown, and the founder of a circus dynasty. He once said of himself, "I am the king of clowns, but not the clown of kings!" His house was opened as a museum in 1901.

Kramskoy Fine Arts Museum, Revolyutsii Prospect 18, in the building of the Coaching Palace, built for Governor Potapov in the 1770s, and reconstructed several times. The museum was opened here in 1911. Ivan Kramskoy (1837–87) was a popular Russian artist. There are a number of his paintings in the museum. Ground floor: ancient Egypt, Greece and Rome; 1st floor: Russian art from the 15th century to the present day (including icons and the works of the 19th–20th century artists Shishkin, Levitan, and Repin); 2nd

floor: west European art, including a Van Dyck self-portrait and some of Rembrandt's etchings. Open 10–5; closed Tues.

Peter the Great Statue, Petrovsky Garden. By Gavrilov and unveiled in 1956. The founder of the Russian navy is shown with one hand resting on an anchor while he points the way forward with the other.

Nikitin Statue, in Nikitin Garden (see above, Nikitin Museum). The seated figure was designed by Shuklin and was unveiled in 1911.

Koltsov's Bust, in Koltsov Garden. Alexei Koltsov (1809–42) was a self-educated Russian poet who was born in Voronezh, and wrote peasant-style poems and songs describing country life. His marble bust by the Italian sculptor Augustin Triskorni was unveiled in 1868.

Lenin Statue, Lenin Square

War Memorial to those who fell in World War II, in the centre of the city, on 20th October Street.

Liberators' (or Glory) Monument, at the entrance to the town from the direction of Moscow. This monument, depicting a soldier all but crushed by the block above him, stands over the common grave of those who fell when the town was liberated at the end of the Second World War. It was unveiled in 1967.

Tank Monument, Patriotov Prospect. The tank, standing on a high granite pedestal, commemorates a tank crew.

Fighter Plane Monument, commemorating the 2nd Air Force Army which fought in the defence of Voronezh during World War II.

Aeroplane Monument, an IL-2 plane, from the Second World War.

Katyusha Rocket-launcher Monument

Rotunda Monument, part of the Regional Hospital, at the end of Transportnaya Street. This was damaged during the war, and left in ruins as it stood as a World War II Monument.

Peschany Log (ravine), Numerous individual graves and a monument to the fallen of World War II.

Koltsov Drama Theatre, Revolyutsii Square 67. The company was founded in 1802 and the building in the 1820s, but it has been reconstructed several times.

Opera and Ballet Theatre, Lenin Square. Performances of opera, ballet, and musical comedy take place here; it can hold 1200.

Youth Theatre, Dzerzhinsky Street

Circus, Pervomaisky Garden, Revolyutsii Prospect

Puppet Theatre, Revolutsii Prospect. The 3-storey building with a winter garden was completed in 1984. It is imaginatively decorated with fairytale characters.

Philharmonia Concert Hall, Lenin Square. Voronezh is famous for its choir which gives concerts all over the country and also abroad.

Detsky Sad (Children's Garden), Universitetskaya Street

Town Park, Lenin Street. Open-air theatre.

Botanical Garden, by the Agricultural Institute.

Hippodrome Racecourse, Begovaya Street 2
Dynamo Stadium, Lenin Street 12
Trud Stadium, Studencheskaya Street 17. This
stadium can seat 20,000.
Yubileyny Palace of Sport, Karl Marx Street
Lysaya Gora, a hill in the suburbs, is a popular
recreation place from which there is a good view
of the town. The Gorky Sanatorium is here.
Voronezh Hotel & Restaurant, Plekhanovskaya
Street 22
Don Hotel & Restaurant, Plekhanovskaya
Street 10
Rossiya Hotel & Restaurant, Teatralnaya Street
23; tel. 6-00-98
Brno Hotel & Restaurant, near Lenin Square
Molodyozhnoye Cafe, Pushkinskaya Street 4
GPO, Revolyutsii Prospect 23
Telegraph Office, Revolyutsii Prospect 35
Bank, Teatralnaya Street 18
Department Stores: Dom Torgovli (House of
Trade), Nikitinskaya Street, Revolyutsii Prospect
and Plekhanovskaya Street 125
Bookshop, Revolyutsii Prospect 33

Uzmansky Forest (40 km/25 miles from town,
and near Grafskaya railway station). There is a museum of the local flora and fauna which is open
10–5; 1 May–10 November; closed Mon. The *Nature Reserve* here was established in 1924, taking
in the territory of the local monastery where there
was a beaver colony, and making use of the monastery buildings. The monastery was a penal one,
and especially undisciplined monks were placed in
niches which had small openings overlooking the
river; watching the activities of the industrious beavers was supposed to have a salutory effect on them.
Many of the monastery buildings were destroyed
by wartime bombing, and the niches have now
been bricked up.

The deer which used to live here were hunted
to extinction in the 18th century. At the beginning
of the 20th century when Princess Oldenburg had
her estate here, deer were brought from Germany
to stock the park. After the Revolution, when the
Princess emigrated, 5 or 6 deer escaped into the
woods and now the herd numbers over 1,000.

Besides the deer, 187 species of birds, 39 species
of fish and 53 types of mammals inhabit the reserve.
Most valuable of the latter are the beavers, and the
reserve was originally formed to protect them. It
used to be the country's largest beaver reserve with
about half the Soviet beaver population in residence. There are now about 200,000 of them, and
from here beavers are sent to found new colonies
in other parts of the country.

Also here are about 900 varieties of plants. Most
of the territory is taken up by pine and aspen, but
stretches of birch and oak are also frequent. Peter
the Great valued the tall, straight oaks for his shipbuilding. An unusual tree here is the cedar-pine,
where a cedar has been grafted onto a pine tree.
No chemicals are used to control harmful insects
in the reserve, but a healthy balance is maintained
by natural means.

VYBORG (Finnish Viipuri; Swedish Viborg)
Population—90,000
Vyborg is situated on the Gulf of Finland about
120 km (75 miles) northwest of Leningrad. Once
a trading point between the people of Novgorod
and the Karelian hunters, it was founded as a castle
in 1293 by Swedish soldiers under Torkel Knutson.
It became a town in 1403 by decree of Erik XIII,
and at that time it, like many other mediaeval
towns, had its own court, council and merchants'
guilds. After Peter the Great's Poltava victory of
1709, he turned his attention to Vyborg. The following year, after a 12-week siege and at the second
attempt, he managed to take the fortress. He is
reported to have said at the time: "Since I have
taken this fortress, St. Petersburg is safe at last."
And he and his retinue climbed to the top of the
castle tower to drink a toast to their victory.

Along with St. Petersburg, Vyborg became a
prominent trading centre. Timber and dairy products were among the more important items handled
and trade ties were maintained with a number of
countries including England and Holland. Perhaps
it was due to foreign trade that Vyborg showed little
Russian influence for at least a century more. A
Swedish system of local government remained and
court proceedings were held in Swedish.

During the reign of Anna Ioannovna (1730–
40) Vyborg was strongly fortified to shield the town
from a possible surprise attack from the west. The
fortifications, among the best examples of 18th-
century Russian engineering skill, were named
after the Empress, Kron St. Anne. The population
tripled due to the influex of both Russians and
Germans, and under Catherine the Great (1726–
96) intensive building produced churches, mansions and impressive municipal structures.

As the town's history began with the founding
of the castle, the road leading to it, Krepostnaya
Street (formerly Linnankatu), is naturally one of
the oldest. Catherine II stayed at No. 3 in 1783
during her visit to Vyborg Province and later, until
the turn of the last century, this same building was
used as a post office. The imposing clocktower
(built in 1494) stands in the courtyard of No. 5 and
at No. 8 Field Marshal Suvorov stayed in 1791–
92. Vyborgskaya Street starts right from the port
where, it is said, Peter I accepted the key to the
town after his victory of 1710. The ancient buildings along this street are Nos. 8, 10, and No.
11 where there is now an electrical instrument
plant. This was built in 1481 and once housed a
Dominican monastery; it was reconstructed in its
present form by Engel in 1828. Also in Vyborgskaya
Street is the 16th-century house of the Merchants'
Guild and the Ratushi Tower (1643). In Teatralnaya Square Workers' School No. 2 used to be the
palace of Paul I's son-in-law, Prince Friedrich Rak-
ensi of Wurttemberg. It afterwards served as the
residence of the military governors; Field Marshal
Kutuzov apparently lived here in 1801.

The old fortress walls also became obsolete and
were destroyed in the 1860s in the course of town
planning. Vyborg was part of independent Finland

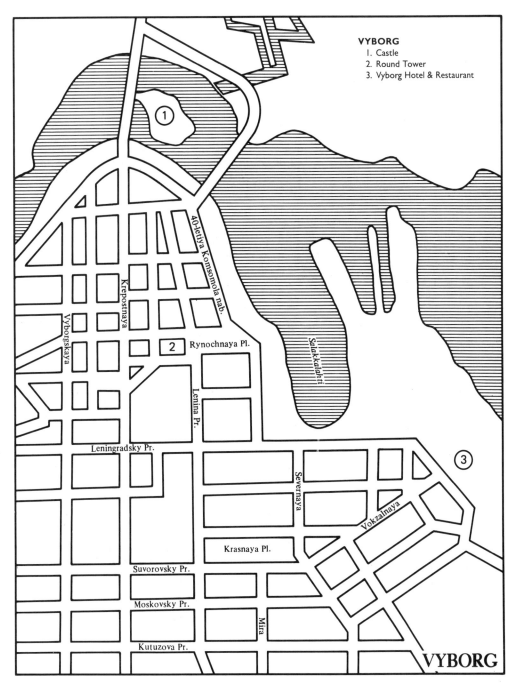

VYBORG
1. Castle
2. Round Tower
3. Vyborg Hotel & Restaurant

from 1818 until 1940 and for a short time during the Second World War, when it was badly damaged, more than half the residential houses being ruined.

The Saimaa Canal, built in 1844–59 to link Vyborg Bay through Vyborg seaport with the huge water basin of the Saimaa Lake 60 km (37 miles) inland, proved of great economic value. Between 1940 and 1962 the Finns were denied the right to use it by the Soviet Union. Besides its port, Vyborg has also an important railway junction where five lines meet. The railway terminal building designed by Saarinen in 1913 was unfortunately destroyed during the war, and in 1953 a new building by the Soviet architects Vasilyev, Goltsgor, Speransky and Berkov was commissioned.

A number of impressive buildings of the beginning of this century are still to be seen. Some of these belonged to banks and business firms as, for example, the 4-storey, Renaissance style building near the Round Tower, designed in 1900 by Aspelin for the Pohjosmaiden Yhdyspankka and now used by the Vyborg District Executive Committee. The bank building next door was constructed by Nystrem in 1901 and an architectural institute is in the former Art Museum designed by Uno Ullberg. The imposing market was built in 1905 by Hard and Segertad.

In the centre of the town Lenin Boulevard (formerly Torkkelinpuistoa) covers the site of the demolished ramparts and bastions of the 16th-century Horned Fortress. The two sculptures adding to its elegance are "The Elk" by Jussi Mantysen (1924) and "Forest Boy" by Yrjo Liipola (1932). At the end of the boulevard stands the City Library by Aalto (1935).

The present population of Vyborg is slightly greater than before the war. The absolute majority are new settlers as the Finns were moved out of Vyborg after 1944.

The *Castle (Viipurilinna)*, the oldest building of Vyborg, was once the most formidable stronghold on the shores of the Baltic Sea and was considered by the Swedes to be the key to the whole of Finland. It was built on a rocky island 170 m (186 yds) long and 122 m (133 yds) wide with two drawbridges connecting it to the shore. Most of the existing structures date from the 16th century. The castle lost its military importance when it became Russian and it was thereafter used as an arsenal, food depot and offices. After the 1825 uprising of the Decembrists in St. Petersburg, it served as a prison. Major reconstruction was undertaken by the experienced Colonel-Engineer Lezedov in 1891–94. The old mediaeval tower of St. Olaf stands in the courtyard, known as Tall Hermann by the soldiers of Peter I. It stands 48.6 m (159 ft) high and its walls at the base are 5 m (16 ft) thick, dating from the time of its foundation in 1293. It was reconstructed in its present octagonal form in 1561–64 and at the time of the castle's reconstruction in 1891 the 10-m (33-ft) cupola was given the form of a Russian helmet.

In April 1918 the castle housed the revolutionary government of Finland, and after the government's defeat there were mass executions of Red Guards in the castle yard.

Pantserlaks Bastion (Pantsarlant Bastionin), at the corner of Leningrad and Vyborg Streets. Built in 1579–81 the bastion is the southeastern "horn" of the so-called Horned Fortress of the 16th century; it is all that remains of the fortress following the demolition of the 1860s.

Kron St. Anne, over the bridge from the castle. Fredrikshamn (Hamina) Gate, with one arch spanning the inner ramparts and another the outer, is the only one of the four gates to have survived. Outside the gate is the common grave of the Russian soldiers who fell in the siege of 1710. Until the 19th century all westbound traffic passed through this gate but then the present road was built.

Round Tower (Pyorea Torni or Runddelag), Rynochnaya (market) Square, near house No. 5. King Vasa of Sweden wished this tower to be built in Italian style, the idea being to build two towers forming a gate to Karelia. The architect Hans von Bergen intended it to be round but it came out oval and was completed in 1550. It was nicknamed Catherina during the reign of Catherine the Great and was used for storage in the 19th century. In 1923 the fashionable Kellotorni Restaurant was opened here.

Transfiguration Russian Orthodox Cathedral, Pionerskaya Square, built in 1787–93 and open for services. Opposite stands the former Rathaus (1643; reconstructed in 1930) and beside it the former Court of Appeal. Also here is the German-Swedish *Cathedral of SS. Peter and Paul*, built in 1793–99 by Felten.

Clock Tower, Krepostnaya Street 5. This was once the belfry for the Agricola Church and because of its great height it also served as a firewatchers' tower. It was built in 1494 upon the order of Prince Michael Agricola of Sweden, who was himself buried here in 1557.

Local Museum, in the castle. Open 11–6; closed Wed.

Lenin Museum, Rubezhnaya Street 14. Here Lenin lived and worked on the eve of the 1917 October Revolution in Russia. His modestly furnished room has been fully restored.

Peter I Monument, on the site of the Russian military headquarters. This monument was erected in 1910 to mark the 200th anniversary of the capture of the town by Peter the Great. The statue by L. Bernstamm was removed after the town became part of Finland in 1918 and instead there was a monument to Finland's independence. Peter I's statue was restored in 1955. The rock just behind the statue bears a monogram which is said to have been cut by Peter himself. The foundations of a military church were also laid in 1910 as part of the anniversary celebrations but nothing came of the idea and instead the provincial archives' building was put up in 1932–34; now there is a library here and the archives of the Leningrad Region.

Finnish Red Guards Monument, at the entrance to the town from Leningrad. Commemorating those who were killed in 1918, this monument by Chebotaryev and Shver was unveiled in 1961. It bears an inscription glorifying the international solidarity of workers.

Lenin Monument, Red Square (formerly Punaisenlahteentori). This monument was designed by Mikatadze and unveiled in 1957.

Mon Repos Park, on the shore of the northern bay, on the west bank of the gulf on the way to Leningrad. The Park was founded by Stupishin, military governor of Finland in the 18th century. Friedrich-Wilhelm-Karl, Governor-General of Finland and later King of Wurttemberg, enlarged and embellished the park. Maria Fyodorovna, wife of the Emperor Paul, continued the landscaping. The 15 hectares (38 acres) are preserved as a typical stretch of northern landscape, and include shady avenues and impressive granite cliffs. The small columned mansion (now a kindergarten) was built in 1820 by Martinelli for Baron Nikolai, who had been given the territory in recognition of his services to the state. On a high granite cliff near the house is a marble obelisk erected in 1827 to commemorate the de Broglio brothers who died during the Napoleonic Wars. *Ludwigstein Castle* (19th century), the family mausoleum, is on the Island of Death on the southwestern side of the park. Also in the park is the Well of Love, otherwise known as the Narcissus Spring, and Paul I's Column, constructed in 1881.

Druzhba (friendship) (Intourist) Hotel & Restaurant, Zheleznodorozhnaya Street 5; tel. 25–744. Intourist office; tel. 23–588.

Vyborg Hotel & Karelia Restaurant, near the railway station, Leningradsky Prospect 19. There is a *Beryozka foreign currency shop* here.

Restaurant, at the railway station

Kruglaya Bashnya Restaurant, Rynochnaya Square; tel. 67–838

Sever (north) Restaurant, Lenin Prospect 13; tel. 20-113

Myak Restaurant, near the Market building

Beryozka (foreign currency) Shop, by the Vyborg Hotel. Open 11–2; 3–8; closed Sat. Other Beryozka shops are at Zheleznodorozhnaya Street 9/15 (open 10–7; closed Mon.), at the seaport and at the railway station.

Filling Station, by the railway station

Intourist organises motorboat trips with a picnic on the site of an ancient settlement, and also excursions from Vyborg to Zelenogorsk, a resort town by the sea.

Zelenogorsk Population—15,000
At the 150/62 km mark on the main road and formerly known as Terioki, the town was frequently visited by Lenin and in 1907 he chaired a conference of the Bolshevik Party here. He also delivered a number of reports in a house which belonged to a certain Ottenen and which stood near the square.

From 1918 to 1940 this resort was on Finnish territory. It lies on the northern shore of the Gulf

of Finland and is backed by pinewoods. Its beach of golden sand is the best in the region and it has long been a favourite place for Leningraders to take their holidays. There are many sanatoria and rest homes here and it is to be further developed.

Lutheran Church, now a cinema

Russian Orthodox Church

Morskoi Priboi Hotel, to the right of the main road. Designed for Finnish motorists and open in summer only.

Hotel, Primorskoye Chaussee 90, in a pinewood at the edge of the sea with a good bathing beach. There is a restaurant, cafe, telephone, baths and showers and a *service station*.

Zhemchuzhina (Pearl) Restaurant

Olen Restaurant & Cafe, on a small hill to the right of the road where it turns towards Leningrad.

Filling Station, Leningradskoye Chaussee 60. Round the clock service.

Some distance to the northwest of Zelenogorsk, by the river Roschinka, is a grove of larch, grown specially for ships' masts. Larches were grown here from seeds brought from the Arkhangelsk Region in 1738, already after the death of Peter the Great but in accordance with an order he had given.

YAKUTSK is the capital of Yakutia.

YAKUTIA

This is a region of vast natural wealth. It covers 3,103.2 sq km—one-seventh of the territory of the USSR, or almost two-thirds of the territory of Western Europe. The population of over 900,000 includes over 70 different nationalities.

It is a land where gold and diamonds are mined, as well as tin, mercury, antimony, coal and natural gas. Already a major producer of these commodities, the completion of BAM (the Baikal-Amur Mainline) and the construction of the AYaM (the Amur-Yakutsk Mainline), linking it by rail with the rest of the country, open up the area to full exploitation. The diamonds were discovered in 1949, and diamond mining was industrialised in 1958. Yakut diamonds are used both for jewellery and technically. Some weigh 100 carats.

The Yakutsk branch of SOAN, the Siberian Department of the Academy of Sciences, is mainly concerned with the problems of developing the north. Its institutes include those of geology, northern mining, biology and the languages, literature and history of the northern ethnic groups. There is a department of environmental protection and a special Permafrost Institute to study the behaviour of the frozen ground. The world's pole of cold is in Yakutia. The winter average is −45–47° C (−49–53°F) while in summer it rises to 17°C (63°F).

Before the Russians came the area was inhabited by Eskimos, Chukchas, Evenks and Yakuts, descendants of southern cattle-breeding tribes who came here from Lake Baikal in the 10th–11th centuries. Their legends say that a rich and powerful man called Omogoy once sailed his raft down the river Lena, and settled on the site of present-day Yakutsk. He had several beautiful daughters but no sons. Then the handsome young Ellai arrived, also from the south and became Omogoy's son-in-law, apparently on a bigamous basis. True or not, certainly the Yakuts are Mongol in appearance, but speak a rich language of Turkic origin. The yurts they used to live in were made of circularly placed inclined logs, meeting at a conical top and fortified by earth and turf. A single window let in the light and inside there was a fireplace for cooking. The Yakuts were hunters, cattle-breeders and skilled craftsmen. They were able blacksmiths and were familiar with iron-smelting. The large accumulations of old slag that are still found near Yakutsk prove the scale of this work. The blacksmith was as highly revered as the shaman-witch doctor; he evoked the same religious awe and was often approached as a medicine-man and fortune-teller.

Their handicrafts included mammoth-bone carving. Mammoths have been found frozen into the ground on the outskirts of Yakutsk. Russia has long been interested in the finds. Peter I decreed that the local authorities should be informed of each mammoth found. From the end of the 16th century until today 30 whole mammoths have been found, the largest near Yakutsk in 1972. But separate bones and tusks are much more common. From the 18th century carved boxes, pipes, chessmen and dagger hilts were exported, and in the 19th century quantities of uncut bone were sold through the Yakutsk fair.

The subjugation of Siberia by the Russians had begun as far back as the end of the 16th century, after the defeat of Tatar Khan Kuchum by the forces of the Don Cossack, Yermak Timofeevich. By 1653 there were 25 small strongholds in Yakutia, a territory which stretches right across to the Pacific. They each consisted of just a few log cabins, a chapel and a watchtower surrounded by a ditch. That at Yakutsk was considered the central one.

The first Russian settlers brought Christianity to Yakutia, and from 1763 missionaries began their work among the local tribes. Yakutia was proclaimed a province in 1775, and an *oblast* in 1783.

The first books in the Yakut language appeared in 1862, but after the 1917 Revolution the Cyrillic alphabet was used.

Counter-revolutionary activity continued until 1922 when, in April, the Yakut Autonomous Socialist Republic was formed.

Yakutsk Population—190,000

Yakutsk is located on the left bank of the river Lena in the northeastern part of Siberia. Opposite, on the right bank, is the village of Bestyyakh. The Lena is 10 km (6 miles) wide in some places, and is ice-free for 152 days each year and navigable from May until the end of September. It is icebound for 213 days, the ice becoming about 213 cm (almost 7 ft) thick.

The first Russian regiments were sent to the river Lena in 1620 to collect taxes from the Yakuts, and in 1630 the military leader Peter Beketov re-ceived instructions from Tobolsk to build a small fortress there. He came here with 100 Cossacks, and in 1632 put up a rough cross on the right bank of the river as a sign that Russians were living there, built a wooden stronghold and sent the following message to Moscow: "I, Petrushka, and my soldiers raised a stronghold on the river Lena in distant lands for His Gracious Majesty . . . against the Yakut Prince."

Soon Beketov realised his mistake. In the thaw the waters rose by 6–8 m (20–26 ft), flooded the stronghold and washed away the earth under the buildings. The fortress was still receiving support from Yeniseisk, but in 1640 it became independent. In 1643 it was resited 70 km (43 miles) upstream, near Saisay Lake and this time on the left bank; it was renamed Yakutsk. The new fortress was quadrangular, and surrounded by wooden walls with towers of solid larch.

Gradually wooden structures sprang up around the Yakutsk fortress. In the 17th century the place was already a real Russian stronghold in northeastern Asia. Expeditions of Cossack explorers, traders and researchers set out from here. In 1648 Semeyon Dezhnev set out on his expedition. He proved the existence of a strait separating Asia from North America. In 1683 the site of Yakutsk was changed for the last time, to its present position, and in 1686 strong wooden walls were built around it with eight defence towers, one of which remains today. In 1690 the expedition organised by Vladimir Atlasov led to the annexation of Kamchatka in 1697. In 1733–43 Yakutsk was the starting point for the Great Northern Expedition when the Laptev brothers and Chelyuskin, among others, mapped the territories lying on the northern seas. In 1790 Yakutsk was granted its coat-of-arms.

Many Yakuts were quickly converted to Christianity. In 1664 the town's first monastery, Spassky Monastery, was founded beside the river Lena by Euphimy. The first monastery school was opened in 1735, and the first parochial school in 1789, but the fires of 1770 and 1781 destroyed the early buildings, churches included. Trinity Cathedral, built in 1708, had been the oldest. New ones were built of stone in the 1820s and reconstructed in the 1860s. The bishopric of Yakutsk and Viluy was established in 1850. The church, especially the missionaries, were influential in helping to open leper colonies. The first hospital was opened here in 1843.

The town developed as a trade centre through which luxurious furs were sent to Russia. Furs began to be brought in from the farthest corners of the region and to be sold once a year at the Yakutsk Fair which eventually took place between July 20 and August 20. An export market developed, but as there was then no telegraph communication with the outside world, the fur prices were fixed according to those of the preceding year without regard to changes in the European market. Yakutsk also grew into the administrative centre for the colonial outskirts and a centre for exile of criminals and political troublemakers.

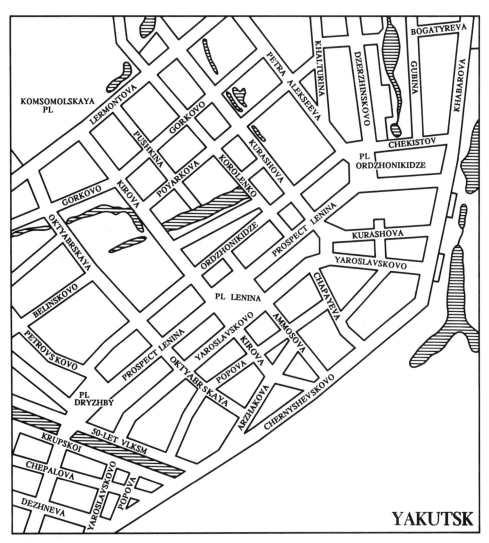

YAKUTSK

At the beginning of the 19th century there were 280 wooden houses in Yakutsk, one of stone, six churches, a monastery, five shops and a dozen taverns. The population of 2,500 included both Yakuts and Russians, and half were already Christians. In 1822 it was officially proclaimed the regional centre, and in 1852 a civil Governor of Yakutia was appointed. In 1827 it became the place of exile for 10 Decembrists, including Bestuzhev-Marlinsky and Muravyev-Apostol. Political prisoners began to be sent here in the 1860s. The Russian writers N. Chernyshevsky and V. Korolenko were sent here, too, and at the end of the 19th century the Dukhobors from the Caucasus. The Dukhobors (the name meaning "spiritual wrestlers") were members of a religious sect organised among the Russian peasantry in the 18th century. In 1801 Tsar Alexander I had settled them along the Molochnaya river near the Sea of Azov.

Then in 1840–41 they were deported to the Caucasus, and in 1895 settled in Georgia. It was from there that they were transferred to Yakutsk, but in 1905 they were allowed to emigrate to Canada, where most of them now live, calling themselves the Union of Spiritual Communities of Christ. Before the revolution, Ordzhonikidze and other Bolsheviks were sent to Yakutsk.

The exiles contributed greatly to the ethnography of the region as well as to local education. It was they who founded the local museum and the library. They researched the history, ethnography and language of the Yakuts, compiling the Yakutian grammar and dictionary. The local printing works opened in 1862 and the first books in the Yakut language appeared. There were many mixed marriages between the exiles and the Yakutian women. They wrote books on the geology of the area and studied the wild life of Yakutia and the climate, interesting for being the coldest place in the world, as discovered by the merchant Neverov in the early 19th century. In 1827 Fyodor Sherghin, a merchant representing a Russian-American trading company, began to dig a *well*. He thought he would get through the frozen earth and strike fresh water, but when he failed to do so, he was asked by some scientists to keep on digging. He dug for 10 years to a depth of 116.4 m (382 ft) and the first geothermal observations on permafrost in the world were conducted here. For the first 2 m (6 ft) the shaft measures 3 × 3 m/yds, and then it continues 1.6 × 1.6 m (5 × 5 ft). There is now a wooden hut over the well, and the walls are lined with wood to a depth of 52 m (171 ft).

By the early 20th century the population was already 7,000. There were still a great number of exiles. In 1904 the Romanov Protest took place; 57 political exiles shut themselves into the house of Fedor Romanov (at Romanovskaya Street 9) demanding an improvement in their conditions. They were besieged for 18 days before being overpowered. One died and others were wounded in the struggle, and the survivors were sentenced to 12 years hard labour. By 1908 the population had risen to 12,000, but an eyewitness wrote: "The town looks more like a village than a town. There is not a single decent building, not one paved street." There were only 24 streets then and 1,200 houses. All the same it was a beginning. 11 merchants had offices here and there were schools, two newspapers, a dramatic society and 8 libraries. Three brickworks, two tanneries and three cigarette factories made up the local industry.

After two years of Civil War Yakutia became Soviet, and in 1922 was proclaimed an autonomous republic. The sawmill, the new brickworks and tannery opened in 1930. Local industry has now increased to include the manufacture of building materials, furniture, clothing and food products. There is also a plant for ship-repairing and shipbuilding in the nearby settlement of Zhatai.

The modern, multi-storey buildings of Yakutzoloto (Gold of Yakutia) emphasise the importance of this organisation. There are many 4–5 storey houses in the centre of the city today. Lenin Prospect is the main thoroughfare. The houses stand on concrete pillars to avoid the irregular thaw of the ground upon which they stand. The pavements are of wood, as the pavements of Leningrad used to be until not so long ago. In 1940 water pipes were laid (for heated water only), and gas was installed. In the 1940s fresh water was finally located below ground.

The university was opened in 1956 with faculties of physics and mathematics, medicine, biology and geography, history and philology, and agriculture; now there are 9 faculties. Also in the city are 16 scientific institutes, and 18 special colleges including the Ordzhonikidze Medical School.

Yaroslavsky Museum of the History & Culture of the Peoples of the North, Lenin Prospect 5/2. Open 11–6; closed Mon. Founded in 1891, and formerly at Lenin Prospect 40 (now a branch of the Pushkin Library). Contains the skull of a fossilised bull known as "the grandfather of Yakutsk Museum" because it was one of the first exhibits, presented in 1886 by Semyon Yegorov.

Gabyshev Fine Arts Museum, Khabarov Street 27. Open 10–6; closed Mon. & Tues. Mainly 19th-century Russian paintings here, and others by modern Yakutian artists. The museum is named after Professor Mikhail Gabyshev (1902–58), agricultural economist, political worker and art collector.

Western European Art Museum, Petrovsky (formerly Pravlenskaya) Street 4. Open 10–6; closed Mon. & Tues. The collection is based upon that of Professor Gabyshev which he left to the state. The museum was opened in 1962.

University Picture Gallery, Lermontov Street 20. Open 10–5; closed Mon.

Oyunsky Literary Museum, Oktyabrskaya Street 10. Open 11–6; closed Mon. Named after Platon Oyunsky (1893–1939), a local revolutionary, politican, linguist, and founder of Yakut Soviet literature. Oyunsky lived in this house from 1935 till 1938, and his study has been restored to look as it did in his lifetime.

Geological Museum, Petrovsky Street 2. Open 9–5; closed Sat. & Sun. The museum belongs to the Academy of Sciences.

Archaeological and Ethnographical Museum, Pavlik Morozov Street 2. Open to groups; closed Mon., Sat. & Sun. The museum belongs to Yakutsk University. As well as the regular exhibits, there is a good collection of slide and film material.

Cossacks' Tower, Lenin Prospect 5/2, in the courtyard of the Yaroslavsky Museum. The wooden tower with its lookout post on the roof was built in 1685–86 as part of the fortress, restored in 1911, moved from its original site in the middle of Druzhby-Narodov Square in 1957 towards the Yakut Theatre, and transferred here in 1967. It is now all that remains of the fortress.

Monastyrevka, in the courtyard of the Yaroslavsky Museum, Lenin Prospect 5/2. This house, which belonged to Monastyrev and stood at Lenin Prospect 21, served as a library and meeting house for 30 political exiles who were sentenced to move on to Kolyma. They protested at the harsh conditions, and when soldiers were sent to imprison them, 6 were killed and 10 wounded. The house was moved to its present position in 1953.

Exiles Museum (Romanovka), Yaroslavsky (formerly Sovietskaya) Street 5. Open 11–6; closed Mon. Fyodor Romanov's house was built in 1890. A plaque commemorates the Romanov Protest of 1904, when a Yakut named Fyodor Romanov sheltered here 57 political exiles who were standing up for their rights, and flying the red flag from the roof. There are exhibits inside about Bolsheviks exiled to Yakutsk.

Governor's Chancery (Voyevoda), Kalandarishvili (formerly Sobornaya) Street 2, in the courtyard of the Yakut Drama Theatre. Built in 1707, and the first building of brick in Yakutsk. In the 18th and 19th centuries the local archives were kept here. The street was renamed after Nestor Kalandarishvili (1876–1922), revolutionary and civil war leader who died in action near Yakutsk.

Sherghin's Well, 50-Let-Komsomol Street 16. The house that stood here belonged to Fyodor Sherghin who, in 1827, began to dig a well in his backyard. There is a wooden hut over the well shaft.

Yaroslavsky's House, in the courtyard of the Yaroslavsky Museum, Lenin Prospect 5/2. Open 11–6; closed Mon. Yemelyan Yaroslavsky (1878–1943) was the pseudonym of Minei Gubelman. The house was built in 1912–13 in the courtyard of the local museum at Lenin Prospect 40. Yaroslavsky lived in it in 1915–17, and it was moved here in 1967. Two of his children were active in setting up the commemorative display in the six rooms inside. The academician was active in the Social Democratic Labour Party, and the founder and first editor of its paper. A firm supporter of Lenin, he was banished here from 1913–17. Later he became known as a militant atheist, and edited the journal, "The Godless."

Petrovsky's House, Yaroslavsky Street 32. Marked with a memorial plaque.

Karl Marx Bust, Dvortsa-Kultury Square. By Lev Kerbel and unveiled in 1982.

Civil War Memorial, eternal flame and bas-relief commemorating the fallen of Yakutia.

Lenin Statue, in front of the regional Party building. The 6-m (20-ft) statue was sculpted by Struchkov and unveiled in 1967.

Petrovsky Statue, Kirov Street, by the Pioneer Palace. Grigory Petrovsky (1878–1958) was a Communist who was exiled here in 1916–17. He was active after the Revolution, holding a number of important posts in Russia and the Ukraine. The cast-iron statue stands 3 m (10 ft) high, and was unveiled in 1982.

Yaroslavsky Monument, by the Museum of the History & Culture of the Peoples of the North. The statue was sculpted by Yaroslavsky's daughter and was unveiled in 1969.

Komsomol Monument, Komsomol Square. Two figures, of a Russian and a Yakut, commemorate the Young Communists of the 1920s. By Neroda and unveiled in 1965.

War Memorial, Pavshikh-Bortsov Square, on the site of Preobrazhenskaya Church, and where a battle took place in 1918, during the Civil War. In 1922–23 the first burials of national heroes took place here. The memorial was reconstructed following the design of V. Karamzin in 1967. A wall was put up inscribed with the names of the 30 revolutionaries who were buried here, and an eternal flame was lit.

Memorial Complex, a decorative wall inscribed with the names of Yakut Heroes of the Soviet Union, a T–34 tank on a pedestal and a flying equestrian statue of a Yakut warrior, in memory of the Yakutian war dead. Unveiled in 1975.

Ilmen Memorial, Ilmen Street. A stone figure grieves for the thousands of Yakutian soldiers who died in the defence of Novgorod during the Second World War. The fiercest battle was on Lake Ilmen,

near Staraya Russa, south of Novgorod, in 1943. The monument was unveiled in 1970.

Yakutsk Monument, at the entrance to the city on the way from the airport. The three posts represent the posts that Yakut horsemen traditionally used to tether their steeds. Designed by Lukin and unveiled in 1982 to mark the 350th anniversary of the foundation of Yakutsk.

Oyunsky Yakut Drama Theatre, Kalandarishvili Street 2. Founded in 1925.

Russian Drama Threatre, Lenin Prospect 21. Founded in 1920.

Yakut Music Theatre, Lenin Prospect 46. Founded in 1971, and rehoused in the new building designed by Isakovich in 1982.

Spartak Stadium, Kirov Street 46

Wrestling Hall, opened in 1976

Park, laid out in 1938 in what were then the western outskirts of the town.

Lena Hotel & Restaurant, Lenin Prospect 8, on Ordzhonikidze Square; tel. 448–90

Yakutsk Hotel & Restaurant, Oktyabrskaya Street 20/1; tel. 921–145

Taiga Hotel, Ordzhonikidze (formerly Krasnoarmeiskaya) Street 23; tel. 245–55

Sever Restaurant, Lenin Prospect 38

GPO, Dzerzhinsky Street 4

Communications House, Lenin Prospect

International Telephone Office, Lenin Prospect 10; tel. 271–43

Bank, Kirov Street 25

Department Store, Ammosov (formerly Komsomolskaya) Street 14. Maxim Ammosov (1897–1939) was an active revolutionary, and important in party and political work in Central Asia and Siberia.

Souvenirs & Jewellery, Lenin Prospect 11

Yakutskiye Promysly, Dzerzhinsky Street 13

Bookshop, Ammosov Street 18

Taxi, Lenin Prospect 7; tel. 207–32 & 295–25

Protok Khatystak

This town was built on the left bank of the Khatystakh in the valley of the Lena. In the spring the river often floods the town, so all houses have to be built on high foundations.

Lenskiye Stolby

About 200 km (124 miles) from Yakutsk, at a point where the river runs through a narrow, steep-sided gorge, there are beautiful limestone columns on either side. Intourist plans to organise excursions here.

GREATER YALTA

The Black Sea coast of the Crimea is a favourite resort area. The central part and that open to foreigners is designated Greater Yalta, after the largest town there. In fact it stretches from Alushta in the east to Foros in the west.

Alushta (Pronounced "alooshta")

This place, at the southern end of the valley of the mountain rivers Ulu-Uzen and Demergi, was originally called Aluston, meaning Valley of the Winds. Aluston Fortress was built by Justinian I of Byzantium (527–565); its walls are 2.1 m (7 ft) thick, and it stood until the 13th century. On the hill in the centre, in Genueskaya Street, a 6th-century stone defence tower and part of a wall remain. In the 14th century Aluston was rebuilt by the Genoese and grew into a considerable town, being ruled by a council until 1475 when it passed into Turkish hands. The Genoese Towers stand on the ruins of part of the old fortress. In 1783, with the rest of the Crimea, Aluston was joined to Russia, and in 1902 it was once again deemed worthy of being proclaimed a town.

Before the revolution one of the houses bore a marble plaque which told how Nicholas II had in October 1894, while still heir apparant, here met his fiancée, the German princess Alix of Hesse-Darmstadt, a granddaughter of Queen Victoria. They were married on 26th November that year.

A long walk westwards towards Yalta follows the old military pass along the coastline as far as Cape Plaka. The cape was once part of the estate of Kuchuk-Lambat, belonging to Princess Gagarin and on the top of it was built a small church and a chapel housing the family sepulchre. The princess's three-storey *palace*, built in 1907 like a castle with mediaeval turrets in old German style, is now the Utyos (cliff) Sanatorium. The old princess bequeathed the estate to her niece and this lady, after the revolution when the palace had been confiscated, was wisely invited to stay on, living in a single room, to work there as librarian, earning her keep by cataloguing the books she knew so well.

Beyond Utyos Sanatorium, to the west is the Skazka (fairytale) Sanatorium, formerly known as Karasan when it belonged to the family of General Rayevsky, friends of Pushkin. The house, in Moorish style, was built at the turn of the century and the splendid *park* covers 18 hectares (45 acres).

There are many sanatoria and rest homes in the Alushta region and the Alushta, Kastel and Taurida state farms grow grapes and process them for wine. The local vineyards were first laid out by German settlers in 1826.

The promenade is officially named after Lenin but it is generally known simply as the Naberezhnaya (embankment). The best shops are here and in Tavricheskaya Street. The Alushta *Geophysical Station* (founded in 1952) is in Partizanskaya Street.

The *bathing beaches* at Alushta are among the best in the Crimea. Recommended are those opposite the Slava (Glory) Sanatorium and below the Naberezhnaya, as well as the town beach.

Local Museum, Lenin Street 8
Natural History Museum, Partisanskaya Street 40
Sergeyev-Tsensky's House, Sergeyev-Tsensky Street 5. Sergei Sergeyev-Tsensky (1875–1958) was a novelist. Among his works was "The Ordeal of Sevastopol," a description of the Crimean War of 1854–55, and three war novels under the collective title of "Transfiguration." This house, now a mu-

seum, is where the novelist lived and worked for half a century. On the slope of Orlinaya Gora (eagle hill) near the house, he planted 400 cypresses and he lies buried there, just as he wished, according to these lines of his:

I would ask of you, as my last request,
A plain warrior's grave without monument
　　　or plaques
In that very same earth which I know best,
Dug with pick and shovel from my soldier's
　　　pack.

Golovkinsky Monument. Rabochy Ugolok (workers' corner), at the foot of Mount Kastel. Prof. Nikolai Golovkinsky (1834–97) was a hydro-geologist who worked in the Crimea in 1886–97. His house is in the street named after him in the village of Lazurnoye. The monument, built in 1905, stands opposite his house. Some other professors had built their houses here from 1872 on, and the place was formerly known as Professors' Corner.
Monument to Gorki in Primorsky Park
On Revolution Square is a *monument* to members of the local government who were shot in 1918.
Monument to Sergeyev-Tsensky, in the park. Made by Tomski.
Magnolia Hotel & Volna (wave) Restaurant, Lenin Street 1
　Tavrida Hotel, Lenin Street 22; tel. 30453
　Chernomorskaya Hotel, Oktybrskaya Street 5
　Morskoy Restaurant, Naberezhnaya 18
　Svetlana Restaurant, Karl Marx Street 3
　Solnyshko Restaurant, Gorky Street 6
　GPO, Lenin Street 15
　Podarki (Gift) Shop, Naberezhnaya 2
　Market, Tavricheskaya Street 29

Nature Reserve (Zapovednik), 18 km (11 miles) from Alushta. Special permission is necessary to visit the 30,000-hectare (75,000-acre) nature reserve which was established in 1923 on former imperial hunting territory. It was said to be to this spot that the two brothers, Kosma and Damian, both doctors, were expelled from the Roman Empire in the time of Diocletian for adopting the Christian faith. An enemy, jealous of their skill in healing, murdered them both and buried their bodies near a spring. Later it was found that the spring had healing powers and it became a place of pilgrimage and was called Savlukh-su Spring meaning Water of Health. The Monastery of SS. Kosma and Damian was founded here in 1856 and converted into a convent in 1898. The remaining buildings were ruined during World War II but the spring rises near the site of the convent. In the reserve there are 36 species of animals including Crimean deer, roe deer and wild sheep (imported in 1913 from Corsica), and 135 species of birds. Interesting plants include the Crimean edelweiss.

From Alushta the main road goes on towards

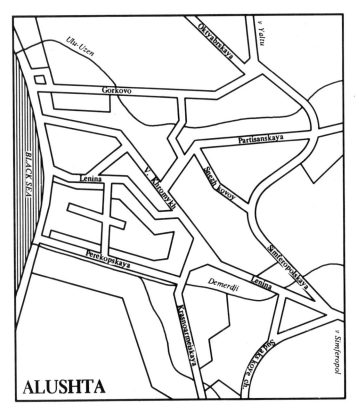

ALUSHTA

Maly Mayak, but a lower road runs near the sea, passes through Lazurnoye and then rejoins the main road.

The boundaries of many of the places along this whole stretch of coastline are almost impossible to define as they run into each other and ramble about, up and down the mountain sides. Sometimes as many as three separate roads run parallel.

In that case the main road is described first.

Maly Mayak Population 1,000
First mentioned in the 13th century and formerly known as Biyuk Lambat. Situated 10 km (6 miles) from Alushta. The main concern of the Tavrida State Farm here is growing grapes.

There are *ruins* of a 10th–12th century monastery near the village.

Memorial plaque at a place of the arrest of members of the first local government by the White Guards and Tatar nationalists; it was unveiled in 1969.

Kiparisnoye
This small village dating back to the 13th century takes its name from the local cypress trees.

Pushkin Bust, outside the village, to the left of the highway, commemorating the poet's visit.

Frunzenskoye Population—5,000
This place, 16 km (10 miles) from Alushta, is situated in the Partenite Valley in the eastern foothills of Mt. Ayu-Dag beside two rivers, the Partenitka and the Ayan. It is named after Mikhail Frunze (1885–1925), the Civil War hero who defeated General Wrangel in the Crimea in 1920.

It was formerly known as Parthenion and the Basilica of SS. Peter and Paul was built here in the 8th century, attached to the nearby monastery on the summit of Ayu-Dag. The settlement flourished in the 13th–15th centuries. There was a harbour and a shipyard and in the middle ages it was one of the principal centres of Christianity on the southern coast of the Crimea but it was destroyed by the Turks in 1475. The church was restored in the 16th century, but it fell into decay and was completely ruined by the 18th century. Excavations made in 1871 and 1907 revealed its history; these cannot now be seen as they are on the private territory of one of the sanatoria. The monastery ruins and the fortifications which surrounded it in the 13th–15th centuries can be seen from the main road; indeed there is a good view over the whole of Frunzenskoye from up above, near Zaprudnoye.

It is a typical urban resort with many shops, a cinema, an open-air cinema, a cafeteria and cafés. There are numerous sanatoria and rest homes in the area.

The local state farm runs a nursery for decorative trees and bushes.

Lenin Monument
Frunze Monument

Artek

Not far from Gurzuf. A large holiday centre for
children, belonging to the Pioneer Organisation,
was opened in 1925 on the site of an estate that
once belonged to Prince Potyomkin's family. Altogether 24,000 children come here each summer
including foreign visitors. The centre's territory
stretches for 7 km (4 miles) along the coast, and
accommodation is divided into 4 camps. More
buildings are now under construction. In the
grounds are the *Pushkin Rock, grottoes* and a *monument* in memory of the poet's three week visit to
the Crimea in 1820.

"Enchanting region! Full of life
Thy hills, thy woods, thy leaping streams,
Ambered and rubied vines, all rife
With pleasure, spot of fairy dreams!
Valleys of verdure, fruits and flowers,
Cool waterfalls and fragrant bowers!
All serve the traveller's heart to fill
With joy . . ."

Gurzuf Population—10,000

On an island rock stand the remains of an ancient
Byzantine *fortress* called Gurzuvit. The fortress
dates back to the time of Justinian I (6th century).
This fortress was taken by the Genoese, and
reconstructed and reinforced by them in the 14th–
15th centuries. When the Crimea became Russian, Catherine the Great gave Gurzuf to her
favourite, Prince Potyomkin, and his family estate
was on the site now occupied by the children's
holiday centre at Artek (see above).

At the beginning of the 19th century a shipyard
for sailing boats was opened here. Chekhov established his holiday home here beside the sea in
1900. It is now a museum (see below). In 1911
Konstantin Korovin, the Russian artist and landscape painter, built a studio on the coast where
Soviet and foreign artists now come for holidays.

The 16-hectare (40-acre) *Pushkin Park* was laid
out by the Duc de Richelieu and Pushkin stayed
in the original chateau when he visited the Rayevsky family in 1820. Today the park contains a
very large sanatorium belonging to the Ministry of
Defence, and other buildings, some dating from
the end of the last century and others added at
different times between 1936 and 1953. The fountains here are reputedly the most beautiful in the
Crimea; one called Night is to be found in front
of Block 2, and the others are Mother Love,
Rachel, and Nymph. Also in the park is *Korovin
House* (see above). In the park's avenues, not far
from the Night fountain, are busts of famous people: Adam Mickiewicz, a Polish writer, Lesya
Ukrainka, a Ukrainian poetess, Chekhov, Gorky,
Mayakovsky and Chaliapin. In 1959 the International Youth Tourist Centre was opened to the west
of Pushkin Park.

Today there are many sanatoria at Gurzuf, besides that of the Ministry of Defence, and the town
is a favourite haunt of artists. The Gurzuf beach
is one of the best along the southern coast and

grapes, fruit and tobacco are grown in the vicinity.

Chekhov Museum, in the little, 4-room house
by the sea which Chekhov used as a holiday home,
while his real house was in Yalta. He bought it in
1900 with a piece of shore for a private beach, and
it was here that he wrote "The Three Sisters." The
museum is run as a branch of the Chekhov Museum in Yalta.

Chaika Hotel

To the west of the valley is a rocky bulge known
as Eagle's Eyrie, where white-headed griffon-vul-
tures nest. To the northeast is the 565 m (1854 ft)
Ayu-Dagh (Bear Mountain). It is 2.5 km (1.5 miles)
long, and on it are the relics of an ancient Taur-
idian settlement and also of a Genoese one. During
the Turkish occupation a garrison was quartered
here. The legend of Ayu-Dagh is as follows:

Once upon a time, when no one lived in the
Crimea except bears and panthers, the bears were
ruled by a very large and cunning old bear. From
time to time they would go out on forays to see
what they could steal, and one day they found a
wreck upon the shore. Wrapped in a bundle was
a tiny baby girl, the sole survivor of the shipwreck,
and they took her back to their den and cared for
her.

She grew up into a beautiful maiden with a
singing voice so sweet that the bears would happily
listen to her songs from morning to night. One day
after a wild storm she was walking along the shore.
She was alone because the bears had gone off hunting and she found a small boat which had been
washed up by the angry waves; lying exhausted in
the bottom of the boat was a handsome young man.
She helped him to a hiding place and nursed and
fed him there in secret. He explained that he had
been sold into slavery and decided to run away,
but had been caught in the storm.

The maiden grew to love him dearly and they
planned to steal away together; they made a mast
and sails, and one night set out across the sea. The
old bear noticed the young girl's absence and
rushed down to the sea, waded in and began to
drink and drink; the other bears joined him and
did likewise until the strong current they made
brought the little boat back to the shore. Then the
maiden sang to them again so sweetly of her love
that they stopped drinking and let them sail away.
But the old bear stood where he was in the sea,
looking out to the horizon, and after thousands of
years he can still be seen, his body full of caves,
his shaggy fur changed to thick woods and his head
a great cliff.

There is another legend of Gurzuf, this time
attached to the two Odolar Rocks which are to be
seen in the sea near the coast. They are the remnants of a cape which once existed, rising 40 m
(131 ft) above the sea. The story runs thus:

Long ago, when Gurzuf was no more than thick
forest, there was a strong fortress on the top of Bear
Mountain. There the twin brothers Prince George
and Prince Peter lived. They loved each other
dearly, fought and played side by side, and were
never apart, for on her deathbed their mother, the

Princess Helen, had asked them to revere the memory of their father and never to quarrel. Their most valued servant was the green-bearded Nimpholis; when he raised his sword in his long arms, hundreds fell, and when he breathed the grass was flattened and little waves appeared on the sea.

One night he came to the brothers and said that he had to leave them, but he gave them two presents "not to be used for any evil purpose, nor to gain anything by force." When he had gone they opened the two mother-of-pearl caskets and in one found an ivory stick with a label: "Raise me and the seas will open; lower me and you will learn the secrets of the seas"; in the second casket was a pair of silver wings and the message, "We will carry you wherever you wish."

Soon after this, news was brought to them of twin sisters of great beauty, and the brothers vowed to win their love. They hurried to the town where the maidens lived, slew the inhabitants and carried off their prizes, but instead of love they were shown scorn. They hoped to change matters by showing off their magic powers, but when they all flew together amidst the clouds and lightning, Nimpholis's voice told them to return, and the sisters laughed at their obedient cowardice. Then they entered the sea to visit the Sea King; again Nimpholis called to them to turn back, but the brothers feared the sisters would jeer at them again, and so went on until the King of the Sea killed them all with two waves of his trident. The bodies floated to the surface and were united to form twin rocks as a reminder of the sad end of all attempts to force the human heart to love.

From Gurzuf a road climbs up to the main road and further along at Botanicheskoye, formerly called Nikita (6 km/4 miles from Yalta), it passes the *Nikitsky Botanical Gardens*. The gardens are closed on Tues. & 4th Thurs. of the month. They were laid out in 1812 by the Swedish botanist Christian Steven (1781–1864) who considered it his duty to collect all the plants that were able to grow in this particular climate. He collected specimens from different parts of Europe and was responsible for the foundation of a scientific library and the museum. The garden was laid out in an area of over 24 hectares (60 acres), formerly covered by woods, and is divided into four parts: Lower, Upper, Primorsky and Cape Montedor. It developed under the supervision of Nicholas Garthvis who collected pines. He served as the director of the Garden until he died in 1860.

The Lower Park, which is the oldest part of the gardens, covers 18 hectares (45 acres); 14 hectares (35 acres) are cultivated and the remaining 4 (10 acres) left to natural woodland growth. In the cultivated part are subtropical fruit trees. The first olive grove was planted here in 1824 and now there are over 60 varieties of olives. Among the Lower Park's attractions is the grove of Cedars of Lebanon, planted in 1844. There are also oriental plane trees and stone oaks.

The Upper Park covers 4 hectares (10 acres) and is a continuation of the Lower Park. It was landscaped by Arnold Regel to provide walks among the trees and shrubs and was turned into a dendrarium at the turn of the century. There is an avenue of pyramidal cypresses, gigantic sequoias of the yew tree type, and weeping blue Atlas cedars, some dating from the earliest planting. The pride of the gardens is perhaps the *giant sequoia*, native of the Sierra Nevada in California. The first one was brought here in 1858. There is also a grove of Himalayan cedars (cedrus deodara). Here also are clematis and the fine rosarium. In the Upper Park a marble bust of Steven was unveiled in 1877; there is also one of Lenin.

To mark the centenary of the Garden in 1912, Primorsky (marine) Park was founded upon 4 hectares (10 acres) in the southern part of the cape which is protected from the cold winds by the summits of Cape Martyan. Subtropicals, including many palms which had only been grown in hothouses before, were planted here and some even manage to bear fruit; there are also some more delicate varieties that are taken inside for the winter.

Montedor Park was founded on Cape Montedor in the 1950s. It covers 7 hectares (18 acres) and stretches down from the colonnade which was built in 1912 to mark the centenary of the founding of the garden. There are coniferous trees here and the main collection of roses, and part of the area is still being developed. There is a way down to the seashore.

Altogether in the gardens there are more than 28,000 different species including over 1,000 species of trees and shrubs, and part of the work of the gardeners is to create new species which can be seen in the gardens. There are over 2,000 species of roses including a number developed here. The gardens have spread to cover more than 1,000 hectares (2,500 acres), including the affiliated experimental stations. Scientific contacts and seed exchange is maintained with 500 establishments in 60 different countries. Of especial interest is the rich herbarium with over 80,000 plants. This was captured by the Nazis during the war, but was found near Berlin and returned. Besides the library, museum and herbarium, the garden management offices and research departments and laboratories are also situated on the grounds.

At the entrance of the Botanical Gardens stands the Sechenov Medical Research Institute where the possibilities of curing tuberculosis in the Crimea are investigated.

Massandra

Today liqueurs, wines and champagne are made in this place. Winemaking began in Massandra in 1785 when winemakers came to the Crimea from the Rhine and Moselle. By 1850 the vineyards had been extended along the entire southern coast of the Crimea. The wines gradually took the place of foreign wines on the Russian market, and even won recognition at international exhibitions. It was here that, at the end of the 19th century, Prince Golitsyn, a friend of Tsar Alexander I and Minister of Education from 1816–1824, began to build up his collection of wines. In 1897 a cellar was excavated in the mountain side to hold 3.5 million litres (nearly one million gallons), apart from storing one million bottles of wine. Radiating from the central hall are seven tunnels, each 150 m (154 yds) long and 4–5 m (13–16 ft) in width, and there is a constant temperature of 10–12° C (50–54°F) in the cellar.

The collection is still preserved, having been saved from invading armies on two occasions, in 1920 and in 1941–43, when 57,000 bottles of the most precious wines were excavated out of harm's way. There are now over 400,000 bottles, the oldest being a Jerez de la Frontera of 1775, Madeira Ribeiro Secci and Muscat Lunelle.

The grounds of the *Magarach Institute* come right down to Massandra. This experimental nursery was founded in 1828 as part of the Nikitsky Botanical Garden; the situation was favourable for vines from Spain, Italy and France. It now possesses 700 different types of vines from all over the world, besides several thousand hybrids.

Massandra Park was laid out upon the orders of Count Vorontsov in the 1840s. In the park stands the 16-storey *Yalta Hotel*. To the east of the hotel stands the Donbass holiday home, one of the largest in the Crimea. Massandra also has a good bathing beach.

From Massandra a winding forest road, built by the Romanovs in 1913, leads up to the Dolossy Sanatorium, high in the pine forests at 486 m (1,594 ft) above sea level. Beyond that and even higher is Grushevaya Polyana (pear field) where there is a small open-air zoo with a family of bears, some deer, mountain sheep and other animals that inhabit the region.

Yalta Population—100,000 (1977)
Intourist organises *boat trips* here from Odessa. Two nights are spent on board, and excursions are made to Livadia and Alupka.

Yalus (the name means shore) was originally an ancient Greek settlement, and modern Yalta lies in a broad amphitheatre between two rivers, river Vodopadnaya or Uchan-su (waterfall) to the west, and river Bystraya or Perekoika (rapid) to the east. The surrounding mountains are between 1,200 m and 1,400 m (3,900–4,600 ft) high and above them towers Ai-Petri. In the valley the average annual temperature is 13.1°C (55.6°F) and in July 24°C (75°F). This is only a little less than in Genoa or Nice. The bathing season here lasts for 4–5 months. There are numerous sanatoria in the Yalta region catering for over 40,000 visitors at a time. There are many holiday homes too, large and small, and altogether the summer holiday makers total more than 2 million each year. Among other towns, Yalta is twinned with Margate and Nice. The town is now best known for the Yalta Conference of February 1945, but this actually took place in one of the most splendid of the sanatoria in Livadia (see below).

All the passenger ships sailing to the Crimea and the Caucasus come to Yalta's port, and so do local boats which ply along the Crimean coast. The quay from which the latter leave is opposite the central polyclinic.

Yalta belonged to Byzantium in the 6th century and was first mentioned in writing at the beginning of the 12th century, by an Arabian geographer, as the Byzantine port and fishing village of Dzhalita. In the 14th century it was known as the Genoese colony of Etalita. In 1475 it passed into Turkish hands, and remained under Turkish domination until it became Russian at the end of the 18th century, when Catherine the Great lavishly gave away land in the newly acquired territories to her nobles. Yalta grew in size and was surrounded by prosperous estates. It is on the site of the village of St. John's Cape which belonged to the Governor General of the area, Prince Vorontsov. With his name are associated many ventures which helped the economic development of these areas when Russia first acquired them. Thanks to him, Yalta received town status in 1837 when there were already many villas in the district, and it was fairly well known. It was proclaimed a town by the order of Nicholas I who was there at the time.

There was a break in development during the Crimean War. In 1854 French ships under Admiral Changarnier landed here and their crews robbed the local population. Yalta really became fashionable much later on when in 1861 Livadia, near Yalta, was acquired by the Imperial family. It soon became the tsar's summer residence. The town's territory was enlarged and the centre moved from Boulevard (now Franklin D. Roosevelt) Street to the embankment. Yalta was comparable to the Riviera; when Anton Chekhov lived in a house near the town, he wrote that in fact Yalta was better than Nice. By the end of the 19th century it was really becoming popular. A number of Russian doctors moved there, including Dr. Botkin, who helped Yalta to become a resort. Special credit is due to Dr. Vladimir Dmitriev who spent 35 years in Yalta; it was largely through his efforts that the resort earned universal acknowledgement. His house at Dmitriev Street 7 is marked with a plaque. Yalta is a twin town with Derby, England.

Most of the streets in Yalta are narrow and many are oneway; some, including the Promenade, are entirely closed to traffic.

Yalta embraces Darsan Hill in a semicircle and stretches up the valleys of the two mountain rivers. One can reach the top of the hill by cable car, the lower station of which is on the promenade next to the Tavrida Hotel. On Darsan Hill is the Glory Memorial with an eternal flame.

The centre of town is the promenade (as in Alushta, officially called Lenin Embankment, but known simply as Naberezhnaya meaning embankment) which runs between the two rivers. The river banks are faced with stone because the waters become rather turbulent in spring. Most of the houses standing in two rows, one behind the other, along the promenade were built at the turn of the century. Among them in the second row, and certainly the most impressive, is the Tavrida Hotel, formerly the

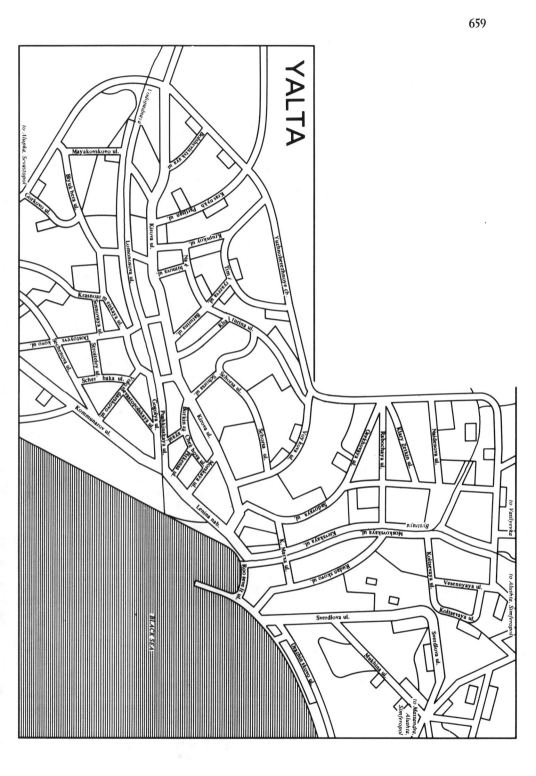

YALTA

Rossia, built in 1875. A constellation of eminent Russian public figures and professionals including writers, actors and artists have stayed there. The resort hospital, built in 1912 as the Villa Helen, stands where the second row is crossed by Kirov Street; it has 60 surgeries and supplies all kinds of medical help and advice.

The central part of the promenade joins the pleasant town garden, which was laid out in the 1880s; here is the local theatre and an open-air stage for concerts. A 12.5 m (41 ft) statue of Lenin, which was unveiled in 1954, stands at the end of the promenade which is a place for shopping and strolling. Parallel to it is Chekhov Street, formerly Vinogradnaya, a name which indicates that vines grew in it before. The building of the Lutheran church serves as a chess club and that of the Commercial Bank at No. 22 is now used by a savings bank. The House of Pioneers opposite was owned by Dr Vasiliyev until 1910. There are small side streets to wander through which give an idea of the old town. Among them is Litkens (formerly Yekaterininskaya) Street with small villas, a bank and a little square. Higher up is Kirov Street, formerly Autskaya, part of the old road which connected Yalta and the village of Autka. Walking along these streets gives a different impression of the town. There are still some quiet corners unspoiled by new construction sites.

Franklin D. Roosevelt (formerly Bulvarnaya) Street, leads from the port at the eastern end to the centre of the town and is one of Yalta's oldest streets. A small bridge over the Bystraya links it with the promenade.

From the Oreanda Hotel the promenade leads to Primorskii Seaside Park where there is a 12.5 m (41 ft) monument to Gorky, unveiled in 1956. There is another Gorky statue and, at the entrance to the park, an obelisk bearing a quotation from Lenin's 1920 decree about the development of the Crimean resorts. This has a column of 10 m (33 ft) and was unveiled in 1951. There is a monument to Chekhov (unveiled in 1953) to be seen in the park, and the local film studios are there as well.

At the end of Primorsky Park, where Yalta runs into Livadia, stands the huge building of the Rossia Sanatorium, built in 1957.

Alexander Nevsky Cathedral, Sadovaya Street 2. This cathedral was built in 1902, with an exterior in old Russian style and an interior in Byzantine style; it is open for services.

Ioanna Zlatoust Belfry, on the top of Polikurovsky Hill. This was built in the middle of the 19th century.

Roman Catholic church, This is to be converted for use as a concert hall.

Local Museum, Pushkin Street 25. Open 10–4; closed Mon. & the last day of each month. This is housed in what was formerly a Roman Catholic church, built in 1914 in late English Gothic style.

History and Archeology Museum, Zagorodnaya Street 3. Open 10–5; closed Mon. This is located in an Armenian church, built in 1914.

Chekhov's House & Museum, Kirov Street 112, in the village of Chekhovo (formerly Autka). Open 9–5; closed Mon. & Tues. & the last day of each month. This is the house called Byelaya Dacha which Chekov had built in 1899. He and his wife laid out the surrounding garden and one can imagine him writing "The Lady With the Lap-Dog" and "The Cherry Orchard" here. It was his home until his final illness in 1904.

Lesya Ukrainka Museum, Litkens Street 8. Open 10–6; closed Mon. A monument to the Ukrainian poetess stands nearby.

Biryukov's House, Krasnoarmeiskaya Street 1a. Open 10–6; closed Mon. Nikolai Biryukov was a modern writer, handicapped by blindness, who lived here.

Wine-tasting Hall, Litkens Street 1. Open 11–8. Lectures on Crimean wine production are given here.

Polyana Skazok (Fairytale Glade), Kirov Street 167, 5 km (3 miles) from the centre of Yalta, at the foot of Mount Stovri-kaya (Cross Cliff). This is an open-air museum of works by sculptors and skilled woodcarvers. Among the characters are Pinocchio, Bagheera and Mowgli. Open 9–5.

Spendiarov Monument, Litkensa Street, opposite the composer's mansion, where he lived from 1901 till 1916 and which is now Medical Workers' House. Alexander Spendiarian (1871–1928) was a classical Armenian composer who is also known by the Russian version of his name. The monument was unveiled in 1971 to mark his centenary.

Lesya Ukrainka Monument, Litkensa Street, near the authoress's house where she lived from 1909 til 1916.

Revolution Memorial, Darsan Hill. This memorial with a stele and an eternal flame was unveiled in 1967 upon the 50th anniversary of the October Revolution.

Civil War Memorial, Lenin Embankment, beyond Primorsky Park

Civil War Memorial, on Darsan Hill, built in 1967

Chekhov Theatre, Litkens Street 11

Yalta Hotel & Restaurant, Drazhinsky Street 50, in Massandra Park; tel: 35-0143. Intourist office; tel. 35–0132. This is an Intourist hotel and the best in Yalta. It stands 16 storeys high with 1,233 rooms and was built by the Yugoslavs. It has all kinds of facilities including a heated swimming pool. There is a private beach and a number of restaurants and bars and it is 1.6 km (1 mile) from the centre along the old Drazhinsky Street.

Oreanda Hotel & Restaurant, Lenin Street 35/32; tel. 32–8276, administrator 32–828. Reconstructed by the Yugoslavs. There is a swimming pool and sauna.

Tavrida Restaurant, in the second row of buildings behind Lenin Embankment, in the old Rossia Hotel. Beside it is the lower station of the cable car.

Gourmand Restaurant, on Lenin Embankment. This is a cooperative restaurant.

Vostok Restaurant, on Lenin Embankment

U Starovo Platana Café, Litkins Street

Motel & Camping Site at Polyana Skazok (Fairytale Glade), Kirov Street 167, 5 km (3 miles) from the centre of Yalta, at the foot of Mount Stovri-kaya (Cross Cliff).

Intourist organises a 4-hour *excursion* through the national park to Lake Karagol and Uchan-su Waterfall; tourists have lunch in the Lesnoi or Uchan-su restaurants.

There are also excursions to Bakhchisarai (q.v.), 125 km (78 miles) from Yalta, with lunch in Simferopol.

Lake Karagol & Uchan-su Waterfall, 7 km (4 miles) north of Yalta, on the way to Ai-Petri. The waterfall is most impressive in spring, after the rains and the thaw, justifying its name which is Tatar for "flying water." It falls from a height of 98.5 m (323 ft) and its source is Lake Karagol. It is surrounded by cliffs and wooded mountains, and Bunin wrote:

Sweeter, sweeter the mountain air.
In the woods, like faintest sighing
Comes the laughing, dancing song from
    where
Down sheer cliffs Uchan-Su's flying.
You look—and it truly frozen seems
But all the while it babbles on,
Never ceasing its tripping run
As, like transparent, snowy dust,
It rushes downwards in a living stream.

From Yalta the main road leads on to Alupka, but a lower road passes through the resorts of Livadia, Oreanda, Gaspra and Koreiz where there is plenty to see on the way.

Livadia Population—2,500

At the end of the 18th century Livadia was a Greek village called Ai-Yan-Su (St. John's Spring), but in 1860 the territory was bought for the imperial family and the place was given its original name of Livadia (Greek for meadow). The present-day buildings took the place of older palaces which were entirely demolished, with the exception of the small Byzantine-style belfry and Church of the Raising of the Cross. This church was built in 1866 and is decorated with frescoes by Monighetti and Professor Grimm.

Livadia Palace, Pushkin Street 25. A cardiological sanatorium since 1925 and, from 4th–11th February, 1945, the venue of the Yalta Conference which took place between the USSR, the USA and Great Britain. At present the palace is used as a Historical Museum and Art Gallery; open 8–8 (in winter 10–5:30), closed Wed. Intourist organises excursions to the palace from Yalta; they last for 3 hours and the distance is 18 km (11 miles).

The large palace, known as the White Palace, was built in 1911 from designs by Krasnov as a summer residence for Nicholas II. The 3-storey palace which is now Sanatorium No. 2 belonged to Baron Frederiks, the tsar's chamberlain, and the third large palace was built in New Renaissance style for the tsar's suite. Like the White Palace, these were designed by Krasnov. All three buildings were completed between April 1910 and September 1911. 2,500 people helped in the construction, sometimes even working at night by the light of bonfires and torches.

The White Palace, which contains altogether 60 rooms, was built in early Italian Renaissance style, the main motifs in the design being taken from Florence. The marble was carved by Italians and the marble decorations around the doors are taken from motifs by Raphael. The building is of white Inkerman granite quarried near Sevastopol. There are two inner courtyards, one in Moorish style and the other a copy of the Monastery Court of St. Mark's in Florence.

Livadia was under enemy occupation from 1941–44; during that time the furniture of the White Palace was badly damaged, the small palace was burnt and the sanatorium building was devastated. The 1945 conference was held in the White Hall, which is now used as the sanatorium dining hall. It was in this palace that President Roosevelt and the American delegation stayed; because of his disability, Roosevelt was allocated a study and bedroom adjoining the White Hall. The windows of the palace are so planned that they each look onto a different view, and the indoor frames are designed to look like picture frames. On a balcony on the left side of the facade is a gargoyle copied from Notre Dame in Paris.

Opposite the entrance is a small marble column inscribed in Arabic, a present to the tsar from the Shah of Persia. There is also a Moorish fountain of exquisite workmanship with "Livadia" written upon it in Arabic. It is built over a natural spring and the water still flows. On a platform in front of the palace are Roman benches of the 1st–3rd centuries A.D., and an ancient Roman well.

From the southern corner of the Livadia's third palace runs the Sunny or Tourist's Path (formerly Horizontal Path and then the Tsar's Path), a mile in length and leading to a semi-circular, columned shelter overlooking Oreanda.

In the park is an open-air theatre seating 1,000 people.

Livadia State Farm Vineyards were organised here in 1922, based on the former imperial vineyards and cellars.

Wrote Mark Twain, who was here in 1867:

"It's a lovely place. The beautiful palace nestles among the grand old groves of the park, the park sits in the lap of the picturesque crags and hills and both look out upon the breezey ocean. In the park are rustic seats, here and there, in secluded nooks that are dark with shade, there are lakelets with inviting grassy banks; there are rivulets of crystal water, there are glimpses of sparkling cascades through openings in the wilderness of foliage, there are streams of clear water gushing from mimic knots on the trunks of forest trees; there are miniature marble temples perched upon old gray crags; there are airy lookouts from which one may gaze upon a broad expanse of landscape and ocean."

Oreanda

Oreanda stretches right down to the sea; its name could be derived from the Greek word meaning "boundary" or it may be of Taurian origin and mean "rocky." There is another explanation of the name saying that it perhaps derives from that of an old fortress, Urgenda, the remains of which can be seen on the top of a cliff, Krestovaya Skala, which overhangs the swimming pool. On the same clifftop are the remains of a Byzantine church. Nicholas I purchased the territory in the 1820s, and by 1852 an imperial palace had been built here for Grand-Duke Konstantin.

The work was begun by the English architect, Henry Hunt, also responsible for the construction of Vorontsov's palace at Alupka and later that of Prince Golitsyn at Gaspra. It was in Italian style from the designs of Stakenschneider. At about the same time a landscaped park was laid out with numerous pergolas, cascades and grottoes. There are ponds shaped like the Black and Caspian Seas and the Sea of Azov. The palace was burnt down in 1882 and the remains were used in the construction of the grey Church of Pokrova Bogoroditsy (the Intercession of the Virgin) which the Academician Avdeyev designed in Byzanto-Georgian style. The interior mosaic decorations are by Salviazzi of Venice.

This church is mentioned in Chekhov's "Lady with Lapdog":

"In Oreanda they sat on a bench not far from the church, looked down on the sea, and were silent. Yalta could scarcely be seen through the morning mist. White clouds lay motionless on the mountain tops. Not a leaf stirred on the trees, the cicadas chirped, and the monotonous, hollow roar of the sea, coming up from below, spoke of rest, of eternal sleep awaiting us all. The sea had roared like that down below when there was no Yalta or Oreanda, it was roaring now, and it would go on roaring as indifferently and hollowly when we were here no more . . ."

The ruins of the palace were finally demolished in the 1940s and a sanatorium was built on the site. The park, which is one of the largest and best on the south coast of the Crimea, has remained.

The resort has been the site of a number of international summit meetings. In July 1974 for a few days it became the site of negotiations during the Soviet-American summit meeting.

Oreanda is divided naturally into two parts, upper and lower. Lower Oreanda Sanatorium was built in 1948–58. Its main building with its flat roof surrounded by a colonnade and its raised central portion embellished by a large vaulted portal, was built to look like a palace and it is one of the best sanatoria on the southern coast. The third

block has a heated indoor swimming pool, 18 m (19.6 yds) long and 2.5 m (8 ft) deep, filled with sea water.

On Khachla-Sayasy Hill on the other side of Oreanda are the ruins of a mediaeval castle and of a small church of the 10th–11th centuries. Besides Chekhov, many other writers visited Oreanda, including Gorky and Tolstoy, who liked to walk along the Tsar's Path.

The *Palace of Kichkine* (Arabic for "a little one") was built here in Oriental style with a tower like a little minaret for Grand-Prince Dmitri Konstantinovich. It was designed by the architect Tarasov in 1912 and now houses a children's sanatorium.

The Oreanda wine-plant produces sherry wines.

Beyond Oreanda stands Mt. Ai-Nikola, covered by dense woods and on the top of which there is an observation platform overlooking Yalta and the sea.

Janetta Co-operative Restaurant, not far from Oreanda, by the main road.

At the foot of the mountain is a small road junction; the upper road leads to Gaspra and further on to the west to Sevastopol. The lower one twists deviously along the coast, passing all the more famous Crimean palaces and parks. The construction of an excellent new road to Sevastopol, running above Ai-Nikola, has relieved both old roads of through traffic.

The locality situated between Krestovy Cliff and Cape Ai-Todor bears the name of Kurpaty. It has three sanatoria. The whole coast from Livadia to Kurpaty inclusive was crown land belonging to the Russian tsars. The land along the shore from the Palace of Kichkine onwards was owned either by the tsars' closest relatives, the grand-dukes, or by distinguished private citizens.

Ferro-concrete plant

Gaspra Population—17,000

Gaspra means "white" in Greek. It is now a town but the site has a long history. In ancient times it was a Tauri settlement. Some 50 tombstones from a Tauri necropolis dating back to 1,000 B.C. have been found. It appeared as a Greek settlement in the Middle Ages, approximately in the 10th century. In the 18th century, when Crimea became Russian, Gaspra was only an insignificant village and in 1865 there were no more than 200 inhabitants. Now in the area there are a great many sanatoria, some housed in new buildings and some in the former royal palaces.

Yasnaya Polyana Sanatorium. Gaspra was the estate of Prince Golitsyn, who ordered the grey stone palace to be built here in the 1830s. He called it his "romantic Alexandria." The architect was Elson (also partly responsible for Leningrad's St. Isaac's Cathedral) and the work was supervised by the Englishman Henry Hunt, who had previously overseen the construction of Vorontsov's palace at Alupka and also the imperial palace at Oreanda. The palace, in English Gothic style with two crenellated towers, is comparatively small. Its northern facade is strict and solemn, while the southern side has numerous verandas and terraces entwined by shrubbery. Building was completed in 1833 but the park was laid out somewhat later. In it is a grotto and a pond shaped like the Black Sea.

Not long after the palace was ready, Princess Golitsyna, accompanied by hundreds of attendants, moved in, taking half a year over her journey from St. Petersburg, whence she had been banished. She was slightly demented, and spent her time in the Crimea preaching Christianity to the Crimean Tatars whom she tracked down, holding a Bible in one hand and a whip in the other. She was locally known as the old she-devil.

The palace was later purchased by Countess Panina, who in 1901–1902 played hostess to Leo Tolstoy; he was in need of medical treatment and lived here for 10 months during which time he received vast numbers of visitors, but apparently never too many for the hospitable countess. They included Gorky, Korolenko, Kuprin and Chekhov. This association accounts for the present name of the Sanatorium; Yasnaya Polyana was Tolstoy's estate near Moscow. There is a memorial plaque to him beside the front door and a bust in front of the sanatorium which was sculpted by Zhuravlyov in 1971.

Lenin Monument, in the park behind the sanatorium.

The Subkhi Sanatorium, named after a Turkish Communist, has a fishpond decorated with marble capitals, brought from excavations in Greece.

The *Rosa Luxemburg Sanatorium*, named after a German Communist, is now a children's sanatorium. Its fine park, known as the second Nikitsky Botanical Garden, contains a marble well decorated with exotic birds and other sculptures. The well, the steps of which are guarded by two ancient lions, was supposedly brought from Greece. Also of interest is the rock called the White Head or Napoleon's Head.

Cape Ai-Todor

The cape, 26 m (85 ft) high, consists of three spurs almost inaccessible from the sea, with the exception of the Ai-Todor Bay, which lies between the Parus (sail) Rock and Lastochkino Gnezdo (swallow's nest). On the top are remains of the mighty Kharaks fortress built by the Taurians. Beginning with the 1st century A.D., when the Crimea was under Roman rule, a Roman garrison was stationed here. Excavations revealed a road, which led to Sevastopol (ancient Khersones), a water-supply system, sanctuaries and fortress walls. These may be seen in the juniper grove behind the lighthouse. In the 3rd century after the departure of the Romans people still lived in Kharaks. In those times Ai-Todor was called Kriumetopon (Ram's Forehead), and this is the name that appears in old navigational directions. Soon the cape was seized by the Byzantines and a monastery built in honor of St. Theodore Tiron ("recruit" in Greek). Thereafter his name was also used for the whole cape, but now nothing remains of the monastery but its foundations.

In the 14th–15th centuries Ai-Todor was known to Italian sailors and a *lighthouse* was erected there. In the 1870s this was replaced by a stone one, which, slightly reconstructed, still stands. Its light can be seen for 27 nautical miles.

The *Dnieper Sanatorium* stands on the western spur of Cape Ai-Todor. The buildings in the style of Swiss chalets date from the last century. There were two estates here belonging to members of the imperial family, and named Kharaks after the ancient Taurian fortress which used to guard the top of the cape. They have housed the Dnieper Sanatorium since 1922. In the park, which was laid out in the 19th century, the *Athenian Summerhouse* at the edge of a precipice merits attention. Its 12 grey marble columns and sandstone cornices, over 2,000 years of age, were brought from Greece at the beginning of the 20th century at the wish of a Greek princess, daughter of King George of Greece, who was married to one of the Romanovs. In the Summerhouse is a central fountain and a Spanish vase also supposed to be over 2,000 years old.

On the way to the lighthouse and on the highest point of the promontory, is an observation platform with a wide view. In 1959 a special lift, 61 m (200 ft) high, was constructed from the beach to the clifftop. A new part of the sanatorium is the pier with summer sleeping accommodation.

The *Zhemchuzhina (pearl) Sanatorium* belongs to the Ministry of Defence, and is situated in a hollow between the central and eastern spurs of the cape. The *Parus (sail) Sanatorium* (named after Sail Rock at the foot of the cape) stands on the highest, eastern spur of the cape. From the small bar next to it a stairway runs up to the *Swallow's Nest* on the central spur.

Lastochkino Gnyezdo clings like a swallow's nest to the 38-m (125-ft) high cliff. Its turrets, spires, crenellations and loopholes give one an impression of unapproachable grandeur. In the last century a general's country house stood there. It was bought by Baron Steingel, a German oil man, who ordered the house to be torn down and another to be built in the style of a Rhine valley castle. The new villa was designed by the architect L. Sherwood and built in 1912. Baron Steigel called it his "castle of love." During the great Crimean earthquake of 1927 part of the base rock crumbled into the sea and access to the castle was closed but the villa survived, in spite of its precarious situation. Between 1968 and 1971 the Swallow's nest was restored and the rock beneath was reinforced with concrete. There is now a restaurant inside the Swallow's Nest where one can see something of the interior.

The *Ukraina Sanatorium* is the largest in Gaspra. It is situated below the Dnieper Sanatorium and has an indoor swimming pool for year-round bathing.

Sosnovaya Roscha (pine grove) Sanatorium is surrounded by 100-year-old trees. A small hunting lodge remains near it.

Koreiz Population—17,000

Koreiz is situated at the foothills of Mt. Ai-Petri, 15 km (9 miles) from Yalta. In Greek the name means "inhabited." It was first mentioned in the 8th century, when it was called Kurasait Market. In the 15th century it was called Kuriz, and when, at the end of the 18th century, the Crimea became a part of Russia, it was such a miserable spot that, in spite of its name, it wasn't even listed among the inhabited places of Crimea. In the middle of the 19th century there were 130 people living here and there was a Tatar mosque, but soon it became one of the busiest settlements of the South coast due to its excellent micro-climate, much drier than that at Miskhor, and many anti-tuberculosis hospitals and dispensaries sprang up.

The *Yusupov Palace*, which was called Koreiz, is a horsehoe-shaped building standing in its own park. It was designed by a local architect, Eshliman, and was completed in 1904. In 1945 during the Yalta Conference the Soviet delegation, headed by Stalin, stayed here, and today it is used by the Soviet Union's foreign guests. Nearby is a pool in the shape of a fallen leaf.

Lenin Monument, in front of the palace; erected in 1954

The *mansion* formerly known as Kleinmichel was built at the beginning of the century. In front of it stands an ancient fountain.

Military Grave of those who fell fighting here in World War II

Next to Koreiz stands the Isar Rock with the ruins of an 11th–12th century fortress.

Miskhor

Miskhor is 12 km (7 miles) from Yalta, to the west of Cape Ai-Todor. The coastline runs down from the cape to the Miskhor health-resort region which is dominated by the rocky heights. The name is derived from the Greek "middle settlement." Miskhor originated in the Middle Ages, but by the 1850s there were only 15 people living there. It is considered to be the warmest resort on the southern coast of the Crimea.

An excellent vantage point for a view of the Cape Ai-Todor is *Kapitansky Mostik* (the Captain's Bridge). This lookout place is 17 m (56 ft) above sea level and is reached after a climb of 315 steps. Looking down one can see the Sail Rock from which seagulls and cormorants dive for fish, and also a sculptured eagle with its wings spread.

Miskhor Park, landscaped from natural woodland in English style in 1790, occupies a territory of 23 hectares (57 acres) at the foot of Ai-Todor. There is a restaurant in the centre of the park and the part nearest to the sea has formal, French-style gardens. Altogether it contains over 300 species of trees and stretches over level ground from the beach to the Kommunari Sanatorium. One of the blocks of the Kommunari Sanatorium was built in the first half of the 19th century and formed part of the estate of Countess Naryshkin.

Krasnoye Znamya (Red Banner) Sanatorium, with its battlements, silver domes and coloured mosaics, has an unusual Moorish appearance. When it was the palace of Grand-Prince Peter Nikolayevich it was called Dyulber (beautiful). It was designed by the architect Nikolai Krasnov (who also planned the tsar's palace of Livadia) and was built in 1895–97. In 1938 a second sanatorium building, designed by Solyanik to harmonise with the original palace, was constructed nearby.

Zolotoi Plyazh (Golden Beach) is considered the best place for bathing on the southern coast of the Crimea. It is 70 m (77 yds) wide and stretches for 400 m (450 yds) along the shore. This is also the site of the Intourist bathing beach. Here is the legend of the origin of the bright pebbles:

The last of the Turkish khans named Hadji-Ahmed-Aga lived in Yalta with his son Del-Balta (Mad Axe). Together they robbed the local population, but were defeated in battle by the Russians in 1771, and planned to flee across the sea to Turkey. The waves, however, refused to bear them, and the wrecked ships with the dead bodies and the rich booty of gold and silver was scattered upon the shore. Since that time it has been known as the Golden Beach.

In the sea near the beach there is a sculptured mermaid ("rusalka" in Russian) which illustrates another Miskhor legend, dating from the middle ages:

When the Crimea was still under the rule of the Turkish sultan there lived in the village of Miskhor a lovely maiden called Arzy. While she was fetching water on her wedding day she was kidnapped by the wicked Ali-Baba and his pirate band, and taken to Istanbul to be sold to the sultan. A year later she threw herself and her tiny baby boy from the tower of the seraglio into the waters of the Bosphorus. That very day a mermaid appeared at Miskhor. She is still supposed to return annually on the day of the kidnapping to visit the spring and drink the water there.

Altogether there are three statues, all executed at the beginning of the 20th century—the fountain group of Arzy fetching water from a natural spring, with the evil turbanned Ali-Baba watching her, and the mermaid with her baby on a low rock in the sea. They were made by the Estonian sculptor, Amandus Adamson (1855–1912), also responsible for the angel monument by the sea near Tallinn.

Gorky Monument. The writer lived in Miskhor in 1901–1902.

Rusalka (mermaid) Restaurant, in Miskhor Park

Miskhor Restaurant, near the quayside

Souvenir Shop, in a pavilion on the Esplanade

Photographers, Miskhor, Krymskaya Street 2 and Zolotoi Plyazh

Boats for Hire, Miskhor beach; also for hire: deck-chairs, cameras, games, towels. Boats coming from Yalta call in at Miskhor.

At the west end of Miskhor there is a pavilion

called the *Tourists' Shelter* which commands a fine view towards Alupka and the Vorontsov Palace.

Alupka Population—17,000

In the region of Alupka the mountains are particularly close to the sea, shielding the shore from the cold winds. The jagged peaks of the 1,400-m (4,590-ft) Ai-Petri hover above all of them, and above the pebbly beach. Alupka's climate is exceptionally mild, with the maximum temperature 24.6°C (76.2°F), and the minimum +3.4°C (38°F).

There are still the remains of some Byzantine structures. On the passes of the main ridge of the Crimean Mountains stand the "long walls," that used to protect the coastlands from raids by the peoples of the inland steppe.

Alupka was first mentioned as Alubik (from the Greek for vixen) in the 10th century. In the 14th–15th centuries it was known as the Genoese harbour of Lupiko. In 1475, after having been conquered by the Turks and Tatars, Alupka fell into a decline. At the end of the 18th century, when it was a picturesque Tatar village, Catherine II presented it to Prince Potemkin. It was bought in 1823 by count (later Prince) Mikhail Vorontsov (1782–1856), Governor-General of Novorossiisk Region which included the Crimea, and one of the richest and best educated men of his time. (Leo Tolstoy mentioned him in his story, "Hadji Murat.") He chose Alupka as the site for his palace which was built here between 1823 and 1846. The stone used was diorite and diabazite, quarried on the estate. They are both very hard and grey-green in colour, and the quarry they came from is now known as the Alupka Chaos.

Vorontsov was brought up in England and returned to Russia at the age of 18. He was a favourite of both Alexandra I and Nicholas I, who appointed him Governor-General of Novorossiisk. Because he was a confirmed anglophile, his contemporaries called him Lord Warrensoff, and all the more so when he decided to build his palace in imitation of an English mansion. The first designs were prepared by the English architect, Thomas Harrison, who planned a series of estates for Vorontsov in the south of Russia. The Italian architect, Francesco Boffo, also took part in the preparations. Construction began in 1830 but stopped after a year. In 1832 another project was drawn up by Edward Blore, the British architect responsible for Sir Walter Scott's Abbotsford in the Scottish lowlands and who had also taken part in the designing of Buckingham Palace. Blore built so strongly that the walls have withstood earthquakes. He implemented his project in Tudor style, uniting in modern form elements of late English Gothic and of eastern style. The towers, turrets and jagged walls follow in silhouette the outline of the Ai-Petri mountain ridge behind it, which itself reminds one of a Gothic abbey. The north facade is strict and primarily of English inspiration, while the southern side is eastern. The south entrance bears a close resemblance to the portal of the Great Mosque in Delhi; the frieze around it bears an Arabic inscription, six times repeated, a quotation from the Koran saying: "There is no happiness, but it comes from Allah." The building was carried out under the English architect, Henry Hunt, also responsible for the imperial palace in Oreanda and that of Prince Golitsyn in Gaspra. Blore's design was nothing if not magnificent. Separate architectural details, as for example the columns for the Winter Garden and the southern terraces of the palace, were brought from England. Marble came from Italy, and masons and sculptors too, to work on it. The final touches to the decorative work were not made until 1852, but even before it was completed, Vorontsov's contemporaries were astonished by the size and splendour of the structure. The three pairs of marble lions beside the steps were specially carved in Italy under the supervision of sculptor Francesco Bonanni; he was personally responsible for the sleeping lion on the right on the way up. The lions were copied from Canova's lions which decorate the tomb of Pope Clement XII in Rome.

Laurence Oliphant, the English author and traveller, was here as a young man and wrote up his impressions of the finished work in 1852 in "The Russian Shores of the Black Sea":

"We descended abruptly to the Castle of Alupka, the residence of Prince Woronzoff, passing through extensive vineyards which belong to this property. The numerous domes and pinnacles which peep out over the trees as we approach, indicate a palace, Oriental in its style and magnitude; while the glittering cupola and tapering minarets of the elegant mosque, which also adjoins it, lead us to imagine that the noble owner of all this magnificence is Hadjy-Selim-Ghiri Khan at least. A few moments more, however, and we find, to our perplexity, that we are driving under the lofty walls and frowning battlements of a feudal chieftain's fortress; and as we passed through the solid gateways into the spacious courtyard, and look up at the massive square tower and belfry to correspond, we find it difficult to decide whether the building before us bears most resemblance to the stronghold of the Black Douglas, or the palace of the Great Mogul.

"Notwithstanding the mixture of such incongruous styles of architecture, the general effect of this splendid chateau is charming."

The palace contains over 150 rooms and, in the eastern and central parts, houses a museum of art and architecture. The collection consists of the 17th–19th century works of art and has copies of some famous paintings, and also a number of Dutch, French, English, Ukrainian and Russian originals. Among them is a portrait of Vorontsov himself, and the winter garden is graced by a bust of William Pitt the Younger. The palace interior has been reconstructed and none of the original furniture is left; Vorontsov's widow took everything to Naples after her husband's death.

In 1945 during the Yalta Conference the British delegation, headed by Sir Winston Churchill, stayed in Alupka palace. Churchill liked the two rooms he used during his stay and reportedly said that the palace reminded him of Blenheim.

In Vorontsov's time a landscaped park was laid out nearby with more than 200 species of plants from all over the world. It covers more than 40 hectares (100 acres) but now the Yalta-Simferopol highway divides it in two, the Upper and the Lower Park. The Upper Park may be reached from the town side by a wide flight of steps, or from the palace side by passing the Izyum-Tash (grape stone) Rock, which got its name from a grapevine pergola that stood here. From the rock a path leads up to a pavilion built in 1848. West of the pavilion an avenue of cypresses leads to Trilbi Fountain, while to the east a path goes to the Small Chaos designed in 1837 as a pile of rocks partly natural, partly artificial, with streams of water rushing down through it. The Great Chaos lies in the northern part of the Upper Park. It is a gigantic heap of boulders, almost devoid of any vegetation. From its top opens out a view over Alupka. Between the Great and Small Chaos lies the Swan Lake with a pyramidal rock and a fountain in the middle. Next to it are two other small ponds. There are many lovely glades in the park, sometimes planted around by a particular species of tree such as chestnut or plane.

The Lower Park is divided into the palace part and the sea part. The palace part, stretching along the southern facade, is in the style of the gardens of Italian palaces, strictly symmetrical, with numerous sculptures. Besides the Lion Steps, there is the Rakovina (shell) Fountain, the Bakhchisarai Dvorik (a summerhouse with a fountain like that at Bakhchisarai), Cupid Fountain, Cat's Eye Fountain and some stone idols discovered in the 1840s in the Crimean steppes. Such idols marked the graves of the Polovets Khans. (The Polovtsy were a Turkic tribe which lived in the South Russian steppes in the 11th–13th centuries.) The sea part of the Lower Park is landscaped. In it is the classical style Tea House built in 1834 by architect Elson.

In the 1860s Alupka became a fashionable health resort and in 1938 it was proclaimed a town.

Lenin Monument, Lenin Square

Monument to the Victims of Civil War (1918–20), in the palace part of the Lower Park.

Obelisk, on the grave of Gaviryn brothers, shot during the German occupation of the Crimea in 1942.

Magnolia Hotel, Letchikov Street 23

Alupka Restaurant, at the corner of Kirov and Rosa Luxembourg Streets

GPO, Voikov Street 26

There is a *car park* near the main bus stop.

On the outskirts of Alupka is the house known as Khoba-Tyubi ("under the rock" in Tatar), which used to be run as a private boarding house for intellectuals. Gorky lived here in 1897. (Mayakovsky also visited Alupka.) At present it is part of the Shakhtyor Sanatorium.

Simeiz Population—6,400

This is the warmest and least windy place on the whole southern coast of the Crimea. From the north it is shielded by the main mountain ridge, the height of which in the Simeiz region is 1,100 m (3,609 ft). In the last century it acquired its present reputation of being an excellent health resort for the relief and cure of pulmonary tuberculosis. In 1885 the village was visited by Tolstoy, and the Ukrainian writer Mikhail Kotsyubinsky lived here from 1895 to 1897.

Local vineyards provide grapes for the Massandra Trust's wine cellars which are located on the outskirts of the village. Here Crimean Tokay, Muskat, Kagor and other wines are made.

Simeiz is still a favourite health resort and there are many sanatoria. The area called Novy (new) Simeiz was built at the turn of the century. Leninsky Prospect is the main street of Simeiz.

The fine bathing beach is protected by towering rocks. At 1,325 m (4,347 ft) the highest of these is Loshadinaya Golova (Horse's Head). To the west Koshka ("cat"—from its shape) Mountain rises 259 m (850 ft) above sea level. Some remains of the ancient Tauri tribe have been found on the mountain top in 70 barrows hidden amidst dense juniper growth; there are also the ruins of some Tauri dwellings and a small fortress. A Byzantine monastery stood here in the 9th–13th centuries but this was destroyed by the Tatars. In the 14th–15th centuries the Genoese built a fortress from the monastery ruins. The remains of both the Byzantine walls and the Genoese fortress are still to be seen in Seaside Park, on Panea Rock. Beside the sea, as a continuation of Koshka Mountain, is Swan's Wing Cliff, 85 m (279 ft) high, and at its foot lie the remains of Monk Cliff which collapsed during a severe storm in 1931. In the sea, but further along to the east, is a rock 50 m (164 ft) high called Diva (maiden) with an observation platform on the top. Koshka Mountain, Monk Cliff, and Diva Rock are all connected in the following legend of Simeiz:

Long ago there lived a wicked man who enjoyed a life of lust and pleasure. However, as he grew older he repented and went to live as a hermit, eventually gaining the reputation of being the holiest monk in this part of the world. His undeserved honour made the devil and the evil spirits very angry; and so the devil came to the old man's cave in the form of a cat and sang songs of love and the joys of married life until the monk took it by the tail and flung it out of the cave. Another day an evil spirit took on the shape of a lovely girl and appeared in the monk's net while he was fishing on the shore. She embraced the old man and he remembered his past life which had been forgotten so long. The devil and the evil spirits laughed to see his real nature showing itself, but the good spirits of the place were angered at such disrespect for all that human beings hold dear and sacred. They turned all three to stone, thus creating Maiden Rock, and, standing back from that, Monk Cliff, and overlooking the whole valley, the hunchbacked Cat Mountain, in the shape that the devil had chosen for himself.

Many Russian writers enjoyed visiting Simeiz including Pushkin, Tolstoy, Gorky and Mayakovsky.

Lenin Monument, Lenin Prospect

Baranov Sanatorium, Baranov Street, on the eastern outskirts of Simeiz. Construction began in 1910 and was completed in the 1920s.

Semashko Sanatorium, to the east of Cape Ai-Panda. Accommodation is located in what were formerly private villas and pavilions. In one of them, Miro-Mare (Block No. 3), the composer Sergei Rakhmaninov once spent a vacation.

Simeiz Observatory, on the top of Mount Koshka, was built by the amateur astronomer Nikolai Maltsev at the turn of century as part of his Ai-Panda estate. In 1906 the domes were spotted by chance by the professional astronomer Alexei Gansky who specialised in making photographs of the sun's corona and who dreamed of setting up an observatory in the Crimea. When the two men met, Maltsev immediately made over his own observatory for the use of the country's main observatory at Pulkovo, near St. Petersburg. The friendship was but short lived for Gansky drowned here two years later at the age of 37. In 1974 most of the astronomical equipment was transferred to the Crimean Observatory in Nauchny, on the way from Simferopol to Bakhchiserai, and Simeiz Observatory was turned into a satellite tracking station.

Pioneer Sanatorium, in the former Ai-Panda estate of Nikolai Maltsev, between Cape Ai-Panda

Krasny Mayak (red lighthouse) Sanatorium, just above Pioneer Sanatorium. It is located in two buildings; one of them is the villa formerly known as Xenia and built by architect Nikolai Krasnov in Gothic style in 1911. The second building is a little higher up. It was built in Moorish style in 1925.

Behind Mount Koshka lies the *Goluboy Zaliv (blue lagoon)* which was formerly called Limena ("harbour" in Greek), and the settlement of Katsiveli. Beyond Simeiz there is a branch of the Crimean Astro-physical Observatory, magnificently sited on Cape Kikineiz. The Polish poet Mikiewicz visited the cape and dedicated one of his Crimean sonnets to it:

Look toward the precipice! The sky below
Is sea. The mountain bird of fabled size,
Shot through with thunder, on that ocean
 lies,
Its mastlike plumage spread to form a bow,
More huge than rainbow's arc. An isle of
 snow
On the blue fields of water, then it flies.
A storm cloud, dropping night from dark-
 ened skies,
You see the ribbons, on its forehead glow.
 (Trans. Dorothea Prall Radin)

Inexpensive Restaurant, Sovietskaya Street
Café, Lenin Propsect
GPO, Sovietskaya Street

Opolznevoye

This is inland from the coast, beside the old road. Formerly known as Kikeneiz, the present name means "landslide" and refers to the incident which occurred nearby in 1786, when a slope 2 km (1 mile) long and 1 km (over half a mile) wide slid down into the sea carrying some houses with it.

Ponizovka

Down by the coast and reached via Katsiveli by a smaller road from Simeiz.

Parkovoye

Formerly Kuchuk-Koy. Its shore is a heap of rocks which appeared after the terrible landslide of 1786. At the end of the 18th century both Chekhov and Gorky visited Kuchuk-Koy. In 1905 Y. Zhukovsky, a collector and patron of the arts, laid out the lovely landscaped park.

Beregovoye

Formerly Kastropol, this is an old health and holiday resort. Its symbol is Iphygenia Rock, called after Agamemnon's daughter, who was sent to these parts to become a priestess in a temple of Artemis. At the top of the rock are the ruins of a small mediaeval fortress, hence the name Kastropol, which is derived from the Greek word for fortress.

Chertova Lestnitsa (Devil's Staircase)

Shatain-Mardven is a pass in the mountains here, a gigantic fissure which may be approached from the Sevastopol chaussée. Besides the blocks of rock obstructing it, there are also pieces of the ancient supporting walls of the road that once ran here, linking the old Sevastopol road with the Foros road. There are some ruins here too, belonging to a small fortress that guarded the entrance. A plaque marks the beginning of the Staircase. The ascent to it is not too steep or difficult. Pushkin climbed it in 1820.

Sanatornoye

The estate known as Melas once belonged to Prince Golitsyn. The main building now serves as a sanatorium and can be identified by its four corner towers.

Foros Population—1,500

40 km (25 miles) from Yalta and the western limit of Greater Yalta. There is a fork in the main road at the 104 km mark, and from here the way runs down to Foros.

Foros is built on the site of the Genoese colony of Foria (the name in Greek meaning tribute, tax or duty) which appears on marine maps of the 13th century. The *park* contains 384 different species of trees and shrubs and its earliest landscaping dates from 1834. The best known owner of the place was the tea millionaire, Alexander Kuznetsov, who purchased it in 1866. Between 1885 and 1892 further planting was done by Professor Klever and a gardener by the name of Albreht, both from the Nikitsky Botanical Gardens, and in 1889 Kuznetsov built a *palace* here above the sea in Russian classical style. Gorky and Chaliapin met here in 1916. The palace is now Korpus 1, the club of the Foros Sanatorium, and houses a library and a billiard room.

To the west of the park stands a *country house* called Tesseli (silence) where Maxim Gorky lived in 1933–36. A bust of the writer by Brodsky stands in front of the house.

The road behind Tesseli leads a little further westwards to *Sarych (cloth-of-gold) Lighthouse* which stands upon Cape Sarych (85 m/280 ft), the most southerly point both of the Crimean peninsula and of the European part of the Soviet Union.

At present Foros is a health resort with many sanatoria, using the buildings of former villas. The building in the shape of a starfish used to house wine cellars; it now serves as a store house for the sanatorium.

The side road which leads up from the sanatorium towards Baydarskiye Vorota has 80 bends over a distance of 7 km (4.5 miles). On the way up it passes a Byzantine church, built in 1892 following a project by the architect Chagin. The frescoes were painted by Konstantin Makovsky and Alexei Korzukhin.

Shalash Restaurant, 6.5 km (4 miles) from the main road. Beyond, the road leads into a border area and is closed.

YAROSLAVL Population—633,000

Yaroslavl stands on either side of the Volga, at the point where the Kotorosl flows into it, and where the Volga is nearly 1 km (0.6 miles) wide. The town covers an area of 200 sq km (77 sq miles) and stretches along the river for about 29 km (18 miles). Its average temperature is $-10.8°C$ ($12°F$) in winter and $18.2°C$ ($64.8°F$) in summer.

Yaroslavl is the oldest town on the Volga, first mentioned in writing in 1071 and said to have been founded by Yaroslav the Wise (978–1054) in 1010. The town emblem is a bear rampant with a halberd on his shoulder. According to legend, when Yaroslav the Wise first came to the place where he later founded the town, the local inhabitants let a bear out of its cage to chase him away, and Yaroslav killed it with his halberd.

Early in the 13th century the first school in northern Russia was established here. In 1238 the town was sacked and burnt by the Tatars, and in 1463 the principality of Yaroslavl was united with Moscow, when Prince Alexander Brukhatyi, "the Paunch," exchanged his ancestral princedom with Tsar Ivan III for some land near Moscow.

During the reign of Ivan the Terrible trade routes were developed with western Europe through the White Sea. Yaroslavl then became prominent as an important trading station for English commerce with the countries of the near east and the Volga; it began to attract foreign investments. During the Time of Troubles it was the temporary capital of the country. It was badly damaged by the Poles and the Cossacks and then, in the middle of the 17th century, was rebuilt and grew in commercial and industrial importance. An 18th-century poet wrote:

"Athens in ancient times boasted of its sciences;
Other towns were proud of the art of their hands
But you have all these in one."

Under Catherine II, in 1777, the town was made a provincial capital. Eventually the Baltic ports took much of its trade but, until the opening of the Moscow-Volga Canal in 1937, Yaroslavl continued to be Moscow's Volga port.

Today Yaroslavl is a big industrial town; its spinning mills still use English and Irish equipment installed in 1906, but apart from making cotton and linen fabric in one of the oldest factories in Russia, it also produces synthetic rubber, motor tyres, diesel engines, electro-machines, chemicals, and leather, and processes tobacco and oil. The university was founded in 1970 and there is also an Agricultural Academy, three institutes—pedagogical (at Respublicanskaya Street 108 in the building of the former seminary), medical and polytechnical—and a drama school.

The oldest part of the town is the Strelka (arrow), where the Kotorosl flows into the Volga. This is where the Kremlin once stood, and where one of the oldest civil buildings, the *Metropolitan's Palace* built in 1690, still survives.

The centre of Yaroslavl is Sovietskaya Square (formerly Ilinskaya Square) with the *Church of Elijah the Prophet* in the centre. The houses around the square were built as regional government buildings in 1781–84. From this square run two streets, Kirovskaya and Bolshaya Oktyabrskaya, which end in two towers, *Znamenskaya*, a lookout tower dating from 1658–59, and *Uglichskaya* (1635), both built onto the town's old earthen wall. Unfortunately Znamenskaya Tower which was built of wood burned down in 1958. Pervomaiskaya (formerly Kazansky) Boulevard, in the centre, is a favourite place for the local inhabitants to take the air and Kirovskaya is a good shopping street.

Yaroslavl is probably the best place for visitors who wish to see *old Russian churches* because it was not damaged at all during World War II. Most of the churches in the town were built by merchants, and in the centre of the town there are still many typical Russian *mansion houses* which add to the special charm of the place. The oldest of the merchant mansions is the 17th-century *Ivanov House* at Tchaikovsky Street 4. The familiar trading arcades used to be very large; all that remains is the western end of the northern block. An unusual feature is the pillared rotunda, built in 1813–18

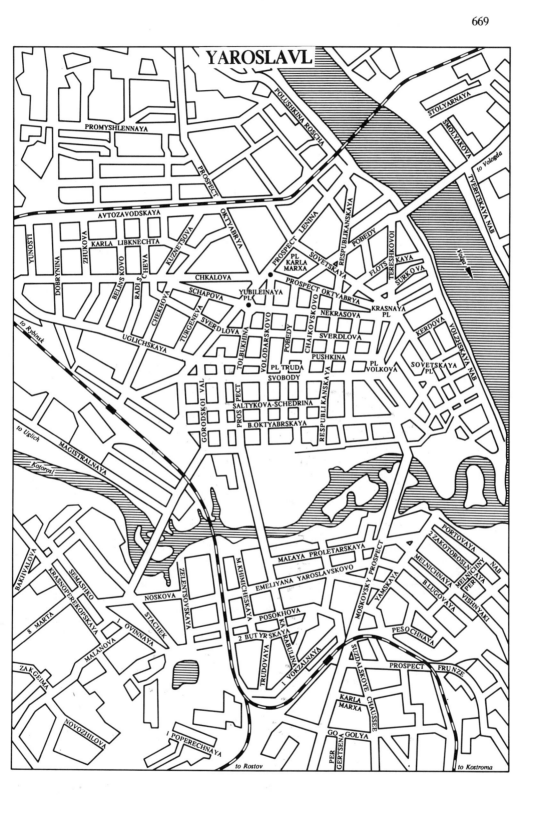

YAROSLAVL

STOLYARNAYA

SMOLYAKOVA

PROMYSHLENNAYA

POLUSHKINA ROSCHA

to Vologda

TVERITSKAYA NAB

PROSPECT

AVTOZAVODSKAYA

OKTYABRYA

Volga

YUNOSTI

KARLA LIBKNECHTA

ZHUKOVA

KUZNETSOVA

PROSPECT LENINA

RESPUBLIKANSKAYA

POBEDY

DOBRYNINA

BELINSCHEVA

RADISCHEVA

PL
KARLA
MARXA

SOVETSKAYA

FLOTSKAYA

TRESHKOVOI

SURKOVA

CHKALOVA

SCHAPOVA

CHEKHOVA

YUBILEINAYA
PL

PROSPECT OKTYABRYA

KRASNAYA
PL

to Rybinsk

UGLICHSKAYA

TURGENEVA

SVERDLOVA

TOLBUKHINA

VOLODARSKOVO

POBEDY

CHAIKOVSKOVO

NEKRASOVA

SVERDLOVA

KERDOVA

VOLZHSKAYA NAB

PUSHKINA

PL
VOLKOVA

SOVETSKAYA
PL

GORODSKOI VAL

PROSPECT

PL TRUDA

SVOBODY

RESPUBLIKANSKAYA

to Uglich

MAGISTRALNAYA

SALTYKOVA-SCHEDRINA

B.OKTYABRSKAYA

Kotorosl

PORTOVAYA

2 ZAKOTOROSLNAYA

BAKIVALOVA

KRASNOPEREKOPSKAYA

SEMASHKO

ZELENTSOVSKAYA

M.KHIMICHESKAYA

MALAYA PROLETARSKAYA

MOSKOVSKY PROSPECT

MELNICHNAYA

MELNICHNAYA
PER

NOSKOVA

EMELIYANA YAROSLAVSKOVO

YAMSKAYA

B.LUGOVAYA

VISHNYAKI

8 MARTA

STACHEK

OVINNAYA

POSOKHOVA

PESOCHNAYA

MALANOVA

2 BUTYRSKAYA

KARAULINAYA

ZAK GEIMA

TRUDOVAYA

VOKZALNAYA

SUZDALSKOYE CHAUSSEE

PROSPECT FRUNZE

NOVOZHILOVA

1 POPERECHNAYA

KARLA
MARXA

GO GOLYA

PER GERTSENA

to Rostov

to Kostroma

but reconstructed after the arcades suffered a fire in 1831. The churches include several from the 16th and 17th centuries which are of considerable interest. In particular the Yaroslavl frescoes are unique for the colossal area they cover; Moscow churches are smaller and consequently have less interior wall space. Yaroslavl is also noted for having the best wood-carvings in Russia.

Spaso-Preobrazhensky (Transfiguration of our Saviour) Monastery, Podbelsky Square 25. This monastery houses the town's main museum complex, open 10–5; closed Mon. and the first Wednesday of each month. It was founded at the end of the 12th century, the first ecclesiastical school in the north of Russia being opened here soon afterwards. When the wall and towers were built in the 16th century, the monastery became important for defence, and it was here that Ivan the Terrible and his court took refuge when, in 1571, the Tatar khan Devlet-Ghirai was approaching Moscow. By the 18th century Yaroslavl was far from the front line, and the monastery lost its defence significance; in 1787 it was closed as a monastery, but in 1788 became the residence of the archbishop.

The wall is 2.8–3 m (9–10 ft) thick and 818 m (895 yds) in circumference. The Holy Gates at the entrance were built in 1516, and the clock that was installed above them in 1624 was purchased from Moscow and brought here from the Spassky Tower of Moscow Kremlin; it was later moved to a more eminent position in the monastery belfry (see below). The frescoes inside the archway illustrating St. John's apocalyptic vision were painted in 1664. Within the walls is the *Transfiguration Cathedral*, built in 1516 by Moscow architects. It was one of the most revered and rich cathedrals in Yaroslavl and through the years has been altered several times. The frescoes were added in 1782. It was in this monastery in 1795 that the manuscript of "The Lay of Igor's Host" was discovered, a medieval epic which provided the subject for the opera "Prince Igor" and about which there is here a permanent exhibition.

Besides the cathedral, the monastery also comprises the adjoining, classical style *Church of Yaroslavl Miracle-Workers* (1831) (now used as a cinema), a lecture hall and the 16th-century *Krestovaya Refectory Church* which houses the Natural History Museum. The *Bell tower of Our Lady of Pechorsk*, also 16th-century, was reconstructed in the 19th century. The clock came from the Spassky Tower of the Moscow Kremlin in 1624, but was first sited in the bell tower over the Holy Gates and only later reinstalled here. The big bell was cast in 1738 and the chimes ring out to mark the hours and the halfhours. The tower is open for groups of visitors; inside is an exhibition of bells and from the top there is an excellent view over the town. The *monks' cells* of the 16th and 17th centuries are now the home of the Historical Museum. Restoration began in 1958 and is still in progress. The *Art Gallery* (open 10–5; closed Fri. and the last Wednesday of each month) contains 18th–19th

century portraits and paintings by leading Russian artists.

The Church of Elijah The Prophet, Sovietskaya Square in the centre of town. Open in summer 10–6; closed Wed. Built in 1647–50 by the richest citizens in the town, this is the most impresive church in Yaroslavl and certainly the one in the best condition; its bell tower stands 36 m (118 ft) high. It is exceptionally well preserved and is open as a museum. Its frescoes were painted in the course of a few months in 1680, the work as usual being in the hands of a whole team of artists. The frescoes are divided into 6 horizontal strips: the first showing Christ arisen, the second the Gospel story of His life on earth, the third the lives of the Apostles, the fourth the life of Elijah (to whom the church is dedicated), the fifth the life of his disciple, Elisha, and the bottom one being purely decorative. The baroque iconostasis dates from 1716 but the icons are older. The tsar's and patriarchs' seats, said to have been made for Alexei Mikhailovich and Patriarch Nikon in the 1760s, were brought here from the Church of St. Nicholas the Wet in 1930. If St. Elijah's is closed, tourists should apply to the museum authorities in the Spaso-Preobrazhensky Monastery to have it opened.

Group of churches in *Korovniki*—Portovaya Naberezhnaya 2. To reach Korovniki, cross the bridge near Spaso-Preobrazhensky Monastery and then turn left onto Malaya Proletarskaya Street, left again onto Melnichnaya Street and left again onto a good new road. The church of *Ioann Zlatoust* (St. John Chrysostom) was built in 1649 and is one of the most picturesque churches in Yaroslavl. It has a 17th-century iconostasis and frescoes painted in 1732–33 by local artists. The outside of the altar window is decorated with coloured tiles. It was built for summer use while the smaller church, *Vladimirskaya* (1669), was heated in winter. Between the two churches stands a 17th-century octagonal *bell tower*; it is 37 m (101 ft) high and is known as the Candle of Yaroslavl. The two churches are linked by a wall with *Holy Gates* (end of the 17th century) in the centre.

While still across the Kotorosl, drive back from Korovniki and over Bolshaya Moskovskaya Street to reach the *churches of Fyodor and Nikoly Penskovo*, Malaya Proletarskaya Street 59. The larger, summer church is closed but the smaller, winter one, built together with its bell tower in 1691, is open for services.

Ioanna Predtechi-v-Tolchekovye (St. John the Baptist), Kotoroslnaya Naberezhnaya 69, is on further in the same direction and beyond the new bridge over the Kotorosyl. The whole population of the region round about contributed either physically or financially to the building of this church in 1671–87. With its 15 domes it is very grand, and is the best church of 17th-century Yaroslavl. The bricks imitate wood-carvings and the impression is that they are made of wood. There are also many coloured tiles in its decoration. The frescoes painted in 1694–95 took only 5 months to complete and they are among the finest of their time. Instead of the usual Last Judgment on the west wall, there are 6 illustrations of the Song of Songs. There is an 18th-century iconostasis, and the 45-m (148-ft) *bell tower* was built in about 1700. The museum is open 10–6; closed Tues.

Go on by the same main road, under the railway bridge and bear right. Here, at No. 56, stands a *church* built about 1900; it is decorated with iridescent tiles and there are art nouveau lilies around the windows. It is now used as a sports hall. Behind it, further on and in to the right, is the small, red-brick church of *Nikola-na-Melenkakh* (meaning "by the little watermills"), Stachek Street 60. The church was built in 1672 and the frescoes were completed by Yaroslavl artists in 1707. On the northern wall is shown the invasion by Tamerlane; Vasily I marched out to meet him, but took the precaution of ordering that the famous icon of Vladimir be sent to Moscow to protect his capital. On the day it arrived, news came that Tamerlane had changed his course. The painting shows the icon being carried from Vladimir to Moscow; even in the grimy fresco one can see in the background Moscow's St. Basil's Cathedral and the Ivan Veliky Bell Tower.

To reach *Peter and Paul Church*, Peter-and-Paul Park, turn back from Stachek and then right. The 57 m (187 ft) bell tower makes a good landmark. The church is painted blue and white, and stands by ponds in the park. It was built in 1736 in honour of Peter the Great by the owner of a Yaroslavl textile factory of which the tsar was patron; the church is in the St. Petersburg baroque style of the 18th century and resembles the Peter-and-Paul Cathedral in Leningrad. The groundfloor church was used in winter, and the upstairs one in summer only. The building now serves as a club. Further on in the park is the mansion that the church belonged to, now used as a hospital building.

Return now across the Kotorosl to see the rest of the town; the following churches are described more or less in the order they come, if one turns to the right and follows the Kotorosl towards the Volga embankment, and then turns to the left along it.

Church of St. Nicholas the Wet, Tchaikovsky Street 1. The church was built by Afanasy Luzin and Andrei Lemin as a summer church in 1665–72. Only in 1986 during restoration work was it discovered that instead of the usual foundations, the church stands upon a single gigantic granite boulder, 12 sq. m in area and over 2 metres thick. The builders simply took advantage of the natural stone and saved themselves a lot of trouble. The architects copied the Church of Ioann Zlatoust in Korovniki, and the outside of the altar window is framed with coloured tiles in the same way. The frescoes were completed in 1673; on the left side of the fresco of the Last Judgement on the west wall, among a group of sinners, are depicted foreigners in 17th-century European dress and Persians in turbans. At the same address is *Tikhvinskaya Church* (1686), designed for winter use. The

Belfry of Nikita-the-Martyr (of Pereslavl-Zalessky fame) is nearby.

Dmitri Solunsky Church, Bolshaya Oktyabrskaya Street 41. This church was built in 1671 and altered in the 18th and 19th centuries. The frescoes were painted by local artists in 1686.

Bogoyavleniye (Epiphany) Church, Podbelsky Square. Built 1684–93 and with its facade decorated with tiles. Inside, the frescoes by local artists date from 1692, and there is a 17th-century iconostasis of beautifully carved wood with icons of the same date.

Church of St. Michael the Archangel, Pervomaiskaya Street 67. This church was bulit in 1657–80 and has a bell tower. Its frescoes were painted by local artists in 1731; they are divided into nine strips and give the impression of brightly coloured tapestry.

Spasa-Na-Gorodu Church, Pochtovaya Street 3. The church was built in 1672 and decorated with frescoes by local artists in 1693; of these the most interesting are the two lower strips which show processions, and battles between the larger towns.

Nikolai Rublenova Church, on the site of the Kremlin. The church was built in 1695; it contains no frescoes.

Iliinsko-Tikhonovskaya Church, Volzhskaya Naberezhnaya 5. This church, built in 1825–31, is the last of a series to stand on the site of the very first one to be built by Yaroslav the Wise. It is now in a bad state of repair.

Nikoly Nadeina Church, Narodnyi Pereulok 2a, inland from the embankment. Open in summer 9–5; closed Tues. This was Yaroslavl's first parish church, built in 1622 from donations from the merchant Nadei. The frescoes of 1640–41 are among the oldest in Russia, painted by a group of 20 artists, but many were subsequently painted over, and the church itself has suffered much alteration. Inside, to the left of the entrance, is a fresco of Adam naming the animals, then comes the story of the Garden of Eden and then that of Noah's ark. Around to the right is Jonah and the whale and the crossing of the Red Sea. Some of the frescoes are reminiscent of miniatures stuck to the wall. The iconostasis (1751) was constructed following a sketch by Fedor Volkov, founder of the Russian national theatre in 1750.

Rozhdestva Khristova (Nativity) Church, Kedrova Street. This church was built in 1644 and reconstructed in the 19th century. The frescoes were painted by local artists in 1683. There is a 17th–18th century iconostasis and the mid-17th century *belfry* is one of the loveliest examples of its kind in Yaroslavl. On the top of a small dome on the southern side is the very ornate and beautiful Korsunsky Cross.

Blagovesheniye (Annunciation) Church, Volzhskaya Naberezhnaya 51. The church was built in 1688–1702. The 18th-century domes resemble flower buds; the frescoes were painted by local artists in 1709.

Vladimirskaya Church, Rubinskaya Street 44. This church was built in 1670–78.

Fyodorovskaya Church, Yaroslavsky Street 74. This church was built in 1687 and contains frescoes painted by local artists in 1715; they are like illustrations to fairy tales, showing the details of secular life in Peter the Great's time. There are battles, architecture and ships depicted.

St. Alexander Nevsky Chapel, Krestyanskaya Street, in front of the modern, 3-storey building of the Regional Administration Office. This is a very decorative little red-brick building.

Kazan Convent Cathedral, Pervomaiskaya Street 19a. Built in 1845, this cathedral used to house the regional archives but is now a planetarium.

Ancient Russian and Applied Art Museum, in the Metropolitan Bishop's Palace (1670), Volzhskaya Naberezhnaya 1. Open 10–5; closed Fri. The house was built as a residence for the Metropolitan Bishop of Rostov. The art works here are designated "ancient and applied" and include icons, embroidery and many other ecclesiastical treasures. Here is the miracle-working icon of Our Lady of Tolga (1314).

Tolgsky Monastery is near Yaroslavl, founded in 1314 by Bishop Trifon of Rostov. The wonder-working icon in the museum came from the Vvedeniye Bogoroditsy Cathedral there, and there is a legend about its appearance. In 1314, when Bishop Trifon was coming from Beloozero, he disembarked on the right bank of the Volga for the night. He was woken by a bright light coming from the left bank of the river, and saw a bridge leading over the water towards it, so taking his crozier in his hand, he set off over the bridge. On the other side he saw the source of light to be an icon of Our Lady suspended in midair, too high for him to reach. He prayed there and then returned to his lodging place. In the morning he found his crozier missing and remembered what he had thought was a dream. There being no bridge, he was taken across the river by boat and there between the trees was the icon he had seen and beside it, his lost crozier. The news quickly reached Yaroslavl, and by midday a crowd had gathered on the spot. It was decided to make a clearing and build a church, and work began without delay. More people came and there were plenty of willing hands. The building took shape throughout the afternoon and by evening was ready for consecration. It was August 8 which ever afterwards was kept as a feast day.

By the embankment and close to the *Metropolitan Palaty* (art museum) are the 19th-century churches *Ilinskaya* and *Tikhinskaya*.

Art Gallery, in the Governor General's House. Open 10–5; closed Fri.

Natural History Museum, in Krestovaya Refectory Church in Spassky Monastery.

Planetarium, in the building of Kazan Convent Cathedral, Pervomaiskaya Street 19a. Open 11–7; closed Tues.

Nekrasov Monument, on the embankment. The poet Nekrasov spent most of his life in this region. His home at Karabikha, 16 km (10 miles) south of Yaroslavl, is now a museum. This monument by Motovilov was unveiled in 1958.

Marx Monument, Karl Marx Square. Made in 1972, by Kerbel (who was also responsible for the Marx bust in Moscow).

Trefolev Monument, Trefolev Street. Leonid Trefolev (1839–1905) was a local newspaper editor, writer and poet, many of whose poems became popular songs. The statue by Chernitsky was made in 1960.

Lenin Statue, Krasnaya Square; by Kozlov, unveiled in 1939.

Lenin Statue, Lenin Prospect. Put up in 1958, designed by Listopad.

Obelisk, in the garden opposite St. Elijah's church. This commemorates Revolutionary Fighters who died during the 16-day White Guard revolt of July 1918; this was largely financed by money given by the French Ambassador Joseph Noulens to coincide with British and French landings in Arkhangelsk. A large part of Yaroslavl was destroyed by fire. The obelisk was made by Kozlova in 1958, replacing the old wooden monument which had stood there for forty years.

Dzerzhinsky Monument, Dzerzhinsky Prospect; sculpted by Kirsanov in 1977.

Tolbukhin Monument, 950-Let-Yaroslavlya Street. Marshal Tolbukhin Fyodor (1894–1949) was born in this region.

Victory Obelisk, Tchaikovsky Street. Erected in 1975 to commemorate the 30th anniversary of VE-Day.

World War II Memorial & eternal flame, off Sovietskaya Street, in Chelyuskintsev Garden; built in 1968. Around the square stands a group of 18th–19th century houses in provincial classical style.

Volkov Drama Theatre, Volkov Square. The theatre was built in 1911 and named after Fedor Volkov (1729–63) who founded the Russian national theatre in 1750. Volkov inherited his stepfather's factories in Yaroslavl, and then organised his own private theatre. His company was the first to stage "Hamlet" in Russia. He wrote and translated a number of plays, but none have survived. In 1752 it was decided to found a court theatre in St. Petersburg and he was summoned to court together with his company. In the same square is a *statue of Volkov* by Solovyov, unveiled in 1973.

Puppet Threatre, Komitetskaya Street 8

Philharmonia Concert Hall, Komitetskaya Street 11

Circus, Svobody Street 69

Butusov Town Park, Tchaikovsky Street

Shinnik Stadium, Trud Square

Yaroslavl (Intourist) Hotel & Medved (bear) Restaurant, Ushinsky Street 40/2, tel. 21–275. There is an Intourist office in Room 203, tel. 21-258.

Volga Hotel & Restaurant, Kirov Street 10. This was formerly the Bristol Hotel.

Tsentralnaya Hotel, Volkov Square

Russky Chai Cafe, Volzhskaya Embankment 43

Bank, Komsomolskaya Street 7. Open 9–12:30; closed Sat. & Sun.

GPO, Podbelsky Square 22/28. The building is that of the old Yaroslavl Hotel, built in 1855.

Yaroslavl Department Store, Trud Square

Souvenirs, Kirov Street 11. Rostov enamelwork is on sale here.

Book Shop, Kirov Street 18

Gift Shop, Lenin Prospect 38

Taxi Rank, Podbelskaya Square; tel. 90081, 90082

Tolgsky Monastery

The monastery is near Yaroslavl, on the left bank of the Volga, where the small river Tolga flows into it. (A bad road leads there, branching off from the way to Vologda; it could more easily be reached by river boat.) Tolgsky is one of the most ancient monasteries in Northern Russia, founded in 1314 by Bishop Trifon of Rostov. Within its walls are *Vvedeniye Bogoroditsy Cathedral* (1681–83), *Vozdvizhenskaya Winter Church* (17th cent.), the summer *Spasskaya Church* and *Nikolskaya Gate-church* (1672).

The monastery has been closed for many years, but in connection with the Millennium of the Baptism of Russ in 1988 it was given back to the Church. After restoration it was reopened as a convent which includes an old people's home.

Intourist organises excursions from Yaroslavl to Karabikha (16 km/10 miles) and Nikulskoye (27 km/17 miles), both described below, and to Rostov Veliki (q.v.) 54 km/34 miles) and Pereslavl-Zalessky (q.v.) (130 km/81 miles).

Karabikha

Here, 16 km (10 miles) to the south of Yaroslavl along the main highway towards Moscow and on the right is *Nekrasov's House*, open 10–5:30; closed Mon. and the last Wednesday of each month.

Nikolai Nekrasov (1821–77) was the leading Russian poet of the second half of the 19th century. He was one of 14 children, of Polish extraction, and destined for a miltiary career. In St. Petersburg he wrote vaudevilles to support himself and his first volume of verse was published when he was 19, but it was not until he was 40 that he was able to support himself comfortably. It was then, in 1861, that he bought Karabikha along with a small distillery (malt house). This was just after the abolition of serfdom and many properties were changing hands.

The estate had once belonged to Prince Golytsin's family; a Golytsin had served at some time as governor of Yaroslavl. Nekrasov later sold it to his brother, Fyodor, and only kept an annex for his own use in the summertime. He spent the summers of 1867–1875 here. The distillery was considerably enlarged. Among Nekrasov's visitors were Saltykov-Schedrin, Alexander Ostrovsky, and Grigorovich. Fyodor's grave is surrounded by bushes, near the carpark at the entrance. The *museum* was

opened in 1949 and there is a *bust* of the writer in front of the main building. Inside is the ticket office and a display of photographs. The annex is to the right of the main building as one comes out. The portrait of Catherine the Great in the dining room belonged to the Golitsyn family. Nekrasov's favourite room, where he worked, was the sitting room with a bust of Walter Scott in the corner. The formal grounds in front of the house were known as the French Park. This area was used by the Soviet Army during the Second World War and the avenues of trees were planted afterwards. Behind the house the grounds slope down to the river Kotorosl which flows about 500 m (550 yds) from the estate. The landscaped grounds on this side were known as the English Park. After visiting the house and Nekrasov's annex, walk downhill to the west of the houses through the park to find the distillery and then climb to the upper pond to see the little cascade running down through the woods.

Nikulskoye

Near this village, 30 km (19 miles) northwest of Yaroslavl along the Uglich road, is the Cosmos branch of the *Yaroslavl History Museum*. Open 10–5:30; closed Mon. and the first Wednesday of each month. Here there is an exposition about Soviet space exploration, and the largest hall tells of the life and achievement of Yaroslavl textile worker Valentina Tereshkova, who was born in the neighbouring village of Maslennikovo in 1937 and who, on June 16, 1963, became the world's first spacewoman. A wooden cottage shows what her childhood was like before the family moved to Yaroslavl in 1945.

Military Glory Museum, Uglichskaya Street 44a

Chaika (seagull) Cafe, "Seagull" was Valentina Tereshkova's identification with ground control while she was making her space flight.

YASNAYA POLYANA

Intourist organises excursions here from Moscow, 195 km (121 miles) away.

This was the birthplace and beloved home of Count Lev Tolstoy (1828–1910). Its name means "bright glade" and of it he wrote: "Without Yasnaya Polyana I can hardly think of Russia or of my attitude to her."

The estate lies 1.5 km (1 mile) to the left of the main road. At 201 km (125 miles) south of Moscow, a visit here may count as a long day trip from the capital; in fact Tolstoy often walked from here to Tula—and on three occasions he went as far as Moscow. He would probably have died in Yasnaya Polyana as well as spending most of his life there if, 10 days before his death, he had not left home and caught pneumonia, so that he died at a small railway station not far away. His grave surrounded by nine oaks is in the park, on Stary Zakaz Hill. The present grounds are only part of the vast estate which Tolstoy inherited from his mother. The large house in which he was born was later dismantled and sold by the family.

Preserved in the existing house are portraits of the writer by Repin and Kramskoy (the latter painted in 1873 while Tolstoy was working on "Anna Karenina"), a library of 22,000 books in more than 20 languages of which Tolstoy himself spoke 13, a phonograph presented by Edison, an English-made grandfather clock, an old Remington typewriter and a portrait of the real Anna Karenina. The desk at which Tolsoy's wife transcribed "War and Peace" many times is in her bedroom. The other simple furnishings remain much as they were during Tolstoy's lifetime. Most of the contents of the house were evacuated to Tomsk during the second world war, which certainly saved them from destruction.

There is now a literary museum in the building where Tolstoy organised a school for the peasants, and one of the curators is his last secretary, Valentin Bulgakov.

The Museum Ticket Office is by the main gates of the estate. The museum is open 10–5:30; closed Mon., Tues. and national holidays.

Restaurant & Cafe, just outside the gates of the estate.

Yasnopolyansky Souvenir Shop, on the main road

YUZHNO-SAKHALINSK (Japanese: Toyohara) Population— 160,000

Yuzhno-Sakhalinsk is in the south of the island of Sakhalin, which is called Karafuto in Japanese; in Manchurian the name means "the rock on the surface of the black river." The town serves as the centre of the Sakhalin Region, which includes the Kuril Islands as well as Sakhalin itself and forms part of the Russian Far East within the Russian Federation.

Sakhalin Island is over 960 km (600 miles) long and between 26 and 201 km (16 and 125 miles) in width. It lies between the Seas of Okhotsk and Japan and is separated from the mainland by the Tatar Straits. La Perouse Strait divides it from the Japanese Island of Hokkaido.

Sakhalin was discovered in 1643 by a Dutch seaman by the name of de Vries, but he thought that it was part of the island of Hokkaido. The first Russian to sail beyond the eastern coastline of Sakhalin was Vasili Poyarkov in 1643–46, but it was the explorer Gennadi Nevelskoi (1813–76) who established that Sakhalin was indeed an island and not a peninsula as had been thought.

From 1855 Sakhalin was ruled jointly by Russia and Japan, then in 1875 it became Russian. Before the Revolution Sakhalin was for many years used

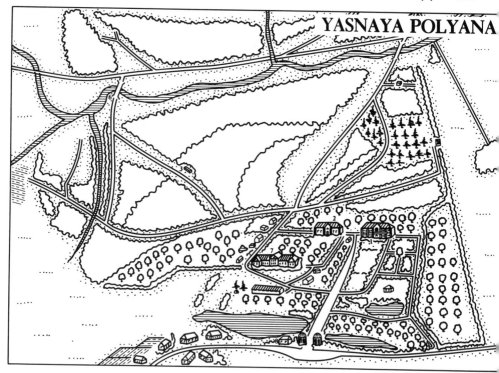

YASNAYA POLYANA

1. Lev Tolstoy's House-Museum
2. Literary Museum
3. Tolstoy's Grave
4. Well
5. Tolstoy's favourite seat
6. Tolstoy's bathing place
7. Volkonsky's House
8. Kamenka Cottage

as a place to which convicts were exiled. Political prisoners served their sentences there together with criminals, so the Russian writer, Anton Chekhov called it "hell on earth." He spent three months in Sakhalin and wrote in his book, "The Island of Sakhalin" (1894): "Undoubtedly, the right of first exploration belongs to the Japanese, and the Japanese were the first to occupy southern Sakhalin."

In 1905 the southern part of the island, up to the 50th parallel, was ceded to Japan. They occupied the northern part, too, from 1920 to 1925, when it was returned to Russia. The southern part was returned to Russia in 1945 according to the Yalta Agreement.

Yuzhno-Sakhalinsk grew up in place of the former settlement of Vladimirovka. In August 1882 Russian settlers built the first wooden houses at the place where the river Bogatka flows into the Susuya.

There is a district in the town called Cheryomushki, with modern 4-storey buildings just as in Moscow and Erevan.

Local Museum, Kommunistichesky Prospect. Distinguished by its stone lion and formerly the Karafuto Historical Museum.

Planetarium and Vostok Cinema, Sakhalinskaya Street. Formerly the Higashi Honganji Temple.

Lenin Monument, Lenin Street. Sculpted by Evgeny Vutetich.

War Memorial, commemorating the 30th anniversary of the victory over Japan.

Obelisk of Friendship

Chekhov Drama Theatre, Kommunistichesky Prospect 27

Sports Palace, Kommunistichesky Prospect

Gagarin Park, laid out by the paper magnate, Fujiwa Ginjiro

Yuzhno-Sakhalinsk Hotel, Kommunistichesky Prospect 36

Sakhalin Hotel, Lenin Street 181, tel. 366–29

Tourist Hotel, at the corner of Sakhalinskaya Street and Prospect Mira

Voskhod Restaurant, Kommunistichesky Prospect 86

Sakhalin Restaurant, Khabarovskaya Street 84

Sakhalin Department Store, on the corner of Sakhalinskaya and Lenin Streets. This neo-classical building was formerly the local branch of the Hokkaido Colonial Bank.

Gorny Vozdukh (mountain air) Tourist Centre, 3 km (2 miles) from town, on the slopes of Rossiiskaya Hill

Singorskiye Mineralniye Vody (Blue Mountains mineral waters) Sanatorium, 17 km (11 miles) from Yuzhno-Sakhalinsk

Intourist organises the following excursions from Yuzhno-Sakhalinsk:

YUZHNO-SAKHALINSK

Kholmsk (Japanese: Maoka) Population—55,000
It is a naval town situated in the southwestern part of Sakhalin on the shore of Tatar Strait, 68 km (42 miles) west of Yuzhno-Sakhalinsk.

The first Russian settlers arrived here in 1870 in the clipper "Vsadnik" (horseman) and later many ex-convicts flocked here from all parts of the island in search of a living.

During the Second World War a considerable part of the town was burnt and destroyed, but restoration was completed by the end of 1974. Among the houses remaining from the 19th century is the brick building of a garage that used to be a warehouse.

Bogatsva Morya (riches of the sea) Museum
Kholmsk Hotel

Nevelsk (Japanese: Honto) Population—30,000
This port is situated on the western part of Sakhalin on the shore of the Sea of Japan. It is 44 km (27 miles) south of Kholmsk and about 100 km (62 miles) from Yuzhno-Sakhalinsk. The Tsushima branch of the warm Kuroshio current flows against the island here, and the area is shielded from the east winds by the mountains of the South-Sakhalinsk Range. The warm climate has earned the Nevelsk Region the name of Sakhalin's Crimea.

Nevelskoi Monument, outside the Seamen's Club

Lenin Monument, sculpted by Leonid Torich
Seamen's Monument, commemorating those who lost their lives.

Poronaisk (Japanese: Shikuka) Population—35,000
The town is 293 km (182 miles) north of Yuzhno-Sakhalinsk on the east coast of Sakhalin. It dates from 1869 when the Russians founded the military post of Tikhmenevsky at the mouth of the river Poronai. The name of the river and consequently of the town, too, comes from the Ainy language in which "poro" means "big" and "nai" means "river." The Ainy people used to live here, but now there are only about 20,000 of them on the Japanese island of Hokkaido.

The growth of Poronaisk as an industrial centre and a commercial port started in 1945.

Molodyozhny Park
Sever (north) Hotel

ZAGORSK Population—120,000
Intourist organises excursions here from Moscow 71 km (44 miles) away.

This town on the rivers Koshura and Glimitsa grew from a small settlement called Sergiyevsky Posad, founded around the monastery in 1762. It kept this name until it received town status in 1925 and was renamed Sergiyev. Then in 1930 it was called Zagorsk, after Vladimir Zagorsky (1883–1919), a revolutionary well known for his political work who was killed by an anarchist's bomb.

The local handmade-toy industry dates back to the 14th century and Zagorsk is particularly renowned for its carved woodwork. Its other factories produce agricultural machinery, furniture, textiles, educational appliances, garage equipment and iron and concrete piping. There are also poultry and fish farms.

The *Troitse-Sergiyeva Lavra (Trinity Monastery of St. Sergius)* is one of the most important architectural and historical monuments of mediaeval Russia, and is also the centre of Russian Orthodoxy today. Founded in 1345, it soon rose to be the religious capital of northern Russia. Its founder, St. Sergius Radonezhsky (1322–92), was the son of a Rostov nobleman named Kirill and his wife Maria. He was christened Bartholomew (Sergius was the name he took when he became a monk) and moved with his parents to live in the small town of Radonezh. The first Troitskaya (Trinity) Church on the site of Zagorsk, and that which subsequently gave the monastery its name, was a small wooden structure in the forest built jointly by Bartholomew and his elder brother, Stephan, who was already a monk and who should, strictly speaking, be considered the real founder of the monastery. The brothers lived here in seclusion for a long time.

Besides this monastery, St. Sergius also founded others around Moscow and elsewhere, and monks from here continued his work; they were responsible for the founding of the Solovetsky Monastery on an island in the White Sea. The history of Russia in mediaeval times is closely connected with that of the Troitse-Sergiyevsky Monastery, for Sergius was influential and played an important role in Grand-Prince Dmitri's rousing of the Russian people against the Tatars; the Russian princes and soldiers were blessed by Abbot Sergius before the Battle of Kulikovo Polye against the Tatars in 1380.

In 1408 the whole region, including the monastery, was again devastated by the Tatars, and afterwards the Abbot Nikon found Sergius's body uninjured among the smoking ruins of the monastery, a sure sign of his sanctity. (St. Sergius is patron saint of Russia, and his feast day is July 18.) Abbot Nikon managed to rebuild the monastery by using much of the treasure he had been able to save.

The monastery grew very rich as the Moscow nobility donated large sums of money and other valuables to it. Its lands included nearly 100 separate estates, and in 1764, when the church was deprived of its right to own serfs, this monastery had 106,000 serf peasants. It conducted such a brisk trade in grain, honey, wax and salt that it even sent its own merchant ships to Norway via Archangelsk. It was also a centre of ancient Russian culture and the second most important educational centre after Kiev. In the 15th century a calligraphic workshop developed here where scribes and artists created their own style of writing, illuminating and illustrating it with colourful miniatures. A famous monk named Maxim the Greek lived here and worked upon his scientific studies, and it is thought that the first Russian printer, Ivan Fyodorov, studied here under him.

The monastery's reserve of fighting men num-

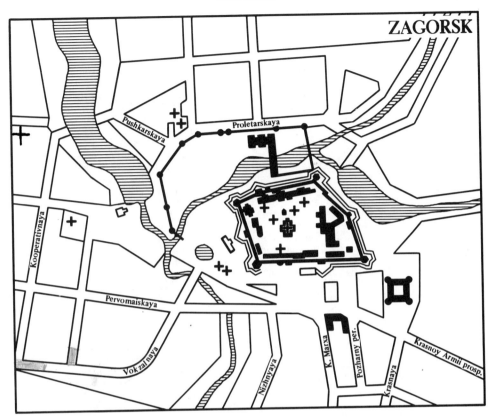

bered 20,000, and in 1540–50 the strong fortress wall was built, 1 km (0.6 miles) in circumference, 15 m (49 ft) thick and with twelve towers. One of the latter was later demolished and the two most westerly ones, Kelarskaya and Pivnaya, were rebuilt into living quarters and no longer served as defence towers. In 1608–10, during the Time of Troubles, the monastery was besieged for 16 months by 30,000 Poles, but although there were only 1500 men to defend it, it never surrendered. The fate of the whole of Russia was dependent upon the outcome of the siege.

It was at this time that the town earned its coat-of-arms, gules St. George and the Dragon of Moscow and below azure fortress walls argent closed by gates sable, while over the wall appears a tower argent roofed by a dome or and protected by two halberds or.

In 1612 an army of volunteers headed by Kosma Minin and Prince Dmitri Pozharsky halted at the monastery for rest and blessing before they set off southwards to liberate Moscow from the Poles, and in 1681 and 1689, during the mutinies of the royal Streltsy guards, the boy-tsars Peter and Ivan sought refuge here from their sister Sophia who was plotting against them. Unfortunately not a single tower is preserved in its original form, but the duck on the top of Utochya (Duck) Tower was mounted there for the young Peter to shoot at for his entertainment. The monastery remained an important fortress defending Moscow until the end of the 17th century.

In 1744 it was granted Lavra status. A Greek word, lavra means "main" or "the most important." Originally it meant a group of hermits, living in separate cells but under the direction of one abbott, as in the Monastery of the Caves in Kiev. As the monastery grew, the community came to include monks of less ascetic inclinations as well. The tradition of isolated living within a larger monastic community is still, however, practiced in Russian Orthodox communities today, for instance at Pechory Monastery near Pskov. There used to be four Lavra in Russia; the other three were Kievo-Pechorskaya in Kiev, Alexandro-Nevskaya in St. Petersburg and Pochayevsko-Uspenskaya in Volyn.

Troitsky (Trinity) Cathedral was built between 1422 and 1427, with a single dome in the Suzdal-Vladimir style. Its frescoes date from the 16th century and there are many icons of value and interest among those in the second, third, and fourth rows of the iconostasis. The icon of the Holy Trinity is a copy of the one painted by Andrei Rublyev especially for this cathedral; the original is now in Moscow's Tretyakov Gallery. Daniil Cherny is another famous icon painter who worked for this cathedral. The present building was erected on the site of the wooden Church of St. Sergius which

Abbot Nikon had built over the founder's grave. The body of St. Sergius, which is still visited by pilgrims, lies inside the cathedral in a dull silver sarcophagus presented by Ivan the Terrible. The silver canopy over it weighs 409 kg. (8 cwt.) and was a gift from Empress Anna. The porch was added to the southern wall of the cathedral in the 18th century.

Dukhovksya Church (The Church of the Descent of the Holy Spirit). This church, built in 1476–77 by architects from Pskov, stands to the east of Troitsky Cathedral. It was among the first of the monastery buildings to be constructed in brick. The top of the single dome was once used as a watchtower.

Church of St. Nikon, adjoining the southern wall of Trinity Cathedral. This church was built in 1548 and reconstructed in 1623.

The *Uspensky (Assumption) Cathedral* reminds one, by its size and shape, of the Uspensky Cathedral in the Moscow Kremlin. It was built in 1559 for Ivan the Terrible to commemorate the capture of Kazan and Astrakhan from the Tatars, and was consecrated in 1585. The frescoes were painted in 1684 by local and Yaroslavl artists. Near the west door of the cathedral, outside, is the tomb of Tsar Boris Godunov, his wife and two of his children. The five domes of the cathedral are painted blue and are decorated with golden stars.

Gate-Church of St. John the Baptist is decorated with frescoes and with an iconostasis in classic style, this church was built in 1692–99. Under the gateway arch are frescoes showing the life of St. Sergei Radonezhsky.

Mikheyevskaya Chapel, built in 1734 over the grave of Mikhei, a disciple of Sergei of Radonezh.

Smolenskaya Church, behind the belfry, is named after the principal icon, Our Lady of Smolensk. With its wide entrance, the church resembles a decorative rotunda. It was designed in 1746–48, probably by Prince Dmitri Ukhtomsky, and was restored in 1955–56. The *Belfry* stands near Smolenskaya Church and, although founded in 1741, was the last of the whole ensemble to be completed, being finished only in 1769. Money for its construction was donated by three tsaritsas; it was founded at the request of Anna Ioanovna, then continued by Elizabeth and completed during the reign of Catherine II. The first plan was by Ivan Michurin, but in 1753 the design was changed by Ukhtomsky who added two more tiers, making it five tiers and 98 m (322 ft) high. At one time it boasted forty bells.

The *Refectory* and *St. Sergius's Church* stand together by the monastery's southern wall. They were built in baroque style in 1686–92 upon the order of Tsars Peter and Ivan. The whole structure is 73 m (80 yds) long and gaily painted. The fact that the enormous refectory hall was roofed by a dome without any supporting pillars demonstrates the advanced architectural knowledge of its Russian builders.

St. Sergius's Well, just outside the Uspensky Cathedral. The small chapel was built in the 17th and 18th centuries to cover the well. Many of the pilgrims who visit the monastery bring bottles to fill with holy water.

The *Hospital Buildings*, with the *Church of SS. Zosim and Savvati*, built in 1635–37, are the oldest of the secular structures in the complex.

Chertogi was built at the end of the 17th century upon the order of Peter the Great and gaily decorated with paintwork and coloured tiles, this was once the tsar's palace. The interior dates from the 1740s and one of the halls has a painted ceiling depicting the victories of Peter the Great. The building, which lies near the northern wall of the monastery, now houses the Theological College (founded in 1749 although the building bears the date 1814) and an Ecclesiastical Academy. It was partly restored in 1950 and 1960. Pokrovskaya Church there is open for services.

The *Metropolitan Bishop's House* is an 18th-century building which was reconstructed from the 17th-century cells of the archimandrites. Stoves decorated with coloured 17th-century tiles can be seen inside.

Other buildings here include the *Treasury* (17th-century and reconstructed in the 19th century), a *sacristy* built in 1781 in early classical style and an *obelisk* built in 1792 upon the order of Metropolitan Platon.

History and Art Museum, in the vestry, the former Palaty of the Metropolitan Bishop Platon (18th-century) and adjoining buildings. At the entrance to the historical department of the museum in the cellar is a necropolis with tombstones. The main collection is displayed in the order in which it was presented to the monastery, and includes 14th–17th century icons and gifts from Russian nobles, and from the tsars Ivan the Terrible and Boris Godunov. The museum contains one of the richest collections of Russian ecclesiastical art with some icons by Simon Ushakov (1626–86). Besides 18th- and 19th-century portraits, there are collections of 17th- to 19th-century furniture, pottery, china and glass. The fabrics are French and Italian of the 14th and 15th centuries, and there are Persian, Syrian, and Turkish tissues of the 17th century. The Russian handicrafts displayed include carving, fabrics, costumes, embroidery, metalwork and toys. There is a good collection of distaffs and other domestic items and also English carriages of the 18th century. Local woodwork may be purchased at the small souvenir stall. The museum is closed Fri. and on the 30th of each month.

Toy Museum, Krasnoi Armyi Prospect 136. This is the only museum of its kind in the Soviet Union. It was founded in Moscow in 1918 but was transferred to Zagorsk in 1931. Its rich collection of more than 30,000 toys spans the centuries, from the Bronze Age to the present day. They are made of all sorts of materials and come from all parts of the world, though many are of local production. There is a laboratory in the town where scientific research on toys is carried out.

The most popular of all Zagorsk toys are the Matryoshka dolls, devised at the end of the last century. A Zagorsk turner, Zvyozdochkin, adapted the construction of the traditional Russian toy—wooden eggs that pack one inside the other and are painted in Russian style. A local artist, Malyutin, painted the first of Zvezdochkin's dolls as a typical Russian peasant girl in apron and headscarf and called her by the popular peasant name of Matryona. Now the dolls are enjoyed in many other parts of the world and one has even made a space flight. As distinct from other Russian Matryoshkas, the Zagorsk Matryoshka is all painted with gouache and covered with varnish. They are from 4–18 cm (1.5–7 in) high and the largest ones have as many as 17 smaller ones in diminishing sizes inside.

Apart from visiting the inside of the monastery and the toy museum, it is worth while driving a little further along Red Army Prospect and then turning left to circle the outside of the monastery walls. In 1-Proletarskaya Street and adjoining the monastery is a red brick hospital in what used to be almshouses and the toy factory is beside this. On the small hill on the right, at Novo-Progonnaya Street 1/5, is *Ilyinskaya (St. Elijah's) Church*, built in 1773 and open for services.

There are three churches on Red Army Prospect. *Vvedenskaya na Podole* was built in 1547 by the noble Ivan Khabarov. It was reconstructed in 1969, but its decor has remained very similar to that of the Dukhovkskaya Church inside the monastery. *Voznesenskaya Church* (1766–79) is the latest example of a baroque church in Zagorsk. It has an impressive belfry and stands on the immediate right on the main road, just before the Zolotoye Koltso Restaurant (which is on the opposite side of the road). *Krasnogorskaya Chapel* (1770) in Red Square is another example of late baroque style, and the *Uspenskaya (Assumption) Church* at Bolotnaya Street 39 was built in 1769. *Nikolskaya Church* is also in Bolotnaya Street, up and back from the main road, on the left on the way into town from Moscow. Once used as a factory, it was under reconstruction at the time of writing.

Lenin Monument, Soviet Square

Druzhba Hotel & Restaurant

Zolotoye Koltso Restaurant, to the left of the main road

Sever Restaurant, to the right of the main road

Rossianochka Cafe, to the right of the road at the beginning of town, just after the level crossing

Beryozka foreign currency shop, on the left, opposite the entrance to the monastery. Credit cards are also accepted here.

Souvenir Shop, in front of the main entrance to the monastery.

ZAPOROZHYE Population—895,000

In the 15th and 16th centuries the Ukrainian Cossacks settled in Zaporozhye Sech on the Island of Khortitsa on the Dnieper. The site of the first settlement is where the Pioneer Garden is today. The island is 12 km (7 miles) long and 2.5 km (1.5 miles) wide with an area of 3,000 hectares (7,500 acres) and can be reached from the old town. It was first mentioned by the Greek Emperor Constantine VII Porphyrogenitus in his manuscript written between 946 and 953. The name Khortitsa derives from that of the pagan god Hors, who was said to protect travellers, and the island formed a resting place on the great Dnieper Way from Constantinople to Kiev.

The Dnieper rapids were well known in ancient times and feature in the manuscript written by Emperor Constantine. Each of the nine rapids had its own name and character. They are Kodatsky, Sursky, Lokhansky, Zvonetsky, Nenasytets, Vovnigsky, Budilovsky, Lishni and Volny. The name of Budilovsky, meaning "awakener" was due to the tragic story of a pilot who, while steering his vessel through the rapids, relaxed for a moment through exhaustion and only awakened to meet his death. Lokhansky means "washtub," because tradition has it that no one has ever passed it without being given a bath. The most terrible of all was Nenasytets the Insatiable: even the most daring pilots said a last prayer as they approached it. Navigation on the Dnieper used to be impossible because of the rapids. The first attempt to avoid them was made in the 18th century, and in the 19th some bypassing channels were built. The river was finally made navigable along the whole of its course by the construction of the Dnieper Hydro-electric Station (known as Dneproges). This was the first big hydropower station to be built in Russia.

The 600-year-old oak, which legend maintains is the one under which the Zaporozhye Cossacks wrote their challenging and insulting letter to the Turkish Sultan, can be seen 5 km (3 miles) outside the town in Gogol Street, Verkhnyaya Khortitsa. There is certainly no doubt about its being the oldest tree in the Ukraine; the girth of its trunk measures 6.32 m (20 ft 9 inches). Another story says that in 1648 Bogdan Khmelnitsky addressed his warriors here with an appeal that in battle against the Poles they should be as strong and firm as this oak tree.

In 1770 a fortress was founded here as part of the Dneprovsky defence line of seven fortresses against the Turks. It was founded in the estuary of the Moskovka river and was called Alexandrovsk after Prince Alexander Golitsyn, commander-in-chief of the 1st Russian Army.

In 1787 Catherine the Great stopped here on her way to the Crimea. She is supposed to have wished to visit the headquarters of Zaporozhye Sech on Khortitsa Island but the Cossack regulations forbade any woman's presence. Catherine had therefore to spend an uncomfortable night in a chair—*Catherine's Armchair*, as the appropriately-shaped cliff opposite the hydro-power station is called. Nice as it is, this is an impossible tale as the Sech was no longer in existence in 1787, and in any case she could never have climbed the cliff.

The fortress was demolished in 1798 when the border with Turkey was at the edge of the Black Sea and the defence line had lost its importance. The military settlement was transformed into a civil one, retaining the original name and many of the demobilised soldiers settled in the town. The site

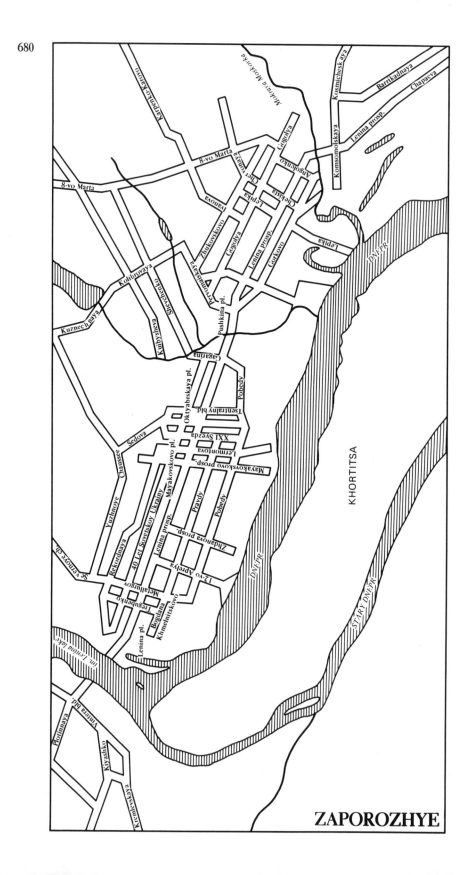

ZAPOROZHYE

of the fortress is near Maly Kolkhozny Rynok, between Kommunarov, Frunze and Khortitskaya Streets where there is now a small garden. In 1806 Alexandrovsk was proclaimed a town. Its coat-of-arms (per fess vert crossed rifles with fixed bayonets and gules a bow sable with three arrows directed downwards) symbolised Russian superiority over the Tatars.

Andrei Zhelyabov (1850–81) was the organiser and leader of the People's Will revolutionary party. In November 1879 he lived here as Timofei Cheremisov from Yaroslavl, a merchant who planned to open a tannery. The long days spent in preparing the site, which was located near the railway, were actually used for digging a tunnel with a view to blowing up Alexander II's train. However, the bomb failed to explode and the train passed Alexandrovsk undamaged. The plot was carried out later in St. Petersburg and most of the revolutionaries were executed.

The records say that before 1917 there was only one 3-storey house in the town and nine with 2 storeys. No more than 120 were brick built. In 1917–21 it was one of the centres of the Makhno Anarchist Movement. The name of Zaporozhye (meaning "beyond the rapids") was given to the town for the first time in 1921.

Zaporozhye saw much fighting in 1918–1919. With the development of industry the new town appeared 10 km (6 miles) away from the old one. Its first streets were laid out in the 1930s and grew up as a model socialist town with multi-storey houses and wide avenues. Metallurgov Prospect is over 30 m (33 yards) from side to side. 70 percent of the town was ruined during the occupation from 1941 to 1943, but it had finally recovered by 1949. Today the local population is 68 per cent Ukrainian and 25.5 per cent Russian, the rest belonging to many different nationalities, including Tatars, Jews, Greeks, Bulgarians, Georgians and Poles.

The main highway leads into the city along Kosmicheskaya Street via the old city and then it joins Lenin Prospect, the main thoroughfare of the town proper. It was formerly known as Cathedral Street, after the cathedral which was demolished in the 1930s. It runs from Yuzhny Vokzal through Svoboda, Zhovtneva and Mayakovsky Squares for a distance of over 15 km (9.5 miles). The old and the new parts of the town are linked by a kilometre-long causeway, 30 m (33 yards) wide and 33 m (108 ft) high. The quay in the old part of the town has been there since boats first plied the Dnieper. In 1880 the artists Repin and Serov visited this place, and Repin made several sketches for his famous painting "The Zaporozhtsi Writing a Letter to the Turkish Sultan," using the dockers as models. Very few old buildings have remained in the city. They are mainly located in the vicinity of Lenin Prospect (formerly Cathedral Street). The building of the former Russian Bank for Foreign Trade stands on Chekista Street. The former college for boys (Zhukovskovo Street 66), as well as that for girls (Leppik and Gogol Streets) are now branches of the Pedagogical Institute. The former

Technical College is now one of the buildings of the Machine-building Engineering Institute (Zhukovskovo Street 64). The Lenin Cinema (at the corner of Gorky and Leppik Streets) was built as the Narodny Dom in 1901. The television centre with its tower was built on the town's highest point, 80 m (262 ft) above sea level; the tower is 194.5 m (638 ft) high.

Local industry in 1861 included a fat-melting factory and three brickworks, but it began to grow with the completion in 1873 of the railway line linking Alexandrovsk with Moscow and, two years later, with the Crimea. Foreign capital, particularly of German origin, poured into this region and helped found local steel production and the development of agricultural machine building. Thus it is that many of the industrial enterprises of Zaporozhye have a pre-revolutionary history. The German-owned Kopp Agricultural Machinery Plant, for instance, was reorganised in 1921 into the Kommunar Plant. The Kirov Aluminium Plant is younger; it went into production in 1933. At present, besides aluminium it produces alumina, silicium and ferro-powder. Other branches of industry here now include chemical, electrical and food production. In all there are 300 industrial enterprises in the town.

Zaporozhets cars are locally made and other factories include Zaporozhstal, a huge steel mill. Before the war it had three blast furnaces, one of them the largest in the world. During the war the equipment was dismantled in 45 days and taken to the Urals. What remained of it was destroyed by the Nazis so it had to be entirely rebuilt. 50,000 workers from all over the country helped in the reconstruction of this plant.

There are pedagogical, medical and machine-building engineering colleges in Zaporozhye. The local railway junction links Moscow and Kharkov with the Crimea and with Krivoi Rog where there are highly developed railway depots and repair yards.

When the Mayor of Lahti in Finland was looking for a Soviet town to twin with his own, he was led by an old guidebook which described Zaporozhye as "a small town, founded by the Cossacks, a daring and honest people." According to this book, there was one mill, an agricultural machine plant and a wood processing factory in the town. All this seemed very similar to Lahti and the Mayor's choice was approved. The Finns were much surprised when they arrived in modern Zaporozhye and saw so much industry and the newly constructed regions of apartment houses. Besides Lahti, Zaporozhye's sister towns include Bellefore (France) and Birmingham (Great Britain).

The Dnieper Hydro-electric Station (Dneproges) was the first big hydropower station to be built in Russia. The plans began in 1905 and construction in 1927, to mark the 10th anniversary of the Revolution. Many foreign firms were consulted before its completion on May 1, 1932, and the General Electric Company supplied most of the equipment to build up its 653,000 kilowatt capacity. Alexandrov was the Russian engineer-hydrologist and Vesnin headed the team of architects.

The dam is 760 m (831 yds) long and 60 m (106 ft) high; it has 49 supports and 47 sluices and the radius of the curve is 600 m (656 yds). Lenin Lake, which formed behind the dam, covers 327 sq. km (126 sq. miles) and in places its depth is as much as 65 m (213 ft). Three-quarters of the whole construction was destroyed during the war when in December 1943 the retreating Germans larded the dam with 25 trainloads of explosives. Three Soviet soldiers managed to cut the cable leading to the fuse, in spite of the ceaseless German fire and the wintery weather. Their names remained unpublished but soon after the liberation of Zaporozhye from the enemy, a monument to the unknown soldier who had saved the dam was put up; only 21 years later was Nikolai Karuzov credited with leading the party on their daring exploit. It took 3 years before Dneproges began to produce current again but it had regained its former capacity by 1950. The completion of a second power house (Dneproges-2) on the left bank of the river doubled its output which is now 1.5 million kilowatts.

Local Museum, Chekista Street 29. Open 10–5; closed Fri. Built in 1913, it used to house the District Council Authority.

Museum of the Zaporozhye Region, Khortitsa Island. The whole island is a historical reserve, but there are sanatoria and children's camps on it.

Art Gallery, 40-Let-Sovetskoy-Ukrainy Street 76. Open 11–7; closed Mon. and the last day of each month.

Exhibition Hall, Zhovtneva Square. Open daily 10–6.

Glinka Monument, Lenin Prospect 183, outside the Glinka concert hall. Mikhail Glinka (1804–57) was a famous Russian composer. This monument was designed by Strakhov.

Monument to Participants in the 1905 Uprising, in Railway Terminal Square. It was unveiled in 1930 in commemoration of the 25th anniversary of the uprising. Zaporozhye has more than 80 monuments commemorating the revolutionary and military exploits of the Zaporozhians.

Revolution Obelisk, in the garden in Svoboda Square; the obelisk was unveiled in 1927 on the common grave of revolutionaries killed in 1917. In 1965 an eternal flame was lit to commemorate the 20th anniversary of VE-Day.

Lenin Monument, at the end of Lenin Prospect; the sculpture by Lysenko and Sukhodolov is faced with pink marble and stands 8 m (25 ft) high. It is mounted on a granite postament which is 12 m (39 ft) high and stands where there is a good panoramic view over Lenin Lake and Dneproges. It was unveiled in 1964.

Dzerzhinsky Monument, Dzerzhinsky Street

Soldier's Monument, in the garden on the right bank of the Dnieper.

Tank Monument, in Radyanska Square commemorating the soldiers who liberated Zaporozhye in 1943; unveiled in 1960. Another tank monument had already been unveiled in 1944.

World War II Victims' Monument, near the Agricultural Research Station and marking the common grave of 36,000 people killed during the German occupation of 1941–43.

Victims' Obelisk, near Shevchenko Club, marking the spot where 6,000 people (mostly Jewish) were killed during the occupation.

Alexander Vinter Monument, on Vinter Boulevard, on the right bank of the Dnieper; unveiled in 1966. Academician Alexander Vinter (1878–1958) was the Soviet power engineer who headed the construction of the Shatura and Dnieper (Dneproges) power stations.

Schors Music & Drama Theatre, Lenin Prospect 41.

Glinka Concert Hall, Lenin Prospect 183. Built in 1952 with seats for 860.

Circus, Rekordnaya Street 41

Kirov Palace of Culture, on Metallurgov Prospect. In front of it stands a monument to Sergei Kirov.

Metallurg Stadium, Sportivnaya Street 21, Metallurgov Park. Room for 30,000.

Zeleny Gai Park, the name means "green grove" and the park, which has an open-air cinema, a children's playground and a boating station, occupies 155 hectares (388 acres). It commands a panoramic view towards the Dnieper, Dneproges and the Island of Khortitsa.

Oak Grove Park, in the old part of the city

Mir Park, there is a restaurant with room for 1,000

Bathing beaches, at Zhdanov Prospect

Zaporozhye Hotel (Intourist) & Restaurant, Lenin Prospect 135, tel. 33–2556. The local Intourist office is here.

Dnepro Hotel & Restaurant, Lenin Prospect 202

Teatralnaya Hotel & Restaurant, Lenin Prospect 41

Yuzhnaya Hotel, 21-Partsyezda Street

Pivdenni Hotel, Pravda Street 53

Camping Site, 22 km (14 miles) from town, on the main road at the 1008 km mark.

Tavria Restaurant, Lenin Prospect 208

Sich Restaurant, Lenin Prospect 234

Zolotoi Kolos Restaurant, Sotsgorodka Market

Marichka Restaurant, Lenin Prospect 48

Pivdenni Restaurant, Gorky Street

Kazachi Dozor (Cossacks' guard) Restaurant, at the entrance to the town on the main road from Moscow. The restaurant is built in old Ukrainian style, to resemble the thatched huts of a fortified Cossack settlement.

Lahti Restaurant, Lenin Prospect 144

Chaika (seagull) Restaurant, on Khortitsa Island, in Oak Grove Park by the river

Bank, Dzerzhinsky Street 23

Kashtan (foreign currency) Shop, Lenin Prospect 147

Bookshop, Lenin Prospect 38

GPO, Lenin Prospect 131

Ukraina Department Store, Lenin Prospect 147

Charovnitsa Souvenir Shop, Lenin Prospect 190

Rubin Jewelry Shop, Lenin Prospect 50

Coral Gift Shop, Lenin Prospect 187

Outside the town a ZIS-5 Lorry mounted on a pedestal stands at the fork where there is a sign to Grigoryovskoye.

Obelisk to the memory of soldier-drivers of 1941–45 with the inscription: "We were on the move day and night, and experienced many difficulties but the driver stuck firmly to the wheel . . ."

Intourist organises *horseback riding excursions* from Zaporozhye.

ZHELEZNOVODSK (Ferruginous springs)

Population—85,000

Intourist organises excursions here from Pyatigorsk, 25 km (16 miles) away.

Zheleznovodsk lies 6 km (3.5 miles) to the right of the main road at the foot of Zheleznaya Mountain. It has a mountainous climate like that of the central Alps, and the average annual temperature is 10°C (50°F). The Zheleznovodsk springs give up to 1,000,000 litres (250,000 gallons) of water a day. The water contains carbonic acid, hydro-carbonate-sulphate, sodium and calcium. The springs have temperatures varying from 10–55°C (50–130°F). The town now has about 15 sanatoria, some located in the old villas and some in new buildings.

When Dr. Friedrich Haaz discovered the first mineral spring here, he proposed calling it Konstantinovskaya Mountain in honour of Grand-Prince Konstantin but the name never caught on. Where Spring No. 1 is now situated, Haaz discovered a massive well built of huge stones which made it clear that the local people knew and used the spring. Haaz also found the remains of baths roughly cut in the rocks and constantly filled with hot mineral water. However, Zheleznovodsk was established as a spa in 1819 when General Alexei Yermolov (1772–1861), then commander of the Russian army in the Caucasus, came here. The first residential house was built here upon his order. Springs Nos. 1 & 2 were faced with stone and wooden pipes were installed for feeding water into the drinking fountains. By 1825 a park was laid out here and in 1842 the Cossack village of Zheleznovodsk grew up around it. By 1856 as many as 24 springs had already been discovered and documented. Many of these were found by Professor Alexander Nelyubin (1785–1858), a Russian pharmacologist, and some of them bear his name. The Zheleznovodsk waters are particularly useful in the cure of metabolic, digestive and kidney diseases. The development of the spa was much accelerated by the construction in 1875 of the railway between Rostov and Vladikavkaz (now Ordzhonikidze) via Mineralnye Vody. In 1898 a direct railway line from Beshtau to Zheleznovodsk was laid which increased the number of people coming here for cures. (To reach Beshtau by road, turn left off the main road.) The existing building of the Slav-

anovskiye Baths was built in 1875, and in 1893 the Ostrovskiye Baths (now mud baths) were built in Mauritanian style by Suzor. In 1912 the building of the New Baths was constructed.

Mount Zheleznaya (Iron) is of typical laccolit rock. A fine park covers the southern foothills of the mountain adjoining the natural forest. A spiral path leads up the mountain side. To the right of the square leading to the Ostrovskiye Baths, a road and then an attractive flight of steps lead up to *Verkhnyaya Ploschadka* (Upper Square) and the *Pushkin Gallery*, gracefully built of ironwork with stained glass windows. It was brought here from Nizhny Novgorod (now Gorky) Fair in 1901 and was named after Pushkin in 1907 in memory of the 70th anniversary of the poet's death. Alexander Pushkin visited Zheleznovodsk twice in 1820 and 1829. The Gallery is open 10–5 when there is an exhibition inside.

Further over and up to the left is the *Tehlmann Sanatorium*, housed in a palace built for the Emir of Bukhara at the turn of the century. Much of it is in his own Muslim, Central Asian style (windows and doors with keyhole arches over them, balconies and terraces with lacey stonework, ceilings faceted like the vaulting in a mosque) but much is also in art nouveau style including windows, doorways, interior decoration and a fine tiled stove.

A chestnut avenue leading to the right from the Pushkin Gallery brings one to the springs. A little further on and to the left under a small bridge is a statue of a group of bears; this is the point at which to turn either up the mountain or around the ring path. The length of the ring road around the Zheleznaya Mountain is 3.6 km (2 miles). The excursion around the Mountain and along the ring road takes 3–3.5 hours.

Alternatively, the same avenue leads on to the *Slavyanovsky Istochnik* (Professor Slavyanov's Spring, discovered in 1913), located in a pleasantly designed pavilion. The spring itself looks like a foaming fountain, and has a temperature of 50°C (132°F); water is served there.

Further on, in the *Bolshaya Ploschadka* (large square), is the colonnade of the three *Smirnov Springs* (45.5°C/114°F). Down from this point run the *Cascade Stairs*, a double staircase with mineral water running down the centre. At the bottom of the Stairs, through the trees, a large artificial pond can be seen. On the slope of the mountains to the left of the stairs is *Nezlobinsky Istochnik* (Nezlobin's Spring) with pleasant tasting and fairly cold water (19°C/66°F). To the right are some other springs.

The uphill spiral path which circles the mountain twice, leads past three springs: *Kegamovsky* (16.5°C/62°F), *Vladimirsky* (26°C/79°F) and *Spring No. 1*. The second path leads to the top of the mountain (852 m/2775 ft) is 3.3 m (2 miles) one way and takes about 1 hour 15 min. to climb. From the top of the mountain there is a good view of Mount Beshtau, and to the left Mount Mashuk can be seen.

Revolutionaries' Memorial Obelisk, in front of the Ostrovskiye Baths

Lenin Statue, Lenin Street

World War II Memorial, on the left of the Lenin Street. There is an eternal flame.

Theatre, in Pushkin Gallery, in the Park

Kavkaz Hotel, Gorky Street 3

Druzhba (friendship) Hotel & Restaurant, Lenin Street

Izbushka Lesnika Restaurant

Beshtau Restaurant, Tchaikovsky Street 11

Cafe, Pushkin Street, in the Park

Ledinka Bar

Bank, Lenin Street 55

GPO, Lenin Street 53

Bookshop, Tchaikovsky Street 9

Zheleznaya Mountain. The two roads leading to the summit are both 3.5 km (2 miles) long.

INDEX

Abakan (*map*), 28
ABKHASIAN AUTONOMOUS S.S.R., 505
Abramtsevo, 33
Abrau-Durso, 392
Academgorodok (*map*), 396
Adler, 494
Agartsin, 137
Ainazi, 451
Akhali-Shuamta, 556
Akhaltsikhe, 85
Akhpat, 140
Akhtala, 140
Ala-Archa Ravine, 80
Alagir, 630
Alaverdi, 139
Alaverdi, 557
Alma-Ata (*map*), 35
Almalyk, 543
Alphabet, Russian, 18
Alupka, 665
Alushta (*map*), 653
Aman-Kutan, 467
Amberd Fortress, 133
Ananuri, 146
Anau, 46
Andizhan (*map*), 39
Angla, 258
Angren, 543
Apsheron Peninsula, 60
Arkhangelskoye, 361
ARMENIA, 121
Artek, 656
Ashe, 486
Ashkhabad (*map*), 41
Ashtarak, 132
Askania-Nova, 208
Ateni, 158
AZERBAIJAN, 152
Azov, 48

Bairam-Ali, 317
Bakharden, 48
Bakhchisarai, 50
Baku (*map*), 52
Bakuriani, 85
BASHKORSTAN, 583
Batumi (*map*), 65
Bauska, 448
Begovat, 543
Belgorod-Dnestrovsky, 69

Beliovezhskaya Puscha, 89
Beltsy (*map*), 71
Bendery (*map*), 72
Beregovoye, 667
Berezhany, 74
Bishkek (*map*), 75
Bogolyubovo, 636
Bolshoy Dub, 264
Borisoglebsk, 460
Borodino (*map*), 81
Borzhomi, 83
Bratsk, 86
Brest (*map*), 86
Bukhara (*map*), 89
Bulduri, 445
Burana, 80
Buron, 632
BURYATIA, 590
BYELORUSSIAN SOVIET SOCIALIST
    REPUBLIC, 320
Byurakan, 133

Cape Ai-Todor, 663
Car Hire, 12
Cesis (*map*), 95
Chakva, 68
Chaltyr, 456
Chardzhou, 97
Chartova Lestuitsa (Devil's Staircase), 667
Cherkassy (*map*), 98
Cherkessk (*map*), 101
Chernigov (*map*), 104
Chernomorka, 403
Chernovtsy (*map*), 107
Chimkent (*map*), 110
Chirchik, 543
Chishma, 587
Chkalovsky, 495
Chufut-Kaleh, 51
Climate, 7
Consulates, 17
CRIMEA (*map*), 474
Currency, 8
Customs regulations, 8

Dagomys (*map*), 487
Dallagkan, 629
Danushavan, 138
Dargavs, 628

Dilijan, 136
Dolinsk, 380
Dombai, 240
Donetsk (map), 111
Druskininkai, 617
Dubosekovo, 361
Dubrovitsi, 422
Dubulti, 447
Dunilovo, 173
Dushanbe (map), 114
Dzhambul (map), 119
Dzintari, 445
Dzizhak, 544
Dzuarikan, 629
Dzveli-Shamta, 556

Echmiadzin (map), 128
Ekheknut, 138
Elbrus, 380
Elektrenai, 616
Embassies, 14
Erevan (map), 121
Essentuki (map), 141
ESTONIAN REPUBLIC, 525

Fergana (map), 143
FERGANA VALLEY, 143
Fioletovo, 138
First Aid, 23
Firyuza Ravine, 47
Food, 9
Foros, 667
Frunzenskoye, 655

Gagra (map), 515
Garni, 133
Gaspra, 662
Gatchina, 298
Gauja National Park, 451
Geguti, 576
GEORGIA, 544
GEORGIAN MILITARY HIGHWAY (map), 145
Ghelati (map), 576
Gizel, 628
Golitsyno, 494
Golovachevka, 120
Golovinka, 487
Gorecha, 109
Gori, 157
Goshavank, 137
Govyany, 603
Goyani, 234
GREATER SOCHI RESORT REGION, 486
GREATER YALTA, 653
Gremi, 557
Grushevo, 234
Gueghard, 133
Guissar, 118
Gurdzhaani, 554
Gurzuf, 656
Gusyra, 629

Hamzaabad, 144
Handos Khevi, 155
History, 3

Ikalto Monastery, 556
Ilyichevsk, 404
Imeni Kosta Khetagurova, 104
Insurance, 23
Irkutsk (map), 158
Itkol, 381
Ivanets, 325
Ivanovo (map), 168
Ivanovskoye, 422
Izborsk, 430

Jakobsen's Estate, 533
Jaundubulti, 447
Juodkrante, 243
Jurmala (map), 446

Kaarma, 258
KABARDINO-BALKARIAN AUTONO-
    MOUS REPUBLIC, 377
KAKHETIA, 552
Kalinin (map), See Tver, 579
Kamenets-Podolsky (map), 174
Kamenka, 100
Kamenka, 177
Kaniv (map), 177
Kara-Kum Canal, 46
Karabikha, 673
KARACHAY-CHERKESS AUTONOMOUS
    REPUBLIC, 101
Karachayevsk, 104
Karaganda, 179
KARELIA, 418
Karja, 258
Karmadon, 628
Kaunas (map), 180
Kazachy Brod, 494
KAZAKHSTAN, 35
Kazan (map), 186
Kazbegi, 156
Kemeri, 447
Kentau, 579
Kepsha, 495
Khabarovsk (map), 195
KHAKASIA, 28
Khala, 69
Kharisdzhin, 629
Kharkov (map), 197
Khatyn, 325
Kherson (map), 204
Khiva (map), 209
Khmelnitsky (map), 213
Khobi, 517
Kholmsk, 676
Khosta (map), 493
Khotin, 216
Kiev (map), 217
Kikhelkonna, 258

Kiparisnoye, 655
KIRGHIZSTAN, 75
Kirovakan, 138
Kishinyov (*map*), 228
Kislovodsk (*map*), 235
Kivach Nature Reserve, 421
Kizhi (*map*), 240
Klaipeda, 242
Klin (*map*), 243
Koban, 628
Kobi, 156
Kobrin (*map*), 244
Kobuleti (*map*), 245
Kobystan, 62
Kokand, 247
Kokushkino, 194
Kola, 376
Kolageran, 138
Kolodyazhne, 306
Koriez, 664
Korostyn, 498
Korsun-Shevchenkovsky, 101
Kostroma (*map*), 248
Krasnaya Polyana, 495
Krasnaya Skala, 495
Krasnodar (*map*), 253
Krasnogorsk, 361
Kuba (*map*), 62
Kumairi, 253
Kuressaare, 256
Kurgan (*map*), 258
Kurgan-Tube, 119
Kursk (*map*), 261
Kutaisi, 574
Kuyalnitsky Resort, 404
Kvareli, 558
Kvesheti, 155

Lake Baikal, 165
Lake Gigidich, 234
Lake Issyk-Kul, 81
Lake Kov-Ata, 47
Lake Ritsa, 512
Lake Sevan, 135
Lats, 629
LATVIA, 438
Lazarevskoye (*map*), 487
Leningrad (*map*), 264
   Art Museums, 290
      Brodsky Museum, 292
      Hermitage, 290
      State Russian Museum (Mikhaliovsky Palace), 292
      Urban Sculpture Museum, 289, 292
   Churches, 294
      Alexander Nevsky Lavra, 294
      Kazan Cathedral, 294
      Peter and Paul Cathedral (Petropavlovsky Sobor), 278, 290
      St Isaac's Cathedral, 286, 294
      St Nicholas's Cathedral, 294
   Circus, 295
   Climate, 265

Consulates, foreign, 296
Gardens, 294
   Dzerzhinsky Gardens, 280
   Field of Mars (Marsovo Polye), 283
   Summer Garden (Lyetny Sad), 283
   Taurida Garden, 283
Historical Museums, 292
   Artillery History Museum, 293
   Central Naval Museum, 293
   Cruiser 'Aurora', 292
   History of Leningrad Museum, 292
   History of Religion & Atheism Museum (Kazan Cathedral), 294
   Lenin Museum, 292
   Military Museum (former Arsenal), 293
   October Revolution Museum, 292
   Suvorov Museum, 293
House Museums, 293
Islands,
   Krestovsky Island, 281
   Trudashchisya (workers') Island, 280
   Vasilyevsky Island, 281
   Yelagin Island, 280
Kirov Sport Stadium, 295
Literary, Musical & Theatrical Museums, 293
   Exhibition of Musical Instruments, 293
   Literary Museum, 293
   Nekrasov Memorial Museum, 293
   Pushkin Museum, 293
   Saltykov-Schedrin Library, 293
Neva, river
   left bank, 282
   right bank (Petrogradskaya Storona), 277
Palaces, etc., 290
   Peter the Great's Cottage (Domik Petra Velikovo), 278, 290
   Mikhailovsky Palace, 284
   Peter and Paul Fortress (Petropavlovskaya Krepost), 277, 290
   Summer Palace (Lyetny Dvoryets), 290
   Winter Palace (Zimny Dvoryets), 286
Petrogradskaya Storona (Petrograd Side), 277
Population, 264
Post Office, 296
Restaurants, 295
Scientific Museums, 293
   Arctic & Antarctic Museum, 293
   Geological Museum, 293
   Kunstkammer (Museum of Anthropology & Ethnology), 293
   Zoological Museum, 293
Shops, 296
Sports Facilities, 295
Statues & Monuments, 294
   Peter the Great (the Bronze Horseman), 294
Streets; major,
   Decembrists' (Dekabristov) Square, 286
   Kirovsky Prospect, 280
   Nevsky Prospect, 287
   Palace (Dvortsovaya) Square, 285
   St Isaac's Square, 286
   Theatre (Teatralnaya) Square, 287

Leningrad (*cont.*)
    Voinova Square, 283
    Vosstaniya Square, 289
    Strelka (Vasilievsky Island), 281
    Telegraph, 296
    Theatres, etc., 295
        Hermitage Theatre, 284
Leninskiye Gorki, 362
Lenskiye Stolby, 653
Lermontovo, 138
Lermontovsky Resort, 403
Letichev, 215
Lielupe, 445
Ligutne, 451
Likany, 84
Lipetsk (*map*), 300
Listvyanka, 166
LITHUANIA, 606
Livadia, 661
Lomonosov, 297
Loo, 487
Lutsk (*map*), 304
Lvov (*map*), 307

Magnitogorsk, 313
Majori, 445
Makhindzhauri, 68
Makopse, 486
Maly Mayak, 655
Mardakyan, 60
Marghilan, 314
Mari (*map*), 315
Mariupol, 320
Martsialnye Vody, 420
Massandra, 657
Matsesta, 493
Medvezhy Ugol, 495
Medzhibozh, 214
Merv (*map*), 317
Metsamor, 131
Michurin State Farm, 121
MINERALNYE VODY, 432
Minsk (*map*), 320
Minusinsk, 31
Minvody, 434
Miskhor, 664
Mizur, 630
Mleti, 155
Mogilyov-Podolsky (*map*), 621
Moldavka, 494
MOLDOVA, 228
Money, 8
Morintsy, 101
Moscow (*map*), 325
    Art Galleries & General Museums, 347
        Andrei Rublov Museum of Ancient Art, 348
        Donskoi Monastery, 349
        House of Boyars Romanov, 329
        Manege (Central Exhibition Hall), 349
        Oriental Culture Museum, 348
        Pushkin Fine Arts Museum, 348, 351
        Russian Chattels of the 17th–19th Century Exhibition, 349

        Russian Decorative Folk Art Exhibition, 349
        Shchusev Architecture Museum, 349, 351
        Tretyakov Gallery, 347
    Bank, 359
    Care Hire, 359
    Churches & Cathedrals, 344
        Annunciation (Blagoveshchensky) Cathedral, 337
        Archangel Gabriel's Church (Menshikov Tower), 347
    Climate, 326
    Economic, Scientific & Technical Museums & Exhibitions, 352
        Botanical Garden, 353
        Darwin Museum, 352
        Durov's Corner, 352
        Korolyov Memorial Museum, 352
        Natural History Museum, 352
        Planetarium, 353
        Polytechnical Museum, 352
        Timiryazev Biological Museum, 352
        USSR Exhibition of Economic Achievements, 352
        Zoo, 353
    Embassies & Consulates, Foreign, 14
        American Embassy, 16
        British Embassy, 16, 331
    Historical Museums, 349
        Battle of Borodino Museum, 351
        History Museum, 350
        Kutuzov's Hut Museum, 351
        Lenin Museum, 349
        Marx & Engels Museum, 350
        Revolution Museum, 350
        Soviet Army Museum, 350
    History, 325
    Hotels, 356
    Kitai-Gorod (Old Moscow), 329
    Kremlin, 336
        Annunciation (Blagoveshchensky) Cathedral, 337
        Archangel Michael's (Arkhangelsky) Cathedral, 338
        Assumption (Uspensky) Cathedral, 338
        Bell Tower of Ivan the Great, 339
        Deposition of the Robe (Rizpolozhenya) Church, 339
        Granovitaya Palata, 340
        Grand Kremlin Palace, 340
        Palace of Chambers, 340
        Patriarch's Palace, 339
        Spassky (Redeemer's) Gate, 337
        Towers, 337, 339
        Tsar Cannon, 339
        Tsar Kolokol (Bell), 339
        Twelve Apostles' Church, 339
    Lenin Hills, 336
    Libraries, 347
    Literary, Theatrical & Musical Museums, 351
        Bakhrushin Theatrical Museum, 352
        Chekhov Museum, 351

Dostoyevsky Museum, 351
Glinka Museum, 352
Gorky's House, 351
Gorky Museum, 351
Herzen Museum, 352
Leo Tolstoy Museum, 351
Monuments, 354
Parks & Recreational Facilities, 353
  Bathing Beaches, 353
  Bitsy Park, 353
  Gorky Park, 333, 353
  Hermitage Garden, 353
  Izmailovo Park, 353
  Sokolniki Park, 353
Population, 325
Post Offices, 359
Public Transport, 353
  Boat Trips, 354
  Metro, 353
Restaurants, 357
Shops, 358
  Gastronom No. 1, 358
  GUM, 358
Sport, 353
  Army Palace of Sports, 353
  Dynamo Sports Stadium, 353
  Hippodrome Racecourse, 353
  Krylatskoye Sports Complex, 353
  Lenin Stadium, 335, 353
  Luzhniki Stadium, 353
  Moskva Open-Air Swimming Pool, 330,
    331
  Sokolniki Palace of Sports, 353
  Young Pioneer Stadium, 353
Statues & Monuments, 354
Streets; Main, 333
  Arbat Square
  Bulvarnoye Koltso (Boulevard Ring),
    330
  Gorky Street, 333, 353
  Herzen Street, 331, 334
  Komsomolsky Prospect, 336
  Kutuzovsky Prospect, 335
  Leninsky Prospect, 336
  Leningradsky Prospect, 334
  Manege Square, 330
  Ostozhenka Street, 335
  Prospect Mira, 336
  Red Square (Krasnaya Ploschad), 328
  Revolution Square, 329
  Sadovoye Koltso (Garden Ring), 332
  Volkhonka Street, 335
Telegraph, 359
Theatres, Concert Halls & Cinemas, 356
  Bolshoi Theatre, 329
  Circus, 356
  Maly Theatre, 356
  Moscow Arts Theatre, 356
  Moscow Theatre of Drama & Comedy on
    Taganka, 356
  Rossiya Cinema, 331
  Tchaikovsky Concert Hall, 356
Tourist Boards
Transport, 353

University, 347
Motsametra Monastery, 576
Mtskheta, 362
Mukachevo, 364
Mukuzani, 554
Murmansk (map), 374

Nakhodka, 376
Nalchik (map), 377
Namangan, 381
Nar, 632
Nardaran, 61
Neftyaniye Kamni, 62
Nemirov, 620
Neringa, 243
Nerubaiskoye, 404
Nesvizh, 382
Nevelsk, 676
Nevinnomyssk, 505
Nevitskoye, 603
Nida, 243
Nikortsminda, 578
Nikulskoye, 673
Ninotsminda Fortress, 552
Ninotsminda, 553
Nisa, 46
Nizhniye Vorota, 604
Nizhnyaya Teberda, 104
Noravank-Gladzor, 141
NORTH OSSETIAN AUTONOMOUS RE-
    PUBLIC, 623
Novaya-Kakhovka, 207
Novgorod (map), 382
Noviye Petrovniye, 228
Novocherkassk, 388
Novorossiisk, 391
Novosibirsk (map), 393
Novospasskoye, 486
Novotalitsa, 170
Novy Afon (map), 509
Nukriani, 553
Nurek, 119
Nuzal, 630

Odessa (map), 398
Odzun, 138
Ogre, 447
Oktemberyan, 131
Olesko, 312
Opolznevoye, 667
Oreanda, 662
Orel (map), 404
Orsha, 409
Oshakan, 132
Otrar, 579
Ozyorki, 304

Palanga, 409
Palekh, 173
Panerai, 616
Panevezys (map), 410

Parkovoye, 667
Parnu (map), 412
Pasanauri, 155
Passports, 8
Pavlovsk, 299
Pechory Monastery, 430
Pendzhikent, 414
Pereslavl-Zalessky (map), 415
Petrodvorets, 296
Petrozavodsk (map), 418
Photography, 13
Pircupis, 616
Pirogovo, 619
Pitsunda (map), 513
Podolsk, 421
Podvolochinsk, 423
Poltava (map), 423
Polyana, 604
Ponizovka, 667
Poronaisk, 676
Protok Khatystak, 653
Pskov (map), 426
Public Holidays, 5
Pushkin, 298
Pushkino, 235
Pushkinskiye Gory (map), 431
Pyatigorsk (map), 432

Raubichi, 325
Rauna, 96
Rava Russkaya, 438
Razliv, 300
Rekom, 632
Repino, 300
Riga (map), 438
Rioni Power Station, 576
Rostov Veliky (map), 456
Rostov-on-Don (map), 451
Rovno (map), 460
Rumsiskes, 617
Russian Orthodox Church, 6
Ryabkova, 261

SAAREMAA, 256
Sagaredzho, 553
Salaspils, 447
Samarkand (map), 462
Sanahin, 139
Sartichale, 552
Sary-Tyuz, 102
Sataplia, 576
Saulkrasty, 451
Seltso, 388
Sevan, 135
Shahr-i Sabz, 468
Shakhtinsk, 180
Sheki, 471
Shemakha (map), 63
Shepetovka, 215
Shevchenkovo, 101
Shopping, 11
Shroma, 555

Shushenskoye (map), 32
Shuya, 172
SIBERIA, 293
Signakhi, 553
Sigulda (map), 449
Simferopol (map), 474
Simiez, 666
Skovorodinovka, 204
Slavyanogorsk, 479
Smiltnye, 243
Smolensk (map), 479
Smolino, 261
Sochi (map), 489
Sokolovo, 203
Solokh Aul, 488
Sortavala, 496
Sosnovka, 100
Spasskoye-Lutovinovo (map),
    408
Staraya Russa (map), 498
Starocherkasskaya Stanitsa, 455
Stavropol (map), 501
Strasheny, 234
Sukhumi (map), 505
Sumgait, 62
Surakhany, 61
Suzdal (map), 517
Svalyava, 604
Sviyazhsk, 194
Svoboda, 264

Taganrog (map), 522
Tagardon, 629
TAJIKISTAN, 114
Talashkino, 486
Tallinn (map), 525
Tamisk, 630
Tanais, 456
Tartu (map), 533
Tashkent (map), 536
TATARSTAN, 186
Tbilisi (map), 544
Teberda, 239
Telavi, 551
Telephone, 12
Temirtau, 180
Ternopol (map), 558
Terskol, 381
Terzhola, 574
Timanovka, 621
Tiraspol (map), 559
Tkibuli, 577
Togliatti, 569
Tokhliauri, 553
Tolgsky Monastery, 673
Torzhok, 570
Trakai, 615
TRANSCARPATHIA, 600
Transport, 12
Travel Agencies, 16
Tsagveri, 85
Tsakhkadzor, 134
Tsaritsyno, 360

Tsei, 630
Tselinograd, 571
Tsikhis-Dziri, 68
Tsinandali, 555
Tskhaltubo (map), 572
Tulchin, 620
Tumanyan, 138
Turkestan, 578
TURKMENISTAN, 600
Tver (map), 579
Tyrnauz, 380

Uch Dere, 487
Ufa (map), 583
Uglich (map), 587
UKRAINIAN SOVIET SOCIALIST
    REPUBLIC, 217
Ulan-Ude, 589
Ulyanovsk (map), 592
Uman (map), 595
Uplis-Tsikhe, 158
Urgench (map), 598
Urvan, 380
Ust-Djiguta, 102
UZBEKISTAN, 536
Uzhgorod (map), 600

Vadu-Lui-Vode, 234
Valaam, 497
Vandra, 533
Varzob Ravine, 118
Vashkovtsy, 109
Vaskhnil, 398
Verkhni Tsei, 632
Veseloye, 496
Viidumyaesky Nature Reserve, 258
Viljandi, 604

Vilnius (map), 606
Vinnitsa (map), 618
Vitebsk, 621
Vladikavkaz (map), 623
Vladimir (map), 632
Vocabulary, 18
Volga-Don Canal, 641
Volgograd (map), 637
Volzhsky (map), 641
Vornichena, 234
Voronezh (map), 641
Voronezh, 641
Voronovitsa, 620
Vyborg (map), 646
Vynzynka, 325

What to Take, 7

Yakovlevo, 264
YAKUTIA, 649
Yakutsk (map), 649
Yalta (map), 658
Yangi-Yul, 543
Yaroslavl (map), 668
Yasnaya Polyana (map), 673
Yuzhno-Sakhalinsk (map), 674

Zagorsk (map), 676
Zakataly (map), 473
Zaporozhye (map), 679
Zdravnevo, 623
Zelenogovsk, 649
Zelyoni Mys, 68
Zheleznogorsk, 264
Zheleznovodsk, 683
Zhinvali, 146
Zvartnots, 131